Test Booklet No. **3947151**

Test Booklet Code **CH1**

MEDACE
NEET (UG)
SELF ASSESSMENT KIT

Electric Charges and Fields

Topics Covered

- Electric Charges and Coulomb's Law
- Electric Field and Electric Dipole
- Electric Flux and Gauss's Law

Important Instructions

- This Booklet Contains – Three Topic Tests and One Test on Complete Chapter.
- Each question carries 4 marks.
- For each correct response, the candidate will get 4 marks and for every incorrect response 1 mark will be additionally deducted from the total score.
- Use **Blue/Black** point pen only for filling the OMR.
- Rough work will be done in the space provided for this purpose within the test booklet only.

Name of the Candidate (In Capitals) ________________

Candidate's Signature ________________

Invigilator's Signature ________________

Facsimile signature stamp of center superintendent________________

Do not open this Booklet until you start attempting the Test

Topical Follow Thru

Test 1

Syllabus

- Conservation of Charge
- Coulomb's Law, Forces between Two Point Charges
- Forces between Multiple Charges
- Superposition Principle

For deeper insight **Scan the QR Code**

Important Instructions

- The test is of 30 minutes duration and contains 15 Multiple Choice Questions. (Four options with a single correct answer).
- Choose the correct option and fill the OMR given on the last page of this test accordingly.
- At some instances, you may find more than 1 option may be correct, in such circumstances you have to judge the most appropriate answer as per the conditions given in the question.

1. Two positive point charges are 3 m apart and their combined charge is 15 μC. If the force between them is 0.050 N, the then charges are

(a) 10 μC, 5 μC (b) 12 μC, 3 μC
(c) 9 μC, 6 μC (d) 8 μC, 7 μC

2. A soap bubble is given -1.6×10^{-19}C charge, then its radius will

(a) increase
(b) decrease
(c) remain same
(d) Information is insufficient

3. What is the Coulomb's force between two β-particles separated by a distance of 1.6×10^{-6} m?

(a) 1.6×10^{-23} N (b) 2.54×10^{-27} N
(c) 9×10^{-17} N (d) 1 N

4. Two charges q_1 and q_2 are separated by a distance r in air. They exert force F on each other. Now, they are placed in a medium of dielectric constant K. What should be the value of charge (keeping the charge q_2 and distance r constant), so that they again experience the same force? (q_1, q_2 are respective charges)

(a) $\frac{q_1}{K}$ (b) $q_1 K$
(c) $\frac{q_1}{\sqrt{K}}$ (d) $q_1\sqrt{K}$

5. A charge q is orbiting around a stationary charge Q in a circular orbit. If T is the time period of revolution, then what would be the radius?

(a) $\left(\frac{4\pi^3 mT^2}{kQq}\right)^{1/3}$

(b) $\left(\frac{Qq}{16\pi^3\varepsilon_0 m}T^2\right)^{1/3}$

(c) $\left(\frac{Qq}{16\pi^2\varepsilon_0 m}T^2\right)^{1/3}$

(d) $\left(\frac{QqT^2}{4\pi^3\varepsilon_0 m}\right)^{1/3}$

6. Two small conducting spheres are connected to the ends of the two identical springs as shown in figure. The spacing between the spheres is 0.05 m. On charging each sphere to 1.6 μC, the separation between the spheres doubles. The spring constant of each spring is approximately

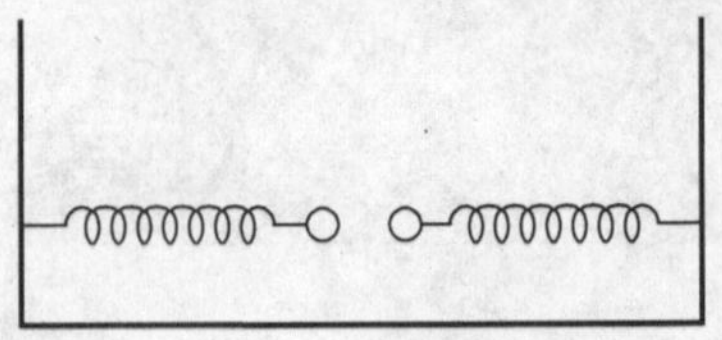

(a) 46 Nm^{-1} (b) 90 Nm^{-1}
(c) 23 Nm^{-1} (d) 92 Nm^{-1}

7. Two charges $+q$ and $-q$ are placed at distance r. Match the following two columns when distance between them is changed to r'.

	Column I	Column II
A.	$r' = 2r$	I. Force between them will become 16 times
B.	$r' = \frac{r}{2}$	II. Force between them will become $\frac{1}{4}$ th
C.	$r' = 4r$	III. Force between them will become four times
D.	$r' = \frac{r}{4}$	IV. Force between them will become $\frac{1}{16}$ th

Choose the correct codes from the options given below.

(a) A-I, B-II, C-III, D-IV
(b) A-IV, B-III, C-II, D-I
(c) A-II, B-III, C-IV, D-I
(d) A-III, B-II, C-I, D-IV

8. Two point charges A and B have charges $+q$ and $-q$, respectively. Now, 50% charge from B to A is transferred. If initial force of attraction was F, then what is the final force of attraction?

(a) $\frac{F}{2}$ (b) $\frac{F}{4}$
(c) $\frac{F}{16}$ (d) F

9. Three equal point charges q are placed at the corners of an equilateral triangle. Another charge Q is placed at the centroid of the triangle. The system of charges will be in equilibrium, if Q equals

(a) $\frac{q}{\sqrt{3}}$
(b) $-\frac{q}{\sqrt{3}}$
(c) $\frac{q}{3}$
(d) $-\frac{q}{3}$

10. The magnitude of electrostatic force between two point charges in air is 100 N. If a medium of dielectric constant K is filled between them, then net electrostatic force is reduced by 20 N. The value of dielectric constant is

(a) 1.2 (b) 1.25
(c) 5 (d) 4

11. Four charges equal to $-Q$ are placed at the four corners of a square and a charge q is at its centre. If the system is in equilibrium, then the value of q is

(a) $-(Q/4)(1+2\sqrt{2})$
(b) $(Q/4)(1+2\sqrt{2})$
(c) $-(Q/2)(1+2\sqrt{2})$
(d) $(Q/2)(1+2\sqrt{2})$

12. A and B are two identical blocks made from a conducting material. These are placed on a horizontal frictionless table and connected by a light conducting spring of force constant k. Unstretched length of the spring is L_0. Charge $Q/2$ is given to each block. Consequently, the spring stretches to an equilibrium length L. Value of Q will be

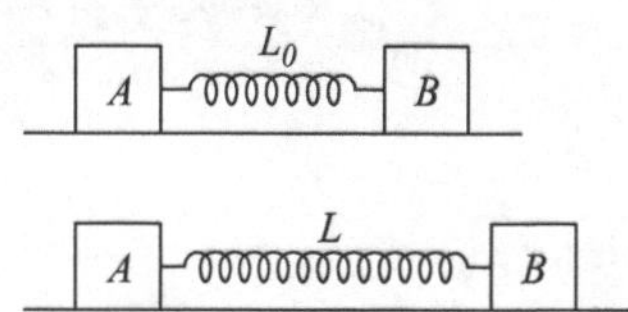

(a) $\sqrt{4\pi\varepsilon_0 kL}$
(b) $L\sqrt{\frac{k}{4\pi\varepsilon_0 (L-L_0)}}$
(c) $2L\sqrt{4\pi\varepsilon_0 k(L-L_0)}$
(d) $4\pi\varepsilon_0 k(L-L_0)$

13. The negative charge possessed by free electrons in 10 g of water is

(a) 6.25×10^4 C (b) 5.35×10^4C
(c) 1.76×10^4C (d) 5.35×10^5C

14. A piece of glass is rubbed with blanket. It is found that -8.9×10^{-6} C charge is on the blanket. Number of electrons on the blanket is

(a) 5.6×10^{13}

(b) 6×10^{3}

(c) 7.8×10^{14}

(d) 9.8×10^{27}

15. Three point charges $4q$, Q and q are placed in a straight line of length l at points distant 0, $l/2$ and l, respectively. The net force on charge q is zero. The value of Q is

(a) $-q$ (b) $-2q$

(c) $-\frac{1}{2}q$ (d) $4q$

Response Index

01	ⓐ	ⓑ	ⓒ	ⓓ	11	ⓐ	ⓑ	ⓒ	ⓓ
02	ⓐ	ⓑ	ⓒ	ⓓ	12	ⓐ	ⓑ	ⓒ	ⓓ
03	ⓐ	ⓑ	ⓒ	ⓓ	13	ⓐ	ⓑ	ⓒ	ⓓ
04	ⓐ	ⓑ	ⓒ	ⓓ	14	ⓐ	ⓑ	ⓒ	ⓓ
05	ⓐ	ⓑ	ⓒ	ⓓ	15	ⓐ	ⓑ	ⓒ	ⓓ
06	ⓐ	ⓑ	ⓒ	ⓓ					
07	ⓐ	ⓑ	ⓒ	ⓓ					
08	ⓐ	ⓑ	ⓒ	ⓓ					
09	ⓐ	ⓑ	ⓒ	ⓓ					
10	ⓐ	ⓑ	ⓒ	ⓓ					

Performance Scanner

> 90% Excellent !	You have mastered these topics. The concepts of these topics are at your fingertips. Move on to the next test and maintain this momentum.
76-90% Very Good !	You have a good command over these topics. Revise them again after a few days and enhance your performance.
60-75% Good !	You have a wide scope to learn for these topics. Revise them again.
<60% Not Satisfactory!	You have a long way ahead of you to master in these topics. Revise them thoroughly.

Test 2

Syllabus

- Electric Field due to a Point Charge
- Electric Field Lines
- Continuous Charge Distribution
- Electric Dipoles
- Electric Field due to a Dipole
- Torque on a Dipole in a Uniform Electric Field

For deeper insight **Scan the QR Code**

Important Instructions

- The test is of 30 minutes duration and contains 15 Multiple Choice Questions. (Four options with a single correct answer).
- Choose the correct option and fill the OMR given on the last page of this test accordingly.
- At some instances, you may find more than 1 option may be correct, in such circumstances you have to judge the most appropriate answer as per conditions given in the question.

1. Two charges 9 μC and 16 μC are separated by a distance 14 cm. Find the point where a 1 μC charge should be placed such that it will remain stationary.

(a) 5 cm (b) 6 cm
(c) 7 cm (d) 8 cm

2. Four charges $q, 2q, 5q, 6q$ are placed on the corners of a square as shown below. The direction of electric field at C is perpendicular to

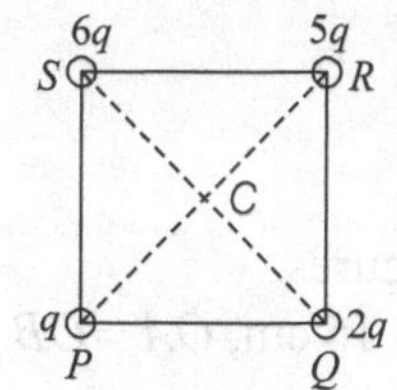

(a) PQ (b) RQ
(c) PS (d) PR

3. The following diagram shows the electric field due to two charges Q and q.

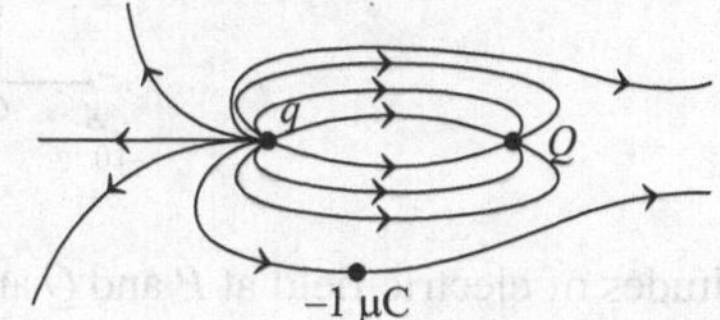

A –1 μC charge is placed as shown. It will move in the

(a) upward direction
(b) downward direction
(c) left direction
(d) right direction

4. An electric dipole of dipole moment $p = 5 \times 10^{-18}$ C-m lying along uniform electric field $E = 4 \times 10^4$ NC^{-1}. The work done in rotating the dipole by 60° is

(a) 0.1 pJ
(b) 0.01 pJ
(c) 1.0 pJ
(d) 10.0 pJ

5. Two point charges $+20q$ and $-5q$ are located at $x = 0$ and $x = M$, respectively. The location of a point on the X-axis, at which the net electric field due to these two point charges is zero, is

(a) $8M$ (b) $4M$
(c) $2M$ (d) $\frac{M}{4}$

6. An infinite number of electric charges each equal to 10 nC (magnitude) are placed along Y-axis at $y = 1$ cm, $y = 2$ cm, $y = 4$ cm, $y = 8$ cm......... and so on. In the setup, if the consecutive charges have opposite sign, then the electric field (in N/C) at $x = 0$ is $\left(\frac{1}{4\pi\varepsilon_0} = 9 \times 10^9 \text{ N-m}^2/\text{C}^2\right)$

(a) 12×10^4
(b) 24×10^4
(c) 36×10^4
(d) 72×10^4

7. Three identical dipoles are arranged as shown below. The electric field at O is

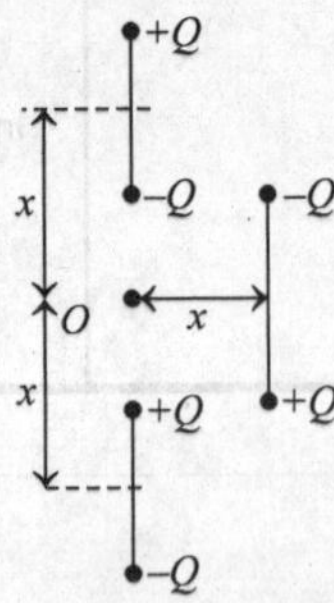

(a) $\frac{5kp}{x^3}$ (b) $\frac{2kp}{x^3}$

(c) zero (d) $\frac{kp}{x^3}$

8. Charges Q_1 and Q_2 are at points A and B of a right angle triangle OAB (see figure). The resultant electric field at point O is perpendicular to the hypotenuse, then Q_1 / Q_2 is proportional to

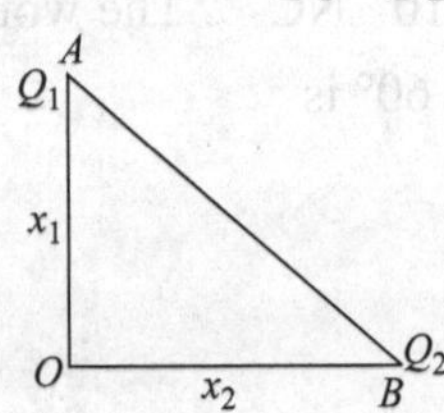

(a) $\frac{x_1^3}{x_2^3}$ (b) $\frac{x_2}{x_1}$

(c) $\frac{x_1}{x_2}$ (d) $\frac{x_2^2}{x_1^2}$

9. An electron revolves around an infinite cylindrical wire having uniform linear charge density 2×10^{-8} Cm^{-1} in circular path under the influence of attractive electrostatic field as shown in the figure. The velocity of electron with which it is revolving, is
(Given, mass of electron $=9\times10^{-31}$ kg)

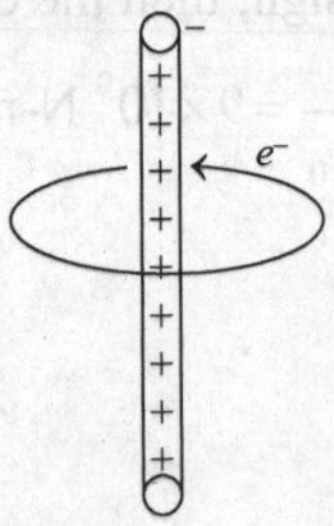

(a) 4×10^6 m/s (b) 6×10^6 m/s

(c) 8×10^6 m/s (d) 12×10^6 m/s

10. An electric dipole has a fixed dipole moment $\mathbf{p}$, which makes angle θ with respect to X-axis. When subjected to an electric field $\mathbf{E}_1 = E\hat{\mathbf{i}}$, it experiences a torque $\tau_1 = \tau\hat{\mathbf{k}}$. When subjected to another electric field $\mathbf{E}_2 = \sqrt{3}E_1\,\hat{\mathbf{j}}$, it experiences torque $\tau_2 = -\tau_1$. The angle θ is

(a) 60° (b) 90°

(c) 30° (d) 45°

11. Two point charges q_1 and q_2 of $+10^{-8}$C and -10^{-8}C respectively, are placed 0.1 m apart.

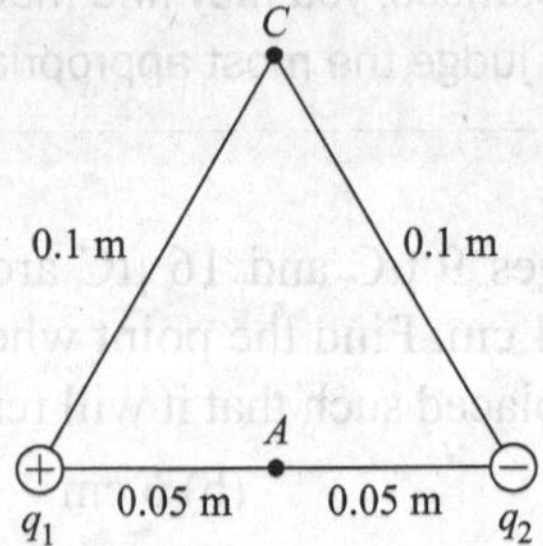

Then, ratio of magnitudes of electric fields at A and C is

(a) 4 : 1

(b) 1 : 4

(c) 8 : 1

(d) 1 : 8

12. In given figures,
$OP = OQ = 15$ cm, $OA = OB = 2.5$ mm.

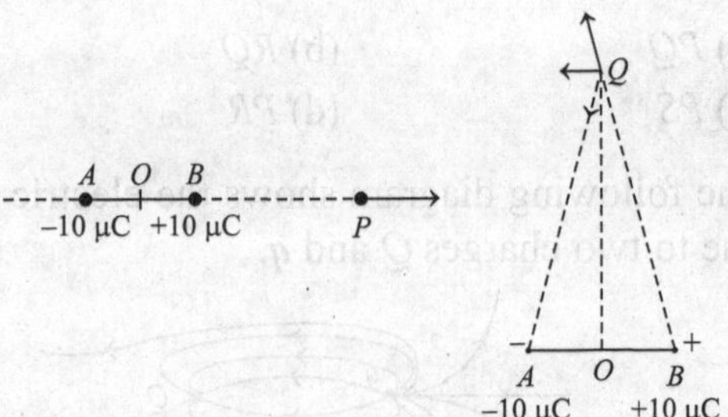

Magnitudes of electric field at P and Q are respectively

(a) 2.6×10^5 NC^{-1}, 2.6×10^5 NC^{-1}

(b) 1.3×10^5 NC^{-1}, 1.3×10^5 NC^{-1}

(c) 2.6×10^5 NC^{-1}, 1.3×10^5 NC^{-1}

(d) 1.3×10^5 NC^{-1}, 2.6×10^5 NC^{-1}

13. p and $64p$ are dipole moments of two dipoles. These are placed in opposite direction on a line at a distance of 0.25 m. The electric field will be zero at point between the dipoles whose distance from the dipole of moment p is

(a) 5 cm

(b) 64 cm

(c) 25 cm

(d) $\frac{4}{13}$ cm

14. Electric field due to two opposite charges of unequal amount is represented by

(a) 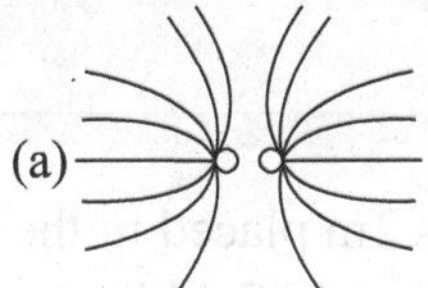

(b) 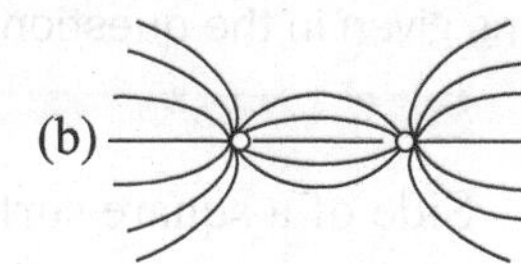

(c) (d) 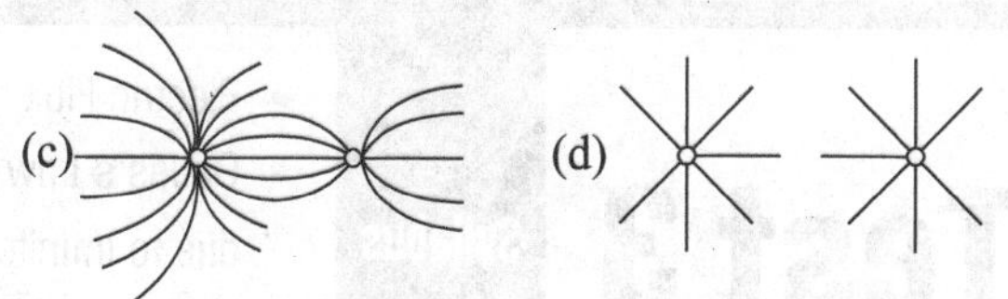

15. Two dipoles are placed as shown,

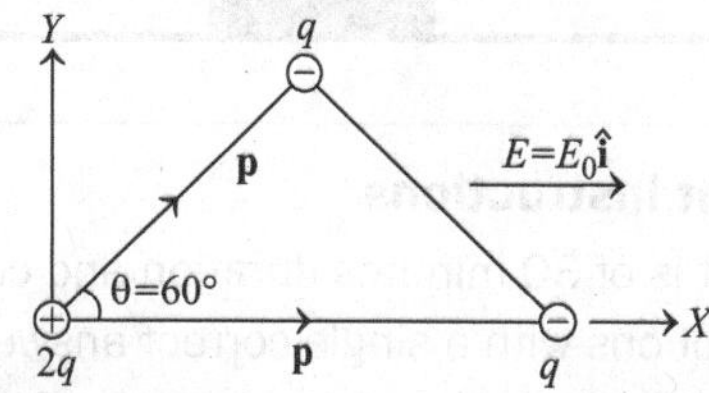

Dipole moment of each dipole is **p**.

An electric field $E_0 \uparrow$ is switched ON in that region. Torque on system of dipoles is

(a) $pE\cos 30°$ (b) $pE\sin 30°$

(c) $pE\cos 60°$ (d) $pE\cos 120°$

Response Index

01	a	b	c	d	11	a	b	c	d
02	a	b	c	d	12	a	b	c	d
03	a	b	c	d	13	a	b	c	d
04	a	b	c	d	14	a	b	c	d
05	a	b	c	d	15	a	b	c	d
06	a	b	c	d					
07	a	b	c	d					
08	a	b	c	d					
09	a	b	c	d					
10	a	b	c	d					

Performance Scanner

> 90% Excellent !	You have mastered these topics. The concepts of these topics are at your fingertips. Move on to the next test and maintain this momentum.
76-90% Very Good !	You have a good command over these topics. Revise them again after a few days and enhance your performance.
60-75% Good !	You have a wide scope to learn for these topics. Revise them again.
<60% Not Satisfactory!	You have a long way ahead of you to master in these topics. Revise them thoroughly.

Test 3

Syllabus

- Electric Flux
- Gauss's Law and Its Application to Find Electric Field due to Infinitely Long Uniformly Charged Straight Wire
- Uniformly Charged Infinite Plane Sheet
- Uniformly Charged Thin Spherical Shell

For deeper insight **Scan the QR Code**

Important Instructions

- The test is of 30 minutes duration and contains 15 Multiple Choice Questions. (Four options with a single correct answer).
- Choose the correct option and fill the OMR given on the last page of this test accordingly.
- At some instances, you may find more than 1 option may be correct, in such circumstances you have to judge the most appropriate answer as per conditions given in the question.

1. A charge q is placed at the centre of the base of a cone. The flux through the curved surface area is

(a) $\frac{q}{\varepsilon_0}$ (b) $\frac{q}{2\varepsilon_0}$

(c) $\frac{q}{3\varepsilon_0}$ (d) $\frac{q}{4\varepsilon_0}$

2. A cone is placed in a uniform electric field **E**. The flux entering the cone is

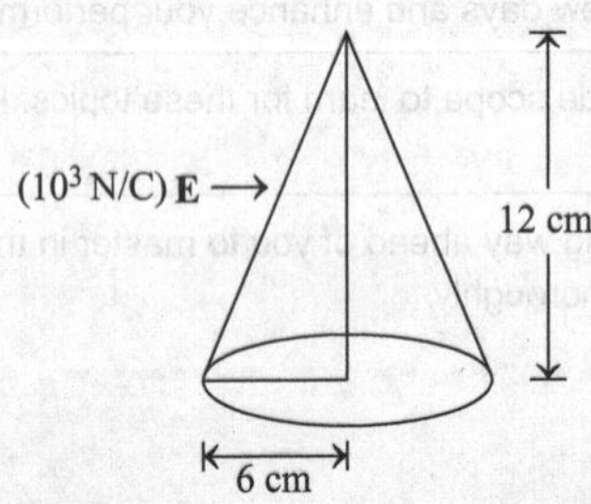

(a) 72×10^{-4} N-m^{2}C^{-1}

(b) 72 N-m^{2}C^{-1}

(c) 7.2 N-m^{2}C^{-1}

(d) 3.6 N-m^{2}C^{-1}

3. An infinite line charge produces field of 9×10^5 N/C at a distance of 0.04 m. The linear charge density is

(a) 10^{-7} C/m (b) 9×10^{-6} C/m

(c) 36×10^{14} C/m (d) 2.0×10^{-6} C/m

4. Side of a square surface is 2 m placed in the plane of the paper. A uniform electric field is also in the plane of the paper as shown in the following diagram. The electric flux in SI units associated with the surface is

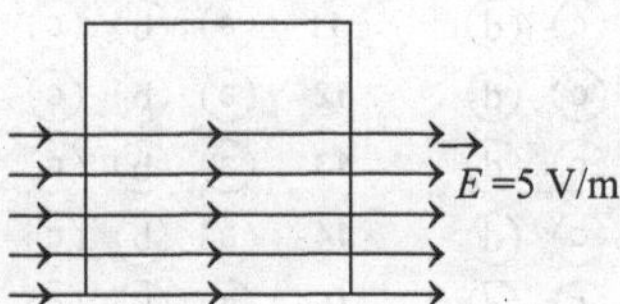

(a) $20 / (2\varepsilon_0)$

(b) 20 / 2

(c) zero

(d) 20

5. The electric flux for Gaussian surface M that encloses the charged particles in free space is (given, $q_1 = -14$ nC, $q_2 = 78.85$ nC, $q_3 = -56$ nC)

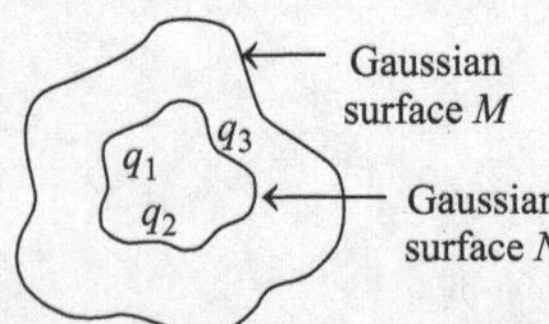

(a) 1000 N-m^{2}C^{-1}

(b) 743 N-m^{2}C^{-1}

(c) 6334 N-m^{2}C^{-1}

(d) 500 N-m^{2}C^{-1}

6. Which of the following statements is not true for the Gauss's theorem in electrostatics?

(a) In a free space, the total normal electric flux over a closed surface is $\frac{\Sigma q}{\varepsilon_0}$.

(b) The closed surface is situated in a uniform electric field, then electric flux will be zero.

(c) A charge q is placed at one of the corners of a cube, then the electric flux will be $\frac{q}{8\varepsilon_0}$.

(d) A charge q is placed at any one of the faces of the cube, then electric flux through cube will be $\frac{q}{6\varepsilon_0}$.

7. An electric field given by $E = 2\hat{\mathbf{i}} + 3(y^3 + 2)\hat{\mathbf{j}}$ is incident on the Gaussian cube of side 1m placed at the origin such that its three sides represent X, Y and Z-axes. The net charge enclosed within the cube is

(a) $4\varepsilon_0$ (b) $2\varepsilon_0$

(c) $3\varepsilon_0$ (d) ε_0

8. Two concentric conducting thin spherical shells R and S having radii r_R and r_S ($r_S > r_R$) are charged to Q_R and $-Q_S$ ($|Q_S| > |Q_R|$). The electric field along a line passing through the centre is

(a)

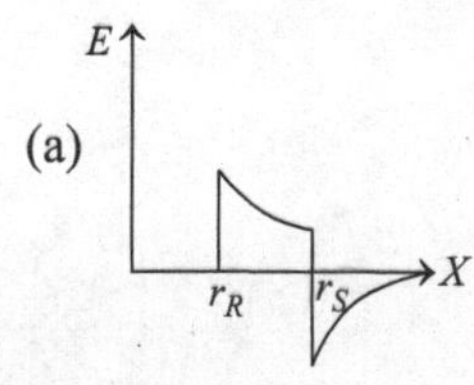

(b)

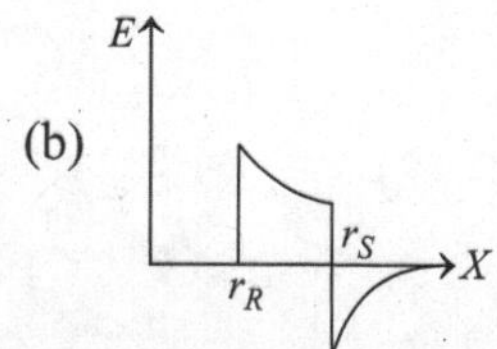

(c)

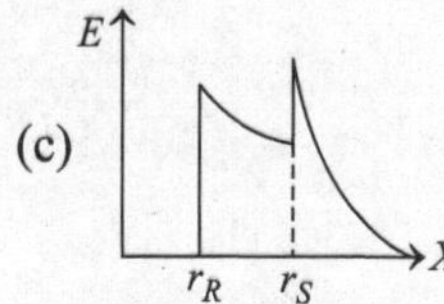

(d)

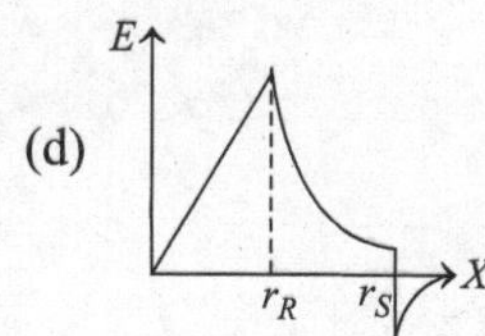

9. A charge 6 nC is located at the centre of a cube. The electric flux through bottom face is

(a) 1.13×10^2 N-m^{2}C^{-1}

(b) 6×10^{-9} N-m^{2}C^{-1}

(c) 6.78×10^{-2} N-m^{2}C^{-1}

(d) 2×10^{-2} N-m^{2}C^{-1}

10. **Statement I** Gauss's law is true for any closed surface, irrespective of its shape and size.
Statement II Gauss's law is based on the inverse square dependence on distance contained in the Coulomb's law.
In the light of above statements, choose the most appropriate answer from the options given below.

(a) Both Statement I and Statement II are correct.

(b) Both Statement I and Statement II are incorrect.

(c) Statement I is correct and Statement II is incorrect.

(d) Statement I is incorrect and Statement II is correct.

11. A cube is placed in an electric field $\mathbf{E} = \frac{E_0 x}{a}\hat{\mathbf{i}}$.
The electric flux passing through the shaded surface of a cube of side length $2a$ is

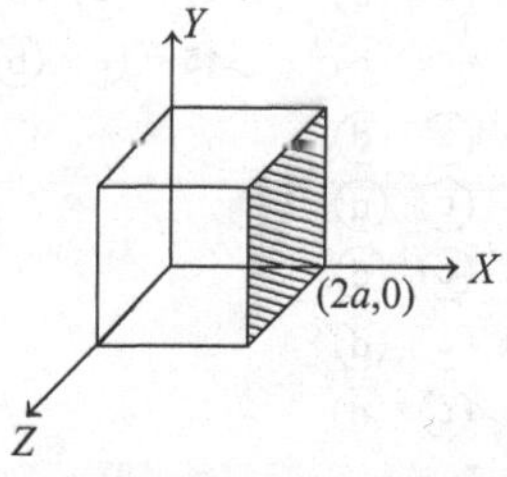

(a) $2E_0a^2$

(b) $4E_0a^2$

(c) $8E_0a^2$

(d) zero

12. A long rod of charge density λ Cm^{-1} passes through a cubical box of side 'a'.
Ratio of minimum and maximum flux through the cube is

(a) 1:1 (b) $1:\sqrt{2}$

(c) $1:\sqrt{3}$ (d) 1:3

13. If the electric field is given by $(5\hat{\mathbf{i}} + 4\hat{\mathbf{j}} + 9\hat{\mathbf{k}})$, then the electric flux through a surface of area 20 unit lying in the YZ- plane will be

(a) 100 units

(b) 80 units

(c) 180 units

(d) 20 units

14. What is the flux through a cube of side a, if a point charge of q is at one of its corner?

(a) $\frac{2q}{\varepsilon_0}$

(b) $\frac{q}{8\varepsilon_0}$

(c) $\frac{q}{\varepsilon_0}$

(d) $\frac{q}{2\varepsilon_0}6a^2$

15. At point P, electric field is due to

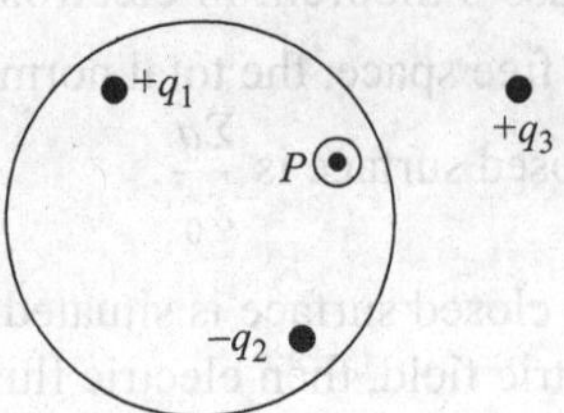

(a) $+q_3$ only

(b) $+q_1$ and $+q_3$

(c) $+q_1, +q_3$ and $-q_2$

(d) $+q_1$ and $-q_2$

Response Index

01	ⓐ	ⓑ	ⓒ	ⓓ	11	ⓐ	ⓑ	ⓒ	ⓓ
02	ⓐ	ⓑ	ⓒ	ⓓ	12	ⓐ	ⓑ	ⓒ	ⓓ
03	ⓐ	ⓑ	ⓒ	ⓓ	13	ⓐ	ⓑ	ⓒ	ⓓ
04	ⓐ	ⓑ	ⓒ	ⓓ	14	ⓐ	ⓑ	ⓒ	ⓓ
05	ⓐ	ⓑ	ⓒ	ⓓ	15	ⓐ	ⓑ	ⓒ	ⓓ
06	ⓐ	ⓑ	ⓒ	ⓓ					
07	ⓐ	ⓑ	ⓒ	ⓓ					
08	ⓐ	ⓑ	ⓒ	ⓓ					
09	ⓐ	ⓑ	ⓒ	ⓓ					
10	ⓐ	ⓑ	ⓒ	ⓓ					

Performance Scanner

> 90% Excellent !	You have mastered these topics. The concepts of these topics are at your fingertips. Move on to the next test and maintain this momentum.
76-90% Very Good !	You have a good command over these topics. Revise them again after a few days and enhance your performance.
60-75% Good !	You have a wide scope to learn more in these topics. Revise them again.
<60% Not Satisfactory!	You have a long way ahead of you to master in these topics. Revise them thoroughly.

Chapter Break Thru

Syllabus	
• Conservation of Charge • Coulomb's Law, Forces between Two Point Charges • Forces between Multiple Charges • Superposition Principle • Electric Field due to a Point Charge • Electric Field Lines • Continuous Charge Distribution • Electric Dipoles	• Electric Field due to a Dipole • Torque on a Dipole in a Uniform Electric Field • Electric Flux • Gauss's Law and Its Application to Find Electric Field due to Infinitely Long Uniformly Charged Straight Wire • Uniformly Charged Infinite Plane Sheet • Uniformly Charged Thin Spherical Shell

Important Instructions

- The test is of 45 minutes duration and contains 30 Multiple Choice Questions (Four options with a single correct answer).
- Choose the correct option and fill the OMR given on the last page of this test accordingly.
- At some instances, you may find more than 1 option may be correct, in such circumstances you have to judge the most appropriate answer as per conditions given in the question.

1. If 10^{10} electrons are transferred from a body per second, then how much time is required to transfer 1C charge?

(a) About 198 yr
(b) About 19.8 yr
(c) About 198 days
(d) About 19.8 days

2. Consider a point mass M is surrounded by a sphere of radius R.
Gravitational flux through the sphere is

(a) $-4\pi GM$ (b) $4\pi GM$
(c) GM (d) $-GM$

3. Six charges, each equal to $+q$, are placed at the corner of a regular hexagon of side a. The electric field at the point of intersection of diagonals is

(a) zero (b) $\frac{1}{4\pi\varepsilon_0}\cdot\frac{q}{a^2}$
(c) $\frac{1}{4\pi\varepsilon_0}\cdot\frac{6q}{a}$ (d) $\frac{1}{4\pi\varepsilon_0}\cdot\frac{\sqrt{3}q}{2a}$

4. Two point charges Q and $4Q$ are held at a separation R. The electric field due to them is zero at a distance

(a) $\frac{R}{\sqrt{3}}$ from charge $4Q$
(b) $\frac{R}{3}$ from charge $4Q$
(c) $\frac{2R}{\sqrt{3}}$ from charge $4Q$
(d) $\frac{2R}{3}$ from charge $4Q$

5. What is the nature of Gaussian surface involved in Gauss's law of electrostatics?

(a) Scalar (b) Electrical
(c) Magnetic (d) Vector

6. Two infinite plane parallel sheets are separated by a distance K. Both plates have equal charge density σ. Electric field at a point between the sheet is

(a) zero

(b) $\frac{\sigma}{\varepsilon_0}$

(c) $\frac{\sigma}{2\varepsilon_0}$

(d) Depends upon the location of the point

7. **Assertion** (A) With the help of Gauss's theorem, we can find electric field at any point.

Reason (R) Gauss's theorem can be applied for any type of charge distribution.

In the light of above statements, choose the most appropriate answer from the options given below.

(a) Both A and R are true and R is the correct explanation of A.

(b) Both A and R are true but R is not the correct explanation of A.

(c) A is true but R is false.

(d) A is false but R is true.

8. A thin conducting ring of radius R is given a charge $+Q$. The electric field at the centre O of the ring due to the charge on the part AKB of the ring is E. The electric field at the centre due to the charge on the part $ACDB$ of the ring is

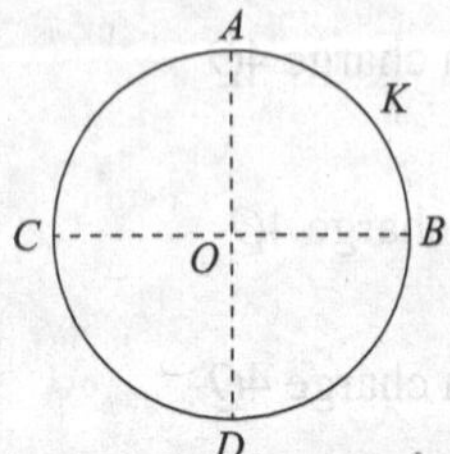

(a) E along KO (b) $3E$ along OK

(c) $3E$ along KO (d) E along OK

9. A point charge q is placed at a distance $x/2$ directly above the centre of a cube of side x. The flux through the cube is

(a) q/ε_0 (b) $q/2\varepsilon_0$

(c) $\frac{q}{4\varepsilon_0}$ (d) q/ε_0

10. A Gaussian surface in the cylinder of cross-sectional area πa^2 and length L is immersed in a uniform electric field **E** with the cylinder axis parallel to the field. The flux ϕ of the electric field through the closed surface is

(a) $2\pi a^2 \mathbf{E}$ (b) $\pi a^2 \mathbf{E} L$

(c) $\pi a^2 (2+L)\mathbf{E}$ (d) zero

11. An electron moves a distance of 3.2 m when accelerated from rest by an electric field of strength 9×10^4 NC^{-1}. The time of travel, when mass of electron and charge of electron are 9×10^{-31} kg and 1.6×10^{-19} C respectively, is

(a) 2×10^{-8} s (b) 4×10^{-8} s

(c) 2×10^{-6} s (d) 4×10^{-6} s

12. The intensity of electric field required to balance a helium nucleus of mass 6.64×10^{-27} kg and charge two times of proton is nearly

(a) 20.3×10^{-8} V/m

(b) 10.3×10^{-8} V/m

(c) 10.3×10^{-7} V/m

(d) 20.3×10^{-7} V/m

13. Two parallel infinite line charges with linear charge density $+10^{-2}$ C/m and -10^{-2} C/m are placed at a distance of 2 m in free space. The electric field mid-way between the two line charges is

(a) 4.5×10^7 N/C (b) 9×10^9 N/C

(c) 36×10^7 N/C (d) 4.5×10^9 N/C

14. Two point electric charges q and $2q$ are separated by distance 2 m in air. You need to place a third charge Q along the same line in such a way that the net force acting on q and $2q$ is zero. The position of charge Q is

(a) $\frac{2}{\sqrt{2}-1}$ (b) $\frac{2}{\sqrt{2}+1}$

(c) $\frac{2}{\sqrt{3}+1}$ (d) $\frac{2}{\sqrt{3}-1}$

15. A wooden block performs SHM on a frictionless surface with frequency ν_0. The block carries a charge $+Q$ on its surface. If now a uniform electric field **E** is switched ON as shown, then SHM of the block will be

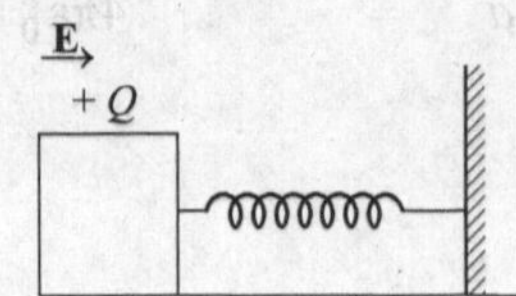

(a) of the same frequency and with shifted mean position
(b) of the same frequency and with the same mean position
(c) of changed frequency and with shifted mean position
(d) of changed frequency and with the same mean position

16. **Statement I** Surface charge density is equal to charge per unit area.
Statement II The surface charge densities of two spherical conductors of different radii are equal. Then, the electric field intensities near their surfaces are also equal.
In the light of above statements, choose the most appropriate answer from the options given below.
(a) Both Statement I and Statement II are true.
(b) Both Statement I and Statement II are false.
(c) Statement I is true but Statement II is false.
(d) Statement I is false but Statement II is true.

17. A particle of mass m and charge $+q$ is located mid-way between two fixed charged particles, each having a charge $+q$ and at a distance $2L$ apart. The middle charge is displaced slightly along the line joining the fixed charges and released. The time period of oscillation is proportional to
(a) $L^{1/2}$ (b) L (c) $L^{3/2}$ d) L^2

18. There is uniform electric field of strength 10^3Vm^{-1} along the Y-axis. A body of mass 1 g and charge 10^{-6}C is projected into the field from the origin along the positive X-axis with a velocity of 10 ms^{-1}. Its speed (in ms^{-1}) after 10 s will be (neglect gravitation)
(a) 10 (b) $5\sqrt{2}$
(c) $10\sqrt{2}$ (d) 20

19. A metallic spherical shell of radius R has a charge $-Q$ distributed uniformly on it. A point charge $+Q$ is placed at the centre of the shell. Which graph shown in figure represents the variation of electric field E with distance r from the centre of the shell?

(a) 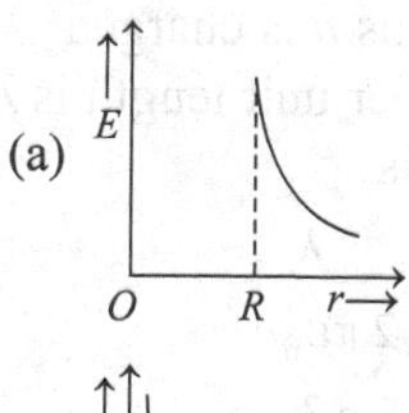

(b) 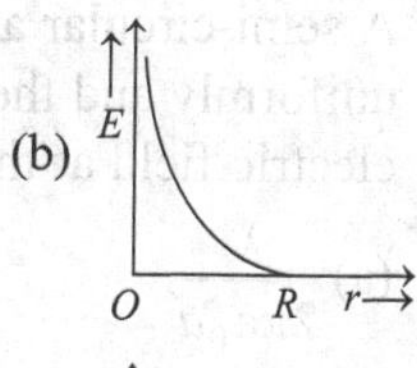

(c) 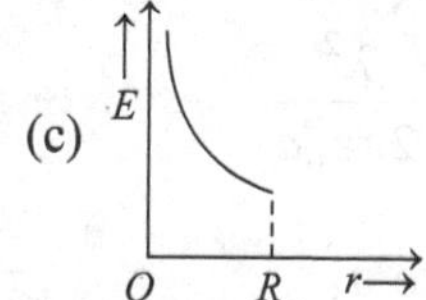

(d) 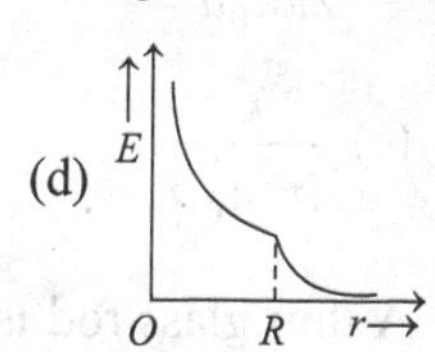

20. Two point charges $q_1 = 2\,\mu\text{C}$ and $q_2 = 1\,\mu\text{C}$ are placed at distances $b = 1$ cm and $a = 2$ cm from the origin on the Y and X-axes as shown in figure. The electric field vector at point $P(a, b)$ will subtend an angle θ with the X-axis given by

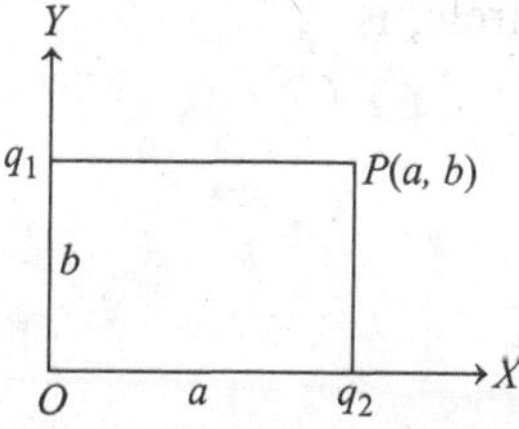

(a) $\tan\theta = 1$ (b) $\tan\theta = 2$
(c) $\tan\theta = 3$ (d) $\tan\theta = 4$

21. A sphere of radius R carries charge density proportional to the square of the distance from the centre given as $\rho = Ar^2$, where A is a positive constant. At a distance of $R/2$ from the centre, the magnitude of the electric field is
(a) $A/4\varepsilon_0$ (b) $AR^3/40\varepsilon_0$
(c) $AR^3/24\varepsilon_0$ (d) $AR^3/5\varepsilon_0$

22. Two equal negative charges $-q$ are fixed at points $(0, a)$ and $(0, -a)$ on the Y-axis. A positive charge Q is released from rest at a point $(2a, 0)$ on the X-axis. The charge Q will
(a) execute simple harmonic motion about the origin
(b) move to the origin and remain at rest there
(c) move to infinity
(d) execute oscillatory but not simple harmonic motion

23. A semi-circular arc of radius a is charged uniformly and the charge per unit length is λ. The electric field at the centre is

(a) $\frac{\lambda}{2\pi\varepsilon_0 a}$ (b) $\frac{\lambda}{2\pi\varepsilon_0 a^2}$

(c) $\frac{\lambda}{4\pi^2\varepsilon_0 a}$ (d) $\frac{\lambda^2}{2\pi\varepsilon_0 a}$

24. A thin glass rod is bent into a semi-circle of radius r. A charge $+Q$ is uniformly distributed along the upper half and a charge $-Q$ is uniformly distributed along the lower half as shown in figure. The electric field E at P, the centre of the semi-circle, is

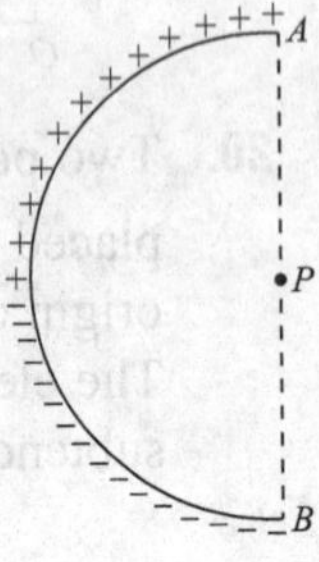

(a) $\frac{Q}{\pi^2\varepsilon_0 r^2}$

(b) $\frac{2Q}{\pi^2\varepsilon_0 r^2}$

(c) $\frac{4Q}{\pi^2\varepsilon_0 r^2}$

(d) $\frac{Q}{4\pi^2\varepsilon_0 r^2}$

25. Four charges Q_1, Q_2, Q_3 and Q_4 of same magnitude are fixed along the X-axis at $x = -2a$, $-a, +a$ and $+2a$ respectively. A positive charge q is placed on the positive Y-axis at a distance $b > 0$. Four options of the signs of these charges are given in List-I.

The direction of the forces on the charge q is given in List-II. Match List-I with List-II and select the correct answer using the codes given below the lists.

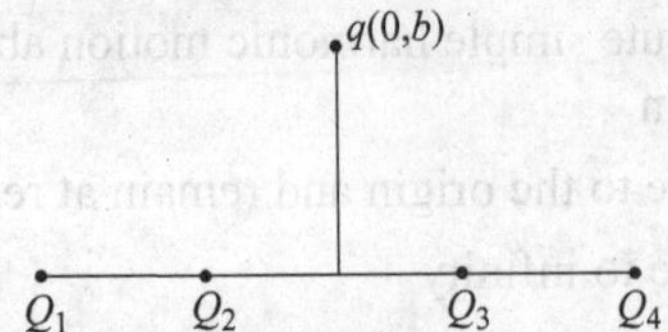

	List-I		List-II
A.	Q_1, Q_2, Q_3, Q_4 all positive	1.	$+x$ direction
B.	Q_1, Q_2 positive; Q_3, Q_4 negative	2.	$-x$ direction
C.	Q_1, Q_4 positive; Q_2, Q_3 negative	3.	$+y$ direction
D.	Q_1, Q_3 positive; Q_2, Q_4 negative	4.	$-y$ direction

Codes

	A	B	C	D
(a)	3	1	4	2
(b)	4	2	3	1
(c)	3	1	2	4
(d)	4	2	1	3

26. The electric field in a region is given by $\mathbf{E} = \frac{E_0}{a} x\, \hat{\mathbf{i}}$. The electric flux passing through a cubical volume bounded by the surfaces $x = 0, x = a, y = 0, y = a, z = 0$ and $z = a$ is

(a) $E_0 a^2$

(b) $-E_0 a^2$

(c) $2E_0 a^2$

(d) $-2E_0 a^2$

27. Two infinite long conducting charged sheets are placed parallel to each other and perpendicular to the plane of paper as shown in the following figure. The electric field at point P will

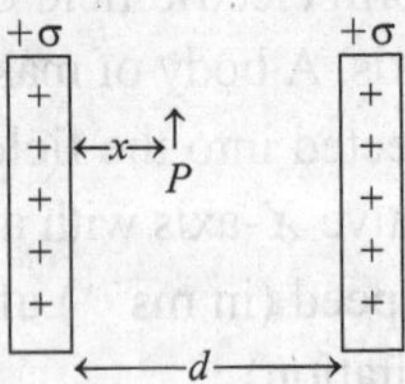

(a) depend only on x and σ

(b) depend on x, σ and d

(c) depend only on σ

(d) not depend on x, σ and d

28. A given charge is situated at a certain distance from an electric dipole in the end-on-position, experiences a force 80×10^{-3} N. If the distance of the charge is doubled, the force acting on the charge is

(a) 160×10^{-3}N

(b) 40×10^{-3} N

(c) 20×10^{-3} N

(d) 10×10^{-3} N

29. Two charges 4.1×10^{-19}C and -4.1×10^{-19}C are placed at 3.2 Å apart to form an electric dipole are placed in a uniform electric field of intensity 5×10^{5} V/m. The electric dipole moment is

(a) 15.36×10^{-29} C-m

(b) 7.68×10^{-19} C-m

(c) 2.62×10^{-28} C-m

(d) 2.62×10^{-19} C-m

30. Two short dipoles $\frac{p}{2}\hat{\mathbf{k}}$ and $\frac{p}{3}\hat{\mathbf{k}}$ are located at (0, 0, 0) and (2 m, 0, 0) respectively. The resultant electric field due to the two dipoles at the point (1 m, 0, 0) is

(a) $\frac{9}{32}\frac{p}{\pi\varepsilon_0}\hat{\mathbf{k}}$

(b) $\frac{5p}{24\pi\varepsilon_0}\hat{\mathbf{k}}$

(c) $\frac{7}{32}\frac{p}{\pi\varepsilon_0}\hat{\mathbf{k}}$

(d) $\frac{-7p}{32\pi\varepsilon_0}\hat{\mathbf{k}}$

Response Index

01 ⓐ ⓑ ⓒ ⓓ	14 ⓐ ⓑ ⓒ ⓓ	27 ⓐ ⓑ ⓒ ⓓ
02 ⓐ ⓑ ⓒ ⓓ	15 ⓐ ⓑ ⓒ ⓓ	28 ⓐ ⓑ ⓒ ⓓ
03 ⓐ ⓑ ⓒ ⓓ	16 ⓐ ⓑ ⓒ ⓓ	29 ⓐ ⓑ ⓒ ⓓ
04 ⓐ ⓑ ⓒ ⓓ	17 ⓐ ⓑ ⓒ ⓓ	30 ⓐ ⓑ ⓒ ⓓ
05 ⓐ ⓑ ⓒ ⓓ	18 ⓐ ⓑ ⓒ ⓓ	
06 ⓐ ⓑ ⓒ ⓓ	19 ⓐ ⓑ ⓒ ⓓ	
07 ⓐ ⓑ ⓒ ⓓ	20 ⓐ ⓑ ⓒ ⓓ	
08 ⓐ ⓑ ⓒ ⓓ	21 ⓐ ⓑ ⓒ ⓓ	
09 ⓐ ⓑ ⓒ ⓓ	22 ⓐ ⓑ ⓒ ⓓ	
10 ⓐ ⓑ ⓒ ⓓ	23 ⓐ ⓑ ⓒ ⓓ	
11 ⓐ ⓑ ⓒ ⓓ	24 ⓐ ⓑ ⓒ ⓓ	
12 ⓐ ⓑ ⓒ ⓓ	25 ⓐ ⓑ ⓒ ⓓ	
13 ⓐ ⓑ ⓒ ⓓ	26 ⓐ ⓑ ⓒ ⓓ	

Performance Scanner

> 90% Excellent !	You have mastered this chapter. The concepts of this chapter are on your fingertips. Move on to the next chapter and maintain this momentum.
76-90% Very Good !	You have a good command over this chapter. Revise the chapter again after a few days and enhance your performance.
60-75% Good !	You have a wide scope to learn for this chapter. Revise this chapter again.
<60% Not Satisfactory!	You have a long way ahead of you to master this chapter. Revise it thoroughly.

For Online Chapter Test **Scan the QR Code**

Space for Rough Work

Test Booklet No. **3947152**

Test Booklet Code **CH2**

MEDACE
NEET (UG)
SELF ASSESSMENT KIT

Electrostatic Potential

Topics Covered

Electrostatic Potential and its Applications

Electric Potential Energy

Important Instructions

- This Booklet Contains – Two Topic Tests and One Test on Complete Chapter.
- Each question carries 4 marks.
- For each correct response, the candidate will get 4 marks and for every incorrect response 1 mark will be additionally deducted from the total score.
- Use **Blue/Black** point pen only for filling the OMR.
- Rough work will be done in the space provided for this purpose within the test booklet only.

Name of the Candidate (In Capitals) ______________________

Candidate's Signature ______________

Invigilator's Signature ______________

Facsimile signature stamp of center superintendent______________

Do not open this Booklet until you start attempting the Test

Topical Follow Thru

Test 1

Syllabus

- Electric Potential and its Calculation for a Point Charge
- Electric Dipole and System of Charges
- Potential Difference
- Equipotential Surfaces

For deeper insight **Scan the QR Code**

Important Instructions

- The test is of 45 minutes duration and contains 25 Multiple Choice Questions. (Four options with a single correct answer).
- Choose the correct option and fill the OMR given on the last page of this test accordingly.
- At some instances, you may find more than 1 option may be correct, in such circumstances you have to judge the most appropriate answer as per the conditions given in the question.

1. Consider the following figure.

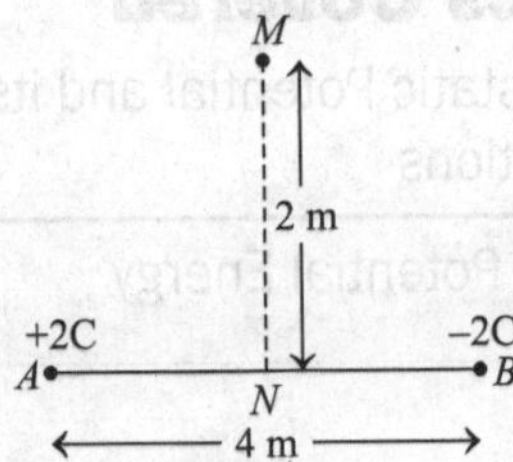

N is the mid-point of line joining the two charges +2C and −2C. The potential at point M is

(a) 12.72×10^9 V

(b) 0

(c) 6.36×10^9 V

(d) 3.18×10^9 V

2. Two spheres of radii 4 cm and 16 cm are charged to the same potential. The ratio of charges on the spheres is

(a) 1 : 2 (b) 1 : 4

(c) 1 : 16 (d) 1 : 64

3. A conducting solid sphere having a charge Q is surrounded by an uncharged concentric conducting hollow spherical shell. You can assume the potential difference between the surface of the solid sphere and that of the outer surface of hollow shell be V. If the shell is given a charge $-7Q$, then the new potential difference between the same two surfaces will be

(a) $\frac{Q}{4\pi\varepsilon_0}\left(\frac{1}{r_2}-\frac{1}{r_1}\right)$ (b) $\frac{Q}{4\pi\varepsilon_0}\left(\frac{1}{r_1}-\frac{1}{r_2}\right)$

(c) $\frac{Q}{4\pi\varepsilon_0}\left(\frac{r}{r_1}-\frac{1}{r_2}\right)$ (d) $\frac{Q}{4\pi\varepsilon_0}\left(\frac{1}{r_1^2}-\frac{1}{r_2^2}\right)$

4. P, Q, R and S are the four points in a uniform electric field as shown in figure given below. The electric potential will be

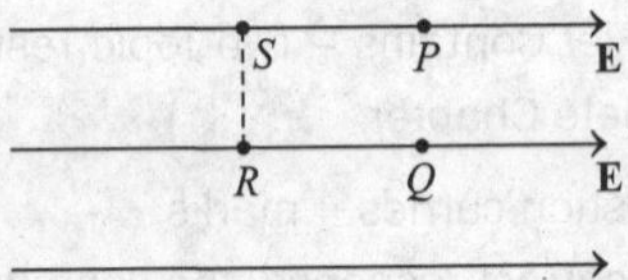

(a) maximum at P

(b) maximum at Q

(c) maximum at SR

(d) maximum at SP

5. A particle M has charge $+q$ and particle N has charge $+4q$ with each of them having the same mass m. When allowed to fall from rest through the same electric potential difference, the ratio of their speeds $\frac{v_N}{v_M}$ will become

(a) 1 : 2

(b) 2 : 1

(c) 1 : 4

(d) 4 : 1

6. A positive charge Q is placed as shown in the figure. Another charge q is moved from R to P by an external force. Work done by external force in this process is

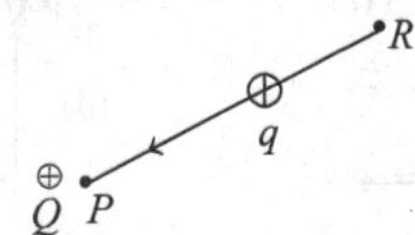

(a) $-\int_R^P \mathbf{F}_E \cdot d\mathbf{r}$ (b) $\int_R^P \mathbf{F}_E \cdot d\mathbf{r}$

(c) $\int_R^P 2\mathbf{F}_E \cdot d\mathbf{r}$ (d) $\int_R^P \frac{\mathbf{F}_E}{2} \cdot d\mathbf{r}$

7. Statement I Electric lines of force always flow from higher potential to lower potential.

Statement II Electric potential is a vector quantity.

In the light of above statements, choose the most appropriate answer from the options given below.

(a) Both Statement I and Statement II are incorrect.

(b) Both Statement I and Statement II are correct.

(c) Statement I is correct but Statement II is incorrect.

(d) Statement I is incorrect but Statement II is correct.

8. What is the work done in moving a 2 μC point charge from corner P to corner O of a square $MNOP$ as given in figure, when a 20 μC charge exists at the centre of the square?

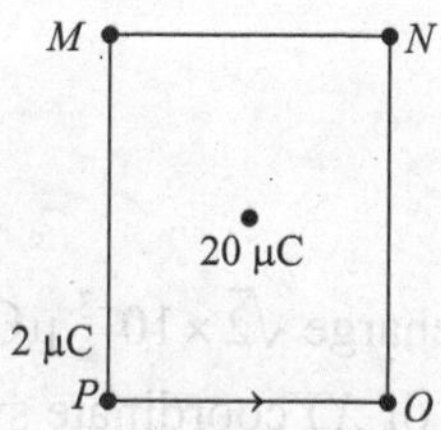

(a) 0 (b) 5 J

(c) 2 J (d) 20 J

9. A region of space have electric field $\mathbf{E} = (2x\hat{\mathbf{i}} + 4y\hat{\mathbf{j}}) \times 10^6$ N/C, where x and y are in metres. A 1 μC charged particle is moved from origin to coordinates (4 m, 6 m) first along the Y-axis and then along the X-axis. The work done by the electric field is

(a) – 88 J (b) + 88 J

(c) 72 J (d) 16 J

10. The electric potential at a point (x, y, z) is given by $V = -x^2y^3 - xz^3 + 4$. The electric field $\mathbf{E}$ at that point is

(a) $\mathbf{E} = \hat{\mathbf{i}}(2xy^3 + z^3) + \hat{\mathbf{j}}(3x^2y^2) + \hat{\mathbf{k}}(3xz^2)$

(b) $\mathbf{E} = \hat{\mathbf{i}}\,2xy + \hat{\mathbf{j}}(x^2 + y^2) + \hat{\mathbf{k}}(3xz - y^2)$

(c) $\mathbf{E} = \hat{\mathbf{i}}\,z^3 + \hat{\mathbf{j}}\,xyz + \hat{\mathbf{k}}z^2$

(d) $\mathbf{E} = \hat{\mathbf{i}}\,(2xy - z^3) + \hat{\mathbf{j}}\,xy^2 + \hat{\mathbf{k}}\,3z^2x$

11. A solid conducting sphere, having a charge Q is surrounded by an uncharged conducting hollow spherical shell. Let the potential difference between the surface of the solid sphere and that of the outer surface of the hollow shell be V. If the shell is now given a charge of $16Q$, then new potential difference between the same two surfaces is

(a) $4V$ (b) V (c) $2V$ (d) $-2V$

12. A point dipole $\mathbf{p} = 3p_0\,\hat{\mathbf{x}}$ is kept at the origin. The potential and electric field due to this dipole on the Y-axis at a distance d respectively, are (Take $V = 0$ at infinity)

(a) $0, \frac{-\mathbf{p}}{4\pi\varepsilon_0 d^3}$ (b) $\frac{|\mathbf{p}|}{4\pi\varepsilon_0 d^2}, \frac{\mathbf{p}}{4\pi\varepsilon_0 d^2}$

(c) $0, \frac{\mathbf{p}}{4\pi\varepsilon_0 d^3}$ (d) $\frac{|\mathbf{p}|}{4\pi\varepsilon_0 d^2}, \frac{-\mathbf{p}}{4\pi\varepsilon_0 d^3}$

13. Assertion (A) Two concentric charged shells are given. The potential difference between the shells depends on charge of inner shell.

Reason (R) Potential due to charge of outer shell remains same at every point inside the sphere.

In the light of above statements, choose the most appropriate answer from the options given below.

(a) Both A and R are true and R is the correct explanation of A.

(b) Both A and R are true but R is not the correct explanation of A.

(c) A is true but R is false.

(d) A is false but R is true.

14. Consider thin spherical insulating shell having radius R carries a uniformly distributed charge q. Its potential at its surface is V_0. Now, charge Q is placed at centre of the shell. The electrostatic potential at a distance $\frac{2R}{3}$ from the centre of the shell is

(a) $V_0\left(\frac{3}{2}\frac{Q}{q}+1\right)$

(b) $\frac{4}{3}V_0\left(\frac{Q}{2}+q\right)$

(c) $\frac{2V_0}{3}(Q+2q)$

(d) $\frac{3}{2}V_0\left(q+\frac{Q}{3}\right)$

15. There is a uniform electrostatic field in a region. The potential at various points on a small sphere centred at P, in the region, is found to vary between the limits 600 V to 600.8 V. What is the potential at a point on the sphere whose radius vector makes an angle of 60° with the direction of the field?

(a) 600.2 (b) 600.6
(c) 600.5 (d) 600.4

16. An electric field $\mathbf{E}=-(60\,\hat{\mathbf{i}}+60\,\hat{\mathbf{j}})\ \text{NC}^{-1}$ exists in a region of space. If the potential at the origin is taken to be zero, then the potential at $x=0$ m, $y=2$ m is

(a) −130 V (b) −120 V
(c) −240 V (d) −110 V

17. Assume that an electric field $\mathbf{E}=30y^2\,\hat{\mathbf{i}}$ exists in space. Then, the potential difference V_A-V_O where V_O is the potential at the origin and V_A the potential at (2, 2) is

(a) 80 V (b) 120 V
(c) −120 V (d) −240 V

18. Consider a thin spherical shell of radius R with its centre at the origin, carrying uniform positive surface charge density. The variation of the magnitude of the electric $E(r)$ field and the electric potential $V(r)$ with the distance r from the centre, is best represented by which graph?

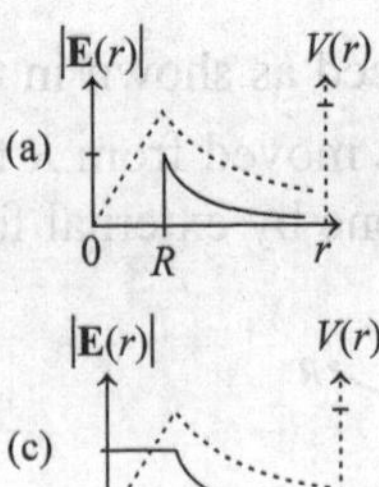

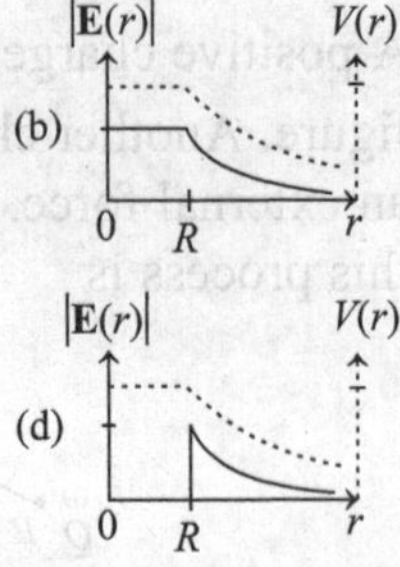

19. The potential at a point x (measured in μm) due to some charges situated on the X-axis is given by $V(x)=30/(x^2-6)\cdot$V.

The electric field E at $x=4\,\mu$m is given by

(a) $\frac{24}{10}$ V/μm and in the +ve x-direction

(b) (5/3) V/μm and in the −ve x-direction

(c) (5/3) V/μm and in the +ve x-direction

(d) $\frac{24}{10}$ V/μm in the −ve x-direction

20. Two thin wire rings each having a radius 3 cm placed at a distance 4 cm apart with their axes coinciding. The charges on the two rings are $+Q$ and $-Q$. The potential difference between the centres of the two rings is

(a) zero

(b) $\frac{Q}{15\pi\varepsilon_0}$

(c) $\frac{2Q}{3\pi\varepsilon_0}$

(d) $\frac{Q}{5\pi\varepsilon_0}$

21. An electric charge $\sqrt{2}\times10^{-3}\ \mu$C is placed at the origin (0, 0) of XY coordinate system. Two points A and B are situated at (2 m, 2 m) and (0, 2m), respectively. The potential difference between the points A and B will be

(a) $\frac{k}{2}\times10^{-9}(1-\sqrt{2})$ V

(b) $\frac{k\sqrt{2}}{2}(1+\sqrt{2})$ V

(c) zero

(d) $3k\left[1+\frac{\sqrt{2}}{3}\right]$ V

22. Charges are placed on the vertices of a square as shown below. Let **E** be the electric field and V the potential at the centre. If the charges on A and B are interchanged with those on C and D respectively, then

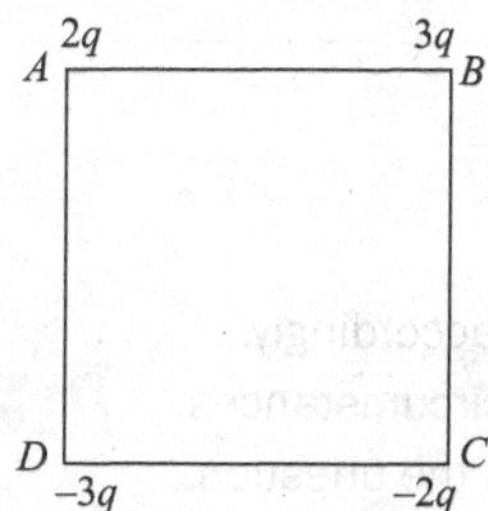

(a) **E** changes, V remains unchanged

(b) **E** remains unchanged, V changes

(c) both **E** and V change

(d) **E** and V remain unchanged

23. Eight liquid drops are combined to form a single liquid drop. Potential of this drop is 20 V. The potential of each single drop was

(a) 10 V (b) 20 V

(c) 5 V (d) 8 V

24. Two point charges $9\,\mu C$ and $16\,\mu C$ are placed 1 m apart in vacuum. The electric potential between the two charges is minimum at a distance of

(a) $\frac{2}{7}$ m from $9\,\mu C$

(b) $\frac{3}{7}$ m from $9\,\mu C$

(c) $\frac{4}{7}$ from $9\,\mu C$

(d) $\frac{3}{7}$ from $16\,\mu C$

25. Ratio of electric potential due to given dipole at points A and B is
(Given, $OA = OB$; $q = 2\,\mu C$ and $d = 2\,Å$)

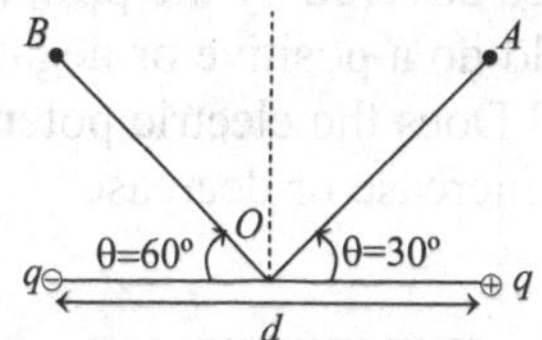

(a) 1.42 (b) 1.58 (c) 1.73 (d) 1

Response Index

01	a	b	c	d	10	a	b	c	d	19	a	b	c	d
02	a	b	c	d	11	a	b	c	d	20	a	b	c	d
03	a	b	c	d	12	a	b	c	d	21	a	b	c	d
04	a	b	c	d	13	a	b	c	d	22	a	b	c	d
05	a	b	c	d	14	a	b	c	d	23	a	b	c	d
06	a	b	c	d	15	a	b	c	d	24	a	b	c	d
07	a	b	c	d	16	a	b	c	d	25	a	b	c	d
08	a	b	c	d	17	a	b	c	d					
09	a	b	c	d	18	a	b	c	d					

Performance Scanner

> 90% Excellent !	You have mastered these topics. The concepts of these topics are on your fingertips. Move on to the next test and maintain this momentum.
76-90% Very Good !	You have a good command over these topics. Revise these topics again after a few days and enhance your performance.
60-75% Good !	You have a wide scope to learn for these topics. Revise them again.
<60% Not Satisfactory!	You have a long way ahead of you to master these topics. Revise them thoroughly.

Test 2

Syllabus

- Electric Potential Energy of a System of Two point Charges
- Potential Energy of Electric Dipole in an Electrostatic Field
- Conductors and Insulators
- Dielectrics and Electric Polarisation

For deeper insight **Scan the QR Code**

Important Instructions

- The test is of 30 minutes duration and contains 15 Multiple Choice Questions. (Four options with a single correct answer).
- Choose the correct option and fill the OMR given on the last page of this test accordingly.
- At some instances, you may find more than 1 option may be correct, in such circumstances you have to judge the most appropriate answer as per the conditions given in the question.

1. A proton is moving in a constant electric field. The distance covered by the proton is d. Does the electric field do a positive or negative work on the proton? Does the electric potential energy of the proton increase or decrease?

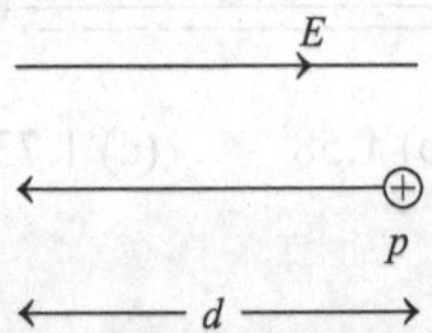

(a) Negative, Increases
(b) Positive, Decreases
(c) Negative, Decreases
(d) Positive, Increases

2. Assertion (A) Electric potential and electric potential energy are different quantities.
Reason (R) For a system of positive test charge and point charge, electric potential energy = electric potential.

In the light of the above statements, choose the most appropriate answer from the options given below.

(a) Both A and R are true and R is the correct explanation of A.
(b) Both A and R are true but R is not the correct expalanation of A.
(c) A is true but R is false.
(d) A is false but R is true.

3. Two free protons are kept at a distance of 1Å and released, then the kinetic energy of each proton at infinite separation is

(a) 5.6×10^{-12} J
(b) 11.5×10^{-19} J
(c) 23×10^{-19} J
(d) 46×10^{-19} J

4. The electric field strength at a distance r from the centre of a positively charged sphere of radius r is E. If $r > R$, work done in bringing a test charge q_0 from r to infinity, is

(a) q_0RE
(b) $\frac{1}{2}q_0RE$
(c) $-q_0rE$
(d) $-\frac{1}{2}q_0rE$

5. Vertices of an equilateral triangle is occupied by three equal charges of magnitude Q. What should be the value of a charge, that when placed at the centroid, reduces the interaction energy of the system to zero?

(a) $\frac{-Q}{6}$
(b) $\frac{-Q}{3}$
(c) $\frac{-Q\varepsilon_0}{2\sqrt{3}}$
(d) $\frac{-Q}{\sqrt{3}}$

6. An electric dipole made up of positive and negative charges each of 3.5 μC and placed at a distance 4.2 cm apart, is placed in an electric field of 5.87×10^5 NC^{-1}. What will be the maximum torque which the field can exert on the dipole? Also, obtain the work that must be done to turn the dipole from 0° to 180°.

(a) 86.289×10^{-3} Nm^{-1}, 1.72×10^{-1} J
(b) 75.26×10^{-3} Nm^{-1}, 1.72×10^{-1} J
(c) 86.289×10^{-3} Nm^{-1}, 3.72×10^{-3} J
(d) 55.26×10^{-3} Nm^{-1}, 1.72×10^{-3} J

7. Three corners of an isosceles triangle is occupied by three charges $Q, +q$ and $+q$ as shown in the figure. The net electrostatic energy of the configuration is zero, if the value of Q is

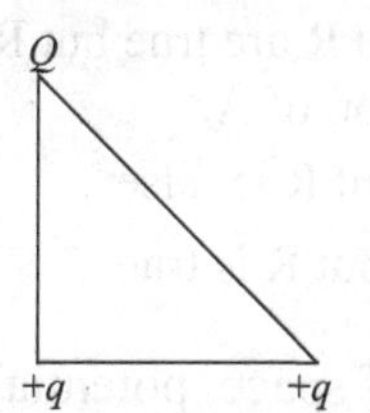

(a) $-2q$ (b) $\frac{2q}{1+\sqrt{2}}$

(c) $+q$ (d) $\frac{-\sqrt{2}q}{\sqrt{2}+1}$

8. Electric dipole moment of a molecule is 10^{-29} C-m. A mole of this substance is polarised (at low temperature) by applying a strong electrostatic field of magnitude 10^6 Vm^{-1}. The direction of the field is suddenly changed from an angle of 60° to 0°. Estimate the heat released from the substance in aligning its dipoles along the new direction of the field.

(a) -3 J (b) 3 J

(c) -9 J (d) 9 J

9. Two identical electric point dipoles have dipole moments $\mathbf{p}_1 = p\hat{\mathbf{i}}$, and $\mathbf{p}_2 = -p\hat{\mathbf{i}}$ and are held on the X-axis at distance a from each other. When released, they move along the X-axis with the direction of their dipole moments remaining unchanged. If the mass of each dipole is m, their speed when they are infinitely far apart is

(a) $\frac{\mathbf{p}}{a}\sqrt{\frac{1}{\pi\varepsilon_0 ma}}$ (b) $\frac{\mathbf{p}}{a}\sqrt{\frac{1}{2\pi\varepsilon_0 ma}}$

(c) $\frac{\mathbf{p}}{a}\sqrt{\frac{2}{\pi\varepsilon_0 ma}}$ (d) $\frac{\mathbf{p}}{a}\sqrt{\frac{3}{2\pi\varepsilon_0 ma}}$

10. A system of three charges are placed as shown in the figure. If $D >> d$, the potential energy of the system is best given by

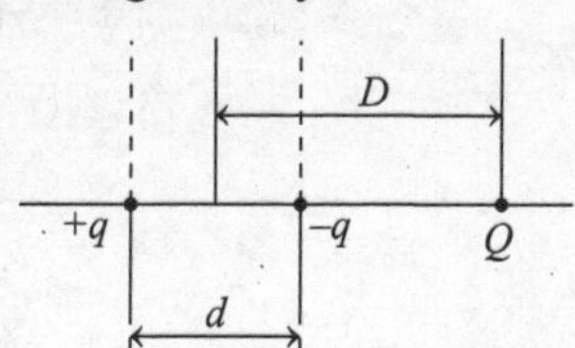

(a) $\frac{1}{4\pi\varepsilon_0}\left[\frac{q^2}{d} - \frac{qQd}{D^2}\right]$

(b) $\frac{1}{4\pi\varepsilon_0}\left[+\frac{q^2}{d} - \frac{qQd}{D^2}\right]$

(c) $\frac{1}{4\pi\varepsilon_0}\left[-\frac{q^2}{d} - \frac{qQd}{2D^2}\right]$

(d) $\frac{1}{4\pi\varepsilon_0}\left[-\frac{q^2}{d} - \frac{2qQd}{D^2}\right]$

11. Statement I A point charge is placed in a uniform field pointing North. There is no change in potential energy of charge when it is moved along East-West.

Statement II Electric field of a point charge is non-uniform.

In the light of the above statements, choose the most appropriate answer from the options given below.

(a) Both Statement I and Statement II are correct.

(b) Both Statements I and Statement II are correct.

(c) Statement I is correct but Statement II is incorrect.

(d) Statement I is incorrect but Statement II is correct.

12. Match the List I with List II and choose the correct option given below.

	List I		List II
A.	Distance between two positive point charges increases	1	PE does not change; $\Delta U = 0$
B.	Distance between two positive point charges decreases	2	PE change; $\Delta U =$–ve
C.	A point charge is moved perpendicular to electric field lines	3	PE change; $\Delta U =$+ve
D.	If reference point of zero PE of changed	4	ΔU remains same

(a) A→2, B→3, C→1, D→4

(b) A→1, B→2, C→3, D→4

(c) A→2, B→1, C→3, D→4

(d) A→3, B→2, C→4, D→1

13. A charge Q is uniformly distributed over a spherical volume of radius R. Expression for energy of system is

(a) $\dfrac{4\pi Q^2 R^5}{15\varepsilon_0}$

(b) $\dfrac{4\pi Q^2 R^5}{3\varepsilon_0}$

(c) $\dfrac{3}{5}\cdot\dfrac{1}{4\pi\varepsilon_0}\left(\dfrac{Q^2}{R}\right)$

(d) $\dfrac{4}{3}\cdot\dfrac{1}{4\pi\varepsilon_0}\left(\dfrac{Q^2}{R}\right)$

14. Assertion (A) If a positive charge comes close to a negative charge, then the potential energy of the system increases.
Reason (R) The potential energy of system of two charges is inversely proportional to the separation between two charges.

In the light of above statements, choose the most appropriate answer from the options given below.

(a) Both A and R are true and R is the correct explanation of A.

(b) Both A and R are true but R is not the correct expalanation of A.

(c) A is true but R is false.

(d) A is false but R is true.

15. In a region of space, potential is given by $V=\left(2\dfrac{\text{V}}{\text{m}^2}\right)x^2$. A dipole of charge 2×10^{-6}C and length 3Å is placed in this region. The net force acting on the dipole when the dipole is placed along the X-axis is

(a) 24×10^{-14} N

(b) 24×10^{-10} N

(c) 24×10^{-16} N

(d) 24×10^{-15} N

Response Index

01	ⓐ	ⓑ	ⓒ	ⓓ	11	ⓐ	ⓑ	ⓒ	ⓓ
02	ⓐ	ⓑ	ⓒ	ⓓ	12	ⓐ	ⓑ	ⓒ	ⓓ
03	ⓐ	ⓑ	ⓒ	ⓓ	13	ⓐ	ⓑ	ⓒ	ⓓ
04	ⓐ	ⓑ	ⓒ	ⓓ	14	ⓐ	ⓑ	ⓒ	ⓓ
05	ⓐ	ⓑ	ⓒ	ⓓ	15	ⓐ	ⓑ	ⓒ	ⓓ
06	ⓐ	ⓑ	ⓒ	ⓓ					
07	ⓐ	ⓑ	ⓒ	ⓓ					
08	ⓐ	ⓑ	ⓒ	ⓓ					
09	ⓐ	ⓑ	ⓒ	ⓓ					
10	ⓐ	ⓑ	ⓒ	ⓓ					

Performance Scanner

> 90% Excellent !	You have mastered these topics. The concepts of these topics are at your fingertips. Move on to the next test and maintain this momentum.
76-90% Very Good !	You have a good command over these topics. Revise them again after a few days and enhance your performance.
60-75% Good !	You have a wide scope to learn for these topics. Revise them again.
<60% Not Satisfactory!	You have a long way ahead of you to master in these topics. Revise them thoroughly.

Chapter Break Thru

Syllabus

- Electric Potential and its Calculation for a Point Charge
- Electric Dipole and System of Charges
- Potential Difference
- Equipotential Surfaces
- Electric Potential Energy of a System of Two Point Charges
- Potential Energy of Electric Dipole in an Electrostatic Field
- Conductors and Insulators
- Dielectrics and Electric Polarisation

Important Instructions

- The test is of 45 minutes duration and contains 30 Multiple Choice Questions (Four options with a single correct answer).
- Choose the correct option and fill the OMR given on the last page of this test accordingly.
- At some instances, you may find more than 1 option may be correct, in such circumstances you have to judge the most appropriate answer as per conditions given in the question.

1. Two charges $+6.4\times10^{-19}$ C and -6.4×10^{-19} C kept at -1.4 Å apart to form a dipole. If it is kept in uniform electric field of intensity 8×10^{5} V/m, then what will be the electrical energy in equilibrium?

(a) $+1.43\times10^{-22}$ J (b) -1.43×10^{-22} J

(c) 7.1×10^{-23} J (d) -7.1×10^{-23} J

2. A thin conducting shell of radius 2 m has a charge 10 μC. Another charge 2 μC is placed at the centre of the shell. The electrostatic potential at a point M, a distance 1 m from the centre of the shell is

(a) 1.08×10^{5} V (b) 9.0×10^{6} V

(c) 7.2×10^{5} V (d) 6.3×10^{4} V

3. Which of the following options is not following the rules of equipotential surface ?

(a) Equipotential surface may be point sized.

(b) Equipotential surface is single valued.

(c) Electric field is always perpendicular to equipotential surface.

(d) Work done to move a point charge q between two points on equipotential surface is zero.

4. A point P lies at a distance of 4.1×10^{-9} m from the centre of a dipole of dipole moment 4.8×10^{-30} C-m. If the point P lies on the axis of the dipole near the positive charge, then potential at point P is

(a) -1.8×10^{-3} V

(b) 1.8×10^{-3} V

(c) 2.6×10^{-3} V

(d) -2.6×10^{-3} V

5. 20 J of work has to be done against an existing electric field to take a charge of 0.08 C from A to B. Then, the potential difference $(V_B - V_A)$ is

(a) 250 V (b) -1500 V

(c) 0.15V (d) -0.15 V

6. Three point charges shown in the figure lie along a straight line. The energy needed to exchange the position of the central positive charge with one of the negative charges is

(a) $\dfrac{Q^2}{8\pi\varepsilon_0 a}$ (b) $\dfrac{3Q^2}{8\pi\varepsilon_0 a}$ (c) $\dfrac{Q^2}{4\pi\varepsilon_0 a}$ (d) $\dfrac{-Q^2}{8\pi\varepsilon_0 a}$

7. An electric point charge 10^{-3} μC is placed at the origin (0, 0) of XY-coordinate system. Two points A and B are situated at $(\sqrt{2}, \sqrt{2})$ and (2, 0) respectively.

The potential difference between the points A and B will be

(a) 9 V (b) zero

(c) 2 V (d) 3.5 V

8. **Statement I** Electric potential is constant within and at the surface of each conductor.

Statement II Electric field just outside a charged conductor is parallel to the surface of the conductor at every point.

In the light of the above statements, choose the most appropriate answer from the options given below.

(a) Both Statement I and Statement II are incorrect.

(b) Both Statement I and Statement II are correct.

(c) Statement I is correct but Statement II is incorrect.

(d) Statement I is incorrect but Statement II is correct.

9. A short electric dipole has a dipole moment of 16×10^{-9} C-m. The electric potential due to the dipole at a point at a distance of 0.6 m from the centre of the dipole, situated on a line making an angle of 60° with the dipole axis is $\left(\frac{1}{4\pi\varepsilon_0} = 9\times 10^9 \text{ Nm}^2/\text{C}^2\right)$

(a) 200 V

(b) 400 V

(c) zero

(d) 50 V

10. A non-conducting ring of radius 1 m carries a total charge of 2×10^{-10}C, distributed non-uniformly on its circumference, producing an electric field E everywhere in space. The value of the integral $\int_{l=\infty}^{l=0} -\mathbf{E}\cdot d\mathbf{l}$ ($l=0$ being centre of the ring) in volt is

(a) 1.8 (b) −1

(c) −1.8 (d) zero

11. A thin spherical conducting shell of radius R has a charge q. Another charge Q is placed at the centre of the shell. The ratio of potential at the centre of shell to that of the point P at distance $R/2$ from the centre of the shell is

(a) zero

(b) $\frac{2Q}{4\pi\varepsilon_0 R} - \frac{2q}{4\pi\varepsilon_0 R}$

(c) $\frac{2Q}{4\pi\varepsilon_0 R} + \frac{q}{4\pi\varepsilon_0 R}$

(d) infinite

12. A circular ring of radius 10 cm is formed from a straight metal wire. A charge of 200 μC is spreaded on the circle uniformly. The electrostatic potential at the centre of circle is

(a) 9×10^4 V

(b) 18×10^6 V

(c) 7×10^4 V

(d) 18×10^{-6} V

13. Two point charges $+q$ and $-q$ are held fixed at $(-d/2, 0)$ and $(d/2, 0)$ respectively, of a XY- coordinates system. Then,

(a) the electric field E at all points on X-axis has the same direction

(b) electric field at all points on Y-axis is along X-axis

(c) work has to be done in bringing a test charge from ∞ to the origin

(d) the dipole moment is $2qd$ along the X-axis

14. A uniform electric field pointing in positive x-direction exists in a region. Let A be the origin, B be the point on the X-axis at $x = +2$ cm and C be the point on the Y-axis at $y = +2$ cm. Then, the potentials at the points A, B and C satisfy

(a) $V_A < V_B$

(b) $V_A > V_B$

(c) $V_A < V_C$

(d) $V_A > V_C$

15. Consider the following statement and match the List I with List II.

Four point charges each having charge Q are located at the corners of a square having side of length a. If the V_C represents the electric potential at the centre of square due to the four charges, F represents the electric force on charge Q, U represents the potential energy of the system and W represents the work required to bring fifth charge q from infinity to the centre of square.

List I		List II
A. V_C	1.	$\frac{5KQ^2}{2a^2}$
B. W	2.	$\frac{KQ^2}{a}(4+\sqrt{2})$
C. F	3.	$\frac{\sqrt{2}Q}{\pi\varepsilon_0 a}$
D. U	4.	$\frac{\sqrt{2}qQ}{\pi\varepsilon_0 a}$

(a) A → 4, B → 3, C → 2, D → 1
(b) A → 3, B → 4, C → 1, D → 2
(c) A → 2, B → 1, C → 3, D → 4
(d) A → 1, B → 3, C → 4, D → 2

16. Consider metallic hollow spheres of radii R and $8R$ hold charges Q_1 and Q_2, respectively. Given that surface charge density of the concentric spheres are equal, the potential difference of both spheres is

(a) $\frac{7Q_1}{32\pi\varepsilon_0 R}$ (b) $\frac{3Q_2}{4\pi\varepsilon_0 R}$
(c) $\frac{Q_2}{4\pi\varepsilon_0 R}$ (d) $\frac{3Q_1}{4\pi\varepsilon_0 R}$

17. A uniformly charged ring of radius $3a$ and total charge Q is placed in XY-plane centred at origin. A point charge q is moving towards the ring along the Z-axis and has speed v at $Z = 4a$. The minimum value of v such that it crosses the origin, is

(a) $\sqrt{\frac{2}{m}}\left(\frac{2}{15}\frac{Qq}{4\pi\varepsilon_0 a}\right)^{1/2}$
(b) $\sqrt{\frac{2}{m}}\left(\frac{1}{5}\frac{qQ}{4\pi\varepsilon_0 a}\right)^{1/2}$
(c) $\sqrt{\frac{2}{m}}\left(\frac{4}{15}\frac{q^2}{4\pi\varepsilon_0 a}\right)^{1/2}$
(d) $\sqrt{\frac{2}{m}}\left(\frac{1}{15}\frac{q^2}{4\pi\varepsilon_0 a}\right)^{1/2}$

18. Twenty seven conducting drops each of radius 0.02 m and each carrying a charge of 10 μC are combined to form a bigger drop. The ratio of surface density of bigger drop to the smaller drop will be

(a) 1:4 (b) 3:1
(c) 1:8 (d) 8:1

19. Two insulating plates are both uniformly charged in such a way that the potential difference between them is $V_2 - V_1 = 20\,\text{V}$ (i.e. plate 2 is at a higher potential).

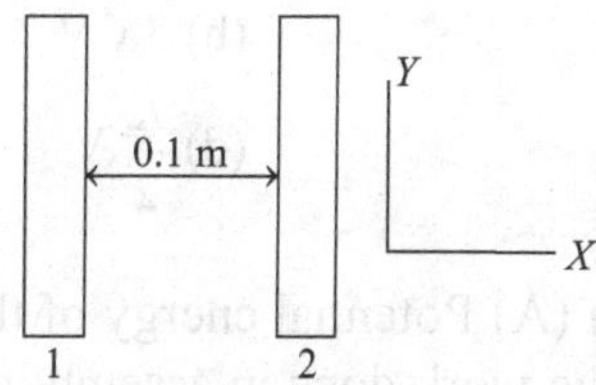

The plates are separated by $d = 0.1\,\text{m}$ and can be treated as infinitely large. An electron is released from rest on the inner surface of plate 1. What is its speed when it hits plate 2?
($e = 1.6\times10^{-19}$ C, $m_e = 9.11\times10^{-31}$ kg)

(a) 32×10^{-19} m/s
(b) 2.65×10^{6} m/s
(c) 7.02×10^{12} m/s
(d) 1.87×10^{6} m/s

20. For a charged spherical ball, electrostatic potential inside the ball varies with r as $V = 2ar^2 + b$. Here, a and b are constants and r is the distance from the centre. The volume charge density inside the ball is $-\beta a\varepsilon$. The value of β is
(ε = permittivity of the medium)

(a) 12 (b) 6
(c) 18 (d) 15

21. Two opposite and equal charge 16×10^{-8}C when placed 12×10^{-2} cm away, form a dipole. If this dipole is placed in an external electric field of 4×10^{8}N/C, the value of maximum torque and the work done in rotating it through 180° from stable equilibrium position will be

(a) 64×10^{-4} N-m and 15.4×10^{-4} J
(b) 32×10^{-4} N-m and 32×10^{-6} J
(c) 64×10^{-4} N-m and 32×10^{-6} J
(d) 768×10^{-4} N-m and 15.4×10^{-6} J

22. A charge 34 mC is distributed over two concentric conducting thin spherical shells of radii 1 cm and 4 cm. If the surface charge densities on the two shells are equal, the electric potential at the common centre is $\left(K = \frac{1}{4\pi\varepsilon_0}\right)$

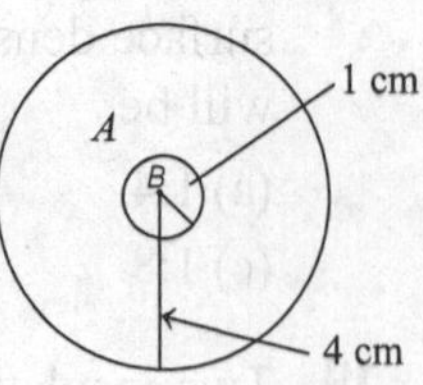

(a) $1K$ V (b) $3K$ V
(c) $2K$ V (d) $\frac{K}{2}$ V

23. Assertion (A) Potential energy of the system is equal to the work done in assembling the configuration.
Reason (R) For a system of positive test charge and point charge, electric potential energy is equal to electric potential.
In the light of the above statements, choose the most appropriate answer from the options given below.
(a) Both A and R are true and R is the correct explanation of A.
(b) Both A and R are true but R is not the correct explanation of A.
(c) A is true but R is false.
(d) A is false but R is true.

24. A solid sphere of radius R carries a charge $Q + q$ distributed uniformly over its volume. A very small point like a piece of it of mass m gets detached from the bottom of the sphere and falls down vertically under gravity. This piece carries charge q. If it acquires a speed v when it has fallen through a vertical height h (see figure), then (assume the remaining portion to be spherical)

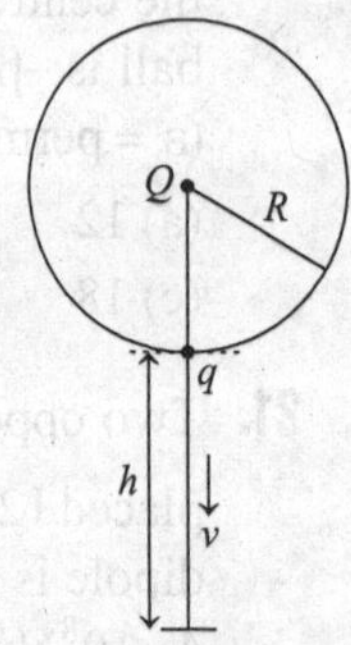

(a) $v^2 = h\left[\frac{qQ}{4\pi\varepsilon_0 R^2 h m} + g\right]$
(b) $v^2 = h\left[\frac{qQ}{4\pi\varepsilon_0 R(R+h)m} + g\right]$
(c) $v^2 = 2h\left[\frac{qQR}{4\pi\varepsilon_0 (R+h)^3 m} + g\right]$
(d) $v^2 = 2h\left[\frac{qQ}{4\pi\varepsilon_0 R(R+h)m} + g\right]$

25. Two point charges $-q$ and $+q$ are located at points $(0, 0, -a)$ and $(0, 0, a)$, respectively. The potential at a point $(0, 0, 2a)$, is
(a) $\frac{qa}{4\pi\varepsilon_0}$ (b) $\frac{q}{4\pi\varepsilon_0 a}$
(c) $\frac{q}{6\pi\varepsilon_0 a}$ (d) $\frac{2q}{6\pi\varepsilon_0 a}$

26. The curve represents the distribution of potential along the straight line joining the two charges Q_1 and Q_2 (separated by a distance r).

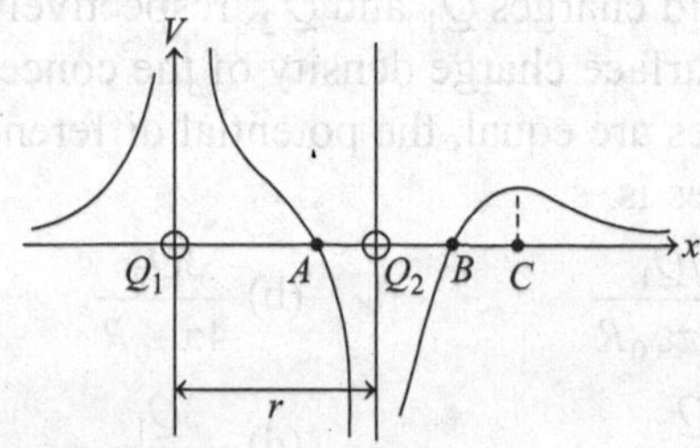

1. $|Q_1| > |Q_2|$
2. Q_1 is positive in nature.
3. A and B are in equilibrium for positive charge.
4. C is a point of unstable equilibrium for negative charge.

Which of the above statements are correct?
(a) 1 and 2 (b) 1, 2 and 3
(c) 1, 2 and 4 (d) 1, 2, 3 and 4

27. Six point charges are kept at the vertices of a regular hexagon of side L and centre O, as shown in the figure.
Given that, $K = \frac{1}{4\pi\varepsilon_0}\frac{q}{L^2}$, which of the following statements is correct?

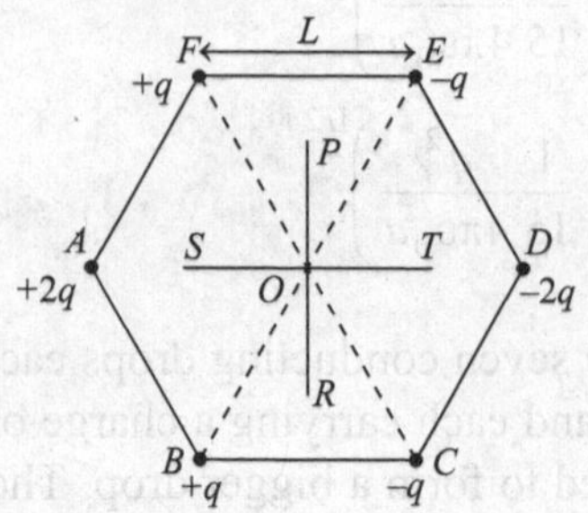

(a) The electric field at O is $6K$ along OD.
(b) The potential at O is K.
(c) The potential at all points on the line PR is not same.
(d) The potential at all points on the line ST is same.

28. The potential function of an electrostatic field is given by $V = 3x^2 + (y^3 - 1)$ V. Then, which of the following statement is correct?
(a) There exist only one point at which potential is zero.
(b) There exist no such point at which electric field is zero.
(c) The direction of electric field does not change throughout the points of space.
(d) The charge $2\sqrt{2}\ \mu C$ experiences a force of $24\ \mu N$ at point $(1\text{m}, \sqrt{2}\text{m})$.

29. A charge of $8\ \mu C$ experiences a force 480 dyne, when placed in a uniform electric field. The potential difference between two points separated by a distance of 3.2 cm along the electric field lines is
(a) 1.86 V
(b) 19.2 V
(c) 186 V
(d) 0 V

30. Consider two concentric conducting shells. The potential of outer shell is 20 V and that of inner shell is 30 V. If the outer shell is grounded, the potential of inner shell is
(a) 50 V
(b) 30 V
(c) 20 V
(d) 10 V

Response Index

01 ⓐ ⓑ ⓒ ⓓ	14 ⓐ ⓑ ⓒ ⓓ	27 ⓐ ⓑ ⓒ ⓓ
02 ⓐ ⓑ ⓒ ⓓ	15 ⓐ ⓑ ⓒ ⓓ	28 ⓐ ⓑ ⓒ ⓓ
03 ⓐ ⓑ ⓒ ⓓ	16 ⓐ ⓑ ⓒ ⓓ	29 ⓐ ⓑ ⓒ ⓓ
04 ⓐ ⓑ ⓒ ⓓ	17 ⓐ ⓑ ⓒ ⓓ	30 ⓐ ⓑ ⓒ ⓓ
05 ⓐ ⓑ ⓒ ⓓ	18 ⓐ ⓑ ⓒ ⓓ	
06 ⓐ ⓑ ⓒ ⓓ	19 ⓐ ⓑ ⓒ ⓓ	
07 ⓐ ⓑ ⓒ ⓓ	20 ⓐ ⓑ ⓒ ⓓ	
08 ⓐ ⓑ ⓒ ⓓ	21 ⓐ ⓑ ⓒ ⓓ	
09 ⓐ ⓑ ⓒ ⓓ	22 ⓐ ⓑ ⓒ ⓓ	
10 ⓐ ⓑ ⓒ ⓓ	23 ⓐ ⓑ ⓒ ⓓ	
11 ⓐ ⓑ ⓒ ⓓ	24 ⓐ ⓑ ⓒ ⓓ	
12 ⓐ ⓑ ⓒ ⓓ	25 ⓐ ⓑ ⓒ ⓓ	
13 ⓐ ⓑ ⓒ ⓓ	26 ⓐ ⓑ ⓒ ⓓ	

Performance Scanner

> 90% Excellent !	You have mastered this chapter. The concepts of this chapter are on your fingertips. Move on to the next chapter and maintain this momentum.
76-90% Very Good !	You have a good command over this chapter. Revise the chapter again after a few days and enhance your performance.
60-75% Good !	You have a wide scope to learn for this chapter. Revise this chapter again.
<60% Not Satisfactory!	You have a long way ahead of you to master this chapter. Revise it thoroughly.

For Online Chapter Test
Scan the QR Code

Space for Rough Work

Space for Rough Work

Space for Rough Work

Test Booklet No. **3947153**

Test Booklet Code **CH3**

MEDACE
NEET (UG)
SELF ASSESSMENT KIT

Capacitance

Topics Covered

Dielectric & Capacitance and their Types

Combination of Capacitors

Energy of Capacitors

Important Instructions

- This Booklet Contains – Three Topic Tests and One Test on Complete Chapter.
- Each question carries 4 marks.
- For each correct response, the candidate will get 4 marks and for every incorrect response 1 mark will be additionally deducted from the total score.
- Use **Blue/Black** point pen only for filling the OMR.
- Rough work will be done in the space provided for this purpose within the test booklet only.

Name of the Candidate (In Capitals) ______________________

____

Candidate's Signature ______________

Invigilator's Signature ______________

Facsimile signature stamp of center superintendent______________

Do not open this Booklet until you start attempting the Test

Topical Follow Thru

Test 1

Syllabus
- Dielectric, Capacitors, Capacitance and their Types

For deeper insight **Scan the QR Code**

Important Instructions
- The test is of 30 minutes duration and contains 15 Multiple Choice Questions. (Four options with a single correct answer).
- Choose the correct option and fill the OMR given on the last page of this test accordingly.
- At some instances, you may find more than 1 option may be correct, in such circumstances you have to judge the most appropriate answer as per conditions given in the question.

1. A parallel plate capacitor is located horizontally such that one of the plates is submerged in a liquid while the other is above the liquid surface. When plates are charged, the level of liquid

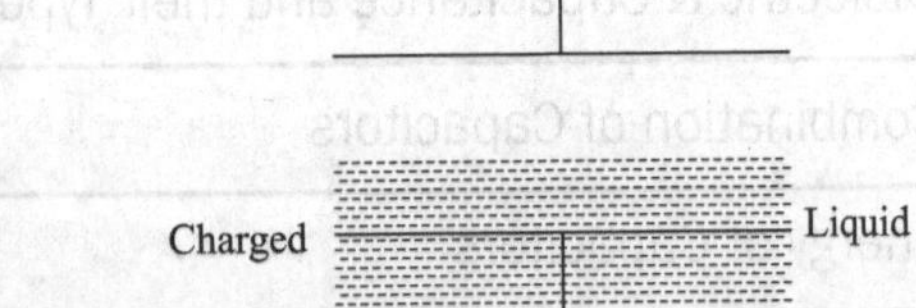

(a) falls

(b) rises

(c) remains unchanged

(d) may rise or fall depending on the amount of charge.

2. The potentials of the two plates of capacitor are +10 V and −10 V. The charge on one of the plates is 40 C. The capacitance of the capacitor is

(a) 2 F (b) 4 F

(c) 0.5 F (d) 0.25 F

3. Consider the situation shown in figure. The capacitor A has a charge q on it whereas B is uncharged. The charge appearing on the capacitor B a long time after the switch is closed is

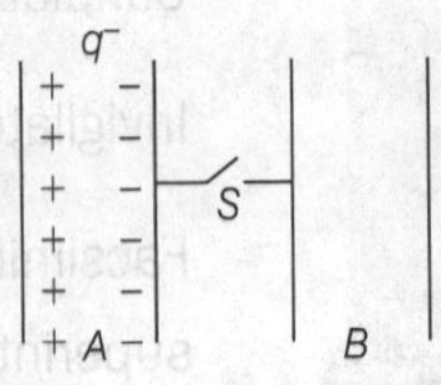

(a) zero (b) $\frac{q}{2}$

(c) q (d) $2q$

4. A dielectric slab is inserted between the plates of a capacitor. The charge on the capacitor is $+50\ \mu C$. What will be the charge induced on the surface A of the dielectric shown below?

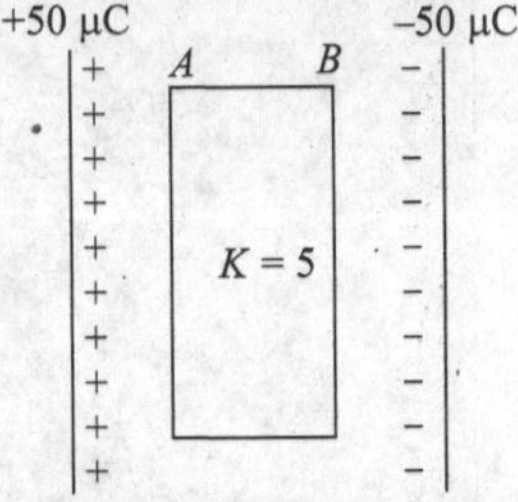

(a) $-50\ \mu C$ (b) $-10\ \mu C$

(c) $-40\ \mu C$ (d) $+40\ \mu C$

5. A parallel plate capacitor with air as dielectric is charged to a potential V. It is then connected to an uncharged parallel plate capacitor filled with wax of dielectric constant K. The common potential of both capacitors is

(a) V (b) KV

(c) $(1+K)V$ (d) $\frac{V}{(1+K)}$

6. The introduction of a metal plate between the plates of a parallel plate capacitor increases its capacitance by 5 times. If d is the separation of the two plates of the capacitor, the thickness of the metal plate introduced is

(a) $\frac{d}{3}$ (b) $\frac{5d}{9}$

(c) $\frac{4d}{5}$ (d) d

7. Two identical metal plates are given positive charges Q_1 and $Q_2\ (<Q_1)$, respectively. If they are brought close together to form a parallel plate capacitor with capacitance C, the potential difference between them is

(a) $\frac{Q_1+Q_2}{2C}$ (b) $\frac{Q_1+Q_2}{C}$

(c) $\frac{Q_1-Q_2}{C}$ (d) $\frac{Q_1-Q_2}{2C}$

8. If n drops, each of capacitance C, coalesce to form a single big drop, the capacitance of the big drop will be

(a) n^3C (b) nC

(c) $n^{1/2}C$ (d) $n^{1/3}C$

9. The capacitance of the capacitor of plate area A_1 and A_2 ($A_2 > A_1$) at a distance $2d$ (in figure) is

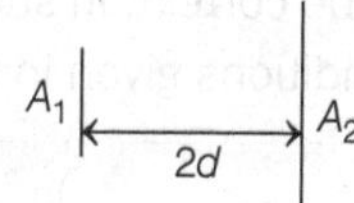

(a) $\frac{\varepsilon_0(A_1+A_2)}{2d}$ (b) $\frac{A_2\varepsilon_0}{2d}$

(c) $\frac{\varepsilon_0\sqrt{A_1A_2}}{2d}$ (d) $\frac{A_1\varepsilon_0}{2d}$

10. The capacity of air capacitor is 20 μF. It is connected to a constant voltage battery of 24 V. Now, the space between the plates is filled with a liquid of dielectric constant 10. The additional charge that now flows from battery to the capacitor will be

(a) 4000 μC (b) 4200 μC

(c) 4300 μC (d) 4320 μC

11. A capacitor filled with a dielectric material ($K=3$), has capacitance C. The capacitance after removing the dielectric is

(a) $\frac{C}{3}$ (b) $3C$

(c) $\sqrt{3}C$ (d) $6C$

12. If a block of mass M is required to keep the right side charged plate of parallel plate capacitor stationary as shown in figure, then the electric field between the plates is

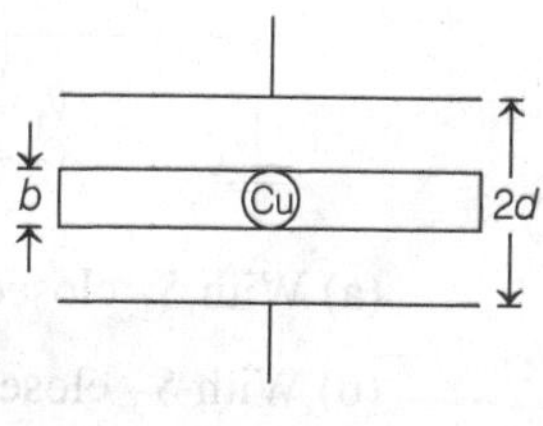

(a) $\sqrt{\frac{2Mg}{A\varepsilon_0}}$ (b) $\sqrt{\frac{Mg}{A\varepsilon_0}}$

(c) $\sqrt{\frac{Mg}{2A\varepsilon_0}}$ (d) $\sqrt{\frac{2Mg}{3A\varepsilon_0}}$

13. A soap bubble of radius r is charged to a potential V. If the radius is increased to n^2r, the potential on the bubbles will become

(a) nV (b) n^2V (c) $\frac{V}{n}$ (d) $\frac{V}{n^2}$

14. A copper slab of thickness b is inserted in between the plates of a parallel plate capacitor as shown in figure. The separation of the plates is $2d$. If $b=\frac{3d}{2}$, then the ratio of capacitance of the capacitor after and before inserting the slab will be

(a) 2 : 1 (b) $1:\sqrt{2}$ (c) 1 : 1 (d) $\sqrt{2}:1$

15. In air, the capacitance of a parallel plate capacitor is 4 μF. In a dielectric medium, the capacitance becomes 8 μF. The permittivity of the dielectric medium will be

(a) $0.17\times10^{-10}\ C^2N^{-1}m^{-2}$

(b) $1.47\times10^{-10}\ C^2N^{-1}m^{-2}$

(c) $0.44\times10^{-10}\ C^2N^{-1}m^{-2}$

(d) $1.1\times10^{-10}\ C^2N^{-1}m^{-2}$

Response Index

01	a	b	c	d	09	a	b	c	d
02	a	b	c	d	10	a	b	c	d
03	a	b	c	d	11	a	b	c	d
04	a	b	c	d	12	a	b	c	d
05	a	b	c	d	13	a	b	c	d
06	a	b	c	d	14	a	b	c	d
07	a	b	c	d	15	a	b	c	d
08	a	b	c	d					

Performance Scanner

> 90% Excellent !	You have mastered these topics. The concepts of these topics are on your fingertips. Move on to the next test and maintain this momentum.
76-90% Very Good !	You have a good command over these topics. Revise them again after a few days and enhance your performance.
60-75% Good !	You have a wide scope to learn for these topics. Revise them again.
<60% Not Satisfactory!	You have a long way ahead of you to master in these topics. Revise them thoroughly.

Test 2

Syllabus

- Combination of Capacitors in Series and Parallel

For deeper insight **Scan the QR Code**

Important Instructions

- The test is of 30 minutes duration and contains 15 Multiple Choice Questions. (Four options with a single correct answer).
- Choose the correct option and fill the OMR given on the last page of this test accordingly.
- At some instances, you may find more than 1 option may be correct, in such circumstances you have to judge the most appropriate answer as per conditions given in the question.

1. For the circuit shown in figure which of the following statements is true?

S_1 + − S_3 + − S_2

$V_1 = 40$ V, $C_1 = 2$ pF; $V_2 = 30$ V, $C_2 = 3$ pF

(a) With S_1 closed, $V_1 = 15$ V, $V_2 = 20$ V

(b) With S_3 closed, $V_1 = V_2 = 35$ V

(c) With S_1 and S_2 closed, $V_1 = V_2 = 0$

(d) With S_1 and S_3 closed, $V_1 = 40$ V and $V_2 = 30$ V

2. Assertion (A) Two condensers of same capacity are connected first is parallel and then in series. The ratio of resultant capacitance in the two cases will be 4 : 1.

Reason (R) In parallel combination capacitance increases and in series combination capacitance decreases.

In the light of above statements, choose the most appropriate answer from the options given below.

(a) Both A and R are true and R is the correct explanation of the A.

(b) Both A and R are true but R is not the correct explanation of the A.

(c) A is true but R is false.

(d) A is false but R is true.

3. Four metal plates numbers 1, 2, 3 and 4 are arranged as shown in figure. The area of each plate is A and the separation between the plates is d.

The capacitance of the arrangement is

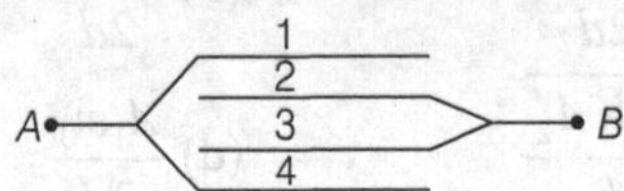

(a) $\frac{\varepsilon_0 A}{d}$ (b) $\frac{2\varepsilon_0 A}{d}$

(c) $\frac{3\varepsilon_0 A}{d}$ (d) $\frac{4\varepsilon_0 A}{d}$

4. In the network shown in figure, $C_1 = 6\,\mu$F and $C = 9\,\mu$F. The equivalent capacitance between points P and Q is

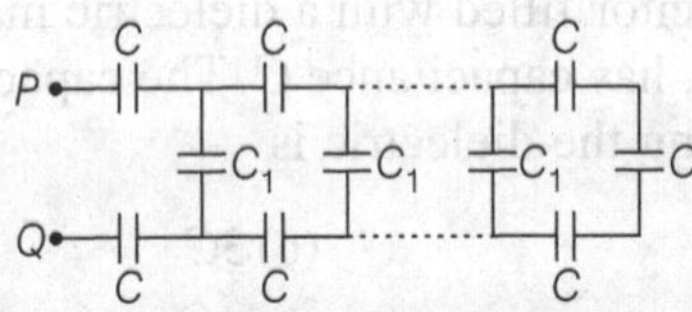

(a) 3 μF (b) 6 μF

(c) 9 μF (d) 12 μF

5. A capacitor of capacitance $C_1 = \frac{C}{2}$ is charged to a voltage V. It is then connected in parallel with a series combination of two uncharged capacitors of capacitances $C_2 = 2C$ and $C_3 = 2C$. The charge that will flow through the connecting wires is

(a) $\frac{CV}{3}$ (b) $\frac{2CV}{5}$

(c) CV (d) zero

6. The equivalent capacitance between points A and B in the network shown in figure is ($C_1 = 6\,\mu F$ and $C_2 = 9\,\mu F$)

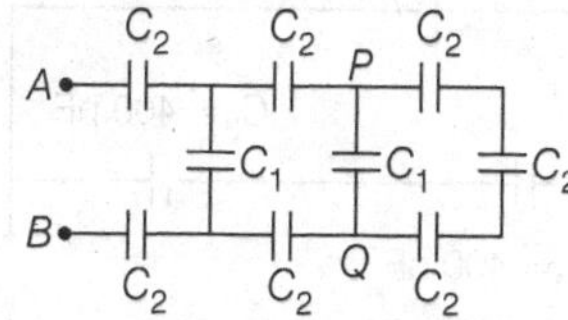

(a) 1 μF (b) 2 μF (c) 3 μF (d) 4 μF

7. The effective capacitance of two capacitors of capacitances C_1 and C_2 (with $C_2 < C_1$) connected in parallel is $\frac{25}{6}$ times the effective capacitance when they are connected in series. The ratio $\frac{C_1}{C_2}$ is

(a) $\frac{3}{2}$ (b) $\frac{4}{3}$ (c) $\frac{5}{3}$ (d) $\frac{25}{6}$

8. In the circuit shown, a potential difference of 90 V is applied across AB. The potential difference between the points P and Q is

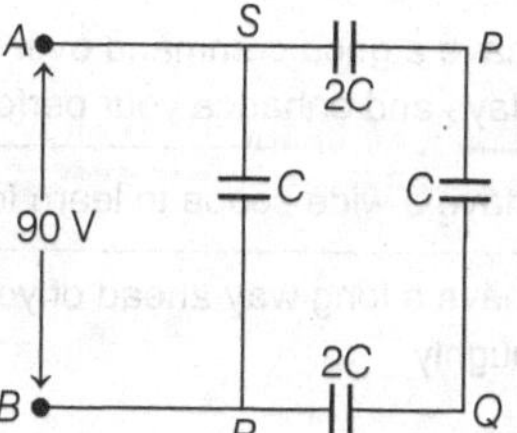

(a) 15 V
(b) 30 V
(c) 45 V
(d) 60 V

9. Three capacitors of capacitances C_1, C_2 and C_3 are connected in series with a battery of emf E as shown below. The graph of electric potential V from point X to point Y has been also shown in figure. The correct relation is

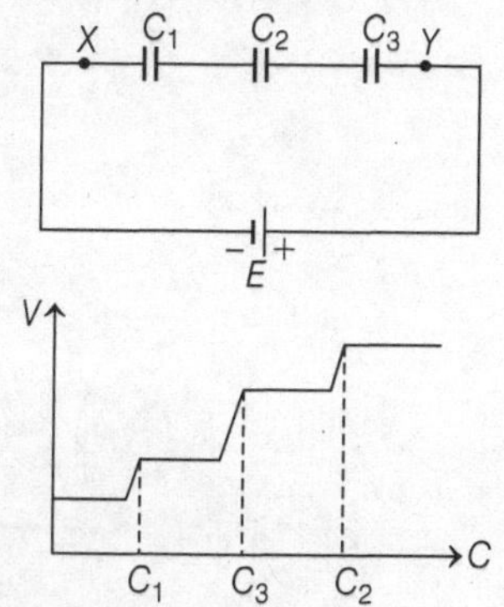

(a) $C_1 > C_2 > C_3$ (b) $C_2 > C_3 > C_1$
(c) $C_3 > C_2 > C_1$ (d) $C_1 > C_3 > C_2$

10. Parallel plate capacitor is made by stacking $(n-2)$ equally spaced plates connected alternatively. If the capacitance between any two plates is $2x$, then the total capacitance will be

(a) $(n+1)x$ (b) $2(n-3)x$
(c) $2(n-2)x$ (d) $2(n-4)x$

11. Charge on both capacitors, when S is open is

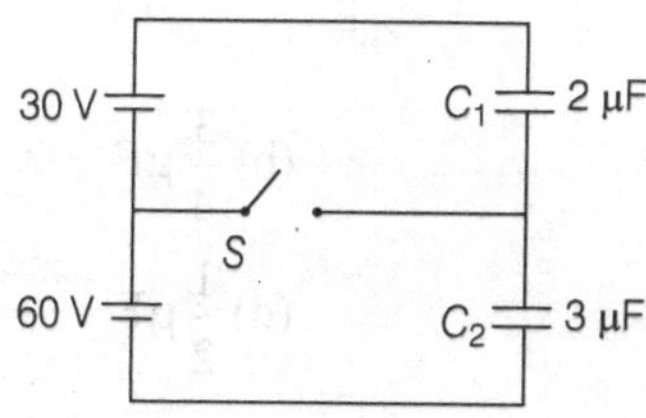

(a) 108 μC
(b) 60 μC
(c) 240 μC
(d) 180 μC

12. Find the effective capacitance between points P and R in the given figure.

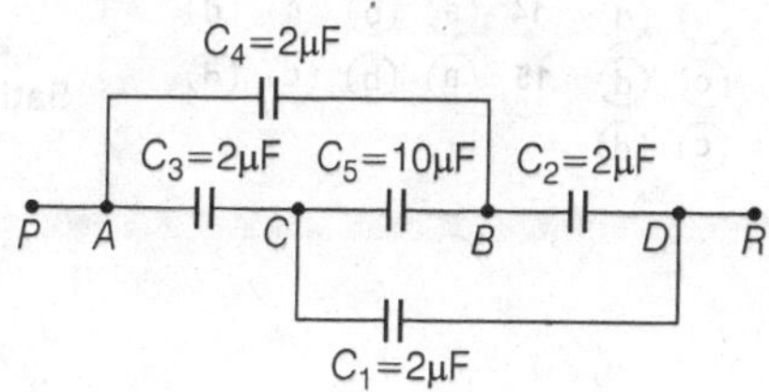

(a) 1 μF (b) 3 μF
(c) 2 μF (d) 4 μF

13. Study the figure given below. Find out the equivalent capacitance of the network between P and Q,

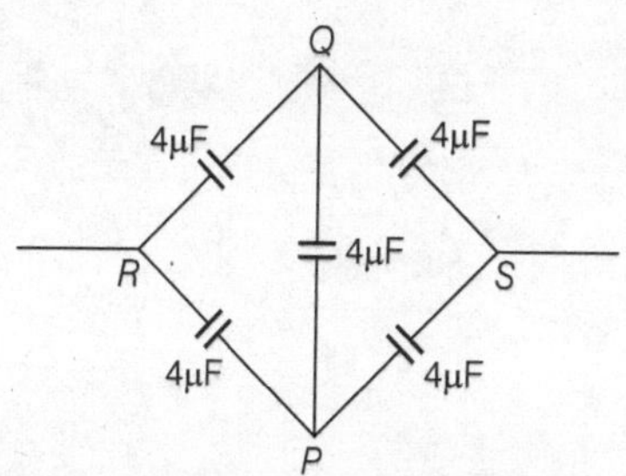

(a) 4 μF (b) 6 μF
(c) 8 μF (d) 7 μF

14. Find the equivalent capacitance between *A* and *B* for the following arrangement.

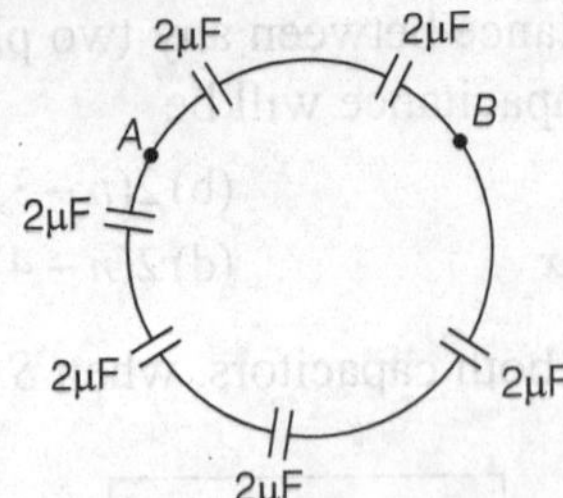

(a) 1 μF
(b) $\frac{3}{4}$ μF
(c) $\frac{3}{2}$ μF
(d) $\frac{1}{2}$ μF

15. What is the equivalent capacitance between *A* and *D* of the network shown in figure?

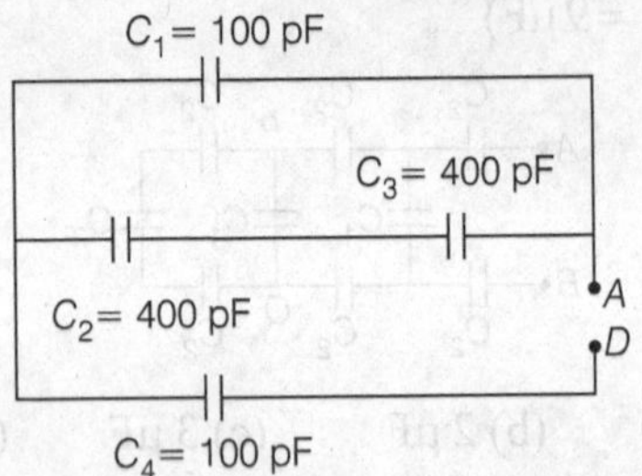

(a) 200 pF
(b) $\frac{300}{4}$ pF
(c) $\frac{200}{3}$ pF
(d) 50 pF

Response Index

01	ⓐ	ⓑ	ⓒ	ⓓ	09	ⓐ	ⓑ	ⓒ	ⓓ
02	ⓐ	ⓑ	ⓒ	ⓓ	10	ⓐ	ⓑ	ⓒ	ⓓ
03	ⓐ	ⓑ	ⓒ	ⓓ	11	ⓐ	ⓑ	ⓒ	ⓓ
04	ⓐ	ⓑ	ⓒ	ⓓ	12	ⓐ	ⓑ	ⓒ	ⓓ
05	ⓐ	ⓑ	ⓒ	ⓓ	13	ⓐ	ⓑ	ⓒ	ⓓ
06	ⓐ	ⓑ	ⓒ	ⓓ	14	ⓐ	ⓑ	ⓒ	ⓓ
07	ⓐ	ⓑ	ⓒ	ⓓ	15	ⓐ	ⓑ	ⓒ	ⓓ
08	ⓐ	ⓑ	ⓒ	ⓓ					

Performance Scanner

> 90% Excellent !	You have mastered these topics. The concepts of these topics are on your fingertips. Move on to the next test and maintain this momentum.
76-90% Very Good !	You have a good command over these topics. Revise them again after a few days and enhance your performance.
60-75% Good !	You have a wide scope to learn for these topics. Revise them again.
<60% Not Satisfactory!	You have a long way ahead of you to master in these topics. Revise them thoroughly.

Test 3

Syllabus • Energy of Capacitors

For deeper insight **Scan the QR Code**

Important Instructions

- The test is of 30 minutes duration and contains 15 Multiple Choice Questions. (Four options with a single correct answer).
- Choose the correct option and fill the OMR given on the last page of this test accordingly.
- At some instances, you may find more than 1 option may be correct, in such circumstances you have to judge the most appropriate answer as per conditions given in the question.

1. The two condensers of capacities 44 μF and 11 μF, respectively are connected in series. The combination is connected across a potential of 6 V. The ratio of energies stored by the condensers will be

(a) $\frac{1}{4}$ (b) $\frac{1}{1}$

(c) $\frac{1}{3}$ (d) $\frac{2}{3}$

2. A capacitor of capacitance C has charge $2Q$ and stored energy is 8 J. If the charge is increased to $3Q$, the stored energy will be

(a) 18 J

(b) 4 J

(c) 6 J

(d) 8 J

3. Capacitance C_1 is charged to a potential V_0. The electrostatic energy stored in it is U_0. It is connected to C_2 in parallel. If C_2 is uncharged. Then, the energy dissipated in this process is

(a) $\frac{C_2}{C_1 + C_2} U_0$

(b) $\frac{C_1}{C_1 + C_2} U_0$

(c) $\left(\frac{C_1 + C_2}{C_1 - C_2}\right) U_0$

(d) $\frac{C_1 C_2}{2(C_1 - C_2)} U_0$

4. Four condensers each of capacity 4 μF are connected as shown in figure. $V_P - V_Q = 15$ V. The energy stored in the system is

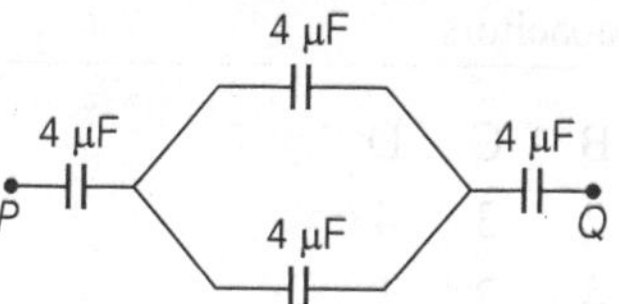

(a) 240 μJ (b) 90 μJ

(c) 360 μJ (d) 180 μJ

5. Statement I As battery remains connected, potential of capacitor will not change.

Statement II If the capacitor is kept connected with the battery and then the dielectric slab is inserted between the plates, both the charges on capacitor and the energy stored in the capacitor gets decreased.

In the light of above statements, choose the most appropriate answer from the options given below.

(a) Both Statement I and Statement II are correct.

(b) Both Statement I and Statement II are incorrect.

(c) Statement I is correct and Statement II is incorrect.

(d) Statement I is incorrect and Statement II is correct.

6. The parallel plates of a capacitor have an area 50 cm^2 each and are separated by 5 mm. The capacitor is charged by connecting it to a 400 V supply. The electrical energy stored by the capacitor will be

(a) 7.08×10^{-7} J (b) 5.60×10^{-6} J

(c) 6.54×10^{-7} J (d) 6.6×10^{-6} J

7. Match the Column I (energy of capacitor) with Column II (value) and select the correct answer from the codes given below.

A capacitor C_1 of capacitance C is charged to a potential difference V_0. The terminals of the charged capacitor are then connected to an uncharged capacitor C_2 of capacitance $C/2$.

Column I	Column II
A. Final energy of capacitor C_1	1. $-(1/6)CV_0^2$
B. Final energy of capacitor C_2	2. $(1/3)CV_0^2$
C. Final energy of the system	3. $(2/9)CV_0^2$
D. Change in energy on joining the capacitors	4. $(1/9)CV_0^2$

	A	B	C	D
(a)	1	2	3	4
(b)	3	4	2	1
(c)	2	4	3	1
(d)	1	2	4	3

8. A capacitor of capacitance C is fully charged by a 400 V supply. It is then discharged through a small coil of resistance wire embedded in a thermally insulated block of specific heat 2.5×10^2 $\text{Jkg}^{-1}\ \text{K}^{-1}$ and of mass 0.1 kg. If the temperature of the block rises by 0.4 K, what is the value of C ?

(a) 125 μF (b) 400 μF
(c) 300 μF (d) 200 μF

9. Three plates A, B and C each of area 50 cm^2 have separation 3 mm between A and B and 3 mm between B and C. The energy stored, when the plates are fully charged is

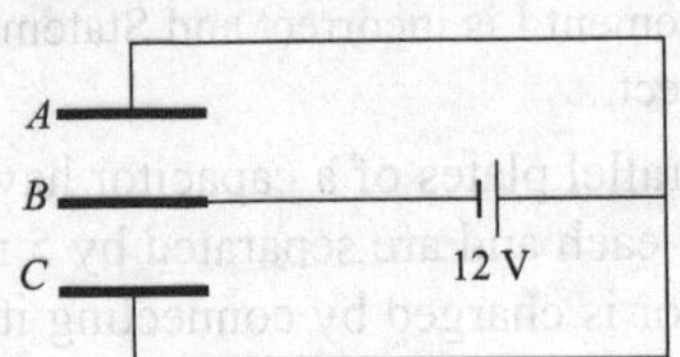

(a) 1.6×10^{-9} J (b) 2.1×10^{-9} J
(c) 5×10^{-9} J (d) 7×10^{-9} J

10. The capacity and the energy stored in a charged parallel plate capacitor with air between its plates are respectively, C_0 and W_0. If the air is replaced by glass (dielectric constant = 5) between the plates, the capacity of the plates and the energy stored in it will respectively be

(a) $5C_0, 5W_0$
(b) $5C_0, \frac{W_0}{5}$
(c) $\frac{C_0}{5}, 5W_0$
(d) $\frac{C_0}{5}, \frac{W_0}{5}$

11. A 2 μF capacitor is charged as shown in the figure. The percentage of its stored energy dissipated after the switch S is turned to position 2 is

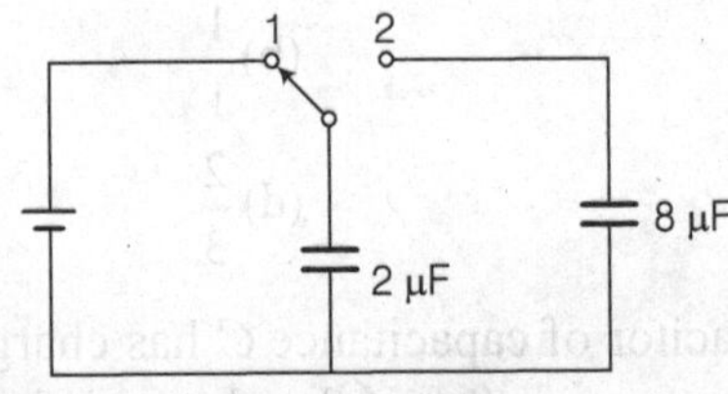

(a) 0% (b) 20%
(c) 75% (d) 80%

12. A parallel plate capacitor of plate area A and plate separation d is charged by a battery of voltage V. The battery is then disconnected. The work needed to pull the plates to a separation $3d$ is

(a) $\frac{AV^2\varepsilon_0}{d}$ (b) $\frac{2AV^2\varepsilon_0}{d}$
(c) $\frac{AV^2\varepsilon_0}{2d}$ (d) $\frac{3AV^2\varepsilon_0}{2d}$

13. A capacitor of capacitance 4 μF is charged to 80 V and another capacitor of capacitance 6 μF is charged to 30 V. When they are connected together, the energy gained by the 6 μF capacitor is

(a) 7.8 mJ (b) 4.8 mJ
(c) 3.2 mJ (d) 2.5 mJ

14. A 650 pF capacitor is charged by a 200 V supply. Then, it is disconnected from the supply and is connected to another uncharged 750 pF capacitor. How much electrostatic energy is lost in this process?

(a) 6.96×10^{-6} J
(b) 6.66×10^{-6} J
(c) 16.96×10^{-6} J
(d) 7.12×10^{-6} J

15. An isolated conducting sphere whose radius is 6.85 cm has a charge $q = 1.25$ nC. The energy density at the surface of the sphere will be

(a) 25 $\mu J/m^3$
(b) 20 $\mu J/m^3$
(c) 15 $\mu J/m^3$
(d) 10 $\mu J/m^3$

Response Index

01	a	b	c	d	09	a	b	c	d
02	a	b	c	d	10	a	b	c	d
03	a	b	c	d	11	a	b	c	d
04	a	b	c	d	12	a	b	c	d
05	a	b	c	d	13	a	b	c	d
06	a	b	c	d	14	a	b	c	d
07	a	b	c	d	15	a	b	c	d
08	a	b	c	d					

Performance Scanner

> 90% Excellent !	You have mastered these topics. The concepts of these topics are on your fingertips. Move on to the next test and maintain this momentum.
76-90% Very Good !	You have a good command over these topics. Revise them again after a few days and enhance your performance.
60-75% Good !	You have a wide scope to learn for these topics. Revise them again.
<60% Not Satisfactory!	You have a long way ahead of you to master in these topics. Revise them thoroughly.

Chapter Break Thru

Syllabus	• Dielectric, Capacitors, Capacitance and their Types	• Combination of Capacitors in Series and Parallel	• Energy of Capacitors

Important Instructions

- The test is of 45 minutes duration and contains 30 Multiple Choice Questions (Four options with a single correct answer).
- Choose the correct option and fill the OMR given on the last page of this test accordingly.
- At some instances, you may find more than 1 option may be correct, in such circumstances you have to judge the most appropriate answer as per conditions given in the question.

1. Four plates 1, 2, 3 and 4 have same area of cross-section. The distance between each plate is d. The equivalent capacity across M and N will be

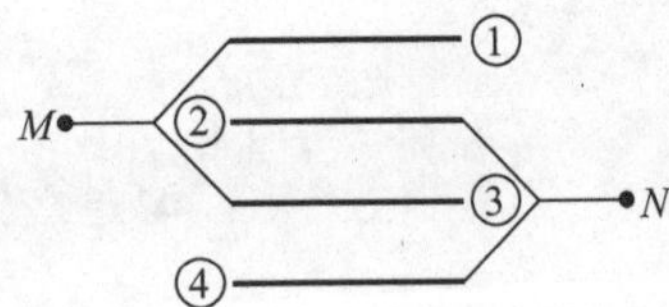

(a) $\frac{4\varepsilon_0 A}{d}$

(b) $\frac{3\varepsilon_0 A}{d}$

(c) $\frac{3\varepsilon_0 A}{2d}$

(d) $\frac{\varepsilon_0 A}{3d}$

2. If the potential difference between the plates of a capacitor is increased by 0.2%, the energy stored in the capacitor increases by

(a) 0.1% (b) 0.11%

(c) 0.144% (d) 0.4%

3. One plate of a parallel plate capacitor of plate area A and plate separation d is connected to the positive terminal of a battery of the voltage V. The negative terminal of the battery and the other plate of the capacitor are earthed as shown in figure.

The charge that flows from the battery to the capacitor plates is

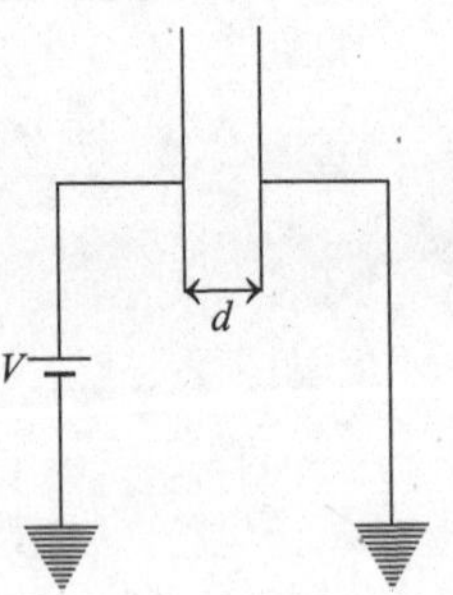

(a) zero (b) $\frac{\varepsilon_0 AV}{d}$

(c) $\frac{Vd}{\varepsilon_0 A}$ (d) $\frac{\varepsilon_0 AV}{2d}$

4. Plates of area A are arranged as shown. The distance between each plate is d, the net capacitance is

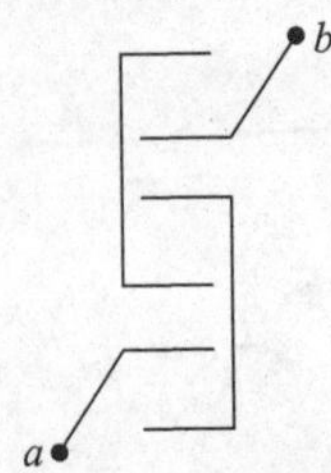

(a) $\frac{\varepsilon_0 A}{d}$ (b) $\frac{7\varepsilon_0 A}{d}$

(c) $\frac{6\varepsilon_0 A}{d}$ (d) $\frac{5\varepsilon_0 A}{d}$

5. A dielectric slab of thickness d is inserted in a parallel plate capacitor whose negative plate is at $x = 0$ and positive plate is at $x = 4d$. The slab is equidistant from the plates. The capacitor is given some charge. As x goes from 0 to $4d$,

(a) the magnitude of the electric field remains the same

(b) the direction of the electric field changes continuously

(c) the electric potential increases continuously

(d) the electric potential increases at first, then decreases and again increases.

6. The equivalent capacitance of combination as shown in figure between points A and B is

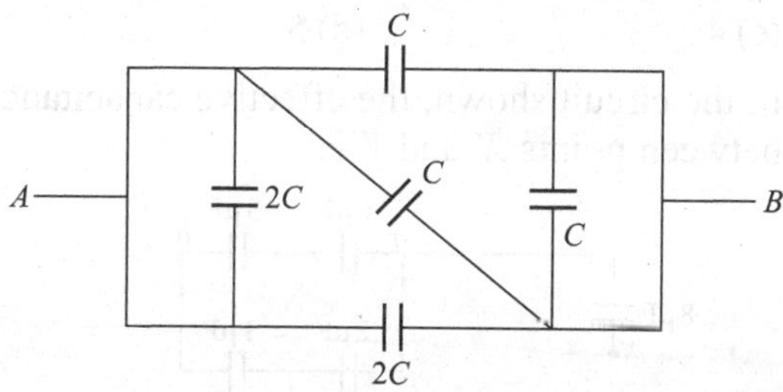

(a) C (b) $3C$

(c) $4C$ (d) $\frac{3C}{2}$

7. Find the capacitance between A and L, if each capacitor in the figure is C.

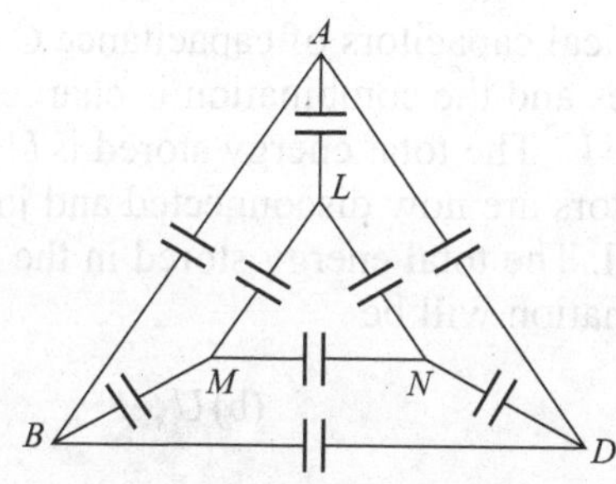

(a) $\frac{2}{3}C$ (b) $\frac{5}{3}C$

(c) $\frac{7}{5}C$ (d) $\frac{7}{3}C$

8. A parallel plate capacitor of capacitance 4 μF and plate separation 6 cm is connected to a 1 V battery and charged. A dielectric of dielectric constant 4 and thickness 4 cm is introduced between the plates of the capacitor. The additional charge that flows into the capacitor from the battery is

(a) 4 μC (b) 3 μC (c) 5 μC (d) 10 μC

9. **Assertion** (A) If the distance between parallel plates of a capacitor is halved and dielectric constant is made three times, then the capacitance become six times.

Reason (R) Capacitance of the capacitor does not depend upon the nature of the material of the plates.

In the light of above statements, choose the most appropriate answer from the options given below.

(a) Both A and R are true and R is the correct explanation of the A.

(b) Both A and R are true but R is not the correct explanation of the A.

(c) A is true but R is false.

(d) A is false but R is true.

10. Two metallic spheres are of radii 1 cm and 2 cm are given charges of 1×10^{-2} C and 5×10^{-2} C respectively.

If these are connected by a copper wire, then final value of charge on smaller sphere is

(a) 1×10^{-2} C

(b) 2×10^{-2} C

(c) 3×10^{-2} C

(d) 4×10^{-2} C

11. It is required to use a 10 μF capacitor with 200 V potential difference. Capacitors of capacitance 10 μF are available but they can withstand only 50 V. Which of these combinations is useful?

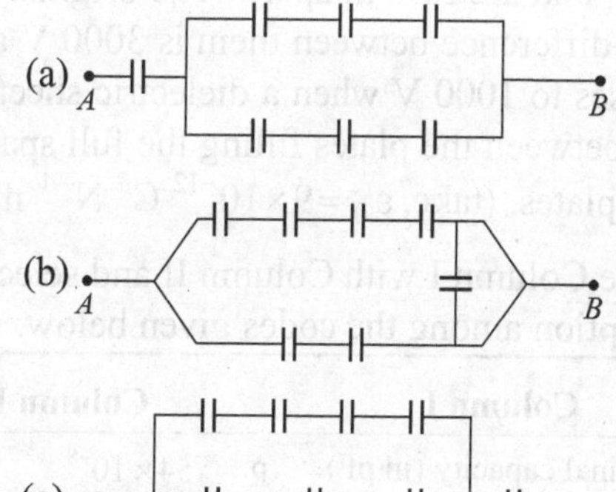

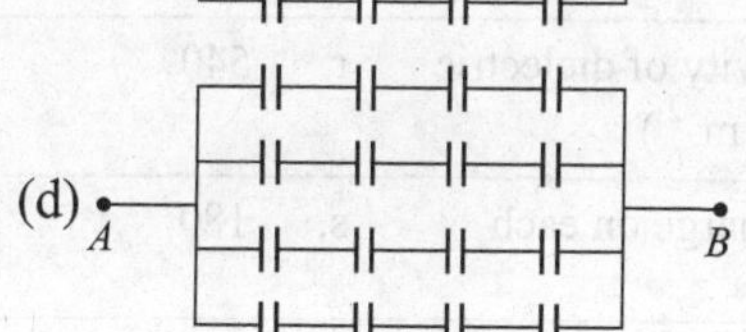

12. **Statement I** If the upper plate of a parallel capacitor is connected to the lower plate, then its capacitance becomes infinity.

Statement II A non-polar molecule develops an induced dipole moment.

In the light of above statements, choose the most appropriate answer from the options given below

(a) Both Statement I and Statement II are incorrect.

(b) Statement I is correct but Statement II is incorrect.

(c) Statement II is correct but Statement I is incorrect.

(d) Both Statement I and Statement II are correct.

13. Two parallel plate capacitors of capacitances C and $2C$ arc connected in parallel and charged to a potential difference V by a battery. The battery is then disconnected and the space between the plates of capacitor C is completely filled with a material of dielectric constant K. The potential difference across the capacitors now becomes

(a) $\frac{V}{K+1}$

(b) $\frac{2V}{K+2}$

(c) $\frac{3V}{K+2}$

(d) $\frac{3V}{K+3}$

14. The parallel plates of a capacitor have an area of 0.2 m^2 and are 10^{-2} m apart . The original potential difference between them is 3000 V and it decreases to 1000 V when a dielectric sheet is inserted between the plates filling the full space between plates. (take, $\varepsilon_0 = 9\times10^{-12} \text{ C}^2 \text{ N}^{-1} \text{ m}^{-2}$).

Match the Column I with Column II and select the correct option among the codes given below.

	Column I		Column II
i.	Original capacity (in pF)	p.	54×10^{-8}
ii.	Capacity after insertion of dielectric (pF)	q.	27×10^{-12}
iii.	Permittivity of dielectric ($\text{C}^2 \text{ N}^{-1} \text{ m}^{-2}$)	r.	540
iv.	Initial charge on each plate	s.	180

Codes

	i	ii	iii	iv
(a)	s	r	q	p
(b)	p	q	r	s
(c)	q	r	p	s
(d)	r	s	t	q

15. A parallel plate capacitor is maintained at a certain potential difference, When a dielectric slab of thickness 4 mm is introduced between the plates, the plate separation had to be increased by 2 mm in order to maintain the same potential difference between the plates, the dielectric constant of the slab is

(a) 2 (b) 3

(c) 4 (d) 5

16. In the circuit shown, the effective capacitance between points X and Y is

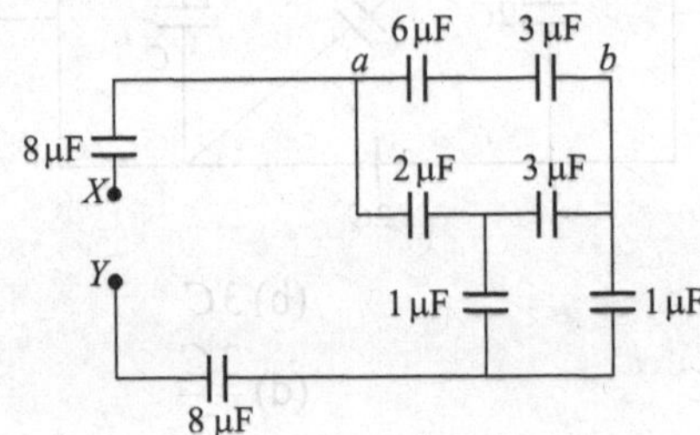

(a) 3.33 μF (b) 1 μF

(c) 0.44 μF (d) 0.88 μF

17. n identical capacitors of capacitance C are joined in series and the combination is charged to voltage V. The total energy stored is U_s. The capacitors are now disconnected and joined in parallel. The total energy stored in the parallel combination will be

(a) $\frac{U_s}{n}$ (b) U_s

(c) nU_s (d) n^2U_s

18. Equivalent capacitance between X and Y points in the given figure is

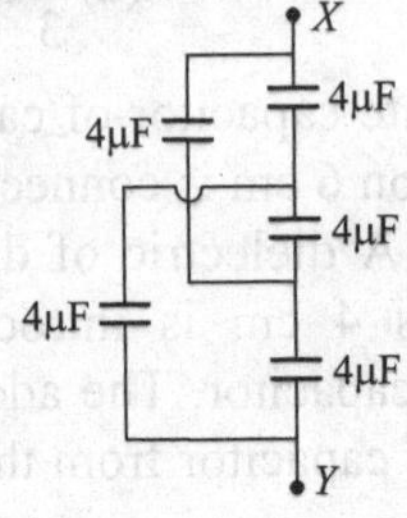

(a) 2 μF (b) 4 μF (c) 3 μF (d) 1 μF

19. Between the plates of a parallel plate capacitor, a dielectric of dielectric constant K_1 and thickness t_1 is placed. In the rest of the space, there is another plate of thickness t_2 and dielectric constant K_2. The potential difference across the condenser will be

(a) $\frac{Q}{A\varepsilon_0}\left(\frac{t_1}{K_1}+\frac{t_2}{K_2}\right)$

(b) $\frac{\varepsilon_0 Q}{A}\left(\frac{t_1}{K_1}+\frac{t_2}{K_2}\right)$

(c) $\frac{Q}{A\varepsilon_0}\left(\frac{K_1}{t_1}-\frac{K_2}{t_2}\right)$

(d) $\frac{\varepsilon_0 Q}{A}(K_1 t_1 - K_2 t_2)$

20. Figure shows a network of capacitors where the numbers indicated capacitances in microfarad. What must be the value of capacitance C if the equivalent capacitance between points A and B is to be 1 μF ?

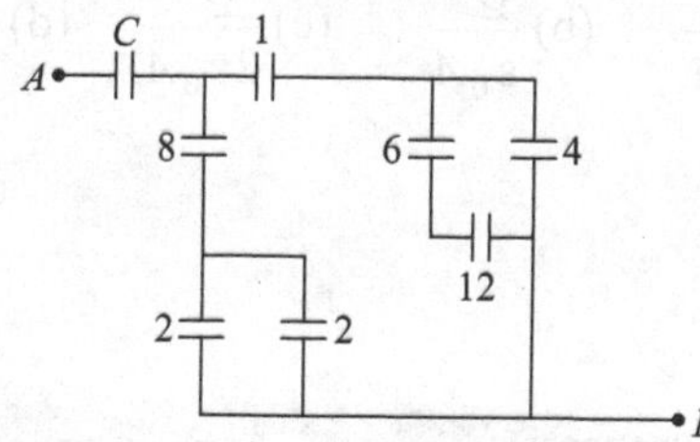

(a) $\frac{31}{23}$ μF (b) $\frac{32}{23}$ μF

(c) $\frac{33}{23}$ μF (d) $\frac{34}{23}$ μF

21. A capacitor of capacitance C_1 is charged by connecting it to a battery. The battery is now removed and this capacitor is connected to a second uncharged capacitor of capacitance C_2. If the charge distributes equally on the two capacitors, the difference of the total energy stored in the capacitors after connection and before connection is

(a) $\frac{Q^2}{C}$ (b) $\frac{-Q^2}{4C}$

(c) $\frac{-Q^2}{3C}$ (d) $\frac{Q^2}{4C}$

22. A battery is used to charge a capacitor. After charging, the battery is removed and capacitor is connected to another similar capacitor. The total electrostatic energy of resulting system

(a) increases by a factor of 16

(b) decreases by a factor of 2

(c) remains the same

(d) increases by a factor of 2

23. The capacitances of the three capacitors 4 μF, 12 μF and 16 μF are connected first in parallel and then in series. The ratio of equivalent capacitance in the two cases will be

(a) $\frac{35}{3}$ (b) $\frac{39}{3}$

(c) $\frac{37}{3}$ (d) $\frac{38}{3}$

24. A capacitor of capacitance 1 μF initially, has charge 2 μC. It is connected to a battery of emf 10V as shown in figure. The work done by battery is

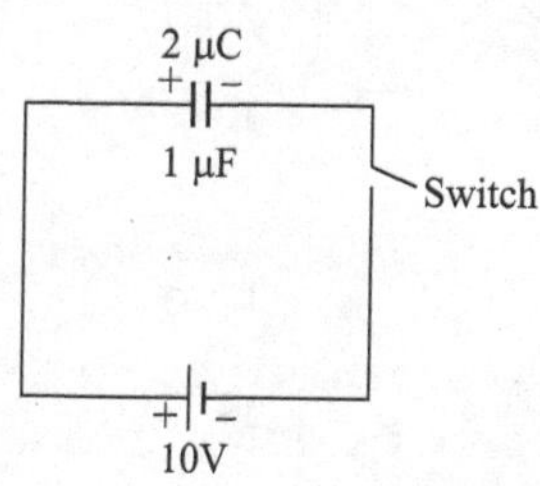

(a) 20 μJ

(b) 30 μJ

(c) 40 μJ

(d) 80 μJ

25. The potential difference between points A and B in the circuit shown in figure is

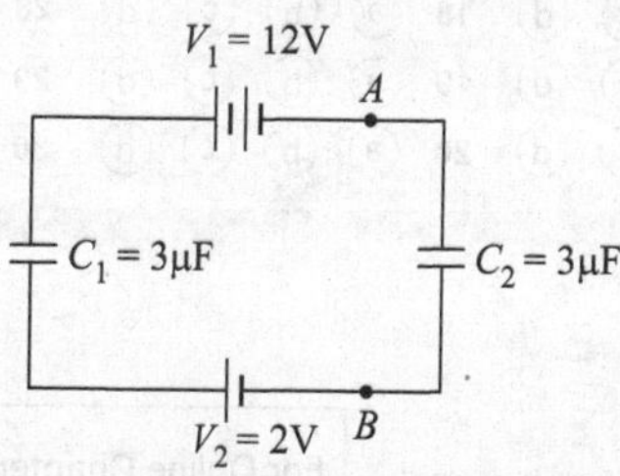

(a) 5 V (b) 2 V (c) 10 V (d) 14 V

26. Calculate energy strored in capacitance C_1 and C_2.

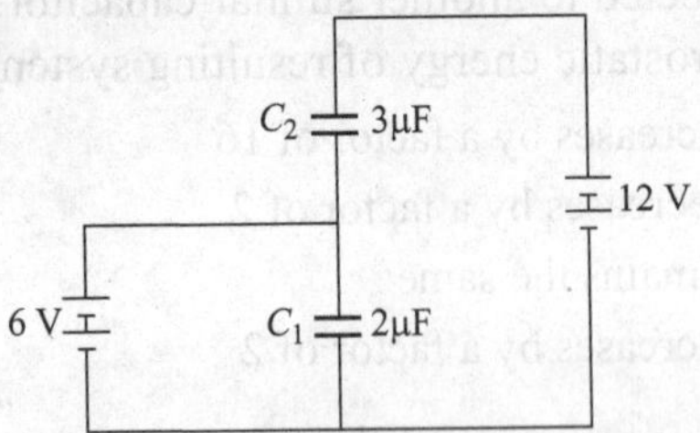

(a) $U_1 = 12\ \mu J, U_2 = 24\ \mu J$
(b) $U_1 = 24\ \mu J, U_2 = 12\ \mu J$
(c) $U_1 = 36\ \mu J, U_2 = 54\ \mu J$
(d) $U_1 = 24\ \mu J, U_2 = 36\ \mu J$

27. The two batteries of 100 V and 50 V are connected to the two capacitors of 5 pF and 10 pF, respectively. If they are connected by the wire, then the common potential of the capacitors will be

(a) 110 V
(b) 77 V
(c) 66.66 V
(d) 220 V

28. A dielectric of dielectric constant K is introduced such that one-third of its area of a capacitor of a capacitance C is occupied by it. The new capacity will be

(a) $\frac{C}{2}(2+K)$ (b) $\frac{C}{3}(2+K)$
(c) $\frac{C}{4}(2+K)$ (d) $C(1+K)$

29. A capacitor is charged with a battery and then its plate separation is increased without disconnecting the battery, then the potential difference across the plates of the capacitor will

(a) increase
(b) decrease
(c) remain same
(d) first increase then decrease

30. The force of attraction between the plates of air filled parallel plate capacitor having charge Q and area of each plate A is given by

(a) $\frac{2Q^2}{\varepsilon_0 A}$ (b) $\frac{Q^2}{\varepsilon_0 A}$ (c) $\frac{Q^2}{2\varepsilon_0 A}$ (d) $\frac{Q^2}{4\varepsilon_0 A}$

Response Index

01	a	b	c	d	11	a	b	c	d	21	a	b	c	d
02	a	b	c	d	12	a	b	c	d	22	a	b	c	d
03	a	b	c	d	13	a	b	c	d	23	a	b	c	d
04	a	b	c	d	14	a	b	c	d	24	a	b	c	d
05	a	b	c	d	15	a	b	c	d	25	a	b	c	d
06	a	b	c	d	16	a	b	c	d	26	a	b	c	d
07	a	b	c	d	17	a	b	c	d	27	a	b	c	d
08	a	b	c	d	18	a	b	c	d	28	a	b	c	d
09	a	b	c	d	19	a	b	c	d	29	a	b	c	d
10	a	b	c	d	20	a	b	c	d	30	a	b	c	d

Performance Scanner

> 90% Excellent !	You have mastered this chapter. The concepts of this chapter are on your fingertips. Move on to the next chapter and maintain this momentum.
76-90% Very Good !	You have a good command over this chapter. Revise the chapter again after a few days and enhance your performance.
60-75% Good !	You have a wide scope to learn more from this chapter. Revise this chapter again.
<60% Not Satisfactory!	You have a long way ahead of you to master this chapter. Revise it thoroughly.

For Online Chapter Test **Scan the QR Code**

For Online Unit Test **Scan the QR Code**

Space for Rough Work

Space for Rough Work

Test Booklet No. **3947154**

Test Booklet Code **CH4**

MEDACE

NEET (UG)

SELF ASSESSMENT KIT

Current Electricity

Topics Covered

Electric Current and Ohm's Law

Combination of Resistors and Cells

Kirchhoff's Laws and Measuring Instruments

Important Instructions

- This Booklet Contains – Three Topic Tests and One Test on Complete Chapter.
- Each question carries 4 marks.
- For each correct response, the candidate will get 4 marks and for every incorrect response 1 mark will be additionally deducted from the total score.
- Use **Blue/Black** point pen only for filling the OMR.
- Rough work will be done in the space provided for this purpose within the test booklet only.

Name of the Candidate (In Capitals)

____

____

Candidate's Signature ____________

Invigilator's Signature ____________

Facsimile signature stamp of center superintendent____________

Do not open this Booklet until you start attempting the Test

Topical Follow Thru

Test 1

Syllabus

- Electric Current
- Drift Velocity, Mobility and their relation with Electric Current
- Ohm's Law
- Electrical Resistance
- *V-I* Characteristics of Ohmic and Non-ohmic Conductors
- Electrical Resistivity and Conductivity
- Temperature Dependence of Resistance

For deeper insight **Scan the QR Code**

Important Instructions

- The test is of 30 minutes duration and contains 15 Multiple Choice Questions (Four options with a single correct answer).
- Choose the correct option and fill the OMR given on the last page of this test accordingly.
- At some instances, you may find more than 1 option may be correct in such circumstances you have to judge the most appropriate answer as per the conditions given in the question.

1. The resistivity *versus* temperature graph of a semiconductor will look like as

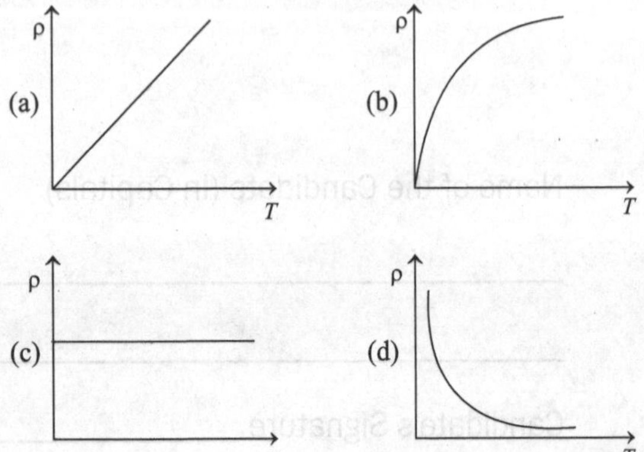

2. The graph of current *versus* time in a wire is given.

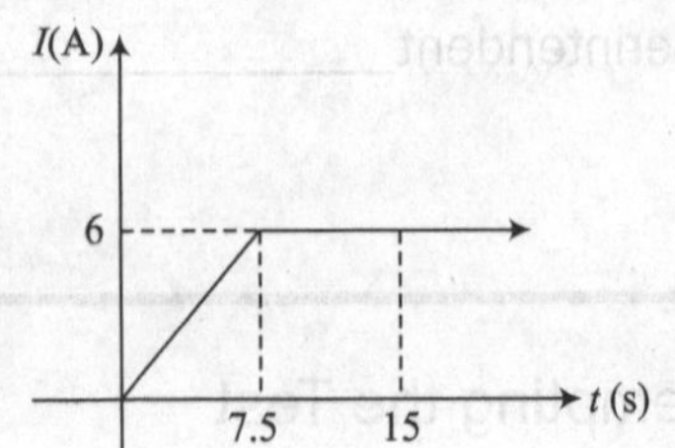

If charge that flows through a wire in 7.5 s is q_1 and that flows through the wire in 15 s is q_2, then ratio $q_1 : q_2$ is

(a) 2 : 1
(b) 1 : 2
(c) 4 : 1
(d) 1 : 4

3. The charge passing through a conductor is a function of time and it is given by $q = (2t^2 - 4t + 3)$ mC. The current through the conductor at $t = 4$ s is

(a) 7 mA
(b) 19 mA
(c) 15 mA
(d) 12 mA

4. A 1.5 V dry cell is tested by connecting it to a low resistance ammeter. The ammeter reads 25 A. Potential drop across ammeter is

(a) 1.5 V
(b) 0.5 V
(c) 1.0 V
(d) 0

5. For the conductor shown below

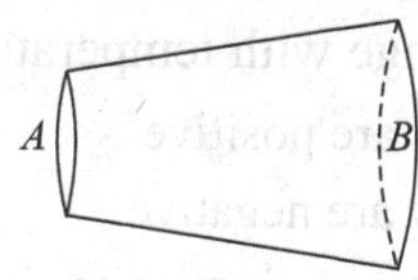

(a) $v_{d(A)} = v_{d(B)}$
(b) $v_{d(A)} > v_{d(B)}$
(c) $v_{d(A)} < v_{d(B)}$
(d) the drift speed varies randomly

6. An electron moving through a wire has an average drift velocity that is very small, (order of drift speed is around 10^{-4} m), because
(a) instantaneous speed of an electron is also very less
(b) electron suffers many collisions
(c) electron is repelled by other electrons
(d) electrons have random velocities

7. The correct relationship between current density (**J**) and electric field (**E**) is (where, σ = conductivity, A = area of cross-section and μ = mobility)
(a) $\mathbf{J} = \sigma\mathbf{E}$
(b) $\mathbf{J} = A\mathbf{E}$
(c) $\mathbf{J} = \sigma^2\mathbf{E}$
(d) $\mathbf{J} = \mu\mathbf{E}$

8. A conducting wire has an electron density of $8 \times 10^{22}\ m^{-3}$. The average time interval between successive collision of electrons is 4×10^{-11} s. The resistivity of the conducting wire is (Take, mass of electron $= 9.1 \times 10^{-31}$ kg)
(a) $1.1 \times 10^{-5}\ \Omega$-m
(b) $1.6 \times 10^{-4}\ \Omega$ - m
(c) $3.2 \times 10^{-5}\ \Omega$ - m
(d) $1.6 \times 10^{-5}\ \Omega$ - m

9. In a particle accelerator, a current of 0.5 mA is carried by a 5 MeV proton beam that has a radius of 1.5 mm. The number of protons in unit volume is
(a) 1.47×10^{13}
(b) 3.10×10^{7}
(c) 2.48×10^{16}
(d) 2.5×10^{8}

10. If electric current i is flowing through a conducting wire of length l, then total momentum of free electrons in conducting wire is (here, m is mass of electron and e is charge on electron)
(a) $\frac{mil^2}{2e}$ (b) $\frac{mil}{e}$ (c) $\frac{mil}{2e}$ (d) $\frac{mi^2l^2}{e}$

11. The relaxation time for collision of electron with ions in a conducting wire is 16.2×10^{-12} s. The mobility of electron inside the conductor is
(a) $4.82\ m^2V^{-1}s^{-1}$
(b) $2.84\ m^2V^{-1}s^{-1}$
(c) $2.84 \times 10^{-2}\ m^2V^{-1}s^{-1}$
(d) $56.8\ m^2V^{-1}s^{-1}$

12. Resistivity of copper is $1.7 \times 10^{-8}\ \Omega$-m. An electric field, $E = 340$ V/m is applied between the two ends of a copper wire. The current density is
(a) $1.7 \times 10^{-8}\ Am^{-2}$
(b) $1.7 \times 10^{-6}\ Am^{-2}$
(c) $2 \times 10^{10}\ Am^{-2}$
(d) $6 \times 10^{7}\ Am^{-2}$

13. **Assertion** (A) Resistivity of a semiconductor decreases with increase in temperature.
Reason (R) Atoms of a semiconductor vibrate with a larger amplitude at higher temperature.

In the light of above statements, choose the most appropriate answer from the options given below.
(a) Both A and R are true and R is the correct explanation of A.
(b) Both A and R are true but R is not the correct explanation of A.
(c) A is true but R is false.
(d) A is false but R is true.

14. V-I graph for a conductor is shown below.

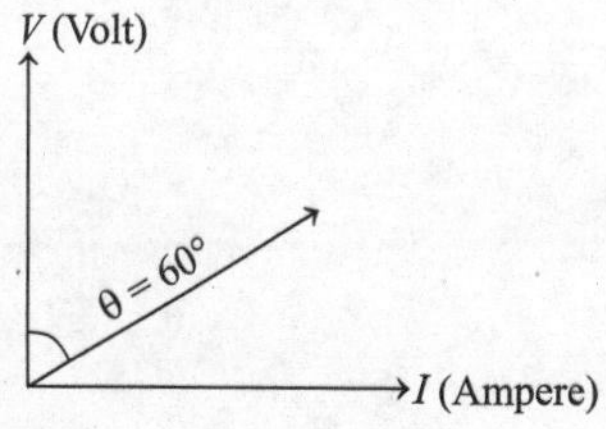

The resistance of the conductor is

(a) $\sqrt{3}\,\Omega$

(b) $\frac{1}{\sqrt{3}}\,\Omega$

(c) $1\,\Omega$

(d) Cannot be predicted

15. Temperature coefficients of resistance of two different materials are α_1 and α_2, respectively. If a new material is made by combining these two materials such that the resistivity of the material does not change with temperature, then

(a) α_1 and α_2 are positive

(b) α_1 and α_2 are negative

(c) α_1 and α_2 are of opposite sign

(d) α_1 and α_2 must have equal value but opposite sign

Response Index

01	ⓐ	ⓑ	ⓒ	ⓓ	11	ⓐ	ⓑ	ⓒ	ⓓ
02	ⓐ	ⓑ	ⓒ	ⓓ	12	ⓐ	ⓑ	ⓒ	ⓓ
03	ⓐ	ⓑ	ⓒ	ⓓ	13	ⓐ	ⓑ	ⓒ	ⓓ
04	ⓐ	ⓑ	ⓒ	ⓓ	14	ⓐ	ⓑ	ⓒ	ⓓ
05	ⓐ	ⓑ	ⓒ	ⓓ	15	ⓐ	ⓑ	ⓒ	ⓓ
06	ⓐ	ⓑ	ⓒ	ⓓ					
07	ⓐ	ⓑ	ⓒ	ⓓ					
08	ⓐ	ⓑ	ⓒ	ⓓ					
09	ⓐ	ⓑ	ⓒ	ⓓ					
10	ⓐ	ⓑ	ⓒ	ⓓ					

Performance Scanner

> 90% Excellent !	You have mastered these topics. The concepts of these topics are at your fingertips. Move on to the next test and maintain this momentum.
76-90% Very Good !	You have a good command over these topics. Revise them again after a few days and enhance your performance.
60-75% Good !	You have a wide scope to learn for these topics. Revise them again.
<60% Not Satisfactory!	You have a long way ahead of you to master in these topics. Revise them thoroughly.

Test 2

Syllabus

- Series and Parallel Combination of Resistors
- Internal Resistance
- Potential Difference and Emf of a Cell
- A Combination of Cells in Series and Parallel

For deeper insight **Scan the QR Code**

Important Instructions

- The test is of 30 mins duration and contains 15 Multiple Choice Questions (Four options with a single correct answer).
- Choose the correct option and fill the OMR given on the last page of this test accordingly.
- At some instances, you may find more than 1 option may be correct in such circumstances you have to judge the most appropriate answer as per the conditions given in the question.

1. Two wires have equal diameters, with resistivities ρ_1 and ρ_2 and lengths l_1 and l_2 respectively. If these two wires are connected in parallel, then the resultant resistance is

(a) $\dfrac{\rho_1 l_2 + \rho_2 l_1}{\rho_1 l_1 \rho_2 l_2}$

(b) $\dfrac{\rho_1 \rho_2 l_1 l_2}{(\rho_1 l_1 + \rho_2 l_2) A}$

(c) $\dfrac{\rho_1 l_1 + \rho_2 l_2}{\rho_1 l_1 \rho_2 l_2}$

(d) $\dfrac{\rho_1 l_1}{A} + \dfrac{\rho_2 l_2}{A}$

2. The equivalent resistance of the following circuit between A and B is

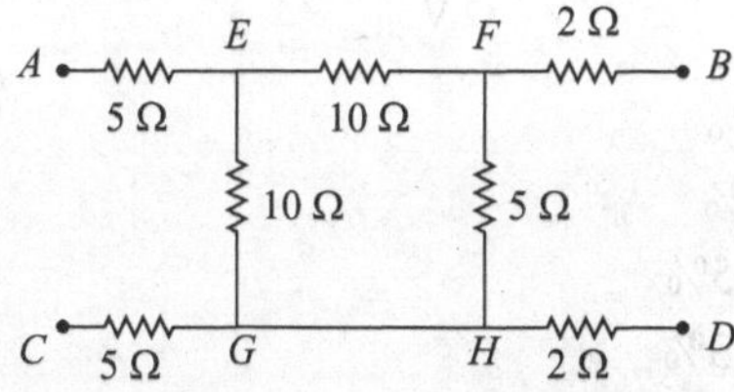

(a) 15 Ω (b) 13 Ω
(c) 20 Ω (d) 7 Ω

3. Internal resistance of a cell depends on

(a) material used for making a cell
(b) output potential of the cell
(c) load resistance
(d) current flowing through the circuit

4. The reading of an ideal voltmeter in the circuit shown is

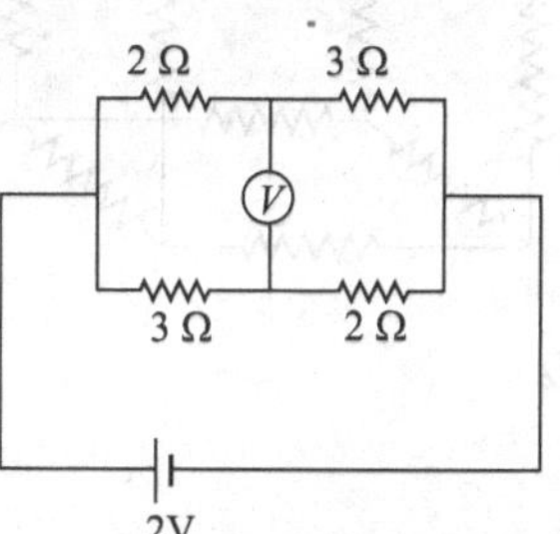

(a) $\dfrac{4}{5}$ V (b) $\dfrac{5}{2}$ V

(c) $\dfrac{6}{5}$ V (d) $\dfrac{2}{5}$ V

5. A heater is labelled as 200 W, 220 V. The coil of the heater is divided into 2 parts and these parts are now connected in parallel to the same source. Now, the energy liberated in 1 min is

(a) 48000 J (b) 800 J
(c) 12000 J (d) 2400 J

6. The power dissipated in 16 Ω resistor is 25 W. The power dissipated in 5 Ω resistor is

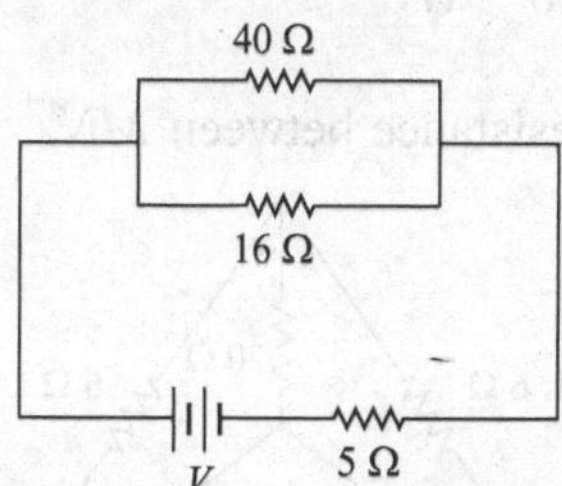

(a) $\dfrac{100}{16}$ W (b) $\dfrac{10000}{(64)^2}$ W

(c) $\dfrac{245}{16}$ W (d) $\dfrac{500}{16}$ W

7. Internal resistances of two cells are 0.6 Ω and 0.3 Ω. They are connected in parallel. The voltage across the battery terminal is 1.8 V. If the emf of the first cell is 1.2 V, then emf of the second cell is

(a) 6 V (b) 1.8 V
(c) 3 V (d) 2.1 V

8. Twelve resistors of equal resistance R are connected in the form of a cube. Effective resistance between diagonals of the cube is

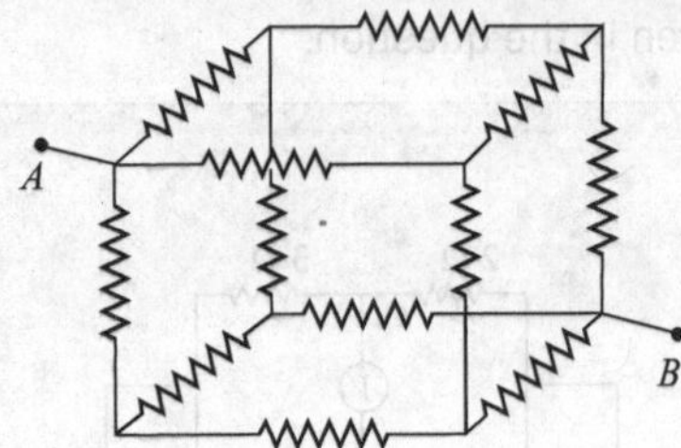

(a) $\frac{12}{5} R\,\Omega$

(b) $\frac{5}{6} R\,\Omega$

(c) $\frac{7}{9} R\,\Omega$

(d) $\frac{11}{6} R\,\Omega$

9. A current of 5 mA was passed through an unknown resistor which dissipated a power of 2.5 W. If the power supply is 25 V, then the power dissipated is

(a) 6.25×10^{-3} W
(b) 2.5×10^{-6} W
(c) 2.5×10^{-3} W
(d) 6.25×10^{-6} W

10. Find the resistance between MN.

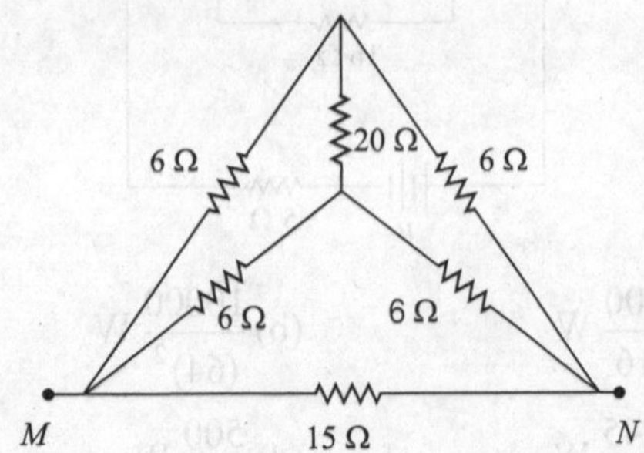

(a) 20 Ω
(b) 15 Ω
(c) 6 Ω
(d) $\frac{30}{7}$ Ω

11. A set of n resistors, each of resistance R are connected in parallel to a battery of emf E and internal resistance R. The current drawn from battery is I. Now, these n resistors are connected in series to the same battery, then the current drawn from the battery becomes $\frac{I}{6}$. The value of n is

(a) 3
(b) 6
(c) 9
(d) 18

12. In the given circuit, the percentage change in potential drop across resistor of resistance 200 Ω in absence of voltmeter and in presence of voltmeter of resistance 200 Ω, is

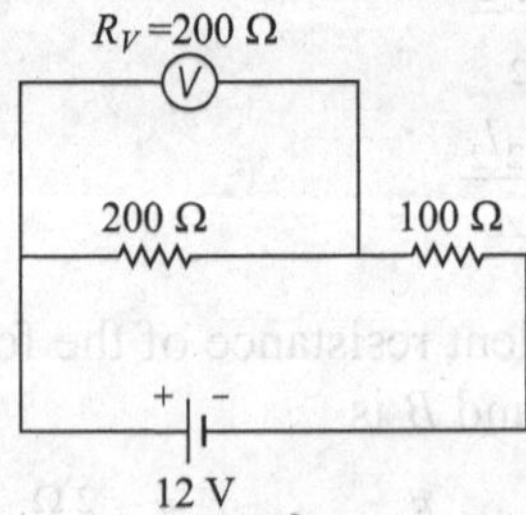

(a) 25%
(b) 50%
(c) 12.5%
(d) 33.3%

13. A cell which has an emf of 1.5 V is connected in series with an external resistance of 10 Ω. If the potential difference across the cell is 1.25 V, then the internal resistance of the cell (in Ω) is

(a) 2
(b) 0.25
(c) 1.5
(d) 0.3

14. Consider the following circuit shown in the figure.

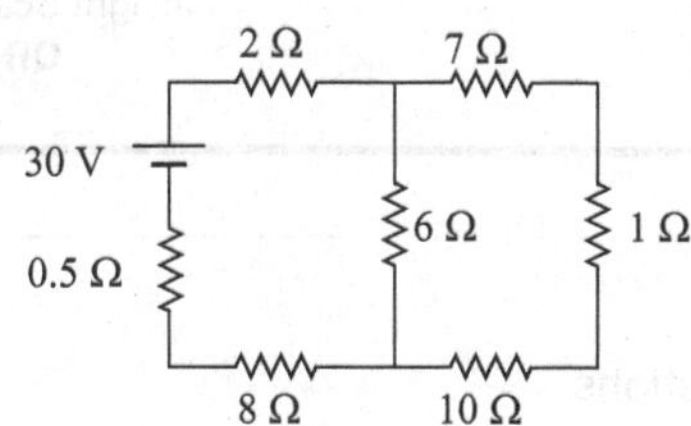

Power consumed by 6 Ω resistor is

(a) 8 W
(b) 13.5 W
(c) 1.75 W
(d) 0 W

15. The figure shows a network of resistors each having value 10 Ω. Find the equivalent resistance between points *A* and *B*.

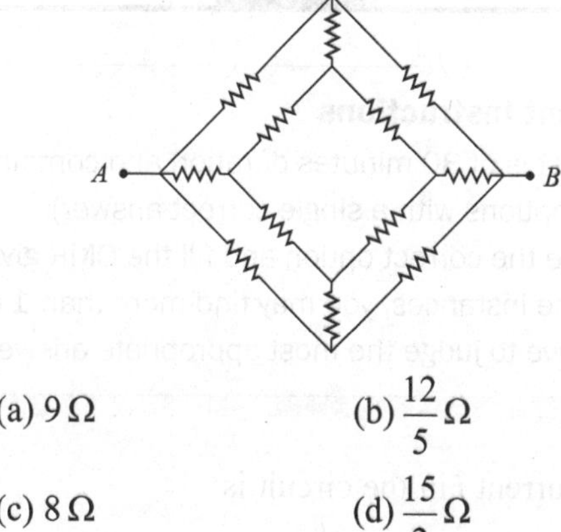

(a) 9 Ω (b) $\frac{12}{5}$ Ω

(c) 8 Ω (d) $\frac{15}{2}$ Ω

■ **Response Index**

01	(a)	(b)	(c)	(d)	11	(a)	(b)	(c)	(d)
02	(a)	(b)	(c)	(d)	12	(a)	(b)	(c)	(d)
03	(a)	(b)	(c)	(d)	13	(a)	(b)	(c)	(d)
04	(a)	(b)	(c)	(d)	14	(a)	(b)	(c)	(d)
05	(a)	(b)	(c)	(d)	15	(a)	(b)	(c)	(d)
06	(a)	(b)	(c)	(d)					
07	(a)	(b)	(c)	(d)					
08	(a)	(b)	(c)	(d)					
09	(a)	(b)	(c)	(d)					
10	(a)	(b)	(c)	(d)					

■ **Performance Scanner**

> 90% Excellent !	You have mastered these topics. The concepts of these topics are at your fingertips. Move on to the next test and maintain this momentum.
76-90% Very Good !	You have a good command over these topics. Revise them again after a few days and enhance your performance.
60-75% Good !	You have a wide scope to learn for these topics. Revise them again.
<60% Not Satisfactory!	You have a long way ahead of you to master in these topics. Revise them thoroughly.

Test 3

Syllabus
- Kirchhoff's Laws and their Applications
- Wheatstone Bridge
- Meter Bridge

For deeper insight **Scan the QR Code** 

Important Instructions

- The test is of 30 minutes duration and contains 15 Multiple Choice Questions (Four options with a single correct answer).
- Choose the correct option and fill the OMR given on the last page of this test accordingly.
- At some instances, you may find more than 1 option may be correct in such circumstances you have to judge the most appropriate answer as per the conditions given in the question.

1. The current i in the circuit is

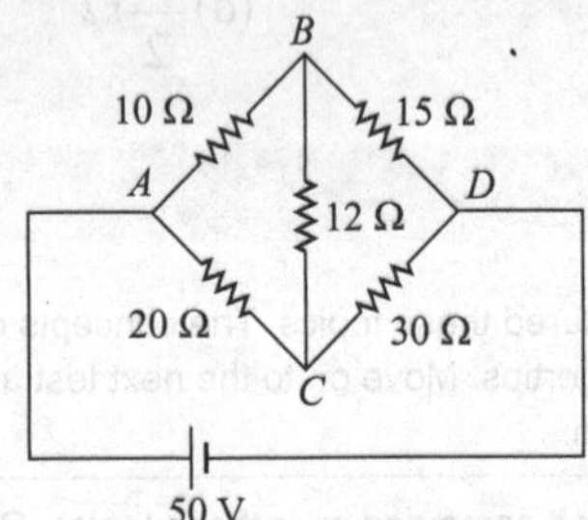

(a) 10 A (b) 3 A
(c) 7 A (d) 12 A

2. Statement I In a meter bridge experiment, a high resistance is always connected in series with a galvanometer.

Statement II When resistance increases in the circuit, current through the circuit also increases.
In the light of above statements, choose the most appropriate answer from the options given below.

(a) Both Statement I and Statement II are correct.
(b) Both Statement I and Statement II are incorrect.
(c) Statement I is correct and Statement II is incorrect.
(d) Statement I is incorrect and Statement II is correct.

3. The following figure shows the current flowing in a circuit. The current I is

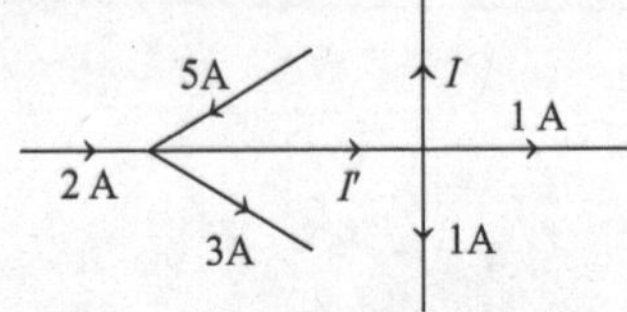

(a) 2 A (b) 4 A
(c) 0 A (d) 3 A

4. We have a meter bridge. The resistance of two arms are 10 Ω and M Ω, respectively. If the resistance M is shunted with an equal resistance, the new balanced point is $1.2\,l_1$. The resistance M is

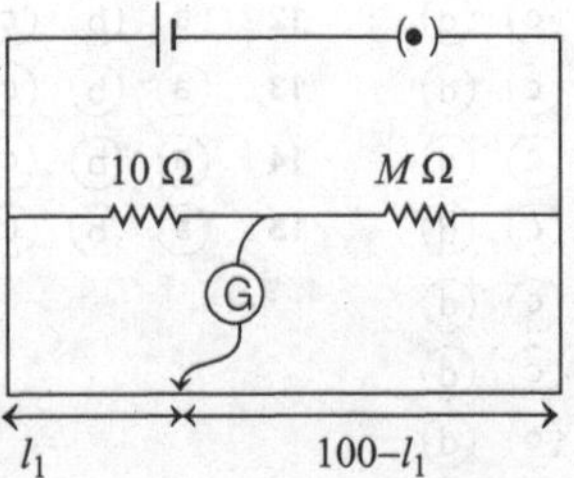

(a) 10 Ω (b) 5 Ω
(c) 20 Ω (d) 15 Ω

5. Find the ratio of currents I_1 and I_2 for the circuit shown below.

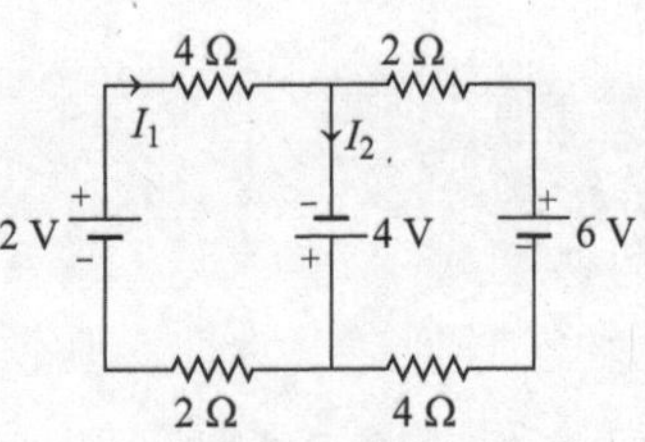

(a) 1 : 3 (b) 5 : 8
(c) 5 : 3 (d) 3 : 8

6. A meter bridge is set-up as shown below. To determine two unknown resistances, X and Y are put in gap. The null point is found to be 40 cm away from the end A, a resistance of 15 Ω is connected in series with Y, then null point is found to shift 10 cm towards the end A of the wire.

The values of X and Y, respectively are

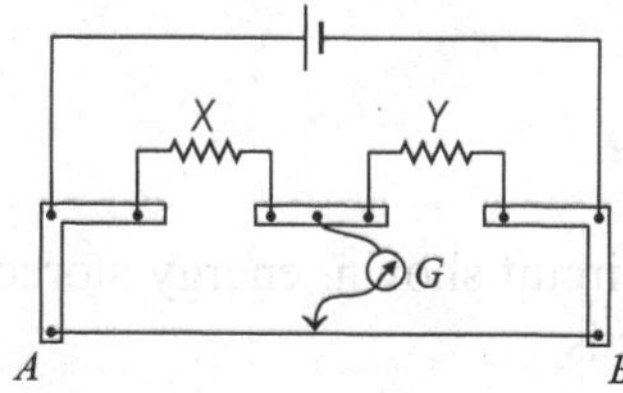

(a) 18 Ω, 27 Ω
(b) 30 Ω, 45 Ω
(c) 50 Ω, 75 Ω
(d) 75 Ω, 50 Ω

7. The resistance G of the galvanometer is being measured in the following circuit. The relation $\frac{P}{Q}=\frac{R}{G}$ will be satisfied only when

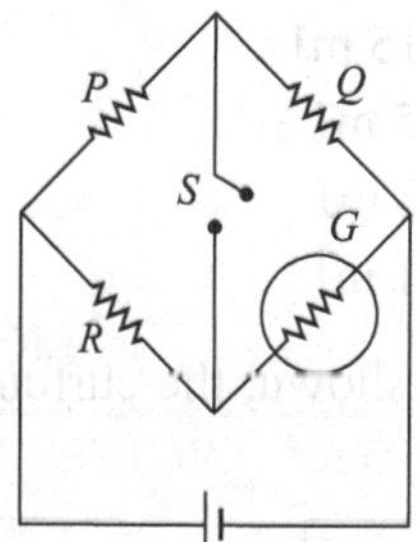

(a) the galvanometer shows no change in deflection whether S is open or closed
(b) the galvanometer shows a deflection when switch S is closed
(c) the galvanometer shows no deflection
(d) the galvanometer shows a deflection when switch S is open

8. Meter bridge experimental set-up is shown in the circuit. The length AC corresponds to null deflection of galvanometer which is represented by x, what would be its value if the radius of the wire AB is halved?

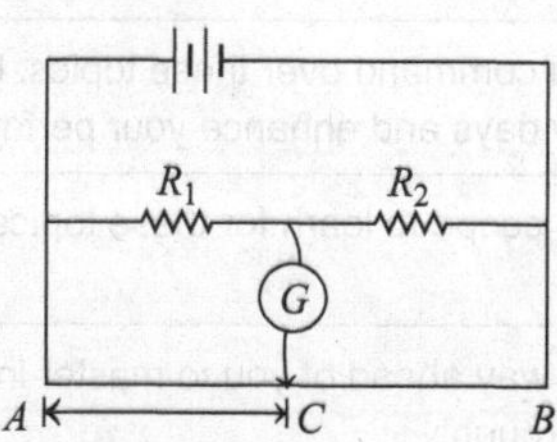

(a) x (b) $\frac{x}{3}$ (c) $4x$ (d) $2x$

9. In the given circuit, points A, B and C are at potentials 70 V, 0 V and 10 V respectively. Then,

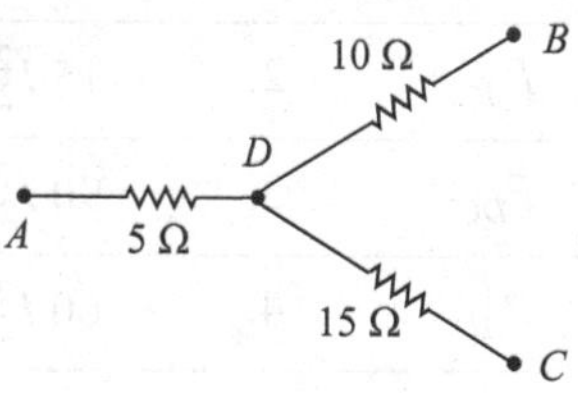

(a) potential at point D is 50 V
(b) potential at point D is 60 V
(c) currents in paths AD, DB and DC are in the ratio of 1 : 2 : 3
(d) currents in the paths AD, DB and DC are in the ratio of 3 : 2 : 1

10. The null point of a meter bridge is 20 cm from zero end. A 15 Ω resistance is connected with the smaller of the two resistances connected in meter bridge. The null point shifts to 40 cm. The smaller resistance is of

(a) 9 Ω (b) 10 Ω
(c) 11 Ω (d) 12 Ω

11. Side wire AB of a meter bridge is 100 cm long. The position of the end of galvanometer for which it will show zero deflection is

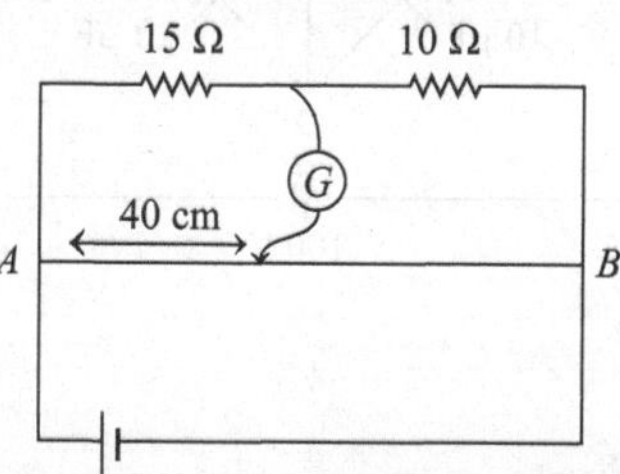

(a) 40 cm (b) 60 cm
(c) 20 cm (d) 80 cm

12. In given circuit, current in branch AD is I_2. Now, match List I with List II.

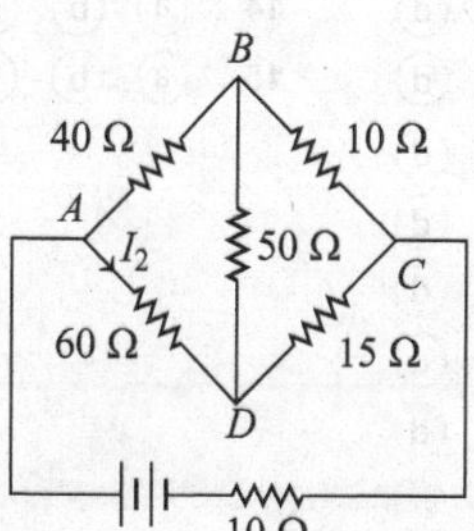

	List I		List II
A.	P_{AB}	1.	$22.5\, I_2^2$
B.	P_{BC}	2.	$15\, I_2^2$
C.	P_{DC}	3.	$90\, I_2^2$
D.	P_{AD}	4.	$60\, I_2^2$

where, P = power dissipated.

Codes

	A	B	C	D
(a)	3	1	2	4
(b)	2	1	3	4
(c)	3	4	1	2
(d)	2	4	3	1

13. Five capacitors of 10 μF capacity each, are connected to a DC potential of 100 V as shown in the adjoining figure. The equivalent capacitance between the points A and B will be equal to

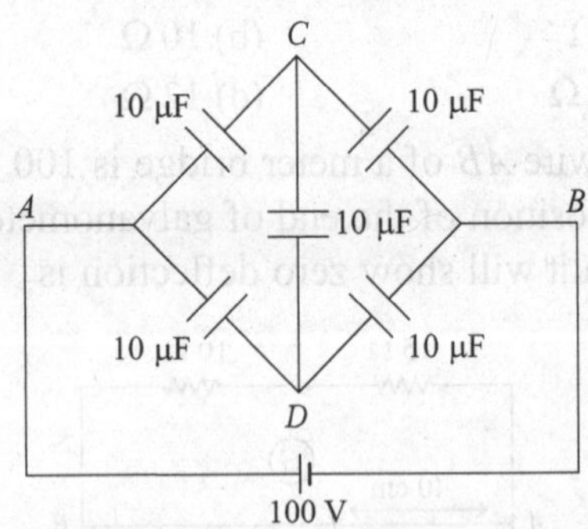

(a) 40 μF
(b) 20 μF
(c) 30 μF
(d) 10 μF

14. For the circuit shown, energy stored by the capacitor is

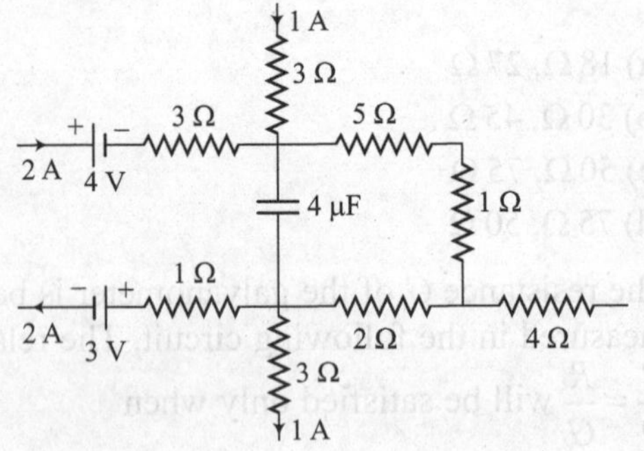

(a) around 1.15 mJ
(b) around 0.5 mJ
(c) around 0.8 mJ
(d) around 0.1 mJ

15. In the circuit shown, the current through 2 Ω resistor is

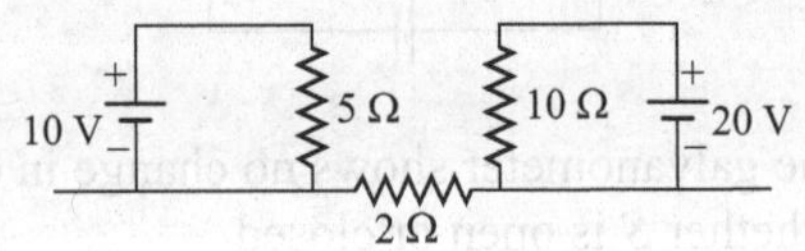

(a) 5 A (b) 2 A
(c) 0 (d) 4 A

Response Index

01	a	b	c	d	11	a	b	c	d
02	a	b	c	d	12	a	b	c	d
03	a	b	c	d	13	a	b	c	d
04	a	b	c	d	14	a	b	c	d
05	a	b	c	d	15	a	b	c	d
06	a	b	c	d					
07	a	b	c	d					
08	a	b	c	d					
09	a	b	c	d					
10	a	b	c	d					

Performance Scanner

> 90% Excellent !	You have mastered these topics. The concepts of these topics are at your fingertips. Move on to the next test and maintain this momentum.
76-90% Very Good !	You have a good command over these topics. Revise them again after a few days and enhance your performance.
60-75% Good !	You have a wide scope to learn for these topics. Revise them again.
<60% Not Satisfactory!	You have a long way ahead of you to master in these topics. Revise them thoroughly.

Chapter Break Thru

Syllabus			
	• Electric Current • Drift Velocity, Mobility and their Relation with Electric Current • Ohm's Law • Electrical Resistance • *V-I* Characteristics of Ohmic and Non-ohmic Conductors	• Electrical Resistivity and Conductivity • Temperature Dependence of Resistance • Series and Parallel Combination of Resistors • Internal Resistance • Potential Difference and Emf of a Cell • A Combination of Cells in Series and Parallel	• Kirchhoff's Rule and their Applications • Wheatstone Bridge • Meter Bridge

Important Instructions

- The test is of 45 minutes duration and contains 30 multiple Choice Questions (Four options with a single correct answer).
- Choose the correct option and fill the OMR given on the last page of this test accordingly.
- At some instances, you may find more than 1 option may be correct, in such circumstances you have to judge the most appropriate answer as per conditions given in the question.

1. Which of the following materials obeys Ohm's law?

(a) GaAs (b) Silicon
(c) Nichrome (d) Ceramic

2. Current flows through the given conductor. Which of these quantities remains constant throughout the complete length of the conductor?

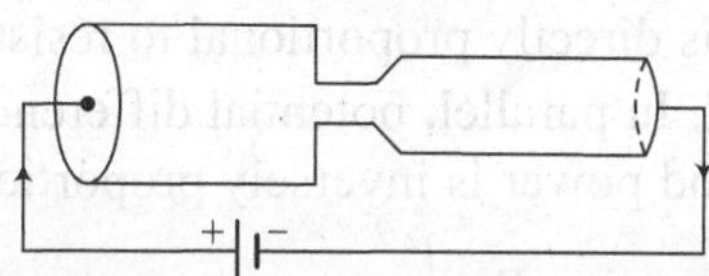

(a) Current
(b) Current density
(c) Electron mobility
(d) Electric field

3. The current through a wire is $I = I_0 + \alpha t$, where $I_0 = 15$ A and $\alpha = 6$ A/s, charge that flows through the wire in 12 s is

(a) 252 C (b) 180 C
(c) 612 C (d) 414 C

4. Two electric bulbs rated (P_1V) and (P_2V) are connected in parallel and V volts are applied to it. Total power (in watt) of this combination is

(a) $P_1 + P_2$ (b) $\sqrt{P_1P_2}$
(c) $\dfrac{P_1P_2}{P_1 + P_2}$ (d) $\dfrac{P_1 + P_2}{P_1P_2}$

5. Length of a copper wire is L and area of cross- section is A. The following graph shows the V-I characteristic of this wire. The slope of the curve becomes

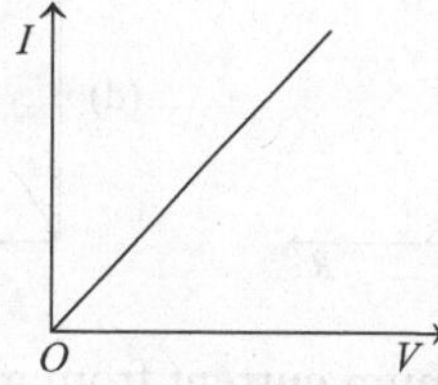

(a) more, if the experiment is performed at higher temperature
(b) more, if a wire of steel of same dimension is used
(c) more, if the length of the wire is increased
(d) less, if the length of the wire is increased

6. In given circuit, reading of voltmeter is nearest to (Take, resistance of voltmeter as 200 Ω.)

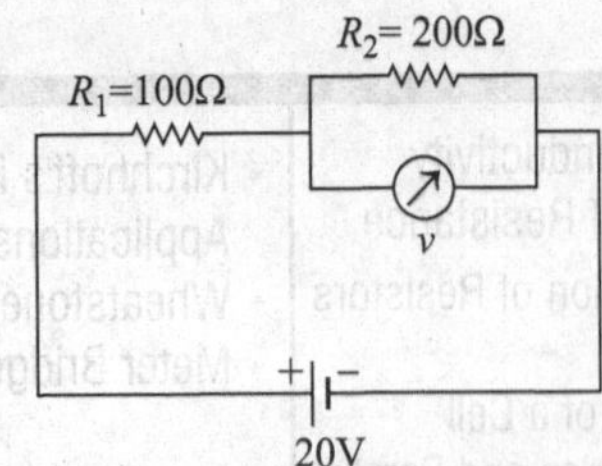

(a) 5 V (b) 15 V
(c) 10 V (d) 13.33 V

7. When a wire carries a current, then an electric field

(a) exists outside the wire
(b) exists outside the wire but perpendicular to its length
(c) exists inside the wire and perpendicular to its length
(d) exists inside the wire along its length

8. A cell of emf E and internal resistance r is connected across a load resistance R. The graph of power (P) *versus* load resistance (R) will look like

(a) 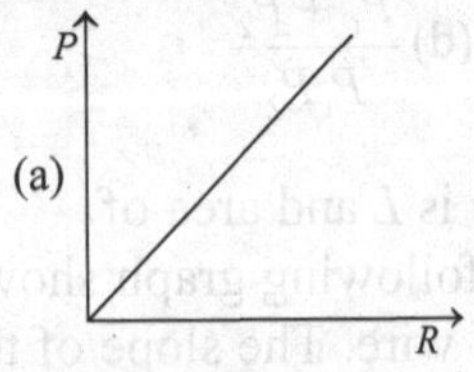

(b) 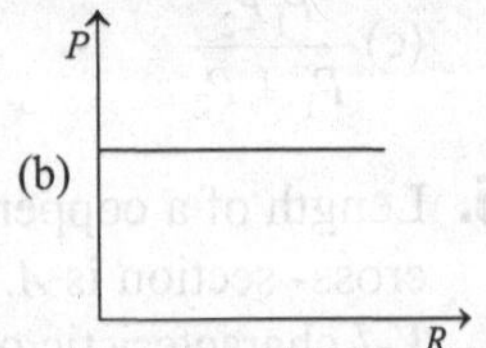

(c) 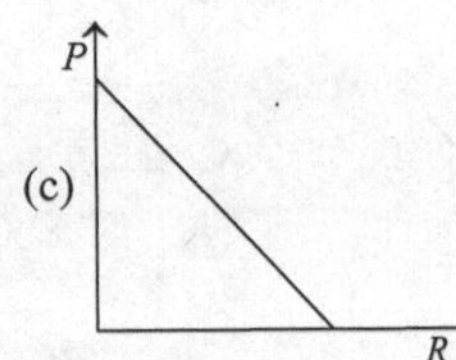

(d) 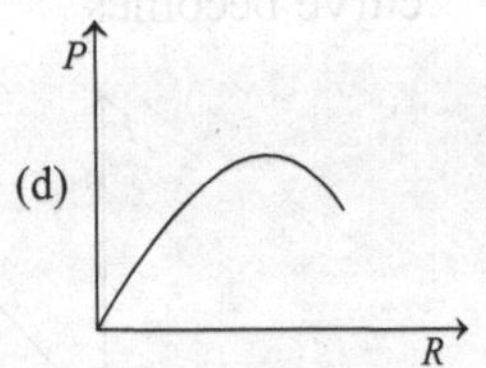

9. To get maximum current from a parallel combination of n identical cells each of internal resistance r connected across external resistance R, when

(a) $\frac{R}{2} >> r$
(b) $R << r$
(c) $R = r$
(d) $R >> r$

10. **Statement I** Electric appliances with metallic body have three pin connections whereas electric bulb has two pin connections.

Statement II Three pin connections reduce the heating of connecting wires.

In the light of above statements, choose the most appropriate answer from the options given below.

(a) Both Statement I and Statement II are incorrect.
(b) Both Statement I and Statement II are correct.
(c) Statement I is correct but Statement II is incorrect.
(d) Statement I is incorrect but Statement I is correct.

11. The figure shown below is a part of a circuit.

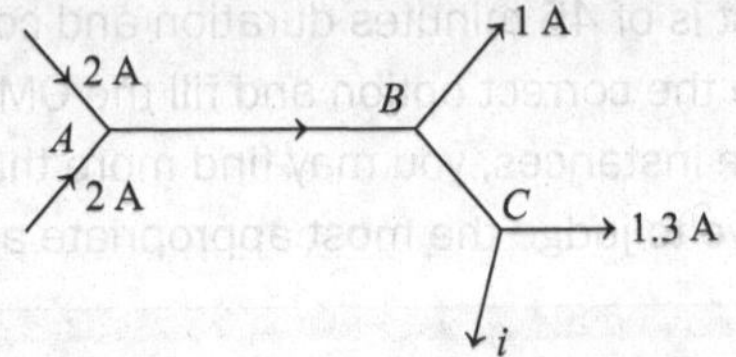

Then, current i is

(a) 1.7 A (b) 3.7 A
(c) 1.3 A (d) 1 A

12. **Assertion** (A) Two electric bulbs of 50 W and 100 W are given. When connected in series, 50 W bulb glows more but when connected in parallel, 100 W bulb glows more.

Reason (R) In series, current remains same and power is directly proportional to resistance, i.e. $P = i^2R$. In parallel, potential difference remains same and power is inversely propórtional to resistance, i.e. $P = \frac{V^2}{R}$.

In the light of above statements, choose the most appropriate answer from the options given below.

(a) Both A and R are true and R is the correct explanation of A.
(b) Both A and R are true but R is not the correct explanation of A.
(c) A is true but R is false
(d) A is false but R is true.

13. Power of a heater is 500 W at 800°C. What will be its power at 200°C, if $\alpha = 4 \times 10^{-4}$/°C?

(a) 484 W (b) 672 W (c) 526 W (d) 611 W

14. Two fuses A and B have following specifications :

Specification	Fuse A (Constantan)	Fuse B (Nichrome)
Length	8.5 m	4.2 m
Width	1 mm	2 mm
Thickness	0.03 mm	0.06 mm
Resistivity	4.9×10^{-7} Ω-m	11×10^{-7} Ω-m
Temperature coefficient	0	0

If you require a more sensitive fuse, then
(a) fuse A is better option
(b) fuse B is better option
(c) both fuses A and B are same in use
(d) both fuses A and B are used together

15. Sixteen resistances each of 5 Ω are connected as shown in the figure.

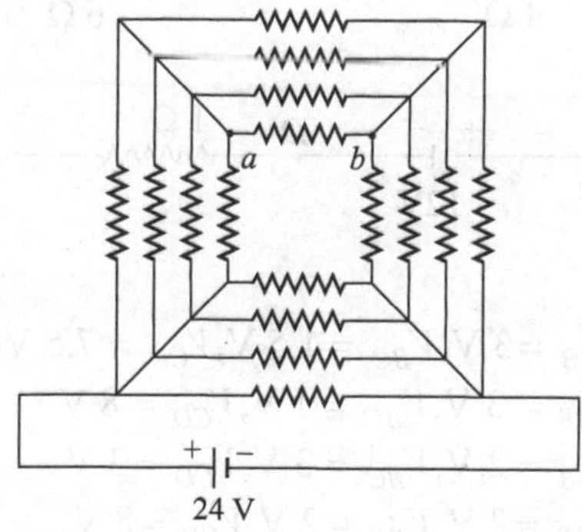

If a battery of 24 V is connected across the network, then current in branch marked ab is
(a) $\frac{8}{5}$ A (b) $\frac{48}{75}$ A
(c) 5 A (d) 13 A

16. A conductor of length l is connected to a DC source of emf E. If length of a conductor is tripled by stretching it and keeping E constant, then drift speed of electrons
(a) is tripled
(b) is doubled
(c) becomes half
(d) becomes one-third

17. The potential difference across 8 Ω resistance is 48 V as shown in the figure. The value of potential difference across X and Y points will be

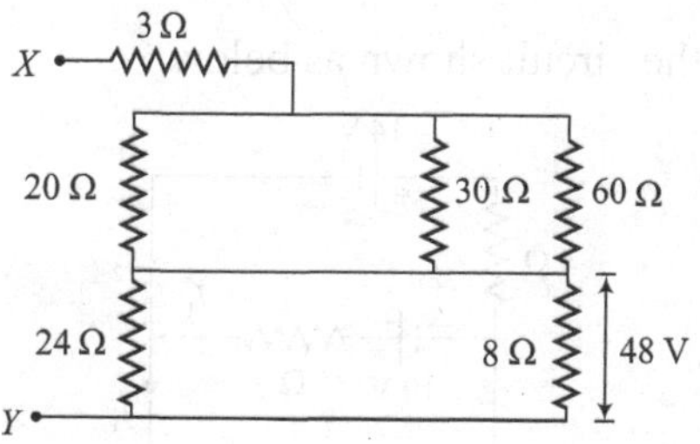

(a) 168 V (b) 100 V
(c) 152 V (d) 48 V

18. When current of 4 A is drawn from a cell, its terminal voltage is 20 V. If current of 1 A is given to same cell, then terminal voltage of cell is 25 V. The internal resistance and emf of cell are
(a) 1 Ω, 22.5 V (b) 2 Ω, 21 V
(c) 1 Ω, 24 V (d) 1 Ω, 22.5 V

19. When a current of 2 A flows through a wire, the drift velocity of electrons is 2.6×10^{-4} m/s. When current of 4 A flows through another wire of same material having double length and double cross-sectional area, then drift velocity of the electrons will be
(a) 2.6×10^{-4} m/s
(b) 1.3×10^{-4} m/s
(c) 6×10^{-5} m/s
(d) 5.2×10^{-4} m/s

20. A current through a wire varies with time as $I=(100+8t)$ A, where t is in second and I is in ampere. The average value of current across the wire in first 10 s is
(a) 140 A (b) 1000 A
(c) 400 A (d) 1400 A

21. For the circuit given below, the charge on the capacitor is

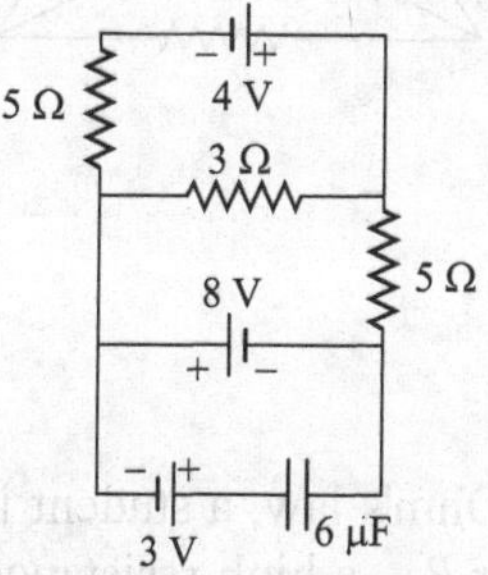

(a) 45 μC (b) 75 μC
(c) 66 μC (d) 78 μC

22. For the circuit shown as below.

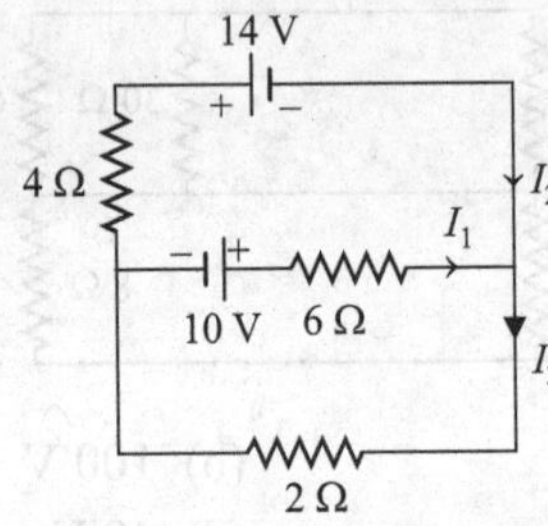

Let I_1, I_2 and I_3 are the currents marked in respective branches, then

(a) $I_1 = 2$ A, $I_2 = -3$ A, $I_3 = -1$ A
(b) $I_1 = -2$ A, $I_2 = 3$ A, $I_3 = -1$ A
(c) $I_1 = 2$ A, $I_2 = -3$ A, $I_3 = -1$ A
(d) $I_1 = -2$ A, $I_2 = 3$ A, $I_3 = 1$ A

23. For the circuit shown in figure,

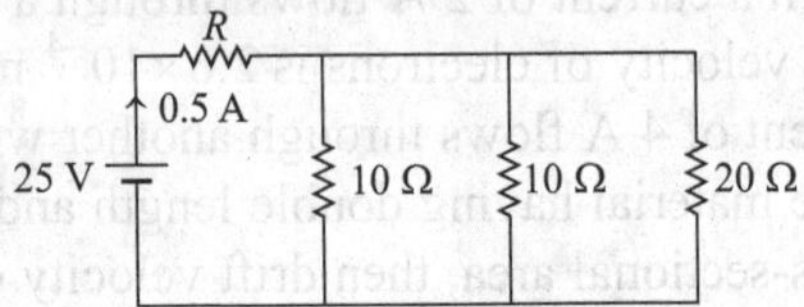

(a) current through 20 Ω resistor is 0.1 A.
(b) potential difference across the middle resistance is 2 V.
(c) R is equal to 46 Ω.
(d) All of the above

24. Five equal resistances of $R\ \Omega$ each are connected as shown in the figure. A battery of 12 V is connected between A and B. If $R = 2\Omega$, then current through the battery will be

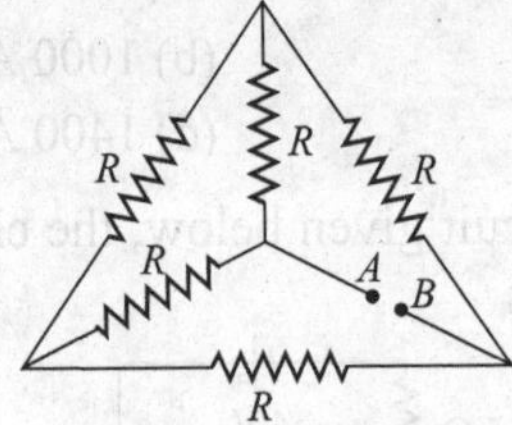

(a) 1 A
(b) 2 A
(c) 4 A
(d) 6 A

25. To verify Ohm's law, a student is provided with a test resistor R_T, a high resistance R_1, a small resistance R_2, two identical galvanometers G_1 and G_2 and a variable voltage source V. The correct circuit to carry out the experiment is

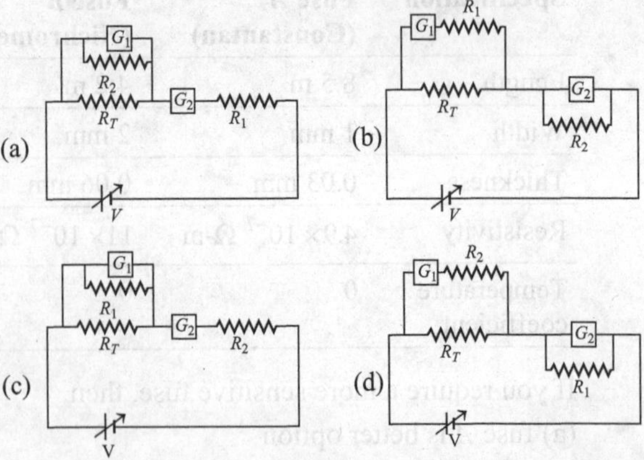

26. A network of resistors is connected with a 12 V battery as shown in figure.

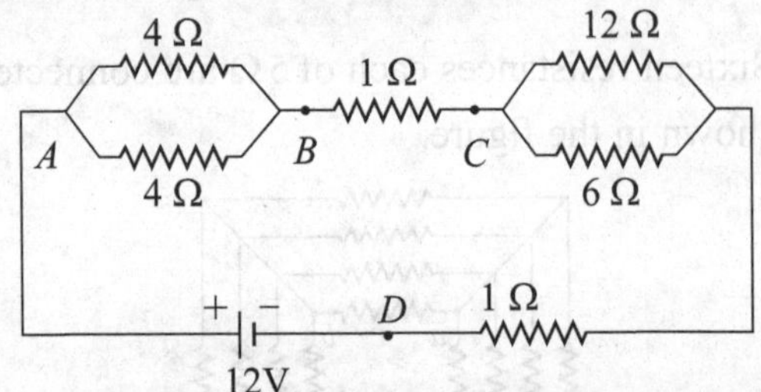

Then,

(a) $V_{AB} = 3$ V, $V_{BC} = 1.5$ V, $V_{CD} = 7.5$ V
(b) $V_{AB} = 3$ V, $V_{BC} = 1$ V, $V_{CD} = 8$ V
(c) $V_{AB} = 2$ V, $V_{BC} = 3$ V, $V_{CD} = 3$ V
(d) $V_{AB} = 2$ V, $V_{BC} = 2$ V, $V_{CD} = 8$ V

27. In given meter bridge experiment balance point is observed at position 1.

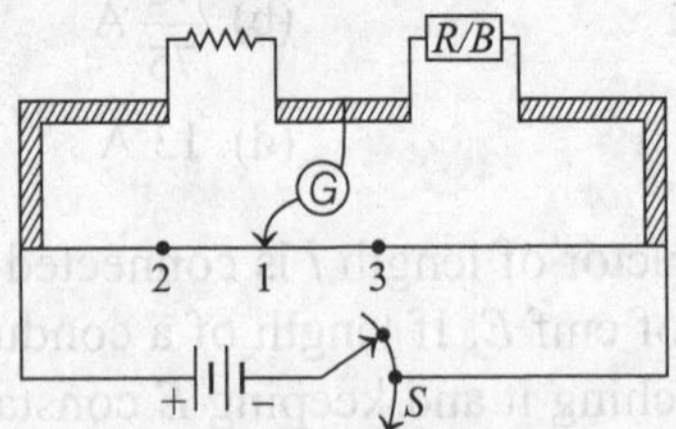

If resistivity of meter bridge wire is slightly increased due to change in temperature of wire, then balance is obtained at

(a) near point 2
(b) near point 3
(c) at point 1
(d) nowhere on wire

28. For the given circuit, potential difference between points c and f is

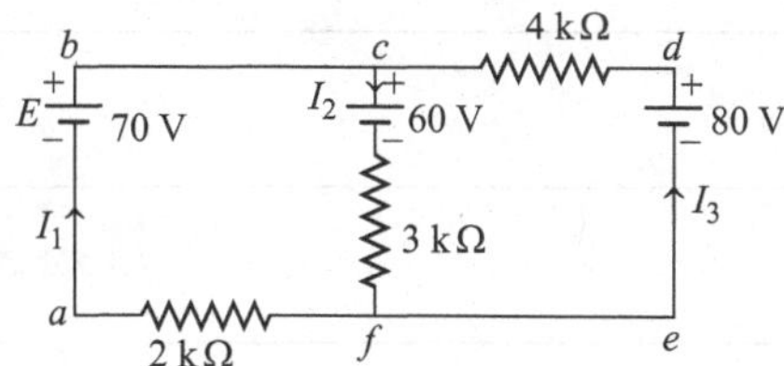

(a) $V_c - V_f = 69.2$ V

(b) $V_c - V_f = -69.2$ V

(c) $V_c - V_f = 48.3$ V

(d) $V_c - V_f = -48.3$ V

29. V-I graph for a conductor at temperatures T_1 and T_2 are given by

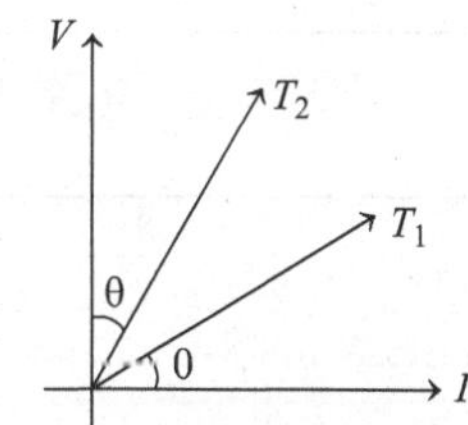

Then, $(T_2 - T_1)$ is proportional to

(a) $\cos 2\theta$ (b) $\sin \theta$

(c) $\cot 2\theta$ (d) $\tan \theta$

30. Match the List I with List II.

	List I		List II
A.	Resistivity of a metal with temperature	1.	
B.	Resistivity of a semiconductor with temperature	2.	
C.	Resistivity of a metal alloy with temperature	3.	
D.	Resistivity of a diamagnetic substance	4.	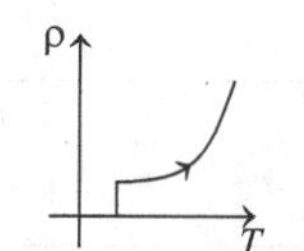

Codes

	A	B	C	D
(a)	2	1	3	4
(b)	1	2	3	4
(c)	2	3	4	1
(d)	2	1	4	3

Response Index

01 ⓐ ⓑ ⓒ ⓓ 14 ⓐ ⓑ ⓒ ⓓ 27 ⓐ ⓑ ⓒ ⓓ
02 ⓐ ⓑ ⓒ ⓓ 15 ⓐ ⓑ ⓒ ⓓ 28 ⓐ ⓑ ⓒ ⓓ
03 ⓐ ⓑ ⓒ ⓓ 16 ⓐ ⓑ ⓒ ⓓ 29 ⓐ ⓑ ⓒ ⓓ
04 ⓐ ⓑ ⓒ ⓓ 17 ⓐ ⓑ ⓒ ⓓ 30 ⓐ ⓑ ⓒ ⓓ
05 ⓐ ⓑ ⓒ ⓓ 18 ⓐ ⓑ ⓒ ⓓ
06 ⓐ ⓑ ⓒ ⓓ 19 ⓐ ⓑ ⓒ ⓓ
07 ⓐ ⓑ ⓒ ⓓ 20 ⓐ ⓑ ⓒ ⓓ
08 ⓐ ⓑ ⓒ ⓓ 21 ⓐ ⓑ ⓒ ⓓ
09 ⓐ ⓑ ⓒ ⓓ 22 ⓐ ⓑ ⓒ ⓓ
10 ⓐ ⓑ ⓒ ⓓ 23 ⓐ ⓑ ⓒ ⓓ
11 ⓐ ⓑ ⓒ ⓓ 24 ⓐ ⓑ ⓒ ⓓ
12 ⓐ ⓑ ⓒ ⓓ 25 ⓐ ⓑ ⓒ ⓓ
13 ⓐ ⓑ ⓒ ⓓ 26 ⓐ ⓑ ⓒ ⓓ

Performance Scanner

> 90% Excellent !	You have mastered this chapter. The concepts of this chapter are on your fingertips. Move on to the next chapter and maintain this momentum.
76-90% Very Good !	You have a good command over this chapter. Revise the chapter again after a few days and enhance your performance.
60-75% Good !	You have a wide scope to learn for this chapter. Revise this chapter again.
<60 Not Satisfactory!	You have a long way ahead of you to master this chapter. Revise it thoroughly.

For Online Chapter Test **Scan the QR Code**

For Online Unit Test **Scan the QR Code**

Space for Rough Work

Test Booklet No. **3947155**

Test Booklet Code **CH5**

MEDACE

NEET (UG)

SELF ASSESSMENT KIT

Moving Charges and Magnetism

Topics Covered

Biot-Savart's Law, Ampere's Circuital Law and their Applications

Motion of Charged Particles and Lorentz Force in Magnetic Field

Force, Torque on Current Carrying Conductor and Moving Coil Galvanometer

Important Instructions

- This Booklet Contains – Three Topic Tests and One Test on Complete Chapter.
- Each question carries 4 marks.
- For each correct response, the candidate will get 4 marks and for every incorrect response, 1 mark will be additionally deducted from the total score.
- Use **Blue/Black** point pen only for filling the OMR.
- Rough work will be done in the space provided for this purpose within the test booklet only.

Name of the Candidate (In Capitals) ____________________

____

Candidate's Signature ____________________

Invigilator's Signature ____________________

Facsimile signature stamp of center superintendent ____________________

Do not open this Booklet until you start attempting the Test

Topical Follow Thru

Test 1

Syllabus

- Biot-Savart's Law and Its Applications to Current Carrying Loop
- Ampere's Law and its Applications to Long Current Carrying Straight Wire
- Solenoid

For deeper insight **Scan the QR Code**

Important Instructions

- The test is of 45 minutes duration and contains 25 Multiple Choice Questions. (Four options with a single correct answer).
- Choose the correct option and fill the OMR given on the last page of this test accordingly.
- At some instances, you may find more than 1 option may be correct, in such circumstances you have to judge the most appropriate answer as per conditions given in the question.

1. The current in straight wire, if the magnetic field is 10^{-4} Wbm^{-2} produced at 0.01 m away from it, is

(a) 0.5 A (b) 0.05 A
(c) 5 A (d) 1.5 A

2. A straight current carrying conductor wire, lying along Y-axis is placed in a plane as shown in figure below. If the magnetic field at a distance r is 0.2 T, then magnetic field at a distance $2r$ will be

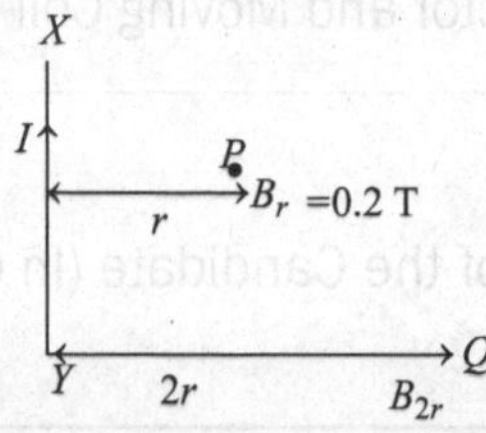

(a) 0.3 T (b) 0.1 T
(c) 0.4 T (d) 0.2 T

3. Two parallel infinitely long current carrying wires are shown in figure. If resultant magnetic field at point P is zero, then the value of current I will be

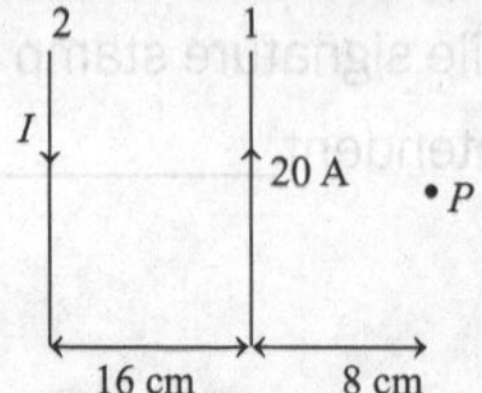

(a) 50 A (b) 60 A
(c) 40 A (d) 30 A

4. A long conducting wire carrying a current I is bent at 60° in given figure. The magnetic field B at a point P on the right bisector of bending angle at a distance d from the bend will be (where, μ_0 = permeability in free space)

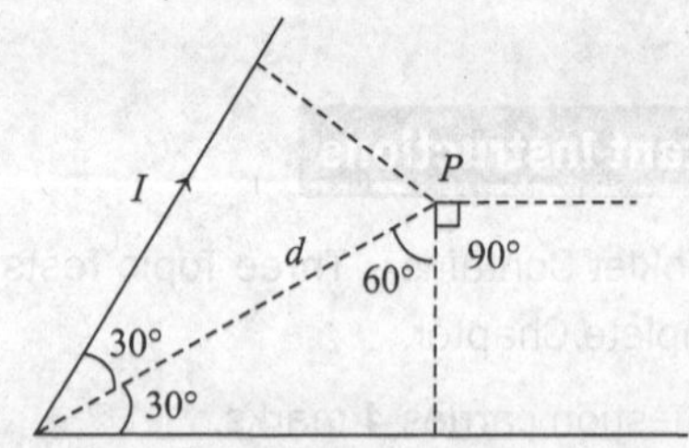

(a) $\frac{\mu_0 I}{2\pi d}(2+\sqrt{3})$ (b) $\frac{\mu_0 I}{2\pi d}$
(c) $\frac{\mu_0 I(2+\sqrt{5})}{2\pi d}$ (d) $\frac{\mu_0 I}{\pi d}$

5. In the given figure, the magnetic field induction at point O will be

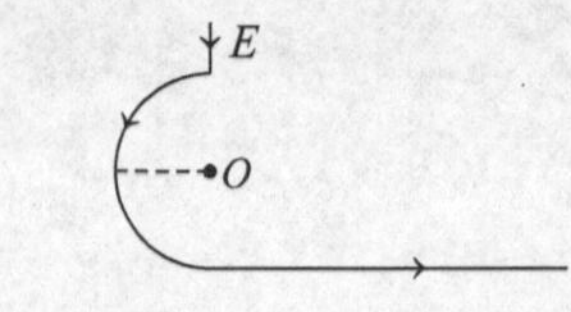

(a) $\frac{\mu_0 I}{4\pi r}$ (b) $\frac{\mu_0 I}{4r}+\frac{\mu_0 I}{2\pi r}$
(c) $\frac{\mu_0 I}{4r}+\frac{\mu_0 I}{4\pi r}$ (d) $\frac{\mu_0 I}{4r}-\frac{\mu_0 I}{4\pi r}$

6. The magnetic field due to a current carrying circular loop of radius 3 cm at a point on the axis at a distance of 4 cm from the centre is 50 μT. Its value at the centre of the loop will be

(a) 100 μT (b) 231 μT
(c) 150 μT (d) 70 μT

7. An element $d\mathbf{l} = dx\hat{\mathbf{i}}$ is placed at the origin and carries a large current $i = 5$A. The magnetic field on the Y-axis at a distance of 0.15 m will be (where, $dx = 2$ cm)

(a) $40.44 \times 10^{-8}\hat{\mathbf{k}}$ (b) $4.4 \times 10^{-8}\hat{\mathbf{k}}$
(c) $44.44 \times 10^{-8}\hat{\mathbf{k}}$ (d) $34.40 \times 10^{-7}\hat{\mathbf{k}}$

8. The magnetic field B due to a current carrying circular loop of radius 12 cm at its centre is 0.5×10^{-4} T. The magnetic field due to this loop at a point on the axis at a distance of 5.0 cm from the centre is

(a) $B_1\left[\frac{R^3}{(R^2+x^2)^{3/2}}\right]$

(b) $B_1\left[\frac{R^3}{(R^2+x^2)^{-3/2}}\right]$

(c) $B_1\left[\frac{R^2}{(R^2+x^2)^{3/2}}\right]$

(d) $B_1\left[\frac{R^2}{(R^2+x^2)^{-3/2}}\right]$

9. A circular coil carrying a certain current produces a magnetic field B_0 at its centre. The coil is now rewound, so as to have 3 turns and the same current is passed through it. The new magnetic field at the centre will be

(a) $B_0/9$ (b) $9B_0$
(c) $3B_0$ (d) $B_0/3$

10. A solenoid has length 0.2 cm, radius 2 cm and 200 turns of wire. If a current of 10 A is passed through this solenoid, the magnetic field inside the solenoid will be

(a) 125.6×10^{-2}T (b) 124.3×10^{-2}T
(c) 126.6×10^{-3}T (d) 120.6×10^{-2}T

11. A current of i ampere is flowing through each of the bent wires as shown in the figure. The magnitude of magnetic field at O is

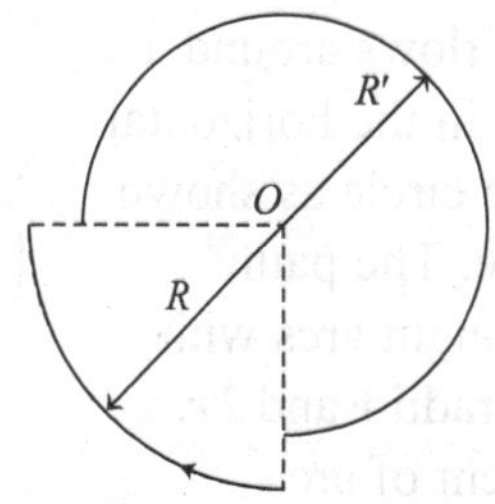

(a) $\frac{\mu_0 i}{4}\left(\frac{1}{R}+\frac{2}{R'}\right)$

(b) $\frac{\mu_0 i}{4}\left(\frac{1}{R}+\frac{3}{R'}\right)$

(c) $\frac{\mu_0 i}{8}\left(\frac{1}{R}-\frac{3}{2R'}\right)$

(d) $\frac{\mu_0 i}{8}\left(\frac{1}{R}+\frac{3}{R'}\right)$

12. Find the magnetic field at point P due to arrangement as shown in the figure.

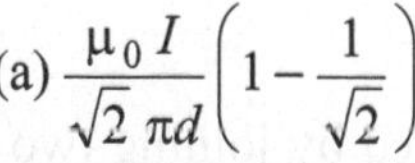

(a) $\frac{\mu_0 I}{\sqrt{2}\pi d}\left(1-\frac{1}{\sqrt{2}}\right)$

(b) $\frac{2\mu_0 I}{\sqrt{2}\pi d}$

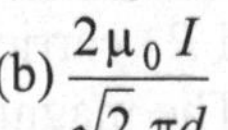

(c) $\frac{\mu_0 I}{\sqrt{2}\pi d}$

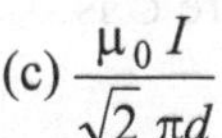

(d) $\frac{\mu_0 I}{\sqrt{2}\pi d}\left(1+\frac{1}{\sqrt{2}}\right)$

13. Ratio of magnetic field due to a straight current-carrying conductor at points P_1 and P_2 is

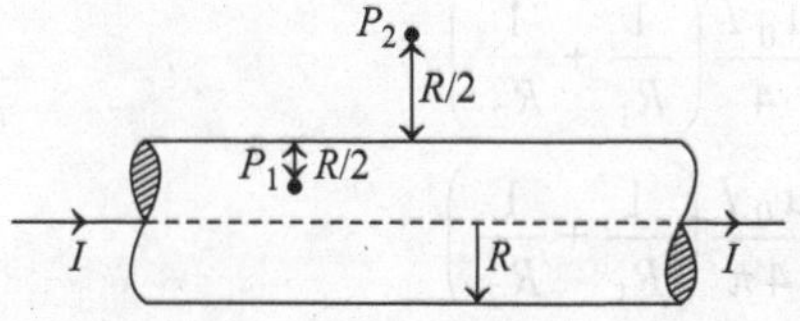

(a) 1:1 (b) 2:1 (c) 3:4 (d) 4:3

14. A current I flows in an infinite long wire with its cross-section in the form of a semi-circular ring of radius R. The magnitude of the magnetic induction along its axis is

(a) $\frac{\mu_0 I}{2\pi^2 R}$ (b) $\frac{\mu_0 I}{2\pi R}$

(c) $\frac{\mu_0 I}{4\pi R}$ (d) $\frac{\mu_0 I}{\pi^2 R}$

15. A current I flows around a closed path in the horizontal plane of the circle as shown in the figure. The path consists of eight arcs with alternating radii r and $2r$. Each segment of arc subtends equal angle at the common centre P. The magnetic field produced by current path at point P is

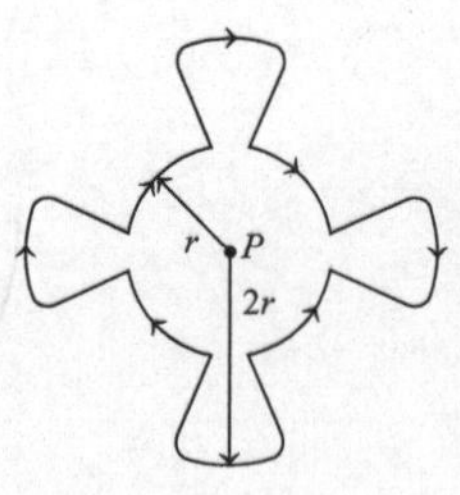

(a) $\frac{3}{8} \cdot \frac{\mu_0 I}{r}$; perpendicular to the plane of the paper and directed inwards

(b) $\frac{3}{8} \cdot \frac{\mu_0 I}{r}$; perpendicular to the plane of the paper and outwards

(c) $\frac{1}{8} \cdot \frac{\mu_0 I}{r}$; perpendicular to the plane of the paper and inwards

(d) $\frac{1}{8} \cdot \frac{\mu_0 I}{r}$; perpendicular to the plane of the paper and outwards

16. A wire loop $PQRSP$ formed by joining two semicircular wires of radii R_1 and R_2 carries a current I as shown in the figure. The magnitude of the magnetic induction at the centre C is

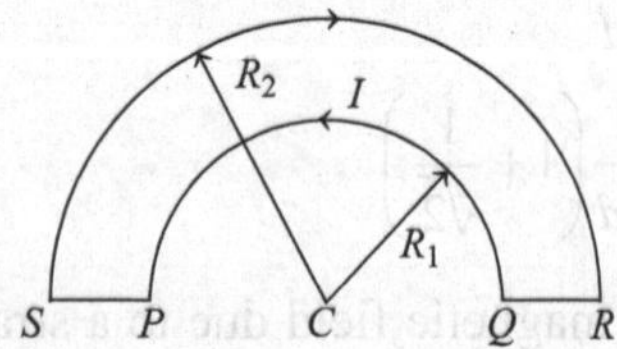

(a) $\frac{\mu_0 I}{4}\left(\frac{1}{R_1}+\frac{1}{R_2}\right)$

(b) $\frac{\mu_0 I}{4\pi}\left(\frac{1}{R_1}+\frac{1}{R_2}\right)$

(c) $\frac{\mu_0 I}{4\pi}\left(\frac{1}{R_1}-\frac{1}{R_2}\right)$

(d) $\frac{\mu_0 I}{4}\left(\frac{1}{R_1}-\frac{1}{R_2}\right)$

17. A hollow cylinder having infinite length and carrying a uniform current per unit length λ along the circumference is shown in the figure. Magnetic field inside the cylinder is

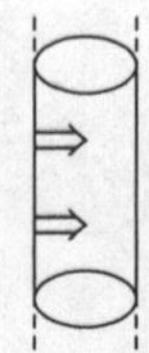

(a) $\frac{\mu_0 \lambda}{2}$ (b) $\mu_0 \lambda$

(c) $2\mu_0 \lambda$ (d) $4\mu_0 \lambda$

18. Figure shows an amperian path $ABCDA$. Part ABC is in vertical plane $PSTU$, while CDA is in horizontal plane $PQRS$. The direction of circulation along the path is shown by an arrow near points B and D. $\oint \mathbf{B} \cdot d\mathbf{l}$ for this path according to Ampere's law will be

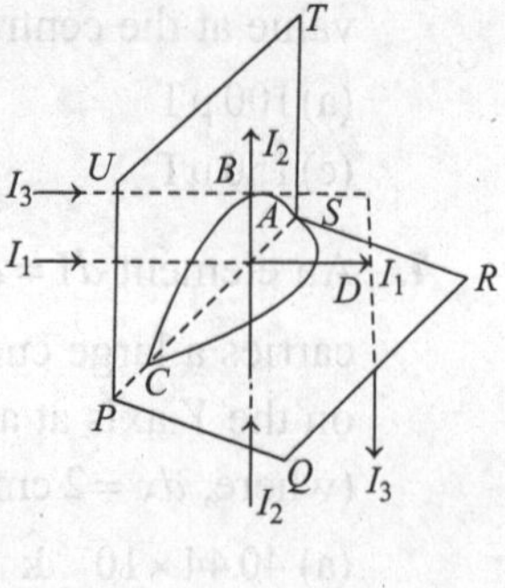

(a) $(I_1 - I_2 + I_3)\mu_0$

(b) $(-I_1 + I_2)\mu_0$

(c) $I_3 \mu_0$

(d) $(I_1 + I_2)\mu_0$

19. A co-axial cable is made up of two conductors. Inner conductor is solid and is of radius R_1 and the outer conductor is hollow of inner radius R_2 and outer radius R_3. The space between conductor is filled with air. The inner and outer conductors are carrying equal and opposite currents. Then, the variation of magnetic field with distance from the axis is best plotted as

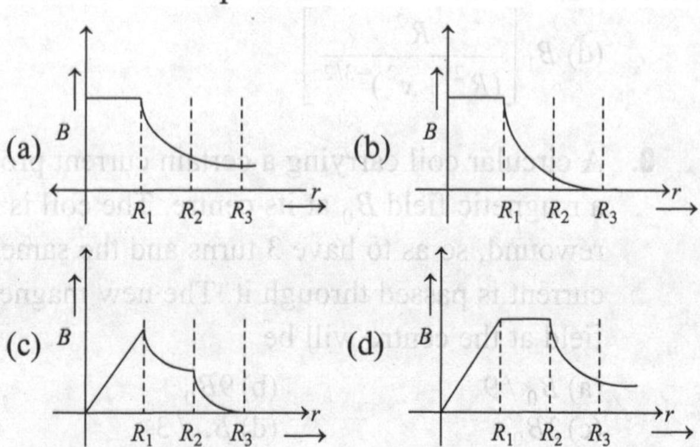

20. A long solenoid has 200 turns/cm and carries a current i. The magnetic field at its centre is 6.28×10^{-2} Wb. Another long solenoid has 100 turns/cm and it carries a current $i/3$. The value of magnetic field at its centre is

(a) 1.05×10^{-4} Wb/m^2 (b) 1.05×10^{-2} Wb/m^2

(c) 1.05×10^{-4} Wb/m^2 (d) 1.05×10^{-3} Wb/m^2

21. A long straight wire of radius a carries a steady current I. The current is uniformly distributed across its cross-section. The ratio of the magnetic field at $a/2$ and $2a$ is

(a) 1/2 (b) 1/4

(c) 4 (d) 1

22. A current I flows along the length of an infinitely long, straight, thin walled pipe. Then,

(a) the magnetic field at all points inside the pipe is the same, but not zero.

(b) the magnetic field is zero only on the axis of the pipe.

(c) the magnetic field is different at different points inside the pipe.

(d) magnetic field at any point inside the pipe is zero.

23. An infinitely long hollow conducting cylinder with inner radius $R/2$ and outer radius R carries a uniform current density along its length. The magnitude of the magnetic field, $|\mathbf{B}|$ as a function of radial distance r from the axis is best represented by

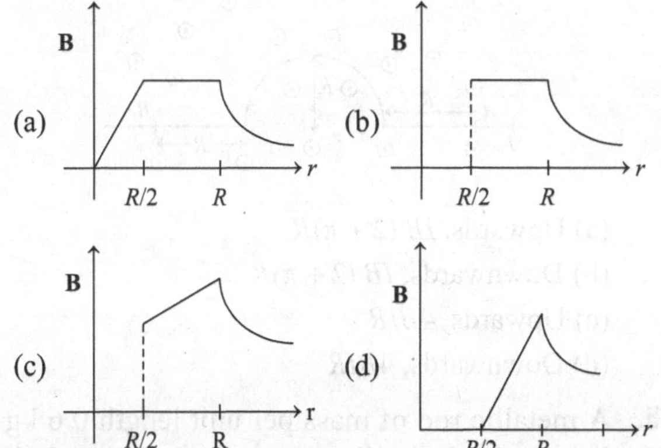

24. A long insulated copper wire is closely wound as a spiral of N turns. The spiral has inner radius a and outer radius b. The spiral lies in the XY-plane and a steady current I flows through the wire. The Z-component of the magnetic field at the centre of the spiral is

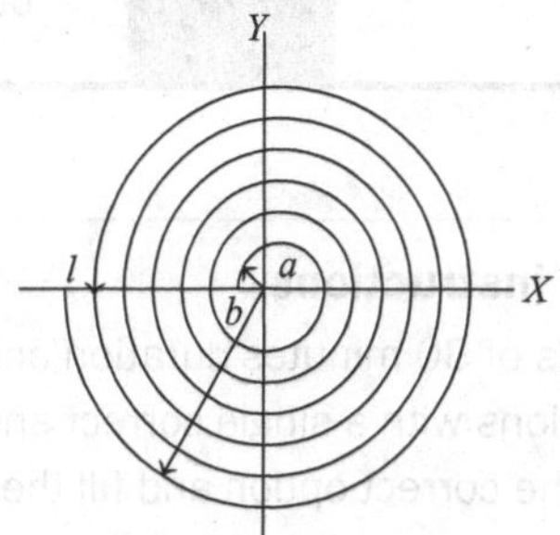

(a) $\dfrac{\mu_0 NI}{2(b-a)} \ln\left(\dfrac{b}{a}\right)$

(b) $\dfrac{\mu_0 NI}{2(b-a)} \ln\left(\dfrac{b+a}{b-a}\right)$

(c) $\dfrac{\mu_0 NI}{2b} \ln\left(\dfrac{b}{a}\right)$

(d) $\dfrac{\mu_0 NI}{2b} \ln\left(\dfrac{b+a}{b-a}\right)$

25. Magnetic field due to a rotating thin ring at its centre is

(Take, charge density of ring $=\lambda$, angular speed of ring $=\omega$, radius of ring $=R$).

(a) $\mu_0\lambda\omega$ (b) $\dfrac{1}{2}\mu_0\lambda\,\omega$

(c) $2\mu_0\lambda\omega$ (d) $\dfrac{1}{3}\mu_0\lambda\omega$

Response Index

01	a	b	c	d	10	a	b	c	d	19	a	b	c	d
02	a	b	c	d	11	a	b	c	d	20	a	b	c	d
03	a	b	c	d	12	a	b	c	d	21	a	b	c	d
04	a	b	c	d	13	a	b	c	d	22	a	b	c	d
05	a	b	c	d	14	a	b	c	d	23	a	b	c	d
06	a	b	c	d	15	a	b	c	d	24	a	b	c	d
07	a	b	c	d	16	a	b	c	d	25	a	b	c	d
08	a	b	c	d	17	a	b	c	d					
09	a	b	c	d	18	a	b	c	d					

Performance Scanner

> 90% Excellent !	You have mastered these topics. The concepts of these topics are on your fingertips. Move on to the next test and maintain this momentum.
76-90% Very Good !	You have a good command over these topics. Revise these topics again after a few days and enhance your performance.
60-75% Good !	You have a wide scope to learn for these topics. Revise them again.
<60% Not Satisfactory!	You have a long way ahead of you to master these topics. Revise them thoroughly.

Test 2

Syllabus

- Force on a Moving Charge in Uniform Magnetic and Electric Fields
- Lorentz' Force
- Force on a Current-Carrying Conductor in a Uniform Magnetic Field
- The Force between Two Parallel Current-Carrying Conductor

For deeper insight **Scan the QR Code**

Important Instructions

- The test is of 30 minutes duration and contains 15 Multiple Choice Questions. (Four options with a single correct answer).
- Choose the correct option and fill the OMR given on the last page of this test accordingly.
- At some instances, you may find more than 1 option may be correct, in such circumstances you have to judge the most appropriate answer as per conditions given in the question.

1. A current of 15 A is flowing in a wire of length 2 m. Force of 45 N acts on it when it is placed in a uniform magnetic field of 3 T. What is the angle between the magnetic field and the direction of current?

(a) 90° (b) 30°
(c) 60° (d) 45°

2. 5 A of current is flowing in a linear conductor having a length of 40 cm. The conductor is placed in a magnetic field of strength 1000 G and makes an angle of 60° with direction of the field. The magnitude of force will be

(a) 1.73×10^{-1} N
(b) 2×10^{-2} N
(c) 1.44×10^{-1} N
(d) 1.6×10^{-2} N

3. A proton carrying 2 MeV kinetic energy is moving in a circular path of radius R in a uniform magnetic field. What should be the energy of an α-particle to describe a circle of same radius in the same field?

(a) 1MeV
(b) 3 MeV
(c) 2 MeV
(d) 1.5 MeV

4. Consider wire segment AB it is bend in middle in form of a semicircle of radius R. Force on segment AB when there is current I in wire and it is surrounded by a magnetic field of strength B is

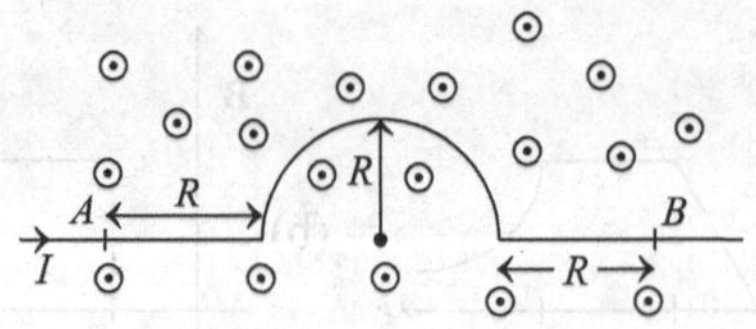

(a) Upwards, $IB(2+\pi)R$
(b) Downwards, $IB(2+\pi)R$
(c) Upwards, $4BIR$
(d) Downwards, $4BIR$

5. A metallic rod of mass per unit length 0.6 kg m^{-1} is lying horizontally on a smooth inclined plane which makes an angle of 60° with the horizontal. The rod is not allowed to slide down by flowing a current through it, when a magnetic field of induction 0.50 T is acting on it in the vertical direction. The current flowing in the rod to keep it stationary will be

(a) 14.78 A
(b) 20.51 A
(c) 15 A
(d) 18.40 A

6. A charged particle of charge $-4\,\mu C$ is moving in a magnetic field of 4 T acting in y-direction. When the particle velocity is $(2\hat{\mathbf{i}}+4\hat{\mathbf{j}})\times 10^6$ m/s, then the magnetic force on it will be

(a) 8 N in z-direction

(b) 12 N in z-direction

(c) 16 N in z-direction

(d) 32 N in z-direction

7. An electron projected in a perpendicular uniform magnetic field of 5×10^{-5} T moves in a circle of radius 4 mm. The linear momentum of electron will be

(a) 3.2×10^{-25} kg-ms^{-1}

(b) 4.3×10^{-25} kg-ms^{-1}

(c) 1.4×10^{-10} kg-ms^{-1}

(d) 1.6×10^{-25} kg-ms^{-1}

8. Assertion (A) A charged particle moves in a circular path under the influence of a perpendicular magnetic field experiences a centripetal force.

Reason (R) The centripetal force acting on the particle is provided by the magnetic Lorentz force.

In the light of the above statements, choose the most appropriate answer from the options given below.

(a) Both A and R are true and R is the correct explanation of A.

(b) Both A and R are true but R is not the correct explanation of A.

(c) A is true but R is false.

(d) A is false but R is true.

9. The resultant force on the current loop $ABCD$ due to a long current carrying conductor will be

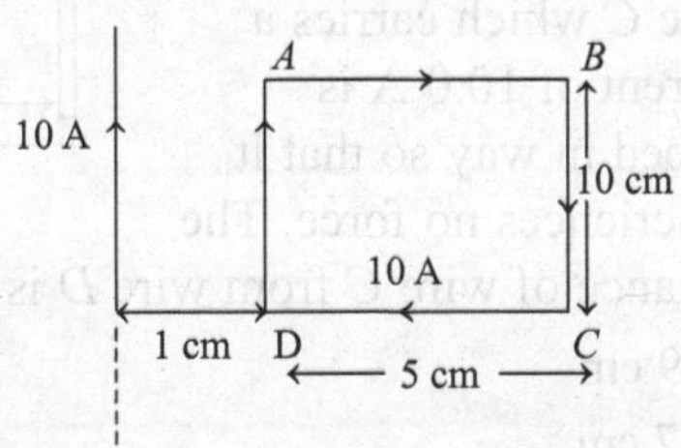

(a) 1.67×10^{-4} N (b) 1.41×10^{-3} N

(c) 2.73×10^{-2} N (d) 2.7×10^{-4} N

10. When a proton has a velocity $\mathbf{v}=(2\hat{\mathbf{i}}+3\hat{\mathbf{j}})\times 10^6$ ms^{-1}, it experiences a force $\mathbf{F}=-(1.28\times 10^{-13}\,\hat{\mathbf{k}})$ N. When its velocity is along the Z-axis, then it experiences a force along the X-axis and its magnetic field is

(a) $(-0.4\,\hat{\mathbf{j}})$ T (b) $(0.4\,\hat{\mathbf{j}})$ T

(c) $(4.0\,\hat{\mathbf{j}})$ T (d) $(-4.0\,\hat{\mathbf{j}})$ T

11. A particle of mass m and charge q is in an electric and magnetic field, given by

$$\mathbf{E}=2\hat{\mathbf{i}}+3\hat{\mathbf{j}},\ \mathbf{B}=4\hat{\mathbf{j}}+6\hat{\mathbf{k}}.$$

The charged particle is shifted from the origin to the point $P(x=1;\,y=1)$ along a straight path. The magnitude of the total work done is

(a) $0.35\,q$ (b) $(0.15)\,q$ (c) $2.5\,q$ (d) $5\,q$

12. An electron is moving along $+x$-direction with a velocity of 6×10^6 ms^{-1}. It enters a region of uniform electric field of 300 V/cm pointing along $+y$-direction. The magnitude and direction of the magnetic field set-up in this region such that the electron keeps moving along the x-direction will be

(a) 3×10^{-4} T, along $+z$-direction

(b) 5×10^{-3} T, along $-z$-direction

(c) 5×10^{-3} T, along $+z$-direction

(d) 3×10^{-4} T, along $-z$-direction

13. A proton beam passes without deviation through a region of space, where there are uniform transverse mutually perpendicular electric and magnetic fields with $E=220$ kV/m and $B=50$ mT. Then, the beam strikes a grounded target. The force imparted by the beam on the target if the beam current is equal to $i=0.80$ mA is

(a) 3.67×10^{-5} N

(b) 36.7×10^{-5} N

(c) 0.36×10^{-5} N

(d) 0.36×10^{-7} N

14. A proton, an electron and a helium nucleus, have the same energy. They are in circular orbits in a plane due to magnetic field perpendicular to the plane. Let r_p, r_e and r_{He} be their respective radii, then

(a) $r_e < r_p = r_{He}$ (b) $r_e > r_p = r_{He}$

(c) $r_e < r_p < r_{He}$ (d) $r_e > r_p > r_{He}$

15. A charged particle carrying charge 1 μC is moving with velocity $(2\hat{i}+3\hat{j}+4\hat{k})\ \text{ms}^{-1}$. If an external magnetic field of $(5\hat{i}+3\hat{j}-6\hat{k})\times10^{-3}$ T exists in the region, where the particle is moving, then the force on the particle is $\mathbf{F}\times10^{-9}$ N. The vector $\mathbf{F}$ is

(a) $-0.30\,\hat{i}+0.32\,\hat{j}-0.09\,\hat{k}$

(b) $-30\,\hat{i}+32\,\hat{j}-9\,\hat{k}$

(c) $-300\,\hat{i}+320\,\hat{j}-90\,\hat{k}$

(d) $-3.0\,\hat{i}+3.2\,\hat{j}-0.9\,\hat{k}$

Response Index

01	(a)	(b)	(c)	(d)	10	(a)	(b)	(c)	(d)
02	(a)	(b)	(c)	(d)	11	(a)	(b)	(c)	(d)
03	(a)	(b)	(c)	(d)	12	(a)	(b)	(c)	(d)
04	(a)	(b)	(c)	(d)	13	(a)	(b)	(c)	(d)
05	(a)	(b)	(c)	(d)	14	(a)	(b)	(c)	(d)
06	(a)	(b)	(c)	(d)	15	(a)	(b)	(c)	(d)
07	(a)	(b)	(c)	(d)					
08	(a)	(b)	(c)	(d)					
09	(a)	(b)	(c)	(d)					

Performance Scanner

> 90% Excellent !	You have mastered these topics. The concepts of these topics are on your fingertips. Move on to the next test and maintain this momentum.
76-90% Very Good !	You have a good command over these topics. Revise these topics again after a few days and enhance your performance.
60-75% Good !	You have a wide scope to learn for these topics. Revise them again.
<60% Not Satisfactory!	You have a long way ahead of you to master these topics. Revise them thoroughly.

Test 3

Syllabus

- Torque Experienced by a Current Loop in a Uniform Magnetic Field
- Moving Coil Galvanometer, its Sensitivity and Conversion to Ammeter and Voltmeter

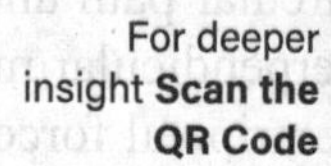

Important Instructions

- The test is of 45 minutes duration and contains 25 Multiple Choice Questions. (Four options with a single correct answer).
- Choose the correct option and fill the OMR given on the last page of this test accordingly.
- At some instances, you may find more than 1 option may be correct, in such circumstances you have to judge the most appropriate answer as per conditions given in the question.

1. Current sensitivity of a moving coil galvanometer is 5 div/mA and its voltage sensitivity (angular deflection per unit voltage applied) is 20 div/V. The resistance of the galvanometer is

(a) 250 Ω (b) 25 Ω (c) 40 Ω (d) 500 Ω

2. A circular coil of radius 20 cm and 200 turns carries a current 4 A. The magnetic moment of the coil will be

(a) 3.142×10^{4} A-m^2

(b) 96.6 A-m^2

(c) 100.48 A-m^2

(d) 106.64 A-m^2

3. Three long straight and parallel wires carrying currents are arranged as shown in the figure. The wire C which carries a current of 10.0 A is placed in way so that it experiences no force. The distance of wire C from wire D is

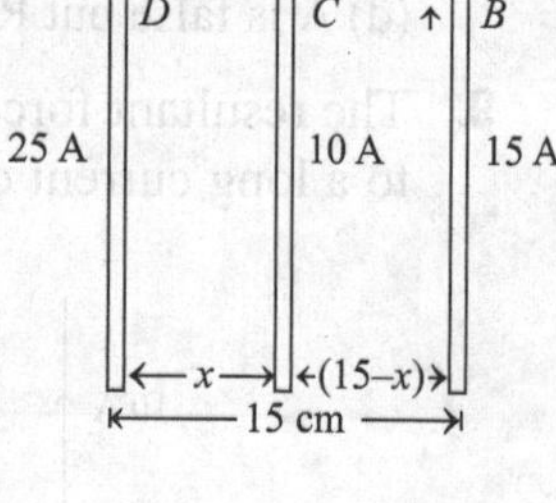

(a) 9 cm

(b) 7 cm

(c) 5 cm

(d) 3 cm

4. In an ammeter, 0.2% of main current passes through the galvanometer. If resistance of galvanometer is G, the resistance of ammeter will be

(a) $\frac{1}{499}G$ (b) $\frac{499}{500}G$

(c) $\frac{1}{500}G$ (d) $\frac{500}{499}G$

5. A coil in the shape of an equilateral triangle of side 0.02 m is suspended from its vertex such that it is hanging in a vertical plane between the pole pieces of permanent magnet producing a uniform field of 6×10^{-2} T. If a current of 0.4 A is passed through the coil, then the couple acting (torque) will be

(a) $5\sqrt{3}\times10^{-7}$ N-m (b) 3.14×10^{-6} N-m

(c) 4.15×10^{-6} N-m (d) 1.16×10^{-6} N-m

6. When a current flows through a conductor placed in a magnetic field, which of the following statement is true regarding the force and torque on the conductor?

(a) The force acting on the conductor is maximum when the current and magnetic field are parallel.

(b) The force acting on the conductor is maximum when the current and magnetic field are anti-parallel.

(c) The torque acting on the conductor is maximum when the current and magnetic field are parallel.

(d) The torque acting on the conductor is maximum when the current and magnetic field are perpendicular.

7. A square loop is carrying a steady current I and the magnitude of its magnetic dipole moment is m. If this square loop is changed to a circular loop and it carries the same current, the magnitude of the magnetic dipole moment of circular loop (in A-m) will be

(a) $\frac{4m}{\pi}$ (b) $\frac{3m}{\pi}$

(c) $\frac{2m}{\pi}$ (d) $\frac{m}{\pi}$

8. A rectangular coil (dimension 5 cm × 2.5 cm) with 100 turns, carrying a current of 3A in the clockwise direction, is kept centred at the origin and in the XZ-plane. A magnetic field of 1 T is applied along X-axis. If the coil is tilted through 45° about Z-axis, then the torque on the coil is

(a) 0.27 N-m (b) 0.38 N-m

(c) 0.42 N-m (d) 0.55 N-m

9. A conducting ring of mass 2 kg and radius 0.5 m is placed on a smooth horizontal plane. The ring carries a current $i = 4$ A. A horizontal magnetic field $B = 10$ T is switched on at time $t = 0$ as shown in figure. The initial angular acceleration of the ring will be

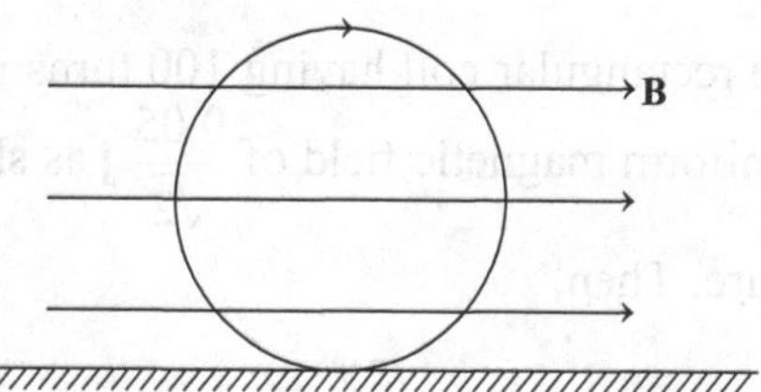

(a) $40\,\pi$ rads^{-2} (b) $20\,\pi$ rads^{-2}

(c) $5\,\pi$ rads^{-2} (d) $15\,\pi$ rads^{-2}

10. A rectangular coil PQ has $2n$ turns, an area $2a$ and carries a current $2I$ (as shown). The plane of the coil is at 60° to a horizontal uniform magnetic field of flux density B. The torque on the coil due to magnetic force is

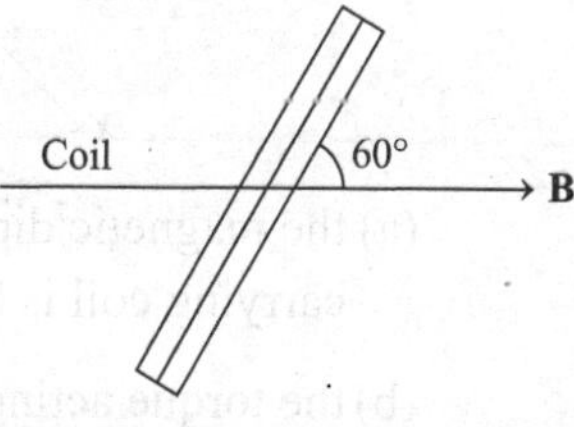

(a) $BnaI \sin 60°$ (b) $8BnaI \cos 60°$

(c) $4naI \sin 60°$ (d) $BnaI \cos 60°$

11. Figure shows a square current carrying loop $ABCD$ of side 10 cm and current $i = 10$ A. The magnetic moment **M** of the loop is

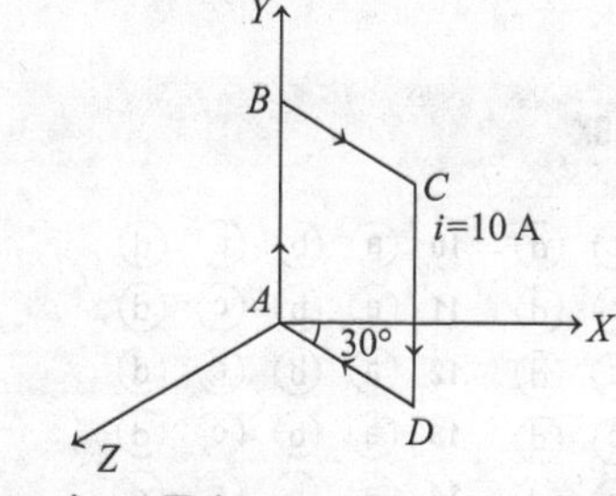

(a) $0.05\,(\hat{\mathbf{i}} - \sqrt{3}\,\hat{\mathbf{k}})$ A-m^2

(b) $0.05\,(\hat{\mathbf{j}} + \hat{\mathbf{k}})$ A-m^2

(c) $0.05\,(\sqrt{3}\,\hat{\mathbf{i}} + \hat{\mathbf{k}})$ A-m^2

(d) $(\hat{\mathbf{i}} + \hat{\mathbf{k}})$ A-m^2

12. A loop carrying current I lies in the XY-plane as shown in the figure. The unit vector $\hat{\mathbf{k}}$ is coming out of the plane of the paper. The magnetic moment of the current loop is

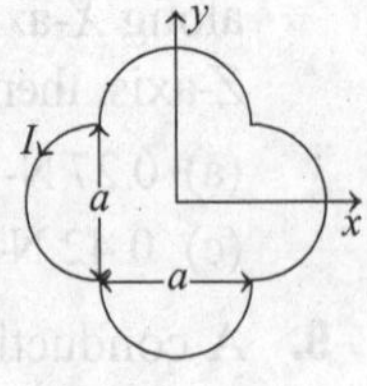

(a) $a^2 I \hat{\mathbf{k}}$ (b) $\left(\frac{\pi}{2}+1\right) a^2 I \hat{\mathbf{k}}$

(c) $-\left(\frac{\pi}{2}+1\right) a^2 I \hat{\mathbf{k}}$ (d) $(2\pi+1) a^2 I \hat{\mathbf{k}}$

13. The rectangular coil having 100 turns is turned in a uniform magnetic field of $\frac{0.05}{\sqrt{2}}\hat{\mathbf{j}}$ as shown in the figure. Then,

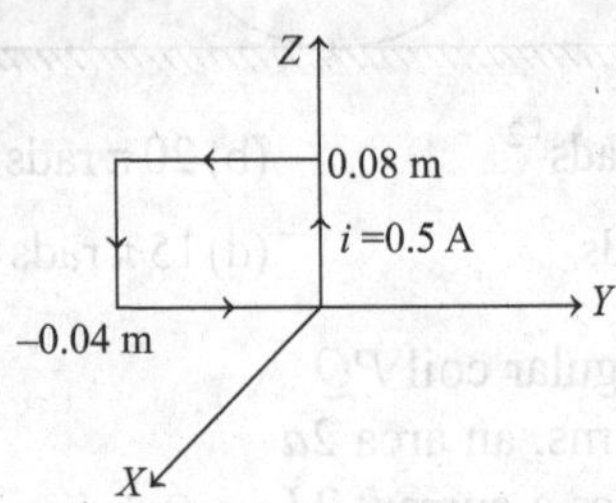

(a) the magnetic dipole moment of the current carrying coil is $1.6\times10^{-2}\ \hat{\mathbf{i}}$ A-m^2

(b) the torque acting on the coil is $5.66\times10^{-5}\ \hat{\mathbf{k}}$ N-m

(c) the torque acting on the coil is $0.566\times10^{-5}\ \hat{\mathbf{k}}$ N-m

(d) the magnetic dipole moment of coil is $160\times10^{-2}\ \hat{\mathbf{i}}$ A-m^2

14. The galvanometer cannot be used as an ammeter to measure the value of current in a given circuit. The following reasons are

(a) galvanometer gives full scale deflection for a small current.

(b) galvanometer has a low resistance.

(c) a linear scale cannot be designed, so that $I \propto \phi$.

(d) a galvanometer can give inaccurate values.

15. Figure shows the construction details of a moving coil galvanometer.

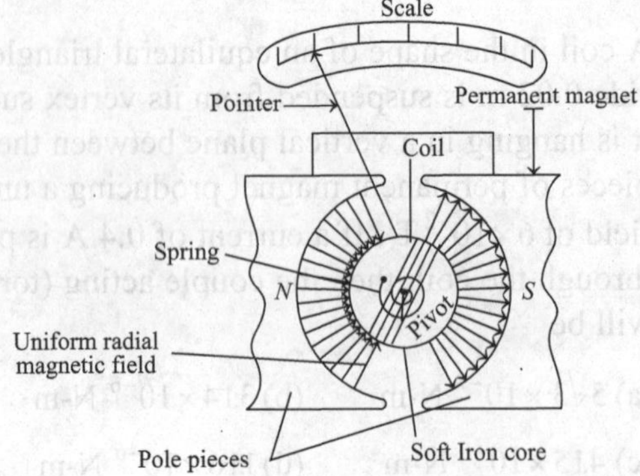

Match the Column I (parts) with Column II (effects) and select the correct answer from the codes given below.

Column I	Column II
A. Soft iron core	1. produces deflecting torque
B. Pole pieces	2. produces restoring torque
C. Spring	3. produce radial field
D. Coil	4. increases field strength

Codes

	A	B	C	D
(a)	1	2	3	4
(b)	1	2	4	3
(c)	2	1	3	4
(d)	4	3	2	1

■ **Response Index**

01	a	b	c	d	10	a	b	c	d
02	a	b	c	d	11	a	b	c	d
03	a	b	c	d	12	a	b	c	d
04	a	b	c	d	13	a	b	c	d
05	a	b	c	d	14	a	b	c	d
06	a	b	c	d	15	a	b	c	d
07	a	b	c	d					
08	a	b	c	d					
09	a	b	c	d					

■ **Performance Scanner**

> 90% Excellent !	You have mastered these topics. The concepts of these topics are on your fingertips. Move on to the next test and maintain this momentum.
76-90% Very Good !	You have a good command over these topics. Revise these topics again after a few days and enhance your performance.
60-75% Good !	You have a wide scope to learn for these topics. Revise them again.
<60% Not Satisfactory!	You have a long way ahead of you to master these topics. Revise them thoroughly.

Chapter Break Thru

Syllabus		
• Biot-Savart's Law and its Applications to Current-Carrying Loop. • Ampere's Law and its Applications to Long Current-Carrying Straight Wire • Solenoid	• Force on a Moving Charge in Uniform Magnetic and Electric Fields • Lorentz Force • Force on a Current-Carrying Conductor in a Uniform Magnetic Field. • The Force between Two Parallel Current-Carrying Conductor	• Torque Experienced by a Current Loop in a Uniform Magnetic Field • Moving Coil Galvanometer, its Sensitivity and Conversion to Ammeter and Voltmeter.

Important Instructions

- The test is of 1 hour duration and contains 50 Multiple Choice Questions (Four options with a single correct answer).
- Choose the correct option and fill the OMR given on the last page of this test accordingly.
- At some instances, you may find more than 1 option may be correct, in such circumstances you have to judge the most appropriate answer as per conditions given in the question.

1. An electron is moving in a circular path of radius 20 cm in a magnetic field of 2×10^{-3} T. The speed of electron is

(a) 1.5×15^5 m/s

(b) 1.6×10^6 m/s

(c) 7×10^7 m/s

(d) 8×10^8 m/s

2. A particle of charge q enters into a magnetic field B with velocity v perpendicular to it. The energy gained by the charged particle in magnetic field when it moves on a circular path of radius r is

(a) $\frac{q^2Br^2}{2m}$ (b) zero

(c) $\frac{q^2B^2r^2}{m}$ (d) $\frac{q^2Br^2}{m}$

3. Calculate the magnetic field at point P in the following diagram.

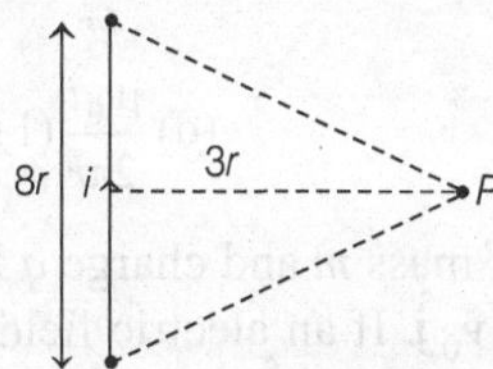

(a) $\frac{2\mu_0 i}{15\pi r}$ (b) $\frac{\mu_0 i}{2\pi r}$

(c) $\frac{\mu_0 i}{4\pi r}$ (d) $\frac{4\mu_0 i}{10\pi r}$

4. A deutron of kinetic energy 100 keV is describing a circular orbit of radius 1 m in a plane perpendicular to magnetic field of 2 T. The kinetic energy of the proton that describes a circular orbit of radius 2 m in the same plane with the same magnetic field is

(a) 200 keV (b) 400 keV

(c) 800 keV (d) 600 keV

5. A current I flowing through the loop is as shown in figure. The magnetic field at the centre O will be

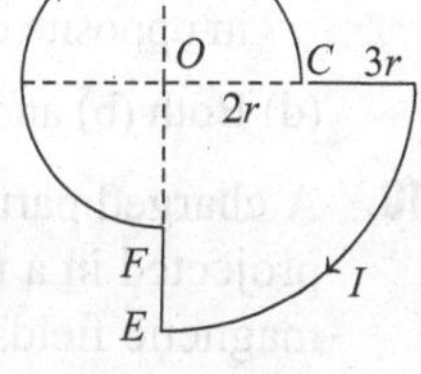

(a) $\frac{17\mu_0 I}{70\ r}$, acting downwards

(b) $\frac{17\mu_0 I}{60\ r}$, acting upwards

(c) $\frac{16\mu_0 I}{50\ r}$, acting upwards

(d) $\frac{17\mu_0 I}{80\ r}$, acting downwards

6. **Statement I** When a charged particle enters into a uniform magnetic field perpendicular to it, it moves on a circular path.

Statement II Higher the range, greater is the resistance of ammeter.

In the light of above statements, choose the most appropriate answer from the options given below.

(a) Both Statement I and Statement II are correct.

(b) Both Statement I and Statement II are incorrect.

(c) Statement I is correct but Statement II is incorrect.

(d) Statement I is incorrect but Statement II is correct.

7. Calculate the magnetic field at point P.

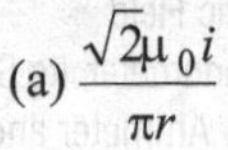

(a) $\frac{\sqrt{2}\mu_0 i}{\pi r}$

(b) $\frac{\mu_0 i}{4r}$

(c) $\frac{2\mu_0 i}{15\pi r}$

(d) $\frac{\mu_0 i}{2\pi r}(1+\pi)$

8. Two long straight current carrying parallel wires are arranged as shown in the following figure.

Where should a third wire (R) having current of 50 A be placed from wire P, so that it may not experience any force?

(a) 12 cm (b) 9 cm (c) 10 cm (d) 7 cm

9. Two current carrying conductors attract each other, if

(a) they are kept perpendicular to each other.

(b) they are kept parallel to each other having currents in same direction.

(c) they are kept parallel to each other having currents in opposite direction.

(d) Both (b) and (c)

10. A charged particle with some initial velocity is projected in a region where non-zero electric and magnetic fields are present. Match the entries of Column I with the entries of Column II and select the correct answer from the codes given below.

Column I	Column II
A. $\mathbf{E}=0, \mathbf{B}\neq 0$ and initial velocity is at any angle with $\mathbf{B}$ $(\theta \neq 90°)$	1. Straight line
B. $\mathbf{E}=0, \mathbf{B}\neq 0$ and initial velocity is perpendicular to $\mathbf{B}$	2. Helical path with uniform pitch
C. $\mathbf{E}\neq 0, \mathbf{B}\neq 0$, $\mathbf{E}\parallel\mathbf{B}$ and initial velocity is $\perp$ to both	3. Circular
D. $\mathbf{E}\neq 0, \mathbf{B}\neq 0$, $\mathbf{E}$ perpendicular to $\mathbf{B}$ and v perpendicular to both $\mathbf{E}$ & $\mathbf{B}$	4. Helical path with non-uniform pitch

Codes

	A	B	C	D
(a)	2	3	4	1
(b)	1	3	4	2
(c)	2	3	1	4
(d)	4	1	2	3

11. A current of 2 A is made to flow through a coil which has only one turn. The magnetic field produced at the centre is $4\pi\times10^{-6}$ Wb/m^2. The radius of the coil is

(a) 0.0001m (b) 0.01m

(c) 0.1m (d) 0.001m

12. A rectangular coil of 500 turns is carrying a current of 2 mA. Its plane is making an angle of 30° with the direction of magnetic field intensity of strength $\sqrt{3}$ T. If the length and width of the coil are 2 cm and 1 cm respectively, then torque on the rectangular coil will be

(a) 3×10^{-4} N-m (b) $\sqrt{3}\times10^{-4}$ N-m

(c) 5×10^{-5} N-m (d) 10^{-4} N-m

13. An ammeter of resistance 0.8 Ω can measure currents upto 1 A. What must be the value of shunt resistance to enable the ammeter to measure current upto 5 A?

(a) 0.5 Ω (b) 0.2 Ω

(c) 0.4 Ω (d) 0.6 Ω

14. Sensitivity of a moving coil galvanometer is increased by increasing the

(a) number of turns in the coil

(b) strength of the magnetic field

(c) the area of the coil

(d) All of the above

15. Find the magnetic field at point P.

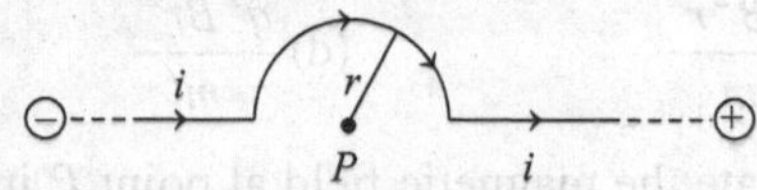

(a) $\frac{\sqrt{2}\mu_0 i}{\pi r}$ (b) $\frac{\mu_0 i}{4r}$

(c) $\frac{2\mu_0 i}{15\pi r}$ (d) $\frac{\mu_0 i}{2\pi r}(1+\pi)$

16. A particle of mass m and charge q has an initial velocity $\mathbf{v}=v_0\hat{\mathbf{j}}$. If an electric field $\mathbf{E}=E_0\hat{\mathbf{i}}$ and magnetic field $\mathbf{B}=B_0\hat{\mathbf{i}}$ act on the particle, its speed will double after a time

(a) $3mv_0/qE_0$ (b) $\sqrt{3}mv_0/qE_0$

(c) $2mv_0/qE_0$ (d) $\sqrt{2}mv_0/qE_0$

17. A 100 turns circular current carrying loop of radius 10 cm is placed in XY-plane. The region is occupied by a uniform magnetic field, $B = (-\hat{i} + \hat{k})$T.

If current in the loop is 5A, then magnitude and direction of torque on the loop are

(a) 2π, along positive Z-axis
(b) 5π, along negative Y-axis
(c) 5π, along positive Z-axis
(d) 2π, along positive Z-axis

18. A straight wire of mass 200 g and length 1.5 m carries a current of 2 A. It is suspended in mid-air by a uniform horizontal magnetic field B. The magnitude of the magnetic field is

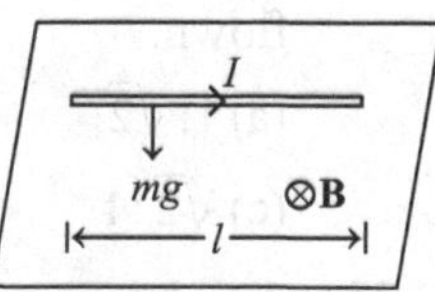

(a) 0.35 T (b) 0.65 T (c) 0.25 T (d) 0.88 T

19. A particle is moving along the X-axis with velocity v having charge q and mass m. It enters a region of electric field E and magnetic field B as shown in figures below. For which figure the net force on the charge may be zero?

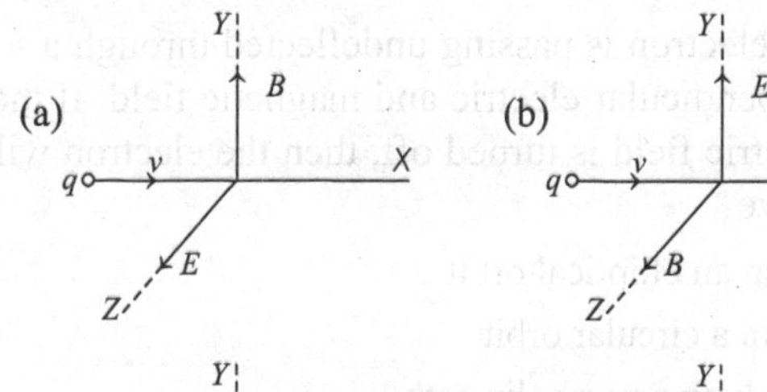

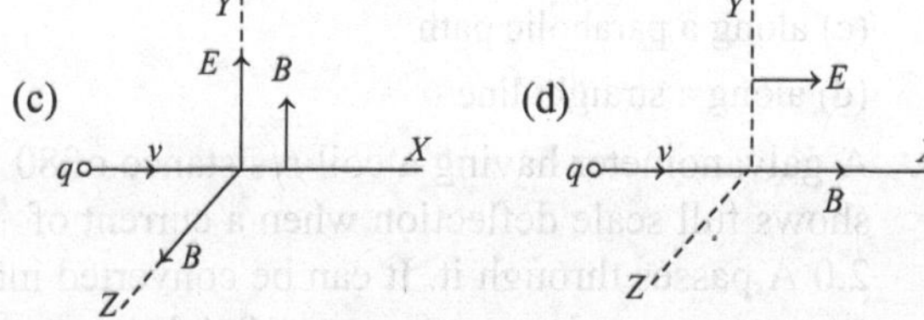

20. An electron is travelling towards east. If there is a magnetic field in the downward direction, then the force on the electron will be towards

(a) east (b) west
(c) north (d) south

21. A long straight wire is carrying a current of 12 A. The magnetic field at a distance of 8 cm is ($\mu_0 = 4\pi \times 10^{-7}$ NA^2)

(a) 2×10^{-4} Wb/m^2
(b) 3×10^{-5} Wb/m^2
(c) 4×10^{-4} Wb/m^2
(d) 4×10^{-5} Wb/m^2

22. Proton and α-particle have same kinetic energy. They enter in a region of uniform magnetic field making an angle 90° with the field. Which one of the following statement(s) will be true?

(a) The α-particle will be bent in a circular path with a radius smaller than that of proton.
(b) The radius of the path of the α-particle will be greater than that of the proton.
(c) The α-particle and the proton will be bent in a circular path with the same radius.
(d) The α-particle and the proton will go through the field in a straight line.

23. Two very long straight parallel wires carry steady currents i and $4i$ in opposite directions. The distance between the wires is d. At a certain instant of time, a point charge q is at a point equidistant from the two wires in the plane of the wires. Its instantaneous velocity **v** is perpendicular to this plane. The magnitude of the force due to the magnetic field acting on the charge at this instant is

(a) $\frac{\mu_0 iqv}{2\pi d}$ (b) $\frac{\mu_0 iqv}{\pi d}$
(c) $\frac{3\mu_0 iqv}{2\pi d}$ (d) zero

24. Two parallel wires in free space are 20 cm apart and each carries a current of 20 A in the same direction. The force one wire exerts on the other per metre of length is

(a) 2×10^{-4} N, attractive
(b) 2×10^{-4} N, repulsive
(c) 2×10^{-7} N, attractive
(d) 2×10^{-7} N, repulsive

25. A wire of radius R is carrying current i uniformly distributed over its cross-section. If a circular loop of radius r is taken as amperian loop, then the variation value of $\oint \mathbf{B} \cdot d\mathbf{l}$ over this loop with radius r of loop will be best represented by

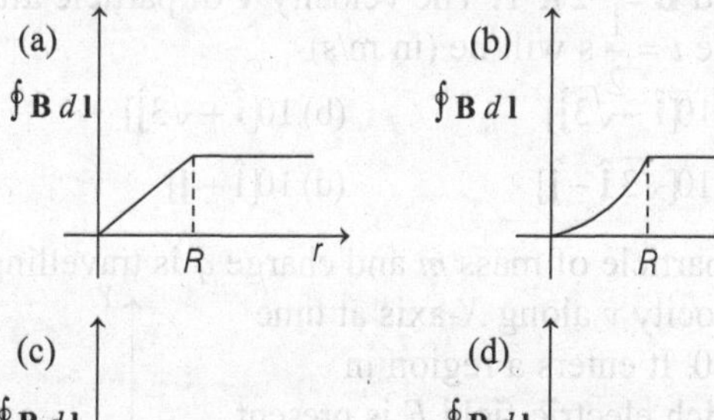

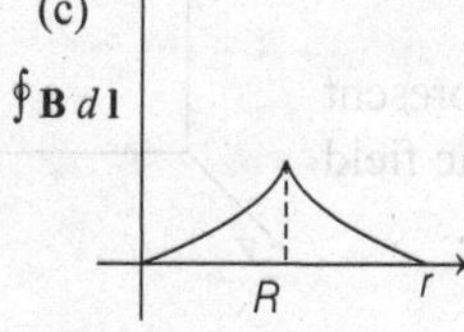

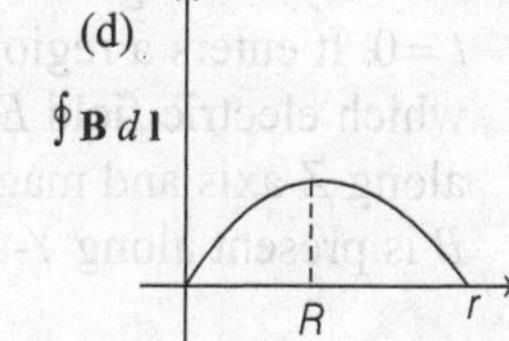

26. If velocity of a charged particle is doubled and strength of magnetic field is same, the radius will be

(a) 2 times (b) 8 times (c) 4 times (d) same

27. In figure, AB is a non-conducting rod. Equal charges of magnitude q are fixed at various points on the rod as shown.

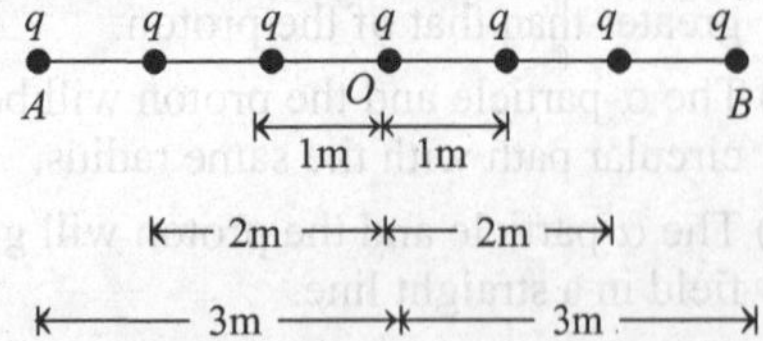

The rod is rotated uniformly about an axis passing through O and perpendicular to its length such that linear speed of the end A or B of the rod is 6 m/s. Magnetic field at O is

(a) $\frac{11\mu_0 q}{6\pi}$ (b) $\frac{3\mu_0 q}{7\pi}$

(c) $\frac{\mu_0 q}{2\pi}$ (d) $\frac{6\mu_0 q}{13\pi}$

28. An electron moving with velocity v along the X-axis is moving away from a circular current carrying loop as shown in the Fig. The magnitude of magnetic force on electron at this instant is

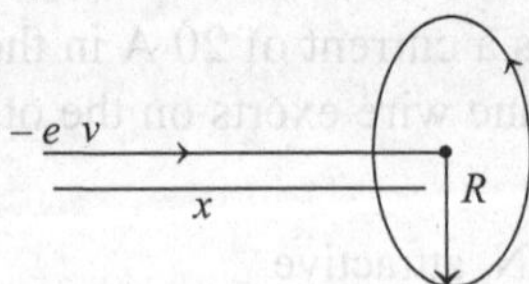

(a) $\frac{\mu_0}{2}\frac{evix^2}{(x^2+R^2)^{3/2}}$ (b) $\mu_0\frac{eviR^2x}{(x^2+R^2)^{3/2}}$

(c) $\frac{\mu_0}{4\pi}\frac{eviR^2x}{(x^2+R^2)^{3/2}}$ (d) zero

29. A particle of specific charge $\frac{q}{m}=2\pi$ C/kg is projected from the origin towards positive X-axis with a velocity of 20 m/s in a uniform magnetic field $\mathbf{B}=-2\hat{\mathbf{k}}$ T. The velocity $\hat{\mathbf{v}}$ of particle after time $t=\frac{1}{2}$ s will be (in m/s)

(a) $10[\hat{\mathbf{i}}-\sqrt{3}\hat{\mathbf{j}}]$ (b) $10[\hat{\mathbf{i}}+\sqrt{3}\hat{\mathbf{j}}]$

(c) $10[\sqrt{3}\,\hat{\mathbf{i}}-\hat{\mathbf{j}}]$ (d) $10[\hat{\mathbf{i}}+\hat{\mathbf{j}}]$

30. A particle of mass m and charge q is travelling at a velocity v along X-axis at time $t=0$. It enters a region in which electric field E is present along Z-axis and magnetic field B is present along Y-axis.

Y X Z

The distance covered in time $t=0.2\times10^{-1}$ s, along X-axis is $v/50$ (in metres). Find the value of v.

(a) $\frac{50E}{B}$ (b) $\frac{E}{50B}$

(c) $\frac{E}{100B}$ (d) $\frac{E}{B}$

31. Two similar coils are kept mutually perpendicular such that their centres coincide. At the centre, find the ratio of resultant magnetic field by both coils, and magnetic field due to one coil, if same current is flown.

(a) $1:\sqrt{2}$ (b) $1:2$

(c) $\sqrt{2}:1$ (d) $\sqrt{3}:1$

32. A galvanometer of 50 Ω resistance has 25 divisions. A current of 4×10^{-4} A gives a deflection of one division. To convert this galvanometer into a voltmeter having a range of 50 V, it should be connected with a resistance of

(a) 2500 Ω as a shunt

(b) 245 Ω as a shunt

(c) 2550 Ω in series

(d) 1200 Ω in series

33. An electron is passing undeflected through a perpendicular electric and magnetic field. If the electric field is turned off, then the electron will move

(a) in an elliptical orbit

(b) in a circular orbit

(c) along a parabolic path

(d) along a straight line

34. A galvanometer having a coil resistance of 80 Ω shows full scale deflection when a current of 2.0 A passes through it. It can be converted into an ammeter to read currents up to 10 A by

(a) putting in parallel a resistance of 240 Ω

(b) putting in series a resistance of 20 Ω

(c) putting in series a resistance of 240 Ω

(d) putting in parallel a resistance of 20 Ω

35. Under the influence of a uniform magnetic field, a charged particle moves with constant speed v in a circle of radius R. The time period of rotation of the particle

(a) depends on v and not on R

(b) depends on R and not on v

(c) is independent of both v and R

(d) depends on both v and R

36. Uniform electric and magnetic fields are produced pointing in the same direction. If an electron is projected with its velocity pointing in the same direction, then

(a) the electron velocity will decrease in magnitude

(b) the electron velocity will increase in magnitude

(c) Neither (a) nor (b)

(d) None of the above

37. Consider the diagram. Three parallel wires are at A, B and C. All carry current I in the same direction. Magnitude of force per unit length on the middle wire B is given by

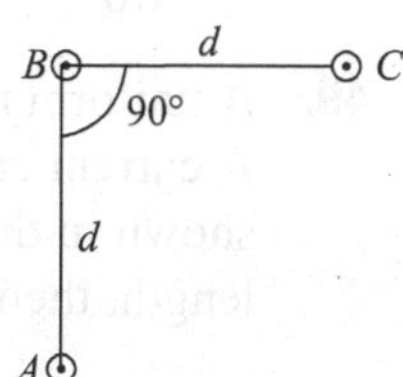

(a) $\frac{2\mu_0 i^2}{\pi d}$ (b) $\frac{\sqrt{2}\mu_0 i^2}{\pi d}$

(c) $\frac{\mu_0 i^2}{\sqrt{2}\pi d}$ (d) $\frac{\mu_0 i^2}{2\pi d}$

38. A galvanometer of resistance G is converted into a voltmeter of range 0-1V by connecting a resistance R_1 in series with it. The additional resistance that should be connected in series with R_1 to increase the range of the voltmeter to 0-2 V will be

(a) $R_1 + G$ (b) R_1

(c) G (d) $R_1 - G$

39. A vertical wire kept in ZX-plane carries a current from P to Q (see figure). The magnetic field due to current will have the direction at the origin O along

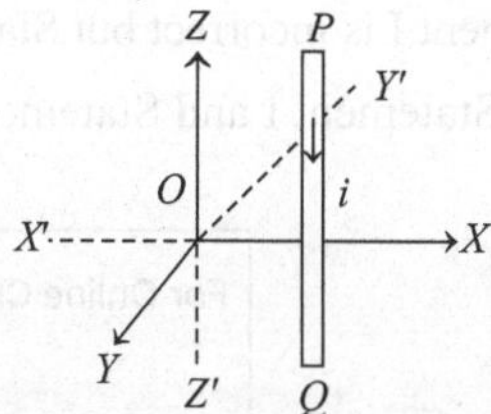

(a) OX (b) OX'

(c) OY (d) OY'

40. Two identical coils A and B each of radius R having currents I and $\sqrt{3}I$ respectively, are lying in perpendicular planes with having same centre. The magnitude of magnetic field at the centre of two coils is

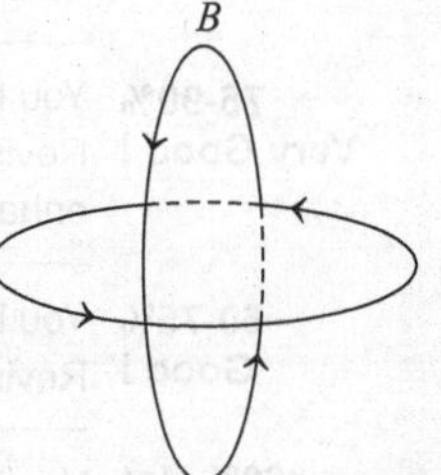

(a) $\frac{\mu_0 I}{2R}$ (b) $\frac{\mu_0 I}{R}$

(c) $\frac{2\mu_0 I}{R}$ (d) $\frac{\mu_0 I}{3R}$

41. An electron moves straight inside a charged parallel plate capacitor. Plates of capacitor have charge density σ. The space between plates is filled with constant magnetic field of induction **B**.

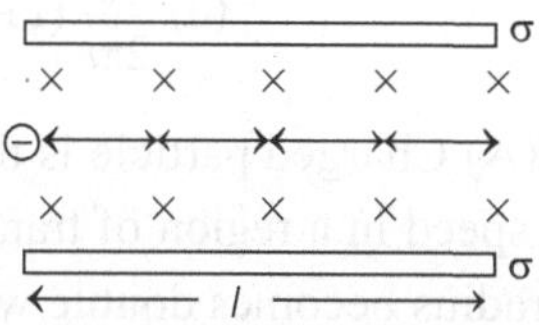

Time taken by electron to pass through the region is

(a) $\frac{\varepsilon_0 e\sigma}{lB}$ (b) $\frac{\varepsilon_0 lB}{\sigma}$

(c) $\frac{\sigma}{eB}$ (d) $\frac{\varepsilon_0 B}{e\sigma}$

42. The force between two parallel current carrying conductor is F. If the current in each conductor is doubled, then the force between them becomes

(a) $4F$ (b) $2F$

(c) F (d) $F/4$

43. Relation between voltage sensitivity S_V and current sensitivity S_i, for a galvanometer of resistance G ohm is

(a) $\frac{S_i}{G} = S_V$ (b) $\frac{S_V}{G} = S_i$

(c) $S_i S_V = \sqrt{G}$ (d) $\sqrt{S_i S_V} = G$

44. A circular coil of 25 turns and radius 4 cm is placed in a uniform magnetic field of 2 T normal to the plane of the coil. If the current in the coil is 6 A, then total torque acting on the coil is

(a) zero (b) 3.4 N-m

(c) 3.8 N-m (d) 4.4 N-m

45. An electron is projected with uniform velocity along the axis inside a current carrying long solenoid, then

(a) the electron path will be circular about the axis

(b) the electron will experience a force at 45° to the axis and execute a helical path

(c) the electron will be accelerated along the axis

(d) the electron will continue to move with uniform velocity along the axis of the solenoid

46. Find the magnetic field at point P.

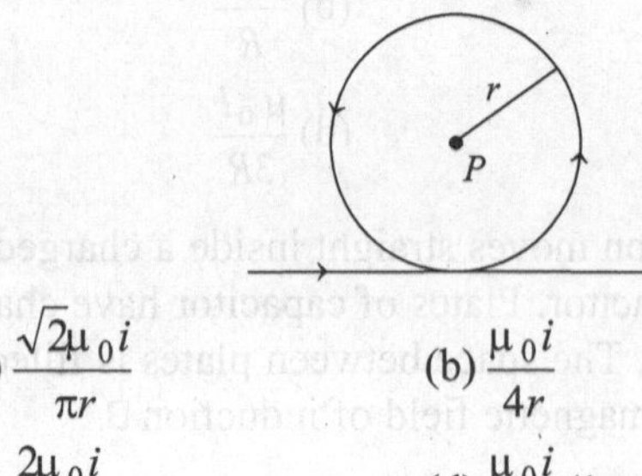

(a) $\frac{\sqrt{2}\mu_0 i}{\pi r}$ (b) $\frac{\mu_0 i}{4r}$

(c) $\frac{2\mu_0 i}{15\pi r}$ (d) $\frac{\mu_0 i}{2\pi r}(1+\pi)$

47. Assertion (A) Charged particle is thrown with double the speed in a region of transverse magnetic field. The radius becomes double while its time period remains the same.

Reason (R) Radius of charged particle is directly proportional to speed while its time period is independent of speed.

In the light of above statements, choose the most appropriate answer from the options given below.

(a) Both A and R are true and R is the correct explanation of A.

(b) Both A and R are true but R is not the correct explanation of A.

(c) A is true but R is false.

(d) A is false but R is true.

48. Three wires of equal length but of different materials are attached to form a loop. The resistance of three parts of a circular loop are as shown in figure. The magnetic field at the centre O is (current enters at A and leaves at B and C as shown)

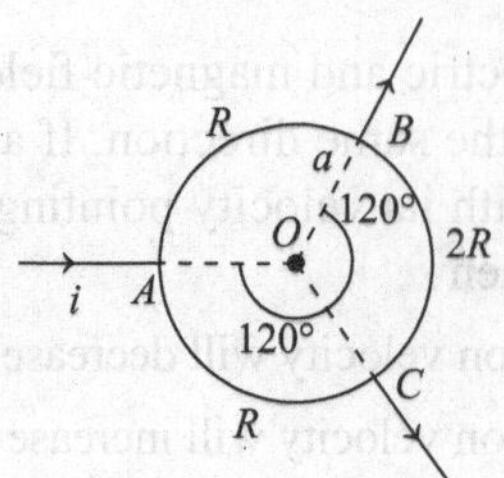

(a) $\frac{\mu_0 I}{6a}$ (b) $\frac{\mu_0 I}{3a}$ (c) $\frac{2}{3}\frac{\mu_0 I}{a}$ (d) zero

49. A uniform magnetic field $\mathbf{B} = B_o\hat{\mathbf{j}}$ exists in a region. A current carrying wire is placed in XY-plane as shown in the diagram. If each segment have equal length, then the force on wire AB is

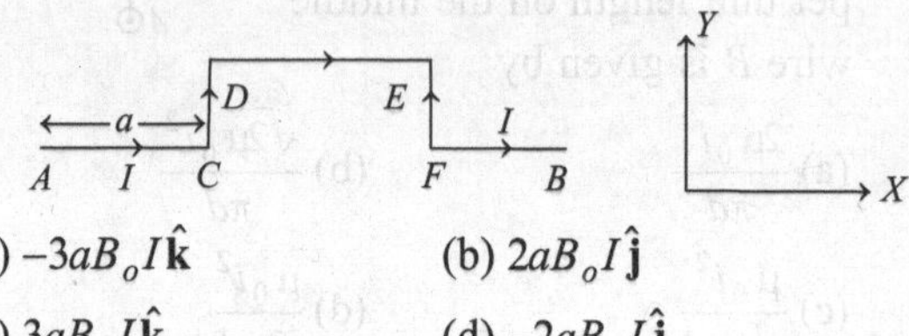

(a) $-3aB_oI\hat{\mathbf{k}}$ (b) $2aB_oI\hat{\mathbf{j}}$

(c) $3aB_oI\hat{\mathbf{k}}$ (d) $-2aB_oI\hat{\mathbf{j}}$

50. Statement I Angular momentum of a charged particle rotating in region of a perpendicular magnetic field is constant in magnitude but not in direction.

Statement II Angular momentum is a vector quantity.

In the light of the above statements, choose the most appropriate answer from the options given below.

(a) Both Statement I and Statement II are correct.

(b) Statement I is correct but Statement II is incorrect.

(c) Statement I is incorrect but Statement II is correct.

(d) Both Statement I and Statement II are incorrect.

For Online Chapter Test **Scan the QR Code**

Response Index

01 ⓐ ⓑ ⓒ ⓓ	14 ⓐ ⓑ ⓒ ⓓ	27 ⓐ ⓑ ⓒ ⓓ	40 ⓐ ⓑ ⓒ ⓓ
02 ⓐ ⓑ ⓒ ⓓ	15 ⓐ ⓑ ⓒ ⓓ	28 ⓐ ⓑ ⓒ ⓓ	41 ⓐ ⓑ ⓒ ⓓ
03 ⓐ ⓑ ⓒ ⓓ	16 ⓐ ⓑ ⓒ ⓓ	29 ⓐ ⓑ ⓒ ⓓ	42 ⓐ ⓑ ⓒ ⓓ
04 ⓐ ⓑ ⓒ ⓓ	17 ⓐ ⓑ ⓒ ⓓ	30 ⓐ ⓑ ⓒ ⓓ	43 ⓐ ⓑ ⓒ ⓓ
05 ⓐ ⓑ ⓒ ⓓ	18 ⓐ ⓑ ⓒ ⓓ	31 ⓐ ⓑ ⓒ ⓓ	44 ⓐ ⓑ ⓒ ⓓ
06 ⓐ ⓑ ⓒ ⓓ	19 ⓐ ⓑ ⓒ ⓓ	32 ⓐ ⓑ ⓒ ⓓ	45 ⓐ ⓑ ⓒ ⓓ
07 ⓐ ⓑ ⓒ ⓓ	20 ⓐ ⓑ ⓒ ⓓ	33 ⓐ ⓑ ⓒ ⓓ	46 ⓐ ⓑ ⓒ ⓓ
08 ⓐ ⓑ ⓒ ⓓ	21 ⓐ ⓑ ⓒ ⓓ	34 ⓐ ⓑ ⓒ ⓓ	47 ⓐ ⓑ ⓒ ⓓ
09 ⓐ ⓑ ⓒ ⓓ	22 ⓐ ⓑ ⓒ ⓓ	35 ⓐ ⓑ ⓒ ⓓ	48 ⓐ ⓑ ⓒ ⓓ
10 ⓐ ⓑ ⓒ ⓓ	23 ⓐ ⓑ ⓒ ⓓ	36 ⓐ ⓑ ⓒ ⓓ	49 ⓐ ⓑ ⓒ ⓓ
11 ⓐ ⓑ ⓒ ⓓ	24 ⓐ ⓑ ⓒ ⓓ	37 ⓐ ⓑ ⓒ ⓓ	50 ⓐ ⓑ ⓒ ⓓ
12 ⓐ ⓑ ⓒ ⓓ	25 ⓐ ⓑ ⓒ ⓓ	38 ⓐ ⓑ ⓒ ⓓ	
13 ⓐ ⓑ ⓒ ⓓ	26 ⓐ ⓑ ⓒ ⓓ	39 ⓐ ⓑ ⓒ ⓓ	

Performance Scanner

> 90% Excellent !	You have mastered this chapter. The concepts of this chapter are on your fingertips. Move on to the next chapter and maintain this momentum.
76-90% Very Good !	You have a good command over this chapter. Revise the chapter again after a few days and enhance your performance.
60-75% Good !	You have a wide scope to learn for this chapter. Revise this chapter again.
<60% Not Satisfactory!	You have a long way ahead of you to master this chapter. Revise it thoroughly.

Test Booklet No. **3947156**

Test Booklet Code **CH6**

MEDACE
NEET (UG)
SELF ASSESSMENT KIT

Magnetism and Matter

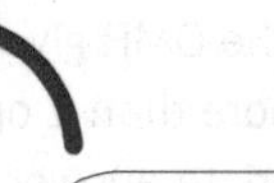

Topics Covered

Magnet, Magnetic Dipole and Magnetic Field

Properties of Magnetic Materials

Important Instructions

- This Booklet Contains – Two Topic Tests and One Test on Complete Chapter.
- Each question carries 4 marks.
- For each correct response, the candidate will get 4 marks and for every incorrect response 1 mark will be additionally deducted from the total score.
- Use **Blue/Black** point pen only for filling the OMR.
- Rough work will be done in the space provided for this purpose within the test booklet only.

Name of the Candidate (In Capitals) ____________________

____

Candidate's Signature __________

Invigilator's Signature __________

Facsimile signature stamp of center superintendent __________

Do not open this Booklet until you start attempting the Test

Topical Follow Thru

Test 1

Syllabus

- Bar Magnet as an Equivalent Solenoid
- Magnetic Field Lines
- Magnetic Field Due to a Magnetic Dipole (Bar Magnet) along its Axis and Perpendicular to Its Axis.
- Torque on a Magnetic Dipole in a Uniform Magnetic Field.

For deeper insight **Scan the QR Code**

Important Instructions

- The test is of 45 minutes duration and contains 25 Multiple Choice Questions. (Four options with a single correct answer).
- Choose the correct option and fill the OMR given on the last page of this test accordingly.
- At some instances, you may find more than 1 option may be correct, in such circumstances you have to judge the most appropriate answer as per the conditions given in the question.

1. A short bar magnet placed with its axis at 30° with a uniform external magnetic field of 2 T, experiences a torque of magnitude 0.04 N-m. The magnetic moment of the bar magnet will be

(a) 0.23 JT^{-1}

(b) zero

(c) 0.40 JT^{-1}

(d) 0.04 JT^{-1}

2. A bar magnet of length 6 cm has points P and Q along its axis at distance of 6 cm and 12 cm on the opposite sides. The ratio of magnetic field at these points will be

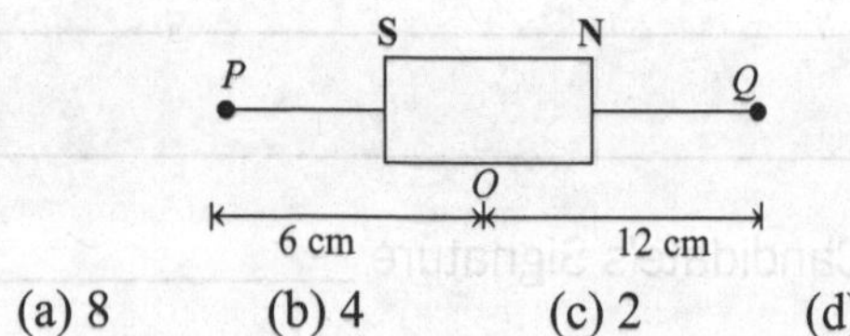

(a) 8 (b) 4 (c) 2 (d) 1

3. A bar magnet having a magnetic moment of $4\times10^4\ JT^{-1}$ is free to rotate in a horizontal plane. A horizontal magnetic field $B=12\times10^{-4}$ T exists in the space. The work done in rotating the magnet slowly from a direction parallel to the field to a direction 30° from the field will be

(a) 4 J (b) 6.48 J

(c) 5.64 J (d) 6 J

4. A bar magnet of 20 cm length is placed on a horizontal table with its south pole pointing towards north pole of earth. Neutral points will be located

(a) on axis of bar magnet

(b) on equatorial axis of bar magnet

(c) There are no neutral points

(d) Depends on material of bar magnet

5. **Assertion** (A) The poles of a magnet cannot be separated by breaking it into two pieces.

Reason (R) The magnetic moment will be reduced to half when a magnet is broken into two equal pieces.

In the light of above statements, choose the most appropriate answer from the options given below.

(a) Both A and R are true and R is a correct explanation of the A.

(b) Both A and R are true and R is not a correct explanation of the A.

(c) A is true but R is false.

(d) Both A and R are true.

6. The following figures show the arrangement of bar magnets in different configurations. Each magnet has magnetic dipole moment *m*. In which configuration has lowest net magnetic dipole moment?

(a) 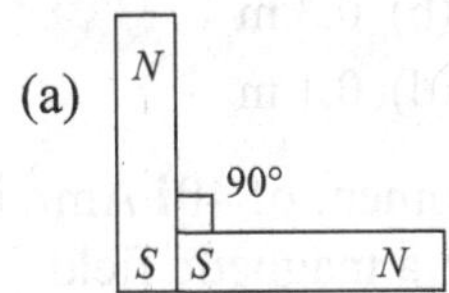

(b) 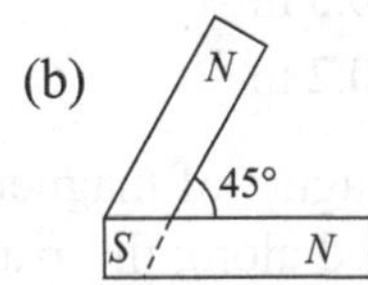

(c) 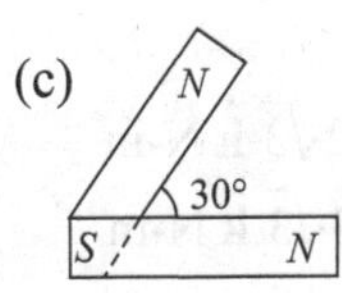

(d) 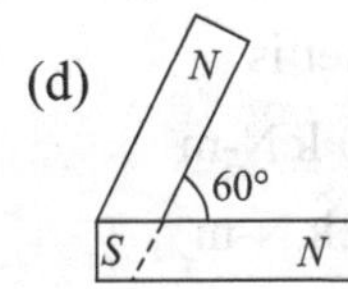

7. A bar magnet is hung by a thin cotton thread in a uniform horizontal magnetic field and is in equilibrium state. The energy required to rotate it by 30° is W. So, the torque required to keep the magnet in this new position will be

(a) $\frac{W}{(2-\sqrt{3})}$ (b) $\frac{W}{2}$

(c) $\frac{W}{\sqrt{3}}$ (d) $\frac{W}{\sqrt{2}}$

8. The time period of a vibration magnetometer is T_0. It's magnet is replaced by another magnet whose moment of inertia is 5 times and magnetic moment is $\frac{1}{5}$ of the initial magnet. The time period now will

(a) $3T_0$ (b) $4T_0$

(c) $6T_0$ (d) $5T_0$

9. A bar magnet suspended freely in an uniform magnetic field is vibrating with a time period of 13 s. If the field strength is increased to 16 times of the earlier field strength, then the time period will be

(a) $\frac{13}{2}$ s (b) 3.25 s

(c) 7.2 s (d) 4.25 s

10. Which of the following statements about the bar magnet, will be false?

(a) The bar magnet has poles similar to the positive and negative charges of an electric dipole.

(b) One pole is designated as north pole and other as south pole.

(c) Like poles repel each other and unlike poles attract each other.

(d) The poles of a magnet can be separated.

11. The pole strength of 12 cm long bar magnet is 20 A-m. The magnetic induction at a point 10 cm away from the centre of the magnet on its axial line is $\left(\text{Take, } \frac{\mu_0}{4\pi} = 10^{-7} \text{ Hm}^{-1}\right)$

(a) 1.17×10^{-3} T (b) 2.20×10^{-2} T

(c) 1.17×10^{-2} T (d) 2.21×10^{-2} T

12. A bar magnet of magnetic moment 1.5 JT^{-1} aligned with direction of uniform magnetic field of 0.22 T.

Match the scenarios (Column I) with corresponding values (Column II).

	Column I		Column II
A.	Work required to align the magnetic moment normal to field direction	I.	0.165 Nm
B.	Work required to align the magnetic moment opposite to the field direction	II.	0
C.	Torque on the magnet when the magnetic moment is 30° to the field direction	III.	0.66 J
D.	Torque on the magnet when the magnetic moment opposite to field direction.	IV.	0.33 J

Choose the correct answer from the options given below.

(a) A-II, B-III, C-IV, D-I

(b) A-III, B-IV, C-II, D-I

(c) A-III, B-IV, C-I, D-II

(d) A-IV, B-III, C-I, D-II

13. A small bar magnet placed with its axis at 30° with an external field of 0.06 T experiences a torque of 0.018 N-m. The minimum work required to rotate it from its stable to unstable equilibrium position is

(a) 9.2×10^{-3} J (b) 7.2×10^{-2} J
(c) 6.4×10^{-2} J (d) 11.7×10^{-3} J

14. A circular coil having N turns and radius r carries a current I. It is held in the XZ-plane in a magnetic field $B\hat{\mathbf{i}}$. The torque on the coil due to the magnetic field (in N-m) is

(a) $\dfrac{Br^2I}{\pi N}$ (b) $B\pi r^2 IN$
(c) $\dfrac{B\pi r^2 I}{N}$ (d) zero

15. Two magnetic dipoles X and Y are placed at a separation d, with their axis perpendicular to each other. The dipole moment of Y is twice that of X. A particle of charge q is passing through their mid-point P, at angle $\theta = 45°$ with the horizontal line, as shown in figure. What would be the magnitude of force on the particle at that instant? (d is much larger than the dimensions of the dipole)

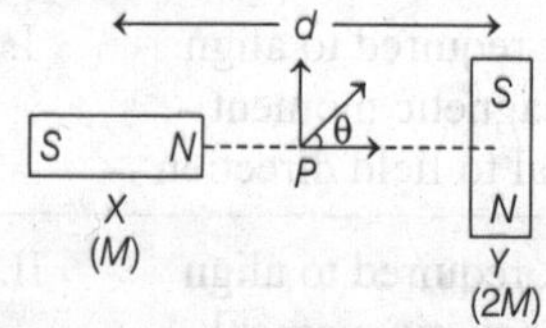

(a) $\left(\dfrac{\mu_0}{4\pi}\right)\dfrac{M}{\left(\dfrac{d}{2}\right)^3} \times qv$

(b) 0

(c) $\sqrt{2}\left(\dfrac{\mu_0}{4\pi}\right)\dfrac{M}{\left(\dfrac{d}{2}\right)^3} \times qv$

(d) $\left(\dfrac{\mu_0}{4\pi}\right)\dfrac{2M}{\left(\dfrac{d}{2}\right)^3} \times qv$

16. Due to a small magnet, intensity at a distance x on the axial position is 9 G, what will be the intensity at a distance $\dfrac{x}{2}$ on the equatorial position?

(a) 9 G
(b) 4 G
(c) 36 G
(d) 4.5 G

17. A bar magnet of magnetic moment 3 A-m^2 is placed in a uniform magnetic induction field of 2×10^{-5} T. If each pole of the magnet experiences a force of 6×10^{-4} N, then the length of the magnet is

(a) 0.5 m (b) 0.3 m
(c) 0.2 m (d) 0.1 m

18. A magnet of magnetic moment of $40\hat{\mathbf{i}}$ Am^2 is placed along the x-axis in a magnetic field $\mathbf{B} = (0.6\hat{\mathbf{i}} + 0.3\hat{\mathbf{j}})$ T. The torque acting on the magnet is

(a) $10\,\hat{\mathbf{k}}$ N-m (b) $12\sqrt{3}\,\hat{\mathbf{k}}$ N-m
(c) $12\hat{\mathbf{k}}$ N-m (d) $11\sqrt{3}\,\hat{\mathbf{k}}$ N-m

19. The magnetic field at a point x on the axis of a smaller magnet is equal to the field at a point y in the equator of the same magnet. The ratio of distance of x and y from the centre of the magnet is

(a) 2^{-3} (b) $2^{-1/3}$
(c) 2^3 (d) $2^{1/3}$

20. Two short magnets of equal dipole moment M are fastened perpendicularly at their centre (see figure). The magnitude of the magnetic field at a distance d from the centre on the bi-sector of the right angle is

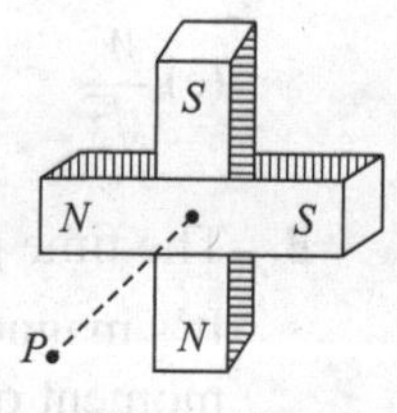

(a) $\dfrac{\mu_0}{4\pi} \cdot \dfrac{M}{d^3}$ (b) $\dfrac{\mu_0}{4\pi} \cdot \dfrac{M\sqrt{2}}{d^3}$
(c) $\dfrac{\mu_0}{4\pi} \cdot \dfrac{2\sqrt{2}\,M}{d^3}$ (d) $\dfrac{\mu_0}{4\pi} \cdot \dfrac{2\,M}{d^3}$

21. A current-carrying loop is placed in a uniform magnetic field in four different orientations as shown in figure. The potential energy increases in order of

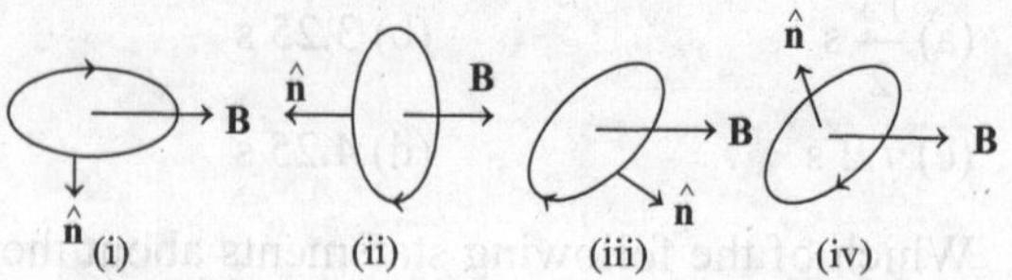

(a) (iii), (i), (iv) and (ii)
(b) (i), (ii), (iii) and (iv)
(c) (ii), (iii), (i) and (iv)
(d) (iv), (iii), (i) and (ii)

22. Two short bar magnets of magnetic moment 8.0 A-m^2 each are arranged at the opposite corners of a square as given in figure. The magnetic induction at corner D is

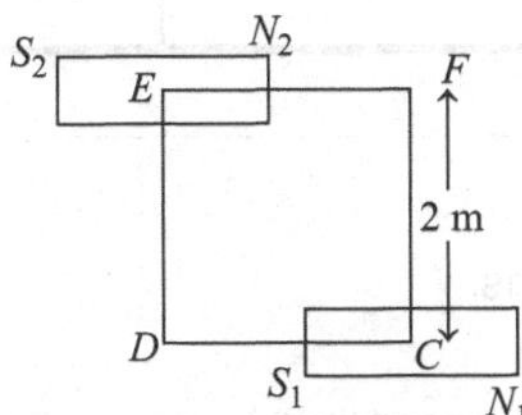

(a) 2 μT (b) 1 μT
(c) 0.1 μT (d) 0.2 μT

23. A small circular coil of 10 turns, area 1 mm^2 and carrying a current of $\left(\frac{21}{44}\right)$ A is in the middle of a long solenoid of 10^3 turns/m with its axis perpendicular to the axis of the solenoid. If torque 1.5×10^{-8} N-m can hold the coil in the solenoid, then current flowing in the solenoid is

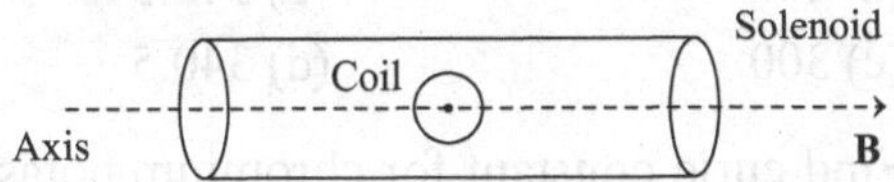

(a) 2.5 A (b) 3.5 A
(c) 1.5 A (d) 2 A

24. A circular coil of 16 turns and radius 10 cm carrying a current of 0.75 A rests with its plane normal to an external field of magnitude 5.0×10^{-2} T. Which of the following statement is correct?

(a) Magnetic moment of the coil is 3.77 JT^{-1}.
(b) If coil oscillates about its stable equilibrium with a frequency of 2s^{-1}, then moment of inertia of the coil will be 1.2×10^{-4} kg-m^2.
(c) If coil oscillates about its stable equilibrium with a frequency of 3s^{-1}, then moment of inertia of the coil will be 3.2×10^{-4} kg-m^2.
(d) If the moment of inertia is 4×10^{-2}, then coil oscillates with frequency of 3s^{-1}.

25. The difference between Gauss's law of magnetism and that for electrostatic is a reflection of the fact that

(a) isolated magnetic poles are not known to exist
(b) isolated magnetic poles are exist
(c) domain of magnetic substance is not align properly
(d) domain of magnetic substance align properly

Response Index

01	ⓐ	ⓑ	ⓒ	ⓓ	10	ⓐ	ⓑ	ⓒ	ⓓ	19	ⓐ	ⓑ	ⓒ	ⓓ
02	ⓐ	ⓑ	ⓒ	ⓓ	11	ⓐ	ⓑ	ⓒ	ⓓ	20	ⓐ	ⓑ	ⓒ	ⓓ
03	ⓐ	ⓑ	ⓒ	ⓓ	12	ⓐ	ⓑ	ⓒ	ⓓ	21	ⓐ	ⓑ	ⓒ	ⓓ
04	ⓐ	ⓑ	ⓒ	ⓓ	13	ⓐ	ⓑ	ⓒ	ⓓ	22	ⓐ	ⓑ	ⓒ	ⓓ
05	ⓐ	ⓑ	ⓒ	ⓓ	14	ⓐ	ⓑ	ⓒ	ⓓ	23	ⓐ	ⓑ	ⓒ	ⓓ
06	ⓐ	ⓑ	ⓒ	ⓓ	15	ⓐ	ⓑ	ⓒ	ⓓ	24	ⓐ	ⓑ	ⓒ	ⓓ
07	ⓐ	ⓑ	ⓒ	ⓓ	16	ⓐ	ⓑ	ⓒ	ⓓ	25	ⓐ	ⓑ	ⓒ	ⓓ
08	ⓐ	ⓑ	ⓒ	ⓓ	17	ⓐ	ⓑ	ⓒ	ⓓ					
09	ⓐ	ⓑ	ⓒ	ⓓ	18	ⓐ	ⓑ	ⓒ	ⓓ					

Performance Scanner

> 90% Excellent !	You have mastered these topics. The concepts of these topics are at your fingertips. Move on to the next test and maintain this momentum.
76-90% Very Good !	You have a good command over these topics. Revise them again after a few days and enhance your performance.
60-75% Good !	You have a wide scope to learn for these topics. Revise them again.
<60% Not Satisfactory!	You have a long way ahead of you to master in these topics. Revise them thoroughly.

Test 2

Syllabus
- Para, Dia and Ferromagnetic Substances with Examples
- Effect of Temperature on Magnetic Properties.

For deeper insight **Scan the QR Code**

Important Instructions
- The test is of 45 minutes duration and contains 25 Multiple Choice Questions. (Four options with a single correct answer).
- Choose the correct option and fill the OMR given on the last page of this test accordingly.
- At some instances, you may find more than 1 option may be correct, in such circumstances you have to judge the most appropriate answer as per the conditions given in the question.

1. A magnetic field of 100 Am^{-1} produces a magnetic flux of 1.4×10^{-4} Wb in a bar of iron of cross-section 2 cm^2. Find permeability of the iron bar used.

(a) 14×10^{-2} TmA^{-1}

(b) 0.071 TmA^{-1}

(c) 2.46×10^{-3} TmA^{-1}

(d) 0.007 TmA^{-1}

2. A magnet of magnetic moment 1.1 A-m^2 and mass 66 g, has density 1000 kg-m^2. Then calculate the intensity of magnetisation.

(a) 2.70×10^4 Am^{-1} (b) 2.54×10^4 Am^{-1}

(c) 1.66×10^4 Am^{-1} (d) 12.54×10^4 Am^{-1}

3. Statement I The permeability of a ferromagnetic material is independent of the magnetic field.
Statement II Permeability of a material is a constant quantity.
In the light of above statements, choose the most appropriate answer from the options given below.

(a) Both Statement I and Statement II are correct.

(b) Both Statement I and Statement II are incorrect.

(c) Statement I is correct but Statement II is incorrect

(d) Statement I is incorrect but Statement II is correct.

4. The percentage increase in magnetic field B. When the space within a current-carrying toroid is filled with aluminium ($\chi = 5.1 \times 10^{-5}$) will be

(a) 2×10^{-2}% (b) 4.3×10^{-4}%

(c) 5.1×10^{-3}% (d) 6.7×10^{-3}%

5. A paramagnetic gas whose atoms have a magnetic dipole moment of about 10^{-24} A-m^2 is placed in an external magnetic field of 5 T. Find the ratio of thermal to magnetic energy at 150 K.

(a) 600 (b) 310.5

(c) 300 (d) 340.5

6. Find curie constant for chromium potassium alum from its graph shown in figure below when $\chi = 0.30$.

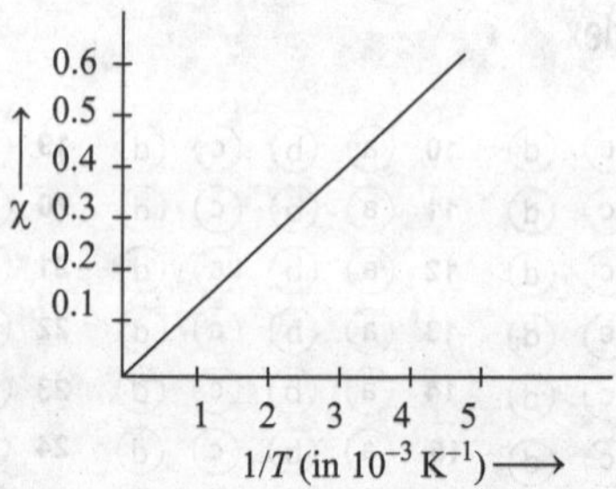

(a) 50 K (b) 30 K

(c) 60 K (d) 40 K

7. A paramagnetic substance in the form of a cube with sides 1 cm has a magnetic dipole moment of 20×10^{-6} J/T when a magnetic intensity of 60×10^3 A/m is applied. Its magnetic susceptibility is

(a) 3.3×10^{-4} (b) 3.3×10^{-2}

(c) 4.3×10^{-2} (d) 2.3×10^{-2}

8. The relative permeability of a substance X is slightly less than unity and that of substance Y is slightly more than unity, then

(a) X is paramagnetic and Y is ferromagnetic
(b) X is diamagnetic and Y is ferromagnetic
(c) X and Y both are paramagnetic
(d) X is diamagnetic and Y is paramagnetic

9. A copper rod is suspended in a non-homogeneous magnetic field region. The rod when in equilibrium will align itself

(a) in the region, where magnetic field is strongest
(b) in the region, where magnetic field is weakest and parallel to direction of magnetic field at that position
(c) in the direction in which it was originally suspended
(d) in the region, where magnetic field is weakest and perpendicular to the direction of magnetic field at that position

10. A uniform magnetic field parallel to the plane of paper, exsisted in space initially directed from left to right. When a bar of soft iron is placed in the field parallel to it, the lines of force passing through it will be represented by figure.

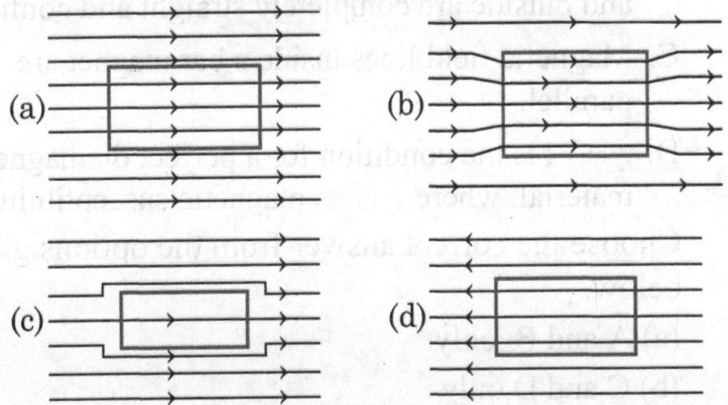

11. A perfectly diamagnetic sphere has a small spherical cavity at its centre,which is filled with a paramagnetic substance. The whole system is placed in a uniform magnetic field **B**. Then, the field inside the paramagnetic substance is

(a) much larger than $|\mathbf{B}|$ and parallel to **B**
(b) **B**
(c) zero
(d) much larger than $|\mathbf{B}|$ but opposite to **B**

12. The variation of the intensity of magnetisation (I) with respect to the magnetising field (H) in a diamagnetic substance is described by the graph in figure.

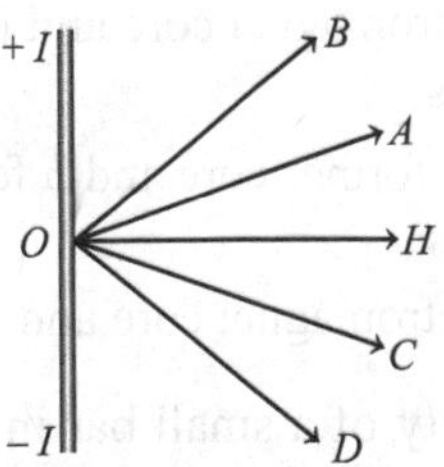

(a) OD (b) OC
(c) OB (d) OA

13. The variation of magnetic susceptibility (χ) with temperature for a diamagnetic substance is best represented by figure

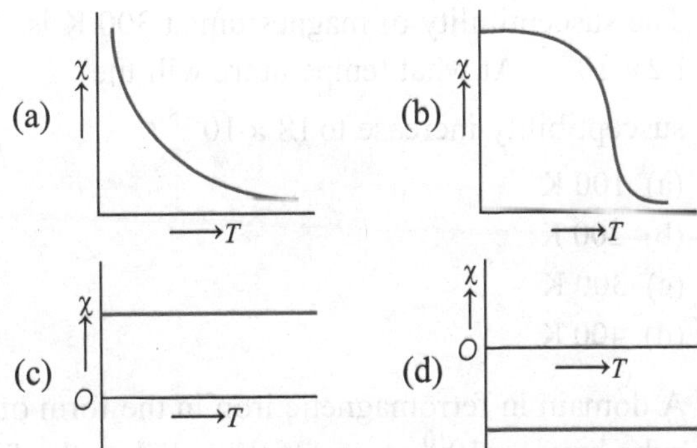

14. A paramagnetic material has 10^{28} atoms/m^3. Its magnetic susceptibility at temperature 350 K is 2.8×10^{-4}. Its susceptibility at 300 K is

(a) 3.726×10^{-4}
(b) 3.672×10^{-4}
(c) 2.672×10^{-4}
(d) 3.267×10^{-4}

15. Hysteresis loops for two magnetic materials a and b are as given below.

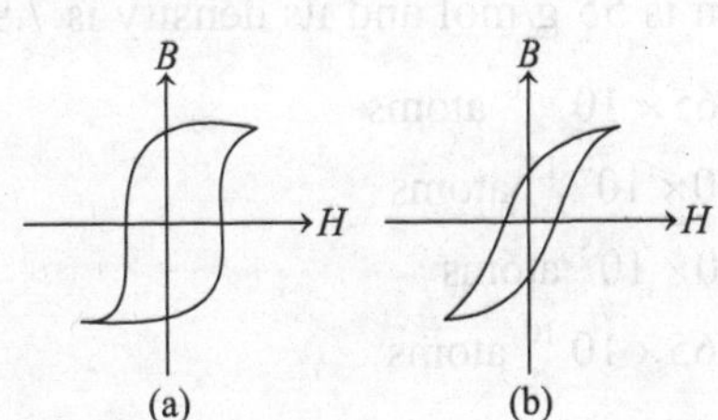

These materials are used to make magnets for electric generators, transformer core and electromagnet core. Then, it is proper to use

(a) *a* for electric generators and transformer core
(b) *a* for electromagnet core and *b* for electric generators
(c) *a* for transformer core and *b* for electric generators
(d) *b* for electromagnet core and transformer core

16. The coercivity of a small bar magnet is 4×10^3 A/m. It is inserted inside a solenoid of 500 turns and length 1 m to demagnetise it. The amount of current to be passed through the solenoid will be

(a) 2.5 A (b) 5 A
(c) 8 A (d) 10 A

17. The susceptibility of magnesium at 300 K is 1.2×10^{-5}. At what temperature will the susceptibility increase to 1.8×10^{-5}?

(a) 100 K
(b) 200 K
(c) 300 K
(d) 400 K

18. A domain in ferromagnetic iron in the form of cube have 8×10^{10} atoms. If the side length of this domain is 2.0 μm and each atom has a dipole moment of 5×10^{-24} Am^2, then magnetisation of domain is

(a) 11.8×10^5 Am^{-1}
(b) 5×10^4 Am^{-1}
(c) 23.5×10^4 Am^{-1}
(d) 5×10^5 Am^{-1}

19. A domain in ferromagnetic iron is in the form of a cube of side length 1 μm. Estimate the number of iron atoms in the domain. The molecular mass of iron is 55 g/mol and its density is 7.9 g cm^{-3}.

(a) 8.65×10^{-10} atoms
(b) 8.0×10^{-13} atoms
(c) 8.0×10^5 atoms
(d) 8.65×10^{10} atoms

20. A paramagnetic material has a magnetic susceptibility of 10^{-5}. When it is placed in a magnetic field of 0.5 T, then the magnetisation of material is

(a) 5×10^{-5} Am^{-1}
(b) 25×10^{-5} Am^{-1}
(c) 5×10^{-6} Am^{-1}
(d) 25×10^{-6} Am^{-1}

21. At temperature of 4K and external field of 0.6 T, a paramagentic sample shows a net magnetisation of 8 Am^{-1}. Magnetisation in Am^{-1} of same sample at 16K when placed in a magnetic field of 0.2 T is

(a) $\frac{32}{3}$ (b) $\frac{2}{3}$
(c) $\frac{6}{5}$ (d) $\frac{12}{7}$

22. Which of the following statement(s) is/are correct?

A. Electric dipole and monopoles exists, whereas magnetic monopoles exist but dipole does not exist.
B. Magnetic field lines due to a solenoid at its ends and outside are completely straight and confined.
C. Magnetic field lines inside a bar magnet are parallel.
D. $\chi=+1$ is the condition for a perfect diamagnetic material, where χ is its magnetic susceptibility.

Choose the correct answer from the options given below.

(a) A and B only
(b) C and D only
(c) B and C only
(d) C only

23. When a piece of a ferromagnetic substance is put in a uniform magnetic field, the flux density inside it is three times the flux density away from the piece. The magnetic permeability of the material is

(a) 1
(b) 3
(c) 4
(d) 2

24. Match the following Columns.

	Column I		Column II
A.	Diamagnetic	I.	$\mu >> \mu_0 \mu_r >> 1$ and $\chi >> 1$
B.	Paramagnetic	II.	$-1 \le \chi < 0$, $0 \le \mu_r < 1$ and $\mu < \mu_0$
C.	Ferromagnetic	III.	$0 < \chi < \varepsilon$, $1 < \mu_r < 1 + \varepsilon$ and $\mu > \mu_0$
D.	Vacuum	IV.	$\mu_r = 1$

Choose the correct answer from the options given below.

(a) A-II, B-III, C-I, D-IV
(b) A-II, B-I, C-III, D-IV
(c) A-III, B-IV, C-I, D-II
(d) A-IV, B-III, C-II, D-I

25. A thin diamagnetic rod is placed vertically between the poles of an electromagnet. When the current in the electromagnet is switched ON, then the diamagnetic rod is pushed up, out of the horizontal magnetic field. Hence, the rod gains gravitational potential energy. The work required to do this, comes from

(a) the lattice structure of the material of the rod
(b) the magnetic field
(c) the current source
(d) the induced electric field due to the changing magnetic field

Response Index

01 ⓐ ⓑ ⓒ ⓓ	10 ⓐ ⓑ ⓒ ⓓ	19 ⓐ ⓑ ⓒ ⓓ
02 ⓐ ⓑ ⓒ ⓓ	11 ⓐ ⓑ ⓒ ⓓ	20 ⓐ ⓑ ⓒ ⓓ
03 ⓐ ⓑ ⓒ ⓓ	12 ⓐ ⓑ ⓒ ⓓ	21 ⓐ ⓑ ⓒ ⓓ
04 ⓐ ⓑ ⓒ ⓓ	13 ⓐ ⓑ ⓒ ⓓ	22 ⓐ ⓑ ⓒ ⓓ
05 ⓐ ⓑ ⓒ ⓓ	14 ⓐ ⓑ ⓒ ⓓ	23 ⓐ ⓑ ⓒ ⓓ
06 ⓐ ⓑ ⓒ ⓓ	15 ⓐ ⓑ ⓒ ⓓ	24 ⓐ ⓑ ⓒ ⓓ
07 ⓐ ⓑ ⓒ ⓓ	16 ⓐ ⓑ ⓒ ⓓ	25 ⓐ ⓑ ⓒ ⓓ
08 ⓐ ⓑ ⓒ ⓓ	17 ⓐ ⓑ ⓒ ⓓ	
09 ⓐ ⓑ ⓒ ⓓ	18 ⓐ ⓑ ⓒ ⓓ	

Performance Scanner

> 90% Excellent !	You have mastered these topics. The concepts of these topics are at your fingertips. Move on to the next test and maintain this momentum.
76-90% Very Good !	You have a good command over these topics. Revise them again after a few days and enhance your performance.
60-75% Good !	You have a wide scope to learn for these topics. Revise them again.
<60% Not Satisfactory!	You have a long way ahead of you to master in these topics. Revise them thoroughly.

Chapter Break Thru

Syllabus	• Bar Magnet as an Equivalent Solenoid • Magnetic Field Lines • Magnetic Field Due to a Magnetic Dipole (Bar Magnet) Along its Axis and Perpendicular to Its Axis • Torque on a Magnetic Dipole in a Uniform Magnetic Field	• Para, Dia and Ferromagnetic Substances with Examples • Effect of Temperature on Magnetic Properties.

Important Instructions

- The test is of 45 minutes duration and contains 30 Multiple Choice Questions (Four options with a single correct answer).
- Choose the correct option and fill the OMR given on the last page of this test accordingly.
- At some instances, you may find more than 1 option may be correct, in such circumstances you have to judge the most appropriate answer as per conditions given in the question.

1. Choose the correct graph of susceptibility *versus* temperature for a paramagnetic material.

(a) 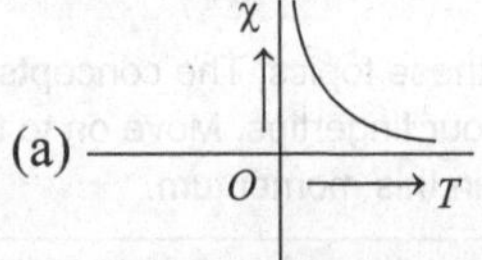

(b) 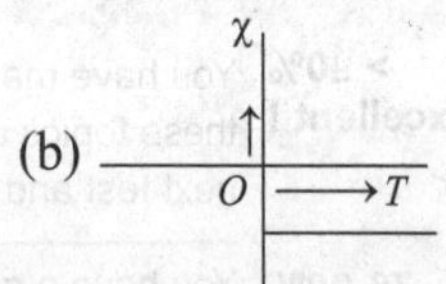

(c) 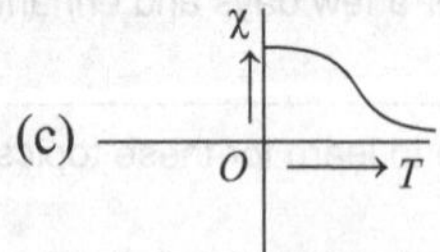

(d) 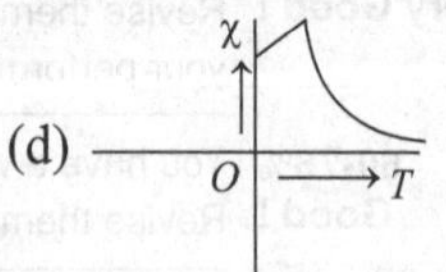

2. Choose incorrect statement.

A. Sodium chloride has negative susceptibility.
B. Superconductors are diamagnetic.
C. Copper chloride is weakly attracted by a strong magnet.
D. Cobalt becomes paramagnetic on heating.
E. Susceptibility of water decreases rapidly with increase in temperature.

(a) A and B (b) B, C and D
(c) D and E (d) E only

3. Statement I Above Curie temperature, a ferromagnetic substance becomes paramagnetic substance.

Statement II On increasing the temperature of a ferromagnetic material, its magnetisation increases.

In light of above statements, choose the most appropriate answer from the options given below.

(a) Both Statement I and Statement II are incorrect.
(b) Both Statement I and Statement II are correct.
(c) Statement I is correct but Statement II is incorrect.
(d) Statement I is incorrect but Statement II is correct.

4. If a long thin magnet of magnetic dipole moment M is bent into a semi-circle, then new value of magnetic dipole moment of the magnet will be

(a) $\frac{M}{2\pi}$ (b) $\frac{2M}{\pi}$
(c) $\frac{3M}{2\pi}$ (d) $\frac{M}{3\pi}$

5. The work done in turning a magnet of magnetic dipole moment M by an angle of 90° from the meridian is n times the corresponding work done to turn it through an angle of 60°. The value of n is given by

(a) 1 (b) 2
(c) 1.5 (d) 0.5

6. Area of B-H curve signifies

(a) strength of magnetic field
(b) induced magnetic dipole moment
(c) heat loss per cycle of magnetisation and demagnetisation
(d) net magnetic dipole moment per unit volume

7. Match the List-I with List-II.

	List-I		List-II
A.	Magnetic field induction	1.	Am^{-1}
B.	1 Gauss	2.	no unit
C.	Unit of intensity of magnetic field	3.	directly proportional to the current flowing through the wire
D.	Unit of magnetic susceptibility	4.	0.0001 S.I. units of magnetic induction

(a) A→2, B→3, C→1, D→4
(b) A→4, B→3, C→2, D→1
(c) A→1, B→2, C→3, D→4
(d) A→3, B→4, C→1, D→2

8. Which of the following statements is incorrect in the case of magnetic field lines?

(a) Magnetic field lines is an imaginary curve, the tangent to which at any point gives direction of magnetic field B at that point.
(b) Two magnetic field lines can intersect each other.
(c) Magnetic lines of force comes out and goes into a magnetic material at any angle.
(d) None of the above

9. The correct graph of susceptibility *versus* temperature for a ferromagnetic substance is

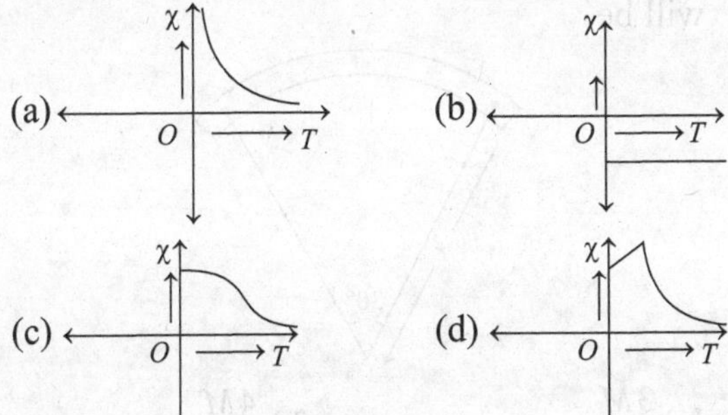

10. The basic magnetisation curve for a ferromagnetic material is shown in figure. The value of magnetic permeability is highest for the point

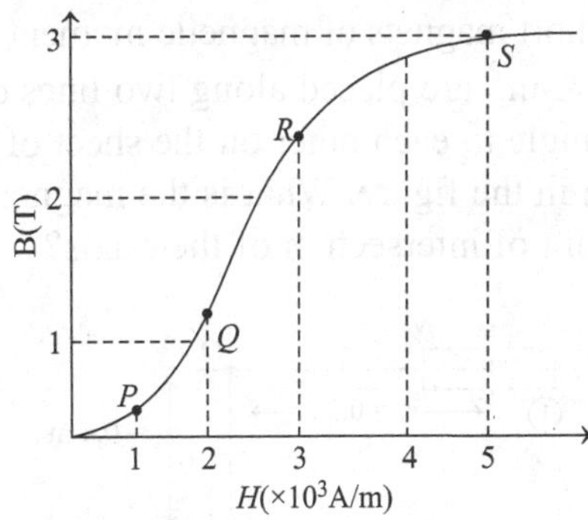

(a) P (b) Q
(c) R (d) S

11. The susceptibility of an anti-ferromagnetic material varies as temperature changes. It is best represented by

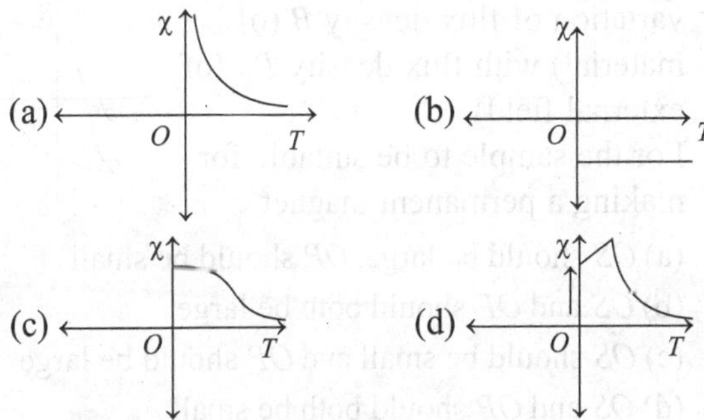

12. Magnetic moment M *versus* temperature T curve for a magnet is

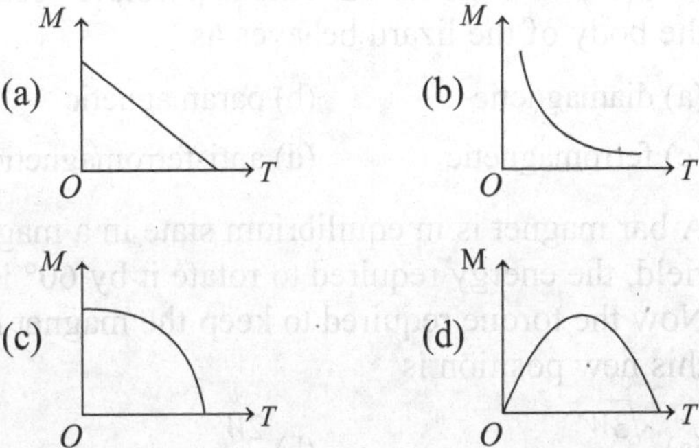

13. A small rod of bismuth is suspended freely between the poles of a strong electromagnet. It is found to arrange itself at right angles to the magnetic field. This observation establishes that bismuth is

(a) diamagnetic
(b) paramagnetic
(c) ferromagnetic
(d) anti-ferromagnetic

14. Two short magnets of magnetic moment 3 A-m^2 and 4 A-m^2 are placed along two lines drawn at right angle to each other on the sheet of paper as shown in the figure. What is the magnetic field at the point of intersection of their axis?

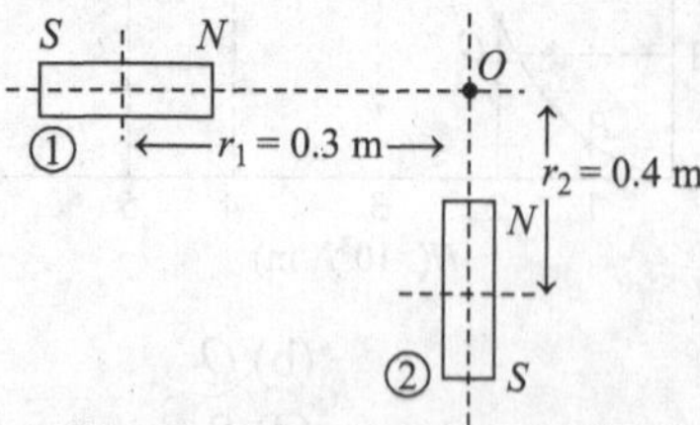

(a) 2.15×10^{-5}T (b) 2.54×10^{-5}T
(c) 2.64×10^{-6}T (d) 2.15×10^{-5}T

15. The following diagram shows the variation of flux density B (of material) with flux density B_0 (of external field).

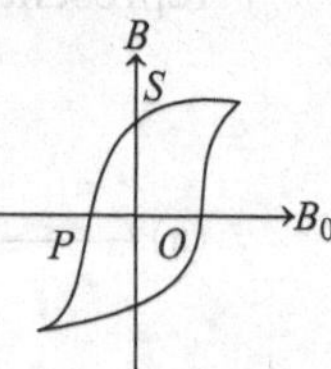

For the sample to be suitable for making a permanent magnet

(a) *OS* should be large, *OP* should be small
(b) *OS* and *OP* should both be large
(c) *OS* should be small and *OP* should be large
(d) *OS* and *OP* should both be small

16. A lizard can be levitated in a magnetic field produced by a current in a vertical solenoid placed below the lizard. This is possible because the body of the lizard behaves as

(a) diamagnetic (b) paramagnetic
(c) ferromagnetic (d) anti-ferromagnetic

17. A bar magnet is in equilibrium state in a magnetic field, the energy required to rotate it by 60° is W. Now the torque required to keep the magnet in this new position is

(a) $\frac{\sqrt{3}W}{2}$ (b) $\frac{2W}{\sqrt{3}}$
(c) $\frac{W}{\sqrt{3}}$ (d) $\sqrt{3}\,W$

18. Choose the correct option for which the magnetic susceptibility is negative.

(a) Diamagnetic material only
(b) Paramagnetic material only
(c) Ferromagnetic material only
(d) Paramagnetic and ferromagnetic materials

19. Cobalt shows ferromagnetic property at room temperature. If the temperature is increased beyond Curie temperature, then it will show

(a) paramagnetism
(b) anti-ferromagnetism
(c) no magnetic property
(d) diamagnetism

20. Soft iron is used for making electromagnets because soft iron has

(a) low retentivity and high coercivity
(b) high retentivity and high coercivity
(c) low retentivity and low coercivity
(d) high retentivity and low coercivity

21. If the magnetic dipole moment of an atom of diamagnetic material, paramagnetic material and ferromagnetic material are denoted by μ_d, μ_p and μ_f respectively, then

(a) $\mu_d \neq 0$ and $\mu_f \neq 0$
(b) $\mu_p = 0$ and $\mu_f \neq 0$
(b) $\mu_d \neq 0$ and $\mu_p \neq 0$
(d) $\mu_d = 0$ and $\mu_p \neq 0$

22. At a certain place, a magnet makes 120 oscillations per minute. At another place where the magnetic field is double, its time period will be

(a) $\frac{1}{\sqrt{2}}$ s (b) $\frac{1}{\sqrt{3}}$ s
(c) $\frac{1}{2\sqrt{2}}$ s (d) $\sqrt{2}$ s

23. A bar magnet of length l and magnetic dipole moment M is bent in the form of an arc as shown in the figure. The new magnetic dipole moment will be

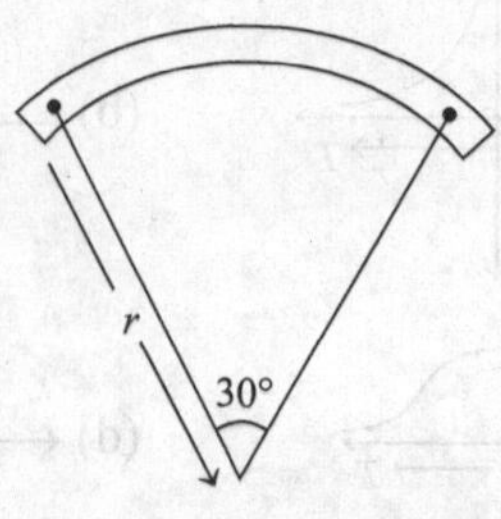

(a) $\frac{3M}{\pi}$ (b) $\frac{4M}{\pi}$
(c) $\frac{6M}{\pi}$ (d) $\frac{M}{\pi}$

24. **Assertion** (A) Repulsion is the sure test for magnetism.
Reason (R) Attraction can occur between two unlike poles of a magnet and also between a magnet and a magnetic material.

In the light of above statements, choose the most appropriate answer from the options given below.

(a) Both A and R are true and R is the correct explanation of A.
(b) Both A and R are true but R is not the correct explanation of A.
(c) A is true but R is false.
(d) A is false but R is true.

25. A thin magnetic needle oscillates in the horizontal plane with a time period of 4.0 s. If the needle is broken into 4 equal parts perpendicular to its length, then the time period of each part will be

(a) 0.5 s (b) 1.0 s
(c) 1.5 s (d) 2.0 s

26. Identify the material in the given figure.

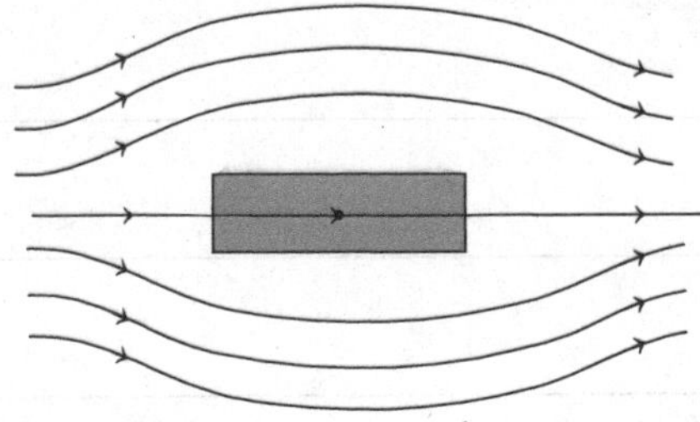

(a) Paramagnetic
(b) Diamagnetic
(c) Ferromagnetic
(d) None of these

27. The correct graph for magnetic susceptibility (χ) *versus* magnetising field (H) for a paramagnetic substance is

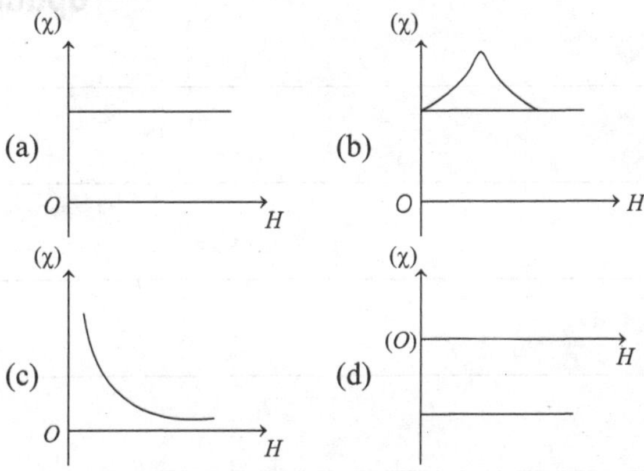

28. Area of hysteresis loop is proportional to

(a) number of turns of coil
(b) permeability of sample
(c) heat produced
(d) magnetisation of sample

29. Two normal uniform magnetic field contain a magnetic needle making an angle 30° with F. Then, the ratio of F/H is

(a) 1 : 2 (b) 2 : 1 (c) $\sqrt{3}:1$ (d) $1:\sqrt{3}$

30. The work done in rotating a magnet of magnetic moment 6 A-m² in a magnetic field of 5×10^{-3} T from the direction along the magnetic field to opposite direction to the magnetic field is

(a) zero (b) 6×10^{-2} J
(c) 10^{-2} J (d) 10 J

For Online Unit Test
Scan the
QR Code

Response Index

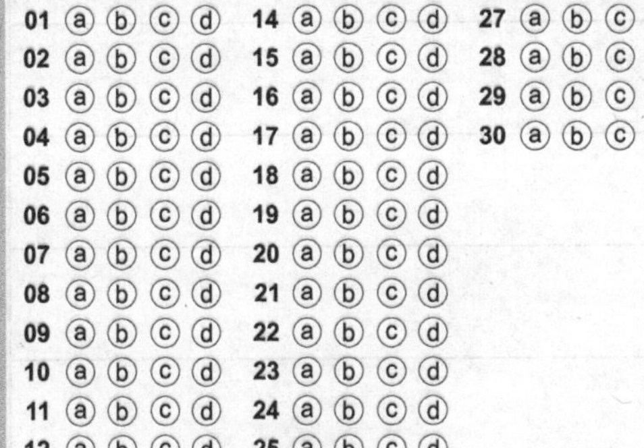

Performance Scanner

> 90% Excellent ! You have mastered this chapter. The concepts of this chapter are on your fingertips. Move on to the next chapter and maintain this momentum.

76-90% Very Good ! You have a good command over this chapter. Revise the chapter again after a few days and enhance your performance.

60-75% Good ! You have a wide scope to learn for this chapter. Revise this chapter again.

<60% Not Satisfactory! You have a long way ahead of you to master this chapter. Revise it thoroughly.

Space for Rough Work

Space for Rough Work

Space for Rough Work

Test Booklet No. **3947157**

Test Booklet Code **CH7**

MED ACE
NEET (UG)
SELF ASSESSMENT KIT

Electromagnetic Induction

Topics Covered

Magnetic Flux and Laws of EMI

Motional EMF and Eddy Current

Inductance

Important Instructions

- This Booklet Contains – Three Topic Tests and One Test on Complete Chapter.
- Each question carries 4 marks.
- For each correct response, the candidate will get 4 marks and for every incorrect response 1 mark will be additionally deducted from the total score.
- Use **Blue/Black** point pen only for filling the OMR.
- Rough work will be done in the space provided for this purpose within the test booklet only.

Name of the Candidate (In Capitals) __________

____

Candidate's Signature __________

Invigilator's Signature __________

Facsimile signature stamp of center superintendent __________

Do not open this Booklet until you start attempting the Test

Topical Follow Thru

Test 1

Syllabus
- Magnetic Flux, Faraday's Law
- Law of Electromagnetic Induction
- Lenz's Law

For deeper insight **Scan the QR Code**

Important Instructions
- The test is of 30 minutes duration and contains 15 Multiple Choice Questions. (Four options with a single correct answer).
- Choose the correct option and fill the OMR given on the last page of this test accordingly.
- At some instances, you may find more than 1 option may be correct, in such circumstances you have to judge the most appropriate answer as per the conditions given in the question.

1. A coil of resistance 100Ω is placed in a magnetic field. If the magnetic flux, ϕ (in Wb) linked with the coil varies with time t (in s) as $\phi = 30t^2 + 5$. The current at $t = 2$ s will be

(a) 6 A (b) 3 A
(c) 1.2 A (d) 1.5 A

2. In a coil of resistance $5\,\Omega$, the induced current developed by changing magnetic flux through it, is shown in figure as a function of time. The magnitude of change in flux through the coil (in Wb) will be

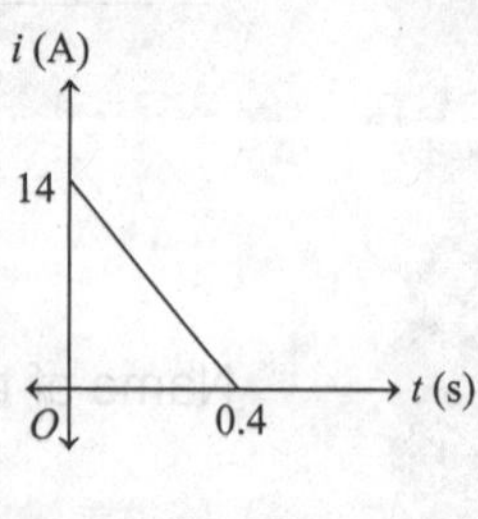

(a) 10 (b) 14
(c) 16 (d) 19

3. A circular disc of radius 0.5 m is placed in a uniform magnetic field of induction $\left(\frac{5}{\pi}\right)$ Wbm^{-2} in such a way that its axis makes an angle of 30° with B(magnetic field). The magnetic flux linked with the disc will be

(a) 0.6 Wb
(b) 2.01 Wb
(c) 1.08 Wb
(d) 4.01 Wb

4. A magnetic field of 4×10^{-4} T acts at right angle to a coil of area 10 m^2 with 100 turns. The average emf induced in the coil is 0.5V, when it is removed from the field in time t s. The value of t will be

(a) 0.5 s (b) 0.4 s
(c) 0.8 s (d) 0.17 s

5. Two co-axial identical circular current-carrying loops are shown in figure, currents in them are in the same direction. Now, match the following two columns.

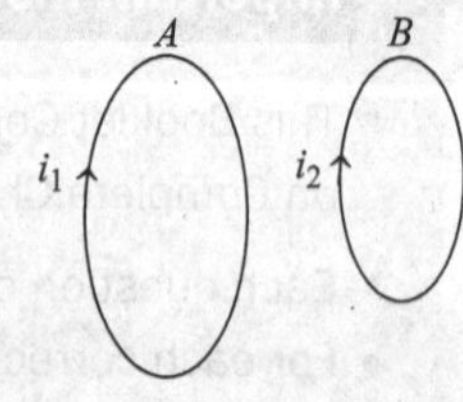

Column I		Column II	
A.	Current i_1 is increased	1.	Loop will attract each other
B.	Current i_2 is decreased	2.	Loop will repel each other
C.	Loop-1 is moved towards loop-2	3.	Loop will attract each other and i_2 will increase
D.	Loop-2 is moved away from loop-1	4.	Loop will repel each other and i_1 will increase

(a) A → 2, B → 1, C → 4, D → 3
(b) A → 1, B → 2, C → 3, D → 4
(c) A → 4, B → 3, C → 2, D → 1
(d) A → 2, B → 3, C → 4, D → 1

6. A constant current flows from P to Q as shown in the figure. The direction of current in circle will be

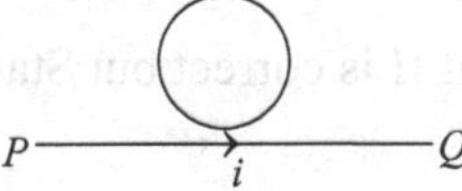

(a) straight line
(b) anti-clockwise
(c) clockwise
(d) No direction

7. The magnetic flux through a coil perpendicular to the plane is varying according to the relation $\phi = (3t^3 + 2t^2 + t - 4)$ Wb. If the induced current through the coil at $t = 2$ s is 7.5 A, then the value of the reistance of coil is
(a) 5 Ω (b) 9 Ω
(c) 6 Ω (d) 7 Ω

8. A small piece of metal wire is dragged across the gap between the pole pieces of a magnet in 1.5 s. If the magnetic flux between the pole pieces is known to be 4×10^{-4} Wb, then calculate the emf induced in the wire.
(a) 2.66×10^{-4} V
(b) 1.64×10^{-2} V
(c) 1.66×10^{-4} V
(d) 4.6×10^{-3} V

9. A coil having 1500 turns of square shape, each of side 5 cm, is placed normal to a magnetic field which is increasing at the reate of 2 Ts^{-1}. The induced emf will be
(a) 7.5 V (b) 2.5 V
(c) 0.5 V (d) 5.5 V

10. A coil of 500 turns, effective area 0.15 m^2 is kept perpendicular to a magnetic field of 1.5×10^{-3} T. When the plane of the coil is rotated by 30° around any of its co-planar axis in time 0.5 s, then the emf induced in the coil will be
(a) 0.03 V
(b) 0.04 V
(c) 0.01 V
(d) 1.2 V

11. The magnetic flux passing through a coil of 40 turns varies as $\phi = (6t^3 - 18t^2)$ mT. If the total resistance of the coil is 5Ω, then maximum current induced in the coil is
(a) 0.0036 A (b) 0.0288 A
(c) 0.144 A (d) 0.288 A

12. A coil of area A, resistance R and number of turns N is held perpendicular to a magnetic field B. Now, it is turned through 120° in time Δt. The average induced emf is
(a) $\frac{3NBA}{2\Delta t}$
(b) $\frac{2NBA}{\Delta t}$
(c) $\frac{NBA}{\Delta t}$
(d) $\frac{NBA}{2\Delta t}$

13. **Assertion** (A) Whenever the magnetic flux linked with a closed coil changes, there will be an induced emf as well as an induced current.
Reason (R) According to Faraday, the induced emf is inversely proportional to the rate of change of magnetic flux linked with a coil.
In the light of above statements, choose the most appropriate answer from the options given below.
(a) Both A and R are true and R is the correct explanation of A.
(b) Both A and R are true but R is not the correct explanation of A.
(c) A is true but R is false.
(d) Both A and R are false.

14.

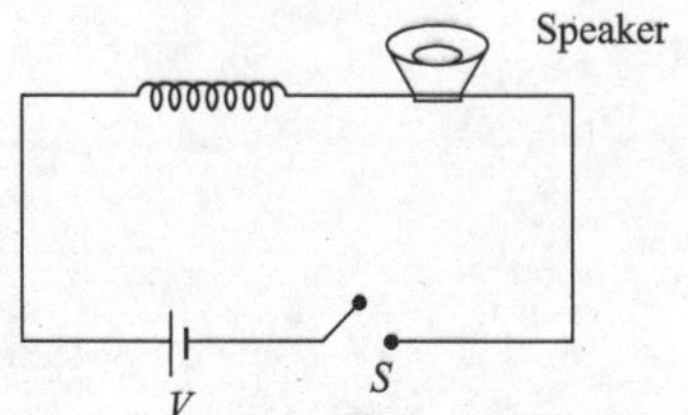

In the given circuit, the sound of speaker is maximum, if
(a) switch is closed or opened
(b) switch is closed
(c) switch is opened
(d) It will remains same always

15. Statement I For a closely wound coil of N-turns, the magnetic flux linked with all turns is different.

Statement II If geometry of the coil vary with time, then $\frac{dB}{dt} \propto \frac{dI}{dt}$

In the light of above statements, choose the most appropriate answer from the options given below.

(a) Both Statement I and Statement II are correct.

(b) Both Statement I and Statement II are incorrect.

(c) Statement I is correct but Statement II is incorrect.

(d) Statement II is correct but Statement I is incorrect.

Response Index

01	a	b	c	d	11	a	b	c	d
02	a	b	c	d	12	a	b	c	d
03	a	b	c	d	13	a	b	c	d
04	a	b	c	d	14	a	b	c	d
05	a	b	c	d	15	a	b	c	d
06	a	b	c	d					
07	a	b	c	d					
08	a	b	c	d					
09	a	b	c	d					
10	a	b	c	d					

Performance Scanner

> 90% Excellent !	You have mastered these topics. The concepts of these topics are at your fingertips. Move on to the next test and maintain this momentum.
76-90% Very Good !	You have a good command over these topics. Revise them again after a few days and enhance your performance.
60-75% Good !	You have a wide scope to learn more in these topics. Revise them again.
<60% Not Satisfactory!	You have a long way ahead of you to master in these topics. Revise them thoroughly.

Test 2

Syllabus • Motional EMF and Eddy Current

For deeper insight **Scan the QR Code**

Important Instructions

- The test is of 45 minutes duration and contains 25 Multiple Choice Questions. (Four options with a single correct answer).
- Choose the correct option and fill the OMR given on the last page of this test accordingly.
- At some instances, you may find more than 1 option may be correct, in such circumstances you have to judge the most appropriate answer as per the conditions given in the question.

1. An aeroplane having a wing space of 15 m flies due north with the speed of 20 ms^{-1}. The induced emf between the tips of the wings will be (take, $B = 5\times10^{-4}$T)

(a) 12.14 V (b) 0.01 V
(c) 0.10 V (d) 0.15 V

2. When a wire loop is rotated in a magnetic field such that it continuously cuts the magnetic field lines, then the direction of induced emf changes once in every

(a) 2 revolutions (b) $\frac{1}{2}$ revolution
(c) $\frac{1}{4}$ revolution (d) 1 revolution

3. **Statement I** Eddy currents are undesirable.

Statement II When coil in galvanometer with metallic core oscillates, then electromagnetic damping occurs.

In the light of above statements, choose the most appropriate answer from the options given below.

(a) Both Statement I and Statement II are incorrect.
(b) Statement I is correct but Statement II is incorrect.
(c) Statement I is incorrect but Statement II is correct.
(d) Both Statement I and Statement II are correct.

4. A copper plate is swinging like a simple pendulum between the pole pieces of a strong magnet. The eddy current produced in the copper plate is

(a) always clockwise as seen from the north pole
(b) always clockwise as seen from the south pole
(c) clockwise and anti-clockwise, changes periodically
(d) constant

5. A cycle wheel have radius 1 m is rotating with 180 rev/min in a magnetic field. The magnetic field is perpendicular to the plane of the wheel and its magnitude is 20 G. The induced emf between the axle and the rim of the wheel is (Take, 1 G $=10^{-4}$ T)

(a) $4\pi\times10^{-3}$ V (b) $6\pi\times10^{-3}$ V
(c) 60π V (d) $2\pi\times10^{-3}$ V

6. A cube is formed by connecting twelve wires of equal lengths (each 12 cm). If the cube is moving with a velocity of 10 m/s in the direction of magnetic field of 0.07 Wbm^{-2}, then the emf induced in each arm of the cube is

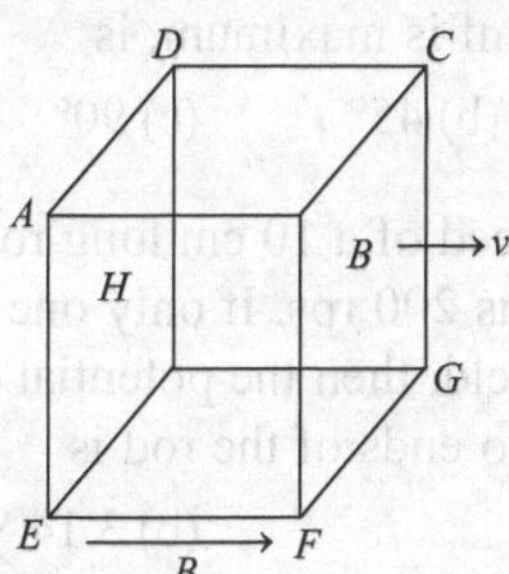

(a) 4 V (b) 0 V
(c) 2 V (d) 3 V

7. A conducting rod of length l is rotating with constant angular speed ω about its perpendicular bisector. A uniform magnetic field B exists parallel to the axis of rotation. The emf induced between the two ends of the rod is

(a) $B\left(\frac{\omega}{2}\right)l^2$ (b) $\frac{1}{2}\left(\frac{B}{2}\right)\omega l^2$

(c) zero (d) $\frac{1}{2}B\omega\left(\frac{l}{2}\right)^2$

8. A wire MN of length $\frac{l}{2}$ and mass $\frac{m}{3}$ is sliding without friction on conducting rails ax and by as shown in figure. The vertical rails are connected to each other with a resistance R between a and b. A uniform magnetic field $\frac{B}{5}$ is applied perpendicular to the plane $abNM$ such that MN moves with a constant velocity of

(a) $\frac{100mgR}{B^2l^2}$ (b) $10\frac{\sqrt{mgR}}{Bl}$

(c) $\frac{mgR}{Bl}$ (d) $\frac{mgR^2}{B^2l^2}$

9. A simple pendulum with bob of mass m and conducting wire of length L swings under gravity through an angle θ. The earth's magnetic field component in the direction perpendicular to swing is B. The angle θ when the emf is maximum, is

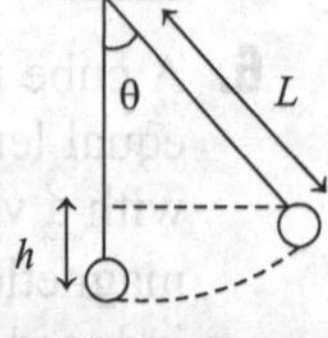

(a) 30° (b) 45° (c) 90° (d) 180°

10. Angular speed of a 10 cm long rod in a magnetic field 0.5 T is 200 rps. If only one end is in the magnetic field, then the potential difference between two ends of the rod is

(a) 6.28 V (b) 3.14 V
(c) 5.23 V (d) 7.95 V

11. The figure shows four wire loops, with edge lengths of either L or $2L$. All four loops will move through a region of uniform magnetic field **B** (directed out of the page) at the same constant velocity. Rank the four loops according to the maximum magnitude of the emf induced as they move through the field, greatest first

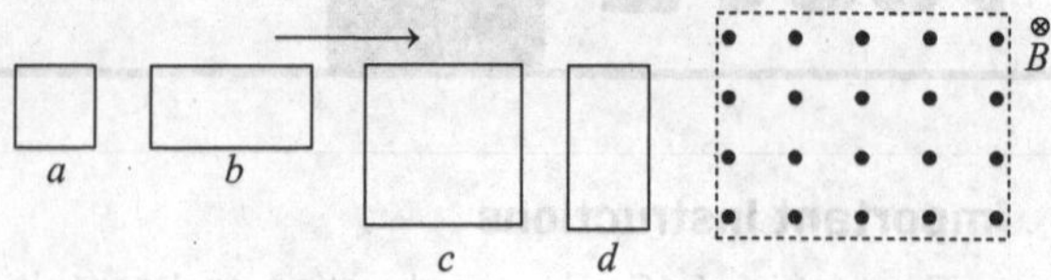

(a) $(e_c = e_d) < (e_a = e_b)$
(b) $(e_c = e_d) > (e_a = e_b)$
(c) $e_c > e_d > e_b > e_a$
(d) $e_c < e_d < e_b < e_a$

12. The rails of a railway track insulated from each other and the ground are connected to a millivoltmeter. Find the reading of voltmeter, when a train travels with a speed of 180 km/h along the track. Given that, the vertical component of the earth's magnetic field is 0.2×10^{-4} Wb/m^2 and the rails are separated by 1 m.

(a) 10^{-4} V (b) 10^{-2} V
(c) 10^{-3} V (d) 1 V

13. **Statement I** When a metal wheel with N spokes is rotated in region of a uniform and perpendicular magnetic field B with angular speed ω, then emf produced is $\frac{1}{2}NB\omega R^2$, where R is radius of wheel.

Statement II Induced emf in a rotating rod of length l in magnetic field B is $\frac{1}{2}B\omega l^2$.

In the light of above statements, choose the most appropriate answer from the options given below.

(a) Both Statement I and Statement II are correct.
(b) Statement I is correct but Statement II is incorrect.
(c) Statement I is incorrect but Statement II is correct.
(d) Both Statement I and Statement II are incorrect.

14. One conducting U-tube can slide inside another as shown in figure, maintaining electrical contacts between the tubes. The magnetic field B is perpendicular to the plane of the figure. If each tube moves towards the other at a constant speed v, then the emf induced in the circuit in terms of B, l and v, where l is the width of each tube, will be

(a) Blv (b) $-Blv$ (c) zero (d) $2Blv$

15. The magnetic field in a region is given by $B = B_0\left(\frac{x}{a}\right)\hat{\mathbf{k}}$. A square loop of side d is placed with its edges along the X and Y-axes. The loop is moved with a constant velocity $\mathbf{v} = v_0\hat{\mathbf{i}}$, then emf induced in the loop is

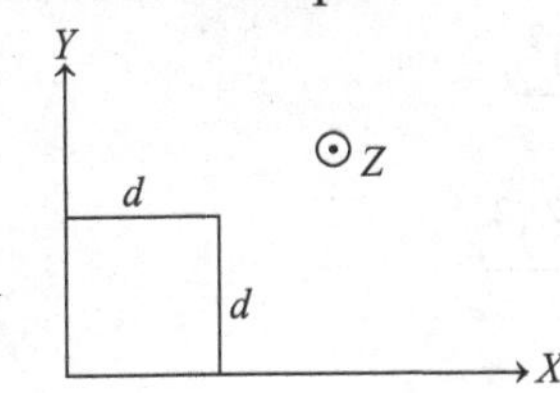

(a) $\frac{B_0 v_0^2 d}{2a}$ (b) $\frac{B_0 v_0 d}{2a}$

(c) $\frac{B_0 v_0 d^2}{a}$ (d) $\frac{B_0 v_0 d^2}{2a}$

16. The loop $ABCD$ is moving with velocity v towards right. The magnetic field is 4 T. The loop is connected to a resistance of 8 Ω. If steady current of 2 A flows in the loop, then value of v, if loop has resistance of 4Ω, is

(Given, $AB = 30$ cm, $AD = 30$ cm, $\sin 37° = \frac{3}{5}$)

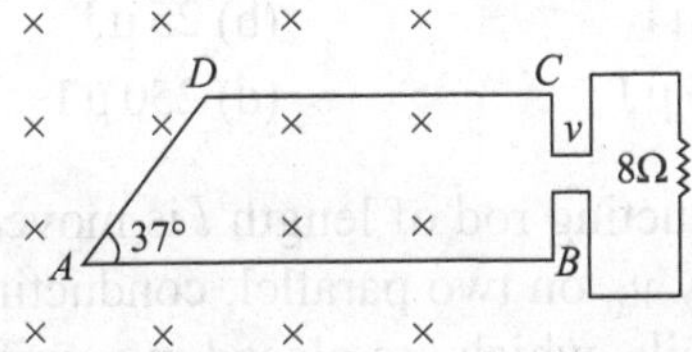

(a) $\frac{50}{3}$ ms^{-1}

(b) 20 ms^{-1}

(c) 10 ms^{-1}

(d) $\frac{100}{3}$ ms^{-1}

17. A rectangular loop has a sliding connector PQ of length l and resistance R Ω and it is moving with a speed v as shown in figure. The setup is placed in a uniform magnetic field going into the plane of the paper. The three currents I_1, I_2 and I are

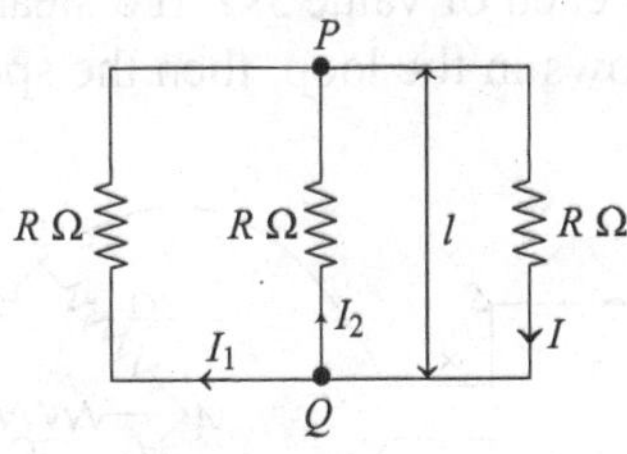

(a) $I_1 = I_2 = \frac{Blv}{6R}, I = \frac{Blv}{3R}$

(b) $I_1 = -I_2 = \frac{Blv}{R}, I = \frac{2Blv}{R}$

(c) $I_1 = I_2 = \frac{Blv}{3R}, I = \frac{2Blv}{3R}$

(d) $I_1 = I_2 = I = \frac{Blv}{R}$

18. A thin wire of length of 2 m is perpendicular to the XY-plane. It is moved with velocity $\mathbf{v} = (2\hat{\mathbf{i}} + 3\hat{\mathbf{j}} + \hat{\mathbf{k}})$ ms^{-1} through a region of magnetic induction $\mathbf{B} = (\hat{\mathbf{i}} + 2\hat{\mathbf{j}})$ Wb/m^2, then potential difference induced between the ends of the wire will be

(a) 2 V (b) 4 V

(c) 0 V (d) None of these

19. A rectangular loop with a sliding connector of length $l = 1.0$ m is situated in a uniform magnetic field $B = 2$ T perpendicular to the plane of loop. Resistances of connector is $R = 2\Omega$. Two resistances of 6 Ω and 3 Ω are connected as shown in figure. The external force required to keep the connector moving with a constant velocity $v = 2$ ms^{-1} is

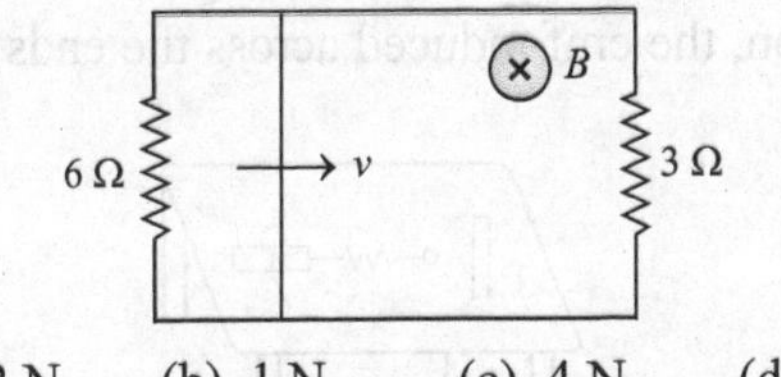

(a) 2 N (b) 1 N (c) 4 N (d) 6 N

20. A square metal of loop $PQRS$ of side 10 cm and resistance 1Ω is moved with a constant velocity partly inside a magnetic field of 2 Wbm^{-2}, directed into the paper, as shown in the figure. This loop is connected to a network $ABCD$ of five resistors each of value 3Ω. If a steady current of 1 mA flows in the loop, then the speed of the loop is

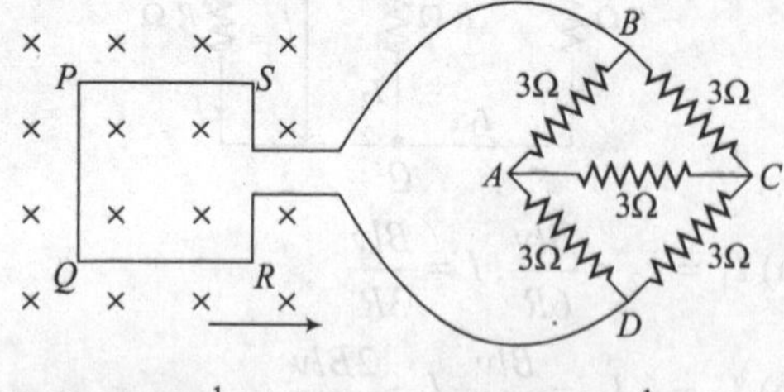

(a) $0.5\ \text{cms}^{-1}$ (b) $1\ \text{cms}^{-1}$

(c) $2\ \text{cms}^{-1}$ (d) $4\ \text{cms}^{-1}$

21. Consider the situation shown in the figure. Where wire PQ with a negligible resistance is sliding on the three rails with a constant speed 5 cm/s. The circuit includes a 10Ω resistor in the circuit. Determine the current flowing through the 10Ω resistor.

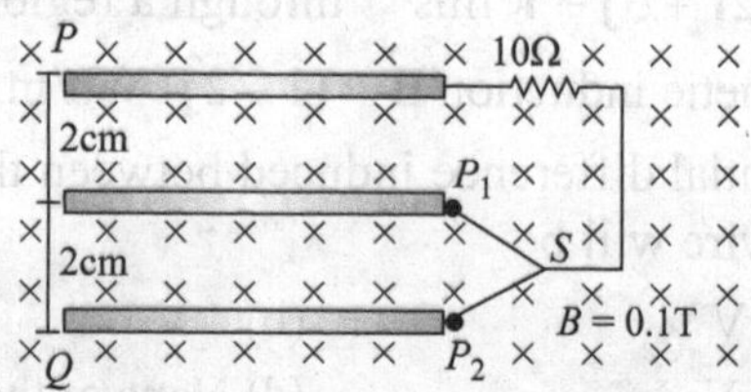

(a) In position P_1, $I = 0.1$ mA

(b) In position P_2, $I = 0.1$ mA

(c) In position P_1, $I = 0.2$ mA

(d) In position P_2, $I = 0.3$ mA

22. A metallic rod of length l is tied to a string of length $2l$ and made to rotate with angular speed ω on a horizontal table with one end of the string fixed. If there is a vertical magnetic field B in the region, the emf induced across the ends of the rod is

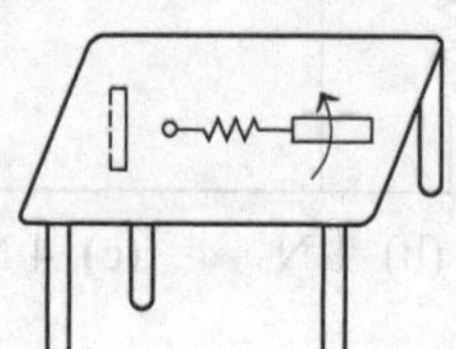

(a) $\frac{2B\omega l^2}{2}$ (b) $\frac{3B\omega l^2}{2}$

(c) $\frac{4B\omega l^2}{2}$ (d) $\frac{5B\omega l^2}{2}$

23. In a uniform magnetic field of induction B, a wire in the form of a semi-circle of radius r rotates about the diameter of the circle with angular frequency ω. If the total resistance of the circuit is R, then the mean power generated per period of rotation is

(a) $\frac{B\pi r^2\omega}{2R}$

(b) $\frac{(B\pi r^2\omega)^2}{8R}$

(c) $\frac{(B\pi r\omega)^2}{2R}$

(d) $\frac{(B\pi r\omega^2)^2}{8R}$

24. A square loop has 50 turns, an area of $2.5\times10^{-3}\ \text{m}^2$ and a resistance of $50\ \Omega$. The perpendicular magnetic field has a magnitude of 0.20 T. If the loop is slowly and uniformly pulled out of the field in 1.0 s, the work done is

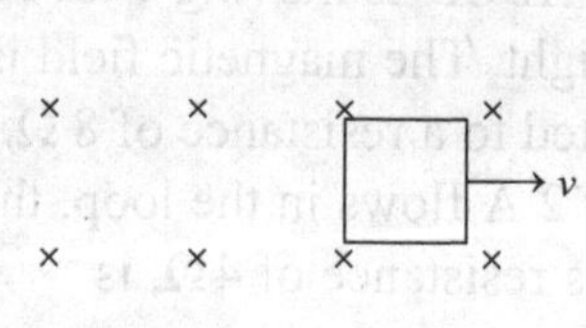

(a) $2.5\ \mu$J (b) $25\ \mu$J

(c) $0.25\ \mu$J (d) $250\ \mu$J

25. A conducting rod of length l is moved at constant velocity v_0 on two parallel, conducting, smooth, fixed rails, which are placed in a uniform constant magnetic field B perpendicular to the plane of rails as shown in the figure. A resistance R is connected between the two ends of the rail. Consider the following statements.

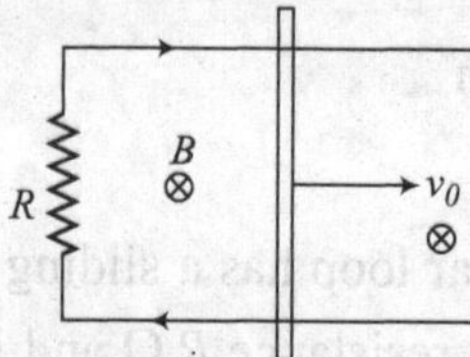

I. The thermal power dissipated in the resistor is equal to the rate of work done by an external person pulling the rod.

II. If applied external force is doubled, then a part of the external power increases the velocity of the rod.

III. Lenz's law is not satisfied, if the rod is accelerated by external force.

IV. If resistance R is doubled, then power required to maintain the constant velocity v_0 becomes half.

Choose the correct option.

(a) I, II
(b) I, II, IV
(c) I
(d) II, III

Response Index

01	a	b	c	d	10	a	b	c	d	19	a	b	c	d
02	a	b	c	d	11	a	b	c	d	20	a	b	c	d
03	a	b	c	d	12	a	b	c	d	21	a	b	c	d
04	a	b	c	d	13	a	b	c	d	22	a	b	c	d
05	a	b	c	d	14	a	b	c	d	23	a	b	c	d
06	a	b	c	d	15	a	b	c	d	24	a	b	c	d
07	a	b	c	d	16	a	b	c	d	25	a	b	c	d
08	a	b	c	d	17	a	b	c	d					
09	a	b	c	d	18	a	b	c	d					

Performance Scanner

> 90% Excellent !	You have mastered these topics. The concepts of these topics are on your fingertips. Move on to the next test and maintain this momentum.
76-90% Very Good !	You have a good command over these topics. Revise these topics again after a few days and enhance your performance.
60-75% Good !	You have a wide scope to learn for these topics. Revise them again.
<60% Not Satisfactory!	You have a long way ahead of you to master these topics. Revise them thoroughly.

Test 3 Syllabus Inductance

For deeper insight **Scan the QR Code**

Important Instructions

- The test is of 30 minutes duration and contains 15 Multiple Choice Questions. (Four options with a single correct answer).
- Choose the correct option and fill the OMR given on the last page of this test accordingly.
- At some instances, you may find more than 1 option may be correct, in such circumstances you have to judge the most appropriate answer as per the conditions given in the question.

1. A long solenoid has 1100 turns. When a current of 2 A flows through it, the magnetic flux linked with each turn of the solenoid is 1.2×10^{-2} Wb. The self-inductance of the solenoid will be

(a) 4.6 H (b) 6.6 H
(c) 2.6 H (d) 1.6 H

2. The inductance of an inductor is 10 H, when the current in the inductor is 50 mA. The magnetic potential energy stored in this inductor will be

(a) 25×10^{-2} J
(b) 5×10^{-3} J
(c) 125×10^{-2} J
(d) 12.5×10^{-3} J

3. A wire of fixed length is wound in such a way that it forms a solenoid of length l and radius r. Its self-inductance is found to be L. Now, if same wire is wound in such a way that it forms a solenoid of length $\frac{l}{2}$ and radius $\frac{r}{2}$, then the self-inductance will be

(a) $4L$ (b) $8L$
(c) L (d) $2L$

4. The current in a self-inductance $L = 20$ mH is to be increased uniformly from 1A to 5A in 2 ms. The induced emf in the inductor during the process will be

(a) 10 V (b) 20 V
(c) 30 V (d) 40 V

5. Two solenoids of equal number of turns have their length and the radii in the same ratio 2 : 3. The ratio of their self-inductances will be

(a) 3 : 4 (b) 2 : 9
(c) 2 : 3 (d) 1 : 2

6. A solenoid whose length is 20.5 cm and area of cross-section 10^{-6} m^2. The total number of turns is 10^4, then the self-inductance of solenoid will be

(a) 2.0 mH (b) 0.10 mH
(c) 4.0 mH (d) 0.61 mH

7. Find the value of self-inductance of an inductor, which is connected to 220 V, 50 Hz supply, so that a maximum current of 0.4 A flows through it.

(a) 11 H (b) 15 H
(c) 12 H (d) 16 H

8. When the current changes from +3 A to –3 A in 0.03 s, an emf of 18 V is induced in a coil. The coefficient of self-induction of the coil will be

(a) 0.09 H (b) 0.03 H
(c) 0.01 H (d) 0.02 H

9. Two metallic coils, X and Y are placed near each other. When the current in coil X changes steadily by 14 A, the magnetic flux linked with coil Y .changes by 0.2 Wb. The mutual inductance of the system of these coils is

(a) 0.014 H (b) 2.01 H
(c) 0.11 H (d) 1.01 H

10. A square coil surrounds a circular coil in same plane as shown. Ratio of areas of coils is 4:1. If mutual inductance of circular coil is M_1, then mutual inductance of square coil is

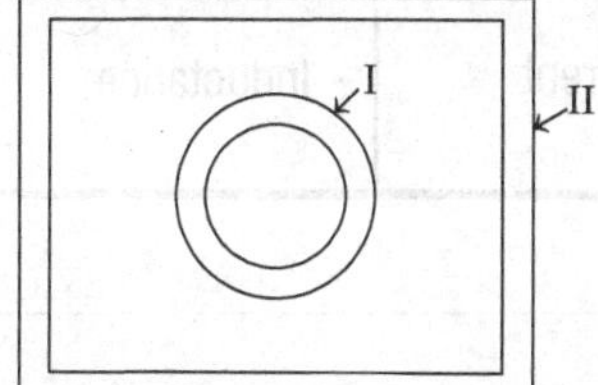

(a) $2M_1$ (b) $4M_1$
(c) $\frac{M_1}{4}$ (d) M_1

11. A coil is wound on a core of rectangular cross-section. If all the linear dimensions of core are increased by a factor of 3 and number of turns per unit length of coil remains same, the self-inductance increases by a factor of
(a) 3 (b) 9
(c) 27 (d) 8

12. A current of 8 A in the primary coil of a circuit is reduced to zero. If the coefficient of mutual inductance is 2 H and emf induced in secondary coil is 20 kV, then time taken for the change of current is
(a) 8 s (b) 0.8 s
(c) 8×10^{-3} s (d) 0.8×10^{-3} s

13. Mutual inductance of two coils is 0.001 H. If current in the first coil is $i = 7\cos(100\pi t)$, then the value of maximum emf in the second coil is
(a) 700 π (b) 100 π
(c) 49 π (d) 0.7 π

14. The current in an inductor is given by $i = (2+3t)$ A, where t is in second. The self induced emf in it is 9 mV, the energy stored in the inductor at $t = 1$ second is
(a) 10 mJ (b) 75 mJ
(c) 37.5 mJ (d) 100 mJ

15. A coil having 500 turns carries a current of 2 A. If magnetic flux per turn is 10^{-4} Tm^{-2}, then the value of inductance is
(a) 25 H (b) 1000 mH
(c) 500 mH (d) 25 mH

Response Index

01	(a)	(b)	(c)	(d)	11	(a)	(b)	(c)	(d)
02	(a)	(b)	(c)	(d)	12	(a)	(b)	(c)	(d)
03	(a)	(b)	(c)	(d)	13	(a)	(b)	(c)	(d)
04	(a)	(b)	(c)	(d)	14	(a)	(b)	(c)	(d)
05	(a)	(b)	(c)	(d)	15	(a)	(b)	(c)	(d)
06	(a)	(b)	(c)	(d)					
07	(a)	(b)	(c)	(d)					
08	(a)	(b)	(c)	(d)					
09	(a)	(b)	(c)	(d)					
10	(a)	(b)	(c)	(d)					

Performance Scanner

> 90% Excellent !	You have mastered these topics. The concepts of these topics are at your fingertips. Move on to the next test and maintain this momentum.
76-90% Very Good !	You have a good command over these topics. Revise them again after a few days and enhance your performance.
60-75% Good !	You have a wide scope to learn for these topics. Revise them again.
<60% Not Satisfactory!	You have a long way ahead of you to master in these topics. Revise them thoroughly.

Chapter Break Thru

Syllabus	• Magnetic Flux and Laws of EMI	• Motional EMF and Eddy Current	• Inductance

Important Instructions

- The test is of 45 minutes duration and contains 30 Multiple Choice Questions (Four options with a single correct answer).
- Choose the correct option and fill the OMR given on the last page of this test accordingly.
- At some instances, you may find more than 1 option may be correct, in such circumstances you have to judge the most appropriate answer as per conditions given in the question.

1. A square loop is placed to the right of large current carrying straight wire as shown in the figure. The current flowing through wire varies with time as $I = (t^2 - 1)$ A. The direction of induced current in the square loop is

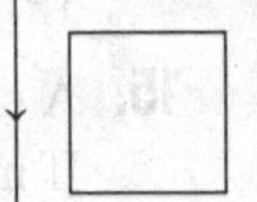

(a) clockwise

(b) anti-clockwise

(c) first clockwise, then anti-clockwise

(d) first anti-clockwise, then clockwise

2. A conducting rod is rotating with a constant angular velocity ω about point O (its centre) in a magnetic field B which is directed into the plane of paper as shown in figure. Due to the rotation, the points of rod, i.e. P, O, Q respectively, are

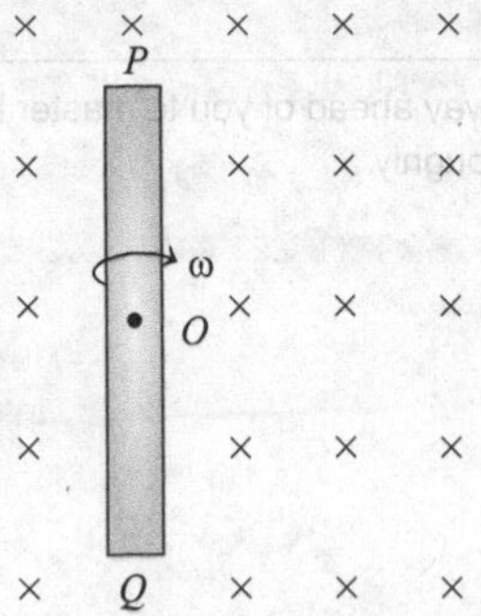

(a) positively, negatively, positively charged

(b) negatively, positively, negatively charged

(c) positively, neutral, negatively charged

(d) negatively, neutral, positively charged

3. The current in a self-inductance, $L = 40$ mH is to be increased uniformly from 1 A to 11 A in 4 ms. The induced emf in the inductor during the process is

(a) 100 V (b) 0.4 V

(c) 40 V (d) 440 V

4. Two coils of self-inductances 2 mH and 8 mH are placed so close together that the effective flux in one coil is completely linked with the other. The mutual inductance between these coils is

(a) 10 mH

(b) 6 mH

(c) 4 mH

(d) 16 mH

5. A long solenoid of length L, cross-section A having N_1 turns wound about its centre by a small coil of N_2 turns as shown in figure. Then, the mutual inductance of two circuits is

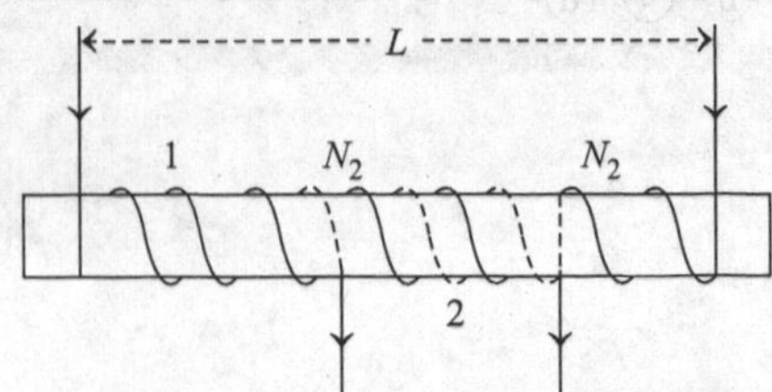

(a) $\frac{\mu_0 A(N_1/N_2)}{L}$ (b) $\frac{\mu_0 N_1 N_2 A}{L}$

(c) $\mu_A N_1 N_2 L$ (d) $\frac{\mu_0 A N_1^2 N_2}{L}$

6. **Assertion** (A) When number of turns in a coil is doubled, coefficient of self-inductance of the coil becomes four times.

Reason (R) Coefficient of self-inductance is proportional to the square of number of turns.

In the light of above statements, choose the most appropriate answer from the options given below.

(a) Both A and R are true and R is the correct explanation of A.

(b) Both A and R are true but R is not the correct explanation of A.

(c) A is true but R is false.

(d) A is false but R is true.

7. At a place, the value of horizontal component of the earth's magnetic field H is 3×10^{-5} Wb/m^2. A metallic rod AB of length 2 m placed in east-west direction, having the end A towards east, falls vertically downward with a constant velocity of 100 m/s. Which end of the rod becomes positively charged and what is the value of induced potential difference between the two ends?

(a) End A, 3×10^{-3} mV

(b) End A, 6 mV

(c) End B, 3×10^{-3} mV

(d) End B, 3 mV

8. The variation of induced emf (E) with time (t) in a coil, if a short bar magnet is moved along its axis with a constant velocity is best represented as

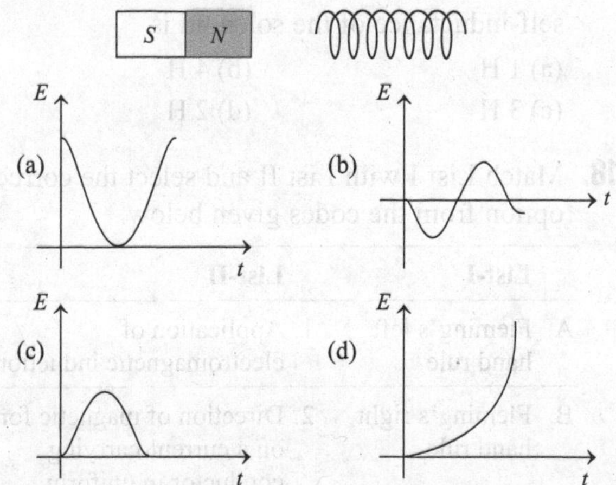

9. The angle made by the plane of eddy currents with the plane of magnetic lines of force is equal to

(a) 60° (b) 30° (c) 90° (d) 180°

10. $ABCD$ is a copper wire frame placed in a magnetic field into plane of paper.

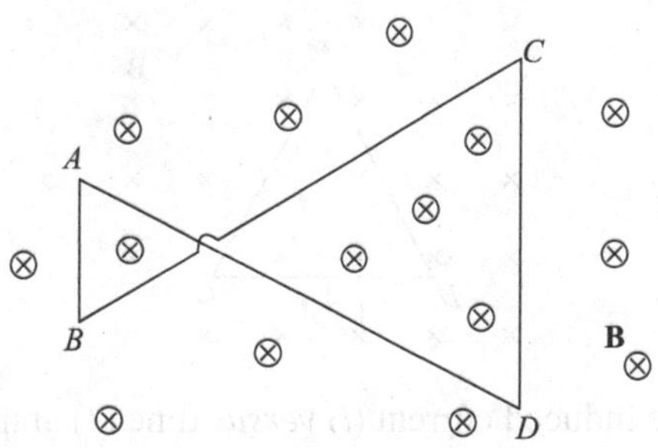

Magnetic field is increasing at constant rate. Directions of current induced in wire AB and CD are

(a) A to B, C to D (b) B to A, C to D

(c) A to D, D to C (d) B to A, D to C

11. A conducting rod PQ of length $l = 1.0$ m is moving with a uniform speed $v = 4.0$ m/s in a uniform magnetic field $B = 4.0$ T directed into the paper. A capacitor of capacity $C = 10\,\mu$F is connected as shown in figure, then

(a) $q_A = +160\,\mu$C and $q_B = -160\,\mu$C

(b) $q_A = -80\,\mu$C and $q_B = +80\,\mu$C

(c) $q_A = 0 = q_B$

(d) charge stored in the capacitor increases exponentially with time

12. A copper rod of mass m slides under gravity on two smooth parallel rails l distance apart set at an angle 30° to the horizontal. At the bottom, the rails are joined by a resistance R.

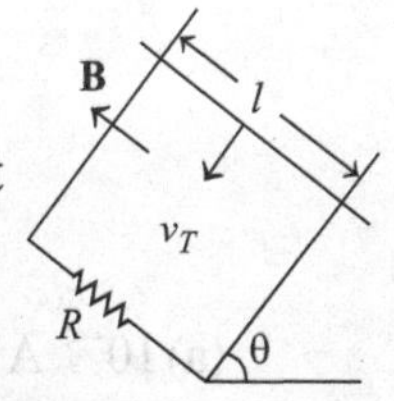

There is a uniform magnetic field perpendicular to the plane of the rails. The terminal velocity of the rod is

(a) $\dfrac{mgR\cos\theta}{B^2l^2}$ (b) $\dfrac{mgR}{2B^2l^2}$

(c) $\dfrac{mgR\tan\theta}{B^2l^2}$ (d) $\dfrac{mgR\cot\theta}{B^2l^2}$

13. An equilateral triangular loop MNO having some resistance is pulled with a constant velocity v out of a uniform magnetic field directed into the paper.

At time $t = 0$, side NO of the loop is at edge of the magnetic field.

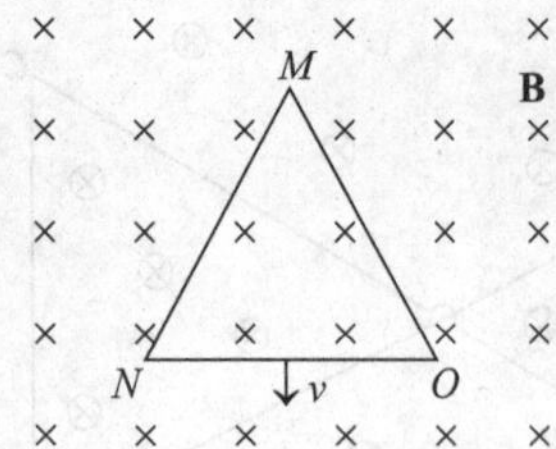

The induced current (i) *versus* time (t) graph will be represented as

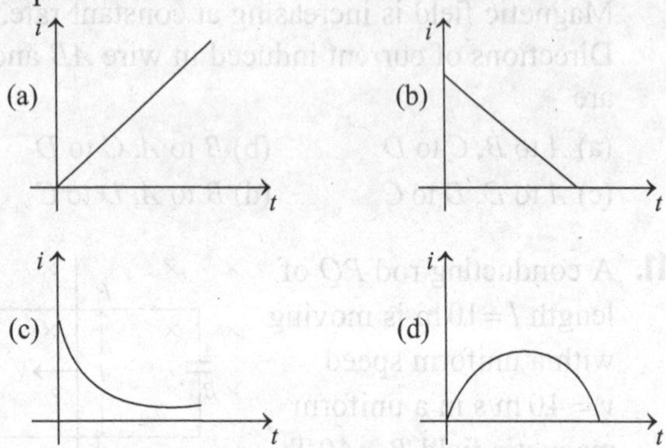

14. A thick coil is made of thin wires of resistance $\rho = 100 \text{ m}\Omega/\text{m}$ are located in a uniform magnetic field perpendicular into the plane of the figures and which decreases at the rate $dB / dt = 0.2 \text{ m T/s}$, then currents in the inner and outer boundary are (The inner radius $a = 10$ cm and outer radius $b = 20$ cm)

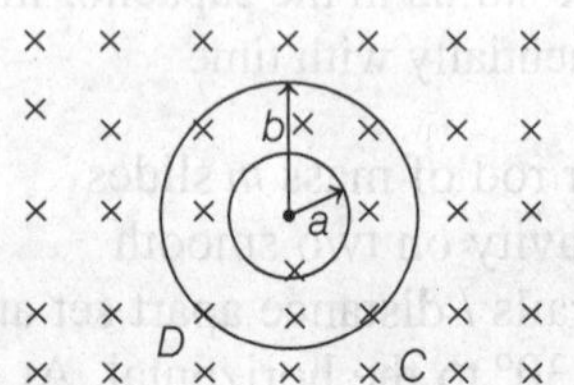

(a) 10^{-4} A (clockwise), 2×10^{-4} A (clockwise)

(b) 10^{-4} A (anti-clockwise), 2×10^{-4} A (clockwise)

(c) 2×10^{-4} A (clockwise), 10^{-4} A (anti-clockwise)

(d) 2×10^{-4} A (anti-clockwise), 10^{-4} A (anti-clockwise)

15. Statement I Self-induction is the phenomenon of production of induced emf in a coil when a changing current passes through it.

Statement II Mutual induction is the phenomenon of production of induced emf in one coil due to a change of current in the neighbouring coil.

In the light of above statements, choose the most appropriate answer from the options given below.

(a) Both Statement I and Statement II are correct.

(b) Both Statement I and Statement II are incorrect.

(c) Statement I is correct and Statement II is incorrect.

(d) Statement I is incorrect and Statement II is correct.

16. A conducting square frame of side a and a long straight wire carrying current I are located in the same plane as shown in the figure. The frame moves to the right with a constant velocity v. The current induced in the frame will be proportional to

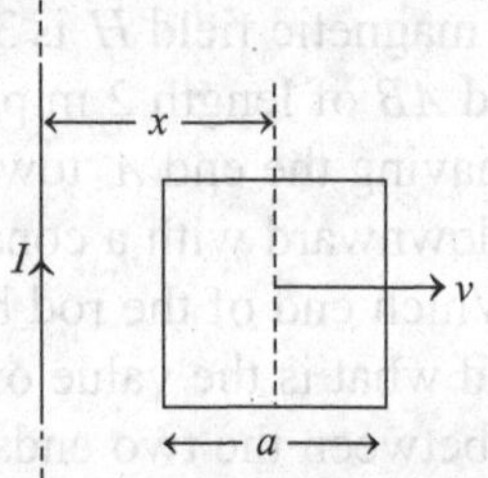

(a) $\dfrac{1}{x^2}$ (b) $\dfrac{1}{(2x - a)^2}$

(c) $\dfrac{1}{(2x + a)^2}$ (d) $\dfrac{1}{(2x - a)(2x + a)}$

17. A long solenoid has 500 turns. When a current of 2 A flows through it, the magnetic flux linked with each turn of the solenoid is 4×10^{-3} Wb. The self-inductance of the solenoid is

(a) 1 H (b) 4 H

(c) 3 H (d) 2 H

18. Match List I with List II and select the correct option from the codes given below.

List-I	List-II
A. Fleming's left hand rule	1. Application of electromagnetic induction.
B. Fleming's right hand rule	2. Direction of magnetic force on a current-carrying conductor in uniform magnetic field
C. Solenoid	3. Similar to bar magnet
D. Generator	4. Direction of induced current

Codes

	A	B	C	D
(a)	3	2	1	4
(b)	2	4	1	3
(c)	4	3	2	1
(d)	2	4	3	1

19. Due to electromagnetic induction an induced current is developed in a coil, which varies with time as shown in figure. If the magnitude of change in flux through the coil is 4 Wb, then the resistance of coil is

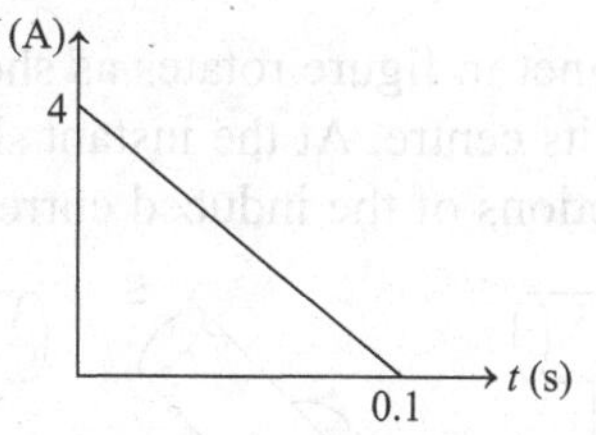

(a) 2 Ω (b) 20 Ω (c) 6 Ω (d) 40 Ω

20. A square loop of side 5 cm enters in a magnetic field with 1 cms^{-1}. The front edge enters the magnetic field at $t = 0$, then which graph best depicts emf?

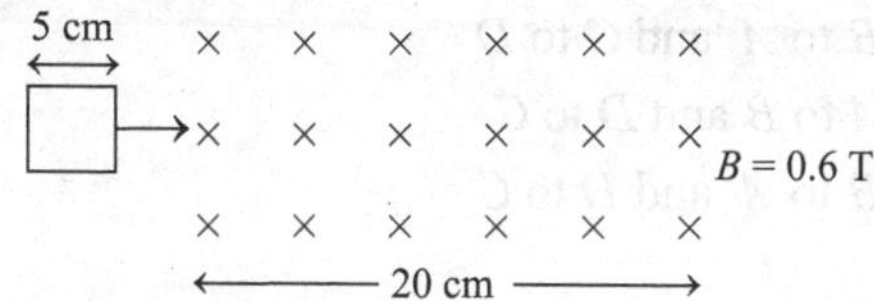

(a)

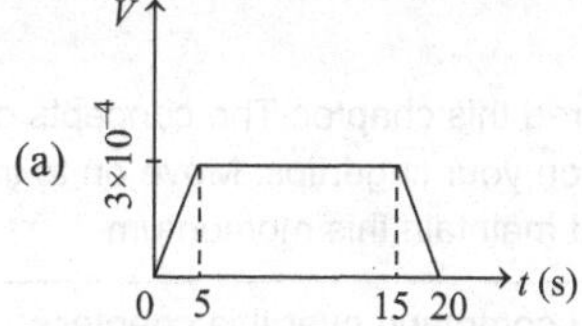

(b)

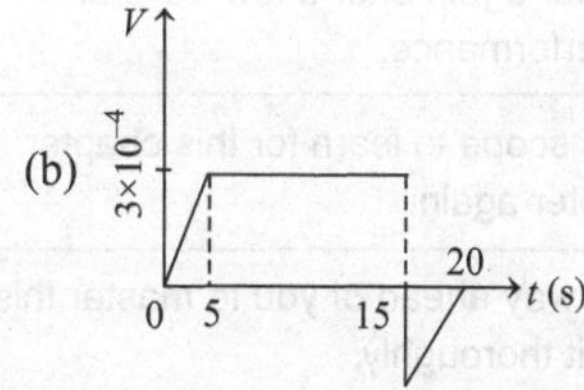

(c)

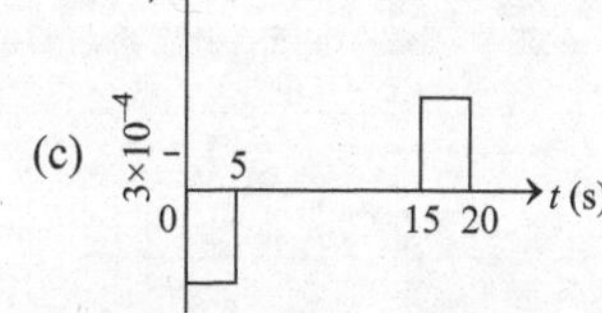

(d)

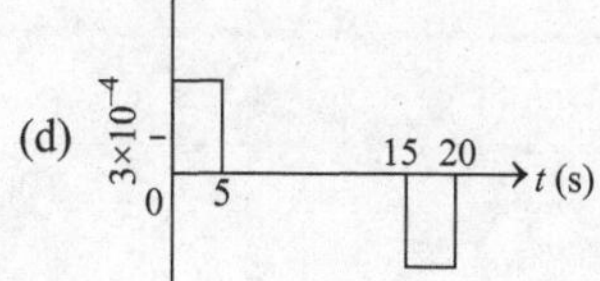

21. The phase difference between the flux linkage and the induced emf in a rotating coil in uniform magnetic field is

(a) π (b) π/2
(c) π/4 (d) π/6

22. A metal conductor of length 2 m rotates vertically about one of its ends at angular velocity 10 rad/s. If the horizontal component of earth's magnetic field is 0.2×10^{-4}T, then the emf developed between the two ends of the conductor is

(a) 5 mV (b) 5×10 V
(c) 200 mV (d) 400 μV

23. A square of side a metre lies in the YZ-plane in a region where the magnetic field is given as $\mathbf{B} = B_0(3\hat{\mathbf{i}} + 6\hat{\mathbf{j}} - 9\hat{\mathbf{k}})$ T, where B_0 is a constant. The magnitude of flux passing through the square (in Wb) is

(a) $2B_0a^2$ (b) $5B_0a^2$
(c) $3B_0a^2$ (d) $4B_0a^2$

24. The flux linked with a circuit is given by $\phi_B = t^3 + 4t - 20$. The graph between time (X-axis) and induced emf (Y-axis) will be a

(a) straight line through the origin
(b) straight line with positive intercept
(c) straight line with negative intercept
(d) parabola, not through the origin

25. If a coil of 80 turns and area 4.0 cm^2 is suddenly removed from a magnetic field, it is observed that a charge of 2.0×10^{-4} C flows into the coil. If the resistance of the coil is 80 Ω, then magnetic flux density (in Wbm^{-2}) is

(a) 0.5 (b) 1.0
(c) 1.5 (d) 2.0

26. A rectangular loop of sides 10 cm and 5 cm with a cut is stationary between the pole pieces of an electromagnet.
The magnetic field of the magnet is normal to the loop. The current feeding the electromagnet is reduced, so that the field is decreased from its initial value of 5 T at the rate of 0.02 Ts^{-1}.

If the cut is joined and the loop has a resistance of 2.0 Ω, the power dissipated by the loop as heat is

(a) 5 nW (b) 4 nW
(c) 3 nW (d) 2 nW

27. The inductance of coil is $L = 20$ H and resistance $R = 5\Omega$. If applied voltage of battery is 20 V and circuit switches off in 1 ms, then find induced emf in inductor.

(a) 8×10^4 V
(b) 1.2×10^4 V
(c) 8×10^{-4} V
(d) 1.2×10^{-4} V

28. An air-cored solenoid with length 30 cm, area of cross-section 25 cm^2 and number of turns 1000, carries a current of 2.5 A. The current is suddenly switched off in a brief time of 10^{-3} s. How much average back emf is induced across the ends of the open switch in the circuit? Ignore the variation in magnetic field near the ends of the solenoid.

(a) 26.2 V (b) 7.5 V
(c) 24.0 V (d) 36.0 V

29. There are two long co-axial solenoids of same length l. The inner and outer coils have radii r_1 and r_2 and number of turns per unit length n. The ratio of mutual inductance to the self-inductance of the inner coil is

(a) $\frac{n_2}{n_1} \cdot \frac{r_1}{r_2}$ (b) $\frac{n_2}{n_1} \cdot \frac{r_2^2}{r_1^2}$
(c) 1 (d) $\frac{n_1}{n_2}$

30. The magnet in figure rotates as shown on a pivot through its centre. At the instant shown, what are the directions of the induced current?

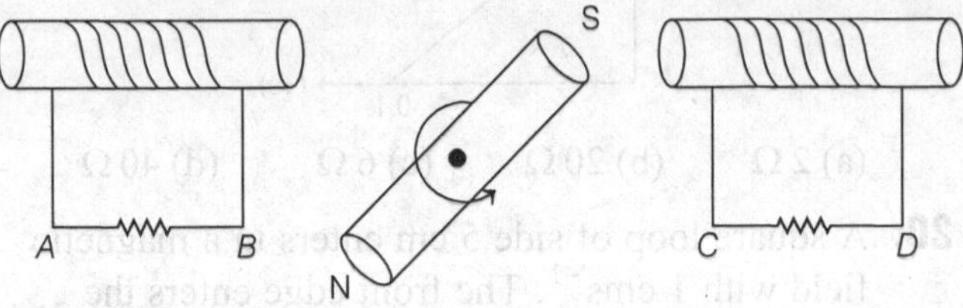

(a) A to B and C to D
(b) B to A and C to D
(c) A to B and D to C
(d) B to A and D to C

Response Index

01	a	b	c	d	11	a	b	c	d	21	a	b	c	d
02	a	b	c	d	12	a	b	c	d	22	a	b	c	d
03	a	b	c	d	13	a	b	c	d	23	a	b	c	d
04	a	b	c	d	14	a	b	c	d	24	a	b	c	d
05	a	b	c	d	15	a	b	c	d	25	a	b	c	d
06	a	b	c	d	16	a	b	c	d	26	a	b	c	d
07	a	b	c	d	17	a	b	c	d	27	a	b	c	d
08	a	b	c	d	18	a	b	c	d	28	a	b	c	d
09	a	b	c	d	19	a	b	c	d	29	a	b	c	d
10	a	b	c	d	20	a	b	c	d	30	a	b	c	d

Performance Scanner

> 90% Excellent !	You have mastered this chapter. The concepts of this chapter are on your fingertips. Move on to the next chapter and maintain this momentum.
76-90% Very Good !	You have a good command over this chapter. Revise the chapter again after a few days and enhance your performance.
60-75% Good !	You have a wide scope to learn for this chapter. Revise this chapter again.
<60% Not Satisfactory!	You have a long way ahead of you to master this chapter. Revise it thoroughly.

For Online Chapter Test **Scan the QR Code**

Test Booklet No. **3947158**

Test Booklet Code **CH8**

MED ACE
NEET (UG)
SELF ASSESSMENT KIT

Alternating Current (AC)

Topics Covered

- Introduction to AC Circuits
- Power in AC Circuits
- AC Based Devices

Important Instructions

- This Booklet Contains – Three Topic Tests and One Test on Complete Chapter.
- Each question carries 4 marks.
- For each correct response, the candidate will get 4 marks and for every incorrect response 1 mark will be additionally deducted from the total score.
- Use **Blue/Black** point pen only for filling the OMR.
- Rough work will be done in the space provided for this purpose within the test booklet only.

Name of the Candidate (In Capitals)

____

____

Candidate's Signature ____________

Invigilator's Signature ____________

Facsimile signature stamp of center superintendent____________

Do not open this Booklet until you start attempting the Test

Topical Follow Thru

Test 1

Syllabus

- Alternating Currents, Peak and RMS Value of Alternating Current/Voltage
- Reactance and Impedance
- *L-C-R* Series Circuit
- Resonance

For deeper insight **Scan the QR Code**

Important Instructions

- The test is of 45 minutes duration and contains 25 Multiple Choice Questions. (Four options with a single correct answer).
- Choose the correct option and fill the OMR given on the last page of this test accordingly.
- At some instances, you may find more than 1 option may be correct, in such circumstances you have to judge the most appropriate answer as per the conditions given in the question.

1. Which graph shows the variation of current and voltage in a purely inductive circuit?

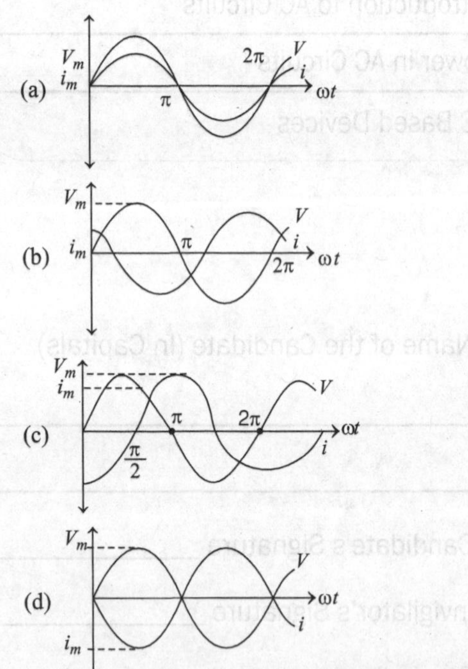

2. A transmitter transmits at a wavelength of 300 m. A condenser of capacitance 3.6 μF is being used. The value of the inductance for the resonant circuit is approximately

(a) 4 nH (b) 6 nH
(c) 8 nH (d) 7 nH

3. Assertion (A) An electric lamp is connected in series with a variable capacitor and AC source, its brightness increases with increase in capacitance.

Reason (R) Capacitive reactance decreases with increase in capacitance of capacitor.

In the light of above statements, choose the most appropriate answer from the options given below.

(a) Both A and R are true and R is the correct explanation of A.
(b) Both A and R are true but R is not the correct explanation of A.
(c) A is true but R is false.
(d) A is false but R is true.

4. A $\frac{20}{\pi}$ μF capacitor is connected to a 110 V, 50 Hz source. The rms value of the current is

(a) 1.53 A (b) 2.56 A
(c) 1.96A (d) 0.22 A

5. Consider the electrical circuit shown in the following figure. The source voltage is $V = 100 \sin (314t)$ V. If the instantaneous potential difference between P and Q points is 30 V, then instantaneous source voltage is

$X_L = 2\ \Omega$ $X_C = 8\ \Omega$ $8\ \Omega$ P Q 100 sin (314t)

(a) 50 V (b) 40 V
(c) 30 V (d) 20 V

6. Current and voltage in an AC circuit is found to be $i = 30\sin 100t$ and $V = 300\sin\left(100t + \frac{\pi}{3}\right)$ respectively. If the resistance is 8 Ω, then the reactance will be

(a) $2\sqrt{7}\,\Omega$
(b) 10Ω
(c) 6Ω
(d) $\sqrt{8}\,\Omega$

7.

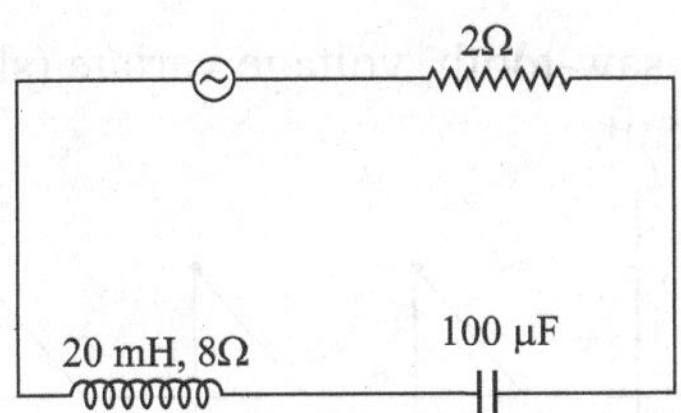

The voltage in the above circuit is $V = 10\cos\omega t$ and $\omega = 1000$ rad/s. The amplitude of current is

(a) 2A (b) 0.707 A
(c) 1 A (d) 1.58 A

8. Match the List I with List II.

	List I		List II
A.	Only inductance	1.	(graph: I, V)
B.	Only capacitance	2.	(graph: V, I)
C.	Only resistance	3.	(graph: V, I)
D.	Inductance and resistance in series	4.	(graph: V, I)

(a) A-2, B-1, C-4, D-3
(b) A-1, B-2, C-3, D-4
(c) A-3, B-1, C-2, D-4
(d) A-2, B-1, C-3, D-4

9. **Statement I** When two alternating currents $i_1 = 20\sin(314\,t + 30°)$ A, $i_2 = 40\sin(314\,t + 45°)$ A are mixed, then resultant current has a magnitude of 60 A.

Statement II In AC, currents are added by using vector addition laws.

In the light of above statements, choose the most appropriate answer from the options given below.

(a) Both Statement I and Statement II are correct.
(b) Both Statement I and Statement II are incorrect.
(c) Statement I is correct but Statement II is incorrect.
(d) Statement II is correct but Statement I is incorrect.

10. Resonant frequency of an *L-C* circuit is ω. If inductance is reduced to half and capacitance is made 8 times, then the new resonant frequency will be

(a) 2ω (b) $\frac{\omega}{2}$
(c) $\sqrt{2}\,\omega$ (d) $\frac{\omega}{\sqrt{2}}$

11. Consider the following *L-C-R* circuit.

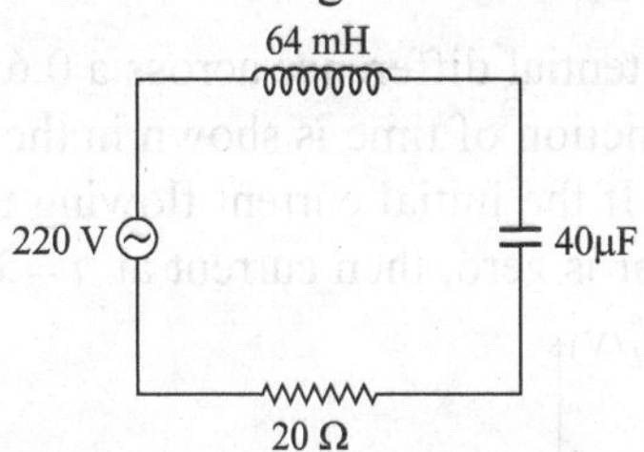

The resonant frequency and amplitude of current of the above circuit are

(a) 6250 rad/s, $11\sqrt{2}$ A
(b) 6250 rad/s, 11 A
(c) 2500 rad/s, $\frac{11}{\sqrt{2}}$ A
(d) 2500 rad/s, 11 A

12. A resistor, a capacitor and a $\frac{20}{\pi^2}$ mH inductor are connected in series to an AC source of frequency 50 Hz. If current and voltage are in phase, then the capacitance will be

(a) 10 μF (b) 200 μF
(c) 5×10^{-3} F (d) 50 μF

13. A 40 μF capacitor is fully charged by a 40 V source. Now, the source is disconnected and the capacitor is connected to a 4 mH coil in series. The equation of variation of charge on the capacitor and current in the inductor are (Take, $t=0$ when capacitor and inductor are connected)

(a) $q(t)=(1.6\times10^{-3})\cos(2.5\times10^{4}t)$
$I(t)=40\cos(2.5\times10^{4}t)$

(b) $q(t)=(0.8\times10^{-3})\cos(2.5\times10^{4}t)$
$I(t)=20\sin(2.5\times10^{4}t)$

(c) $q(t)=(2\times10^{-3})\cos(5\times10^{4}t)$
$I(t)=100\cos(5\times10^{4}t)$

(d) $q(t)=(1.6\times10^{-3})\cos(2.5\times10^{3}t)$
$I(t)=4\sin(2.5\times10^{3}t)$

14. An alternating voltage $V=100\sqrt{2}\sin(100t)$ V is connected to a 1 μF capacitor through an AC ammeter. The reading of the ammeter is

(a) 10 mA (b) $10\sqrt{2}$ mA
(c) 20 mA (d) $20\sqrt{2}$ mA

15. The potential difference across a 0.6 H inductor as a function of time is shown in the following figure. If the initial current flowing through the inductor is zero, then current at $t=3$ s will be

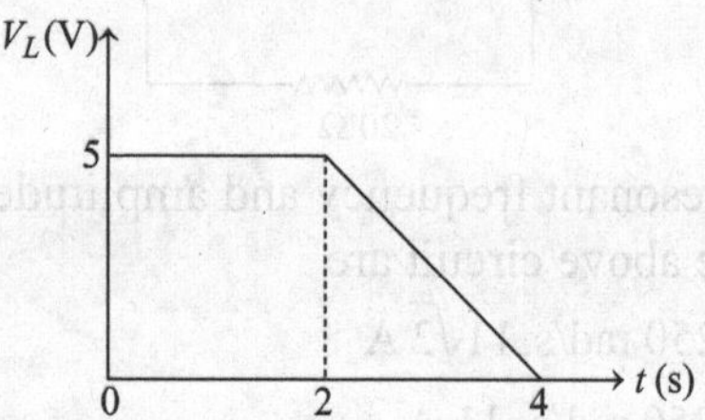

(a) 33.33 A (b) 22.9 A
(c) 21.5 A (d) None of these

16. The ratio of rms value of current $I=4\sin\omega t$ from

I. $t=0$ to $t=\frac{\pi}{\omega}$

II. $t=\frac{\pi}{2\omega}$ to $t=\frac{3\pi}{2\omega}$ is given by $k:1$.

The value of k is equal to

(a) 1 (b) 2
(c) 3 (d) 5

17. An arc lamp requires a direct current of 10 A at 80 V to function. If it is connected to a 220 V (rms), 50 Hz AC supply, the series inductor needed for it to work is close to

(a) 80 H (b) 0.08 H
(c) 0.044 H (d) 0.065 H

18. Household electricity is supplied at 220 V rms and 50 Hz frequency. Time in which voltage can change from the rms value to zero is $N\times2.5$ ms. The value of N is equal to

(a) 3 (b) 2
(c) 4 (d) 6

19. For the saw-tooth, voltage variate (shown) for an AC circuit.

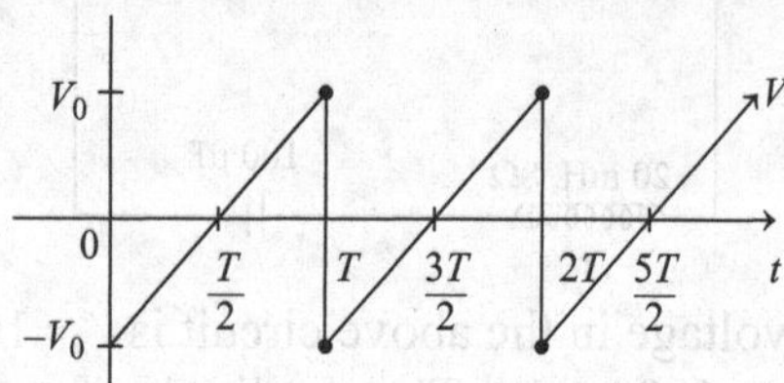

Choose the correct option.

(a) $V=V_0\left(\frac{3t}{T}-1\right)$

(b) $V_{av}\left(\frac{1}{2}\text{cycle}\right)=\frac{V_0}{4}$

(c) $V_{rms}=\frac{V_0}{\sqrt{3}}$

(d) $V_0<<V_{rms}<V_{av}$

20. An alternating voltage $V=200\sqrt{2}\sin(100t)$ V is connected to a 1 μF capacitor through an AC ammeter. The reading of the ammeter will be

(a) 20 mA (b) 25 mA
(c) 30 mA (d) 40 mA

21. The rms value of the signal is

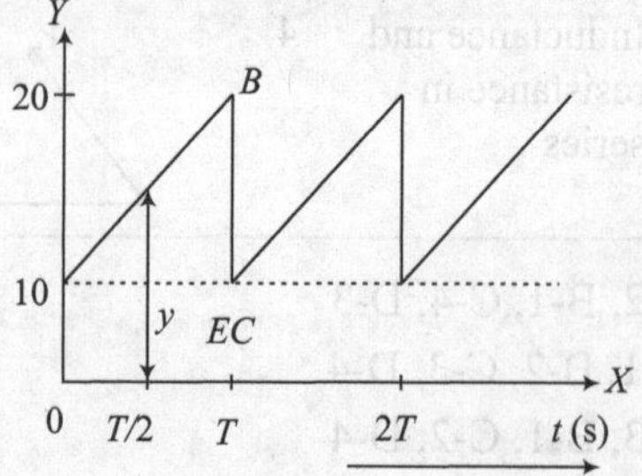

(a) $10\sqrt{\frac{7}{3}}$ (b) $\frac{10}{\sqrt{3}}$

(c) $10\sqrt{7}$ (d) $10\sqrt{3}$

22. An AC current is given by $I = I_0 + I_1 \sin \omega t$, then its rms value will be

(a) $\sqrt{I_0^2 + 0.5 I_1^2}$ (b) $\sqrt{I_1^2 + 0.5 I_0^2}$

(c) 0 (d) $\frac{I_0}{\sqrt{2}}$

23. Two alternating voltage generators produce emf of the same amplitude E_0 but with a phase difference of $\pi/3$. The resultant emf is

(a) $E_0 \sin [\omega t + (\pi/3)]$

(b) $E_0 \sin [\omega t + \pi/6)]$

(c) $\sqrt{3}\, E_0 \sin [\omega t + (\pi/6)]$

(d) $\sqrt{3}\, E_0 \sin [\omega t + (\pi/2)]$

24. The average value of current from $t = 0$ to $t = \frac{2\pi}{\omega}$, if the current varies as $I = I_0 \sin \omega t$ is

(a) 0 (b) $\frac{I_0}{\pi}$

(c) $\frac{2I_0}{\pi}$ (d) $\frac{I_0}{\sqrt{2}}$

25. The rms value of current $i = 2 \sin 100\pi t + 2 \cos (100\pi t + 30°)$ is

(a) 2 A (b) $2\sqrt{2}$ A

(c) $\frac{1}{\sqrt{2}}$ A (d) $\sqrt{2}$ A

Response Index

01	a	b	c	d	10	a	b	c	d	19	a	b	c	d
02	a	b	c	d	11	a	b	c	d	20	a	b	c	d
03	a	b	c	d	12	a	b	c	d	21	a	b	c	d
04	a	b	c	d	13	a	b	c	d	22	a	b	c	d
05	a	b	c	d	14	a	b	c	d	23	a	b	c	d
06	a	b	c	d	15	a	b	c	d	24	a	b	c	d
07	a	b	c	d	16	a	b	c	d	25	a	b	c	d
08	a	b	c	d	17	a	b	c	d					
09	a	b	c	d	18	a	b	c	d					

Performance Scanner

> 90% Excellent !	You have mastered these topics. The concepts these topics are on your fingertips. Move on to the next test and maintain this momentum.
76-90% Very Good !	You have a good command over these topics. Revise them again after a few days and enhance your performance.
60-75% Good !	You have a wide scope to learn for these topics. Revise them again.
<60% Not Satisfactory!	You have a long way ahead of you to master these topics. Revise them thoroughly.

Test 2

Syllabus
- Power in AC Circuits
- Wattless Current

For deeper insight **Scan the QR Code**

Important Instructions
- The test is of 30 minutes duration and contains 15 Multiple Choice Questions. (Four options with a single correct answer).
- Choose the correct option and fill the OMR given on the last page of this test accordingly.
- At some instances, you may find more than 1 option may be correct, in such circumstances you have to judge the most appropriate answer as per the conditions given in the question.

1. Current $i = 5\sin\omega t$ and voltage $V = 10\cos\omega t$ is applied across an instrument. The frequency of AC circuit is f. Power consumed by the device is

(a) 50 W (b) 0
(c) 2 W (d) 25 W

2. If 4 A is the rms current in an AC circuit and wattless current is 2A, then the power factor is

(a) $\frac{1}{2}$ (b) $\frac{1}{\sqrt{2}}$
(c) $\frac{\sqrt{3}}{2}$ (d) 1

3. **Statement I** A glowing bulb becomes dim when an iron bar is put in the inductor in series L-R circuit.

Statement II In series L-R circuit, current increases.

In the light of above statements, choose the most appropriate answer from the options given below.

(a) Both Statement I and Statement II are correct.
(b) Both Statement I and Statement II are incorrect.
(c) Statement I is correct and Statement II is incorrect.
(d) Statement I is incorrect but Statement II is correct.

4. In a series L-C-R circuit, at resonance, the bandwidth frequency can be represented as

(a) $\frac{R}{LC}$ (b) $\frac{R}{C}$ (c) $\frac{RL}{2\pi}$ (d) $\frac{R}{2\pi L}$

5. At 180 Hz frequency, a choke coil has power factor of 0.5 lagging. Then, at 60 Hz frequency, power factor of same choke coil will be

(a) 0.6 (b) 0.8 (c) 0.866 (d) 0.707

6. In an AC circuit, when applied voltage is $V = 200\sin\left(\omega t + \frac{\pi}{3}\right)$ V, current flowing through it is $I = 5\sqrt{2}\cos\left(\omega t - \frac{\pi}{6}\right)$ A, then power consumption by it will be

(a) 0 (b) 500 W
(c) 1000 W (d) $500\sqrt{2}$ W

7. An inductor 20 mH, a capacitor 50 μF and a resistor 40 Ω are connected in series across a source of emf $V = 25\sin 340t$. The power loss in AC circuit is

(a) 1.7 W (b) 0.51 W
(c) 0.67 W (d) 2.90 W

8. For series R-L-C circuit, $R = 100\,\Omega$, $C = \frac{100}{\pi}\,\mu F$ and $L = \frac{100}{\pi}$ mH are connected to an AC source as shown in the figure. The rms value of AC voltage is 220 V and its frequency is 50 Hz. In List I, some physical quantities are mentioned while in List II, information about quantities are provided.

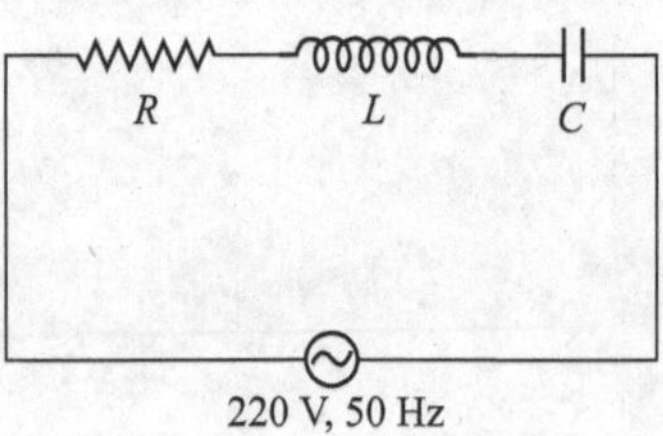

Match the following lists and select the correct option from the codes given below.

	List I		List II
A.	Average power dissipated in the resistor is	1.	0
B.	Average power dissipated in the inductor is	2.	1.63 SI units
C.	rms value of current through the inductor is	3.	163 SI units
D.	rms voltage across the capacitor is	4.	265.7 SI units

Codes

(a) A-4, B-1, C-2, D-3
(b) A-2, B-3, C-4, D-1
(c) A-2, B-3, C-1, D-4
(d) A-3, B-2, C-1, D-4

9. Maximum value of power factor in an *L-C-R* circuit is, when

(a) $X_L = X_C$ (b) $R = 0$
(c) $X_L = 0$ (d) $X_C = 0$

10. An *L-C-R* series circuit with 100 Ω resistance is connected to an AC source of 200 V and angular frequency 300 rad/s. When only the capacitor is removed, the current lags behind the voltage by 60°. When only the inductor is removed, the current leads the voltage by 60°. Calculate the average power (in watt) dissipated in *L-C-R* circuit.

(a) 100 (b) 150
(c) 200 (d) 250

11. An inductor of inductance *L* and resistor of resistance *R* are joined in series and connected by a source of frequency ω. Power dissipated in the circuit is

(a) $\frac{(R^2+\omega^2L^2)}{V}$ (b) $\frac{V^2R}{(R^2+\omega^2L^2)}$
(c) $\frac{V}{(R^2+\omega^2L^2)}$ (d) $\frac{\sqrt{R^2+\omega^2L^2}}{V^2}$

12. A lamp consumes 89% of peak power in an AC circuit. The phase difference between applied voltage and current is

(a) 27° (b) 50°
(c) 89° (d) 35°

13. An inductor of reactance 2Ω and a resistor of resistance 4Ω are connected in series. If voltage source is of 6 V AC, then power dissipated in the circuit is

(a) 7.2 W (b) 36 W
(c) 12 W (d) 24 W

14. A capacitor is connected to a lamp rated 50 V, 10 W. If the capacitor is connected in series with an AC source of emf 240 V and frequency 50 cycles/s, then what should be the value of capacitor to run this lamp ?

(a) 5.79 μF (b) 3.20 μF
(c) 4.86 μ F (d) 2.65 μF

15. If a lamp rated at 60 V and 10 W is to be operated at AC source of 100 V and 50 Hz, then required value of inductance is

(a) 2.28 H (b) 0.76 H
(c) 1.52 H (d) 3.04 H

Response Index

01	a	b	c	d	10	a	b	c	d
02	a	b	c	d	11	a	b	c	d
03	a	b	c	d	12	a	b	c	d
04	a	b	c	d	13	a	b	c	d
05	a	b	c	d	14	a	b	c	d
06	a	b	c	d	15	a	b	c	d
07	a	b	c	d					
08	a	b	c	d					
09	a	b	c	d					

Performance Scanner

> 90% Excellent !	You have mastered these topics. The concepts of these topics are on your fingertips. Move on to the next test and maintain this momentum.
76-90% Very Good !	You have a good command over these topics. Revise them again after a few days and enhance your performance.
60-75% Good !	You have a wide scope to learn more from these topics. Revise them again.
<60% Not Satisfactory!	You have a long way ahead of you to master these topics. Revise them thoroughly.

Test 3

Syllabus

- AC Generator and Transformer

For deeper insight **Scan the QR Code**

Important Instructions

- The test is of 30 minutes duration and contains 15 Multiple Choice Questions. (Four options with a single correct answer).
- Choose the correct option and fill the OMR given on the last page of this test accordingly.
- At some instances, you may find more than 1 option may be correct, in such circumstances you have to judge the most appropriate answer as per the conditions given in the question.

1. The lamination of core of a transformer helps in

(a) preventing the rusting of core

(b) reduction of energy loss due to eddy currents

(c) reducing the cost of making

(d) prevention from short-circuit

2. A step-down transformer operates on a 220 V line and supplies 1 A current. The ratio of primary and secondary winding is 1 : 50. The current in the primary coil is

(a) 25 A

(b) 100 A

(c) 2 A

(d) 50 A

3. A 1100 W, 220 V lamp is lighted up by a transformer. If source voltage is 110 V and current is 0.5 A, then the efficiency of the transformer is

(a) 80% (b) 60%

(c) 40% (d) 20%

4. A transformer of 100% efficiency has 200 turns in the primary and 40000 turns in secondary. It is connected to a 220 V main supply and secondary feeds to a 100 kΩ resistance. The potential difference per turn is

(a) 1.1 V (b) 25 V

(c) 18 V (d) 11 V

5. The primary and secondary coils of transformer have 50 and 1500 turns, respectively. If the magnetic flux ϕ linked with the primary coil is given by $\phi = \phi_0 + 4t$, where ϕ is in weber, t is time in second and ϕ_0 is a constant, then the output voltage across the secondary coil is

(a) 90 V (b) 120 V

(c) 220 V (d) 30 V

6. Input voltage of a step-down transformer is 1100 V with 2000 primary windings. The output power is delivered at 220 V by the transformer. If current in the primary coil is 6 A and its efficiency is 95%, then the output current is

(a) 28.5 A (b) 63.2 A

(c) 15 A (d) 12 A

7. Transformation ratio of a transformer is $\frac{N_1}{N_2} = \frac{40}{1}$. It is connected to 160 V AC supply. If resistances of primary and secondary circuits are 2.4 Ω and 1 Ω respectively, then the output power is

(a) 1600 W (b) 400 W

(c) 1200 W (d) 500 W

8. A transformer is used to light a 140 W, 24 V lamp from 240 V AC mains. The current in the main cable is 0.7 A. The efficiency of the transformer is

(a) 48% (b) 63.8%

(c) 83.3% (d) 90%

9. An ideal transformer is used to step up an alternating emf of 220 V to 3.3 kV to transmit 6.6 kW of power. The current rating of the secondary coil is

(a) 1.5 A (b) 3 A

(c) 2 A (d) 1 A

10. A hydroelectric power plant generating electrical power at 440 V supply to a small scale industrial area. Industrial area gets power from a 4000 -220 V step-down transformer. Power station is 15 km away from industrial area and resistance of two wire lines used for transmission is $0.5\Omega\,km^{-1}$. Industrial area requires 800 kW of electric power at 220 V. Then, line power loss (in kW) is

(a) 100 (b) 450 (c) 200 (d) 600

11. The number of turns in the primary and secondary coils of an ideal transformer are 2000 and 50, respectively. Then, the primary coil is connected to a main supply of 120 V and secondary to a night bulb of 0.6 Ω. The power in primary and secondary coils is

(a) 15 W (b) 12W

(c) 10 W (d) 20 W

12. A power transmission line feeds input power at 2300 V to a step-down transformer with its primary winding having 4000 turns. The output power is delivered at 230 V by the transformer. If the current in the primary coil of the transformer is 5A and its efficiency is 90%, then output current would be

(a) 45 A (b) 50 A
(c) 25 A (d) 35 A

13. The turns ratio of transformer is given as 3 : 2. If the current passing through the primary coil is 3 A, find the current through the load resistance.

(a) 4.5 A (b) 1.5 A
(c) 2 A (d) 1 A

14. In a step-up transformer, the turns ratio of primary and secondary coils is 1:3. A Leclanche cell of emf 2 V is connected across the primary coil. The voltage developed across the secondary coil would be

(a) 0 (b) 6 V
(c) 1.5 V (d) 0.66 V

15. A transformer consisting of 300 turns in the primary coil and 150 turns in the secondary coil, gives output power of 2.2 kW. If the current in the secondary coil is 10 A, then the input voltage and current in the primary coil are

(a) 440 V and 5 A
(b) 220 V and 20 A
(c) 220 V and 10 A
(d) 440 V and 20 A

Response Index

01	(a)	(b)	(c)	(d)	10	(a)	(b)	(c)	(d)
02	(a)	(b)	(c)	(d)	11	(a)	(b)	(c)	(d)
03	(a)	(b)	(c)	(d)	12	(a)	(b)	(c)	(d)
04	(a)	(b)	(c)	(d)	13	(a)	(b)	(c)	(d)
05	(a)	(b)	(c)	(d)	14	(a)	(b)	(c)	(d)
06	(a)	(b)	(c)	(d)	15	(a)	(b)	(c)	(d)
07	(a)	(b)	(c)	(d)					
08	(a)	(b)	(c)	(d)					
09	(a)	(b)	(c)	(d)					

Performance Scanner

> 90% Excellent !	You have mastered these topics. The concepts of these topics are on your fingertips. Move on to the next test and maintain this momentum.
76-90% Very Good !	You have a good command over these topics. Revise them again after a few days and enhance your performance.
60-75% Good !	You have a wide scope to learn more from these topics. Revise them again.
<60% Not Satisfactory!	You have a long way ahead of you to master these topics. Revise them thoroughly.

Chapter Break Thru

Syllabus

- Alternating Currents, Peak and RMS Value of Alternating Current/Valtege.
- Reactance and Impedance
- *L-C-R* Series Circuit
- Resonance
- Power in AC Circuits
- Wattless Current
- AC Generator and Transformer

Important Instructions

- The test is of 1 hour duration and contains 50 Multiple Choice Questions (Four options with a single correct answer).
- Choose the correct option and fill the OMR given on the last page of this test accordingly.
  At some instances, you may find more than 1 option may be correct, in such circumstances you have to judge the most appropriate answer as per conditions given in the question.

1. In a series *L-C-R* circuit, when $X_L = 2X_C$ and $R = X_C$, then phase difference will be

(a) 30° (b) 90° (c) 0° (d) 45°

2. Impedance (Z) *verus* frequency of generator (w_d) for given circuit is

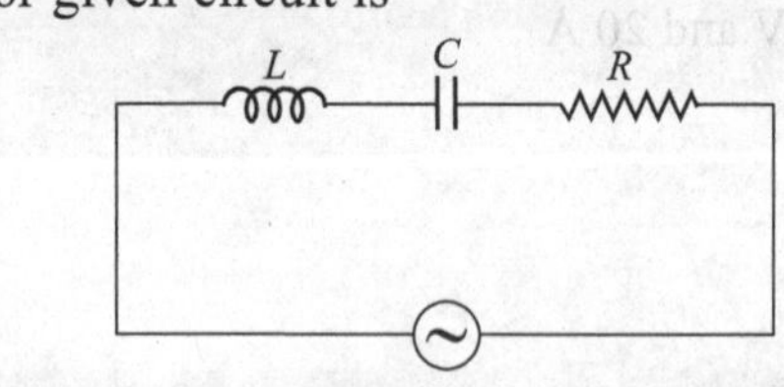

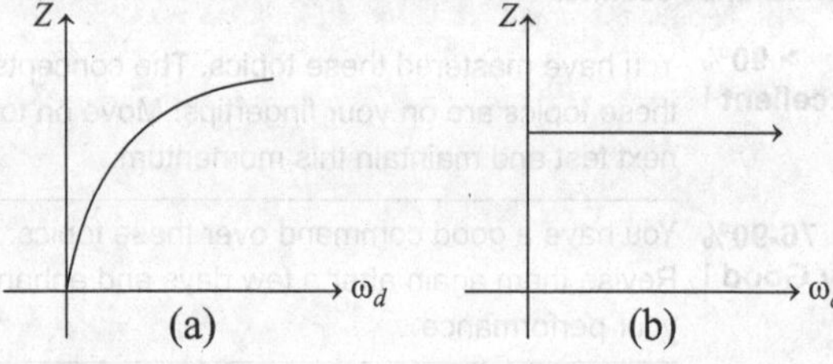

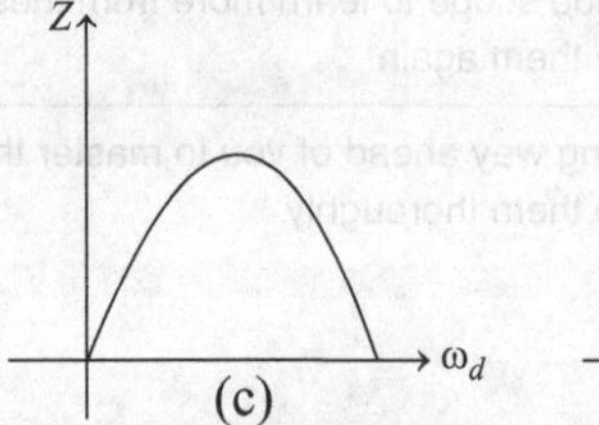

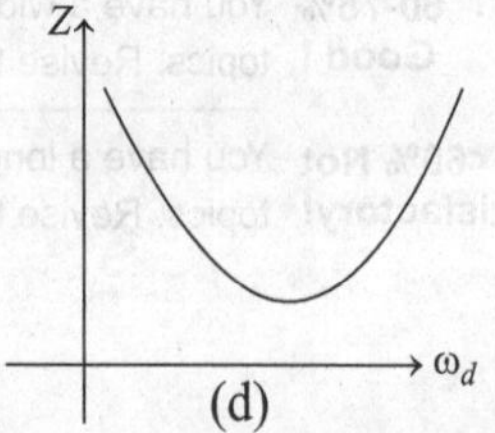

3. A sinusoidal voltage $V(t) = 210 \sin 3000t$ volt is applied to a series *L-C-R* circuit in which $L = 10$ mH, $C = 25\,\mu$F and $R = 100\,\Omega$.

The phase difference (ϕ) between the applied voltage and resultant current will be

(a) $\tan^{-1}(0.17)$ (b) $\tan^{-1}(9.46)$

(d) $\tan^{-1}(0.30)$ (d) $\tan^{-1}(13.33)$

4. Statement I The current in a capacitive circuit is $i = i_m \sin(\omega t - \pi/2)$, where the amplitude of the oscillating current is $i_m = \dfrac{V_m}{\omega C}$.

Statement II The impedance triangle is a right angled triangle with Z as its base.

In the light of above statements, choose the most appropriate answer from the options given below.

(a) Both Statement I and Statement II are correct.

(b) Both Statement I and Statement II are incorrect.

(c) Statement I is correct but Statement II is incorrect.

(d) Statement I is incorrect but Statement II is correct.

5. An alternating voltage (in volts) is given by $V = 100\sqrt{2} \sin(50t)$, is connected to a 2 μF capacitor through an ideal AC ammeter in series. The reading of the ammeter and the average power consumed in the circuit will be

(a) 10 mA, 10 W (b) $20\sqrt{2}$ mA, 4 W

(c) $20\sqrt{2}$ mA, 8 W (d) 10 mA, 0

6. At very high frequencies, impedance of given circuit will be

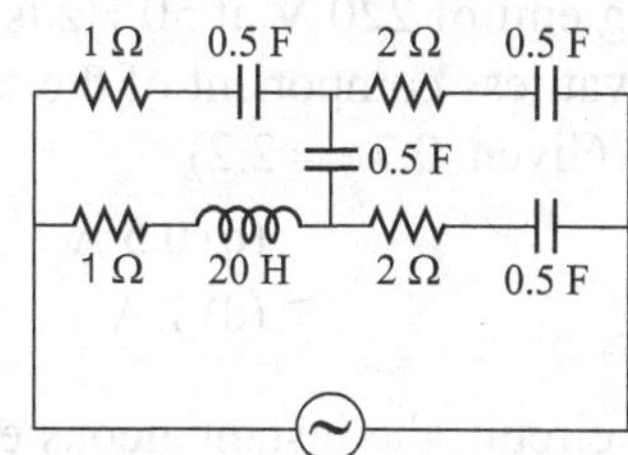

(a) 2 Ω (b) 1 Ω
(c) 4 Ω (d) ∞

7. In an *L-C-R* circuit having $L = 18$ H, $C = 2$ μF and $R = 100\,\Omega$ in series. The resonance frequency is
(a) 192 rad/s (b) 166 rad/s
(c) 128 rad/s (d) 270 rad/s

8. An electric bulb and a capacitor are connected in series with an AC source. On increasing the frequency of the source, the brightness of the bulb will
(a) increase
(b) decrease
(c) remain unchanged
(d) None of the above

9. The rms value of potential difference V shown in the figure is

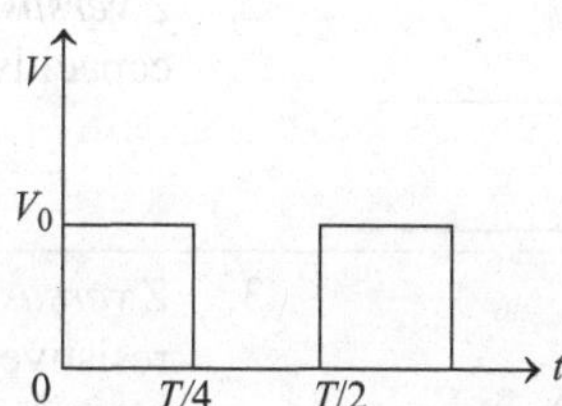

(a) V_0 (b) $\frac{V_0}{\sqrt{2}}$
(c) $\frac{V_0}{2}$ (d) $\frac{V_0}{\sqrt{3}}$

10. A coil has resistance 30 Ω and inductive reactance 20 Ω at 50 Hz frequency. If an AC source of 100 V, 100 Hz is connected across the coil, the current in the coil will be
(a) 4.0 A (b) 8.0 A
(c) $\frac{20}{\sqrt{13}}$ A (d) 2.0 A

11. A coil of 100 Ω resistance and 1.0 H inductance is connected to an AC source of frequency $100/2\pi$ Hz. Then, Phase angle between potential and current will be
(a) 30° (b) 90°
(c) 45° (d) 0°

12. A direct current of 10 A is superimposed on an alternating current $I = 12 \sin \omega t$ flowing through a wire. The effective value of the resulting current will be
(a) (15/2) A (b) $5\sqrt{3}$ A
(c) $5\sqrt{5}$ A (d) 13 A

13. Match List-I with List-II.

	List-I		List-II
A.	Phase difference between current and voltage in a purely resistive AC circuit.	1.	Zero
B.	Phase difference between current and voltage in a pure inductive AC circuit.	2.	$\frac{\pi}{2}$, current leads voltage
C.	Phase difference between current and voltage in a pure capacitive AC circuit.	3.	$\frac{\pi}{2}$, current lags voltage
D.	Phase difference between current and voltage in an *L-C-R* series circuit.	4.	$\tan^{-1}\left(\frac{X_C - X_L}{R}\right)$

Codes

	A	B	C	D
(a)	1	3	2	4
(b)	1	3	4	2
(c)	2	3	4	1
(d)	2	4	3	1

14. A resistor R, an inductor L and a capacitor C are connected in series to an oscillator of frequency n, if the resonant frequency is n_r, then the current will lag behind voltage when
(a) $n = 0$
(b) $n < n_r$
(c) $n = n_r$
(d) $n > n_r$

15. A sinusoidal AC of peak value I_0 passes through a heater of resistance R. What is the mean power output of the heater?

(a) $I_0^2 R$ (b) $\frac{I_0^2 R}{2}$

(c) $2I_0^2 R$ (d) $\sqrt{2}\, I_0^2 R$

16. The number of turns in the primary coil of a transformer is 200 and the number of turns in secondary coil is 10. If 240 V AC is applied to the primary coil, the output from secondary coil will be

(a) 48 V (b) 24 V (c) 12 V (d) 6 V

17. For an *L-C-R* circuit, the power transferred from the driving source to the driven oscillator is $P = I^2 Z \cos\phi$.

I. Here, the power factor $\cos\phi \geq 0, P \geq 0$.
II. The driving force can give no energy to the oscillator ($P = 0$) in some cases.
III. The driving force cannot syphon out $P \not< 0$ the energy of oscillator.
IV. The driving force can take away energy out of the oscillator.

Select the correct option.

(a) I,II,III (b) II, IV

(c) IV (d) III, IV

18. **Assertion** (A) An alternating current does not show any magnetic effect.
Reason (R) Alternating current vary with time.
In the light of above statements, choose the most appropriate answer from the options given below.

(a) Both A and R are ture and R is the correct explanation of A.

(b) Both A and R are true but R is not the correct explanation of A.

(c) A is true but R is false.

(d) A is false but R is true.

19. A current of 4 A flows in a coil when connected to a 12 V DC source. If the same coil is connected to a 12 V, 50 rad/s AC source, a currentof 2.4 A flows in the circuit. The inductance (in henry) of the coil is

(a) 0.06 (b) 0.02

(c) 0.08 (d) 0.04

20. A coil has an inductance of 0.7 H and is joined in series with a resistance of 220 Ω. When an alternating emf of 220 V at 50 Hz is applied to it, then the wattless component of the current in the circuit is (Given, $0.7\pi = 2.2$)

(a) 5 A (b) 0.5 A

(c) 0.7 A (d) 7 A

21. In an AC circuit, the instantaneous emf and current are given by $e = 100 \sin 30t$, $i = 20 \sin\left(30t - \frac{\pi}{4}\right)$. In one cycle of AC, the average power consumed by the circuit and the wattless current are, respectively

(a) $\frac{1000}{\sqrt{2}}$, 10 (b) 50, 0

(c) 50, 10 (d) $\frac{50}{\sqrt{2}}$, 0

22. Match the following graphs in List I with the correct entries in List II. In List II, first quantity listed is shown on Y-axis and second quantity listed is on X-axis of the graph.

List I	List II
A.	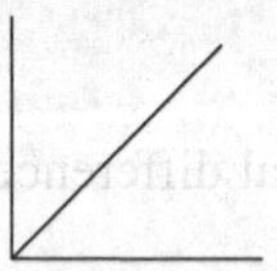 1. *Z versus f* for *L-C-R* circuit
B.	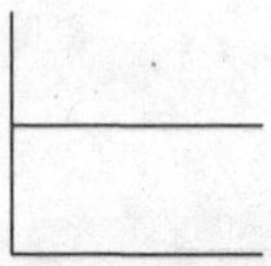 2. *Z versus f* for purely capacitive circuit
C.	 3. *Z versus f* for purely resistive circuit
D.	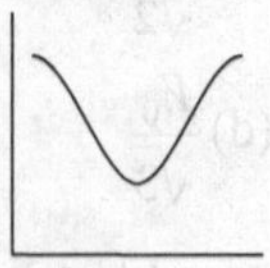 4. *Z versus f* for purely inductive circuit

Codes

	A	B	C	D
(a)	1	2	3	4
(b)	4	3	2	1
(c)	4	3	1	2
(d)	3	4	2	1

23. Primary coil of a transformer has a current of 5 A. The resulting fluxes linked with primary and secondary are 0.2 mWb and 0.4 mWb, respectively. If primary has 500 turns and secondary has 1500 turns and self-inductance of secondary coil is $90k$ mH, then find the value of k.

(a) 20 (b) 8 (c) 10 (d) 16

24. Electrical energy is transmitted over large distances at high alternating voltages. Which of the following statement(s) is/are incorrect?

(a) For a given power level, there is a lower current.

(b) Lower current implies less power loss.

(c) Transmission line can be made thinner.

(d) It is easy to reduce the voltage at the receiving end using step-down transformer.

25. For the given figures, choose the correct options.

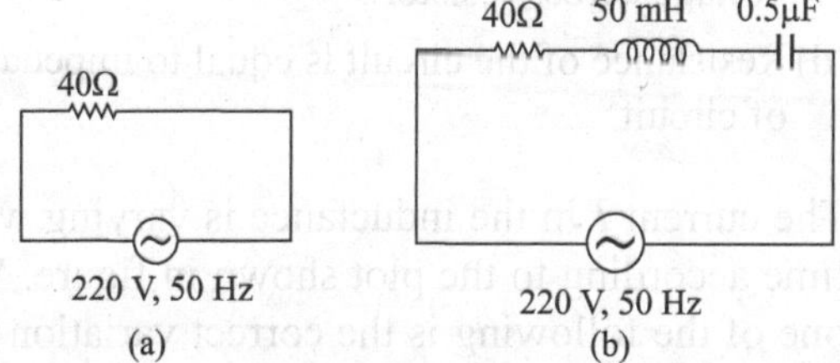

(a) The rms current in circuit (b) is always larger than that in (a).

(b) The rms current in circuit (a) is always equal to that in circuit (b).

(c) At resonance, current in circuit (b) is less than that in circuit (a).

(d) The rms current in circuit (b) can never be larger than that in circuit (a).

26. For the circuit as shown in figure, if the value of rms current is 2.2 A, the power factor of the box is

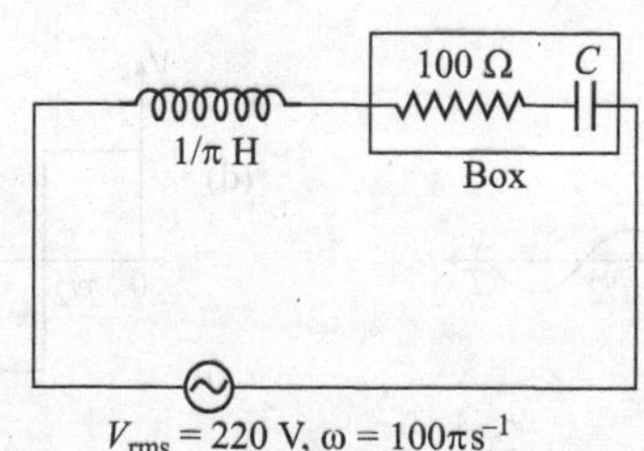

(a) $\frac{1}{\sqrt{2}}$ (b) 1 (c) $\frac{\sqrt{3}}{2}$ (d) $\frac{1}{2}$

27. A small DC motor operating at 200 V draws a current of 5.0 A at its full speed of 3000 rpm. The resistance of the armature of the motor is 8.5 Ω. Determine the efficiency of motor.

(a) 85% (b) 78.75%
(c) 76% (d) 72%

28. In a series L-C-R circuit, $R = 200\,\Omega$ and the voltage and the frequency of the main supply is 220 V and 50 Hz, respectively. On taking out the capacitance from the circuit, the current lags behind the voltage by 30°. On taking out the inductor from the circuit, the current leads the voltage by 30°. The power dissipated in the L-C-R circuit is

(a) 305 W

(b) 210 W

(c) zero

(d) 242 W

29. In the circuit shown in figure, the voltage across inductor L and capacitor C are

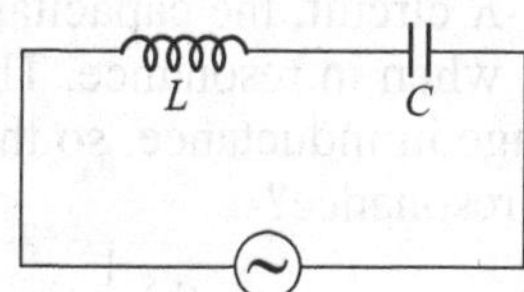

(a) in a phase difference which depends upon the value of L and C

(b) in same phase

(c) out of phase by 90°

(d) out of phase by 180°

30. When 100 V DC is applied across a solenoid, a current of 1 A flows in it. When 100 V AC is applied across the same coil, the current drops to 0.5 A. If the frequency of the AC source is 50 Hz, the impedance and inductance of solenoid are

(a) 100Ω, 0.93 H

(b) 200 Ω, 1.0 H

(c) 10Ω, 0.86 H

(d) 200 Ω, 0.55 H

31. The self-inductance of a choke coil is 10 mH. When it is connected with a 10 V DC source, then the loss of power is 20 W. When it is connected with 10 V AC source, loss of power is 10 W. The frequency of AC source will be

(a) 80 Hz (b) 100 Hz
(c) 120 Hz (d) 220 Hz

32. A 110 V, 60 W lamp is run from a 220 V AC mains using a capacitor in series with the lamp instead of a resistor, then the voltage across the capacitor is about

(a) 110 V (b) 190 V
(c) 220 V (d) 311 V

33. The instantaneous emf in an AC circuit is given by $E = 50 \sin(314t)$ V, where t is in seconds. In how much time, the emf will become 25 V starting from zero?

(a) $\frac{1}{50}$ s (b) $\frac{1}{200}$ s (c) $\frac{1}{314}$ s (d) $\frac{1}{600}$ s

34. For an *L-C-R* circuit, the capacitance is made one-fourth, when in resonance. Then, what should be the change in inductance, so that the circuit remains in resonance?

(a) 4 times (b) $\frac{1}{4}$ times
(c) 8 times (d) 2 times

35. For a series *R-L-C* circuit, $R = X_L = 2X_C$. The impedance of the circuit and phase difference (between) V and i will be

(a) $\frac{\sqrt{5}R}{2}, \tan^{-1}(2)$ (b) $\frac{\sqrt{5}R}{2}, \tan^{-1}\left(\frac{1}{2}\right)$
(c) $\sqrt{5}X_C, \tan^{-1}(2)$ (d) $\sqrt{5}R, \tan^{-1}\left(\frac{1}{2}\right)$

36. For the series *L-C-R* circuit, the voltmeter and ammeter readings are

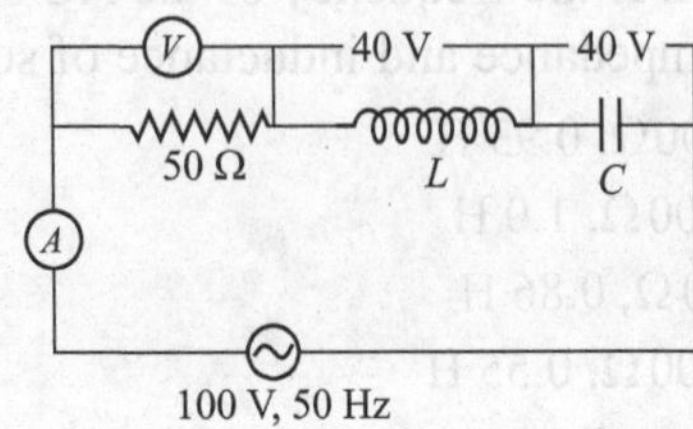

(a) $V = 100$ V, $I = 2$ A
(b) $V = 100$ V, $I = 5$ A
(c) $V = 1000$ V, $I = 2$ A
(d) $V = 300$ V, $I = 1$ A

37. For the given AC circuit, which of the following options is incorrect?

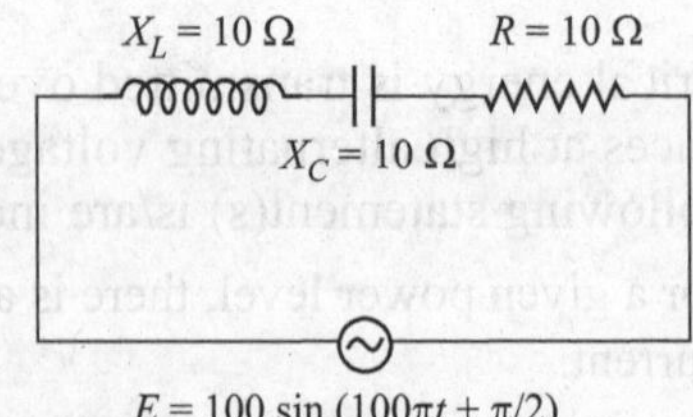

(a) Voltage across resistance is lagging by 90° than voltage across capacitor.
(b) Voltage across capacitor is lagging by 180° than voltage across inductor.
(c) Voltage across inductor is leading by 90° than voltage across resistor.
(d) Resistance of the circuit is equal to impedance of circuit.

38. The current I in the inductance is varying with time according to the plot shown in figure. Which one of the following is the correct variation of voltage with time in the coil?

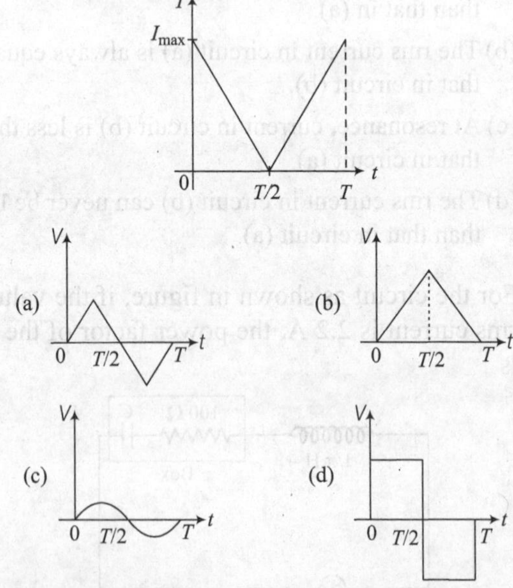

39. **Statement I** Resonance frequency will decrease in a series *L-C-R* circuit, if a dielectric slab is inserted in between the plates of capacitor.

Statement II Due to dielectric slab, capacity of capacitor will increase.

In the light of above statements, choose the most appropriate answer from the options given below.

(a) Both Statement I and Statement II are correct.
(b) Both Statement I and Statement II are incorrect.
(c) Statement I is correct but Statement II is incorrect.
(d) Statement I is incorrect but Statement II is correct.

40. A group of electric lamps having a total power rating of 1000 W is connected by an AC voltage $E = 200\sin(310t + 60°)$, then the rms value of the circuit current is

(a) 10 A (b) $10\sqrt{2}$ A (c) 20 A (d) $20\sqrt{2}$ A

41. The average power dissipated in a pure inductor L carrying an alternating current of rms value i is

(a) $\frac{1}{4}Li^2$ (b) $\frac{1}{3}Li^2$ (c) zero (d) $\frac{1}{2}Li^2$

42. The impedance of the given circuit is

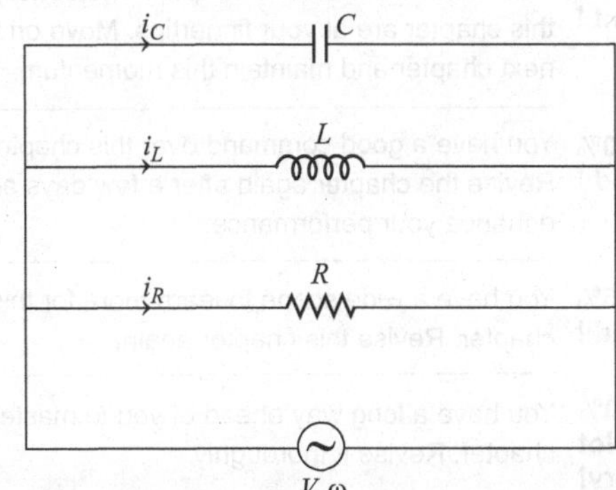

(a) $\left[\frac{1}{R} + \left(\omega C - \frac{1}{\omega L}\right)^2\right]^{-\frac{1}{2}}$

(b) $\left[R^2 + \left(\omega C - \frac{1}{\omega L}\right)^2\right]^{\frac{1}{2}}$

(c) $\left[\frac{1}{R^2} + \left(\omega C - \frac{1}{\omega L}\right)^2\right]^{-\frac{1}{2}}$

(d) $\left[R^2 + \left(\omega C - \frac{1}{\omega L}\right)^2\right]^{\frac{1}{3}}$

43. In an L-C-R circuit, $R = 100\,\Omega$. When capacitance C is removed, the current lags behind the voltage by $\pi/3$. When inductance L is removed, the current leads the voltage by $\pi/3$. The impedance of the circuit is

(a) 50 Ω (b) 100 Ω
(c) 200 Ω (d) 400 Ω

44. An AC source rated 220 V, 50 Hz is connected to a resistor. The time taken by the current to change from its maximum to the rms value is

(a) 2.5 ms (b) 25 ms
(c) 2.5 s (d) 0.25 ms

45. For the given circuit, the type of transformer used is

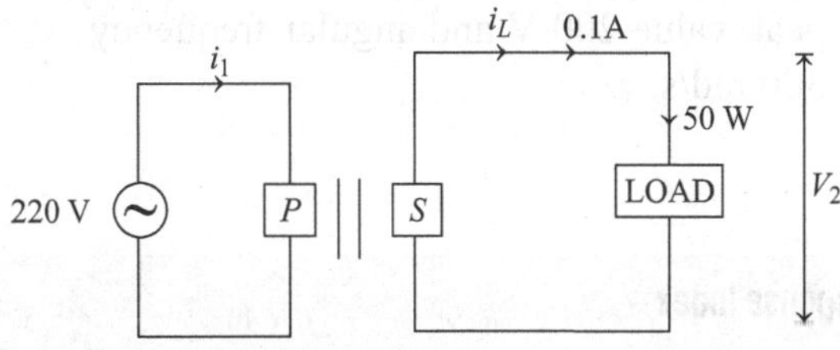

(a) auxilliary transformer
(b) step-down transformer
(c) step-up transformer
(d) auto transformer

46. A step-down transformer operates on a 2.5 kV line and supplies 80 A to a load. The ratio of the primary winding to the secondary winding is 20 : 1. Assuming 100 % efficiency, the output power is

(a) 200 kW (b) 100 kW
(c) 10 kW (d) None of these

47. The potential differences across the resistance, capacitance and inductance are 50 V, 20 V and 120 V respectively, in an L-C-R circuit. The power factor of this circuit is

(a) 0.8 (b) 1.0
(c) 0.4 (d) 0.6

48. As given in the figure, a series circuit connected across a 200 V, 60 Hz line consists of a capacitor of capacitive reactance 30 Ω, a non-inductive resistor of 44 Ω and a coil of inductive reactance 90 Ω and resistance 36 Ω. The power dissipated in the coil is

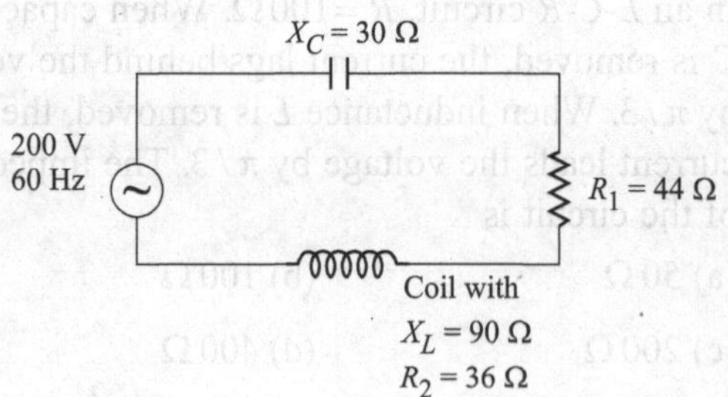

(a) 320 W
(b) 176 W
(c) 144 W
(d) 0

49. Kanha wants to calculate the current and power dissipated in an *L-C-R* series circuit. He connected $100\,\Omega$ resistance to an AC source of peak value 200 V and angular frequency 300 rad/s. When he removed the capacitance only, the current was found to be lagging behind the voltage by 60°. While on removing the inductance, he found the current leading the voltage by 60°. The value of peak current and the power dissipated obtained by him will be

(a) 2 A, 200 W (b) 4 A, 100 W
(c) 3 A, 120 W (d) None of thse

50. An *L-C-R* circuit has $L = 10\,\text{mH}$, $R = 3\,\Omega$ and $C = 1\,\mu\text{F}$ connected in series to a source of $15\cos\omega t$ V. The current amplitude and the average power dissipated per cycle at a frequency 10% lower than the resonant frequency will be respectively,

(a) 0.704 A, 0.744 W
(b) 0.704 A, 0.704 W
(c) 7.04 A, 7.44 W
(d) 70.4 A, 74.4 W

Response Index

01	ⓐ ⓑ ⓒ ⓓ	14	ⓐ ⓑ ⓒ ⓓ	27	ⓐ ⓑ ⓒ ⓓ	40	ⓐ ⓑ ⓒ ⓓ
02	ⓐ ⓑ ⓒ ⓓ	15	ⓐ ⓑ ⓒ ⓓ	28	ⓐ ⓑ ⓒ ⓓ	41	ⓐ ⓑ ⓒ ⓓ
03	ⓐ ⓑ ⓒ ⓓ	16	ⓐ ⓑ ⓒ ⓓ	29	ⓐ ⓑ ⓒ ⓓ	42	ⓐ ⓑ ⓒ ⓓ
04	ⓐ ⓑ ⓒ ⓓ	17	ⓐ ⓑ ⓒ ⓓ	30	ⓐ ⓑ ⓒ ⓓ	43	ⓐ ⓑ ⓒ ⓓ
05	ⓐ ⓑ ⓒ ⓓ	18	ⓐ ⓑ ⓒ ⓓ	31	ⓐ ⓑ ⓒ ⓓ	44	ⓐ ⓑ ⓒ ⓓ
06	ⓐ ⓑ ⓒ ⓓ	19	ⓐ ⓑ ⓒ ⓓ	32	ⓐ ⓑ ⓒ ⓓ	45	ⓐ ⓑ ⓒ ⓓ
07	ⓐ ⓑ ⓒ ⓓ	20	ⓐ ⓑ ⓒ ⓓ	33	ⓐ ⓑ ⓒ ⓓ	46	ⓐ ⓑ ⓒ ⓓ
08	ⓐ ⓑ ⓒ ⓓ	21	ⓐ ⓑ ⓒ ⓓ	34	ⓐ ⓑ ⓒ ⓓ	47	ⓐ ⓑ ⓒ ⓓ
09	ⓐ ⓑ ⓒ ⓓ	22	ⓐ ⓑ ⓒ ⓓ	35	ⓐ ⓑ ⓒ ⓓ	48	ⓐ ⓑ ⓒ ⓓ
10	ⓐ ⓑ ⓒ ⓓ	23	ⓐ ⓑ ⓒ ⓓ	36	ⓐ ⓑ ⓒ ⓓ	49	ⓐ ⓑ ⓒ ⓓ
11	ⓐ ⓑ ⓒ ⓓ	24	ⓐ ⓑ ⓒ ⓓ	37	ⓐ ⓑ ⓒ ⓓ	50	ⓐ ⓑ ⓒ ⓓ
12	ⓐ ⓑ ⓒ ⓓ	25	ⓐ ⓑ ⓒ ⓓ	38	ⓐ ⓑ ⓒ ⓓ		
13	ⓐ ⓑ ⓒ ⓓ	26	ⓐ ⓑ ⓒ ⓓ	39	ⓐ ⓑ ⓒ ⓓ		

Performance Scanner

> 90% Excellent !	You have mastered this chapter. The concepts of this chapter are at your fingertips. Move on to the next chapter and maintain this momentum.
76-90% Very Good !	You have a good command over this chapter. Revise the chapter again after a few days and enhance your performance.
60-75% Good !	You have a wide scope to learn more for this chapter. Revise this chapter again.
<60% Not Satisfactory!	You have a long way ahead of you to master this chapter. Revise it thoroughly.

For Online Chapter Test **Scan the QR Code**

For Online Unit Test **Scan the QR Code**

Test Booklet No. **3947159**

Test Booklet Code **CH9**

MEDACE
NEET (UG)
SELF ASSESSMENT KIT

Electromagnetic Waves

Topics Covered

Electromagnetic Waves and their Characteristics

Electromagnetic Spectrum and Applications of EM Waves

Important Instructions

- This Booklet Contains – Two Topic Tests and One Test on Complete Chapter.
- Each question carries 4 marks.
- For each correct response, the candidate will get 4 marks and for every incorrect response 1 mark will be additionally deducted from the total score.
- Use **Blue/Black** point pen only for filling the OMR.
- Rough work will be done in the space provided for this purpose within the test booklet only.

Name of the Candidate (In Capitals) ________________

____

Candidate's Signature ________

Invigilator's Signature ________

Facsimile signature stamp of center superintendent________

Do not open this Booklet until you start attempting the Test

Topical Follow Thru

Test 1

Syllabus

- Displacement Current
- Electromagnetic Waves and their Characteristics
- Transverse Nature of Electromagnetic Waves

For deeper insight **Scan the QR Code**

Important Instructions

- The test is of 30 minutes duration and contains 15 Multiple Choice Questions. (Four options with a single correct answer).
- Choose the correct option and fill the OMR given on the last page of this test accordingly.
- At some instances, you may find more than 1 option may be correct, in such circumstances you have to judge the most appropriate answer as per conditions given in the question.

1. Electromagnetic waves can be produced by

(a) an electron in rest position.

(b) an accelerating neutron.

(c) a proton moving in a non-uniform electric field.

(d) a wire carrying constant current.

2. Total current in a circuit is given by $i = i_c + i_d$. Here, i_c is conduction current and i_d is displacement current. The quantity which is zero inside a capacitor is

(a) conduction current

(b) displacement current

(c) direct current

(d) alternating current

3. Assertion (A) An electromagnetic wave is a self-sustaining oscillating wave.

Reason (R) An oscillating charge produces an electric field in space, which produces an oscillating magnetic field, which in turn, is a source of electric field and so on.

In the light of above statements, choose the most appropriate answer from the options given below.

(a) Both A and R are true and R is the correct explanation of A.

(b) Both A and R are true but R is not the correct explanation of A.

(c) A is true but R is false.

(d) A is false but R is true.

4. A parallel plate capacitor with plate area A and separation between the plates d, is charged by a constant current I. Consider a plane surface of area $2A/3$ parallel to the plates and between the plates. The displacement current through the area is

(a) $\frac{2I}{3}$

(b) $\frac{I}{2}$

(c) $\frac{I}{4}$

(d) $\frac{I}{8}$

5. Relative permittivity ε_r and relative permeability μ_r are 1.69 and 0.8, respectively. The velocity of light in that medium is
(a) 2.58×10^8 m/s
b) 3×10^8 m/s
(c) 0.86×10^8 m/s
(d) 1.5×10^8 m/s

6. Electric field associated with an electromagnetic wave is $\mathbf{E} = 9\sin(1.6 \times 10^3 x + 48 \times 10^{10} t)\,\hat{\mathbf{k}}$ V/m. The direction of propagation of electromagnetic wave and its frequency is
(a) $48 \times 10^8\,\hat{\mathbf{i}}$ Hz
(b) $7.64 \times 10^{10}\,(-\hat{\mathbf{i}})$ Hz
(c) $2.46 \times 10^8\,\hat{\mathbf{j}}$ Hz
(d) $1.6 \times 10^{10}\,(-\hat{\mathbf{i}})$ Hz

7. An electromagnetic wave is represented by $B_y = 4\times10^{-6}\sin(10^3\pi x - 2\times10^{11}\pi t)$ T. Then, speed of the wave is
(a) 1×10^8 m/s (b) 3×10^8 m/s
(c) 2×10^8 m/s (d) 1.5×10^8 m/s

8. The light of energy flux 50×10^4 W/m^2 falls on a perfectly reflecting surface at normal incidence. If the surface area is 30 cm^2, then the average force exerted on the surface is
(a) 2×10^{-5} N (b) 1×10^{-5} N
(c) 2.5×10^{-6} N (d) 1×10^{-6} N

9. An oscillating electromagnetic field is given by the following expression, $B_y = 2\times10^{-9}\sin(100\pi x - 2\times10^{11}\pi t)$T. The energy density of the wave is
(a) 4.77×10^{-4} W/m^2
(b) 2×10^{-3} W/m^2
(c) 5.6×10^{-3} W/m^2
(d) 7×10^{-3} W/m^2

10. Electric field of plane electromagnetic wave propagating through a non-magnetic medium is given by $E = 20\cos(2\times10^{10}t - 200x)$ V/m. The dielectric constant of the medium is equal to (Take, $\mu_r = 1$)
(a) 9
(b) 2
(c) 1/3
(d) 3

11. An instantaneous displacement current of 1 A in the space between the parallel plates of 1 μF capacitor can be established by changing the potential difference at the rate of
(a) 10^5 Vs^{-1}
(b) 10^6 Vs^{-1}
(c) 10^{-6} Vs^{-1}
(d) 10^7 Vs^{-1}

12. A large parallel plate capacitor, whose plates have an area of 1 m^2 and are separated from each other by 1 mm, is being charged at a rate of 25 Vs^{-1}.

If the dielectric between the plates has the dielectric constant 10, then the displacement current at this instant is
(a) 25 μA
(b) 11 μA
(c) 2.2 μA
(d) 1.1 μA

13. A parallel plate capacitor consists of two circular plates each of radius 2 cm, separated by a distance of 0.1 mm. If the potential difference across the plates is varying at the rate of 5×10^6 Vs^{-1}, then the value of displacement current is
(a) 0.228 mA
(b) 5.56 mA
(c) 0.556 mA
(d) 2.28 mA

14. The electromagnetic wave travelling along Z-axis is given as $E = E_0\cos(kz - \omega t)$. Choose the incorrect option from the following.
(a) The associated magnetic field is given as $\mathbf{B} = 1/c\,\hat{\mathbf{k}} \times \mathbf{E}$
(b) The electromagnetic field can be written in terms of the associated magnetic field as $\mathbf{E} = c\,(\mathbf{B} \times \hat{\mathbf{k}})$
(c) $\hat{\mathbf{k}} \cdot \mathbf{E} = 0, \hat{\mathbf{k}} \cdot \mathbf{B} = 0$
(d) $\hat{\mathbf{k}} \times \mathbf{E} = 0, \hat{\mathbf{k}} \times \mathbf{B} = 0$

15. The amplitude of the electric field in a parallel beam of plane electromagnetic waves of intensity $53.1\ Wm^{-2}$ is

(Permittivity of free space $= 8.85 \times 10^{-12}\ C^2N^{-1}m^{-2}$)

(a) $400\ NC^{-1}$

(b) $50\ NC^{-1}$

(c) $100\ NC^{-1}$

(d) $200\ NC^{-1}$

Response Index

01	a	b	c	d	10	a	b	c	d
02	a	b	c	d	11	a	b	c	d
03	a	b	c	d	12	a	b	c	d
04	a	b	c	d	13	a	b	c	d
05	a	b	c	d	14	a	b	c	d
06	a	b	c	d	15	a	b	c	d
07	a	b	c	d					
08	a	b	c	d					
09	a	b	c	d					

Performance Scanner

> 90% Excellent !	You have mastered these topics. The concepts of these topics are on your fingertips. Move on to the next chapter and maintain this momentum.
76-90% Very Good !	You have a good command over these topics. Revise these topics again after a few days and enhance your performance.
60-75% Good !	You have a wide scope to learn for these topics. Revise these topics again.
<60 Not Satisfactory!	You have a long way ahead of you to master these topics. Revise it thoroughly.

Test 2

Syllabus

- Electromagnetic Spectrum (Radio waves, Microwaves, Infrared, Visible, Ultraviolet, X-rays, Gamma rays)
- Applications of EM Waves

For deeper insight **Scan the QR Code**

Important Instructions

- The test is of 30 minutes duration and contains 15 Multiple Choice Questions. (Four options with a single correct answer).
- Choose the correct option and fill the OMR given on the last page of this test accordingly.
- At some instances, you may find more than 1 option may be correct, in such circumstances you have to judge the most appropriate answer as per conditions given in the question.

1. The waves used for TV communication system are

(a) γ-rays
(b) X-rays
(c) infrared rays
(d) radio waves

2. The secret writings on the ancient walls can be revealed by

(a) radio waves
(b) X-rays
(c) infrared rays
(d) γ-rays

3. The structure of molecules and arrangement of electrons in the external shells can be studied by

(a) visible light
(b) X-rays
(c) γ-rays
(d) radio waves

4. Which visible light has the shortest wavelength?

(a) Ultraviolet
(b) Green
(c) Yellow
(d) Orange

5. The frequency that can be used in RADAR and satellite communication is

(a) 4×10^{14} Hz
(b) 5×10^{17} Hz
(c) 3×10^{10} Hz
(d) 9×10^{2} Hz

6. Which of the following statements is incorrect about UV-rays?

(a) UV-rays cover wavelengths ranging from 4×10^{-7} m (400 nm) to 6×10^{-10} m (0.6 nm).
(b) UV radiation is produced by special lamps and very hot bodies.
(c) The sun is an important source of ultraviolet rays.
(d) The ozone layer in the atmosphere cannot absorb UV-rays.

7. Match the Column I with Column II and mark the correct option from the codes given below.

	Column I		Column II
A.	Electromagnetic wave used in communication satellite	1.	Ultraviolet
B.	Electromagnetic wave used to kill germs in water purifiers	2.	Infrared
C.	Electromagnetic wave used to detect leakage of oil in underground pipelines	3.	Microwave
D.	Electromagnetic wave used to improve visibility in runways during fog and mist conditon	4.	X-ray

Codes

	A	B	C	D
(a)	1	2	3	4
(b)	3	1	4	2
(c)	3	4	1	2
(d)	4	1	2	3

8. The ray used in radio therapy for the treatment of tumor and cancer is

(a) X-ray
(b) radio wave
(c) γ-ray
(d) UV-ray

9. Arrange the following electromagnetic radiation in the order of increasing energy

A : Blue light
B : Yellow light
C : X-ray
D : Radio wave

(a) C, A, B, D
(b) B, A, D, C
(c) D, B, A, C
(d) A, B, D, C

10. The rays used in cricket to measure the speed of ball are

(a) X-rays (b) radio waves
(c) γ-rays (d) infrared rays

11. Match Table I (electromagnetic wave type) with Table II (its association/application) and select the correct option from the codes given below.

	Table I		Table II
A.	Infrared waves	1.	To treat muscular strain
B.	Radio waves	2.	For broadcasting
C.	X-rays	3.	To detect fracture of bones
D.	Ultraviolet rays	4.	Absorbed by the ozone layer of the atmosphere

Codes

	A	B	C	D
(a)	4	3	2	1
(b)	1	2	4	3
(c)	3	2	1	4
(d)	1	2	3	4

12. Microwave oven can heat food items, if

(a) the frequency of microwave is equal to the resonant frequency of water molecules.
(b) the food items are placed at the centre of the microwave.
(c) the food items contain 90% water.
(d) food items are covered with an aluminium foil.

13. Choose the correct option relating speed of different parts of electromagnetic wave spectrum.

(a) $v_{\text{X-rays}} < v_{\text{microwaves}} < v_{\text{radio waves}} < v_{\text{visible}}$
(b) $v_{\text{visible}} > v_{\text{X-rays}} > v_{\text{radio waves}} > v_{\text{microwaves}}$
(c) $v_{\text{radio waves}} = v_{\text{microwaves}} = v_{\text{visible}} = v_{\text{X-rays}}$
(d) $v_{\text{visible}} < v_{\text{microwaves}} < v_{\text{radio waves}} < v_{\text{X-rays}}$

14. **Statement I** Microwave oven heats up a food item containing water most efficiently.
Statement II The frequency of the microwave matches the resonant frequency of water molecules.

In the light of above statements, choose the most appropriate answer from the options given below.

(a) Both Statement I and Statement II are correct.
(b) Both Statement I and Statement II are incorrect
(c) Statement I is correct but Statement II is incorrect.
(d) Statement II is correct but Statement I is incorrect.

15. The correct sequence of the increasing wavelength of the given radiation sources is

(a) radioactive source, X-ray tube, crystal oscillator, sodium vapour lamp

(b) radioactive source, X-ray tube, sodium vapour lamp, crystal oscillator

(c) X-ray tube, radioactive source, crystal oscillator, sodium vapour lamp

(d) X-ray tube, crystal oscillator, radioactive source, sodium vapour lamp

Response Index

01	a	b	c	d	10	a	b	c	d
02	a	b	c	d	11	a	b	c	d
03	a	b	c	d	12	a	b	c	d
04	a	b	c	d	13	a	b	c	d
05	a	b	c	d	14	a	b	c	d
06	a	b	c	d	15	a	b	c	d
07	a	b	c	d					
08	a	b	c	d					
09	a	b	c	d					

Performance Scanner

> 90% Excellent !	You have mastered these topics. The concepts of these topics are on your fingertips. Move on to the next test and maintain this momentum.
76-90% Very Good !	You have a good command over these topics. Revise these topics again after a few days and enhance your performance.
60-75% Good !	You have a wide scope to learn for these topics. Revise these topics again.
<60 Not Satisfactory!	You have a long way ahead of you to master these topics. Revise it thoroughly.

Chapter Break Thru

Syllabus	• Displacement Current • Electromagnetic Waves and their Characteristics • Transverse Nature of Electromagnetic Waves	• Electromagnetic Spectrum (Radio waves, Microwaves, Infrared, Visible, Ultraviolet, X-rays, Gamma rays) • Applications of EM Waves

Important Instructions

- The test is of 45 minutes duration and contains 30 Multiple-Choice Questions (Four options with a single correct answer).
- Choose the correct option and fill the OMR given on the last page of this test accordingly.
- At some instances, you may find more than 1 option may be correct, in such circumstances you have to judge the most appropriate answer as per conditions given in the question.

1. Displacement current between the two plates of the capacitor during charging or discharging, arises due to

(a) time rate of change of electric field.
(b) time rate of change of magnetic field.
(c) space rate of change of electric field.
(d) space rate of change of magnetic field.

2. Conducting plates of a parallel plate capacitor having plate area $10^{-2}\ m^2$ are separated by a short distance. If the displacement current between the plates is 15 A, then rate of change of electric field with respect to time between the capacitor plates is

(a) 1.69×10^{12} V/m
(b) 1.69×10^{13} V/m
(c) 1.69×10^{14} V/m
(d) 1.69×10^{15} V/m

3. A capacitor made of two circular plates each of radius 10 cm and separated by 4 cm is shown in the figure below. The capacitor is being charged by an external source. The charging current is constant and is equal to 0.2 A. The displacement current across the plates is

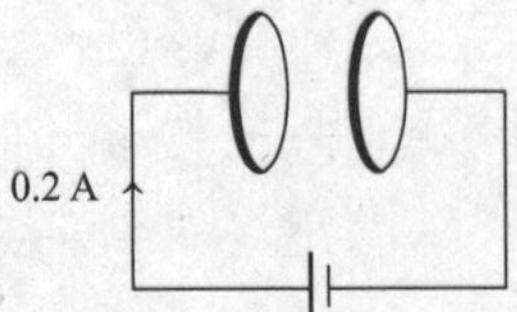

(a) 0
(b) 0.2 A
(c) 0.4 A
(d) 0.3 A

4. A capacitor is made of two square shaped conducting plates each of side 8 cm and separated by a distance of 2 cm. If the capacitor is being charged by an external source and the charging current equals to 0.5 A, then the rate of change of potential difference between the plates is

(a) 17.65×10^{10} V/s
(b) 17.65×10^{11} V/s
(c) 3.53×10^{11} V/s
(d) 3.53×10^{12} V/s

5. Which of these is not Maxwell's equation?

(a) $\oint \mathbf{E}\cdot d\mathbf{s} = \frac{q}{\varepsilon_0}$
(b) $\oint \mathbf{B}\cdot d\mathbf{s} = 0$
(c) $\oint \mathbf{E}\cdot d\mathbf{l} = -\frac{d\phi_B}{dt}$
(d) $\oint \mathbf{B}\cdot d\mathbf{l} = \mu_0 I$

6. The electric field of a plane electromagnetic wave propagating along the x-direction in vacuum is $\mathbf{E} = E_0\cos(\omega t - kx)\hat{\mathbf{j}}$. The magnetic field $\mathbf{B}$, at the moment $t = 0$ is

(a) $\mathbf{B} = \frac{E_0}{\sqrt{\mu_0\varepsilon_0}} \cos(kx)\,\hat{\mathbf{k}}$

(b) $\mathbf{B} = E_0\sqrt{\mu_0\varepsilon_0} \cos(kx)\,\hat{\mathbf{j}}$

(c) $\mathbf{B} = E_0\sqrt{\mu_0\varepsilon_0} \cos(kx)\,\hat{\mathbf{k}}$

(d) $\mathbf{B} = \frac{E_0}{\sqrt{\mu_0\varepsilon_0}} \cos(kx)\,\hat{\mathbf{j}}$

7. Consider an electromagnetic wave which is travelling in a medium with a speed of 6×10^7 m/s. The relative magnetic permeability of the medium is 5. The relative electrical permittivity of the medium will be

(a) 2.25
(b) 4
(c) 4.67
(d) 5

8. A charged particle oscillates about its mean position with a frequency of 2×10^{10} Hz. The produced electromagnetic waves

(a) will have frequency of 2×10^{16} Hz
(b) will have wavelength of 1.5 cm
(c) lie in the ultravoilet region
(d) will have frequency of 3 Hz

9. An electromagnetic wave going through vacuum is described by electric field $E = E_0 \sin(px + qt)$ and magnetic field $B = B_0 \sin(px + qt)$, then which of the following relation is true?

(a) $E_{rms}\,p = B_0 q$
(b) $qE_0 = pB_0$
(c) $pE_{rms} = qB_{rms}$
(d) $pE_0 = qB_{rms}$

10. The plane electromagnetic wave of frequency 6 MHz travels in free space along the y-direction. At a particular point in space and time, $\mathbf{E} = 8\,\hat{\mathbf{k}}$ V/m. The magnetic field $\mathbf{B}$ at that point will be

(a) $2\times10^{-8}(\hat{\mathbf{i}})$ T
(b) $2.33\times10^{-8}(-\hat{\mathbf{i}})$ T
(c) $2.33\times10^{-8}\,\hat{\mathbf{i}}$ T
(d) $3\times10^{-8}\,\hat{\mathbf{i}}$ T

11. The magnetic field in a plane EM wave is given by $B_x = 6\times10^{-8} \sin(2\times10^3 y - 3\times10^{10} t)$ T where, y is in metre and t is in second. The expression of the electric field for the given wave is

(a) $2\times10^{-8} \sin(2\times10^3 y - 3\times10^{10} t)$ V/m
(b) $2\times10^{-8} \sin(2\times10^3 y + 3\times10^{10} t)$ V/m
(c) $18 \sin(2\times10^3 y - 3\times10^{10} t)$ V/m
(d) $12.73 \sin(2\times10^3 y - 3\times10^{10} t)$ V/m

12. An electromagnetic wave enters from air in a non-magnetic material medium. The electric field in air is $E_1 = E_{01} \sin\left[\pi\nu\left(\frac{x}{c} - t\right)\right]$ and in medium $E_2 = E_{02} \sin[k(2x - ct)]$, where k and ν represent wave number and frequency in air respectively. The relative permittivity of the medium is

(a) 2
(b) 3
(c) 4
(d) 6

13. Travelling in x-direction, the equation of electric field component of a light beam is given as $E_y = 200 \sin\omega\left(t - \frac{x}{c}\right)$ V/m. A charge of 2 μC is constrained to move along the y-direction with speed 400 m/s. The maximum magnetic force on charge is

(a) 5.33×10^{-10} N
(b) 5.33×10^{-11} N
(c) 3.77×10^{-10} N
(d) 3.77×10^{-11} N

14. A linearly polarised EM wave given as $\mathbf{E} = \hat{\mathbf{k}}\ 40 \cos(kx - 6\times10^8 t)$ V/m is incident normally on a perfectly reflecting infinite wall at $x = a$. Assuming that the material of the wall is optically inactive, the reflected wave $\mathbf{E}_r$ is given as

(a) $\mathbf{E}_r = \hat{\mathbf{k}} 40 \sin(kx - 6\times10^8 t)$ V/m
(b) $\mathbf{E}_r = -\hat{\mathbf{k}}\ 40 \sin(kx - 6\times10^8 t)$ V/m
(c) $\mathbf{E}_r = \hat{\mathbf{k}}\ 40 \cos(kx + 6\times10^8 t)$ V/m
(d) $\mathbf{E}_r = -\hat{\mathbf{k}}\ 40 \cos(kx + 6\times10^8 t)$ V/m

15. **Assertion** (A) Microwaves are used in RADAR.

Reason (R) Because, microwaves have very small wavelength.

In the light of above statements, choose the most appropriate answer from the options given below.

(a) Both A and R are true and R is the correct explanation of A.

(b) Both A and R are true but R is not the correct explanation of A.

(c) A is true but R is false.

(d) A is false but R is true.

16. If an electromagnetic wave is travelling through a material medium, then its wavelength can never be equal to

(a) 0.5 m (b) 1.2 m

(c) 2 m (d) 8.5 m

17. An electromagnetic wave is travelling in positive x-direction, where amplitude of electric field is $E_0 = 80$ N/C and frequency is 30 MHz. The expression of magnetic field will be

(a) $2.67 \times 10^{-8} \sin \{6\pi \times 10^7 \text{(rad/s)}t - 0.4 (\text{cm}^{-1})x\}$ T

(b) $2.67 \times 10^{-7} \sin \{6\pi \times 10^7 \text{(rad/s)}t - 0.4 (\text{cm}^{-1})x\}$ T

(c) $2.67 \times 10^{-8} \sin \{6\pi \times 10^7 \text{(rad/s)}t - 0.6 (\text{m}^{-1})x\}$ T

(d) $2.67 \times 10^{-7} \sin \{6\pi \times 10^7 \text{(rad/s)}t - 0.6 (\text{m}^{-1})x\}$ T

18. An electromagnetic wave is travelling in a material medium whose oscillating electric field is described by the equation $E(x,t) = 0.1 \sin \pi (3 \times 10^4 x - 7.5 \times 10^{14} t)$ V/m, where x is in centimetre and t is in second. The refractive index of the medium is

(a) 1 (b) 1.2

(c) 1.25 (d) 1.33

19. The maximum value of electric field produced by the radiation coming from a 60 W bulb at a distance of 3 m is

(Take, efficiency of bulb 5% and is a point source)

(a) 3.16 V/m

(b) 4.46 V/m

(c) 2.23 V/m

(d) 6.30 V/m

20. The intensity of a plane electromagnetic wave travelling in space is 5.9×10^{-4} W/m^2. Then, rms value of component of electric field is

(a) 0.235 V/m

(b) 0.333 V/m

(c) 0.471 V/m

(d) 0.667 V/m

21. **Statement I** Both electric field and magnetic field components of electromagnetic wave vibrate parallel to the direction of propogation of electromagnetic wave.

Statement II Electromagnetic waves exert radiation pressure.

In the light of above statements, choose the most appropriate answer from the options given below.

(a) Both Statement I and Statement II are incorrect.

(b) Statement I is correct but Statement II is incorrect.

(c) Statement I is incorrect but Statement II is correct.

(d) Both Statement I and Statement II are correct.

22. An electromagnetic wave is represented by the electric field $\mathbf{E} = E_0 \hat{\mathbf{n}} \sin[\omega t + (6y - 8z)]$. Taking unit vectors in x, y and z-directions to be $\hat{\mathbf{i}}, \hat{\mathbf{j}}$ and $\hat{\mathbf{k}}$ respectively, the direction of propagation $\hat{\mathbf{s}}$ is

(a) $\hat{\mathbf{s}} = \frac{3\hat{\mathbf{i}} - 4\hat{\mathbf{j}}}{5}$ (b) $\hat{\mathbf{s}} = \frac{-4\hat{\mathbf{k}} + 3\hat{\mathbf{j}}}{5}$

(c) $\hat{\mathbf{s}} = \left(\frac{-3\hat{\mathbf{j}} + 4\hat{\mathbf{k}}}{5}\right)$ (d) $\hat{\mathbf{s}} = \frac{4\hat{\mathbf{j}} - 3\hat{\mathbf{k}}}{5}$

23. **Statement I** In a microwave oven, a magnetron produces radiations of nearly 3 GHz to heat food items.

Statement II Water molecules absorb microwaves and emit infrared radiations or heat waves.

In the light of above statements, choose the most appropriate answer from the options given below.

(a) Both Statement I and Statement II are correct.

(b) Both Statement I and Statement II are incorrect.

(c) Statement I is correct but Statement II is incorrect.

(d) Statement I is incorrect but Statement II is correct.

24. Match the columns.

	Column I		Column II
A.	$\mathbf{E} \times \mathbf{B}$	1.	Momentum
B.	E/B	2.	Mass
C.	$h\nu/c$	3.	Poynting vector
D.	$h\nu/c^2$	4.	Speed of electromagnetic wave

(a) A $\rightarrow$ 3, B $\rightarrow$ 4, C $\rightarrow$ 1, D $\rightarrow$ 2
(b) A $\rightarrow$ 1, B $\rightarrow$ 2, C $\rightarrow$ 3, D $\rightarrow$ 4
(c) A $\rightarrow$ 4, B $\rightarrow$ 1, C $\rightarrow$ 3, D $\rightarrow$ 2
(d) A $\rightarrow$ 1, B $\rightarrow$ 2, C $\rightarrow$ 4, D $\rightarrow$ 3

25. Electric field vector of a light beam is $E = 800 \sin\left(\omega t - \frac{x}{c}\right)$ V/m.

An electron is projected perpendicular to direction of propagation of light beam with speed of 3×10^7 m/s. What is the maximum force experienced by electron due to light beam?

(a) 1.8×10^{-16} N
(b) 1.8×10^{-17} N
(c) 1.8×10^{-19} N
(d) Zero

26. Faraday's law of electromagnetic induction in integral form is represented by

(a) $\oint \mathbf{B} \cdot d\mathbf{l} = \mu_0 \left(I + \varepsilon_0 \frac{d\phi_E}{dt} \right)$

(b) $\oint \mathbf{E} \cdot d\mathbf{l} = -\frac{d}{dt} \oint_S \mathbf{B} \cdot d\mathbf{S}$

(c) $\oint \mathbf{B} \cdot d\mathbf{l} = \mu_0 I$

(d) $\oint \mathbf{E} \cdot d\mathbf{S} = \frac{1}{\varepsilon_0} \oint_S \rho dS$

27. The electric field intensity produced by the radiation coming from a 100 W bulb at a distance of 3 m is E. The electric field intensity produced by the radiation coming from 55 W at the same distance is

(a) $\sqrt{\frac{11}{20}} \cdot E$

(b) $\sqrt{\frac{20}{11}} \cdot E$

(c) $\sqrt{\frac{11}{20}} \cdot 3E$

(d) $\sqrt{\frac{20}{11}} \cdot 33E$

28. The value of μ_r and ε_r for a transparent medium are 1.3 and 0.9, respectively. The speed of light in this medium is

(a) 1.66×10^8 m/s
(b) 2.77×10^8 m/s
(c) 2.02×10^8 m/s
(d) 1.92×10^8 m/s

29. The average wavelength of sodium light is 5893 Å. If it will fall perpendicular on a surface, then the momentum transferred to the surface will be

(a) 1.1×10^{-27} kg-m/s
(b) 2.3×10^{-16} kg-m/s
(c) 11 kg-m/s
(d) 9.7×10^{-27} kg-m/s

30. Equation of an electromagnetic wave travelling through air is $E = E_0 \sin(kx - \omega t)$.
As it undergoes refraction in water, change does not occur in
A. wave speed (v)
B. wave number (k)
C. angular frequency (ω)
D. phase (ϕ)
(a) Only D
(b) Only C
(c) Only B
(d) Both C and D

Response Index

01	a	b	c	d	11	a	b	c	d	21	a	b	c	d
02	a	b	c	d	12	a	b	c	d	22	a	b	c	d
03	a	b	c	d	13	a	b	c	d	23	a	b	c	d
04	a	b	c	d	14	a	b	c	d	24	a	b	c	d
05	a	b	c	d	15	a	b	c	d	25	a	b	c	d
06	a	b	c	d	16	a	b	c	d	26	a	b	c	d
07	a	b	c	d	17	a	b	c	d	27	a	b	c	d
08	a	b	c	d	18	a	b	c	d	28	a	b	c	d
09	a	b	c	d	19	a	b	c	d	29	a	b	c	d
10	a	b	c	d	20	a	b	c	d	30	a	b	c	d

Performance Scanner

> 90% Excellent !	You have mastered this chapter. The concepts of this chapter are on your fingertips. Move on to the next test and maintain this momentum.
76-90% Very Good !	You have a good command over this chapter. Revise this chapter again after a few days and enhance your performance.
60-75% Good !	You have a wide scope to learn for this chapter. Revise this topic again.
<60 Not Satisfactory!	You have a long way ahead of you to master this chapter. Revise it thoroughly.

For Online Chapter Test **Scan the QR Code**

For Online Unit Test **Scan the QR Code**

Space for Rough Work

Space for Rough Work

Space for Rough Work

Space for Rough Work

Test Booklet No. 3947160

Test Booklet Code CH10

MED ACE
NEET (UG)
SELF ASSESSMENT KIT

Ray Optics and Optical Instruments

Topics Covered

Reflection

Refraction, Lens and Prism

Optical Instruments

Important Instructions

- This Booklet Contains – Three Topic Tests and One Test on Complete Chapter.
- Each question carries 4 marks.
- For each correct response, the candidate will get 4 marks and for every incorrect response 1 mark will be additionally deducted from the total score.
- Use **Blue/Black** point pen only for filling the OMR.
- Rough work will be done in the space provided for this purpose within the test booklet only.

Name of the Candidate (In Capitals) ______________

Candidate's Signature ______________

Invigilator's Signature ______________

Facsimile signature stamp of center superintendent ______________

Do not open this Booklet until you start attempting the Test

Topical Follow Thru

Test 1

Syllabus
- Reflection of Light
- Spherical Mirrors
- Mirror Formula

For deeper insight **Scan the QR Code**

Important Instructions

- The test is of 30 minutes duration and contains 15 Multiple Choice Questions. (Four options with a single correct answer).
- Choose the correct option and fill the OMR given on the last page of Booklet accordingly.
- At some instances, you may find more than 1 option may be correct in such circumstances you have to judge the most appropriate answer as per the conditions given in the question.

1. A beam of light, from a source L is incident normally on a plane mirror fixed at a certain distance x from the source. The beam is reflected back as a spot on a scale placed just above the source L. When the mirror is rotated through a small angle θ, the spot of the light is found to move through a distance y on the scale. The angle θ is given by

(a) $\frac{y}{2x}$ (b) $\frac{y}{x}$ (c) $\frac{x}{2y}$ (d) $\frac{x}{y}$

2. Lower half of concave mirror's reflecting surface is covered with an opaque (non-reflective) material. The intensity of an image of an object placed in front of the mirror is

(a) one-third the original image
(b) half the original image
(c) same as the original image
(d) one-fourth the original image

3. A rod MN of length 2 cm lies along the principal axis of a concave mirror of focal length 20 cm. The end of the rod closer to pole is 40 cm away from it. The length of image is

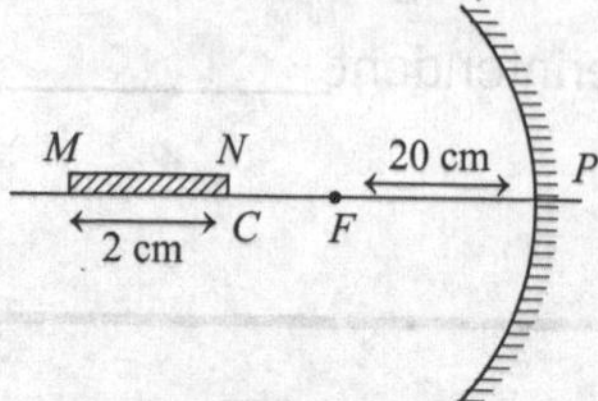

(a) 2.2 cm (b) 2 cm
(c) 4 cm (d) 4.2 cm

4. Assertion (A) The image formed by a concave mirror is certainly real if the object is virtual.

Reason (R) The image formed by a concave mirror is certainly virtual if the object is real.

In the light of above statements, choose the most appropriate answer from the options given below.

(a) Both A and R are true and R is the correct explanation of A.
(b) Both A and R are true but R is not the correct explanation of A.
(c) A is true but R is false.
(d) A is false but R is true.

5. If two mirrors are inclined at 20°, then total number of images formed of a body placed at the middle is

(a) 17 (b) 20 (c) 18 (d) 6

6. A convex mirror of focal length f forms an image which is $\frac{1}{m}$ times the object. The distance of object from the mirror is

(a) $\left(\frac{m+1}{m}\right)f$ (b) $(m+1)f$

(c) $-(m-1)f$ (d) $\left(\frac{m}{m+1}\right)f$

7. An object of height 5 cm is placed at a distance of 10 cm from a concave mirror of radius of curvature 10 cm. The size of image is

(a) 0.03 cm
(b) 0.15 cm
(c) 5 cm
(d) 2.5 cm

8. A soldier directs a laser beam on an enemy by reflecting the beam from a mirror. If the mirror is rotated by an angle θ, then by what angle it will reflected beam rotate?

(a) $\theta/2$ (b) θ
(c) 2θ (d) $\frac{3\theta}{2}$

9. A candle is placed before a thick plane mirror. When looked obliquely in the mirror, a number of images are seen from the surfaces of the plane mirror. Then,

(a) first image is brightest
(b) second image is brightest
(c) third image is brightest
(d) all images beyond second are brighter

10. A car is moving with at a constant speed of 60 km h^{-1} on a straight road. Looking at the rear view mirror, the driver finds that the car following him is at distance of 100 m and is approaching with a speed of 5 km h^{-1}. In order to keep track of the car in the rear, the driver begins to glance alternatively at the rear and side mirror of his car after every 2 s till the other car overtakes. If the two cars were maintaining their speeds, which of the following statement is correct?

(a) The speed of the car in the rear is 65 km h^{-1}.
(b) In the side mirror, the car in the rear would appear to approach with a speed of 5 km h^{-1} to the driver of the leading car.
(c) In the rear view mirror, the speed of the approaching car would appear to decrease as the distance between the cars decreases.
(d) In the side mirror, the speed of the approaching car would appear to increase as the distance between the cars decreases.

11. Find velocity of image when object and mirror both are moving towards each other with velocity 2 ms^{-1} and 3 ms^{-1}, respectively.

(a) 8 ms^{-1} (b) –8 ms^{-1}
(c) –5 ms^{-1} (d) 5 ms^{-1}

12. Two plane mirrors are inclined at 30° as shown in figure. A light ray is incident at angle 45°. Find total deviation produced by combination of mirror after two successive reflections.

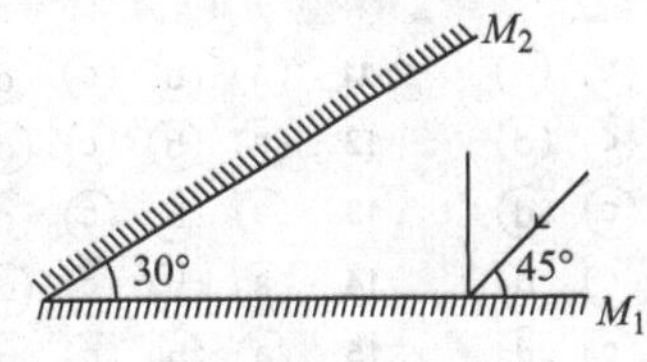

(a) 60°↑ (b) 58°↑
(c) 50°↑ (d) 68°↑

13. An object A is placed at a distance d in front of a plane mirror of length L. An observer O is walking with a uniform velocity v in front of mirror at a dsitance $2d$ as shown.

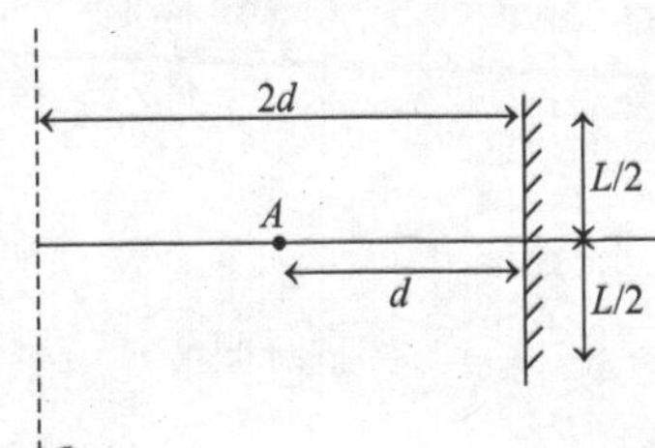

Time for which observer is able to see image of A in mirror is

(a) $\frac{3L}{v}$ (b) $\frac{3L}{2v}$
(c) $\frac{5L}{v}$ (d) $\frac{5L}{2v}$

14. An object of length 2.5 cm is placed at $1.5f$ from a concave mirror, where f is the focal length of the mirror. The length of the object is perpendicular to the principal axis. Find the length of the image. Is the image erected or inverted?

(a) 5 cm, inverted
(b) 4 cm, erected
(c) 6 cm, inverted
(d) 3 cm, erected

15. A concave mirror of focal length 10 cm and a convex mirror of focal length 15 cm are placed facing each other 40 cm apart. A point object is placed between the mirrors, on their common axis and 15 cm from the concave mirror. Find the position of the image produced by the successive reflections, first at concave mirror and then at convex mirror.

(a) –30cm, +6 cm

(b) –30 cm, +10 cm

(c) +30 cm, +15 cm

(d) +6 cm, +30 cm

Response Index

01	ⓐ	ⓑ	ⓒ	ⓓ	11	ⓐ	ⓑ	ⓒ	ⓓ
02	ⓐ	ⓑ	ⓒ	ⓓ	12	ⓐ	ⓑ	ⓒ	ⓓ
03	ⓐ	ⓑ	ⓒ	ⓓ	13	ⓐ	ⓑ	ⓒ	ⓓ
04	ⓐ	ⓑ	ⓒ	ⓓ	14	ⓐ	ⓑ	ⓒ	ⓓ
05	ⓐ	ⓑ	ⓒ	ⓓ	15	ⓐ	ⓑ	ⓒ	ⓓ
06	ⓐ	ⓑ	ⓒ	ⓓ					
07	ⓐ	ⓑ	ⓒ	ⓓ					
08	ⓐ	ⓑ	ⓒ	ⓓ					
09	ⓐ	ⓑ	ⓒ	ⓓ					
10	ⓐ	ⓑ	ⓒ	ⓓ					

Performance Scanner

> 90% Excellent !	You have mastered these topics. The concepts of these topics are at your fingertips. Move on to the next test and maintain this momentum.
76-90% Very Good !	You have a good command over these topics. Revise them again after a few days and enhance your performance.
60-75% Good !	You have a wide scope to learn for these topics. Revise them again.
<60% Not Satisfactory!	You have a long way ahead of you to master in these topics. Revise them thoroughly.

Test 2

Syllabus

- Refraction of Light at Plane and Spherical Surfaces
- Thin Lens Formula and Lens Maker's Formula
- Total Internal Reflection and its Applications
- Magnification
- Power of a Lens
- Combination of Thin Lenses in Contact
- Refraction of Light Through a Prism

For deeper insight **Scan the QR Code**

Important Instructions

- The test is of 45 minutes duration and Contains 25 Multiple Choice Questions (Four options with a single correct answer).
- Choose the correct option and fill the OMR given on the last page of Booklet accordingly.
- At some instances, you may find more than 1 option may be correct in such circumstances you have to judge the most appropriate answer as per the conditions given in the question.

1. The refractive index of a material with respect to water is $\frac{7}{2}$. If the velocity of light in water is 21×10^8 m/s, then the velocity of light in that medium is

(a) 6×10^7 m/s (b) 2×10^8 m/s

(c) 3×10^8 m/s (d) 3×10^7 m/s

2. A light ray is travelling from denser to rarer medium. The angle of incidence is 30° and reflected and refracted rays makes angle 90° with each other. The critical angle is

(a) $\sin^{-1}(1)$ (b) $\sin^{-1}\left(\frac{\sqrt{3}}{2}\right)$

(c) $\sin^{-1}(1/2)$ (d) $\sin^{-1}\left(\frac{1}{\sqrt{3}}\right)$

3. Light takes T_1 second to travel a distance y m in vacuum and takes T_2 second to travel $20y$ m in a medium. The critical angle for the medium is

(a) $\sin^{-1}\left(\frac{20T_2}{T_1}\right)$ (b) $\sin^{-1}\left(\frac{T_1}{20T_2}\right)$

(c) $\sin^{-1}\left(\frac{20T_1}{T_2}\right)$ (d) $\sin^{-1}\left(\frac{T_2}{20T_1}\right)$

4. An object is placed infront of a sphere of radius M and refractive index μ at a distance y from the first surface. The value of y for which the light after refraction from the first surface becomes parallel to the axis is

(a) $\frac{M}{(\mu-1)}$ (b) $\frac{M}{\mu+1}$

(c) $\frac{2M}{(1+\mu)}$ (d) $\frac{M\mu}{(\mu+1)}$

5. Two similar thin equi-convex lenses, of focal length f each are kept co-axially in contact with each other such that the focal length of the combination is F_2. When the space between the two lenses is filled with glycerine (which has the same refractive index μ as that of glass), then the equivalent focal length is F_1. The ratio of $F_1 : F_2$ will be

(a) 1 : 2 (b) 2 : 3

(c) 3 : 4 (d) 2 : 1

6. A lens having focal length f and aperture of diameter d forms an image of intensity I. Aperture of diameter $d/2$ in central region of lens is covered by a black paper. Focal length of lens and intensity of image now will be, respectively

(a) f and $\frac{I}{4}$ (b) $\frac{3f}{4}$ and $\frac{I}{2}$

(c) f and $\frac{3I}{4}$ (d) $\frac{f}{2}$ and $\frac{I}{2}$

7. A lens of refractive index K is put in a liquid of refractive index K'. If focal length of lens in air is F, then its focal length in liquid will be

(a) $\dfrac{-FK'(K-1)}{K'-K}$ (b) $\dfrac{-F(K'-K)}{K'(K-1)}$

(c) $\dfrac{-K'(K-1)}{F(K'-K)}$ (d) $\dfrac{FK'K}{K-K'}$

8. A convex lens of focal length 20 cm produces a virtual image 5 times the size of the object. Then, the distance of the object from the lens is

(a) 80 cm (b) 120 cm

(c) 16 cm (d) 24 cm

9. Plane surface of a plano-convex lens is silvered. Its radius of curvature is 6 cm and refractive index is 1.2. If parallel rays are incident on this lens, then they will converge at a distance of

(a) 15 cm (b) 3 cm

(c) 12 cm (d) 10 cm

10. The radius of curvature of a convex surface is 20 cm. It separates two media of refractive indices 2/3 and 1.50. An object is placed in the first medium at a distance of 10 cm from the surface. The distance of image from the surface is

(a) 60 cm in the first medium

(b) 60 cm in the second medium

(c) 20 cm in the first medium

(d) 20 cm in the second medium

11. If refractive index of medium is μ_m and refractive index of lens is μ_g such that $\mu_m > \mu_g$. If the lens is immersed in medium, then

(a) nature of lens remains same but focal length increases

(b) nature of lens changes and focal length remains same

(c) nature of lens remains same but focal length decreases

(d) nature of lens changes and focal length decreases

12. Distance of a screen from an object is 100 cm. The image on the screen is formed by a convex lens at two different locations, separated by 20 cm. The focal length of the lens is

(a) 24 cm (b) 20 cm

(c) 100 cm (d) 80 cm

13. Angle of minimum deviation of a prism is given by (D_m = angle of minimum deviation, A = angle of prism)

(a) $D_m = (\mu - 1)A$ (b) $D_m = \dfrac{\sin\left(\dfrac{A+\mu}{2}\right)}{\sin(A/2)}$

(c) $D_m = (\mu + 1)A$ (d) $D_m = \dfrac{\cos\left(\dfrac{A+\mu}{2}\right)}{\cos(A/2)}$

14. Refractive index of glass with respect to water is 9/8. Refractive index of glass with respect to air is 3/2. Find the refractive index of water with respect to air.

(a) 3/4 (b) 4/3

(c) 9/8 (d) 8/9

15. A hollow double concave lens is made of very thin transparent material. It can be filled with air or either of two liquids L_1 or L_2 having refractive indices n_{L_1} and n_{L_2}, respectively (such that $n_{L_1} > n_{L_2} > 1$). The lens will diverge a parallel beam of light, if it is filled with

(a) air and placed in air

(b) air and immersed in L_1

(c) L_1 and immersed in L_2

(d) L_2 and immersed in L_1

16. A plane surface separates two media of refractive indices, $\mu_1 = 2$ and $\mu_2 = 1$. A converging beam of light incident on the surface, whose converging point is 10 cm behind the surface as shown in the figure. The new converging point is

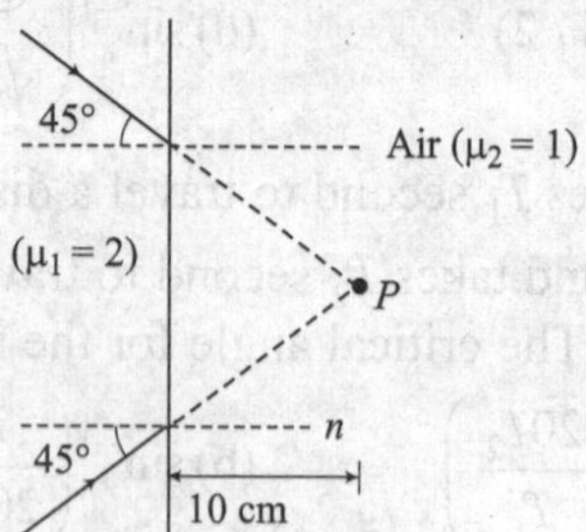

(a) before the surface at a distance 10 cm.

(b) behind the surface at a distance less than 10 cm.

(c) behind the surface at a distance greater than 10 cm.

(d) before the surface at a distance greater than 10 cm.

17. A solid glass sphere of radius 10 cm is placed in air. The refractive index of glass is $\mu = 2$. The beam converges

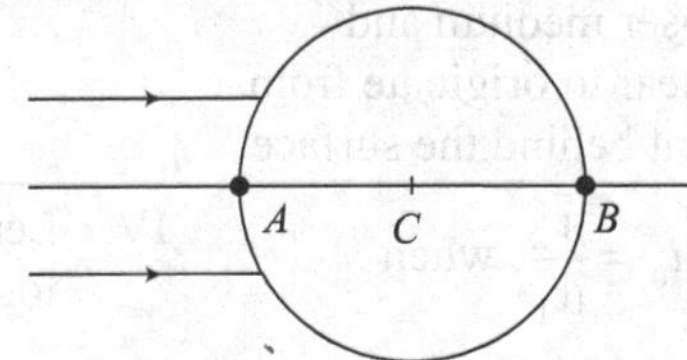

(a) between points C and B
(b) at point B
(c) beyond point B
(d) at point C

18. A fish in an aquarium, approaches the left wall at a rate of 3 ms^{-1} and observes a fly approaching it at 8 ms^{-1}. If the refractive index of water is 4/3, find the actual velocity of the fly.

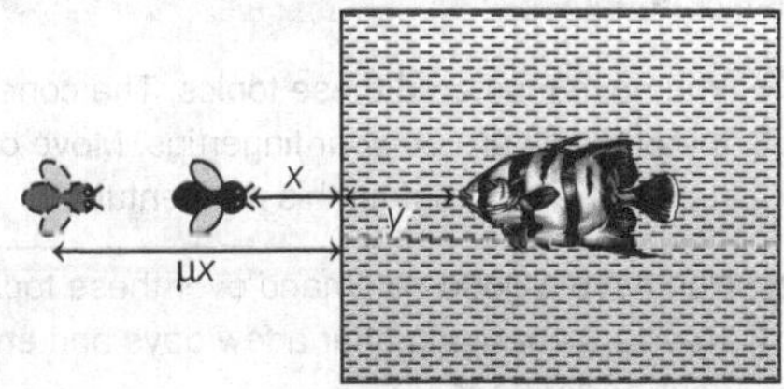

(a) 3.75 ms^{-1} (b) 2.75 ms^{-1}
(c) 0.75 ms^{-1} (d) 4.75 ms^{-1}

19. A convex refracting surface of radius of curvature 40 cm separates two media of refractive indices 4/3 and 2. An object is placed in the first medium $\left(\mu = \frac{4}{3}\right)$ at a distance of 2 m from the refracting surface. The position of image is

(a) 100 cm
(b) – 150 cm
(c) 200 cm
(d) – 80 cm

20. Two thin convex lens are kept in contact. If focal length of first lens is twice of second lens and their combined power is 10 D, then the focal length of both lenses are

(a) 5 cm, 10 cm
(b) 10 cm, 20 cm
(c) 2.5 cm, 5 cm
(d) 15 cm, 30 cm

21. A spherical surface of radius 20 cm separates two media of refractive indices $\mu_1 = \frac{4}{3}$ and $\mu_2 = \frac{3}{2}$. A linear object is placed at distance 80 cm from the refractive surface as shown in the figure. The magnification of the object is

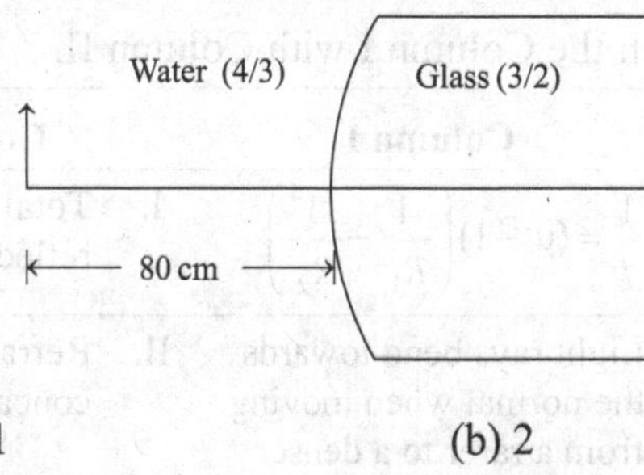

(a) 1 (b) 2
(c) 3 (d) 4

22. When ray propagates from denser medium to rarer medium, deviation in ray (δ) *versus* angle of incidence (i) graph is

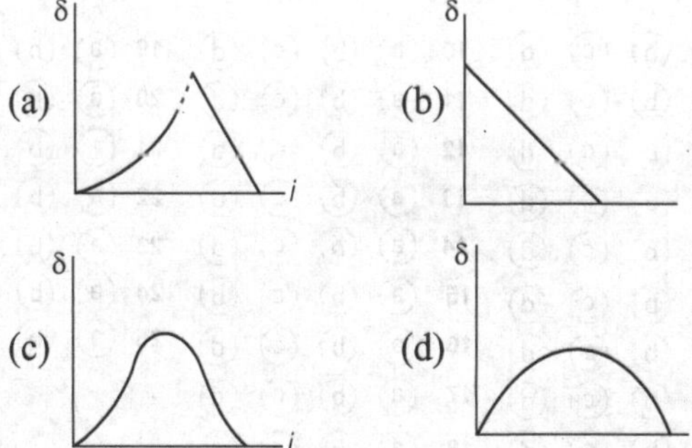

23. The radii of curvature of the faces of a double convex lens are 10 cm and 15 cm and its focal length is 12 cm.The refractive index of glass lens is

(a) 1.33
(b) 1.05
(c) 1.5
(d) 1.0

24. **Statement I** The formula $\frac{\mu_2}{v} - \frac{\mu_1}{u} = \frac{\mu_2 - \mu_1}{R}$ is applicable for only paraxial rays.

Statement II The laws of refraction is applicable for plane refractive surface as well as curved refractive surface.

Choose the most appropriate answer from the options given below

(a) Both Statement I and Statement II are correct.

(b) Both Statement I and Statement II are incorrect.

(c) Statement I is correct but Statement II is incorrect.

(d) Statement I is incorrect but Statement II is correct.

25. Match the Column I with Column II.

	Column I		Column II
A.	$\frac{1}{f} = (\mu - 1)\left(\frac{1}{R_1} - \frac{1}{R_2}\right)$	I.	Total internal reflection
B.	Light rays bend towards the normal when moving from a rarer to a denser medium.	II.	Refraction at a concave surface
C.	Light rays diverge when passing through rarer to denser medium and appear to originate from a point behind the surface	III.	Refraction at a convex surface
D.	$\sin i_c = \frac{\mu_2}{\mu_1}$, when $\mu_1 > \mu_2$	IV.	Lens maker's formula

Choose the correct answer from the options given below.

(a) A-(IV), B-(III), C-(II), D-(I)

(b) A-(III), B-(IV), C-(II) D-(I)

(c) A-(II), B-(III), C-(IV), D-(I)

(d) A-(I), B-(IV), C-(II), D, (III)

Response Index

01	a	b	c	d	10	a	b	c	d	19	a	b	c	d
02	a	b	c	d	11	a	b	c	d	20	a	b	c	d
03	a	b	c	d	12	a	b	c	d	21	a	b	c	d
04	a	b	c	d	13	a	b	c	d	22	a	b	c	d
05	a	b	c	d	14	a	b	c	d	23	a	b	c	d
06	a	b	c	d	15	a	b	c	d	24	a	b	c	d
07	a	b	c	d	16	a	b	c	d	25	a	b	c	d
08	a	b	c	d	17	a	b	c	d					
09	a	b	c	d	18	a	b	c	d					

Performance Scanner

> 90% Excellent !	You have mastered these topics. The concepts of these topics are on your fingertips. Move on to the next test and maintain this momentum.
76-90% Very Good !	You have a good command over these topics. Revise them again after a few days and enhance your performance.
60-75% Good !	You have a wide scope to learn for these topics. Revise them again.
<60% Not Satisfactory!	You have a long way ahead of you to master in these topics. Revise them thoroughly.

Test 3

Syllabus
- Microscope and Astronomical Telescope (Reflecting and Refracting) and their Magnifying Powers.

For deeper insight **Scan the QR Code**

Important Instructions
- The test is of 30 minutes Duration and Contains 15 Multiple Choice Question (Four options with a single correct answer).
- Choose the correct option and fill the OMR given on the last page of Booklet accordingly.
- At some instances, you may find more than 1 option may be correct in such circumstances you have to judge the most appropriate answer as per the conditions given in the question.

1. Magnification of a compound microscope is 10. To get overall magnification of 100 when image is formed at 25 cm from the eye, the focal length of the eye lens should be

(a) $\frac{25}{9}$ cm (b) 25 cm
(c) 10 cm (d) 100 cm

2. In compound microscope, magnifying power is 95 and the distance of object from objective lens is $\frac{1}{3.8}$ cm. The focal length of objective lens is $\frac{1}{4}$ cm. What is the magnification of eyepiece?

(a) 5 (b) 10
(c) 100 (d) 200

3. The focal lengths of objective and eyepiece of a microscope are 2 cm and 8 cm. If least distance of distinct vision is 20 cm and object distance is 3 cm from the objective lens, then the magnifying power of the microscope will be

(a) 16 (b) 40
(c) 15 (d) 7

4. The diameter of the moon is 3.5×10^3 km and its distance from the earth is 3.8×10^5 km. It is seen by a telescope having the focal lengths of the objective and the eyepiece as 4 m and 10 cm, respectively. The diameter of the image of the moon will be approximately

(a) 2° (b) 20°
(c) 40° (d) 50°

5. Focal length of objective of a compound microscope is $f_0 = 1.0$ cm, and focal length of eyepiece is 2.0 cm. If tube length is 20 cm, then the magnification is

(a) 250 (b) 150
(c) 200 (d) 100

6. If F_1 and F_2 are focal lengths of objective and eyepiece respectively, of the telescope. The angular magnification of the given telescope is

(a) $\frac{F_2}{F_1}$ (b) $\frac{F_1F_2}{F_1+F_2}$
(c) $\frac{F_1}{F_2}$ (d) $\frac{F_1+F_2}{F_1F_2}$

7. An astronomical telescope has a converging eyepiece of focal length 5 cm and objective of focal length 80 cm. When the final image is formed at the least distance of distinct vision 25 cm, the separation between the two lenses is

(a) 75.0 cm (b) 80.0 cm
(c) 84.2 cm (d) 85.0 cm

8. If we need a magnification of 375 from a compound microscope of tube length 150 mm and an objective of focal length 5 mm, the focal length of the eyepiece should be close to

(a) 22 mm (b) 2 mm
(c) 12 mm (d) 33 mm

9. The magnifying power of a telescope is 9. When it is adjusted for parallel rays, the distance between the objective and the eyepiece is found to be 20 cm. The focal lengths of the lenses are

(a) 18 cm, 2 cm
(b) 11 cm, 9 cm
(c) 10 cm, 10 cm
(d) 15 cm, 5 cm

10. The magnifying power of a telescope with tube length 60 cm is 5. What is the focal length of its eyepiece?
(a) 10 cm (b) 20 cm
(c) 30 cm (d) 40 cm

11. The focal lengths of objective and eye lens of an astronomical telescope are 2 m and 5 cm, respectively. Final image is formed at least distance of distinct vision in case I and at infinity in case II, then magnifying powers in two cases will be
(a) $-48, -40$ (b) $-40, 48$
(c) $-40, +48$ (d) $-48, +40$

12. A simple microscope consists of a concave lens of power $-10D$ and a convex lens of power $+20D$ in contact. If the image is formed at infinity, then the magnifying power when $D = 25$ cm is
(a) 2.5 (b) 3.5
(c) 2.0 (d) 3.0

13. A telescope has an objective of focal length 50 cm and an eyepiece of focal length 5 cm. The least distance of distinct vision is 25 cm. The telescope is focussed for distinct vision on a scale 200 cm away. The separation between the objective and eyepiece is
(a) 74 cm (b) 75 cm
(c) 60 cm (d) 71 cm

14. The focal lengths of the objective and the eyepiece of a microscope are 4 mm and 25 mm, respectively. If the final image is formed at infinity and the length of the tube is 16 cm, then the magnifying power of microscope will be
(a) -337.5 (b) -3.75
(c) 3.375 (d) 33.75

15. A planet is observed by an astronomical refracting telescope having an objective of focal length 16 m and an eyepiece of focal length 2 cm, then
(a) the distance between the objective and the eyepiece is 16.02 m
(b) the angular magnification of the planet is -800
(c) the image of the planet is inverted
(d) All of the above

Response Index

01	(a)	(b)	(c)	(d)	11	(a)	(b)	(c)	(d)
02	(a)	(b)	(c)	(d)	12	(a)	(b)	(c)	(d)
03	(a)	(b)	(c)	(d)	13	(a)	(b)	(c)	(d)
04	(a)	(b)	(c)	(d)	14	(a)	(b)	(c)	(d)
05	(a)	(b)	(c)	(d)	15	(a)	(b)	(c)	(d)
06	(a)	(b)	(c)	(d)					
07	(a)	(b)	(c)	(d)					
08	(a)	(b)	(c)	(d)					
09	(a)	(b)	(c)	(d)					
10	(a)	(b)	(c)	(d)					

Performance Scanner

> 90% Excellent !	You have mastered these topics. The concepts of these topics are on your fingertips. Move on to the next test and maintain this momentum.
76-90% Very Good !	You have a good command over these topics. Revise them again after a few days and enhance your performance.
60-75% Good !	You have a wide scope to learn for these topics. Revise them again.
<60% Not Satisfactory!	You have a long way ahead of you to master in these topics. Revise them thoroughly.

Chapter Break Thru

Syllabus	• Reflection of Light • Spherical Mirrors • Mirror Formula	• Refraction of Light at Plane and Spherical Surfaces • Thin Lens Formula and Lens Maker's Formula • Total Internal Reflection and its Applications • Magnification • Power of a Lens • Combination of Thin Lenses in Contact • Refraction of Light through a Prism	• Microscope and Astronomical Telescope (Reflecting and Refracting) and their Magnifying Powers.

Important Instructions

- The test is of 1 hour duration and contains 50 Multiple Choice Questions (Four options with a single correct answer).
- Choose the correct option and fill the OMR given on the last page of this test accordingly.
- At some instances, you may find more than 1 option may be correct, in such circumstances you have to judge the most appropriate answer as per conditions given in the question.

1. **Statement I** A small angled prism is not able to produce a clear spectrum.

Statement II Angular dispersion produced by a prism depends on refractive indices of different colours.

In the light of the above statements, choose the most appropriate answer from the options given below.

(a) Both Statement I and Statement II are correct.

(b) Statement I is correct but Statement II is incorrect.

(c) Statement I is incorrect but Statement II is correct.

(d) Both Statement I and Statement II are incorrect.

2. If the speed of light in vacuum is c, then the velocity of light in a medium of refractive index 2 is

(a) $2 \times c$ (b) c

(c) $\frac{c}{2}$ (d) $\frac{3c}{2}$

3. A boy is trying to start a fire by focusing sunlight on a piece of paper using an equiconvex lens of focal length 20 cm. The diameter of the sun is 1.39×10^9 m and its mean distance from the earth is 1.5×10^{11} m. What is the diameter of the sun's image on the paper?

(a) 9.2×10^{-4} m (b) 6.5×10^{-4} m

(c) 1.8×10^{-3} m (d) 12.4×10^{-4} m

4. A biconvex lens has a radius of curvature of magnitude 20 cm and the refractive index of the lens is 1.5. Which one of the following options describes best image formed of an object of height 6 cm placed 30 cm from the lens?

(a) Virtual, upright, height = 3 cm

(b) Real, inverted, height = 12 cm

(c) Real, upright, height = 12 cm

(d) Virtual, upright, height = 6 cm

5. A thin prism of angle 20° made of glass of refractive index $\mu_1 = 1.5$ is combined with another prism of glass of refractive index $\mu_2 = 1.40$. The combination of the prism produces dispersion without deviation. The angle of the second prism should be

(a) 7° (b) 10° (c) 12° (d) 25°

6. A plano-convex lens is placed on a plano-concave lens, so that both fits exactly. Plane surfaces of both lenses are parallel to each other. If lenses are made of different materials of refractive indices μ_1 and μ_2 and R is the radius of curvature of the curved surface of the lenses, then the focal length of the combination is

(a) $\frac{R}{2(\mu_1 + \mu_2)}$ (b) $\frac{R}{2(\mu_1 - \mu_2)}$

(c) $\frac{R}{(\mu_1 - \mu_2)}$ (d) $\frac{R}{(\mu_2 + \mu_1)}$

7. A microscope is focused on a mark on a piece of paper and then a slab of glass of thickness 6 cm and refractive index 2 is placed over the mark. How should the microscope be moved to get the mark in focus again?
(a) 3 cm downward
(b) 4.5 cm downward
(c) 1 cm downward
(d) 3 cm upward

8. A ray of light travelling in glass $\left(\mu=\frac{3}{2}\right)$ is incident on a horizontal glass-air surface at the critical angle θ_C. If thin layer of water $\left(\mu=\frac{4}{3}\right)$ is now poured on the glass-air surface, then angle at which the ray emerges into air at the water-air surface is
(a) 60° (b) 45° (c) 90° (d) 180°

9. A person who can see things most clearly at a distance of 10 cm requires spectacles to enable to him to see clearly things at a distance of 20 cm. What should be the focal length of the spectacles ?
(a) 20 cm (Concave)
(b) 20 cm (Convex)
(c) 10 cm (Concave)
(d) 15 (Convex)

10. A short linear object of length b lies along the axis of a concave mirror of focal length f at a distance u from the pole of the mirror. The size of the image is approximately equal to
(a) $b\left(\frac{u-f}{f}\right)^{1/2}$
(b) $b\left(\frac{f}{u-f}\right)^{1/2}$
(c) $b\left(\frac{u-f}{f}\right)$
(d) $b\left(\frac{f}{u-f}\right)^{2}$

11. The angle of incidence for a ray of light at a refracting surface of a prism is 45°. The angle of prism is 60°. If the ray suffers minimum deviation through the prism, the angle of minimum deviation and refractive index of the material of the prism respectively, are
(a) 45°, $\frac{1}{\sqrt{3}}$ (b) 30°, $\sqrt{2}$
(c) 45°, $\sqrt{3}$ (d) 30°, $\frac{1}{\sqrt{3}}$

12. A person can see objects clearly only when they lie between 100 cm and 400 cm from his eyes. In order to increase the maximum distance of distinct vision to infinity, the type and power of the correcting lens, the person has to use will be
(a) concave, – 1.5 D
(b) convex, + 0.15 D
(c) convex, + 2.25 D
(d) concave, – 0.25 D

13. Consider the following diagram.

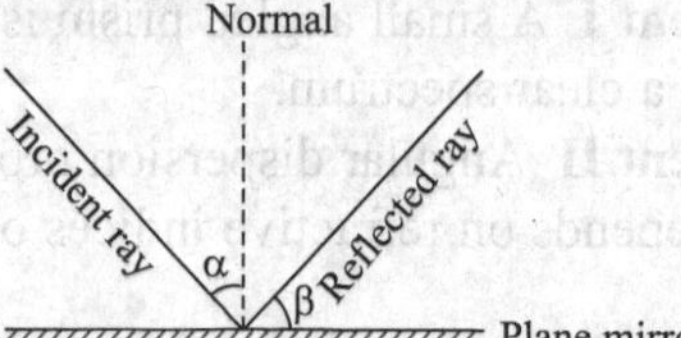

Angle of deviation of the incident ray is
(a) α (b) $\pi/2-\alpha$
(c) $\pi-2\alpha$ (d) $2\pi-\alpha$

14. A microscope is focused on a coin lying at the bottom of a beaker. The microscope is now raised up by 2 cm. To what depth should the water be poured into the beaker, so that coin is again in focus ? (Refractive index of water is 4/3)
(a) 1 cm (b) 4/3 cm (c) 8 cm (d) 4 cm

15. The difference between angle of minimum deviation of violet and red rays in the spectrum of white light from a prism is 3°. If angle of minimum deviation of mean ray is 48°, then the dispersive power of the material is
(a) 16 (b) 8
(c) 0.0215 (d) 0.0625

16. Choose the correct option for the following lens.

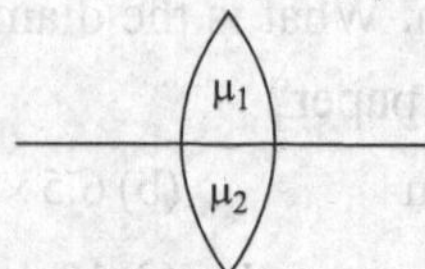

(a) Continuous image is formed between focal points of upper and lower lens.
(b) One image is formed.
(c) Two images are formed.
(d) No image will be formed.

17. The focal lengths of the object and eyepiece of a telescope are 40 cm and 5 cm, respectively. The magnifying power P for normal adjustment is
(a) 8 (b) 200 (c) 4 (d) 100

18. A telescope is made up of two thin lenses of focal length 0.3 m and 3 cm, respectively. When it is focused on moon, it subtends 0.5° angle at the objective. The angle subtended at the eye by the final image is
(a) 2° (b) 5° (c) 4° (d) 0.5°

19. The power of biconvex lens is 25 D and the radius of curvature of each surface is 4 cm. The refractive index of the lens is
(a) $\frac{3}{2}$ (b) $\frac{7}{4}$
(c) $\frac{5}{2}$ (d) $\frac{9}{4}$

20. A beaker contains water (refractive index n_1) up to height h_1 and oil (of refractive index n_2) up to height h_2. The apparent shift in the position of the bottom as viewed from above is
(a) $\left(1+\frac{1}{n_1}\right)h_1+\left(1-\frac{1}{n_2}\right)h_2$
(b) $\left(1-\frac{1}{n_1}\right)h_1+\left(1-\frac{1}{n_2}\right)h_2$
(c) $\left(1+\frac{1}{n_1}\right)h_1+\left(1+\frac{1}{n_2}\right)h_2$
(d) $\left(1-\frac{1}{n_1}\right)h_1+\left(1+\frac{1}{n_2}\right)h_2$

21. For the angle of minimum deviation of a prism to be equal to its prism angle, the prism must be made of material whose refractive index
(a) lies between $\sqrt{2}$ and 1
(b) lies between 2 and $\sqrt{2}$
(c) is less than 1
(d) is greater than 2

22. An object of length 1 cm lies along the axis of a concave mirror of focal length 4 cm at a distance 6 cm from the pole of the mirror. The size of the image is approximately equal to
(a) $\frac{1}{\sqrt{2}}$ cm (b) $\frac{1}{4}$ cm
(c) $\sqrt{2}$ cm (d) 4 cm

23. An object viewed from a near point distance of 30 cm, using a microscopic lens with magnification 7, gives an unresolved image. A resolved image is observed at infinite distance with a total magnification of double the earlier using an eyepiece along with the given lens and a tube of length 0.7 m, if the focal length of the eyepiece is equal to
(a) 30 cm (b) 50 cm
(c) 60 cm (d) 80 cm

24. The light rays from an object have been reflected towards an observer from a standard flat mirror, the image observed by the observer are
A. real
B. erect
C. smaller in size than object
D. laterally inverted
Choose the most appropriate answer from the options given below.
(a) B and C only
(b) B and D only
(b) A, C and D only
(c) A and D only

25. A layer of ice ($n = 4/3$) lies on a glass plate ($n = 3/2$). A ray of light makes an angle of incidence 60° on the surface of ice as shown in the figure below.

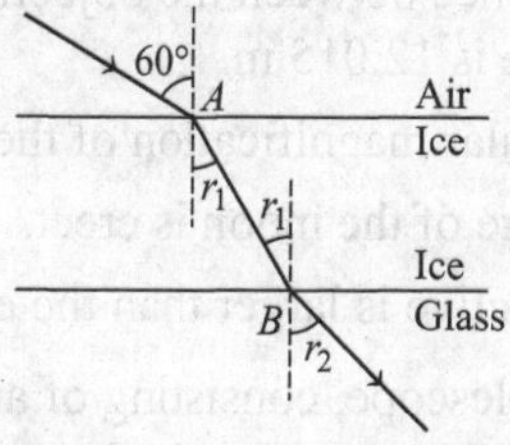

The value of $\sin r_2$ is
(a) $\frac{1}{\sqrt{3}}$ (b) $\frac{3\sqrt{3}}{8}$ (c) $\frac{8}{9}$ (d) $\frac{1}{\sqrt{2}}$

26. A converging beam of light is incident on a concave lens of focal length 40 cm. In the absence of lens, the beam converges at a point 20 cm behind the lens. After refraction, the beam

(a) converges to 10 cm behind the lens
(b) diverges to 20 cm behind the lens
(c) behind the lens
(d) converges to 40 cm behind the lens

27. A small air bubble is inside a glass cube of side 12 cm. When looking the top face, the bubble appears to be at a distance of 3 cm. However, when it is seen from the opposite face, it appears to be at a distance of 5 cm. The bubble distance from the top face of cube and refractive index of the glass, respectively are

(a) 7.5 cm, 1.4 (b) 7.5 cm, 1.5
(c) 4.5 cm, 1.4 (d) 4.5 cm, 1.5

28. A concave mirror of radius 15 cm is kept on a horizontal surface. A transparent liquid is poured in it upto a height of 3 cm. When the distance of object from the surface of liquid is 9 cm, it is seen that image of object is formed on itself, then refractive index of liquid is

(a) 1.2 (b) 1.33
(c) 1.5 (d) 1.6

29. For a convex lens , radius of curvature is 30 cm and refractive index of medium is 1.5, then focal length of the lens is

(a) – 30 cm (b) 30 cm
(c) 60 cm (d) – 60 cm

30. Moon is observed by an astronomical refracting telescope having an objective of focal length 12m and an eyepiece of focal length of 1.5 cm. The incorrect statement is

(a) the distance between the objective and the eyepiece is 12.015 m.
(b) the angular magnification of the moon is 800.
(c) the image of the moon is erect.
(d) the objective is larger than the eyepiece.

31. A simple telescope, consisting of an objective of focal length 50 cm and a single eyepiece of focal length 4 cm is focused on a distant object in such a way that parallel rays comes out from the eyepiece. If the object subtends an angle 2° at the objective, then angular width of the images is

(a) 8° (b) 25°
(c) $\frac{4°}{25}$ (d) 50°

32. In a compound microscope, the focal length of the objective and the eyepiece are 4 cm and 5 cm, respectively. The distance between the objective and eyepiece is 20 cm. The final image formed by the eyepiece is at infinity. The distances of the object and the image produced by the objective measured from the objective lens, respectively are

(a) 5.33 cm, 16 cm (b) 5.33 cm, 20 cm
(c) 5 cm, 16 cm (d) 5 cm, 20 cm

33. Match the Column I with Column II.

Column I	Column II
A. Rays through centre of curvature	I. reflected parallel rays to principal axis in mirror
B. Rays through focus	II. converges at principal focus
C. Rays from infinite distance	III. emerge through principal focus
D. Refracted rays to infinity	IV. retrace in mirrors

Choose the correct answer from the given options.

(a) A - IV, B - I, C - II, D- III
(b) A - III, B - IV, C - I, D- II
(c) A - II, B - I, C - IV, D- III
(d) A - IV, B - II, C - I, D- III

34. There are four spherical lenses of focal lengths +10 cm, +20 cm, +140 cm and +200 cm which are available for making an astronomical telescope. If someone wants to produce largest magnification, then focal length of objective and eyepiece are, respectively

(a) +200 cm, +10 cm
(b) +200 cm, +15 cm
(c) +20 cm, +140 cm
(d) +140 cm, +20 cm

35. Radius of curvature of the following lens is $R = 30$ cm and refractive index of the medium is $\mu = 1.5$. The focal length is

(a) – 30 cm (b) 60 cm
(c) – 60 cm (d) 30 cm

36. For a prism of refractive index 1.732, the angle of minimum deviation is equal to the angle of the prism. The angle of the prism is

(a) 80° (b) 70°
(c) 60° (d) 50°

37. **Assertion** (A) The images formed by total internal reflections are much brighter than those formed by mirrors or lenses.

Reason (R) There is no loss of intensity in total internal reflection.

(a) Both A and R are true and R is the correct explanation of A.
(b) Both A and R are true but R is not the correct explanation of A.
(c) A is true but R is false.
(d) A is false but R is true.

38. The sun makes 0.5° angle on earth surface. Its image is made by convex lens of 50 cm focal length. The diameter of the image will be

(a) 5 mm (b) 4.36 mm
(c) 7 mm (d) 43.6 mm

39. The chromatic aberration in lenses is due to

(a) dissimilarity of main axis of rays
(b) dissimilarity of radii of curvature
(c) variation of focal length of lenses with wavelength
(d) None of the above

40. The apparent depth of water in cylindrical water tank of diameter $4R$ cm is reducing at the rate $2x$ cm/min when water is being drained out at a constant rate. The amount of water drained in cc per minute is (n_1 = refractive index of air, n_2 = refractive index of water)

(a) $8x\pi R^2 n_1 / n_2$ (b) $8x\pi R^2 n_2 / n_1$
(c) $2\pi R n_1 / n_2$ (d) $4\pi R^2 x$

41. An optical fibre consists of core of μ_1 surrounded by a cladding of $\mu_2 < \mu_1$. A beam of light enters from air at an angle β with axis of fibre. The highest β for which ray can be travelled through fibre is

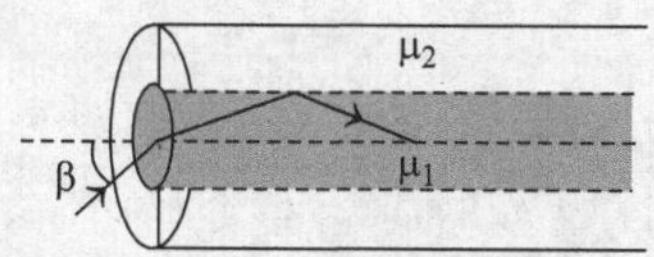

(a) $\cos^{-1}\sqrt{\mu_2^2 - \mu_1^2}$
(b) $\sin^{-1}\sqrt{\mu_1^2 - \mu_2^2}$
(c) $\tan^{-1}\sqrt{\mu_1^2 - \mu_2^2}$
(d) $\sec^{-1}\sqrt{\mu_1^2 - \mu_2^2}$

42. **Statement I** In compound microscope objective lens forms a real, inverted, magnified image of the object.

Statement II Eyepiece lens, produces a final image which is enlarged and virtual.

In the light of above statements, choose the most appropriate answer from the options given below.

(a) Both Statement I and Statement II are correct.
(b) Statement I is correct but Statement II is incorrect.
(c) Statement II is correct but Statement I is incorrect.
(d) Both Statement I and Statement II are incorrect.

43. In a compound microscope, the focal length of the objective and the eye lens are 2.5 cm and 10 cm, respectively. If an object is placed at 3.75 cm before the objective and image is formed at the least distance of distinct vision, then the distance between two lenses will be (i.e. length of the microscopic tube)

(a) 11.67 cm (b) 12.67 cm
(c) 14.64 cm (d) 12.00 cm

44. The plot between magnification of real image and the distance of concave mirror from the focus is

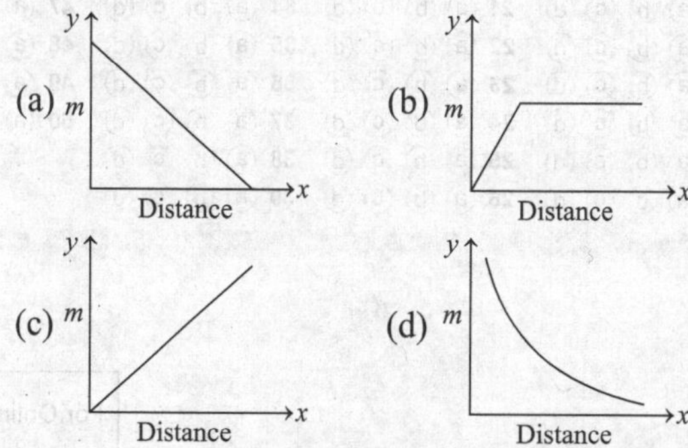

45. A pole is vertically submerged in a swimming pool, such that it gives a length of shadow 2.15 m within water when sunlight is incident at an angle of 30° with the surface of water. If swimming

pool is filled to a height of 1.5 m, then the height of the pole above the water surface (in cm) is ($n_w = 4/3$)

(a) 20 (b) 30
(c) 50 (d) 60

46. A convex lens of focal length 0.25 m and a concave lens of focal length 0.1 m are 0.1 m apart. A parallel beam of light is incident in the convex lens. The beam emerging after refraction from both lenses is

(a) parallel to principle axis
(b) convergent
(c) divergent
(d) None of the above

47. The focal length of objective and eye piece of a microscope are 2 cm and 10 cm, respectively. If the magnifying power for relaxed eye is 50, then length of the tube is

(a) 6 cm (b) 42 cm
(c) 52 cm (d) 15 cm

48. A ray of light undergoes deviation of 30° when incident on an equilateral prism of refractive index $\sqrt{2}$. The angle made by the ray inside the prism with the base of the prism is

(a) zero (b) 30°
(c) 60° (d) 90°

49. A concave spherical surface of radius of curvature 50 cm separate two media of refractive indices 1.2 and 2. An object is placed at a distance of 20 cm from the surface in medium 1. Position of the image from the object is (medium 1 is one the left side)

(a) 6.3 cm right to the object
(b) 56.3 cm left to the object
(c) 6.3 cm left to object
(d) 56.3 cm right to the object

50. A lens of refractive index $\frac{3}{2}$ has focal length 10 cm is immersed in water $\left(\mu = \frac{4}{3}\right)$. Now, the focal length is

(a) 10 cm (b) 20 cm
(c) 40 cm (d) 30 cm

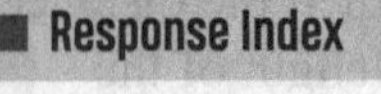

01 ⓐ ⓑ ⓒ ⓓ	14 ⓐ ⓑ ⓒ ⓓ	27 ⓐ ⓑ ⓒ ⓓ	40 ⓐ ⓑ ⓒ ⓓ
02 ⓐ ⓑ ⓒ ⓓ	15 ⓐ ⓑ ⓒ ⓓ	28 ⓐ ⓑ ⓒ ⓓ	41 ⓐ ⓑ ⓒ ⓓ
03 ⓐ ⓑ ⓒ ⓓ	16 ⓐ ⓑ ⓒ ⓓ	29 ⓐ ⓑ ⓒ ⓓ	42 ⓐ ⓑ ⓒ ⓓ
04 ⓐ ⓑ ⓒ ⓓ	17 ⓐ ⓑ ⓒ ⓓ	30 ⓐ ⓑ ⓒ ⓓ	43 ⓐ ⓑ ⓒ ⓓ
05 ⓐ ⓑ ⓒ ⓓ	18 ⓐ ⓑ ⓒ ⓓ	31 ⓐ ⓑ ⓒ ⓓ	44 ⓐ ⓑ ⓒ ⓓ
06 ⓐ ⓑ ⓒ ⓓ	19 ⓐ ⓑ ⓒ ⓓ	32 ⓐ ⓑ ⓒ ⓓ	45 ⓐ ⓑ ⓒ ⓓ
07 ⓐ ⓑ ⓒ ⓓ	20 ⓐ ⓑ ⓒ ⓓ	33 ⓐ ⓑ ⓒ ⓓ	46 ⓐ ⓑ ⓒ ⓓ
08 ⓐ ⓑ ⓒ ⓓ	21 ⓐ ⓑ ⓒ ⓓ	34 ⓐ ⓑ ⓒ ⓓ	47 ⓐ ⓑ ⓒ ⓓ
09 ⓐ ⓑ ⓒ ⓓ	22 ⓐ ⓑ ⓒ ⓓ	35 ⓐ ⓑ ⓒ ⓓ	48 ⓐ ⓑ ⓒ ⓓ
10 ⓐ ⓑ ⓒ ⓓ	23 ⓐ ⓑ ⓒ ⓓ	36 ⓐ ⓑ ⓒ ⓓ	49 ⓐ ⓑ ⓒ ⓓ
11 ⓐ ⓑ ⓒ ⓓ	24 ⓐ ⓑ ⓒ ⓓ	37 ⓐ ⓑ ⓒ ⓓ	50 ⓐ ⓑ ⓒ ⓓ
12 ⓐ ⓑ ⓒ ⓓ	25 ⓐ ⓑ ⓒ ⓓ	38 ⓐ ⓑ ⓒ ⓓ	
13 ⓐ ⓑ ⓒ ⓓ	26 ⓐ ⓑ ⓒ ⓓ	39 ⓐ ⓑ ⓒ ⓓ	

Performance Scanner

> 90% Excellent !	You have mastered this chapter. The concepts of this chapter are on your fingertips. Move on to the next chapter and maintain this momentum.
76-90% Very Good !	You have a good command over this chapter. Revise the chapter again after a few days and enhance your performance.
60-75% Good !	You have a wide scope to learn for this chapter. Revise it again.
<60 Not Satisfactory!	You have a long way ahead of you to master this chapter. Revise it thoroughly.

For Online Chapter Test
Scan the QR Code

Test Booklet No. 3947161

Test Booklet Code CH11

MEDACE
NEET (UG)
SELF ASSESSMENT KIT

Wave Optics

Topics Covered

- Huygens' Principle and Interference
- Diffraction and Polarisation

Important Instructions

- This Booklet Contains – Two Topic Tests and One Test on Complete Chapter.
- Each question carries 4 marks.
- For each correct response, the candidate will get 4 marks and for every incorrect response 1 mark will be additionally deducted from the total score.
- Use **Blue/Black** point pen only for filling the OMR.
- Rough work will be done in the space provided for this purpose within the test booklet only.

Name of the Candidate (In Capitals) ________________

Candidate's Signature ________________

Invigilator's Signature ________________

Facsimile signature stamp of center superintendent ________________

Do not open this Booklet until you start attempting the Test

Topical Follow Thru

Test 1

Syllabus

- Wavefront and Huygens' Principle
- Laws of Reflection and Refraction using Huygens' Principle
- Interference
- Young's Double Slit Experiment and Expression for Fringe Width, Coherent Sources and Sustained Interference of Light

For deeper insight **Scan the QR Code**

Important Instructions

- The test is of 45 minutes duration and contains 25 Multiple Choice Questions. (Four options with a single correct answer).
- Choose the correct option and fill the OMR given on the last page of this test accordingly.
- At some instances, you may find more than 1 option may be correct, in such circumstances you have to judge the most appropriate answer as per the conditions given in the question.

1. Two coherent sources of intensity ratio β interfere, then the value of $\frac{(I_{max} - I_{min})}{(I_{max} + I_{min})}$ is

(a) $\frac{1+\beta}{2\sqrt{\beta}}$ (b) $\frac{1+\beta}{\sqrt{\beta}}$ (c) $\sqrt{\frac{(1+\beta)}{\beta}}$ (d) $\frac{2\sqrt{\beta}}{1+\beta}$

2. Two identical light sources emit light of same wavelength λ. These light rays will exhibit interference, if

(a) their phase difference remain constant
(b) their path difference are varying
(c) their light intensities change randomly
(d) their penetration power remain constant

3. A monochromatic light of wavelength λ_1 is travelling in a medium of refractive index n_1, enters a denser medium of refractive index n_2. The wavelength in the denser medium is

(a) $n_2\lambda_1$ (b) $n_1\lambda_1$
(c) $\left(\frac{n_2}{n_1}\right)\lambda_1$ (d) $\left(\frac{n_1}{n_2}\right)\lambda_1$

4. If two waves are represented by

$y_1 = a\sin\left(\omega t - \frac{\pi}{6}\right)$ and $y_2 = b\cos\left(\omega t - \frac{\pi}{3}\right)$, then

phase difference between these two waves is

(a) $\frac{\pi}{2}$ (b) π
(c) $\frac{\pi}{3}$ (d) 2π

5. Three waves of equal frequency having amplitudes 8 μm, 3 μm and 12 μm meet at a point with successive phase difference of $\frac{\pi}{2}$. The amplitude of resultant wave (in μm) is

(a) 5 (b) 26
(c) 2 (d) 8

6. In YDSE, the ratio of slit width is 49:64. The ratio of intensity of minima to maxima is

(a) 5:9 (b) 15:113
(c) 1:15 (d) 7:8

7. In YDSE, two coherent sources are placed 0.80 mm apart and the fringes are observed one metre away. If distance of 3rd dark fringe from the central fringe is 0.9 cm, then the wavelength of the interfering lights is

(a) 352×10^{-6} m
(b) 288×10^{-6} m
(c) 196×10^{-6} m
(d) 624×10^{-8} m

8. In YDSE, how many maxima can be obtained on a screen (including central maxima) on both sides of the central fringe, if $\lambda = 4000$ Å and $d = 6000$ Å ?

(a) 3 (b) 5
(c) 7 (d) 1

9. In a double slit experiment, sodium light ($\lambda = 589$ nm) have angular separation of 4.2×10^{-3} rad. If angular separation is increased by 20%, then the wavelength will be

(a) 648 nm (b) 706.8 nm
(c) 449 nm (d) 527 nm

10. In Young's double slit experiment, intensity of light at a point on the screen, where path difference is λ, is I (λ being the wavelength of light used). The intensity of light where path difference becomes $\frac{\lambda}{4}$ is

(a) 0 (b) $\frac{I}{4}$
(c) $\frac{I}{2}$ (d) $\frac{I}{16}$

11. If the first order minima in Young's double slit experiment occurs direct by in front of one of the slits. If distance between slits is d and the distance between slits and screen is D, then the wavelength of used light is

(a) $\frac{d^2}{2D}$ (b) $\frac{d^2}{D}$
(c) $\frac{d^2}{3D}$ (d) $\frac{d^2}{4D}$

12. Let AB is incident wavefront and DC is its position after time t. Then, refractive index of medium 2 with respect to medium 1 is

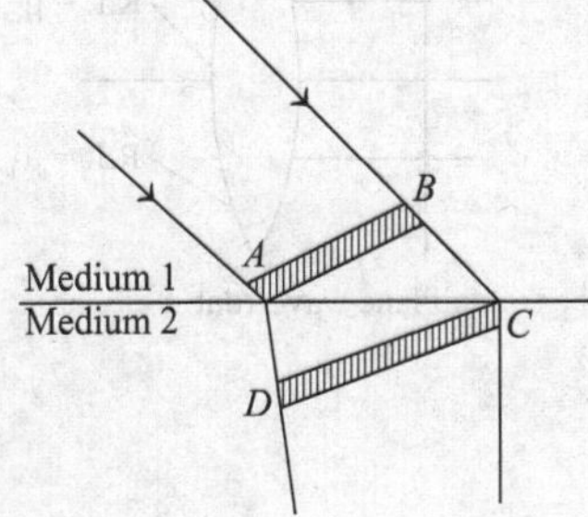

(a) $\frac{BC}{AD}$ (b) $\frac{AB}{DC}$
(c) $\frac{DC}{AB}$ (d) $\frac{AD}{BC}$

13. In a Young's double slit experiment, if there is no initial phase difference between the light from the two slits, then a point on the screen corresponding to the fifth minimum has path difference

(a) $5\frac{\lambda}{2}$ (b) $10\frac{\lambda}{2}$
(c) $9\frac{\lambda}{2}$ (d) $11\frac{\lambda}{2}$

14. In Young's double slit experiment, the slit S_1 and S_2 are illuminated with coherent microwave sources, each of frequency 10^6 Hz. The initial phase difference between them is zero. The separation between slits is $d = 150$ m. The intensity on screen due to each source is 1 Wm^{-2}. Find intensity on screen for $\theta = 30°$.

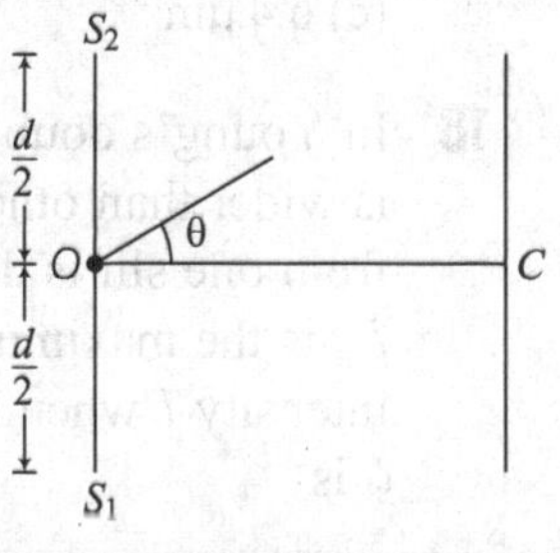

(a) 1 Wm^{-2} (b) 2 Wm^{-2}
(c) 3 Wm^{-2} (d) 4 Wm^{-2}

15. The following figure represents a wavefront AB which passes from air to another transparent medium and produces a new wavefront CD after refraction. The refractive index of the medium is (PQ is the boundary between air and the medium)

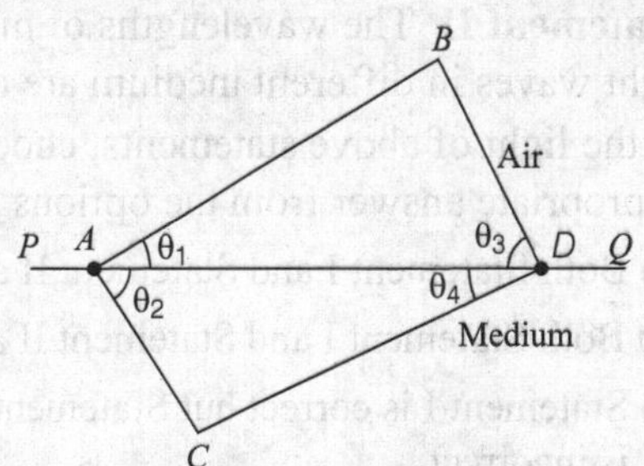

(a) $\frac{\cos\theta_1}{\cos\theta_4}$ (b) $\frac{\cos\theta_4}{\cos\theta_1}$
(c) $\frac{\sin\theta_1}{\sin\theta_4}$ (d) $\frac{\sin\theta_2}{\sin\theta_3}$

16. The maximum number of possible interference maxima, for slit separation equal to twice the wavelength in Young's double slit experiment, is

(a) infinite (b) five
(c) three (d) zero

17. In YDSE, fringes are produced using light of wavelength 4800Å. If one slit is covered by a thin plate of glass of refractive index 1.4 and the other with another glass plate of same thickness but of refractive index 1.7, then the central bright shifts to original 4th bright fringe from centre. What is the thickness of the glass plate?

(a) 6.8 m (b) 9.2 m
(c) 6.4 μm (d) 9.2 μm

18. In Young's double slit experiment, one of the slits is wider than other, so that amplitude of the light from one slit is double of that from other slit. If I_m is the maximum intensity, then the resultant intensity I when they interfere at phase difference ϕ is

(a) $\frac{I_m}{9}(4+5\cos\phi)$

(b) $\frac{I_m}{3}\left(1+2\cos^2\frac{\phi}{2}\right)$

(c) $\frac{I_m}{5}\left(1+4\cos^2\frac{\phi}{2}\right)$

(d) $\frac{I_m}{9}\left(1+8\cos^2\frac{\phi}{2}\right)$

19. **Statement I** The colour of a monochromatic light wave is different in different medium.

Statement II The wavelengths of monochromatic light waves in different medium are different.

In the light of above statements, choose the most appropriate answer from the options given below.

(a) Both Statement I and Statement II are correct.
(b) Both Statement I and Statement II are incorrect.
(c) Statement I is correct but Statement II is incorrect.
(d) Statement I is incorrect but Statement II is correct.

20. **Statement I** If the optical path between points A and B in first medium is same as the optical path between two points D and E in second medium. Then, time taken by light to travel from point A to B is same as that of from point D to E.

Statement II The speed of light in denser medium is same as that of in rarer medium.

In the light of above statements, choose the most appropriate answer from the options given below.

(a) Both Statement I and Statement II are correct.
(b) Both Statement I and Statement II are incorrect.
(c) Statement I is correct but Statement II is incorrect.
(d) Statement I is incorrect but Statement II is correct.

21. Due to interference between direct and reflected light from mirror, maxima is formed at point P. By what minimum distance mirror is shifted downward to find minima at point P? (Assume that, wavelength of light is 600 nm)

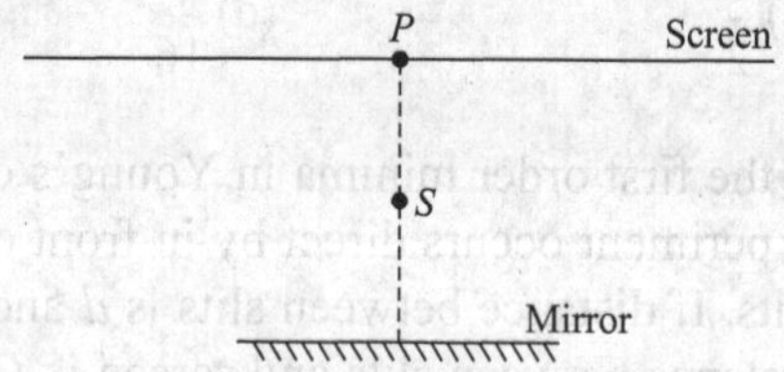

(a) 100 nm (b) 200 nm
(c) 300 nm (d) 400 nm

22. For the situation as shown in the figure, Column I relates the values of μ_1, μ_2 and μ_3 and Column II shows the possible shapes of wavefronts. Match the Column I with Column II and mark the correct option from the codes given below.

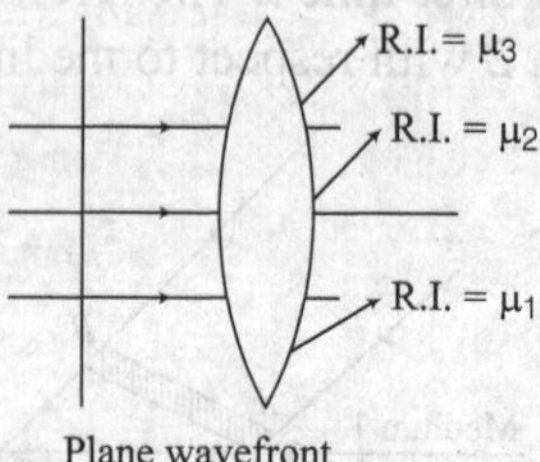

Column I	Column II
A. $\mu_1 = 1.4, \mu_2 = 1.5, \mu_3 = 1.6$	1. 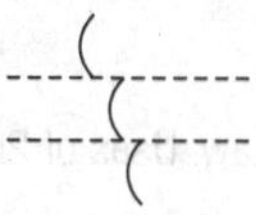
B. $\mu_1 = 1.6, \mu_2 = 1.5, \mu_3 = 1.4$	2. 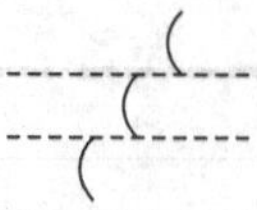
C. $\mu_1 = 1.7, \mu_2 = 1.5, \mu_3 = 1.7$	3. 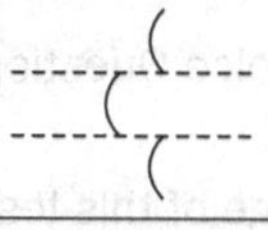
D. $\mu_1 = 1.3, \mu_2 = 1.5, \mu_3 = 1.3$	4. 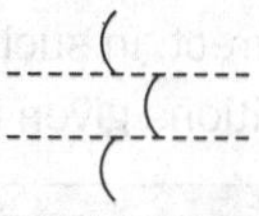

Codes

	A	B	C	D
(a)	1	4	2	3
(b)	3	1	2	4
(c)	2	1	3	4
(d)	2	1	4	3

23. In Young's double slit experiment, interference fringes $1°$ apart are produced on the screen, the slit separation is (Take, $\lambda = 589$ nm)

(a) 0.546 mm
(b) 0.0337 mm
(c) 0.246 mm
(d) 0.0927 mm

24. In the Young's double slit experiment, the intensity of light at a point on the screen, where the path difference is λ is K (λ being the wavelength of light used). The intensity at a point, where the path difference is $\lambda/3$ will be

(a) K
(b) $\frac{K}{2}$
(c) $\frac{K}{4}$
(d) zero

25. When one of the slits in Young's experiment is covered with a transparent sheet of thickness 3.6×10^{-3} cm, the central fringe shifts to a position originally occupied by 30th bright fringe. If $\lambda = 6000$ Å, then what is the refractive index of the sheet?

(a) 0.5
(b) 2.0
(c) 1.5
(d) 3.0

Response Index

01	a	b	c	d	10	a	b	c	d	19	a	b	c	d
02	a	b	c	d	11	a	b	c	d	20	a	b	c	d
03	a	b	c	d	12	a	b	c	d	21	a	b	c	d
04	a	b	c	d	13	a	b	c	d	22	a	b	c	d
05	a	b	c	d	14	a	b	c	d	23	a	b	c	d
06	a	b	c	d	15	a	b	c	d	24	a	b	c	d
07	a	b	c	d	16	a	b	c	d	25	a	b	c	d
08	a	b	c	d	17	a	b	c	d					
09	a	b	c	d	18	a	b	c	d					

Performance Scanner

> 90% Excellent ! You have mastered these topics. The concepts of these topics are on your fingertips. Move on to the next test and maintain this momentum.

76-90% Very Good ! You have a good command over these topics. Revise the topics again after a few days and enhance your performance.

60-75% Good ! You have a wide scope to learn for these topic. Revise them again.

<60% Not Satisfactory! You have a long way ahead of you to master these topics. Revise them thoroughly.

Test 2

Syllabus

- Diffraction due to a Single Slit
- Width of Central Maximum
- Polarisation
- Plane Polarised Light : Brewster's Law, Uses of Plane Polarised Light and Polaroid

For deeper insight **Scan the QR Code**

Important Instructions

- The test is of 45 minutes duration and contains 25 Multiple Choice Questions. (Four options with a single correct answer).
- Choose the correct option and fill the OMR given on the last page of this test accordingly.
- At some instances, you may find more than 1 option may be correct, in such circumstances you have to judge the most appropriate answer as per the conditions given in the question.

1. A diffraction pattern is obtained by a wire. If diameter of the wire is increased, then the fringe width will

(a) increase

(b) decrease

(c) remain unchanged

(d) increase or decrease depends on the length of the wire

2. In YDSE, green light (5303 Å) is incident on double slit. Slit separation is 19.44 μm and width is 4.05 μm. The number of bright fringes between the first and second diffraction minima is

(a) 7 (b) 5 (c) 6 (d) 9

3. Converging lens of focal length f is placed after a single slit and distance of lens from the slit is f. The size of screen should be

(a) $\frac{f\lambda}{a}$ (b) $\frac{\lambda}{a}$ (c) $\frac{2f\lambda}{a}$ (d) $\frac{2\lambda}{a}$

4. Let an unpolarised light beam with electric vector $E = E_0 \sin(kx - \omega t)$ is incident over a polaroid, then the transmitted beam will be

(a) $E_0 \sin(kx - \omega t)$

(b) $E_0 \cos(kx - \omega t)$

(c) $\frac{E_0}{\sqrt{2}} \sin(kx - \omega t)$

(d) $\frac{E_0}{\sqrt{2}} \cos(kx - \omega t)$

5. Wavelength of parallel beam is $\lambda = 500 \times 10^{-9}$ m. It passes through a long slit of width 5×10^{-4} m. The angular divergence for which most of the light is diffracted, is

(a) 5×10^{-3} rad

(b) 4.5×10^{-3} rad

(c) 3×10^{-3} rad

(d) 2×10^{-3} rad

6. In the far field diffraction pattern of a single slit under polychromatic illumination, the first minimum with the wavelength λ_1, is formed to be coincident with the fourth maximum at λ_2. So,

(a) $3\lambda_1 = 2\lambda_2$

(b) $2\lambda_1 = 9\lambda_2$

(c) $\lambda_1 = 3.5\lambda_2$

(d) $\lambda_1 = 2.5\lambda_2$

7. A beam of light of wavelength 450 nm from a distant source falls on a single slit 0.5 mm wide and resulting diffraction pattern is observed on a screen placed at 2 m. The distance between the first dark fringes on either side of the central bright fringe is

(a) 1.8 mm

(b) 3.6 mm

(c) 5.4 mm

(d) 0.9 mm

8. A single slit of width a is illuminated by blue light of wavelength 500 nm and the width of diffraction pattern is measured as x. If half of the slit width is covered and blue light is replaced by green light of wavelength 550 nm, the width of diffraction pattern is

(a) $\frac{11}{5}x$ (b) $\frac{x}{5}$

(c) $5x$ (d) $\frac{x}{11}$

9. A parallel monochromatic beam of light is incident normally on a narrow slit. A diffraction pattern is formed on a screen placed perpendicular to the direction of the incident beam. At the first minima of the diffraction pattern, the phase difference between the rays coming from the two edges of the slit is

(a) zero (b) $\pi/2$

(c) π (d) 2π

10. In a single slit diffraction experiment, first minima for $\lambda_1 = 660$ nm coincides with first maxima for wavelength λ_2, then λ_2 will be equal to

(a) 240 nm (b) 345 nm

(c) 440 nm (d) 330 nm

11. The distance between the first and the sixth minima in the diffraction pattern of a single slit is 0.5 mm. The screen is 0.5 m away from the slit. If the wavelength of light used is 5000 Å, then the slit width will be

(a) 5 mm (b) 2.5 mm

(c) 1.25 mm (d) 1.0 mm

12. In a single slit diffraction pattern, the distance between first minima on the right and first minima on the left of central maximum is 4 mm. The screen on which the pattern is displaced is 2 m from the slit and wavelength of light used is 6000 Å. Find width of the slit and width of the central maximum.

(a) 4 mm, 6 mm

(b) 0.4 mm, 6 mm

(c) 0.6 mm, 4 mm

(d) 0.6 mm, 0.4 mm

13. Visible light of wavelength 6000×10^{-8} cm falls normally on a single slit and produces a diffraction pattern. It is found that the second diffraction minimum is at 60° from the central maximum. If the first minimum is produced at θ_1, then θ_1 is close to

(a) 25° (b) 30°

(c) 20° (d) 45°

14. **Statement I** Scattered light seen in a direction perpendicular to the direction of incidence is plane polarised. This is called polarisation by scattering.

Statement II The angle of incidence at which the reflected light is completely plane polarised is called polarising angle or Brewster's angle i_B.

In the light of above statements, choose the most appropriate answer from the options given below.

(a) Both Statement I and Statement II are correct.

(b) Both Statement I and Statement II are incorrect.

(c) Statement I is correct but Statement II is incorrect.

(d) Statement I is incorrect but Statement II is correct.

15. Choose the option which is not due to polarisation.

(a) Formation of 3-D movies.

(b) Study of earthquakes in seismology.

(c) Making hologram.

(d) Testing of chirality of organic compounds in chemistry.

16. A beam of plane polarised light is incident normally on a polariser of cross-sectional area $3 \times 10^{-4} \text{m}^2$, which rotates about the axis of the ray with an angular velocity 10π rad s^{-1}. The power of incident ray is 10^{-3} W. Find the intensity of emergent beam.

(a) $\frac{1}{3}$ Wm^{-2}

(b) $\frac{5}{3}$ Wm^{-2}

(c) $\frac{4}{3}$ Wm^{-2}

(d) $\frac{10}{3}$ Wm^{-2}

17. A ray of light is incident on a glass plate at an angle of 45°. Then, the refractive index of glass, if the reflected and refracted rays are perpendicular to each other is

(a) tan 30°
(b) cot 45°
(c) sin 60°
(d) cos 60°

18. A light has an amplitude A and angle between analyser and polariser is 45°. If light is reflected by an analyser, then its amplitude is

(a) $\frac{\sqrt{3}A}{2}$
(b) $\frac{A}{\sqrt{2}}$
(c) $\frac{A}{2}$
(d) $A\sqrt{2}$

19. Intensity of an unpolarised light is 30 Wm^{-2}. It passes through three polarisers such that transmission axes of the first and second polariser makes an angle 30° with each other and the transmission axis of the last polariser is crossed with that of the first. The intensity of final emerging light will be

(a) $\frac{45}{16}$ Wm^{-2}
(b) $\frac{21}{4}$ Wm^{-2}
(c) $\frac{15}{2}$ Wm^{-2}
(d) 4 Wm^{-2}

20. A polariser-analyser set is adjusted such that the intensity of light coming out of the analyser is just 10% of the original intensity. Assuming that the polariser-analyser set does not absorb any light, the angle by which the analyser need to be rotated further to reduce the output intensity to be zero, is

(a) 71.6°
(b) 90°
(c) 45°
(d) 18.4°

21. A plane polarised light is incident on a polariser with its pass axis making angle θ with X-axis as shown in the figure. At four different values of θ, θ = 8°, 38°, 188° and 218°, the observed intensities are same. What is the angle between the direction of polarisation and X-axis?

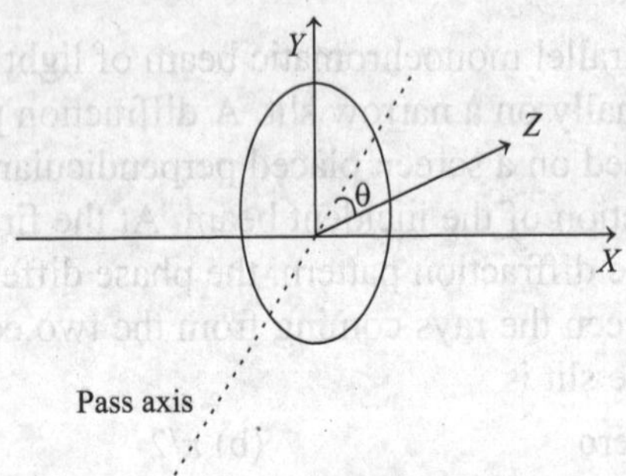

(a) 98°
(b) 128°
(c) 203°
(d) 45°

22. Two beams A and B of plane polarised light with mutually perpendicular planes of polarisation are seen through a polaroid. From the position, when the beam A has maximum intensity (and beam B has zero intensity), a rotation of polaroid through 30° makes the two beams appear equally bright. If the initial intensities of the two beams are I_A and I_B respectively, then I_A/I_B equals

(a) 3
(b) 3/2
(c) 1
(d) 1/3

23. Light reflected from the surface of glass plate of refractive index 1.57 is linearly polarised. What is the angle of refraction of glass ?

(a) 32.5°
(b) 42.5°
(c) 30.2°
(d) 44.5°

24. An unpolarised light beam is made to pass through a polariser and an analyser. Which of these graphs represents intensity of light *versus* angle between pass axis of polariser and analyser?

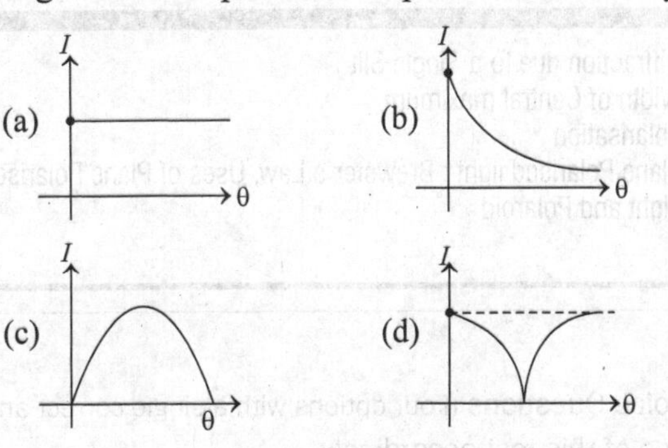

25. When a polaroid sheet is rotated between two crossed polaroids, the intensity of the transmitted light will be maximum, when angle θ between pass axes is

(a) $\frac{\pi}{2}$

(b) $\frac{3\pi}{4}$

(c) $\frac{\pi}{4}$

(d) $\frac{2\pi}{3}$

Response Index

01	a	b	c	d	10	a	b	c	d	19	a	b	c	d
02	a	b	c	d	11	a	b	c	d	20	a	b	c	d
03	a	b	c	d	12	a	b	c	d	21	a	b	c	d
04	a	b	c	d	13	a	b	c	d	22	a	b	c	d
05	a	b	c	d	14	a	b	c	d	23	a	b	c	d
06	a	b	c	d	15	a	b	c	d	24	a	b	c	d
07	a	b	c	d	16	a	b	c	d	25	a	b	c	d
08	a	b	c	d	17	a	b	c	d					
09	a	b	c	d	18	a	b	c	d					

Performance Scanner

> 90% Excellent !	You have mastered these topics. The concepts of these topics are on your fingertips. Move on to the next test and maintain this momentum.
76-90% Very Good !	You have a good command over these topics. Revise the topics again after a few days and enhance your performance.
60-75% Good !	You have a wide scope to learn for these topic. Revise them again.
<60% Not Satisfactory!	You have a long way ahead of you to master these topics. Revise them thoroughly.

Chapter Break Thru

Syllabus

- Wavefront and Huygens' principle
- Laws of Reflection and Refraction using Huygens' Principle
- Interference
- Young's Double Slit Experiment and Expression for Fringe Width, Coherent Sources and Sustained Interference of Light
- Diffraction due to a Single Slit
- Width of Central maximum
- Polarisation
- Plane Polarised light : Brewster's Law, Uses of Plane Polarised
- Light and Polaroid

Important Instructions

- The test is of 45 minutes duration and contains 30 Multiple Choice Questions (Four options with a single correct answer).
- Choose the correct option and fill the OMR given on the last page of this test accordingly.
- At some instances, you may find more than 1 option may be correct, in such circumstances you have to judge the most appropriate answer as per conditions given in the question.

1. YDSE is performed in a medium whose refractive index μ can be varied. Which among the following graphs best represents the variation of angular width θ with μ?

(a) 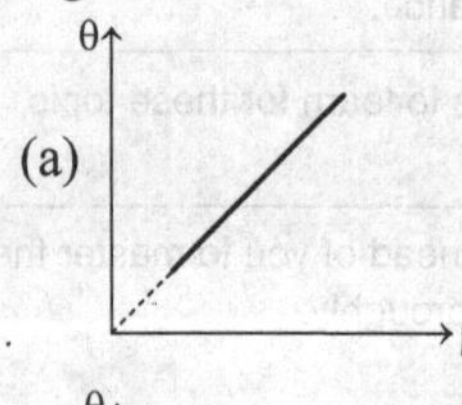

(b) 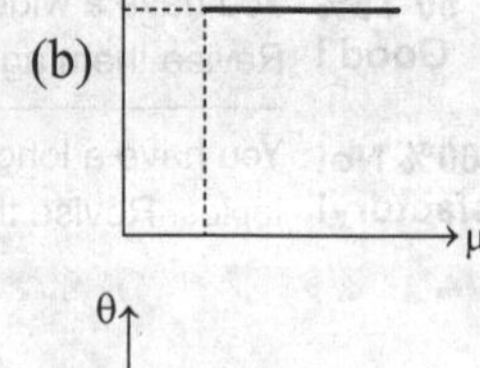

(c) 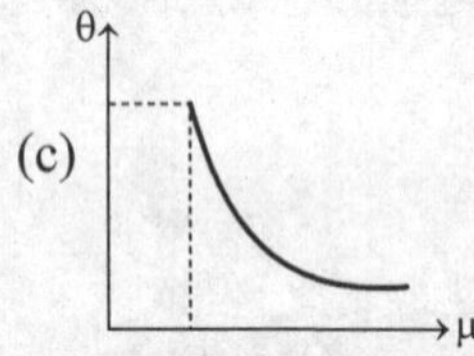

(d) 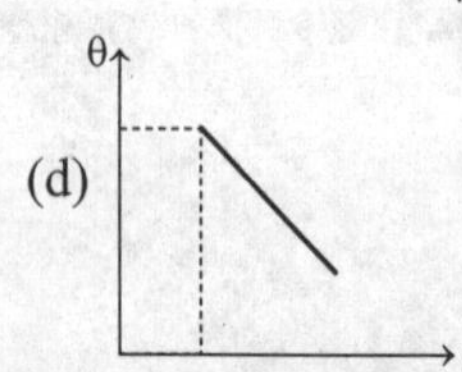

2. Two coherent waves having amplitudes in ratio of 2 : 1 interfere. The value of $\dfrac{I_{max}-I_{min}}{I_{max}+I_{min}}$ is

(a) 1 : 1 (b) 3 : 2
(c) 4 : 5 (d) 4:1

3. In YDSE, laser light of wavelength 5800 Å incident on pair of identical slits, produces an interference pattern where dark fringes are separated by 7.25 mm. If another laser light produces interference pattern where bright fringes are separated by 5.075 mm, then wavelength of second light is

(a) 4060 Å (b) 5075 Å
(c) 6090 Å (d) None of these

4. The slits are 0.24 mm apart from each other and illuminated with a light of wavelength λ. If the distance of screen from slit's plane is 0.8 m, then the distance between ninth dark fringe to sixth bright fringe is obtained to be 5.4 mm, then value of λ is

(a) 4628 Å
(b) 5490 Å
(c) 6480 Å
(d) None of the above

5. In Young's double slit experiment, the intensity of light at a point on the screen where path difference λ is I. If intensity at a point is $I/4$, then possible path differences at this point are

(a) $\dfrac{\lambda}{2}, \dfrac{\lambda}{3}$ (b) $\dfrac{\lambda}{3}, \dfrac{2\lambda}{3}$
(c) $\dfrac{\lambda}{3}, \dfrac{\lambda}{4}$ (d) $\dfrac{2\lambda}{3}, \dfrac{\lambda}{4}$

6. A parallel beam of monochromatic light of wavelength 6000 Å passes through a slit of width 0.24 mm and diffraction pattern is observed on screen 1 m away from slit. The width of central maxima and first secondary maxima respectively, are

(a) 0.25 cm, 0.25 cm
(b) 0.5 cm, 0.25 cm
(c) 0.25 cm, 0.5 cm
(d) 0.5 cm, 0.5 cm

7. Diffraction pattern due to a single slit has been shown in the following figure.

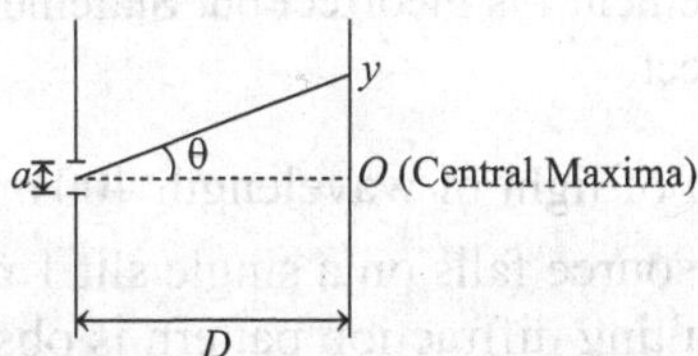

Which among the following graphs best represents the intensity I variation with $\sin\theta$?

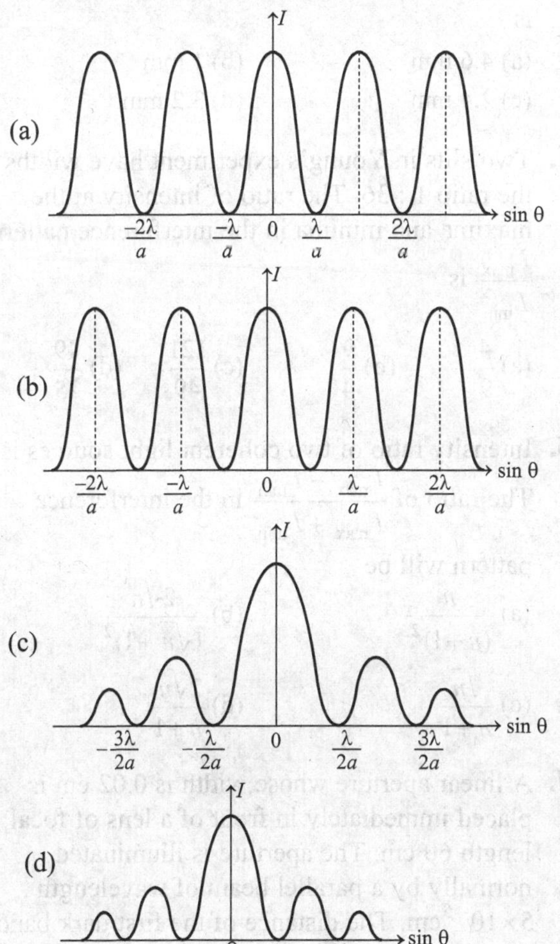

8. Two identical polaroids are placed in the path of unpolarised beam of intensity I such that no light is emitted from the second polaroid. If a third identical polaroid whose polarisation axis makes an angle θ with the polarisation axis of first polaroid, is placed between these polaroids, then the intensity of light emerging from the last polaroid is

(a) $\left(\frac{I}{8}\right)\sin^2 2\theta$

(b) $\left(\frac{I}{4}\right)\sin^2 2\theta$

(c) $\left(\frac{I}{2}\right)\cos^4 \theta$

(d) $I\cos^4\theta$

9. A beam of light is incident on the surface of transparent medium as shown in following figure. (Here, θ_P is angle of polarisation)

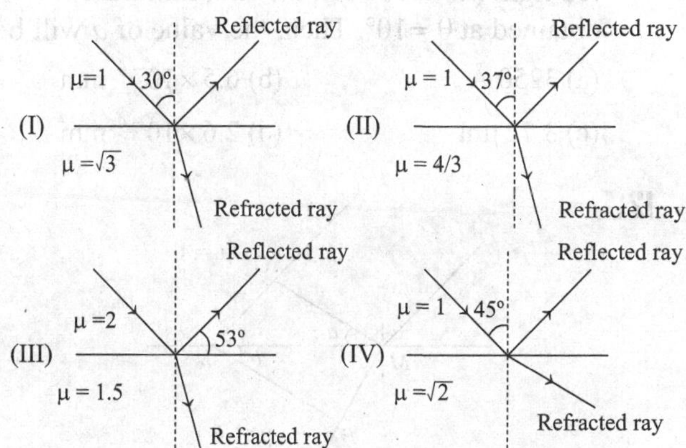

Match List I with List II.

	List I		List II
(A)	θ_P for I	1.	54.74°
(B)	θ_P for II	2.	53°
(C)	θ_P for III	3.	60°
(D)	θ_P for IV	4.	37°

Choose the correct answer from options given below.

Codes

	A	B	C	D
(a)	1	3	4	2
(b)	3	2	1	4
(c)	3	2	4	1
(d)	4	1	3	2

10. **Assertion** (A) For sustained interference, the interfering waves should be in the same state of polarisation.

Reason (R) In sustained interference, the positions of maxima and minima of intensity on the observation screen slightly changes with time.

In the light of above statements, choose the most appropriate answer from the options given below.

(a) Both A and R are true and R is the correct explanation of A.
(b) Both A and R are true but R is not the correct explanation of A.
(c) A is true but R is false.
(d) A is false but R is true.

11. A slit of width a is illuminated by white light. For red light ($\lambda = 6500$ Å), the first minima is obtained at $\theta = 10°$. Then, the value of a will be

(a) 3250 Å
(b) 6.5×10^{-4} mm
(c) 3.72 μm
(d) 2.6×10^{-4} mm

12.

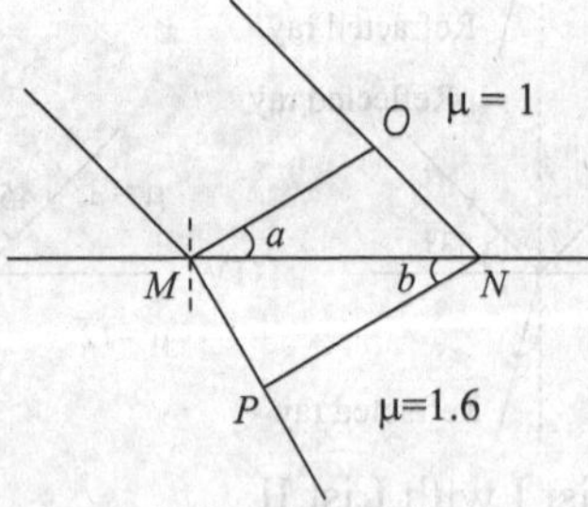

If MO is incident wavefront and PN is refracted wavefront, then $\frac{\sin a}{\sin b}$ is

(a) $\frac{3}{8}$
(b) $\frac{8}{5}$
(c) $\frac{1}{2}$
(d) $\frac{3}{7}$

13. **Statement I** The reflected light is not linearly polarised.

Statement II Transmitted intensity will be zero when the axis of the analyser is in the plane of the figure, i.e. the plane of incidence.

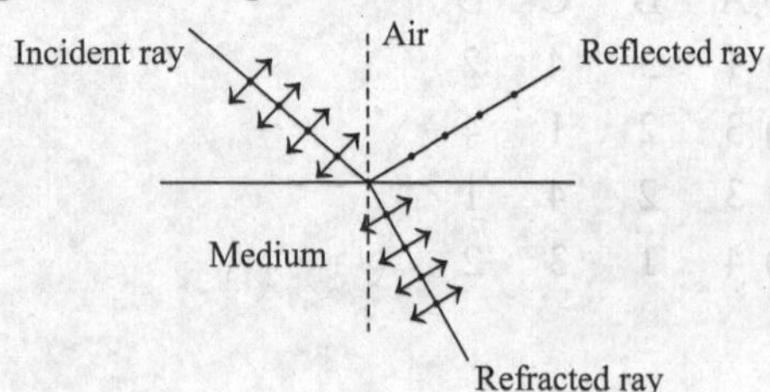

In the light of above statements, choose the most appropriate answer from the options given below.

(a) Both Statement I and Statement II are correct.
(b) Both Statement I and Statement II are incorrect.
(c) Statement I is correct but Statement II is incorrect.
(d) Statement I is incorrect but Statement II is correct.

14. A beam of light of wavelength 400 nm from a distant source falls on a single slit 1 mm wide and the resulting diffraction pattern is observed on a screen 4 m away. The distance between first dark fringes on either side of the central bright fringe is

(a) 4.6 mm
(b) 1 mm
(c) 2.4 mm
(d) 3.2 mm

15. Two slits in Young's experiment have widths in the ratio 1 : 36. The ratio of intensity at the maxima and minima in the interference pattern $\frac{I_{max}}{I_{min}}$ is

(a) $\frac{4}{9}$
(b) $\frac{9}{4}$
(c) $\frac{121}{49}$
(d) $\frac{49}{25}$

16. Intensity ratio of two coherent light sources is n. The ratio of $\frac{I_{max} - I_{min}}{I_{max} + I_{min}}$ in the interference pattern will be

(a) $\frac{n}{(n+1)^2}$
(b) $\frac{2\sqrt{n}}{(\sqrt{n}+1)^2}$
(c) $\frac{\sqrt{n}}{n+1}$
(d) $\frac{2\sqrt{n}}{n+1}$

17. A linear aperture whose width is 0.02 cm is placed immediately in front of a lens of focal length 60 cm. The aperture is illuminated normally by a parallel beam of wavelength 5×10^{-5} cm. The distance of the first dark band of the diffraction pattern from the centre of the screen is

(a) 0.20 cm
(b) 0.15 cm
(c) 0.10 cm
(d) 0.09 cm

18. Wavelength of blue light is 0.6 μm. In air, it suffers reflection in a medium in which velocity of light is 2.4×10^8 m/s. Wavelength of light in that medium is

(a) 0.6 μm (b) 0.3 μm

(c) 0.48 μm (d) 0.5 μm

19. Two polaroids P_1 and P_2 are placed with their axis perpendicular to each other. Unpolarised light I_0 is incident on P_1. A third polariod P_3 is kept in between P_1 and P_2 such that its axis makes an angle 30° with that of P_1. The intensity of transmitted light through P_2 is

(a) $\frac{5I_0}{24}$ (b) $\frac{I_0}{18}$

(c) $\frac{I_0}{16}$ (d) $\frac{3I_0}{32}$

20. A monochromatic light undergoes destructive interference, then the path difference is

(a) $n\lambda$ (b) $n(\lambda+1)$

(c) $\frac{(n+2)\lambda}{2}$ (d) $\frac{(2n+1)\lambda}{2}$

21. A plane wavefront is incident at an angle of 40° with horizontal boundary of refractive medium from air to a medium of refractive index $\mu = \frac{4}{3}$. The angle of refracted wavefront with horizontal is

(a) 30° (b) 26°

(c) 28.8° (d) 24.2°

22. In the ideal double-slit experiment, when a glass plate (refractive index 1.8) of thickness t is introduced in the path of one of the interfering beams (wavelength λ), the intensity at the position where the central maximum occurred previously remains unchanged. The minimum thickness of the glass plate is

(a) 1.25 λ (b) $\frac{2\lambda}{3}$

(c) $\frac{\lambda}{3}$ (d) 1.5λ

23. In Young's double slit experiment, the y-coordinates of central maxima and 6th maxima are 6 cm and 9 cm, respectively. When the YDSE apparatus is immersed in a liquid of refractive index 1.5, the corresponding y-coordinates will be

(a) 4 cm, 7.5 cm

(b) 8 cm, 6 cm

(c) 6 cm, 8 cm

(d) $\frac{4}{3}$ cm, $\frac{10}{3}$ cm

24. In Young's double slit experiment, the slits are 0.5 mm apart and interference pattern is observed on a screen placed at a distance of 1.0 m from the plane containing the slits. If wavelength of the incident light is 6000 Å, then the separation between the fourth bright fringe and the central maxima is

(a) 4.0 mm (b) 4.8 mm

(c) 3.0 mm (d) 2.5 mm

25. Light is incident on a polariser with intensity I_0. A second prism called analyser is kept at an angle of 22.5° from the first polariser, then the intensity of final emergent light will be

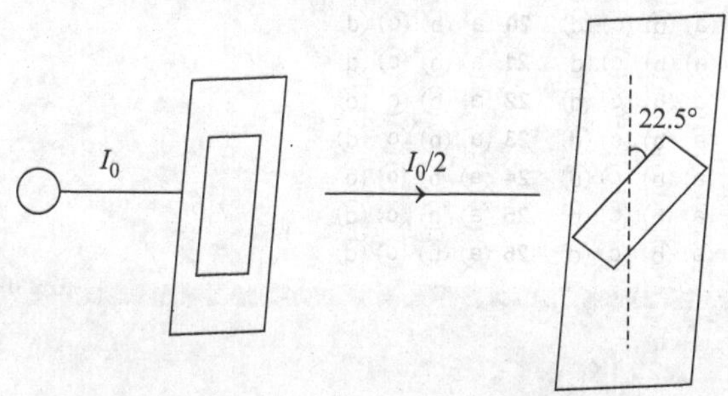

(a) 0.5 I_0 (b) 0.6 I_0

(c) 0.46 I_0 (d) 0.83 I_0

26. In Young's experiment, the distance between the slits is doubled and the distance between the slit and screen is reduced to half, then the fringe width

(a) will not change

(b) will become half

(c) will be doubled

(d) will become one-fourth

27. A double slit arrangement produces fringes for light $\lambda = 5890$ Å which are 0.2° apart. If the whole arrangement is fully dipped in a liquid of refractive index $\mu = \frac{5}{3}$, then the angular fringes separation is

(a) 0.15° (b) 0.30°
(c) 0.10° (d) 0.12°

28. A beam of light of wavelength 800 nm from a distant source falls on a single slit 2 mm wide and the resulting diffraction pattern is observed on a screen 4 m away. The distance between the first dark fringes on either side of the central bright fringe is

(a) 1.2 mm (b) 1.8 cm
(c) 2.8 cm (d) 3.2 mm

29. In YDSE, two parallel slits are illuminated by two wavelengths 400 nm and 700 nm. The fourth dark fringe resulting from 400 nm wavelength of light coincides on screen with *n*th order fringe of 700 nm wavelength, then value of *n* is

(a) 3 (b) 2
(c) 1 (d) 4

30. In a single slit diffraction experiment, the width of the slit is made double of its original width. Then, the central maximum on the diffraction pattern will become

(a) narrower and fainter
(b) narrower and brighter
(c) broader and brighter
(d) broader and fainter

Response Index

01 ⓐ ⓑ ⓒ ⓓ	14 ⓐ ⓑ ⓒ ⓓ	27 ⓐ ⓑ ⓒ ⓓ
02 ⓐ ⓑ ⓒ ⓓ	15 ⓐ ⓑ ⓒ ⓓ	28 ⓐ ⓑ ⓒ ⓓ
03 ⓐ ⓑ ⓒ ⓓ	16 ⓐ ⓑ ⓒ ⓓ	29 ⓐ ⓑ ⓒ ⓓ
04 ⓐ ⓑ ⓒ ⓓ	17 ⓐ ⓑ ⓒ ⓓ	30 ⓐ ⓑ ⓒ ⓓ
05 ⓐ ⓑ ⓒ ⓓ	18 ⓐ ⓑ ⓒ ⓓ	
06 ⓐ ⓑ ⓒ ⓓ	19 ⓐ ⓑ ⓒ ⓓ	
07 ⓐ ⓑ ⓒ ⓓ	20 ⓐ ⓑ ⓒ ⓓ	
08 ⓐ ⓑ ⓒ ⓓ	21 ⓐ ⓑ ⓒ ⓓ	
09 ⓐ ⓑ ⓒ ⓓ	22 ⓐ ⓑ ⓒ ⓓ	
10 ⓐ ⓑ ⓒ ⓓ	23 ⓐ ⓑ ⓒ ⓓ	
11 ⓐ ⓑ ⓒ ⓓ	24 ⓐ ⓑ ⓒ ⓓ	
12 ⓐ ⓑ ⓒ ⓓ	25 ⓐ ⓑ ⓒ ⓓ	
13 ⓐ ⓑ ⓒ ⓓ	26 ⓐ ⓑ ⓒ ⓓ	

Performance Scanner

> 90% Excellent !	You have mastered this chapter. The concepts of this chapter are on your fingertips. Move on to the next chapter and maintain this momentum.
76-90% Very Good !	You have a good command over this chapter. Revise the chapter again after a few days and enhance your performance.
60-75% Good !	You have a wide scope to learn more from this chapter. Revise this chapter again.
<60% Not Satisfactory!	You have a long way ahead of you to master this chapter. Revise it thoroughly.

For Online Chapter Test **Scan the QR Code**

For Online Unit Test **Scan the QR Code**

Space for Rough Work

Space for Rough Work

Test Booklet No. 3947162

Test Booklet Code CH12

MEDACE

NEET (UG)

SELF ASSESSMENT KIT

Dual Nature of Radiation and Matter

Topics Covered

- Photoelectric Effect
- Particle Nature of Light : The Photon
- Matter Waves and de-Broglie Relation

Important Instructions

- This Booklet Contains – Three Topic Tests and One Test on Complete Chapter.
- Each question carries 4 marks.
- For each correct response, the candidate will get 4 marks and for every incorrect response, 1 mark will be additionally deducted from total score.
- Use **Blue/Black** point pen only for filling the OMR.
- Rough work is to be done in the space provided for this purpose within the test booklet only.

Name of the Candidate (In Capitals) ____________________

____

Candidate's Signature ____________

Invigilator's Signature ____________

Facsimile signature stamp of center superintendent ____________

Do not open this Booklet until you start attempting the Test

Topical Follow Thru

Test 1

Syllabus

- Photoelectric Effect
- Einstein's Photoelectric Equation
- Hertz and Lenard's Observations

For deeper insight **Scan the QR Code**

Important Instructions

- The test is of 30 minutes duration and contains 15 Multiple Choice Questions. (Four options with a single correct answer).
- Choose the correct option and fill the OMR given on the last page of this test accordingly.
- At some instances, you may find more than 1 option may be correct, in such circumstances you have to judge the most appropriate answer as per conditions given in the question.

1. The threshold frequency of a metal is f_0. When the light of frequency $2f_0$ is incident on the metal plate, the maximum velocity of photoelectrons is v_1. When the frequency of incident radiation is increased to $5f_0$, the maximum velocity of photoelectrons emitted is v_2. The ratio of v_1 to v_2 is

(a) $\frac{v_1}{v_2} = \frac{1}{4}$

(b) $\frac{v_1}{v_2} = \frac{1}{2}$

(c) $\frac{v_1}{v_2} = \frac{1}{8}$

(d) $\frac{v_1}{v_2} = \frac{1}{16}$

2. In the context of the photoelectric effect, the concept of stopping potential V_0 can be analysed from multiple perspectives. Considering its theoretical implications and experimental observations, which of the following statements accurately describes the dependency of V_0?

(a) It is independent of the intensity of the incident light.

(b) It depends upon the surface nature of the substance.

(c) It depends upon the intensity of incident light.

(d) It depends upon the angle of incident light.

3. A photon of energy 3.4 eV is incident on a metal having work function 3 eV. The maximum kinetic energy of photoelectrons is equal to

(a) 1.4 eV (b) 1.7 eV

(c) 0.4 eV (d) 6.8 eV

4. **Assertion** (A) The strength of photoelectric current depends upon the intensity of incident radiation.

Reason (R) A photon of energy E possesses a mass equal to $\frac{E}{c^2}$ and momentum equal to $\frac{E}{c}$.

In the light of above statements, choose the most appropriate answer from the options given below.

(a) Both A and R are true and R is the correct explanation of A.

(b) Both A and R are true but R is not the correct explanation of A.

(c) A is true but R is false.

(d) A is false but R is true.

5. If the work function of a photometal is 5.825 eV, then the threshold wavelength will be (Take, speed of light, $c = 3 \times 10^8$ m/s)

(a) 1200 Å
(b) 2124.4 Å
(c) 2400 Å
(d) 3600 Å

6. According to Einstein's photoelectric equation, the graph between the kinetic energy of photoelectrons ejected and the frequency of incident radiation is

(a) 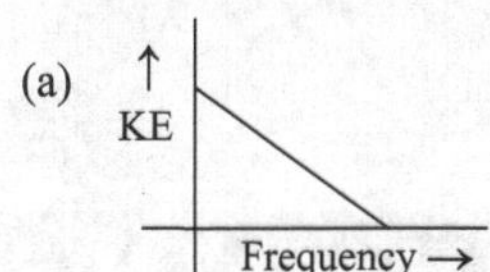

(b) 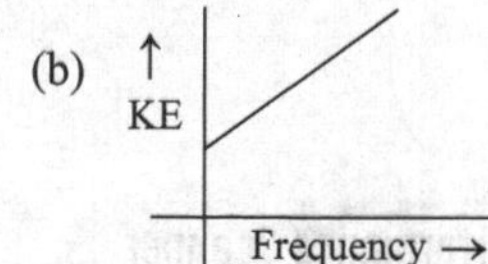

(c) 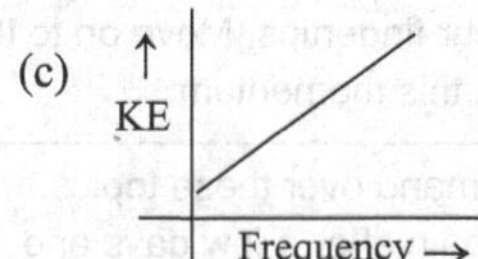

(d) 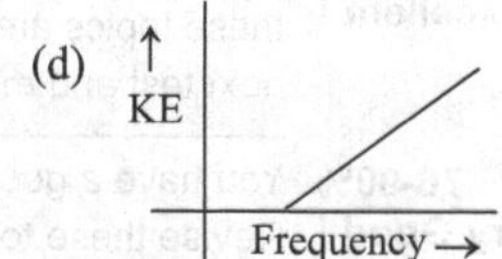

7. Two metals, one is sodium and other is copper, have work functions 4.6 eV and 8.5 eV, respectively. Then, the ratio of their wavelength is nearest to

(a) 1:2 (b) 1.847 : 1
(c) 2:1 (d) 1:4

8. When light falls on a metal surface, the maximum kinetic energy of the emitted photoelectrons depends upon

(a) frequency of incident light
(b) velocity of the incident light
(c) intensity of the incident light
(d) the time for which light falls on the metal

9. The work function of metals is in the range of 3 eV to 6 eV. Which of the following wavelength of light cannot be used for photoelectric effect ?

(a) 310 nm
(b) 250 nm
(c) 400 nm
(d) 440 nm

10. The threshold wavelength for a metal having work function ϕ_0 is λ_0. Then, threshold wavelength for a metal whose work function is $\phi_0/2$ will be

(a) $4\lambda_0$ (b) $2\lambda_0$
(c) $\frac{\lambda_0}{2}$ (d) $\frac{\lambda_0}{4}$

11. In a photoemissive cell with exciting wavelength λ, the maximum kinetic energy of the electron is K. If the exciting wavelength is changed to $\frac{2\lambda}{3}$, the kinetic energy of the fastest emitted electron will be

(a) $\frac{2K}{3}$
(b) $\frac{3K}{2}$
(c) less than $\frac{3K}{2}$
(d) more than $\frac{3K}{2}$

12. A light beam, $E = 100[\sin(\omega_1 t) + \sin(\omega_2 t)]\,\text{Vm}^{-1}$ with $\omega_1 = 5 \times 10^{15}\,\text{s}^{-1}$ and $\omega_2 = 10 \times 10^{15}\,\text{s}^{-1}$, falls on a metal surface of work function 4.0 eV. Maximum KE of emitted photoelectrons is

(a) 2.50 eV (b) 1.50 eV
(c) 2.59 eV (d) 2.3 eV

13. Estimate the value of work function of cesium from the experimental results plotted on the graph given below.

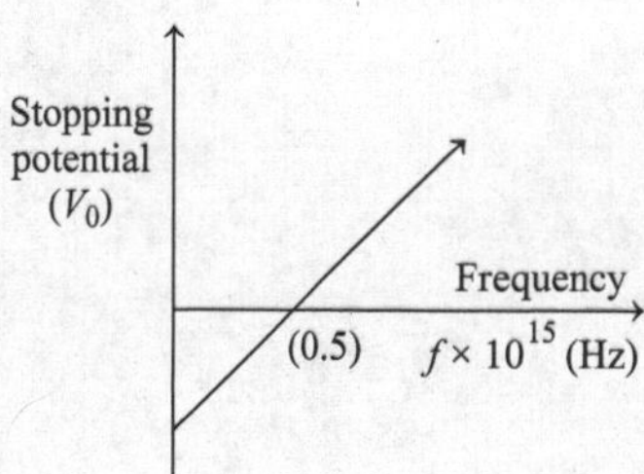

(a) 2.50 eV
(b) 2.30 eV
(c) 2.06 eV
(d) 3.20 eV

14. Let K_1 and K_2 be the maximum kinetic energies of photoelectrons emitted when two monochromatic beams of wavelength λ_1 and λ_2 respectively, are incident on a metallic surface. If $\lambda_1 = 3\lambda_2$, then

(a) $K_1 > \frac{K_2}{3}$

(b) $K_1 < \frac{K_2}{3}$

(c) $K_1 = \frac{K_2}{3}$

(d) $K_2 = \frac{K_1}{3}$

15. A metal surface is illuminated by light of two different wavelengths 248 nm and 310 nm. The maximum speeds of the photoelectrons corresponding to these wavelengths are u_1 and u_2, respectively. If the ratio $u_1 : u_2 = 2:1$ and $hc = 1240$ eV nm, the work function of the metal is nearly

(a) 3.7 eV

(b) 3.2 eV

(c) 2.8 eV

(d) 2.5 eV

Response Index

01	ⓐ	ⓑ	ⓒ	ⓓ	10	ⓐ	ⓑ	ⓒ	ⓓ
02	ⓐ	ⓑ	ⓒ	ⓓ	11	ⓐ	ⓑ	ⓒ	ⓓ
03	ⓐ	ⓑ	ⓒ	ⓓ	12	ⓐ	ⓑ	ⓒ	ⓓ
04	ⓐ	ⓑ	ⓒ	ⓓ	13	ⓐ	ⓑ	ⓒ	ⓓ
05	ⓐ	ⓑ	ⓒ	ⓓ	14	ⓐ	ⓑ	ⓒ	ⓓ
06	ⓐ	ⓑ	ⓒ	ⓓ	15	ⓐ	ⓑ	ⓒ	ⓓ
07	ⓐ	ⓑ	ⓒ	ⓓ					
08	ⓐ	ⓑ	ⓒ	ⓓ					
09	ⓐ	ⓑ	ⓒ	ⓓ					

Performance Scanner

> 90% Excellent !	You have mastered these topics. The concepts of these topics are on your fingertips. Move on to the next test and maintain this momentum.
76-90% Very Good !	You have a good command over these topics. Revise these topics again after a few days and enhance your performance.
60-75% Good !	You have a wide scope to learn for these topics. Revise them again.
<60% Not Satisfactory!	You have a long way ahead of you to master in these topics. Revise them thoroughly.

Test 2

Syllabus • Particle Nature of Light : The Photon

For deeper insight **Scan the QR Code**

Important Instructions

- The test is of 30 minutes duration and contains 15 Multiple Choice Questions. (Four options with a single correct answer).
- Choose the correct option and fill the OMR given on the last page of this test accordingly.
- At some instances, you may find more than 1 option may be correct, in such circumstances you have to judge the most appropriate answer as per conditions given in the question.

1. In an accelerator experiment on high-energy collisions of electrons with positrons, a certain event is interpreted as annihilation of an electron-positron pair of total energy 10.2 eV into two γ-rays of equal energy. What is the wavelength associated with each γ-ray?

(a) 2.436×10^{-7} m
(b) 1.436×10^{-7} m
(c) $2.436\times 10^{+7}$ m
(d) $1.436\times 10^{+7}$ m

2. A photon of wavelength 4400 Å is passing through vacuum. The effective mass and momentum of the photon are respectively, (Take, speed of light, $c = 2.8\times 10^{8}$ m/s)

(a) 5×10^{-36} kg, 1.5×10^{-27} kg-m/s
(b) 5×10^{-35} kg, 1.5×10^{-26} kg-m/s
(c) zero, 1.5×10^{-26} kg-m/s
(d) 5×10^{-36} kg, 1.67×10^{-43} kg-m/s

3. The energy of a photon of light with wavelength 8000 Å is approximately 8.5 eV. The energy of X-ray photon with wavelength 1 Å would be

(a) 64 keV (b) 68 keV
(c) 20 keV (d) 24 keV

4. If we express the energy of a photon in keV and the wavelength in angstroms, then energy of a photon can be calculated from the relation

(a) $12.4\, h\nu$ (b) $12.4\dfrac{h}{\lambda}$
(c) $12.4/\lambda$ (d) $h\nu$

5. A wireless radio operates at a frequency of 10 kHz and using power of 10 kW. Then, number of photons emitted per second are

(a) 1.72×10^{31}
(b) 0.15×10^{34}
(c) 13.27×10^{34}
(d) 0.75×10^{-20}

6. A material undergoes photoelectric emission for a threshold wavelength of 4800 Å. Photoelectrons will be emitted from the material, when it is illuminated with light from a

(a) 40 W green lamp
(b) 40 W blue lamp
(c) 2 W green lamp
(d) 2 W yellow lamp

7. If 3% of the energy supplied to a bulb is irradiated as visible light, how many photons are emitted per second by a 100 W lamp? (Given, wavelength of visible light as 6.6×10^{-5} cm)

(a) 4×10^{19} (b) 4×10^{3}
(c) 1×10^{21} (d) 1×10^{14}

8. A monochromatiç source of light emits photons of frequency 6×10^{14} Hz. The power emitted by the source is 8×10^{-3} W. The number of photons emitted per second is (Take, $h = 6.63\times 10^{-34}$ J-s)

(a) 6×10^{14}
(b) 4×10^{15}
(c) 2×10^{16}
(d) 1×10^{17}

9. A light having wavelength of 840 nm incident on a metal surface and power of incident light is 100 W, then number of emitted photons is ($h = 6 \times 10^{-34}$ J-s)

(a) 4890×10^{16} (b) 4826×10^{10}
(c) 4666×10^{17} (d) 4822×10^{18}

10. A radio station is broadcasting the waves of wavelength 3×10^{8} m. If the radiating power of the transmitter is 10 kW, then the number of photons radiated per second is

(a) 1.5×10^{29} (b) 0.50×10^{36}
(c) 1.5×10^{33} (d) 1.5×10^{37}

11. How many photons are emitted per second by a 10 mW laser source operating at 632.8 nm?

(a) 1.6×10^{16} (b) 4.8×10^{16}
(c) 3.2×10^{16} (d) 1×10^{16}

12. A beam of 10.6 eV photons of intensity 2.0 Wm^{-2} falls on a surface of platinum of surface area 1.0×10^{-4} m^2 and the work function of the material is 5.6 eV. Given that, 0.53% of the incident photons eject photoelectrons. The number of photoelectrons emitted per second and their maximum kinetic energy is respectively,

(a) 7×10^{11}, 0 eV
(b) 6.25×10^{11}, 5.0 eV
(c) 9×10^{10}, 6.0 eV
(d) 11×10^{11}, 2.5 eV

13. A source of monochromatic light liberates 9×10^{20} photons per second with wavelength 600 nm when operated at 400 W. The number of photons emitted per second with wavelength of 800 nm by the source of monochromatic light operating at same power will be

(a) 12×10^{20} (b) 6×10^{20}
(c) 9×10^{20} (d) 24×10^{20}

14. The energy flux of sunlight reaching the surface of the earth is 1.52×10^{3} Wm^{-2}. The photons in the sunlight have an average wavelength of 520 nm. How many photons per square metre are incident on the earth per second?

(a) 4×10^{21} (b) 4×10^{34}
(c) 4×10^{31} (d) 4×10^{28}

15. Match the Column I (quantities) with Column II (expression of the values) and select the correct answer from the codes given below.

Column I	Column II
A. Maximum number of photons absorbed by an electron	1. $\frac{\phi_0}{\nu_0}$
B. Number of photons emitted by a source per second	2. $\frac{P}{E}$
C. Energy of a photon E	3. $h\nu$
D. Planck's constant h	4. 1

Codes

	A	B	C	D
(a)	2	4	1	3
(b)	4	2	3	1
(c)	2	4	3	1
(d)	3	1	2	4

Response Index

01 (a) (b) (c) (d)
02 (a) (b) (c) (d)
03 (a) (b) (c) (d)
04 (a) (b) (c) (d)
05 (a) (b) (c) (d)
06 (a) (b) (c) (d)
07 (a) (b) (c) (d)
08 (a) (b) (c) (d)
09 (a) (b) (c) (d)
10 (a) (b) (c) (d)
11 (a) (b) (c) (d)
12 (a) (b) (c) (d)
13 (a) (b) (c) (d)
14 (a) (b) (c) (d)
15 (a) (b) (c) (d)

Performance Scanner

> 90% Excellent !	You have mastered these topics. The concepts of these topics are on your fingertips. Move on to the next test and maintain this momentum.
76-90% Very Good !	You have a good command over these topics. Revise these topics again after a few days and enhance your performance.
60-75% Good !	You have a wide scope to learn for these topics. Revise them again.
<60% Not Satisfactory!	You have a long way ahead of you to master these topics. Revise them thoroughly.

Test 3

Syllabus
- Matter Waves
- Wave Nature of Particle
- de-Broglie Relation

For deeper insight **Scan the QR Code**

Important Instructions
- The test is of 30 minutes duration and contains 15 Multiple Choice Questions. (Four options with a single correct answer).
- Choose the correct option and fill the OMR given on the last page of this test accordingly.
- At some instances, you may find more than 1 option may be correct, in such circumstances you have to judge the most appropriate answer as per conditions given in the question.

1. An α-particle of mass 1 mg has the same wavelength as an electron moving with a velocity of 5×10^{6} ms^{-1}. The velocity of the particle is (mass of electron = 9.1×10^{-31} kg)

(a) 3×10^{-31} ms^{-1}
(b) 2.7×10^{-21} ms^{-1}
(c) 4.5×10^{-18} ms^{-1}
(d) 9×10^{-2} ms^{-1}

2. When a potential difference of V is applied to an electron of mass m, it gets accelerated and gains wavelength λ. The de-Broglie wavelength associated with a proton of mass M accelerated through the same potential difference will be

(a) $\lambda\dfrac{m}{M}$ (b) $\lambda\sqrt{\dfrac{m}{M}}$
(c) $\lambda\dfrac{M}{m}$ (d) $\lambda\sqrt{\dfrac{M}{m}}$

3. The kinetic energy of electron and proton is 10^{-32} J. Then, relation between their de-Broglie wavelength is

(a) $\lambda_p<\lambda_e$ (b) $\lambda_p>\lambda_e$
(c) $\lambda_p=\lambda_e$ (d) $\lambda_p=2\lambda_e$

4. A neutron particle is moving with de-Broglie wavelength λ, at 27°C. Then, wavelength of neutron particle at 927°C will be

(a) $\dfrac{\lambda}{2}$ (b) $\dfrac{\lambda}{3}$
(c) $\dfrac{\lambda}{4}$ (d) $\dfrac{\lambda}{9}$

5. The de-Broglie wavelengths of electron, proton and α-particle are λ_e, λ_p and λ_α, respectively. If all are accelerated by same potential, then

(a) $\lambda_e>\lambda_p>\lambda_\alpha$ (b) $\lambda_e<\lambda_p<\lambda_\alpha$
(c) $\lambda_e<\lambda_p>\lambda_\alpha$ (d) $\lambda_e=\lambda_p>\lambda_\alpha$

6. A proton accelerated through a potential V has de-Broglie wavelength λ. Then, the de-Broglie wavelength of an α-particle, when accelerated through the same potential V is

(a) $\dfrac{\lambda}{2}$ (b) $\dfrac{\lambda}{\sqrt{2}}$
(c) $\dfrac{\lambda}{2\sqrt{2}}$ (d) $\dfrac{\lambda}{8}$

7. Statement I A particle at rest breaks into two particles of different mass. They fly-off in different direction. Their de-Broglie wavelength will be different.

Statement II Their speed will be different.

In the light of above statements, choose the most appropriate answer from the options given below.

(a) Both Statement I and Statement II are true.
(b) Both Statement I and Statement II are false.
(c) Statement I is true but Statement II is false.
(d) Statement I is false but Statement II is true.

8. When the momentum of a proton is changed by an amount p_0, the corresponding change in de-Broglie wavelength is found to be 0.40%.

Then, the original momentum of the proton was

(a) 400 p_0 (b) 250 p_0 (c) 200 p_0 (d) 125 p_0

9. In a system of two particles in which electron and photon both have same mass m and energy E, when they are moving. The ratio of their de-Broglie wavelength is

(a) $\frac{1}{c}\left(\frac{E}{2m}\right)^{\frac{1}{2}}$ (b) $\left(\frac{E}{2m}\right)^{\frac{1}{2}}$

(c) $c(2mE)^{\frac{1}{2}}$ (d) $\frac{1}{4c}\left(\frac{2m}{E}\right)^{\frac{1}{2}}$

10. A particle is moving with kinetic energy of x initially and it is increased to 64 times. The percentage change in the de-Broglie wavelength of the particle is

(a) 62.6% (b) 53.2%
(c) −87.5% (d) −62.6%

11. A particle of mass $4m$ at rest, decays into two particles of masses $2m$ and $2m$ having non-zero speeds. What is the ratio of de-Broglie wavelengths of the particles ?

(a) 2 : 1 (b) 3 : 2 (c) 2 : 3 (d) 1 : 1

12. If de-Broglie wavelength of a moving electron is decreased from 2 Å to 1 Å, then calculate change in its KE (in eV).

(a) 100 eV (b) 200 eV
(c) 115.6 eV (d) 112.5 eV

13. In which of the following situations, the heavier of the two particles has smaller de-Broglie wavelength? The two particles

(i) move with same linear momentum
(ii) move with same kinetic energy
(iii) have fallen through the same height
(iv) move with same speed

(a) (i), (ii), (iii) (b) (ii), (iii), (iv)
(c) (i), (iii), (iv) (d) (i), (ii), (iv)

14. Match the Column I with Column II when KE of an electron is 100 eV.

	Column I		Column II
A.	Momentum (in kg-ms^{-1})	I.	1.22×10^{-10}
B.	Speed (in ms^{-1})	II.	5.9×10^{6}
C.	de-Broglie wavelength (in m)	III.	5.4×10^{-24}
D.	Frequency (in s^{-1})	IV.	2.46×10^{18}

Choose the correct answer from the given options.

(a) A-II, B-I, C-III, D-IV
(b) A-III, B-II, C-I, D-IV
(c) A-I, B-II, C-III, D-IV
(d) A-II, B-I, C-IV, D-III

15. A photocell is illuminated by a bright source of frequency greater than threshold frequency. On increasing distance of source from photocell, minimum value of de-Broglie wavelength emitted photoelectrons

(a) remains same
(b) increases
(c) decreases
(d) at first decreases and then becomes constant

Response Index

01	(a)	(b)	(c)	(d)	10	(a)	(b)	(c)	(d)
02	(a)	(b)	(c)	(d)	11	(a)	(b)	(c)	(d)
03	(a)	(b)	(c)	(d)	12	(a)	(b)	(c)	(d)
04	(a)	(b)	(c)	(d)	13	(a)	(b)	(c)	(d)
05	(a)	(b)	(c)	(d)	14	(a)	(b)	(c)	(d)
06	(a)	(b)	(c)	(d)	15	(a)	(b)	(c)	(d)
07	(a)	(b)	(c)	(d)					
08	(a)	(b)	(c)	(d)					
09	(a)	(b)	(c)	(d)					

Performance Scanner

> 90% Excellent !	You have mastered these topics. The concepts of these topics are on your fingertips. Move on to the next test and maintain this momentum.
76-90% Very Good !	You have a good command over these topics. Revise these topics again after a few days and enhance your performance.
60-75% Good !	You have a wide scope to learn for these topics. Revise them again.
<60% Not Satisfactory!	You have a long way ahead of you to master in these topics. Revise them thoroughly.

Chapter Break Thru

Syllabus	• Photoelectric Effect • Einstein's Photoelectric Equation • Hertz and Lenard's Observations	• Particle Nature of Light : The Photon	• Matter Waves • Wave Nature of Particle • de-Broglie Relation

Important Instructions

- The test is of 45 minutes duration and contains 30 Multiple Choice Questions. (Four options with a single correct answer).
- Choose the correct option and fill the OMR given on the last page of this test accordingly.
- At some instances, you may find more than 1 option may be correct, in such circumstances you have to judge the most appropriate answer as per conditions given in the question.

1. If an electron and a photon propagate in the form of waves having the same wavelength, it implies that they have the same

(a) energy
(b) momentum
(c) velocity
(d) angular momentum

2. Which of the following graphs represents the variation of particle momentum and the associated de-Broglie wavelength?

(a) 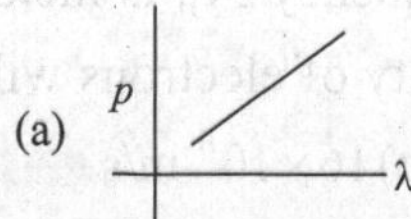

(b) 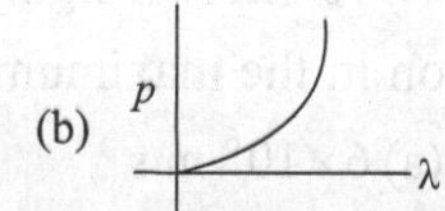

(c) 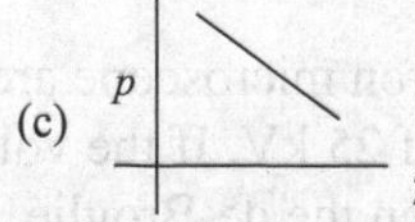

(d) 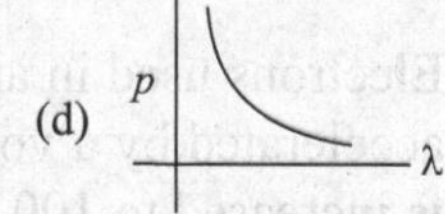

3. The kinetic energy of an electron which is accelerated through a potential of 200 V is

(a) 3.2×10^{-17} J
(b) 418.6×10^{-12} J
(c) 1.16×10^{4} J
(d) 6.626×10^{-34} J

4. Assertion (A) Though monochromatic light is incident on a metal surface, the energies of emitted photoelectrons are different.

Reason (R) The energy of electrons emitted from inside the metal surface is lost in collision with the other atoms in the metal.

In the light of above statements, choose the most appropriate answer from the options given below.

(a) Both A and R are true and R is the correct explanation of A.
(b) Both A and R are true but R is not the correct explanation of A.
(c) A is true but R is false.
(d) A is false but R is true.

5. In a photoelectric experiment, if both the intensity and frequency of the incident light are doubled, then the saturation photoelectric current

(a) remains constant
(b) becomes half
(c) becomes double
(d) becomes four times

6. The de-Broglie wavelength for electron in an orbit of hydrogen atom is 10^{-10} m and radius of orbit is 5.3×10^{-11} m. The principal quantum number for this electron is

(a) 1 (b) 2 (c) 3 (d) 4

7. A particle is moving with a velocity 2.25×10^8 m/s and de-Broglie wavelength equal to the wavelength of photon. Then, ratio of kinetic energy of the particle to the energy of the photon is
(Take, speed of light, $c = 3 \times 10^8$ m/s)

(a) $\frac{1}{8}$ (b) $\frac{3}{8}$

(c) $\frac{5}{8}$ (d) $\frac{7}{8}$

8. A particle A of mass m and initial velocity v collides with a particle B of mass $\frac{m}{2}$ which is at rest. The collision is head-on and elastic. The ratio of the de-Broglie wavelengths λ_A to λ_B after the collision is

(a) 2 (b) $\frac{2}{3}$

(c) $\frac{1}{2}$ (d) $\frac{1}{3}$

9. When a monochromatic point source of light is at a distance of 0.4 m from a photoelectric cell, the cut-off voltage and the saturation current are respectively 0.6 V and 27 mA. If the same source is placed 0.6 m away from the photoelectric cell, then

(i) $V_S = 0.3$ V
(ii) $V_S = 0.6$ V
(iii) $i = 6$ mA
(iv) $i = 12$ mA

(a) (i), (iii) (b) (ii), (iii) (c) (ii), (iv) (d) (i), (iv)

10. A box contains n photons having wavelength λ which are absorbed by a body of mass m. The momentum gained by the body is

(a) $\frac{nh}{\lambda}$ (b) $\frac{mnh}{\lambda}$

(c) $\frac{nh}{m\lambda}$ (d) $\frac{h}{m\lambda}$

11. The work function of a metal is 2 eV. Light of wavelength 4000 Å is incident on this metal surface. The velocity of emitted photoelectrons will be

(a) 10 m/s (b) 1×10^3 m/s

(c) 1×10^4 m/s (d) 0.618×10^6 m/s

12. An electron with initial velocity $v_0\hat{\mathbf{i}}$ is in the region of electric and magnetic fields, $-E_0\hat{\mathbf{i}}$ and $B_0\hat{\mathbf{j}}$, respectively. The de-Broglie wavelength of the electron at time t is given by

(a) $\lambda = \frac{h}{mv_0}$

(b) $\lambda = \frac{h}{qt(E_0)}$

(c) $\lambda = \frac{h}{qt(E_0^2 + B_0^2)^{1/2}}$

(d) $\lambda = \frac{h}{qt(E_0^2 + v_0^2 B_0^2)^{1/2}}$

13. **Statement I** If wavelength of incident photons is halved, then maximum kinetic energy of photoelectrons will become two times.
Statement II Energy of photon is inversely proportional to the wavelength.
In the light of above statements, choose the most appropriate answer from the options given below.

(a) Both Statement I and Statement II are true.
(b) Both Statement I and Statement II are false.
(c) Statement I is true but Statement II is false.
(d) Statement I is false but Statement II is true.

14. For a certain metal, the threshold frequency is ν_0. If light of frequency $2\nu_0$ is incident on it, the electrons come out with a maximum velocity of 4×10^6 m/s. If light of frequency $5\nu_0$ is incident on it, the maximum velocity of electrons will be

(a) 6×10^6 m/s (b) 16×10^6 m/s

(c) 8×10^6 m/s (d) 4×10^6 m/s

15. Electrons used in an electron microscope are accelerated by a voltage of 25 kV. If the voltage is increased to 100 kV, then the de-Broglie wavelength associated with the electrons would

(a) increase by 4 times
(b) increase by 2 times
(c) decrease by 2 times
(d) decrease by 4 times

16. The de-Broglie wavelength of a proton having charge 1.6×10^{-19} C and mass 1.6×10^{-27} kg accelerated through potential difference of 1 kV is

(a) 600 Å
(b) 0.9×10^{-12} m
(c) 7 Å
(d) 0.9 nm

17. Threshold wavelength for lithium metal is 6250 Å. For photoemission, the wavelength of the incident light must be

(a) more than 6250 Å
(b) exactly equal to 6250 Å
(c) equal to or more than 6250 Å
(d) equal to or less than 6250 Å

18. A substance is placed at the ground surface and having work function of 19.2 eV. The longest wavelength of light that cause photoelectrons emission from this substance is approximately

(a) 540 nm (b) 645.8 nm
(c) 310 nm (d) 220 nm

19. The kinetic energy of an electron is 6 eV. The de-Broglie wavelength associated with it, is ($h = 6.6 \times 10^{-34}$ J-s, $m_e = 9.1 \times 10^{-31}$ kg)

(a) 4.99 Å
(b) 5.67 Å
(c) 3.99 Å
(d) 7.61 Å

20. During photoelectric effect, the stopping potential V for photoelectric emission from a metal surface is plotted along Y-axis and frequency ν of incident light along X-axis. As a result, a straight line is obtained as shown. Planck's constant is given by

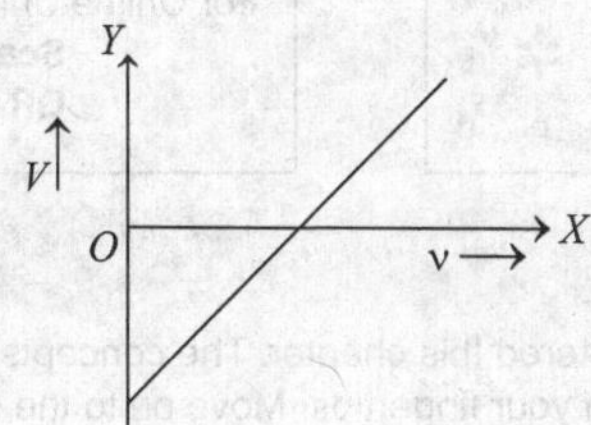

(a) slope of the line
(b) product of slope on the line and charge on the electron
(c) product of intercept along Y-axis and mass of the electron
(d) product of slope and mass of electron

21. In an experiment on photoelectric effect, the slope of the cut-off voltage *versus* frequency of incident light is found to be 2.14×10^{-14} V-s. The value of Planck's constant will be

(a) 1.12×10^{-34} J-s
(b) 6.592×10^{-34} J-s
(c) 3.42×10^{-33} J-s
(d) 1.46×10^{-29} J-s

22. For photosensitive material, match the Column I with Column II and choose the correct combination from options given below.

	Column I	Column II
A.	Photocurrent *versus* Intensity	1.
B.	Photocurrent *versus* Collector potential	2.
C.	Kinetic energy of photoelectrons *versus* Intensity	3.
D.	Stopping potential *versus* Frequency	4.

(a) A-2, B-4, C-1, D-3
(b) A-3, B-2, C-4, D-1
(c) A-4, B-3, C-2, D-1
(d) A-1, B-2, C-3, D-4

23. A metal exposed to light of wavelength 800 nm emits photoelectrons with a certain kinetic energy. The maximum kinetic energy of photoelectrons doubles when light of wavelength 500 nm is used. The work function of the metal is (Take, $hc = 1230$ eV-nm)

(a) 1.537 eV
(b) 2.46 eV
(c) 0.615 eV
(d) 1.23 eV

24. Two streams of photons, possessing energies equal to five and ten times the work function of metal, are incident on the metal surface successively. The ratio of maximum velocities of the photoelectron emitted, in the two cases respectively, will be

(a) 1 : 2 (b) 1 : 3 (c) 2 : 3 (d) 3 : 2

25. In an experiment, the threshold wavelength of light is 580 nm. If the wavelength of incident light is 460 nm, the maximum kinetic energy will be

$$\left(\text{Given, } E(\text{in eV}) = \frac{1237}{\lambda(\text{in nm})}\right)$$

(a) 0.5 eV (b) 4.5 eV
(c) 15.1 eV (d) 3.0 eV

26. An electron of mass m_e and a proton of mass m_p are accelerated through the same potential difference. The ratio of the de-Broglie wavelength associated with the electron to that with the proton is

(a) $\frac{m_p}{m_e}$ (b) 1 (c) $\sqrt{\frac{m_p}{m_e}}$ (d) $\frac{m_e}{m_p}$

27. The difference between threshold wavelengths for two metal surfaces A and B having work functions $\phi_A = 8$ eV and $\phi_B = 4.5$ eV (in nm) is
(Given, $hc = 1242$ eV-nm)

(a) 180.75 nm (b) 260.75 nm
(c) 120.75 nm (d) 220.75 nm

28. In a photocell, a lens is placed and light beam is focused over photosensitive metal. Then, maximum kinetic energy of emitted electrons

(a) increases
(b) decreases
(c) remains same
(d) either increases or decreases

29. The graph between $1/\lambda$ and stopping potential V of three metals having work functions ϕ_1, ϕ_2 and ϕ_3 in an experiment of photoelectric effect is plotted as shown in the figure given below. Which of the following statement(s) is/are correct? (Here, λ is the wavelength of the incident ray).

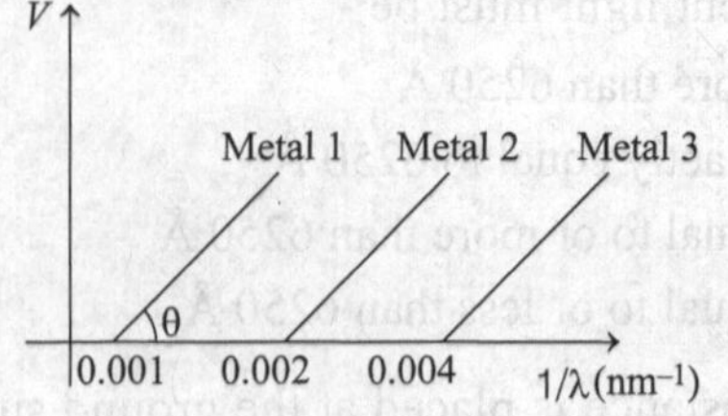

(a) Ratio of work functions $\phi_1 : \phi_2 : \phi_3 = 1 : 3 : 4$
(b) Ratio of work functions $\phi_1 : \phi_2 : \phi_3 = 4 : 2 : 1$
(c) Tan θ is directly proportional to hc/e, where h is Planck's constant and c is the speed of light.
(d) The violet colour light can eject photoelectrons from metals 2 and 3.

30. The magnetic field associated with a light wave is given at the origin by
$B = B_0 [\sin(3.14 \times 10^7)\, ct + \sin(6.28 \times 10^7) ct]$.
If this light falls on a silver plate having a work function of 4.7 eV, then what will be the maximum kinetic energy of the photoelectrons?
(Take, $c = 3 \times 10^8$ ms^{-1} and $h = 6.6 \times 10^{-34}$ J-s)

(a) 7.72 eV (b) 6.82 eV
(c) 8.52 eV (d) 12.5 eV

For Online Chapter Test **Scan the QR Code**

For Online Unit Test **Scan the QR Code**

Response Index

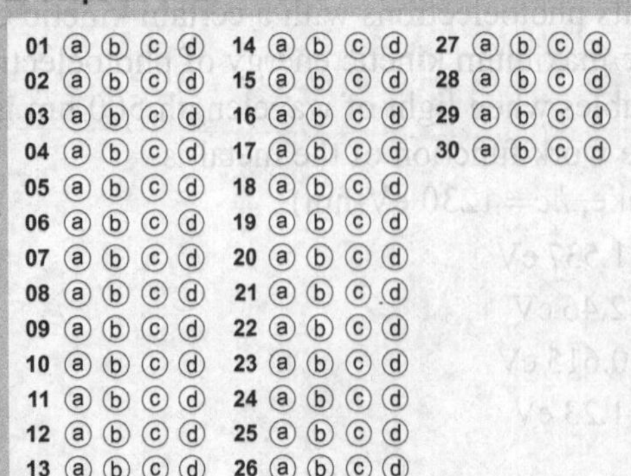

Performance Scanner

> 90% Excellent !	You have mastered this chapter. The concepts of this chapter are on your fingertips. Move on to the next chapter and maintain this momentum.
76-90% Very Good !	You have a good command over this chapter. Revise this chapter again after a few days and enhance your performance.
60-75% Good !	You have a wide scope to learn for this chapter. Revise it again.
<60% Not Satisfactory!	You have a long way ahead of you to master in this chapter. Revise it thoroughly.

Space for Rough Work

Space for Rough Work

Space for Rough Work

Space for Rough Work

Test Booklet No. **3947163**

Test Booklet Code **CH13**

MEDACE
NEET (UG)
SELF ASSESSMENT KIT

Atoms

Topics Covered

α-particle Scattering Experiment and Rutherford's Model of Atom

Bohr's Model and Hydrogen Spectra

Important Instructions

- This Booklet contains-Two Topic Tests and one Test on Complete Chapter.
- Each question carries 4 Marks. For each correct response, the candidate will get 4 marks.
- For every incorrect response, 1 mark will be additionally deducted from total score.
- Use **Blue/Black** point pen only for filling the OMR.
- Rough work to be done in the space provided for this purpose within the test booklet only.

Name of the Candidate (In Capitals)

____

____

Candidate's Signature __________

Invigilator's Signature __________

Facsimile signature stamp of center superintendent__________

Do not open this Booklet until you start attempting the Test

Topical Follow Thru

Test 1

Syllabus
- α-particle Scattering Experiment and Rutherford's Model of Atom

For deeper insight **Scan the QR Code**

Important Instructions
- The test is of 45 min duration and contains 25 Multiple Choice Questions. (Four options with a single correct answer).
- Choose the correct option and fill the OMR given on the last page of this test accordingly.
- At some instances, you may find more than 1 option may be correct, in such circumstances you have to judge the most appropriate answer as per conditions given in the question.

1. In α-particle scattering experiment, for a small thickness of gold foil and keeping other parameters constant, the number of α-particles scattered at moderate angles is proportional to thickness ($N \propto t$). This is due to the fact that

(a) increase in thickness is proportional to number of collisions of particle

(b) increase in thickness is inversely proportional to number of collisions of particle

(c) scattering is predominantly due to single collision and chance of a single collision increases with the number of target atoms

(d) scattering in thick sheets is due to multiple collision of α-particles

2. J.J. Thomson's cathode ray experiment demonstrated

(a) that the (e/m) ratio of cathode-ray particle changes when a different gas is placed in the discharge tube

(b) that all the mass of an atom is essentially in the nucleus

(c) that cathode rays are streams of negatively charged ions

(d) that the (e/m) ratio of electrons is much greater than the (e/m) ratio of protons

3. A beam of fast moving α-particles were directed towards a thin film of gold. The parts A', B' and C' of the transmitted and reflected beams corresponding to the incident parts A, B and C of the beam, are shown in the given diagram. The number of α-particles in

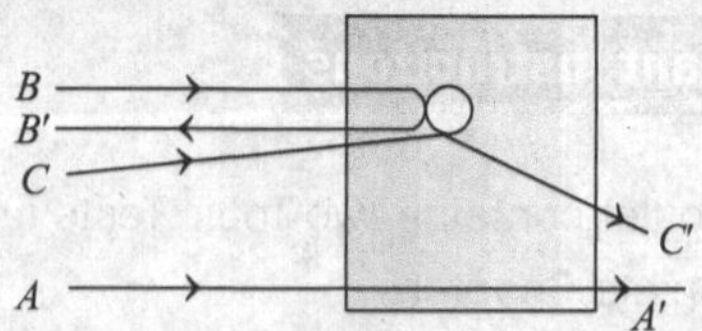

(a) B' will be minimum and in C' maximum

(b) A' will be maximum and in B' minimum

(c) A' will be minimum and in B' maximum

(d) C' will be minimum and in B' maximum

4. In Rutherford's α-particle experiment, an α-particle is noticed to trace its path backwards. Which of the following is most likely its probability?

(a) 1%

(b) 10%

(c) 40%

(d) 90%

5. In a Rutherford's scattering experiment, when a projectile of charge Z_1 and mass M_1 approaches a target nucleus of charge Z_2 and mass M_2, the distance of closest approach is r_0. The energy of the projectile is

(a) directly proportional to $Z_1 \times Z_2$
(b) inversely proportional to Z_1
(c) directly proportional to mass M_1
(d) directly proportional to $M_1 \times M_2$

6. An α-particle of energy 5 MeV is scattered through 180° by a fixed uranium nucleus. The distance of closest approach is the order of

(a) 1 Å
(b) 10^{-10} cm
(c) 10^{-11} cm
(d) 10^{-15} cm

7. Which of the following options is correct regarding atom of same element?

(a) Size of atom in Thomson's model is larger than the Rutherford's model.
(b) Size of atom in Rutherford's model is larger than the Thomson's model.
(c) Size of atom is same in both Rutherford's and Thomson's model.
(d) No comparison can be made for both models.

8. In a head-on collision between an α-particle and gold nucleus, the closest distance of approach is 2×10^{-14} m. The kinetic energy of α-particle is

(a) 9.1×10^{-3} J (b) 9.1×10^{-13} J
(c) 1.8×10^{-12} J (d) zero

9. Statement I In Rutherford's α-scattering experiment, only one among the 20000 α-particles is deflected.

Statement II Most of the space in the atom in Rutherford's experiment is vacant.

In the light of above statements, choose the most appropriate answer from the options given below.

(a) Both Statement I and Statement II are correct.
(b) Both Statement I and Statement II are incorrect.
(c) Statement I is correct but Statement II is incorrect.
(d) Statement I is incorrect but Statement II is correct.

10. Spectrum of Rutherford's atom is

(a) line emission spectrum
(b) line absorption spectrum
(c) band emission spectrum
(d) No emission by Rutherford's atom

11. The distance of closest approach of an α-particle fired towards a nucleus with momentum p is r. Then, the distance of closest approach when the momentum of α-particle is $2p$, will be

(a) $2r$ (b) $4r$
(c) $r/2$ (d) $r/4$

12. In Rutherford's scattering experiment, if impact $b = 0$, then the correct angle for α-scattering for an impact parameter is

(a) 90° (b) 270°
(c) 0° (d) 180°

13. Assertion (A) Most of an atom is an empty space.

Reason (R) From Rutherford's experiment, size of the nucleus is 10^{-10} m and from kinetic theory, size of the atom is 10^{-15} m.

In the light of above statements, choose the most appropriate answer from the options given below.

(a) Both A and R are true and R is the correct explanation of A.
(b) Both A and R are true but R is not the correct explanation of A.
(c) A is true but R is false.
(d) A is false but R is true.

14. When an α-particle of mass m moving with velocity v bombards a heavy nucleus of charge Ze, its distance of closest approach from the nucleus depends on m as

(a) $\frac{1}{\sqrt{m}}$ (b) $\frac{1}{m^2}$
(c) m (d) $\frac{1}{m}$

15. Total energy of electron in Rutherford's model is
(a) positive
(b) negative
(c) zero
(d) initially positive then negative

16. In Thomson's experiment, the potential difference between cathode and anode in the accelerating column is same as the potential difference between the deflecting plates (in the region of crossed **E** and **B**). If potential difference is doubled, then by what factor should the magnetic field be increased to ensure that the electron beam remains undeflected?
(a) $\sqrt{2}$ (b) $2\sqrt{2}$
(c) 2 (d) 4

17. In α-particle scattering experiment for a given angle θ, fraction of α-particles scattered by angle θ or more by a foil of thickness t and containing n atoms per unit volume will be
(a) $nt\pi b^2$ (b) $nt^2\pi b$
(c) $n^2t^3b^3$ (d) $n\pi$

18. **Statement I** Rutherford's model proposses a stable orbit.
Statement II A negative total energy is necessary for a stationary stable orbit.
In the light of above statements, choose the most appropriate answer from the options given below.
(a) Both Statement I and Statement II are correct.
(b) Both Statement I and Statement II are incorrect.
(c) Statement I is correct but Statement II is incorrect
(d) Statement I is incorrect but Statement II is correct.

19. Choose the correct option from the following options given below.
(a) In the ground state of Rutherford's model, electrons are in stable equilibrium. While in Thomson's model, electrons always experience a net force.
(b) An atom has a nearly continuous mass distribution in a Rutherford's model but has a highly non-uniform mass distribution in Thomson's model.
(c) A classical atom based on Rutherford's model is doomed to collapse.
(d) The positively charged part of the atom possesses most of the mass in Rutherford's model but not in Thomson's model.

20. $\sqrt{d_1}$ and $\sqrt{d_2}$ are the impact parameters corresponding to scattering angles 60° and 90° respectively, when an α-particle is approaching a gold nucleus. The ratio of d_1 and d_2 is
(a) 3 (b) 6
(c) 2 (d) 4

21. An alpha particle of initial energy 10 MeV is scattered by an inverse square field produced by a nucleus of $Z = 79$. For the scattering angle 90°, the impact parameter is
(a) 15×10^{-15} m (b) 11×10^{-15} m
(c) 1.5×10^{-15} m (d) 1.1×10^{-15} m

22. An α-particle is scattered by a nucleus as shown in the figure.

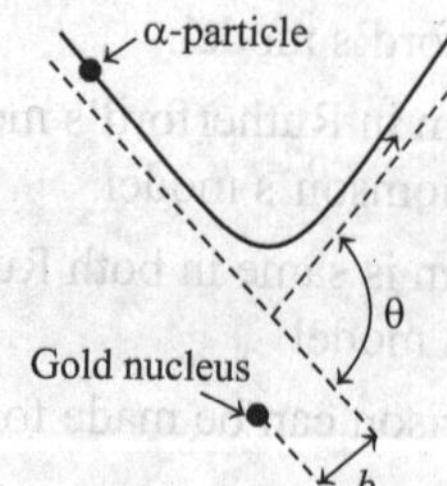

Let mass of α-particle is m and its speed is v. Assuming nucleus remains stationary, change in momentum of α-particle is
(a) $2mv\sin\theta$
(b) $2mv\cos\theta$
(c) $2mv\cos\frac{\theta}{2}$
(d) $2mv\sin\frac{\theta}{2}$

23. In Thomson's experiment of finding specific charge of electrons, if electrons are replaced by muons ($m = 208\times$ mass of an electron, $q =$ same as electron), then the no deflection is observed when
(a) B is increased 208 times
(b) B is increased 14.4 times
(c) E is increased 208 times
(d) E is increased 14.4 times

24. The distance of closest approach of an α-particle is fired at a nucleus with momentum p is r_0. When the α-particles are fired at the same nucleus with momentum $5p$, the distance of closest approach will be

(a) $5r_0$ (b) $\frac{1}{5}r_0$ (c) $25\,r_0$ (d) $\frac{1}{25}r_0$

25. Thomson's model cannot explain

(a) photoemission

(b) neutrality of matter

(b) presence of two types of charges in matter

(d) backward scattering of α-particle

Response Index

01	a	b	c	d	10	a	b	c	d	19	a	b	c	d
02	a	b	c	d	11	a	b	c	d	20	a	b	c	d
03	a	b	c	d	12	a	b	c	d	21	a	b	c	d
04	a	b	c	d	13	a	b	c	d	22	a	b	c	d
05	a	b	c	d	14	a	b	c	d	23	a	b	c	d
06	a	b	c	d	15	a	b	c	d	24	a	b	c	d
07	a	b	c	d	16	a	b	c	d	25	a	b	c	d
08	a	b	c	d	17	a	b	c	d					
09	a	b	c	d	18	a	b	c	d					

Performance Scanner

> 90% Excellent !	You have mastered these topics. The concepts of these topics are on your fingertips. Move on to the next test and maintain this momentum.
76-90% Very Good !	You have a good command over these topics. Revise these topics again after a few days and enhance your performance.
60-75% Good !	You have a wide scope to learn for these topics. Revise them again.
<60% Not Satisfactory!	You have a long way ahead of you to master these topics. Revise them thoroughly.

Test 2

Syllabus
- Bohr's Model
- Hydrogen Spectrum
- Energy Levels

For deeper insight **Scan the QR Code**

Important Instructions
- The test is of 45 min duration and contains 25 Multiple Choice Questions. (Four options with a single correct answer).
- Choose the correct option and fill the OMR given on the last page of this test accordingly.
- At some instances, you may find more than 1 option may be correct, in such circumstances you have to judge the most appropriate answer as per the conditions given in the question.

1. A hydrogen atom changes its state from $n=3$ to $n=2$. Due to recoil, the percentage loss in energy of photon is

(a) 10^{-7}
(b) 10^{-9}
(c) 10^{-5}
(d) 10^{-11}

2. Statement I Bohr's model cannot be extended to two or more electron atoms.

Statement II Each electron in the atom interacts not only with the positively charged nucleus but also with all other electrons.

In the light of above statements, choose the most appropriate answer from the options given below.

(a) Both Statement I and Statement II are correct.
(b) Statement I is correct but Statement II is incorrect.
(c) Statement I is incorrect but Statement II is correct.
(d) Both Statement I and Statement II are incorrect.

3. If E_P and E_K are the potential energy and kinetic energy of the electron in stationary orbit in the hydrogen, then value of $\frac{E_P}{E_K}$ will be

(a) 2
(b) -1
(c) 1
(d) -2

4. In hydrogen atom, electron jumps from second to first orbit, the energy emitted is

(a) -13.6 eV
(b) 27.2 eV
(c) -6.8 eV
(d) 10.2 eV

5. In hydrogen atom, electron making transition between different states.

Column I (Initial and final state)	Column II (No. of spectral lines)	
A. $n=4$ to $n_1=1$	(i)	10
B. $n_2=5$ to $n_1=3$	(ii)	6
C. $n_2=6$ to $n_1=2$	(iii)	15
D. $n_2=6$ to $n_1=1$	(iv)	3

(a) A→ iv, B→ i, C→ iii, D→ ii
(b) A→ ii, B→ iv, C→ i, D→ iii
(c) A→ ii, B→ iii, C→ i, D→ iv
(d) A→ iii, B→ ii, C→ iv, D→ i

6. The ionisation energy of hydrogen atom is 13.6 eV. Following Bohr's theory, the energy corresponding to a transition between 3rd and 4th orbit is

(a) 3.40 eV
(b) 1.51 eV
(c) 0.85 eV
(d) 0.66 eV

7. $\frac{x}{x+4}$ is the ratio of energies of photons produced due to transition of an electron of hydrogen atom from its third permitted energy level to the second level and the highest permitted energy level to the second permitted level. The value of x will be

(a) 4 (b) 5
(c) 6 (d) 9

8. Taking the Bohr radius as $a_0 = 53$ pm, the radius of Li^{++} ion in its ground state, on the basis of Bohr's model will be about

(a) 53 pm (b) 27 pm
(c) 18 pm (d) 13 pm

9. If the wavelength of the first line of the Balmer series of hydrogen is 6561 Å, the wavelength of the second line of the series should be

(a) 13122 Å (b) 3280 Å
(c) 4860 Å (d) 2187 Å

10. For a hydrogen atom, λ_1 and λ_2 are the wavelengths corresponding to the transitions 1 and 2, respectively as shown in figure. The ratio of λ_1 and λ_2 is

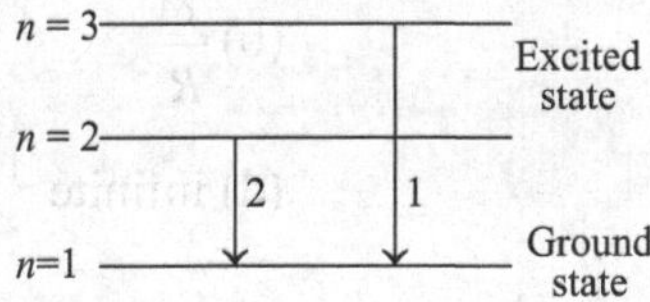

(a) $\frac{15}{32}$ (b) $\frac{17}{32}$
(c) $\frac{27}{32}$ (d) $\frac{25}{32}$

11. A 10 kg satellite circles earth once every 2h in an orbit having a radius of 8000 km. Assuming that Bohr's angular momentum postulate applies to satellites just as it does to an electron in hydrogen atom, then the quantum number of the orbit of satellite is

(a) 10×10^{40}
(b) 5.3×10^{45}
(c) 4×10^{10}
(d) 3.2×10^{25}

12. Calculate the radius of the third Bohr orbit of the electron of the hydrogen atom. (Take, $h = 6.625\times10^{-34}$ Js, $e = 1.6\times10^{-19}$ C, $m = 9.1\times10^{-31}$ kg, $c = 3\times10^8$ ms^{-1}, $\varepsilon_0 = 8.85\times10^{-12}$ C^{2}N^{-1}m^{-2})

(a) 2.48 Å
(b) 3.68 Å
(c) 2.68 Å
(d) 4.77 Å

13. Some energy levels of a molecule are shown in the figure. The ratio of the wavelengths, $r = \lambda_1 / \lambda_2$ is given by

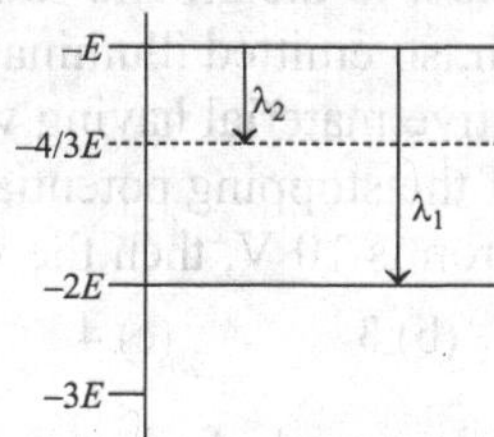

(a) $r = \frac{2}{3}$ (b) $r = \frac{3}{4}$
(c) $r = \frac{1}{3}$ (d) $r = \frac{4}{3}$

14. Hydrogen atom from excited state comes to the ground state by emitting a photon of wavelength λ. If R is the Rydberg constant, then the principal quantum number n of the excited state is

(a) $\sqrt{\frac{\lambda R}{\lambda R - 1}}$
(b) $\sqrt{\frac{\lambda}{\lambda R - 1}}$
(c) $\sqrt{\frac{\lambda R^2}{\lambda R - 1}}$
(d) $\sqrt{\frac{\lambda R}{\lambda - 1}}$

15. If the shortest wavelength in the Lyman series is 911.6 Å, the longest wavelength in the same series will be

(a) 1600 Å
(b) 2430 Å
(c) 1215 Å
(d) ∞

16. Energy levels A, B and C of a certain atom correspond to increasing values of energy i.e. $E_A < E_B < E_C$. If λ_1, λ_2 and λ_3 are the wavelengths of radiation corresponding to the transitions C to B, B to A and C to A respectively, which of the following relation is correct?

(a) $\lambda_3 = \lambda_1 + \lambda_2$

(b) $\lambda_3 = \dfrac{\lambda_1 \lambda_2}{\lambda_1 + \lambda_2}$

(c) $\lambda_1 + \lambda_2 + \lambda_3 = 0$

(d) $\lambda_3^2 = \lambda_1^2 + \lambda_2^2$

17. An electron in the hydrogen atom jumps from excited state n to the ground state. The wavelength, so emitted illuminates a photosensitive material having work function 2.75 eV. If the stopping potential of the photoelectron is 10 V, then the value of n is

(a) 2 (b) 3 (c) 4 (d) 5

18. In the Bohr's model of a hydrogen atom, the centripetal force is furnished by the coulomb attraction between the proton and the electron. If a_0 is the radius of the ground state orbit, m is the mass and e is the charge on the electron, ε_0 is the vacuum permittivity, the speed of the electron is

(a) zero

(b) $\dfrac{e}{\sqrt{\varepsilon_0 a_0 m}}$

(c) $\dfrac{e}{\sqrt{4\pi\varepsilon_0 a_0 m}}$

(d) $\dfrac{\sqrt{4\pi\varepsilon_0 a_0 m}}{e}$

19. An electron of a stationary hydrogen atom passes from the fifth energy level to the ground level. The velocity that the atom acquired as a result of photon emission will be

(a) $\dfrac{24\,hR}{25\,m}$ (b) $\dfrac{25\,hR}{24\,m}$

(c) $\dfrac{25\,m}{24\,hR}$ (d) $\dfrac{24\,m}{25\,hR}$

(m is the mass of electron, R is Rydberg's constant and h is Planck's constant)

20. The angular speed of the electron in the nth orbit of Bohr's hydrogen atom is

(a) inversely proportional to $\sqrt{n}$

(b) inversely proportional to n^2

(c) inversely proportional to n^3

(d) directly proportional to n

21. Suppose an electron is attracted towards the origin by a force $\frac{k}{r}$, where k is a constant and r is the distance of the electron from the origin. By applying Bohr model to this system. The radius of the nth orbital of the electron is found to be r_n and the kinetic energy of the electron to be T_n. Then, which of the following is true?

(a) $T_n \propto \frac{1}{n^2}$, $r_n \propto n^2$

(b) T_n independent of n, $r_n \propto n$

(c) $T_n \propto \frac{1}{n}$, $r_n \propto n$

(d) $T_n \propto \frac{1}{n}$, $r_n \propto n^2$

22. The series limit wavelength of lyman series for the hydrogen atom is given by

(a) $\dfrac{1}{R}$ (b) $\dfrac{8}{R}$

(c) $\dfrac{16}{R}$ (d) infinite

23. Ground state energy of hydrogen atom is E_0. Match the following two columns.

	Column I		Column II
A.	Electrostatic potential energy in ground state of hydrogen atom	I.	$4E_0$
B.	Total energy in first excited state of He^+ ion	II.	$-2E_0$
C.	Kinetic energy of electron in first excited state of He^+ ion	III.	$2E_0$
D.	Kinetic energy of electron in ground state of hydrogen atom	IV.	$\dfrac{-E_0}{2}$

Choose the correct answer from the options given below.

(a) A→I, B→II, C→III, D→IV
(b) A→II, B→IV, C→III, D→I
(c) A→IV, B→III, C→I, D→II
(d) A→III, B→I, C→II, D→IV

24. Consider 3rd orbit of He^+ (Helium), using non-relativistic approach, the speed of electron in this orbit will be (given $K = 9 \times 10^9$ constant, $Z = 2$ and h (Planck's constant) $= 6.6 \times 10^{-34}$ J-s)

(a) 2.92×10^6 m/s (b) 1.46×10^6 m/s
(c) 0.73×10^6 m/s (d) 3.0×10^8 m/s

25. An electron jumps from the second excited state to the first excited state of the hydrogen atom, the wavelength of photon emitted is λ_0 and then jumps from the third excited state to the second excited state of the hydrogen atom, the wavelength of the photon emitted λ'. The ratio of the wavelength λ' and λ_0 is

(a) $\frac{7}{20}$
(b) $\frac{9}{20}$
(c) $\frac{20}{9}$
(d) $\frac{20}{7}$

Response Index

01	a	b	c	d	10	a	b	c	d	19	a	b	c	d
02	a	b	c	d	11	a	b	c	d	20	a	b	c	d
03	a	b	c	d	12	a	b	c	d	21	a	b	c	d
04	a	b	c	d	13	a	b	c	d	22	a	b	c	d
05	a	b	c	d	14	a	b	c	d	23	a	b	c	d
06	a	b	c	d	15	a	b	c	d	24	a	b	c	d
07	a	b	c	d	16	a	b	c	d	25	a	b	c	d
08	a	b	c	d	17	a	b	c	d					
09	a	b	c	d	18	a	b	c	d					

Performance Scanner

> 90% Excellent !	You have mastered these topics. The concepts of these topics are on your fingertips. Move on to the next test and maintain this momentum.
76-90% Very Good !	You have a good command over these topics. Revise these topics again after a few days and enhance your performance.
60-75% Good !	You have a wide scope to learn for these topics. Revise them again.
<60% Not Satisfactory!	You have a long way ahead of you to master these topics. Revise them thoroughly.

Chapter Break Thru

Syllabus	• α-particle Scattering Experiment and Rutherford Model of Atom	• Bohr's Model • Hydrogen Spectrum • Energy levels

Important Instructions

- The test is of 45 minutes duration and contains 30 Multiple Choice Questions (Four options with a single correct answer).
- Choose the correct option and fill the OMR given on the last page of this test accordingly.
- At some instances, you may find more than 1 option may be correct, in such circumstances you have to judge the most appropriate answer as per conditions given in the question.

1. The ground state energy of hydrogen atom is 13.6 eV. The energy required to ionise the target atom by knocking its electron out from $n=3$ state is

(a) 27.2 eV (b) 13.6 eV
(c) 6.8 eV (d) 1.51 eV

2. If m is mass of electron, v its velocity, r is the radius of stationary circular orbit around a nucleus with charge Ze, then from Bohr's first postulate, the kinetic energy $K=\frac{1}{2}mv^2$ of the electron in CGS system is equal to

(a) $\frac{1}{2}\frac{Ze^2}{r}$

(b) $\frac{1}{2}\frac{Ze^2}{r^2}$

(c) $\frac{Ze^2}{r}$

(d) $\frac{Ze}{r}$

3. The figure indicates the energy level diagram of an atom and the origin of six spectral lines in emission (e.g line no. 5 arises from the transition from level B to A).

The following spectral lines will also occur in the absorption spectrum.

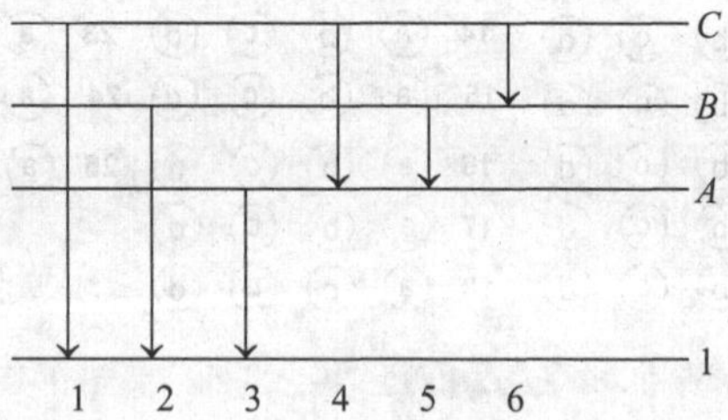

(a) 1, 4, 6 (b) 4, 5, 6
(c) 1, 2, 3 (d) 1, 2, 3, 4, 5, 6

4. The Rutherford α-particle experiment shows that the most of the α-particles pass through almost unscattered while some are scattered through large angle which means that

(a) atom is hollow
(b) the whole mass of the atom is concentrated in a small centre
(c) nucleus is positively charged
(d) All of the above

5. According to Bohr's theory, angular momentum of an electron in excited state of hydrogen atom is

(a) 1.11×10^{34} J-s (b) 1.51×10^{-31} J-s
(c) 2.11×10^{-34} J-s (d) 3.72×10^{-34} J-s

6. According to Bohr's theory, a hydrogen atom consists of a nucleus with a positive charge Ze, and single electron of charge $-e$, which revolves around it in a circular orbit of radius r. Then, radius of the second orbit of helium atom is
(a) 0.53 Å (b) 2.38 Å (c) 2.12 Å (d) 0.265 Å

7. An electron has a mass of 9.1×10^{-31} kg. It revolves around the nucleus in a circular orbit of radius 0.529×10^{-10} m at a speed of 2.2×10^{8} m/s. The magnitude of its linear momentum in this motion is
(a) 1.1×10^{-34} kg-m/s
(b) 20.02×10^{-23} kg-m/s
(c) 4.0×10^{-24} kg-m/s
(d) 4.0×10^{-31} kg-m/s

8. Assertion (A) According to classical theory, the proposed path of an electron in Rutherford atom model will be parabolic.
Reason (R) According to electromagnetic theory, an accelerated particle continuously emits radiation.
In the light of above statements, choose the most appropriate answer from the options given below.
(a) Both A and R are true and R is the correct explanation of A.
(b) Both A and R are true but R is not the correct explanation of A.
(c) A is true but R is false.
(d) A is false but R is true.

9. Figure shows the energy levels P, Q, R, S and G of an atom where G is the ground state. A red line in the emission spectrum of the atom can be obtained by an energy level change from Q to S. A blue line can be obtained by following energy level change.

(a) P to Q (b) Q to R
(c) R to S (d) R to G

10. As the electron in Bohr's orbit of hydrogen atom passes from states $n = 2$ to $n = 1$. The kinetic energy K and potential energy U change as
(a) K two fold, U four fold
(b) K four fold, U two fold
(c) K four fold, U also four fold
(d) K two fold, U also two fold

11. In Rutherford α-particle experiment, the number of particles scattered at 90° angle are 28 per min, then number of scattered particles at an angle 60° and 120° will be
(a) 112/min, 12.5/min
(b) 100/min, 200/min
(c) 50/min, 12.5min
(d) 117/min, 25/min

12. In a boron atom, if a_0 be the radius of the first orbit, then the radius of the second orbit will be in general.
(a) na_0 (b) a_0 (c) $n^2 a_0$ (d) $\frac{a_0}{n^2}$

13. Hydrogen atom is excited from ground state to another state with principal quantum number equal to 6. Then, the number of spectral lines in the emission spectra will be
(a) 8 (b) 10 (c) 12 (d) 15

14. An α-particle of 5 MeV energy strikes with a nucleus of uranium at stationary at an scattering angle of 180°. The nearest distance upto which α-particle reaches the nucleus will be of the order of
(a) 1 Å (b) 10^{-10} cm
(c) 10^{-12} cm (d) 10^{-15} cm

15. A particle of mass m moves in a circular orbit in a central potential field $U(r) = \frac{1}{2} kr^2$. If Bohr's quantization conditions are applied, radii of possible orbitals and energy levels vary with quantum number n as
(a) $r_n \propto n, E_n \propto n$
(b) $r_n \propto n^2, E_n \propto \frac{1}{n^2}$
(c) $r_n \propto \sqrt{n}, E_n \propto n$
(d) $r_n \propto \sqrt{n}, E_n \propto \frac{1}{n}$

16. An electron makes a transition from orbit $n = 4$ to the orbit $n = 2$ of H-atom. Then, wave number of the emitted radiation will be (R = Rydberg's constant)

(a) $\frac{3R}{16}$ (b) $\frac{4R}{16}$
(c) $\frac{2R}{16}$ (d) $\frac{16}{3R}$

17. A doubly ionised lithium atom is hydrogen like with atom number 3. Find the wavelength of the radiation required to excite the electron in Li^{2+} from the first to the third Bohr orbit, if the ionisation energy of the hydrogen atom is 13.6 eV.

(a) 132.52 Å (b) 4.25 Å
(c) 133.5 A (d) 113.74 Å

18. In Bohr's atomic model of hydrogen, let K, P and E are the kinetic energy, potential energy and total energy of the electron respectively. Choose the correct option when the electron undergoes transition to a higher level.

(a) All K, P and E increase
(b) K decreases, P and E increase
(c) P decreases, K and E increase
(d) K increases, P and E decrease

19. The energy level of hydrogen spectrum is shown in figure. There are some transition A, B, C, D and E. Transition A, B and C respectively, are

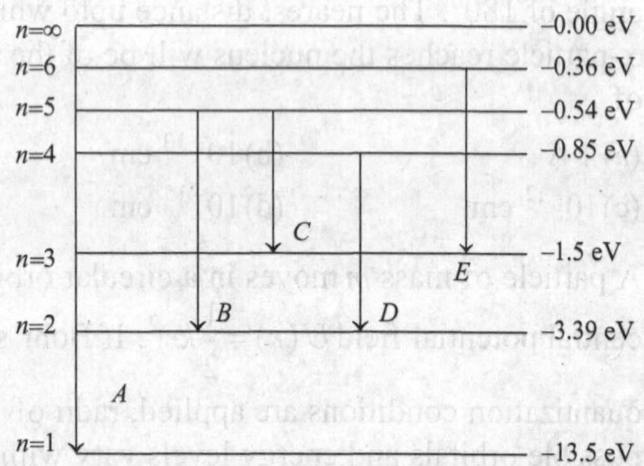

(a) First member of Lyman series, third spectral line of Balmer series and the second spectral line of Paschen series.
(b) Series limit of Lyman series, third spectral line of Balmer series and second spectral line of Paschen series.
(c) Ionisation potential of hydrogen, second spectral line of Balmer series and third spectral line of Paschen series.
(d) None of the above

20. Ionisation potential of hydrogen atom is 13.6 eV. Hydrogen atoms in the ground state are excited by monochromatic radiation of photon energy 12.1 eV. The spectral lines emitted by hydrogen atoms according to Bohr' will be

(a) one (b) two
(c) three (d) four

21. It is found experimentally that 13.6 eV energy is required to separate a hydrogen atom into a proton and an electron. The orbital radius of the electron in hydrogen atom is

(a) 5.3×10^{-11} m (b) 3.2×10^{-12} m
(c) 3.8×10^{-11} m (d) 4.5×10^{-12} m

22. An electron is present in the nth orbit of a hydrogen atom in the Bohr model. The circumference of the orbit can be expressed in terms of the de-Broglie wavelength of that electron as

(a) (0.259) $n\lambda$ (b) $\sqrt{n}\lambda$
(c) (13.6) λ (d) $n\lambda$

23. **Statement I** It is essential that all the lines available in the emission spectrum will also be available in the absorption spectrum.

Statement II The spectrum of hydrogen atom is only absorption spectrum.

(a) Both Statement I and Statement II are correct.
(b) Statement I is correct but Statement II is incorrect.
(c) Statement I is incorrect but Statement II is correct.
(d) Both Statement I and Statement II are incorrect.

24. The wavelength of the energy emitted when electrons come from fourth orbit in hydrogen is 28.397 cm. Then the wavelength of energy for the same transition in He^{+} is

(a) 5.099 cm (b) 20.947 cm
(c) 40.997 cm (d) 14.199 cm

25. The transition from the state $n=4$ to $n=3$ in a hydrogen like atom results in ultraviolet radiation. Infrared radiation will be obtained in the transition from

(a) $2 \rightarrow 1$ (b) $3 \rightarrow 2$ (c) $4 \rightarrow 2$ (d) $5 \rightarrow 4$

26. The ratio of the longest to shortest wavelength in Lyman series of H-atom is

(a) $\frac{25}{9}$ (b) $\frac{17}{6}$

(c) $\frac{9}{5}$ (d) $\frac{4}{3}$

27. Match the List-I and List-II.

List-I	List-II
P. The de-Broglie wavelength of electron in nth Bohr's orbit of hydrogen atom	1. $\propto \frac{1}{n^5}$
Q. Magnetic moment of electron in nth Bohr's orbit of hydrogen atom	2. $\propto n$
R. Magnetic field at the centre of hydrogen atom due to motion of electron in nth orbit	3. $\propto r^{1/2}$
S. Angular momentum of an electron in nth orbit of hydrogen atom	4. $\propto r^2$

Codes

	P	Q	R	S
(a)	2	1	4	3
(b)	1	3	2	4
(c)	2	4	1	3
(d)	4	1	2	3

28. The ratio of minimum to maximum wavelength in Balmer series is

(a) 5 : 9

(b) 5 : 36

(c) 1 : 4

(d) 3 : 4

29. If scattering particles are 56 for 90° angle, then scattering particles will be at 60° angle are

(a) 224

(b) 256

(c) 98

(d) 108

30. Energy required for the electron excitation in Li^{++} from the first to the third Bohr's orbit is

(a) 12.1 eV

(b) 36.3 eV

(c) 108.8 eV

(d) 122.4 eV

Response Index

01	a	b	c	d	11	a	b	c	d	21	a	b	c	d
02	a	b	c	d	12	a	b	c	d	22	a	b	c	d
03	a	b	c	d	13	a	b	c	d	23	a	b	c	d
04	a	b	c	d	14	a	b	c	d	24	a	b	c	d
05	a	b	c	d	15	a	b	c	d	25	a	b	c	d
06	a	b	c	d	16	a	b	c	d	26	a	b	c	d
07	a	b	c	d	17	a	b	c	d	27	a	b	c	d
08	a	b	c	d	18	a	b	c	d	28	a	b	c	d
09	a	b	c	d	19	a	b	c	d	29	a	b	c	d
10	a	b	c	d	20	a	b	c	d	30	a	b	c	d

Performance Scanner

> 90% Excellent !	You have mastered this chapter. The concepts of this chapter are on your fingertips. Move on to the next chapter and maintain this momentum.
76-90% Very Good !	You have a good command over this chapter. Revise the chapter again after a few days and enhance your performance.
60-75% Good !	You have a wide scope to learn for this chapter. Revise it again.
<60% Not Satisfactory!	You have a long way ahead of you to master this chapter. Revise it thoroughly.

For Online Chapter Test **Scan the QR Code**

Space for Rough Work

Space for Rough Work

Space for Rough Work

Test Booklet No. 3947164

Test Booklet Code CH14

MED ACE
NEET (UG)
SELF ASSESSMENT KIT

Nuclei

Topics Covered

- Composition of Nuclei
- Nuclear Reactions and Energy

Important Instructions

- This Booklet Contains – Two Topic Tests and One Test on Complete Chapter.
- Each question carries 4 marks.
- For each correct response, the candidate will get 4 marks and for every incorrect response 1 mark will be additionally deducted from the total score.
- Use **Blue/Black** point pen only for filling the OMR.
- Rough work will be done in the space provided for this purpose within the test booklet only.

Name of the Candidate (In Capitals)

____

____

Candidate's Signature ____________

Invigilator's Signature ____________

Facsimile signature stamp of center superintendent ____________

Do not open this Booklet until you start attempting the Test

Topical Follow Thru

Test 1

Syllabus
- Composition of Nuclei
- Atomic Mass
- Mass-Energy Relation

For deeper insight **Scan the QR Code**

Important Instructions

- The test is of 30 minutes duration and contains 15 Multiple Choice Questions. (Four options with a single correct answer).
- Choose the correct option and fill the OMR given on the last page of this test accordingly.
- At some instances, you may find more than 1 option may be correct, in such circumstances you have to judge the most appropriate answer as per the conditions given in the question.

1. 1 atomic mass unit is expressed as

(a) 1.67×10^{-27} g

(b) 6.023×10^{-23} kg

(c) 1.67×10^{-27} kg

(d) 6.023×10^{-23} g

2. Ratio of masses of nuclei of hydrogen, tritium and deuterium are

(a) 1 : 2 : 3 (b) 1 : 1 : 1

(c) 1 : 3 : 2 (d) 2 : 3 : 1

3. Arrange electron, proton and neutron in decreasing order of stability in free state.

(a) Electron > Proton > Neutron

(b) Proton > Electron > Neutron

(c) Neutron > Proton > Electron

(d) Neutron > Electron > Proton

4. Ratio of radii of $^{235}_{92}$U and $^{107}_{47}$Ag is

(a) 1.4 (b) 1.6

(c) 1.8 (d) 1.3

5. The natural boron of atomic weight 10.81 is found to have two isotopes ^{10}B and ^{11}B. The ratio of abundance of isotopes of natural boron should be

(a) 11 : 10 (b) 81 : 19

(c) 10 : 11 (d) 19 : 81

6. Using electrons as probe, radius of $^{27}_{13}$Al is estimated around 3.6 fm. Radius of $^{197}_{97}$Au using same probe will be

(a) 6 fm (b) 7 fm

(c) 8 fm (d) 9 fm

7. The mass of silver nucleus is 107.8682 u and $A = 107$. The nuclear density of silver nucleus will be (Given, $R_0 = 1.2\times10^{-15}$)

(a) 2.32×10^{17} g / cm^3

(b) 10 g / cm^3

(c) 2.32×10^{17} kg / m^3

(d) 2.16×10^{17} kg / m^3

8. If Avogadro number is 6×10^{23}, then number of protons, neutrons and electrons in 14 g of $_6C^{14}$ are respectively

(a) 36×10^{23}, 48×10^{23}, 36×10^{23}

(b) 36×10^{23}, 36×10^{23}, 36×10^{23}

(c) 48×10^{23}, 36×10^{23}, 48×10^{23}

(d) 48×10^{23}, 48×10^{23}, 36×10^{23}

9. r_1 and r_2 are the radii of atomic nuclei of mass numbers 64 and 27, respectively. The ratio (r_1/r_2) is

(a) $\frac{64}{27}$ (b) $\frac{27}{64}$

(c) $\frac{4}{3}$ (d) 1

10. The radius R of a nucleus of mass number A can be estimated by the formula $R = (1.3 \times 10^{-15})\,A^{1/3}$ m. It follows that the mass density of a nucleus is the order of $(M_{\text{proton}} \cong M_{\text{neutron}} \cong 1.67 \times 10^{-27}$ kg)

(a) 10^{17} kg m^{-3} (b) 10^{24} kg m^{-3}

(c) 10^{10} kg m^{-3} (d) 10^{3} kg m^{-3}

11. Highly energetic electrons are bombarded on a target of an element containing 30 neutrons. The ratio of radii of nucleus to that of Helium nucleus is $(14)^{1/3}$. The atomic number of nucleus will be

(a) 25 (b) 26

(c) 56 (d) 30

12. Radius of ${}^{X}_{32}$Ge (germanium) nuclide is measured to be twice the radius of ${}^{9}_{4}$Be. Number of neutrons in Ge are

(a) 38 (b) 40

(c) 42 (d) 44

13. Consider the plot of N (neutron number) *versus* Z (photon number) for the different nuclei. Let three nuclides A, B and C are at the positions as shown in the figure.

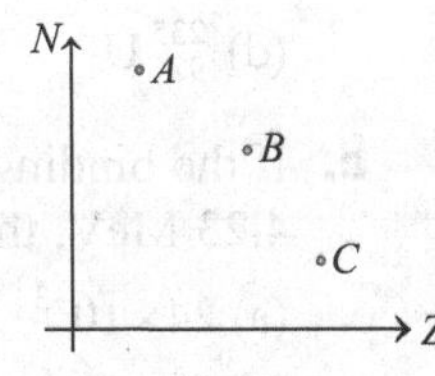

The order of their stability may be

(a) $A > B > C$

(b) $A < B < C$

(c) $B > A > C$

(d) $C < A < B$

14. The radius of oxygen nucleus ${}_{8}O^{16}$ is 2.8×10^{-15} m. The radius of the lead nucleus is

(a) 6.56×10^{-15} m

(b) 7.52×10^{-15} m

(c) 6.2×10^{-12} m

(d) 2×10^{-12} m

15. **Assertion** (A) Density of all the nuclei is same.

Reason (R) Radius of nucleus is directly proportional to the cube root of mass number.

In the light of above statements, choose the most appropriate answer from the options given below.

(a) Both A and R are true and R is the correct explanation of A.

(b) Both A and R are true but R is not the correct explanation of A.

(c) A is true but R is false.

(d) A is false but R is true.

Response Index

01	(a)	(b)	(c)	(d)	10	(a)	(b)	(c)	(d)
02	(a)	(b)	(c)	(d)	11	(a)	(b)	(c)	(d)
03	(a)	(b)	(c)	(d)	12	(a)	(b)	(c)	(d)
04	(a)	(b)	(c)	(d)	13	(a)	(b)	(c)	(d)
05	(a)	(b)	(c)	(d)	14	(a)	(b)	(c)	(d)
06	(a)	(b)	(c)	(d)	15	(a)	(b)	(c)	(d)
07	(a)	(b)	(c)	(d)					
08	(a)	(b)	(c)	(d)					
09	(a)	(b)	(c)	(d)					

Performance Scanner

> 90% Excellent !	You have mastered these topics. The concepts of these topics are on your fingertips. Move on to the next test and maintain this momentum.
76-90% Very Good !	You have a good command over these topics. Revise these topics again after a few days and enhance your performance.
60-75% Good !	You have a wide scope to learn. Revise them again.
<60% Not Satisfactory!	You have a long way ahead of you to master these topics. Revise them thoroughly.

Test 2

Syllabus
- Mass Defect
- Binding Energy per Nucleon and Its Variation with Mass Number
- Nuclear Fission and Fusion

For deeper insight **Scan the QR Code**

Important Instructions

- The test is of 30 minutes duration and contains 15 Multiple Choice Questions. (Four options with a single correct answer).
- Choose the correct option and fill the OMR given on the last page of this test accordingly.
- At some instances, you may find more than 1 option may be correct, in such circumstances you have to judge the most appropriate answer as per the conditions given in the question.

1. Which of the following is a fusion reaction ?

(a) ${}_1H^2 + {}_1H^2 \rightarrow {}_2He^4$

(b) ${}_0n^1 + {}_7N^{14} \rightarrow {}_6C^{14} + {}_1H^1$

(c) ${}_1H^3 \rightarrow {}_2He^3 + \beta^{-1} + \gamma$

(d) ${}_0n^1 + {}_{92}U^{238} \rightarrow {}_{93}Np^{239} + \beta^{-1} + \gamma$

2. The energy generation in stars is mainly due to

(a) chemical reactions

(b) fission of heavy nuclei

(c) fusion of light nuclei

(d) fusion of heavy nuclei

3. Nucleus A is having mass number 220 and its binding energy per nucleon is 5.6 MeV. It splits in two fragments B and C of mass numbers 105 and 115. The binding energy of nucleons in B and C is 6.4 MeV per nucleon.
The energy Q released per fission will be

(a) 0.8 MeV (b) 275 MeV

(c) 220 MeV (d) 176 MeV

4. In a fission reaction ${}^{236}_{92}U \rightarrow {}^{117}X + {}^{117}Y + n + n$, the binding energy per nucleon of X and Y is 7.5 MeV, whereas of ${}^{236}U$ is 6.6 MeV. The total energy liberated will be about

(a) 200 keV

(b) 197.4 MeV

(c) 200 MeV

(d) 2000 MeV

5. The binding energy per nucleon is maximum in the case of

(a) ${}^{56}_{26}Fe$

(b) ${}^{4}_{2}He$

(c) ${}^{141}_{56}Ba$

(d) ${}^{235}_{92}U$

6. If the binding energy of the deuterium is 4.23 MeV, the mass defect given in amu is

(a) 24×10^{-3}

(b) 12×10^{-5}

(c) 12×10^{-3}

(d) 4.5×10^{-3}

7. Statement I The binding energy curve has almost, a flat maximum roughly from $A = 50$ to $A = 80$ corresponding to an average binding energy per nucleon of about 8.5 MeV.

Statement II The nuclei having mass number between 50 to 80 are most stable. Iron, Fe^{56} $(A = 56)$ having a binding energy per nucleon about 8.8 MeV has maximum stability.

In the light of above statements, choose the most appropriate answer from the options given below.

(a) Both Statement I and Statement II are correct.

(b) Both Statement I and Statement II are incorrect.

(c) Statement I is correct but Statement II is incorrect.

(d) Statement I is incorrect but Statement II is correct.

8. If a proton and anti-proton come close to each other and annihilate, then amount of energy released is

(a) 1.5×10^{-10} J

(b) 4.5×10^{-10} J

(c) 3×10^{-10} J

(d) 3.8×10^{-16} J

9. Find the binding energy of an α-particle from the following data.

Mass of He nucleus = 4.001265 amu
Mass of proton = 1.007277 amu
Mass of neutron = 1.00866 amu

(a) 1850 MeV

(b) 296 MeV

(c) 28.512 MeV

(d) 285.12 MeV

10. When a slow neutron goes sufficiently close to a U^{235} nucleus, then the process takes place is

(a) fission of U^{235}

(b) fusion of neutron

(c) fusion of U^{235}

(d) Both (a) and (b)

11. Consider the binding energy of ${}_{17}Cl^{35}$ and ${}_{15}P^{31}$ are 287.67 MeV and 262.48 MeV, respectively. Then,

(a) ${}_{17}Cl^{35}$ is more stable than ${}_{15}P^{31}$

(b) ${}_{15}P^{31}$ is more stable than ${}_{17}Cl^{35}$

(c) stability of both the elements is equivalent

(d) stability cannot be estimated from the given data

12. A heavy nucleus P of mass number 240 and binding energy 7.6 MeV per nucleon splits into two nuclei Q and R of mass number 110, 130 and binding energy per nucleon 8.5 MeV and 8.4 MeV, respectively.

On the basis of above condition, match Column I (energies) with Column II (values in MeV).

Column I	Column II
A. Binding energy of nucleus P	I. 935
B. Binding energy of nucleus Q	II. 1092
C. Binding energy of nucleus R	III. 203
D. Energy released per fission	IV. 1824

Choose the correct answer from the options given below.

(a) A-IV, B-II, C-I, D-III
(b) A-IV, B-II, C-III, D-I
(c) A-IV, B-I, C-II, D-III
(d) A-II, B-IV, C-I, D-III

13. Binding energy for nuclei P, Q and R are E_P, E_Q and E_R, respectively.
In the fusion processes,

$$3P \longrightarrow Q + \text{Energy } (E_1)$$
$$2Q \longrightarrow R + \text{Energy } (E_2)$$

Total energy released in the fusion process

$$6P \longrightarrow R + \text{Energy } (E_3) \text{ is}$$

(a) $E_1 + E_2$
(b) $E_1 - E_2$
(c) $E_1 - 2E_2$
(d) $2E_1 + E_2$

14. M_1 and M_2 represent the masses of ${}^{20}_{10}Ne$ nucleus and ${}^{40}_{20}Ca$ respectively, then the correct option is

(a) $M_1 = 2M_2$
(b) $M_2 = 2M_1$
(c) $M_2 > 2M_1$
(d) $M_2 < 2M_1$

15. The mass of ${}^{7}_{3}Li$ nucleus is $0.042u$ less than the sum of the masses of all its nucleons. The binding energy per nucleon of ${}^{7}_{3}Li$ nucleus is nearly

(a) 46 MeV
(b) 23 MeV
(c) 5.6 MeV
(d) 3.8 MeV

Response Index

01	a	b	c	d	10	a	b	c	d
02	a	b	c	d	11	a	b	c	d
03	a	b	c	d	12	a	b	c	d
04	a	b	c	d	13	a	b	c	d
05	a	b	c	d	14	a	b	c	d
06	a	b	c	d	15	a	b	c	d
07	a	b	c	d					
08	a	b	c	d					
09	a	b	c	d					

Performance Scanner

> 90% Excellent !	You have mastered these topics. The concepts of these topics are on your fingertips. Move on to the next test and maintain this momentum.
76-90% Very Good !	You have a good command over these topics. Revise these topics again after a few days and enhance your performance.
60-75% Good !	You have a wide scope to learn for these topics. Revise them again.
<60% Not Satisfactory!	You have a long way ahead of you to master these topics. Revise them thoroughly.

Chapter Break Thru

Syllabus	• Composition of Nuclei • Atomic Mass • Mass-Energy Relation	• Mass Defect • Binding Energy per Nucleon and Its Variation with Mass Number • Nuclear Fission and Fusion

Important Instructions

- The test is of 45 minutes duration and contains 30 Multiple Choice Questions (Four options with a single correct answer).
- Choose the correct option and fill the OMR given on the last page of this test accordingly.
- At some instances, you may find more than 1 option may be correct, in such circumstances you have to judge the most appropriate answer as per conditions given in the question.

1. The mass number of a nucleus is

(a) always less than its atomic number

(b) always more than its atomic number

(c) always equal to its atomic number

(d) sometimes more than and sometimes equal to its atomic number

2. In $_{88}Ra^{226}$ nucleus, there are

(a) 138 protons and 88 neutrons

(b) 138 neutrons and 88 protons

(c) 226 neutrons and 88 electrons

(d) 226 neutrons and 138 electrons

3. The radius of a nucleus of mass number A is directly proportional to

(a) A^3 (b) A (c) $A^{2/3}$ (d) $A^{1/3}$

4. For a nucleus to be stable, the correct relation between neutron number N and proton number Z for light nuclei is

(a) $N > Z$ (b) $N = Z$

(c) $N < Z$ (d) $N \geq Z$

5. Nuclear forces are

(a) short ranged, attractive and charge independent

(b) short ranged, attractive and charge depende

(c) long ranged, repulsive and charge independent

(d) long ranged, repulsive and charge dependent

6. In the given nuclear reaction A, B, C, D, E represent

$$_{92}U^{238} \xrightarrow{\alpha} {}_BZ^A \xrightarrow{\beta} {}_DY^C \xrightarrow{E} {}_{92}X^{234}$$

(a) $A = 234, B = 90, C = 234, D = 91, E = \beta$

(b) $A = 234, B = 90, C = 238, D = 94, E = \alpha$

(c) $A = 238, B = 93, C = 234, D = 91, E = \beta$

(d) $A = 234, B = 90, C = 234, D = 93, E = \alpha$

7. How does the binding energy per nucleon vary with increase in the number of nucleons?

(a) Decrease continuously with mass number.

(b) First decreases and then increases with increase in mass number.

(c) First increases and then decreases with increase in mass number.

(d) Increase continuously with mass number.

8. Heavy nuclei are stable only when they have more neutrons than protons because

(a) neutrons decay into protons through beta decay

(b) neutrons are heavier than proton

(c) electrostatic force between protons are repulsive

(d) nuclear forces between neutrons are weaker than that between protons

9. Two lighter nuclei combine to form a comparatively heavier nucleus by the relation given below

$${}^2_1X + {}^2_1X = {}^4_2Y$$

The binding energies per nucleon for ${}^2_1X$ and ${}^4_2Y$ are 1.1 MeV and 7.6 MeV, respectively. The energy released in this process is

(a) 26 MeV (b) 30.2 MeV

(c) 34.6 MeV (d) 28.4 MeV

10. Fusion process, like combining two deutrons to form a He nucleus are impossible at ordinary temperature and pressure. The reasons for this can be traced to the fact

(a) nuclear forces have short range

(b) the original nuclei must be completely ionized before fusion can take place

(c) the original nuclei must first break up before combining with each other

(d) nuclear forces have long range

11. The energy equivalent of 1 g of a substance is

(a) 4.5×10^{13} J (b) 4×10^{13} J

(c) 9×10^{13} J (d) 9.5×10^{13} J

12. If m, m_n and m_p are the masses of $_ZX^A$ nucleus, neutron and proton respectively, then

(a) $m<(A-Z)m_n+Zm_p$

(b) $m=(A-Z)m_n+Zm_p$

(c) $m=(A-Z)m_p+Zm_p$

(d) $m>(A-Z)m_n+Zm_p$

13. If 400 MeV energy is released in the fission of a single U^{235} nucleus, the number of fissions required per second to produce 2 kW power will be

(a) 3.1×10^{13} (b) 4.2×10^{10}

(c) 5.2×10^{12} (d) 7.2×10^{14}

14. If the energy released in the fission of one nucleus is 200 MeV. The number of nuclei required per second in power plant of 16 kW will be

(a) 0.5×10^{14} (b) 5×10^{14}

(c) 50×10^{14} (d) 30×10^{12}

15. A nucleus disintegrates into two nuclear parts which have velocities in ratio 2 : 1. Ratio of their nuclear sizes is

(a) $1:3^{\frac{1}{2}}$ (b) $1:2^{\frac{1}{3}}$ (c) $3^{\frac{1}{2}}:1$ (d) $2^{\frac{1}{3}}:1$

16. The by product of $^{235}_{92}U$ with ^1_0n reaction is

(a) $^{235}_{92}U+^1_0n\longrightarrow ^{140}_{54}Xe+^{94}_{38}Sr+2^1_0n$

(b) $^{235}_{92}U+^1_0n\longrightarrow ^{95}_{43}Mo+^{139}_{57}La+2^1_0n$

(c) $^{235}_{92}U+^1_0n\longrightarrow ^{137}_{56}I+^{97}_{39}Y+2^1_0n$

(d) $^{235}_{92}U+^1_0n\longrightarrow ^{144}_{56}Cs+^{90}_{37}Pb+2^1_0n$

17. In the reaction $^2_1H+^3_1H\rightarrow ^4_2He+^1H_0$. If the binding energies of ^2_1H, ^3_1H and ^4_2He are respectively a, b and c (in MeV), then the energy (in MeV) released in this reaction is

(a) $c+a-b$ (b) $c-a-b$

(c) $a+b+c$ (d) $a+b-c$

18. The fusion reaction in the sun is a multi-step process in which the

(a) helium is burned into deuterons

(b) helium is burned into hydrogen

(c) deuteron is burned into helium

(d) hydrogen is burned into helium

19. The mass of proton is 1.0073 u and that of neutron is 1.0087 u (u = atomic mass unit). The binding energy of ^4_2He is

(Mass of helium nucleus = 4.0015 u)

(a) 28.4 MeV (b) 0.061 u

(c) 0.0305 erg (d) 32 MeV

20. The BE per nucleon of $^{56}_{26}Fe$ is
[Given, $m(^{56}_{26}Fe)=55.934939$
$m_{proton}=1.007825$ u, $m_{neutron}=1.008665$ u]

(a) 7.8 MeV (b) 8.1 MeV

(c) 7.250 MeV (d) 8.790 MeV

21. **Assertion (A)** Positive value of packing fraction implies a large value of binding energy.

Reason (R) The ratio of the difference between the atomic mass of nucleus and the mass number of the nucleus to that of atomic mass is called packing fraction.

In the light of above statements, choose the most appropriate answer from the options given below.

(a) Both A and R are true and R is the correct explanation of A.

(b) Both A and R are true but R is not the correct explanation of A.

(c) A is true but R is false.

(d) A is false but R is true.

22. An electron in the ground state of He-atom having binding energy $E_0=24.6$ eV. The energy required to remove both electrons from the atom is

(a) 24.6 eV (b) 79.0 eV (c) 54.4 eV (d) 89.0 eV

23. 1 g of $^{235}_{92}U$ undergoes fission and energy per fission is 200 MeV. Then, energy released by the fission is

(a) 2.278×10^4 kWh

(b) 2.68×10^5 kWh

(c) 4.68×10^4 kWh

(d) 4.68×10^5 kWh

24. The energy released in fusion reaction $^2_1H+^2_1H\longrightarrow ^3_2He+n$, where binding energy of $^2_1H=2.23$ MeV and $^3_2He=7.73$ MeV is

(a) 3.62 MeV (b) 3.27 MeV

(c) 4.62 MeV (d) 4.27 MeV

25. When 240 MeV energy is released in the fission of a single nucleus of $^{235}_{92}U$. Then, fission occur to produce a power of 1 kW is

(a) 3.125×10^{13} (b) 4.125×10^{13}

(c) 0 (d) 2.60×10^{13}

26. In fission reaction, the percentage of mass converted into energy is about

(a) 10% (b) 1% (c) 0.1% (d) 0.01%

27. In the nuclear fusion reaction $^2_1H+^3_1H\rightarrow ^4_2He+^1_0n$, given that the repulsive potential energy between the two nuclei is -7.7×10^{-14} J. The temperature at which the gases must be heated to initiate the reaction is of the order of [Boltzmann's constant, $k=1.38\times10^{-23}$ J/K]

(a) 10^9 K (b) 10^7 K

(c) 10^5 K (d) 10^3 K

28. Nuclear energy required to separate all the neutrons and protons of a 3g copper coin is (Take, mass of $^{63}_{29}Cu=62.92960$ u)

(a) 1.6×10^{16} MeV (b) 1.6×10^{19} MeV

(c) 1.6×10^{25} MeV (d) 1.6×10^{31} MeV

29. **Statement I** In both fission and fusion processes, energy is released.

Statement II BE per nucleon on reactants is less than BE per nucleon of products in both cases.

In the light of above statements, choose the most appropriate answer from the options given below.

(a) Both Statement I and Statement II are correct.

(b) Both Statement I and Statement II are incorrect.

(c) Statement I is correct but Statement II is incorrect.

(d) Statement I is incorrect but Statement II is correct.

30. The binding energy per nucleon (in MeV) of a carbon nucleus $^{12}C_6$ is

(Given, Mass of proton = 1.00783 u

Mass of neutron = 1.00867 u

Mass of carbon nucleus = 12 u)

(a) 7.68 MeV (b) 6.59 MeV

(c) 8.59 MeV (d) 4.59 MeV

For Online Chapter Test **Scan the QR Code**

For Online Unit Test **Scan the QR Code**

Response Index

01	ⓐ ⓑ ⓒ ⓓ	14	ⓐ ⓑ ⓒ ⓓ	27	ⓐ ⓑ ⓒ ⓓ
02	ⓐ ⓑ ⓒ ⓓ	15	ⓐ ⓑ ⓒ ⓓ	28	ⓐ ⓑ ⓒ ⓓ
03	ⓐ ⓑ ⓒ ⓓ	16	ⓐ ⓑ ⓒ ⓓ	29	ⓐ ⓑ ⓒ ⓓ
04	ⓐ ⓑ ⓒ ⓓ	17	ⓐ ⓑ ⓒ ⓓ	30	ⓐ ⓑ ⓒ ⓓ
05	ⓐ ⓑ ⓒ ⓓ	18	ⓐ ⓑ ⓒ ⓓ		
06	ⓐ ⓑ ⓒ ⓓ	19	ⓐ ⓑ ⓒ ⓓ		
07	ⓐ ⓑ ⓒ ⓓ	20	ⓐ ⓑ ⓒ ⓓ		
08	ⓐ ⓑ ⓒ ⓓ	21	ⓐ ⓑ ⓒ ⓓ		
09	ⓐ ⓑ ⓒ ⓓ	22	ⓐ ⓑ ⓒ ⓓ		
10	ⓐ ⓑ ⓒ ⓓ	23	ⓐ ⓑ ⓒ ⓓ		
11	ⓐ ⓑ ⓒ ⓓ	24	ⓐ ⓑ ⓒ ⓓ		
12	ⓐ ⓑ ⓒ ⓓ	25	ⓐ ⓑ ⓒ ⓓ		
13	ⓐ ⓑ ⓒ ⓓ	26	ⓐ ⓑ ⓒ ⓓ		

Performance Scanner

> 90% Excellent !	You have mastered this chapter. The concepts of this chapter are on your fingertips. Move on to the next chapter and maintain this momentum.
76-90% Very Good !	You have a good command over this chapter. Revise the chapter again after a few days and enhance your performance.
60-75% Good !	You have a wide scope to learn for this chapter. Revise it again.
<60% Not Satisfactory!	You have a long way ahead of you to master this chapter. Revise it thoroughly.

Test Booklet No. **3947165**

Test Booklet Code **CH15**

MEDACE
NEET (UG)
SELF ASSESSMENT KIT

Electronic Devices

Topics Covered

Semiconductors and Energy Band Theory

Logic Gates

Important Instructions

- This Booklet Contains – Three Topic Tests and One Test on Complete Chapter.
- Each question carries 4 marks.
- For each correct response, the candidate will get 4 marks and for every incorrect response 1 mark will be additionally deducted from the total score.
- Use **Blue/Black** point pen only for filling the OMR.
- Rough work will be done in the space provided for this purpose within the test booklet only.

Name of the Candidate (In Capitals) __________

Candidate's Signature __________

Invigilator's Signature __________

Facsimile signature stamp of center superintendent __________

Do not open this Booklet until you start attempting the Test

Topical Follow Thru

Test 1

Syllabus

- Semiconductors
- Semiconductor diode
- *I-V* characteristics in forward and reverse bias
- Diode as a rectifier
- *I-V* characteristics of LED
- Photodiode, Solar cell, Zener diode
- Zener diode as a voltage regulator

For deeper insight **Scan the QR Code**

Important Instructions

- The test is of 45 minutes duration and contains 25 Multiple Choice Questions. (Four options with a single correct answer).
- Choose the correct option and fill the OMR given on the last page of this test accordingly.
- At some instances, you may find more than 1 option may be correct, in such circumstances you have to judge the most appropriate answer as per the conditions given in the question.

1. When germanium is doped with phosphorus, the doped material has

(a) more positive current carriers
(b) more negative current carriers
(c) excess negative charge
(d) excess positive charge

2. The forbidden gap in the energy bands of germanium at room temperature is about

(a) 1.1 eV (b) 0.1 eV
(c) 0.67 eV (d) 6.7 eV

3. A pure semiconductor has equal electron and hole concentration of $10^{16}\,m^{-3}$. Doping by indium increases n_h to 4.5×10^{16}. The value of n_e in the doped semiconductor is

(a) $10^{6}\,m^{-3}$ (b) $10^{22}\,m^{-3}$
(c) $0.22 \times 10^{16}\,m^{-3}$ (d) $4.5 \times 10^{22}\,m^{-3}$

4. If n_e and n_h are the number of electrons and holes in a semiconductor heavily doped with phosphorus, then

(a) $n_e >> n_h$ (b) $n_e << n_h$
(c) $n_e \leq n_h$ (d) $n_e = n_h$

5. **Statement I** In a *p-n* junction, if we increase the doping, then width of junction decreases.

Statement II Electric field in junction decreases with increase in doping.

In the light of above statements, choose the most appropriate answer from the options given below.

(a) Both Statement I and Statement II are correct.
(b) Both Statement I and Statement II are incorrect.
(c) Statement I is correct but Statement II is incorrect.
(d) Statement I is incorrect but Statement II is correct.

6. If the two ends p and n of a *p-n* junction diode are joined by a wire, then

(a) there will not be a steady current in the circuit.
(b) there will be a steady current from *n*-side to *p*-side.
(c) there will be steady current from *p*-side to *n*-side.
(d) there may not be a current depending upon the resistance of the connecting wire.

7. In the circuit given below, the value of the current is

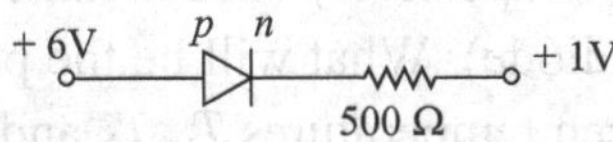

(a) 0 A (b) 10^{-2} A (c) 10^{2} A (d) 10^{-4} A

8. In *p-n* junction, the barrier potential offers resistance to

(a) only free electrons in *n* -region
(b) only holes in *p*-region
(c) free electrons in *p*-region and holes in *n*-region
(d) free electrons in *n* -region and holes in *p*-region

9. Assertion (R) No important electronic devices can be developed using intrinsic semiconductors.
Reason (A) The conductivity of an intrinsic semiconductor depends on its temperature.
In the light of above statements, choose the most appropriate answer from the options given below.

(a) Both A and R are true and R is the correct explanation of A.
(b) Both A and R are true but R is not the correct explanation of A.
(c) A is true but R is false.
(d) A is false but R is true.

10. Regarding a semiconductor, which one of the following is incorrect?

(a) There are no free electrons at 0 K.
(b) There are no free electrons at room temperature.
(c) The number of free electrons increases at high temperature.
(d) The charge carriers are electrons and holes.

11. When a large number (N) of identical atoms come closer uniformly, we get a band consisting of closely spaced level which are

(a) N in number (b) $2N$ in number
(c) N^2 in number (d) 2^N in number

12. Energy band in solid sodium metal is as shown in the figure?

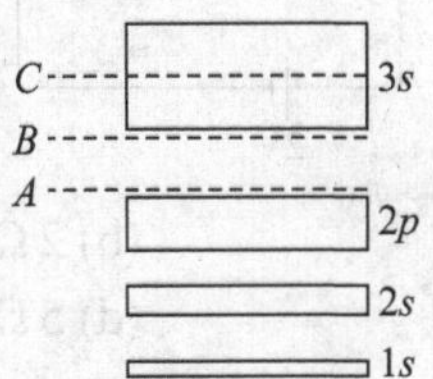

What will be the position of fermi energy level in sodium?

(a) A (b) B
(c) C (d) Below B

13. In an insulator, the forbidden energy gap between the valence band and the conduction band is of the order of

(a) 2 MeV (b) 1 MeV
(c) 1 eV (d) 4 eV

14. An *n*-type silicon sample of width 4×10^{-3} m thickness and length 6×10^{-2} m carries a current of 4.8 mA. If the free electron density is 10^{22} m^{-3}, then how much time it takes for the electrons to travel the full length of the sample.

(a) 4.8 s (b) 6.8 s (c) 7.2 s (d) 3.6 s

15. In figure, V_0 is the potential barrier across a *p-n* junction when no battery is connected across the junction. Then, choose the correct option.

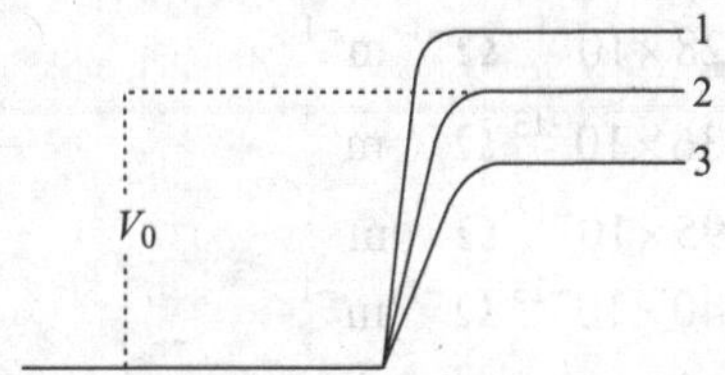

(a) 1 and 3 both correspond to forward bias of junction.
(b) 3 corresponds to forward bias of junction and 1 corresponds to reverse bias of junction.
(c) 1 corresponds to forward bias and 3 corresponds to reverse bias of junction.
(d) 1 and 3 both correspond to reverse bias of junction.

16. Match the List I with List II.

	List I		List II
A.	Conductivity of intrinsic semiconductor	1.	low at room temperature
B.	Conductivity of *n*-type semicondctor	2.	higher due to excess electrons
C.	Conductivity of *p*-type semiconductor	3.	higher due to excess holes
D.	Conductivity of degenerate semiconductor	4.	very high similar to metals

(a) A-1, B-2, C-3, D-4
(b) A-4, B-3, C-2, D-1
(c) A-2, B-1, C-4, D-3
(d) A-3, B-4, C-1, D-2

17. In the following circuit, find I_1 and I_2.

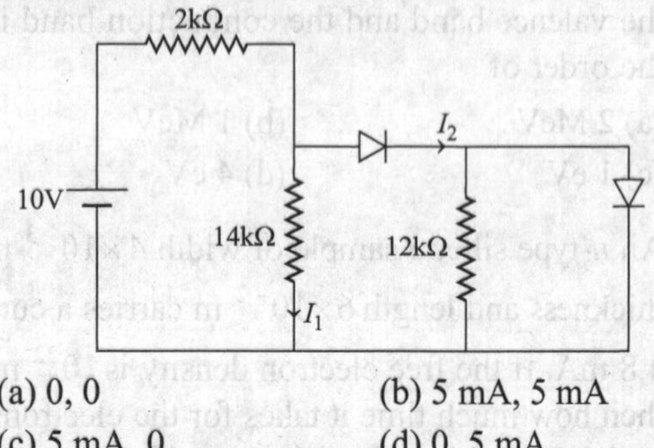

(a) 0, 0 (b) 5 mA, 5 mA
(c) 5 mA, 0 (d) 0, 5 mA

18. Concentration of carriers in pure germanium at room temperature is $1.6 \times 10^6\ m^{-3}$. The mobilities of electrons and holes are $0.4\ m^2V^{-1}s^{-1}$ and $0.2\ m^2V^{-1}s^{-1}$ respectively. The conductivity of germanium is
(a) $1.428 \times 10^{-13}\ \Omega^{-1}\ m^{-1}$
(b) $1.536 \times 10^{-13}\ \Omega^{-1}\ m^{-1}$
(c) $1.295 \times 10^{-13}\ \Omega^{-1}\ m^{-1}$
(d) $1.840 \times 10^{-13}\ \Omega^{-1}\ m^{-1}$

19. Current supplied by the battery in the circuit given below, is

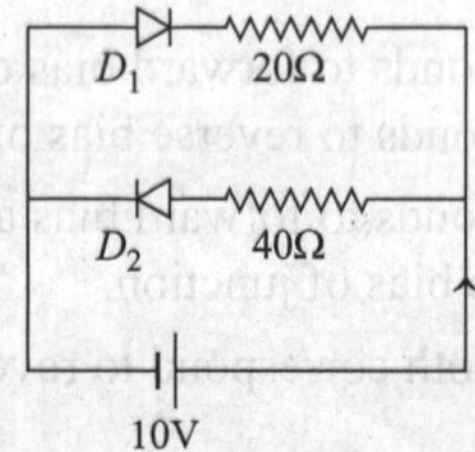

(a) 0.5 A (b) 0.75 A (c) 0.25 A (d) 1 A

20. A typical diode characteristics curve A is drawn at temperature T_2(K).

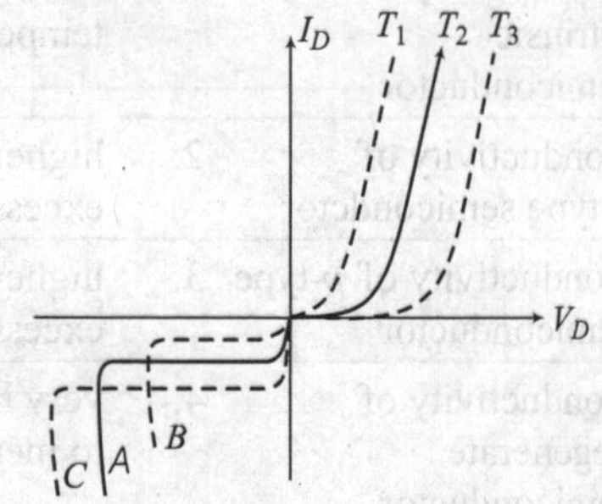

Let curves B and C are drawn at temperatures T_3 and T_1 respectively (under same setup and for same diode). What will be the possible relation between temperatures T_1, T_2 and T_3?
(a) $T_1 > T_2 > T_3$
(b) $T_1 < T_2 < T_3$
(c) $T_2 = \dfrac{T_1 + T_3}{2}$
(d) $T_1 = T_2 = T_3$

21. Choose the correct option for a p-n junction diode.
(a) A p-n junction diode is formed by joining together n-type and p-type silicon crystals, using a suitable glue.
(b) To from p-n junction a semiconductor crystal is doped simultaneously with suitable impurities to make one side p-type and other n-type.
(c) Depletion zone appears in a p-n junction, when p-type silicon is given a negative potential and n-type silicon is given a positive potential.
(d) Diffusion of electrons in a newly formed p-n junction creates a junction field that stops further diffusion of electrons from n to p-side.

22. An n-type silicon sample of width 8×10^{-3} m and length 12×10^{-2} m carries a current of 9.6 mA when the voltage is applied across the length of the sample. If the free electron density is $10^{22}\ m^{-3}$, then the drift speed of electron will be
(a) 12.5×10^{-3} m/s (b) 6.25×10^{-3} m/s
(c) 1.6×10^{-3} m/s (d) 25×10^{-3} m/s

23. The diode used in the circuit shown in the figure has a constant voltage drop of 1 V at all currents and a maximum power rating of 200 milliwatts. What should be the value of the resistor R, connected in series with the diode for obtaining maximum current?

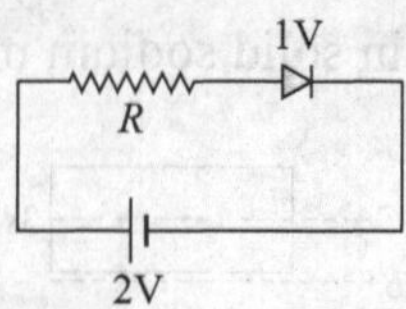

(a) 1 Ω (b) 2 Ω
(c) 10 Ω (d) 5 Ω

24. A silicon diode has a knee voltage or threshold voltage value of 0.7 V. This Si diode is connected in a circuit as shown in the figure.

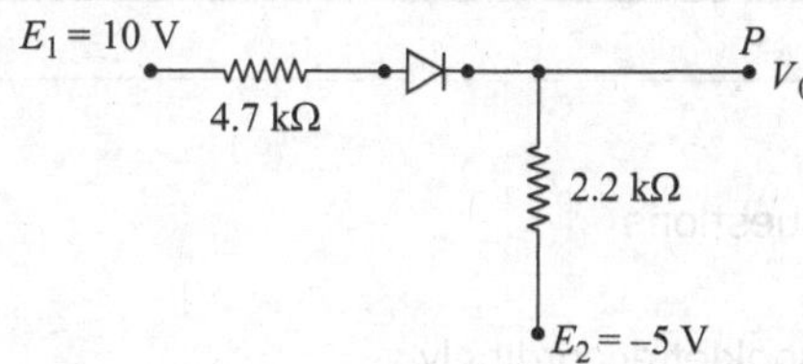

Potential V_0 of point P in the circuit will be

(a) – 0.44 V
(b) 0.44 V
(c) 4.4 V
(d) – 4.4 V

25. Consider the given circuit.

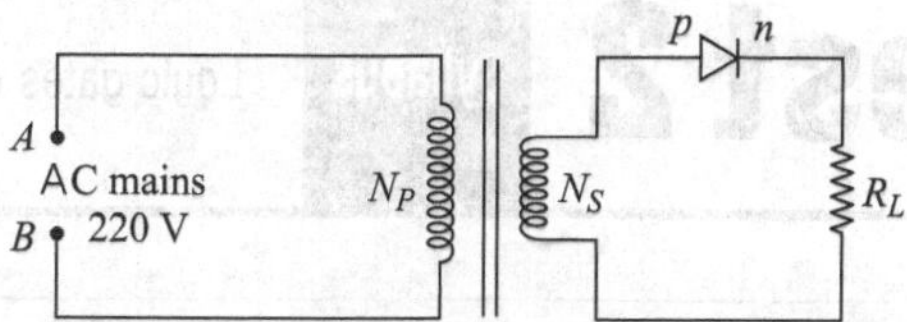

Given, supply voltage (AC mains) = 220 V
Number of turns of primary coil, $N_P = 1000$
Number of turns of secondary coil, $N_s = 50$
Current in primary coil = 0.25 A
Diode is ideal. Average value of current flowing through load resistance R_L is

(a) 5 A (b) $\frac{5}{\pi}$ A
(c) $\frac{5}{\sqrt{2}}$ A (d) $\frac{5\sqrt{2}}{\pi}$ A

Response Index

01	a	b	c	d	10	a	b	c	d	19	a	b	c	d
02	a	b	c	d	11	a	b	c	d	20	a	b	c	d
03	a	b	c	d	12	a	b	c	d	21	a	b	c	d
04	a	b	c	d	13	a	b	c	d	22	a	b	c	d
05	a	b	c	d	14	a	b	c	d	23	a	b	c	d
06	a	b	c	d	15	a	b	c	d	24	a	b	c	d
07	a	b	c	d	16	a	b	c	d	25	a	b	c	d
08	a	b	c	d	17	a	b	c	d					
09	a	b	c	d	18	a	b	c	d					

Performance Scanner

> 90% Excellent !	You have mastered these topics. The concepts of these topic are on your fingertips. Move on to the next test and maintain this momentum.
76-90% Very Good !	You have a good command over these topics. Revise them again after a few days and enhance your performance.
60-75% Good !	You have a wide scope to learn for these topics. Revise them again.
<60% Not Satisfactory!	You have a long way ahead of you to master in these topics. Revise them thoroughly.

Test 2

Syllabus Logic gates (OR, AND, NOT, NAND and NOR)

For deeper insight **Scan the QR Code**

Important Instructions

- The test is of 45 minutes Duration and Contains 25 Multiple Choice Questions (Four options with a single correct answer).
- Choose the correct option and fill the OMR given on the last page of Booklet accordingly.
- At some instances, you may find more than 1 option may be correct in such circumstances you have to judge the most appropriate answer as per the conditions given in the question.

1. The output of a NAND gate is 0,

(a) if both inputs are 0

(b) if one input is 0 and the other input is 1

(c) if both inputs are 1

(d) either if both inputs are 1 or if one of the inputs is 1 and the other is 0

2. The inputs to the digital circuit are shown below. The output Y is

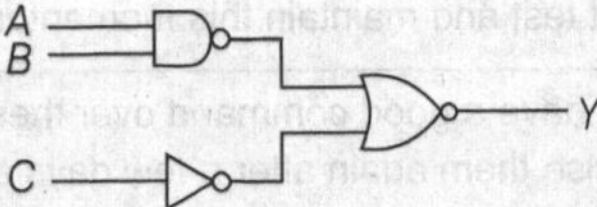

(a) $A \cdot B \cdot C$ (b) $(A+B)\overline{C}$

(c) $\overline{A}+\overline{B}+\overline{C}$ (d) $\overline{A}+\overline{B}+C$

3. The output of the given logic circuit is

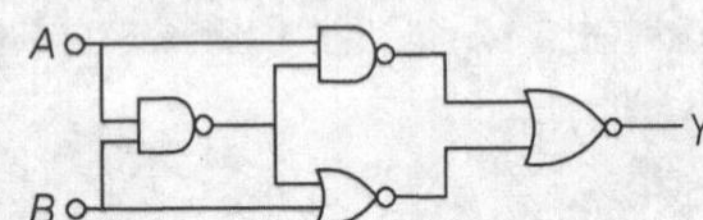

(a) $A\overline{B}$ (b) $A+B$

(c) $AB+\overline{AB}$ (d) $A\overline{B}+\overline{A}B$

4. Statement I NOT gate is also called inverter circuit.

Statement II NOT gate inverts the input order.

In the light of above statements, choose the most appropriate answer from the options given below.

(a) Both Statement I and Statement II are correct.

(b) Both Statement I and Statement II are incorrect.

(c) Statement I is correct but Statement II is incorrect.

(d) Statement I is incorrect but Statement II is correct.

5. Which logic gate is realised in given circuit?

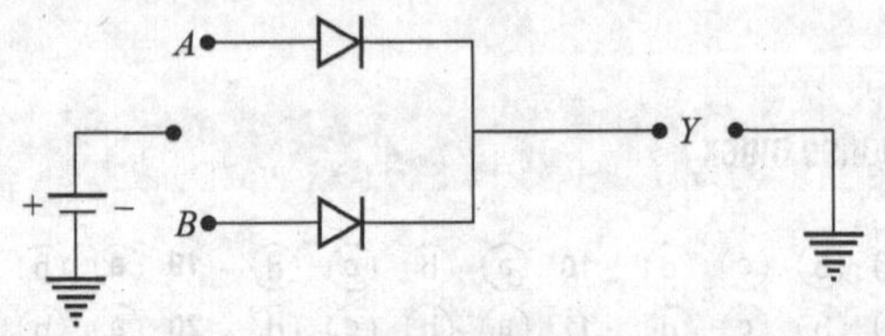

(a) OR (b) AND

(c) NOT (d) NAND

6. Which logic gate is represented by the following combination of logic gates?

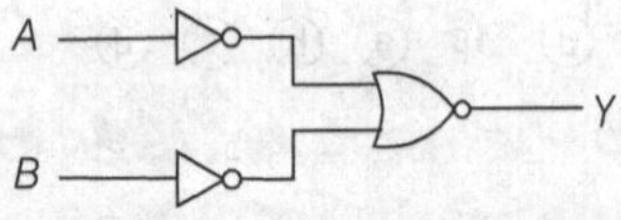

(a) OR (b) NAND

(c) AND (d) NOR

7. To get an output $Y=1$ in given circuit, which of the following input will be correct?

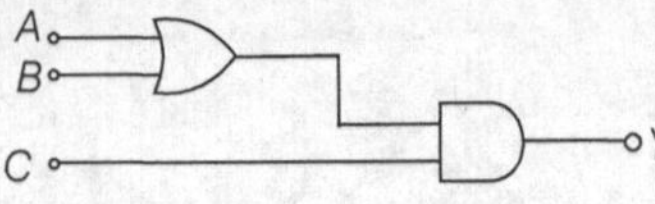

(a) A = 1 B = 0 C = 0

(b) A = 1 B = 0 C = 1

(c) A = 1 B = 1 C = 0

(d) A = 0 B = 1 C = 0

8. In the following combinations of logic gates, the outputs of A, B and C are, respectively.

A. 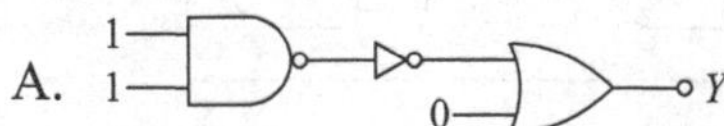

B. 0 1 Y

C. 0 1 Y

(a) 1, 1, 0 (b) 1, 0, 1
(c) 0, 1, 0 (d) 0, 1, 1

9. The truth table for the circuit given in the figure is

A B Y

(a)

A	B	Y
0	0	1
0	1	1
1	0	0
1	1	0

(b)

A	B	Y
0	0	0
0	1	0
1	0	1
1	1	1

(c)

A	B	Y
0	0	1
0	1	0
1	0	0
1	1	0

(d)

A	B	Y
0	0	1
0	1	1
1	0	1
1	1	1

10. The truth table for the logical function is

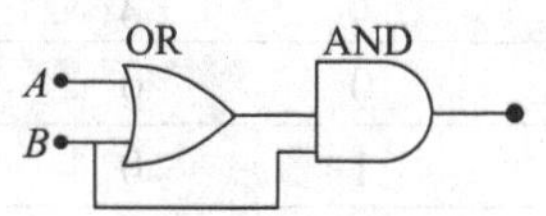

(a)

A	B	D
1	0	0
0	1	1
0	0	0
1	1	1

(b)

A	B	D
1	0	1
0	1	1
0	0	0
1	1	0

(c)

A	B	D
1	0	0
0	1	1
0	0	1
1	1	0

(d)

A	B	D
1	0	0
0	1	0
0	0	0
1	1	1

11. The truth table for the circuit given in figure is

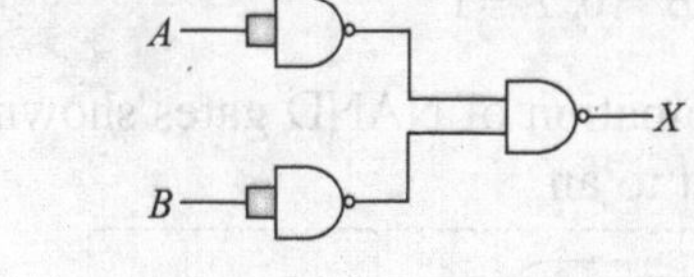

(a)

A	B	X
0	0	0
0	1	1
1	0	1
1	1	1

(b)

A	B	X
0	0	0
0	1	0
1	0	1
1	1	1

(c)

A	B	X
0	1	0
1	0	1
0	0	1
1	1	0

(d)

A	B	X
1	0	0
1	1	0
0	1	1
0	0	1

12. In given logic circuit,

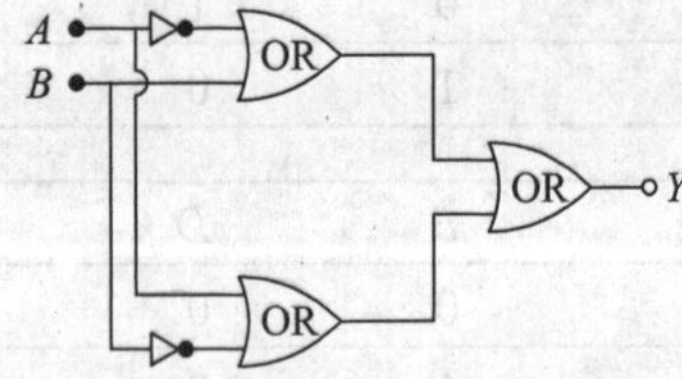

Which of these is correct?

(a) $A=0, B=0, Y=0$
(b) $A=1, B=0, Y=0$
(c) $A=1, B=1, Y=0$
(d) $A=0, B=0, Y=1$

13. The combination of NAND gates shown here are equivalent to an

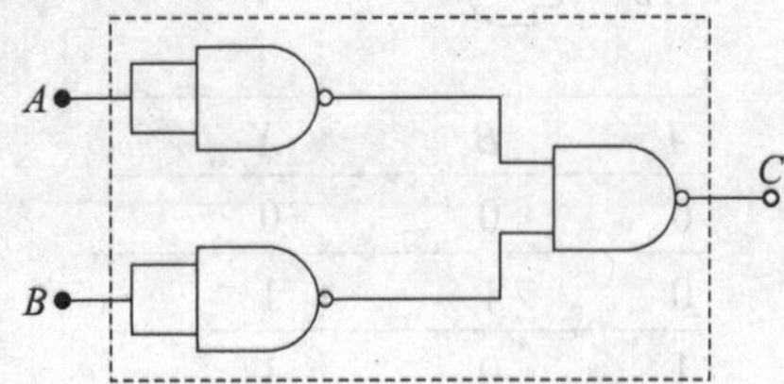

(a) OR gate and an AND gate, respectively
(b) AND gate and a NOT gate, respectively
(c) AND gate and an OR gate, respectively
(d) OR gate and a NOT gate, respectively

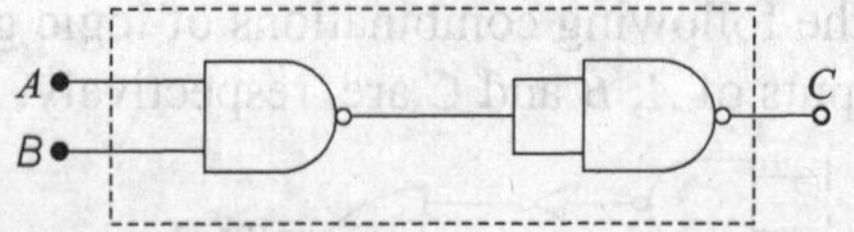

14. Consider given input waveforms A and B,

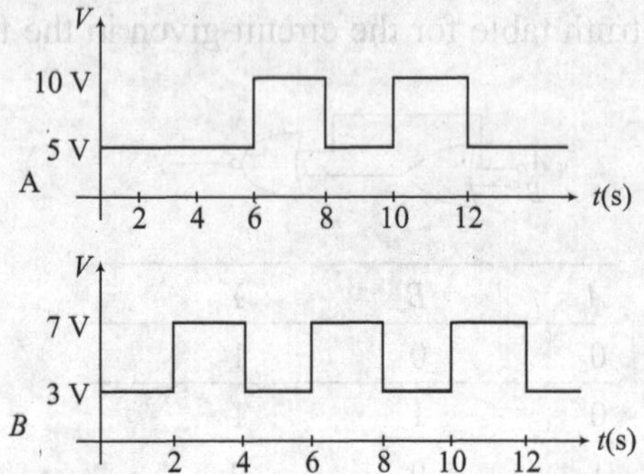

When the inputs are fed to a NAND gate with a negative logic, output in binary form is

(a) 111010
(b) 111111
(c) 000101
(d) 000100

15. The truth table for the gate shown in the following figure will be

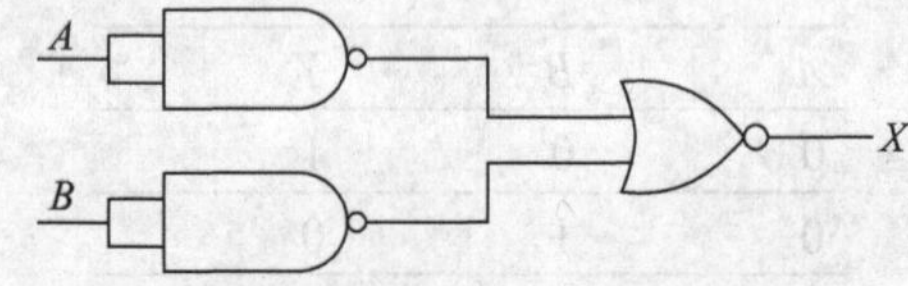

(a)

A	B	X
0	0	0
0	1	1
1	0	1
1	1	0

(b)

A	B	X
0	0	0
0	1	1
1	0	1
1	1	1

(c)

A	B	X
0	0	1
0	1	1
1	0	1
1	1	0

(d)

A	B	X
0	0	0
0	1	0
1	0	0
1	1	1

16. A researcher wants an alarm to sound when the temperature of air in his controlled research chamber rises above 40°C or falls below 20°C. The alarm can be triggered by the output of a

(a) NOT gate
(b) AND gate
(c) NAND gate
(d) OR gate

17. The logic circuit shown below has the input waveforms A and B as shown. Pick out the correct output waveform.

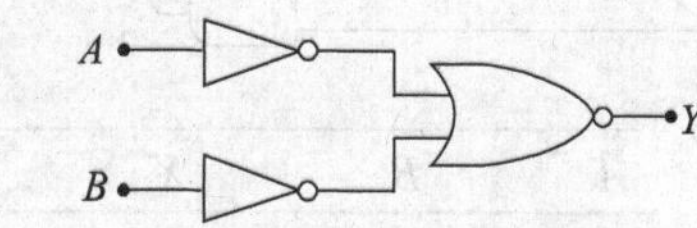

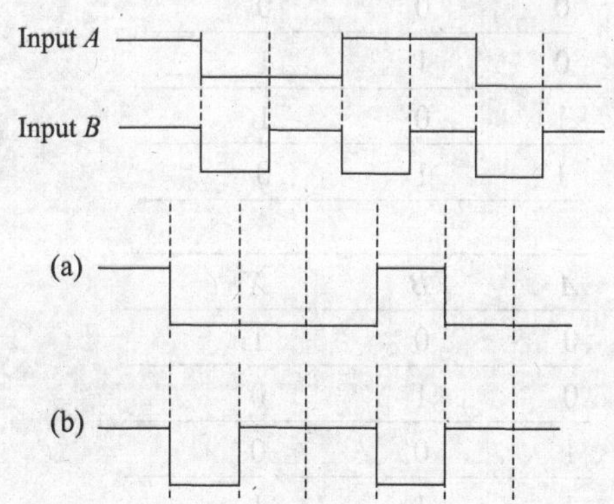

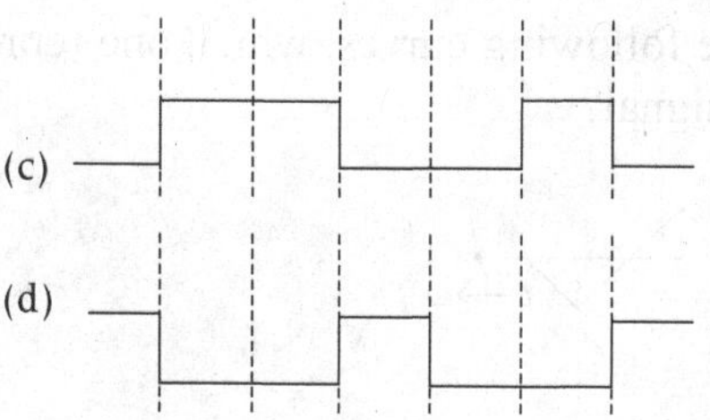

18. Given gate is a

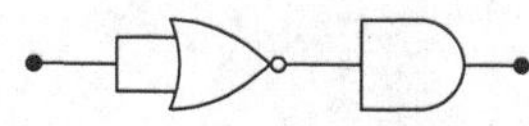

(a) XOR gate
(b) NOR gate
(c) AND gate
(d) NOT gate

19. Following circuit is realisation of

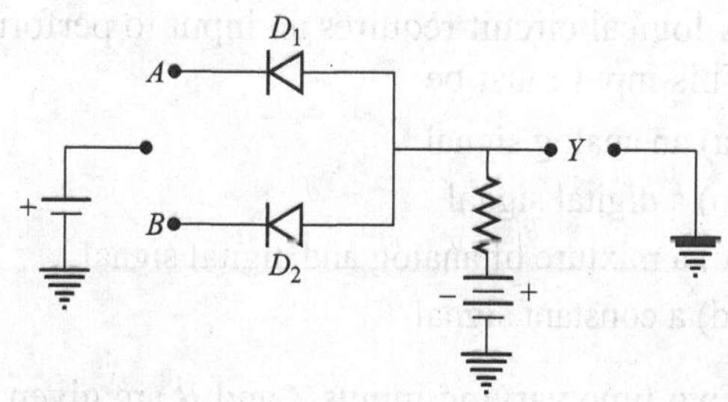

(a) OR gate
(b) NOT gate
(c) AND gate
(d) NAND gate

20. There are four entries for the truth table of two point input OR gate given below. Which two are wrong?

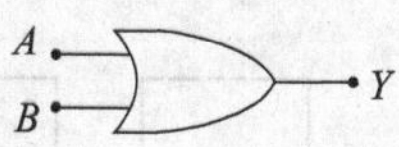

	A	B	Y
i	1	0	1
ii	1	1	0
iii	0	0	1
iv	0	1	1

(a) i, ii
(b) ii, iii
(c) iii, iv
(d) iv, i

21. Out of the following curves, which one represents a digital signal?

(a) 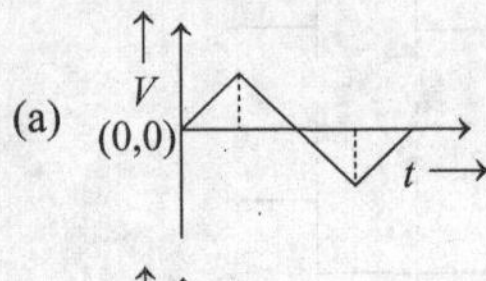

(b) 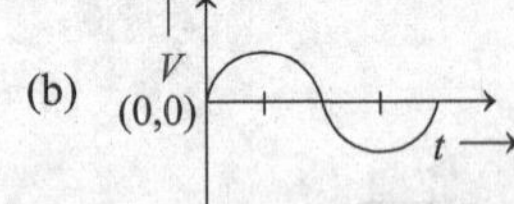

(c) 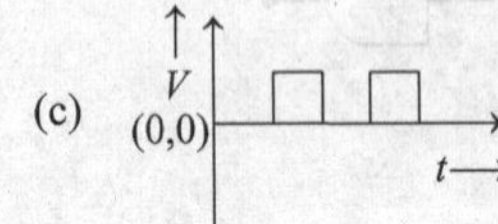

(d) 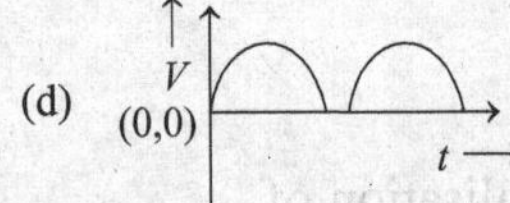

22. A logical circuit requires an input to perform. This input must be

(a) an analog signal
(b) a digital signal
(c) a mixture of analog and digital signal
(d) a constant signal

23. Two time varying inputs A and B are given below.

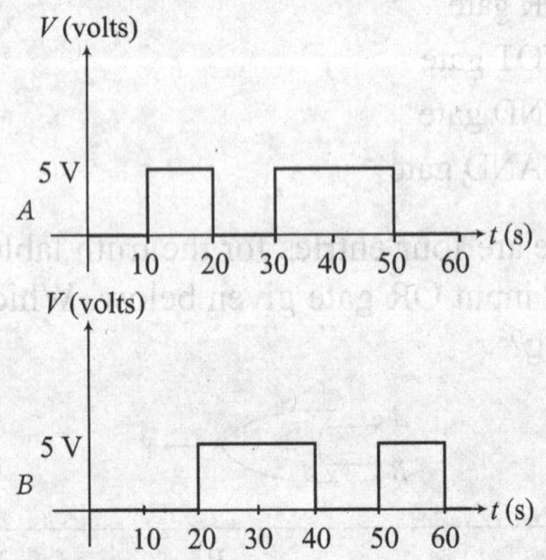

If they are fed to a two input OR gate, then output will be

(a) $V = \begin{cases} 0, & 0 \le t \le 10 \\ 1\text{V}, & 10 \le t \le 20 \\ 0, & 20 \le t \end{cases}$

(b) $V = \begin{cases} 0, & 0 \le t \le 20 \\ 5\text{V}, & 20 \le t \end{cases}$

(c) $V = \begin{cases} 0, & 0 \le t \le 10 \\ 5\text{V} & 10 \le t \le 60 \end{cases}$

(d) $V = \begin{cases} 0, & 0 \le t < 10 \\ 5\text{V} & 10 \le t \le 60 \end{cases}$

24. Two time varying functions are as follows.

$$A = \begin{cases} 0, & 0 \le t < 1, \\ 1, & 1 \le t \le 2, \\ 0, & 2 < t \le 3, \end{cases} \quad B = \begin{cases} 0, & 0 \le t < \frac{1}{2} \\ 1, & \frac{1}{2} \le t \le \frac{5}{2} \\ 0, & \frac{5}{2} < t \le 3 \end{cases}$$

Output of a NAND gate will be

(a) 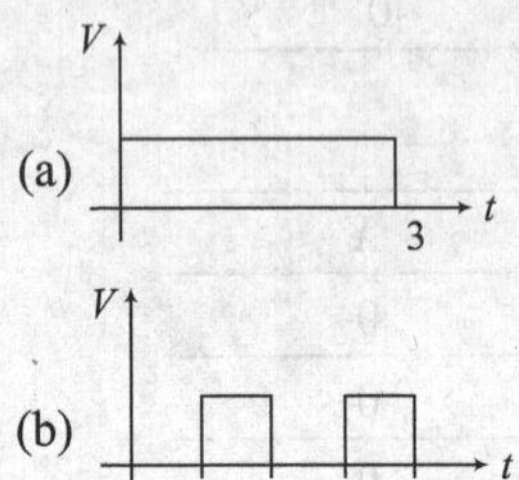

(b)

(c) 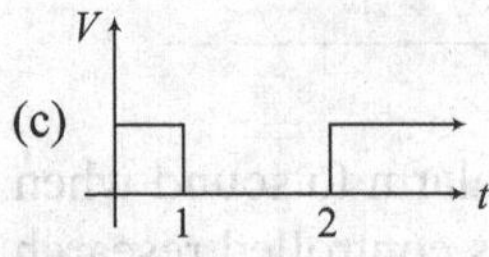

(d) 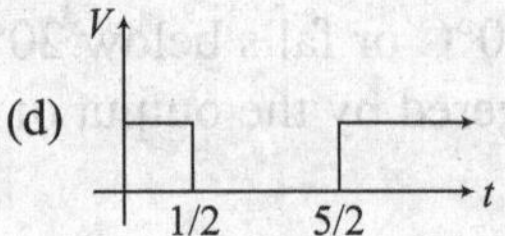

25. The truth table for the circuit given in figure is

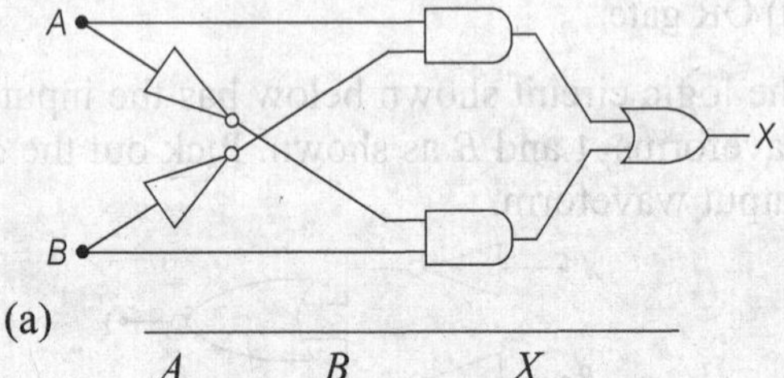

(a)

A	B	X
0	0	0
0	1	1
1	0	1
1	1	0

(b)

A	B	X
0	0	1
0	1	0
1	0	0
1	1	1

(c)

A	B	X
0	0	0
0	1	1
1	0	0
1	1	1

(d)

A	B	X
0	0	1
0	1	0
1	0	0
1	1	0

Response Index

01	a	b	c	d	10	a	b	c	d	19	a	b	c	d
02	a	b	c	d	11	a	b	c	d	20	a	b	c	d
03	a	b	c	d	12	a	b	c	d	21	a	b	c	d
04	a	b	c	d	13	a	b	c	d	22	a	b	c	d
05	a	b	c	d	14	a	b	c	d	23	a	b	c	d
06	a	b	c	d	15	a	b	c	d	24	a	b	c	d
07	a	b	c	d	16	a	b	c	d	25	a	b	c	d
08	a	b	c	d	17	a	b	c	d					
09	a	b	c	d	18	a	b	c	d					

Performance Scanner

> 90% Excellent !	You have mastered these topics. The concepts of these topic are on your fingertips. Move on to the next test and maintain this momentum.
76-90% Very Good !	You have a good command over these topics. Revise them again after a few days and enhance your performance.
60-75% Good !	You have a wide scope to learn for these topics. Revise them again.
<60% Not Satisfactory!	You have a long way ahead of you to master in these topics. Revise them thoroughly.

Chapter Break Thru

Syllabus		
	• Semiconductors • Semiconductor diode • *I-V* characteristics in forward and reverse bias • Diode as a rectifier • *I-V* characteristics of LED	• Photodiode, Solar cell, Zener Diode • Zener diode as a voltage regulator • Logic gates (OR, AND, NOT, NAND and NOR)

Important Instructions

- The test is of 45 minutes duration and contains 30 multiple-Choice Questions (Four option with a single correct answer).
- Choose the correct option and fill the OMR given on the last page of this test accordingly.
- At some instances, you may find more than 1 option may be correct, in such circumstances you have to judge the most appropriate answer as per conditions given in the question.

1. In a *p-n* junction photocell, the value of the photo-electromotive force produced by monochromatic light is proportional to

(a) the barrier voltage at the *p-n* junction
(b) the intensity of the light falling on the cell
(c) the voltage applied at the *p-n* junction
(d) the frequency of the light falling on the cell

2. Solids having highest energy level and partially filled with electrons are

(a) semiconductor
(b) conductor
(c) insulator
(d) None of these

3. In a semiconductor, the concentration of electrons is given $9\times10^{14}/\text{cm}^3$ and that of the holes is $4\times10^{12}\ \text{cm}^3$, then the semiconductor is of

(a) *p*-type
(b) *n*-type
(c) intrinsic
(d) *pnp*-type

4. The valency of the impurity atom that is to be added to the germanium crystal so as to make it an *n*-type semiconductor, is

(a) 6 (b) 5
(c) 4 (d) 3

5. If the electrical conductivity of a semiconductor is due to the breaking of its covalent bonds, then the semiconductor is said to be

(a) donor (b) acceptor
(c) intrinsic (d) extrinsic

6. To obtain *p*-type Si semiconductor, we need to dope pure Si with

(a) aluminium (b) phosphorus
(c) oxygen (d) germanium

7. **Assertion** (A) The probability of electrons to be found in the conduction band of an intrinsic semiconductor at a finite temperature, decreases exponentially with increasing band gap.

Reason (R) It will be more difficult for the electrons to cross over the large band gap while going from valence band to conduction band.

In the light of above statements, choose the most appropriate answer from the options given below.
(a) Both A and R are true and R is the correct explanation of A.
(b) Both A and R are true but R is not the correct explanation of A.
(c) A is true but R is false.
(d) A is false but R is true.

8. In *p-n* junction diode, the approximate ratio of resistance in the forward and reverse bias is
(a) $10^2:1$
(b) $10^{-2}:1$
(c) $1:10^{-4}$
(d) $1:10^4$

9. When a semiconductor is heated, the value of its resistance is
(a) increases
(b) decreases
(c) remains unchanged
(d) Nothing is define

10. In *p*-type semiconductor, the majority and minority charge carriers are, respectively
(a) protons and electrons
(b) electrons and protons
(c) electrons and holes
(d) holes and electrons

11. The depletion layer in silicon diode is 1 μm wide and the knee potential is 0.5 V, then the electric field in the depletion layer will be
(a) zero
(b) 0.6 Vm^{-1}
(c) 6×10^4 V/m
(d) 5×10^5 V/m

12. A *p*-type semiconductor has acceptor levels 57 meV above the valence band. The maximum wavelength of light required to create a hole is (Planck's constant, $h=6.6\times10^{-34}$ J-s)
(a) 57×10^{-3} Å
(b) 217100 Å
(c) 57 Å
(d) 11.61×10^{-33} Å

13. In a *p-n* junction,
(a) *p* and *n* are at same potential.
(b) higher potential is at *n*-side and lower potential is at *p*-side.
(c) higher potential is at *p*-side and lower potential is at *n*-side.
(d) lower potential is at *n*-side and zero potential is at *p*-side.

14. A photodetector is used in reverse bias because
(a) reverse current is of higher magnitude
(b) reverse current is of lower magnitude
(c) fractional change of reverse current is low
(d) fractional change of forward current is low

15. The output waveform of AND gate for the following input waveforms is

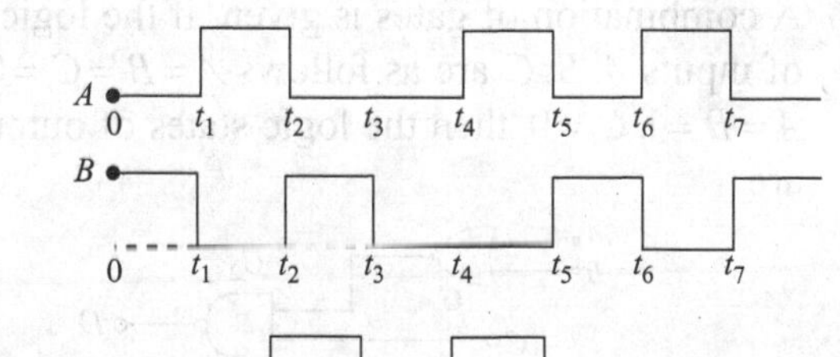

(a) 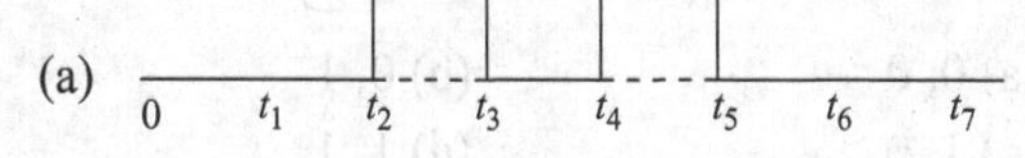

(b) 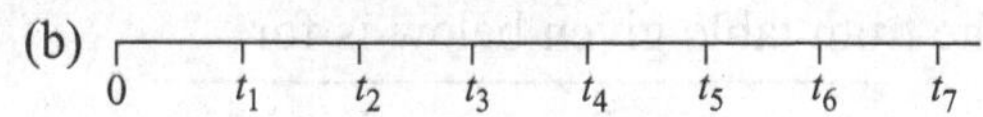

(c) 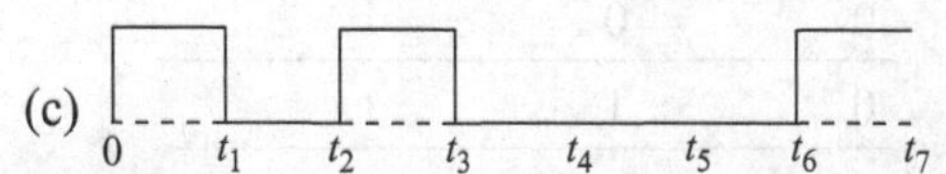

(d) 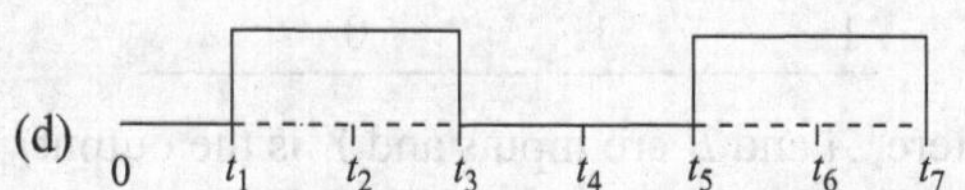

16. What is the current in the circuit shown below?

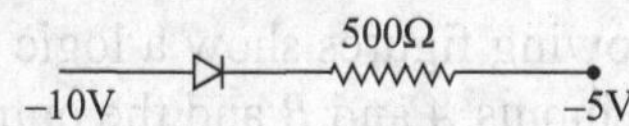

(a) 100 A
(b) 33.33 A
(c) 0
(d) 50 A

17. In the circuit shown, $V(t)$ is the sinusoidal voltage source. Voltage drop $V_{AB}(t)$ across the resistance R

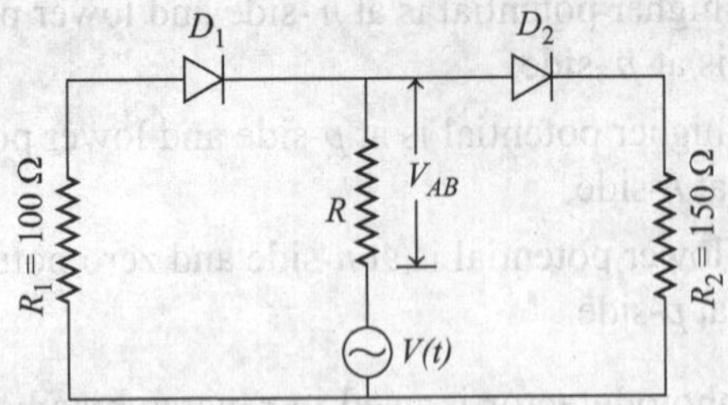

(a) is half-wave rectified
(b) is full wave rectified
(c) has the same peak value in the positive and negative half-cycles
(d) has different peak values during positive and negative half-cycles

18. A combination of gates is given, if the logic states of inputs A, B, C are as follows $A = B = C = 0$ and $A = B = 1$, $C = 0$, then the logic states of output D are

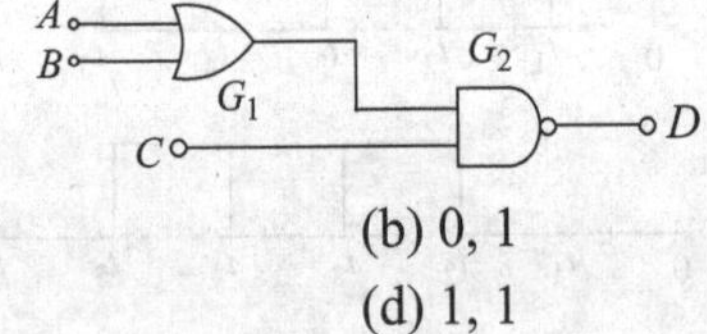

(a) 0, 0 (b) 0, 1
(c) 1, 0 (d) 1, 1

19. The truth table given below is for

A	B	Y
0	0	1
0	1	1
1	0	1
1	1	0

(Here, A and B are inputs and Y is the output)
(a) NOR (b) AND
(c) XOR (d) NAND

20. Two following figures show a logic gate circuit with two inputs A and B and the output Y.

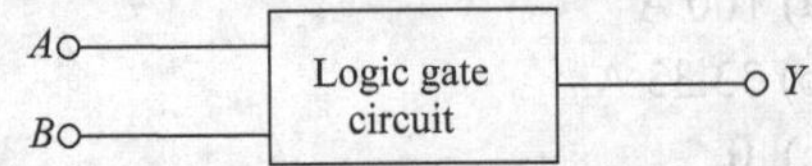

The voltage waveforms of A, B and Y are given. The logic gate is

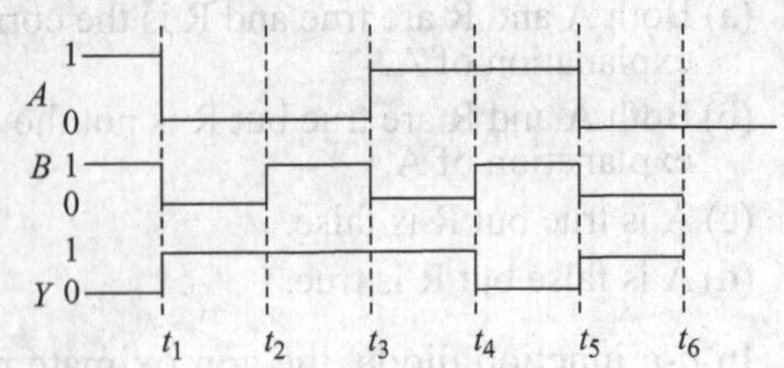

(a) NOT gate
(b) OR gate
(c) AND gate
(d) NAND gate

21. Statement I NAND gate and NOR gate are building blocks of digital circuit.

Statement II The repeated use of NOR and NAND gates can produce all the basic complicated gates.

In the light of above statements, choose the most appropriate answer from the options given below.

(a) Both Statement I and Statement II are correct.
(b) Both Statement I and Statement II are incorrect.
(c) Statement I is correct but Statement II is incorrect.
(d) Statement I is incorrect but Statement II is correct.

22. An LED is a
(a) *p-n* junction in forward bias
(b) *p-n* junction in reverse bias
(c) Both (a) and (b)
(d) is a Zener diode

23. Which of the following gates will have an output of 1?

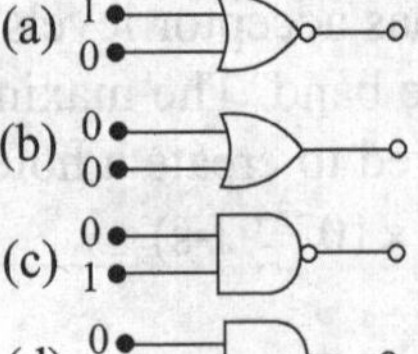

24. Match the List I with List II.

	List I		List II
A.	Rectifier	1.	used either for stepping up or stepping down the AC voltage
B.	Stabilizer	2.	used to convert AC voltage into DC voltage
C.	Transformer	3.	used to remove any ripple in the rectified output voltage
D.	Filter	4.	used for constant output voltage even when the input voltage or load current change

(a) A-1, B-2, C-3, D-4
(b) A-4, B-3, C-2, D-1
(c) A-2, B-4, C-1, D-3
(d) A-2, B-3, C-4, D-1

25. Consider the circuit diagram shown below. Two ammeters A_1 and A_2 are connected across a diode and resistor, respectively. The amount of current flowing through these two ammeters is (Neglect the resistance of the ammeters).

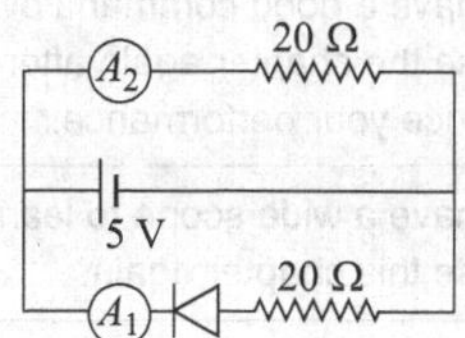

(a) 0A, 0.25 A
(b) 0.25 A, 0A
(c) 0A, 0A
(d) 0.25 A, 0.25

26. **Statement I** Ionisation energy of isolated pentavalent atom of phosphorus is very large, so in an n-type semiconductor, there are no free charge carriers at room temperature.
Statement II When current flows through a $p-n$ junction diode, it becomes hot.
In the light of above statements, choose the most appropriate answer from the options given below.

(a) Both Statement I and Statement II are incorrect.
(b) Both Statement I and Statement II are correct.
(c) Statement I is correct but Statement II is incorrect.
(d) Statement I is incorrect but Statement II is correct.

27. The truth table for the circuit given in the figure is

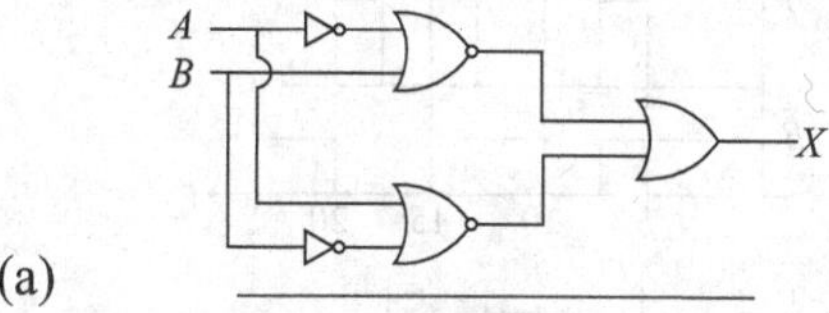

(a)

A	B	X
0	0	0
0	1	0
1	0	0
1	1	0

(b)

A	B	X
0	0	0
0	1	1
1	0	0
1	1	0

(c)

A	B	X
0	0	1
0	1	0
1	0	0
1	1	1

(d)

A	B	X
0	0	0
0	1	1
1	0	1
1	1	0

28. A Zener diode, having breakdown voltage equal to 20 V, is used in a voltage regulator circuit as shown in figure. The current through diode is

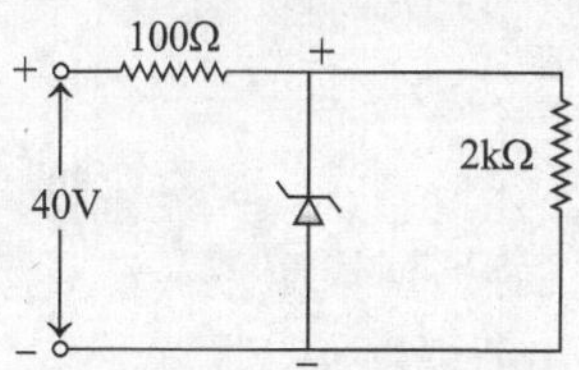

(a) 20 mA
(b) 200 mA
(c) 190 mA
(d) 5 mA

29. Identify the correct output signal Y in the given combination of gates (as shown) for the given inputs A and B.

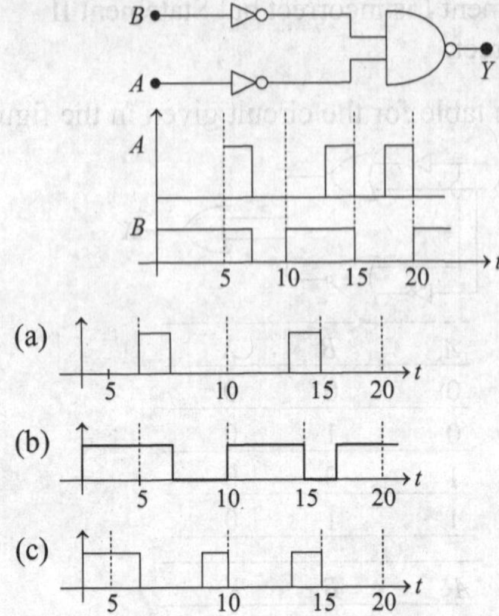

(d) 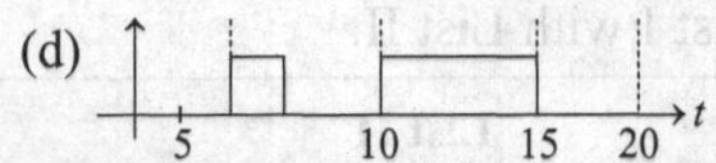

30. In the given circuit, the value of output Y is

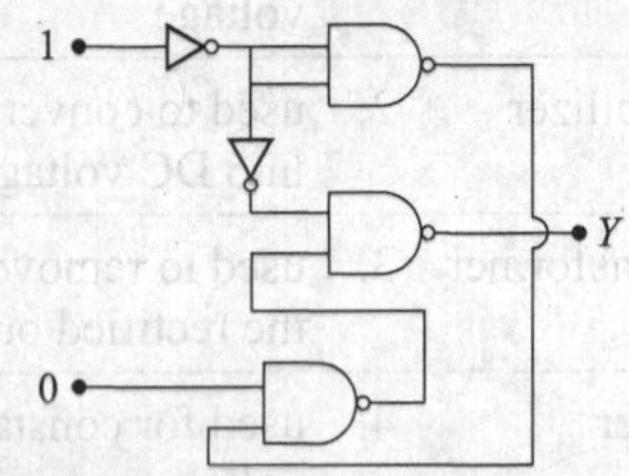

(a) toggles between 0 and 1
(b) 1
(c) 0
(d) Will not execute

Response Index

01	a	b	c	d	11	a	b	c	d	21	a	b	c	d
02	a	b	c	d	12	a	b	c	d	22	a	b	c	d
03	a	b	c	d	13	a	b	c	d	23	a	b	c	d
04	a	b	c	d	14	a	b	c	d	24	a	b	c	d
05	a	b	c	d	15	a	b	c	d	25	a	b	c	d
06	a	b	c	d	16	a	b	c	d	26	a	b	c	d
07	a	b	c	d	17	a	b	c	d	27	a	b	c	d
08	a	b	c	d	18	a	b	c	d	28	a	b	c	d
09	a	b	c	d	19	a	b	c	d	29	a	b	c	d
10	a	b	c	d	20	a	b	c	d	30	a	b	c	d

Performance Scanner

> 90% Excellent !	You have mastered this chapter. The concepts of this chapter are on your fingertips. Move on to the next chapter and maintain this momentum.
76-90% Very Good !	You have a good command over this chapter. Revise the chapter again after a few days and enhance your performance.
60-75% Good !	You have a wide scope to learn for this chapter. Revise this chapter again.
<60% Not Satisfactory!	You have a long way ahead of you to master this chapter. Revise it thoroughly.

For Online Chapter Test **Scan the QR Code**

For Online Unit Test **Scan the QR Code**

Test Booklet No. **3947166**

Test Booklet Code **CH16**

MED ACE
NEET (UG)
SELF ASSESSMENT KIT

Experimental Skills

Topics Covered

Vernier Callipers, Screw Gauge, Simple Pendulum, Meter Scale, Young's Modulus, Surface Tension and Coefficient of Viscosity

Resonance Tube, Specific Heat Capacity, Meter Bridge, Resistance using Ohm's Law and Galvanometer

Focal Length of Mirrors and Lenses, Triangular Prism, Travelling Microscope, Semiconductor and Electronic Devices

Important Instructions

- This Booklet Contains – Three Topic Tests and One Test on Complete Chapter.
- Each question carries 4 marks.
- For each correct response, the candidate will get 4 marks and for every incorrect response, 1 mark will be additionally deducted from the total score.
- Use **Blue/Black** point pen only for filling the OMR.
- Rough work will be done in the space provided for this purpose within the test booklet only.

Name of the Candidate (In Capitals) ____________________

____

Candidate's Signature ____________

Invigilator's Signature ____________

Facsimile signature stamp of center superintendent____________

Do not open this Booklet until you start attempting the Test

Topical Follow Thru

Test 1

Syllabus

- Vernier Callipers, Screw Gauge, Simple Pendulum
- Meter Scale, Young's Modulus, Surface Tension
- Coefficient of Viscosity

For deeper insight **Scan the QR Code**

Important Instructions

- The test is of 30 min duration and Contains 15 Multiple Choice Questions. (Four options with a single correct answer).
- Choose the correct option and fill the OMR given on the last page of Booklet accordingly.
- At some instances, you may find more than 1 option may be correct in such circumstances you have to judge the most appropriate answer as per the conditions given in the question.

1. Least count of an instrument using two scales, a main scale and a vernier scale, is

(a) 1 MSD ÷ 1 VSD

(b) 1 VSD + 1 MSD

(c) 1 MSD ÷ Number of divisions on vernier scale

(d) 1 MSD – 1 VSD

2. In a screw gauge when the edge of the circular scale lies to the above of the zero mark on the main scale when the stud and the spindle touch each other, then the

(a) zero correction is negative

(b) zero error is negative

(c) zero error does not exist

(d) zero correction is positive

3. If 1 main scale division of a vernier calliper is of measure 1 mm and there are 10 divisions on vernier scale, then least count of vernier is

(a) 0.1 cm (b) 0.1 mm

(c) 0.01 mm (d) 1 mm

4. Two instruments *A* and *B* have equal zero error of 4 VSD. Least count of both *A* and *B* is 0.1 mm.

The scales of *A* and *B* are shown with jaws closed as below

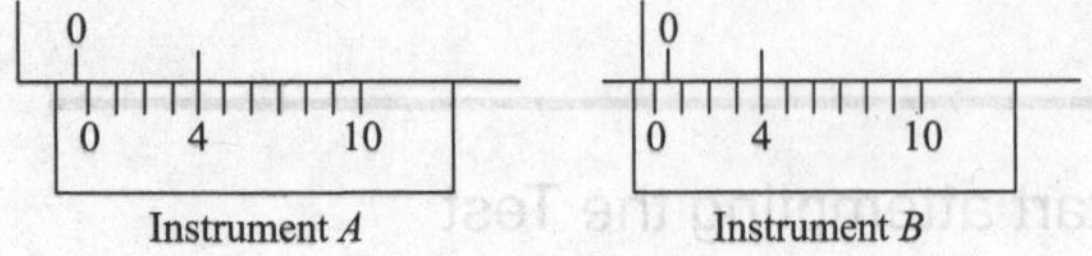

Now, choose correct statement.

(a) Zero correction for *A* is 0.4 mm and for *B* is – 0.4 mm.

(b) Zero correction for *A* is – 0.4 mm and for *B* is 0.4 mm.

(c) Zero correction for *A* is 4 mm and for *B* is – 4 mm.

(d) Zero correction for *A* is – 4 mm and for *B* is 4 mm.

5.

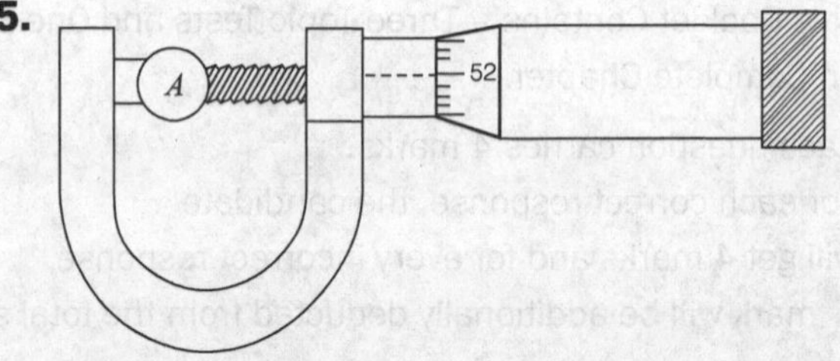

A screw gauge is used to measure diameter of a spherical ball *A*.

Given, 1 MSD = 1 mm

Negative zero error of 4 divisions of circular scale

Number of divisions on circular scale is 100.

While taking reading, instrument is shown in diagram.

Diameter of spherical ball is closest to

(a) 2.48 mm

(b) 2.52 mm

(c) 2.56 mm

(d) 2.50 mm

6. In an experiment of simple pendulum, L *versus* T^2 graph is drawn.

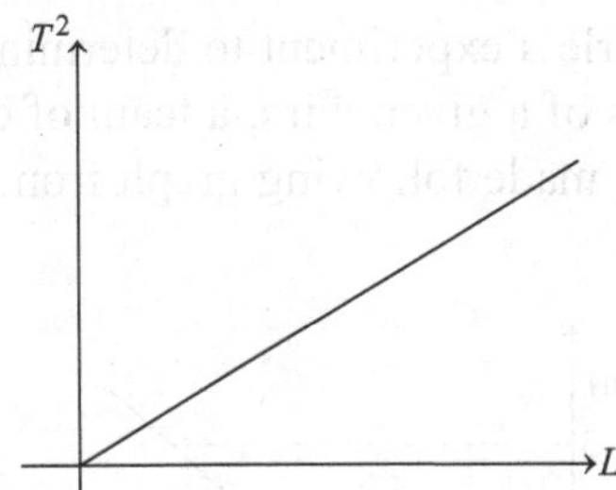

Slope of this graph is nearly

(a) 1 (b) $\sqrt{3}$
(c) 4 (d) $\tan^{-1}(2)$

7. In an experiment of surface tension when a glass capillary tube of radius 0.015 cm is dipped in water, the water rises to a height of 15 cm within it. Assuming contact angle between water and glass to be 0°, the surface tension of water is $[\rho_{water} = 1000 \text{ kg-m}^{-3}, g = 9.8 \text{ ms}^{-2}]$

(a) 0.11 N-m^{-1}
(b) 0.7 N-m^{-1}
(c) 0.072 N-m^{-1}
(d) 0.011 N-m^{-1}

8. The least count of vernier callipers is 0.1 mm. The main scale reading before the zero of the vernier scale is 20 mm and the zeroth division of the vernier scale coincides with the main scale division. Given that each main scale division is 2 mm, then the measured value should be equal to

(a) 2 cm (b) 3 cm
(c) 0.2 cm (d) 2 m

9. In experiment for measuring surface tension by capillary rise method, readings for positions A, B, C and D for internal diameter of capillary tube are given as under. Mean internal radius of capillary is

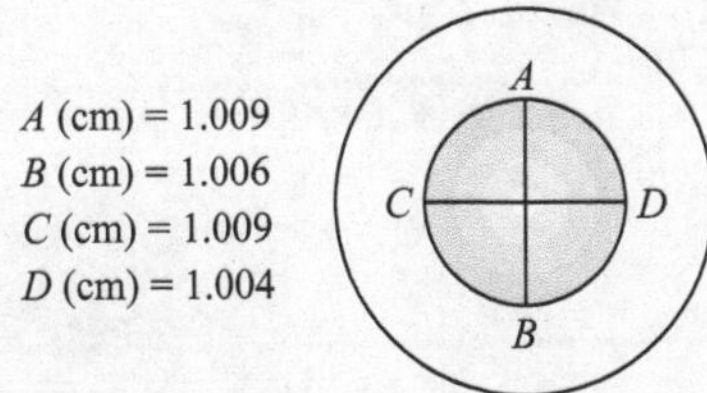

(a) 0.002 cm (b) 0.003 cm
(c) 0.004 cm (d) 0.005 cm

10. The pitch of a screw gauge is 2 mm and there are 50 divisions on the circular scale. When nothing is put in between the jaws, the zero of the circular scale lies 6 divisions below the reference line. When a wire is placed between the jaws, the first linear scale division is clearly visible while 70th division on the circular scale coincides with the reference line. The radius of the wire is

(a) 4.56 mm
(b) 1.64 mm
(c) 0.82 mm
(d) 2.28 mm

11. A glass capillary tube is lowered vertically into liquid in a vessel. Now, match the Column I with Column II and choose the correct option given below.

	Column I		Column II
A.	Contact angle for concave meniscus	(I)	ascends
B.	Contact angle for convex meniscus	(II)	greater than 90°
C.	Liquid in capillary tube for concave meniscus	(III)	descends
D.	Liquid in capillary tube for convex meniscus	(IV)	less than 90°

(a) A - (IV), B - (II), C- (I), D - (III)
(b) A - (I), B - (II), C- (III), D - (IV)
(c) A - (II), B - (IV), C- (III), D - (I)
(d) A - (II), B - (I), C- (III), D - (IV)

12. **Statement I** The time period of a simple pendulum of infinite length is infinite.
Statement II The time period of a simple pendulum is directly proportional to the square root of length.
In the light of above statements, choose the most appropriate answer from the options given below.

(a) Both Statement I and Statement II are correct.
(b) Both Statement I and Statement II are incorrect.
(c) Statement I is correct but Statement II is incorrect.
(d) Statement I is incorrect but Statement II is correct.

13. **Statement I** A screw gauge gives more precise reading than a vernier calliper.

Statement II A vernier calliper gives more precise reading than a screw gauge.

In the light of above statements, choose the most appropriate answer from the options given below.

(a) Both statement I and statement II are correct.

(b) Both statement I and statement II are incorrect.

(c) Statement I is correct but statement II is incorrect.

(d) Statement I is incorrect but statement II is correct.

14. In an experiment to determine viscosity of given oil, a student collected following data,

Radius of iron ball = 0.3 cm

Density of iron ball = 7.8 g cm^{-3}

Density of oil = 0.94 g cm^{-3}

Terminal velocity attained by ball = 0.5 cm s^{-1}

Viscosity of oil (in CGS units), she measures, is around

(a) 270 (b) 289

(c) 301 (d) 254

15. In a Searle's experiment to determine Young's modulus of a given wire, a team of class 11th students made following graph from collected data.

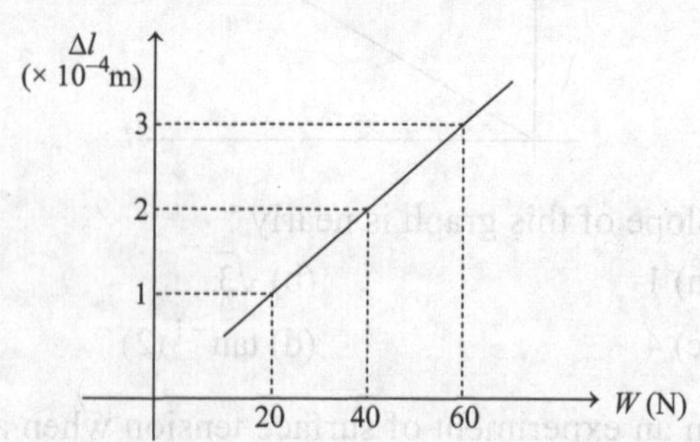

Length of wire is 1 m and area of wire is 10^{-6} m^2 Young's modulus of wire is

(a) 2×10^{11} Nm^{-2}

(b) 2×10^{-11} Nm^{-2}

(c) 2×10^{12} Nm^{-2}

(d) 2×10^{-12} Nm^{-2}

Response Index

01	a	b	c	d	11	a	b	c	d
02	a	b	c	d	12	a	b	c	d
03	a	b	c	d	13	a	b	c	d
04	a	b	c	d	14	a	b	c	d
05	a	b	c	d	15	a	b	c	d
06	a	b	c	d					
07	a	b	c	d					
08	a	b	c	d					
09	a	b	c	d					
10	a	b	c	d					

Performance Scanner

> 90% Excellent !	You have mastered these topics. The concepts of these topic are on your fingertips. Move on to the next test and maintain this momentum.
76-90% Very Good !	You have a good command over these topics. Revise these topic again after a few days and enhance your performance.
60-75% Good !	You have a wide scope to learn more for topics. Revise them again.
<60% Not Satisfactory!	You have a long way ahead of you to master in these topics. Revise them thoroughly.

Test 2

Syllabus Resonance Tube, Specific Heat Capacity, Meter Bridge, Resistance using Ohm's Law and Galvanometer.

For deeper insight **Scan the QR Code**

Important Instructions

- The test is of 30 min duration and contains 15 Multiple Choice Questions. (Four options with a single correct answer).
- Choose the correct option and fill the OMR given on the last page of Booklet accordingly.
- At some instances, you may find more than 1 option may be correct in such circumstances you have to judge the most appropriate answer as per the conditions given in the question.

1. In an experiment of meter bridge as the temperature of metallic resistor is increased, the product of resistivity and conductivity

(a) increases

(b) decreases

(c) may decrease or increase

(d) remains constant

2. **Assertion (A)** In meter bridge experiment, a high resistance is connected in series with the galvanometer.

Reason (R) As resistance increases, current through the circuit increases.

In the light of above statements, choose the most appropriate answer from the options given below.

(a) Both A and R are true and R is the correct explanation of A.

(b) Both A and R are true but R is not the correct explanation of A.

(c) A is true but R is false.

(d) A is false but R is true.

3. In a resonance tube experiment tube of length 1.0 m is initially filled completely with water. A tuning fork of frequency 500 Hz is kept near open end of tube and water is simultaneously drained slowly from bottom of tube.

Total number of resonances that are heard, is (Velocity of sound = 330 m/s)

(a) 1

(b) 2

(c) 3

(d) 4

4. In an experiment of determining the specific heat 200 g of a solid ball at 15°C is dropped in an equal amount of water at 105°C. The resulting temperature is 45°C. This means that specific heat of solid is

(a) one-third of water (b) same as water

(c) twice of water (d) three times of water

5. Current sensitivity of a moving coil galvanometer is 6 div/mA and its voltage sensitivity (angular deflection per unit voltage applied) is 30 div/V. The resistance of the galvanometer is

(a) 100 Ω (b) 150 Ω

(c) 200 Ω (d) 250 Ω

6. **Statement I** If we use tuning fork of smaller frequency, then we require a large tube in resonance column method.

Statement II In resonance column method $v = 2f(l_2 - l_1)$

Here, v = velocity of sound in air,

f = frequency of tuning fork,

l_1 = first resonance length of air column,

l_2 = second resonance length of air column.

In the light of above statements, choose the most appropriate answer from the options given below.

(a) Both Statement I and Statement II are correct.

(b) Both Statement I and Statement II are incorrect.

(c) Statement I is correct but Statement II is incorrect.

(d) Statement I is incorrect but Statement II is correct.

7. In the measurement of resistance of a wire using Ohm's law, the plot between V and I is drawn as shown. The resistance of the wire is

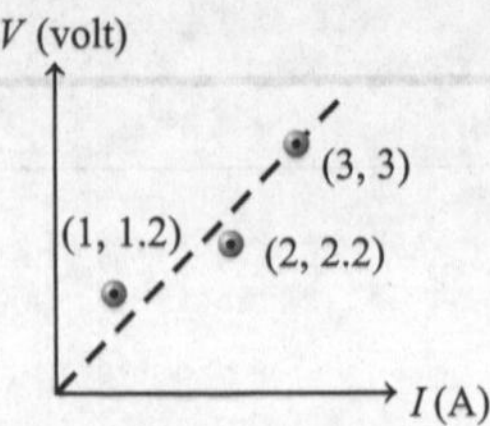

(a) 0.833 Ω
(b) 0.9 Ω
(c) 1 Ω
(d) 1.12 Ω

8. In a calorimeter experiment when 0.15 kg of ice at 0°C is mixed with 0.30 kg of water at 50°C in a container, the resulting temperature is 6.7°C. The heat of fusion of ice is
(Given, $S_{water} = 4186$ J/kg k)
(a) 3.34×10^5 J kg^{-1}
(b) 2.34×10^{-5} J kg^{-1}
(c) 4.34×10^4 J kg^{-1}
(d) 3.34×10^6 J kg^{-1}

9. Resistance in the two gaps of a meter bridge are 12 ohms and 24 ohms, respectively. If the resistance are interchanged, the balance point shifts by
(a) 33.33 cm (b) 25 cm
(c) 66.66 cm (d) 50 cm

10. The scale of a galvanometer of resistance 100 Ω contains 60 divisions. It gives a deflection of 1 division on passing a current of 5×10^{-4} A. The resistance in ohm to be added to it, so that it may become a voltmeter of range 6 V is
(a) 50 Ω (b) 75 Ω
(c) 25 Ω (d) 100 Ω

11. The temperature coefficient of resistance of a wire is 0.00145°C^{-1}. At 100°C, its resistance is 3 Ω. At what temperature the resistance of the wire will be 5 Ω?
(a) 900 K
(b) 567.5 K
(c) 928.3 K
(d) 727.56 K

12. In a circuit for finding the resistance of a galvanometer by half deflection method, a 7.26 V battery and a high resistance of 15 kΩ are used. The figure of merit of the galvanometer is 60 μA per division.
In the absence of shunt resistance, the galvanometer produces a deflection of $\theta = 8$ divisions when current flows in the circuit. The value of the shunt resistance that can cause the deflection of $\frac{\theta}{2}$ is closest to
(a) 110 Ω
(b) 124 Ω
(c) 248 Ω
(d) 220 Ω

13. In an experiment, a sphere of aluminium of mass 0.90 kg is heated upto 170°C. Immediately, it is put into water of volume 170 cc at 27°C kept in a calorimeter of water equivalent to 0.050 kg. Final temperature of the system is 70°C. The specific heat of aluminium is (take 4.2 J = 1 cal)
(a) 952 J/kg°C
(b) 993 J/kg°C
(c) 864 J/kg°C
(d) 964 J/kg°C

14. The meter bridge shown in the balance position with $\frac{P}{Q} = \frac{l_1}{l_2}$. If we now interchange the positions of galvanometer and cell, will the bridge work?

If yes, then the balanced condition will be

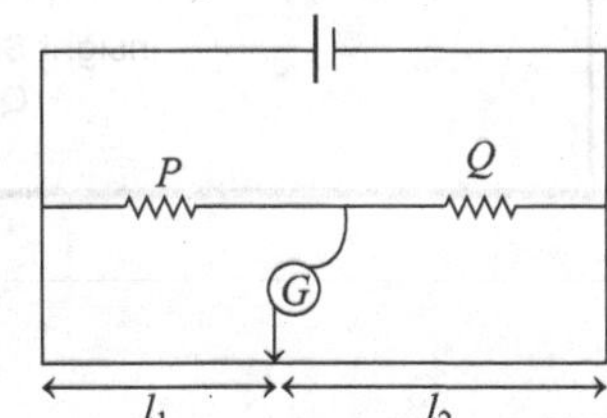

(a) yes, $\frac{P}{Q} = \frac{l_2 - l_1}{l_2 + l_1}$ (b) no, no null point

(c) yes, $\frac{P}{Q} = \frac{l_2}{l_1}$ (d) yes, $\frac{P}{Q} = \frac{l_1}{l_2}$

15. The internal radius of a 1 m long resonance tube is measured as 3.0 cm. A tuning fork of frequency 2000 Hz is used. The first resonating length is measured as 4.6 cm and the second resonating length is measured as 14.0 cm. Percentage error in calculation of end correction e is

(a) 100% (b) 80%
(c) 94% (d) 75%

Response Index

01	a	b	c	d	11	a	b	c	d
02	a	b	c	d	12	a	b	c	d
03	a	b	c	d	13	a	b	c	d
04	a	b	c	d	14	a	b	c	d
05	a	b	c	d	15	a	b	c	d
06	a	b	c	d					
07	a	b	c	d					
08	a	b	c	d					
09	a	b	c	d					
10	a	b	c	d					

Performance Scanner

> 90% Excellent !	You have mastered these topics. The concepts of these topics are on your fingertips. Move on to the next test and maintain this momentum.
76-90% Very Good !	You have a good command over these topics. Revise these topics again after a few days and enhance your performance.
60-75% Good !	You have a wide scope to learn for these topics. Revise them again.
<60% Not Satisfactory!	You have a long way ahead of you to master in these topics. Revise them thoroughly.

Test 3

Syllabus
- Focal Length of Mirrors and Lenses, Triangular Prism, Travelling Microscope,
- Semi conductor and Electronic Devices

For deeper insight **Scan the QR Code**

Important Instructions
- The test is of 30 minutes duration and contains 15 Multiple Choice Questions. (Four options with a single correct answer).
- Choose the correct option and fill the OMR given on the last page of Booklet accordingly.
- At some instances, you may find more than 1 option may be correct in such circumstances you have to judge the most appropriate answer as per the conditions given in the question.

1. For practical use, the colour we take for the refractive index of a material of lens and glass slab, is

(a) red
(b) yellow
(c) blue
(d) green

2. Observation taken by an student in a Zener diode experiment are

Voltage (V)	3	4	5	6	7	8	8.4	8.8	9	9.3
Current (I)	0	0	0	0	0	0	0.1	0.2	0.4	3.0

Zener breakdown voltage is nearly

(a) 8.5 V (b) 8.4 V
(c) 9 V (d) 9.2 V

3. A given ray of light suffers minimum deviation in an equilateral prism P. If refractive index increases slightly, then the ray will suffer

(a) greater deviation
(b) no deviation
(c) same deviation as before
(d) lesser deviation

4. An experiment is performed to find the refractive index of glass using a travelling microscope. In this experiment distances are measured by

(a) vernier scale from microscope
(b) a standard laboratory scale
(c) a meter scale provided on the microscope
(d) a screw gauge provided on the microscope

5. A Zener diode normally operates under reverse bias condition, the major use of this fact is in the applications where we require

(a) large value of current
(b) a constant voltage
(c) a current that is increasing without any change in applied voltage
(d) All of the above

6. **Statement I** When colour of light changes, the focal length of thin lens change but that of spherical mirror does not change.

Statement II Refractive index of material depends on wavelength of light.

In the light of above statements, choose the most appropriate answer from the options given below.

(a) Both Statement I and Statement II are correct.
(b) Both Statement I and Statement II are incorrect.
(c) Statement I is correct but Statement II is incorrect.
(d) Statement I is incorrect but Statement II is correct.

7. **Assertion (A)** If angles of base of a prism are equal, then in the position of minimum deviation, the refracted ray will pass parallel to the base of prism.
Reason (R) In the case of minimum deviation, the angle of incidence is equal to the angle of emergence.
In the light of above statements, choose the most appropriate answer from the options given below.
(a) Both A and R are true and R is the true explanation of A.
(b) Both A and R are true but R is not the true explanation of A.
(c) A is true but R is false.
(d) A is false but R is true.

8. A microscope is focused on a mark on a piece of paper and then a slab of glass of thickness 6 cm and refractive index 1.5 is placed over the mark. How should the microscope be moved to get the mark in focus again.
(a) 2 cm upward
(b) 2 cm downward
(c) 4 cm upward
(d) 4 cm downward

9. The forward bias characteristics of two diodes D_1 and D_2 are shown. The knee voltages for D_1 and D_2 are respectively (approx.)

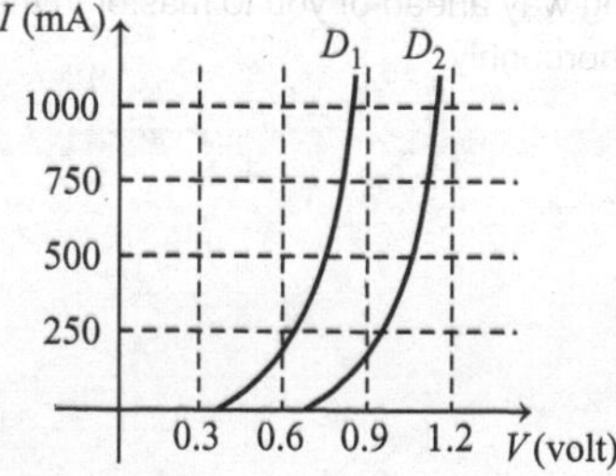

(a) 0.4 V and 0.7 V
(b) 0.6 V and 0.9 V
(c) 0.6 V and 0.8 V
(d) 0.4 V and 0.9 V

10. The readings corresponding to Zener diode are given below in the table. From given table, determine the reverse breakdown voltage of the Zener diode.

Forward bias		Reverse bias	
V (volt)	I (mA)	V (volt)	I (μA)
0.5	5	0.5	2.0
0.7	20	1.0	2.0
0.8	40	3.0	2.0
1.0	250	5.0	2.0
		5.5	100.0
		5.5	120.0

(a) It is lying between 1.0 V to 5.0 V
(b) 1.0 V
(c) Approx. 5.3 V
(d) Less than 1.0 V

11. A ray of light passes through an equilateral prism such that the angle of incidence is equal to angle of emergence and later is equal to $\left(\frac{3}{4}\right)$th the angle of prism. The angle of deviation is
(a) 45°
(b) 20°
(c) 40°
(d) 30°

12. A travelling microscope is used to determine the refractive index of a glass slab. If 50 divisions are there in 1 cm on main scale and 60 vernier scale divisions are equal to 58 main scale divisions, the least count of the travelling microscope is
(a) 5×10^{-6} m
(b) 6.66×10^{-6} m
(c) 8×10^{-6} m
(d) 2×10^{-6} m

13. Choose the incorrect answer from the given options by considering the convex lens characteristics

(a) If position of object at infinity, then size of image is extremely diminished.

(b) If position of object at $2F_1$, then size of image is same as object.

(c) If position of object at F_1 then size of image is highly magnified.

(d) If position of object beyond $2F_1$, then size of image is magnified.

14. Find the current through the Zener diode when the load resistance is 4 kΩ. Use diode approximation.

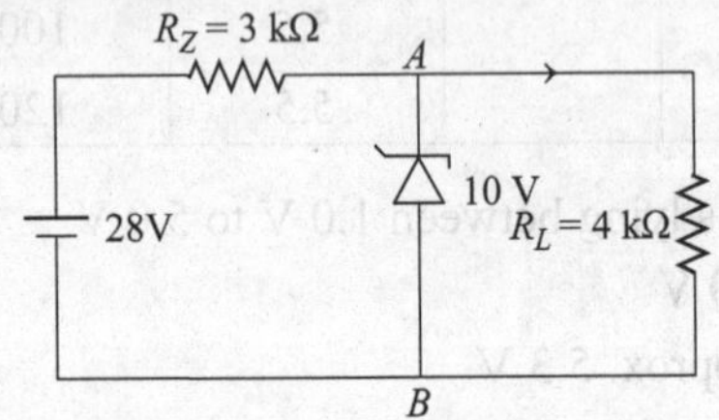

(a) 1 mA

(b) 2 mA

(c) 3.5 mA

(d) 2.5 mA

15. In the figure, potential difference between A and B is

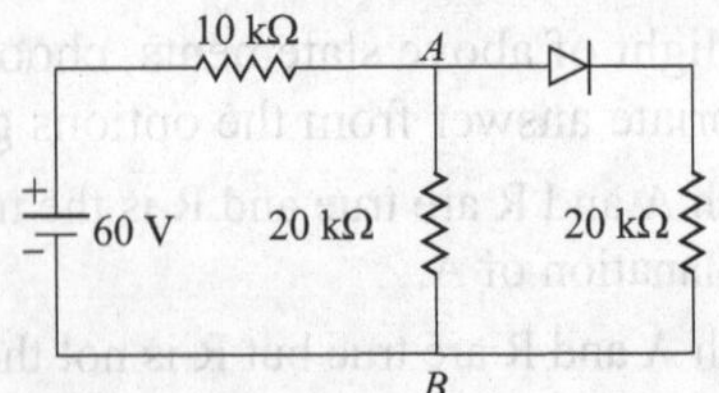

(a) zero

(b) 30 V

(c) 5 V

(d) 15 V

Response Index

01	a	b	c	d	11	a	b	c	d
02	a	b	c	d	12	a	b	c	d
03	a	b	c	d	13	a	b	c	d
04	a	b	c	d	14	a	b	c	d
05	a	b	c	d	15	a	b	c	d
06	a	b	c	d					
07	a	b	c	d					
08	a	b	c	d					
09	a	b	c	d					
10	a	b	c	d					

Performance Scanner

> 90% Excellent !	You have mastered these topics. The concepts of these topics are on your fingertips. Move on to the next test and maintain this momentum.
76-90% Very Good !	You have a good command over these topics. Revise these topics again after a few days and enhance your performance.
60-75% Good !	You have a wide scope to learn for these topics. Revise them again.
<60% Not Satisfactory!	You have a long way ahead of you to master in these topics. Revise them thoroughly.

Chapter Break Thru

Syllabus		
	• Vernier Callipers, Screw Gauge, Simple Pendulum • Meter Scale, Young's Modulus, Surface Tension • Coefficient of Viscosity • Resonance Tube, Specific Heat Capacity, Meter Bridge, Resistance using Ohm's Law and Galvanometer.	• Focal Length of Mirrors and Lenses • Triangular Prism, Travelling Microscope • Semi conductor and Electronic Devices

Important Instructions

- The test is of 45 min duration and contains 30 Multiple-Choice Questions (Four options with a single correct answer).
- Choose the correct option and fill the OMR given on the last page of this test accordingly.
- At some instances, you may find more than 1 option may be correct, in such circumstances you have to judge the most appropriate answer as per conditions given in the question.

1. In meter bridge experiment, we try to obtain the null point at the middle. This
(a) reduces systematics error as well as random error
(b) reduces systematics error but not the random error
(c) reduces random error but not the systematics error
(d) reduces neither systematic error nor the random error

2. The electrical resistance of depletion layer is large because
(a) it has no charge carriers
(b) it has large number of charge carriers
(c) it contains electrons as charge carriers
(d) it has holes as charge carriers

3. Two masses M and m are tied to two ends of a meter scale. If a balanced point is obtained at point P and $M > m$, then

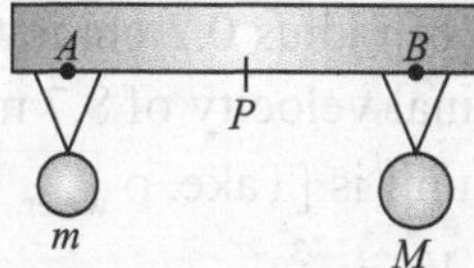

(a) $PA = PB$
(b) $PA > PB$
(c) $PB > PA$
(d) $PA = 3PB$

4. In the experiment of measuring speed of sound by resonance tube, it is observed that for tuning fork of frequency $\nu = 480$ Hz, length of air column $l_1 = 30$ cm, $l_2 = 70$ cm, then v_1 is equal to
(a) 338 ms^{-1}
(b) 379 ms^{-1}
(c) 384 ms^{-1}
(d) 332 ms^{-1}

5. A sphere of mass m and radius r is falling in a viscous fluid. The square of the terminal velocity attained by the falling object will be proportional to
(a) $\frac{m}{r}$
(b) $\frac{m}{r^2}$
(c) mr^2
(d) $\frac{m^2}{r^2}$

6. Match the following columns.

	Column I		Column II
A.	The difference between one main scale division and one vernier scale division, used to measure with high precision.	I.	Main scale
B.	The part of the vernier callipers that provides the primary reading usually in millimetres or centimetres.	II.	Vernier scale
C.	A correction needed when the zero mark of the vernier scale does not coincide with the zero mark of the main scale when the jaws are closed.	III.	Zero error
D.	The part of the vernier callipers that provides the additional decimal places to the main scale reading.	IV.	Least count

Choose the correct answer from the options given below.

(a) A-II, B-I, C-IV, D-III
(b) A-IV, B-I, C-III, D-II
(c) A-III, B-IV, C-II, D-I
(d) A-I, B-IV, C-III, D-II

7. The characteristic curve for a diode is shown in the figure for forward bias mode. The cut-off voltage for this diode is approximately

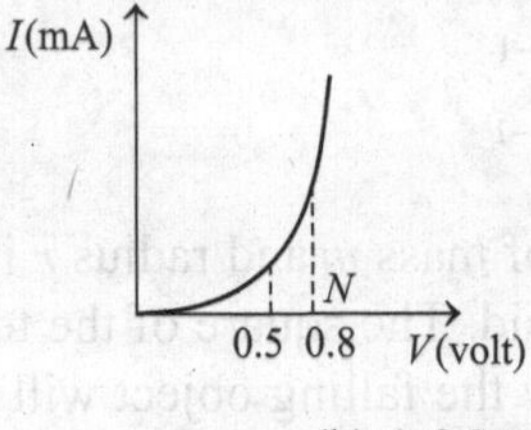

(a) 0.5 V
(b) 0.8 V
(c) 1 V
(d) > 1 V

8. A screw gauge has 100 divisions on its circular scale. The circular scale is 5 units ahead of the pitch scale marking, prior to use. Upon one complete rotation of the circular scale, a displacement of 1.0 mm is noticed on the pitch scale. The nature of zero error involved and the least count of the screw gauge are respectively

(a) positive, 10 μm
(b) negative, 0.1 mm
(c) positive 5 μm
(d) negative, 10 μm

9. Two wires A and B have same length and made of the same material but A is thicker than B. Both are subjected to the same extending load. Which will extend more?

(a) A
(b) B
(c) Same extension
(d) Can't predict

10. **Statement I** The value of Young's modulus (Y) increases, if the diameter of the wire decreases.
Statement II The value of Young's modulus (Y) decreases with the rise in temperature.
In the light of above statements, choose the most appropriate answer from the options given below.

(a) Both Statement I and Statement II are correct.
(b) Both Statement I and Statement II are incorrect.
(c) Statement I is correct but Statement II is incorrect.
(d) Statement I is incorrect but Statement II is correct.

11. While measuring surface tension of water using capillary rise method, height of the lower meniscus from free surface of water is 3 cm while inner radius of capillary tube is found to be 0.5 cm. Then, compute surface tension of water using this data. [Take, contact angle between glass and water as 0° and $g = 9.81 \text{ ms}^{-2}$]

(a) 0.72 Nm^{-1}
(b) 0.77 Nm^{-1}
(c) 1.67 Nm^{-1}
(d) 0.92 Nm^{-1}

12. A rain drop of radius 0.2 cm is falling through air with a terminal velocity of 8.7 ms^{-1}. The viscosity of air in SI unit is [Take, $\rho_{water} = 1000 \text{ kg m}^{-3}$ and $\rho_{air} = 1 \text{ kg m}^{-3}$]

(a) 10^{-4} poise
(b) 1×10^{-3} poise
(c) 8.6×10^{-3} poise
(d) 1.02×10^{-3} poise

13. The angle of minimum deviation for a glass prism with $\mu = \sqrt{3}$ is equal to the refracting angle of the prism. The angle of the prism is
(a) 60° (b) 30°
(c) 45° (d) 90°

14. A uniform meter scale is balanced at 60 cm mark, when weight of 5 gf and 40 gf are suspended at 10 cm and 80 cm mark, respectively. The weight of meter scale is
(a) 65 gf (b) 60 gf
(c) 75 gf (d) 55 gf

15. A wide jar is filled with glycerine having specific gravity 1.26×10^3 kg/m^3. In this jar, a steel ball of radius 0.25 cm has been dropped. After some time it has been observed that ball is taking equal interval of time (1.8 s) to cover equal successive distances, of 20 cm. [Take, $\rho_{steel} = 7.8\times10^3$ kg - m^{-3}, $g = 9.81$ ms^{-2}]. The viscosity of glycerine (in N-sm^{-2}) is
(a) 0.802 (b) 1.67
(c) 0.76 (d) 0.963

16. **Statement I** In the measurement of specific heat of a liquid using calorimeter, while performing the experiment, we keep the value of current constant by adjusting rheostat.
Statement II Charging current damages the coil of heater.
In the light of above statements, choose the most appropriate answer from the options given below.
(a) Both Statement I and Statement II are correct.
(b) Both Statement I and Statement II are incorrect.
(c) Statement I is correct but Statement II is incorrect.
(d) Statement I is incorrect but Statement II is correct.

17. The length of a given cylindrical wire is increased by 100%. Due to consequent decrease in diameter the change in the resistance of the wire will be
(a) 100%
(b) 300%
(c) 200%
(d) 250%

18. **Assertion** (A) Solids have the highest heat capacity as compared to liquids.
Reason (R) Gases have the least value of specific heat capacity.
In the light of above statements, choose the most appropriate answer from the options given below.
(a) Both A and R are true and R is the true explanation of A.
(b) Both A and R are true but R is not the true explanation of A.
(c) A is true but R is false.
(d) A is false but R is true.

19. The minimum deviation produced by a glass prism of angle 60° is 30°. If the velocity of light in vacuum is 3×10^8 m/s, then the velocity of light in glass (in m/s) is
(a) 2.9×10^8 (b) 2.72×10^8
(c) 3.1×10^8 (d) 2.121×10^8

20. A Zener diode is operating in its normal region *i.e.*, the breakdown region for which the circuit diagram is as shown in the figure. Here, take $V_Z = 7$ V and $R = 10$ kΩ. For potential difference equal to 8 V across *AB*, what is the current through microammeter?

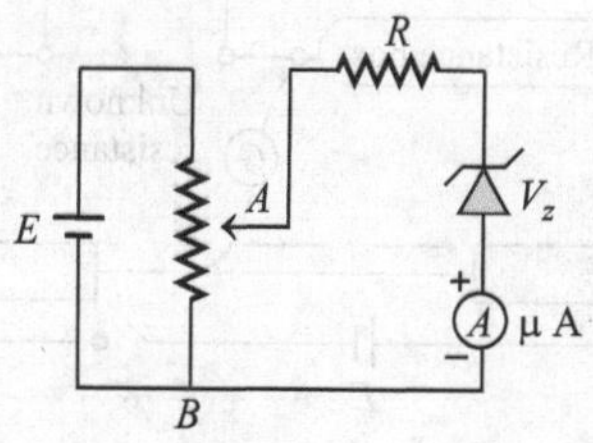

(a) 1000 μA
(b) 1 mA
(c) 10 μA
(d) 100 μA

21. Three students S_1, S_2 and S_3 perform an experiment for determining the acceleration due to gravity (g) using a simple pendulum. They use different lengths of pendulum and record time for different number of oscillations. The observations are as shown in the table.

Student no.	Length of pendulum (cm)	No. of oscillations (n)	Total time for n oscillations (t)	Time period (s)
1.	50	7	95	12
2.	55	8	80	10
3.	70	8	85	12

(Least count of length = 0.1 cm, least count for time = 0.1 s)

If E_1, E_2 and E_3 are the percentage errors in g for students 1, 2 and 3 respectively, then the minimum percentage error is obtained by student number is

(a) 3 (b) 2
(c) Both 1 and 2 (d) 1

22. In meter bridge experiment, the observation table and circuit diagram are shown in figure.

R (Ω)	l (cm)
1000	60 cm
100	13 cm
10	1.5 cm
1	1.0 cm

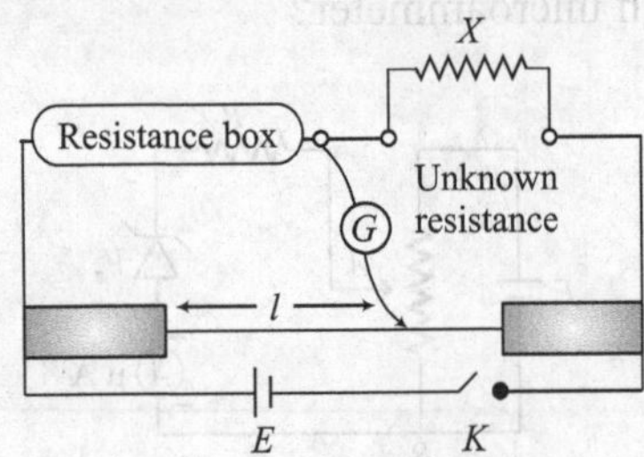

Which of the readings is not taken correctly?

(a) 1 (b) 2
(c) 3 (d) 4

23. For the angle of minimum deviation of a prism to be equal to its refracting angle, the prism must be made of a material whose refractive index

(a) lies between 2 and $\sqrt{2}$
(b) lies between $\sqrt{2}$ and 1
(c) is greater than 2
(d) is less than 1

24. In a meter bridge experiment, balance is observed at 27 cm from left end.
A student changes positions of supply cell and galvanometer and again try to find balance. Now, balance is obtained at

(a) 29 cm
(b) 25 cm
(c) 27 cm
(d) No balance is obtained

25. In a meter bridge experiment, S is a standard resistance and R is a resistance wire. It is found that, balancing length is $l = 40$ cm. If R is replaced by a wire of half length and half diameter that of R of same material, then find the balancing distance l'.

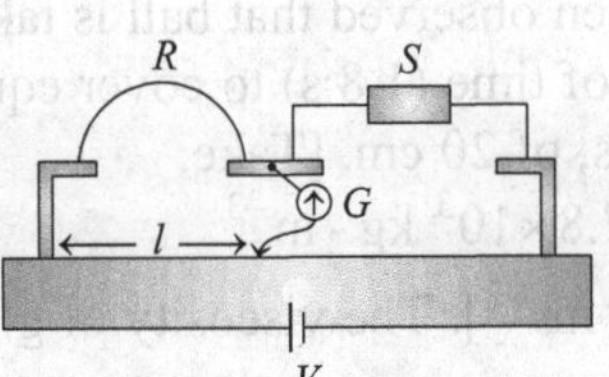

(a) 20 cm (b) 30 cm
(c) 57 cm (d) 50 cm

26. Four silicon diodes and a 15 Ω resistor are connected as shown in figure below. Each diode has a resistance of 5 Ω. Find the current flows through the 15 Ω resistor?

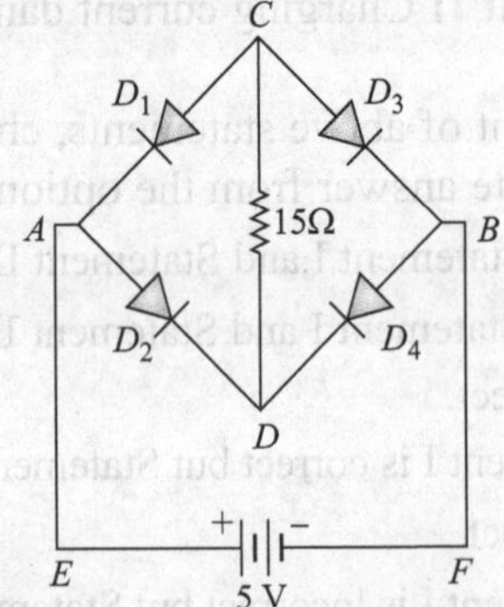

(a) 0.144 A (b) 0.2 A
(c) 0.3 A (d) 0.4 A

27. The density of a cube is measured by measuring its mass and length of its sides. If the maximum error in the measurement of mass and lengths are 4% and 3% respectively, the maximum error in the measurement of density is

(a) 15% (b) 13%
(c) 11% (d) 9%

28. The amount of energy evolved when 64 droplets of mercury (surface tension = 0.55 N/m) of radius 0.4 mm each combine into one drop, is

(a) 53.05 μJ (b) 37.7 μJ
(c) 35.3 μJ (d) 29.9 μJ

29. For the same density of impurity atoms, Zener voltage is

(a) higher for Ge than for Si
(b) higher for Si than for Ge
(c) same for both Ge and Si
(d) zero for both Ge and Si

30. In an experiment, the angle are required to be measured using an instrument. 44 divisions of the main scale exactly coincide with the 45 divisions of the vernier scale. If the smallest division of main scale is 0.3°, then the least count of the instrument in degrees is

(a) $\frac{1}{100}$ (b) $\frac{1}{75}$
(c) $\frac{1}{125}$ (d) $\frac{1}{150}$

Response Index

01	ⓐ ⓑ ⓒ ⓓ	14	ⓐ ⓑ ⓒ ⓓ	27	ⓐ ⓑ ⓒ ⓓ
02	ⓐ ⓑ ⓒ ⓓ	15	ⓐ ⓑ ⓒ ⓓ	28	ⓐ ⓑ ⓒ ⓓ
03	ⓐ ⓑ ⓒ ⓓ	16	ⓐ ⓑ ⓒ ⓓ	29	ⓐ ⓑ ⓒ ⓓ
04	ⓐ ⓑ ⓒ ⓓ	17	ⓐ ⓑ ⓒ ⓓ	30	ⓐ ⓑ ⓒ ⓓ
05	ⓐ ⓑ ⓒ ⓓ	18	ⓐ ⓑ ⓒ ⓓ		
06	ⓐ ⓑ ⓒ ⓓ	19	ⓐ ⓑ ⓒ ⓓ		
07	ⓐ ⓑ ⓒ ⓓ	20	ⓐ ⓑ ⓒ ⓓ		
08	ⓐ ⓑ ⓒ ⓓ	21	ⓐ ⓑ ⓒ ⓓ		
09	ⓐ ⓑ ⓒ ⓓ	22	ⓐ ⓑ ⓒ ⓓ		
10	ⓐ ⓑ ⓒ ⓓ	23	ⓐ ⓑ ⓒ ⓓ		
11	ⓐ ⓑ ⓒ ⓓ	24	ⓐ ⓑ ⓒ ⓓ		
12	ⓐ ⓑ ⓒ ⓓ	25	ⓐ ⓑ ⓒ ⓓ		
13	ⓐ ⓑ ⓒ ⓓ	26	ⓐ ⓑ ⓒ ⓓ		

Performance Scanner

> 90% Excellent !	You have mastered this chapter. The concepts of this chapter are on your fingertips. Move on to the next chapter and maintain this momentum.
76-90% Very Good !	You have a good command over this chapter. Revise the chapter again after a few days and enhance your performance.
60-75% Good !	You have a wide scope to learn for this chapter. Revise it again.
<60% Not Satisfactory!	You have a long way ahead of you to master this chapter. Revise it thoroughly.

For Online Chapter Test **Scan the QR Code**

For Online Unit Test **Scan the QR Code**

Space for Rough Work

Test Booklet No. **3947167**

Test Booklet Code **SPT1**

MEDACE
NEET (UG)
SELF ASSESSMENT KIT

Syllabus Part Thru 1
(Based on 12th Syllabus)

Chapters Covered

- Electric Charges and Fields
- Electrostatic Potential
- Capacitance
- Current Electricity
- Moving Charges and Magnetism
- Magnetism and Matter
- Electromagnetic Induction
- Alternating Current

Important Instructions

- The test is of 45 minute and the Test Booklet contains 45 multiple choice questions (four options with a single correct answer) from Physics.
- Candidates are advised to read all questions before they start attempting the question paper.
- Each question carries 4 marks. For each correct response, the candidate will get 4 marks. For each incorrect response, one mark will be deducted from the total scores. The maximum marks are 180.
- In the event of candidate marking more than one option, one mark will be deducted.
- Use **Blue/Black Point Pen** only for writing particular on this page/ marking response on answer sheet.

Name of the Candidate (In Capitals) ____________________

____

Candidate's Signature ____________________

Invigilator's Signature ____________________

Facsimile signature stamp of center superintendent ____________________

Do not open this Booklet until you start attempting the Test

Physics (Q. No. 1-45)

1. Two similar bar magnets P and Q, each of magnetic moment M, are taken. If P is cut along its axial line and Q is cut along its equatorial line, all the four pieces obtained have

(a) magnetic moment $\frac{M}{4}$

(b) magnetic moment $\frac{M}{2}$

(c) magnetic moment M

(d) equal pole strength

2. The work done in moving an electric charge of 10 C from a point A at potential -20 V to another point B at V volt is 200 J. The value of V is

(a) 15 V (b) 0

(c) 40 V (d) 20 V

3. Four capacitors of capacity $30\,\mu\text{F}$, each are connected in a certain manner such that their effective capacitance is $40\,\mu\text{F}$. This can be achieved by

(a) connecting all the capacitors in series.

(b) connecting two in series and two in parallel.

(c) connecting three of them in series and one in parallel.

(d) connecting three of them in parallel and one in series.

4. Assertion (A) Surface of symmetrical conductor can be treated as equipotential surface.

Reason (R) Charges can easily flow in a conductor.

In the light of above statements, choose the most appropriate answer from the options given below.

(a) Both A and R are true and R is the correct explanation of A.

(b) Both A and R are true but R is not the correct explanation of A.

(c) A is true but R is false.

(d) A is false but R is true.

5. In the following figure, X, Y and Z are ammeters and Y reads 0.5 A. The reading in ammeters X and Z are .

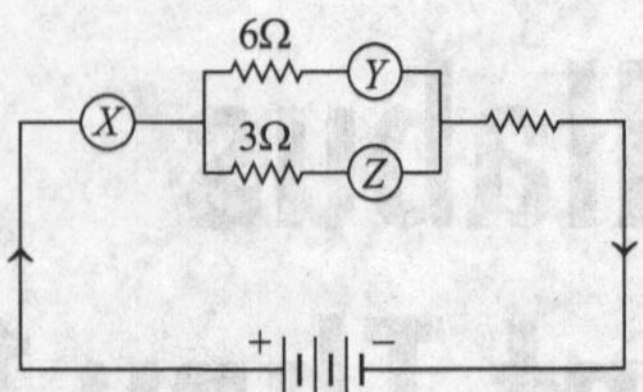

(a) 1.5 A, 1.0 A (b) 2 A, 4 A

(c) 1.2 A, 1.4 A (d) 3 A, 1 A

6. Three identical bulbs are connected as shown in figure. If bulb B_3 gets fused suddenly, how will the brightness of bulbs B_1 and B_2 change?

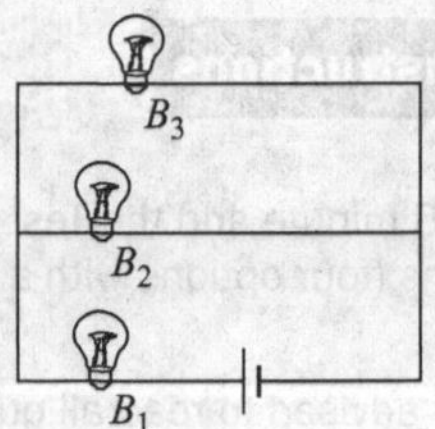

(a) Brightness of bulb B_1 will increase whereas B_2 will decrease.

(b) Brightness of bulb B_2 will increase whereas B_1 will decrease.

(c) Brightness of both bulbs B_1 and B_2 will increase.

(d) Brightness of bulb B_1 will increase whereas brightness of bulb B_2 will remain the same.

7. A moving coil galvanometer has 150 equal divisions. Its current sensitivity is 10 divisions per milliampere and voltage sensitivity is 2 divisions per millivolt. In order that each division reads 1 V, the resistance in ohms needed in series with the coil is

(a) 10^3 (b) 10^5

(c) 99995 (d) 9995

8. A network of inductance and resistance is shown below. If current at certain instant is 10 A and decreasing at the rate of 10^3 A/s, then $V_B - V_A$ is

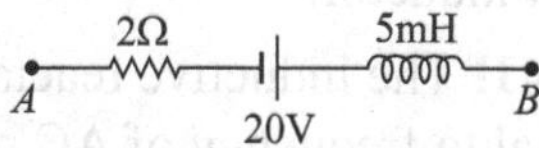

(a) 5V (b) 20V
(c) 10V (d) 30V

9. The rms value of an AC current that, when passes through a resistor, produces four times the heat generated by a 4A DC current in the same resistor, is

(a) 8 A (b) 16 A
(c) 4 A (d) 2 A

10. Consider the following circuit in which instantaneous current through inductor and capacitor are 0.8 A and 0.4 A, respectively. The instantaneous current through resistor is

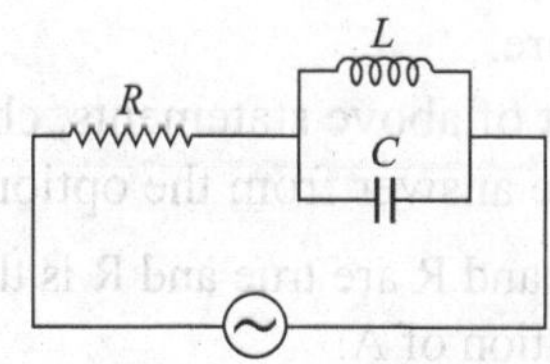

(a) 0.4 A (b) 0.8 A
(c) 1.2 A (d) $2\sqrt{0.8}$ A

11. Two coils of self inductances 4 mH and 36 mH are placed so close together that the effective flux in one coil is completely linked with the other. The mutual inductance between these coils is

(a) 16 mH (b) 10 mH
(c) 6 mH (d) 12 mH

12. A circular current loop of magnetic moment M is in an arbitrary orientation in an external magnetic field **B**. The work done to rotate the loop by 30° about an axis perpendicular to its plane is

(a) $\sqrt{3}\,MB$ (b) zero
(c) MB (d) $\frac{MB}{2}$

13. The capacity of a parallel plate capacitor is 10 μF. When a glass plate is inserted between plates of conductor, its potential becomes one-third of the original value. The value of dielectric constant is

(a) 3 (b) 2
(c) 4 (d) 8

14. A bar magnet is demagnetised by inserting it inside a solenoid of length 0.2 m, 100 turns and carrying current of 5.2 A. Magnetising intensity of solenoid is

(a) 1200 A/m (b) 2850 A/m
(c) 2600 A/m (d) 520 A/m

15. A bar magnet used in a vibration magnetometer is heated so as to reduce its magnetic moment by 19%. The periodic time of the magnetometer will

(a) decrease by 19%
(b) increase by 19%
(c) decrease by 11%
(d) increase by 11%

16. A loss free transformer has 1000 turns on its primary winding and 3000 turns in secondary. The secondary coil draws 200 V at 8 A. The voltage and current in primary are

(a) 200 V, 20 A
(b) $\frac{200}{3}$ V, 24 A
(c) $\frac{100}{3}$ V, 30 A
(d) 80 V, 20 A

17. The south pole of magnet is brought near to metal ring attached to the wall. The induced current in the ring will be

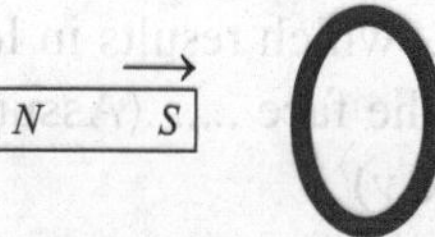

(a) first clockwise and then anti-clockwise
(b) in the clockwise direction
(c) in the anti-clockwise direction
(d) first anti-clockwise and then clockwise

18. The magnitude of flux passing through the square of side a placed in XZ-plane having magnetic field $\mathbf{B} = B_0(2\hat{\mathbf{i}} + 3\hat{\mathbf{j}} - 8\hat{\mathbf{k}})$, where B_0 is constant, is given as

(a) $5B_0a^2$ (b) $2B_0a^2$
(c) $4B_0a^2$ (d) $3B_0a^2$

19. Figure shows a small magnetised needle A placed at point O. The arrow represents the direction of its magnetic moment. The configurations in which the system have stable equilibrium are

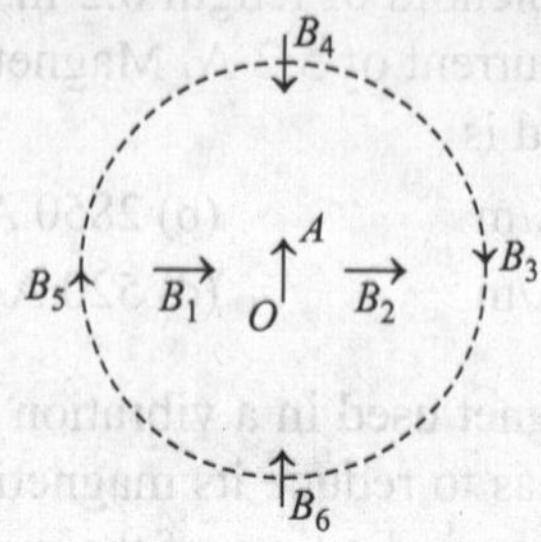

(a) AB_3, AB_6 (b) AB_3, AB_5
(c) AB_4, AB_5 (d) AB_4, AB_6

20. Two identical bar magnets each of dipole moment M and length L are perpendicular to each other. The magnetic field at point P is

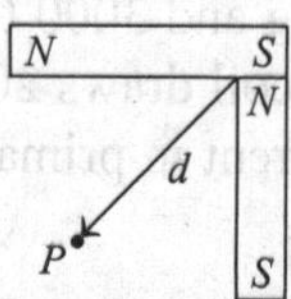

(a) $\frac{\mu_0 m}{4\pi d^2}$ (b) $\frac{2\mu_0 m}{4\pi d^2}$
(c) $\frac{2\sqrt{2}\mu_0 m}{4\pi d^2}$ (d) $\frac{3\mu_0 m}{4\pi d^2}$

21. A metallic block carrying current I is subjected to a uniform magnetic induction **B** as shown in figure. The moving charges experience a force F given by ...... which results in lowering of the potential of the face ....(Assume the speed of the carriers to be v)

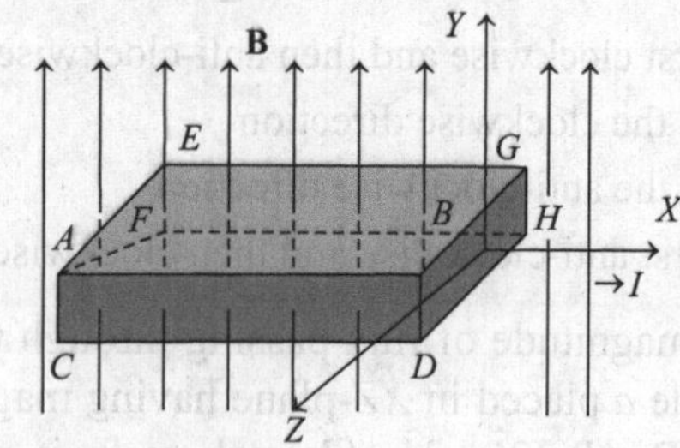

(a) $ev B\hat{\mathbf{k}}$, $ABCD$
(b) $-ev B \hat{\mathbf{k}}$, $ABCD$
(c) $evB \hat{\mathbf{k}}$, $EFGH$
(d) $-ev B \hat{\mathbf{k}}$, $EFGH$

22. **Statement I** The alternating current lags behind the emf by a phase angle of $\frac{\pi}{2}$, when AC flows through an inductor.

Statement II The inductive reactance is directly proportional to frequency of AC source.

In the light of above statements, choose the most appropriate answer from the options given below.

(a) Both Statement I and Statement II are correct.
(b) Both Statement I and Statement II are incorrect.
(c) Statement I is correct but Statement II is incorrect.
(d) Statement I is incorrect but Statement II is correct.

23. **Assertion** (A) A 60 W - 120 V bulb glows more than a 100 W -120 V bulb when they are connected in series across a potential difference.

Reason (R) The resistance of 100 W – 120 V bulb will be more.

In the light of above statements, choose the most appropriate answer from the options given below.

(a) Both A and R are true and R is the correct explanation of A.
(b) Both A and R are true but R is not the correct explanation of A.
(c) A is true but R is false.
(d) A is false but R is true.

24. The distance between Noida and Delhi is 150 km. Electric power is sent from Delhi to Noida through copper wires. The fall of potential per km is 8 V and the average resistance per km is 0.5 Ω. The power loss in the wire is

(a) 19.2 W (b) 12.2 kW
(c) 19.2 kW (d) 12.2 W

25. The cell has an emf of 4 V and internal resistance of this cell is 0.2 Ω. If it is connected to 4.8 Ω resistor, then voltage across the cell is

(a) 1.95 V (b) 3.84 V
(c) 2.06 V (d) 4.73 V

26. A current of 3 mA was passed through an unknown resistor which dissipated power of 36.0 W. Dissipated power when an ideal power supply of 10 V is connected across it is

(a) 25×10^{-3} W (b) 25×10^{4} W
(c) 25×10^{6} W (d) 25×10^{-6} W

27. Free electrons are drifting with velocity v in a conductor and current I is flowing in conductor. What will be the drift velocity, if radius and current both are doubled?

(a) v (b) $2v$
(c) $v/2$ (d) $v/3$

28. A slab of dielectric constant K having same area as that of plates of parallel plate capacitor but thickness is $\frac{2}{3}d$, where d is distance between the plates. If this slab is inserted between the plates, then capacitance is changed to

(a) $\frac{4KC_0}{K+3}$ (b) $\frac{K-3C_0}{4K}$
(c) $\frac{3KC_0}{K+2}$ (d) $\frac{4KC_0}{K+2}$

29. Flux through faces of cube, if charge is placed at edge-centre is

(a) $\frac{q}{\varepsilon_0}$ (b) $\frac{q}{16\varepsilon_0}$
(c) $\frac{q}{4\varepsilon_0}$ (d) $\frac{q}{8\varepsilon_0}$

30. Four charges are arranged at the corner of a square $PQRS$ as shown below. The force on positive charge Q kept at centre O is

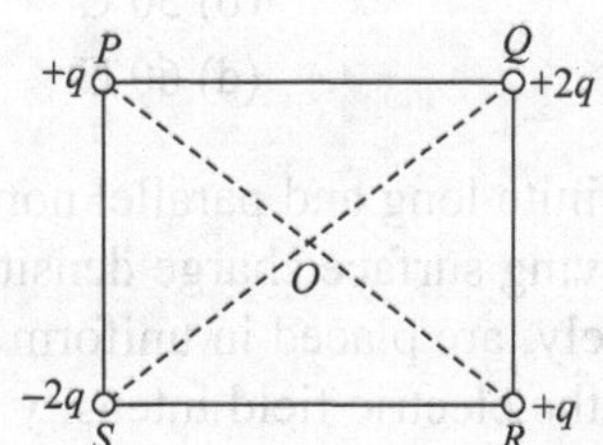

(a) along QS (b) along PR
(c) zero (d) along PQ

31. Induced emf can be produced in a coil by

A. moving coil with uniform speed inside uniform magnetic field..
B. moving coil with acceleration inside uniform magnetic field.
C. rotating the coil in uniform field.
D. changing area of coil in uniform field.

Choose correct answer.

(a) B and C (b) A and C
(c) B and D (d) C and D

32. The variation of electric field along bisector of two equal and opposite charges separated by distance d is given as

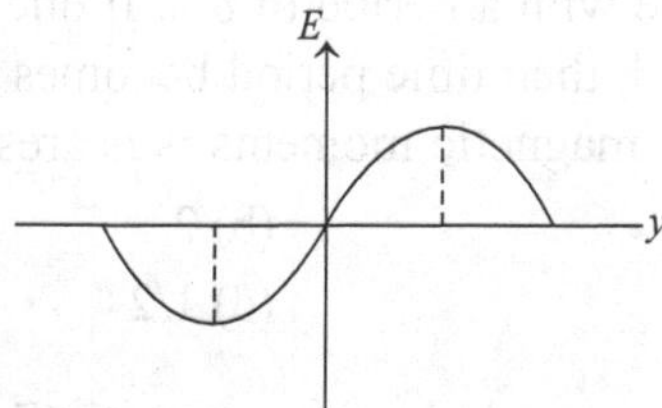

The maxima of E is at

(a) $y=\frac{d}{2\sqrt{2}}$ (b) $y=\frac{d}{2}$
(c) $y=\frac{d}{\sqrt{2}}$ (d) $y=\frac{d}{2\sqrt{3}}$

33. The electric field intensity produced by the radiation coming from a 200 W bulb at a distance of 4 m is E. The electric field intensity produced by the radiation coming from 100 W at the same distance $\sqrt{\frac{X}{20}}E$. The value of X is

(a) 11 (b) 21
(c) 10 (d) 12

34. When an AC voltage of 220 V is applied to capacitor C.

I. The maximum voltage between plates is 200 V.
II. The current is in phase with the applied voltage.
III. The charge on the plates is in phase with applied voltage.
IV. Power delivered to the capacitor is zero.

Choose the correct option.

(a) (I, III) (b) (II, IV)
(c) (I, IV) (d) (III, IV)

35. Two concentric circular coils with radii 4 cm and 400 cm and number of turns 10 and 100 respectively, are placed coaxially with centres coinciding. The neutral inductance is (in 10^{-9} H)

(a) 400 (b) 789
(c) 100 (d) 635

36. A coil having diameter 0.04 m is perpendicularly placed in a magnetic field of 4000 T. The induced emf is 10 V when the magnetic field changes to 2000 T in 2 s. The number of turns in the coil is

(a) 8 (b) 10
(c) 20 (d) 7

37. Two magnets placed one above the other, oscillate with a period of 8 s. If one of them is reversed, then time period becomes 16 s. The ratio of their magnetic moments is nearest to

(a) 2/3 (b) 2
(c) 5/3 (d) 1/2

38. A long solenoid having magnetic field $B = 0.168$ T at its centre. The radius of solenoid is 0.01 m and wire carries current of 2 A. If solenoid is 1.4 m long, then the length of the wire needed in nearest integer (in m) is

(a) 4220 (b) 5842
(c) 2550 (d) 5880

39. In the meter bridge, point D is a neutral point as shown below.

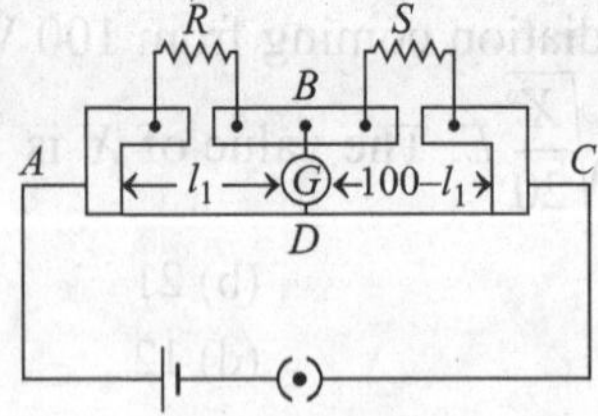

I. The meter bridge can have no other neutral point for this set of resistance.
II. When the jockey contacts a point on the meter wire to the left of D, current flows to B from the wire.
III. When the jockey contacts a point on the meter wire to the right of D, current flows from B to the wire through the galvanometer.
IV. When R is increased, the neutral point shifts to left.

Which of the above statements is correct?

(a) (I, III)
(b) (II, III)
(c) (I, IV)
(d) (III, IV)

40. In the given figure, the value of X resistance when the potential difference between B and D is zero, will be

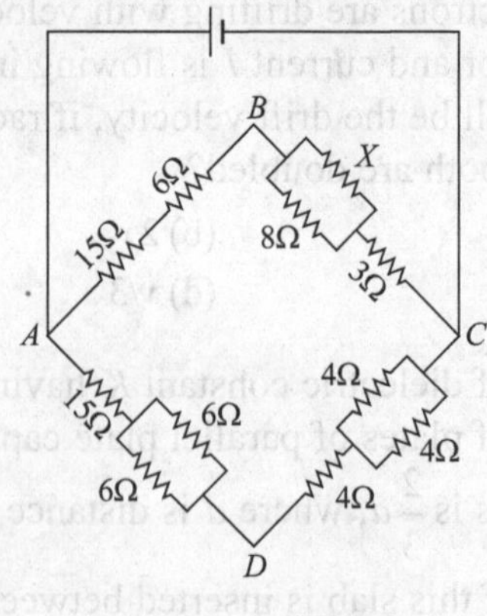

(a) 4 Ω (b) 8 Ω
(c) 6 Ω (d) 9 Ω

41. Three wires are made up of same material. The ratio of their length and radii are 2 : 3 : 4 and 3 : 4 : 5, respectively. Later they are connected in parallel in a circuit having 5 A current. The current in each wire respectively, is

(a) 1.3 A, 1.23 A, 1.43 A
(b) 1.67 A, 1.52 A, 1.80 A
(c) 1.4 A, 1.66 A, 1.94 A
(d) 2.1 A, 1.32 A, 1.76 A

42. Current flowing in a wire is given as $I = (6 + 2t + 3t^2)$ A, where t is in second. The value of charge passing through a cross-section of the wire during time $t = 2$ s to $t = 4$ s will be

(a) 80 C (b) 50 C
(c) 48 C (d) 60 C

43. Three infinite long and parallel non-conducting sheets having surface charge densities $\sigma, -2\sigma, 3\sigma$ respectively, are placed in uniform electric field. Find out the electric field intensity in regions II and III (between the sheets).

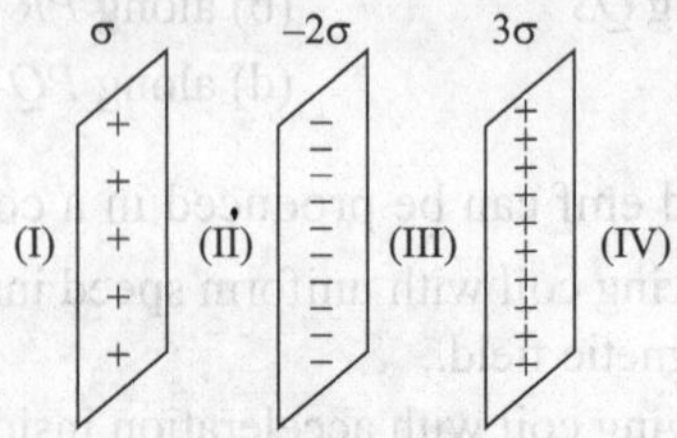

(a) $0, -\frac{2\sigma}{\varepsilon_0}$ (b) 0, 0

(c) $\frac{\sigma}{\varepsilon_0}, \frac{\sigma}{\varepsilon_0}$ (d) $\frac{\sigma}{3\varepsilon_0}, \frac{\sigma}{\varepsilon_0}$

44. There are five balls labelled as A, B, C, D and E, are suspended using separate threads. Pairs $(A, B), (B, D), (D, A)$ show electrostatic attraction, while (B, C) and (D, E) show repulsion. What is the nature of charge on ball A?

(a) Positive
(b) Negative
(c) Neutral
(d) Information deficit

45. Consider the circuit shown in figure. The sliding contact is being pulled towards the right, so that the resistance in the circuit is increasing. Its value at the instant shown is $12\,\Omega$. The current flowing in the circuit is I. Then,

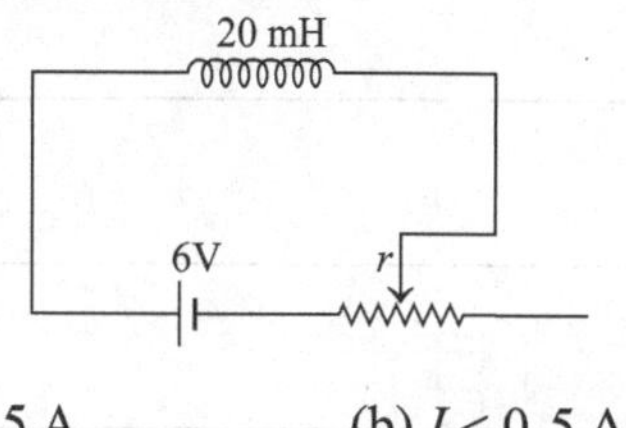

(a) $I > 0.5$ A (b) $I < 0.5$ A
(c) $I = 0.5$ A (d) $I = 0$ A

For Online Syllabus Part Thru
Scan the QR Code

Response Index

01	ⓐ	ⓑ	ⓒ	ⓓ	14	ⓐ	ⓑ	ⓒ	ⓓ	27	ⓐ	ⓑ	ⓒ	ⓓ	40	ⓐ	ⓑ	ⓒ	ⓓ
02	ⓐ	ⓑ	ⓒ	ⓓ	15	ⓐ	ⓑ	ⓒ	ⓓ	28	ⓐ	ⓑ	ⓒ	ⓓ	41	ⓐ	ⓑ	ⓒ	ⓓ
03	ⓐ	ⓑ	ⓒ	ⓓ	16	ⓐ	ⓑ	ⓒ	ⓓ	29	ⓐ	ⓑ	ⓒ	ⓓ	42	ⓐ	ⓑ	ⓒ	ⓓ
04	ⓐ	ⓑ	ⓒ	ⓓ	17	ⓐ	ⓑ	ⓒ	ⓓ	30	ⓐ	ⓑ	ⓒ	ⓓ	43	ⓐ	ⓑ	ⓒ	ⓓ
05	ⓐ	ⓑ	ⓒ	ⓓ	18	ⓐ	ⓑ	ⓒ	ⓓ	31	ⓐ	ⓑ	ⓒ	ⓓ	44	ⓐ	ⓑ	ⓒ	ⓓ
06	ⓐ	ⓑ	ⓒ	ⓓ	19	ⓐ	ⓑ	ⓒ	ⓓ	32	ⓐ	ⓑ	ⓒ	ⓓ	45	ⓐ	ⓑ	ⓒ	ⓓ
07	ⓐ	ⓑ	ⓒ	ⓓ	20	ⓐ	ⓑ	ⓒ	ⓓ	33	ⓐ	ⓑ	ⓒ	ⓓ					
08	ⓐ	ⓑ	ⓒ	ⓓ	21	ⓐ	ⓑ	ⓒ	ⓓ	34	ⓐ	ⓑ	ⓒ	ⓓ					
09	ⓐ	ⓑ	ⓒ	ⓓ	22	ⓐ	ⓑ	ⓒ	ⓓ	35	ⓐ	ⓑ	ⓒ	ⓓ					
10	ⓐ	ⓑ	ⓒ	ⓓ	23	ⓐ	ⓑ	ⓒ	ⓓ	36	ⓐ	ⓑ	ⓒ	ⓓ					
11	ⓐ	ⓑ	ⓒ	ⓓ	24	ⓐ	ⓑ	ⓒ	ⓓ	37	ⓐ	ⓑ	ⓒ	ⓓ					
12	ⓐ	ⓑ	ⓒ	ⓓ	25	ⓐ	ⓑ	ⓒ	ⓓ	38	ⓐ	ⓑ	ⓒ	ⓓ					
13	ⓐ	ⓑ	ⓒ	ⓓ	26	ⓐ	ⓑ	ⓒ	ⓓ	39	ⓐ	ⓑ	ⓒ	ⓓ					

Performance Scanner

> 90% Excellent !	You have mastered the first half of NEET syllabus (12th). The concepts of this syllabus are on your fingertips. Maintain this momentum.
76-90% Very Good !	You have a good command over the first half of NEET syllabus (12th). Revise it again after a few days and enhance your performance.
60-75% Good !	You have a wide scope to learn for the first half of NEET syllabus (12th). Revise it again.
<60% Not Satisfactory!	You have a long way ahead of you to master the first half of NEET syllabus (12th). Revise it thoroughly.

Space for Rough Work

Test Booklet No. **3947168**

Test Booklet Code **SPT2**

MEDACE
NEET (UG)
SELF ASSESSMENT KIT

Syllabus Part Thru 2

(Based on 12th Syllabus)

Chapters Covered

Electromagnetic Waves

Ray Optics and Optical Instruments

Wave Optics

Dual Nature of Radiation and Matter

Atom

Nuclei

Electronic Devices

Experimental Skills

Important Instructions

- The test is of 45 minute and the Test Booklet contains 45 multiple choice questions (four options with a single correct answer) from Physics.
- Candidates are advised to read all questions before they start attempting the question paper.
- Each question carries 4 marks. For each correct response, the candidate will get 4 marks. For each incorrect response, one mark will be deducted from the total scores. The maximum marks are 180.
- In the event of candidate marking more than one option, one mark will be deducted.
- Use **Blue/Black Point Pen** only for writing particular on this page/ marking response on answer sheet.

Name of the Candidate (In Capitals) ____________

Candidate's Signature ____________

Invigilator's Signature ____________

Facsimile signature stamp of center superintendent ____________

Do not open this Booklet until you start attempting the Test

Physics (Q. No. 1-45)

1. A light ray enters into equilateral prism, suffers minimum deviation at an angle 60°. The speed of light in the prism is given as

(a) $\sqrt{3} \times 10^8$ m/s (b) 2×10^8 m/s
(c) 3×10^8 m/s (d) $\sqrt{2} \times 10^8$ m/s

2. The magnification of a book held 7.50 cm from a 10.0 cm focal length lens was found to be 3.00. The magnification for the book when it is held 8.50 cm from the magnifier is

(a) 3.00 (b) 6.67
(c) 4.82 (d) 5.67

3. A Zener diode when used as a voltage regulator is connected

I. in forward bias
II. in reverse bias
III. in parallel with the load
IV. in series with the load

Choose the correct option.

(a) I and II are correct.
(b) II and III are correct.
(c) Only II is correct.
(d) Only IV is correct.

4. Consider the following statements regarding conditions required for the phenomenon of total internal reflection to occur.

Statement I Light must travel from optical denser medium to an optically rarer medium.

Statement II The angle of incidence in the rarer medium must be greater than the critical angle for the media.

In the light of above statements, choose the correct answer from the options given below.

(a) Both Statement I and Statement II are correct.
(b) Both Statement I and Statement II are incorrect.
(c) Statement I is correct but Statement II is incorrect.
(d) Statement I is incorrect but Statement II is correct.

5. When white light is passed through an unexcited gas, then transmitted light consists of

(a) few bright lines in dark background
(b) few dark lines in bright background
(c) alternate dark and bright lines
(d) alternate dark and bright bands

6. The electric field of a plane electromagnetic wave propagating along x-direction in vacuum is $E = E_0 \hat{\mathbf{k}} \cos(\omega t - kx)$. The magnetic field at the moment of $t = 2$s is

(a) $\mathbf{B} = E_0 \sqrt{\mu_0 \varepsilon_0} \cos(kx) \hat{\mathbf{j}}$
(b) $\mathbf{B} = E_0 \sqrt{\mu_0 \varepsilon_0} \cos(2\omega - kx) \hat{\mathbf{k}}$
(c) $\mathbf{B} = \dfrac{E_0}{\sqrt{\mu_0 \varepsilon_0}} \cos(kx) \hat{\mathbf{k}}$
(d) $\mathbf{B} = E_0 \sqrt{\mu_0 \varepsilon_0} \cos(2\omega - kx) \hat{\mathbf{j}}$

7. The temperature of equal masses of three different liquids A, B and C are 12°C, 19°C and 28°C, respectively. The temperature when A and B are mixed is 16°C and when B and C are mixed is 23°C. The temperature when A and C are mixed, will be

(a) 18.2°C (b) 22°C
(c) 20.2°C (d) 25.2°C

8. Maximum number of possible interference maxima for slit separation equals to twice the wavelength in YDSE is

(a) ∞ (b) 5
(c) 3 (d) 1

9. In given situation, distance L_1L_2 is

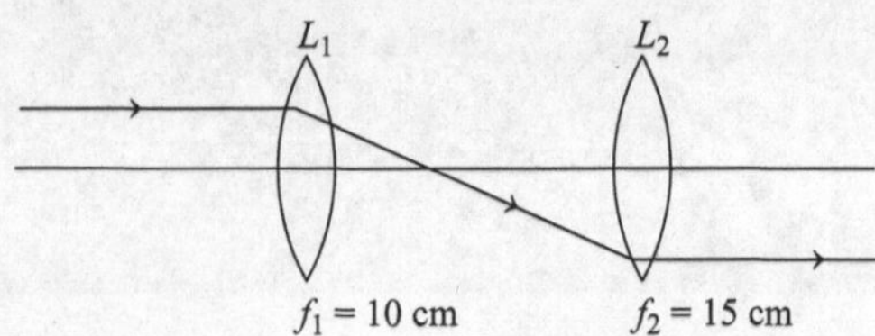

(a) 15 cm (b) 10 cm
(c) 35 cm (d) 25 cm

10. When a light enters a prism with a 60° refracting angle, what angle must it strike the opposing face of the prism to first cause complete internal reflection? (Considering that the prism's material has a refractive index of 1.524).

(a) 25.34° (b) 35.12°
(c) 29.54° (d) 45.00°

11. Which of the following energy diagram represents energy band diagram for semiconductors?

(a) 

(b) 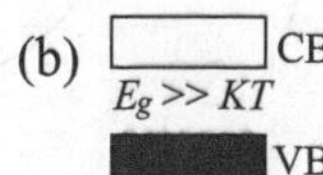

(c) 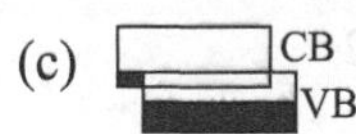

(d) 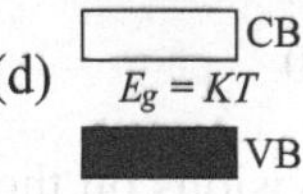

12. A light ray is entering a glass slab of thickness 5 cm with a refractive index of $\frac{3}{2}$. The angle of incidence is 30°. The lateral displacement of the ray as it emerges from the other side of the slab will be

(a) 0.9 cm (b) 2 cm
(c) 1.5 cm (d) 0.5 cm

13. At which angle, the intensity of transmitted light is maximum when a polaroid sheet is rotated between two crossed polaroids?

(a) $\pi/4$ (b) $\pi/2$
(c) $\pi/3$ (d) π

14. A convex lens of focal length F is placed somewhere in between an object and a screen. The distance between the object and the screen is y. If the numerical value of the magnification produced by the lens is m_1, then the focal length of the lens is

(a) $\frac{my}{(m-1)^2}$ (b) $\frac{(m+1)^2 y}{m}$
(c) $\frac{(m-1)^2}{m}$ (d) $\frac{my}{(m+1)^2}$

15. Binding energy per nucleon *versus* mass number curve for nuclei is shown in the figure. W, X, Y and Z are four nuclei indicated on the curve. The process that would release energy is

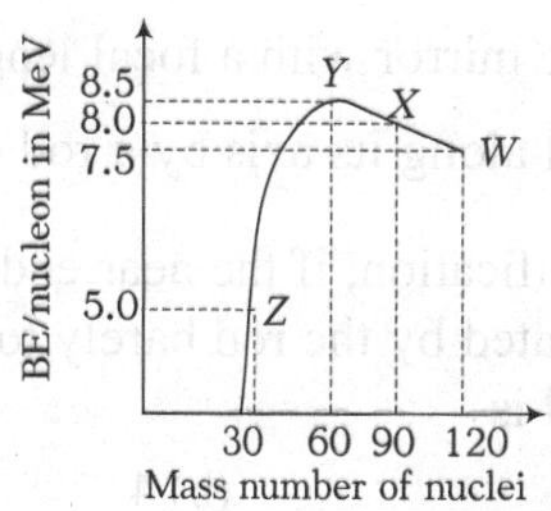

(a) $Y \to 2Z$ (b) $W \to X + Y$
(c) $W \to 2Y$ (d) $X \to Y + Z$

16. The diagram shows the energy levels for an electron in a certain atom. Which transition represents the emission of a photon with the most energy?

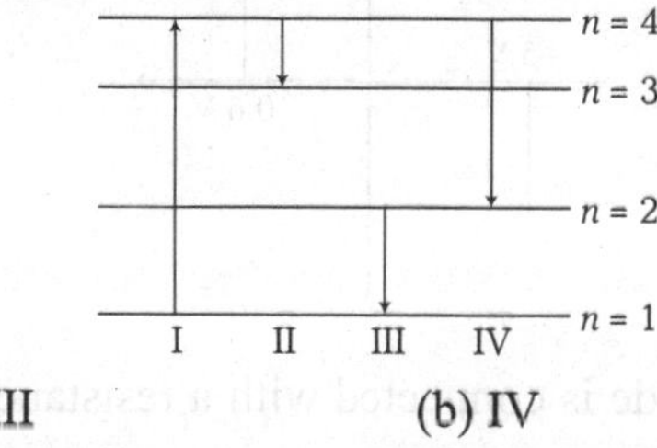

(a) III (b) IV
(c) I (d) II

17. Particle A of mass $m_A = \frac{m}{3}$, moving along the X-axis with velocity v_0, collides elastically with another particle B at rest having mass $m_B = \frac{m}{4}$. If both the particles move along the X-axis after the collision, the change in de-Broglie wavelength $\Delta\lambda$ of particle A in terms of its de-Broglie wavelength λ_0 before collision is

(a) $\Delta\lambda = 3\lambda_0$ (b) $\Delta\lambda = 6\lambda_0$
(c) $\Delta\lambda = \frac{5}{2}\lambda_0$ (d) $\Delta\lambda = \frac{7}{2}\lambda_0$

18. **Assertion** (A) When light travels from a rarer to a denser medium, the speed of light decreases.
Reason (R) The reduction in the speed of light implies a reduction in its energy.
In the light of above statements, choose the correct answer from the options given below.

(a) Both A and R are correct and R is the correct explanation of A.
(b) Both A and R are correct but R is not the correct explanation of A.
(c) A is correct but R is incorrect.
(d) A is incorrect but R is correct.

19. A concave mirror with a focal length f of its positioned along its axis by a rod of length $\frac{f}{2}$. The magnification, if the near end of the real image created by the rod barely touches the far end of rod is

(a) 3 (b) 4

(c) 2 (d) 1

20. The current-voltage characteristic of an ideal *p-n* junction diode is given by the graph as shown in figure.

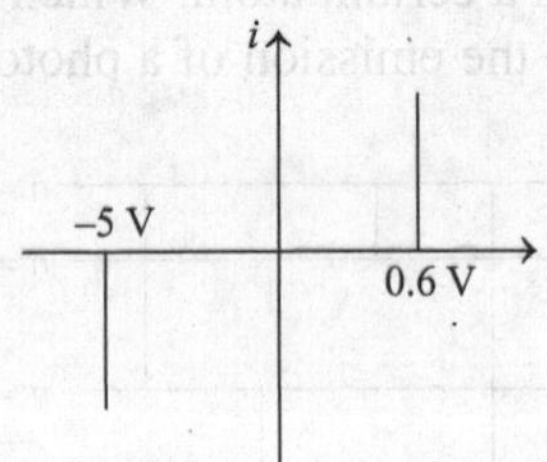

This diode is connected with a resistance of 5Ω in series.

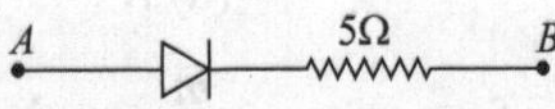

Which of the following shows the dependence of the voltage V_{AB} and the current I, when the diode is forward biased?

(a) $V_{AB} = 5I + 0.6$

(b) $V_{AB} = 5I - 0.6$

(c) $V_{AB} = 5I + (0.6 - 5)$

(d) $V_{AB} = 5I + (0.6 + 5)$

21. The *I-V* characteristic of *p-n* junction diode is shown below. The approximate dynamic resistance of *p-n* junction when a forward bias of 2 V is applied, is

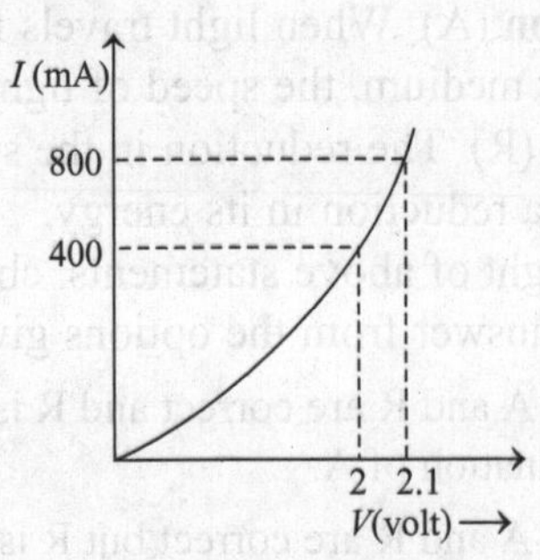

(a) 1Ω (b) 0.25Ω

(c) 0.5Ω (d) 5Ω

22. Two point sources separated by 2 m are radiating in phase with $\lambda = 0.50$ m. A detector moves in a circular path around the two sources in a plane containing them. The maximum number of maxima detected are

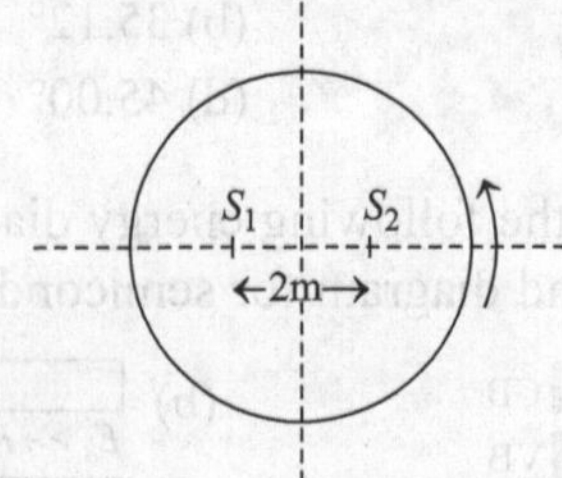

(a) 24 (b) 16

(c) 20 (d) 32

23. N divisions on the main scale of a vernier callipers coincide with $N+1$ divisions of the vernier scale. If each division of main scale is a unit, then least count of the instrument is

(a) a unit

(b) $\frac{a}{N}$ unit

(c) $\frac{a}{N+1}$ unit

(d) $\frac{N}{N+1} \times a$ unit

24. A stationary He^+ ion emitted a photon corresponding to the first line of Lyman series. This photon liberated a photoelectron from a stationary H-atom in the ground state. The velocity of the photoelectron will be (in m/s)

(a) 3.9×10^6

(b) 4.5×10^6

(c) 2.5×10^6

(d) 3.1×10^6

25. Monochromatic radiation of wavelength 640.2 nm (1 nm $= 10^{-9}$ m) from a neon lamp irradiates photosensitive material made of caesium on tungsten. The stopping voltage is measured to be 0.54 V. The source is replaced by an iron source and its wavelength 427.2 nm line irradiates the same photocell. Predict the new stopping voltage.

(a) 1.51 V (b) 3.5 V (c) 0.05 V (d) 2.03 V

26. In the fusion reaction ${}_1^2\text{H} + {}_1^2\text{H} \longrightarrow {}_2^3\text{He} + {}_0^1 n$, the masses of deuteron, helium and neutron expressed in amu are 2.05, 3.017 and 1.00 respectively. If 1 kg deuterium undergoes complete fusion, then amount of total energy released is (1 amu = 931.5 MeV/c^2)

(a) 9×10^{13} J

(b) 6×10^{14} J

(c) 9×10^{14} J

(d) 6×10^{13} J

27. An empty cylindrical beaker whose height is equal to its diameter is kept on a table. An observer's eye (E) looking towards S (line of sight ES) can see the point Q on the lower right. The angle of view θ, is the angle the line of sight ES, makes with the vertical RS-extended. A transparent liquid is now slowly poured into the beaker. As the liquid level rises in the beaker, the line of sight has to be continually adjusted (by increasing angle θ) in order to keep Q visible. When the liquid fills the beaker to the brim, Q can no more be seen by adjusting the line of sight ES. The minimum refractive index of the liquid should be

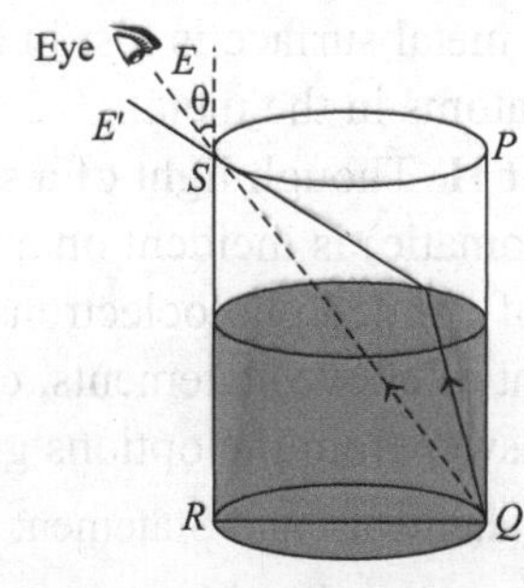

(a) $\frac{3}{2}$ (b) 2

(c) $\sqrt{\frac{3}{2}}$ (d) $\sqrt{2}$

28. An electric field associated with electromagnetic wave is given as $\mathbf{E} = E_0 \hat{\mathbf{n}} \sin[\omega t + (8y - 4z)]$. The direction of propagation vector **s** is

(a) $\frac{-8\hat{\mathbf{i}} + 4\hat{\mathbf{k}}}{\sqrt{80}}$ (b) $\frac{2\hat{\mathbf{i}} + 3\hat{\mathbf{k}}}{\sqrt{13}}$

(c) $-8\hat{\mathbf{j}} + 4\hat{\mathbf{k}}$ (d) $\frac{8\hat{\mathbf{k}} + 3\hat{\mathbf{j}}}{\sqrt{5}}$

29. The minimum input voltage required for regulation to be established in below figure is (Assume ideal Zener diode with $I_{ZK} = 1.5$ mA, $R_Z = 20\,\Omega$ $V_Z = 14$ V, at 30 mA)

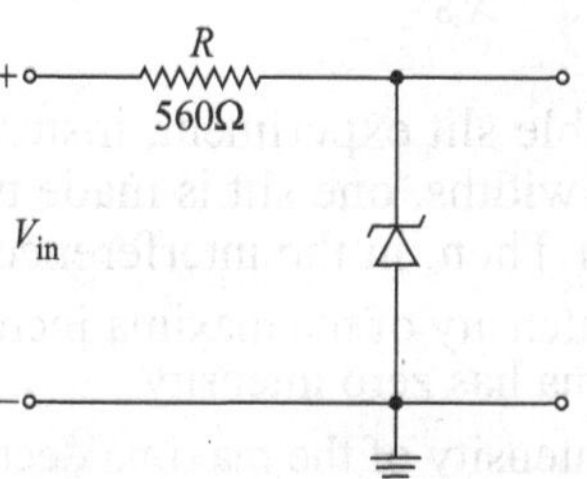

(a) 14.27 V (b) 15 V

(c) 14 V (d) 10 V

30. While measuring surface tension of water using capillary rise method, height of the lower meniscus from free surface of water is 3 cm while inner radius of capillary tube is found to be 0.5 cm. If we add some detergent to water, then

(a) liquid level in capillary tube is greater than 3 cm

(b) liquid level in capillary tube is less than 3 cm

(c) liquid level in capillary tube is equal to 3 cm

(d) anything may happen

31. Given the masses of ^{14}N, ^{4}He, ^{1}H and ^{17}O are respectively 14.00307 u, 4.00260 u, 1.00783 u and 16.99913 u. The minimum kinetic energy of an α-particle to cause the reaction $^{14}\text{N}(\alpha, p)^{17}\text{O}$ will be

(a) 1.66 MeV (b) 1.54 MeV

(c) 1.98 MeV (d) 2.25 MeV

32. An electron of a hydrogen atom has orbital radius r. Angular momentum of electron is proportional to

(a) r (b) $\frac{1}{r}$

(c) $\frac{1}{\sqrt{r}}$ (d) $\sqrt{r}$

33. Light of wavelength 0.6 μm from a sodium lamp falls on a photocell and causes the emission of photoelectrons for which the stopping potential is 0.5 V. With light of wavelength 0.4 μm from a sodium lamp, stopping potential is 1.5 V. With this data, the value of h/e is

(a) 4×10^{-19} Vs
(b) 0.25×10^{15} Vs
(c) 4×10^{-15} Vs
(d) 4×10^{-8} Vs

34. In a double slit experiment, instead of taking slits of same widths, one slit is made twice or wide as the other.Then, in the interference pattern,
(a) the intensity of the maxima increases and the minima has zero intensity
(b) the intensity of the maxima decreases and that of the minima increases
(c) the intensity of both maxima and the minima increases
(d) the intensity of the maxima decreases and the minima has zero intensity

35. A glass prism of refractive index 1.5 is immersed in a liquid of refractive index of 1.3. The angle of minimum deviation δ
(a) decreases in liquid with $\delta = 9°$
(b) increases in liquid with $\delta = 30°$
(c) increases in liquid with $\delta = 41°$
(d) remains unaffected

36. The combination of NAND gates shown here is

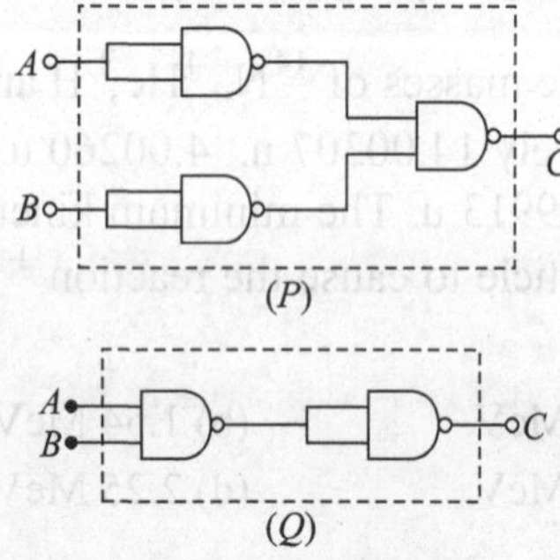

(a) P = OR gate, Q = AND gate
(b) P = AND gate, Q = NOT gate
(c) P = AND gate, Q = OR gate
(d) P = OR gate, Q = NOT gate

37. A ray of light passes through a triangular prism. Which among the following is correct?
(a) Angle of deviation increases with increase in angle of incidence.
(b) Angle of deviation decreases with increase in angle of incidence till minimum deviation.
(c) Angle of deviation increases with increase in angle of incidence till minimum deviation.
(d) Angle of deviation always decreases with increase in angle of incidence.

38. The intensity of each of the two slits in Young's double slit experiment is I_0. Calculate the minimum separation between the two points on the screen where intensities are $2I_0$ and I_0. (Given, fringe width $=\alpha$)

(a) $\frac{\alpha}{4}$ (b) $\frac{\alpha}{3}$ (c) $\frac{\alpha}{12}$ (d) $\frac{\alpha}{9}$

39. In the experiment of measuring speed of sound by resonance tube, it is observed that for tuning fork of frequency $\nu = 480$ Hz, length of air column $l_1 = 20$ cm and $l_2 = 70$ cm. The v_1 is equal to
(a) 380 ms^{-1} (b) 484 ms^{-1}
(c) 384 ms^{-1} (d) 480 ms^{-1}

40. A nucleus disintegrates into two nuclear parts which have their velocities in the ratio 2 : 1. The ratio of their nuclear sizes will be
(a) $3^{\frac{1}{2}}:1$ (b) $1:2^{\frac{1}{3}}$
(c) $2^{\frac{1}{3}}:1$ (d) $1:3^{\frac{1}{2}}$

41. **Statement I** The energy of electrons emitted from inside the metal surface is lost in collision with the other atoms in the metal.
Statement II Though light of a single frequency (monochromatic) is incident on a metal, the energies of emitted photoelectrons are different.
In the light of above statements, choose the correct answer from the options given below.
(a) Both Statement I and Statement II are correct.
(b) Both Statement I and Statement II are incorrect.
(c) Statement I is correct but Statement II is incorrect.
(d) Statement II is correct but Statement I is incorrect.

42. If energy of an electron in the second orbit of hydrogen atom is E, then the energy of electron in 3rd orbit of He will be
(a) $E_3 = \frac{4E}{9}$ (b) $E_3 = \frac{4E}{3}$
(c) $E_3 = \frac{16E}{3}$ (d) $E_3 = \frac{16E}{9}$

43. Match the following columns.

	Column I		Column II
A.	p- type semiconductor	1.	$\frac{n_h}{n_e}=1$
B.	n- type semiconductor	2.	$n_i^2=n_e n_h$
C.	Extrinsic semiconductor	3.	$\frac{n_h}{n_e}>1$
D.	Intrinsic semiconductor	4.	$\frac{n_h}{n_e}<1$

	A	B	C	D
(a)	1	2	4	3
(b)	2	1	3	4
(c)	3	4	2	1
(d)	4	2	3	1

44. The voltage $V_{AB}=20\,\text{V}$ at its peak value, and is sinusoidal in time.The current i (in amperes), when plotted as a function of time, is given by

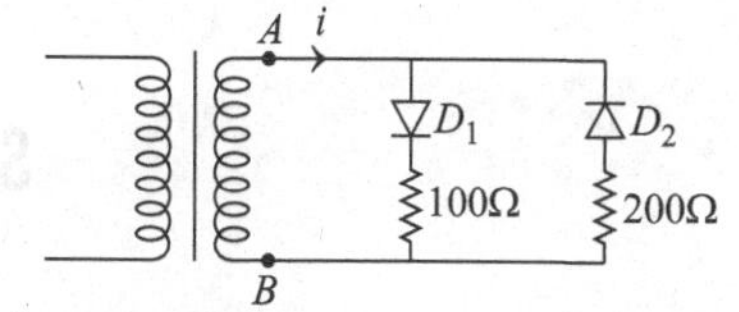

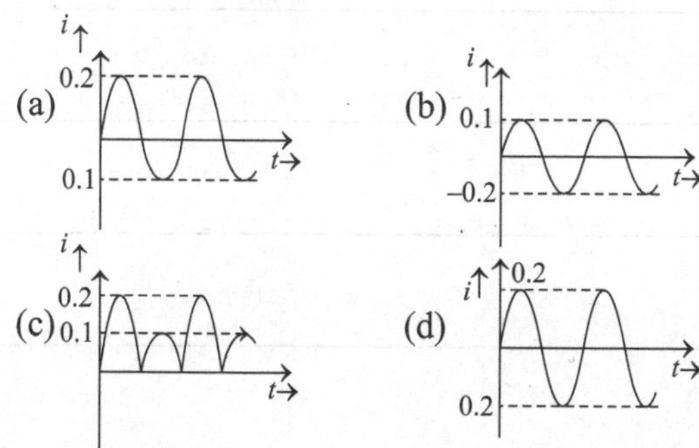

45. Electrical conductivity of a semiconductor increases when a beam of radiation of wavelength $\lambda=2480$ nm shines it's surface.

Energy gap of semiconductor is

(a) 1.1 eV
(b) 2.5 eV
(c) 0.5 eV
(d) 0.7 eV

For Online Syllabus Part Thru
Scan the QR Code

Response Index

01 ⓐ ⓑ ⓒ ⓓ	14 ⓐ ⓑ ⓒ ⓓ	27 ⓐ ⓑ ⓒ ⓓ	40 ⓐ ⓑ ⓒ ⓓ
02 ⓐ ⓑ ⓒ ⓓ	15 ⓐ ⓑ ⓒ ⓓ	28 ⓐ ⓑ ⓒ ⓓ	41 ⓐ ⓑ ⓒ ⓓ
03 ⓐ ⓑ ⓒ ⓓ	16 ⓐ ⓑ ⓒ ⓓ	29 ⓐ ⓑ ⓒ ⓓ	42 ⓐ ⓑ ⓒ ⓓ
04 ⓐ ⓑ ⓒ ⓓ	17 ⓐ ⓑ ⓒ ⓓ	30 ⓐ ⓑ ⓒ ⓓ	43 ⓐ ⓑ ⓒ ⓓ
05 ⓐ ⓑ ⓒ ⓓ	18 ⓐ ⓑ ⓒ ⓓ	31 ⓐ ⓑ ⓒ ⓓ	44 ⓐ ⓑ ⓒ ⓓ
06 ⓐ ⓑ ⓒ ⓓ	19 ⓐ ⓑ ⓒ ⓓ	32 ⓐ ⓑ ⓒ ⓓ	45 ⓐ ⓑ ⓒ ⓓ
07 ⓐ ⓑ ⓒ ⓓ	20 ⓐ ⓑ ⓒ ⓓ	33 ⓐ ⓑ ⓒ ⓓ	
08 ⓐ ⓑ ⓒ ⓓ	21 ⓐ ⓑ ⓒ ⓓ	34 ⓐ ⓑ ⓒ ⓓ	
09 ⓐ ⓑ ⓒ ⓓ	22 ⓐ ⓑ ⓒ ⓓ	35 ⓐ ⓑ ⓒ ⓓ	
10 ⓐ ⓑ ⓒ ⓓ	23 ⓐ ⓑ ⓒ ⓓ	36 ⓐ ⓑ ⓒ ⓓ	
11 ⓐ ⓑ ⓒ ⓓ	24 ⓐ ⓑ ⓒ ⓓ	37 ⓐ ⓑ ⓒ ⓓ	
12 ⓐ ⓑ ⓒ ⓓ	25 ⓐ ⓑ ⓒ ⓓ	38 ⓐ ⓑ ⓒ ⓓ	
13 ⓐ ⓑ ⓒ ⓓ	26 ⓐ ⓑ ⓒ ⓓ	39 ⓐ ⓑ ⓒ ⓓ	

Performance Scanner

> 90% Excellent !	You have mastered the first half of NEET syllabus (12th). The concepts of this syllabus are on your fingertips. Maintain this momentum.
76-90% Very Good !	You have a good command over the first half of NEET syllabus (12th). Revise it again after a few days and enhance your performance.
60-75% Good !	You have a wide scope to learn for the first half of NEET syllabus (12th). Revise it again.
<60% Not Satisfactory!	You have a long way ahead of you to master the first half of NEET syllabus (12th). Revise it thoroughly.

Space for Rough Work

Test Booklet No. **3947169**

Test Booklet Code **NSS 1**

NEET Stepping Stones 1

(Based on 12th Syllabus)

Name of the Candidate (In Capitals)

____

____

____

Candidate's Signature ____________

Invigilator's Signature ____________

Facsimile signature stamp of center superintendent________________

Important Instructions

- The test is of 45 minute and the Test Booklet contains 45 multiple choice questions (four options with a single correct answer) from Physics.
- Candidates are advised to read all questions before they start attempting the question paper.
- Each question carries 4 marks. For each correct response, the candidate will get 4 marks. For each incorrect response, one mark will be deducted from the total scores. The maximum marks are 180.
- In the event of candidate marking more than one option, one mark will be deducted.
- Use **Blue/Black Point Pen** only for writing particular on this page/ marking response on answer sheet.

Do not open this Booklet until you start attempting the Test

Physics (Q. No. 1-45)

1. A charged particle enters in a uniform magnetic field with velocity vector at an angle of 45° with the magnetic field. The pitch of the helical path followed by the particle is P. The radius of the helix will be

(a) $\frac{P}{\sqrt{2}\pi}$ (b) $\sqrt{2}P$

(c) $\frac{P}{2\pi}$ (d) $\frac{\sqrt{2}P}{\pi}$

2. The binding energy of ${}_1^2H$ is 1.15 MeV per nucleon. An alpha particle ${}_2^4He$ has a binding energy of 7.1 MeV per nucleon. The Q-value of the following reaction is

$${}_1^2H + {}_1^2H \rightarrow {}_2^4He + Q$$

(a) 5.95 MeV (b) 23.8 MeV

(c) 26.1 MeV (d) 28.9 MeV

3. In the circuit given below, V_{in} is the sinusoidal voltage source. The voltage drop across R $(R_1 \neq R_2)$

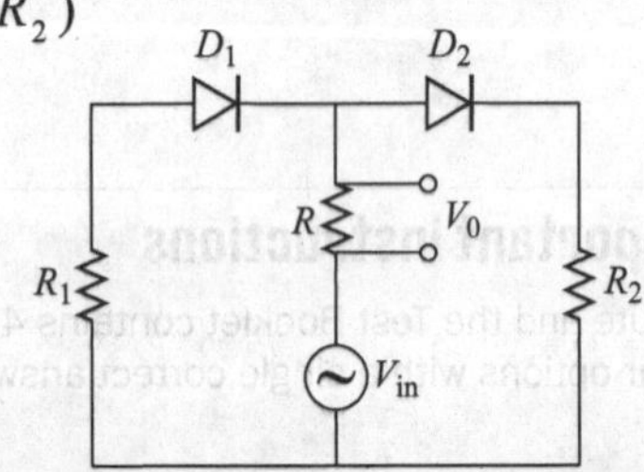

(a) is half-wave rectified

(b) is pure DC

(c) has same peak values in the positive and negative half-cycles

(d) has different peak values in the positive and negative half-cycles

4. In Fraunhofer diffraction from a narrow slit, a screen is positioned 2 m away from the slit to observe the diffraction pattern. The slit width is 0.2 mm and the first minimum of the diffraction pattern is located 5 mm away on either side of the central maximum. The wavelength of the light used in the experiment is

(a) 4000 Å (b) 6000 Å

(c) 5000 Å (d) 7000 Å

5. An electron and a positron, each with an energy of 0.5 MeV collide head-on and annihilate, resulting in the emission of two photons. If the rest mass energy of an electron is 0.2 MeV, then the wavelength of each photon produced during annihilation will be

(a) 1.78×10^{-12} m (b) 1.78×10^{-6} m

(c) 1.78×10^{-15} m (d) 1.78×10^{-9} m

6. Two spherical conductors of radii r_1 and r_2 having charge densities σ_1 and σ_2 respectively, are separated by a distance much greater than the radius of either sphere. The spheres are connected by a connecting wire, as shown in the following figure. If there is no flow of charge through connecting wire, then true condition is

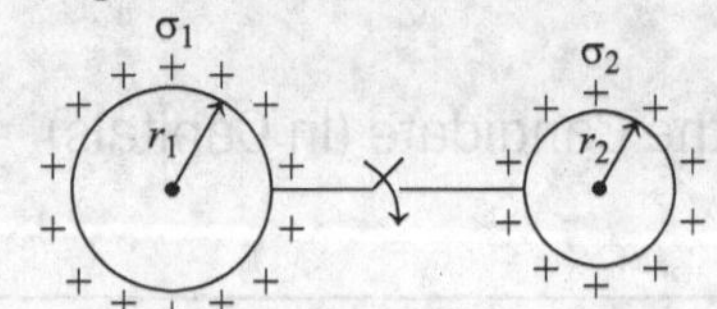

(a) $\frac{\sigma_1}{r_1} = \frac{\sigma_2}{r_2}$ (b) $\sigma_1 = \sigma_2$

(c) $\sigma_1 r_1 = \sigma_2 r_2$ (d) $\frac{\sigma_1}{r_1^2} = \frac{\sigma_2}{r_2^2}$

7. Experimental observations of time period of a pendulum are 2.63 s, 2.56 s, 2.42 s, 2.71 s and 2.80 s, then reported value of time period will be

(a) $(2.62 + 0.11)$ s (b) $(2.62 - 0.11)$ s

(c) (2.62 ± 0.11) s (d) All of these

8. **Assertion (A)** The refractive index of diamond is $\sqrt{6}$ and that of liquid is $\sqrt{3}$. If the light travels from diamond to the liquid, it will totally get reflected when the angle of incidence is 30°.

Reason (R) $n = \frac{1}{\sin i_C}$, where n is the refractive index of diamond with respect to liquid and i_C is the critical angle.

In the light of above statements, choose the most appropriate answer from the options given below.

(a) Both A and R are true and R is the correct explanation of A.

(b) Both A and R are true but R is not the correct explanation of A.

(c) A is true but R is false.

(d) A is false but R is true.

9. An electric dipole of moment **p** is placed in a uniform electric field **E**, then

(i) the torque on the dipole is $\mathbf{p} \times \mathbf{E}$.

(ii) the potential energy of the system is $\mathbf{p} \cdot \mathbf{E}$.

(iii) the resultant force on the dipole is zero.

Choose the correct option, based on above statements.

(a) (i), (ii) and (iii) are correct

(b) (i) and (iii) are correct and (ii) is wrong

(c) Only (i) is correct

(d) (i) and (ii) are correct and (iii) is wrong

10.

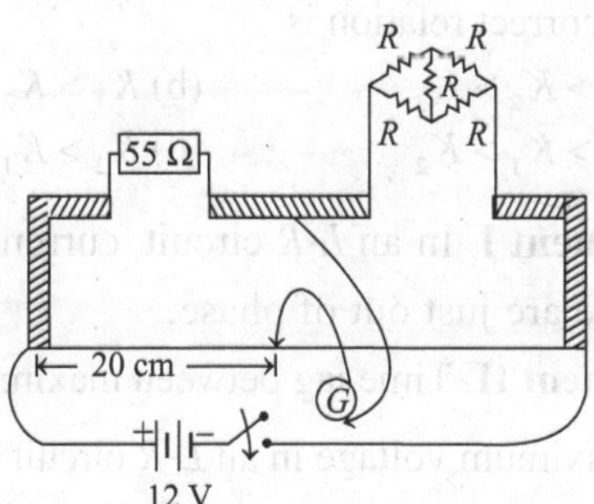

In above arrangement, value of R is (balance length is 20 cm)

(a) $110\,\Omega$ (b) $220\,\Omega$

(c) $55\,\Omega$ (d) $72\,\Omega$

11. An α-particle of energy $\frac{1}{2}mv^2$ is bombarded on a heavy nuclear target of charge Ze, then the minimum distance of closest approach is proportional to

(a) $\frac{1}{Ze}$ (b) v^2

(c) $\frac{1}{m}$ (d) $\frac{1}{v^4}$

12. A naturally occurring liquid is filled in a narrow U-tube and one limb is placed in between the pole pieces of an electromagnet. When switch is ON for the electromagnet, the situation hence obtained is shown in figure. From this figure, predict the nature of material.

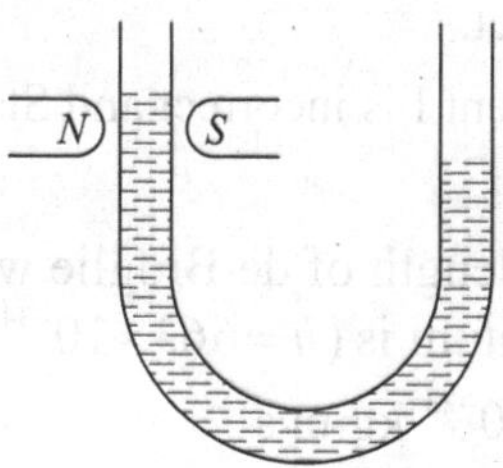

(a) Paramagnetic

(b) Ferromagnetic

(c) Diamagnetic

(d) Can be (a) or (b)

13. An electric dipole consists of a positive charge of $+1\ \mu C$ and an equal negative charge of $-1\ \mu C$, separated by a distance of 2 cm. This dipole is placed in an electric field with a strength of 10^5 N/C. Then, the work done in rotating the dipole from the position of stable equilibrium through an angle of 180° is

(a) 2×10^{-3} J (b) 4×10^{-3} J

(c) 10^{-3} J (d) zero

14. Two circular coils A and B have the same radius and are made from wire of the same material. However, the radius of the wire used for coil B is twice that of the wire used for coil A. To ensure that the magnetic field induction at the centre of both coils is the same, the ratio of the potential difference across coil A to that across coil B, will be

(a) 2 (b) 1

(c) 4 (d) $\frac{1}{4}$

15. Radiowaves of constant amplitude can be produced by using

(a) LED (b) rectifier

(c) logic gates (d) oscillator

16. **Statement I** A dead beat galvanometer contains a coil wrapped with aluminium foil.

Statement II Eddy currents dissipate oscillation energy as heat.

In the light of above statements, choose the most appropriate answer from the options given below.

(a) Both Statement I and Statement II are correct.

(b) Both Statement I and Statement II are incorrect.

(c) Statement I is correct and Statement II is incorrect.

(d) Statement I is incorrect and Statement II is correct.

17. The wavelength of de-Broglie wave is $2\mu m$, then its momentum is ($h = 6.63 \times 10^{-34}$ J-s)

(a) 3.31×10^{-28} kg-m/s

(b) 1.66×10^{-28} kg-m/s

(c) 4.97×10^{-28} kg-m/s

(d) 9.9×10^{-28} kg-m/s

18. Two metal spheres of radii r_1 and r_2 (where $r_2 > r_1$) are placed far apart from each other. The capacitance of this system is

(a) $\frac{4\pi\varepsilon_0 r_1 r_2}{r_2 - r_1}$ (b) $\frac{4\pi\varepsilon_0 r_1 r_2}{r_2 + r_1}$

(c) zero (d) $4\pi\varepsilon_0 r_1$

19. **Assertion** (A) Two infinitely long wires *A* and *B* carry unequal currents both in inward direction.

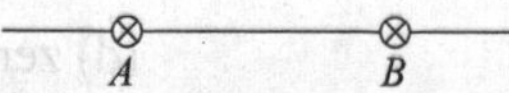

Then, there is only one point (excluding the points at infinity), where net magnetic field is zero.

Reason (R) That point lies between points *A* and *B*.

In light of above statements, choose the most appropriate answer from the options given below.

(a) Both A and R are true and R is the correct explanation of A.

(b) Both A and R are true but R is not the correct explanation of A.

(c) A is true but R is false.

(d) A is false but R is true.

20. Two particles each of mass *M* and charge *q* are fixed at the two ends of a light rigid rod of length $2l$. The rod rotates at a constant angular speed about a perpendicular axis passing through its centre. The ratio of the magnitudes of the magnetic moment of the system to its angular momentum about the centre of the rod is

(a) $\frac{q}{kM}$ (b) $\frac{q}{M}$

(c) $\frac{q}{2M}$ (d) $\frac{2q}{M}$

21. Two H-atoms in the ground state collide inelastically. The maximum amount by which their combined kinetic energy is reduced, is

(a) 10.20 eV (b) 20.40 eV

(c) 13.6 eV (d) 27.2 eV

22. Three thin dielectric slabs of dielectric constants K_1, K_2 and K_3 are inserted between the plates of a parallel plate capacitor as shown in the following figure. The variation of electric field between the plates with distance *x* is shown below.

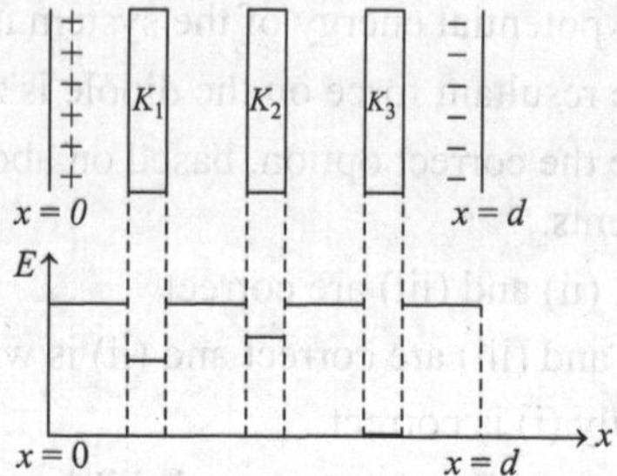

Then, correct relation is

(a) $K_1 > K_2 > K_3$ (b) $K_1 > K_3 > K_2$

(c) $K_3 > K_1 > K_2$ (d) $K_2 > K_1 > K_3$

23. **Statement I** In an *L-R* circuit, current and voltage are just out of phase.

Statement II Time lag between maximum current and maximum voltage in an *L-R* circuit is $\tau = \frac{\phi}{\omega}$, where ϕ is phase difference and ω is angular frequency.

In the light of above statements, choose the most appropriate answer from the options given below.

(d) Both Statement I and Statement II are correct.

(b) Both Statement I and Statement II are incorrect.

(c) Statement I is correct and Statement II is incorrect.

(d) Statement I is incorrect and Statement II is correct.

24. An electric bulb is rated as 200 W. What will be the peak magnetic field at 4 m distance produced by the radiations coming from this bulb? Consider this bulb as a point source wth 3.5% efficiency.

(a) 1.19×10^{-8} T (b) 1.71×10^{-8} T

(c) 0.84×10^{-8} T (d) 3.36×10^{-8} T

25. The energy flux of sunlight reaching the surface of earth is about $1300 \frac{\text{W}}{\text{m}^2}$. Number of photons reaching per square metre in 1 s of earth's surface is around (Given, average wavelength of photons in the sunlight is 550 nm)

(a) 4×10^{19} (b) 4×10^{16}
(c) 4×10^{21} (d) 4×10^{25}

26. Three resistance of 1 Ω each are connected in parallel, such connection is again connected with (2/3)Ω resistance in series. The resultant resistance will be

(a) (5/3) Ω (b) (3/2) Ω
(c) 1 Ω (d) (2/3) Ω

27. A 100 μF capacitor is in series with a 40 Ω resistance. It is connected with a supply of 110 V and 60 Hz. Time lag between maximum current and maximum voltage is

(a) 1 ms (b) 2.55 ms
(c) 3 ms (d) 1.55 ms

28. Both a proton and an electron are launched with equal initial velocities perpendicular to a uniform electric field. Then

(a) both trajectories will be equally curved
(b) both trajectories will be rectilinear
(c) the electron's trajectory will be more curved than the proton's trajectory
(d) the electron's trajectory will be less curved than the proton's trajectory

29. When a photosensitive surface is illuminated by light of wavelength λ, the stopping potential observed is V. When the same surface is illuminated by light of wavelength 2λ, the stopping potential decreases to $\frac{V}{3}$. The threshold wavelength λ_0 of the surface is

(a) $\frac{5\lambda}{2}$ (b) $\frac{3\lambda}{2}$ (c) $\frac{7\lambda}{2}$ (d) 4λ

30. A system of three charges is shown below.

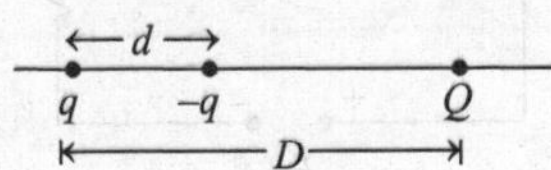

Now, $-q$ charge is shifted near Q charge as shown.

D q −q d Q

Work done in the process is (Take, $Q = 2q$ and $D = 3d$)

(a) $\frac{kq^2}{d}$ (b) $\frac{-kq^2}{d}$
(c) $\frac{-kq^2}{2d}$ (d) $\frac{kq^2}{2d}$

31. In a YDSE, a beam of electrons is used. If speed of electrons is made 4 times, then central bright fringe width becomes

(a) 1/4 times
(b) 2 times
(c) $\frac{1}{2}$ times
(d) No fringes are obtained with electrons

32. In a two slit interference pattern, the intensity of light at a point on the screen is I' when the path difference is λ. The intensity of light at a point where the path difference is $\frac{\lambda}{3}$ will be (Given, λ is the wavelength of the light used)

(a) $\frac{I'}{3}$ (b) $3I'$
(c) $\frac{I'}{4}$ (d) $\frac{I'}{2}$

33. In a displacement method experiment, a convex lens is moved between fixed positions of an object and a screen, which are separated by a distance d. If the magnifications of the images at the two conjugate positions of the lens are m_1 and m_2, the focal length of the lens is

(a) $d\left(\frac{m_1}{m_2}\right)$
(b) $\frac{d}{m_2 - m_1}$
(c) $\frac{d}{m_1 + m_2}$
(d) $d\left(\frac{m_1 m_2}{m_1 + m_2}\right)$

34. A 2 μF capacitor is being charged through a 4 MΩ resistor. The time, when the capacitor acquires half of its maximum energy will be

(a) 2.44 s (b) 4.88 s
(c) 9.76 s (d) 1.22 s

35. Two identical small conducting spheres have charges q_1 and q_2 (with $q_2 << q_1$). The spheres are placed at a certain distances. The electrostatic force between them is F_1. The spheres are made to touch each other and then placed at same distance. Now force acting between them is F_2, then $\frac{F_1}{F_2}$ is

(a) $\frac{q_1}{4q_2}$ (b) $\frac{4q_1}{q_2}$
(c) $\frac{4q_2}{q_1}$ (d) $\frac{q_1}{q_2}$

36. In an interference experiment using sodium light, interference bands with a width of 0.194 mm are observed at a distance of 100 cm from the coherent slits. A convex lens is placed between the slits and the eyepiece to form an image of the slits at a distance of 100 cm from the slits. The distance between the images of the two slits is found to be 7 mm, with the lens positioned 30 cm from the slits. The wavelength of sodium light used is

(a) 5850 Å (b) 5820 Å
(c) 5890 Å (d) 5900 Å

37. An object 2.4 m in front of a lens forms a sharp image on a film 12 cm behind the lens. A glass plate 1 cm thick, of refractive index 1.50 is interposed between lens and film with its plane faces parallel to the film. At what distance (from lens) should object shifted to be in sharp focus on film?

(a) 7.2 m (b) 2.4 m
(c) 3.2 m (d) – 5.6 m

38. A resistor of resistance $r/2$ and n resistors of resistance r are connected to a battery. If internal resistance of the battery is negligible. At what value of n, would the amount of power consumed by all resistors of resistance r be the largest?

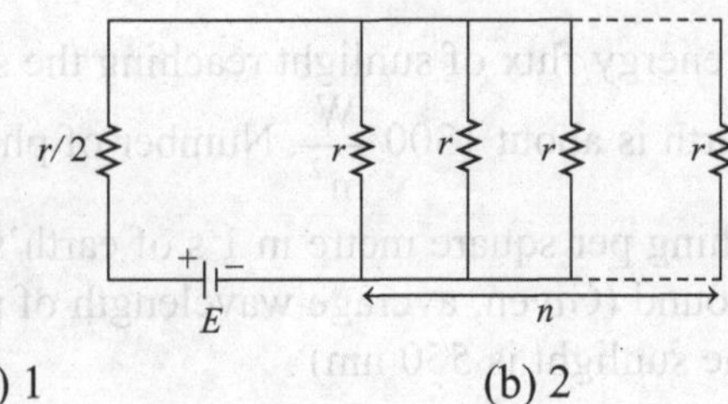

(a) 1 (b) 2
(c) 3 (d) 4

39. A short-circuited coil is placed in a time varying magnetic field, causing electrical power to be dissipated due to the induced current. If the number of turns in the coil is quadrupled and the wire radius is halved, then charge in electrical power dissipation will be

(a) halved (b) doubled
(c) the same (d) quadrupled

40. An inductor coil stores 64 J of magnetic field energy and dissipates energy at the rate of 640 W when a current of 8 A is passed through it. If this coil is joined across an ideal battery, find the time constant of the circuit in seconds.

(a) 0.4 (b) 0.8
(c) 0.125 (d) 0.2

41. The magnetic flux (ϕ) linked with a conducting coil depends on time t as $\phi = 4t^n - 3^n$, where n is a positive constant. If the magnitude of emf induced in the coil is e, then which of the following is incorrect about induced emf e ?

(a) If $n = 1$, then e is constant.
(b) If $n > 1$, then e increases with time.
(c) If $n > 1$, then e decreases with time.
(d) If $0 < n < 1$, then e decreases with time.

42. In the given circuit, the charge supplied by a battery with emf varied with time t according to the equation $q = \alpha t - \beta t^2$, where α and β are constants. The total heat produced in the resistor $2R$ is

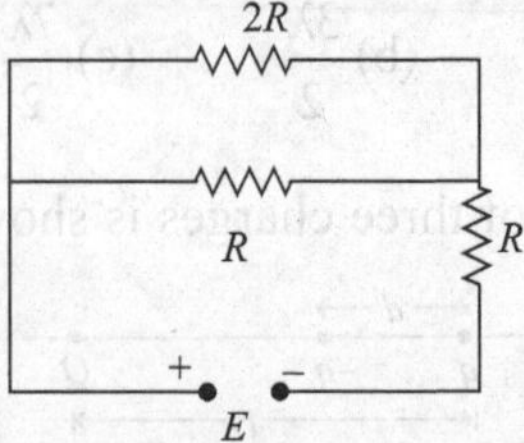

(a) $\dfrac{\alpha^2 R}{27\beta}$ (b) $\dfrac{\alpha^3 R}{27\beta}$

(c) $\dfrac{\alpha^2 R}{\beta}$ (d) $\dfrac{\alpha^3 R}{\beta}$

43. In the circuit shown in the figure, cells E, F, G and H have emfs of 2 V, 1 V, 3 V and 1 V, respectively and internal resistances of 2 Ω, 1 Ω 3 Ω and 1 Ω respectively. The potential difference between points B and D is

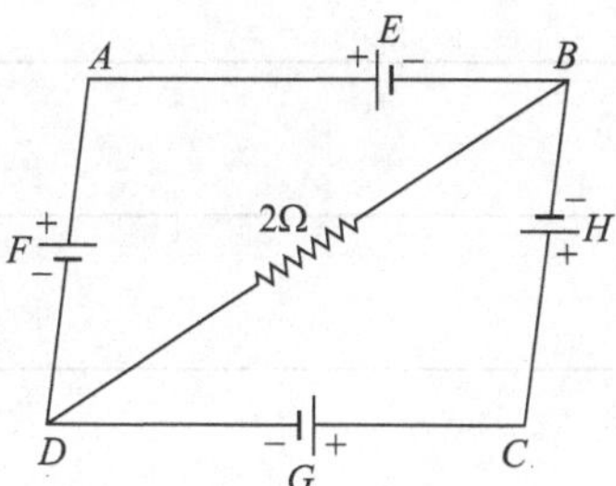

(a) $\dfrac{2}{13}$ V (b) $\dfrac{3}{13}$ V

(c) $\dfrac{1}{13}$ V (d) $\dfrac{4}{13}$ V

44. The area of parallel plates of an air-filled capacitor is $0.20\,m^2$ and the distance between them is 0.01 m. The potential difference across the plates is 3000 V. When a 0.01 m thick dielectric sheet is introduced between the plates, then the potential difference decreases to 1000 V.

Now, match the two columns (all in SI units) and choose the correct code.

	Column I		Column II
A.	Capacitance of air-filled capacitor	(1)	5.31×10^{-7}
B.	Charge on each plate	(2)	5.31×10^{-10}
C.	Dielectric constant of the material	(3)	3
D.	Capacitance after the dielectric sheet is introduced	(4)	1.77×10^{-10}

Codes

	A	B	C	D
(a)	2	4	1	3
(b)	4	3	1	2
(c)	4	1	3	2
(d)	2	3	1	4

45. Two equal negative charges, each of magnitude q are fixed at the coordinates $(0, -a)$ and $(0, a)$ on the XY-plane. A positive charge, Q is initially at rest at the point $(2a, 0)$. The charge Q will

(a) move to infinity

(b) execute oscillatory motion not SHM

(c) move to the origin and remain at rest there

(d) execute SHM about the origin

Response Index

01 ⓐ ⓑ ⓒ ⓓ	14 ⓐ ⓑ ⓒ ⓓ	27 ⓐ ⓑ ⓒ ⓓ	40 ⓐ ⓑ ⓒ ⓓ
02 ⓐ ⓑ ⓒ ⓓ	15 ⓐ ⓑ ⓒ ⓓ	28 ⓐ ⓑ ⓒ ⓓ	41 ⓐ ⓑ ⓒ ⓓ
03 ⓐ ⓑ ⓒ ⓓ	16 ⓐ ⓑ ⓒ ⓓ	29 ⓐ ⓑ ⓒ ⓓ	42 ⓐ ⓑ ⓒ ⓓ
04 ⓐ ⓑ ⓒ ⓓ	17 ⓐ ⓑ ⓒ ⓓ	30 ⓐ ⓑ ⓒ ⓓ	43 ⓐ ⓑ ⓒ ⓓ
05 ⓐ ⓑ ⓒ ⓓ	18 ⓐ ⓑ ⓒ ⓓ	31 ⓐ ⓑ ⓒ ⓓ	44 ⓐ ⓑ ⓒ ⓓ
06 ⓐ ⓑ ⓒ ⓓ	19 ⓐ ⓑ ⓒ ⓓ	32 ⓐ ⓑ ⓒ ⓓ	45 ⓐ ⓑ ⓒ ⓓ
07 ⓐ ⓑ ⓒ ⓓ	20 ⓐ ⓑ ⓒ ⓓ	33 ⓐ ⓑ ⓒ ⓓ	
08 ⓐ ⓑ ⓒ ⓓ	21 ⓐ ⓑ ⓒ ⓓ	34 ⓐ ⓑ ⓒ ⓓ	
09 ⓐ ⓑ ⓒ ⓓ	22 ⓐ ⓑ ⓒ ⓓ	35 ⓐ ⓑ ⓒ ⓓ	
10 ⓐ ⓑ ⓒ ⓓ	23 ⓐ ⓑ ⓒ ⓓ	36 ⓐ ⓑ ⓒ ⓓ	
11 ⓐ ⓑ ⓒ ⓓ	24 ⓐ ⓑ ⓒ ⓓ	37 ⓐ ⓑ ⓒ ⓓ	
12 ⓐ ⓑ ⓒ ⓓ	25 ⓐ ⓑ ⓒ ⓓ	38 ⓐ ⓑ ⓒ ⓓ	
13 ⓐ ⓑ ⓒ ⓓ	26 ⓐ ⓑ ⓒ ⓓ	39 ⓐ ⓑ ⓒ ⓓ	

Performance Scanner

> 90% Excellent !	You have mastered the NEET syllabus (12th). The concepts of this syllabus are on your fingertips. Maintain this momentum.
76-90% Very Good !	You have a good command over the NEET syllabus (12th). Revise it again after a few days and enhance your performance.
60-75% Good !	You have a wide scope to learn for the NEET syllabus (12th). Revise it again.
<60% Not Satisfactory!	You have a long way ahead of you to master the NEET syllabus (12th). Revise it thoroughly.

Space for Rough Work

Test Booklet No. 3947170

Test Booklet Code NSS 2

MEDACE

NEET (UG)

SELF ASSESSMENT KIT

NEET Stepping Stones 2

(Based on 12th Syllabus)

Name of the Candidate (In Capitals)

____

____

____

Candidate's Signature ____________

Invigilator's Signature ____________

Facsimile signature stamp of center superintendent____________

Important Instructions

- The test is of 45 minute and the Test Booklet contains 45 multiple choice questions (four options with a single correct answer) from Physics.
- Candidates are advised to read all questions before they start attempting the question paper.
- Each question carries 4 marks. For each correct response, the candidate will get 4 marks. For each incorrect response, one mark will be deducted from the total scores. The maximum marks are 180.
- In the event of candidate marking more than one option, one mark will be deducted.
- Use **Blue/Black Point Pen** only for writing particular on this page/ marking response on answer sheet.

Do not open this Booklet until you start attempting the Test

Physics (Q. No. 1-45)

1. A small loop Q is kept coaxially with a bigger loop P.

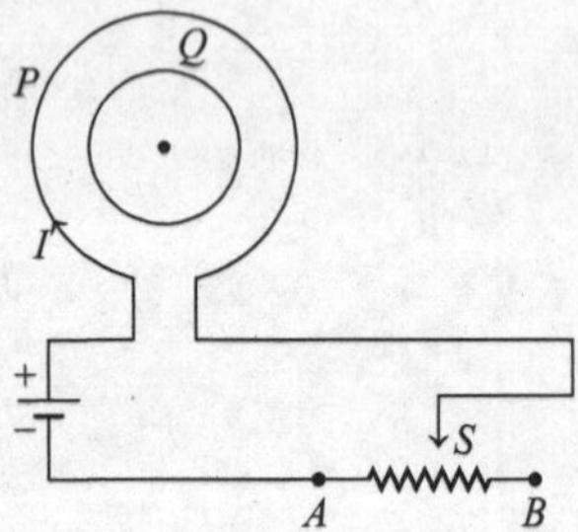

As slider S moves from B to A, then current in Q

(a) is zero
(b) flows clockwise
(c) flows anti-clockwise
(d) flows initially clockwise then anti-clockwise

2. A metallic rod of length l is tied to a string of length $2l$ and rotated with constant angular speed ω in region of a perpendicular magnetic field of strength B. Induced emf in rod is

(a) $\frac{7}{2}Bl^2\omega$ (b) $\frac{5}{3}Bl^2\omega$
(c) $\frac{5}{2}Bl^2\omega$ (d) $\frac{3}{5}Bl^2\omega$

3. A plane mirror reflects a beam of light to form a real image, then the beam of light incident on the mirror is

(a) parallel
(b) convergent
(c) divergent
(d) vertical

4. The average power dissipated in a pure inductor of inductance L when an AC current is passing through it, is

(a) $\frac{1}{2}LI^2$ (b) $\frac{1}{4}LI^2$
(c) $2LI^2$ (d) zero

5. **Assertion** (A) When we produce charge q_1 on a body by rubbing it against another body which gets a charge q_2 in the process, then $q_1 + q_2 = 0$.

Reason (R) Charge on an isolated system remains constant.

In the light of the above statements, choose the most appropriate answer from the options given below.

(a) Both A and R are correct and R is the correct explanation of A.
(b) Both A and R are correct but R is not the correct explanation of A.
(c) A is correct but R is incorrect.
(d) A is incorrect but R is correct.

6. Two resistors 400Ω and 800Ω are connected in series with a 6 V battery. The potential difference measured by voltmeter of $10\,k\Omega$ across 400Ω resistor is

(a) 2 V (b) 1.95 V
(c) 3.8 V (d) 4 V

7. The length of a magnet is large compared to its width and breadth. The time period of its oscillation in a vibration magnetometer is 2 s. The magnet is cut along its length into three equal parts and these parts are placed on each other with their like poles together. The time period of this combination will be

(a) 2 s (b) $\frac{2}{3}$ s
(c) $2\sqrt{3}$ s (d) $\frac{2}{\sqrt{3}}$ s

8. An EM wave of wavelength λ is incident on a photosensitive surface of negligible work function. If the photoelectrons emitted from the surface have de-Broglie wavelength λ_0, then λ is equal to

(a) $\lambda_0\sqrt{\frac{2mc}{h}}$ (b) $\lambda_0^2\left(\frac{2mc}{h}\right)$
(c) $\sqrt{\lambda_0\frac{h}{2mc}}$ (d) $\lambda_0\left(\frac{2mc}{h}\right)^2$

9. The graph shows how the magnification m produced by a convex thin lens varies with image distance v. What was focal length of the used lens?

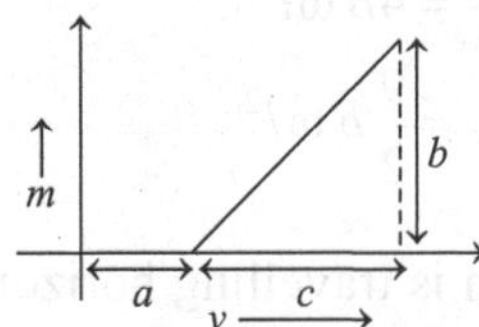

(a) $\frac{b}{c}$ (b) $\frac{bc}{a}$

(c) $\frac{b}{ca}$ (d) $\frac{c}{b}$

10. **Statement I** The reactance of an AC circuit is zero. It is possible that the circuit contains a capacitor and an inductor.

Statement II In purely inductive circuit, voltage lags the current by $\frac{\pi}{2}$.

In the light of above statements, choose the most appropriate answer from the options given below.

(a) Both Statement I and Statement II are correct.

(b) Both Statement I and Statement II are incorrect.

(c) Statement I is correct but Statement II is incorrect.

(d) Statement I is incorrect but Statement II is correct.

11. Light with an energy flux of 20 W/cm^2 strikes a non-reflective surface perpendicularly. If the surface area is 30 cm^2, then the total momentum transferred (assuming complete absorption) after a duration of 30 minutes is

(a) 36×10^{-4} kg-m/s

(b) 36×10^{-5} kg-m/s

(c) 108×10^{4} kg-m/s

(d) 1.08×10^{7} kg-m/s

12. The output of the given circuit would be

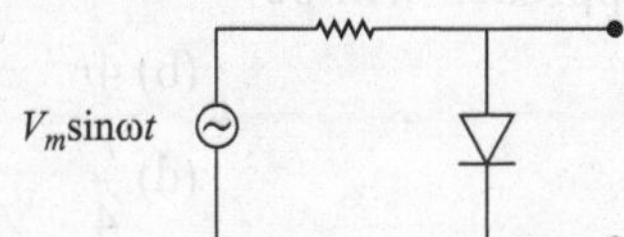

(a) zero at all times

(b) like that of a full wave rectifier

(c) like a half-wave rectifier with positive cycles in output

(d) like a half-wave rectifier with negative cycles in output

13. Two charges $+4e$ and $+e$ are at a distance x apart. At what distance, a charge q must be placed from charge $+e$, so that it is in equilibrium?

(a) $x/2$ (b) $2x/3$

(c) $x/3$ (d) $x/6$

14. In YDSE, ratio of intensity at centre of bright fringe to the intensity at a point (1/4)th of distance between two fringes from the centre is

(a) 2 (b) $\frac{1}{2}$

(c) 4 (d) 16

15. While examining the magnetic properties of substances, it is found that a hydrogen atom is paramagnetic. The hydrogen molecule is

(a) diamagnetic

(b) paramagnetic

(c) ferromagnetic

(d) May be anything depends upon temperature

16. In the standard Young's double slit experiment, the intensity on the screen, at a point distant 1.25 fringe widths from the central maximum, is (assuming slits to be identical)

(a) I_{max} (b) $\frac{I_{max}}{2}$

(c) $\frac{I_{max}}{3}$ (d) $\frac{I_{max}}{4}$

17. **Assertion** (A) If the distance between parallel plates of a capacitor is halved and dielectric constant is made three times, then the capacitance becomes 6 times.

Reason (R) Capacity of the capacitor depends upon the nature of the medium between the plates.

In the light of above statements, choose the most appropriate answer from the options given below.

(a) Both A and R are true and R is the correct explanation of A.
(b) Both A and R are true but R is not the correct explanation of A.
(c) A is true but R is false.
(d) A is false but R is true.

18. When a 20 Ω resistor is connected in parallel with a moving coil galvanometer, then its deflection reduces from 75 divisions to 25 divisions, then the resistance of galvanometer will be

(a) 10 Ω (b) 20 Ω
(c) 40 Ω (d) 60 Ω

19. A conducting triangular frame made of thin wire is kept in XY-plane as shown in the following figure. If magnetic field is applied as $\mathbf{B} = 4x^2\hat{\mathbf{i}}$ T, where x is in metre, then induced emf in the loop will be

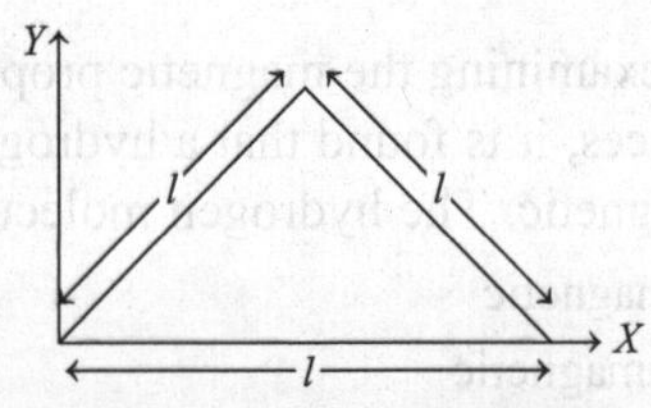

(a) $\sqrt{3}l^2$ (b) $\frac{\sqrt{3}}{2}l^2$
(c) $\frac{1}{2}l^2$ (d) zero

20. A magnetic dipole of moment M is placed in external uniform magnetic field B. If magnetic dipole is rotated from field direction to a position θ very slowly, then work done by external source is

(a) $2MB\sin\theta$ (b) $2MB\sin\frac{\theta}{2}$
(c) $MB\cos^2\frac{\theta}{2}$ (d) $2MB\sin^2\frac{\theta}{2}$

21. A conducting rod AC of length $4l$ is rotated about a point O in a uniform magnetic field $\mathbf{B}$ directed into the paper. If $AO = l$ and $OC = 3l$, then

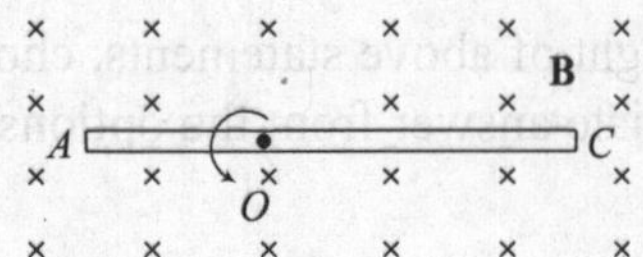

(a) $V_A - V_O = \frac{B\omega l^2}{2}$
(b) $V_O - V_C = \frac{7}{2}B\omega l^2$
(c) $V_A - V_C = 4B\omega l^2$
(d) $V_C - V_O = \frac{9}{2}B\omega l^2$

22. An electron is travelling horizontally towards east. A magnetic field in vertically downward direction exerts a force on the electron along

(a) east (b) west
(c) north (d) south

23. To decrease cut-off wavelength of continuous X-rays by 25%, potential difference of a coolidge tube must be

(a) increased by 34%
(b) decreased by 34%
(c) increased by 25%
(d) decreased by 25%

24. A star initially contains 10^{40} deuterons and generates energy through the reactions

${}_1H^2 + {}_1H^2 \longrightarrow {}_1H^3 + p$ and

${}_1H^2 + {}_1H^3 \longrightarrow {}_2He^4 + n$, where the masses of the nuclei are $m({}_1^2H) = 2.014$ amu, $m(p) = 1.007$ amu, $m(n) = 1.008$ amu and $m({}_2^1He) = 4.001$ amu.

If the average power radiated by the star is 10^{16} W, then the deuteron supply of the star is exhausted in a time of the order of

(a) 10^{28} s (b) 10^{12} s
(c) 10^{16} s (d) 10^{20} s

25. An alpha particle is fixed towards a nucleus with momentum p and its minimum distance of closest approach is r. If the momentum of the alpha particle is doubled to $2p$, then the new distance of closest approach will be

(a) $2r$ (b) $4r$
(c) $\frac{r}{2}$ (d) $\frac{r}{4}$

26. A semiconductor diode is used as a half-wave rectifier having internal resistance 150Ω. The voltage applied is given by $V = (50\sin\omega t)$ V and load resistance is 850Ω, then the maximum output current is

(a) 50 mA (b) 60 mA
(c) 80 mA (d) 40 mA

27. If a centre tap transformer is used with 2 diodes for full wave rectification, then output voltage of rectifier w.r.t. each diode is

(a) $2 \times$ secondary voltage of transformer
(b) $(2/3) \times$ secondary voltage of transformer
(c) $(1/2) \times$ secondary voltage of transformer
(d) $(3/2) \times$ secondary voltage of transformer

28. If $\mathbf{E}_1$ and $\mathbf{E}_2$ be respective electric fields at equipotential position and axial position of electric dipole at same distance, then

(a) $\mathbf{E}_1 \cdot \mathbf{E}_2 = 0$
(b) $|\mathbf{E}_1 + \mathbf{E}_2| = 0$
(c) $|\mathbf{E}_1 \times \mathbf{E}_2| = 0$
(d) $|\mathbf{E}_1 - \mathbf{E}_2| = 0$

29. A coil of inductance $L = 50\,\mu$H and resistance $= 0.5\,\Omega$ is connected to a battery of emf $= 5$ V. A resistor of $10\,\Omega$ is connected parallel to the coil. Now at same instant, the connection of the battery is switched OFF. Then, the amount of heat generated in the coil after switching OFF the battery is

(a) 0.65 mJ
(b) 0.12 mJ
(c) 2.5 mJ
(d) 1.25 mJ

30. An electron moving with a speed u along the positive X-axis at $Y = 0$ enters a region of uniform magnetic field which exists to the right of Y-axis. The electron exits from the region after some time with the speed v at coordinate y, then

(a) $v > u$, $y < 0$ (b) $v = u$, $y > 0$
(c) $v > u$, $y > 0$ (d) $v = u$, $y < 0$

31. If two lenses of +5 D are mounted at same distance apart, the equivalent power will always be negative, if the distance is

(a) greater than 40 cm
(b) equal to 40 cm
(c) equal to 10 cm
(d) less than 10 cm

32. An object O and a mirror M are moving with the velocities shown in the figure. The velocity of the image of the object in the mirror is

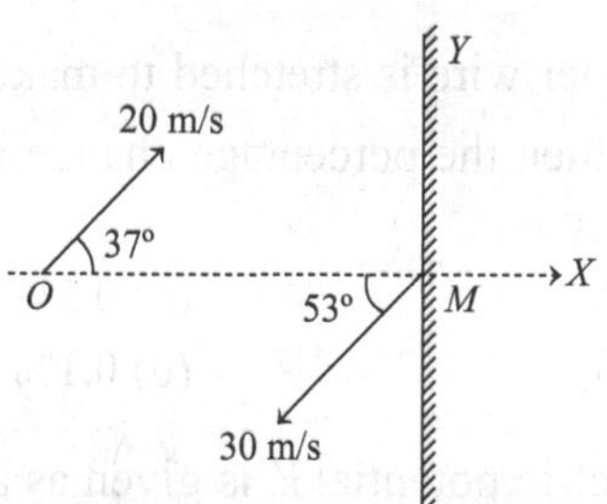

(a) $(-34\,\hat{\mathbf{i}} + 12\,\hat{\mathbf{j}})$ m/s
(b) $(-34\,\hat{\mathbf{i}} + 16\,\hat{\mathbf{j}})$ m/s
(c) $(-52\,\hat{\mathbf{i}} + 12\,\hat{\mathbf{j}})$ m/s
(d) $(52\,\hat{\mathbf{i}} + 12\,\hat{\mathbf{j}})$ m/s

33. Three long, straight and parallel wires carrying currents are arranged as shown in figure. The force experienced by 10 cm length of wire Q is

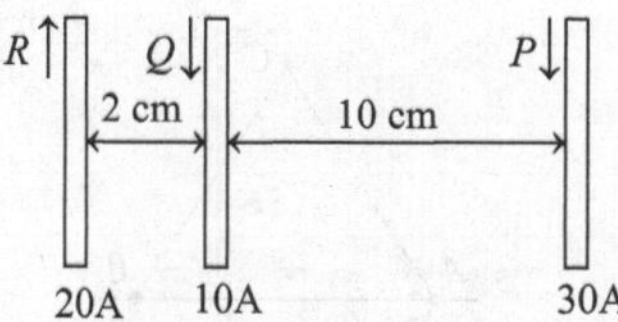

(a) 1.4×10^{-4} N towards the right
(b) 1.4×10^{-4} N towards the left
(c) 2.6×10^{-4} N towards the right
(d) 2.6×10^{-4} N towards the left

34. A potential difference V is applied to a copper wire of diameter d and length L, then match the statements given in Column I with the statements given in Column II.

Column I	Column II
A. Voltage V is doubled	P. Drift speed will decrease
B. Length L is doubled	Q. Drift speed will be doubled
C. Diameter d is doubled	R. Drift speed will be halved
D. Temperature of wire is increased	S. Drift speed will not change

(a) A → Q; B → R; C → S, D → P
(b) A → Q; B → R; C → P D → S
(c) A → S; B → P; C → Q; D → R
(d) A → P; B → Q; C → R; D → S

35. If a copper wire is stretched to make it $n = 0.2\%$ longer, then the percentage change in its resistance is

(a) 0.4% (b) 0.3%
(c) 0.2% (d) 0.1%

36. The electric potential V is given as a function of distance as $V = (10x^2 + 5x + 2)$ V, where x is in metres. The difference of electrostatic potential energy of a charge +2 μC at $x = 1$ m and $x = 2$ m is

(a) 7 μJ (b) 3.5 μJ
(c) 70 μJ (d) 35 μJ

37. Two point charges $+10^{-7}$C and -10^{-7}C are placed at A and B, 20 cm apart as shown in the figure. Calculate the electric field at C, 20 cm apart from both A and B

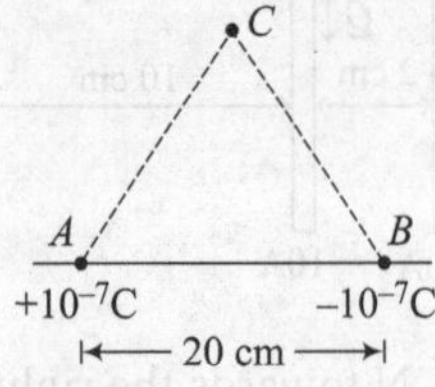

(a) 1.5×10^{-5} N C^{-1}
(b) 2.2×10^{4} NC^{-1}
(c) 3.5×10^{6} NC^{-1}
(d) 3.0×10^{5} NC^{-1}

38. Two conducting spheres of radii 3 cm and 1 cm are separated by a distance of 10 cm in free space. If the spheres are charged to same potential of 10 V each, then the force of repulsion between them will be

(a) $\left(\frac{1}{3}\right) \times 10^{-9}$ N (b) $\left(\frac{2}{9}\right) \times 10^{-9}$ N
(c) $\left(\frac{1}{9}\right) \times 10^{-9}$ N (d) $\left(\frac{4}{9}\right) \times 10^{-9}$ N

39. The value of current I_0 for the circuit given below is (Assume that diodes are ideal)

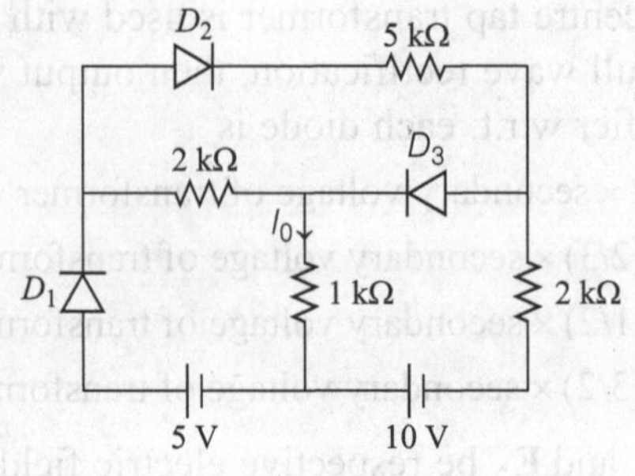

(a) 1mA
(b) 0.66 mA
(c) 1.25 mA
(d) 1.66 mA

40. For a telescope, focal length of objective is 144 cm and that of eyepiece is 6 cm. If image is formed at infinity, separation of objective and eyepiece is

(a) 138 cm (b) 155 cm
(c) 150 cm (d) 135 cm

41. An arc lamp requires a direct current of 10 A at 80 V to function. If it is connected to a 220 V(rms), 50 Hz AC supply, the series inductor needed for it to work is close to

(a) 0.08 H (b) 0.044 H
(c) 0.064 H (d) 80 H

42. A DC battery of 2 V emf and internal resistance 1 Ω are connected through the external load. Current of 1 A is flowing through the external load. If this type of battery is connected twice in series, then the value of current through same load is

(a) 1.33 A (b) 2.7 A
(c) 0.67 A (d) 1.11 A

43. The angular width of the central maximum in Fraunhofer diffraction for light with a wavelength of 6000 Å is θ_0. If the same slit is illuminated with another monochromatic light and the angular width is decreased by 30% , then the wavelength of this new light is

(a) 1800 Å (b) 3000 Å
(c) 4200 Å (d) 6000 Å

44. A body with a mass of 1 g and a charge of 10^{-8} C moves between two points, P and Q. The electric potentials at P and Q are 600 V and 0 V respectively. If the body's velocity at point Q is 20 cm/s, then its velocity at point P (in m/s) is

(a) $\sqrt{0.56}$ (b) $\sqrt{0.056}$
(c) $\sqrt{5.6}$ (d) $\sqrt{0.028}$

45. In the nuclear reaction stated below.

$${}^{23}_{10}\text{Ne} \longrightarrow {}^{23}_{11}\text{Na} + {}^{0}_{-1}e + Q$$

The maximum kinetic energy of the electrons emitted will be

$(m({}^{23}_{10}\text{Ne}) = 22.994466$ u,

$m({}^{23}_{11}\text{Na}) = 22.989770$ u)

(a) 4.374 MeV (b) 0.4374 MeV
(c) 43.74 MeV (d) 220 MeV

Response Index

01 ⓐ ⓑ ⓒ ⓓ	14 ⓐ ⓑ ⓒ ⓓ	27 ⓐ ⓑ ⓒ ⓓ	40 ⓐ ⓑ ⓒ ⓓ
02 ⓐ ⓑ ⓒ ⓓ	15 ⓐ ⓑ ⓒ ⓓ	28 ⓐ ⓑ ⓒ ⓓ	41 ⓐ ⓑ ⓒ ⓓ
03 ⓐ ⓑ ⓒ ⓓ	16 ⓐ ⓑ ⓒ ⓓ	29 ⓐ ⓑ ⓒ ⓓ	42 ⓐ ⓑ ⓒ ⓓ
04 ⓐ ⓑ ⓒ ⓓ	17 ⓐ ⓑ ⓒ ⓓ	30 ⓐ ⓑ ⓒ ⓓ	43 ⓐ ⓑ ⓒ ⓓ
05 ⓐ ⓑ ⓒ ⓓ	18 ⓐ ⓑ ⓒ ⓓ	31 ⓐ ⓑ ⓒ ⓓ	44 ⓐ ⓑ ⓒ ⓓ
06 ⓐ ⓑ ⓒ ⓓ	19 ⓐ ⓑ ⓒ ⓓ	32 ⓐ ⓑ ⓒ ⓓ	45 ⓐ ⓑ ⓒ ⓓ
07 ⓐ ⓑ ⓒ ⓓ	20 ⓐ ⓑ ⓒ ⓓ	33 ⓐ ⓑ ⓒ ⓓ	
08 ⓐ ⓑ ⓒ ⓓ	21 ⓐ ⓑ ⓒ ⓓ	34 ⓐ ⓑ ⓒ ⓓ	
09 ⓐ ⓑ ⓒ ⓓ	22 ⓐ ⓑ ⓒ ⓓ	35 ⓐ ⓑ ⓒ ⓓ	
10 ⓐ ⓑ ⓒ ⓓ	23 ⓐ ⓑ ⓒ ⓓ	36 ⓐ ⓑ ⓒ ⓓ	
11 ⓐ ⓑ ⓒ ⓓ	24 ⓐ ⓑ ⓒ ⓓ	37 ⓐ ⓑ ⓒ ⓓ	
12 ⓐ ⓑ ⓒ ⓓ	25 ⓐ ⓑ ⓒ ⓓ	38 ⓐ ⓑ ⓒ ⓓ	
13 ⓐ ⓑ ⓒ ⓓ	26 ⓐ ⓑ ⓒ ⓓ	39 ⓐ ⓑ ⓒ ⓓ	

Performance Scanner

> 90% Excellent !	You have mastered the NEET syllabus (12th). The concepts of this syllabus are on your fingertips. Maintain this momentum.
76-90% Very Good !	You have a good command over the NEET syllabus (12th). Revise it again after a few days and enhance your performance.
60-75% Good !	You have a wide scope to learn for the NEET syllabus (12th). Revise it again.
<60% Not Satisfactory!	You have a long way ahead of you to master the NEET syllabus (12th). Revise it thoroughly.

Space for Rough Work

Test Booklet No. **3947171**

Test Booklet Code **NSS 3**

MEDACE

NEET (UG)

SELF ASSESSMENT KIT

NEET Stepping Stones 3

(Based on 12th Syllabus)

Name of the Candidate (In Capitals)

____

____

____

Candidate's Signature __________

Invigilator's Signature __________

Facsimile signature stamp of center superintendent__________

Important Instructions

- The test is of 45 minute and the Test Booklet contains 45 multiple choice questions (four options with a single correct answer) from Physics.
- Candidates are advised to read all questions before they start attempting the question paper.
- Each question carries 4 marks. For each correct response, the candidate will get 4 marks. For each incorrect response, one mark will be deducted from the total scores. The maximum marks are 180.
- In the event of candidate marking more than one option, one mark will be deducted.
- Use **Blue/Black Point Pen** only for writing particular on this page/ marking response on answer sheet.

Do not open this Booklet until you start attempting the Test

Physics (Q. No. 1-45)

1. Which of the following is a wrong description about the binding energy of a stable nucleus?
(a) It is the energy required to break a nucleus into its constituent nucleons.
(b) It is the energy released, when free nucleons combine to form a nucleus.
(c) It is the sum of rest mass energies of its nucleons minus the rest mass energy of the nucleus.
(d) It is the sum of kinetic energy of all the nucleons in the nucleus.

2. Total energy density of electromagnetic waves in vacuum is given by the relation
(a) $\frac{1}{2}\frac{E^2}{\varepsilon_0}+\frac{B^2}{2\mu_0}$
(b) $\frac{1}{2}\varepsilon_0 E^2+\frac{1}{2}\mu_0 B^2$
(c) $\frac{E^2+B^2}{2}$
(d) $\frac{1}{2}\varepsilon_0 E^2+\frac{1}{2}\frac{B^2}{\mu_0}$

3. **Statement I** In two consecutive readings of a meter bridge experiment, null point cannot be obtained at same length.
Statement II Temperature coefficient of meter bridge wire and wires of resistance box may be different.
In the light of above statements, choose the most appropriate answer from the options given below.
(a) Both Statement I and Statement II are incorrect.
(b) Statement I is correct and Statement II is incorrect.
(c) Statement I is incorrect and Statement II is correct.
(d) Both Statement I and Statement II are correct.

4. Which of the following waves are used to detect fault or crack on bridges?
(a) Microwaves (b) Infrared waves
(c) X-rays (d) Gamma rays

5. An electron with a mass of 9×10^{-31} kg and a charge of 1.6×10^{-19} C moves initially with a velocity of 5×10^6 m/s parallel to an electric field of intensity 1×10^3 N/C. If the electric field causes the electron to decelerate, then the distance travelled by the electron before it comes to rest for an instant will be
(a) 7 m (b) 7 cm
(c) 0.7 m (d) 0.7 cm

6. A 3 m long wire of uniform thickness with a resistance of 100Ω is connected to a 6 V battery. The potential difference between two points on the wire that are 50 cm apart, will be
(a) 3 V (b) 2 V
(c) 1.5 V (d) 1 V

7. The coil has an inductance $L=10\,\text{H}$ and resistance $R=5\Omega$. When a 10 V battery is applied, it causes the circuit to switch off in 1 ms, then the induced electromotive force (emf) across the inductor is
(a) 2×10^{-4} V (b) 2×10^{4} V
(c) 1.2×10^{4} V (d) 1.2×10^{-4} V

8. If an uncharged capacitor is connected across another charged capacitor, then the energy stored in the combination can be
(a) equal to the energy in the initial capacitor
(b) less than the energy in the initial capacitor
(c) more than the energy in initial capacitor
(d) more or less than the energy in initial capacitor depending on the relative capacities of the both capacitors

9. **Assertion (A)** Reflecting type telescopes give much sharper image than refracting type telescopes.

Reason (R) Dust trapped between tube of telescope makes image dull.

In the light of above statements, choose the most appropriate answer from the options given below.

(a) Both A and R are true and R is the correct explanation of A.

(b) Both A and R are true and R is not the correct explanation of A.

(c) A is true but R is false.

(d) Both A and R are true.

10. In a series electrical circuit containing resistors (R), inductors (L), capacitors (C) and an AC voltage source, the phase difference between voltage and current is $\frac{\pi}{3}$ when either the inductor L or the capacitor C is removed from the circuit. The power factor of the circuit is

(a) 0.5 (b) $\frac{3}{4}$ (c) $\frac{\sqrt{3}}{2}$ (d) 1

11. In free space, a plane electromagnetic wave propagates along the x-direction. Given that the magnetic field **B** at a specific point in space and time is 1.2×10^{-8}T in the $\hat{\mathbf{k}}$-direction, then the electric field **E** (in $\mathrm{Vm^{-1}}$) at that same point will be

(a) $3.6\,\hat{\mathbf{k}}$ (b) $3.6\,\hat{\mathbf{j}}$

(c) $1.2\,\hat{\mathbf{j}}$ (d) $1.2\,\hat{\mathbf{k}}$

12. Given that the Brewster angle for the interface between glass and air is 53.74°. If a ray of light travels from air into glass at an incident angle of 45°, then the angle of refraction is $(\tan 53.74° = \sqrt{2})$

(a) 30° (b) 45°

(c) 60° (d) 54.74°

13. The equivalent output of the given logic circuit is

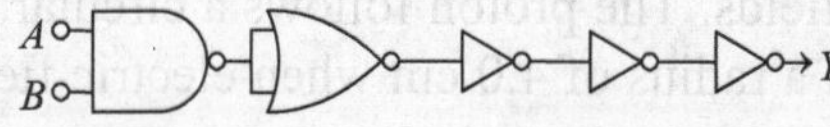

(a) NOR gate (b) NAND gate

(c) OR gate (d) AND gate

14. Two lenses are placed in contact with each other and the focal length of combination is 80 cm. If the focal length of one is 20 cm, then the power of the other will be

(a) 1.66 D (b) 4.00 D

(c) −1.00 D (d) −3.75 D

15. Two similar plano-convex lenses are combined together in three different ways as shown in the adjoining figure. The ratio of the focal lengths in three cases will be

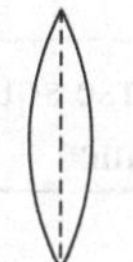  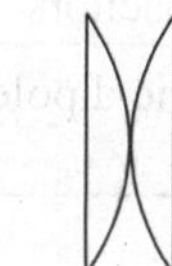

(a) 2:2:1 (b) 1:1:1

(c) 1:2:2 (d) 2:1:1

16. Given the mass of a $_{20}\mathrm{Ca}^{40}$ nucleus is 39.9625894u, the mass of a neutron is 1.008665u and the mass of a proton is 1.007825u, then binding energy per nucleon for the $_{20}\mathrm{Ca}^{40}$ nucleus is

(a) 9.54 MeV / N

(b) 8.34 MeV / N

(c) 8.12 MeV / N

(d) 7.94 MeV / N

17. In a full wave junction diode rectifier, an AC voltage with an rms value of 20V is applied to the primary winding of a step-up transformer with a turn ratio of 1 : 2. The DC voltage of the rectified output is

(a) 24 V (b) 30 V

(c) 42 V (d) 36 V

18. The impedance of the given L-C-R circuit is

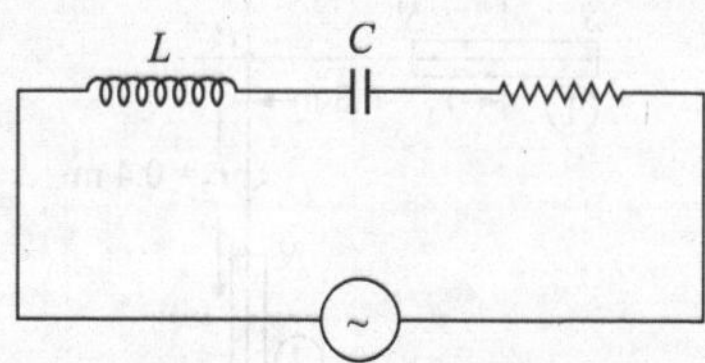

(a) 200 Ω (b) 300 Ω

(c) 500 Ω (d) 800 Ω

19. Match the Column I with Column II and select the correct answer from the codes given below.

Column I	Column II
A. Coulomb force and gravitational force, both follow	1. charge on each capacitor is same
B. In series combination of capacitors	2. potential difference across each capacitor is same
C. In parallel combination of capacitors	3. stable equilibrium
D. Electric dipole	4. inverse square law of distance

Codes

	A	B	C	D
(a)	4	1	2	3
(b)	1	2	3	4
(c)	2	3	4	1
(d)	4	1	3	1

20. In a thermal power plant, electric power is produced at 4000 V. It is transferred using a step-up transformer with number of turns of primary to that in the secondary is 1 : 10. If power is to be supplied at 200 V, then ratio of number of turns of primary to that of secondary in the step-down transformer is

(a) 200 : 1 (b) 150 : 1
(c) 100 : 1 (d) 50 : 1

21. Two short magnets of magnetic moment 2 Am^2 and 5 Am^2 are placed along two lines drawn at right angle to each other on the sheet of paper as shown in the figure. What is the magnetic field at the point of intersection of their axis?

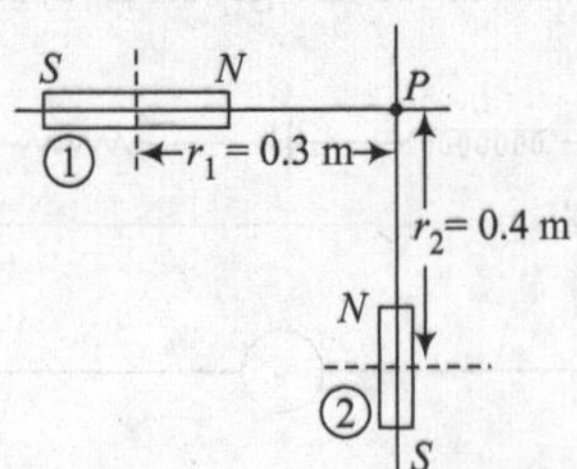

(a) 2.15×10^{-5} T (b) 215×10^{-5} T
(c) 2.15×10^{-3} T (d) 21.5×10^{-5} T

22. In a Young's experiment, one of the slit is covered with a transparent sheet of thickness 3.6×10^{-3}cm due to which position of central fringe shifts to a position originally occupied by 30th bright fringe. Find the refractive index of the sheet, if $\lambda = 6000$ Å.

(a) 1.5 (b) 1.2 (c) 1.3 (d) 1.7

23. An infinite series of point charges, each with a magnitude of q coulombs is arranged along the X-axis at positions $x = 1, 2, 4, 8, \ldots\ldots$ metres. The electric potential and electric field at the origin ($x = 0$) in SI units due to this set of charges are respectively $\frac{1}{4\pi\varepsilon_0}$ times

(a) $2q, \frac{4q}{3}$ (b) $\frac{2q}{3}, \frac{4q}{3}$
(c) $\frac{2q}{3}, 4q$ (d) $2q, 4q$

24. When an electric heater is switched ON, the current flowing through it is plotted against time t. Taking into account, the variation of resistance with temperature, which of the following best represent the variation?

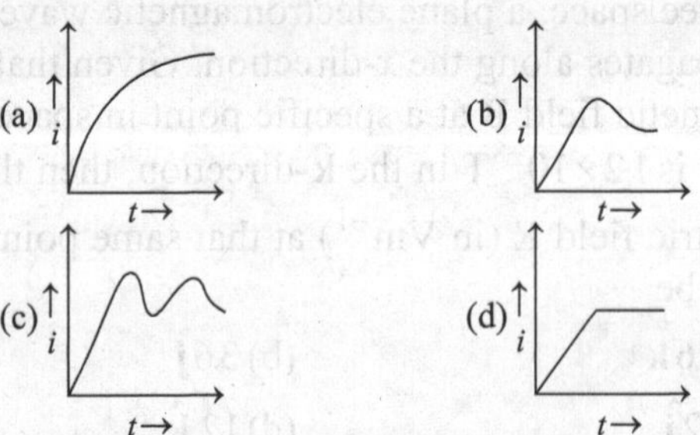

25. The maximum number of possible interference maxima for slit separation equal to thrice the wavelength in YDSE is

(a) 3 (b) 4 (c) 7 (d) 8

26. A proton initially travels without any deflection through a region where perpendicular electric and magnetic fields co-exist, with a velocity of 2×10^5 m / s. The velocity is perpendicular to both the fields. The proton follows a circular trajectory with a radius of 4.0 cm when electric field is deactivated. If mass of proton $= 1.6\times10^{-27}$ kg, then the magnitudes of the electric and the magnetic fields are

(a) 10^{-4} N / C, 0.05 T
(b) 10^{4} N / C, 0.05 T
(c) 10^{5} N / C, 0.04 T
(d) 10^{-5} N / C, 0.04 T

27. An air-cored solenoid with length 30 cm, area of cross-section 25 cm^2 and number of turns 500, carries a current of 2.5 A. The current is suddenly switched-off in a brief time of 10^{-3} s. How much average back emf induced across the ends of the open switch in the circuit? Ignore the variation in magnetic field near the ends of the solenoid.

(a) 6.5 V (b) 7.4 V
(c) 8.2 V (d) 9.3 V

28 A square loop *PQRS* is placed in *XY*- plane with its centre at the origin and carrying a current *I* along the direction as shown in figure. If it is placed in a magnetic field, $\mathbf{B} = B_0(\hat{\mathbf{i}} - \hat{\mathbf{j}})$ and loop is released from rest, then loop will rotate about an axis along

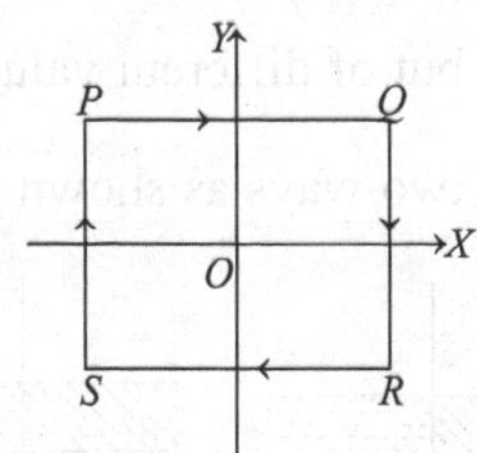

(a) *X*-axis (b) *Z*-axis
(c) *PR* (d) *QS*

29. The magnetic field at the origin due to the current flowing in the wire *ABCD* as shown in figure below is

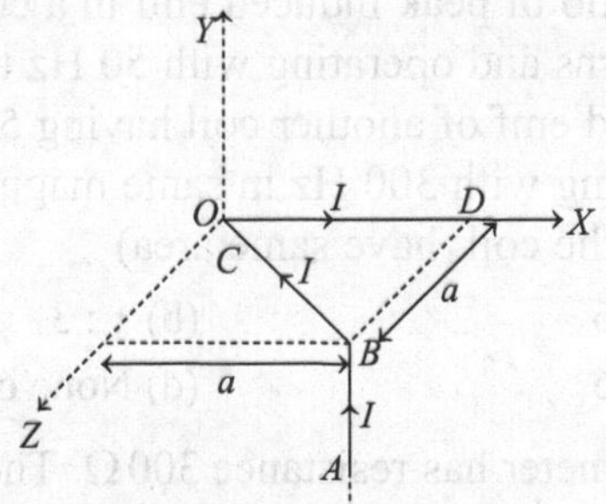

(a) $-\frac{\mu_0 I}{8\pi a}(\hat{\mathbf{i}} + \hat{\mathbf{k}})$ (b) $\frac{\mu_0 I}{2\pi a}(\hat{\mathbf{i}} + \hat{\mathbf{k}})$
(c) $\frac{\mu_0 I}{8\pi a}(-\hat{\mathbf{i}} + \hat{\mathbf{k}})$ (d) $\frac{\mu_0 I}{4\pi a\sqrt{2}}(\hat{\mathbf{i}} + \hat{\mathbf{k}})$

30. Two charges q_1 and q_2 are positioned 30 cm apart, as depicted in the diagram. A third charge q_3 is displaced along an arc of a circle with a radius of 40 cm from point *C* to *D*. The change in the potential energy of the system given by $\frac{q_3}{4\pi\varepsilon_0} \cdot K$, where *K* is

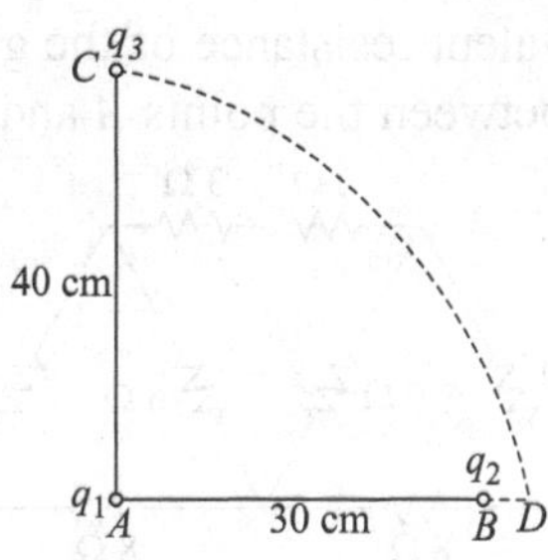

(a) $8q_1$ (b) $6q_1$
(c) $8q_2$ (d) $6q_2$

31. An α-particle, with a mass of 6.4×10^{-27} kg undergoes acceleration by a potential difference of 10^4 V. When it enters perpendicular to a magnetic field of 0.1T over a width of 0.1m, then the change in its direction of motion will be

(a) 60° (b) 45°
(c) 30° (d) 90°

32. In an experiment of resonance tube for finding speed of sound, tuning fork of frequency 480 Hz is used. Resonance occurs at two successive lengths of air column $l_1 = 30$ cm and $l_2 = 70$ cm. Speed of sound obtained will be

(a) 332 m/s (b) 340 m/s
(c) 384 m/s (d) 379 m/s

33. Six 1.1 V cells with internal resistance 3 Ω each, are connected in three parallel branches of two cell each. If the resistance of external circuit is 2Ω, then power consumed by external circuit is

(a) 0.66 W (b) 0.88 W
(c) 0.605 W (d) 0.871 W

34. A solenoid with a uniform winding having a self inductance of 1.8×10^{-4}H and a resistance of 6Ω, is divided into two equal coils. These coils are connected in parallel to a 12V battery with negligible internal resistance. The time constant and the steady state current for this configuration will be
(a) 30 μs, 8 A (b) 10 μs, 8A
(c) 10 μs, 6A (d) 30 μs, 6A

35. The equivalent resistance of the given electrical network between the points *A* and *B* is

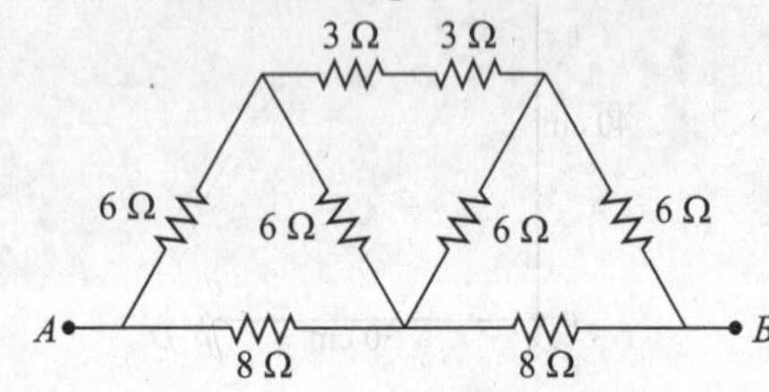

(a) 3 Ω (b) 12 Ω (c) 23 Ω (d) 8 Ω

36. A bi-convex lens composed of two thin plano-convex lenses as shown in figure each with a refractive index of 1.5 and 1.2, respectively. Both lenses having curved surfaces of radius 14 cm. The image distance when the object is positioned at a distance of 40 cm from the lens system, will be

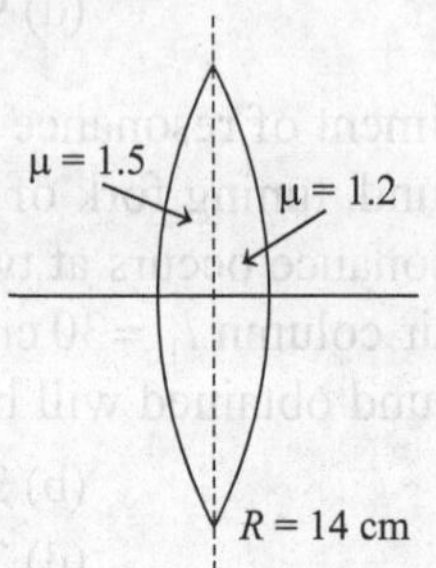

(a) 20 cm (b) – 280 cm
(c) 40 cm (d) 16.5 cm

37. The de-Broglie wavelength of a photon is double that of an electron's de-Broglie wavelength. The speed of the electron is $v_e = \frac{c}{100}$. Then the ratio of the energy of the electron to that of the photon is

(a) $\frac{E_e}{E_p} = 10^{-2}$ (b) $\frac{E_e}{E_p} = 10^{-3}$
(c) $\frac{E_e}{E_p} = 10^{-1}$ (d) $\frac{E_e}{E_p} = 10^{-4}$

38. A laser with an average power output of 16 mW puts out a narrow beam 4.00 mm in diameter. If the rms field are $1/\sqrt{2}$ times of their maximum value, then rms values of *E* and *B* in the beam, respectively are
(a) 978.48 V/m, 3.252 μT
(b) 978.48 V/m, 3.252 mT
(c) 692×10^2 V/m, 2.3 μT
(d) 692 V/m, 2.3 mT

39. The ratio of wavelengths of 1st line of Lyman series to that of 1st line of Balmer series is
(a) 3 : 8 (b) 5 : 27
(c) 7 : 31 (d) 2 : 27

40. Calculate the ratio of capacitance of two capacitors, filled with dielectrics of same dimensions but of different values *K* and $\frac{K}{4}$ arranged in two ways as shown in Fig. (i) and (ii).

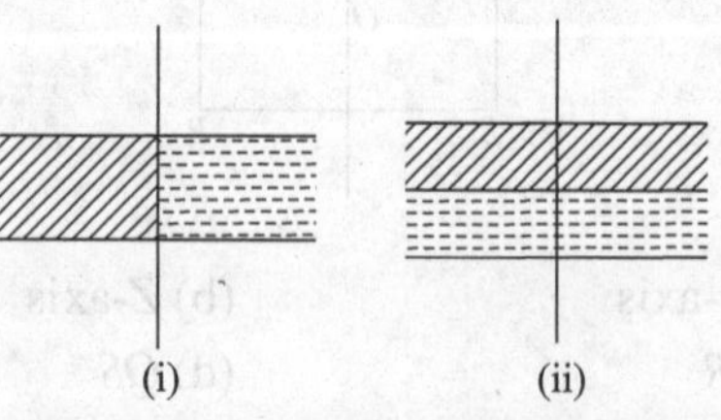

(a) 5 : 2 (b) 25 : 16
(c) 5 : 4 (d) 2 : 5

41. The ratio of peak induced emf in a coil having 100 turns and operating with 50 Hz to that of induced emf of another coil having 50 turns and operating with 300 Hz in same magnetic field is (Both the coil have same area)
(a) 5 : 6 (b) 1 : 3
(c) 1 : 6 (d) None of these

42. A voltmeter has resistance 300 Ω. The operating range of voltmeter is 5 V. If it is to be converted into an ammeter of 5 A, then value of required resistance is
(a) 6.3 Ω (b) 1.5 Ω
(c) 1 1 Ω (d) 1 Ω

43. If the accelerating voltage of electron is multiplied by constant five, then new de-Broglie wavelength

(a) increases 1.8 times

(b) decreases 0.4 times

(c) decreases 0.44 times

(d) increases 0.4 times

44. Two charged particles of charge $+2q$ and $+q$ have masses m and $2m$, respectively. They are kept in uniform electric field and allowed to move for the same time. Find the ratio of their kinetic energies.

(a) 1 : 8 (b) 16 : 1

(c) 2 : 1 (d) 3 : 1

45. Refractive index of a prism is $\sqrt{2}$ and angle of prism is 30°.

One of its refracting face is polished. An incident beam which enters prism from first surface is found reflected back on its path by polished surface. Angle of incidence of incident ray will be

(a) 0° (b) 45°

(c) 60° (d) 90°

Scan for online stepping stones

Response Index

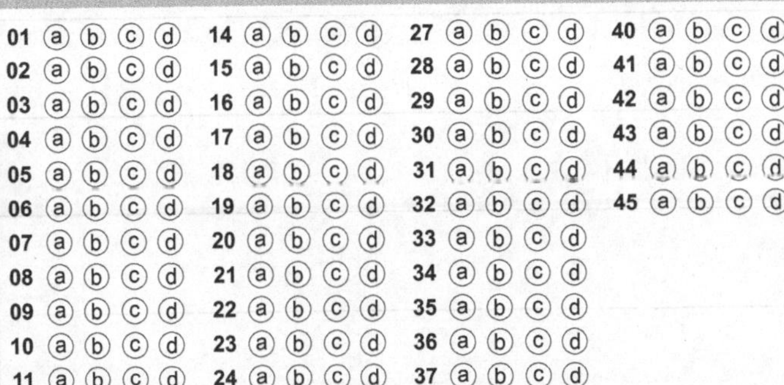

01 ⓐ ⓑ ⓒ ⓓ	14 ⓐ ⓑ ⓒ ⓓ	27 ⓐ ⓑ ⓒ ⓓ	40 ⓐ ⓑ ⓒ ⓓ
02 ⓐ ⓑ ⓒ ⓓ	15 ⓐ ⓑ ⓒ ⓓ	28 ⓐ ⓑ ⓒ ⓓ	41 ⓐ ⓑ ⓒ ⓓ
03 ⓐ ⓑ ⓒ ⓓ	16 ⓐ ⓑ ⓒ ⓓ	29 ⓐ ⓑ ⓒ ⓓ	42 ⓐ ⓑ ⓒ ⓓ
04 ⓐ ⓑ ⓒ ⓓ	17 ⓐ ⓑ ⓒ ⓓ	30 ⓐ ⓑ ⓒ ⓓ	43 ⓐ ⓑ ⓒ ⓓ
05 ⓐ ⓑ ⓒ ⓓ	18 ⓐ ⓑ ⓒ ⓓ	31 ⓐ ⓑ ⓒ ⓓ	44 ⓐ ⓑ ⓒ ⓓ
06 ⓐ ⓑ ⓒ ⓓ	19 ⓐ ⓑ ⓒ ⓓ	32 ⓐ ⓑ ⓒ ⓓ	45 ⓐ ⓑ ⓒ ⓓ
07 ⓐ ⓑ ⓒ ⓓ	20 ⓐ ⓑ ⓒ ⓓ	33 ⓐ ⓑ ⓒ ⓓ	
08 ⓐ ⓑ ⓒ ⓓ	21 ⓐ ⓑ ⓒ ⓓ	34 ⓐ ⓑ ⓒ ⓓ	
09 ⓐ ⓑ ⓒ ⓓ	22 ⓐ ⓑ ⓒ ⓓ	35 ⓐ ⓑ ⓒ ⓓ	
10 ⓐ ⓑ ⓒ ⓓ	23 ⓐ ⓑ ⓒ ⓓ	36 ⓐ ⓑ ⓒ ⓓ	
11 ⓐ ⓑ ⓒ ⓓ	24 ⓐ ⓑ ⓒ ⓓ	37 ⓐ ⓑ ⓒ ⓓ	
12 ⓐ ⓑ ⓒ ⓓ	25 ⓐ ⓑ ⓒ ⓓ	38 ⓐ ⓑ ⓒ ⓓ	
13 ⓐ ⓑ ⓒ ⓓ	26 ⓐ ⓑ ⓒ ⓓ	39 ⓐ ⓑ ⓒ ⓓ	

Performance Scanner

> 90% Excellent !	You have mastered the NEET syllabus (12th). The concepts of this syllabus are on your fingertips. Maintain this momentum.
76-90% Very Good !	You have a good command over the NEET syllabus (12th). Revise it again after a few days and enhance your performance.
60-75% Good !	You have a wide scope to learn for the NEET syllabus (12th). Revise it again.
<60% Not Satisfactory!	You have a long way ahead of you to master the NEET syllabus (12th). Revise it thoroughly.

Space for Rough Work

Test Booklet No. **3947172**

Test Booklet Code **NK01**

NEET Knock Offs 1

(NEET Simulator Test)

Name of the Candidate (In Capitals)

____

____

____

Candidate's Signature ______________

Invigilator's Signature ______________

Facsimile signature stamp of center superintendent______________

Important Instructions

- The test is of 45 minute and the Test Booklet contains 45 multiple choice questions (four options with a single correct answer) from Physics.
- Candidates are advised to read all questions before they start attempting the question paper.
- Each question carries 4 marks. For each correct response, the candidate will get 4 marks. For each incorrect response, one mark will be deducted from the total scores. The maximum marks are 180.
- In the event of candidate marking more than one option, one mark will be deducted.
- Use **Blue/Black Point Pen** only for writing particular on this page/ marking response on answer sheet.

Do not open this booklet until you start attempting the test

Physics (Q. No. 1-45)

1. An electron travels with velocity $\mathbf{v} = 60\,\hat{\mathbf{i}}$ m/s through a point in space, where $\mathbf{B} = 0.1\,\hat{\mathbf{j}}$ T.

The force on the electron at this point is $\mathbf{F} = (9.6 \times 10^{-19}\,\hat{\mathbf{i}} - 9.6 \times 10^{-19}\,\hat{\mathbf{k}})$ N. The electric field $\mathbf{E}$ will be

(a) $-6\,\hat{\mathbf{i}}$ N/C

(b) $(6\,\hat{\mathbf{i}} - 12\,\hat{\mathbf{k}})$ N/C

(c) $(-12\,\hat{\mathbf{i}} + 6\,\hat{\mathbf{k}})$ N/C

(d) $(-6\,\hat{\mathbf{i}} - 6\,\hat{\mathbf{j}} + 6\,\hat{\mathbf{k}})$ N/C

2. Angle between two unit vectors $\hat{\mathbf{a}}$ and $\hat{\mathbf{b}}$ is θ. A unit vector along angle bi-sector of $\hat{\mathbf{a}}$ and $\hat{\mathbf{b}}$ is

(a) $\dfrac{\hat{\mathbf{a}} + \hat{\mathbf{b}}}{\left(2\cos\dfrac{\theta}{2}\right)}$ (b) $\dfrac{\hat{\mathbf{a}} - \hat{\mathbf{b}}}{\left(2\cos\dfrac{\theta}{2}\right)}$

(c) $\dfrac{\hat{\mathbf{a}} + \hat{\mathbf{b}}}{\left(4\cos\dfrac{\theta}{2}\right)}$ (d) $\dfrac{\hat{\mathbf{a}} - \hat{\mathbf{b}}}{\left(4\cos\dfrac{\theta}{2}\right)}$

3. A particle moves in a straight line and its position x at time t is given by $x^2 = 4 + t$. The acceleration of the particle is given by

(a) $\dfrac{1}{x^3}$ (b) $-\dfrac{2}{x^3}$

(c) $\dfrac{1}{4x^3}$ (d) $-\dfrac{1}{4x^3}$

4. If a variable frequency AC source is connected to a capacitor, then with decrease in frequency, the displacement current will

(a) decrease

(b) increase

(c) remains same

(d) depend on the shape of AC waveform

5. Focal length of a convex lens of refractive index 1.5 is 20 cm. Focal length of the lens when immersed in a liquid of refractive index of 1.25 will be

(a) 8 cm (b) 25 cm

(c) 75 cm (d) 50 cm

6. **Statement I** Infrared wave is absorbed by the ozone layer of the atmosphere.

Statement II During the propagation of EM waves in a medium, the electric energy density is equal to magnetic energy density.

In the light of above statements, choose the most appropriate answer from the options given below.

(a) Both Statement I and Statement II are correct.

(b) Both Statement I and Statement II are incorrect.

(c) Statement I is correct but Statement II is incorrect.

(d) Statement I is incorrect but Statement II is correct.

7. Which of the following units denotes the dimensions $[ML^2 / Q^2]$, where Q denotes the electric charge ?

(a) $\dfrac{\text{Wb}}{\text{m}}$

(b) $\dfrac{\text{H}}{\text{m}^3}$

(c) Henry (H)

(d) Weber (Wb)

8. What should be the value of distance d, so that final image is formed on the object itself ?

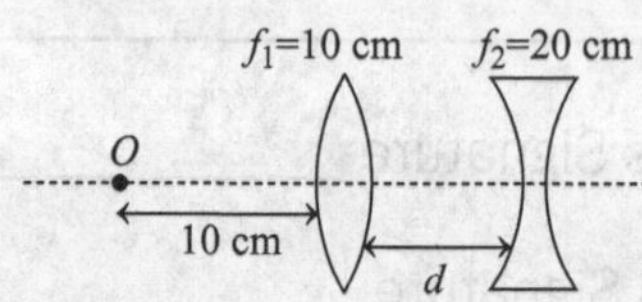

(a) 5 cm (b) 10 cm

(c) 20 cm (d) 25 cm

9. What will be the escape velocity v of a rocket of mass m, if it is situated at mid-point of line joining two planets each of mass M at a distance r ?

(a) $2\sqrt{\dfrac{2GM}{r}}$ (b) $\sqrt{\dfrac{2GM}{r}}$

(c) $\sqrt{\dfrac{GM}{2r}}$ (d) $\dfrac{1}{2}\sqrt{\dfrac{GM}{2r}}$

10. In the given cycle $ABCDA$, the heat required for an ideal monoatomic gas will be

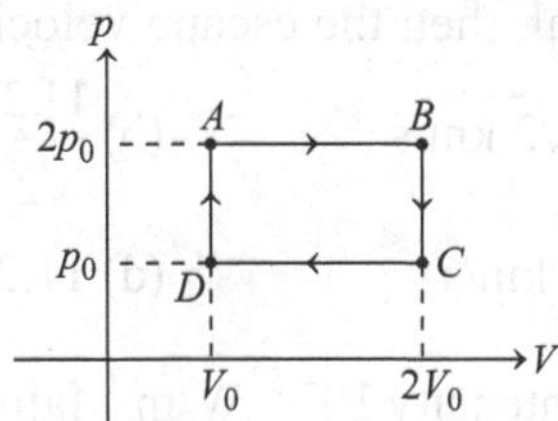

(a) p_0V_0 (b) $\frac{13}{2}p_0V_0$ (c) $\frac{11}{2}p_0V_0$ (d) $4p_0V_0$

11. In the circuit shown below, the diode has 20 Ω forward bias resistance. When V_i increases from 8 V to 12 V, the change in the current will be

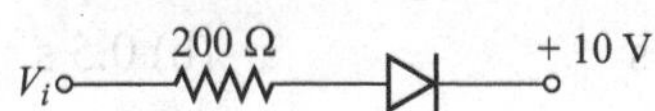

(a) 9 mA (b) 50 mA
(c) 47 mA (d) 40 mA

12. If λ_1, λ_2 and λ_3 are the wavelengths of the waves giving resonance to the fundamental, first and second overtone modes respectively, in a string fixed at both ends. The ratio of the wavelengths, $\lambda_1 : \lambda_2 : \lambda_3$ is

(a) 1 : 2 : 3 (b) 1 : 3 : 5
(c) 6 : 3 : 2 (d) 15 : 5 : 3

13. The drift velocity of free electrons in a conducting wire is of order of 10^{-4} m/s. Yet, the bulb glows very quickly after the switch is turn ON because

(a) the random speed of electrons is very high of order of 10^6 m/s.
(b) the electrons transfer their energy very quickly through collisions.
(c) electric field is set-up in the wire with a speed of light producing a current through each cross-section, almost instantaneously.
(d) the random speed of electrons is very low of order of 10^{-6} m/s.

14. A short bar magnet of magnetic moment 0.15 J/T is placed in a uniform magnetic field of 0.4 T. The potential energy of the magnet in unstable equilibrium is

(a) 6×10^{-4} J (b) -6×10^{-2} J
(c) 6×10^{-2} J (d) -6×10^{-4} J

15. Match List I with List II.

List I	List II
A. Steradian	1. $[ML^3T^{-3}A^{-2}]$
B. Permittivity of free space	2. $[M^{-1}L^{-3}T^4A^2]$
C. Frequency	3. $[M^0L^0T^0]$
D. Resistivity	4. $[M^0L^0T^{-1}]$

Choose the correct option from the codes given below.

Codes

	A	B	C	D
(a)	3	4	2	1
(b)	3	2	4	1
(c)	1	2	4	3
(d)	3	4	1	2

16. For a cell, V-I graph is given below.

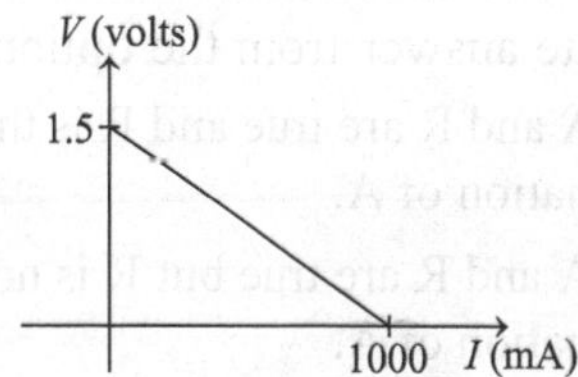

Which of the following options gives correct value of emf of cell and its internal resistance?

(a) 1.5 V, 1.0 Ω (b) 1.5 V, 2.0 Ω
(c) 1.0 V, 1.5 Ω (d) 1.5 V, 1.5 Ω

17. Two co-axial solenoids are made by winding thin insulated wire over a pipe of cross-sectional area $A = 10\,\text{cm}^2$ and length $= 20$ cm. If one of the solenoids has 500 turns and the other has 300 turns, then their mutual inductance is ($\mu_0 = 4\pi \times 10^{-7}\,\text{TmA}^{-1}$)

(a) $2.4\pi \times 10^{-5}$ H (b) $3.0\pi \times 10^{-4}$ H
(c) $4.8\pi \times 10^{-5}$ H (d) $2.4\pi \times 10^{-4}$ H

18. Consider charges and surface S shown below.

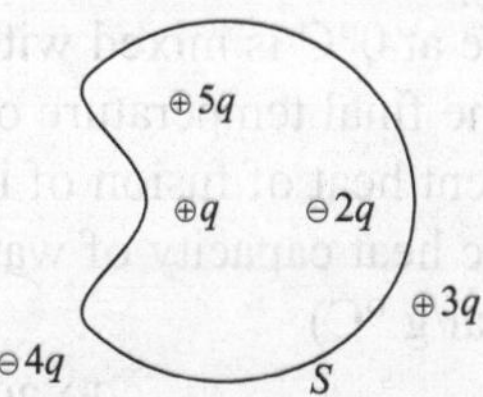

Electric flux through the surface is

(a) $\frac{3q}{\varepsilon_0}$ (b) $\frac{5q}{\varepsilon_0}$

(c) $\frac{4q}{\varepsilon_0}$ (d) $\frac{q}{\varepsilon_0}$

19. A hydrogen atom is given an energy of 10.2 eV. How many spectral lines will be emitted due to transition of electron?

(a) zero (b) 1

(c) 3 (d) 4

20. **Assertion** (A) Moment of inertia of a circular disc of mass M and radius R about X and Y-axes (passing through its plane) and Z-axis which is perpendicular to its plane were found to be I_X, I_Y and I_Z, respectively. The respective radii of gyration about all the three axes will be the same.

Reason (R) A rigid body making rotational motion has fixed mass and shape.

In the light of above statements, choose the most appropriate answer from the options given below.

(a) Both A and R are true and R is the correct explanation of A.

(b) Both A and R are true but R is not the correct explanation of A.

(c) A is true but R is false.

(d) A is false but R is true.

21. The stress *versus* strain graphs for wires of two materials A and B are as shown in the figure. If Y_A and Y_B are the Young's modulii of the materials, then

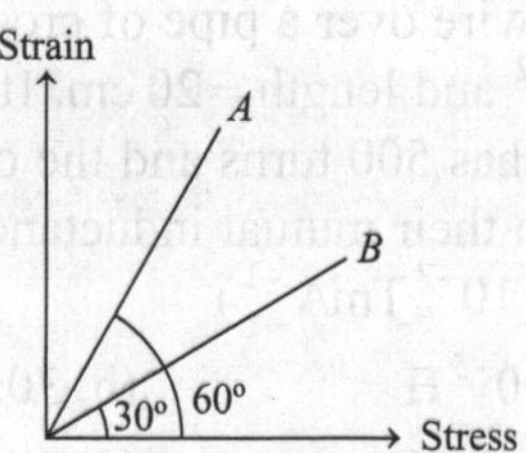

(a) $Y_B = 2Y_A$ (b) $Y_A = Y_B$

(c) $Y_B = 3Y_A$ (d) $Y_A = 3Y_B$

22. 100 g of ice at 0°C is mixed with 100 g of water at 80°C. The final temperature of the mixture is (Given, latent heat of fusion of ice, $L_f = 80$ cal/g and specific heat capacity of water, $S_{water} = 1$ cal/g °C)

(a) 0°C (b) 20°C

(c) 40°C (d) 60°C

23. The escape velocity is 11.2 km/s. If a body is to be projected in a direction making an angle 60° to the vertical, then the escape velocity will be

(a) $11.2 \times \sqrt{2}$ km/s (b) $\frac{11.2}{\sqrt{2}}$ km/s

(c) $11.2\sqrt{3}$ km/s (d) 11.2 km/s

24. Light of intensity 10^{-5} W/m^2 falls on sodium photocell of surface area 2 cm^2 and work function 2 eV. Assume that only top 5-layers of sodium absorbs the incident energy and effective atomic area of sodium atom is 10^{-20} m^2. The time required for photo emission considering wave picture of light will be nearly

(a) 10.5 s (b) 0.5 s

(c) 0.5 h (d) 0.5 yr

25. If an electron in $n = 4$ orbit of hydrogen atom jumps down to $n = 3$ orbit, the amount of energy released and the wavelength of radiation emitted are

(a) 0.66 eV; 1.88×10^{-6} m

(b) 1.89 eV; 1.98×10^{-7} m

(c) 0.29 eV; 1.78×10^{-5} m

(d) 0.98 eV; 0.93×10^{-6} m

26. At the time of an adiabatic process, the pressure of a gas is proportional to the cube of its absolute temperature. The value of $\frac{C_p}{C_V}$ for that gas is

(a) $\frac{9}{2}$ (b) $\frac{7}{2}$

(c) $\frac{5}{3}$ (d) $\frac{3}{2}$

27. If the frequency of incident photon on metal surface is doubled, then stopping potential will become

(a) doubled

(b) less than double

(c) more than double

(d) less than existing value

28. If the coefficient of volume expansion of brass is 6×10^{-5} °C^{-1}, then fractional change in its density for a 60°C rise in temperature will be

(a) 2×10^{-6}
(b) 10^{-6}
(c) 3.6×10^{-5}
(d) -3.6×10^{-3}

29. The equivalent resistance between points P and Q, if value of each resistor is R, is $\frac{NR}{6}$. The value of N is

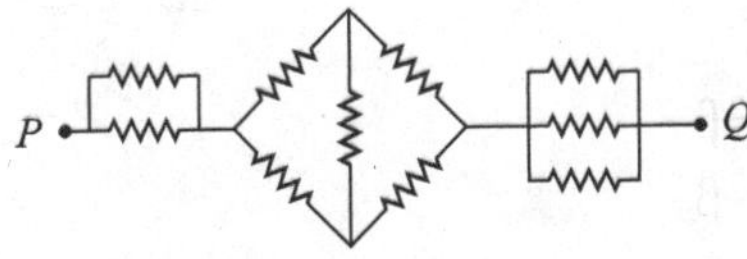

(a) 3
(b) 2
(c) 11
(d) 6

30. In the network shown below, the value of V_0 and I_D is

+12V Si Ge V_0 5.6 kΩ

(a) 12 V, 0 A
(b) 12 V, 1.96 mA
(c) 0 V, 0 A
(d) 11 V, 1.96 mA

31. **Assertion** (A) For an electric bulb connected in series with a variable capacitor and AC source, its brightness increases with increase in capacitance.

Reason (R) Capacitive reactance decreases with increase is capacitance of capacitor.

In the light of above statements, choose the most appropriate answer from the options given below.

(a) Both A and R are true and R is the correct explanation of A.
(b) Both A and R are true but R is not the correct explanation of A.
(c) A is true but R is false.
(d) A is false but R is true.

32. In YDSE, monochromatic light falls on a screen 1.80 m from two slits separated by 2.08 mm. The first and second order bright fringes are separated by 0.553 mm. The wavelength of light used is

(a) 520 nm
(b) 639 nm
(c) 715 nm
(d) 579 nm

33. Infinite long wire have a linear charge density of 0.2 C/m. Find the electric field intensity at a distance of 2 m from wire.

(a) 1.8×10^9 V/m
(b) 0.9×10^9 V/m
(c) 2.7×10^9 V/m
(d) 0.3×10^5 V/m

34. The three wire loops shown in the figure below have same width and vertical edge lengths of $L, 2L$ and $3L$. They will move with the same speed into a region of uniform magnetic field **B** directed in to page. Rank them according to the maximum magnitude of the induced emf, greatest to least.

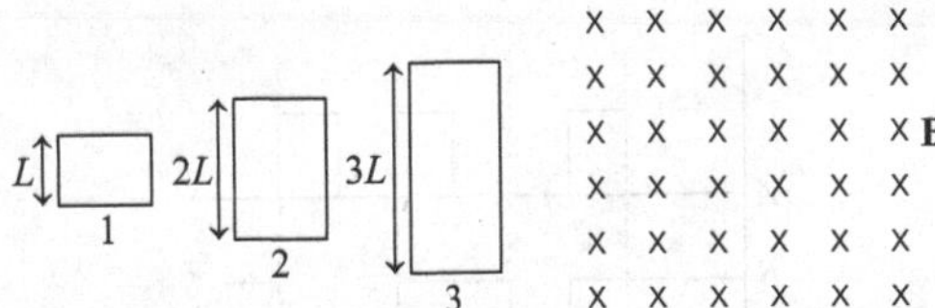

(a) $e_1 > e_2 > e_3$
(b) $e_3 > e_1 > e_2$
(c) $e_3 > e_2 > e_1$
(d) $e_2 > e_3 > e_1$

35. A block is attached to one end of a spring which executes harmonic motion about an equilibrium position with an amplitude A. Its speed as it passes through the equilibrium position is v. If spring is extended to $2A$ and released, then the speed of the block passing through the equilibrium position will be

(a) $2v$
(b) $4v$
(c) $\sqrt{3}v$
(d) $3v$

36. A resistance of 10Ω draws power 150 W when connected to an AC source. If an inductor is now placed in series with the resistance, such that the impedance of the circuit becomes 20Ω, then the power drawn and inductive reactance are respectively,

(a) 37.5 W, 10Ω (b) 37.5 W, $10\sqrt{3}\ \Omega$
(c) 75 W, 10Ω (d) 75 W, $10\sqrt{3}\ \Omega$

37. In an *L-R* series circuit, resistance is *R* and inductive reactance $X_L = 3R$. When a capacitor is added in a circuit such that $X_C = 2R$, the ratio of initial and final power factors of circuit is

(a) $\sqrt{3}$ (b) $\sqrt{5}$
(c) $1/\sqrt{3}$ (d) $1/\sqrt{5}$

38. Identify the correct output signal *Y* in the given combination of gates for the given inputs *A* and *B* shown in the figure.

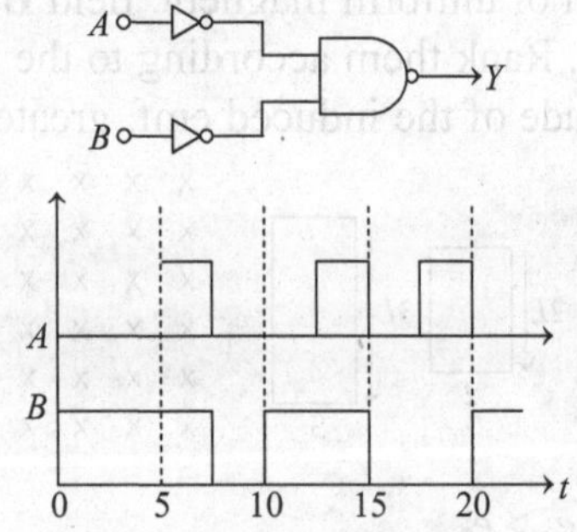

(a)

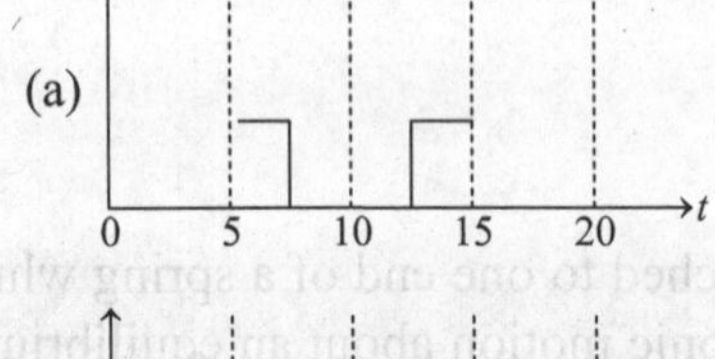

(b)

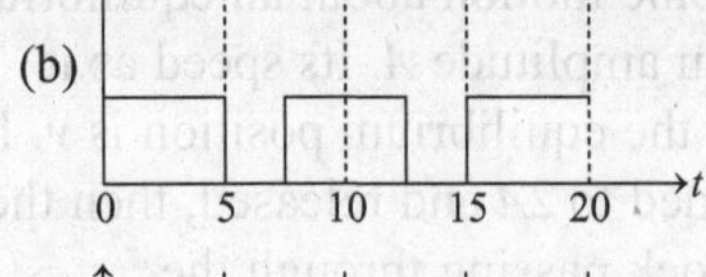

(c)
(d)

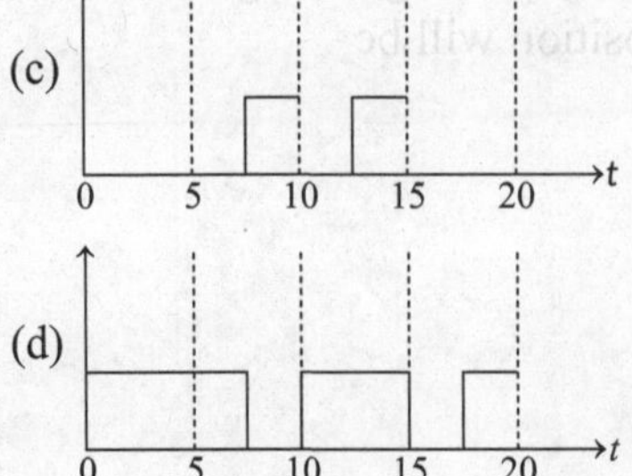

39. Two pith balls with mass *m* are suspended from insulating threads. The charges on the left pith ball and right pith ball are *Q* and 2*Q*, respectively. The situation of equilibrium of both balls has been shown in the following figure. So, correct relation between α and β is

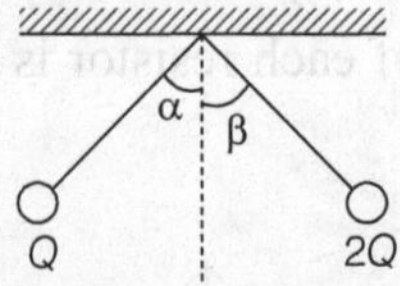

(a) $\alpha = \beta$
(b) $\alpha > \beta$
(c) $\alpha < \beta$
(d) None of the above

40. The equivalent capacitance of the arrangement shown in the figure below is $\frac{3\varepsilon_0 A}{d}$. The value of K_3 is

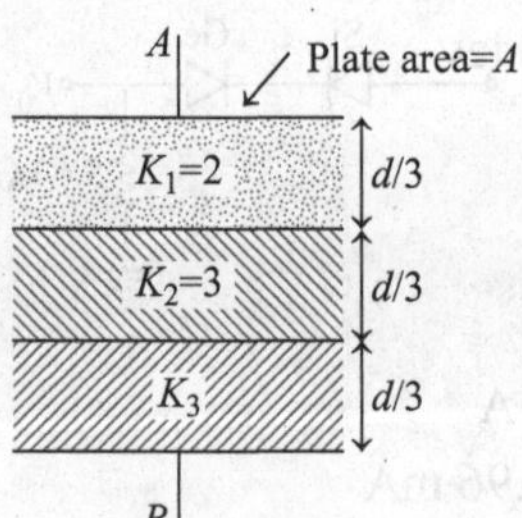

(a) 1 (b) 2
(c) 3 (d) 18

41. The rms current in an AC circuit is 4 A. If the wattless current be 2 A. What is power factor?

(a) 1/2
(b) $\sqrt{3}/2$
(c) $1/\sqrt{3}$
(d) $\sqrt{3}$

42. A block of mass *m* slides down on an inclined plane of slope angle θ with constant velocity. If block is projected up the same plane with an initial velocity v_0, then distance travelled by block along the incline in upward motion before coming to rest is

(a) $\frac{v_0^2}{2g\sin\theta}$ (b) $\frac{v_0^2}{4g\sin\theta}$

(c) $\frac{v_0^2}{4g}$ (d) $\frac{v_0^2}{8\sin\theta}$

43. A ball of mass 0.5 kg is thrown vertically upwards with a speed u from a tower of height 80 m. The time taken by the particle to hit the ground is 4 times the time taken by it to reach the highest point of its path. The initial kinetic energy of ball is (Take, $g = 9.8 \text{ m/s}^2$)

(a) 14 J (b) 24.5 J

(c) 39.2 J (d) 49 J

44. The trajectory of a stone that has been launched from ground is shown in figure given below. It flies just over the wall in 1 s which is 30 m away from the projection. If the time of flight of the stone is 8 s, then its projection velocity is (take, $g = 10 \text{ m/s}^2$)

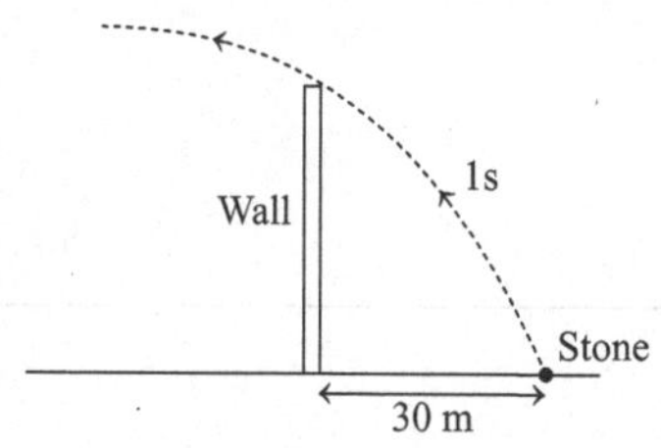

(a) 30 m/s

(b) 40 m/s

(c) 50 m/s

(d) $10\sqrt{3}$ m/s

45. A boy sits stationary at one end of a long trolley moving uniformly with a speed 20 km/h on a smooth horizontal floor. If the boy gets up and runs with a speed 3 km/h on the trolley in the same direction, then speed of the centre of mass of the (trolley + boy) system is

(a) 3 km/h (b) 17 km/h

(c) 20 km/h (d) 23 km/h

Response Index

01 ⓐ ⓑ ⓒ ⓓ	14 ⓐ ⓑ ⓒ ⓓ	27 ⓐ ⓑ ⓒ ⓓ	40 ⓐ ⓑ ⓒ ⓓ
02 ⓐ ⓑ ⓒ ⓓ	15 ⓐ ⓑ ⓒ ⓓ	28 ⓐ ⓑ ⓒ ⓓ	41 ⓐ ⓑ ⓒ ⓓ
03 ⓐ ⓑ ⓒ ⓓ	16 ⓐ ⓑ ⓒ ⓓ	29 ⓐ ⓑ ⓒ ⓓ	42 ⓐ ⓑ ⓒ ⓓ
04 ⓐ ⓑ ⓒ ⓓ	17 ⓐ ⓑ ⓒ ⓓ	30 ⓐ ⓑ ⓒ ⓓ	43 ⓐ ⓑ ⓒ ⓓ
05 ⓐ ⓑ ⓒ ⓓ	18 ⓐ ⓑ ⓒ ⓓ	31 ⓐ ⓑ ⓒ ⓓ	44 ⓐ ⓑ ⓒ ⓓ
06 ⓐ ⓑ ⓒ ⓓ	19 ⓐ ⓑ ⓒ ⓓ	32 ⓐ ⓑ ⓒ ⓓ	45 ⓐ ⓑ ⓒ ⓓ
07 ⓐ ⓑ ⓒ ⓓ	20 ⓐ ⓑ ⓒ ⓓ	33 ⓐ ⓑ ⓒ ⓓ	
08 ⓐ ⓑ ⓒ ⓓ	21 ⓐ ⓑ ⓒ ⓓ	34 ⓐ ⓑ ⓒ ⓓ	
09 ⓐ ⓑ ⓒ ⓓ	22 ⓐ ⓑ ⓒ ⓓ	35 ⓐ ⓑ ⓒ ⓓ	
10 ⓐ ⓑ ⓒ ⓓ	23 ⓐ ⓑ ⓒ ⓓ	36 ⓐ ⓑ ⓒ ⓓ	
11 ⓐ ⓑ ⓒ ⓓ	24 ⓐ ⓑ ⓒ ⓓ	37 ⓐ ⓑ ⓒ ⓓ	
12 ⓐ ⓑ ⓒ ⓓ	25 ⓐ ⓑ ⓒ ⓓ	38 ⓐ ⓑ ⓒ ⓓ	
13 ⓐ ⓑ ⓒ ⓓ	26 ⓐ ⓑ ⓒ ⓓ	39 ⓐ ⓑ ⓒ ⓓ	

Performance Scanner

> 90% Excellent !	You have mastered the NEET syllabus. The concepts of this entire syllabus are on your fingertips. Maintain this momentum.
76-90% Very Good !	You have a good command over the entire NEET syllabus. Revise it again after a few days to enhance your performance.
60-75% Good !	You have a wide scope to learn for the entire NEET syllabus. Revise it again.
<60% Not Satisfactory!	You have a long way ahead of you to master the entire NEET syllabus. Revise it thoroughly.

Scan to fill up online OMR and get AI based Rank prediction on performance

Space for Rough Work

Test Booklet No. 3947173

Test Booklet Code NK02

MEDACE

NEET (UG)

SELF ASSESSMENT KIT

NEET Knock Offs 2

(NEET Simulator Test)

Name of the Candidate (In Capitals)

____

____

____

Candidate's Signature ____________

Invigilator's Signature ____________

Facsimile signature stamp of center superintendent____________

Important Instructions

- The test is of 45 minute and the Test Booklet contains 45 multiple choice questions (four options with a single correct answer) from Physics.
- Candidates are advised to read all questions before they start attempting the question paper.
- Each question carries 4 marks. For each correct response, the candidate will get 4 marks. For each incorrect response, one mark will be deducted from the total scores. The maximum marks are 180.
- In the event of candidate marking more than one option, one mark will be deducted.
- Use **Blue/Black Point Pen** only for writing particular on this page/ marking response on answer sheet.

Do not open this booklet until you start attempting the test

Physics (Q. No. 1-45)

1. Two bodies, A of mass 2 kg and B of mass 5 kg, are dropped from heights 9 m and 25 m, respectively. The ratio of the time taken by them to reach the ground is
(a) 4/5 (b) 3/5 (c) 5/3 (d) 5/4

2. A pipe, 20 cm long, is open at both ends, harmonic mode of the pipe which resonates at 1.6 kHz source is (speed of sound in air is 330 ms^{-1})
(a) fifth (b) second
(c) third (d) sixth

3. If momentum p, area A and time t are taken as fundamental quantities, then the dimensional formula for energy is
(a) $[p^2At^{-2}]$
(b) $[pA^{-1}t^{-2}]$
(c) $[pA^{1/2}t^{-1}]$
(d) $[p^{1/2}At^{-1}]$

4. **Statement I** In adiabatic expansion, temperature of gas always decreases.
Statement II In adiabatic process, exchange of heat is zero.
In the light of above statements, choose the most appropriate answer from the options given below.
(a) Both Statement I and Statement II are correct.
(b) Both Statement I and Statement II are incorrect.
(c) Statement I is correct and Statement II is incorrect.
(d) Statement I is incorrect and Statement II is correct.

5. Surface area of $_{13}Al^{27}$ is S_0, then surface area of Zn^{64} is
(a) $\frac{4}{3}S_0$ (b) $\frac{7}{3}S_0$
(c) $\frac{16}{9}S_0$ (d) $\frac{8}{9}S_0$

6. An electron is moving along positive direction of X-axis with a speed of 6×10^6 ms^{-1}. It enters a region of uniform electric field of 300 V/cm $\hat{\mathbf{j}}$. Magnitude and direction of magnetic field needed to keep electron moving in x-direction will be
(a) 5×10^{-4} T along $-z$-direction
(b) 5×10^{-3} T along $+z$-direction
(c) 5×10^{-3} T along $-y$-direction
(d) 5×10^{-4} T along $+y$-direction

7. When p-n junction diode is forward biased, then
(a) both the depletion region and barrier height are reduced
(b) the depletion region is widened and barrier height is reduced
(c) the depletion region is reduced and barrier height is increased
(d) both the depletion region and barrier height are increased

8. A 27 mW laser beam has an area of cross-section of 20 mm^2. Magnitude of maximum electric field in laser is
(Take, $\varepsilon_0 = 9\times10^{-12}$ SI unit and $c = 3\times10^8$ m/s)
(a) 1 kV/m (b) 0.7 kV/m
(c) 2 kV/m (d) 1.4 kV/m

9. The curve between v_{rms}^2 and absolute temperature T is
(a)
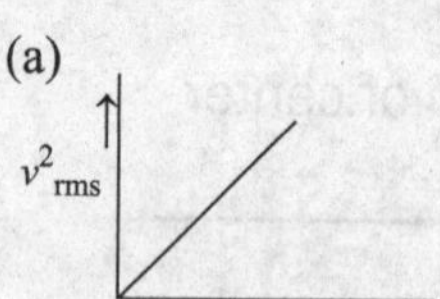

(b)
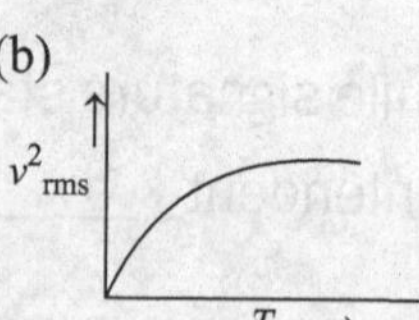

(c)
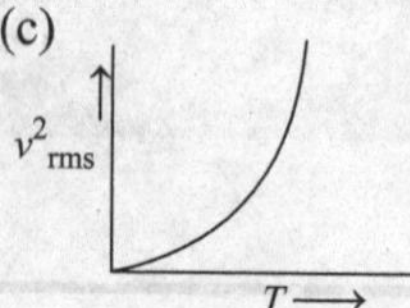

(d)
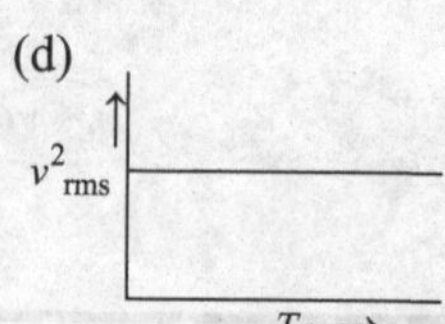

10. A source of 6.6 kW produces 10^{20} photons per second, then source is
(a) an incandescent bulb
(b) a red LED
(c) coolidge tube
(d) a hot iron rod

11. A hydrogen atom emits a photon as its electron jumps from $n=5$ to $n=1$ state. Recoil speed of hydrogen atom will be
(a) 4.17 m/s (b) 2.19 m/s
(c) 3.25 m/s (d) 4.34 m/s

12. In the middle of the depletion layer of reverse biased *p-n* junction, the
(a) electric field is zero
(b) potential is maximum
(c) electric field is maximum
(d) potential is zero

13. In the figure shown below, box of two inputs *A* and *B* consists arrangement of logic gate(s). The input waveforms *A* and *B* and output waveform *Y* has been shown. The Boolean output *Y* is

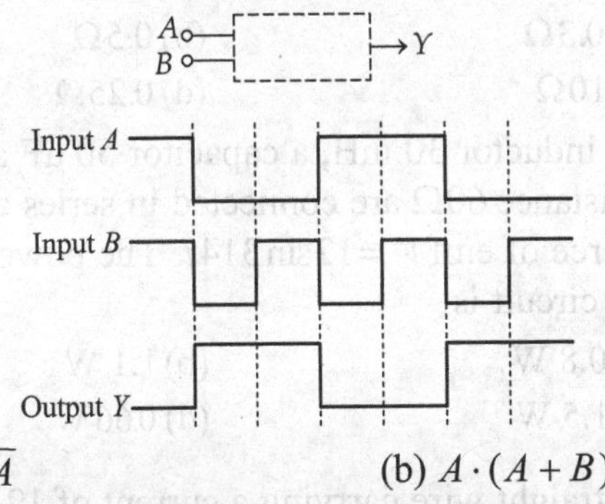

(a) $\overline{A}$ (b) $A \cdot (A+B)$
(c) $A+B$ (d) $A\,\overline{B}+\overline{A}B$

14. **Assertion** (A) Body *P* having mass *M* moving with speed *u* has head-on collision elastically with another body *Q* having mass *m* initally at rest. If $m << M$, body *Q* will have a maximum speed equal to $2u$ after collision.

Reason (R) During elastic collision, the momentum and kinetic energy both are conserved.

In the light of above statements, choose the most appropriate answer from the options given below.
(a) Both A and R are true and R is the correct explanation of A.
(b) Both A and R are true but R is not the correct explanation of A.
(c) A is true but R is false.
(d) A is false but R is true.

15. A spring of stiffness constant *k* and natural length *l* is cut into two parts $\frac{3l}{4}$ and $\frac{l}{4}$ respectively, and an arrangement is made as shown below. If the mass is slightly displaced and then released, the time period of oscillations will be

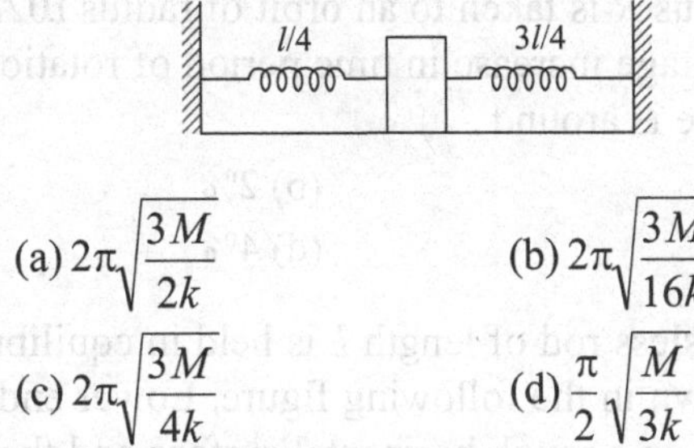

(a) $2\pi\sqrt{\frac{3M}{2k}}$ (b) $2\pi\sqrt{\frac{3M}{16k}}$
(c) $2\pi\sqrt{\frac{3M}{4k}}$ (d) $\frac{\pi}{2}\sqrt{\frac{M}{3k}}$

16. Four plates of equal area *A* are separated by equal distances *d* and arranged as shown in the following figure. The equivalent capacitance is

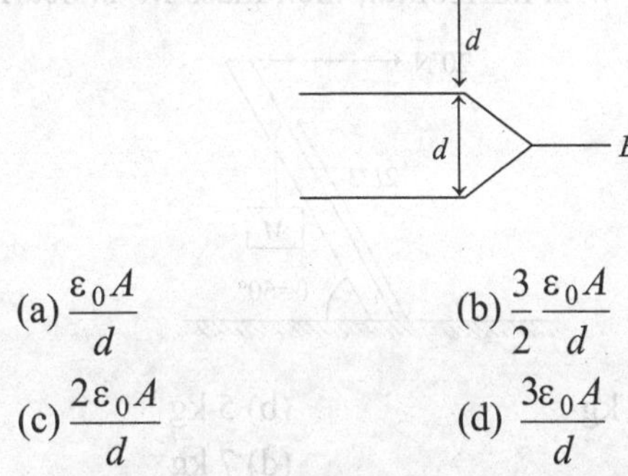

(a) $\frac{\varepsilon_0 A}{d}$ (b) $\frac{3}{2}\frac{\varepsilon_0 A}{d}$
(c) $\frac{2\varepsilon_0 A}{d}$ (d) $\frac{3\varepsilon_0 A}{d}$

17. A particle is projected from ground. The graph between its vertical velocity v_y and time *t* is shown in the figure. The maximum height attained by particle is (Take, $g=10\text{ m/s}^2$)

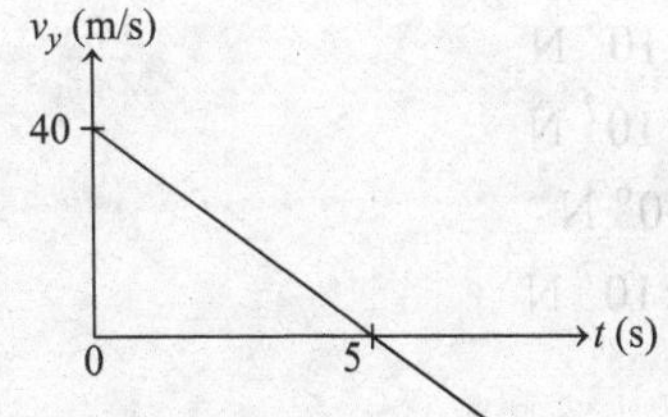

(a) 40 m (b) 80 m
(c) 100 m (d) 200 m

18. The water drops fall at regular intervals from a tap 20 m above the ground. The third drop is leaving the tap at instant the first drop touches the ground. The height of second drop at that instant is
(a) 5 m (b) 15 m
(c) 8 m (d) 7 m

19. A satellite revolving around the earth in an orbit of radius R is taken to an orbit of radius $1.02R$. Percentage increase in time period of rotation of satellite is around
(a) 1% (b) 2%
(c) 3% (d) 4%

20. A massless rod of length L is held in equilibrium as shown in the following figure. Lower end is placed on a rough horizontal surface and the upper end of the rod is attached to an ideal spring that exerts a force of magnitude of 20 N in negative x-direction. A block of mass M is suspended from the rod at a distance $\frac{2L}{3}$ from bottom end along the rod. If rod makes an angle of 60° with horizontal, then mass M is nearly

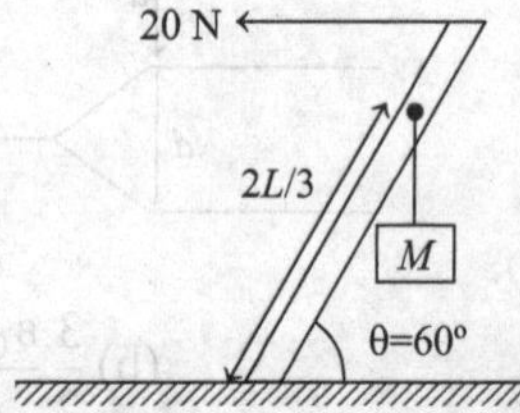

(a) 2.5 kg (b) 5 kg
(c) 0 (d) 7 kg

21. A metal cable with radius 3 cm supports a chairlift at a ski area. If the maximum stress does not to exceed 10^{10} N/m^2, then maximum load the cable can support is
(a) 2.8×10^6 N
(b) 2.8×10^7 N
(c) 4×10^6 N
(d) 4.0×10^7 N

22. The moment of inertia of a body about the given axis is 10 kg-m^2. Initially, the body is at rest. In order to produce a rotational kinetic energy of 980 J, an angular acceleration of 28 rad/s^2 must be applied about that axis for duration of
(a) 0.5 s
(b) 2 s
(c) 4 s
(d) None of these

23. An electric field $\mathbf{E} = 2x\,\hat{\mathbf{i}}\,\text{NC}^{-1}$ exists in a region. A cubical metal box is placed with one of its vertices at origin and sides parallel to coordinate planes. If side of cube is 2 cm, then net flux through the cube will be
(a) 4×10^{-2} Ncm^{2}C^{-1}
(b) 8×10^{-2} Ncm^{2}C^{-1}
(c) 0.5×10^{-2} Ncm^{2}C^{-1}
(d) zero

24. A battery of emf 12 V and internal resistance 0.3Ω is connected across a variable resistance R. The value of R for which the power delivered in it is maximum, is
(a) 0.3Ω (b) 0.5Ω
(c) 1.0Ω (d) 0.25Ω

25. An inductor 30 mH, a capacitor 50 μF and a resistance 60Ω are connected in series across a source of emf $V = 12\sin 314t$. The power loss in the circuit is
(a) 0.8 W (b) 1.1 W
(c) 1.5 W (d) 0.66 W

26. A straight wire carrying a current of 12 A is bent into a semi-circular loop of radius 2 cm. What will be magnetic field at the centre of the semi-circular loop?

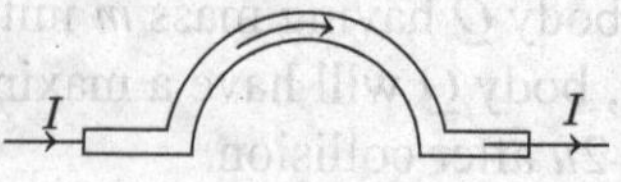

(a) $\mathbf{B} = 1.9 \times 10^{-4}$ T, ⊙
(b) $\mathbf{B} = 1.9 \times 10^{4}$ T, ⊙
(c) $\mathbf{B} = 1.9 \times 10^{-4}$ T, ⊗
(d) $\mathbf{B} = 1.9 \times 10^{4}$ T, ⊗

27. A charge passing through a resistor is varying with time as shown in the figure. The amount of heat generated H in time t as a function of time is best represented by

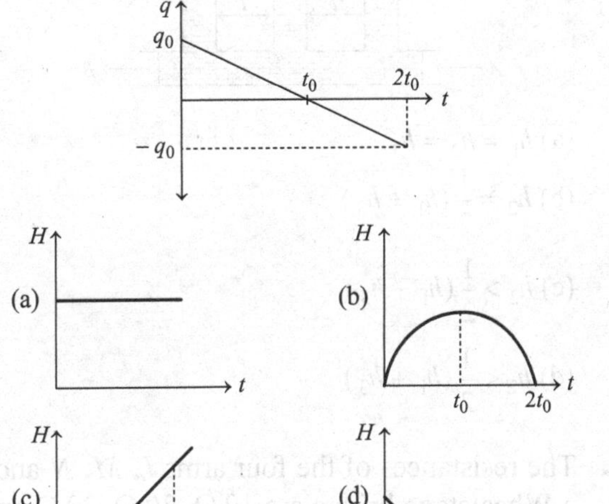

28. Which of the following is not a characteristic of diamagnetic materials?

(a) The diamagnetic materials are repelled by a magnetic field.

(b) Susceptibility of diamagnetic materials is inversely proportional to the absolute temperature.

(c) Magnetic susceptibility of diamagnetic materials is small and negative.

(d) Diamagnetic materials move from a region of strong magnetic field to weak magnetic field.

29. A planar loop of wire rotates in a uniform magnetic field. Initially at $t = 0$, the plane of the loop is perpendicular to the magnetic field. If it rotates with a period of 10 s about an axis in its plane, then the magnitude of induced emf will be maximum at

(a) 10.0 s (b) 2.5 s

(c) 3.0 s (d) 5.0 s

30. The intensity of light through each slit in Young's double slit experiment is I_0. The minimum separation between the two points on the screen where intensities are $2I_0$ and I_0 is (Here, β is fringe width)

(a) $\frac{\beta}{4}$ (b) $\frac{\beta}{3}$

(c) $\frac{\beta}{6}$ (d) $\frac{\beta}{12}$

31. Four rods of different masses and lengths are arranged in XY-plane as shown in the following figure. The centre of mass of such arrangement lies in which of the following mentioned region?

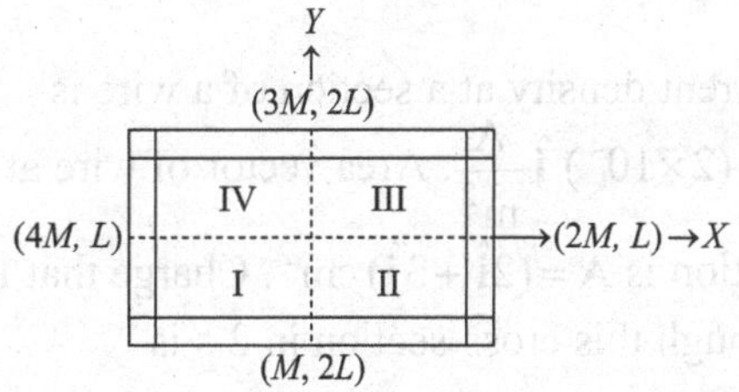

(a) I (b) II

(c) III (d) IV

32. A series L-C-R circuit with $L = 10$ H, $C = 10\,\mu$F and $R = 50\,\Omega$ is connected to a variable frequency 200 V AC source. Column I listed quantities and Column II listed the value of quantities (in SI units) at resonance frequency. Then, match Column I with Column II.

Column I	Column II
A. Impedance $\lvert Z \rvert$ ____ Ω	I. 4000
B. I_{rms} ____ A	II. 200
C. $V_{R_{rms}}$ ____ V	III. 4
D. $V_{L_{rms}}$ ____ V	IV. 50

(a) A-IV, B-III, C-II, D-I

(b) A-II, B-III, C-I, D-IV

(c) A-III, B-II, C-IV, D-I

(d) A-I, B-IV, C-II, D-III

33. If source of light used in YDSE is changed from red to violet, then

(a) fringes come closer

(b) central fringe will be dark

(c) fringes become bright

(d) maxima intensity increases

34. The relation between R and r (internal resistance of the battery) for which the power consumed in the external part of the circuit is maximum?

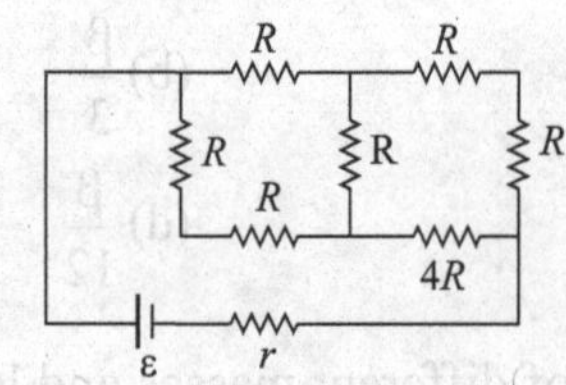

(a) $R = r$
(b) $R = \frac{r}{2}$
(c) $R = 2r$
(d) $R = \frac{3}{2}r$

35. Current density at a section of a wire is $\mathbf{J} = (2\times10^4)\,\hat{\mathbf{j}}\,\frac{\text{A}}{\text{m}^2}$. Area vector of wire at this section is $\mathbf{A} = (2\hat{\mathbf{i}} + 3\hat{\mathbf{j}})\ \text{cm}^2$. Charge that flows through this cross-section in 2 s is
(a) 12 μC
(b) 12 nC
(c) 12 mC
(d) 12 C

36. A block slides on rough horizontal surface with a velocity of 20 m/s. It comes to rest after travelling a distance of 80 m. The coefficient of kinetic friction between block and surface is (Take, $g = 10\ \text{m/s}^2$)
(a) 0.20
(b) 0.25
(c) 0.125
(d) 0.05

37. From top of a tower, two particles are simultaneously projected horizontally in opposite directions. If 30 m/s and 40 m/s are the initial velocities, then the time after which their velocities are mutually perpendicular, is given by (Take, $g = 10\ \text{m/s}^2$)
(a) 5 s
(b) $\sqrt{21}$ s
(c) $2\sqrt{3}$ s
(d) $2\sqrt{7}$ s

38. An electric dipole with dipole moment $\mathbf{p} = (3\hat{\mathbf{i}} + 4\hat{\mathbf{j}})\times10^{-30}$ C-m is placed in an electric field $\mathbf{E} = 4000\,\hat{\mathbf{i}}$ N/C. The dipole is rotated very slowly until its electric dipole moment becomes $(-4\hat{\mathbf{i}} + 3\hat{\mathbf{j}})\times10^{-30}$ C-m. The work done by external torque is equal to
(a) -4×10^{-28} J
(b) 4×10^{-28} J
(c) 2.8×10^{-26} J
(d) -2.8×10^{-26} J

39. An ideal liquid flows through the horizontal pipe *AB*, which is of uniform cross-section. The vertical pipes 1, 2 and 3 are equispaced. The liquid levels in these pipes are at heights h_1, h_2 and h_3 respectively, above *AB*. Liquid flows from *A* to *B* in *AB*. Then, correct relation is

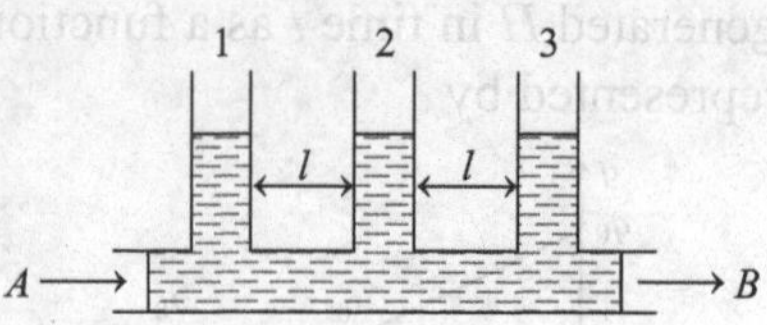

(a) $h_1 = h_2 = h_3$
(b) $h_2 = \frac{1}{2}(h_1 + h_3)$
(c) $h_2 > \frac{1}{2}(h_1 + h_3)$
(d) $h_2 < \frac{1}{2}(h_1 + h_3)$

40. The resistances of the four arms *L*, *M*, *N* and *P* in a Wheatstone bridge are 10 Ω, 30 Ω, 20 Ω and 60 Ω, respectively. The emf and internal resistance of the cell are 7 V and 5Ω, respectively. If the galvanometer resistance is 50 Ω, the current drawn from the cell will be

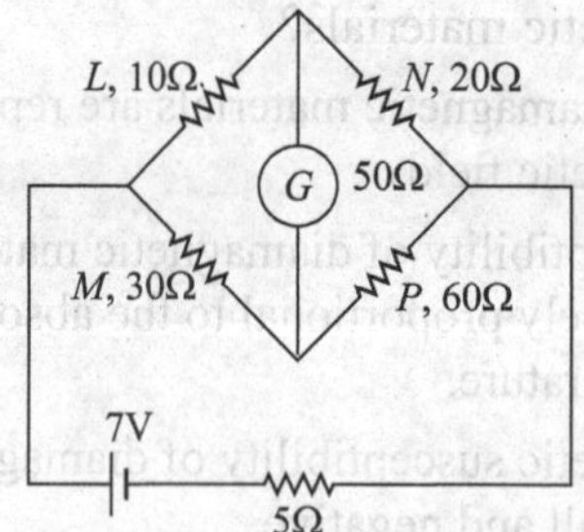

(a) 1.5 A
(b) 2.3 A
(c) 0.25 A
(d) 4.6 A

41. A concave mirror of focal length 48 cm produces a real image which is 12 times the size of the object. The distance of the image from the mirror is
(a) 6.24 m
(b) 7.2 m
(c) 6.24 cm
(d) 7.2 cm

42. A metal surface is illuminated with photons of energies $E_1 = 4$ eV and $E_2 = 2.5$ eV, respectively. The ratio of maximum speeds of the photoelectrons in two cases is 2. Work function of metal surface will be
(a) 2.5 eV
(b) 5 eV
(c) 4 eV
(d) 2 eV

43. When the jaws of a standard vernier are together, the 6th vernier scale division coincides with the 6th main scale division, then the zero error is

(a) – 0.4 mm (b) 0.6 mm
(c) – 0.6 mm (d) 0.4 mm

44. **Statement I** When temperature of a gas is increased 3 times, its pressure also increases 3 times keeping volume constant.

Statement II Pressure of N molecules of an ideal gas contained in a volume V is $p = \frac{2}{3}\frac{N}{V}\left(\frac{1}{2}mv^2\right)$.

In light of above statements, choose the most appropriate answer from the options given below.

(a) Both Statement I and Statement II are correct.
(b) Both Statement I and Statement II are incorrect.
(c) Statement I is correct and Statement II is incorrect.
(d) Statement I is incorrect and Statement II is correct.

45. A bent tube is lowered into a water stream as shown in the following figure. The velocity of the stream relative to the tube is 2.5 m/s. The closed upper end of the tube located at the height 12 cm has a small orifice. The height h up to which water jet spurt is ($g = 9.8 \text{ m/s}^2$)

(a) 0.32 m
(b) 0.2 m
(c) 0.44 m
(d) 0 m

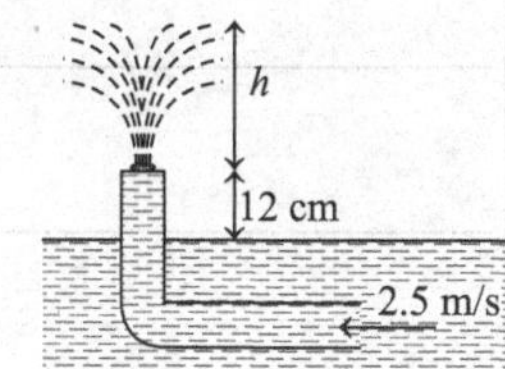

Scan to fill up online OMR and get AI based Rank prediction on performance

Response Index

01 ⓐ ⓑ ⓒ ⓓ	14 ⓐ ⓑ ⓒ ⓓ	27 ⓐ ⓑ ⓒ ⓓ	40 ⓐ ⓑ ⓒ ⓓ
02 ⓐ ⓑ ⓒ ⓓ	15 ⓐ ⓑ ⓒ ⓓ	28 ⓐ ⓑ ⓒ ⓓ	41 ⓐ ⓑ ⓒ ⓓ
03 ⓐ ⓑ ⓒ ⓓ	16 ⓐ ⓑ ⓒ ⓓ	29 ⓐ ⓑ ⓒ ⓓ	42 ⓐ ⓑ ⓒ ⓓ
04 ⓐ ⓑ ⓒ ⓓ	17 ⓐ ⓑ ⓒ ⓓ	30 ⓐ ⓑ ⓒ ⓓ	43 ⓐ ⓑ ⓒ ⓓ
05 ⓐ ⓑ ⓒ ⓓ	18 ⓐ ⓑ ⓒ ⓓ	31 ⓐ ⓑ ⓒ ⓓ	44 ⓐ ⓑ ⓒ ⓓ
06 ⓐ ⓑ ⓒ ⓓ	19 ⓐ ⓑ ⓒ ⓓ	32 ⓐ ⓑ ⓒ ⓓ	45 ⓐ ⓑ ⓒ ⓓ
07 ⓐ ⓑ ⓒ ⓓ	20 ⓐ ⓑ ⓒ ⓓ	33 ⓐ ⓑ ⓒ ⓓ	
08 ⓐ ⓑ ⓒ ⓓ	21 ⓐ ⓑ ⓒ ⓓ	34 ⓐ ⓑ ⓒ ⓓ	
09 ⓐ ⓑ ⓒ ⓓ	22 ⓐ ⓑ ⓒ ⓓ	35 ⓐ ⓑ ⓒ ⓓ	
10 ⓐ ⓑ ⓒ ⓓ	23 ⓐ ⓑ ⓒ ⓓ	36 ⓐ ⓑ ⓒ ⓓ	
11 ⓐ ⓑ ⓒ ⓓ	24 ⓐ ⓑ ⓒ ⓓ	37 ⓐ ⓑ ⓒ ⓓ	
12 ⓐ ⓑ ⓒ ⓓ	25 ⓐ ⓑ ⓒ ⓓ	38 ⓐ ⓑ ⓒ ⓓ	
13 ⓐ ⓑ ⓒ ⓓ	26 ⓐ ⓑ ⓒ ⓓ	39 ⓐ ⓑ ⓒ ⓓ	

Performance Scanner

> 90% Excellent !	You have mastered the NEET syllabus. The concepts of this entire syllabus are on your fingertips. Maintain this momentum.
76-90% Very Good !	You have a good command over the entire NEET syllabus. Revise it again after a few days to enhance your performance.
60-75% Good !	You have a wide scope to learn for the entire NEET syllabus. Revise it again.
<60% Not Satisfactory!	You have a long way ahead of you to master the entire NEET syllabus. Revise it thoroughly.

Space for Rough Work

Test Booklet No. **3947174**

Test Booklet Code **NK03**

MEDACE
NEET (UG)
SELF ASSESSMENT KIT

NEET Knock Offs 3

(NEET Simulator Test)

Name of the Candidate (In Capitals)

____

____

____

Candidate's Signature ____________

Invigilator's Signature ____________

Facsimile signature stamp of center superintendent____________

Important Instructions

- The test is of 45 minute and the Test Booklet contains 45 multiple choice questions (four options with a single correct answer) from Physics.
- Candidates are advised to read all questions before they start attempting the question paper.
- Each question carries 4 marks. For each correct response, the candidate will get 4 marks. For each incorrect response, one mark will be deducted from the total scores. The maximum marks are 180.
- In the event of candidate marking more than one option, one mark will be deducted.
- Use **Blue/Black Point Pen** only for writing particular on this page/ marking response on answer sheet.

Do not open this booklet until you start attempting the test

Physics (Q. No. 1-45)

1. The length and breadth of a rectangular sheet are 16.2 cm and 10.1 cm, respectively. The area of the sheet in appropriate significant figures and error is

(a) $(163.62 \pm 3)\ cm^2$ (b) $(163.6 \pm 2.6)\ cm^2$
(c) $(163.6 \pm 2.6)\ cm^2$ (d) $(164 \pm 3)\ cm^2$

2. Which of the following cannot be changed by an ideal transformer that has different number of turns in its primary and secondary coils?

(a) Resistive loads
(b) Electric current
(c) Electric power
(d) Electric potential difference or voltage

3. If two soap bubbles of different radii are connected by a tube, then

(a) air flows from the smaller bubble to the bigger bubble.
(b) air flows from bigger bubble to the smaller bubble till the sizes are interchanged.
(c) air flows from the bigger bubble to the smaller bubble till the sizes becomes equal.
(d) there is no flow of air.

4. An ideal gas of given mass is kept at constant pressure. By what percentage should the pressure be increased, so as to decrease its volume by 5%?

(a) 2.5% (b) 3.6%
(c) 5% (d) 5.26%

5. Assertion (A) When current flows through a *p-n* junction in forward bias its temperature increases.

Reason (R) In forward bias due to resistance of semiconductor, part of electrical energy is converted into heat energy.

(a) Both A and R are true and R is the correct explanation of A.
(b) Both A and R are true but R is not the correct explanation of A.
(c) A is true but R is false.
(d) A is false but R is true.

6. Two liquids are at temperatures 20°C and 40°C. When same amount of mass of both of them is mixed, the temperature of the mixture is 32°C. The ratio of their specific heats is

(a) 4 : 3 (b) 2 : 5 (c) 3 : 2 (d) 2 : 3

7. Match List I with List II.

	List I		List II
A.	$C - A - B = 0$	1.	
B.	$A - C - B = 0$	2.	
C.	$B - A - C = 0$	3.	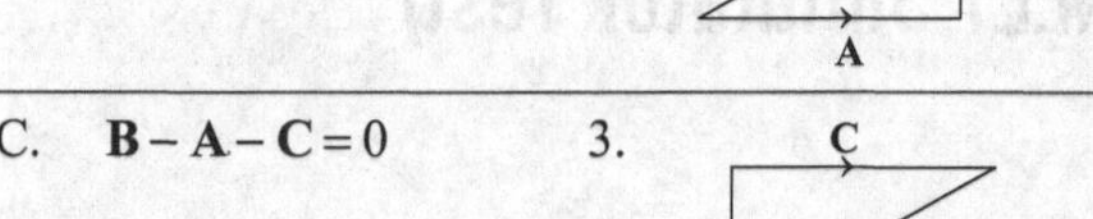
D.	$A + B = -C$	4.	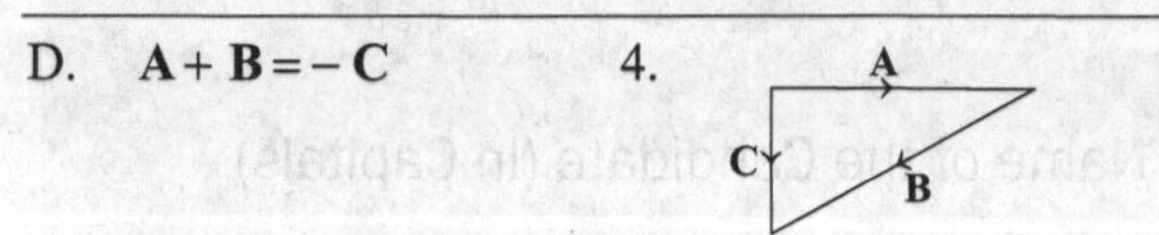

	A	B	C	D
(a)	4	1	3	2
(b)	4	3	1	2
(c)	3	2	4	1
(d)	1	4	2	3

8. The electric field lines due to positive charge has been shown in the following figure. If a small negative charge is released at point *B*, then the difference of potential energy of negative charge between the points *B* and *A* is

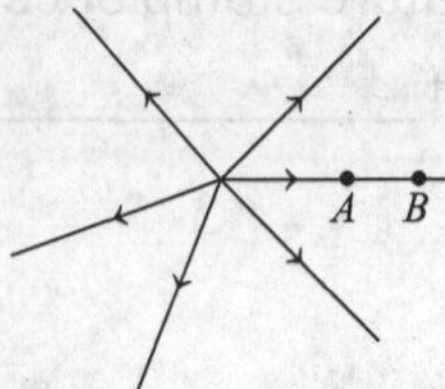

(a) positive
(b) negative
(c) zero
(d) either positive or negative

9. In the circuit shown in the below figure, the current between B and D is zero, the unknown resistance X is of

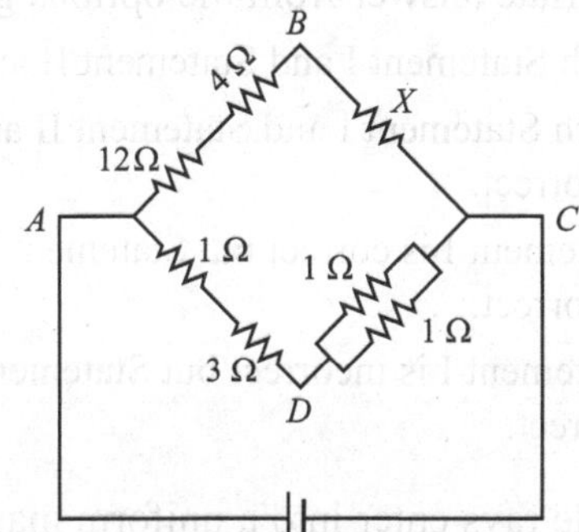

(a) 4Ω
(b) 2Ω
(c) 3Ω
(d) emf of a cell is required to find the value of X

10. A thin lens made of glass $\left(n_g = \frac{3}{2}\right)$ of focal length f_1 in air. This lens when dipped in a liquid of refractive index $\frac{7}{5}$, focal length of lens will become f_2. Ratio of $\frac{f_2}{f_1}$ will be

(a) 1 (b) 5
(c) 7 (d) 9

11. If E and B are the electric field and magnetic field at any instant in an electromagnetic wave, then rate of flow of energy across a unit area at any instant is given as

(a) EB (b) $\frac{EB}{\mu_0}$
(c) $\frac{EB}{\sqrt{\mu_0 \varepsilon_0}}$ (d) $\frac{EB}{c^2}$

12. A particle is at height h from the surface of the earth. If it is fired with a velocity greater than escape velocity parallel to the surface of earth, then trajectory of the projectile is

(a) straight line (b) parabolic
(c) elliptical (d) hyperbolic

13. What will be the minimum radial distance between first orbit and second orbit in He^+ ion, if the de-Broglie wavelength of an electron in first orbit is λ,

(a) 2λ (b) $\frac{2\lambda}{\pi}$
(c) $\frac{\lambda}{2\pi}$ (d) $\frac{\lambda}{4\pi}$

14. If a container filled with liquid is heated, the level of liquid in container is

(a) increases
(b) decreases
(c) remains same
(d) depends on coefficient of volume expansion of container and liquid

15. Position of a particle moving along X-axis is $x = (t^3 - 6t^2 + 9t)$ m, where t is in seconds. Ratio of distance and displacement of particle in first 5 s of journey is

(a) 1:1 (b) 3:5
(c) 7:5 (d) 5:9

16. A charge q is enclosed by an imaginary Gaussian surface.

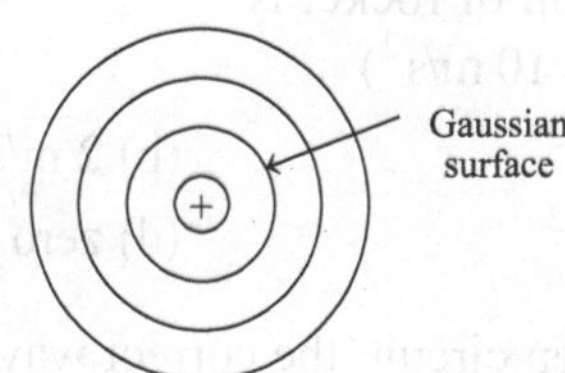

If the radius of Gaussian surface is increasing at a rate $\frac{dr}{dt} = \alpha$, then flux linked with surface is

(a) increasing at a rate, $\frac{d\phi}{dt} = \alpha$
(b) decreasing at a rate, $\frac{d\phi}{dt} = -\alpha$
(c) decreasing at a rate, $\frac{d\phi}{dt} = \frac{1}{k}$
(d) $\frac{q}{\varepsilon_0}$

17. A particle is executing SHM about origin. It has time period of 8 s and amplitude 6 cm. At $t = 0$, particle is at right extreme position, then displacement from origin at $t = 10$ s, is

(a) 0 cm (b) -3 cm
(c) $+3$ cm (d) $+2$ cm

18. If width of one slit in YDSE is slightly increased, then

(a) maximum intensity will decrease and minimum intensity will increase.

(b) maximum intensity will increase and minimum intensity will decrease.

(c) both maximum and minimum intensities will increase.

(d) both maximum and minimum intensities will decrease.

19. A generator produces a voltage that is given by $V = 240\sin 120t$, where t is in seconds. The frequency and rms voltage are

(a) 60 Hz and 240 V

(b) 19 Hz and 120 V

(c) 19 Hz and 170 V

(d) 754 Hz and 70 V

20. The initial mass of a rocket is 2000 kg. If the fuel is burning at the rate of 60 kg/s and gases come out at a speed of 400 m/s relative to rocket, then acceleration of rocket is (Take, $g = 10 \text{ m/s}^2$)

(a) 12 m/s^2 (b) 2 m/s^2

(c) 22 m/s^2 (d) zero

21. In the given circuit, the correct waveform depicting voltage across resistance V_R with time t, is

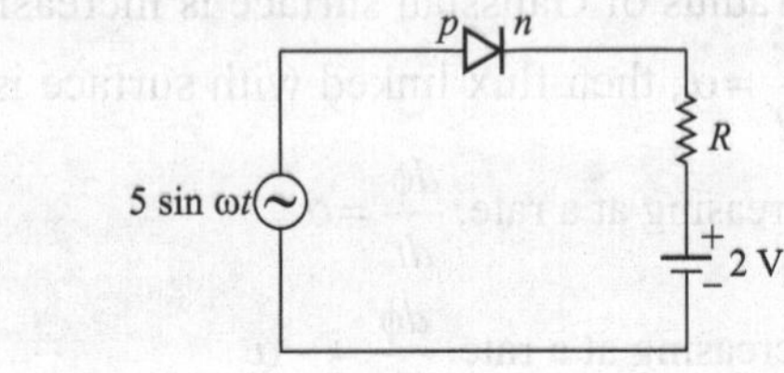

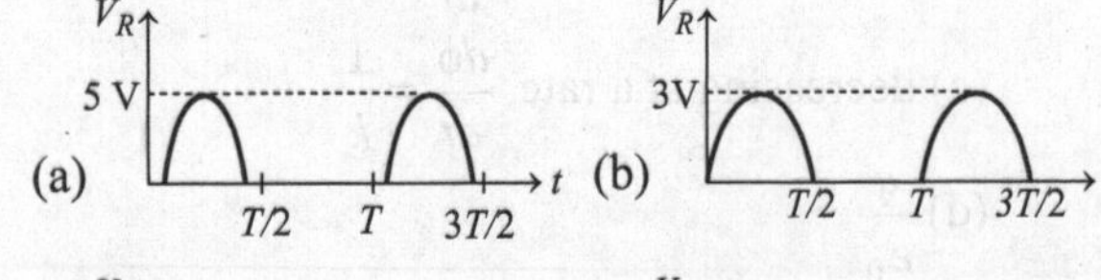

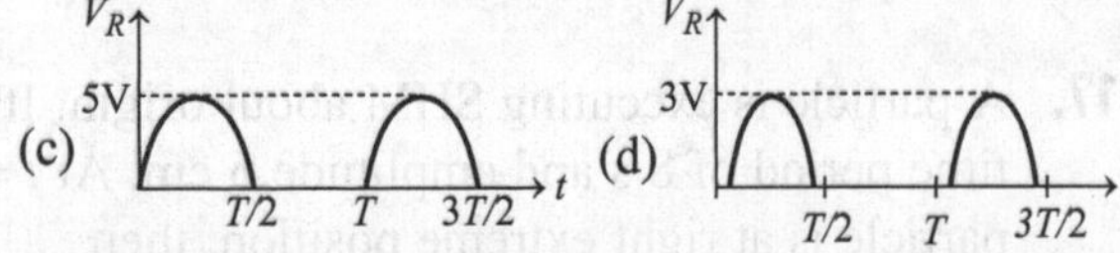

22. Two non-ideal batteries are connected in parallel. Consider the following statements.

Statement I The equivalent emf is smaller than either of the two emf's.

Statement II The equivalent internal resistance is smaller than either of the two internal resistances.

In the light of above statements, choose the most appropriate answer from the options given below.

(a) Both Statement I and Statement II are correct.

(b) Both Statement I and Statement II are incorrect.

(c) Statement I is correct but Statement II is incorrect.

(d) Statement I is incorrect but Statement II is correct.

23. Cathode rays enter into a uniform magnetic field perpendicular to the direction of the field. In the magnetic field their path will be

(a) straight line (b) circle

(c) parabolic (d) ellipse

24. The phase difference between the two particles situated on both the sides of a node is

(a) 0° (b) 90°

(c) 180° (d) 360°

25. A small bar magnet has a magnetic moment 1.2 A-m^2. The magnetic field at a distance 0.1 m on its axis will be ($\mu_0 = 4\pi \times 10^{-7} \text{ T-m/A}$)

(a) 1.2×10^{-4} T

(b) 2.4×10^{-4} T

(c) 2.4×10^{4} T

(d) 12×10^{4} T

26. An aluminium slab of thickness equals to the one-third distance between the plates of capacitor is inserted between the plates. The ratio of capacitances after and before the insertion of slab is

(a) 1 : 3 (b) 3 : 1

(c) 2 : 3 (d) 3 : 2

27. If dimensional formula of critical velocity v_c of a liquid flowing through a tube is expressed as $[\eta^\alpha \rho^\beta r^\gamma]$, where η, ρ, r are the coefficients of viscosity of liquid, density of liquid and radius of the tube respectively, then $\alpha + \beta + \gamma$ is

(a) 0 (b) 1

(c) −1 (d) 2

28. A metal wire of linear mass density 5×10^{-4} kg/m^3 is stretched by a tension force of 80 N is fixed at both ends. If it resonates at frequencies 450 Hz and 500 Hz consecutively, then length of the wire is

(a) 2.5 m (b) 4 m
(c) 4.6 m (d) 6 m

29. Statement I Binding energy of electron (mono-electronic species) is equal to negative of potential energy in that orbit.

Statement II Binding energy of electron in ground state is equal to ionisation energy in same state.

In the light of above statements, choose the most appropriate answer from the options given below.

(a) Both Statement I and Statement II are correct.
(b) Both Statement I and Statement II are incorrect.
(c) Statement I is correct but Statement II is incorrect.
(d) Statement I is incorrect but Statement II is correct.

30. Three long straight wires parallel and equally spaced carrying equal amount of currents as shown in the figure. If net magnetic force experienced by wire A, B and C due to the other are F_A, F_B and F_C respectively, then

A B C
⊙ ⊙ ⊗

(a) $F_A > F_B > F_C$ (b) $F_B > F_C > F_A$
(c) $F_C > F_A > F_B$ (d) $F_A = F_B = F_C$

31. Moment of inertia of a uniform quarter disc of mass M and radius R about an axis passing through its centre and perpendicular to plane is

(a) $\frac{MR^2}{2}$ (b) $\frac{MR^2}{4}$
(c) $\frac{MR^2}{8}$ (d) $\frac{MR^2}{16}$

32. The figure shown a logic circuit having two inputs A, B and output C. The voltage waveforms across A, B and C are as given. The logic circuit gate is

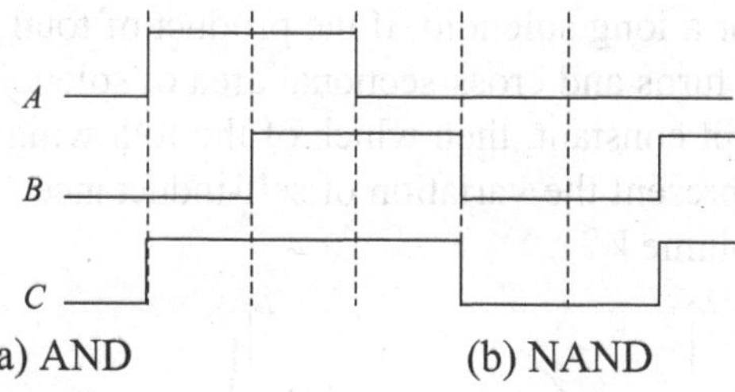

(a) AND (b) NAND
(c) OR (d) NOR

33. An aeroplane is flying horizontally with constant speed u at height h from the surface of the earth. At some instant, a person is standing on ground just below it. At that instant, aeroplane drops a food packet which has to be catched by man. What should be the minimum acceleration of man, so that man just catches the food packet?

(a) $2u\sqrt{\frac{g}{h}}$ (b) $\frac{u}{2}\sqrt{\frac{g}{h}}$
(c) $u\sqrt{\frac{2g}{h}}$ (d) $u\sqrt{\frac{g}{2h}}$

34. An α-particle enters in a region of uniform magnetic field. If the velocity makes an angle 37° with the magnetic field and pitch of the helical path followed by α-particle is P, then radius of helix is (Given, $\cot 37° = \frac{4}{3}$)

(a) $\frac{P}{\pi}$ (b) $\frac{3P}{8\pi}$
(c) $\frac{2P}{3\pi}$ (d) $\frac{3P}{4\pi}$

35. Consider an air capacitor with capacity C_0. It is filled with dielectrics of dielectric constants $K_1 = 2$, $K_2 = 3$ and $K_3 = 5$ as shown. If C_0 is 2 μF, then capacity of shown capacitor is

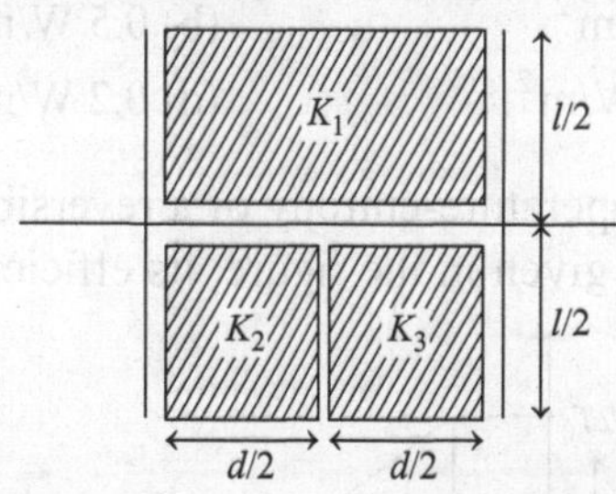

(a) $\left(\frac{23}{4}\right)$ μF (b) $\left(\frac{27}{4}\right)$ μF
(c) $\left(\frac{29}{4}\right)$ μF d) $\left(\frac{31}{4}\right)$ μF

36. For a long solenoid, if the product of total number of turns and cross-sectional area of solenoid is kept constant, then which of the following graph represent the variation of self-inductance L and volume V?

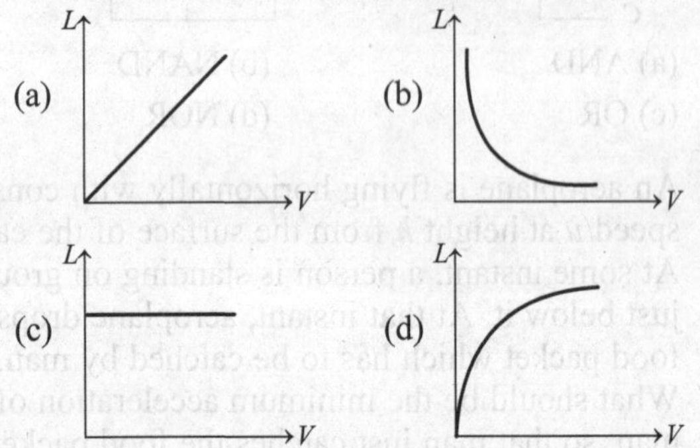

37. A germanium crystal is doped with arsenic atoms and indium atoms, simultaneously. Number of arsenic atoms used $= 5 \times 10^{22}$ per m^3 and number of indium atoms used $= 5 \times 10^{20}$ per m^3, then resulting crystal is a/an

(a) p-n junction
(b) p-type semiconductor
(c) n-type semiconductor
(d) depends on number of germanium atoms in given sample.

38. A charged shell has a potential of 5 V at its centre. Radius of shell is 1 m. Potential at a point at a distance of 1 m from its surface is

(a) 2.5 V (b) 5 V (c) 7.5 V (d) 1.25 V

39. About 5% of power of a 100 W light bulb is converted to visible radiation. Average intensity of light at a distance of 1 m from the bulb is nearly

(a) 1 W/m^2 (b) 0.5 W/m^2
(c) 0.4 W/m^2 (d) 0.2 W/m^2

40. The temperature-entropy of a reversible engine cycle is given in the figure, its efficiency is

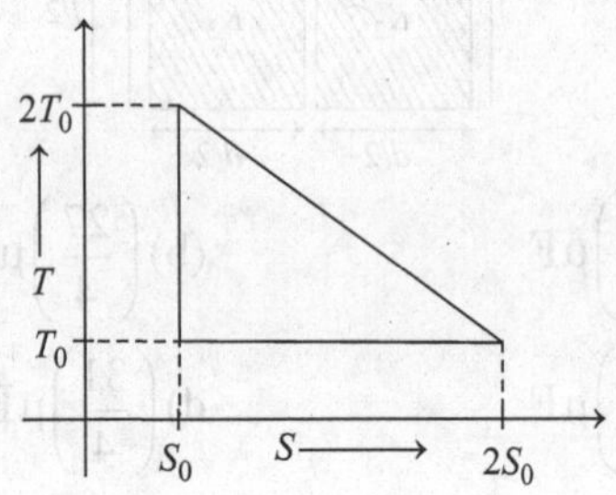

(a) 1/3 (b) 2/3
(c) 1/2 (d) 1/4

41. While executing simple harmonic motion, at a certain instant of time the displacement, velocity and acceleration of a particle are y, α and β, respectively. Then according to dimensional formula analysis, which of the following expression for amplitude is correct?

(a) $y\sqrt{\dfrac{\alpha^2 - \beta^2}{\beta}}$ (b) $\sqrt{\dfrac{y(\alpha^2 - \beta y)}{\beta}}$

(c) $\sqrt{\dfrac{\beta(\beta y - \alpha^2)}{y}}$ (d) $\dfrac{y}{\beta}\sqrt{\beta y - \alpha^2}$

42. A string is stretched between fixed points separated by 75.0 cm. It is observed to have resonant frequencies of 420 Hz and 315 Hz. There are no other resonant frequencies between them. The lowest resonant frequency for this string is

(a) 205 Hz (b) 10.5 Hz
(c) 105 Hz (d) 155 Hz

43. A thin equiconvex lens of glass has radii of curvature of each surface 30 cm. The lens has different medium on its left and right side of refractive indices 1.2 and 1.6, respectively. If the refractive index of the glass is 1.5, then focal length of this lens for parallel beam incident from left is

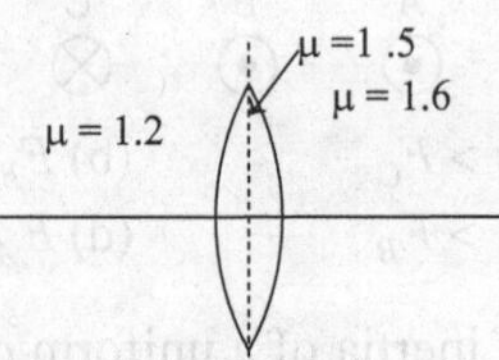

(a) 30 cm (b) 60 cm (c) 120 cm (d) 240 cm

44. Two light waves having same wavelength of 550 nm are travelling through vacuum are in phase initially.

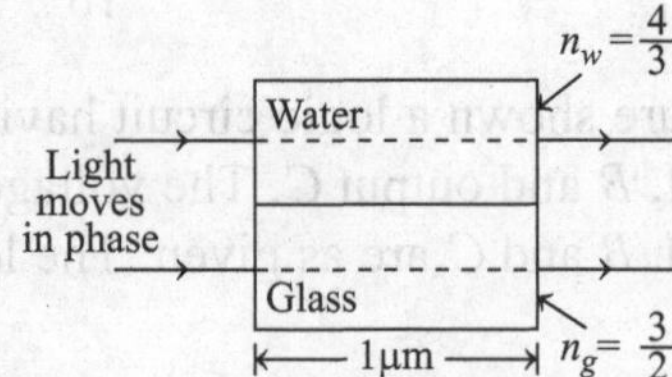

They pass through 1 μm blocks of water and glass, respectively as shown above. Phase difference between waves as they emerge out is

(a) 0.4 π rad

(b) 0.5 π rad

(c) 0.7 π rad

(d) 0.6 π rad

45. A uniform sphere of mass 500 g rolls without slipping on a plane horizontal surface with its centre moving at a speed of 5.00 cm/s. Its kinetic energy is

(a) 6.25×10^{-4} J (b) 1.13×10^{-3} J

(c) 8.75×10^{-4} J (d) 8.75×10^{-3} J

Scan to fill up online OMR and get AI based Rank prediction on performance

Response Index

01 ⓐ ⓑ ⓒ ⓓ	14 ⓐ ⓑ ⓒ ⓓ	27 ⓐ ⓑ ⓒ ⓓ	40 ⓐ ⓑ ⓒ ⓓ
02 ⓐ ⓑ ⓒ ⓓ	15 ⓐ ⓑ ⓒ ⓓ	28 ⓐ ⓑ ⓒ ⓓ	41 ⓐ ⓑ ⓒ ⓓ
03 ⓐ ⓑ ⓒ ⓓ	16 ⓐ ⓑ ⓒ ⓓ	29 ⓐ ⓑ ⓒ ⓓ	42 ⓐ ⓑ ⓒ ⓓ
04 ⓐ ⓑ ⓒ ⓓ	17 ⓐ ⓑ ⓒ ⓓ	30 ⓐ ⓑ ⓒ ⓓ	43 ⓐ ⓑ ⓒ ⓓ
05 ⓐ ⓑ ⓒ ⓓ	18 ⓐ ⓑ ⓒ ⓓ	31 ⓐ ⓑ ⓒ ⓓ	44 ⓐ ⓑ ⓒ ⓓ
06 ⓐ ⓑ ⓒ ⓓ	19 ⓐ ⓑ ⓒ ⓓ	32 ⓐ ⓑ ⓒ ⓓ	45 ⓐ ⓑ ⓒ ⓓ
07 ⓐ ⓑ ⓒ ⓓ	20 ⓐ ⓑ ⓒ ⓓ	33 ⓐ ⓑ ⓒ ⓓ	
08 ⓐ ⓑ ⓒ ⓓ	21 ⓐ ⓑ ⓒ ⓓ	34 ⓐ ⓑ ⓒ ⓓ	
09 ⓐ ⓑ ⓒ ⓓ	22 ⓐ ⓑ ⓒ ⓓ	35 ⓐ ⓑ ⓒ ⓓ	
10 ⓐ ⓑ ⓒ ⓓ	23 ⓐ ⓑ ⓒ ⓓ	36 ⓐ ⓑ ⓒ ⓓ	
11 ⓐ ⓑ ⓒ ⓓ	24 ⓐ ⓑ ⓒ ⓓ	37 ⓐ ⓑ ⓒ ⓓ	
12 ⓐ ⓑ ⓒ ⓓ	25 ⓐ ⓑ ⓒ ⓓ	38 ⓐ ⓑ ⓒ ⓓ	
13 ⓐ ⓑ ⓒ ⓓ	26 ⓐ ⓑ ⓒ ⓓ	39 ⓐ ⓑ ⓒ ⓓ	

Performance Scanner

> 90% Excellent !	You have mastered the NEET syllabus. The concepts of this entire syllabus are on your fingertips. Maintain this momentum.
76-90% Very Good !	You have a good command over the entire NEET syllabus. Revise it again after a few days to enhance your performance.
60-75% Good !	You have a wide scope to learn for the entire NEET syllabus. Revise it again.
<60% Not Satisfactory!	You have a long way ahead of you to master the entire NEET syllabus. Revise it thoroughly.

Space for Rough Work

Test Booklet No. **3947175**

Test Booklet Code **NK04**

MEDACE
NEET (UG)
SELF ASSESSMENT KIT

NEET Knock Offs 4

(NEET Simulator Test)

Name of the Candidate (In Capitals)

____

____

____

Candidate's Signature __________

Invigilator's Signature __________

Facsimile signature stamp of center superintendent__________

Important Instructions

- The test is of 45 minute and the Test Booklet contains 45 multiple choice questions (four options with a single correct answer) from Physics.
- Candidates are advised to read all questions before they start attempting the question paper.
- Each question carries 4 marks. For each correct response, the candidate will get 4 marks. For each incorrect response, one mark will be deducted from the total scores. The maximum marks are 180.
- In the event of candidate marking more than one option, one mark will be deducted.
- Use **Blue/Black Point Pen** only for writing particular on this page/ marking response on answer sheet.

Do not open this booklet until you start attempting the test

Physics (Q. No. 1-45)

1. A uniform rod of mass 1.5 kg is hung with one end attached to ceiling. The rod is 60 cm long and has $100\,cm^2$ area of cross-section. If the Young's modulus of the rod is $1.2\times10^{11}\,N/m^2$, then elongation of the rod due to its weight is

   (a) 3.67×10^{-9} m

   (b) 7.35×10^{-11} m

   (c) 1.47×10^{-10} m

   (d) 7.35×10^{-9} m

2. A pipe, 30 cm long is open at both ends, harmonic mode of the pipe which resonates at 1.65 kHz source is (speed of sound is 330 ms^{-1})

   (a) third (b) fourth (c) first (d) second

3. Two persons *A* and *B* perform the same amount of work in moving a body through same distance *d* with application of forces acting at angles 45° and 60°, respectively with the direction of displacement. The ratio of force applied by person *A* to the force applied by person *B* is

   (a) 1 : 1 (b) $1:\sqrt{2}$

   (c) $\sqrt{2}:1$ (d) $\sqrt{3}:2$

4. Force acting on a particle is 5 N. If unit of length and time are doubled and unit of mass is halved, then the numerical value of the force in the new unit will be

   (a) 4 times (b) 2 times

   (c) 1/4 time (d) 1/2 time

5. If a rigid body rolls on a surface without slipping, then

   (a) angular speed is different at different points of rigid body.

   (b) linear speed is minimum at the highest point but maximum at the point of contact.

   (c) linear speed is same at all points of the rigid body.

   (d) linear speed is maximum at the highest point but minimum at the point of contact.

6. A bar magnet is oscillating in magnetic field with a period *T*. What happens to its period of motion, if its mass is quadrupled?

   (a) Motion remains simple harmonic with new period = $T/2$.

   (b) Motion remains simple harmonic with new period = $2T$.

   (c) Motion remains simple harmonic with new period = $4T$.

   (d) Motion remains simple harmonic with new period = $6T$.

7. **Assertion** (A) Photosensitivity of metal is high, if its work function is small.

   Reason (R) Work function = hf_0, where f_0 is the threshold frequency.

   In light of above statements, choose the most appropriate answer from the options given below.

   (a) Both A and R are true and R is the correct explanation of A.

   (b) Both A and R are true but R is not the correct explanation of A.

   (c) A is true but R is false.

   (d) A is false but R is true.

8. **Statement I** The resistance of *p-n* junction diode decreases when it is forward biased and increases when it is reverse biased.

   Statement II In forward bias, the potential barrier is supported by the battery and in reverse bias, potential barrier is opposed by battery.

   In the light of above statements, choose the most appropriate answer from the options given below.

   (a) Both Statement I and Statement II are correct.

   (b) Both Statement I and Statement II are incorrect.

   (c) Statement I is correct and Statement II is incorrect.

   (d) Statement I is incorrect and Statement II is correct.

9. The heat given to a body to raise its temperature is given by $Q = ms\Delta\theta$, where Q = heat given, m = mass of body, s = specific heat and $\Delta\theta$ = change in temperature.
The dimensional formula of specific heat is
(a) $[M^1L^2T^{-2}K^{-1}]$
(b) $[M^0L^2T^{-2}K^0]$
(c) $[M^0L^1T^{-2}K^{-2}]$
(d) $[M^0L^2T^{-2}K^{-1}]$

10. Six identical charged particles are placed on the vertices of a regular hexagon of side 0.9 m. One of the charged particle is released from hexagon. When it reaches infinity, another particle adjacent to the first particle is released. If the difference of kinetic energies of both the particles at infinity is 90 mJ, then magnitude of the charge is
(a) 3 μC (b) 2 μC
(c) 0.284 C (d) 0.1C

11. The angle between two vectors **P** and **Q** is 60°. If $|\mathbf{P}+2\mathbf{Q}|=|3\mathbf{P}-2\mathbf{Q}|$ and $\frac{\mathbf{P}}{4}$ is a unit vector, then magnitude of **Q** is
(a) 2 (b) 4
(c) 8 (d) $2\sqrt{3}$

12. The displacement-time graph of a moving particle is shown below.

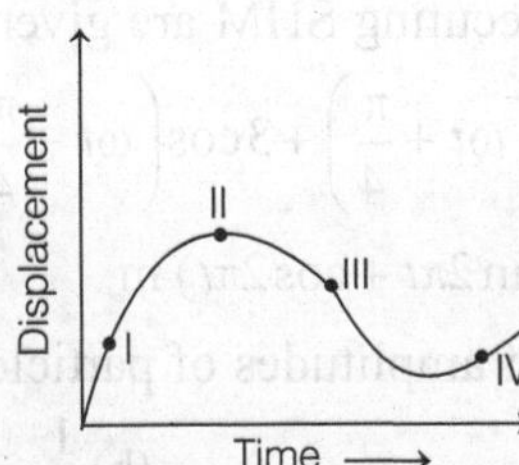

The instantaneous velocity of the particle is negative at the point
(a) IV (b) I
(c) II (d) III

13. A cubical block of density 400 kg/m^3 and weight 80 N is floating on liquid of density 1200 kg/m^3 as shown in the figure. If the container starts moving with an upward acceleration of 2 m/s^2, then buoyant force acting on the block is
(Take, acceleration due to gravity, g = 10 m/s^2)

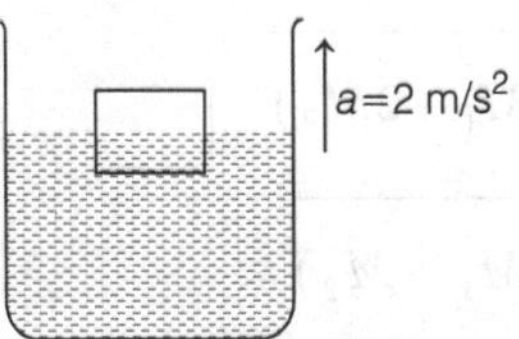

(a) 640 N (b) 64 N
(c) 80 N (d) 96 N

14. The straight wire AB carries a current I. The ends of the wire subtend angles θ_1 and θ_2 at the point P as shown in figure. The magnetic field at the point P is

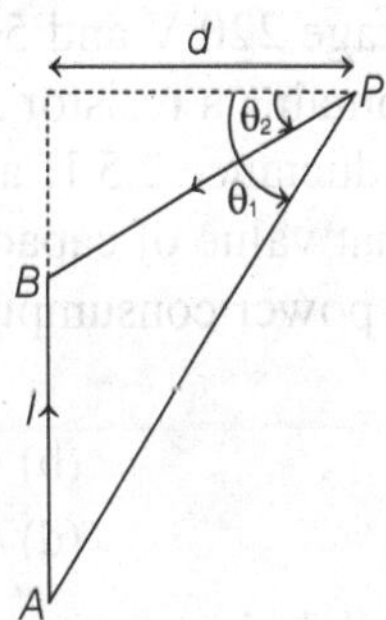

(a) $\frac{\mu_0 I}{4\pi d}(\sin\theta_1 - \sin\theta_2)$
(b) $\frac{\mu_0 I}{4\pi d}(\sin\theta_1 + \sin\theta_2)$
(c) $\frac{\mu_0 I}{4\pi d}(\cos\theta_1 - \cos\theta_2)$
(d) $\frac{\mu_0 I}{4\pi d}(\cos\theta_1 + \cos\theta_2)$

15. An object of mass m is kept at a point on the line joining the centres of two planets of masses M_1, M_2 and radii R_1, R_2, respectively. Centres of the planets are separated by a distance r. If the object is $\frac{r}{3}$ distance away from the centre of planet having mass M_1, then what minimum velocity should be given to the object, so that it can just overcome the gravitational force of mass of two planets?

(a) $\sqrt{\frac{3G}{r}(2M_1 + M_2)}$

(b) $\sqrt{\frac{3G}{2r}(2M_1 + M_2)}$

(c) $\sqrt{\frac{3G}{r}(M_1 + 2M_2)}$

(d) $\sqrt{\frac{3G}{r}(M_1 + M_2)}$

16. Areal speed of a planet around sun is proportional to (r is mean distance of planet from sun)

(a) r^0 (b) r^1

(c) $r^{\frac{1}{2}}$ (d) $r^{\frac{3}{2}}$

17. A series R-L-C circuit is subjected to an AC source of voltage 220 V and 50 Hz frequency. The circuit contains a resistor $R = 10\,\text{k}\Omega$, an inductor of inductance 2.5 H and an unknown capacitor. What value of capacitance should be taken, so that power consumption in circuit can be maximum?

(a) 4 μF (b) 40 μF

(c) 25 μF (d) 400 μF

18. A 5.80 μF parallel plate air capacitor has a plate separation of 5 mm and is charged to a potential difference of 400 V. The energy density in the region between the plates is

(a) $2.83 \times 10^{-2}\ \text{J/m}^3$

(b) $2.83\ \text{J/m}^3$

(c) $2.83 \times 10^{-4}\ \text{J/m}^3$

(d) $2.83 \times 10^{6}\ \text{J/m}^3$

19. The volume occupied by the molecules containedin 3.6 kg water at STP, if the intermolecular force vanishes away, is

(a) $2.8\ \text{m}^3$ (b) $4.48\ \text{m}^3$

(c) $5.44\ \text{m}^3$ (d) $6.0\ \text{m}^3$

20. In photoelectric experiment, a light of wavelength 4800 nm is incident on a metal surface of work function 1.67 eV, then photoelectrons are emitted. A fastest photoelectron combines with an excited He^{+2} ion in its third excited state to form He^{+} ion. What is energy of photon emitted by de-excitation of He^{+} ion?

(a) 4.5 eV (b) 4.3 eV

(c) 6.9 eV (d) 0.9 eV

21. A sphere encloses an electric dipole with charges $\pm 2.5 \times 10^{-6}$C. What is the total electric flux across the sphere ?

(a) $6 \times 10^{-5}\ \text{Nm}^2/\text{C}$

(b) $-2.5 \times 10^{-6}\ \text{Nm}^2/\text{C}$

(c) 0

(d) $2.5 \times 10^{-6}\ \text{Nm}^2/\text{C}$

22. Match List I (electromagnetic wave type) with List II (its association/application).

List I	List II
A. Infrared rays	1. To treat muscular strain
B. Radio waves	2. For broadcasting
C. X-rays	3. To detect fracture of bones
D. Ultraviolet rays	4. Absorbed by the ozone layer of the atmosphere

Codes

	A	B	C	D
(a)	4	3	2	1
(b)	1	2	4	3
(c)	3	2	1	4
(d)	1	2	3	4

23. The displacement time equations of two particles A and B executing SHM are given as

$$x_A = 4\sin\left(\omega t + \frac{\pi}{4}\right) + 3\cos\left(\omega t - \frac{\pi}{4}\right)\ \text{m}$$

$$x_B = 5\sqrt{2}(\sin 2\pi t + \cos 2\pi t)\ \text{m}$$

The ratio of amplitudes of particles A and B is

(a) 1 (b) $\frac{1}{2}$

(c) $\frac{1}{\sqrt{3}}$ (d) $\frac{7}{10}$

24. The output of an AC generator is given by $e = e_0 \sin\left(\omega t - \frac{\pi}{4}\right)$ and current is given by $i = i_0 \sin\left(\omega t - \frac{3\pi}{4}\right)$. The circuit contains a single element other than the generator. The element is

(a) capacitor
(b) resistor
(c) inductor
(d) capacitor and inductor

25. Two conducting spheres A and B of radii 4 cm and 2 cm carry charges of 18×10^{-8} stat coulomb and 9×10^{-8} stat coulomb respectively, of positive electricity. When they are put in electrostatic contact, then the charge will
(a) not flow at all
(b) flow from A to B
(c) flow from B to A
(c) disappear

26.

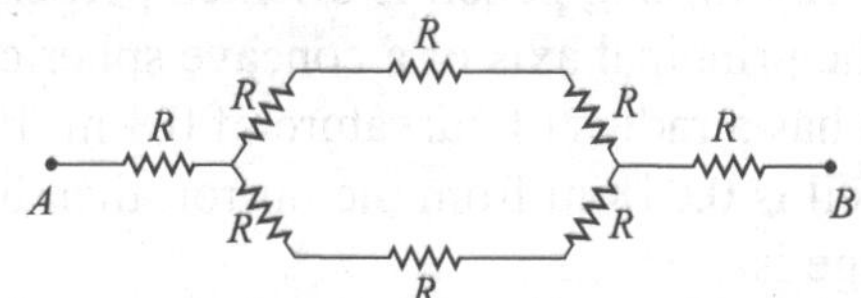

Consider the above figure consists of 8 resistors each of 10 Ω resistance, connected between points A and B. The equivalent resistance between A and B is
(a) 10 Ω (b) 35 Ω
(c) 20 Ω (d) 25 Ω

27. A parallel beam of light of all wavelengths greater than 3000 Å falls on a double slit in a YDSE. It was found that wavelengths 3600 Å and 6000 Å are absent at a distance of 31.5 mm from the position of the central maximum and orders of the interference at this point for the two wavelengths differ by 7. If the distance between the slits and the screen is 1 m, then separation between the two slits is
(a) 0.08 mm (b) 0.1 mm
(c) 0.13 mm (d) 0.2 mm

28. Consider the arrangement given below.

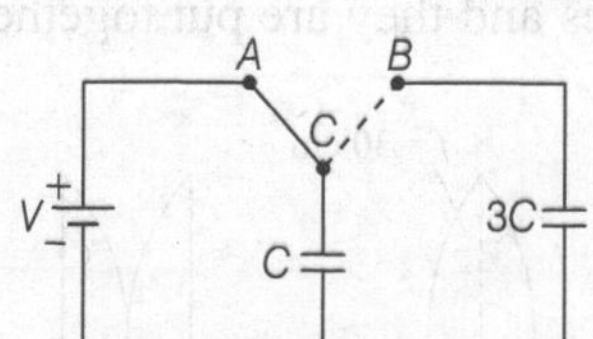

When C and A are in contact, charge on capacitor of capacity C is q. Energy dissipated when C is connected to B will be
(a) $\frac{3}{4}\frac{q^2}{C}$ (b) $\frac{5}{8}\frac{q^2}{C}$
(c) $\frac{1}{8}\frac{q^2}{C}$ (d) $\frac{3}{8}\frac{q^2}{C}$

29. **Statement I** The net work done by a conservative force on an object moving along a closed loop is always non-zero.
Statement II For a charged particle moving from point P to point Q, the net work done by electric field on the particle is independent of path.
In the light of above statements, choose the most appropriate answer from the options given below.
(a) Both Statement I and Statement II are correct.
(b) Both Statement I and Statement II are incorrect.
(c) Statement I is correct and Statement II is incorrect.
(d) Statement I is incorrect and Statement II is correct.

30. Magnetic field in a region is changing at a constant rate. As a result, an induced electric field appears in the region which gives rise to an emf. Induced electric field lines are
(a) open loops
(b) closed loops
(c) can be open or closed depending on magnetic field
(d) no field lines are produced

31. In context of diamagnetic material, the correct graphs for intensity of magnetisation *versus* magnetic field strength is

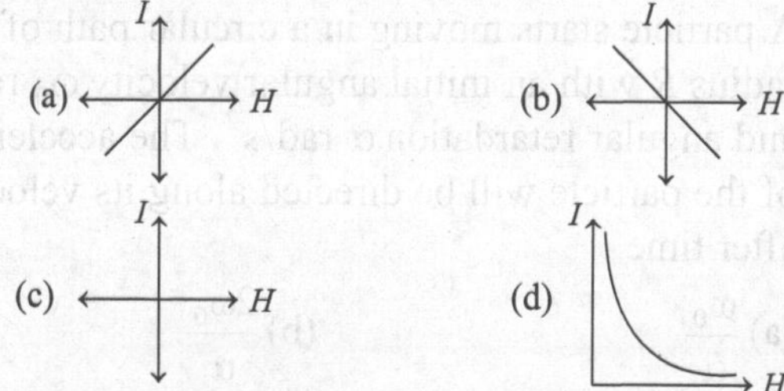

32. In a helium ion, if potential energy of electron in ground state is assumed to be zero, then its energy in first excited state is equal to

(a) 13.6 eV (b) 27.2 eV
(c) 54.4 eV (d) 95.2 eV

33. Which of the following component(s) a thermistor can have?

I. A low resistance at high temperature
II. A high resistance at high temperature
III. Zero resistance at 0°C
IV. Resistance depends on temperature coefficient

(a) I, II are correct
(b) I, II, IV are correct
(c) III, IV are correct
(d) IV is correct

34. An unknown resistance R is connected to left gap of a meter bridge and another unknown resistance S is connected to right gap, such that the balance point from left end is at 30 cm. If a resistance of 2Ω is connected in parallel with S, the null point occurs at 40 cm. The value of S is

(a) 1.1Ω (b) 2Ω
(c) 3.2Ω (d) 4Ω

35. An electric bulb is rated at 220 V and 100 W. Power consumed by bulb when operated at 110 V will be

(a) 50 W (b) 75 W
(c) 100 W (d) 25 W

36. A particle is projected with initial speed of 30 m/s making an angle 60° with horizontal. The velocity of particle when its velocity makes angle of 30° with horizontal is

(a) 10 m/s (b) $10\sqrt{2}$ m/s
(c) $10\sqrt{3}$ m/s (d) 20 m/s

37. A particle starts moving in a circular path of radius R with an initial angular velocity ω_0 rad/s and angular retardation α rad/s^2. The acceleration of the particle will be directed along its velocity after time

(a) $\frac{\omega_0}{\alpha}$ (b) $\frac{2\omega_0}{\alpha}$
(c) $\frac{\omega_0}{2\alpha}$ (d) $\frac{3\omega_0}{2\alpha}$

38. A mass m is attached to a string of length L which makes 90° angle with the vertical as shown in figure. The mass is released from rest and swings through a circular arc. The tension in the string, when the mass reaches the bottom of the arc is

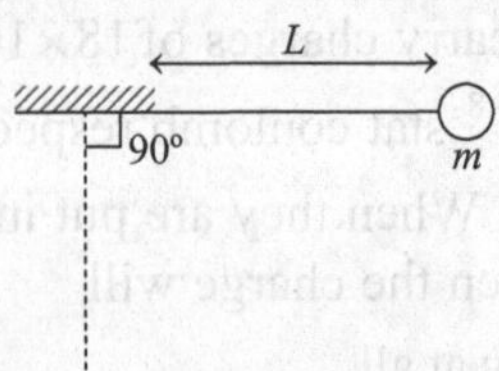

(a) zero (b) mg
(c) $2mg$ (d) $3mg$

39. A 0.124 m long pencil is oriented perpendicular to the principal axis of a concave spherical mirror that has a radius of curvature of 0.3 m. If the pencil is 0.018 m from the mirror, then height of image is

(a) 2.13 cm (b) 16.5 cm
(c) 9.3 cm (d) 1.6 cm

40. Inside a solenoid of radius 0.5 m, magnetic field is changing at a rate of 50×10^{-6} T/s. Acceleration of an electron placed at a distance of 0.3 m from axis of solenoid will be

(a) 23×10^6 ms^{-2}
(b) 2.6×10^6 m/s^2
(c) 1.3×10^9 ms^{-2}
(d) 2.6×10^9 m/s^2

41. A particle is executing SHM on a straight line starting from its mean position. It passes through the mean position at successive intervals 1.5 s and 3 s with a speed of 1.57 m/s. The amplitude of the motion is

(a) 0.5 m (b) 0.75 m
(c) 1 m (d) 1.5 m

42. A biconvex lens of focal length 30 cm is cut into two halves and they are put together as shown in figure.

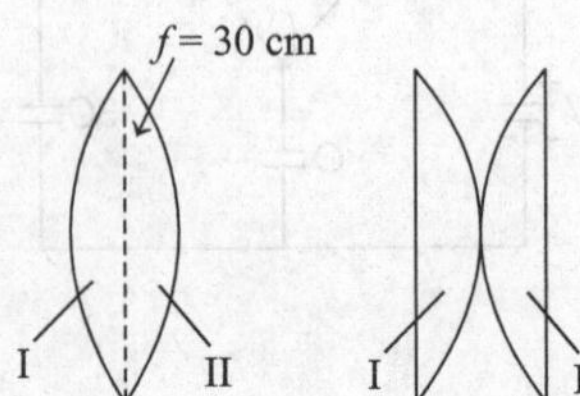

What is focal length of given arrangement?

(a) 30 cm

(b) 15 cm

(c) 45 cm

(d) 60 cm

43. Given diagram shows a p-n junction immediately after formation of the junction.

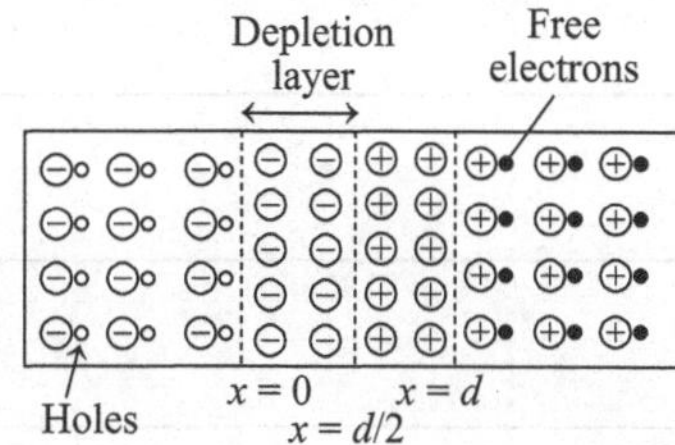

If a graph between charge density and distance from $x = 0$ to $x = d$ is plotted, then it is best represented as

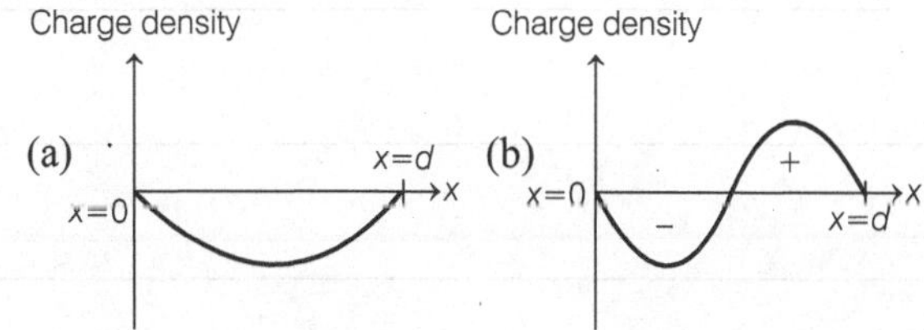

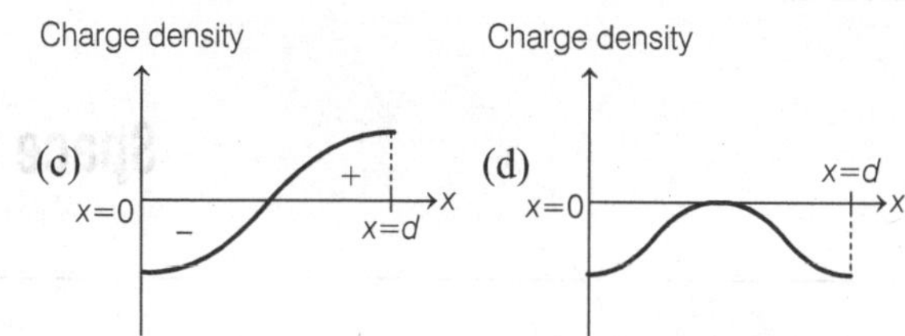

44. The significant result(s) deduced from the Rutherford's scattering experiment is that

I. electrons are embedded in the atom.

II. whole of the positive charge is concentrated at the centre of atom.

III. there are neutrons inside the nucleus.

IV. α-particles are helium nuclei.

(a) I and IV are correct. (b) Only I is correct.

(c) Only II is correct. (d) III and IV are correct.

45. Two nuclei have mass numbers in the ratio $1:8$. Which of the following statements is correct?

(a) Ratio of their nuclear radii is $1:2$.

(b) Ratio of their nuclear radii is $2:1$.

(c) Nuclear density ratio is $1:2$.

(d) Nuclear density ratio is $2:1$.

Scan to fill up online OMR and get AI based Rank prediction on performance

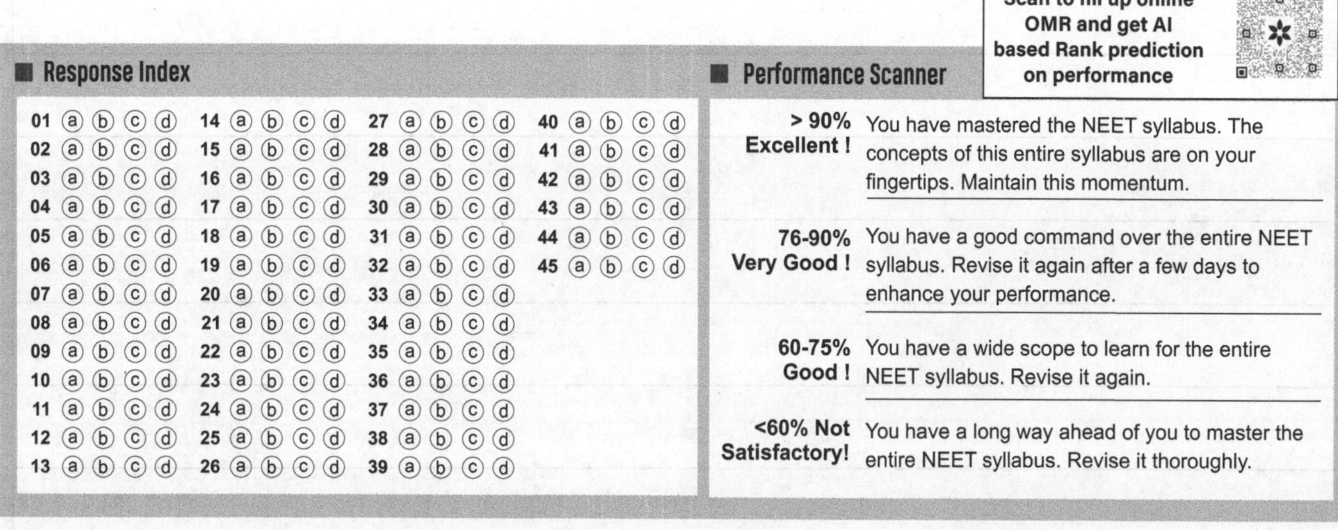

Response Index

01 ⓐ ⓑ ⓒ ⓓ	14 ⓐ ⓑ ⓒ ⓓ	27 ⓐ ⓑ ⓒ ⓓ	40 ⓐ ⓑ ⓒ ⓓ
02 ⓐ ⓑ ⓒ ⓓ	15 ⓐ ⓑ ⓒ ⓓ	28 ⓐ ⓑ ⓒ ⓓ	41 ⓐ ⓑ ⓒ ⓓ
03 ⓐ ⓑ ⓒ ⓓ	16 ⓐ ⓑ ⓒ ⓓ	29 ⓐ ⓑ ⓒ ⓓ	42 ⓐ ⓑ ⓒ ⓓ
04 ⓐ ⓑ ⓒ ⓓ	17 ⓐ ⓑ ⓒ ⓓ	30 ⓐ ⓑ ⓒ ⓓ	43 ⓐ ⓑ ⓒ ⓓ
05 ⓐ ⓑ ⓒ ⓓ	18 ⓐ ⓑ ⓒ ⓓ	31 ⓐ ⓑ ⓒ ⓓ	44 ⓐ ⓑ ⓒ ⓓ
06 ⓐ ⓑ ⓒ ⓓ	19 ⓐ ⓑ ⓒ ⓓ	32 ⓐ ⓑ ⓒ ⓓ	45 ⓐ ⓑ ⓒ ⓓ
07 ⓐ ⓑ ⓒ ⓓ	20 ⓐ ⓑ ⓒ ⓓ	33 ⓐ ⓑ ⓒ ⓓ	
08 ⓐ ⓑ ⓒ ⓓ	21 ⓐ ⓑ ⓒ ⓓ	34 ⓐ ⓑ ⓒ ⓓ	
09 ⓐ ⓑ ⓒ ⓓ	22 ⓐ ⓑ ⓒ ⓓ	35 ⓐ ⓑ ⓒ ⓓ	
10 ⓐ ⓑ ⓒ ⓓ	23 ⓐ ⓑ ⓒ ⓓ	36 ⓐ ⓑ ⓒ ⓓ	
11 ⓐ ⓑ ⓒ ⓓ	24 ⓐ ⓑ ⓒ ⓓ	37 ⓐ ⓑ ⓒ ⓓ	
12 ⓐ ⓑ ⓒ ⓓ	25 ⓐ ⓑ ⓒ ⓓ	38 ⓐ ⓑ ⓒ ⓓ	
13 ⓐ ⓑ ⓒ ⓓ	26 ⓐ ⓑ ⓒ ⓓ	39 ⓐ ⓑ ⓒ ⓓ	

Performance Scanner

> 90% Excellent !	You have mastered the NEET syllabus. The concepts of this entire syllabus are on your fingertips. Maintain this momentum.
76-90% Very Good !	You have a good command over the entire NEET syllabus. Revise it again after a few days to enhance your performance.
60-75% Good !	You have a wide scope to learn for the entire NEET syllabus. Revise it again.
<60% Not Satisfactory!	You have a long way ahead of you to master the entire NEET syllabus. Revise it thoroughly.

Space for Rough Work

Test Booklet No. 3947176

Test Booklet Code NK05

NEET Knock Offs 5

(NEET Simulator Test)

Name of the Candidate (In Capitals)

____

____

____

Candidate's Signature ____________

Invigilator's Signature ____________

Facsimile signature stamp of center superintendent____________

Important Instructions

- The test is of 45 minute and the Test Booklet contains 45 multiple choice questions (four options with a single correct answer) from Physics.
- Candidates are advised to read all questions before they start attempting the question paper.
- Each question carries 4 marks. For each correct response, the candidate will get 4 marks. For each incorrect response, one mark will be deducted from the total scores. The maximum marks are 180.
- In the event of candidate marking more than one option, one mark will be deducted.
- Use **Blue/Black Point Pen** only for writing particular on this page/ marking response on answer sheet.

Do not open this booklet until you start attempting the test

Physics (Q. No. 1-45)

Section-A

1. A system consisting of two masses connected by a massless rod lies along the X-axis. A 0.4 kg mass is at a distance $x = 2$ m while a 0.6 kg mass is at a distance $x = 7$ m. The x-coordinate of the centre of mass is

(a) 5 m (b) 3.5 m
(c) 4.5 m (d) 4 m

2. Side of a cube measured using a vernier calliper is $L = (30.0 \pm 0.1)$ mm. Percentage uncertainty in volume is about

(a) 0.1% (b) 0.3%
(c) 1% (d) 3%

3. In the following circuit diagram, potential difference across 4μF capacitor is

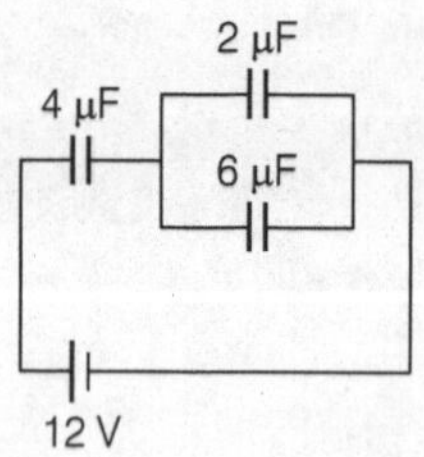

(a) 19 V (b) 14 V
(c) 16 V (d) 8 V

4. If the number of turns of a current-carrying solenoid is decreased to half of its previous value, then its self-inductance is

(a) increased to double
(b) decreased to one-fourth
(c) increased to four times
(d) decreased to half

5. **Statement I** When lengths of 123 cm and 5.35 cm are added, reported length (sum) is found to be 128 cm instead of 128.35 cm.

Statement II If length of a room is 13.8 m and width is 9 m, then recorded area of room is 100 m^2.

In the light of above statements, choose the most appropriate answer from the options given below.

(a) Both Statement I and Statement II are correct.
(b) Both Statement I and Statement II are incorrect.
(c) Statement I is correct and Statement II is incorrect.
(d) Statement I is incorrect and Statement II is correct.

6. Two diodes of silicon and germanium are connected in series as shown below. The current flowing through the circuit will be around

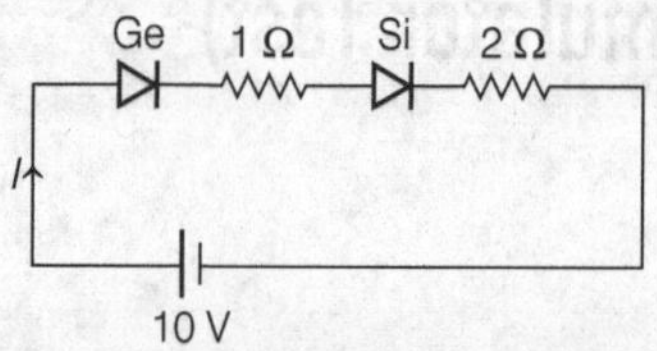

(a) 0 (b) 3 A
(c) 4 A (d) 3.5 A

7. A car turns on a banked road of radius 300 m. If the coefficient of friction between the tyres and the road is 0.3, then maximum speed of the car on the turn is (Take, $g = 10\ m/s^2$)

(a) 10 m/s (b) 30 m/s
(c) 40 m/s (d) 50 m/s

8 The graph between angle of deviation (δ) and angle of incidence (i) for a triangular prism is represented by

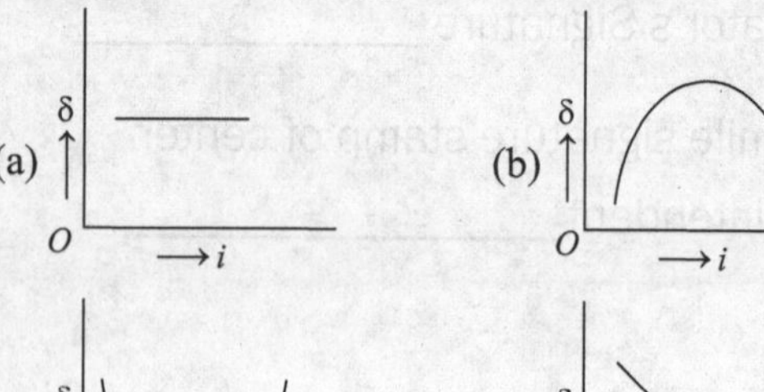

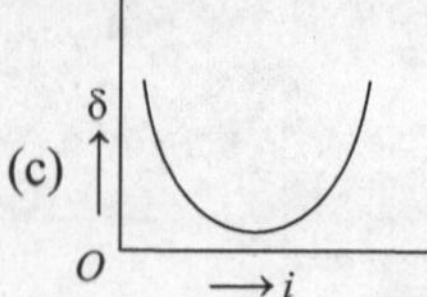

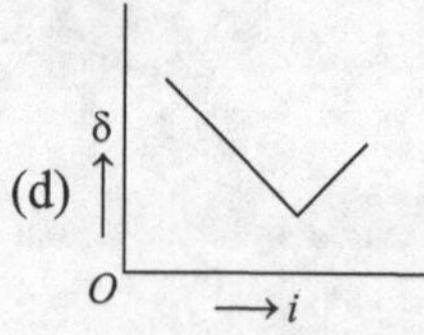

9. A spring is vibrating with frequency n under some mass. It is cut into two equal parts and same mass is suspended from one part, then the new frequency of vibration is

(a) n (b) $\frac{n}{\sqrt{2}}$

(c) $\frac{n}{2}$ (d) $n\sqrt{2}$

10. If a car at rest accelerates uniformly to a speed of 72 km/h for 25 s, then it covers a distance of

(a) 450 m (b) 250 m

(c) 800 m (d) 20 m

11. Two moles of oxygen is mixed with eight moles of helium. The effective specific heat of the mixture at constant volume will be

(a) 2.5 R (b) 1.7 R

(c) 1.4 R (d) 1.8 R

12. A motor is producing a torque of 180 N-m to rotate a flour mill at constant speed of 200 rad s^{-1}. Assuming 50% efficient molar, electrical power consumed by motor is

(a) 36 kW (b) 72 kW

(c) 18 kW (d) 54 kW

13. A body floats with one-third of its volume outside water and 3/4th of its volume outside another liquid. The density of liquid is

(a) $\frac{9}{4}$ g/cc (b) $\frac{4}{9}$ g/cc

(c) $\frac{8}{3}$ g/cc (d) $\frac{3}{8}$ g/cc

14. Electric field in a region is $\mathbf{E} = (20x + 10)\,\hat{\mathbf{i}}$ N/C, where x is in metre. Find potential difference $[V_1(x=1) - V_2(x=-5)]$.

(a) −48 V

(b) −520 V

(c) 180 V

(d) 320 V

15. In forward biasing of a p-n junction,

(a) electrons move from lower to higher energy level

(b) electrons move from higher to lower energy level

(c) holes in valence band move from higher to lower energy level

(d) None of the above

16. A rectangular film of liquid is extended from (4 cm × 2 cm) to (5 cm × 4 cm). If the work done is 6×10^{-4} J, then the value of the surface tension of the liquid is

(a) 0.25 N/m (b) 0.50 N/m

(c) 0.75 N/m (d) 1.25 N/m

17. The ratio of escape velocity at earth to the escape velocity at another planet, whose radius and mean density are half as that of the earth, is

(a) $1:2\sqrt{2}$ (b) $2\sqrt{2}:1$

(c) 1:1 (d) 2:1

18. **Assertion** (A) An emf can be induced by moving a conductor in a magnetic field.

Reason (R) An emf can be induced by changing the magnetic field.

In the light of above statements, choose the most appropriate answer from the options given below.

(a) Both A and R are true and R is the correct explanation of A.

(b) Both A and R are true but R is not the correct explanation of A.

(c) A is true but R is false.

(d) A is false but R is true.

19. A conducting wire is stretched by applying a deforming force, so that its diameter decreases to 40% of original value. The percentage change in its resistance will be

(a) 0.9% (b) 0.12%

(c) 1.6% (d) 0.5%

20. T_1 is the time period of simple pendulum at a place. If the length of pendulum is doubled of its original value, then the modified time period is

(a) $\sqrt{2}T_1$ (b) $\frac{T_1}{2}$

(c) $2T_1$ (d) $3T_1$

21. Match List-I and List-II.

List I	List II
A. Moment of inertia of the rod (length L and mass M) about an axis perpendicular to the rod passing through the mid-point	1. $\frac{8ML^2}{3}$
B. Moment of inertia of the rod (length L and mass $2M$) about an axis perpendicular to the rod passing through one of its end	2. $\frac{ML^2}{3}$
C. Moment of inertia of the rod (length $2L$ and mass M) about an axis perpendicular to the rod passing through its mid-point	3. $\frac{ML^2}{12}$
D. Moment of inertia of the rod (length $2L$ and mass $2M$) about an axis perpendicular to the rod passing through one of its end	4. $\frac{2ML^2}{3}$

Codes

	A	B	C	D
(a)	2	3	1	4
(b)	2	1	3	4
(c)	3	4	2	1
(d)	3	4	1	2

22. A particle moves in XY-plane, its position, velocity and acceleration are $\mathbf{r} = x\hat{\mathbf{i}} + y\hat{\mathbf{j}}$, $\mathbf{v} = v_x\hat{\mathbf{i}} + v_y\hat{\mathbf{j}}$ and $\mathbf{a} = a_x\hat{\mathbf{i}} + a_y\hat{\mathbf{j}}$, respectively. If particle is slowing down, then choose the correct option.

(a) $xv_x + yv_y < 0$
(b) $xv_x + yv_y > 0$
(c) $a_xv_x + a_yv_y < 0$
(d) $a_xv_x + a_yv_y > 0$

23. A thin glass prism placed in air produces deviation of 10° in a light ray. If the prism is immersed in water of refractive index $\frac{4}{3}$, then what will be the deviation produced by it?

(Take, ${}_a\mu_g = 1.5$)

(a) 1.5° (b) 4.5°
(c) 7.5° (d) 2.5°

24.

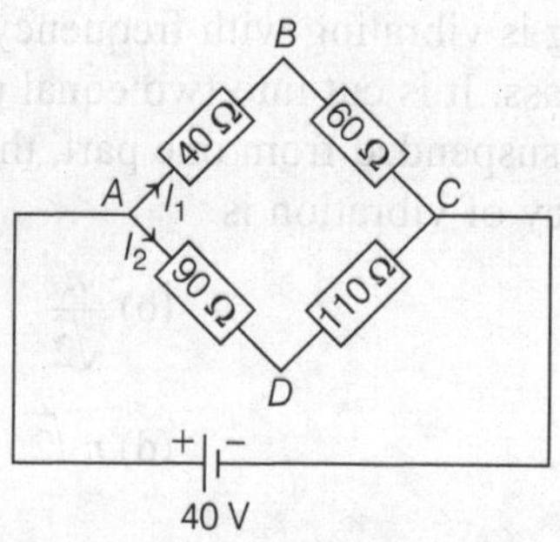

In above circuit, potential drop $V_B - V_D$ (in V) is

(a) 0 (b) 2 (c) 3 (d) 4

25. A constant magnetic field of 1 T exists in the $x > 0$ region.

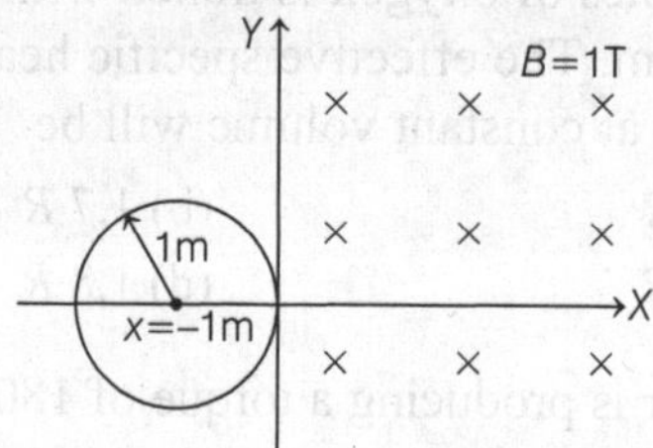

At $t = 0$, centre of a conducting ring of radius 1 m is at $x = -1$ m and ring is moving with a constant velocity of $v = 1\,\hat{\mathbf{i}}$ m/s. Value of induced emf in ring at $t = 1$ s will be

(a) 1 V (b) 1.5 V
(c) 2 V (d) 0

26. A proton and an α-particle, both are accelerated from rest with same energy. The ratio of de-Broglie wavelength of α-particle to that of proton is

(a) 1 : 4 (b) 4 : 1
(c) 1 : 2 (d) 2 : 1

27. The volume (V) of a monoatomic gas varies with its temperature (T), as shown in the graph. The ratio of work done by the gas to the heat absorbed by it, when it undergoes a change from state A to state B is

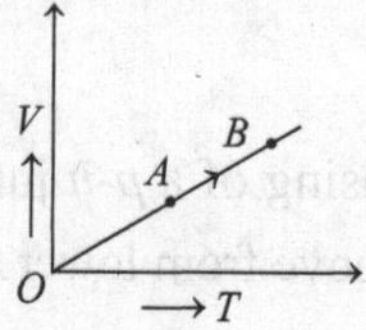

(a) $\frac{1}{3}$ (b) $\frac{2}{3}$

(c) $\frac{2}{5}$ (d) $\frac{2}{7}$

28. A semiconductor sample has electron concentration of $5\times10^{18}\ m^{-3}$, hole concentration of $5\times10^{19}\ m^{-3}$; electron mobility $2 m^2\ V^{-1}s^{-1}$ and hole mobility $0.01\ m^2\ V^{-1}s^{-1}$. Conductivity of semiconductor sample is

(a) $1.68\ (\Omega m)^{-1}$

(b) $1.83\ (\Omega m)^{-1}$

(c) $0.59\ (\Omega m)^{-1}$

(d) $1.20\ (\Omega m)^{-1}$

29. In Young's double slit experiment, if the distance between the slits and screen is increased to double and distance between the slits is decreased to half, then fringe width is

(a) increased to four times

(b) decreased to one-third

(c) decreased to half

(d) decreased to one-fourth

30. A new system of units is proposed in which , the unit of mass is α kg, unit of length is β m, and unit of time is γ s. What will be the value of 5 J in the new system?

(a) $5\alpha^{-2}\beta^{-1}\gamma^{-2}$

(b) $5\alpha^{-1}\beta^{-2}\gamma^{2}$

(c) $5\alpha^{-1}\beta^{2}\gamma^{2}$

(d) $5\alpha\beta^{2}\gamma^{-2}$

31. A beam of alpha and electron particles are projected along $+X$-axis, experiences a force due to a magnetic field along $+Y$-axis. The direction of magnetic field for alpha particles and electrons are respectively,

(a) $-Z, -Z$

(b) $-Z, +Z$

(c) $+Z, -Z$

(d) $+Z, +Z$

32. If K_e, K_p, K_n and K_d are the respective kinetic energies of electron, proton, neutron and deuteron having same de-Broglie wavelength λ, then

(a) $K_e > K_p > K_n > K_d$

(b) $K_e = K_p = K_n = K_d$

(c) $K_e < K_p < K_n < K_d$

(d) $K_e > K_p \simeq K_n > K_d$

33. The temperature of two outer surfaces of composite slab, consisting of two materials having coefficient of thermal conductivity k and $\frac{k}{2}$ and thickness x and $\frac{x}{4}$, respectively are T_2 and T_1 ($T_2 > T_1$). The rate of heat transfer through the slab in a steady state is $\frac{2kA}{x}f$, where f is equal to

(a) $T_2 - T_1$

(b) $T_2 - 3T_1$

(c) $2T_2 - T_1$

(d) $\frac{T_2 - T_1}{3}$

34. A battery of emf E is connected across a conductor AB of variable cross-section (as shown).

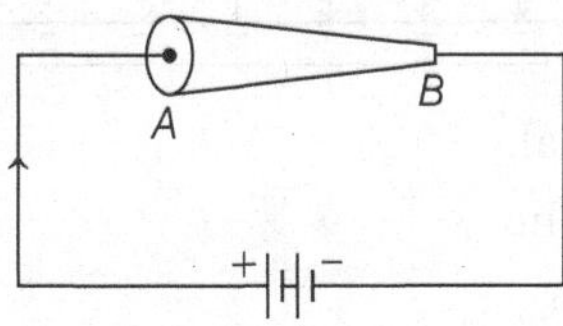

As, we move from A to B,

(a) drift velocity increases

(b) current increases

(c) electric field decreases

(d) electric potential increases

35. Two wires A and B are of the same material. Their lengths are in the ratio 2:1 and the diameter are in the ratio 1:2. If they are pulled by same force, then change in length will be in the ratio of

(a) 1:2 (b) 2:1

(c) 8:1 (d) 1:8

36. A rectangular coil of 800 turns carrying a current of 10 A when its plane making an angle of 60° with the direction of magnetic field of 5 T. If the area of the coil is 800 cm^2, then torque on the rectangular coil will be

(a) 1600 N-m
(b) 1200 N-m
(c) 1300 N-m
(d) 1400 N-m

37. A body is whirled in a horizontal circle of radius 40 cm. It has an angular velocity of 15 rad/s. Its linear velocity at any point on circular path is

(a) 2 m/s
(b) 4 m/s
(c) 8 m/s
(d) 6 m/s

38. An electron enters into an electric field E as shown below. Path of electron in electric field will be

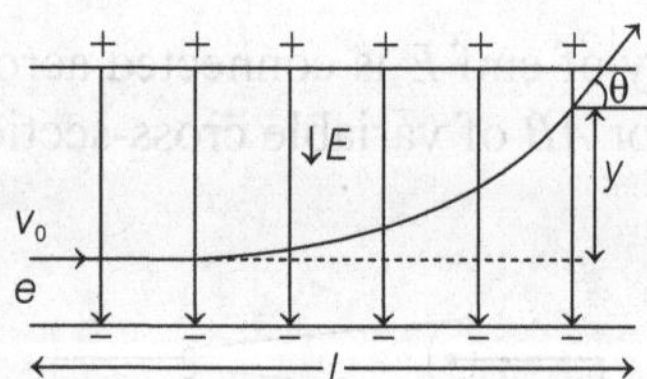

(a) elliptical
(b) parabolic
(c) circular
(d) straight line

39. A stone is thrown vertically upward with velocity u_0. It reaches a maximum height upto h. If one wishes to triple the maximum height, then the ball should be thrown with velocity

(a) $\sqrt{2}u_0$
(b) $\sqrt{3}u_0$
(c) $\sqrt{\frac{2}{3}}u_0$
(d) $\frac{\sqrt{3}}{2}u_0$

40. A current-carrying wire of length l is bent first in the shape of square and then in the shape of circle, then the ratio of their magnetic moment is

(a) $\pi:2$ (b) $\pi:1$
(c) $\pi:3$ (d) $\pi:4$

41. Eight small liquid drops of potential 16 V each are combined to form a single large drop. The potential of large drop is

(a) 32 V (b) 16 V (c) 48 V (d) 64 V

42. When an alternating voltage source $V = 100\sin\left(100\pi t + \frac{\pi}{6}\right)$ is applied to a pure capacitor of 1 μF, then the instantaneous value of current through capacitor is

(a) $0.01\,\pi\sin\left(100\pi t + \frac{\pi}{3}\right)$
(b) $0.01\,\pi\sin\left(100\pi t + \frac{\pi}{6}\right)$
(c) $0.04\,\pi\sin\left(100\pi t + \frac{\pi}{3}\right)$
(d) $0.04\,\pi\sin\left(100\pi t + \frac{\pi}{6}\right)$

43. In an electromagnetic wave, average energy density of electric field vector and magnetic field vector are u_E and u_M, then

(a) $u_E > u_M$
(b) $u_E < u_M$
(c) $u_E = u_M$
(d) $u_E = \frac{1}{u_M}$

44. Two bodies of masses m and M are situated in air and the gravitational force between them is F. The space around the masses is now filled with a liquid of specific gravity 8. The gravitational force will be

(a) $F/8$
(b) $2\sqrt{2}F$
(c) F
(d) $8\,F$

45. If ν_1 is the frequency of the series limit of Lyman series, ν_2 is the frequency of the first line of Lyman series and ν_3 is the frequency of the series limit of the Balmer series. Then,

(a) $\nu_1 = \nu_2 = \nu_3$

(b) $\nu_1 = \nu_2 + \nu_3$

(c) $\frac{1}{\nu_2} = \frac{1}{\nu_1} + \frac{1}{\nu_3}$

(d) $\frac{1}{\nu_1} = \frac{1}{\nu_2} + \frac{1}{\nu_3}$

Scan to fill up online OMR and get AI based Rank prediction on performance

Response Index

01 ⓐ ⓑ ⓒ ⓓ	14 ⓐ ⓑ ⓒ ⓓ	27 ⓐ ⓑ ⓒ ⓓ	40 ⓐ ⓑ ⓒ ⓓ
02 ⓐ ⓑ ⓒ ⓓ	15 ⓐ ⓑ ⓒ ⓓ	28 ⓐ ⓑ ⓒ ⓓ	41 ⓐ ⓑ ⓒ ⓓ
03 ⓐ ⓑ ⓒ ⓓ	16 ⓐ ⓑ ⓒ ⓓ	29 ⓐ ⓑ ⓒ ⓓ	42 ⓐ ⓑ ⓒ ⓓ
04 ⓐ ⓑ ⓒ ⓓ	17 ⓐ ⓑ ⓒ ⓓ	30 ⓐ ⓑ ⓒ ⓓ	43 ⓐ ⓑ ⓒ ⓓ
05 ⓐ ⓑ ⓒ ⓓ	18 ⓐ ⓑ ⓒ ⓓ	31 ⓐ ⓑ ⓒ ⓓ	44 ⓐ ⓑ ⓒ ⓓ
06 ⓐ ⓑ ⓒ ⓓ	19 ⓐ ⓑ ⓒ ⓓ	32 ⓐ ⓑ ⓒ ⓓ	45 ⓐ ⓑ ⓒ ⓓ
07 ⓐ ⓑ ⓒ ⓓ	20 ⓐ ⓑ ⓒ ⓓ	33 ⓐ ⓑ ⓒ ⓓ	
08 ⓐ ⓑ ⓒ ⓓ	21 ⓐ ⓑ ⓒ ⓓ	34 ⓐ ⓑ ⓒ ⓓ	
09 ⓐ ⓑ ⓒ ⓓ	22 ⓐ ⓑ ⓒ ⓓ	35 ⓐ ⓑ ⓒ ⓓ	
10 ⓐ ⓑ ⓒ ⓓ	23 ⓐ ⓑ ⓒ ⓓ	36 ⓐ ⓑ ⓒ ⓓ	
11 ⓐ ⓑ ⓒ ⓓ	24 ⓐ ⓑ ⓒ ⓓ	37 ⓐ ⓑ ⓒ ⓓ	
12 ⓐ ⓑ ⓒ ⓓ	25 ⓐ ⓑ ⓒ ⓓ	38 ⓐ ⓑ ⓒ ⓓ	
13 ⓐ ⓑ ⓒ ⓓ	26 ⓐ ⓑ ⓒ ⓓ	39 ⓐ ⓑ ⓒ ⓓ	

Performance Scanner

> 90% Excellent !	You have mastered the NEET syllabus. The concepts of this entire syllabus are on your fingertips. Maintain this momentum.
76-90% Very Good !	You have a good command over the entire NEET syllabus. Revise it again after a few days to enhance your performance.
60-75% Good !	You have a wide scope to learn for the entire NEET syllabus. Revise it again.
<60% Not Satisfactory!	You have a long way ahead of you to master the entire NEET syllabus. Revise it thoroughly.

Scan for online NEET knock offs

Space for Rough Work

Test Booklet No. **3947177**

Test Booklet Code **NC1**

NEET Chronicles 1

(2023 Paper)

Name of the Candidate (In Capitals)

____

____

____

Candidate's Signature ______________

Invigilator's Signature ______________

Facsimile signature stamp of center superintendent________________

Important Instructions

- The test is of **1 hour** duration and the Test Booklet contains **50** multiple choice questions (four options with a single correct answer) from **Physics.** The test is divided into two sections (A and B) as per details given below
  - **Section A** shall consist of **35 (Thirty-five)** questions (Questions Nos - 1 to 35). All questions are compulsory.
  - **Section B** shall consist of **15 (Fifteen)** questions (Question Nos- 36 to 50). In Section B, a candidate needs to attempt any 10 (Ten) questions out of 15 (Fifteen) in each subject. **Candidates are advised to read all 15 questions in each subject of Section B** before they start attempting the question paper. In the event of a candidate attempting more than ten questions, **the first ten questions answered by the candidate shall be evaluated.**
- Each question carries 4 marks. For each correct response, the candidate will get 4 marks. For each incorrect response, one mark will be deducted from the total scores.
- Rough work is to be done in the space provided for this purpose within the Test Booklet only.

Do not open this booklet until you start attempting the test

Physics (Q. No. 1-50)

Section-A

1. If the galvanometer (G) does not sany deflection in the circuit shown, the value of R is given by

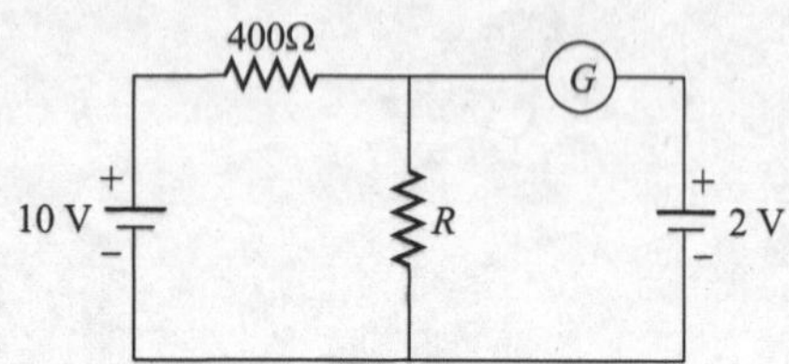

(a) 50 Ω (b) 100 Ω
(c) 400 Ω (d) 200 Ω

2. A full wave rectifier circuit consists of two *p-n* junction diodes, a centre-tapped transformer, capacitor and a load resistance. Which of these components remove the AC ripple from the rectified output?

(a) *p-n* junction diodes
(b) Capacitor
(c) Load resistance
(d) A centre-tapped transformer

3. A Carnot engine has an efficiency of 50% when its source is at a temperature 327°C. The temperature of the sink is

(a) 15°C
(b) 100°C
(c) 200°C
(d) 27°C

4. Light travels a distance x in time t_1 in air and $10x$ in time t_2 in another denser medium. What is the critical angle for this medium?

(a) $\sin^{-1}\left(\frac{10\,t_2}{t_1}\right)$ (b) $\sin^{-1}\left(\frac{t_1}{10\,t_2}\right)$

(c) $\sin^{-1}\left(\frac{10\,t_1}{t_2}\right)$ (d) $\sin^{-1}\left(\frac{t_2}{t_1}\right)$

5. The angular acceleration of a body, moving along the circumference of a circle, is

(a) along the radius towards the centre
(b) along the tangent to its position
(c) along the axis of rotation
(d) along the radius, away from centre

6. The venturimeter works on

(a) Bernoulli's principle
(b) the principle of parallel axes
(c) the principle of perpendicular axes
(d) Huygen's principle

***7.** The half-life of a radioactive substance is 20 minutes. In how much time, the activity of substance drops to (1/16)th of its initial value?

(a) 40 minutes (b) 60 minutes
(c) 80 minutes (d) 20 minutes

8. The errors in the measurement which arise due to unpredictable fluctuations in temperature and voltage supply are

(a) personal errors
(b) least count errors
(c) random error
(d) instrumental errors

9. An electric dipole is placed at an angle of 30° with an electric field of intensity 2×10^5 NC^{-1}. It experiences a torque equal to 4 N m. Calculate the magnitude of charge on the dipole, if the dipole length is 2 cm.

(a) 6 mC (b) 4 mC
(c) 2 mC (d) 8 mC

10. A football player is moving southward and suddenly turns eastward with the same speed to avoid an opponent. The force that acts on the player while turning is

(a) along northward (b) along north-east
(c) along south-west (d) along eastward

11. In hydrogen spectrum, the shortest wavelength in the Balmer series is λ. The shortest wavelength in the Bracket series is

(a) 4λ (b) 9λ
(c) 16λ (d) 2λ

12. The magnitude and direction of the current in the following circuit is

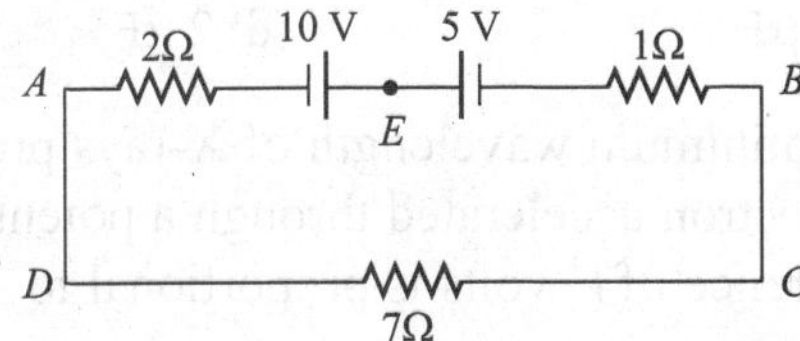

(a) 0.5 A from A to B through E
(b) $\frac{5}{9}$ A from A to B through E
(c) 1.5 A from B to A through E
(d) 0.2 A from B to A through E

13. A 12 V, 60 W lamp is connected to the secondary of a step down transformer, whose primary is connected to AC mains of 220 V. Assuming the transformer to be ideal, what is the current in the primary winding?

(a) 2.7 A (b) 3.7 A
(c) 0.37 A (d) 0.27 A

14. The work functions of caesium (Cs), Potassium (K) and sodium (Na) are 2.14 eV, 2.30 eV and 2.75 eV respectively. If incident electromagnetic radiation has an incident energy of 2.20 eV. Which of these photosensitive surfaces may emit photoelectrons?

(a) Both Na and K
(b) K only
(c) Na only
(d) Cs only

15. The potential energy of a long spring when stretched by 2 cm is U. If the spring is stretched by 8 cm, potential energy stored in it will be

(a) 4 U
(b) 8 U
(c) 16 U
(d) 2 U

16. The net magnetic flux through any closed surface is

(a) positive (b) infinity
(c) negative (d) zero

17. The amount of energy required to form a soap bubble of radius 2 cm from a soap solution is nearly (surface tension of soap solution = 0.03 N m^{-1})

(a) 5.06×10^{-4} J (b) 3.01×10^{-4} J
(c) 50.1×10^{-4} J (d) 30.16×10^{-4} J

18. Let a wire be suspended from the ceiling (rigid support) and stretched by a weight w attached at its free end. The longitudinal stress at any point of cross-sectional area A of the wire is

(a) w/A (b) $w/2A$
(c) zero (d) $2w/A$

19. Two bodies of mass m and $9m$ are placed at a distance R. The gravitational potential on the line joining the bodies where the gravitational field equals zero, will be (G = gravitational constant)

(a) $-\frac{12\,Gm}{R}$ (b) $-\frac{16\,Gm}{R}$
(c) $-\frac{20\,Gm}{R}$ (d) $-\frac{8\,Gm}{R}$

20. The temperature of a gas is $-50°$C. To what temperature the gas should be heated so that the rms speed is increased by 3 times?

(a) 3295°C (b) 3097 K
(c) 223 K (d) 669°C

21. Given below are two statements.

Statement I Photovoltaic devices can convert optical radiation into electricity.

Statement II Zener diode is designed to operate under reverse bias in breakdown region.

In the light of the above statements, choose the *most appropriate* answer from the options given below.

(a) Both Statement I and Statement II are incorrect.
(b) Statement I is correct but Statement II is incorrect.

(c) Statement I is incorrect but Statement II is correct.

(d) Both Statement I and Statement II are correct.

22. If $\oint E \cdot dS = 0$ over a surface, then:

(a) the magnitude of electric field on the surface is constant.

(b) all the charges must necessarily be inside the surface.

(c) the electric field inside the surface is necessarily uniform.

(d) the number of flux lines entering the surface must be equal to the number of flux lines leaving it.

23. In a series *L-C-R* circuit, the inductance *L* is 10 mH, capacitance *C* is $1\,\mu F$ and resistance *R* is $100\,\Omega$. The frequency at which resonance occurs is

(a) 15.9 kHz (b) 1.59 rad/s
(c) 1.59 kHz (d) 15.9 rad/s

24. An AC source is connected to a capacitor *C*. Due to decrease in its operating frequency

(a) displacement current increases.

(b) displacement current decreases.

(c) capacitive reactance remains constant.

(d) capacitive reactance decreases.

25. A bullet is fired from a gun at the speed of 280 m s^{-1} in the direction 30° above the horizontal. The maximum height attained by the bullet is ($g = 9.8\ m\,s^{-2}$, $\sin 30° = 0.5$)

(a) 2000 m (b) 1000 m
(c) 3000 m (d) 2800 m

26. A vehicle travels half the distance with speed *v* and the remaining distance with speed 2*v*. Its average speed is

(a) $\frac{2v}{3}$ (b) $\frac{4v}{3}$
(c) $\frac{3v}{4}$ (d) $\frac{v}{3}$

***27.** Resistance of a carbon resistor determined from colour codes is $(22000 \pm 5\%)\,\Omega$. The colour of third band must be

(a) green (b) orange
(c) yellow (d) red

28. The equivalent capacitance of the system shown in the following circuit is

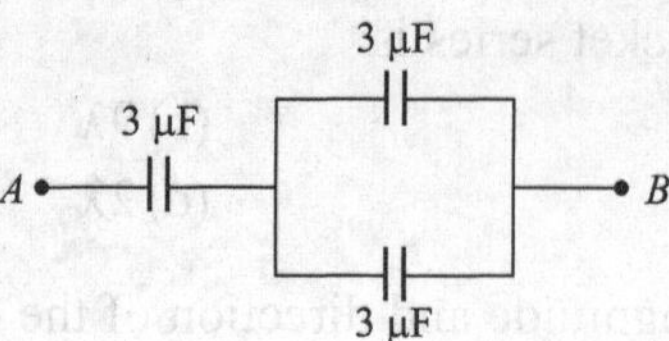

(a) $3\,\mu F$ (b) $6\,\mu F$
(c) $9\,\mu F$ (d) $2\,\mu F$

29. The minimum wavelength of X-rays produced by an electron accelerated through a potential difference of *V* volts is proportional to

(a) $\frac{1}{V}$ (b) $\frac{1}{\sqrt{V}}$
(c) V^2 (d) $\sqrt{V}$

30. The magnetic energy stored in an inductor of inductance $4\,\mu H$ carrying a current of 2 A is

(a) 4 mJ (b) 8 mJ
(c) 8 μJ (d) 4 μJ

31. For Young's double slit experiment, two statements are given below:

Statement I If screen is moved away from the plane of slits, angular separation of the fringes remains constant.

Statement II If the monochromatic source is replaced by another monochromatic source of larger wavelength, the angular separation of fringes decreases.

In the light of the above statements, choose the correct answer from the options given below.

(a) Both Statement I and Statement II are false.

(b) Statement I is true but Statement II is false.

(c) Statement I is false but Statement II is true.

(d) Both Statement I and Statement II are true.

32. The ratio of radius of gyration of a solid sphere of mass *M* and radius *R* about its own axis to the radius of gyration of the thin hollow sphere of same mass and radius about its axis is

(a) 5 : 3

(b) 2 : 5

(c) 5 : 2

(d) 3 : 5

33. In a plane electromagnetic wave travelling in free space, the electric field component oscillates sinusoidally at a frequency of 2.0×10^{10} Hz and amplitude 48 V m^{-1}. Then the amplitude of oscillating magnetic field is (Speed of light in free space $= 3 \times 10^8$ m s^{-1})

(a) 1.6×10^{-8}T
(b) 1.6×10^{-7} T
(c) 1.6×10^{-6} T
(d) 1.6×10^{-9} T

34. A metal wire has mass (0.4 ± 0.002) g, radius (0.3 ± 0.001) mm and length (5 ± 0.02) cm. The maximum possible percentage error in the measurement of density will nearly be

(a) 1.3% (b) 1.6%
(c) 1.4% (d) 1.2%

35. The ratio of frequencies of fundamental harmonic produced by an open pipe to that of closed pipe having the same length is

(a) 2:1 (b) 1:3
(c) 3:1 (d) 1:2

Section-B

36. Two thin lenses are of same focal lengths f, but one is convex and the other one is concave. When they are placed in contact with each other, the equivalent focal length of the combination will be

(a) $f / 4$
(b) $f / 2$
(c) infinite
(d) Zero

37. A satellite is orbiting just above the surface of the earth with period T. If d is the density of the earth and G is the universal constant of gravitation, the quantity $\frac{3\pi}{Gd}$ represents

(a) T^2 (b) T^3
(c) $\sqrt{T}$ (d) T

38. In the figure shown here, what is the equivalent focal length of the combination of lenses (Assume that, all layers are thin)?

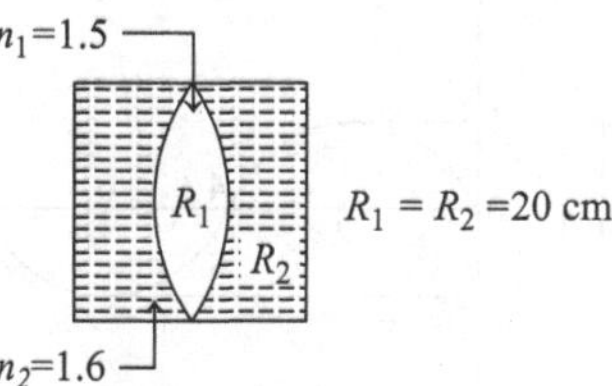

(a) – 40 cm (b) – 100 cm
(c) – 50 cm (d) 40 cm

39. A bullet from a gun is fired on a rectangular wooden block with velocity u. When bullet travels 24 cm through the block along its length horizontally, velocity of bullet becomes $\frac{u}{3}$. Then it further penetrates into the block in the same direction before coming to rest exactly at the other end of the block. The total length of the block is

(a) 24 cm (b) 28 cm
(c) 30 cm (d) 27 cm

40. 10 resistors, each of resistance R are connected in series to a battery of emf E and negligible internal resistance. Then those are connected in parallel to the same battery, the current is increased n times. The value of n is

(a) 100 (b) 1
(c) 1000 (d) 10

41. The net impedance of circuit (as shown in figure) will be

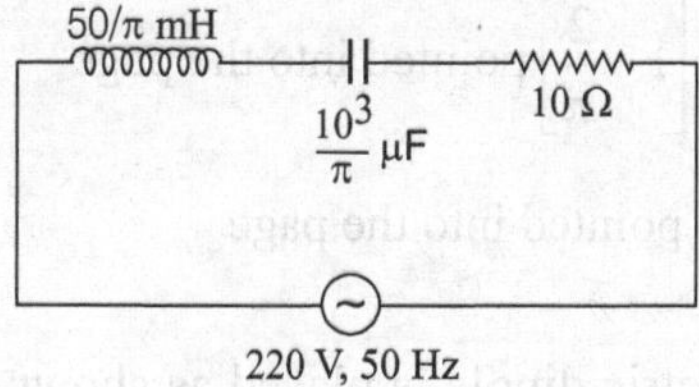

(a) 15 Ω (b) $5\sqrt{5}$ Ω
(c) 25 Ω (d) $10\sqrt{2}$ Ω

42. The x-t graph of a particle performing simple harmonic motion is shown in the figure. The acceleration of the particle at $t = 2$ s is

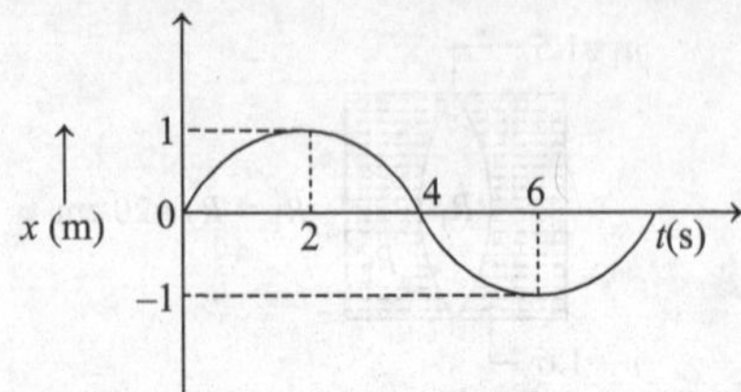

(a) $-\frac{\pi^2}{8}$ m s^{-2}

(b) $\frac{\pi^2}{16}$ m s^{-2}

(c) $-\frac{\pi^2}{16}$ m s^{-2}

(d) $\frac{\pi^2}{8}$ m s^{-2}

43. A very long conducting wire is bent in a semi-circular shape from A to B as shown in figure. The magnetic field at point P for steady current configuration is given by

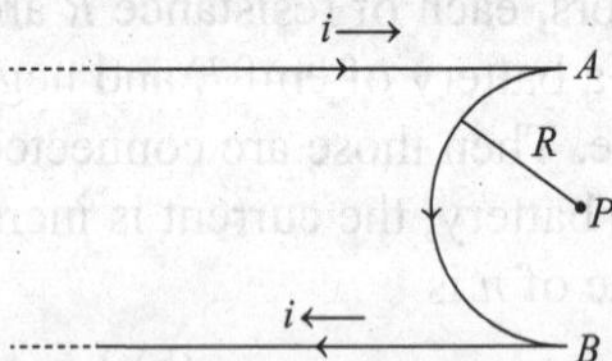

(a) $\frac{\mu_0 i}{4R}$ pointed away from the page

(b) $\frac{\mu_0 i}{4R}\left[1-\frac{2}{\pi}\right]$ pointed away from page

(c) $\frac{\mu_0 i}{4R}\left[1-\frac{2}{\pi}\right]$ pointed into the page

(d) $\frac{\mu_0 i}{4R}$ pointed into the page

44. An electric dipole is placed as shown in the figure.

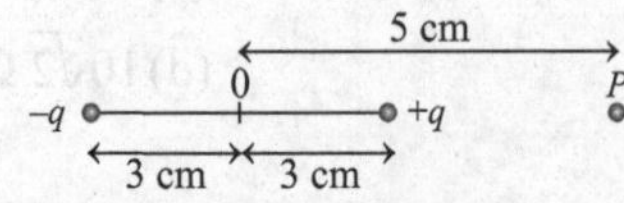

The electric potential (in 10^2 V) at point P due to the dipole is (ε_0 = permittivity of free space and $\frac{1}{4\pi\varepsilon_0} = K$)

(a) $\left(\frac{5}{8}\right)qk$ (b) $\left(\frac{8}{5}\right)qk$

(c) $\left(\frac{8}{3}\right)qk$ (d) $\left(\frac{3}{8}\right)qk$

45. The resistance of platinum wire at 0°C is 2 Ω and 6.8 Ω at 80°C. The temperature coefficient of resistance of the wire is

(a) 3×10^{-3} °C^{-1}

(b) 3×10^{-2} °C^{-1}

(c) 3×10^{-1} °C^{-1}

(d) 3×10^{-4} °C^{-1}

46. A wire carrying a current I along the positive X-axis has length L. It is kept in a magnetic field $\mathbf{B} = (2\hat{\mathbf{i}} + 3\hat{\mathbf{j}} - 4\hat{\mathbf{k}})$ T. The magnitude of the magnetic force acting on the wire is

(a) $\sqrt{5}\, IL$ (b) $5\, IL$

(c) $\sqrt{3}\, IL$ (d) $3\, IL$

47. Calculate the maximum acceleration of a moving car so that a body lying on the floor of the car remains stationary. The coefficient of static friction between the body and the floor is 0.15 ($g = 10$ m s^{-2}).

(a) 150 m s^{-2} (b) 1.5 m s^{-2}

(c) 50 m s^{-2} (d) 1.2 m s^{-2}

48. The radius of inner most orbit of hydrogen atom is 5.3×10^{-11} m. What is the radius of third allowed orbit of hydrogen atom?

(a) 1.06 Å (b) 1.59 Å

(c) 4.77 Å (d) 0.53 Å

49. For the following logic circuit, the truth table is

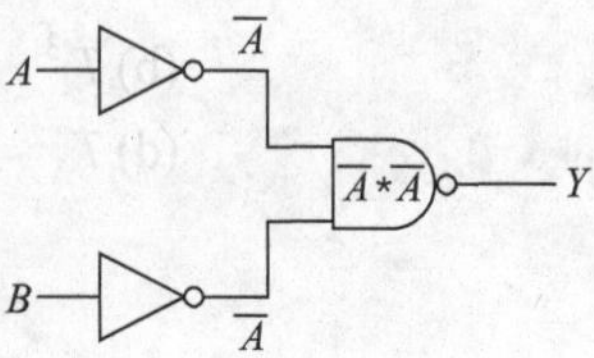

(a)

A	B	Y
0	0	0
0	1	1
1	0	1
1	1	1

(b)

A	B	Y
0	0	1
0	1	0
1	0	1
1	1	0

(c)

A	B	Y
0	0	0
0	1	0
1	0	0
1	1	1

(d)

A	B	Y
0	0	1
0	1	1
1	0	1
1	1	0

50. A horizontal bridge is built across a river. A student standing on the bridge throws a small ball vertically upwards with a velocity 4 ms^{-1}. The ball strikes the water surface after 4 s. The height of bridge above water surface is (Take, $g = 10 \text{ m s}^{-2}$)

(a) 60 m (b) 64 m
(c) 68 m (d) 56 m

Response Index

01 ⓐ ⓑ ⓒ ⓓ	14 ⓐ ⓑ ⓒ ⓓ	27 ⓐ ⓑ ⓒ ⓓ	40 ⓐ ⓑ ⓒ ⓓ
02 ⓐ ⓑ ⓒ ⓓ	15 ⓐ ⓑ ⓒ ⓓ	28 ⓐ ⓑ ⓒ ⓓ	41 ⓐ ⓑ ⓒ ⓓ
03 ⓐ ⓑ ⓒ ⓓ	16 ⓐ ⓑ ⓒ ⓓ	29 ⓐ ⓑ ⓒ ⓓ	42 ⓐ ⓑ ⓒ ⓓ
04 ⓐ ⓑ ⓒ ⓓ	17 ⓐ ⓑ ⓒ ⓓ	30 ⓐ ⓑ ⓒ ⓓ	43 ⓐ ⓑ ⓒ ⓓ
05 ⓐ ⓑ ⓒ ⓓ	18 ⓐ ⓑ ⓒ ⓓ	31 ⓐ ⓑ ⓒ ⓓ	44 ⓐ ⓑ ⓒ ⓓ
06 ⓐ ⓑ ⓒ ⓓ	19 ⓐ ⓑ ⓒ ⓓ	32 ⓐ ⓑ ⓒ ⓓ	45 ⓐ ⓑ ⓒ ⓓ
07 ⓐ ⓑ ⓒ ⓓ	20 ⓐ ⓑ ⓒ ⓓ	33 ⓐ ⓑ ⓒ ⓓ	46 ⓐ ⓑ ⓒ ⓓ
08 ⓐ ⓑ ⓒ ⓓ	21 ⓐ ⓑ ⓒ ⓓ	34 ⓐ ⓑ ⓒ ⓓ	47 ⓐ ⓑ ⓒ ⓓ
09 ⓐ ⓑ ⓒ ⓓ	22 ⓐ ⓑ ⓒ ⓓ	35 ⓐ ⓑ ⓒ ⓓ	48 ⓐ ⓑ ⓒ ⓓ
10 ⓐ ⓑ ⓒ ⓓ	23 ⓐ ⓑ ⓒ ⓓ	36 ⓐ ⓑ ⓒ ⓓ	49 ⓐ ⓑ ⓒ ⓓ
11 ⓐ ⓑ ⓒ ⓓ	24 ⓐ ⓑ ⓒ ⓓ	37 ⓐ ⓑ ⓒ ⓓ	50 ⓐ ⓑ ⓒ ⓓ
12 ⓐ ⓑ ⓒ ⓓ	25 ⓐ ⓑ ⓒ ⓓ	38 ⓐ ⓑ ⓒ ⓓ	
13 ⓐ ⓑ ⓒ ⓓ	26 ⓐ ⓑ ⓒ ⓓ	39 ⓐ ⓑ ⓒ ⓓ	

Performance Scanner

> 90% Excellent !	You have mastered the NEET syllabus. The concepts of this syllabus are on your fingertips. Maintain this momentum.
76-90% Very Good !	You have a good command over the NEET syllabus. Revise it again after a few days and enhance your performance.
60-75% Good !	You have a wide scope to learn for the NEET syllabus. Revise it again.
<60% Not Satisfactory!	You have a long way ahead of you to master the NEET syllabus. Revise it thoroughly.

Space for Rough Work

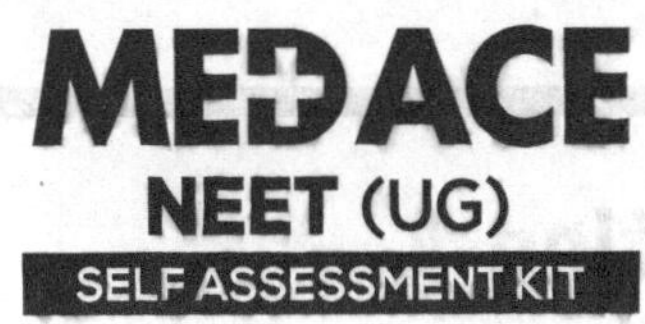

Test Booklet No. 3947178

Test Booklet Code NC2

NEET Chronicles 2

(2024 Paper)

Name of the Candidate (In Capitals)

____

____

____

Candidate's Signature ____________

Invigilator's Signature ____________

Facsimile signature stamp of center superintendent____________

Important Instructions

- The test is of **1 hour** duration and the Test Booklet contains **50** multiple choice questions (four options with a single correct answer) from **Physics**. The test is divided into two sections (A and B) as per details given below
  - **Section A** shall consist of **35 (Thirty-five)** questions (Questions Nos - 1 to 35). All questions are compulsory.
  - **Section B** shall consist of **15 (Fifteen)** questions (Question Nos- 36 to 50). In Section B, a candidate needs to attempt any 10 (Ten) questions out of 15 (Fifteen) in each subject. **Candidates are advised to read all 15 questions in each subject of Section B** before they start attempting the question paper. In the event of a candidate attempting more than ten questions, **the first ten questions answered by the candidate shall be evaluated.**
- Each question carries 4 marks. For each correct response, the candidate will get 4 marks. For each incorrect response, one mark will be deducted from the total scores.
- Rough work is to be done in the space provided for this purpose within the Test Booklet only.

Do not open this booklet until you start attempting the test

Physics (Q. No. 1-50)

Section-A

1. A bob is whirled in a horizontal plane by means of a string with an initial speed of ω rpm. The tension in the string is T. If speed becomes 2ω while keeping the same radius, the tension in the string becomes

(a) T (b) $4T$
(c) $T/4$ (d) $\sqrt{2}T$

2. A particle moving with uniform speed in a circular path maintains

(a) constant velocity
(b) constant acceleration
(c) constant velocity but varying acceleration
(d) varying velocity and varying acceleration

3. A logic circuit provides the output Y as per the following truth table.

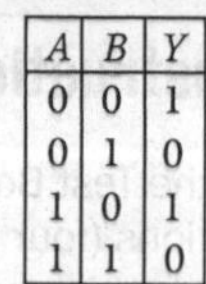

A	B	Y
0	0	1
0	1	0
1	0	1
1	1	0

The expression for the output Y is

(a) $A.B + \bar{A}$ (b) $A.\bar{B} + \bar{A}$
(c) $\bar{B}$ (d) B

4.

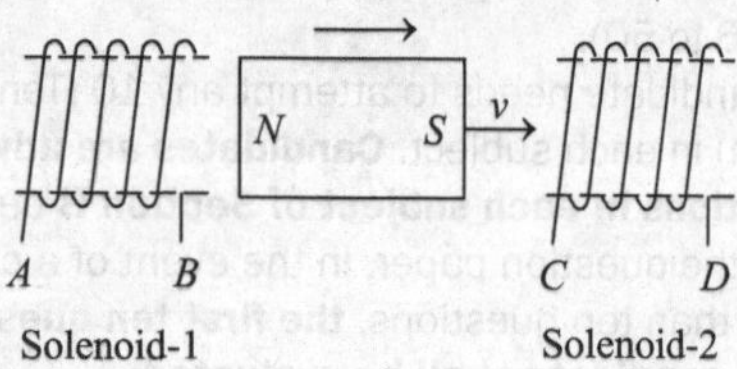

In the above diagram, a strong bar magnet is moving towards solenoid-2 from solenoid-1. The direction of induced current in solenoid-1 and that in solenoid-2, respectively, are through the directions.

(a) AB and DC (b) BA and CD
(c) AB and CD (d) BA and DC

5. Given below are two statements. One is labelled as Assertion (A) and the other is labelled as Reason (R).

Assertion (A) The potential V at any axial point, at 2 m distance r from the centre of the dipole of dipole moment vector **p** of magnitude, 4×10^{-6} C m, is $\pm 9 \times 10^3$ V.

(Take, $\frac{1}{4\pi\varepsilon_0} = 9 \times 10^9$ SI units)

Reason (R) $V = \pm \frac{2p}{4\pi\varepsilon_0 r^2}$, where r is the distance of any axial point, situated at 2 m from the centre of the dipole.

In the light of the above statements, choose the correct answer from the options given below.

(a) Both A and R are true and R is the correct explanation of A.
(b) Both A and R are true but R is not the correct explanation of A.
(c) A is true but R is false.
(d) A is false but R is true.

6. Match List-I with List-II.

List-I (Material)	List-II (Susceptibility (χ))
A Diamagnetic	I. $\chi = 0$
B Ferromagnetic	II. $0 > \chi \geq -1$
C Paramagnetic	III. $\chi >> 1$
D Non-magnetic	IV. $0 < \chi < \varepsilon$ (a small positive number)

Choose the correct answer from the options given below.

(a) A-II, B-III, C-IV, D-I
(b) A-II, B-I, C-III, D-IV
(c) A-III, B-II, C-I, D-IV
(d) A-IV, B-III, C-II, D-I

7. In a uniform magnetic field of 0.049 T, a magnetic needle performs 20 complete oscillations in 5 s as shown. The moment of inertia of the needle is 9.8×10^{-6} kg m^2. If the magnitude of magnetic moment of the needle is $x \times 10^{-5}$ Am^2, then the value of x is

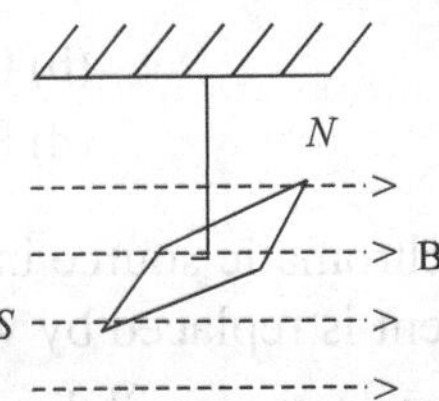

(a) $5\pi^2$ (b) $128\pi^2$
(c) $50\pi^2$ (d) $1280\pi^2$

8. In an ideal transformer, the turns ratio is $\frac{N_p}{N_s} = \frac{1}{2}$. The ratio $V_s : V_p$ is equal to (the symbols carry their usual meaning)

(a) 1 : 2 (b) 2 : 1
(c) 1 : 1 (d) 1 : 4

9. In a vernier callipers, $(N + 1)$ divisions of vernier scale coincide with N divisions of main scale. If 1 MSD represents 0.1 mm, the vernier constant (in cm) is

(a) $\frac{1}{10N}$ (b) $\frac{1}{100(N+1)}$
(c) $100N$ (d) $10(N + 1)$

10. A horizontal force 10 N is applied to a block A as shown in figure. The mass of blocks A and B are 2 kg and 3 kg, respectively. The blocks slide over a frictionless surface. The force exerted by block A on block B is

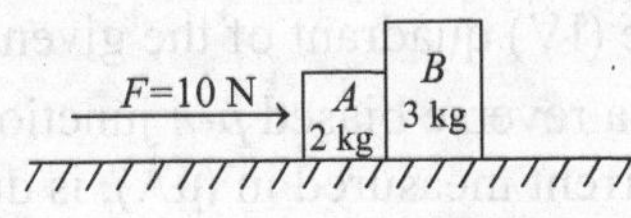

(a) zero (b) 4 N
(c) 6 N (d) 10 N

11. If $x = 5 \sin\left(\pi t + \frac{\pi}{3}\right)$ m represents the motion of a particle executing simple harmonic motion, the amplitude and time period of motion, respectively, are

(a) 5 cm, 2 s (b) 5 m, 2 s
(c) 5 cm, 1 s (d) 5 m, 1 s

12. The terminal voltage of the battery, whose emf is 10 V and internal resistance 1Ω when connected through an external resistance of 4 Ω as shown in the figure is

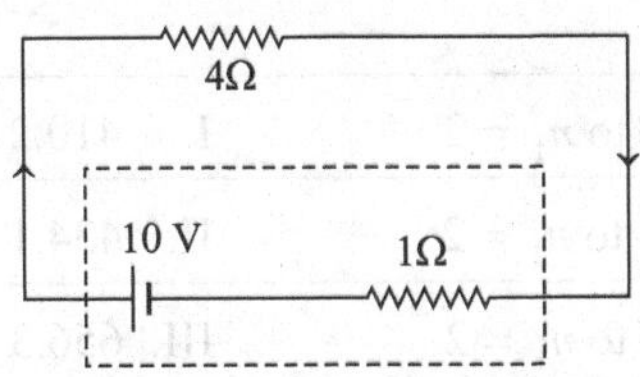

(a) 4 V (b) 6 V
(c) 8 V (d) 10 V

13. Given below are two statements.

Statement I Atoms are electrically neutral as they contain equal number of positive and negative charges.

Statement II Atoms of each element are stable and emit their characteristic spectrum.

In the light of the above statements, choose the most appropriate answer from the options given below.

(a) Both Statement I and Statement II are correct.
(b) Both Statement I and Statement II are incorrect.
(c) Statement I is correct but Statement II is incorrect.
(d) Statement I is incorrect but Statement II is correct.

14. If c is the velocity of light in free space, the correct statements about photon among the following are

A. The energy of a photon is $E = h\nu$.
B. The velocity of a photon is c.
C. The momentum of a photon, $p = \frac{h\nu}{c}$
D. In a photon-electron collision, both total energy and total momentum are conserved.
E. Photon possesses positive charge.

Choose the correct answer from the options given below

(a) A and B only
(b) A, B, C and D only
(c) A, C and D only
(d) A, B, D and E only

15. Match List I with List II.

List I (Spectral lines of Hydrogen for transitions from)	List II (Wavelengths (nm))
A. $n_2 = 3$ to $n_1 = 2$	I. 410.2
B. $n_2 = 4$ to $n_1 = 2$	II. 434.1
C. $n_2 = 5$ to $n_1 = 2$	III. 656.3
D. $n_2 = 6$ to $n_1 = 2$	IV. 486.1

Choose the correct answer from the options given below.

(a) A-II, B-I, C-IV, D-III
(b) A-III, B-IV, C-II, D-I
(c) A-IV, B-III, C-I, D-II
(d) A-I, B-II, C-III, D-IV

16. A tightly wound 100 turns coil of radius 10 cm carries a current of 7 A. The magnitude of the magnetic field at the centre of the coil is (Take, permeability of free space as $4\pi \times 10^{-7}$ SI units)

(a) 44 mT (b) 4.4 T
(c) 4.4 mT (d) 44 T

17. The output Y of the given logic gate is similar to the output of an/a

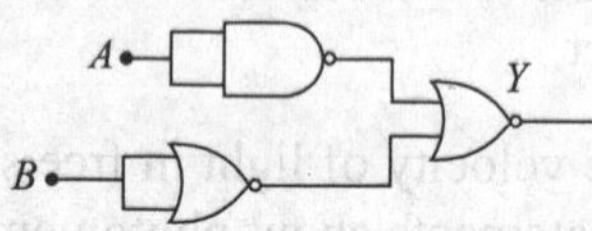

(a) NAND gate (b) NOR gate
(c) OR gate (d) AND gate

18. A wire of length l and resistance 100 Ω is divided into 10 equal parts. The first 5 parts are connected in series while the next 5 parts are connected in parallel. The two combinations are again connected in series. The resistance of this final combination is

(a) 26 Ω (b) 52 Ω
(c) 55 Ω (d) 60 Ω

19. $^{290}_{82}X \xrightarrow{\alpha} {}^{286}_{80}Y \xrightarrow{e^+} Z \xrightarrow{\beta^-} P \xrightarrow{e^-} Q$

In the nuclear emission stated above, the mass number and atomic number of the product Q respectively are

(a) 280, 81 (b) 286, 80
(c) 288, 82 (d) 286, 81

20. The maximum elongation of a steel wire of 1 m length if the elastic limit of steel and its Young's modulus, respectively, are 8×10^8 Nm^{-2} and 2×10^{11} Nm^{-2}, is

(a) 4 mm (b) 0.4 mm
(c) 40 mm (d) 8 mm

21. If the monochromatic source in Young's double slit experiment is replaced by white light, then

(a) interference pattern will disappear
(b) there will be a central dark fringe surrounded by a few coloured fringes
(c) there will be a central bright white fringe surrounded by a few coloured fringes
(d) all bright fringes will be of equal width

22. At any instant of time t, the displacement of any particle is given by $2t - 1$ (SI unit) under the influence of force of 5 N. The value of instantaneous power is (in SI unit)

(a) 10 (b) 5
(c) 7 (d) 6

23. Consider the following statements A and B and identify the correct answer.

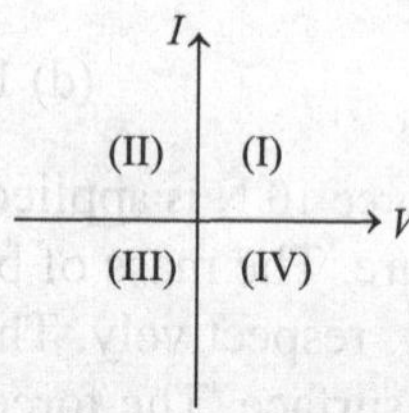

A. For a solar-cell, the I-V characteristics lies in the (IV) quadrant of the given graph.
B. In a reverse biased p-n junction diode, the current measured in (μA), is due to majority charge carriers.

(a) A is correct but B is incorrect.
(b) A is incorrect but B is correct.
(c) Both A and B are correct.
(d) Both A and B are incorrect.

24. Two bodies A and B of same mass undergo completely inelastic one dimensional collision. The body A moves with velocity v_1 while body B is at rest before collision. The velocity of the system after collision is v_2. The ratio is

(a) 1 : 2 (b) 2 : 1
(c) 4 : 1 (d) 1 : 4

25. A light ray enters through a right angled prism at point P with the angle of incidence 30° as shown in figure. It travels through the prism parallel to its base BC and emerges along the face AC. The refractive index of the prism is

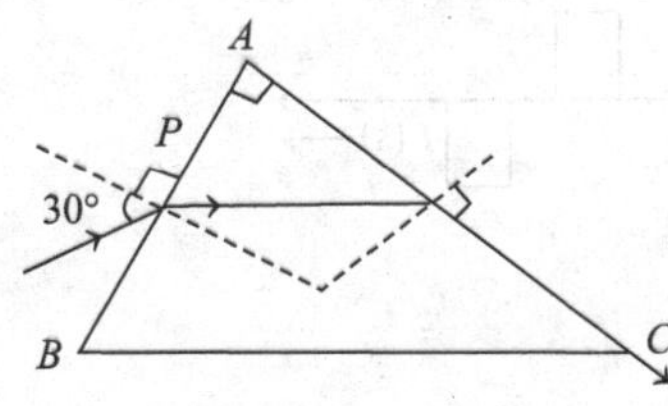

(a) $\frac{\sqrt{5}}{4}$ (b) $\frac{\sqrt{5}}{2}$

(c) $\frac{\sqrt{3}}{4}$ (d) $\frac{\sqrt{3}}{2}$

26. The graph which shows the variation of $\frac{1}{\lambda^2}$ and its kinetic energy, E is (where, λ is de-Broglie wavelength of a free particle)

(a) 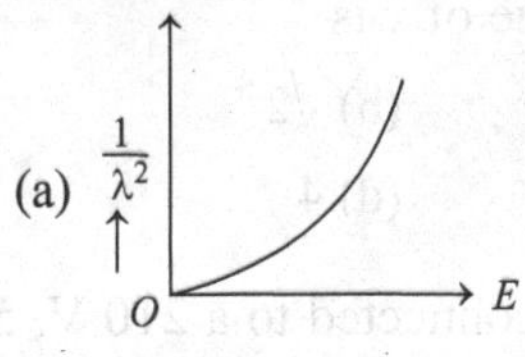

(b) 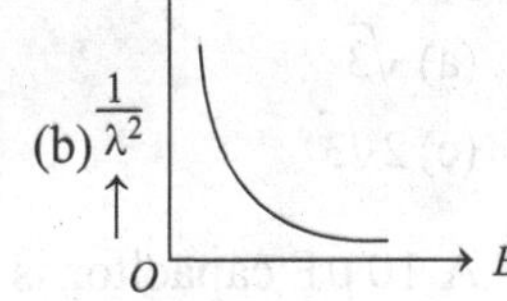

(c) 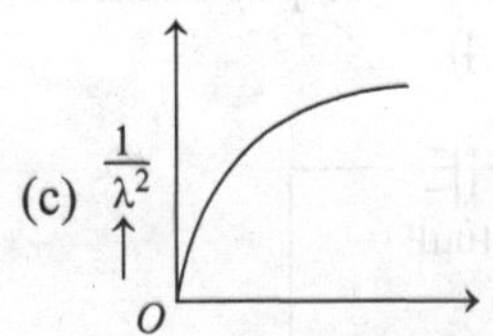

(d) 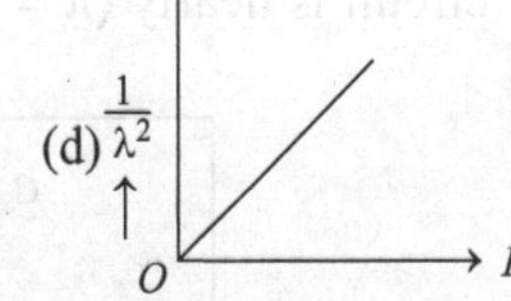

27. The quantities which have the same dimensions as those of solid angle are
(a) strain and angle
(b) stress and angle
(c) strain and arc
(d) angular speed and stress

28. An unpolarised light beam strikes a glass surface at Brewster's angle. Then
(a) the reflected light will be partially polarised.
(b) the refracted light will be completely polarised.
(c) both the reflected and refracted light will be completely polarised.
(d) the reflected light will be completely polarised but the refracted light will be partially polarised.

29. The moment of inertia of a thin rod about an axis passing through its mid-point and perpendicular to the rod is 2400 g cm^2. The length of the 400 g rod is nearly
(a) 8.5 cm (b) 17.5 cm
(c) 20.7 cm (d) 72.0 cm

30. A thin flat circular disc of radius 4.5 cm is placed gently over the surface of water. If surface tension of water is 0.07 Nm^{-1}, then the excess force required to take it away from the surface is
(a) 19.8 mN (b) 198 N
(c) 1.98 mN (d) 99 N

31. A thermodynamic system is taken through the cycle $abcda$. The work done by the gas along the path bc is

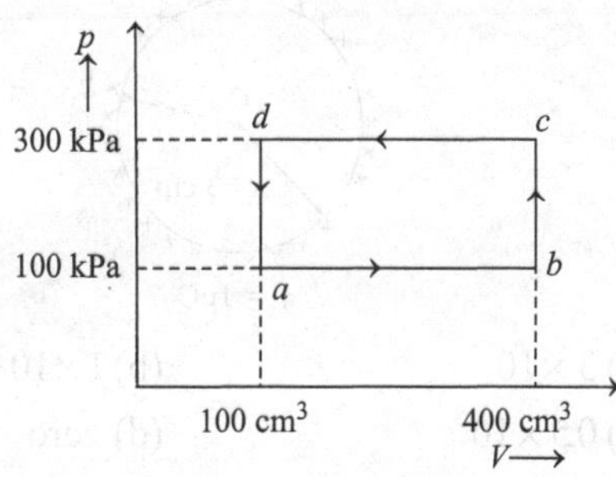

(a) zero (b) 30 J
(c) −90 J (d) −60 J

32. A wheel of a bullock cart is rolling on a level road as shown in the figure below. If its linear speed is v in the direction shown, which one of the following options is correct (P and Q are any highest and lowest points on the wheel, respectively)?

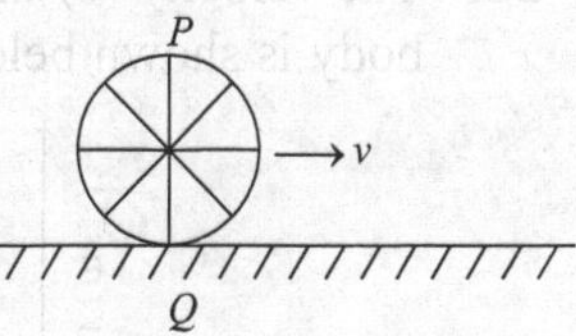

(a) Point P moves slower than point Q
(b) Point P moves faster than point Q
(c) Both the points P and Q move with equal speed
(d) Point P has zero speed

33. The mass of a planet is $1/10$ th that of the earth and its diameter is half that of the earth. The acceleration due to gravity on that planet is

(a) 19.6 ms^{-2} (b) 9.8 ms^{-2}
(c) 4.9 ms^{-2} (d) 3.92 ms^{-2}

34. In the following circuit, the equivalent capacitance between terminal A and terminal B is

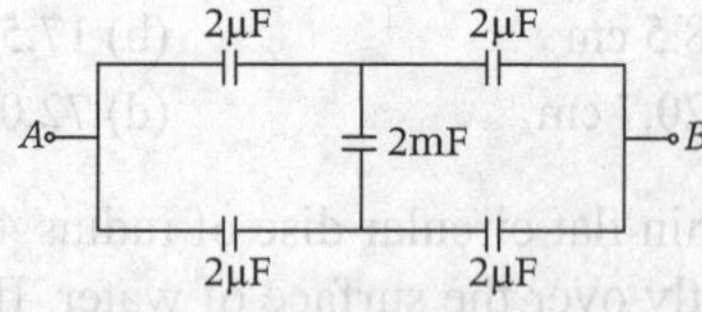

(a) 2 μF (b) 1 μF
(c) 0.5 μF (d) 4 μF

35. A thin spherical shell is charged by some source. The potential difference between the two points C and P (in V) shown in the figure is

(Take, $\frac{1}{4\pi\varepsilon_0} = 9 \times 10^9$ SI units)

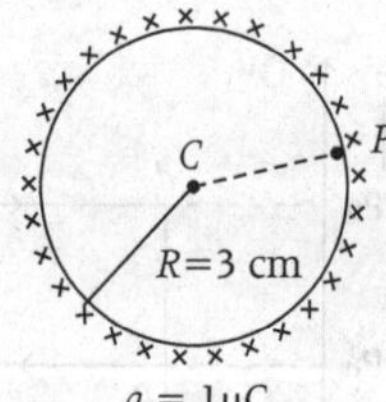

(a) 3×10^5 (b) 1×10^5
(c) 0.5×10^5 (d) zero

Section-B

36. The velocity (v)-time (t) plot of the motion of a body is shown below

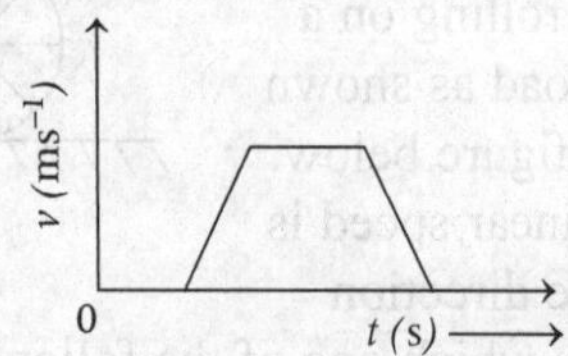

The acceleration (a)- time (t) graph that best suits this motion is

(a)
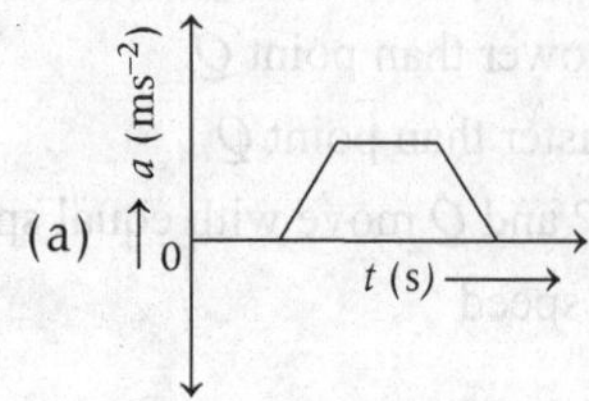

(b)
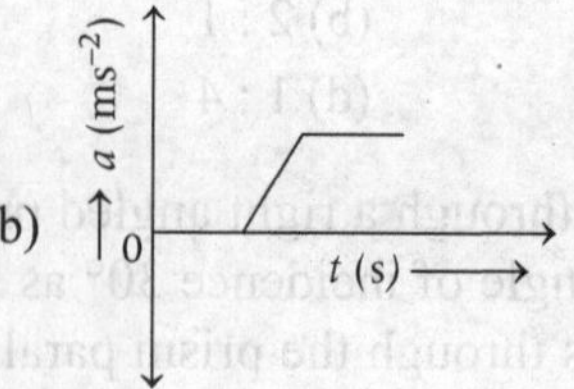

(c)
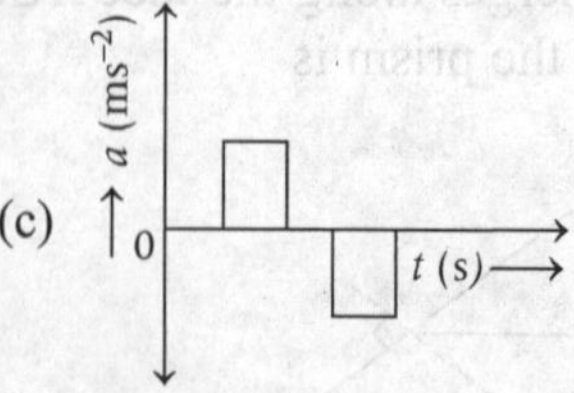

(d)
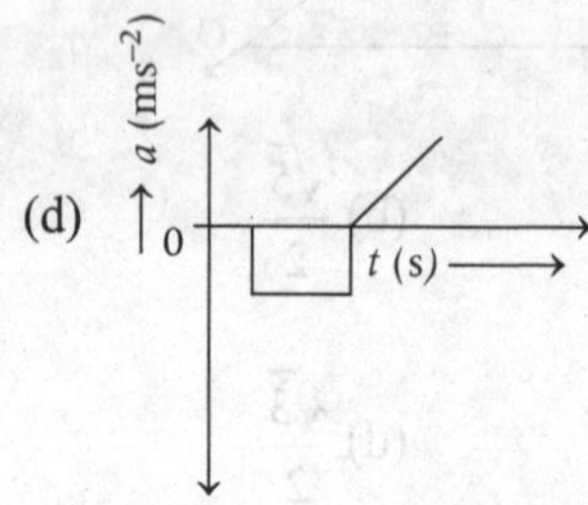

37. If the mass of the bob in a simple pendulum is increased to thrice its original mass and its length is made half its original length, then the new time period of oscillation is $x/2$ times its original time period. Then, the value of x is

(a) $\sqrt{3}$ (b) $\sqrt{2}$
(c) $2\sqrt{3}$ (d) 4

38. A 10 μF capacitor is connected to a 210 V, 50 Hz source as shown in figure. The peak current in the circuit is nearly ($\pi = 3.14$).

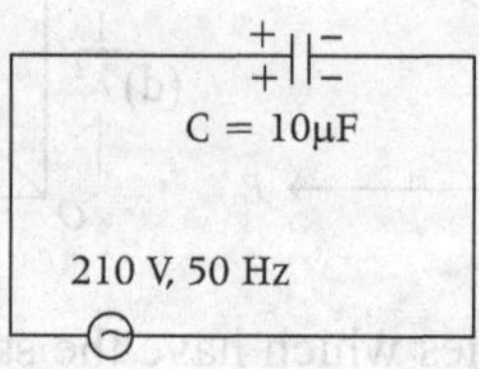

(a) 0.58 A
(b) 0.93 A
(c) 1.20 A
(d) 0.35 A

39. The following graph represents the T-V curves of an ideal gas (where T is the temperature and V the volume) at three pressures p_1, p_2 and p_3 compared with those of Charles's law represented as dotted lines.

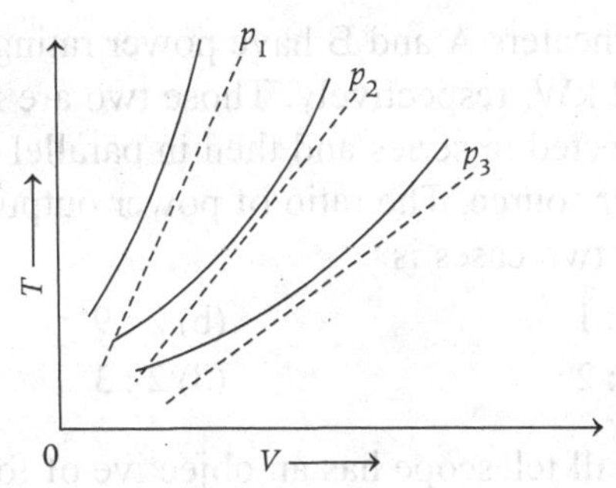

Then the correct relation is.

(a) $p_3 > p_2 > p_1$
(b) $p_1 > p_3 > p_2$
(c) $p_2 > p_1 > p_3$
(d) $p_1 > p_2 > p_3$

40. An iron bar of length L has magnetic moment M. It is bent at the middle of its length such that the two arms make an angle 60° with each other. The magnetic moment of this new magnet is

(a) M (b) $\frac{M}{2}$
(c) $2M$ (d) $\frac{M}{\sqrt{3}}$

41. The minimum energy required to launch a satellite of mass m from the surface of earth of mass M and radius R in a circular orbit at an altitude of $2R$ from the surface of the earth is

(a) $\frac{5GmM}{6R}$
(b) $\frac{2GmM}{3R}$
(c) $\frac{GmM}{2R}$
(d) $\frac{GmM}{3R}$

42. A parallel plate capacitor is charged by connecting it to a battery through a resistor. If I is the current in the circuit, then in the gap between the plates.

(a) There is no current.
(b) Displacement current of magnitude equal to I flows in the same direction as I.
(c) Displacement current of magnitude equal to I flows in a direction opposite to that of I.
(d) Displacement current of magnitude greater than I flows but can be in any direction.

43. The property which is not of an electromagnetic wave travelling in free space is that

(a) They are transverse in nature
(b) The energy density in electric field is equal to energy density in magnetic field
(c) They travel with a speed equal to $\frac{1}{\sqrt{\mu_0 \varepsilon_0}}$
(d) They originate from charges moving with uniform speed

44. A metallic bar of Young's modulus, 0.5×10^{11} N m^{-2} and coefficient of linear thermal expansion 10^{-5} °C^{-1}, length 1 m and area of cross-section 10^{-3} m^2 is heated from 0°C to 100°C without expansion or bending. The compressive force developed in it is

(a) 5×10^3 N (b) 50×10^3 N
(c) 100×10^3 N (d) 2×10^3 N

45. Choose the correct circuit which can achieve the bridge balance.

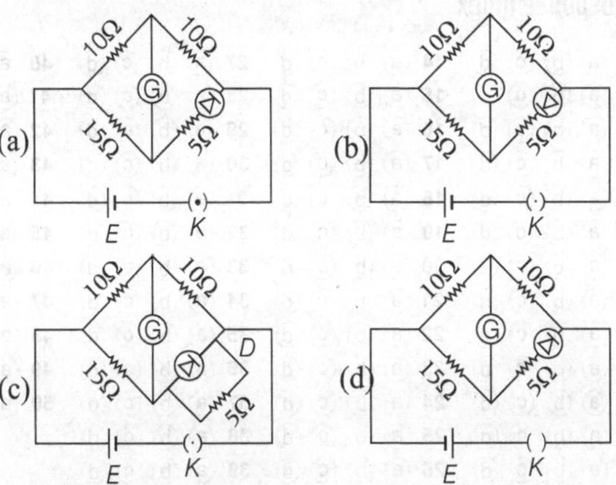

46. A sheet is placed on a horizontal surface in front of a strong magnetic pole. A force is needed to

A. hold the sheet there if it is magnetic.
B. hold the sheet there if it is non-magnetic.
C. move the sheet away from the pole with uniform velocity if it is conducting.
D. move the sheet away from the pole with uniform velocity if it is both, non-conducting and non-polar.

Choose the correct statement(s) from the options given below

(a) B and D only
(b) A and C only
(c) A, C and D only
(d) C only

47. If the plates of a parallel plate capacitor connected to a battery are moved close to each other, then

A. the charge stored in it, increases.
B. the energy stored in it, decreases.
C. its capacitance increases.
D. the ratio of charge to its potential remains the same.
E. the product of charge and voltage increases.

Choose the most appropriate answer from the options given below

(a) A, B and E only
(b) A, C and E only
(c) B, D and E only
(d) A, B and C only

48. Two heaters A and B have power rating of 1 kW and 2 kW, respectively. Those two are first connected in series and then in parallel to a fixed power source. The ratio of power outputs for these two cases is

(a) 1 : 1 (b) 2 : 9
(c) 1 : 2 (d) 2 : 3

49. A small telescope has an objective of focal length 140 cm and an eyepiece of focal length 5.0 cm. The magnifying power of telescope for viewing a distant object is

(a) 34 (b) 28
(c) 17 (d) 32

50. A force defined by $F = \alpha t^2 + \beta t$ acts on a particle at a given time t. The factor which is dimensionless, if α and β are constants, is

(a) $\frac{\beta t}{\alpha}$ (b) $\frac{\alpha t}{\beta}$
(c) $\alpha\beta t$ (d) $\frac{\alpha\beta}{t}$

Response Index

01	ⓐ ⓑ ⓒ ⓓ	14	ⓐ ⓑ ⓒ ⓓ	27	ⓐ ⓑ ⓒ ⓓ	40	ⓐ ⓑ ⓒ ⓓ
02	ⓐ ⓑ ⓒ ⓓ	15	ⓐ ⓑ ⓒ ⓓ	28	ⓐ ⓑ ⓒ ⓓ	41	ⓐ ⓑ ⓒ ⓓ
03	ⓐ ⓑ ⓒ ⓓ	16	ⓐ ⓑ ⓒ ⓓ	29	ⓐ ⓑ ⓒ ⓓ	42	ⓐ ⓑ ⓒ ⓓ
04	ⓐ ⓑ ⓒ ⓓ	17	ⓐ ⓑ ⓒ ⓓ	30	ⓐ ⓑ ⓒ ⓓ	43	ⓐ ⓑ ⓒ ⓓ
05	ⓐ ⓑ ⓒ ⓓ	18	ⓐ ⓑ ⓒ ⓓ	31	ⓐ ⓑ ⓒ ⓓ	44	ⓐ ⓑ ⓒ ⓓ
06	ⓐ ⓑ ⓒ ⓓ	19	ⓐ ⓑ ⓒ ⓓ	32	ⓐ ⓑ ⓒ ⓓ	45	ⓐ ⓑ ⓒ ⓓ
07	ⓐ ⓑ ⓒ ⓓ	20	ⓐ ⓑ ⓒ ⓓ	33	ⓐ ⓑ ⓒ ⓓ	46	ⓐ ⓑ ⓒ ⓓ
08	ⓐ ⓑ ⓒ ⓓ	21	ⓐ ⓑ ⓒ ⓓ	34	ⓐ ⓑ ⓒ ⓓ	47	ⓐ ⓑ ⓒ ⓓ
09	ⓐ ⓑ ⓒ ⓓ	22	ⓐ ⓑ ⓒ ⓓ	35	ⓐ ⓑ ⓒ ⓓ	48	ⓐ ⓑ ⓒ ⓓ
10	ⓐ ⓑ ⓒ ⓓ	23	ⓐ ⓑ ⓒ ⓓ	36	ⓐ ⓑ ⓒ ⓓ	49	ⓐ ⓑ ⓒ ⓓ
11	ⓐ ⓑ ⓒ ⓓ	24	ⓐ ⓑ ⓒ ⓓ	37	ⓐ ⓑ ⓒ ⓓ	50	ⓐ ⓑ ⓒ ⓓ
12	ⓐ ⓑ ⓒ ⓓ	25	ⓐ ⓑ ⓒ ⓓ	38	ⓐ ⓑ ⓒ ⓓ		
13	ⓐ ⓑ ⓒ ⓓ	26	ⓐ ⓑ ⓒ ⓓ	39	ⓐ ⓑ ⓒ ⓓ		

Performance Scanner

> 90% Excellent !	You have mastered the NEET syllabus. The concepts of this syllabus are on your fingertips. Maintain this momentum.
76-90% Very Good !	You have a good command over the NEET syllabus. Revise it again after a few days and enhance your performance.
60-75% Good !	You have a wide scope to learn for the NEET syllabus. Revise it again.
<60% Not Satisfactory!	You have a long way ahead of you to master the NEET syllabus. Revise it thoroughly.

MED ACE

NEET (UG) SELF ASSESSMENT KIT

Exactly as per the Latest Pattern of NTA

Released on 25 Jan 2025

PHYSICS - XIIth

Hints, Solutions & Mind Maps Booklet

Authors
Sunny Kumar,
Anshuman & Kajal

ARIHANT PRAKASHAN (SERIES), MEERUT

卐 **Administrative & Production Offices**

Regd. Office

'Ramchhaya' 4577/15, Agarwal Road, Darya Ganj, New Delhi -110002
Tele: 011- 47630600, 43518550

卐 **Head Office**

Kalindi, TP Nagar, Meerut (UP) - 250002
Tel: 0121-7156203, 7156204

卐 **Sales & Support Offices**

Agra, Ahmedabad, Bengaluru, Bareilly, Chennai, Delhi, Guwahati, Hyderabad, Jaipur, Jhansi, Kolkata, Lucknow, Nagpur & Pune.

卐 **PRICE** ₹ 1200.00

卐 **PO No :** TXT-59-T063622-03-25

Published by Arihant Publications (India) Ltd.

For further information about the books published by Arihant, log on to www.arihantbooks.com or e-mail at info@arihantbooks.com

PHYSICS XIIth

CONTENT LIST

MEDACE

Hints & Solutions

Ch-01 Electric Charges and Fields

Topical Follow Thru

Test-1

1. (a) Given, $q_1 + q_2 = 15\mu C$ ...(i)

From Coulomb's law,

$$F = \frac{1}{4\pi\varepsilon_0} \cdot \frac{q_1 q_2}{r^2}$$

$$0.050 = \frac{9\times 10^9 \times q_1 q_2}{(3)^2}$$

$$q_1 q_2 = 50\times 10^{-12} \quad ...(ii)$$

Now, $(q_1 - q_2)^2 = (q_1 + q_2)^2 - 4q_1 q_2$

From Eqs. (i) and (ii), we get

$$(q_1 - q_2)^2 = (15\times 10^{-6})^2 - 4\times 50\times 10^{-12}$$

$$(q_1 - q_2)^2 = (225 - 200)\times 10^{-12}$$

$$(q_1 - q_1)^2 = 25\times 10^{-12}$$

$$q_1 - q_2 = 5\times 10^{-6} = 5\mu C \quad ...(iii)$$

From Eqs. (i) and (iii), we get

$$q_1 = 10\mu C$$

$$q_2 = 5\mu C$$

2. (a) When a soap bubble is given a negative charge, its radius will increase.

3. (c) $\because F = k\frac{q_1 q_2}{r^2}$

$$= (9\times 10^9)\frac{(1.6\times 10^{-19})(1.6\times 10^{-19})}{(1.6\times 10^{-6})^2}$$

$$= 9\times 10^{-17} N$$

4. (b) Force in air, $F_{air} = \frac{q_1 q_2}{4\pi\varepsilon_0 r^2}$

Force in medium,

$$F_m = \frac{q_1' q_2}{4\pi\varepsilon_0 K(r^2)}$$

According to question, $F = F_m$

It is possible only when the new charge,

$$q_1' = Kq_1$$

5. (b) Coulomb's force = Centripetal force

$$\frac{1}{4\pi\varepsilon_0}\frac{Qq}{r^2} = mr\omega^2$$

$$= \frac{4\pi^2 mr}{T^2} \quad \left(\because \omega = \frac{2\pi}{T}\right)$$

$$r^3 = \frac{Q\cdot q}{16\pi^3\varepsilon_0 m}T^2$$

$$\Rightarrow \quad r = \left(\frac{Q\cdot q}{16\pi^3\varepsilon_0 m}T^2\right)^{1/3}$$

6. (d) Repulsion = Spring force

$$\frac{1}{4\pi\varepsilon_0}\frac{q^2}{r^2} = kx$$

$$\frac{(9\times 10^9)(1.6\times 10^{-6})^2}{(0.1)^2} = k\left(\frac{0.05}{2}\right)$$

$$\therefore \quad k = 92.16 \text{ N/m} \approx 92 \text{ Nm}^{-1}$$

7. (c) From Coulomb's law,

$$F = \frac{k\, q_1 q_2}{r^2} \text{ or } F \propto \frac{1}{r^2}$$

When the distance between the charges changes to

A. $r' = 2r$, then force between them will become $\frac{1}{4}$th.

B. $r' = \frac{r}{2}$, then force between them will become 4 times.

C. $r' = 4r$, then force between them will become $\frac{1}{16}$ th.

D. $r' = \frac{r}{4}$, then force between them will become 16 times.

Hence, A → (II), B → (III), C → (IV), D → (I).

8. (b) Initial force of attraction,

$$F = k\frac{(q)(-q)}{r^2}$$

Now, 50% charge from B is transferred to A,

$$q_B = -\frac{q}{2}$$

$$q_A = +q + \left(-\frac{q}{2}\right) = +\frac{q}{2}$$

New force of attraction,

$$F' = \frac{k\left(\frac{q}{2}\right)\left(\frac{-q}{2}\right)}{r^2} = \frac{F}{4}$$

9. (b)

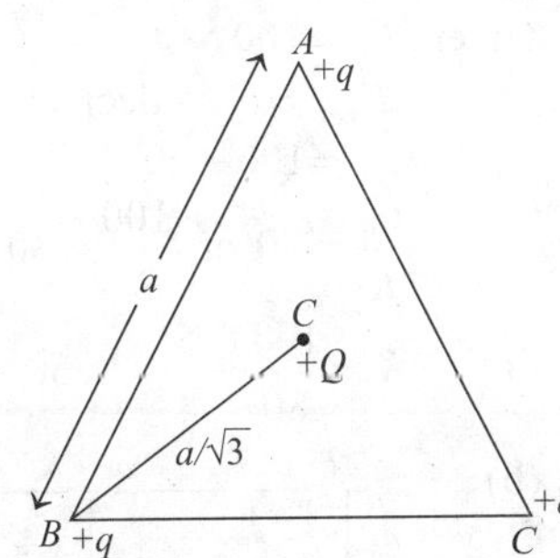

Let equilateral triangle has side a. The distance from the centroid to any vertex is $\frac{a}{\sqrt{3}}$. For an equilateral triangle, the force between two charges $+q$ separated by a distance a is given by Coulomb's law, $F = \frac{kq^2}{a^2}$

The resultant force due to the other two charges,

$$F_{net} = \sqrt{F_1^2 + F_2^2 + 2F_1F_2\cos\theta}$$

$$F_{net} = \sqrt{F_1^2 + F_2^2 + 2F_1F_2\cos 60°}$$

∴Charge on vertex and distance between them is same.

So, $F = F_1 = F_2$

$$F_{net} = \sqrt{F^2 + F^2 + F^2}$$

$$= \sqrt{3}F = \sqrt{3}\frac{kq^2}{a^2}$$

The force due to charge Q at the centroid on the charge at vertex B is

$$F_{centroid} = \frac{k|Q|q}{\left(\frac{a}{\sqrt{3}}\right)^2} = \frac{3k|Q|q}{a^2}$$

For equilibrium condition,

$$\sqrt{3}\frac{kq^2}{a^2}=\frac{3k|Q|q}{a^2}$$

$$|Q|=\frac{q}{\sqrt{3}}$$

Charge at the centroid must be attractive to balance the repulsive force, it must be negative.

$$Q=-\frac{q}{\sqrt{3}}$$

10. (b) Let the magnitude of electrostatic force be F_0 in air. The net electrostatic force between the both charges in medium is equal to $\frac{F_0}{K}$, where K is dielectric constant.

Given, $F_0=100$ N

$$F_{net}=F_0-\text{decrease in force}$$

$$F_{net}=100-20$$

$$\frac{F_0}{K}=80 \text{ or } \frac{100}{K}=80$$

or $$K=\frac{100}{80}=\frac{5}{4}=1.25$$

11. (b)

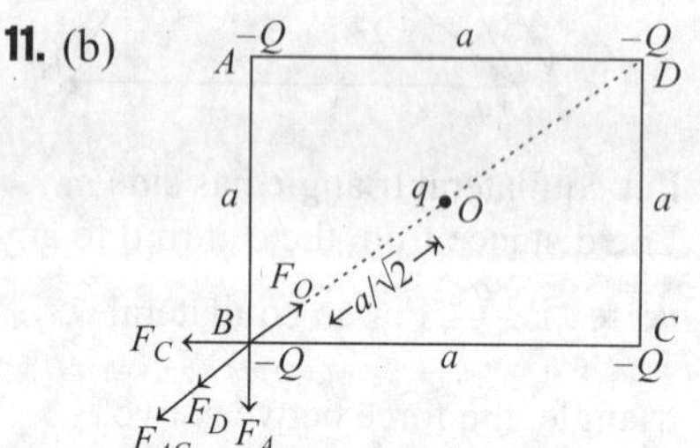

For the system to be in equilibrium, net force must be zero.

Forces at B away from the centre = Forces at B towards the centre

$$F_{AC}+F_D=F_O$$

$$F_{AC}+F_D-F_O=0$$

$$\sqrt{2}\frac{kQ^2}{a^2}+\frac{kQ^2}{2a^2}-\frac{kQq}{(a/\sqrt{2})^2}=0$$

we get, $$q=\frac{Q}{4}(1+2\sqrt{2})$$

12. (c) Electrostatic force must be balanced by spring force, therefore

$$F=\frac{1}{4\pi\varepsilon_0}\frac{\left(\frac{Q}{2}\right)\left(\frac{Q}{2}\right)}{L^2}=k(L-L_0)$$

On solving, we get

$$Q=2L\sqrt{4\pi\varepsilon_0 k(L-L_0)}$$

13. (d) One molecule of water (H_2O) contains $2+8=10$ electrons.

Number of molecules in 1 g of water,

$$n=\frac{\text{Avogadro number}}{\text{Atomic weight}}$$

For 10 g of water,

$$n=\frac{6.02\times10^{23}}{18}\times10=3.344\times10^{23}$$

Therefore, number of electrons in 10 g of water,

$$n'=n\times10=3.344\times10^{23}\times10$$

$$=3.344\times10^{24}$$

The negative charge possessed by 10 g of water,

$$q=n'e=3.344\times10^{24}\times1.6\times10^{-19}$$

$$=5.35\times10^5\text{ C}$$

14. (a) Charge on one electron

$$=-1.6\times10^{-19}\text{ C}$$

Number of electrons transferred

$$=\frac{-8.9\times10^{-6}\text{ C}}{-1.6\times10^{-19}\text{ C}}=5.6\times10^{13}$$

15. (a) 4q ——— Q ——— q (with $\frac{l}{2}$ between 4q and Q, and l between 4q and q)

The net force on q will be zero, if

$$\frac{q\cdot4q}{4\pi\varepsilon_0 l^2}+\frac{qQ}{4\pi\varepsilon_0\left(\frac{l}{2}\right)^2}=0$$

$$4q^2+4qQ=0$$

or $$4q(q+Q)=0$$

$$Q=-q$$

Hence, the correct option is (a).

Test-2

1. (b) A point charge will remain stationary at a point where the electric field is zero. Consider electric field is zero at point M in the following figure.

9μC ——— M ——— 16μC (with x between 9μC and M)

Electric field at M due to 9μC should be equal to electric field due to 16μC.

$$E=k\frac{q_1}{r^2}$$

$$\frac{k\cdot9}{x^2}=\frac{k\cdot16}{(14-x)^2}$$

$$\left(\frac{14-x}{x}\right)^2=\frac{16}{9}$$

$$\frac{14-x}{x}=\sqrt{\frac{16}{9}}$$

$$\frac{14-x}{x}=\frac{4}{3}$$

$$14-x=\frac{4}{3}x$$

$$\frac{4}{3}x+x=14$$

$$x=\frac{14}{\frac{4}{3}+1}=6\text{ cm}$$

2. (a) Consider, E is the electric field at C due to q, then $2E$ due to $2q$, $5E$ due to $5q$ and $6E$ due to $6q$.

The direction of electric field is shown in the following figure.

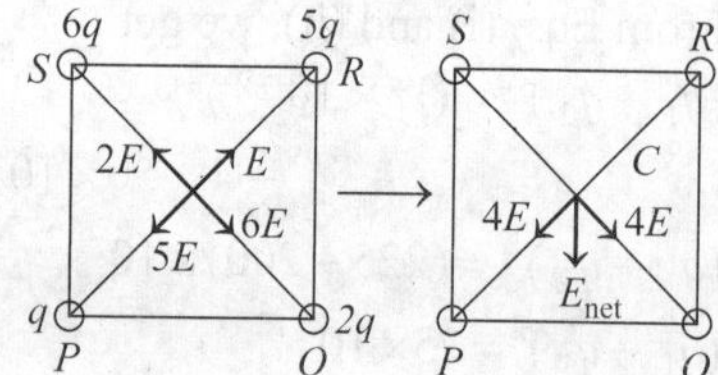

Hence, among the options, the direction of net electric field is perpendicular to PQ.

3. (c) The tangent in the direction of electric field at $-1\,\mu$C shows the direction of motion of a + ve charge. Hence, $-1\,\mu$C will move in the left direction.

4. (a) It is given that, electric dipole moment, $p=5\times10^{-18}$ C-m

Electric field strength,

$E=4\times10^4$ NC^{-1}

When the electric dipole is placed in an electric field **E**, a torque $\tau=\mathbf{p}\times\mathbf{E}$ acts on it. This torque tries to rotate the dipole through an angle θ.

If the dipole is rotated from an angle θ_1 to θ_2, then work done by external force is given by

$$W=pE(\cos\theta_1-\cos\theta_2)\quad\ldots(\text{i})$$

Putting $\theta_1=0°, \theta_2=60°$ in the Eq. (i), we get

$$W=pE(\cos0°-\cos60°)$$

$$= pE\,(1-1/2) = \frac{pE}{2}$$

$$= \frac{5\times 10^{-18} \times 4\times 10^{4}}{2} = 10^{-13}\ \text{J}$$

$$\Rightarrow W = 0.1\times 10^{-12}\ \text{J} = 0.1\,\text{pJ}$$

5. (c) The net electric field will be zero at a point outside the charges and near the charge which is smaller in magnitude.

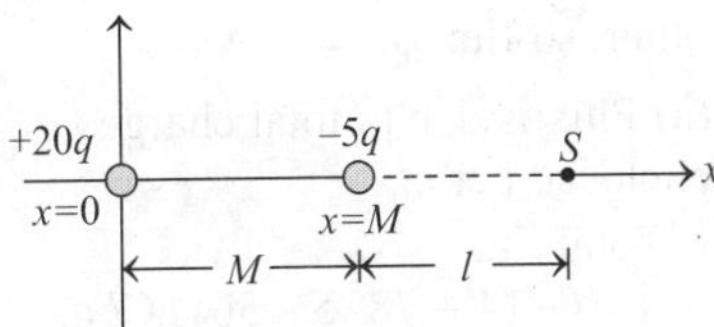

Suppose, electric field is zero at S as shown.

Hence, at S,

$$k\cdot\frac{20q}{(M+l)^2} = \frac{k\cdot(5q)}{l^2} \Rightarrow l = M$$

So, distance of S from origin is

$$M + M = 2M$$

6. (d) $$E = \frac{1}{4\pi\varepsilon_0}\cdot\left[\frac{10\times 10^{-9}}{(1\times 10^{-2})^2} - \frac{10\times 10^{-9}}{(2\times 10^{-2})^2} + \frac{10\times 10^{-9}}{(4\times 10^{-2})^2} - \frac{(10\times 10^{-9})}{(8\times 10^{-2})^2} + \ldots\right]$$

$$\Rightarrow E = \frac{9\times 10^{9} \times 10\times 10^{-9}}{10^{-4}}\left[1 - \frac{1}{(2)^2} + \frac{1}{(4)^2} - \frac{1}{(8)^2} + \ldots\right]$$

$$\Rightarrow E = 90\times 10^{4}\left[1 + \frac{1}{(4)^2} + \frac{1}{(16)^2} + \ldots\right] - 90\times 10^{4}\left[\frac{1}{(2)^2} + \frac{1}{(8)^2} + \frac{1}{(32)^2} + \ldots\ldots\right]$$

$$\Rightarrow E = 90\times 10^{4}\left[\frac{1}{1-\frac{1}{16}}\right] - \frac{90\times 10^{4}}{(2)^2}\left[1 + \frac{1}{4^2} + \frac{1}{(16)^2} + \ldots\right]$$

$$E = 96\times 10^{4} - 24\times 10^{4}$$

$$= 72\times 10^{4}\ \text{N/C}$$

7. (a) Point O is at axial position for upper and lower dipole while it is at equitorial position for the dipole on the right.

Electric field due to upper and lower dipole,

$$E_U = E_L = \frac{2k\,(2p)}{x^3}\ \text{(upward)}$$

Electric field due to dipole on right is

$$E_R = \frac{kp}{x^3}\ \text{(upward)}$$

Total electric field due to dipole

$$= \frac{2k(2p)}{x^3} + \frac{kp}{x^3} = \frac{5kp}{x^3}$$

8. (c) Electric field due to charge Q_2 at O,

$$E_2 = \frac{kQ_2}{x_2^2}$$

Electric field due to charge Q_1 at O, $E_1 = \dfrac{kQ_1}{x_1^2}$

From figure,

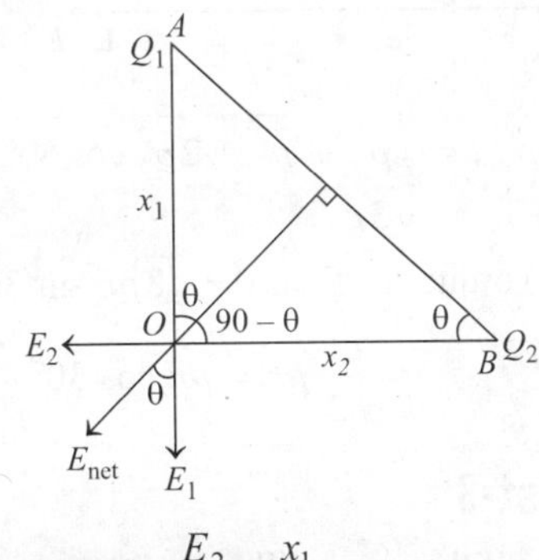

$$\tan\theta = \frac{E_2}{E_1} = \frac{x_1}{x_2}$$

$$\Rightarrow \frac{kQ_2 \times x_1^2}{kQ_1 \times x_2^2} = \frac{x_1}{x_2}$$

$$\Rightarrow \frac{Q_2}{Q_1} = \frac{x_2}{x_1} \Rightarrow \frac{Q_1}{Q_2} = \frac{x_1}{x_2}$$

9. (c) Given, linear charge density,

$$\lambda = \frac{q}{l} = 2\times 10^{-8}\ \text{Cm}^{-1}$$

F=eE

Forces of electron will be in equilibrium when electrostatic force will be equal to centripetal force.

i.e., $$eE = \frac{mv^2}{r} \Rightarrow e\cdot\frac{2k\lambda}{r} = \frac{mv^2}{r}$$

$$\Rightarrow \quad v = \sqrt{\frac{e\cdot 2k\lambda}{m}}$$

$$= \sqrt{\frac{1.6\times 10^{-19} \times 2\times 9\times 10^{9} \times 2\times 10^{-8}}{9\times 10^{-31}}}$$

$$= 8\times 10^{6}\ \text{m/s}$$

10. (a) Torque on a dipole placed in an external electric field,

$$\tau = \mathbf{p}\times\mathbf{E} \text{ or } \tau = pE\sin\theta$$

$$\mathbf{p} = p\cos\theta\,\hat{\mathbf{i}} + p\sin\theta\,\hat{\mathbf{j}};\ \mathbf{E}_1 = E\hat{\mathbf{i}}$$

$$\tau = \mathbf{p}\times\mathbf{E}_1 = (p\cos\theta\,\hat{\mathbf{i}} + p\sin\theta\,\hat{\mathbf{j}}) \times E(\hat{\mathbf{i}})$$

$$\tau\hat{\mathbf{k}} = pE\sin\theta(-\hat{\mathbf{k}})$$

$$\tau\hat{\mathbf{k}} = -\,pE\sin\theta\hat{\mathbf{k}}$$

$$\mathbf{E}_2 = \sqrt{3}\,E\,\hat{\mathbf{j}};$$

$$\tau_2 = (p\cos\theta\hat{\mathbf{i}} + p\sin\theta\hat{\mathbf{j}})\times\sqrt{3}\,E\hat{\mathbf{j}}$$

$$\tau\hat{\mathbf{k}} = \sqrt{3}\ pE\cos\theta\hat{\mathbf{k}}$$

According to question,

$$pE\sin\theta = \sqrt{3}pE\cos\theta,$$

$$\tan\theta = \sqrt{3}$$

$$\therefore \quad \theta = 60°$$

11. (c) $$E_1 = \frac{kq_1}{r^2} = \frac{(9\times 10^{9})\times(10^{-8})}{(0.05)^2}$$

$$= 3.6\times 10^{4}\ \text{NC}^{-1}$$

$$E_2 = \frac{kq_2}{r^2} = \frac{(9\times 10^{9})\times(-10^{-8})}{(0.05)^2}$$

$$= 3.6\times 10^{4}\ \text{NC}^{-1}$$

The magnitude of the total electric field at A,

$$E_A = E_1 + E_2$$

$$= 7.2\times 10^{4}\ \text{NC}^{-1} \qquad \ldots\text{(i)}$$

Thus $\mathbf{E}_A$ is directed towards the right.

Now, consider the following given figure.

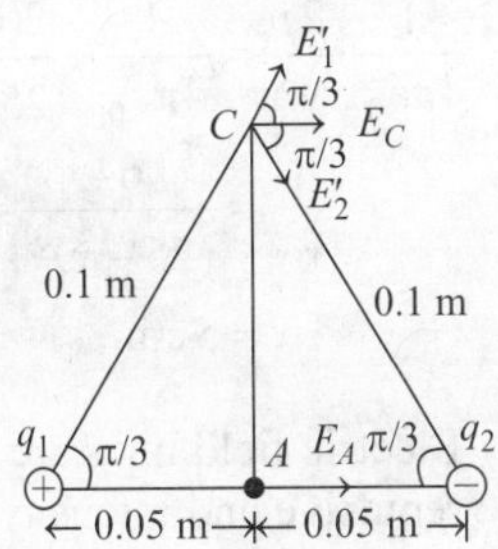

The magnitude of each electric field vector at point C, due to charges q_1 and q_2 is

$$E_1' = E_2'$$
$$= \frac{(9\times 10^9)(10^{-8})}{(0.1)^2}$$
$$= 9\times 10^3 \text{ NC}^{-1}$$

The resultant of these two vectors is

$$E_C = E_1' \cos\frac{\pi}{3} + E_2' \cos\frac{\pi}{3}$$
$$= 9\times 10^3 \text{ NC}^{-1} \quad \text{...(ii)}$$

This $\mathbf{E}_C$ points towards the right.

Dividing Eq. (i) by Eq. (ii), we get

$$\frac{E_A}{E_C} = \frac{7.2\times 10^4}{9\times 10^3} = \frac{8}{1} \text{ or } 8:1$$

12. (c) Electric field at a point P on dipole axis is

$$E_P = \frac{2p}{4\pi\varepsilon_0 r^3} = \frac{2(2a\times q)}{4\pi\varepsilon_0 r^3}$$
$$= \frac{2(5\times 10^{-3}\times 10\times 10^{-6})\times(9\times 10^9)}{(15\times 10^{-2})^3}$$
$$= 2.6\times 10^5 \text{ NC}^{-1}$$

Now, electric field at a point Q on equatorial plane is

$$E_Q = \frac{p}{4\pi\varepsilon_0 r^3} = \frac{1}{2}E_P$$
$$= \frac{1}{2}\times 2.6\times 10^5$$
$$= 1.3\times 10^5 \text{ NC}^{-1}$$

13. (a) Suppose neutral point N lies at a distance x from dipole of moment p or at a distance $(25-x)$ from dipole of $64p$.

$\vec{p}$ ① —— N —— $\overleftarrow{64p}$ ②
$\leftarrow x \rightarrow \leftarrow 25-x \text{ cm} \rightarrow$
$\leftarrow$ 25 cm $\rightarrow$

At N, electric field due to dipole 1 = electric field due to dipole 2

$$\Rightarrow \frac{1}{4\pi\varepsilon_0}\cdot\frac{2p}{x^3} = \frac{1}{4\pi\varepsilon_0}\cdot\frac{2(64p)}{(25-x)^3}$$
$$\Rightarrow \frac{1}{x^3} = \frac{64}{(25-x)^3}$$
$$\Rightarrow x = 5 \text{ cm}$$

14. (c) (a) Electric field lines are repulsive and intensity of field lines is same for both charges. It is possible for two like charges.

(b) Electric field originates from one charge and ends on other charge. Also, intensity of electric field lines is same for both the charges. It is possible for two opposite charges of equal amount.

(c) It is same as (b) but intensity of electric field lines is less for charge on the right than charge on the left, which shows the unequal amount of charges.

(d) If charges are at large distance then they do not affect the electric field of each other.

15. (a) Resultant dipole moment of system is

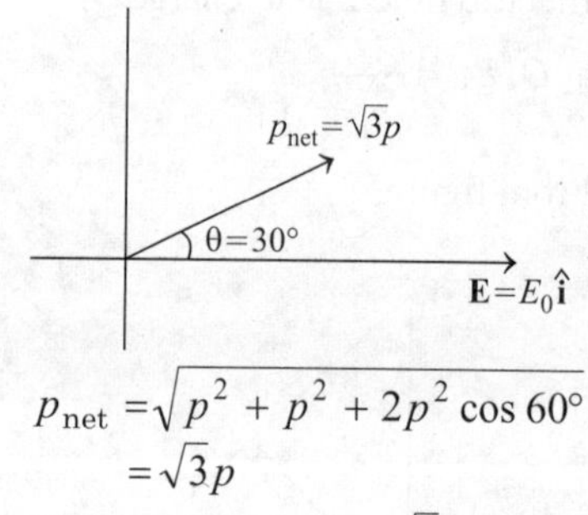

$$p_{net} = \sqrt{p^2 + p^2 + 2p^2\cos 60°}$$
$$= \sqrt{3}p$$

$$\therefore \text{Torque} = pE\sin\theta = \sqrt{3}pE\sin 30°$$
$$= \sqrt{\frac{3}{2}}\,pE = pE\cos 30°$$

Test-3

1. (b) If the cone will cover the whole charge, then the flux will be $\frac{q}{\varepsilon_0}$ but it covers only half of the charge, hence flux is $\frac{q}{2\varepsilon_0}$.

2. (c) Plane normal to electric field is a triangle having base = 2 times of radius of cone and height of triangle is same as height of cone.

$$\text{Area, } A = \frac{1}{2}(2\times 6)(12)$$
$$= 72 \text{ cm}^2 = 72\times 10^{-4} \text{ m}^2$$

Electric flux

$$= EA = 10^3 \times (72\times 10^{-4} \text{ m}^2)$$
$$= 7.2 \text{ N-m}^2\text{C}^{-1}$$

3. (d) $E = \frac{\lambda}{2\pi\varepsilon_0 r} = \frac{2\lambda}{4\pi\varepsilon_0 r}$

$$\Rightarrow \lambda = \frac{E\cdot 4\pi\varepsilon_0 r}{2}$$
$$= \frac{(9\times 10^5)(0.04)}{9\times 10^9\times 2}$$
$$= 2.0\times 10^{-6} \text{ C/m}$$

4. (c) As the area vector **A** and field vector **E** are perpendicular to each other, so flux $\phi_E = \mathbf{E}\cdot\mathbf{A} = 0$

5. (a) Flux is due to total charges enclosed per ε_0.

$\therefore$ Total flux

$$= (-14 + 78.85 - 56) \text{ nC}/\varepsilon_0$$
$$= 8.85\times 10^{-9} \text{ C}\times\frac{4\pi}{4\pi\varepsilon_0}$$
$$= 8.85\times 10^{-9}\times 9\times 10^9\times 4\pi$$
$$= 1000.4 \text{ N-m}^2/\text{C}$$
$$\approx 1000 \text{ N-m}^2/\text{C}$$

6. (d) The statement in option (d) is not correct because if charge q is placed at any of the faces of the cube, then electric flux will be $q/2\varepsilon_0$.

7. (c) The x-component of electric field is constant, hence it will not contribute to the flux.

$$\phi_E = E\cdot A$$

Incoming flux due to y-component

$$= -3(y^3 + 2)(1)$$
$$= -3(0^3 + 2)(1)$$
$$= -6 \text{ (at } y = 0)$$

Outgoing flux at $y = 1$

$$= 3(1^3 + 2)(1) = 9$$

Total flux, $\phi = 9 - 6 = 3$

Now, by Gauss's law,

$$\phi = \frac{q}{\varepsilon_0}$$
$$\Rightarrow q = \phi\varepsilon_0 = 3\varepsilon_0$$

8. (a) At the surface of shell R,

$$E_R = \frac{kQ_R}{r_R^2}$$

(a fixed positive value)

Between the shell R and S, at a distance x from the common centre,

$$E = \frac{kQ_R}{x^2}$$

(as x increases, E decreases)

At the surface of shell S,

$$E = \frac{k(Q_R - Q_S)}{r_S^2}$$

(a fixed negative value because $|Q_R| < Q_S|$)

Outside the both shells, at distance x' from the common centre,

$$E = k\frac{(Q_R - Q_S)}{x'^2}$$

As x' increases, negative value of E decreases and it becomes zero at $x' = \infty$.

So, option (a) is the correct interpretation of the graph.

9. (a) Total flux passing through the cube $= \frac{q}{\varepsilon_0}$.

Flux passing through 1 side

$$= \frac{\phi}{6} = \frac{q}{6\varepsilon_0}$$

$$= \frac{6 \times 10^{-9}}{6 \times 8.85 \times 10^{-12}}$$

$$= 1.13 \times 10^2 \text{ N-m}^2\text{C}^{-1}$$

10. (d) **Gauss's law** The net electric flux (due to the charge enclosed by the surface as well as the charges outside it) through any imaginary closed surface (called Gaussian surface) of any arbitrary shape is equal to the total charge enclosed by the surface divided by ε_0.

$$\phi = \frac{\Sigma q_{\text{enclosed}}}{\varepsilon_0} \quad \ldots\text{(i)}$$

$\therefore$ The above law is true for any closed surface irrespective of its shape.

The derivation of this law can be obtained from Coulomb's law and we know that, Coulomb's law follows inverse square law. Thus, Gauss's law is also based on the inverse square dependence on distance contained in the Coulomb's law. Any violation of Gauss' law will indicate departure from the inverse square law.

Hence, both Statement I and Statement II are correct.

11. (c) Electric field at shaded surface $(x = 2a)$,

$$\mathbf{E} = \frac{E_0(2a)}{a}\hat{\mathbf{i}} \quad \left[\because \mathbf{E} = \frac{E_0 x}{a}\hat{\mathbf{i}}\right]$$

$$\Rightarrow \quad \mathbf{E} = 2E_0\hat{\mathbf{i}}$$

Area of shaded surface, $\mathbf{A} = (2a)^2\hat{\mathbf{i}}$

$$\Rightarrow \quad \mathbf{A} = 4a^2\hat{\mathbf{i}}$$

Electric flux,

$$\phi = \mathbf{E} \cdot \mathbf{A}$$

$$= (2E_0\hat{\mathbf{i}}) \cdot (4a^2\hat{\mathbf{i}}) = 8E_0 a^2$$

12. (c) $\frac{\phi_{\max}}{\phi_{\min}} = \frac{\sqrt{3}a \times \lambda}{a\lambda} = \frac{\sqrt{3}}{1}$

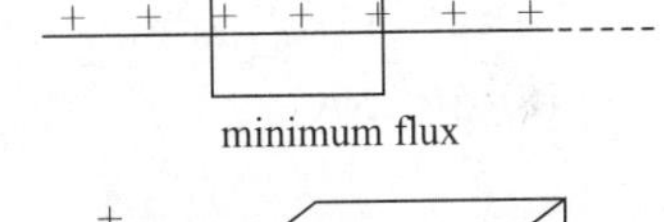

minimum flux

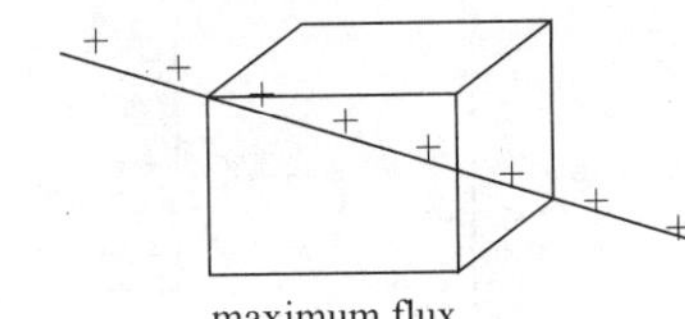

maximum flux

$$\Rightarrow \quad \frac{\phi_{\min}}{\phi_{\max}} = \frac{1}{\sqrt{3}}$$

13. (a) Electric flux is equal to the product of an area element and the perpendicular component of **E**. As the surface is lying in YZ-plane,

$\therefore \quad \mathbf{E} \cdot d\mathbf{A} = \phi = (5)(20) = 100$ units

14. (b) Charge enclosed $= q/8$

Therefore, flux, $\phi = \frac{q_{\text{enclosed}}}{\varepsilon_0}$

$$\Rightarrow \quad \phi = \frac{q}{8\varepsilon_0}$$

15. (c) The electric field is due to all charges present whether inside or outside the given surface. So, option (c) is correct.

Chapter Break Thru

1. (b) Number of electrons in 1 C charge,

$$n = \frac{q}{e} = \frac{1\,\text{C}}{1.6 \times 10^{-19}\,\text{C}}$$

$$= 6.25 \times 10^{18} \text{ electrons}$$

Time required to transfer 10^{10} electrons

$$= \frac{6.25 \times 10^{18}}{10^{10}}$$

$$= 6.25 \times 10^8 \text{ s}$$

$$\approx 19.8 \text{ yr}$$

2. (a) Gravitational flux $= \int \mathbf{E}_g \cdot d\mathbf{A}$

$$= \int -\frac{GM}{R^2} \cdot dA = -\frac{GM}{R^2}\int dA$$

$$= -4\pi GM$$

3. (a) The net electric field at the point of intersection of diagonals is zero because the electric field at this point due to equal charges at opposite corners will cancel each other in pairs.

4. (d) Let the electric field be zero at a distance x from charge $4Q$, then

$$\frac{1}{4\pi\varepsilon_0} \cdot \frac{4Q}{x^2} = \frac{1}{4\pi\varepsilon_0} \cdot \frac{Q}{(R - x)^2}$$

or $2(R - x) = x$

or $x = \frac{2R}{3}$

5. (d) The Gauss's law in electrostatics gives a relation between electric flux through any closed hypothetical surface (called a Gaussian surface) and the charge enclosed by the surface.

So, the nature of Gaussian surface is vector.

6. (a) Electric field due to plate A at point P,

$$E_A = \frac{\sigma}{2\varepsilon_0}$$

Electric field due to plate B at point P,

$$E_B = \frac{\sigma}{2\varepsilon_0}$$

But both are in opposite direction. Hence, total electric field,

$$E = \frac{\sigma}{2\varepsilon_0} - \frac{\sigma}{2\varepsilon_0} = 0$$

7. (c) With the help of Gauss's theorem, we can find electric field at any point and it is true that Gauss's theorem can't be applied for any symmetry of charge distribution due to the complexity of calculations involved.

8. (d) Electric field at the centre of charged circular ring is zero. Hence, electric field at O due to the part $ACDB$ is equal in magnitude and opposite in direction that due to the part AKB.
Therefore, the electric field at the centre due to the charge on part $ACDB$ of the ring is E along OK.

9. (b) If a point charge q is placed at a distance $\frac{x}{2}$ directly above the centre of a cube of side x, it will be at the face of a cube.
As we know, if charge q is placed at any of the faces of the cube, then electric flux will be $q/2\varepsilon_0$.

10. (d) Gaussian surface is given below.

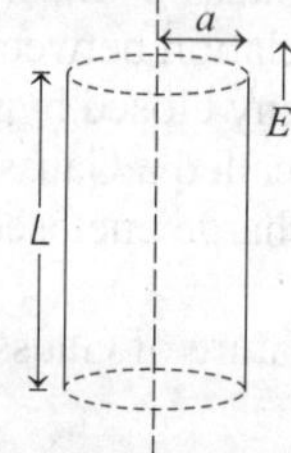

Net flux crossing through surface of cylinder is given by

$$\phi = \text{Flux through upper disc} + \text{Flux through lower disc} + \text{Flux through curved surface}$$
$$= E(\pi a^2) + (-E\pi a^2) + 0$$
$$= \pi a^2 E - \pi a^2 E = 0$$

11. (a) Force exerted on the electron by the electric field, $F = eE$

$\therefore$ Acceleration,

$$a = \frac{F}{m} = \frac{eE}{m}$$
$$= \frac{1.6\times 10^{-19} \times 9\times 10^4}{9\times 10^{-31}}$$
$$a = 1.6\times 10^{16}\ \text{ms}^{-2}$$

Now, $u = 0$, $s = 3.2$ m,

$$\because \quad s = ut + \frac{1}{2}at^2$$
$$3.2 = 0 + \frac{1}{2}\times 1.6\times 10^{16}\, t^2$$
$$t = \sqrt{\frac{6.4}{1.6\times 10^{16}}} = \frac{2}{10^8}$$
$$t = 2\times 10^{-8}\ \text{s}$$

12. (a) Since, $qE = mg$

or $E = \frac{mg}{q} = \frac{6.64\times 10^{-27} \times 9.8}{2\times 1.6\times 10^{-19}}$

$= 20.3\times 10^{-8}$ V/m

13. (c) Electric field due to $+10^{-2}$ C/m,

$$|E_A| = \frac{\lambda}{2\pi\varepsilon_0 R}$$
$$= \frac{10^{-2}\times 2\times 9\times 10^9}{1}$$
$$= 18\times 10^7\ \text{N/C}$$

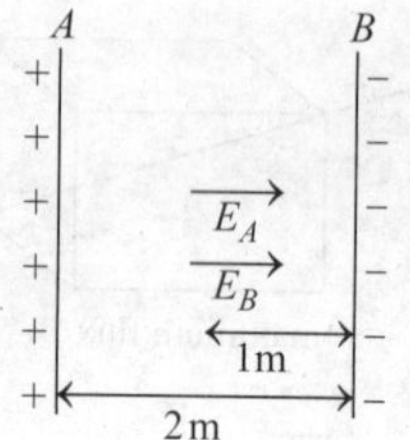

Electric field due to -10^{-2} C/m,

$$|E_B| = \frac{\lambda}{2\pi\varepsilon_0 R}$$
$$= \frac{10^{-2}\times 2\times 9\times 10^9}{1}$$
$$= 18\times 10^7\ \text{N/C}$$

Total electric field is

$$|E_A| + |E_B| = 36\times 10^7\ \text{N/C}$$

14. (b) Suppose that the charges q, $2q$ and Q are placed as shown in the figure.

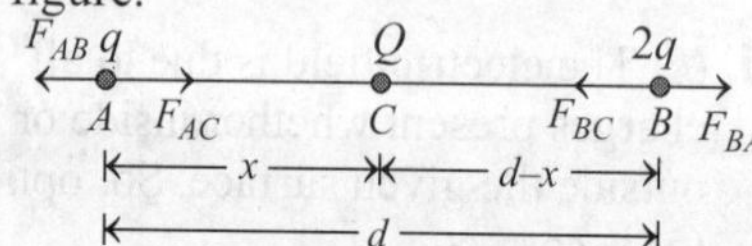

It follows that the net force on charges q and $2q$ can be zero, only if the charge Q is of opposite sign to those of charges q and $2q$. Therefore, if charges q and $2q$ are positive, then charge Q must be negative in nature.
Let the distance of charge Q (negative) from q be equal to x.
For force on charge q to zero,

$$F_{AB} = F_{AC}$$

or $$\frac{1}{4\pi\varepsilon_0}\cdot\frac{q(2q)}{d^2} = \frac{1}{4\pi\varepsilon_0}\cdot\frac{qQ}{x^2}$$

or $$\frac{Q}{q} = \frac{2x^2}{d^2} \quad \text{...(i)}$$

For force on charge $2q$ to be zero,

$$F_{BA} = F_{BC}$$

or $$\frac{1}{4\pi\varepsilon_0}\cdot\frac{q(2q)}{d^2} = \frac{1}{4\pi\varepsilon_0}\cdot\frac{(2q)Q}{(d-x)^2}$$

or $$\frac{Q}{q} = \frac{(d-x)^2}{d^2} \quad \text{...(ii)}$$

From Eqs. (i) and (ii), we get

$$x = \frac{d}{\sqrt{2}+1} \text{ or } -\frac{d}{\sqrt{2}-1}$$

Substitute $d = 2$, we get

$$x = \frac{2}{\sqrt{2}+1} \text{ or } -\frac{2}{\sqrt{2}-1}$$

$\because$ Distance cannot be negetive, so option (b) is correct.

15. (a) The frequency will be same, $\nu_0 = \frac{1}{2\pi}\sqrt{\frac{k}{m}}$ but due to the constant force qE, the equilibrium position gets shifted by $\frac{qE}{k}$ in forward direction. So, option (a) is correct.

16. (a) As, surface charge densities are equal,

$$\sigma_1 = \sigma_2$$
$$\therefore \quad \frac{q_1}{4\pi r_1^2} = \frac{q_2}{4\pi r_2^2}$$
$$\frac{q_1}{q_2} = \left(\frac{r_1}{r_2}\right)^2 \quad \text{...(i)}$$

where, q_1, q_2 and r_1, r_2 are charges and radii of two spheres.
Now, ratio of electric fields,

$$\frac{E_1}{E_2} = \frac{kq_1}{r_1^2}\times\frac{r_2^2}{kq_2} = \frac{q_1}{q_2}\times\left(\frac{r_2}{r_1}\right)^2$$

Using Eq. (i),

$$\frac{E_1}{E_2} = 1$$

then, $E_1 = E_2$

So, both Statement I and Statement II are correct.

17. (c) If the middle charge is displaced by a distance x, the net force acting when it is released, is

$$F = \frac{1}{4\pi\varepsilon_0}\times\frac{q^2}{(L+x)^2} - \frac{1}{4\pi\varepsilon_0}\times\frac{q^2}{(L-x)^2}$$

$$= \frac{-4q^2 Lx}{4\pi\varepsilon_0 (L^2 - x^2)^2}$$

For $x << L$, $F = \frac{-q^2 x}{\pi\varepsilon_0 L^3} = -kx$

where, $k = \frac{q^2}{\pi\varepsilon_0 L^3}$

Now, $T = 2\pi\sqrt{\frac{m}{k}}$

Time period of oscillation is proportional to $L^{3/2}$.

18. (c) Given, $v_x = 10 \text{ ms}^{-1}$. Since, the electric field is directed along the Y-axis, the acceleration of the body will be along the y-direction,

$$a_y = \frac{qE}{m} = \frac{10^{-6} \times 10^3}{10^{-3}} = 1 \text{ ms}^{-2}$$

Therefore, the velocity of the body along the Y-axis at time $t = 10$ s,

$v_y = a_y t = 1 \times 10 = 10 \text{ ms}^{-1}$

$\therefore$ Resultant velocity, $v = \sqrt{v_x^2 + v_y^2}$

$$= \sqrt{(10)^2 + (10)^2}$$

$$= 10\sqrt{2} \text{ ms}^{-1}$$

19. (c) Electric field due to charge $-Q$ on the shell at a distance r from its centre (for $r < R$),

$$E_1 = \frac{Q}{4\pi\varepsilon_0 r^2}$$

directed towards the centre.

Electric field due to charge $+Q$ at the centre at a distance r,

$$E_2 = \frac{Q}{4\pi\varepsilon_0 r^2}$$

directed away from the centre.

$\therefore$ Net electric field E (for $r > R$)

$= E_1 - E_2 = 0$.

For $r > R$, the electric field due to the shell is zero. In this region, the electric field due to charge $+Q$ at the centre decreases as $\frac{1}{r^2}$. Hence, the correct graph is (c).

20. (b) The electric field at point $P(a, b)$ due to q_1 has a magnitude,

$$E_1 = \frac{1}{4\pi\varepsilon_0} \cdot \frac{q_1}{a^2}$$

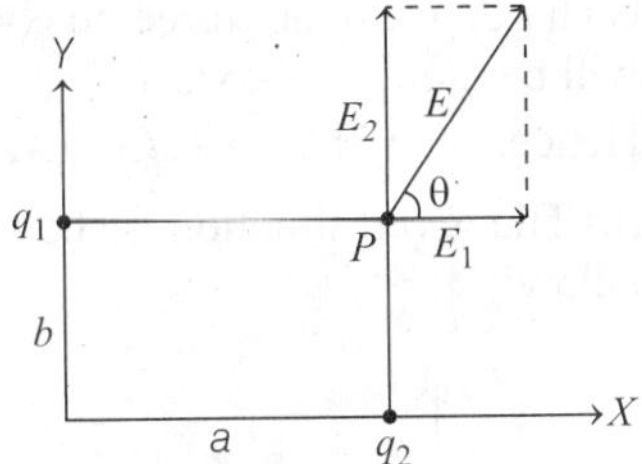

and is directed along $+X$-axis.

The electric field at (a, b) due to q_2 has a magnitude,

$$E_2 = \frac{1}{4\pi\varepsilon_0} \cdot \frac{q_2}{b^2}$$

and is directed along $+Y$-axis. The angle θ subtended by the resultant field E with the X-axis is given by

$$\tan\theta = \frac{E_2}{E_1} = \frac{q_2}{q_1} \cdot \frac{a^2}{b^2}$$

$$= \frac{1}{2} \times \left(\frac{2}{1}\right)^2 = 2$$

21. (b) $E = \frac{1}{4\pi\varepsilon_0} \cdot \frac{q_{in}}{r^2}$ ...(i)

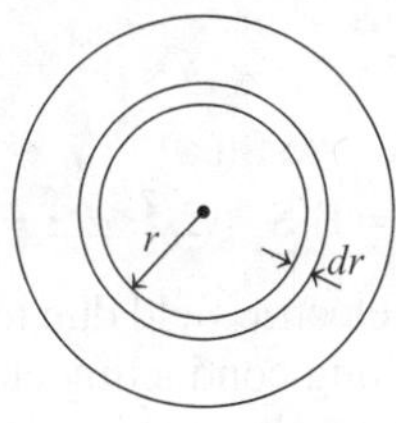

$$dq = \rho \cdot dV = (Ar^2)(4\pi r^2)\, dr$$

Integrating from 0 to r, we get

q_{in} from 0 to $r = \frac{4\pi A r^5}{5}$

Substituting in Eq. (i), we get

$$E = \frac{Ar^3}{5\varepsilon_0}$$

At $r = \frac{R}{2}$

$$E = \frac{AR^3}{40\,\varepsilon_0}$$

22. (d) Let the charge Q be at point P, with $OP = x$. The resultant force F is along the X-axis directed towards the origin. The charge Q moves to O and acquires kinetic energy. It will cross O and move to negative X-axis until it comes to rest. It is again attracted towards O and cross it and this process continues.

Therefore, charge Q exceutes periodic motion.

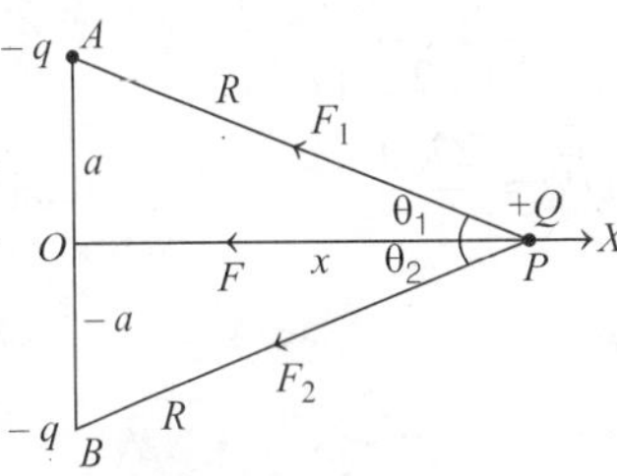

Let $AP = BP = R$, then

$$F_1 = F_2 = \frac{qQ}{4\pi\varepsilon_0 R^2}$$

The resultant force on Q,

$$F = F_1 \cos\theta + F_2 \cos\theta$$

$$= \frac{2qQ}{4\pi\varepsilon_0 R^2} \cos\theta$$

$$F = 2\frac{qQx}{4\pi\varepsilon_0 R^3}$$

$$= \frac{2qQ}{4\pi\varepsilon_0} \frac{x}{(a^2 + x^2)^{3/2}}$$

Thus, F is not of the form $F = kx$ (where $k =$ constant) and hence the motion is not simple harmonic. Hence, the correct option is (d).

23. (a) Electric field intensity at centre O, due to small element dl of charged ring,

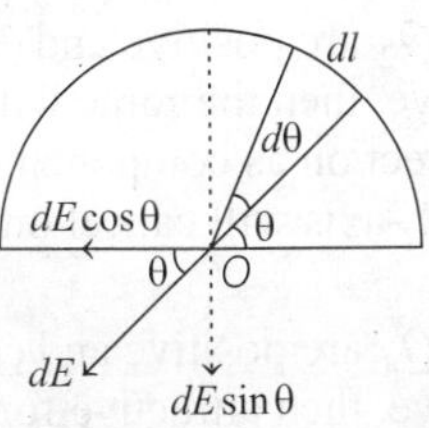

$$dE = \frac{\lambda dl}{4\pi\varepsilon_0 a^2} = \frac{\lambda(a d\theta)}{4\pi\varepsilon_0 a^2}$$

$\because$ It is clear from figure, horizontal components of dE will cancel out in pairs and vertical components will add.

$$\therefore \quad E = \int_0^\pi dE \sin\theta$$

$$= \int_0^\pi \frac{\lambda}{4\pi\varepsilon_0 a} \cdot \sin\theta\, d\theta$$

$$= \frac{\lambda}{4\pi\varepsilon_0 a}[-\cos\theta]_0^\pi$$

$$\Rightarrow \quad E = \frac{\lambda}{4\pi\varepsilon_0 a}[-\cos\pi + \cos 0]$$

$$= \frac{\lambda}{2\pi\varepsilon_0 a}$$

24. (a) $dq = \frac{2Q d\theta}{\pi}$ ...(i)

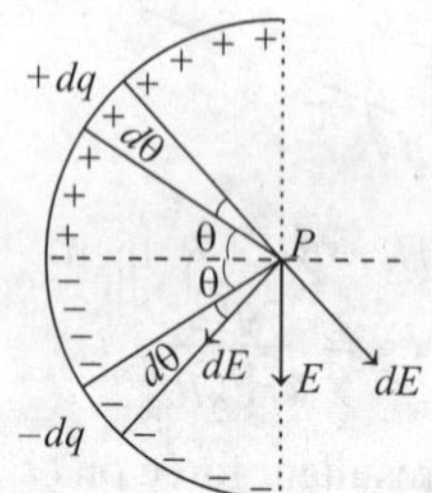

Net electric field at point P,

$$dE_{\text{net}} = 2dE \sin\theta$$

$$dE_{\text{net}} = \frac{2kdq}{r^2}\sin\theta$$

Substituting value of dq and then integrating dE from $\theta = 0°$ to $\theta = 90°$, we get

$$E_{\text{net}} = \frac{Q}{\pi^2 \varepsilon_0 r^2}$$

25. (a) If Q_1, Q_2, Q_3 and Q_4 are all positive, then the force will be along $+y$-direction as components of forces along X-axis will cancel out each other.

If Q_1, Q_2 are positive and Q_3, Q_4 are negative, then the force will act along $+x$-direction as components of forces along Y-axis will cancel out each other.

If Q_1, Q_4 are positive and Q_2, Q_3 are negative, then attractive force will dominate repulsive force and the force will be along $-y$ direction.

If Q_1, Q_3 are positive and Q_2, Q_4 are negative, then the components of forces along Y-axis will cancel out each other. So, net force on charge q will be along $-X$-axis.

Hence, A → 3; B → 1; C → 4; D → 2

26. (a) The given situation is shown below.

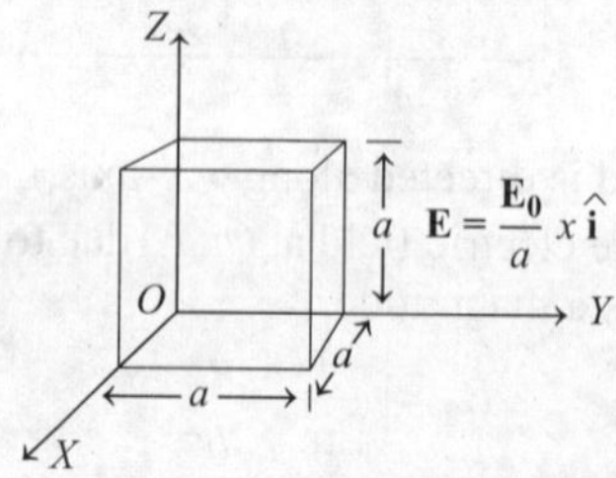

On four faces, electric field and area vector are perpendicular, hence there will be no flux. One face is at origin, *i.e.* $x = 0$

$\Rightarrow E = 0$, hence there will be no flux.

On the sixth face, $x = a$

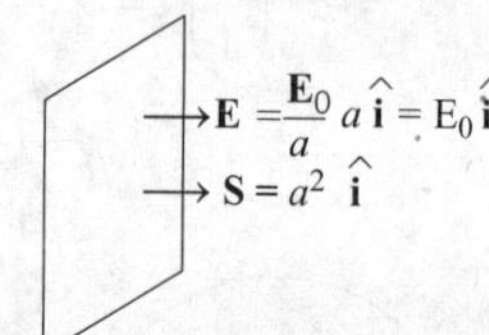

∴ Net electric flux,

$$\phi = \mathbf{E} \cdot \mathbf{S} = E_0 \hat{\mathbf{i}} \cdot a^2 \hat{\mathbf{i}} = E_0 a^2$$

27. (d) The electric field due to an infinite long conducting charged sheet, which have charge on one side is $E = \frac{\sigma}{2\varepsilon_0}$, where σ is surface charge density.

The direction of field due to charged sheets in given question can be shown as

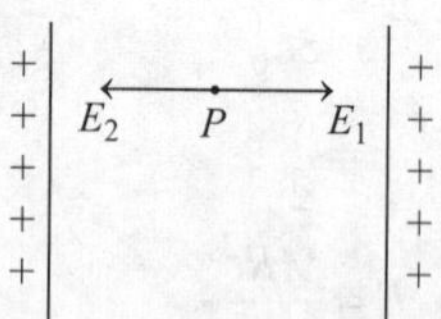

Electric field at point P,

$$E_P = E_1 - E_2 = \frac{\sigma}{2\varepsilon_0} - \frac{\sigma}{2\varepsilon_0}$$

$$E_P = 0$$

Hence, electric field at point P does not depend on the position of point P and charge density σ.

28. (d) Force on a charge is

$$F = qE_a = q \cdot \frac{k \cdot 2p}{r^3} \Rightarrow F \propto \frac{1}{r^3}$$

Hence, at $r \to 2r, F' \to \frac{1}{8}F$ or

$$F' = \frac{1}{8} \times 80 \times 10^{-3} = 10 \times 10^{-3}\,\text{N}$$

29. (c) $p = 2ql$

$$= 2(4.1 \times 10^{-19}\,\text{C})\,(3.2 \times 10^{-10}\,\text{m})$$

$$= 26.24 \times 10^{-29}\,\text{C-m}$$

$$= 2.62 \times 10^{-28}\,\text{C-m}$$

30. (b) The given point is on the equitorial line for both the dipoles.

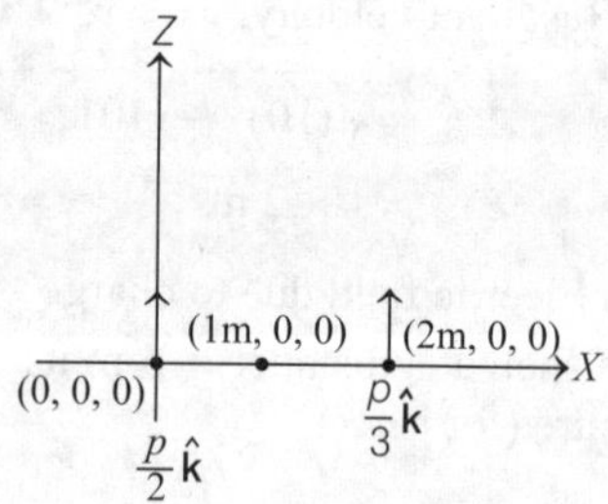

Electric field due to a dipole on the equitorial line is as follows

$$E = \frac{kp}{r^3}$$

Hence, the total electric field is

$$\mathbf{E} = \left(\frac{k\,p/2}{(1)^3}\right) + \left(\frac{k\,p/3}{(1)^3}\right)\hat{\mathbf{k}}$$

$$= \frac{5kp}{6}\hat{\mathbf{k}} = \frac{5p}{24\pi\varepsilon_0}\hat{\mathbf{k}}$$

Ch-2 Electrostatic Potential

Topical Follow Thru

Test-1

1. (b) Potential due to a charge q, $V = \dfrac{kq}{r}$

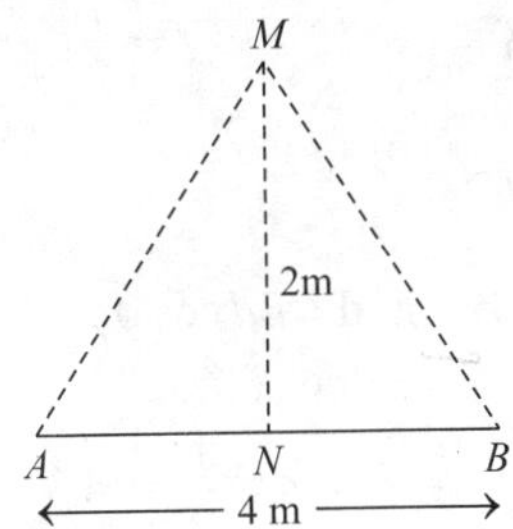

From the figure,

$$BM = AM = \sqrt{2^2 + 2^2} = 2\sqrt{2}\text{ m}$$

Potential at point M due to charge at A and B is

$$V_M = V_A + V_B$$
$$= \frac{k(2)}{2\sqrt{2}} + \frac{k(-2)}{2\sqrt{2}} = 0$$

2. (b) Potential on the surface of charged sphere is $V = \dfrac{kQ}{R}$

Since, spheres have same potential,

$$\frac{kQ_1}{4} = \frac{kQ_2}{16} \Rightarrow \frac{Q_1}{Q_2} = \frac{4}{16} = \frac{1}{4} \text{ or}$$

1:4

3. (b) If r_1 and r_2 are the radii of solid sphere and spherical shell respectively, potential at their surfaces will be

$$V_{\text{Sphere}} = \frac{1}{4\pi\varepsilon_0}\frac{Q}{r_1}$$

and $$V_{\text{Shell}} = \frac{1}{4\pi\varepsilon_0}\frac{Q}{r_2}$$

Since, $V = V_{\text{Sphere}} - V_{\text{Shell}}$

$$\Rightarrow \quad V = \frac{1}{4\pi\varepsilon_0}\frac{Q}{r_1} - \frac{1}{4\pi\varepsilon_0}\frac{Q}{r_2}$$

$$\Rightarrow \quad V = \frac{Q}{4\pi\varepsilon_0}\left[\frac{1}{r_1} - \frac{1}{r_2}\right]$$

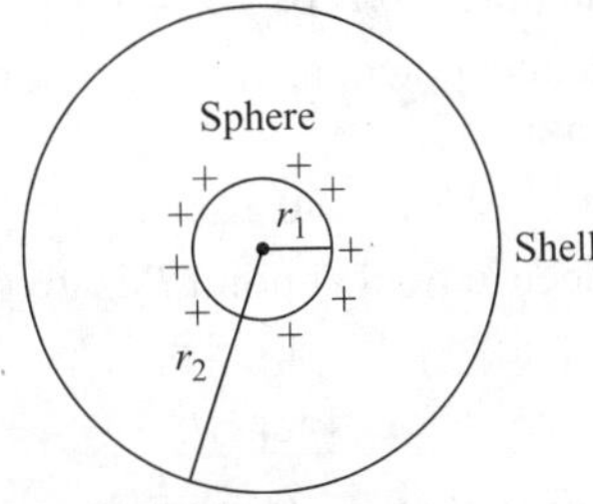

Now, when the shell is given a charge $-7Q$, the potential at its surface and also inside will get changed by a potential V_0.

$$\therefore \quad V_0 = \frac{1}{4\pi\varepsilon_0}\left[\frac{-7Q}{r_2}\right]$$

Therefore, we can write from above information,

$$V'_{\text{Sphere}} = \frac{1}{4\pi\varepsilon_0}\left(\frac{Q}{r_1}\right) + V_0$$

and $$V'_{\text{Shell}} = \frac{1}{4\pi\varepsilon_0}\left(\frac{Q}{r_2}\right) + V_0$$

Hence,

$$V'_{\text{Sphere}} - V'_{\text{Shell}} = \frac{Q}{4\pi\varepsilon_0}\left(\frac{1}{r_1} - \frac{1}{r_2}\right) = V$$

Therefore, we can say that, if any charge is given to an external shell, then the potential difference between sphere and shell will not change.

4. (c) We know that, electric potential decreases in the direction of electric field, therefore electric potential is maximum at SR.

5. (b) Kinetic energy of the particle will be equal to electrostatic potential energy. Therefore,

$$\frac{1}{2}mv_M^2 = qV$$

$$\frac{1}{2}mv_N^2 = 4qV$$

$$\frac{v_M^2}{v_N^2} = \frac{qV}{4qV}$$

or $$\frac{v_M^2}{v_N^2} = \frac{1}{4}$$

or $$\frac{v_N}{v_M} = \frac{2}{1}$$

6. (a) According to the question, a charge q is brought from point R to point P against the repulsive force on it due to charge Q. In bringing the charge q from R to P, an external force $\mathbf{F}_{\text{ext}}$ is applied just to counter the repulsive electric force $\mathbf{F}_E$ (i.e., $\mathbf{F}_{\text{ext}} = -\mathbf{F}_E$).

In this situation, work done by the external force is negative of the work done by the electric force. Thus, the work done by external force in moving the charge q from R to P is

$$W_{RP} = \int_R^P \mathbf{F}_{\text{ext}} \cdot d\mathbf{r} = -\int_R^P \mathbf{F}_E \cdot d\mathbf{r}$$

7. (c) Electric lines of forces always flow from higher to lower potential regions.

Electric potential is a scalar quantity because it doesn't have any direction.

8. (a) As corners P and O are at equal distance from $20\,\mu\text{C}$ at the centre, so potential at P and O due to $20\,\mu\text{C}$ charge are equal.

$\therefore$ Potential difference, $V_P - V_O = 0$

Thus, work done,

$W_{PO} = q(V_O - V_P) = 0$

9. (b)

Y
4 m
A
B(4 m, 6 m)
6 m
O
X

Work dm is given by $W = q\int \mathbf{E} \cdot d\mathbf{r}$

Work done in moving from O to A,

$$W_{OA} = \int_0^6 4y\,dy = 72\text{ J}$$

Work done in moving from A to B

$$W_{AB} = \int_0^4 2x\,dx = 16\text{ J}$$

$\therefore$ Net work done $= (72+16)$ J $= 88$ J

10. (a) Potential gradient relates with electric field according to the following relation, $E = \frac{-dV}{dr}$

$$E = \left[-\frac{\partial V}{\partial x}\hat{\mathbf{i}} - \frac{\partial V}{\partial y}\hat{\mathbf{j}} - \frac{\partial V}{\partial z}\hat{\mathbf{k}}\right]$$

$$= [\hat{\mathbf{i}}\,(2xy^3 + z^3) + \hat{\mathbf{j}}\,(3x^2y^2) + \hat{\mathbf{k}}\,(3xz^2)]$$

11. (b) **Case I :**

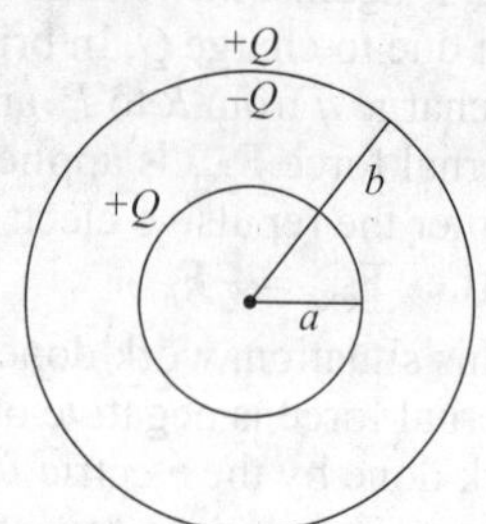

$$V_a - V_b = k\left(\frac{Q}{a} - \frac{Q}{b}\right) = V \text{ (Given)}$$

Case II :

$$V_a' = \frac{kQ}{a} + \frac{k(-16Q)}{b}$$

$$V_b' = \frac{kQ}{b} + \frac{k(-16Q)}{b}$$

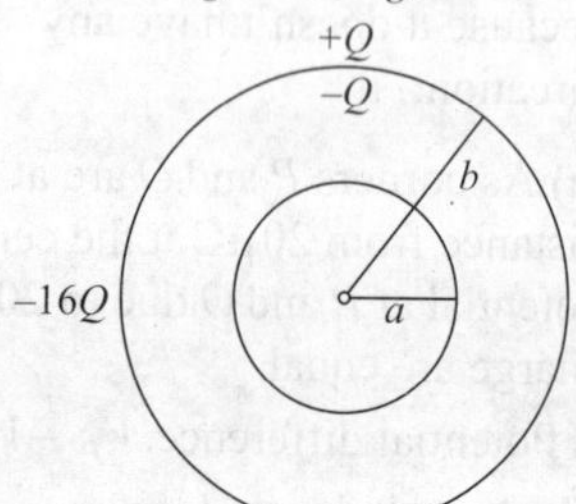

$$V_a' - V_b' = \frac{kQ}{a} - \frac{kQ}{b}$$

$$= V_a - V_b = V$$

12. (c)

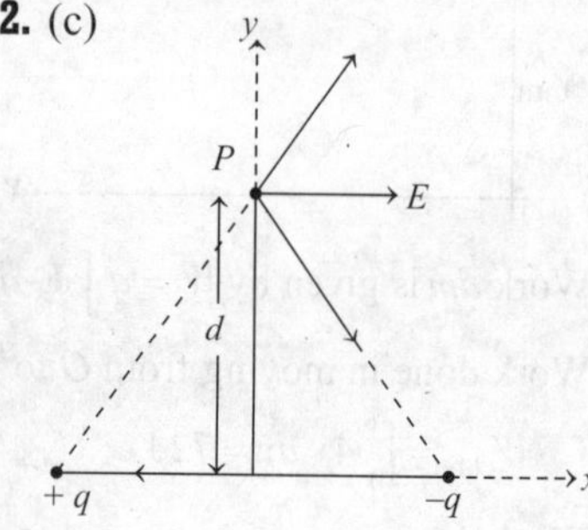

The potential **V** at a point P due to a dipole is given by

$$\mathbf{V} = \frac{1}{4\pi\varepsilon_0}\frac{\mathbf{p}\cdot\mathbf{r}}{r^2}$$

Since, the dipole is aligned along x-axis and P is along y-axis, thus $\mathbf{p}\cdot\mathbf{r} = pr\cos 90° = 0$

Hence, potential at any point on y-axis is V.

$$V_P = 0$$

Electric field at point P is given by

$$E = \frac{1}{4\pi\varepsilon_0}\frac{|\mathbf{p}|}{d^3}$$

Potential at $P = 0$ and field

$$\mathbf{E} = \frac{\mathbf{p}}{4\pi\varepsilon_0 d^3}$$

13. (a) Potential on surface or any point inside

$$V_1 = \frac{KQ_1}{R_1}, V_2 = \frac{KQ_2}{R_2}$$

Potential at inner shell,

$$V_i = \frac{KQ_1}{R_1} + \frac{KQ_2}{R_2}$$

Potential at outer shell,

$$V_o = \frac{KQ_1}{R_2} + \frac{KQ_2}{R_2}$$

Potential difference,

$$V_o - V_i = \frac{KQ_1}{R_1} - \frac{KQ_1}{R_2}$$

The outer shells charge does not affect the potential inside it, the potential difference between the shell is determined by the inner shell's charge alone and remains same at every point.

14. (a) Potential initially at surface,

$$V_0 = \frac{q}{4\pi\varepsilon_0 R} \quad \ldots\text{(i)}$$

Potential at $\frac{2R}{3}$ distance due to charge Q,

$$V' = \frac{3Q}{4\pi\varepsilon_0\, 2R} = \frac{3Q}{8\pi\varepsilon_0 R}$$

Potential at $\frac{2R}{3}$ distance due to sphere $V'' = \frac{q}{4\pi\varepsilon_0 R}$

So, net potential at $\frac{2R}{3}$ distance from the centre,

$$V = V' + V'' = \frac{3Q}{8\pi\varepsilon_0 R} + \frac{q}{4\pi\varepsilon_0 R}$$

$$= \frac{3QV_0}{2q} + V_0 \quad \text{[From Eq.(i)]}$$

$$= V_0\left(\frac{3Q}{2q} + 1\right)$$

15. (d) $E = -\frac{dV}{dx}$

$$|E| = \frac{0.8}{d}$$

$$\Delta V = \mathbf{E}\cdot\mathbf{d} = Ed\cos\theta$$

$$= Ed\cos 60°$$

$$= \frac{0.8}{d} \times d \times \frac{1}{2} = 0.4\text{ V}$$

$$V + \Delta V = 600 + 0.4 = 600.4\text{ V}$$

16. (b) $E = -(60\hat{\mathbf{i}} + 60\hat{\mathbf{j}})\,\text{NC}^{-1}$

$$\Delta V = -\mathbf{E}\cdot\mathbf{r}$$

Here, $\mathbf{r} = 2\hat{\mathbf{j}}$

$$\therefore \quad \Delta V = -(60\hat{\mathbf{i}} + 60\hat{\mathbf{j}})\cdot(2\hat{\mathbf{j}})$$

$$= -(120)$$

$$V_P - V_O = -(120)$$

$$V_O = 0$$

$$V_P - 0 = -(120)\text{ V}$$

$$V_P = -120\text{ V}$$

17. (d) Here, $\mathbf{E} = 30y^2\,\hat{\mathbf{i}}$

V_O is at (0, 0) and V_A is at (2, 2)

As, $\quad dV = -\mathbf{E}\cdot dx$

or $\quad \int_{V_O}^{V_A} dV = -\int_{0,0}^{2,2} 30y^2\,dx$

$$[V]_{V_o}^{V_A} = -[-30\,y^2x]_{(0,0)}^{(2,2)}$$

$$= -[(30(2)^2 \times 2)]$$

$$= -240\text{ V}$$

18. (d) For uniform spherical surface charge distribution,

$$\mathbf{E} = 0 \text{ for } (r < R)$$

$$\propto \frac{1}{r^2} \text{ for } (r > R)$$

$$\mathbf{V} = \text{constant for } (r < R)$$

$$\propto \frac{1}{r} \text{ for } r > R$$

Therefore, option (d) is correct.

19. (a) Given, potential,

$$V(x) = \frac{30}{x^2 - 6} \text{ V}$$

Electric field,

$$E = \frac{-dV}{dx}$$

$$= \frac{-d}{dx}\left(\frac{30}{x^2 - 6}\right)$$

$$= \frac{60x}{(x^2 - 6)^2}$$

At $x = 4\,\mu\text{m}$,

$$E = \frac{60 \times 4}{(16 - 6)^2}$$

$$= \frac{240}{100} = \frac{24}{10} \text{ V/}\mu\text{m}$$

Positive sign indicates E is in the +ve x-direction.

Hence, option (a) is correct.

20. (b)

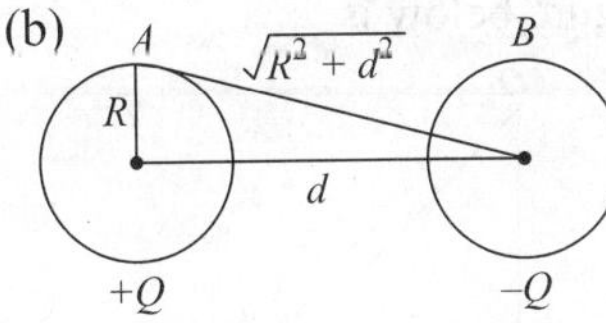

$$V_A = \frac{1}{4\pi\varepsilon_0}\frac{Q}{R} - \frac{1}{4\pi\varepsilon_0}\frac{Q}{\sqrt{R^2 + d^2}}$$

$$V_B = \frac{1}{4\pi\varepsilon_0}\frac{-Q}{R} + \frac{1}{4\pi\varepsilon_0}\frac{Q}{\sqrt{R^2 + d^2}}$$

$\therefore$

$$V_A - V_B = \frac{1 \times Q}{4\pi\varepsilon_0}\left[\frac{2}{R} - \frac{2}{\sqrt{R^2 + d^2}}\right]$$

$$= \frac{Q}{2\pi\varepsilon_0}\left[\frac{1}{R} - \frac{1}{\sqrt{R^2 + d^2}}\right]$$

$$= \frac{Q}{2\pi\varepsilon_0}\left[\frac{1}{3} - \frac{1}{\sqrt{9 + 16}}\right]$$

$$= \frac{Q}{2\pi\varepsilon_0}\left[\frac{1}{3} - \frac{1}{5}\right] = \frac{Q}{2\pi\varepsilon_0}\frac{2}{15}$$

$$= \frac{Q}{15\pi\varepsilon_0}$$

21. (a)

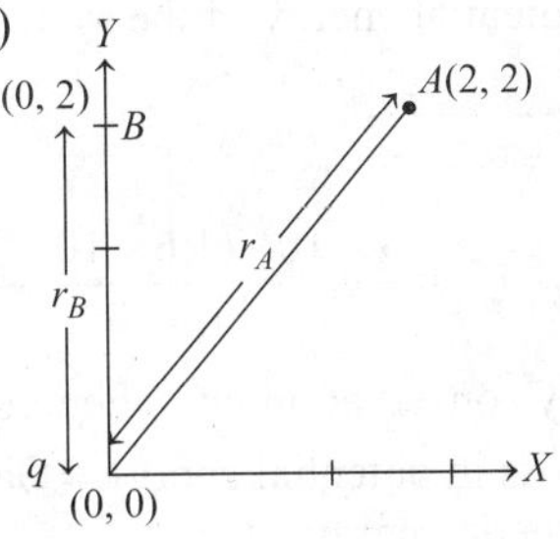

$$\mathbf{r}_A = 2\hat{\mathbf{i}} + 2\hat{\mathbf{j}}$$

$$\mathbf{r}_B = 2\hat{\mathbf{j}}$$

$$|\mathbf{r}_A| = \sqrt{2^2 + 2^2} = \sqrt{8} = 2\sqrt{2} \text{ m}$$

$$|\mathbf{r}_B| = 2 \text{ m}$$

$$V_A = \frac{kq}{r_A} = \frac{k \times \sqrt{2} \times 10^{-3} \times 10^{-6}}{2\sqrt{2}}$$

$$= \frac{k}{2} \times 10^{-9} \text{ V}$$

$$V_B = \frac{kq}{r_B} = \frac{k \times \sqrt{2} \times 10^{-3} \times 10^{-6}}{2}$$

$$= \frac{\sqrt{2}k}{2} \times 10^{-9} \text{ V}$$

$$V_A - V_B = \frac{k}{2} \times 10^{-9}(1 - \sqrt{2}) \text{ V}$$

22. (a) Let d be the distance between vertex and centre of square.

$$V_{\text{centre}} = \frac{k2q}{d} + \frac{k3q}{d} - \frac{k3q}{d} - \frac{-k2q}{d}$$

Potential at centre before and after the charges are interchanged, will remain same, since potential is a scalar quantity.

After interchange

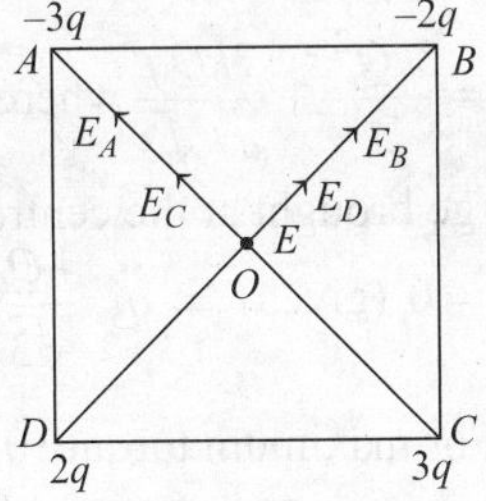

Since, electric field is a vector quantity, the direction of electric field got changed.

So, option (a) is correct.

23. (c) Volume of eight drops

= Volume of a big drop

$$\therefore \quad \left(\frac{4}{3}\pi r^3\right) \times 8 = \frac{4}{3}\pi R^3$$

$$\Rightarrow \quad 2r = R \quad \ldots\text{(i)}$$

According to charge conservation,

$$8q = Q \quad \ldots\text{(ii)}$$

Potential of one small drop,

$$V' = \frac{q}{4\pi\varepsilon_0 r}$$

Similarly, potential of big drop,

$$V = \frac{Q}{4\pi\varepsilon_0 R}$$

Now, $\frac{V'}{V} = \frac{q}{Q} \times \frac{R}{r}$

$$\Rightarrow \quad \frac{V'}{20} = \frac{q}{8q} \times \frac{2r}{r}$$

[from Eqs. (i) and (ii)]

$$\therefore \quad V' = 5 \text{ V}$$

So, the potential of each single drop was 5 V.

24. (b) Let the minimum potential at point P be at x distance away from $9\,\mu\text{C}$.

The potential due to a point charge q at a distance r is given as

$$V = \frac{kq}{r}$$

So, potential at point P of given system of charge can be written as

$$V_P = \frac{k \times 9 \times 10^{-6}}{x} + \frac{k \times 16 \times 10^{-6}}{1 - x}$$

$$= k \times 10^{-6}\left(\frac{9}{x} + \frac{16}{1 - x}\right)$$

To find the distance from the charges where V is minimum,

$$\frac{dV_P}{dx} = 0$$

$$\frac{dV_P}{dx} = k \times 10^{-6}\left(-\frac{9}{x^2} + \frac{16}{(1-x)^2}\right) = 0$$

$$\Rightarrow -\frac{9}{x^2} + \frac{16}{(1-x)^2} = 0$$

$$\Rightarrow \left(\frac{3}{x}\right)^2 = \left(\frac{4}{1-x}\right)^2$$

$$\Rightarrow \frac{3}{x} = \frac{4}{1-x}$$

$$\Rightarrow 3 - 3x = 4x$$

or $x = \frac{3}{7}$ m

Thus, potential is minimum at a distance of $\frac{3}{7}$ m from 9 μC.

25. (c) Potential due to a dipole is

$$V = \frac{kp\cos\theta}{r^2}$$

$$\Rightarrow \frac{V_A}{V_B} = \frac{\cos\theta_A}{\cos\theta_B} = \frac{\cos 30°}{\cos 120°}$$

$$= \frac{\frac{\sqrt{3}}{2}}{-\frac{1}{2}} = \sqrt{3} \approx 1.73$$

Test-2

1. (a) Since, the proton is moving against the direction of electric field, so work is done on the proton against electric field. It implies that electric field does negative work on the proton.

Again, proton is moving in electric field from low potential region to high potential region, hence its potential energy increases.

2. (c) Electric potential and electric potential energy are different quantities. If test charge $= Q$ and point charge $= q$, the electric potential is $V = Kq/r$ and potential energy is $W = QV = KQ\,q/r$.

Thus, $V \neq W$.

3. (b) The masses of protons are same, so they will have the same velocities.

Total KE at infinite separation of the two protons is the electrostatic potential energy of the system

$$= \frac{1}{4\pi\varepsilon_0}\frac{e^2}{r}$$

$$= \frac{9\times 10^9\,(1.6\times 10^{-19})^2}{10^{-10}}$$

By conservation law of energy,

Loss in potential energy = Gain in kinetic energy

$$U - 0 = 2\times\frac{1}{2}mv^2$$

$$\frac{9\times 10^9\,(1.6\times 10^{-19})^2}{10^{-10}} = 2\times\frac{1}{2}mv^2$$

So, KE of one proton $= \frac{1}{2}mv^2$

$$= \frac{9\times 10^9\,(1.6\times 10^{-19})^2}{2\times 10^{-10}}$$

$$= 11.5\times 10^{-19}\text{ J}$$

4. (c) As we know that,

$$E = \frac{V}{r}$$

or $V = rE$, $U = q_0V = q_0rE$

U will be negative because the test charge is moving in direction of electric field.

$\therefore\ U = -q_0rE,\ W = -q_0rE$

5. (d) Initially electrostatic energy of the equilateral triangle will be

$U_i = \frac{3kQ^2}{a}$ where, $a =$ side of equilateral triangle.

When charge q is brought at centroid,

$U_f = \frac{3kQ^2}{a} + \frac{3kQq}{a/\sqrt{3}}$ where, q is the charge brought at the centre.

$U_f = 0$ (given) $\Rightarrow q = \frac{-Q}{\sqrt{3}}$.

6. (a) For maximum torque, $\theta = 90°$

$$\tau_{max} = pE\sin 90°$$

i.e. $\tau_{max} = pE$

$$\Rightarrow \tau_{max} = q\times 2l\times E$$

$$= (3.5\times 10^{-6})\times 4.2 \times 10^{-2}\times 5.87\times 10^5$$

$$= 86.289\times 10^{-3}\text{ Nm}^{-1}$$

Work done in rotating the dipole from an angle θ_0 to θ,

$$W = \int_{\theta_0}^{\theta} pE\sin\theta\,d\theta$$

$$= pE[\cos\theta_0 - \cos\theta]$$

Here, $\theta_0 = 0°$ and $\theta = 180°$

$$W = pE(\cos 0° - \cos 180°)$$

$$\Rightarrow W = 2pE = 2\times q\times 2l\times E$$

$$= 2\times(3.5\times 10^{-6})\times(4.2\times 10^{-2})\times 5.87\times 10^5$$

$$= 1.725\times 10^{-1}\text{ J}$$

$$\simeq 1.72\times 10^{-1}\text{ J}$$

7. (d) Electrostatic energy between two charges q_1 and q_2 such that the distance between them is r, is given as

$$U = \frac{K\,q_1q_2}{r}$$

In accordance to the principle of superposition, total energy of the charge system as shown in the figure below is

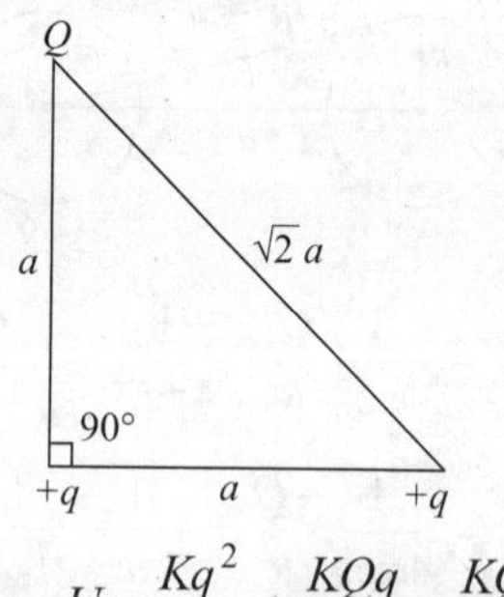

$$U = \frac{Kq^2}{a} + \frac{KQq}{a} + \frac{KQq}{\sqrt{2}a}$$

It is given that, $U = 0$

$$\therefore \frac{Kq}{a}\left[q + Q + \frac{Q}{\sqrt{2}}\right] = 0$$

$$\Rightarrow Q = \frac{-\sqrt{2}\times q}{(\sqrt{2}+1)}$$

8. (b) Given, dipole moment of a molecule $= 10^{-29}$ C-m

Number of molecules in 1 mole of the substance $= 6\times 10^{23}$

Therefore, total dipole moment of all molecules,

$$p = 6\times 10^{23}\times 10^{-29}\text{ C-m}$$

$$= 6\times 10^{-6}\text{ C-m}$$

Initial potential energy,

$$U_i = -pE\cos\theta$$

$= -6 \times 10^{-6} \times 10^{6} \times \cos 60°$

$= -6 \times \frac{1}{2} = -3\text{ J}$

Final potential energy (when $\theta = 0°$) (finally p and E are aligned in the same direction),

$U_f = -6 \times 10^{-6} \times 10^{6} \times \cos 0° = -6\text{ J}$

Change in potential energy

$= -6\text{ J} - (-3\text{ J}) = -3\text{ J}$

So, there is a loss in potential energy. This must be the energy released by the substances in the form of heat in aligning its dipole.

$\therefore$ Heat energy

$= -\text{PE} = -(-3\text{ J}) = 3\text{ J}$

9. (b) As, $U = -\mathbf{p} \cdot \mathbf{E}$

and $\mathbf{E} = \dfrac{2p}{4\pi\varepsilon_0 \times a^3}$

$\Delta U_{\text{loss}} = \dfrac{2\mathbf{p}^2}{4\pi\varepsilon_0 a^3} = 2 \times \dfrac{1}{2} mv^2$

$v = \dfrac{\mathbf{p}}{a}\sqrt{\dfrac{1}{2\pi\varepsilon_0 ma}}$

10. (a) $U_{q,-q} = \dfrac{1}{4\pi\varepsilon_0}\dfrac{-q^2}{d}$

$U_{Q,-q} = \dfrac{1}{4\pi\varepsilon_0}\dfrac{-qQ}{(D-d/2)}$

$U_{Q,q} = \dfrac{1}{4\pi\varepsilon_0}\dfrac{qQ}{(D+d/2)}$

Total potential energy

$U = U_{q,-q} + U_{Q,q} + U_{Q,-q}$

$= \dfrac{-q}{4\pi\varepsilon_0}\left[\dfrac{q}{d} - 2Q\left(\dfrac{1}{(2D+d)} - \dfrac{1}{(2D-d)}\right)\right]$

$= \dfrac{-q}{4\pi\varepsilon_0}\left[\dfrac{q}{d} - 2Q\left(\dfrac{-2d}{4D^2 - d^2}\right)\right]$

$= \dfrac{1}{4\pi\varepsilon_0}\left[\dfrac{-q^2}{d} - \dfrac{qQd}{D^2}\right] \quad (\because D >> d)$

11. (b) Line along East-West is an equipotential line.

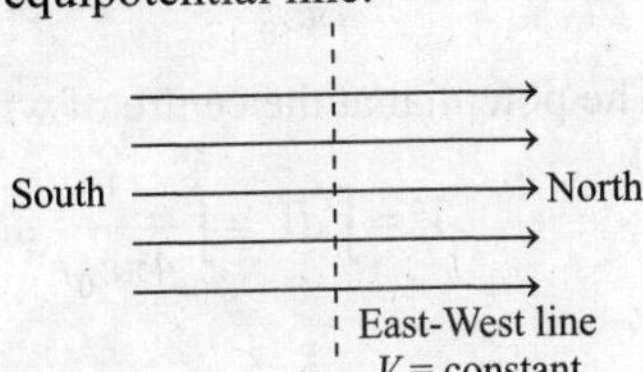

As V = constant along East-West line,

qV or PE of charge remains constant along this line.

Also, field of a point charge is non-uniform.

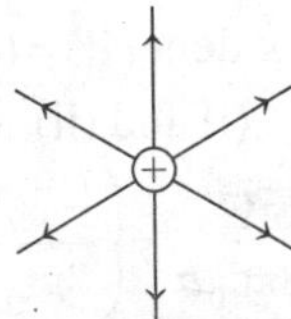

12. (a) When distance between two like charges increases, the PE decreases because they repel each other.

So, $\Delta U = (-)$ve

When distance between two like charges decreases, the PE increases because the charges repel each other more strongly. So, $\Delta U = (+)$ve

When a charge is moved perpendicular to the electric field lines, there is no change in PE because the work done is zero.

So, $\Delta U = 0$

Changing the reference point for PE does not change the actual potential energy difference between points.

So, ΔU remains same.

13. (c) Let the spherical charge distribution of radius R has been assembled by bringing one by one infinite small thin spherical charge layers.

Work done in bringing a charge layer of radius r, thickness dr and charge dq,

$dU = \dfrac{1}{4\pi\varepsilon_0}\dfrac{q}{r} \times dq$

Using, $U = \dfrac{kq_1q_2}{r} = \dfrac{1}{4\pi\varepsilon_0} \cdot \dfrac{q}{r} dq$

If ρ = volume charge density,

then $q = \dfrac{4}{3}\pi r^3 \rho$

and $dq = 4\pi r^2 dr\rho$

$\therefore \quad dU = \dfrac{1}{4\pi\varepsilon_0} \times \dfrac{4\pi r^2 \rho}{3} \times 4\pi r^2 dr\rho$

$= \dfrac{4}{3}\dfrac{\pi}{\varepsilon_0}\rho^2 r^4 dr$

Total energy,

$U = \int_0^R dU = \dfrac{4\pi\rho^2}{3\varepsilon_0}\int_0^R r^4 dr$

$= \dfrac{4\pi\rho^2 R^5}{15\varepsilon_0} \left(\because \rho = \dfrac{Q}{\frac{4}{3}\pi R^3}\right)$

$= \dfrac{3}{5} \times \dfrac{1}{4\pi\varepsilon_0} \times \dfrac{Q^2}{R}$

14. (d) The potential energy of system of two charges is

$U = \dfrac{1}{4\pi\varepsilon_0} \cdot \dfrac{q_1q_2}{r} \Rightarrow U \propto \dfrac{1}{r}$

When a positive charge comes close to a negative charge, then its potential energy decreases.

15. (c) Field in the region is given by

$E_x = -\dfrac{\partial V}{\partial x}\hat{\mathbf{i}} = \left(-\dfrac{\partial}{\partial x}2x^2\right)\hat{\mathbf{i}}$

$= -4x\,\hat{\mathbf{i}}\left(\dfrac{\text{N}}{\text{C}}\right)$

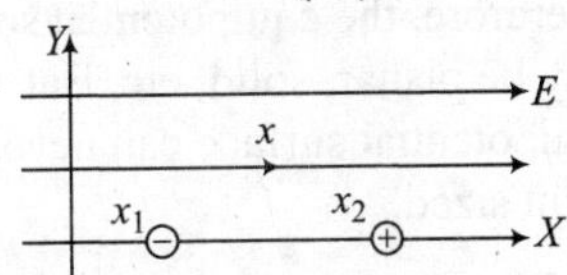

When field is uniform in direction, there is no component of field in any other direction except along X-axis.

So, force on dipole,

F_{net} = Force on positive charge − Force on negative charge

$= qE_{(x_2)} - qE_{(x_1)}$

$= q(-4x_2 - (-4x_1))$

$= 4q(x_1 - x_2)$

$= 4 \times 2 \times 10^{-6} \times 3 \times 10^{-10}$

$= 24 \times 10^{-16}\text{ N}$

Chapter Break Thru

1. (b) Potential energy of electric dipole is

$U = -pE\cos\theta = -2qlE\cos\theta$

$= -(2)(6.4 \times 10^{-19})(1.4 \times 10^{-10})(8 \times 10^{5})\cos 0°$

$= -1.43 \times 10^{-22}\text{ J}$

2. (d) Potential inside a charged spherical shell, $V = \frac{kq}{R}$

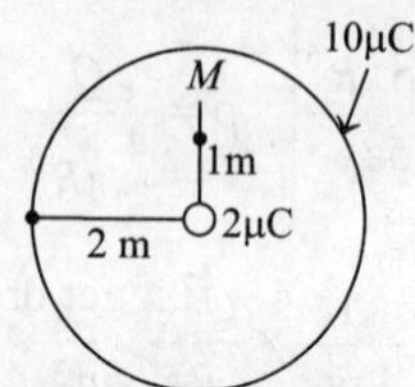

Potential at M = Potential inside a shell + Potential due to charge $2\,\mu C$

$$= \frac{k(10\times10^{-6})}{2} + \frac{k(2\times10^{-6})}{1}$$

$$= \frac{(9\times10^9)(10\times10^{-6})}{2} + \frac{(9\times10^9)(2\times10^{-6})}{1}$$

$$= 6.3\times10^4\ \text{V}$$

3. (a) Equipotential surface is an imaginary surface joining the points of same potential in an electric field. Therefore, the equipotential surface may be planar, solid, etc. But equipotential surface can never be point sized.

4. (c) The situation is shown below.

Given, distance of point OP is

$$r = 4.1\times10^{-9}\ \text{m}$$

dipole moment, $\mathbf{p} = 4.8\times10^{-30}$ C-m

Potential at axial line of dipole is given as

$$V = \frac{kp}{r^2} = \frac{9\times10^9\times4.8\times10^{-30}}{(4.1\times10^{-9})^2}$$

$$= 2.6\times10^{-3}\ \text{V}$$

5. (a) As, $W_{AB} = q\times\Delta V_{BA}$

$$20 = 0.08\times\Delta V_{BA}$$

$$\Delta V_{BA} = \frac{20}{0.08} = 250\,\text{V}$$

6. (c) For initial condition,

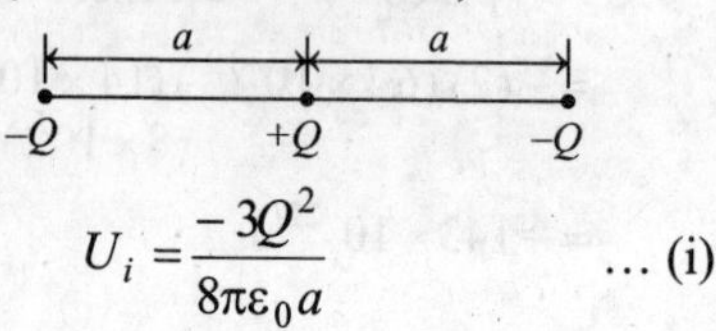

$$U_i = \frac{-3Q^2}{8\pi\varepsilon_0 a} \quad \ldots\text{(i)}$$

For final condition,

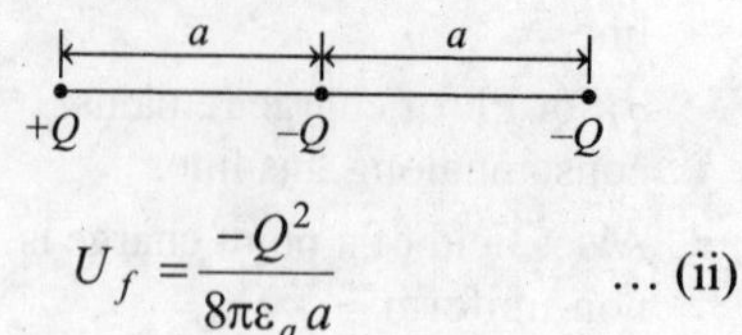

$$U_f = \frac{-Q^2}{8\pi\varepsilon_a a} \quad \ldots\text{(ii)}$$

Now, work done, $W = U_f - U_i$

Using Eqs. (i) and (ii), we get

$$W = \frac{-Q^2}{8\pi\varepsilon_0 a} - \left(\frac{-3Q^2}{8\pi\varepsilon_0 a}\right)$$

$$= \frac{Q^2}{4\pi\varepsilon_0^a}$$

7. (b)

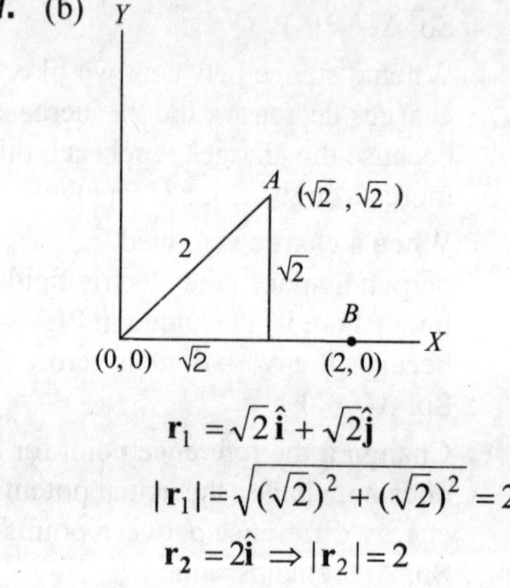

$$\mathbf{r}_1 = \sqrt{2}\,\hat{\mathbf{i}} + \sqrt{2}\,\hat{\mathbf{j}}$$

$$|\mathbf{r}_1| = \sqrt{(\sqrt{2})^2 + (\sqrt{2})^2} = 2$$

$$\mathbf{r}_2 = 2\hat{\mathbf{i}} \Rightarrow |\mathbf{r}_2| = 2$$

Potential at point A,

$$V_A = \frac{kq}{r_1}$$

$$= \frac{9\times10^9\times10^{-9}\ \text{C}}{2}$$

Potential at point B,

$$V_B = \frac{kq}{r_2}$$

$$V_B = \frac{9\times10^9\times10^{-9}\ \text{C}}{2}$$

$$V_{AB} = V_A - V_B = \frac{Kq}{2} - \frac{Kq}{2}$$

$$\therefore \quad V_{AB} = 0$$

8. (c) Electric field is zero inside the conductor, therefore electric potential is constant within conductor as $E = -\frac{dV}{dr}$.

Surface of conductor is equipotential surface, therefore electric field just outside a charged conductor is perpendicular to the surface of the conductor at every point.

9. (a) Electric potential at a point which is at a distance r at some angle θ from electric dipole is

$$V = \frac{p\cos\theta}{4\pi\varepsilon_0 r^2}$$

$$= \frac{9\times10^9\times16\times10^{-9}\times\frac{1}{2}}{(0.6)^2} \quad (\because \theta = 60°)$$

$$= 2\times10^2 = 200\,\text{V}$$

10. (a) As $-\int_{l=\infty}^{l=0} \mathbf{E}\cdot d\mathbf{r}$ = Potential at the centre of ring

$$= \frac{1}{4\pi\varepsilon_0}\frac{q}{r} = \frac{(9\times10^9)\times(2\times10^{-10})}{1}$$

$$= 1.8\,\text{V}$$

11. (d) Potential at any internal point of charged shell $= \frac{q}{4\pi\varepsilon_0 R}$

Potential at P due to Q at centre

$$= \frac{1}{4\pi\varepsilon_0}\frac{Q}{R/2} = \frac{1}{4\pi\varepsilon_0}\frac{2Q}{R}$$

$\therefore$ Total potential at point P,

$$V_p = \frac{q}{4\pi\varepsilon_0 R} + \frac{2Q}{4\pi\varepsilon_0 R}$$

$$= \frac{1}{4\pi\varepsilon_0 R}(q + 2Q)$$

Potential at centre,

$$V_C = \frac{q}{4\pi\varepsilon_0 R} + \frac{Q}{4\pi\varepsilon_0\times0} = \infty$$

$$\text{Ratio of } V_C / V_P = \frac{\infty}{V_P} = \infty$$

12. (b) Let circular wire be made of a large number of elementary charges dq. The potential due to such charge is

$$dV = \frac{1}{4\pi\varepsilon_0}\frac{dq}{r}$$

The potential at the centre of wire is

$$V = \int dV = \int_0^q \frac{1}{4\pi\varepsilon_0 r}\,dq$$

$$= \frac{1}{4\pi\varepsilon_0 r}\int_0^q dq = \frac{1}{4\pi\varepsilon_0}\frac{q}{r}$$

$$= \frac{9\times 10^9 \times 2\times 10^{-4}}{0.10}$$

$$= 18\times 10^6 \text{ V}$$

13. (b)

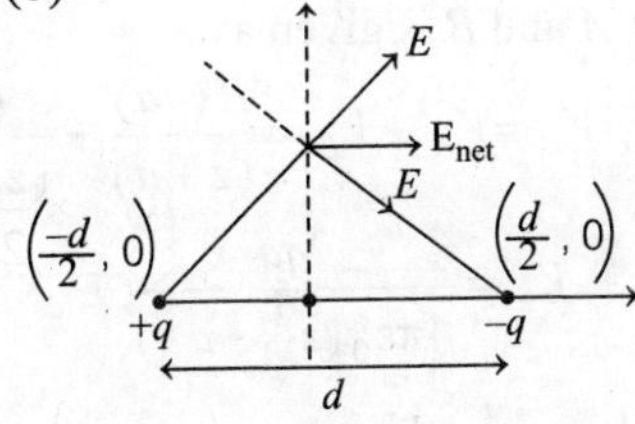

Electric field on X-axis has not same direction for all points on X-axis.

Electric field at all points on Y-axis is along X-axis is either positive or negative.

Dipole moment $= qd$ along negative X-axis.

14. (b)

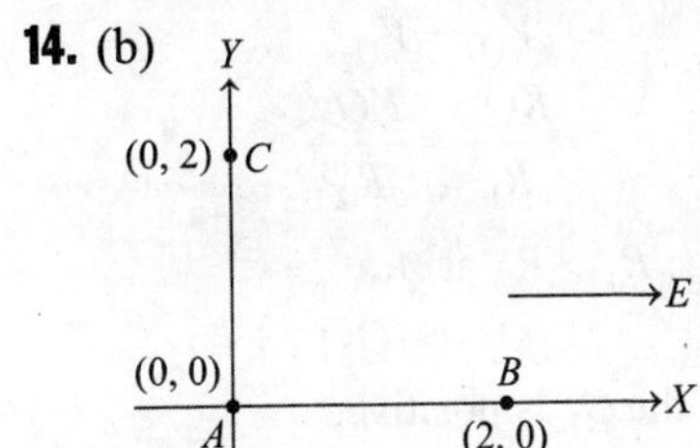

Potential decreases as we move along the direction of electric field. The field E is uniform and runs parallel to X-axis..

Any line perpendicular to X-axis will be equipotential line.

$$V_A = V_C$$

$V_A > V_B$, as E points in positive x-direction.

15. (b) $V_C = 4\times \frac{KQ}{r}$

and $r = \frac{\sqrt{2}a}{2} = \frac{a}{\sqrt{2}}$

$$\therefore \quad V_C = 4\times \frac{1}{4\pi\varepsilon_0}\frac{Q\sqrt{2}}{a}$$

$$V_C = \frac{\sqrt{2}Q}{\pi\varepsilon_0 a}$$

$\therefore \quad A\to 3$

Workdone, $W = qV = \frac{\sqrt{2}\,qQ}{\pi\varepsilon_0 a}$

$\therefore \quad B\to 4$

Force on charge Q,

$$F = \frac{KQQ}{a^2} + \frac{KQQ}{a^2} + \frac{KQQ}{(\sqrt{2}a)^2}$$

$$= \frac{2KQ^2}{a^2} + \frac{KQ^2}{2a^2} = \frac{5KQ^2}{2a^2}$$

$\therefore \quad C\to 1$

Potential energy,

$$U = \frac{4KQQ}{a} + \frac{KQ^2}{\sqrt{2}a} + \frac{KQ^2}{\sqrt{2}a}$$

$$= \frac{4KQ^2}{a} + \sqrt{2}\frac{KQ^2}{a}$$

$$= \frac{KQ^2}{a}(4+\sqrt{2})$$

$\therefore \quad D\to 2$

16. (a) Since, surface charge density of concentric spheres are equal i.e.,

$$\sigma_R = \sigma_{8R}$$

$$\frac{Q_1}{4\pi\varepsilon_0 R^2} = \frac{Q_2}{4\pi\varepsilon_0 (8R)^2}$$

$$\frac{Q_1}{Q_2} = \frac{R^2}{(8R)^2} = \frac{1}{64}$$

Potential difference between the spheres is

$$\therefore \quad V(R) - V(8R)$$

$$= K\left[\frac{Q_1}{R} + \frac{Q_2}{8R}\right] - K\left[\frac{Q_1}{8R} + \frac{Q_2}{8R}\right]$$

$$= KQ_1\left[\frac{1}{R} - \frac{1}{8R}\right]$$

$$= \frac{7kQ_1}{8R} = \frac{7Q_1}{32\pi\varepsilon_0 R}$$

17. (a) (Total energy)$_{\text{initial}}$ = (Total energy)$_{\text{final}}$

$$\Rightarrow (\text{PE}+\text{KE})_{\text{initial}} = (\text{PE}+\text{KE})_{\text{final}}$$

$$\Rightarrow \frac{1}{4\pi\varepsilon_0}\times\frac{qQ}{\sqrt{(4a)^2+(3a)^2}} + \frac{1}{2}mv^2$$

$$= \frac{1}{4\pi\varepsilon_0}\frac{qQ}{3a} + 0$$

$$\Rightarrow \frac{1}{4\pi\varepsilon_0}\frac{Qq}{5a} + \frac{1}{2}mv^2 = \frac{1}{4\pi\varepsilon_0}\frac{Qq}{3a}$$

$$\Rightarrow \frac{1}{2}mv^2 = \frac{Qq}{4\pi\varepsilon_0 a}\left(\frac{1}{3}-\frac{1}{5}\right)$$

$$\Rightarrow v = \sqrt{\frac{2}{m}}\left(\frac{2}{15}\frac{Qq}{4\pi\varepsilon_0 a}\right)^{1/2}$$

18. (b) Given, $n = 27$, $r = 0.02$ m, $q = 10\ \mu$C

Let the radius of bigger drop be R.

$$\Rightarrow \quad n\frac{4}{3}\pi r^3 = \frac{4}{3}\pi R^3$$

$$\Rightarrow 27\times(0.02)^3 = R^3$$

$$\Rightarrow \quad R = 3\times 0.02 = 0.06 \text{ m}$$

$$\sigma_r = \frac{q}{4\pi r^2},\ \sigma_R = \frac{nq}{4\pi R^2}$$

$$\frac{\sigma_R}{\sigma_r} = \frac{nq}{4\pi R^2}\times\frac{4\pi r^2}{q}$$

$$= n\times\frac{(0.02)^2}{(0.06)^2}$$

$$\frac{\sigma_R}{\sigma_r} = 27\times\frac{1}{9} = 3:1$$

19. (b) An electron on plate 1 has electrostatic potential energy. When it moves, potential energy is converted into kinetic energy.

$\therefore$ Kinetic energy = Electrostatic potential energy

or $\quad \frac{1}{2}mv^2 = e\Delta V$

or $v = \sqrt{\frac{2e\times\Delta V}{m}}$

$$= \sqrt{\frac{2\times 1.6\times 10^{-19}\times 20}{9.11\times 10^{-31}}}$$

$$\approx 2.65\times 10^6 \text{ m/s}$$

20. (a)

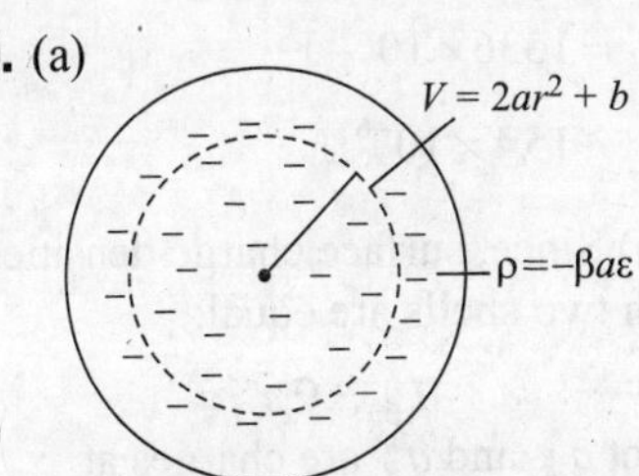

Given, volume charge density inside a charged spherical ball, $\rho = -\beta a\varepsilon$

As, charge density is constant, charge enclosed in a Gaussian sphere of radius r is

$$q = \rho \cdot V = -\beta a \varepsilon\left(\frac{4}{3}\pi r^3\right)$$

By Gauss's law, electric field on surface of Gaussian sphere is

$$E = \frac{1}{4\pi\varepsilon}\frac{q_{\text{enclosed}}}{r^2}$$

$$= \frac{1}{4\pi\varepsilon}\frac{-\beta a \varepsilon \frac{4}{3}\pi r^3}{r^2} = -\frac{\beta}{3}ar$$

Now, using $E = \frac{-dV}{dr}$, we get

$$V = \int_0^V dV = -\int_0^r (Edr)$$

or $V = \int_0^r \frac{\beta}{3} ar\, dr = \frac{\beta a}{3}\cdot\left(\frac{r^2}{2}\right)$

or $V = \frac{\beta}{6}ar^2$ ...(i)

But potential is given,

$V = 2ar^2 + b$ ...(ii)

On comparing Eq. (i) and Eq. (ii), we get

$$\frac{\beta}{6} = 2 \text{ or } \beta = 12$$

21. (d) Maximum torque,

$$\tau = pE$$
$$= (q \times L)E$$
$$= (16 \times 10^{-8} \times 12 \times 10^{-4}) \times 4 \times 10^8$$
$$= 768 \times 10^{-4} \text{ N-m}$$

Work done in rotating dipole through 180° is

$$W = pE(\cos\theta_1 - \cos\theta_2)$$
$$= (q \times L)E(\cos 0° - \cos 180°)$$
$$= 768 \times 10^{-4} \times [1 - (-1)]$$
$$= 1536 \times 10^{-4} \text{ J}$$
$$\simeq 15.4 \times 10^{-6} \text{ J}$$

22. (a) Since, surface charge densities on two shells are equal.

i.e. $\sigma_A = \sigma_B$

Let q_A and q_B are charges at spheres A and B, then $\frac{q_A}{r_A^2} = \frac{q_B}{r_B^2}$

$$\frac{q_A}{q_B} = \frac{r_A^2}{r_B^2} = \frac{4^2}{1^2} = 16 \text{ ...(i)}$$

$q_A + q_B = Q$ [Given]

$q_A + q_B = 34 \text{ mC}$ ...(ii)

Solving Eqs. (i) and (ii), we get

$$q_A = 32 \text{mC}$$
$$q_B = 2 \text{mC}$$

Potential at common centre,

$$V = \frac{Kq_A}{r_A} + \frac{Kq_B}{r_B}$$
$$= \frac{K \times 32 \times 10^{-3}}{4 \times 10^{-2}} + \frac{K \times 2 \times 10^{-3}}{1 \times 10^{-2}}$$
$$= \left[\frac{8K}{10^{-2}} + \frac{2K}{10^{-2}}\right] \times 10^{-3}$$
$$= \frac{10^{-2}K}{10^{-2}} = 1K \text{ V}$$

23. (c) Let, test charge $= Q$

Point charge $= q$

The electric potential,

$$V = \frac{kq}{r}$$

Electric potential energy,

$$W = QV = \frac{kQq}{r}$$

Thus, V is not equal to W.

24. (d) Radius of sphere $= R$

Mass of the piece $= m$

Charge on the piece $= q$

Speed $= v$

Height $= h$

By using law of conservation of energy,

$$\Delta\text{KE} + (\Delta\text{PE})_{\text{electrical}} + (\Delta\text{PE})_{\text{gravitational}} = 0$$

$$\frac{1}{2}mv^2 + \left(\frac{KQq}{R+h} - \frac{KQq}{R}\right) + (-mgh) = 0$$

$$\frac{1}{2}mv^2 = mgh + KQq\left(\frac{1}{R} - \frac{1}{R+h}\right)$$

$$v^2 = 2gh + \frac{2KQq}{m}\frac{h}{R(R+h)}$$

$$v^2 = 2h\left[\frac{qQ}{4\pi\varepsilon_0 R(R+h)m} + g\right]$$

25. (c)

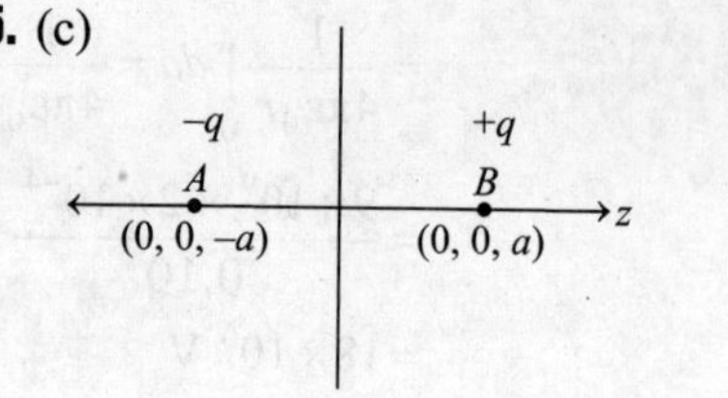

Potential at z due to charges present at A and B is given as

$$V_z = V_A + V_B = \frac{K(-q)}{(z+a)} + \frac{Kq}{(z-a)}$$

$$V_z = \frac{2qa}{4\pi\varepsilon_0(z^2 - a^2)}$$

At, $z = 2a$

$$V_{2a} = \frac{2qa}{4\pi\varepsilon_0(4a^2 - a^2)}$$
$$= \frac{2qa}{4\pi\varepsilon_0 3a^2} = \frac{q}{6\pi\varepsilon_0 a}$$

26. (a) From the graph, r is more for Q_1 than the Q_2.

At point A,

$$V_{Q_1} = V_{Q_2}$$
$$\frac{KQ_1}{R_1} = \frac{KQ_2}{R_2}$$

As, $R_1 > R_2$ at A.

$\therefore$ $|Q_1| > |Q_2|$

If the Q_1 is positive,

$$V_A = \frac{KQ_1}{R_1} + \frac{KQ_2}{R_2}$$

For the equilibrium, net force must be zero, $F = -\frac{dU}{dx}$

Since, the slope is not zero. Hence, they are not the equilibrium points. Point C has the maximum potential energy. So, C is the point of unstable equilibrium for positive charge.

27. (a)

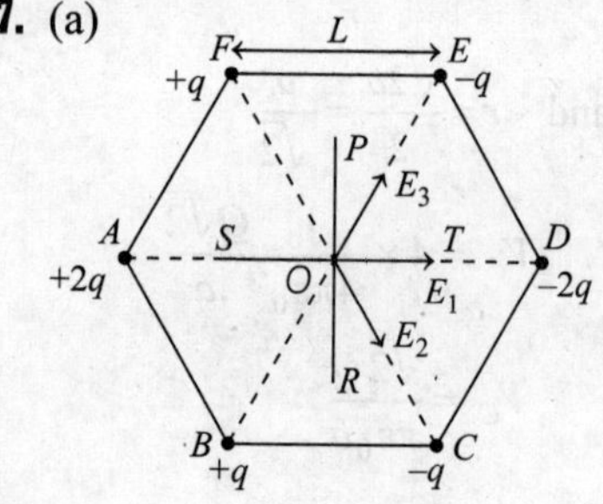

The electric field along OE and OC are same.

i.e., $E_2 = E_3 = \frac{2Kq}{L^2}$ and $E_1 = \frac{4Kq}{L^2}$

$\therefore \; E_{all} = \frac{6Kq}{L^2} = 6 \times \frac{1}{4\pi\varepsilon_0} \frac{q}{L^2} = 6K$

(along OD)

Potential at centre O is zero.

Potential at line PR is zero because this line is equatorial axis for three dipole.

28. (d) Given, potential,

$V = 3x^2 + (y^3 - 1)\,\text{V}$

When, $V = 0$

$\Rightarrow \quad 3x^2 + (y^3 - 1) = 0$

or $\quad 3x^2 + y^3 = 1 \quad \ldots\text{(i)}$

There can be many combinations of x and y which can satisfy the above equation, so statement given in option (a) is incorrect.

As, $\quad \mathbf{E} = -\frac{\partial V}{\partial x}\hat{\mathbf{i}} - \frac{\partial V}{\partial y}\hat{\mathbf{j}}$

$\Rightarrow \quad = -6x\hat{\mathbf{i}} - 3y^2\hat{\mathbf{j}}$

[using Eq. (i)]

From above, $\mathbf{E}$ is zero at (0, 0) and this implies electric field is zero at point (0, 0). So, statement given in option (b) is incorrect.

The direction of electric field from X-axis is given as

$\tan\alpha = \frac{E_y}{E_x} = \frac{-3y^2}{-6x} = \frac{y^2}{2x}$

Now, if we change values of x and y, then value of $\tan\alpha$ will also be changed and the direction of electric field also changes. Thus, the direction of electric field is not same in space, so statement given in option (c) is incorrect.

α depends on values of x and y, so direction changes.

At point $(1\text{ m}, \sqrt{2}\text{m})$, electric field,

$\mathbf{E} = -6 \times 1\hat{\mathbf{i}} - 3 \times (\sqrt{2})^2\,\hat{\mathbf{j}}$

$= -6\hat{\mathbf{i}} - 6\hat{\mathbf{j}}\,\text{V/m}$

or $|\mathbf{E}| = E = 6\sqrt{2}$ V/m

Electric force on charge q,

$F = qE = 2\sqrt{2} \times 10^{-6} \times 6\sqrt{2}$

$= 24 \times 10^{-6}\,\text{N} = 24\,\mu\text{N}$

Therefore, statement given in option (d) is correct.

29. (b) Given, force, $F = 480$ dyne

$= 480 \times 10^{-5}$ N

Charge, $q = 8\,\mu\text{C} = 8 \times 10^{-6}$ C

Distance, $d = 3.2$ cm$= 3.2 \times 10^{-2}$ m

As we know, electric field,

$E = \frac{\text{Force}}{\text{Charge}} = \frac{480 \times 10^{-5}}{8 \times 10^{-6}}$

$= 600$ N/C

Potential difference between two points (say A and B) along the electric field is given by

$V_A - V_B = Ed$

$= 600 \times 3.2 \times 10^{-2}$

$= 19.2$ V

30. (d) Let the charges on inner shell and outer shell be Q_1 and Q_2, respectively.

According to the question, potential of inner sphere is

$\frac{KQ_1}{R_1} + \frac{KQ_2}{R_2} = 30 \quad \ldots\text{(i)}$

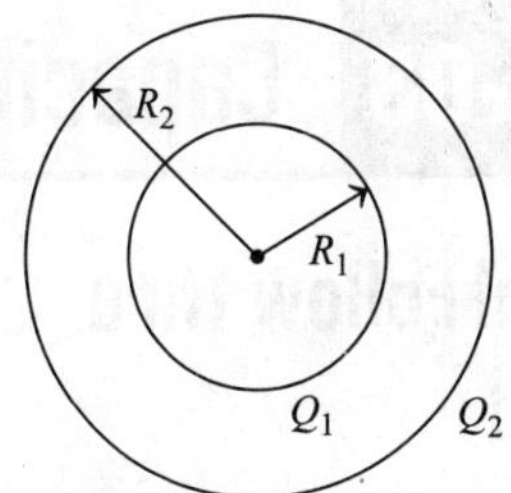

and potential of outer sphere is

$\frac{kQ_1}{R_2} + \frac{kQ_2}{R_2} = 20 \quad \ldots\text{(ii)}$

Subtracting Eq. (i) from Eq. (ii), we get

$\frac{kQ_1}{R_2} - \frac{kQ_1}{R_1} = -10 \quad \ldots\text{(iii)}$

When outer shell is grounded.

Let Q_3 be the charge on outer sphere,

$V_{outer} = \frac{kQ_1}{R_2} + \frac{kQ_3}{R_2} = 0$

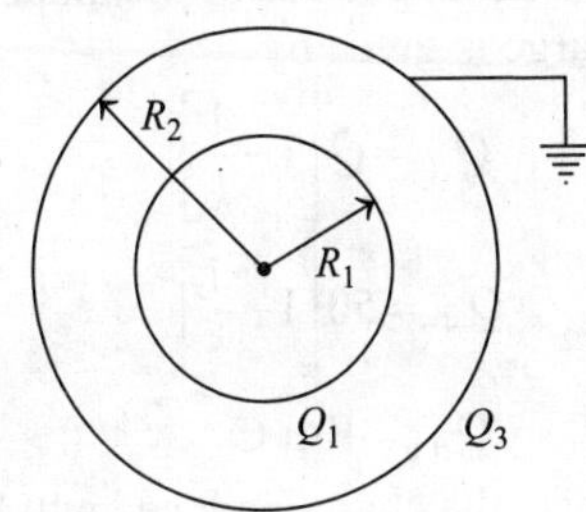

or $\quad Q_3 = -Q_1 \quad \ldots\text{(iv)}$

Now, $V_{inner} = \frac{kQ_1}{R_1} + \frac{kQ_3}{R_2}$

$= \frac{kQ_1}{R_1} - \frac{kQ_1}{R_2}$ [using Eq. (iv)]

$= +10$ V [From Eq. (iii)]

Ch-03 Capacitance

Topical Follow Thru

Test-1

1. (b) When plates of the capacitor are charged, opposite charges are induced on water (dielectric). So, due to attractive forces, level of liquid rises.

2. (a) The potential difference across the parallel plate capacitor,

$$V = 10-(-10) = 20\,V$$

$$\therefore \text{ Capacitance} = \frac{Q}{V} = \frac{40}{20} = 2\,F$$

3. (a) Since, the outer plate of B is free, charge cannot flow from A to B. Hence, the correct option is (a).

4. (c) The magnitude of the induced charge is given by

$$Q_A = Q\left[1-\frac{1}{k}\right]$$

$$Q_A = 50\left[1-\frac{1}{5}\right]$$

$$\therefore \quad Q_A = 40\,\mu C$$

Since, the charge induced will be opposite of actual charge, so charge on A will be $-40\,\mu C$.

5. (d) If C is the capacitance of the air-filled capacitor, the total charge on its plates before connection is $Q = CV$. After it is connected with an uncharged capacitor, let V' be the common potential and Q_1 be the charge on capacitor C and Q_2 on the other capacitor $Q_1 = V'C$

$$Q_2 = V'KC$$

Also $\quad Q = Q_1 + Q_2$

Therefore,

$$CV = V'C + V'KC$$

or $\quad V = V'(1+K)$

or $\quad V' = \dfrac{V}{(1+K)}$

6. (c) Initial capacitance $C = \dfrac{\varepsilon_0 A}{d}$.

When a metal plate of thickness t is introduced, the capacitance becomes $C' = \dfrac{\varepsilon_0 A}{(d-t)}$.

Given, $\quad C' = 5C$

Thus, $\quad \dfrac{\varepsilon_0 A}{d-t} = \dfrac{\varepsilon_0 A}{d} \times 5$

$$d = 5(d-t)$$

$$d = 5d - 5t$$

$$5t = 4d$$

$$t = \frac{4d}{5}$$

7. (d) Within the plates electric fields due to charges Q_1 and Q_2 are

$$E_1 = \frac{Q_1}{2\varepsilon_0 A} \text{ and } E_2 = \frac{Q_2}{2\varepsilon_0 A}$$

As these fields are in opposite directions and $Q_1 > Q_2$, the net electric field between the plates is

$$E = E_1 - E_2 = \frac{1}{2\varepsilon_0 A}(Q_1 - Q_2)$$

Hence, $V = Ed = \dfrac{d}{2\varepsilon_0 A}(Q_1 - Q_2)$

$$= \frac{Q_1 - Q_2}{2C}$$

8. (d) If ρ is the density of a small drop and r its radius, then the mass of each small drop is $m = \dfrac{4\pi}{3} r^3 \rho$. If n such drops coalesce to form a big drop of radius R, then the mass of the big drop is $nm = \dfrac{4\pi}{3} R^3 \rho$.

Hence, $R = n^{1/3} r$. Now, the capacitance of a sphere is proportional to its radius. Hence, the capacitance of the big drop will be $C' = n^{1/3} C$. Hence, the correct option is (d).

9. (b) Electric field between the two plates is perpendicular to the surface of the conductor as shown in figure. Therefore, the effective area of the capacitor is A_2.

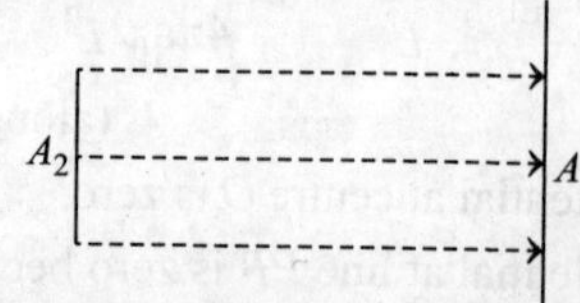

Hence, $C = \dfrac{A_2 \varepsilon_0}{2d}$

10. (d) In first stage, capacitor is connected to a battery, then charge on capacitor

$$q_1 = C_1 V = 20 \times 24 = 480\,\mu C$$

and when space between the plates is filled with liquid of dielectric constant 10, then charge on capacitor, $q_2 = C_2 V = KC_1 \times V$

$$= 10 \times 20 \times 24$$

$$= 4800\,\mu C$$

The additional charge that flows

$$= q_2 - q_1 = 4800 - 480$$

$$= 4320\,\mu C$$

11. (a) Capacitance,

$$C = \frac{K\varepsilon_0 A}{d} \quad (\because K = 3)$$

$$C = \frac{3\varepsilon_0 A}{d} \quad \ldots(i)$$

When dielectric is removed,

$$C' = \frac{\varepsilon_0 A}{d} \quad \ldots(ii)$$

From Eqs. (i) and (ii), we get

$$C = 3C'$$

$$\Rightarrow \quad C' = \frac{C}{3}$$

12. (a) Let the surface charge density on plate be $+\sigma$ and $-\sigma$.

Force on right side plate.

$F = q \times$ Electric field of left plate

$$= (\sigma \times A) \times \left(\frac{\sigma}{2\varepsilon_0}\right)$$

$$F = \frac{\sigma^2 A}{2\varepsilon_0}$$

Tension in string, $T = Mg$

FBD of right side plate,

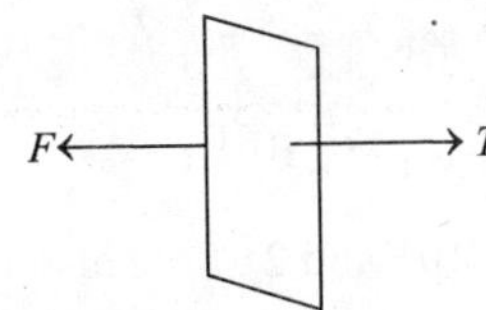

At stationary position, $F = T$

or $\frac{\sigma^2 A}{2\varepsilon_0} = Mg$ or $\sigma = \sqrt{\frac{2Mg\varepsilon_0}{A}}$

As we know that, electric field between the plates, $E = \frac{\sigma}{\varepsilon_0}$

or $E = \frac{\sqrt{\frac{2Mg\varepsilon_0}{A}}}{\varepsilon_0} = \sqrt{\frac{2Mg}{A\varepsilon_0}}$

13. (d) If the radius of a bubble is increased by a factor n^2, its capacitance is also increased by a factor n^2, i.e. $C' = n^2 C$. Since, the charge Q on the bubble remains unchanged, we have $Q = CV = C'V'$

or $V' = \frac{CV}{C'} = \frac{CV}{n^2 C} = \frac{V}{n^2}$

14. (a) Before inserting the slab,

$$C_1 = \frac{A\varepsilon_0}{d}$$

After inserting the slab, capacitance will be

$$\Rightarrow C_2 = \frac{A\varepsilon_0}{d-b} = \frac{A\varepsilon_0}{2d - \frac{3d}{2}} = \frac{2A\varepsilon_0}{d}$$

Therefore, the ratio of capacitances is $\frac{C_2}{C_1} = \frac{2}{1}$

15. (a) Capacitance of a parallel plate capacitor with air,

$$C = \frac{A\varepsilon_0}{d} \quad \text{...(i)}$$

Capacitance of the same parallel plate capacitor with the introduction of a dielectric medium,

$$C' = \frac{KA\varepsilon_0}{d} \quad \text{...(ii)}$$

where, K = dielectric constant

Dividing Eq. (ii) by Eq. (i), we get

$$\frac{C'}{C} = K$$

$$\Rightarrow \quad K = \frac{8}{4} = 2$$

and $K = \frac{\varepsilon}{\varepsilon_0}$

$$\Rightarrow \quad \varepsilon = K\varepsilon_0 = 2 \times 8.85 \times 10^{-12}$$

$$\Rightarrow \quad \varepsilon = 17.708 \times 10^{-12}$$

$$\Rightarrow \quad \varepsilon = 0.17 \times 10^{-10} \text{ C}^2 \text{ N}^{-1} \text{m}^{-2}$$

Test-2

1. (b) When switch S_3 is closed, the potential difference across C_1 and C_2 will become equal to the average of V_1 and V_2, i.e. $(40+30)/2 = 35$ V. Hence, the correct option is (b).

2. (b) The equivalent capacitance in parallel combination,

$$C_P = C + C = 2C$$

Equivalent capacitance in series combination,

$$\frac{1}{C_S} = \frac{1}{C} + \frac{1}{C} \Rightarrow C_S = \frac{C}{2}$$

So, required ratio

$$\frac{C_P}{C_S} = \frac{2C}{\frac{C}{2}} \Rightarrow \frac{C_P}{C_S} = \frac{4}{1}$$

$$C_P : C_S = 4 : 1$$

3. (b) The inner plates 2 and 3 are connected together. Hence, they act as a single conductor. Since, the outer plates 1 and 4 are connected together, there are effectively two capacitors (between plates 1 and 2 and plates 3 and 4) in parallel. Each of capacitance $C = \varepsilon_0 A/d$ as shown in figure. Thus, the equivalent capacitance is

$$C' = 2C = \frac{2\varepsilon_0 A}{d}, \text{ which is option (b).}$$

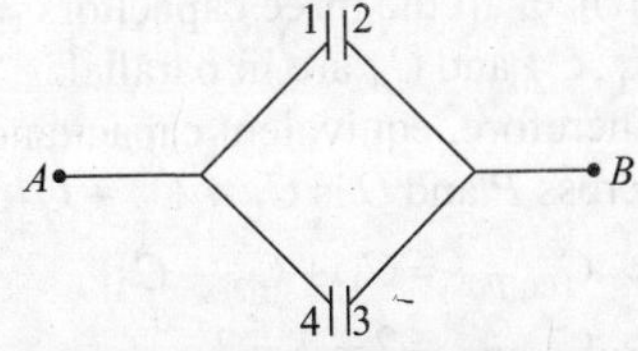

4. (a) The last three capacitors on the right, each of capacitance, $C = 9\,\mu\text{F}$ are in series and are equivalent to a capacitance C' given by

$$\frac{1}{C'} = \frac{1}{9} + \frac{1}{9} + \frac{1}{9} = \frac{1}{3} \text{ or } C' = 3\,\mu\text{F}$$

Since, C is in parallel with C_1, the equivalent capacitance of the last part of the network is $C'' = C' + C_1 = 3 + 6 = 9\,\mu\text{F}$. Continuing this process of calculation towards the left, we notice that we are finally left with the combination whose equivalent capacitance is 3 μF.

5. (a) Charge on C_1, $Q_1 = C_1 V = \frac{CV}{2}$.

This charge is shared by the three capacitors. The equivalent capacitance of the series combination of C_2 and C_3 is

$$C' = \frac{C_2 C_3}{C_2 + C_3} = \frac{4C}{4} = C$$

$$(C_2 = C_3 = 2C)$$

The common potential of C_1 and C' is

$$V' = \frac{Q_1}{C_1 + C'} = \frac{C_1 V}{C_1 + C'}$$

$$= \frac{\frac{CV}{2}}{\frac{C}{2} + C} = \frac{V}{3}$$

∴ Final charge on C_1 is

$$Q'_1 = C_1 V' = \frac{C}{2} \times \frac{V}{3} = \frac{CV}{6}$$

∴Charge that will flow through connecting wires is

$$Q' = Q_1 - Q_1' = \frac{CV}{2} - \frac{CV}{6}$$

$$= \frac{2CV}{6} = \frac{CV}{3}$$

6. (c) The network reduces to that shown in fig.

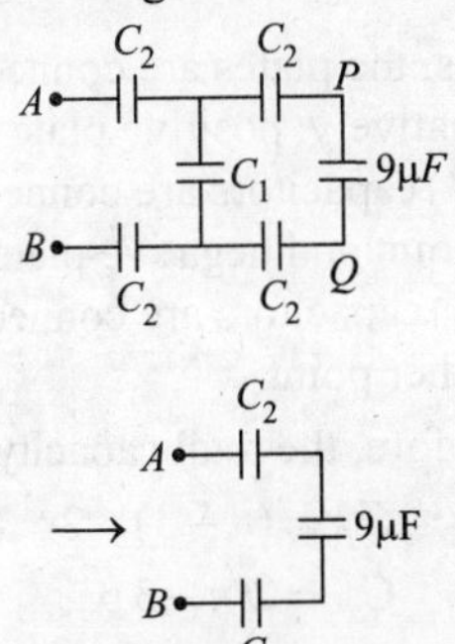

$$C_{eq} = \frac{C_2}{3} = \frac{9}{3} = 3\,\mu\text{F}$$

7. (a) Given, $C_1 + C_2 = \frac{C_1C_2}{C_1 + C_2} \times \frac{25}{6}$

or $6(C_1 + C_2)^2 = 25C_1C_2$

or $6C_1^2 + 6C_2^2 + 12C_1C_2 = 25C_1C_2$

or $6C_1^2 + 6C_2^2 - 13C_1C_2 = 0$

Let $C_1 = XC_2$. Then, we have

$6X^2C_2^2 + 6C_2^2 - 13XC_2^2 = 0$

$6X^2 - 13X + 6 = 0$

$X = \frac{2}{3}$ or $\frac{3}{2}$

$\because C_1 > C_2$

$\therefore x = \frac{3}{2}$ is only possible.

8. (c)

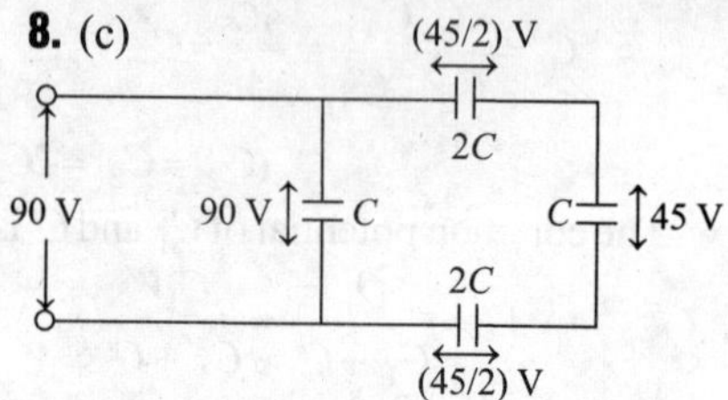

In parallel, potential difference is same.

In series, it distributes in inverse ratio of capacity.

9. (d) From the graph, it is clear that, potential difference across capacitor C_2 is maximum and that for C_1 is minimum,

i.e., $V_2 > V_3 > V_1$ ...(i)

As we know that, in series, charge on each capacitor remains same.

$Q = CV =$ constant

or $C \propto \frac{1}{V}$

$\therefore$ $C_1 > C_3 > C_2$ [using Eq. (i)]

10. (b) As, the plates are connected alternatively, positive plate of all $(n-3)$ capacitors are connected to one point and negative plate of all $(n-3)$ capacitors are connected to the other point.

Therefore, the total capacity,

$C_P = (n-3) \times 2x$

$\Rightarrow$ $C_P = 2(n-3)x$

11. (a) When S is opened, then

$C_{eq} = \frac{C_1C_2}{C_1 + C_2}$

$= \frac{(2\,\mu F)(3\,\mu F)}{(2\,\mu F + 3\,\mu F)} = \frac{6}{5}\,\mu F$

Charge on both capacitors will be same because both are connected in series i.e.,

$q = C_{eq}\,V = \left(\frac{6}{5}\,\mu F\right)(30 + 60)$

$= 108\,\mu C$

12. (c) The circuit is equivalent to Wheatstone bridge.

As $\frac{C_1}{C_2} = \frac{C_3}{C_4}$, the bridge is balanced, C_5 is ineffective.

Here, C_1 and C_2 are in series

$\Rightarrow$ $\frac{1}{C_{S_1}} = \frac{1}{C_1} + \frac{1}{C_2} = \frac{1}{2} + \frac{1}{2} = 1\,\mu F$

$\therefore$ $C_{S_1} = 1\,\mu F$

Similarly, C_3 and C_4 are also in series.

$\Rightarrow$ $\frac{1}{C_{S_2}} = \frac{1}{C_3} + \frac{1}{C_4} = \frac{1}{2} + \frac{1}{2} = 1\,\mu F$

$\therefore$ $C_{S_2} = 1\,\mu F$

Therefore, the effective capacitance between points P and R will be C_P.

$\Rightarrow$ $C_{PR} = C_{S_1} + C_{S_2} = 1 + 1 = 2\,\mu F$

13. (c) Capacitance of branch

QSP, $\frac{1}{C_1} = \frac{1}{4} + \frac{1}{4} = \frac{2}{4} = \frac{1}{2}\,\mu F$

$\Rightarrow$ $C_1 = 2\,\mu F$

Capacitance between Q and P

$C_2 = 4\,\mu F$

Capacitance of branch

PRQ, $\frac{1}{C_3} = \frac{1}{4} + \frac{1}{4} = \frac{2}{4} = \frac{1}{2}\,\mu F$

$\Rightarrow$ $C_3 = 2\,\mu F$

Hence, all the three capacitors C_1, C_2 and C_3 are in parallel. Therefore, equivalent capacitance across P and Q is $C_1 + C_2 + C_3$.

$\Rightarrow C_{eq\,PQ} = C_1 + C_2 + C_3$

$\Rightarrow C_{eq\,PQ} = 2 + 4 + 2$

$\Rightarrow C_{eq\,PQ} = 8\,\mu F$

14. (c) Here, $2\,\mu F$, $2\,\mu F$, $2\,\mu F$ and $2\,\mu F$ capacitors are in series. Therefore,

$\frac{1}{C_{eq_1}} = \frac{1}{2} + \frac{1}{2} + \frac{1}{2} + \frac{1}{2} = 2\,\mu F$

$\Rightarrow$ $C_{eq_1} = \frac{1}{2}\,\mu F$

Now, $2\,\mu F$ and $2\,\mu F$ are also is series.

$\frac{1}{C_{eq_2}} = \frac{1}{2} + \frac{1}{2} = 1\,\mu F$

$\Rightarrow C_{eq_2} = 1\,\mu F$

Since, $1/2\,\mu F$ and $1\,\mu F$ are in parallel, so we have

$C_{eq} = C_{eq_1} + C_{eq_2}$

$= \frac{1}{2} + 1 = \frac{3}{2}\,\mu F$

15. (b) The series combination of C_2 and C_3 is equivalent to a capacitance C' given by

$\frac{1}{C'} = \frac{1}{C_2} + \frac{1}{C_3}$

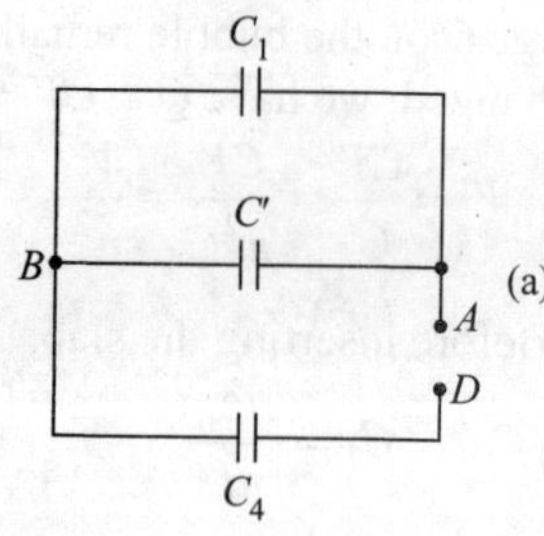

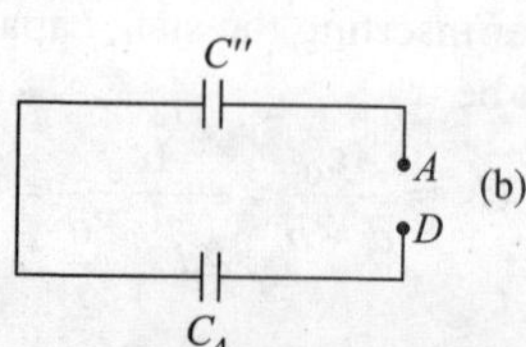

Or $C' = \frac{C_2C_3}{C_2 + C_3} = \frac{400 \times 400}{400 + 400}$

$= 200\,pF$

Therefore, the circuit reduces to the one shown in Fig. (a). The equivalent capacitance between points A and B is

$C'' = C_1 + C = 200 + 100 = 300\,pF$

The circuit may be further simplified to that in Fig. (b). The equivalent capacitance C of the entire network, i.e., between points A and D, is now that of the series combination of C'' and C_4. Thus,

$\frac{1}{C} = \frac{1}{C''} + \frac{1}{C_4}$

$$=\frac{1}{300}+\frac{1}{100}=\frac{4}{300}$$

or $C=\frac{300}{4}$ pF

Test-3

1. (a) In series combination, charge Q on each condenser is same.

$$\therefore \quad \frac{E_1}{E_2}=\frac{Q^2/2C_1}{Q^2/2C_2}$$

$$=\frac{C_2}{C_1}=\frac{11}{44}=\frac{1}{4}$$

2. (a) The energy stored will be,

$$U=\frac{Q^2}{2C}$$

In first condition,

$$U=\frac{(2Q)^2}{2C}=\frac{4Q^2}{2C}$$

$$U=\frac{4Q^2}{2C}=8\,\text{J} \quad \text{(given)}$$

$$\Rightarrow \quad \frac{Q^2}{2C}=2\,\text{J}$$

Second condition, when the charge is increasing,

$$U'=\frac{(3Q)^2}{2C}$$

$$\Rightarrow \quad U'=\frac{9Q^2}{2C} \Rightarrow U'=18\,\text{J}$$

3. (a) Loss of energy during sharing

$$=\frac{C_1C_2(V_1-V_2)^2}{2(C_1+C_2)}$$

In the equation, put $V_2=0, V_1=V_0$

$$\therefore \text{ Loss of energy}=\frac{C_1C_2V_0^2}{2(C_1+C_2)}$$

$$=\frac{C_2U_0}{C_1+C_2} \quad \left[\because U_0=\frac{1}{2}C_1V_0^2\right]$$

4. (d) Total capacitance of given system,

$$\frac{1}{C_{eq}}=\frac{1}{4}+\frac{1}{8}+\frac{1}{4}$$

$$=\frac{2+1+2}{8}=\frac{5}{8}$$

$$C_{eq}=\frac{8}{5}\,\mu\text{F}$$

$$U=\frac{1}{2}C_{eq}V^2=\frac{1}{2}\times\frac{8}{5}\times 10^{-6}\times 225$$

$$=180\times 10^{-6}\,\text{J}=180\,\mu\text{J}$$

5. (c) On inserting a dielectric slab, the capacitance of capacitor C_0 is increased to C_0K or KC_0, therefore charge $(q_0=C_0V)$ will increase to $(q=Kq_0)$.

Initial potential energy,

$U_0=\frac{1}{2}C_0V^2$. Hence, final potential energy,

$$U=\frac{1}{2}CV^2=\frac{1}{2}KC_0V^2=KU_0$$

6. (a) Given,

$$A=50\text{ cm}^2=50\times 10^{-4}\text{ m}^2$$

$$d=5\text{ mm}=5\times 10^{-3}\text{m}$$

$$V=400\text{ V}$$

Electrical energy stored by capacitor

$$=\frac{1}{2}CV^2=\frac{1}{2}\frac{A\varepsilon_0}{d}V^2$$

$$=\frac{1}{2}\times\frac{8.85\times 10^{-12}\times 50\times 10^{-4}}{5\times 10^{-3}}(400)^2$$

$$=7.08\times 10^{-7}\,\text{J}$$

7. (b)

A. As, $\frac{Q_1}{C_1}=\frac{Q_2}{C_2}, Q_2=\left(\frac{C_2}{C_1}\right)Q_1$

$$=\frac{(C/2)}{C}Q_1=\frac{Q_1}{2}$$

Further as,

$$Q=Q_1+Q_2=Q_1+\frac{Q_1}{2}=\frac{3}{2}Q_1$$

$$Q_1=\frac{2}{3}Q \text{ and } Q_2=\frac{1}{3}Q$$

Final energy of capacitor C_1,

$$U_1=\frac{Q_1^2}{2C_1}=\frac{\left(\frac{2}{3}Q\right)^2}{2C}$$

$$=\frac{2}{9}\left(\frac{Q^2}{C}\right)=\frac{2}{9}\left(\frac{C^2V_0^2}{C}\right)$$

$$=\frac{2}{9}CV_0^2 \quad (\text{as } Q=CV_0)$$

B. Final energy of capacitor C_2,

$$U_2=\frac{Q_2^2}{2C_2}=\frac{\left(\frac{1}{3}Q\right)^2}{2(C/2)}$$

$$=\frac{1}{9}\left(\frac{Q^2}{C}\right)=\frac{1}{9}CV_0^2$$

C. Final energy of system,

$$U_{final}=U_1+U_2=\frac{1}{3}CV_0^2$$

D. Inital energy of system,

$$U_{initial}=\frac{Q^2}{2C}=\frac{(CV_0)^2}{2C}=\frac{1}{2}CV_0^2$$

$\therefore$ Change in energy,

$$\Delta U=U_{final}-U_{initial}=-\frac{1}{6}CV_0^2$$

Hence, A $\rightarrow$ 3, B $\rightarrow$ 4, C $\rightarrow$ 2 and D $\rightarrow$ 1.

8. (a) Energy stored in the capacitor is

$$\frac{1}{2}CV^2=\frac{1}{2}\times C\times(400)^2$$

$$=8\times 10^4 C\,\text{J}$$

Energy appearing as heat in the block is

$$mc\theta=0.1\times 2.5\times 10^2\times 0.4=10\,\text{J}$$

$$8\times 10^4\times C=10$$

$$\text{or } C=\frac{10}{8}\times 10^{-4}$$

$$=125\,\mu\text{F}$$

9. (b) $C=\frac{A\varepsilon_0}{d}$

$$=\frac{50\times 10^{-4}\times 8.85\times 10^{-12}}{3\times 10^{-3}}$$

$$=1.475\times 10^{-11}$$

$$U_{AB}=U_{BC}=\frac{1}{2}CV^2$$

$$=\frac{1.475\times 10^{-11}}{2}(12)^2$$

$$U_{AB}=1.06\times 10^{-9}\,\text{J}$$

So, total energy stored

$$=2\times 1.06\times 10^{-9}$$

$$=2.1\times 10^{-9}\,\text{J}$$

10. (b) On introducing dielectric K in a parallel plate capacitor, its capacity becomes,

$$C' = KC_0$$

$$\therefore \quad C' = 5C_0$$

Also, energy stored, $W_0 = \dfrac{q^2}{2C_0}$

$$\therefore \quad W' = \frac{q^2}{2C'} = \frac{q^2}{2 \times 5C_0}$$

$$\therefore \quad \frac{W_0}{W'} = \frac{5}{1}$$

$$\therefore \quad W' = \frac{W_0}{5}$$

11. (d) $q_i = C_i V = 2V = q$

This charge will remain constant after switch S is shifted from position 1 to position 2.

$$U_i = \frac{1}{2}\frac{q^2}{C_i} = \frac{q^2}{2 \times 2} = \frac{q^2}{4}$$

$$U_f = \frac{1}{2}\frac{q^2}{C_f} = \frac{q^2}{2 \times 10} = \frac{q^2}{20}$$

Energy dissipated $= U_i - U_f = \dfrac{q^2}{5}$

So, % decrease in energy

$$= \frac{U_i - U_f}{U_i} \times 100\% = \frac{q^2/5}{q^2/4} \times 100\%$$

$$= \frac{4}{5} \times 100\% = 80\%$$

The energy dissipated is 80% of the initial stored energy.

12. (a) Energy stored initially is $U_i = \dfrac{Q^2}{2C}$. If d is tripled, C becomes $C/3$. Hence, energy stored when d is tripled is

$$U_f = \frac{3Q^2}{2C}$$

$\therefore$ Work needed is

$$W = U_f - U_i$$

$$= \frac{3Q^2}{2C} - \frac{Q^2}{2C} = \frac{Q^2}{C}$$

Now, $C = \dfrac{A\,\varepsilon_0}{d}$ and $Q = CV$

Hence, $W = \dfrac{A\varepsilon_0 V^2}{d}$

13. (b) Common potential is

$$V = \frac{C_1V_1 + C_2V_2}{C_1 + C_2}$$

$$= \frac{(4 \times 10^{-6}) \times 80 + (6 \times 10^{-6}) \times 30}{4 \times 10^{-6} + 6 \times 10^{-6}}$$

$$= 50 \text{ V}$$

$\therefore$ Energy gained by 6 μF capacitor

$$= \frac{1}{2}C_1V^2 - \frac{1}{2}C_1V_1^2$$

$$= \frac{1}{2}C_1(V^2 - V_1^2)$$

$$= \frac{1}{2} \times (6 \times 10^{-6}) \times \{(50)^2 - (30)^2\}$$

$$= 4.8 \times 10^{-3} \text{ J}$$

$$= 4.8 \text{ mJ}$$

14. (a) Capacitance of capacitor,

$$C_1 = 650 \text{ pF} = 650 \times 10^{-12} \text{ F}$$

Supply voltage, $V_1 = 200$ V

Also, $C_2 = 750$ pF

$$= 750 \times 10^{-12} \text{ F}$$

and $V_2 = 0$

Loss in energy,

$$E = \frac{C_1C_2(V_1 - V_2)^2}{2(C_1 + C_2)}$$

$$\Rightarrow E = \frac{650 \times 10^{-12} \times 750 \times 10^{-12}(200 - 0)^2}{2(650 + 750) \times 10^{-12}}$$

$$\Rightarrow E = 6.96 \times 10^{-6} \text{ J}$$

15. (a) Electric filed at surface,

$$E = \frac{1}{4\pi\varepsilon_0}\frac{q}{R^2}$$

Energy density,

$$u = \frac{1}{2}\varepsilon_0 E^2$$

$$= \frac{q^2}{32\pi^2\varepsilon_0 R^4}$$

$$= \frac{(1.25 \times 10^{-9})^2}{32\pi^2 (8.85 \times 10^{-12})(0.0685)^4}$$

$$= 2.54 \times 10^{-5} \text{ J/m}^3$$

$$\simeq 25 \ \mu\text{J/m}^3$$

Chapter Break Thru

1. (b) The given arrangement is equivalent to the parallel combination of three identical capacitors. Hence, equivalent capacitance $= 3C = 3\dfrac{\varepsilon_0 A}{d}$

2. (d) $U_1 = \dfrac{1}{2}CV^2$.

Therefore, $\delta U = CV\,\delta V$. Therefore

$$\frac{dU}{U} \times 100 = \frac{CV\delta V}{\frac{1}{2}CV^2} \times 100$$

$$= \frac{2\delta V}{V} \times 100$$

$$= \frac{2 \times 0.2 \times 100}{100} = 0.4\%$$

3. (b) The circuit can be redrawn as shown in Fig.

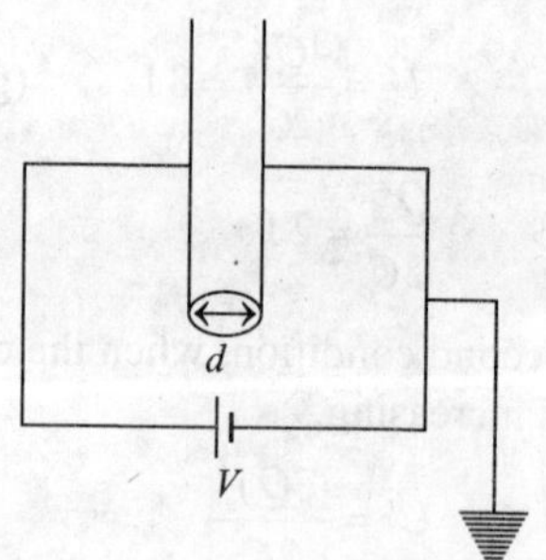

The charge on the capacitor plates is

$$Q = CV = \frac{A\varepsilon_0 V}{d}$$

4. (a) Equivalent circuit can be redrawn as

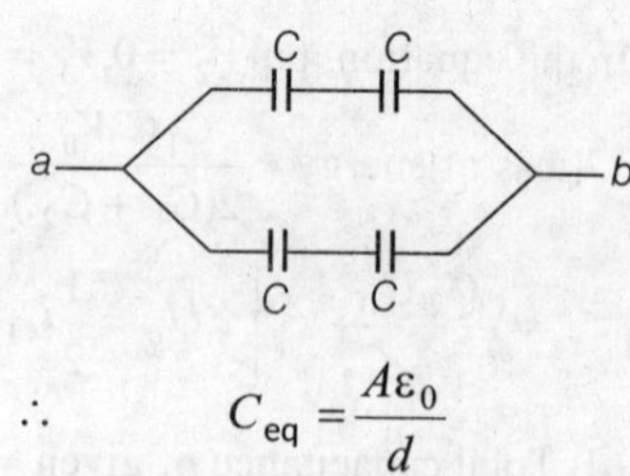

$$\therefore \quad C_{eq} = \frac{A\varepsilon_0}{d}$$

5. (c) The insertion of the dielectric slab decreases the electric field without changing its direction. The electric potential increases as we go from the negative to the positive plate. Hence, the correct option is (c).

6. (c) Two capacitors $2C$ and C are short-circuited. Remaining three, C, C and $2C$ are in parallel.

So, equivalent capacitance $= 4\,C$

7. (b) $V_M = V_N$ and $V_B = V_D$ (from symmetry)

Therefore, capacitors between M and N or between B and D can be removed.

Resultant circuit becomes

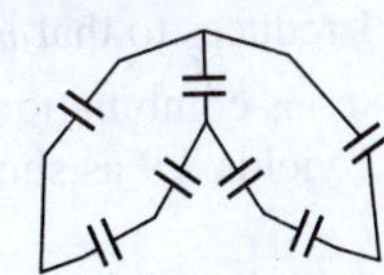

$$C_{eq} = \frac{C}{3} + \frac{C}{3} + C = \frac{5}{3}C$$

8. (a) Charge on capacitor plates without the d_1 electric is

$Q = CV = 4 \times 10^{-6} \times 1 = 4 \times 10^{-6}\ Q = 4\,\mu C$

The capacitance after the dielectric is introduced is

$$C' = \frac{\varepsilon_0 A}{d - \left(t - \frac{t}{K}\right)} = \frac{\frac{\varepsilon_0 A}{d}}{1 - \left(\frac{t - \frac{t}{K}}{d}\right)}$$

$$= \frac{4\mu\,F}{1 - \left(\frac{4-1}{6}\right)}$$

$\therefore$ Charge on capacitor plates now will be

$Q' = C'V = 8 \times 1 = 8\,\mu C$

Additional charge transferred

$= Q' - Q = 8\,\mu C - 4\,\mu C = 4\,\mu C.$

9. (c) The capacitance C, with dielectric between the plates is given as

$$C = \frac{KA\varepsilon_0}{d}$$

As $d' = \frac{d}{2}, K' = 3K$

Then, new capacitance becomes

$$C' = \frac{\varepsilon_0 3KA}{\frac{d}{2}} = 6\frac{\varepsilon_0 KA}{d} = 6C$$

The capacitance C depends only on the geometrical configuration (shape, size, separation) of the system of two conductors.

10. (b) Common potential after joining is

$$V = \frac{q_1 + q_2}{C_1 + C_2}$$

Charge on smaller sphere after redistribution of charges is

$$q_1' = C_1 V = \frac{C_1 (q_1 + q_2)}{C_1 + C_2}$$

$$= \frac{4\pi\varepsilon_0 r_1 (q_1 + q_2)}{4\pi\varepsilon_0 (r_1 + r_2)}$$

After substituting given values we have,

$$q_1 = \frac{r_1 (q_1 + q_2)}{(r_1 + r_2)}$$

$$= \frac{6 \times 10^{-2} \times 10^{-2}}{(10^{-2} + 2 \times 10^{-2})} = \frac{6 \times 10^{-4}}{3 \times 10^{-2}}$$

$$= 2 \times 10^{-2}\,C$$

11. (d) As capacitor cannot withstand 50 V, we need at least 4 capacitors in series.

To make 10 pF capacity with $\frac{10}{4}$ pF capacitors, we need 4 rows in parallel.

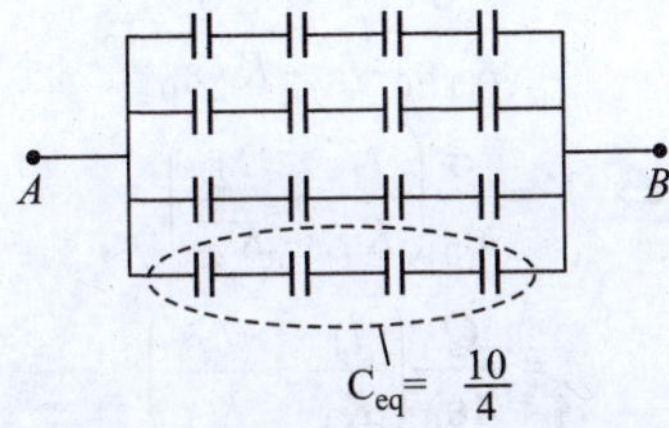

12. (b) As, $C = \frac{\varepsilon_0 A}{d} = \frac{\varepsilon_0 A}{0} = \infty$

The polar molecules develope an induced dipole moment in presence of external electric field. Hence, Statement I is correct and Statement II is incorrect.

13. (c) Original capacitance of the parallel combination of C and $2C = C + 2C = 3C$. Total charge $Q = 3CV$. When the capacitor C is filled with dielectric, its capacitance becomes KC. Therefore, the capacitance of the combination after the capacitor C is filled with dielectric,

$C' = KC + 2C = (K + 2)C$. Since the charge remains the same, $Q = 3CV$, the potential difference across the capacitors will be

$$\frac{Q}{C'} = \frac{3CV}{(K+2)C} = \frac{3V}{K+2}$$

14. (a) Original capacitance,

$$C_0 = \frac{\varepsilon_0 A}{d}$$

$$= \frac{9 \times 10^{-12} \times 0.2}{10^{-2}} = 180\,\text{pF}$$

Initial potential difference,

$V_0 = 3000\,\text{V}$

Initial charge, $Q_0 = C_0 V_0$

$= 180 \times 10^{-12} \times 3000$

$= 18 \times 3 \times 10^{-8}$

$= 54 \times 10^{-8}\,C$

Final value of capacity after insertion of dielectric

$$= \frac{Q_0}{V'} = \frac{54 \times 10^{-8}}{1000} = 540\,\text{pF}$$

Final capacity $= \frac{\varepsilon_0 KA}{d} = K \times 180$

$\Rightarrow \quad 540 = K \times 180$

$\Rightarrow \quad K = 3$

So, permittivity of dielectric

$= \varepsilon_0 K = 3 \times 9 \times 10^{-12}$

$= 27 \times 10^{-12}\,C^2\,N^{-1}\,m^{-2}$

(i) $\rightarrow$ (s), (ii) $\rightarrow$ (r), (iii) $\rightarrow$ (q), (iv) $\rightarrow$ (p)

15. (a) The capacitance before the introduction of the slab is $C = \frac{\varepsilon_0 A}{d}$.

If Q is the charge on the plates, the potential difference is

$$V = \frac{Q}{C} = \frac{Qd}{\varepsilon_0 A} \quad \text{...(i)}$$

Let d' be the new separation between the plates. When a slab of thickness t and dielectric constant K is introduced, the new capacitance is

$$C' = \frac{\varepsilon_0 A}{d' - t\left(1 - \frac{1}{K}\right)}$$

Since, charge Q remains the same, the new potential difference is

$$V' = \frac{Q}{C'} = \frac{Q\left[d' - t\left(1 - \frac{1}{K}\right)\right]}{\varepsilon_0 A} \quad \text{...(ii)}$$

Given $V' = V$. Equating Eqs. (1) and (2), we get

$$d = d' - t\left(1 - \frac{1}{K}\right)$$

or $$d' - d = t\left(1 - \frac{1}{K}\right)$$

Given $d' - d = 2$ mm and $t = 4$ mm. Thus,

$$2 = 4\left(1 - \frac{1}{K}\right)$$

$$\frac{1}{2} = 1 - \frac{1}{K}$$

$$\frac{1}{K} = \frac{1}{2}$$

$$K = 2$$

16. (b)

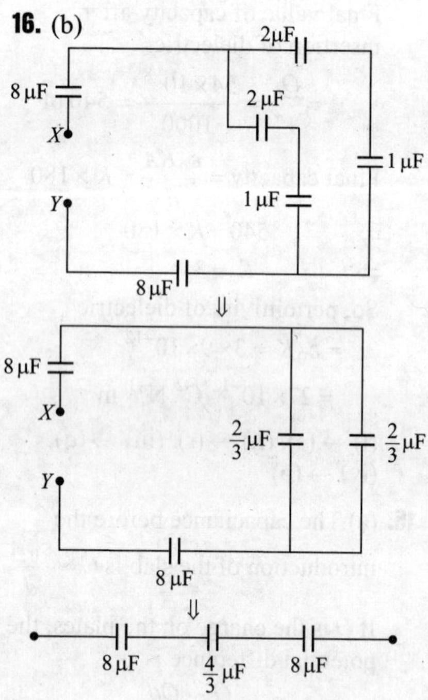

$\therefore \quad C_{eq} = 1 \mu F$

17. (b) Net capacitance for series combination is $C_s = \frac{C}{n}$

Voltage, $V_s = nV$

Energy, $U_s = \frac{1}{2} C_s V_s$

$$= \frac{1}{2} \times \frac{C}{n} \times n^2 V^2$$

$$= \frac{CV^2 n}{2}$$

For parallel combination, $C_p = nC$

$$V_p = V$$

$$U_p = \frac{1}{2} C_p V_p^2 = \frac{1}{2} nCV^2$$

$$= \frac{1}{2} nCV^2 = U_s$$

18. (b) As, the circuit is Wheatstone balanced, circuit can be redrawn as,

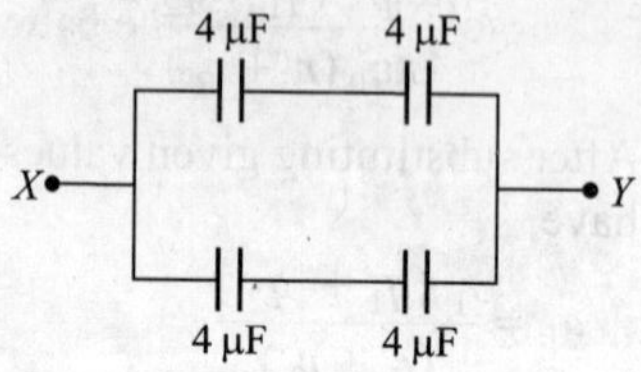

In both the half, capacitors are in series. So, their equivalent,

$$C_{eq} = \frac{4 \times 4}{4 + 4} = 2 \mu F$$

Now, $2 \mu F$ is in parallel with another $2 \mu F$.

So, $C_{eq} = 2 + 2 = 4 \mu F$

19. (a) Potential difference across the condenser,

$$V = V_1 + V_2 = E_1 t_1 + E_2 t_2$$

$$= \frac{\sigma}{K_1 \varepsilon_0} t_1 + \frac{\sigma}{K_2 \varepsilon_0} t_2$$

$$\Rightarrow V = \frac{\sigma}{\varepsilon_0}\left(\frac{t_1}{K_1} + \frac{t_2}{K_2}\right)$$

$$= \frac{Q}{A\varepsilon_0}\left(\frac{t_1}{K_1} + \frac{t_2}{K_2}\right)$$

20. (b)The series combination of 6 and 12 is equivalent to 4 and the parallel combination of 2 and 2 is also equivalent to 4. Therefore the network can be simplified as shown in figure

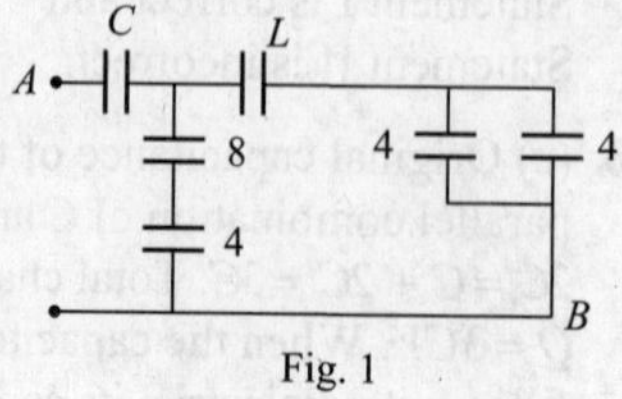

Fig. 1

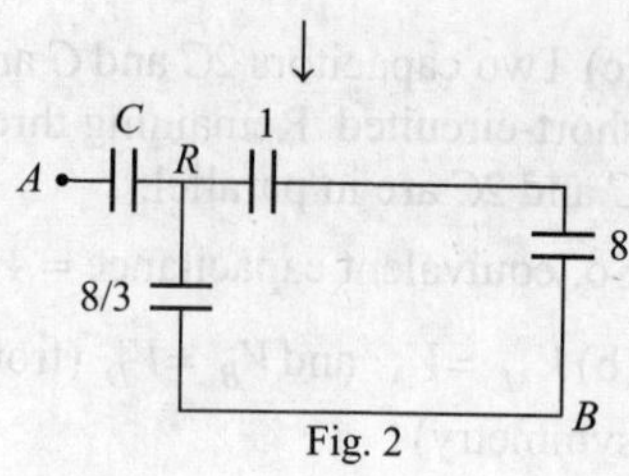

Fig. 2

The parallel combination of 4 and 4 is equivalent to 8 and the series combination of 8 and 4 is equivalent to 8/3. Thus the combination in Fig. 1 reduces to that in Fig. 2

The series combination of 1 and 8 in Fig. 2 yields 8/9 as shown in Fig. 3.

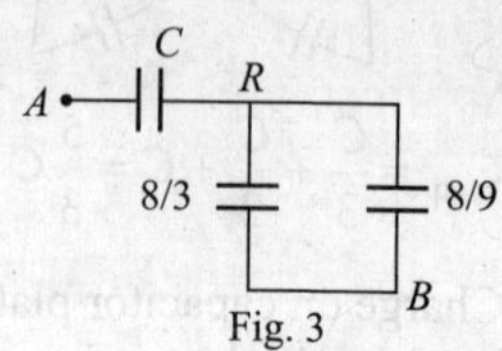

Fig. 3

$$C_{RB} = \frac{8}{3} + \frac{8}{9} = \frac{32}{9} \mu F$$

$$C_{AB} = 1 \mu F = \frac{1}{C} + \frac{9}{32} = \frac{32 + 9C}{32C}$$

$$\Rightarrow \quad C = \frac{32}{23} \mu F$$

21. (b) If Q is the initial charge on capacitor C_1, the initial energy is given by $U_i = \frac{Q^2}{2C_1}$

When the two capacitors are connected together, and as the charge is distributed equally, the charge on each capacitor is $Q/2$. Since, the potential difference (in a parallel connection) across the two capacitors is also the same, it follows that their capacitances are equal (since $C = Q/V$). Thus , $C_1 = C_2 = C$ (say). Also $Q_1 = Q_2 = Q/2$

Therefore, final energy stored in the two capacitors is

$$U_f = \frac{Q_1^2}{2C_1} + \frac{Q_2^2}{2C_2} = \frac{\left(\frac{Q}{2}\right)^2}{2C} + \frac{\left(\frac{Q}{2}\right)^2}{2C}$$

$$= \frac{Q^2}{4C}$$

But, $U_i = \frac{Q^2}{2C}$

$$U_f - U_i = \frac{Q^2}{4C} - \frac{Q^2}{2C}$$

$$= \frac{Q^2 - 2Q^2}{4C} = \frac{-Q^2}{4C}$$

22. (b) Charge on capacitor when it is connected with battery, $q = CV$

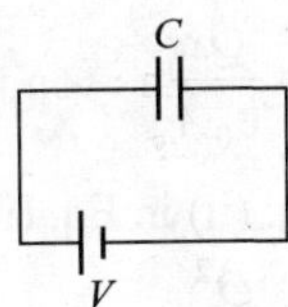

When it is connected with another uncharged capacitor.

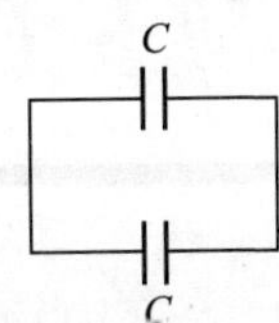

Common potential difference across capacitors,

$$V_C = \frac{q_1 + q_2}{C_1 + C_2} = \frac{q + 0}{C + C} = \frac{q}{2C}$$

$$V_C = \frac{V}{2}$$

Initial energy, $U_i = \frac{1}{2}CV^2$

Final energy, $U_f = \frac{1}{2}[2C]\left[\frac{V}{2}\right]^2$

$$= \frac{1}{2} \cdot \frac{1}{2} CV^2 = \frac{1}{2} U_i$$

Hence, total electrostatic energy of resulting system is decreased by a factor of 2.

23. (d) In series capacitance,

$$\frac{1}{C_S} = \frac{1}{4} + \frac{1}{12} + \frac{1}{16}$$

$$\Rightarrow \frac{1}{C_S} = \frac{12 + 4 + 3}{48}$$

$$\Rightarrow \frac{1}{C_S} = \frac{19}{48}$$

$$\Rightarrow C_S = \frac{48}{19} \mu F$$

In parallel capacitance,

$$C_P = 4 + 12 + 16$$

$$C_P = 32 \mu F$$

The ratio of capacitors will be $\frac{C_P}{C_S}$

$$\Rightarrow \frac{C_P}{C_S} = \frac{32}{\frac{48}{19}} = \frac{32 \times 19}{48} = \frac{38}{3}$$

24. (d) Initial charge on left plate, $Q = 2 \mu C$

Final charge on left plate i.e., after switch is ON,

$$Q' = CV = 10^{-6} \times 10 C$$

$$= 10 \mu C$$

Charge delivered by the battery,

$$\Delta Q = Q' - Q$$

$$= 10 - 2 = 8 \mu C$$

Work done by battery,

$$W_{battery} = (\Delta Q) V$$

$$= (8 \times 10^{-6}) \times 10$$

$$= 80 \times 10^{-6}$$

$$= 80 \mu J$$

25. (a) The batteries are in opposition as their positive terminals are connected together. Hence, the effective voltage is

$$V = V_1 - V_2 = 12 - 2 = 10 V$$

As the capacitors C_1 and C_2 are in series, the effective capacitance of the circuit is given by

$$\frac{1}{C} = \frac{1}{C_1} + \frac{1}{C_2} = \frac{1}{3} + \frac{1}{3} = \frac{2}{3}$$

or $C = \frac{3}{2} = 1.5 \mu F$

Therefore, charge on capacitors is

$$Q = CV = 1.5 \mu F \times 10 V = 15 \mu C$$

$\therefore$ Potential difference across A and B = potential difference across capacitor C_2,

$$= \frac{Q}{C_2} = \frac{15}{3} = 5 V$$

26. (c) Capacitors $C_1 = 2 \mu F$ and $C_2 = 3 \mu F$ are connected in the parallel.

$$C_{eq} = 3 + 2 = 5 \mu F$$

Now, the charge flown through battery,

$$Q = C_{eq} V = 5 \times 6 = 30 \mu C$$

We know in parallel connection, charge distributes in the direct ratio of capacity

Charge on $C_1 = \frac{2 \times 30}{2 + 3} = 12 \mu C$

Charge on $C_2 = \frac{3 \times 30}{2 + 3} = 18 \mu C$

Energy stored in capacitor C_1,

$$U_1 = \frac{(12)^2}{2(2)} = 36 \mu J \quad \left(\because E = \frac{Q^2}{2C}\right)$$

Energy stored in capacitor C_2,

$$U_2 = \frac{(18)^2}{2(3)} = 54 \mu J$$

27. (c) Given, $C_1 = 5 pF = 5 \times 10^{-12}$ F

$$C_2 = 10 pF = 10 \times 10^{-12} F$$

$$V_1 = 100 V \text{ and } V_2 = 50 V$$

We know that,

$$V_1 = \frac{q_1}{C_1} \text{ and } V_2 = \frac{q_2}{C_2}$$

$$\Rightarrow q_1 = V_1 C_1 \quad ...(i)$$

$$\Rightarrow q_2 = V_2 C_2 \quad ...(ii)$$

$$q_{net} = q_1 + q_2$$

$$C_{eq} = C_1 + C_2$$

$$\Rightarrow V = \frac{q_{net}}{C_{eq}} = \frac{q_1 + q_2}{C_1 + C_2}$$

$$= \frac{V_1 C_1 + V_2 C_2}{C_1 + C_2}$$

$$\Rightarrow V = \frac{100 \times 5 \times 10^{-12} + 50 \times 10^{-12} \times 10}{5 \times 10^{-12} + 10 \times 10^{-12}}$$

$$= \frac{10^{-12}(500 + 500)}{10^{-12}(5 + 10)}$$

$$\Rightarrow V = \frac{1000}{15} = 66.66 V$$

28. (b) The dielectric is introduced such that one-third of its area is occupied by it. In the given case, the three capacitors are in parallel.

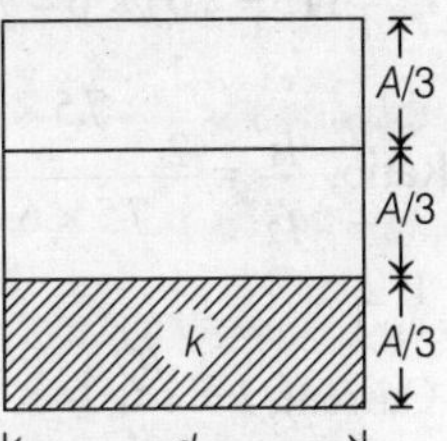

Therefore, $C' = C_1 + C_2 + C_3$

$$C_1 = \frac{A\varepsilon_0}{3d}$$

$$C_2 = \frac{A\varepsilon_0}{3d}$$

$$C_3 = \frac{KA\varepsilon_0}{3d}$$

Thus, $C' = \frac{A\varepsilon_0}{3d} + \frac{A\varepsilon_0}{3d} + \frac{KA\varepsilon_0}{3d}$

$$= \frac{2A\varepsilon_0}{3d} + \frac{KA\varepsilon_0}{3d}$$

$$= \frac{A\varepsilon_0}{3d}(2+K)$$

$$= \frac{C}{3}(2+K)$$

29. (c) The potential difference across the plates of the capacitor will remain same because the battery remains connected.

30. (c) The capacitance of the capacitor is $C = \frac{\varepsilon_0 A}{x}$, where x is the distance between the plates. The energy stored in the capacitor is

$$U = \frac{1}{2}CV^2 = \frac{\varepsilon_0 AV^2}{2x}$$

Differentiating w.r.t x, we get

$$\frac{dU}{dx} = \frac{\varepsilon_0 AV^2}{2}\frac{d}{dx}\left(\frac{1}{x}\right)$$

$$= -\frac{\varepsilon_0 AV^2}{2x^2}$$

The force of attraction between the plates is

$$F = -\frac{dU}{dx} = \frac{\varepsilon_0 AV^2}{2x^2} \quad \text{...(i)}$$

Now $Q = CV = \frac{\varepsilon_0 AV}{x}$

or $V = \frac{Qx}{\varepsilon_0 A}$ ...(ii)

Using Eq. (ii) in Eq. (i), we get

$$F = \frac{Q^2}{2\varepsilon_0 A}$$

Ch-04 Current Electricity

Topical Follow Thru

Test-1

1. (d) As temperature rises, more number of covalent bond of a semiconductor breaks which gives more number of free electrons. The increase in number of free electrons is exponential. Hence, resistivity decreases exponentially with increase in temperature.

2. (b) As, $q = I \times t$

$\therefore$ Charge = Area under graph of I *versus* t

$\Rightarrow q_1$ = Area of triangle

$$= \frac{1}{2} \times 7.5 \times 6$$

q_2 = Area of rectangle

$$= (15 - 7.5) \times 6 = 7.5 \times 6$$

$$\Rightarrow \text{Ratio, } \frac{q_1}{q_2} = \frac{\frac{1}{2} \times 7.5 \times 6}{7.5 \times 6} = \frac{1}{2}$$

or 1 : 2

3. (d) Current, $I = \frac{dQ}{dt}$

$$= \frac{d}{dt}(2t^2 - 4t + 3) \times 10^{-3}$$

$$= (4t - 4) \times 10^{-3}$$

At $t = 4$ s,

$$I = (4 \times 4 - 4) \times 10^{-3} \text{ A}$$

$$= 12 \text{ mA}$$

4. (d) As, $V = IR$

So, when ammeter has very low resistance ($R \approx 0$), then there is no potential drop across ammeter. Hence, option (d) is correct.

5. (b) $I = nev_d A$

$$\Rightarrow v_d = \frac{I}{neA} \Rightarrow v_d \propto \frac{1}{A}$$

$$\therefore v_{d(A)} > v_{d(B)}$$

6. (d) Due to randomly moving electrons, drift velocity is very less as

$$v_d = \frac{v_1 + v_2 + \ldots + v_n}{N}$$

7. (a) The correct relationship is $\mathbf{J} = \sigma \mathbf{E}$.

8. (a) Given, electron density,

$$n = 8 \times 10^{22} \text{ m}^{-3}$$

Collision time, $\tau = 4 \times 10^{-11}$ s

Mass of electron,

$$m = 9.1 \times 10^{-31} \text{ kg}$$

Charge on electron,

$$e = 1.6 \times 10^{-19} \text{ C}$$

As, resistivity,

$$\rho = \frac{m}{ne^2\tau}$$

$$= \frac{9.1 \times 10^{-31}}{8 \times 10^{22} \times (1.6 \times 10^{-19})^2 \times 4 \times 10^{-11}}$$

$$= 1.1 \times 10^{-5} \ \Omega\text{-m}$$

9. (a) $E = 5$ MeV

$$= 5 \times 1.6 \times 10^{-13} \text{ J}$$

$$v_d = \sqrt{\frac{2E}{m}} = \sqrt{\frac{2 \times 5 \times 1.6 \times 10^{-13}}{1.67 \times 10^{-27}}}$$

$$\simeq 3 \times 10^7 \text{ m/s}$$

$$A = \pi r^2$$

$$= \pi \times (1.5 \times 10^{-3})^2$$

Current,

$I = Anev_d$

$n = \frac{I}{Aev_d}$

$= \frac{0.5 \times 10^{-3}}{(1.5 \times 10^{-3})^2 \times \pi \times 1.6 \times 10^{-19} \times 3 \times 10^7}$

$= 1.47 \times 10^{13}$

Number of protons in unit volume $= 1.47 \times 10^{13}$

10. (b) In a conductor, free electrons move with drift velocity.

So, total momentum of free electrons,

$p =$ mass of free electron $\times$ velocity $= mv_d$

Momentum of N number of free electrons $= (Nm)v_d$

$- Nm \times \frac{i}{neA} \quad \left(\because v_d = \frac{i}{neA}\right)$

$= nVm \times \frac{i}{neA} \quad (\because N = nV)$

$= Vm\frac{i}{e} \times \frac{l}{V} \quad (\because A \times l = V)$

$\Rightarrow \quad p = \frac{mil}{e}$

11. (b) Given that, relaxation time,

$\tau = 16.2 \times 10^{-12}$ s

Electric charge, $e = 1.6 \times 10^{-19}$ C

Mass of electron,

$m_e = 9.1 \times 10^{-31}$ kg

As we know that, mobility,

$\mu = \frac{e\tau}{m}$

Substituting the given values, we get

$\mu = \frac{1.6 \times 10^{-19} \times 16.2 \times 10^{-12}}{9.1 \times 10^{-31}}$

$= 2.84\ m^2V^{-1}s^{-1}$

12. (c) Current density, $J = \sigma E$

where, σ is conductivity.

$J = \frac{1}{\rho}E \quad \left(\because \sigma = \frac{1}{\rho}\right)$

$= \frac{1}{1.7 \times 10^{-8}\ \Omega} \times 340$

$= 2 \times 10^{10}\ Am^{-2}$

13. (b) Resistivity of semiconductor decreases with increase in temperature because number of electrons thermally agitated to conduction band. The atoms of a semiconductor vibrate with large amplitudes at higher temperatures. Reason is also correct but it does not explain why reristivity decreases.

14. (b) $V = IR$

On comparing with $y = mx + c$, we have,

Slope = Resistance of wire

In given graph,

Slope = tan (angle with X-axis)

$= \tan(90° - 60°) = \tan 30° = \frac{1}{\sqrt{3}}$

$\therefore$ Resistance of conductor is $\frac{1}{\sqrt{3}}\ \Omega$.

15. (c) Let at temperature T_0, resistivities of the given two materials be ρ_1 and ρ_2 and at temperature T, resistivities are ρ_1' and ρ_2', respectively.

So, we have, for material 1,

$\rho_1' = \rho_1[1 + \alpha_1(T - T_0)]$

or $\rho_1' - \rho_1 = \rho_1\alpha_1(T - T_0)$

or $\quad \Delta\rho_1 = \rho_1\alpha_1(T - T_0) \quad$ ...(i)

Similarly, for material 2,

$\Delta\rho_2 = \rho_2\alpha_2(T - T_0) \quad$ ...(ii)

As it is given in the question that, resistivity of the new material does not change with temperature, it means sum of change in resistivity should be zero.

$\therefore$ Adding Eqs. (i) and (ii), we get

$\Delta\rho_1 + \Delta\rho_2 = \rho_1\alpha_1(T - T_0) + \rho_2\alpha_2(T - T_0)$

$0 = (\rho_1\alpha_1 + \rho_2\alpha_2)(T - T_0)$

or $\rho_1\alpha_1 + \rho_2\alpha_2 = 0$

or $\quad \alpha_1 = \frac{-\rho_2}{\rho_1}\alpha_2$

Here, materials are different, so $\rho_1 \neq \rho_2$.

Thus, $|\alpha_1| \neq |\alpha_2|$, but they are of opposite sign.

Test-2

1. (b) $\because R = \rho\frac{l}{A}$

$\therefore \quad R_1 = \rho_1\frac{l_1}{A}$

and $R_2 = \rho_2\frac{l_2}{A}$

$R = \frac{R_1R_2}{R_1 + R_2}$

$= \frac{\rho_1\frac{l_1}{A} \cdot \rho_2\frac{l_2}{A}}{\rho_1\frac{l_1}{A} + \rho_2\frac{l_2}{A}}$

$= \frac{\rho_1 l_1 \rho_2 l_2}{(\rho_1 l_1 + \rho_2 l_2)A}$

2. (b) The equivalent circuit is

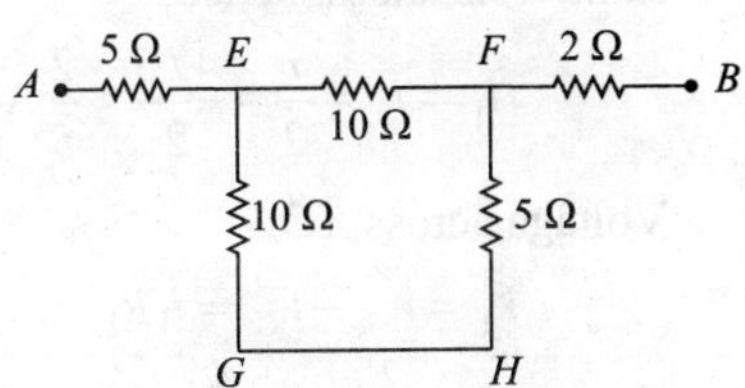

In the loop $EFHG$, 5 Ω and 10 Ω are in series. hence, their equivalent resistance is

$R_1 = 5 + 10 = 15\ \Omega$

Now, this R_1 is parallel with 10 Ω.

$R_2 = \frac{R_1 \times 10}{R_1 + 10}$

$= \frac{15 \times 10}{15 + 10}$

$= \frac{15 \times 10}{25} = 6\ \Omega$

Now, this R_2 is in series with 5 Ω and 2 Ω.

Hence, equivalent resistance

$R = 5 + 6 + 2 = 13\ \Omega$

3. (a) Internal resistance is the internal property of a cell, hence it depends on the material used for making a cell.

4. (d) The equivalent resistance of the circuit,

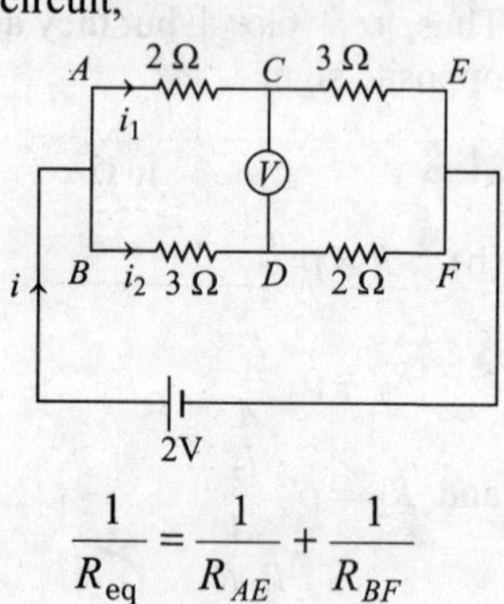

$$\frac{1}{R_{eq}} = \frac{1}{R_{AE}} + \frac{1}{R_{BF}}$$

$$= \frac{1}{(2+3)} + \frac{1}{(3+2)}$$

$$R_{eq} = \frac{5}{2}\,\Omega$$

$$\text{Current, } i = \frac{V}{R_{eq}} = \frac{2}{5/2} = \frac{4}{5}\text{ A}$$

Since, branch AE and BF have same resistances, hence

$$i_1 = i_2 = \frac{i}{2} = \frac{4/5}{2} = \frac{2}{5}\text{ A}$$

Voltage across AC,

$$V_1 = V_A - V_C = i_1 R_1$$

$$= \frac{2}{5} \times 2 = \frac{4}{5}\text{ V}$$

Voltage across BD,

$$V_2 = V_B - V_D$$

$$= i_2 R_2 = \frac{2}{5} \times 3 = \frac{6}{5}\text{ V}$$

Voltmeter reading

$$= V_C - V_D$$

$$= \frac{6}{5} - \frac{4}{5} = \frac{2}{5}\text{ V}$$

5. (a) Consider the new resistance as R' and old resistance as R.

$$R' = \frac{\frac{R}{2}\cdot\frac{R}{2}}{\frac{R}{2}+\frac{R}{2}}$$

$$\Rightarrow \quad R' = \frac{R}{4}$$

Hence, new resistance is $\frac{1}{4}$th of the old resistance.

Now, $P = \frac{V^2}{R}$

Since, power supply is same, hence V is same.

$$\Rightarrow \quad P \propto \frac{1}{R}$$

Hence, new power is 4 times of the old power.

$$P' = 4 \times 200\text{ W} = 800\text{ W}$$

Energy liberated in 1 min is

$$E = P' \times t = P' \times 60$$

$$= (800)(60)$$

$$= 48000\text{ J}$$

6. (c) $P = \frac{V^2}{R}$

$$\Rightarrow V = \sqrt{PR} = \sqrt{25 \times 16} = 20\text{ V}$$

Current in 16 Ω resistor,

$$I_1 = \frac{V}{R} = \frac{20}{16} = \frac{5}{4}\text{ A}$$

Consider the total current in the circuit is I, then current through 16 Ω resistor is given by

$$I_1 = \frac{40}{40+16} \times I$$

$$I = I_1 \frac{56}{40} = \frac{5}{4} \times \frac{56}{40} = \frac{7}{4}\text{ A}$$

Power dissipated through 5 Ω,

$$P = I^2 R = \left(\frac{7}{4}\right)^2 \times 5 = \frac{245}{16}\text{ W}$$

7. (d) 1.2 V, 0.6 Ω

E, 0.3 Ω

If E_1, E_2 are emfs and r_1, r_2 are internal resistances, then the equivalent emf of the battery is given by

$$E_{eq} = \frac{\frac{E_1}{r_1} + \frac{E_2}{r_2}}{\frac{1}{r_1} + \frac{1}{r_2}}$$

$$= \frac{\frac{1.2}{0.6} + \frac{E}{0.3}}{\frac{1}{0.6} + \frac{1}{0.3}} = 1.8$$

$$2 + \frac{E}{0.3} = 1.8\left(\frac{3}{0.6}\right)$$

$$E = 2.1\text{ V}$$

8. (b) Given circuit is a network equivalent to

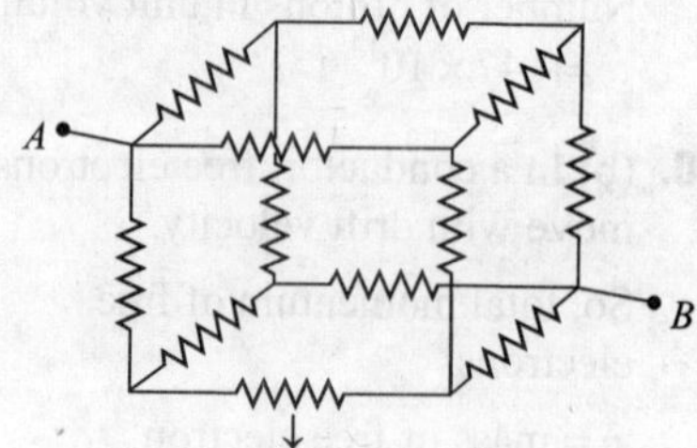

To redraw circuit, we join resistors across points which are at same potentials. This can be judged on the basis of symmetry of circuit.

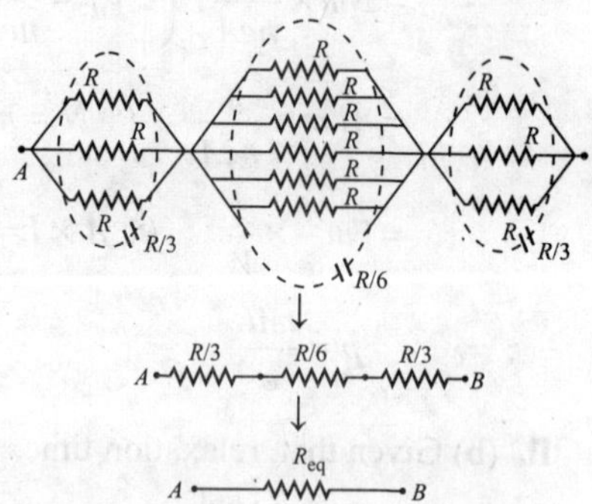

$$R_{eq} = \frac{R}{3} + \frac{R}{6} + \frac{R}{3}$$

$$= \frac{2R + R + 2R}{6} = \frac{5R}{6}\,\Omega$$

9. (a) $P = I^2 R$

$$\Rightarrow \quad R = \frac{P}{I^2} = \frac{2.5}{(5 \times 10^{-3})^2}\,\Omega$$

$$\text{Now, } P = \frac{V^2}{R} = \frac{(25)^2}{2.5/(5 \times 10^{-3})^2}$$

$$= \frac{25 \times 25 \times (5 \times 10^{-3})^2}{2.5}$$

$$= 6.25 \times 10^{-3}\text{ W}$$

10. (d) All 6 Ω resistors and 20 Ω resistor are forming Wheatstone bridge. Since, the bridge is in balanced condition, hence 20 Ω resistor can be removed.

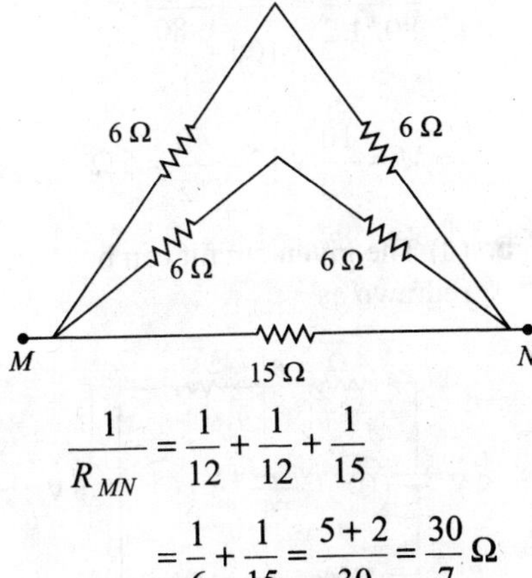

$$\frac{1}{R_{MN}} = \frac{1}{12} + \frac{1}{12} + \frac{1}{15}$$

$$= \frac{1}{6} + \frac{1}{15} = \frac{5+2}{30} = \frac{30}{7}\,\Omega$$

11. (b) In parallel connection, equivalent resistance of n equal resistors of resistance R each, is

$$R_{eq} = \frac{R}{n}$$

As, current, $I = \frac{E}{R_{eq} + r} = \frac{E}{\frac{R}{n} + r}$

(where, r is internal resistance of battery)

Here, $r = R$

$$\Rightarrow \quad I = \frac{E}{\frac{R}{n} + R}$$

$$\Rightarrow \quad I = \frac{nE}{(n+1)R}$$

$$\Rightarrow \quad \frac{I}{n} = \frac{E}{(n+1)R} \quad \ldots\text{(i)}$$

In series connection, equivalent resistance of n equal resistors is

$$R_{eq} = nR$$

and total emf $= E$

As, current, $I' = \frac{E}{nR + r}$

$$= \frac{E}{nR + R} \quad (\because r = R)$$

$$\frac{I}{6} = \frac{E}{(n+1)R} \quad \ldots\text{(ii)}$$

$$\left[\text{given, } I' = \frac{I}{6}\right]$$

On comparing Eqs. (i) and (ii), we get

$$\frac{I}{n} = \frac{I}{6}$$

$$\Rightarrow \quad n = 6$$

12. (a) In absence of voltmeter (actual potential difference), the circuit is as shown below

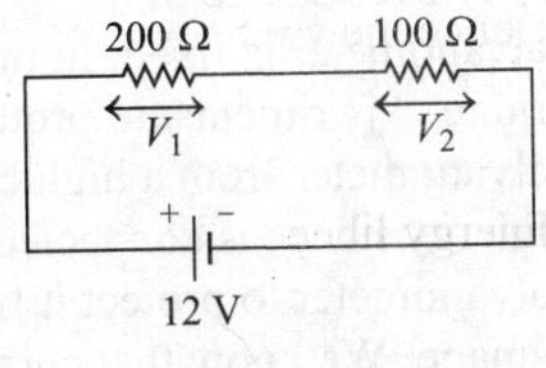

$$V_1 = \frac{R_1}{R_1 + R_2} \times V$$

$$= \frac{200}{200 + 100} \times 12 = 8\text{ V}$$

In presence of voltmeter (measured potential difference), the circuit is as shown below

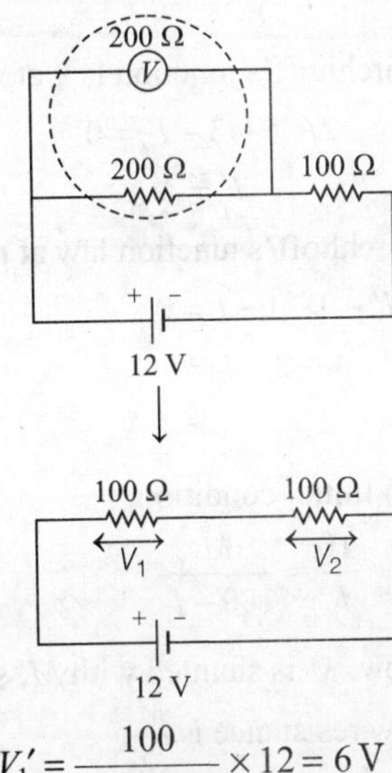

$$V_1' = \frac{100}{100 + 100} \times 12 = 6\text{ V}$$

$\therefore$ Percentage change

$$= \frac{V_1 - V_1'}{V_1} \times 100$$

$$= \frac{8 - 6}{8} \times 100 = 25\%$$

13. (a) Internal resistance,

$$r = R\left(\frac{E}{V} - 1\right)$$

$$= (10)\left(\frac{1.5}{1.25} - 1\right) = 2\,\Omega$$

14. (b) To find the current flown by the battery, we will reduce the given circuit as

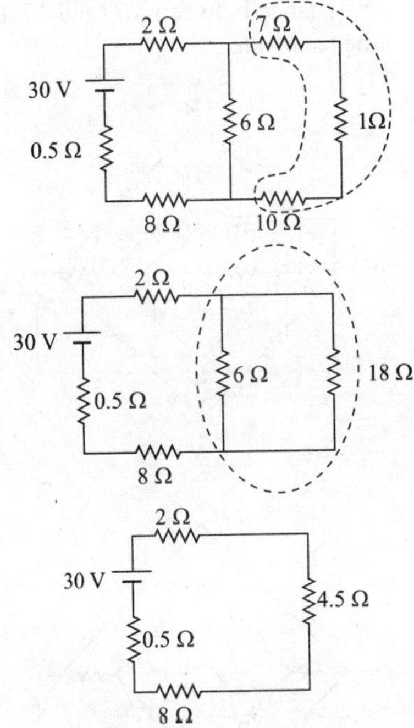

Equivalent resistance,

$$R_{eq} = 0.5 + 8 + 2 + 4.5 = 15\,\Omega$$

Current through battery,

$$I = \frac{E}{R_{eq}} = \frac{30}{15} = 2\text{ A}$$

From the given figure,

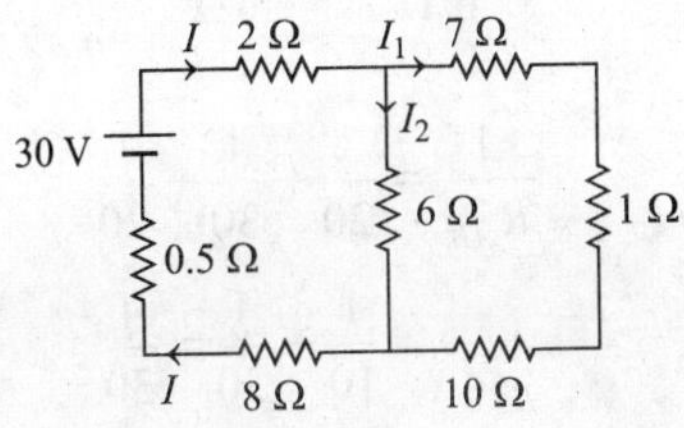

$$I_1 = \frac{R_2}{R_1 + R_2} \times I$$

$$= \frac{6}{(7+1+10)+6} \times 2$$

$$I_1 = 0.5\text{ A}$$

$$I_2 = I - I_1 = 2 - 0.5$$

$$I_2 = 1.5\text{ A}$$

Power consumed by 6 Ω resistor,

$$P_{6\,\Omega} = I_2^2 R = (1.5)^2 \times 6$$

$$= 13.5\text{ W}$$

15. (d) By applying perpendicular axis symmetry, points lying on the line *MN* have same potential, therefore resistance between *MO* and *NP* can be removed.

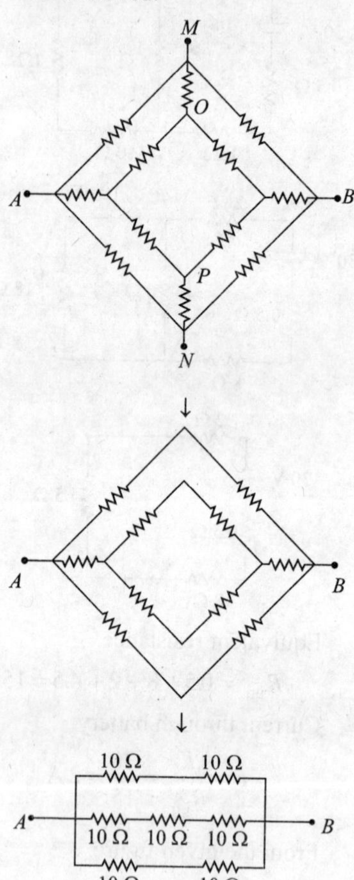

$$\frac{1}{R_{AB}} = \frac{1}{20} + \frac{1}{30} + \frac{1}{20}$$

$$= \frac{1}{10} + \frac{1}{30} = \frac{4}{30}$$

$$R_{AB} = \frac{15}{2}\,\Omega$$

Test-3

1. (b) The circuit satisfies the Wheatstone bridge condition, hence no current will flow through *BC*.

Now, equivalent resistance of the circuit,

$$\frac{1}{R_{eq}} = \frac{1}{(10+15)} + \frac{1}{(20+30)}$$

$$= \frac{1}{25} + \frac{1}{50}$$

$$R_{eq} = \frac{25 \times 50}{25+50} = \frac{25 \times 50}{75} = \frac{50}{3}\,\Omega$$

$$i = \frac{50}{\frac{50}{3}} = 3\text{ A}$$

2. (c) The resistance of a galvanometer is fixed. In meter bridge experiments, to protect the galvanometer from a high current, high resistance is connected to the galvanometer to protect it from any damage. We know that current *I* is inversely proportional to resistance *R*.

Thus, Statement I is correct and Statement II is incorrect.

3. (a)

Kirchhoff's junction law at node 1,

$$2 + 5 - 3 - I' = 0$$

$$I' = 4\text{ A}$$

Kirchhoff's junction law at node 2,

$$I' - 1 - 1 - I = 0$$

$$4 - 2 - I = 0$$

$$I = 2\text{ A}$$

4. (b) Initial condition,

$$\frac{10}{l_1} = \frac{M}{100 - l_1} \quad \text{...(i)}$$

Now, *M* is shunted with *M*, so the new resistance is $\frac{M}{2}$.

Now, new balanced condition,

$$\frac{10}{1.2l_1} = \frac{M/2}{100 - 1.2l_1} \quad \text{...(ii)}$$

Divide Eqs. (i) by (ii), we get

$$\frac{1.2}{1} = \frac{100 - 1.2l_1}{100 - l_1} \times 2$$

$$120 - 1.2l_1 = 200 - 2.4l_1$$

$$l_1 = \frac{80}{1.2}\text{ A}$$

Substitute value in Eq. (i),

$$\frac{10}{80/1.2} = \frac{M}{100 - \frac{80}{1.2}}$$

$$\Rightarrow M = \frac{10}{80} \times 1.2 \times \frac{40}{1.2} = 5\,\Omega$$

5. (d) The given circuit can be redrawn as

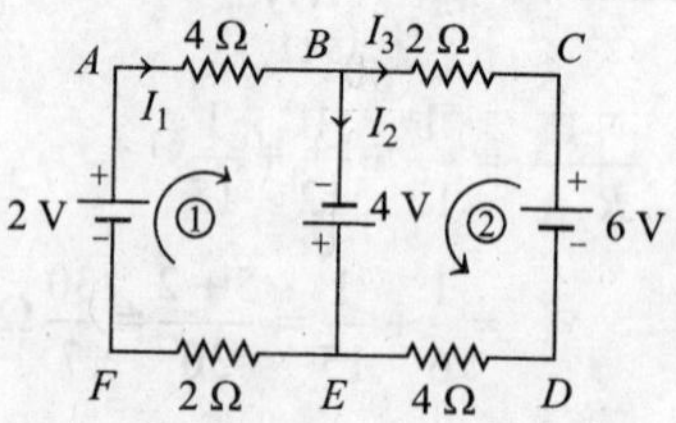

At junction *B*,

$$I_1 = I_2 + I_3 \quad \text{...(i)}$$

Applying KVL in loop (1) as shown the direction,

$$2 - 4I_1 + 4 - 2I_1 = 0$$

or $6I_1 = 6$

or $I_1 = 1\text{ A}$

Applying KVL in loop (2) as shown the direction,

$$6 + 2I_3 + 4 + 4I_3 = 0$$

$$6I_3 = -10$$

or $I_3 = -\frac{5}{3}\text{ A}$

From Eq. (i), we get

$$I_2 = I_1 - I_3 = 1 - \left(-\frac{5}{3}\right) = \frac{8}{3}\text{ A}$$

So, $\frac{I_1}{I_2} = \frac{1}{\frac{8}{3}} = \frac{3}{8} = 3:8$

6. (a) At the balancing situation of meter bridge, the relation between *X* and *Y* is given as

$$\frac{X}{Y} = \frac{l}{100 - l} \quad \text{...(i)}$$

where, *X* resistance is connected in left gap, *Y* resistance is connected in right gap and *l* is balancing length.

In first case, $\frac{X}{Y} = \frac{40}{60}$

or $\frac{X}{Y} = \frac{2}{3}$ ...(ii)

In second case, 15 Ω resistance is connected in series with Y, then equivalent resistance in right gap becomes $15 + Y$. So, we can write from Eq. (i),

$$\frac{X}{15+Y} = \frac{(40-10)}{60+10}$$

$$\Rightarrow \frac{X}{15+Y} = \frac{3}{7} \quad ...(iii)$$

On solving Eqs. (ii) and (iii), we get

$$X = 18\,\Omega \text{ and } Y = 27\,\Omega$$

7. (a) In balance condition, no current will flow through the branch containing S.
Same current will flow through the galvanometer whether switch S is open or closed.

8. (a) Balancing length is independent of the cross-sectional area of the wire.

9. (d) Apply Kirchhoff's junction law at point D.

$$i_1 = i_2 + i_3$$

$$\frac{V_A - V_D}{5} = \frac{V_D - V_B}{10} + \frac{V_D - V_C}{15}$$

$$\Rightarrow 70 - V_D = \frac{V_D}{2} + \frac{V_D - 10}{3}$$

$$\Rightarrow V_D = 40\text{ V}$$

Now, $i_1 = \frac{V_A - V_D}{5} = \frac{70-40}{5} = 6\text{ A}$

$$i_2 = \frac{V_D - V_B}{10} = \frac{40-0}{10} = 4\text{ A}$$

$$i_3 = \frac{V_D - V_C}{15} = \frac{40-10}{15} = 2\text{ A}$$

$$i_1 : i_2 : i_3 = 3:2:1$$

10. (a) Consider S and R are two resistances out of which R is smaller.

$$S = \left(\frac{100-l}{l}\right)R$$

$$= \left(\frac{100-20}{20}\right)R = 4R \quad ...(i)$$

Now, 15 Ω resistance is connected with R.

$$S = \left(\frac{100-40}{40}\right)(R+15)$$

$$= \frac{3}{2}(R+15) \quad ...(ii)$$

From Eq. (i) and (ii), we get

$$4R = \frac{3}{2}(R+15)$$

$$R = 9\,\Omega$$

11. (b) Consider $AC = l$ cm

and $CB = (100 - l)$ cm

For zero deflection,

$$\frac{l}{100-l} = \frac{15}{10}$$

$$\Rightarrow l = 60\text{ cm}$$

12. (a) Wheatstone bridge is balanced,

$$\frac{P}{Q} = \frac{R}{S}$$

$$\Rightarrow \frac{40}{10} = \frac{60}{15} = \frac{4}{1}$$

$$\Rightarrow V_{AB} = V_{AD}$$

Assuming, I_1 current is flowing through branch AB, so

$$40I_1 = 60I_2$$
$$I_1 = 1.5I_2$$

Power in AB

$$= I_1^2 R = (1.5I_2)^2 \times 40$$
$$= 90\,I_2^2$$

Power in BC

$$= I_1^2 R = (1.5I_2)^2 \times 10$$
$$= 22.5\,I_2^2$$

Power in DC

$$= I_2^2 R = I_2^2 \times 15 = 15I_2^2$$

Power in AD

$$= I_2^2 R = I_2^2 \times 60 = 60I_2^2$$

So, (A) → (3), (B) → (1), (C) → (2), (D) → (4)

13. (d) Given circuit is balanced Wheatstone bridge circuit.

For branch ACB,

$$C' = \frac{10 \times 10}{10+10} = 5\,\mu\text{F}$$

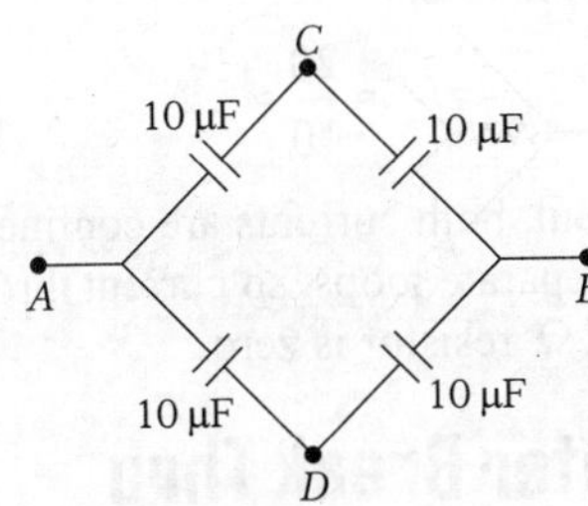

For branch ADB,

$$C'' = \frac{10 \times 10}{10+10} = 5\,\mu\text{F}$$

Their is no flow of charge in branch CD.

So, equivalent capacitance between AB is

$$C_{AB} = C' + C'' = 5 + 5 = 10\,\mu\text{F}$$

14. (a)

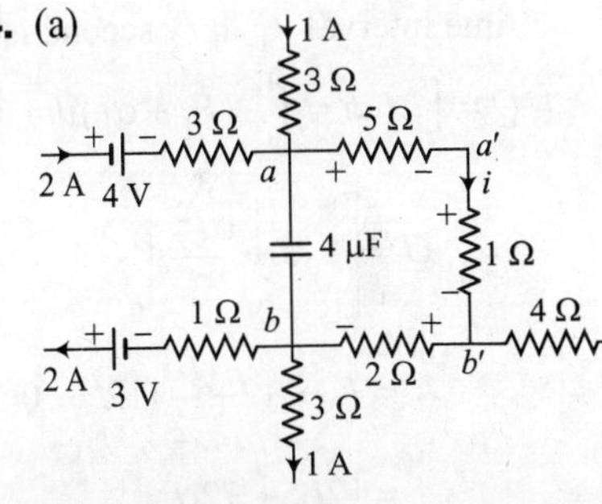

By Kirchhoff's junction law, at junction a and b

$$i = 3\text{A}$$

and also current through corner 4 Ω resistor is zero.

Now, for path $aa'b'b$,

$$-3\times 5 - 3\times 1 - 3\times 2 = V_{ab} = V_b - V_a$$

$$\Rightarrow V_{ab} = V_b - V_a = -24\text{ V}$$

So, potential drop across capacitor $= 24$ V

Hence, energy stored

$$= \frac{1}{2}CV^2 = \frac{1}{2} \times 4 \times 10^{-6} \times 24^2\text{ J}$$

$$= 1.15\text{ mJ}$$

15. (c) In loop 1,

$$i_1 = \frac{10}{5} = 2\text{ A}$$

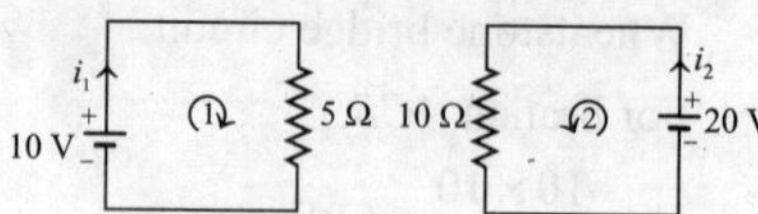

In loop 2,

$$i_2 = \frac{20}{10} = 2\text{ A}$$

But, both currents are confined to separate loops, so current through 2 Ω resistor is zero.

Chapter Break Thru

1. (c) Nichrome is a material made up of Ni and Cr. Its resistance remains same for a wide range of temperature, hence called ohmic material. All others do not follow Ohm's law.

2. (a) Current through any cross-section remains same.

3. (c) Charge that flows in a wire in time interval t_1 to t_2 second is

$$Q = \int_{t_1}^{t_2} I\,dt = \int_0^{12} (I_0 + \alpha t)\,dt$$

$$\Rightarrow \quad Q = \left[I_0 t + \frac{\alpha t^2}{2}\right]_0^{12}$$

$$= I_0 \times 12 + \frac{\alpha}{2}(12^2 - 0^2)$$

$$= 12I_0 + 72\alpha$$
$$= 12 \times 15 + 72 \times 6$$
$$= 180 + 432 = 612\text{ C}$$

4. (a) If resistances of bulbs are R_1 and R_2 respectively, then in parallel, $\frac{1}{R_P} = \frac{1}{R_1} + \frac{1}{R_2}$

$$\Rightarrow \frac{1}{\left(\frac{V^2}{P_p}\right)} = \frac{1}{\left(\frac{V^2}{P_1}\right)} + \frac{1}{\left(\frac{V^2}{P_2}\right)}$$

$$\Rightarrow \quad P_p = P_1 + P_2$$

5. (d) Slope of given curve $= \frac{1}{R}\left(= \frac{A}{\rho l}\right)$ i.e. with the increase in length of the wire, slope of the curve will decrease.

6. (c) Resistance of voltmeter $= 200\,\Omega$

So, circuit has two parts R_1 and R_2 with voltmeter. Both are of same resistance, so potential drop of voltmeter is 10 V.

7. (d) An electric field exists inside the wire along its length which accelerates electrons till they move with an average velocity v_d and $I = nev_d A$.

8. (d) Current through the load,

$$I = \frac{E}{R + r}$$

Power, $P = I^2 R = \frac{E^2}{(R + r)^2} R$

Maximum power is delivered when

$$\frac{dP}{dR} = 0$$

$$\Rightarrow \frac{-2E^2}{(R + r)^3} R + \frac{E^2}{(R + r)^2} = 0$$

$$\Rightarrow \quad \frac{-2R}{R + r} + 1 = 0$$

$$-2R = -R - r$$

$$R = r$$

$$P_{\max} = \frac{E^2 r}{(r + r)^2} = \frac{E^2}{4r}$$

Power is maximum when $r = R$, hence option (d) is correct.

9. (b) Cells are joined in parallel.

The current in the circuit is given by

$$i = \frac{E}{R + \frac{r}{n}}$$

The current in the circuit will be maximum when $R << \frac{r}{n} \Rightarrow R << r$.

10. (c) Third pin is connected to metal box, covering the instrument or appliance and the wall socket connects third pin to ground. In case of a leakage current or short circuit, current is conducted to the earth and instrument does not give any shock to user.

11. (a) At junction A, $i_{AB} = 2 + 2 = 4\text{ A}$

At junction B, $i_{BC} = i_{AB} - 1$

$\Rightarrow i_{BC} = 4 - 1 = 3\text{ A}$

At junction C,

$i = i_{BC} - 1.3 = 3 - 1.3 = 1.7\text{ A}$

12. (a) Resistance of 50 W bulb is two times the resistance of 100 W bulb. When bulbs are connected in series, 50 W bulb will glow more because in series combination $P = i^2 R$ (current remains same in series combination). In parallel combination the 100 W bulb $P = \frac{V^2}{R}$ (potential difference remain same in parallel combination) will glow more. Hence, both Assertion and Reason are correct and Reason is the correct explanantion of Assertion.

13. (d) $P = \frac{V^2}{R} \Rightarrow \frac{P_{200}}{P_{800}} = \frac{V^2 / R_{200}}{V^2 / R_{800}}$

$$= \frac{R_{800}}{R_{200}} = \frac{R_{200}(1 + \alpha\Delta T)}{R_{200}}$$

$$\Rightarrow \quad P_{200} = P_{800} \times (1 + 4 \times 10^{-4} \times 600)$$

$$= 500(1 + 4 \times 10^{-4} \times 600) = 620\text{ W}$$

So, most close option is 611 W.

14. (b) Using, $R = \rho\frac{l}{A}$, resistance of nichrome is more, so rate of heat loss $(I^2 R)$ is higher. So, fuse B is better option.

15. (a) Given circuit is

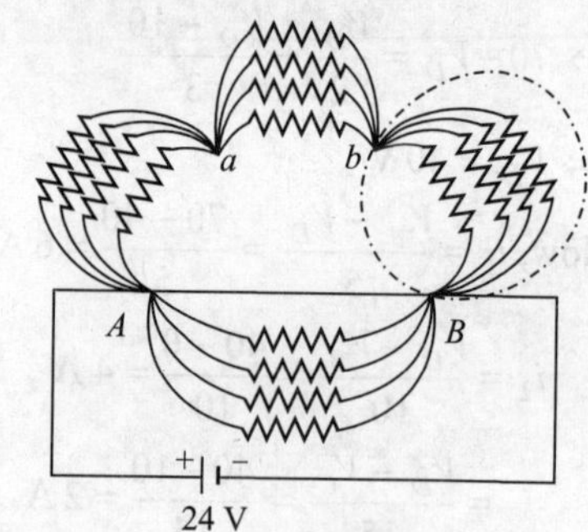

$$\frac{1}{R}=\frac{1}{5}+\frac{1}{5}+\frac{1}{5}+\frac{1}{5} \Rightarrow R=\frac{5}{4}\,\Omega$$

So, circuit can be redrawn as

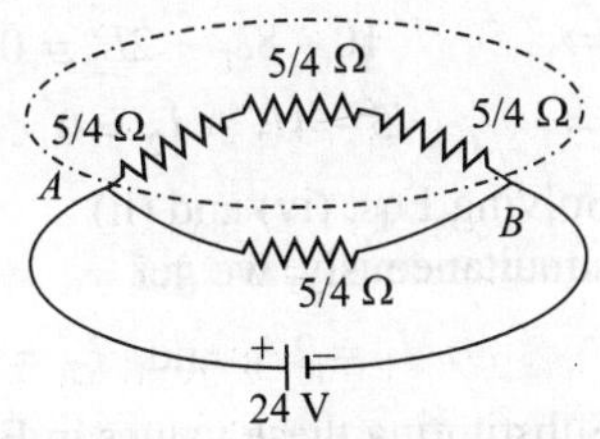

$$R=3\times\frac{5}{4}=\frac{15}{4}\,\Omega$$

15/4 Ω
A B
5/4 Ω
⇒
24 V

$$\Rightarrow R_{\text{total}}=R_{AB}=\frac{\frac{15}{4}\times\frac{5}{4}}{\frac{15}{4}+\frac{5}{4}}=\frac{15\times5\times4}{20\times16}$$

$$=\frac{15}{4\times4}=\frac{15}{16}\,\Omega$$

Now, as $V = 24$ V

Current through arm of resistance $\frac{15}{4}\,\Omega$,

$$I_1=\frac{V}{R}=\frac{24}{15/4}=\frac{24\times4}{15}\,\text{A}$$

Now, $I'=\frac{1}{4}$ of I_1

$$=\frac{1}{4}\times\frac{24\times4}{15}=\frac{8}{5}\,\text{A}$$

16. (d) As, volume of conductor remains constant.

$$\therefore \quad l_iA_i=l_fA_f$$

Given, $l_f=3l_i$ or $\frac{l_i}{l_f}=\frac{1}{3}$

$$\Rightarrow \quad A_f=\frac{l_i}{l_f}\cdot A_i=\frac{A_i}{3}$$

Also, $R_i=\rho\frac{l_i}{A_i}$

and $R_f=\rho\frac{l_f}{A_f}=\rho\frac{3l_i}{A_i/3}=9R_i$

As, $E=IR$

$$\Rightarrow \quad I=\frac{E}{R}$$

$$\therefore \quad I_i=\frac{E}{R_i}$$

$$I_f=\frac{E}{9R_i}=\frac{I_i}{9}$$

$$I_i=nev_{d_i}A_i$$

$$I_f=nev_{d_f}A_f$$

$$\Rightarrow \quad \frac{I_i}{I_f}=9=\frac{nev_{d_i}A_i}{nev_{d_f}A_f}$$

$$\Rightarrow \quad 9=\frac{v_{d_i}}{v_{d_f}}\cdot 3$$

$$\Rightarrow \quad v_{d_f}=\frac{1}{3}v_{d_i}$$

17. (c) Given circuit is

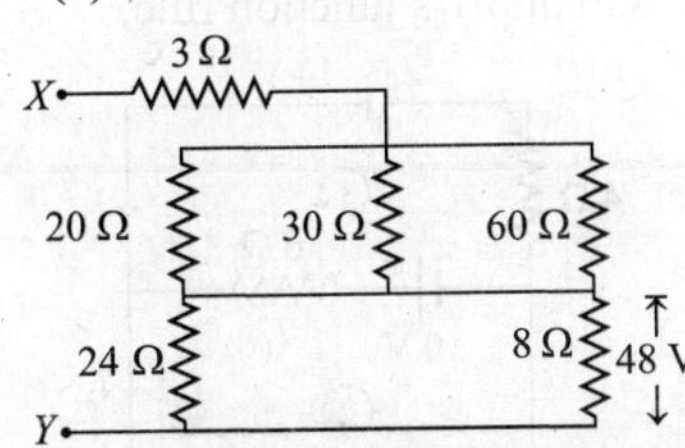

The circuit is equivalent to

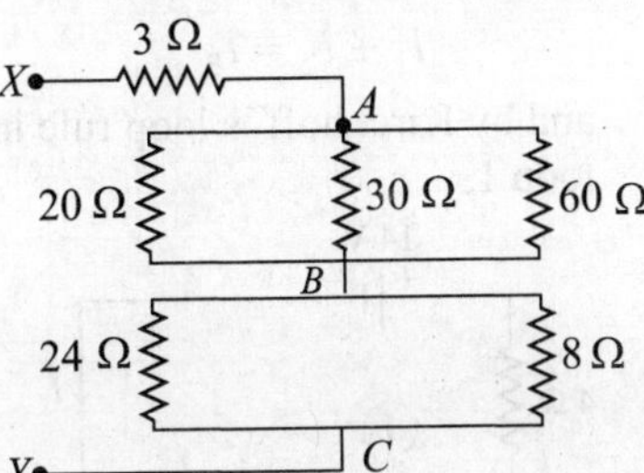

Given, $V_{BC}=48$ V

So, current through 8 Ω resistor,

$$I_1=\frac{V_{BC}}{R_{BC}}=\frac{48}{8}=6\,\text{A}$$

and current through 24 Ω resistor,

$$I_2=\frac{V}{R}=\frac{48}{24}=2\,\text{A}$$

Hence, current flowing out of network is

$$I_1+I_2=6+2=8\,\text{A}$$

∴ Current flowing through XY is 8 A.

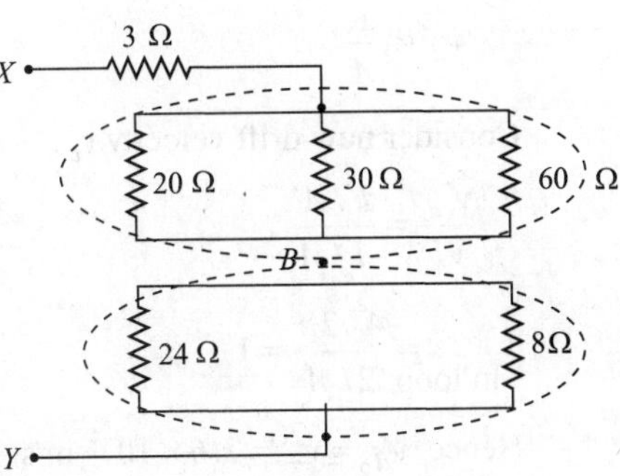

Now, $\frac{1}{R'_{\text{eq}}}=\frac{1}{20}+\frac{1}{30}+\frac{1}{60}$

$$=\frac{3+2+1}{60}$$

$$\Rightarrow \quad R'_{\text{eq}}=\frac{60}{6}=10\,\Omega$$

$$\frac{1}{R''_{\text{eq}}}=\frac{1}{24}+\frac{1}{8}=\frac{1+3}{24}$$

$$\Rightarrow \quad R''_{\text{eq}}=\frac{24}{4}=6\,\Omega$$

So, $R_{XY}=3+10+6=19\,\Omega$

Hence, $V_{XY}=IR_{XY}=8\times19$
$=152$ V

18. (c) Cell equation in discharging mode,

$$V=E-Ir$$

$$20=E-4r \quad \ldots\text{(i)}$$

Cell equation in charging mode,

$$V=E+Ir$$

$$25=E+Ir$$

$$25=E+r\ (\because I=1\,\text{A}) \quad \ldots\text{(ii)}$$

On subtracting Eq. (ii) from Eq. (i), we get

$$-5=-5r$$

or $r=1\,\Omega$

Putting the value of r in Eq. (i), we get

$$20=E-4\times1$$

or $E=20+4$

$$E=24\text{ V}$$

19. (a) As we know, $I=neAv_d$

$$v_d=\frac{I}{neA}$$

$$v_d \propto \frac{I}{A}$$

Consider new drift velocity v'_d.

$$\frac{v'_d}{v_d} = \frac{I'/A'}{I/A}$$

$$= \frac{4/2A}{2/A} = 1$$

Hence, $v'_d = v_d = 2.6 \times 10^{-4}$ m/s

20. (a) As given current,

$$I = (100 + 8t)\text{ A} \quad \ldots\text{(i)}$$

$\therefore$ Net charge, $q = \int I\,dt$

$$q = \int_0^{10} (100 + 8t)\,dt \quad \text{[using Eq. (i)]}$$

$$= \int_0^{10} 100\,dt + \int_0^{10} 8t\,dt$$

$$= 100\int_0^{10} dt + 8\int_0^{10} t\,dt$$

$$= 100[t]_0^{10} + 8\left[\frac{t^2}{2}\right]_0^{10}$$

$$= 100[10 - 0] + 4[(10)^2 - 0^2]$$

$$= 1000 + 4 \times 100$$

$$\Rightarrow q = 1400$$

Average value of current,

$$I_{avg} = \frac{q}{t}$$

Here, $t = 10$ s

$$I_{avg} = \frac{1400}{10} = 140\text{ A}$$

21. (c) Current distribution in the given circuit is taken as below.

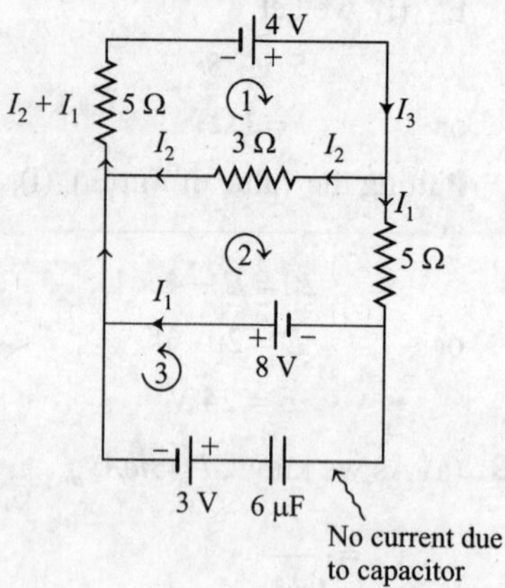

Using equations of Kirchhoff's law as given below

$$I_1 + I_2 = I_3$$

$$4 - 3I_2 - 5I_3 = 0 \text{ (loop 1)}$$

$$3I_2 - 5I_1 + 8 = 0 \text{ (loop 2)}$$

On solving these equations, we get

$$I_2 = -0.364\text{ A},$$

$$I_1 = 1.38\text{ A},$$

$$I_3 = 1.02\text{ A}$$

Now, going clockwise direction in loop 3,

$$\Sigma V = 0$$

$$\Rightarrow 8 + 3 - \Delta V_{\text{capacitor}} = 0$$

$$\Rightarrow \Delta V_{\text{capacitor}} = 11\text{ V}$$

So, charge on a capacitor,

$$Q = C\Delta V = 6\,\mu\text{F} \times 11\text{ V} = 66\,\mu\text{C}$$

22. (a) As per marked currents, by Kirchhoff's junction rule,

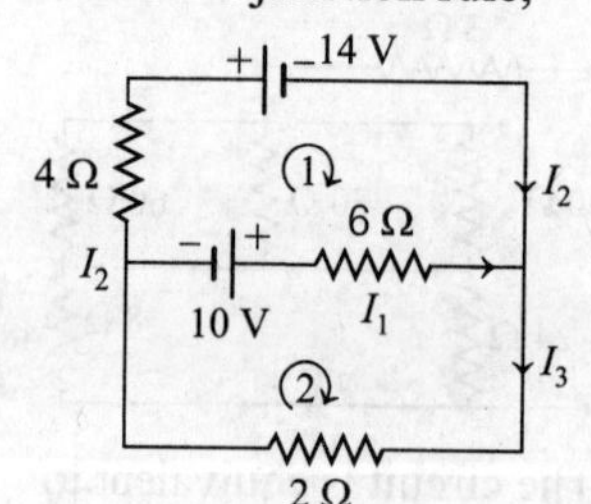

$$I_1 + I_2 = I_3 \quad \ldots\text{(i)}$$

and by Kirchhoff's loop rule in loop 1,

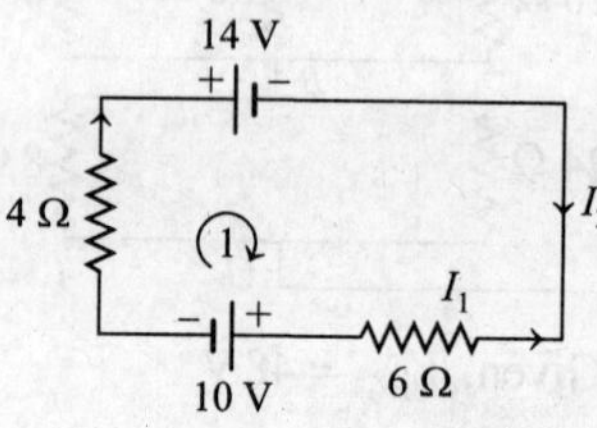

$$\Sigma V = 0$$

$$\Rightarrow -14 + 6I_1 - 10 - 4I_2 = 0$$

$$\Rightarrow -24 + 6I_1 - 4I_2 = 0 \quad \ldots\text{(ii)}$$

In loop 2,

$$\Sigma V = 0$$

$$\Rightarrow 10 - 6I_1 - 2I_3 = 0 \quad \ldots\text{(iii)}$$

From Eqs. (i) and (iii), we have

$$10 - 6I_1 - 2(I_1 + I_2) = 0$$

$$\Rightarrow 10 - 8I_1 - 2I_2 = 0$$

$$\Rightarrow 5 - 4I_1 - I_2 = 0 \quad \ldots\text{(iv)}$$

Solving Eqs. (iv) and (ii) simultaneously, we get

$$I_1 = 2\text{ A and } I_2 = -3\text{ A}$$

Substituting these values in Eq. (i), we get

$$I_3 = -1\text{ A}$$

23. (d) First we shall find the equivalent resistance R' of 10 Ω, 10 Ω and 20 Ω resistors. Since, all are connected in parallel,

$$\frac{1}{R'} = \frac{1}{10} + \frac{1}{10} + \frac{1}{20}$$

$$\frac{1}{R'} = \frac{2+2+1}{20}$$

$$= \frac{5}{20} = \frac{1}{4}$$

or $R' = 4\,\Omega$

Now, the circuit, can be redrawn as

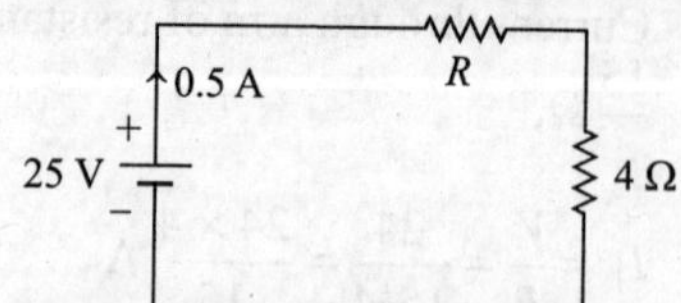

Using Ohm's law,

$$i = \frac{25}{R+4}$$

$$\Rightarrow 0.5 = \frac{25}{R+4}$$

$$\Rightarrow 0.5R + 2 = 25$$

$$\Rightarrow 0.5R = 23$$

or $R = \frac{23}{0.5} = 46\,\Omega$

Current through 20 Ω resistor

$$= \frac{5}{20+5} \times 0.5 = 0.1\text{ A}$$

and potential difference across middle resistor

= potential difference across 20 Ω

$= 20 \times 0.1 = 2$ V

24. (d) Circuit can be redrawn as follows.

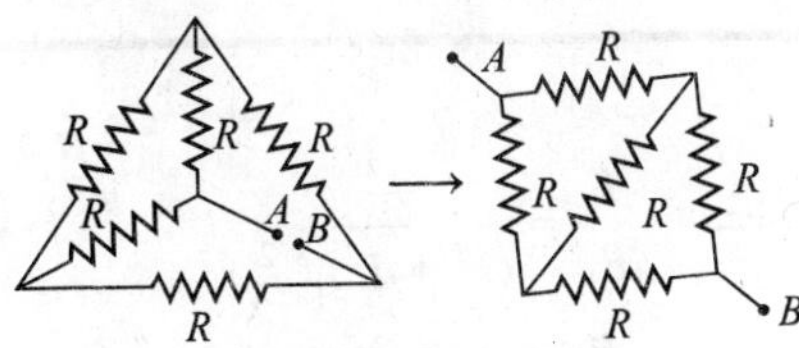

So, given circuit is a balanced Wheatstone bridge and hence, above circuit is equivalent to

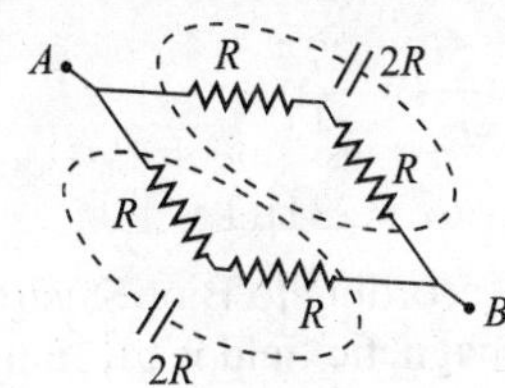

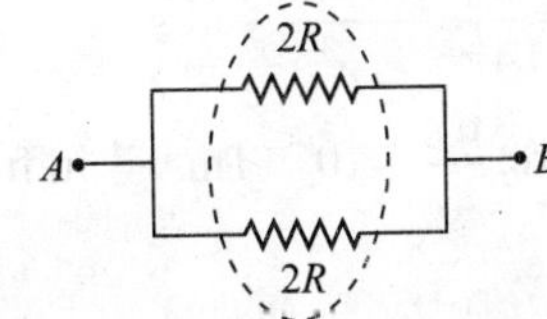

$$\Rightarrow \quad R_{eq} = \frac{2R \times 2R}{2R + 2R}$$

$$\Rightarrow \quad R_{eq} = R$$

$R = 2\,\Omega$, A, B, 12 V

So, using $V = IR$

$$I = \frac{12}{2} = 6\text{ A}$$

25. (b) We will require a voltmeter, an ammeter, a test resistor and a variable battery to verify Ohm's law.

Voltmeter which is made by connecting a high resistance with a galvanometer (G_1) is connected in parallel with the test resistor.

Further, an ammeter which is formed by connecting a low resistance in parallel with galvanometer (G_2) is required to measure the current through test resistor.

26. (a)

Total resistance of circuit = resistance of two $4\,\Omega$ resistance in parallel + resistance of $1\,\Omega$ + resistance of $12\,\Omega$ and $6\,\Omega$ in parallel + $1\,\Omega$ resistance

$$= \frac{4 \times 4}{4 + 4} + 1 + \frac{12 \times 6}{12 + 6} + 1 = 8\,\Omega$$

So, current through cell,

$$I = \frac{V}{R} = \frac{12}{8} = \frac{3}{2}\text{ A}$$

Now, $V_{AB} = I \times R_{AB}$

$$= \frac{3}{2} \times 2 = 3\text{ V}$$

$$V_{BC} = I \times R_{BC} = \frac{3}{2} \times 1 = 1.5\text{ V}$$

$$V_{CD} = I \times R_{CD} = \frac{3 \times 5}{2} = \frac{15}{2} = 7.5\text{ V}$$

27. (c) Change of resistivity of meter bridge wire does not shifts balance point.

28. (a) Let currents in branches are I_1, I_2 and I_3.

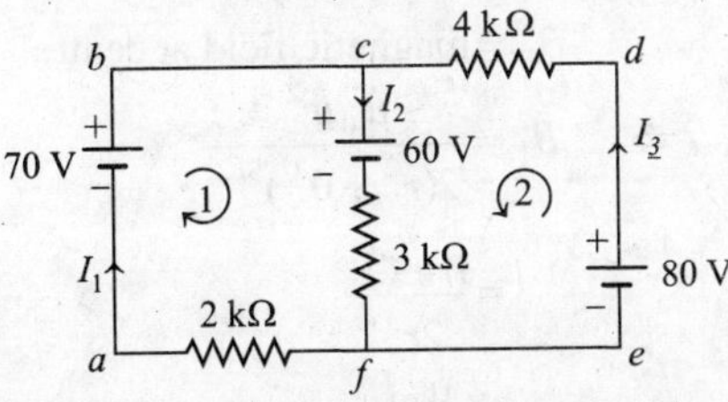

Then, from loops 1 and 2, we have

$$70 - 60 - I_2 \times 3 - I_1 \times 2 = 0 \quad \ldots(\text{i})$$

$$80 - I_3 \times 4 - 60 - I_2 \times 3 = 0 \ldots(\text{ii})$$

and $\quad I_2 = I_1 + I_3 \quad \ldots(\text{iii})$

On solving, we get

$$I_1 = 0.385\text{ mA}$$

$$I_2 = 3.08\text{ mA}$$

$$I_3 = 2.69\text{ mA}$$

and $V_{cf} = 60 + 3.08 \times 3$

i.e. $V_c - V_f = 69.2\text{ V}$

Point c is at higher potential.

29. (c) As, resistance $\propto$ temperature

$$\Rightarrow \quad R_1 \propto T_1$$

$$\Rightarrow \quad \tan\theta \propto T_1$$

$$\Rightarrow \quad \tan\theta = KT_1$$

and $\quad R_2 \propto T_2$

$$\Rightarrow \quad \tan(90^\circ - \theta) \propto T_2$$

$$\Rightarrow \quad \cot\theta = KT_2$$

$$\Rightarrow T_2 - T_1 \propto \left(\frac{\cos\theta}{\sin\theta} - \frac{\sin\theta}{\cos\theta}\right)$$

$$\propto \frac{\cos^2\theta - \sin^2\theta}{\sin\theta\cos\theta}$$

$$\propto \frac{2\cos 2\theta}{\sin 2\theta} = 2\cot 2\theta$$

$$\Rightarrow \quad (T_2 - T_1) \propto \cot 2\theta$$

30. (a) Resistivity of metal increases with temperature. Resistivity of a semiconductor decreases with temperature.

Resistivity of metal alloys is nearly constant with temperature.

Resistivity of some diamagnetic substances fall to zero or it exhibits superconductivity.

(A) → (2), (B) → (1), (C) → (3), (D) → (4)

Ch-05 Moving Charges and Magnetism

Topical Follow Thru

Test-1

1. (c) $B = \frac{\mu_0}{4\pi} \times \frac{2i}{a}$

$10^{-4} = \frac{4\pi \times 10^{-7} \times 2 \times i}{4\pi \times 0.01}$

$i = 5\,A$

2. (b) $B_r = \frac{\mu_0 I}{2\pi d} = \left(\frac{\mu_0 I}{2\pi r}\right)$

$= 0.2\,T \quad \text{...(i)}$

$B_{2r} = \frac{\mu_0 I}{2\pi d} = \frac{\mu_0 I}{2\pi(2r)}$

$= \frac{1}{2}\left(\frac{\mu_0 I}{2\pi r}\right) \quad \text{...(ii)}$

By using Eqs. (i) and (ii), we get

$B_{2r} = \frac{1}{2} B_r$

$B_{2r} = \frac{1}{2} \times 0.2\,T = 0.1\,T$

3. (b) The resultant magnetic field due to current carrying parallel wire1 (20A) and wire 2 (1A) at point P is zero.

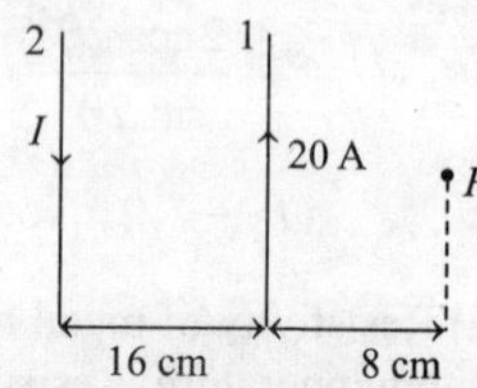

i.e. $B_1 = B_2$

$\Rightarrow \frac{I_1}{r_1} = \frac{I_2}{r_2}$

$\Rightarrow \frac{20}{8 \times 10^{-2}} = \frac{I}{24 \times 10^{-2}}$

$\Rightarrow I = 60\,A$

4. (a)

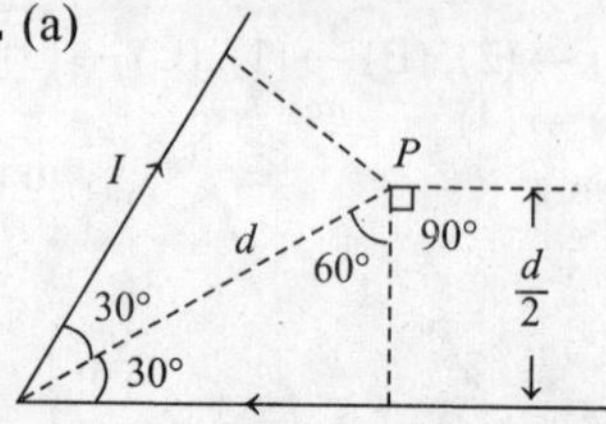

$B_{net} = 2\left[\frac{\mu_0 I}{4\pi r}(\sin\theta_1 + \sin\theta_2)\right]$

$= 2\left[\frac{\mu_0}{4\pi} \times \frac{I}{\frac{d}{2}} \times (\sin 90° + \sin 60°)\right]$

$= 2\left[\frac{\mu_0}{4\pi} \times \frac{2I}{d} \times \left(1 + \frac{\sqrt{3}}{2}\right)\right]$

$= \frac{\mu_0 I}{2\pi d}(2 + \sqrt{3})$

5. (c) The magnetic field due to straight wire above O is zero.

Therefore, $B_1 = 0$ (since, $\theta = 0°$)

The magnetic field due to semi-circular part,

$B_2 = \left(\frac{\mu_0 nI}{2r}\right)$

$= \frac{\mu_0 \times 1/2 \times I}{2r} = \frac{\mu_0 I}{4r}$

The magnetic field due to lower straight portion,

$B_3 = \frac{\mu_0 I}{4\pi r}(\sin\theta° + \sin 90°)$

$= \frac{\mu_0 I}{4\pi r} \quad \text{(upward)}$

Net magnetic field,

$B_{net} = B_1 + B_2 + B_3$

$B_{net} = 0 + \frac{\mu_0 I}{4r} + \frac{\mu_0 I}{4\pi r}$

$B = \frac{\mu_0 I}{4r} + \frac{\mu_0 I}{4\pi r} \quad \text{(upward)}$

6. (b) As magnetic field at an axis of current carrying loop is given by

$B = \frac{\mu_0 i r^2}{2(r^2 + d^2)^{3/2}} \quad \text{...(i)}$

B_1 = magnetic field at centre.

$\Rightarrow B_1 = \frac{\mu_0 i r^2}{2(r^2 + 0^2)^{3/2}}$

$= \frac{\mu_0 i r^2}{2r^3}$

$= \frac{\mu_0 i}{2r} \quad \text{...(ii)}$

Dividing Eq. (i) by Eq. (ii), we get

$\Rightarrow \frac{B}{B_1} = \frac{\mu_0 i r^2 \times 2 \times r}{2(r^2 + d^2)^{3/2} \times \mu_0 i}$

$\Rightarrow \frac{B}{B_1} = \frac{r^3}{(r^2 + d^2)^{3/2}}$

$\Rightarrow \frac{B}{B_1} = \frac{(3)^3}{(3^2 + 4^2)^{3/2}}$

$\Rightarrow \frac{50}{B_1} = \frac{27}{(25)^{3/2}}$

$\Rightarrow \frac{50}{B_1} = \frac{27}{5^3}$

$\Rightarrow B_1 = 231\,\mu T$

7. (c) According to Biot-Savart's law, the magnetic field is given by

$dB = \frac{\mu_0}{4\pi} \cdot \frac{i(d\mathbf{l} \times \mathbf{r})}{r^3}$

where, $\frac{\mu_0}{4\pi} = 10^{-7}\ \text{TmA}^{-1}$ in free space.

$= \frac{\mu_0}{4\pi} \cdot \frac{idl}{r^2}(\hat{\mathbf{i}} \times \hat{\mathbf{j}})$

$= \frac{10^{-7} \times 5 \times 2 \times 10^{-2}}{(0.15)^2}\hat{\mathbf{k}}$

$= 44.44 \times 10^{-8}\,\hat{\mathbf{k}}$

8. (a) Magnetic field at the centre of a circular loop, $B_1 = \frac{\mu_0 i}{2R}$

and that at an axial point,

$B_2 = \frac{\mu_0 i R^2}{2(R^2 + x^2)^{3/2}}$

Thus, $\frac{B_2}{B_1} = \frac{R^3}{(R^2 + x^2)^{3/2}}$

or $B_2 = B_1\left[\frac{R^3}{(R^2 + x^2)^{3/2}}\right]$

9. (b) The magnetic field produced at the centre of the circular coil carrying current is given by

$B = \frac{\mu_0 NI}{2r}$

For one turn, $N = 1$

$B_0 = \frac{\mu_0 I}{2r}$

As the coil is rewound,

$r' = \frac{r}{3}, N' = 3$

$$B' = \frac{\mu_0 I \times 3}{2\times\left(\frac{r}{3}\right)} = \frac{9\mu_0 I}{2r} = 9B_0$$

10. (a) The magnetic field inside the solenoid is given by

$$B = \mu_0 nI$$

$\because$ Number of turns per unit length,

$$n = \frac{N}{L} = \frac{200}{0.2\times 10^{-2}} = 10^5$$

$$B = 4\pi\times 10^{-7}\times 10^5\times 10$$
$$= 4\times 3.14\times 10^{-7}\times 10^6$$
$$= 1.256$$
$$= 125.6\times 10^{-2}\ \text{T}$$

11. (d) Magnetic field at current carrying wire of radius R, i.e.

$$B_1 = \frac{\mu_0 i}{4\pi R}\times\frac{\pi}{2}$$

Similarly, magnetic field at current carrying wire of radius R', i.e.

$$B_2 = \frac{\mu_0}{4\pi}\times\frac{i}{R'}\times\frac{3\pi}{2}$$

Net magnetic field at point O, i.e.

$$B = B_1 + B_2$$
$$B = \frac{\mu_0 i}{4\pi R}\times\frac{\pi}{2} + \frac{\mu_0}{4\pi}\cdot\frac{i}{R'}\times\frac{3\pi}{2}$$
$$= \frac{\mu_0 i}{8}\left(\frac{1}{R} + \frac{3}{R'}\right)$$

12. (a) As we know,

$$\frac{x}{d} = \sin 45°$$
$$\Rightarrow \quad x = \frac{d}{\sqrt{2}}$$

We can extend the wire and then subtract the field of extended part.

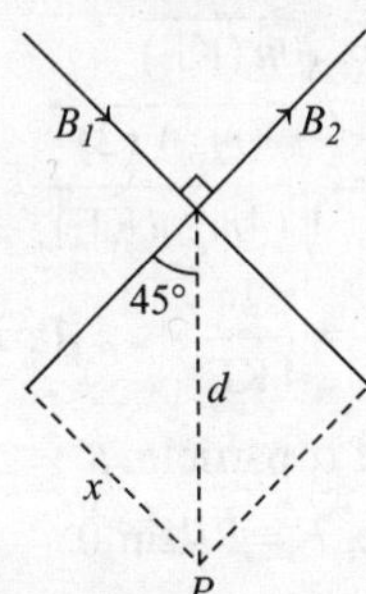

Magnetic field, i.e.

$$B_1 = \frac{\mu_0 I}{4\pi d/\sqrt{2}}(\sin 0° + \sin 90°) - \frac{\mu_0 I}{4\pi d/\sqrt{2}}(\sin 0° + \sin 45°)$$

$$= \frac{\mu_0 I}{2\sqrt{2}\pi d}\left(1 - \frac{1}{\sqrt{2}}\right)$$

and similarly,

$$B_2 = \frac{\mu_0 I}{2\sqrt{2}\pi d}\left[1 - \frac{1}{\sqrt{2}}\right]$$

Then, net magnetic field at point P,

$$B = (B_1 + B_2) = 2B$$
$$= \frac{\mu_0 I}{\sqrt{2}\pi d}\left(1 - \frac{1}{\sqrt{2}}\right)$$

13. (c) By Ampere's rule, fields at P_1 and P_2 are

$$B_1 = \frac{\mu_0 i}{2\pi R^2}\cdot r$$

Here, $r = \frac{R}{2} \Rightarrow B_1 = \frac{\mu_0 i}{4\pi R}$

and $B_2 = \frac{\mu_0 i}{2\pi r}$

Here, $r = \frac{3R}{2} \Rightarrow B_2 = \frac{\mu_0 i}{3\pi R}$

$$\therefore \frac{B_1}{B_2} = \frac{\mu_0 i}{4\pi R}\times\frac{3\pi R}{\mu_0 i} = \frac{3}{4}$$

14. (d) Consider wire to be made up of large number of thin wires of infinite lengths.

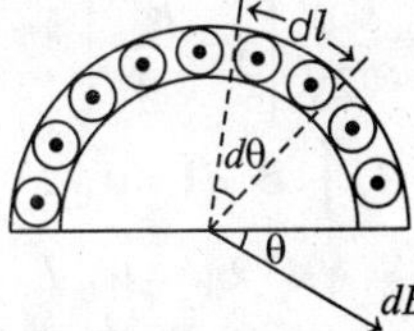

Consider thickness dl making an angle $d\theta$ at centre.

Current through dl, $dI = \frac{d\theta}{\pi} I$

$\therefore$ Magnetic field at the centre,

$$dB = \frac{\mu_0}{4\pi}\cdot\frac{2dI}{R} = \frac{\mu_0 I}{2\pi^2 R}d\theta$$

$$\therefore B = \int_{-\pi/2}^{\pi/2} dB\cos\theta\, d\theta$$
$$= \int_{-\pi/2}^{\pi/2}\frac{\mu_0 I}{2\pi^2 R}\cos\theta\, d\theta$$
$$= \frac{\mu_0 I}{\pi^2 R}$$

15. (a) Magnetic field along a current carrying wire of radius r, i.e.

$$\mathbf{B}_1 = \frac{\mu_0}{4\pi}\times\frac{I}{r}\times\pi = \frac{\mu_0 I}{4r}$$

Similarly, magnetic field along a current carrying wire of radius $2r$, i.e.

$$\mathbf{B}_2 = \frac{\mu_0}{4\pi}\times\frac{I}{2r}\times\pi = \frac{\mu_0 I}{8r}$$

So, net magnetic field at point P,

$$\mathbf{B} = \mathbf{B}_1 + \mathbf{B}_2$$
$$= \frac{\mu_0 I}{4r} + \frac{\mu_0 I}{8r} = \frac{3}{8}\cdot\frac{\mu_0 I}{r}$$

i.e. perpendicular to the plane of the paper and directed inwards.

16. (d) At the centre C, magnetic field due to wires RQ and PS will be zero. Due to wire QP,

$$B_1 = \frac{1}{2}\left[\frac{\mu_0 I}{2R_1}\right] = \frac{\mu_0 I}{4R_1}\odot$$

(perpendicular to paper and directed outwards)

and due to wire SR,

$$B_2 = \frac{1}{2}\left[\frac{\mu_0 I}{2R_2}\right] = \frac{\mu_0 I}{4R_2}\otimes$$

(perpendicular to paper and directed inwards)

$\therefore$ Net magnetic field would be,

$$B = B_1 - B_2$$
$$B = \frac{\mu_0 I}{4}\left[\frac{1}{R_1} - \frac{1}{R_2}\right]\odot$$

(perpendicular to paper and directed outwards)

17. (b) According to Ampere's circuital law, we get

$$\int \mathbf{B}\cdot d\mathbf{l} = \mu_0\times dI$$

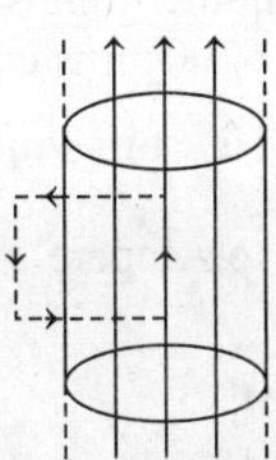

$\because$ Linear density i.e. $\lambda = \frac{dI}{dl}$,

so $dI = \lambda\, dl$

Magnetic field inside the cylinder,

$$B = \mu_0\lambda$$

18. (d) According to Ampere's circuital law, we have

$$\oint \mathbf{B}\cdot d\mathbf{l} = \mu_0 nI$$

$$\oint_{ABCD} \mathbf{B}\cdot d\mathbf{l} = \oint_{ABCA} \mathbf{B}\cdot d\mathbf{l} + \oint_{CDAC} \mathbf{B}\cdot d\mathbf{l}$$
$$= \mu_0 I_1 + \mu_0 I_2 = \mu_0 (I_1 + I_2)$$

19. (c) As we know, magnetic field **B** varies with respect to radius R, such that

(i) $0 < x < R_1,\ B \propto x$

(ii) $R_1 < x < R_2,\ B \propto \frac{1}{x}$

(iii) $R_2 < x < R_3,\ B \propto \frac{1}{x}$

So, (ii) and (iii) decrease hyperbolically but with different slopes as the media are different. Only plot (c) matches this description.

20. (b) ***Case* I** A long solenoid is having $n_1 = 200$ turns/cm,
$= 200 \times 10^{-2}$ turns/m

$B_1 = 6.28 \times 10^{-2}$ Wb

According to Ampere's circuital law, we get

$$B_1 = \mu_0 n_1 I_1$$
$$6.28 \times 10^{-2} = 4\pi \times 10^{-7} \times 200 \times 10^{-2} \times I_1$$
$$\Rightarrow I_1 = \frac{6.28 \times 10^{-2}}{4\pi \times 10^{-7} \times 200 \times 10^{-2}} \quad ...(i)$$

***Case* II** Another long solenoid is having $n_2 = 100$ turns/cm,

$n_2 = 100 \times 10^{-2}$ turns/m, $I_2 = \frac{i}{3}$

According to Ampere's circuital law, we have

$B_2 = \mu_0 n_2 I_1$

From Eq. (i),

$$B_2 = \frac{4\pi \times 10^{-7} \times 100 \times 10^{-2} \times 6.28 \times 10^{-2}}{4\pi \times 10^{-7} \times 200 \times 10^{-2} \times 3}$$
$$= 1.046 \times 10^{-2}\ \text{T}$$
$$\approx 1.05 \times 10^{-2}\ \text{Wb/m}^2$$

21. (d) A long straight wire of radius a is carrying a steady current I. The magnetic field is given by

$$\mathbf{B} = \frac{\mu_0 I}{2\pi a^2} \times r$$

***Case* I** Magnetic field at $r = \frac{a}{2}$ is

$$B_1 = \frac{\mu_0 I}{2\pi a^2} \times \frac{a}{2} = \frac{\mu_0 I}{4\pi a} \quad ...(i)$$

***Case* II** Magnetic field at $r = 2a$ is

$$B_2 = \frac{\mu_0 I}{2\pi r} = \frac{\mu_0 I}{2\pi (2a)} = \frac{\mu_0 I}{4\pi a} \quad ...(ii)$$

On dividing Eq. (i) by Eq. (ii), we get

$$\frac{B_1}{B_2} = 1$$

22. (d) Take any point P inside the thin walled pipe. Consider a circular loop through this point and apply Ampere's circuital law. As, net current inside the loop is zero, the magnetic field at any point inside the pipe will be zero.

$$\oint \mathbf{B}\cdot d\mathbf{l} = \mu_0 nI = \mu_0 \times 0 = 0$$

23. (d) For $x < \frac{R}{2}$, $|\mathbf{B}| = 0$

For $\frac{R}{2} \le x < R$

According to Ampere's circuital law,

$$\int \mathbf{B}\cdot d\mathbf{l} = \mu_0 I$$
$$|\mathbf{B}|\, 2\pi x = \mu_0 \left[\pi r^2 - \pi\left(\frac{R}{2}\right)^2\right]\hat{\mathbf{i}}$$
$$|\mathbf{B}| = \frac{\mu_0 I}{2x}\left[x - \frac{R^2}{4}\right]$$

For $x \ge R$, $\int \mathbf{B}\cdot d\mathbf{l} = \mu_0 I$

$$|\mathbf{B}|\, 2\pi r = \mu_0 I$$
$$|\mathbf{B}| = \frac{\mu_0 I}{2xr}$$

Thus, graph is

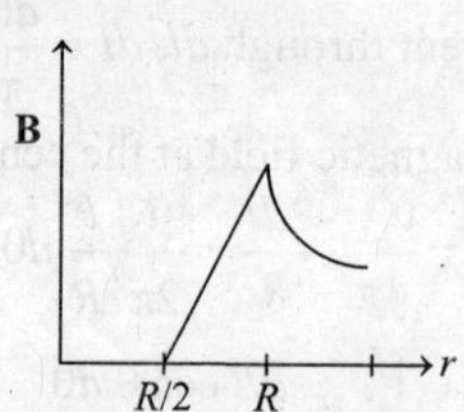

24. (a) If we take a small strip of dr at distance r from centre, then number of turns in this strip would be

$$dN = \left(\frac{N}{b-a}\right) dr$$

Magnetic field due to this element at the centre of the coil will be

$$dB = \frac{\mu_0 (dN) I}{2r} = \frac{\mu_0 NI}{(b-a)} \cdot \frac{dr}{r}$$

$$\therefore B = \int_{r=a}^{r=b} dB = \frac{\mu_0 NI}{2(b-a)} \ln\left(\frac{b}{a}\right)$$

25. (b) A charged rotating ring constitutes a current.

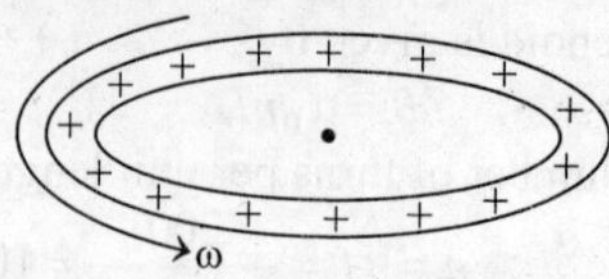

$$\text{Current, } I = \frac{Q}{T} = \frac{2\pi R\lambda}{\frac{2\pi}{\omega}} = \lambda R\omega$$

Magnetic field due to this current,

$$B = \frac{\mu_0 I}{2R} = \frac{\mu_0 \lambda R\omega}{2R} = \frac{1}{2}\mu_0 \lambda\omega$$

Test-2

1. (b) $F = ILB\sin\theta$

or $\sin\theta = \frac{F}{ILB}$

$\Rightarrow \sin\theta = \frac{45}{15 \times 2 \times 3}$

$\Rightarrow \sin\theta = \frac{1}{2}$

$\Rightarrow \theta = \sin^{-1}\left(\frac{1}{2}\right) \Rightarrow \theta = 30°$

2. (a) $F = Bil\sin\theta = 1000 \times 10^{-4} \times 5 \times (40 \times 10^{-2})\sin 60°$

$$= 1000 \times 10^{-4} \times 5 \times 40 \times 10^{-2} \times \frac{\sqrt{3}}{2}$$
$$= 1.73 \times 10^{-1}\ \text{N}$$

3. (c) Radius of circular path,

$$R = \frac{\sqrt{2m(\text{KE})}}{(qB)}$$

So, $q \propto \sqrt{m(\text{KE})}$

$$\therefore \frac{e}{2e} = \sqrt{\frac{(m_p)(2)}{(4m_e)(\text{KE})}}$$
$$\frac{1}{4} = \frac{2}{4\,\text{KE}} \quad (\because m_R = m_e)$$

Energy of α-particle, $K = 2$ MeV

4. (c) Force, $F = BIl\sin\theta$

Here, $\theta = 90°$

and $l = R + 2R + R = 4R$

$\therefore$ Force, $F = 4BIR$

From Fleming's left hand rule, this force is upwards.

5. (b) As the system is in equilibrium,

$$\Sigma Fx = 0$$

According to the question,

$\Rightarrow \quad mg \sin\theta = F\cos\theta \quad$ ...(i)

$\Rightarrow \quad F = ILB \quad$ ...(ii)

Substitute the value of F in Eq. (i),

$$\Rightarrow \quad mg\sin\theta = ILB\cos\theta$$

$$\Rightarrow I = \frac{mg\sin\theta}{LB\cos\theta} = \frac{mg}{LB}\tan\theta$$

$$\Rightarrow \quad I = \left(\frac{m}{L}\right)\frac{g\tan\theta}{B}$$

Here, $\frac{m}{L} = 0.6\,\text{kg m}^{-1}$

$g = 9.80\,\text{m/s}^2$

$$\Rightarrow \quad I = 0.6 \times \frac{9.80\times\tan 60^\circ}{0.50}$$

$$I = 20.51\,\text{A}$$

6. (d) $q = -4\mu\text{C}$

$v = (2\hat{\mathbf{i}} + 4\hat{\mathbf{j}}) \times 10^6\,\text{ms}^{-1}$

$B = 4\hat{\mathbf{j}}$

Magnetic force, $\mathbf{F} = q(\mathbf{v}\times\mathbf{B})$

$= (-4\times10^{-6})[(2\hat{\mathbf{i}} + 4\hat{\mathbf{j}})\times10^6\times4\hat{\mathbf{j}}]$

$= (-4\times10^{-6})[8(\hat{\mathbf{i}}\times\hat{\mathbf{j}})\times10^6]$

$= -4\times8\hat{\mathbf{k}}$

$= -32\hat{\mathbf{k}}\,\text{N}$

$= 32\,\text{N}$ in $-z$-direction

7. (a) $\frac{mv^2}{r} = evB$

$$r = \frac{mv}{eB}$$

As for a particle in motion, $p = mv$

$$\therefore \quad r = \frac{mv}{eB} = \frac{p}{eB} \Rightarrow p = eBr$$

$$\Rightarrow \quad p = 1.6\times10^{-19}\times5\times10^{-5}\times4\times10^{-2}$$

$$= 3.2\times10^{-25}\,\text{kg-ms}^{-1}$$

8. (a) A charged particle moving in a magnetic field perpendicular to its velocity experiences a Lorentz force $F = qvB$ which acts as the centripetal force keeping the particle in a circular path.

Thus, the magnetic force indeed provides the necessary centripetal force.

9. (a) $F = \frac{\mu_0}{2\pi}\frac{I_1 I_2 l}{r}$

$$\Rightarrow F_{DA} = \frac{10^{-7}\times2\times10\times10\times10\times10^{-2}}{1\times10^{-2}}$$

$$= 2\times10^{-4}\,\text{N}$$

$$\Rightarrow F_{CB} = \frac{10^{-7}\times2\times10\times10\times10\times10^{-2}}{6\times10^{-2}}$$

$$= 3.3\times10^{-5}\,\text{N}$$

$$\Rightarrow F_{\text{net}} = F_{DA} - F_{CB}$$

$$= 2\times10^{-4} - 0.33\times10^{-4}$$

$$= 1.67\times10^{-4}\,\text{N}$$

10. (a) Magnetic force, $\mathbf{F}_m = q(\mathbf{v}\times\mathbf{B})$

For $\mathbf{F}_m$ to be along $(-\hat{\mathbf{k}})$, magnetic field must be along $(-\hat{\mathbf{j}})$.

Now, substituting all the values in above equation, we get

$$-(1.28\times10^{-13}\hat{\mathbf{k}}) = (1.6\times10^{-19})[(2\hat{\mathbf{i}} + 3\hat{\mathbf{j}})\times(-B\hat{\mathbf{j}})]\times10^6$$

$\therefore \quad 1.28 = 1.6\times2\times B$

or $\quad B = \frac{1.28}{3.2} = 0.4$

Therefore, the magnetic field,

$$\mathbf{B} = -B\hat{\mathbf{j}} = (-0.4\hat{\mathbf{j}})\,\text{T}$$

11. (d) Here,

$\mathbf{E} = 2\hat{\mathbf{i}} + 3\hat{\mathbf{j}}$, $\mathbf{B} = 4\hat{\mathbf{j}} + 6\hat{\mathbf{k}}$,

$q =$ charge on a particle. [Given]

Initial position, $r_1 = (0,0)$

Final position, $r_2 = (1,1)$

Net force experienced by charge particle inside electromagnetic field is

$$\mathbf{F}_{\text{net}} = q\mathbf{E} + q(\mathbf{v}\times\mathbf{B})$$

$$= q(2\hat{\mathbf{i}} + 3\hat{\mathbf{j}}) \text{ [here, } \mathbf{v}\times\mathbf{B} = 0]$$

$$= (2q\,\hat{\mathbf{i}} + 3q\,\hat{\mathbf{j}})$$

$$\therefore \quad dW = \mathbf{F}_{\text{net}}\cdot d\mathbf{r}$$

$$\Rightarrow \int dW = \int_{r_1}^{r_2}(2q\,\hat{\mathbf{i}} + 3q\,\hat{\mathbf{j}})\cdot(dx\,\hat{\mathbf{i}} + dy\,\hat{\mathbf{j}})$$

[here $d\mathbf{r} = dx\,\hat{\mathbf{i}} + dy\,\hat{\mathbf{j}}$]

$$\Rightarrow \quad W = 2q\int_0^1 dx + 3q\int_0^1 dy$$

or $\quad W = 2q + 3q$

or $\quad W = 5q$

12. (c) Given that, $\mathbf{v} = 6\times10^6\,\hat{\mathbf{i}}$ m/s,

$\mathbf{E} = 300\,\hat{\mathbf{j}}$ V/cm

$= 3\times10^4\,\hat{\mathbf{j}}$ V/m

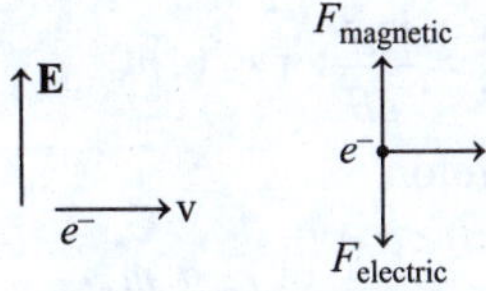

To keep the electron moving along x-direction,

$$\mathbf{F}_{\text{net}} = 0$$

or $\quad \mathbf{F}_{\text{electric}} + \mathbf{F}_{\text{magnetic}} = 0$

$$q\mathbf{E} + q(\mathbf{v}\times\mathbf{B}) = 0$$

or $\quad \mathbf{E} + \mathbf{v}\times\mathbf{B} = 0$

It is possible when magnetic field $\mathbf{B}$ is along $+z$-direction and magnitude is

$$\mathbf{B} = \frac{\mathbf{E}}{\mathbf{v}} = \frac{3\times10^4\,\hat{\mathbf{j}}}{6\times10^6\,\hat{\mathbf{i}}} = 5\times10^{-3}\,\hat{\mathbf{k}}\,\text{T}$$

13. (a) Since, proton is moving in a straight line, hence net force is zero.

$$\therefore \quad qE = Bqv \Rightarrow v = \frac{E}{B}$$

Also, current associated with the beam,

$$i = ne \Rightarrow n = i/e$$

where, n is number of protons/time.

Momentum of a proton $= mv$

Force, $F = nmv$

$$\Rightarrow F = \frac{imE}{eB}$$

$$= \frac{0.80\times10^{-3}\times1.67\times10^{-27}\times220\times10^3}{1.6\times10^{-19}\times50\times10^{-3}}$$

$$= 3.67\times10^{-5}\,\text{N}$$

14. (c) When a moving charged particle is placed in a magnetic field $\mathbf{B}$, then the net magnetic force acting on it is

$$\mathbf{F}_m = q(\mathbf{v}\times\mathbf{B})$$

$$\mathbf{F}_m = q\,vB\sin\theta$$

Here, $\theta = 90^\circ$

$$\mathbf{F}_m = q\,vB$$

Also, due to this net force, the particle transverses a circular path, whose necessary centripetal force is being provided by F_m, i.e.

$$\frac{mv^2}{r} = q\,vB$$

$$\Rightarrow \quad r = \frac{mv^2}{qvB} = \frac{mv}{qB}$$

$$\Rightarrow \quad r \propto m$$

So, for electron

$$r_e = \frac{m_e v}{eB} \text{ or } r_e \propto m_e$$

For proton

$$r_p = \frac{m_p v}{eB} \text{ or } r_p \propto m_p$$

For He-particle

$$r_{He} = \frac{4m_p v}{2eB} = \frac{2m_p v}{eB}$$

Clearly, $r_{He} > r_p \quad (\because r_{He} = 2r_p)$

and we know that, $m_p > m_e$ $\left(\begin{array}{l}\because m_p \approx 10^{-27} \text{ kg}, \\ m_e \approx 10^{-31} \text{ kg}\end{array}\right)$

$$\therefore r_p > r_e \Rightarrow r_{He} > r_p > r_e$$

15. (b) Force on a charged particle moving in region of a magnetic field is given by

$$\mathbf{F} = q(\mathbf{v} \times \mathbf{B})$$

Here, $q = 1\,\mu\text{C} = 1 \times 10^{-6}$ C,

$$\mathbf{v} = (2\hat{\mathbf{i}} + 3\hat{\mathbf{j}} + 4\hat{\mathbf{k}})\,\text{ms}^{-1}$$

and $\quad \mathbf{B} = (5\hat{\mathbf{i}} + 3\hat{\mathbf{j}} - 6\hat{\mathbf{k}}) \times 10^{-3}$ T

So, force on the particle is

$$\mathbf{F} \times 10^{-9} = 1 \times 10^{-6} \begin{vmatrix} \hat{\mathbf{i}} & \hat{\mathbf{j}} & \hat{\mathbf{k}} \\ 2 & 3 & 4 \\ 5\times 10^{-3} & 3\times 10^{-3} & -6\times 10^{-3} \end{vmatrix}$$

$$= 10^{-9} \begin{vmatrix} \hat{\mathbf{i}} & \hat{\mathbf{j}} & \hat{\mathbf{k}} \\ 2 & 3 & 4 \\ 5 & 3 & -6 \end{vmatrix}$$

$$\Rightarrow \quad \mathbf{F} = -30\hat{\mathbf{i}} + 32\hat{\mathbf{j}} - 9\hat{\mathbf{k}}$$

Test- 3

1. (a) Current sensitivity of a moving coil galvanometer is the deflection (θ) per unit current (i) flowing through it, i.e.

$$i_S = \frac{\theta}{i} = \frac{NAB}{k} \quad \ldots(i)$$

where, N = number of turns in the coil,

A = area of each turn of coil,

B = magnetic field

and k = restoring torque per unit twist of the fibre strip.

Similarly, voltage sensitivity is the deflection per unit voltage, i.e.

$$V_S = \frac{\theta}{V} = \left(\frac{NAB}{k}\right)\frac{i}{V} = \frac{NAB}{kR_G} \quad \ldots(ii)$$

where, R_G is the resistance of the galvanometer.

From Eqs. (i) and (ii), we get

$$R_G = \frac{i_S}{V_S} \quad \ldots(iii)$$

Here, $i_S = 5 \text{ div/mA} = 5 \times 10^3$ div/A

and $V_S = 20$ div/V

Substituting the given values in Eq. (iii), we get

$$R_G = \frac{5 \times 10^3}{20} = 250\,\Omega$$

$\therefore$ The resistance of the galvanometer is 250 Ω.

2. (c) The magnetic dipole moment of current loop,

$$M = NiA$$

$$M = Ni\pi r^2 \qquad [\because A = \pi r^2]$$

$$= 200 \times 4 \times 3.14 \times (20 \times 10^{-2})^2$$

$$M = 100.48 \text{ A-m}^2$$

3. (a) For no force on wire C, force on wire C due to wire D = force on wire C due to wire B

$$\Rightarrow \quad \frac{\mu_0}{4\pi} \times \frac{2 \times 25 \times 10}{x} \times l = \frac{\mu_0}{4\pi} \times \frac{2 \times 15 \times 10}{(15 - x)} \times l$$

$$\Rightarrow \quad x = 9.1 \text{ cm}$$

$$x \approx 9 \text{ cm}$$

4. (c) For ammeter,

[Circuit: $0.002\,i$ through ammeter A and G; $0.9988\,i$ through shunt r_s]

$$0.002i \times G = 0.9988i \times r_s$$

$$r_s = \frac{0.002}{0.998} G$$

$$\Rightarrow \quad r_s = 0.002004\,G$$

$$= \frac{1}{499} \times G$$

Equivalent resistance of ammeter,

$$\frac{1}{R} = \frac{1}{G} + \frac{1}{r_s}$$

$$\therefore \quad \frac{1}{R} = \frac{1}{G} + \frac{1}{G/499} \Rightarrow R = \frac{G}{500}$$

5. (c) Torque, $\tau = iAB \sin\theta$

where, $A = \frac{1}{2} \times \text{base} \times \text{height}$

$$\Rightarrow \quad A = \frac{1}{2} \times a \times \frac{a\sqrt{3}}{2}$$

$$= \frac{\sqrt{3}}{4} a^2 = \frac{\sqrt{3} \times (0.02)^2}{4}$$

$$= \sqrt{3} \times 10^{-4} \text{ m}^2$$

Now, $\tau = iAB \sin\theta$

$$\tau = 0.4 \times \sqrt{3} \times 10^{-4} \times 6 \times 10^{-2} \sin 90°$$

$$= 4.15 \times 10^{-6} \text{ N-m}$$

6. (a) Given, $\tau = mB$

A = Area of coil

B = magnetic field

$$K\theta = IANB \quad [\because \tau = K\theta, m = NIA]$$

$$\frac{\theta}{I} = \frac{ANB}{K}$$

$$\frac{\theta}{I} = \text{Current sensitivity}$$

$$1.25\left(\frac{\theta}{I}\right)_1 = \left(\frac{\theta}{I}\right)_2 \quad \ldots(i)$$

$$1.25\left[\frac{AN_1B}{K}\right] = \left[\frac{AN_2B}{K}\right]$$

$$\Rightarrow \quad 1.25 = \frac{N_2}{N_1}$$

$$\frac{N_2}{N_1} = \frac{125}{100} = \frac{5}{4} \quad \ldots(ii)$$

$$R = \rho\frac{l}{a} = \text{constant } l \propto a$$

Voltage sensitivity

$$= \frac{\theta}{V} = \frac{\theta}{IR}$$

$$= \frac{\text{Current sensitivity}}{R}$$

R = constant

Voltage sensitivity ∝ Current sensitivity + 25%

7. (d) If the direction of current and magnetic field are perpendicular to each other ($\theta = 90°$), then $\sin\theta$ term becomes 1. It will maximise both the force and torque. The torque acting on the conductor is given by the formula $\tau = BIL \sin\theta \times d$

8. (d) Given, current passing through galvanometer, $I = 6\,\text{mA}$
Deflection, $\theta = 2°$
We know that, figure of merit of galvanometer is I/θ.

$$\Rightarrow \frac{I}{\theta} = \frac{6\times10^{-3}}{2} \Rightarrow = 3\times10^{-3}\,\text{A/div.}$$

9. (d) Given, deflection in the coil,
$\theta = 0.05\,\text{rad}$
Current, $I = 10\,\text{mA} = 10^{-2}\,\text{A}$
Magnetic field,
$B = 0.01\,\text{T}, n = 200$
Torsional constant,
$C = 4\times10^{-5}\,\text{N-m rad}^{-1}$

We know that, $\frac{\theta}{I} = \frac{nBA}{C}$

$$\Rightarrow A = \frac{C\theta}{nBI} = \frac{4\times10^{-5}\times0.05}{200\times0.01\times10^{-2}}$$
$$= 1\times10^{-4}\,\text{m}^2$$
$$= 1\times10^{-4}\times10^{4}\,\text{cm}^2$$
$$= 1\,\text{cm}^2$$

10. (a) $m = Ia^2$
When square is converted into a circular loop of radius r, then length of wire will be same in both areas.

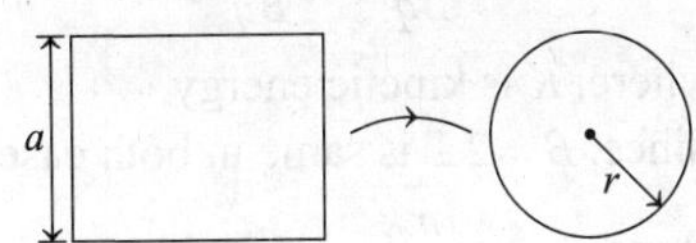

$$\Rightarrow 4a = 2\pi r \Rightarrow r = \frac{4a}{2\pi} = \frac{2a}{\pi}$$

Hence, area of circular loop formed,

$$A' = \pi r^2 = \pi\left(\frac{2a}{\pi}\right)^2 = \frac{4a^2}{\pi}$$

Magnitude of magnetic dipole moment of circular loop will be

$$m' = IA' = I\frac{4a^2}{\pi}$$

Ratio of magnetic dipole moments of both shapes,

$$\frac{m'}{m} = \frac{I\cdot\frac{4a^2}{\pi}}{Ia^2} = \frac{4}{\pi} \Rightarrow m' = \frac{4m}{\pi}$$

11. (b) Given, $G = 100\,\Omega$,
$I_g = 10^{-5}\,\text{A}, I = 1\,\text{A}, S = ?$
As, $I_g\times G = (I - I_g)\times S$

$$\therefore S = \frac{I_g}{I - I_g}G = \frac{10^{-5}}{1-10^{-5}}\times100$$

$$S = \frac{10^{-3}}{1-0.00001} = 10^{-3}\,\Omega \text{ in parallel}$$

12. (a) Given,
Area of the rectangular coil,
$A = 5\,\text{cm}\times2.5\,\text{cm}$
$\Rightarrow A = 12.5\,\text{cm}^2 = 12.5\times10^{-4}\,\text{m}^2$
Number of turns, $N = 100$ turns
Current through the coil, $I = 3\,\text{A}$
Magnetic field applied, $B = 1\,\text{T}$
Angle between the magnetic field and area vector of the coil, $\theta = 45°$
As we know that, when a coil is tilted by an angle θ in the presence of some external magnetic field, then the net torque experienced by the coil,
$$\tau = \mathbf{M}\times\mathbf{B} = NI(\mathbf{A}\times\mathbf{B})$$
$$= NIAB\sin\theta$$
Substituting the given values, we get
$$\tau = 100\times3\times12.5\times10^{-4}\times1\times\sin45°$$
$$\tau = 0.707\times100\times3\times12.5\times10^{-4}$$
$$= 2.651\times10^{-1}\approx0.27\,\text{N-m}$$

13. (b) We know that, resistance across voltmeter is $R = \frac{V'}{I_g} - G$

The voltmeter gives full scale deflection for potential difference of V volts. Its resistance is G.
Hence, $I_g = V/G$, given that $V' = nV$

$$R = \frac{nV}{(V/G)} - G = (n-1)G$$

14. (a) $\tau = I\alpha$
$$iAB = I\alpha \quad (\because \tau = \mathbf{M}\times\mathbf{B})$$
$$i\pi R^2 B = \frac{MR^2}{2}\alpha \quad \left(\because I = \frac{MR^2}{2}\right)$$
or
$$\alpha = \frac{2i\pi B}{M}$$
$$= 40\,\pi\,\text{rads}^{-2}$$

15. (b) $\tau = NIAB\sin\theta$
$[\tau = \mathbf{M}\times\mathbf{B} \text{ or } |\tau| = MB\sin\theta]$

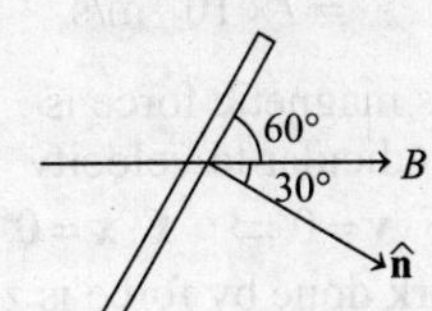

$$\Rightarrow \tau = (2n)(2I)\times(2a)\times B\sin30°$$
$$= 4nIB \text{ or } 8BnaI\cos60°$$

16. (a) Here, current across ammeter,
$I_g = 0.5\% \text{ of } I = 0.005\,I$
And current across shunt resistance,
$I_s = I - I_g = I - 0.005\,I = 0.995I$
$\therefore$ Resistance across shunt,

$$S = \frac{I_g G}{I_s} = \frac{0.005\,I\times G}{0.995\,I} = \frac{G}{199}$$

Thus, resistance of ammeter will be

$$= \frac{GS}{G+S} = \frac{\frac{G}{199}\times G}{G + \frac{G}{199}} = \frac{G}{200}$$

17. (b) Here, $I_1 = 200\,\mu\text{A}, \theta_1 = 30°$,
$\theta_2 = \frac{\pi}{10}\,\text{rad} = 18°, \quad I_2 = ?$

So, $I_1 = \frac{k}{NBA}.\theta_1$

and $I_2 = \frac{k}{NBA}.\theta_2$

$$\Rightarrow \frac{I_2}{I_1} = \frac{\theta_2}{\theta_1}$$
$$\Rightarrow I_2 = \frac{\theta_2}{\theta_1}\times I_1$$
$$= \frac{18}{30}\times200 = 120\,\mu\text{A}$$

Current sensitivity of the galvanometer,

$$= \frac{18°}{120\,\mu\text{A}} = 0.15°\,\mu\text{A}^{-1}$$

18. (a) Area vector will be perpendicular to plane. Area vector is at 60° angle with X-axis and 30° angle with $-Z$-axis.

−Z M 60° 30° X Z

$$M = iAN = 10\times(0.1)^2$$
$$= 0.1\,\text{A-m}^2$$
$$\mathbf{M} = M\cos60\hat{\mathbf{i}} - M\sin60°\,\hat{\mathbf{k}}$$
$$\Rightarrow \mathbf{M} = \left(\frac{M}{2}\right)\hat{\mathbf{i}} - \left(\frac{M\sqrt3}{2}\right)\hat{\mathbf{k}}$$
$$= \frac{M}{2}[\hat{\mathbf{i}} - \sqrt3\,\hat{\mathbf{k}}]$$
$$= 0.05[\hat{\mathbf{i}} - \sqrt3\,\hat{\mathbf{k}}]\,\text{A-m}^2$$

19. (b) Area of the given loop

A = (area of two circles of radius $a/2$ + area of a square of side a)

$$= 2\pi\left(\frac{a}{2}\right)^2 + a^2 = \left(\frac{\pi}{2}+1\right)a^2$$

$$|\mathbf{M}| = IA = \left(\frac{\pi}{2}+1\right)a^2 I$$

From screw law, direction of **M** is outwards or in positive z-direction.

$$\therefore\ \mathbf{M} = \left(\frac{\pi}{2}+1\right)a^2 I\,\hat{\mathbf{k}}$$

20. (b) Resistance of the galvanometer,

$$G = \frac{\text{Current sensitivity}}{\text{Voltage sensitivity}} = \frac{10}{2} = 5\,\Omega$$

Number of divisions on the galvanometer scale, $n = 150$.

Current required for full scale deflection,

$$I_g = \frac{n}{\text{Current sensitivity}} = \frac{150}{10} = 15\text{ mA} = 15\times 10^{-3}\text{ A}$$

Required range of voltmeter $= 150 \times 1 = 150\text{ V}$

Required series resistance,

$$R = \frac{V}{I_g} - G = \frac{150}{15\times 10^{-3}} - 5 = 9995\,\Omega$$

21. (a) In moving coil galvanometer,

$G = 100\,\Omega$, $S = 0.1\,\Omega$

$I_g = 100\,\mu\text{A} = 100\times 10^{-6}$ A

So, minimum current in the circuit so that ammeter shows maximum deflection.

$$I = \frac{G+S}{S}\times I_g = \left[\frac{100+0.1}{0.1}\right]\times 100\,\mu\text{A} = 100100\,\mu\text{A} = 100.1\text{ mA}$$

22. (b) The magnetic dipole moment of the current carrying coil is given by

$$\mathbf{M} = NiA\hat{\mathbf{n}} = 100\times 0.5\times(0.08\times 0.04)\,\hat{\mathbf{i}}$$

or $\mathbf{M} = 16\times 10^{-2}$

The torque acting on the coil is

$$\tau = \mathbf{M}\times\mathbf{B} = MB\,(\hat{\mathbf{i}}\times\hat{\mathbf{j}}) = 1.6\times 10^{-2}\times\frac{0.05}{\sqrt{2}}\,\hat{\mathbf{k}}$$

or $\tau = 5.66\times 10^{-5}\ \hat{\mathbf{k}}$ N-m

23. (a) The galvanometer cannot be used as an ammeter to measure the value of the current in a given circuit. This supports two reasons

(i) Galvanometer is a very sensitive device, it gives a full scale deflection for a current of the order of μA.

(ii) For measuring currents, the galvanometer has to be connected in series and as it has a large resistance, this will change the value of the current in the circuit.

24. (d) A → 4, B → 3, C → 2, D → 1

25. (a) $\tau_1 = NBIA\cos\theta$

$$\tau_2 = NBIA\cos(90°+\theta) = NBIA\sin\theta$$

$$\Rightarrow \tau_1^2 + \tau_2^2 = (NBIA)^2 \quad (\because \cos^2\theta + \sin^2\theta = 1)$$

$$\Rightarrow B = \frac{\sqrt{\tau_1^2+\tau_2^2}}{NIA}$$

Chapter Break Thru

1. (c) Here, $B = 2\times 10^{-3}$ T

$r = 20\text{ cm} = 0.2\text{ m}$,

$e = 1.6\times 10^{-19}$ C

and $m = 9.1\times 10^{-31}$ kg

We know that, radius of circular path,

$$r = \frac{mv}{Bq}$$

$$\Rightarrow v = \frac{rBq}{m} = \frac{rBe}{m} \quad [\because q = e]$$

$$v = \frac{0.2\times 2\times 10^{-3}\times 1.6\times 10^{-19}}{9.1\times 10^{-31}} = 7\times 10^7\text{ m/s}$$

2. (b) As magnetic force is perpendicular to velocity

$\Rightarrow \mathbf{F}\cdot\mathbf{v} = 0 \Rightarrow \mathbf{F}\cdot\mathbf{x} = 0$

or work done by force is zero.

Hence, no gain in KE occurs due to acceleration (rotation) produced by magnetic field.

3. (a) Magnetic field at point P due to a straight current carrying wire is given by

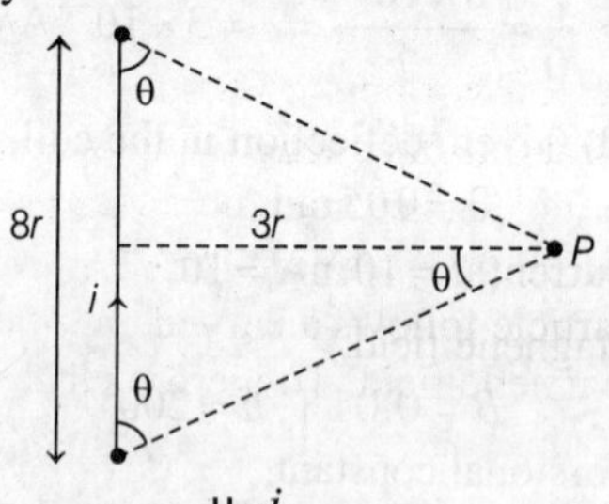

$$B_p = \frac{\mu_0 i}{4\pi d}(\cos\theta_1 + \cos\theta_2)$$

where, $d = 3r$, $\theta_1 = \theta_2 = \theta$

$$\therefore\ B_p = \frac{\mu_0 i}{6\pi r}\cos\theta$$

From the figure,

$$\cos\theta = \frac{4}{5}$$

$$\therefore\ B_p = \frac{2\mu_0 i}{15\pi r}$$

4. (c) We know that, radius of a charged particle in magnetic field is

$$r = \frac{mv}{Bq} = \frac{\sqrt{2mK}}{Bq}$$

where, K is kinetic energy.

Since, $B = 2$ T is same in both cases.

Hence, $r \propto \sqrt{\frac{mk}{q}}$

$$\therefore\ \frac{r_p}{r_d} = \sqrt{\frac{m_p}{m_d}\times\frac{K_p}{K_d}\times\frac{q_d}{q_p}}$$

$$\Rightarrow \frac{2}{1} = \sqrt{\frac{m_p}{2m_p}\times\frac{K_p}{K_d}\times\frac{q_p}{q_p}}$$

$$\Rightarrow 2 = \sqrt{\frac{K_p}{2K_d}}$$

$$\Rightarrow 8K_d = K_p$$

$$\Rightarrow K_p = 8K_d = 8\times 100 = 800\text{ keV}$$

5. (d) The effective magnetic field at O,

$$B = B_{DE} + B_{FC} = \frac{\mu_0}{4\pi}\frac{I}{5r}\times\frac{\pi}{2} + \frac{\mu_0}{4\pi}\frac{I}{2r}\times\left(\frac{3\pi}{2}\right)$$

$$= \frac{\mu_0 I}{8r}\left[\frac{1}{5} + \frac{3}{2}\right]$$

$$= \frac{17\mu_0 I}{80r}, \text{ acting downwards}$$

6. (c) When a charged particle moves perpendicular to uniform magnetic field, according to Fleming's left hand rule, magnetic force on charged particle acts perpendicular to its direction of motion. Hence, charged particle follows a curved path in magnetic field. To increase the range of ammeter, smaller value of shunt is used.

7. (a)

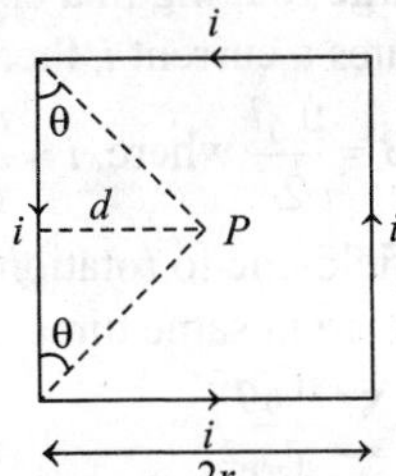

Magnetic field at point P due to one side of square is given by

$$B_P = \frac{\mu_0 i}{4\pi d}(\cos\theta + \cos\theta)$$

(Here, $\theta = 45°$ from geometry)

$$= \frac{\mu_0 i}{4\pi r}.2\left(\frac{1}{\sqrt{2}}\right) \quad (\because d = r)$$

$$\Rightarrow \quad = \frac{\mu_0 i}{2\sqrt{2}\pi r}$$

Magnetic field at point P due to square box,

$$B_P = 4B = 4 \times \frac{\mu_0 i}{2\sqrt{2}\pi r} = \frac{\sqrt{2}\mu_0 i}{\pi r}$$

8. (b) The given situation is shown below.

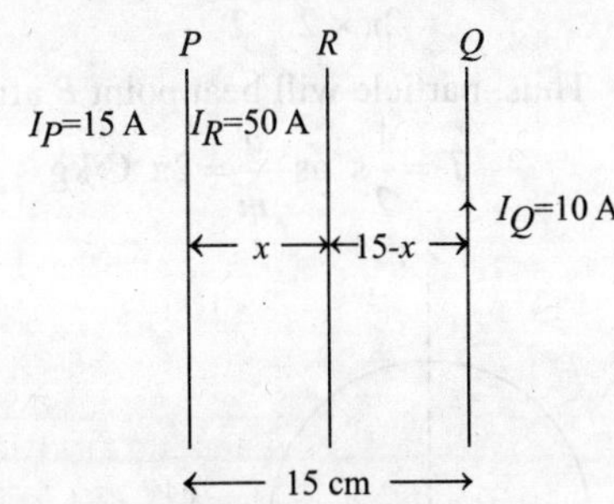

Since, wire R is placed such that it experiences no force, $\frac{F_{PR}}{l} = \frac{F_{RQ}}{l}$

$$\Rightarrow \quad \frac{\mu_0 I_P I_R}{2\pi x} = \frac{\mu_0 I_R I_Q}{2\pi(15-x)}$$

$$\frac{I_P}{x} = \frac{I_Q}{15-x}$$

$$\frac{15}{x} = \frac{10}{15-x}$$

$$225 - 15x = 10x$$

$$25x = 225$$

$$x = 9\,\text{cm}$$

9. (b) Two parallel current carrying conductors having currents in same direction attract each other, while those having currents in opposite direction repel each other.

10. (a)

A. Since $\mathbf{E} = 0$ and $\mathbf{B} \neq 0$, the magnetic force will act on it and the path will be helical (with uniform pitch) if $\mathbf{v}$ is at any angle to $\mathbf{B}$ ($\theta \neq 90°$).

B. Since $\mathbf{E} = 0$, $\mathbf{B} \neq 0$ and $\mathbf{v} \perp \mathbf{B}$, then a force called Lorentz force, $F = q\,(\mathbf{v} \times \mathbf{B})$, acts on charged particle, which provides centripetal force to it and hence, the path will be circular.

C. Since $\mathbf{E} \neq 0$, $\mathbf{B} \neq 0$, $\mathbf{E} \,||\, \mathbf{B}$, so path will be helical with non-uniform pitch as both electric and magnetic forces act on it.

D. Since $\mathbf{E} \neq 0$, $\mathbf{B} \neq 0$, $\mathbf{E} \perp \mathbf{B}$ and $\mathbf{v}$ is perpendicular to both $\mathbf{E}$ and $\mathbf{B}$, then the particle will move in a straight line due to the resultant force of magnetic and electric fields.

Hence, A → 2, B → 3, C → 4 and D → 1.

11. (c) The magnetic field at centre of a coil, $B = \frac{\mu_0 Ni}{2R}$

Given, $i = 2\,\text{A}$, $N = 1$

$$\text{So,} \quad R = \frac{\mu_0 Ni}{2B}$$

$$R = \frac{4\pi \times 10^{-7} \times 1 \times 2}{2 \times 4\pi \times 10^{-6}}$$

$$\Rightarrow \quad R = \frac{1}{10} = 0.1\,\text{m}$$

12. (a) Given, $N = 500$ turns,

$$I = 2\,\text{mA} = 2 \times 10^{-3}\,\text{A}, B = \sqrt{3}\,\text{T}$$

$$\theta = 30°, l = 2\,\text{cm} = 2 \times 10^{-2}\,\text{m}.$$

$$b = 1\,\text{cm} = 10^{-2}\,\text{m}$$

Area of the coil, $A = l \times b$

$$= 2 \times 10^{-2} \times 10^{-2} = 2 \times 10^{-4}\,\text{m}^2$$

Angle made by normal of rectangular coil with the direction of magnetic field,

$$\alpha = 90° - \theta = 90° - 30° = 60°$$

$\therefore$ Torque, $\tau = NIAB \sin\alpha$

$$= 500 \times 2 \times 10^{-3} \times 2 \times 10^{-4} \times \sqrt{3} \times \sin 60°$$

$$= 1000 \times 10^{-3} \times 2 \times 10^{-4} \times \sqrt{3} \times \frac{\sqrt{3}}{2}$$

$$= 3 \times 10^{-4}\,\text{N-m}$$

13. (b) The given ammeter can be regarded as the galvanometer

$$\therefore \quad I_g = 1\text{A}, R_g = 0.8\,\Omega$$

Total current, $I = 5\,\text{A}$

$\therefore$The required value of shunt resistance,

$$R_s = \left(\frac{I_g}{I - I_g}\right) \times R_g = \left(\frac{1}{5-1}\right) \times 0.8$$

$$= 0.2\,\Omega$$

14. (d) Sensitivity of a moving coil galvanometer is given by

$$S = \frac{\theta}{i} = \frac{NBA}{C}$$

Since, $S \propto N, S \propto B$ and $S \propto A$.

15. (b)

$-\infty$ — i — r — i — $+\infty$, P

Magnetic fields at point P due to straight wire will cancel out each other. Thus, magnetic field due to a semi-circular wire is given by

$$B_P = \frac{\mu_0 i}{4r}$$

16. (b) Acceleration produced by electric field, $\mathbf{a} = \frac{qE_0}{m}\hat{\mathbf{i}}$

After time t, velocity of the particle,

$$\mathbf{v} = \mathbf{u} + \mathbf{a}t$$

$$\Rightarrow \quad \mathbf{v} = v_0\hat{\mathbf{j}} + \left(\frac{qE_0 t}{m}\right)\hat{\mathbf{i}}$$

$$[\because \mathbf{u} = \mathbf{v} = v_0\hat{\mathbf{j}}]$$

So, speed of the particle,

$$|\mathbf{v}| = \sqrt{v_0^2 + \left(\frac{qE_0t}{m}\right)^2}$$

Now, given $|\mathbf{v}| = 2v_0$ after time t,

so $$2v_0 = \sqrt{v_0^2 + \left(\frac{qE_0t}{m}\right)^2}$$

$$\Rightarrow \quad 4v_0^2 = v_0^2 + \left(\frac{qE_0t}{m}\right)^2$$

$$\Rightarrow \quad 3v_0^2 = \left(\frac{qE_0t}{m}\right)^2$$

So, time interval, $t = \frac{\sqrt{3}\, mv_0}{qE_0}$

Here, we must note that no change in magnitude of velocity is caused by a perpendicular magnetic field. So, we are not taking effect of magnetic field while calculating change in speed.

17. (b) $\tau = n\ |M|\,|B|\sin\theta$

Here, n is number of turns in the coil.

$$|M| = I\pi r^2 = 5 \times \pi(0.1)^2$$

$$|B| = \sqrt{(-1)^2 + (1)^2} = \sqrt{2}\ \text{T}$$

$$\tau = (100)\{5\pi(0.1)^2\}\sqrt{2} \times \sin 45^\circ$$

$= 5\pi$, along negative Y-axis.

18. (b) Applying Fleming's rule, we find that upward force F is of magnitude IlB. For mid-air suspension, this must be balanced by the force due to gravity.

$$\therefore \quad mg = i\,lB$$

$$\Rightarrow \quad B = \frac{mg}{i\,l}$$

Given, $m = 200\ \text{g} = 0.2\ \text{kg}$, $g = 9.8\ \text{m/s}^2$, $I = 2\ \text{A}, l = 1.5\ \text{m}$

we have,

$$B = \frac{0.2 \times 9.8}{2 \times 1.5} = 0.65\ \text{T}$$

19. (b) The charge will not experience any force ,if $|\mathbf{F}_e| = |\mathbf{F}_m|$. Hence, the correct option is (b).

20. (d) According to Fleming's left hand rule, the direction of force is towards south.

21. (b) Magnetic field, $B = \frac{\mu_0 I}{2\pi r}$

Given, $\mu_0 = 4\pi \times 10^{-7}\ \text{N/A}^2$, $r = 8\ \text{cm} = 8 \times 10^{-2}\ \text{m}, I = 12\ \text{A}$

$$B = \frac{4\pi \times 10^{-7}}{2\pi} \times \frac{12}{8 \times 10^{-2}}$$

$$\Rightarrow B = 3 \times 10^{-5}\ \text{Wb/m}^2$$

22. (c) $r = \frac{\sqrt{2mk}}{qB} \Rightarrow r \propto \frac{\sqrt{m}}{q}$

Take ratio of radius.

$$\Rightarrow \quad \frac{r_p}{r_\alpha} = \frac{\sqrt{m_p}}{\sqrt{m_\alpha}} \cdot \frac{q_\alpha}{q_p} = \frac{\sqrt{m}}{\sqrt{4m}} \cdot \frac{2e}{e} = 1$$

23. (d)

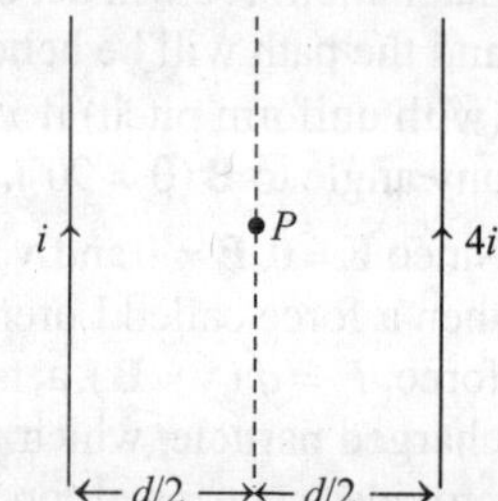

According to right hand thumb rule, magnetic field at P is perpendicular to paper inwards due to both the wires. Charged particle is also projected in the same direction. So, force on charged particle is zero.

As, $\mathbf{v} \parallel \mathbf{B}$ and $\mathbf{F}_m = q\ (\mathbf{v} \times \mathbf{B})$

$= qvB\sin\theta = qvB\sin 0 = 0$

24. (a) $F = \frac{\mu_0}{2\pi} \times \frac{2I_1I_2}{a}$

$$= 10^{-7} \times \frac{2 \times 20 \times 20}{0.2} = 2 \times 10^{-4}\ \text{N}$$

Direction of current is same, so force is attractive.

25. (b) Current enclosed by an Amperial loop of radius $r \le R$

$$I_{\text{in}} = \frac{i}{\pi R^2}\pi r^2 = \frac{ir^2}{R^2}$$

For $r < R$, $\oint \mathbf{B} \cdot d\mathbf{l} = \mu_0 I_{\text{in}} = \frac{\mu_0 ir^2}{R^2}$

$\Rightarrow$ Parabolic

For $r > R$, $\oint \mathbf{B} \cdot d\mathbf{l} = \mu_0 I_{in} = \mu_0 I$

$\Rightarrow$ Constant

26. (a) $qvB = \frac{mv^2}{r}$

$$\Rightarrow \quad r = \frac{mv}{qB}$$

$$r' = \frac{m \times 2v}{q \times B} = 2r$$

27. (a) Since, the rod is a rigid body, every point has same angular velocity, $\omega = 1\ \text{rad/s}$.

For points at a distance of 1 m, $v_1 = 2\ \text{m/s}$

For points at a distance of 2 m, $v_2 = 4\ \text{m/s}$

If a charge rotating in a circle constitutes a current i, then

$$B = \frac{\mu_0 i}{2r} \text{ where, } i = \frac{q}{t} = \frac{qv}{2\pi r}$$

Since, field due to rotation of all charges are in same direction.

$$B = \sum \frac{\mu_0 qv}{4\pi r^2}$$

$$B = \frac{\mu_0 q}{4\pi}\left(\frac{2}{(1)^2} + \frac{2}{(1)^2} + \frac{4}{(2)^2} + \frac{4}{(2)^2} + \frac{6}{(3)^2} + \frac{6}{(3)^2}\right)$$

$$= \frac{\mu_0 q}{4\pi}\left(2 + 2 + 1 + 1 + \frac{2}{3} + \frac{2}{3}\right)$$

$$\Rightarrow B = \frac{11\mu_0 q}{6\pi}$$

28. (d) $\mathbf{F} = q(v\hat{\mathbf{i}}) \times B(-\hat{\mathbf{i}}) = 0$

Because, B as well as v are along X-axis.

29. (b) Time period, $T = \frac{2\pi m}{qB}$

$$T = \frac{2\pi}{2\pi \times 2} = \frac{1}{2}\ \text{s}$$

Thus, particle will beat point P after,

$$T = \frac{1}{2}\ \text{s as } \frac{q}{m} = 2\pi\ \text{C/kg}$$

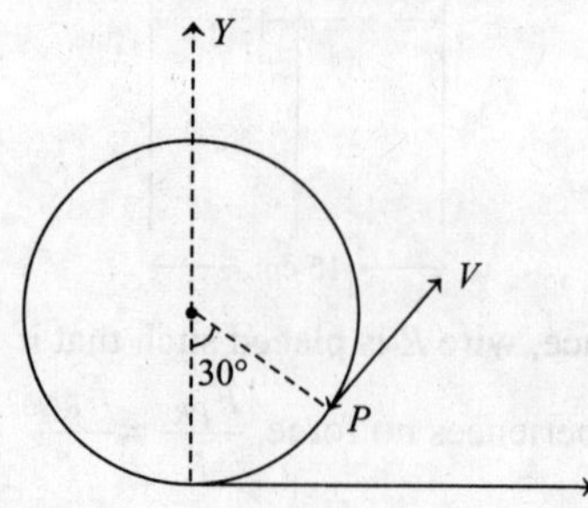

$$\mathbf{v} = 20[\cos 60\hat{\mathbf{i}} + \sin 60\hat{\mathbf{j}}]$$

$$\mathbf{v} = 20\left[\frac{1}{2}\hat{\mathbf{i}} + \frac{\sqrt{3}}{2}\hat{\mathbf{j}}\right]$$

$$= 10[\hat{\mathbf{i}} + \sqrt{3}\hat{\mathbf{j}}] \text{ m/s}$$

30. (d) Distance covered in time $t = v/50$ (given)

$\because x = vt = v \times 0.02 = v/50$

Thus, acceleration of particle = 0

So, $F_{\text{net}} = 0$

$$F_e = F_m$$

$$qE = qvB$$

$$v = \frac{E}{B}$$

31. (c)

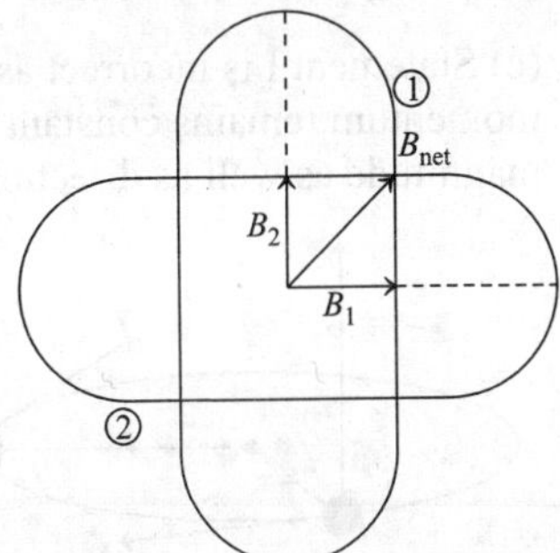

$$B_1 = B_2 = B = \frac{\mu_0}{4\pi} \times \frac{2\pi i}{r}$$

$$B_{\text{net}} = \sqrt{B_1^2 + B_2^2}$$

$$= \sqrt{B^2 + B^2} = \sqrt{2}B$$

$$\Rightarrow \quad \frac{B_{\text{net}}}{B_1} = \frac{\sqrt{2}}{1}$$

32. (d) To convert a galvanometer into voltmeter, high resistance should be connected in series with it. Let R be the resistance connected in series with the galvanometer.

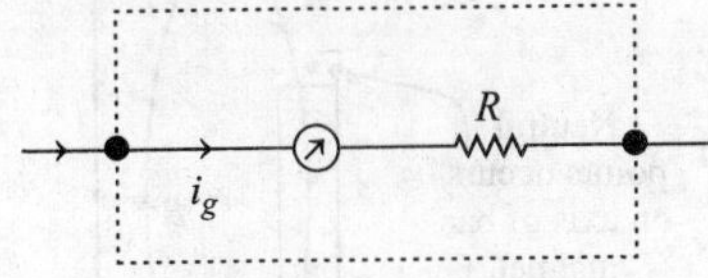

$$i_g = \frac{V}{G+R} \text{ or } R = \frac{V}{i_g} - G$$

Given, $G = 50\,\Omega$

$i_g = 50 \times 4 \times 10^{-4} = 2 \times 10^{-2}$ A

$V = 25$ V

$$\therefore \quad R = \frac{25}{2 \times 10^{-2}} - 50$$

$$= 1250 - 50 = 1200\,\Omega$$

33. (b) If beam of electrons passes undeflected, then force due to electric field should be balanced with force due to magnetic fields, i.e. $F_e = F_m$. But if electric field becomes zero, then only force due to magnetic field exists. Under this force, the charge moves along a circle.

34. (d) A small resistance is connected in parallel to the coil of the galvanometer to convert it into ammeter.

$$I_g G_I = (I - I_g)S$$

$$S = \frac{I_g G_I}{I - I_g} = \frac{2}{10-2} \times 80$$

$$= 20\,\Omega$$

35. (c) The time period of circular motion of the charged particle is given by

$$T = \frac{2\pi r}{v} = \frac{2\pi}{v} \times \frac{mv}{Bq}$$

or $\quad T = \dfrac{2\pi m}{Bq}$

Hence, time period of rotation of the charged particle in uniform magnetic field is independent of both v and R.

36. (a) Since, electron is moving parallel to the magnetic field, hence magnetic force on it. $F_m = 0$

$-e$ ⟶ v, **E** ⟶, $F = eE$ ⟵

So, the only force which is acting on electron in the direction is electric force which reduces its speed.

37. (c) $F = \dfrac{\mu_0 i_1 i_2}{2\pi d}$ = force per unit length

F_1 (due to wire A) ⟶, F_2 (due to wire C) ↓

$$F_1 = \frac{(\mu_0 i)i}{2\pi d} = \frac{\mu_0 i^2}{2\pi d} = F_2$$

$$F_{\text{net}} = \sqrt{F_1^2 + F_2^2} = \frac{\mu_0 i^2}{\sqrt{2}\pi d}$$

38. (a) According to question,

i_g — G — R_1 — 1V

From Ohm's law, $V = IR$

$$\therefore \quad i_g(R_1 + G) = 1\text{V} \quad \ldots\text{(i)}$$

Let x be the required resistance.

Now, $i_g(R_1 + G + x) = 2$ V

i_g — R_1+G — x — 2V

Using Eq. (i) in above equation, we get

$$\frac{1}{(R_1+G)}(R_1 + G + x) = 2$$

$$R_1 + x + G = 2(R_1 + G)$$

$$x = R_1 + G$$

39. (c) Using Right hand palm rule, the magnetic field will be along OY.

40. (b) $\mathbf{B}_A = \dfrac{\mu_0 I}{2R}$, vertically upward

$\mathbf{B}_B = \dfrac{\mu_0\sqrt{3}I}{2R}$, along horizontal

Resultant field at the centre is given by

$$B = \sqrt{B_A^2 + B_B^2}$$

$$= \sqrt{\left(\frac{\mu_0 I}{2R}\right)^2 + \left(\frac{\mu_0\sqrt{3}I}{2R}\right)^2}$$

$$= \frac{\mu_0 I}{2R}\sqrt{(1+3)}$$

$$= \frac{\mu_0 I}{2R} \times 2 = \frac{\mu_0 I}{R}$$

41. (b) Velocity of particle,

$$v = \frac{E}{B} = \frac{\sigma}{\varepsilon_0 B}$$

$$\left(\because E = \frac{\sigma}{\varepsilon_0} \text{ for parallel plate capacitor}\right)$$

Time taken by electron to pass the region,

$$t = \frac{l}{v} = \frac{\varepsilon_0 l B}{\sigma}$$

42. (a) The force between two parallel current carrying conductor is

$$F = \frac{\mu_0}{4\pi}\frac{I_1 I_2}{d} \times l$$

When current in each conductors are doubled, then force will be

$$F' = \frac{\mu_0}{2\pi}\frac{2I_1 \times 2I_2}{d} \times l$$

$$= 4\frac{\mu_0}{2\pi}\frac{I_1 I_2}{d} \times l = 4F$$

43. (a) As we know, current sensitivity

$$S_i = \frac{NBA}{k} \quad ...(i)$$

and voltage sensitivity,

$$S_V = \frac{NBA}{kR} \quad ...(ii)$$

From Eqs. (i) and (ii), we get

$$\frac{S_i}{S_V} = R$$

$$\Rightarrow \quad \frac{S_i}{G} = S_V \ (\because R = G)$$

44. (a) The torque acting on the coil

$$|\tau| = |\mathbf{m} \times \mathbf{B}| = mB \sin\theta$$

Here, the circular coil is placed normal to the direction of magnetic field, then the angle between the direction of magnetic moment **m** and magnetic field **B** is zero, so

$$\tau = mB\sin\theta = mB\sin 0° = 0$$

45. (d) Since, electron is moving uniformly along magnetic field inside a current carrying solenoid.

i.e. $\theta = 0°$

Then, using Lorentz force formula,

$$F_{net} = qvB\sin\theta = 0$$

Hence, electron will move in direction of its initial velocity along the axis of the solenoid without changing its motion and speed.

46. (d)

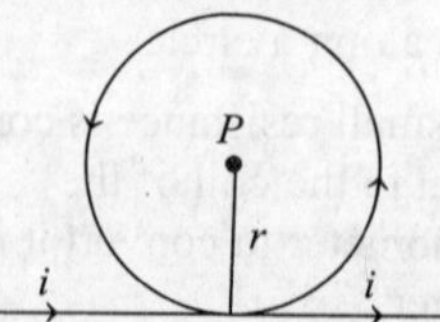

Magnetic field due to a straight wire,

$$B_s = \frac{\mu_0 i}{2\pi r}$$

Magnetic field due to circular wire,

$$B_c = \frac{\mu_0 i}{2r}$$

Magnetic field at point P is given as

$$B_P = B_s + B_c$$

$$= \frac{\mu_0 i}{2\pi r} + \frac{\mu_0 i}{2r}$$

$$= \frac{\mu_0 i}{2\pi r}(1+\pi).$$

47. (a) As, $R = \frac{mv}{qB}$, since $R \propto v$.

Hence, radius becomes double.

$T = \frac{2\pi m}{qB}$, since T is independent of v.

Hence, T remains same.

48. (d) No current will flow through the section BC, as the potentials are same.

Magnetic field to the sections AB and AC are equal and opposite. Hence, they cancel out. So, the magnetic field at O is zero.

49. (c) Effective length of wire from point A to B is $3a$. The net force acting on the wire of length $3a$ is

$$\mathbf{F} = I(3a\hat{\mathbf{i}} \times B_0) = 3aB_0 I\,\hat{\mathbf{k}}$$

50. (c) Statement I is incorrect as angular momentum remains constant in magnitude as well as direction.

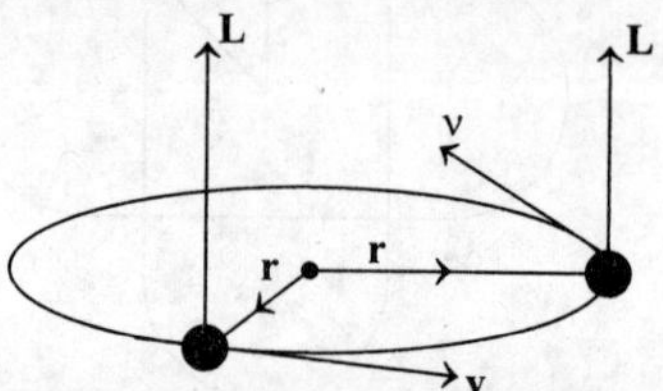

Statement II is correct as angular momentum is a vector quantity,

$$\mathbf{L} = \mathbf{r} \times \mathbf{p}$$

Ch-06 Magnetism and Matter

Topical Follow Thru

Test-1

1. (d) Magnetic moment is given by

$$M = \frac{\tau}{B\sin\theta} = \frac{0.04}{2\sin 30°}$$

$$\Rightarrow \quad M = \frac{0.04}{2 \times \frac{1}{2}}$$

$$M = 0.04\ \text{JT}^{-1}$$

2. (a) Magnetic field due to a bar magnet at a distance r from the centre of magnet on axial position is

$$B = \frac{\mu_0}{4\pi}\cdot\frac{2M}{r^3}$$

Now, $\frac{B_1}{B_2} = \left(\frac{r_2}{r_1}\right)^3$

$$= \left(\frac{12}{6}\right)^3 = 8$$

3. (b) Work done in rotating the bar magnet from angular position 0° to 30°,

$$W = -MB(\cos 30° - \cos 0°)$$

$$= -MB\left(\frac{\sqrt{3}}{2} - 1\right)$$

$$= \frac{4 \times 10^4 \times 12 \times 10^{-4} \times 0.27}{2}$$

$$= 6.48\ \text{J}$$

4. (a)

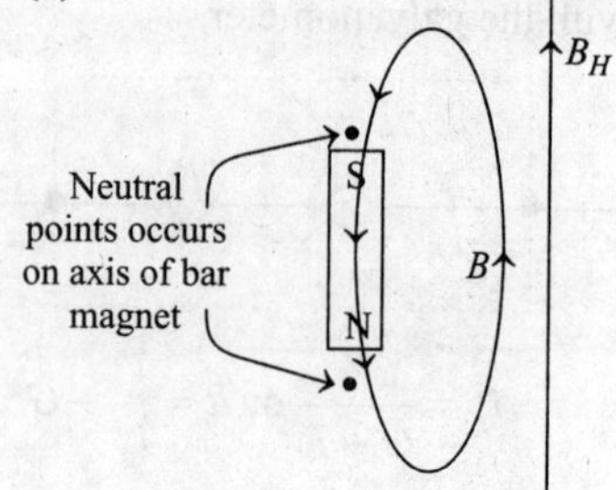

Neutral points occurs on axis of bar magnet.

5. (b) When we break magnet into two pieces, its poles do not get separated as it again becomes a magnet.

Also, when magnet is broken into two equal pieces, its magnetic moment gets reduced to half.

6. (a) Magnetic dipole moment is from S to N,

$$m_{\text{net}} = \sqrt{m^2 + m^2 + 2m^2 \cos\theta}$$

m_{net} will be minimum, if $\cos\theta$ is minimum. $\cos\theta$ will be minimum when θ will be maximum.

Hence, at $\theta = 90°$, m_{net} will be minimum.

7. (a) Work done to rotate a bar magnet from 0° to 30° is given as

$$\Rightarrow \quad W = MB(\cos 0° - \cos 30°)$$

$$\Rightarrow \quad W = MB\left(1 - \frac{\sqrt{3}}{2}\right)$$

$$\Rightarrow \quad W = MB\left(\frac{2-\sqrt{3}}{2}\right)$$

$$\Rightarrow \quad MB = \frac{2W}{(2-\sqrt{3})} \quad \text{...(i)}$$

Torque on a magnet in this position is given by

$$\tau = \mathbf{M} \times \mathbf{B} = MB \sin\theta$$

$$= \frac{2W}{(2-\sqrt{3})} \times \sin 30° \text{ [from Eq. (i)]}$$

$$= \frac{2W}{(2-\sqrt{3})} \times \frac{1}{2} = \frac{W}{(2-\sqrt{3})}$$

8. (d) $T = 2\pi\sqrt{\dfrac{I}{MB}}$

$I \rightarrow 5$ times of initial value

$M \rightarrow \dfrac{1}{5}$ time of initial value

$$T' = 2\pi\sqrt{\frac{5I_0}{\frac{1}{2}M_0 B}}$$

$$T' = 5T_0$$

9. (b) As, the time period of a bar magnet of magnetic moment M in a magnetic field B is given by

$$T = 2\pi\sqrt{\frac{I}{MB}}$$

or $T \propto \dfrac{1}{\sqrt{B}}$

Therefore, $\dfrac{T_2}{T_1} = \sqrt{\dfrac{B_1}{B_2}}$

Now, $\dfrac{T_2}{13} = \sqrt{\dfrac{1}{16}}$

$$T_2 = \frac{13}{4}$$

$$T_2 = 3.25 \text{ s}$$

10. (d) The poles of a magnet can never be separated because the magnetic field of a magnet forms closed loops, connecting the north and south poles. Breaking a magnet creates two smaller magnets with their own closed magnetic field. Opposite poles attract, and like poles repel, each other.

11. (a) Here, $2l = 12 \text{ cm} = 0.12$ m,

$m = 20$ A-m, $d = 10 \text{ cm} = 0.1$ m

On axial line, $B = \dfrac{\mu_0}{4\pi}\dfrac{2Md}{(d^2 - l^2)^2}$

$$= \frac{\mu_0}{4\pi}\frac{2m(2l)d}{(d^2 - l^2)^2}$$

$$= 10^{-7} \times \frac{2(20)(0.12) \times 0.1}{[(0.1)^2 - (0.06)^2]^2}$$

$$= 1.17 \times 10^{-3} \text{ T}$$

12. (d) $\theta_1 = 0°$ as the dipole is aligned with B.

A. When the bar magnet is displaced to perpendicular position, then $\theta_2 = 90°$.

$W = MB(\cos\theta_1 - \cos\theta_2)$, we get

$$W = 1.5 \times 0.22 (\cos 0° - \cos 90°)$$

$$= 0.33 \text{ J}$$

B. When the magnet is displaced, so as to align M opposite to B, then

$$\theta_2 = 180°$$

$$W = MB(\cos\theta_1 - \cos\theta_2)$$

$$= 1.5 \times 0.22 (\cos 0° - \cos 180°)$$

$$= 0.66 \text{ J}$$

C. Let τ_1 be the torque on the magnet when it is aligned perpendicular to B, then using the relation

$\tau = MB\sin\theta$, we get

$$\tau_1 = MB\sin\theta_1$$

$$= 1.5 \times 0.22 \times \sin 30°$$

$$= 0.165 \text{ N-m} \qquad (\because \theta_1 = 30°)$$

D. Let τ_2 be the torque on the magnet when the magnetic moment opposite to B, then

$$\theta_2 = 180°$$

$$\tau_2 = MB\sin\theta_2$$

$$= 1.5 \times 0.22 \times \sin 180° = 0$$

Hence, A-(IV), B-(III), C-(I), D-(II).

13. (b) Torque on a bar magnet,

$$\tau = MB\sin\theta$$

$$0.018 = M \times 0.06 \times \sin 30°$$

$$\Rightarrow M = 0.6 \text{ A-m}^2$$

Now, work done to rotate bar magnet,

$$W = MB[\cos\theta_1 - \cos\theta_2]$$

Here, $\theta_1 = 0°$ (for stable equilibrium position)

and $\theta_2 = 180°$ (for unstable equilibrium position).

So, $W = 0.6 \times 0.06[\cos(0°) - \cos(180°)]$

$$= 0.036[(1) - (-1)] = 0.036(2)$$

$$= 0.072 = 7.2 \times 10^{-2} \text{ J}$$

14. (b) According to the question, the situation can be drawn as

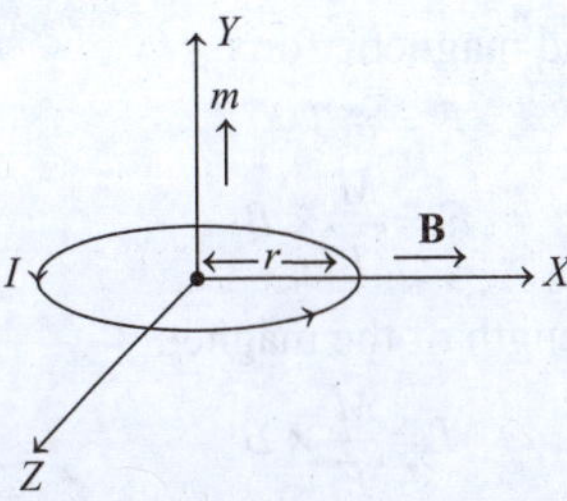

Let the current I is flowing in anti-clockwise direction, then the magnetic moment of the coil is $M = NIA$.

where, N = number of turns in coil and A = area of each coil $= \pi r^2$.

Its direction is perpendicular to the area of coil and is along Y-axis.

Then, torque on the current coil is

$$\tau = \mathbf{M} \times \mathbf{B} = mB\sin 90°$$

$$= NIAB = NI\pi r^2 B \text{ (N-m)}$$

15. (b)

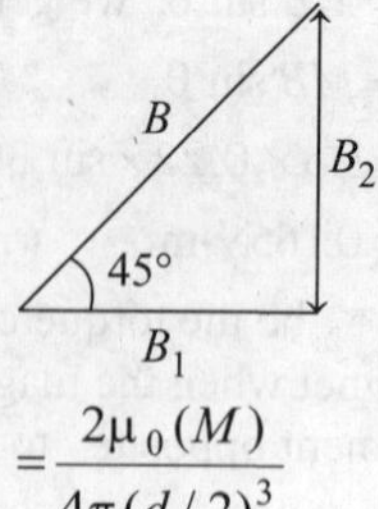

$$B_1 = \frac{2\mu_0 (M)}{4\pi (d/2)^3}$$

$$B_2 = \frac{\mu_0 (2M)}{4\pi (d/2)^3}$$

$$B_1 = B_2$$

Resultant magnetic field (B_{net}) will be 45° with the horizontal.

As **v** is along **B**, thus $\mathbf{F}_{net} = 0$

16. (c) As, magnetic field on axial position,

$$B_{equatorial} = 9 = \frac{2M}{x^3} \quad \ldots(i)$$

and magnetic field on equatorial position

$$B_{equatoriall} = \frac{M}{\left(\frac{x}{2}\right)^3} = \frac{8M}{x^3} \quad \ldots(ii)$$

On comparing Eqs. (i) and (ii), we get

$$B_{equatorial} = 36 \text{ G}$$

17. (d) As, magnetic moment of a bar magnet $M = mL$

and magnetic force,

$$F = mB$$

$$\Rightarrow \quad F = \frac{M}{L} \times B$$

Length of the magnet,

$$L = \frac{M}{F} \times B$$

$$= \frac{3 \text{ A-m}^2}{6 \times 10^{-4} \text{ N}} \times 2 \times 10^{-5} \text{ T}$$

$$= 0.1 \text{ m}$$

18. (c) $\tau = \mathbf{M} \times \mathbf{B}$

$$= 40\hat{\mathbf{i}} \times (0.6\hat{\mathbf{i}} + 0.3\hat{\mathbf{j}})$$

$$= 40 \times 0.3 (\hat{\mathbf{i}} \times \hat{\mathbf{j}})$$

$$= 12 \hat{\mathbf{k}} \text{ N-m}$$

19. (d) Magnetic field at a point x on a axial plane,

$$B_{axial} = \frac{\mu_0}{4\pi} \times \frac{2M}{x^3} \quad \ldots(i)$$

Magnetic field at an equatorial plane,

$$B_{equatorial} = \frac{\mu_0}{4\pi} \times \frac{M}{y^3} \quad \ldots(ii)$$

Given, $B_{axial} = B_{equatorial}$ ...(iii)

On comparing Eqs. (i), (ii) and (iii), we get

$$\frac{\mu_0}{4\pi} \times \frac{M}{y^3} = \frac{\mu_0}{4\pi} \times \frac{2M}{x^3}$$

or $\quad \frac{x}{y} = (2)^{1/3}$

20. (c) Net magnetic moment of the couple of magnets is

$\sqrt{M^2 + M^2} = M\sqrt{2}$ at 45° (mid-way). So, point P lies on axial line of net magnetic moment. Therefore,

$$B = \frac{\mu_0}{4\pi} \frac{2\sqrt{2}\, M}{d^3}$$

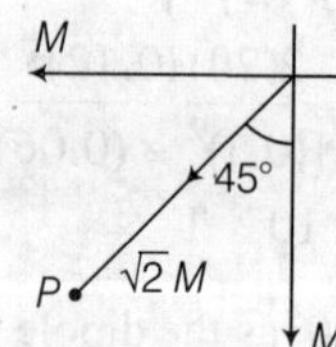

21. (a) In given cases,

(i) $U = -MB \cos 90° = 0$ $\quad [\because \cos 90° = 0]$

(ii) $U = -MB \cos 180° = mB$ $\quad [\because \cos 180° = -1]$

(iii) $U = -MB \cos (360° - \theta)$

$= -MB \cos \theta$

$[\because \cos (360° - \theta) = +\cos \theta]$

(iv) $U = -MB \cos (90° + \theta)$

$= MB \sin \theta$

$[\because \cos (90° + \theta) = -\sin \theta]$

So, correct order of potential energy in increasing order is (iii) < (i) < (iv) < (ii).

22. (c) The magnetic induction at point D due to magnet at C [axial point],

$$B_1 = \frac{\mu_0}{4\pi} \cdot \frac{2M_1}{d^3}$$

$$= \frac{10^{-7} \times 2 \times 8.0}{(2.0)^3}$$

$= 2 \times 10^{-7}$ T along D to C ...(i)

Magnetic induction at point D due to magnet at E [equatorial point],

$$B_2 = \frac{\mu_0}{4\pi} \cdot \frac{M_2}{d^3} = \frac{10^{-7} \times 8.0}{(2.0)^3}$$

$= 1 \times 10^{-7}$ T along C to D ...(ii)

Now, total magnetic induction at point D,

$$B = B_1 - B_2$$

From Eqs. (i) and (ii), we get

$$B = 2 \times 10^{-7} - (1 \times 10^{-7})$$

$$= 1 \times 10^{-7} \text{ T}$$

$$= 0.1 \mu\text{T}$$

23. (a) Magnetic field due to a long solenoid on its axis,

$$B = \mu_0 n I_2 \quad \ldots(i)$$

Magnetic moment of a circular coil,

$$M = NAI_1 \quad \ldots(ii)$$

Torque, $\tau = \mathbf{M} \times \mathbf{B}$

$\tau = MB \sin \theta = MB$

$[\because \theta = 90° \text{ (Given)}]$

$\tau = (NAI_1)(\mu_0 n I_2)$

[Using Eqs. (i) and (ii)]

$$\Rightarrow \quad I_2 = \frac{\tau}{NAI_1 \mu_0 n}$$

$$= \frac{1.5 \times 10^{-8}}{(10)(1 \times 10^{-6})\left(\frac{21}{44}\right)(4\pi \times 10^{-7})(10^3)}$$

$$= 2.5 \text{ A}$$

24. (b) Magnetic moment, $M = NIA$

$$= 16 \times 0.75 \times \pi \times (0.1)^2$$

$$= 0.377 \text{ JT}^{-1}$$

Frequency of oscillation of the coil,

$$f = \frac{1}{2\pi} \sqrt{\frac{M \times B}{I}}$$

Squaring on both the sides, we get

$$f^2 = \frac{1}{4\pi^2} \cdot \frac{MB}{I}$$

$$\Rightarrow \quad I = \frac{MB}{4\pi^2 f^2}$$

$$= \frac{0.377 \times 5 \times 10^{-2}}{4 \times 3.14 \times 3.14 \times 2 \times 2}$$

$$\Rightarrow \quad I = 1.2 \times 10^{-4} \text{ kg-m}^2$$

25. (a) Here, both laws of magnetism and electrostatic are different but in isolated magnetic poles are not known to exist by Gauss's law of magnetism.

Test-2

1. (d) Magnetic induction,

$$B = \frac{\phi_B}{A} = \frac{1.4 \times 10^{-4} \text{ Wb}}{2 \times 10^{-4} \text{ m}^2}$$

$$\Rightarrow \quad B = 0.7 \text{ Wb-m}^{-2}$$

Now, permeability $(\mu) = \frac{B}{H}$

$$\mu = \frac{0.7}{100}$$

$$\mu = 0.007 \text{ TmA}^{-1}$$

2. (c) We know that

$$\text{Volume, } V = \frac{\text{Mass}}{\text{Density}} = \frac{66 \times 10^{-3}}{1000}$$

$$= 66 \times 10^{-6} \text{ m}^3$$

Intensity of Magnetisation,

$$I = \frac{M}{V} = \frac{1.1}{66 \times 10^{-6}}$$

$$I = 1.66 \times 10^4 \text{ Am}^{-1}$$

3. (b) Both Statement I and Statement II are incorrect.

The permeability of a ferromagnetic material is not independent of magnetic field, $\mathbf{B} = K_m \mathbf{B}_0$. where, B_0 is applied field. The total magnetic field **B** inside a ferromagnetic material may be 10^3 or 10^4 times the applied fieldB_0.

The permeability K_m of a ferromagnetic material is not constant, neither the field **B** nor the magnetisation **M**. **M** increases linearly with **B** even at small value of B_0.

4. (c) From $B = \mu_0(H + I)$

$$\Rightarrow \quad B = \mu_0 H\left(1 + \frac{I}{H}\right)$$

$$\Rightarrow \quad B = \mu_0 H(1+\chi) = B_0(1+\chi)$$

Since, $\quad B = B_0(1+\chi)$

$$B - B_0 = B_0 \chi$$

$$\chi = \frac{B - B_0}{B_0}$$

Multiply by 100 on both sides in above expression,

$$100\chi = \frac{B - B_0}{B_0} \times 100$$

$$\frac{B - B_0}{B_0} \times 100 = 100 \times 5.1 \times 10^{-5}$$

$$= 5.1 \times 10^{-3} \%$$

5. (b) Average kinetic energy of molecules at temperature T,

$$\text{KE} = \frac{3}{2} KT$$

Magnetic energy $= 2MB$

Thus according to question,

$$\frac{\text{Thermal energy}}{\text{Magnetic energy}} = \frac{\frac{3}{2}KT}{2MB} = \frac{3KT}{4MB}$$

$$= \frac{3}{4} \times \frac{1.38 \times 10^{-23} \times 150}{10^{-24} \times 5} = 310.5$$

6. (c) According to Curie's law,

$$\chi = \frac{C}{T}$$

$$\therefore \quad C = \chi T \quad \text{...(i)}$$

From the given graph,

$$\frac{1}{T} = 5.0 \times 10^{-3} \text{ K}^{-1}$$

$$T = 200 \text{ K}$$

Then, $C = 0.30 \times 200$ (from Eq. (i))

$$C = 60 \text{ K}$$

7. (a) Given, side of cube

$$= 1 \text{ cm} = 10^{-2} \text{ m}$$

$\therefore$ Volume, $V = 10^{-6} \text{ m}^3$

Dipole moment,

$$M = 20 \times 10^{-6} \text{ J/T}$$

Applied magnetic intensity,

$$H = 60 \times 10^3 \text{ A/m}$$

Intensity of magnetisation,

$$I = \frac{M}{V} = \frac{20 \times 10^{-6}}{10^{-6}} = 20 \text{ A/m}$$

Now, magnetic susceptibility χ is

$$\chi = \frac{\text{Intensity of magnetisation}}{\text{Applied magnetic intensity}} = \frac{I}{H}$$

$$= \frac{20}{60 \times 10^3}$$

$$\Rightarrow \chi = \frac{1}{3} \times 10^{-3} = 3.3 \times 10^{-4}$$

8. (d) As, $\mu_r < 1$ for substance X, it must be diamagnetic and $\mu_r > 1$ for substance Y, so it is must be paramagnetic.

9. (d) Copper is a diamagnetic material, therefore its rod align itself, where magnetic field is weakest and perpendicular to the direction of magnetic field at that position.

10. (b) Because of large permeability of soft iron, magnetic lines of force prefer to pass through it. Concentration of lines in soft iron bar increases as shown in Fig. (b).

11. (c) As, the sphere is perfectly diamagnetic, it completely expels field as shown below

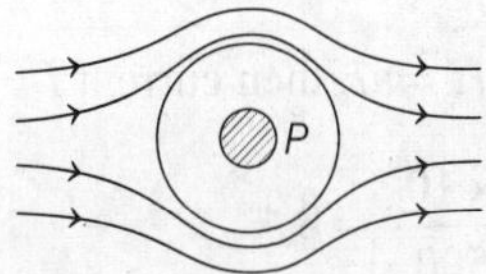

Therefore, there will be no magnetic field inside the cavity of sphere.

So, the paramagnetic sample in the spherical cavity at the centre of sphere remains uneffected by external field and field inside paramagnetic sample is zero.

12. (b) For a diamagnetic substance, I is negative and $-I \propto H$. Therefore, the variation is represented by OC or OD. As magnetisation is small, so OC is the better choice.

13. (d) For diamagnetic substances, the magnetic susceptibility is negative and it is independent of temperature.

14. (d) From Curie's law for paramagnetic substance, we have

Magnetic susceptibility, $\chi \propto \frac{1}{T}$

$\therefore \quad \frac{\chi_2}{\chi_1} = \frac{T_1}{T_2} \Rightarrow \chi_2 = \frac{\chi_1 \cdot T_1}{T_2}$

$\Rightarrow \quad \chi_2 = \frac{2.8 \times 10^{-4} \times 350}{300}$

$= 3.267 \times 10^{-4}$

15. (d) Area of hysteresis loop is proportional to the net energy absorbed per unit volume by the material, as it is taken over a complete cycle of magnetisation. For electromagnets and transformers, energy loss should be low.

i.e. Thin hysteresis curves.

Also, $|B| \to 0$ when $H = 0$ and $|H|$ should be small when $B \to 0$.

Hence, option (d) is correct.

16. (c) Here, coercivity of a small bar magnet is 4×10^3 Am^{-1}.

$n = 500, l = 1$ m

So, $n = \frac{500}{1} = 500$ turns/m

As, $H = nI$, then current $I = \frac{H}{n}$

$= \frac{4 \times 10^3}{500} = 8$ A

17. (b) As magnetic susceptibility,

$\chi = \frac{C}{T}$

$\Rightarrow \frac{\chi}{\chi'} = \frac{T'}{T}$

$\Rightarrow T' = \left(\frac{\chi}{\chi'}\right) T = \left(\frac{1.2 \times 10^{-5}}{1.8 \times 10^{-5}}\right) 300$

$= 200$ K

18. (b) Now, volume of cubic domain,

$V = l^3 = (2.0 \times 10^{-6})^3$

$= 8.0 \times 10^{-18}$ m^3

Total dipole moment of all atoms

$M_{max} = N \times M$

$= 8 \times 10^{10} \times 5 \times 10^{-24}$

$= 40 \times 10^{-14}$

$= 4 \times 10^{-13}$ Am^2

The magnetisation of domain,

$I = \frac{M_{max}}{V}$

$= \frac{4 \times 10^{-13}}{8 \times 10^{-18}} = 5 \times 10^4$ Am^{-1}

19. (d) The volume of cubic domain is

$V = (10^{-6})^3$ m^3

$= 10^{-18}$ m^3 $= 10^{-12}$ cm^3

[$\because$ side = 1 μm]

Mass = Density × Volume

($\because$ Density = 7.9 gcm^{-3})

$= 7.9$ gcm^{-3} $\times 10^{-12}$ cm^3

$= 7.9 \times 10^{-12}$ g

It is given that Avogadro's number i.e. $N_A = (6.023 \times 10^{23})$ of iron atoms have a mass of 55 g. Hence, the number of atoms in the domain is

$N = \frac{\text{Mass} \times N_A}{\text{Molecular mass}}$

$= \frac{7.9 \times 10^{-12} \times 6.023 \times 10^{23}}{55}$

$= 8.65 \times 10^{10}$ atoms

20. (c) Magnetisation,

$I = \chi B = 10^{-5} \times 0.5$

$= 5 \times 10^{-6}$ Am^{-1}

21. (b) As, $M \propto \frac{B_0}{T}$

$\Rightarrow \quad \frac{M_2}{M_1} = \frac{\frac{B_2}{T_2}}{\frac{B_1}{T_1}} = \frac{B_2}{B_1} \cdot \frac{T_1}{T_2}$

$\Rightarrow \quad M_2 = 8 \times \left(\frac{0.2}{0.6}\right) \times \left(\frac{4}{16}\right)$

$= \frac{2}{3}$ Am^{-1}

22. (d)

A. Magnetic dipole exists but magnetic monopole does not exist.

B. Magnetic field lines at the ends of the solenoid are not straight and confined.

C. Yes, magnetic field lines inside a bar magnet are parallel.

D. For a perfectly diamagnetic material, $\chi = -1$.

23. (b) Magnetic permeability is defined as the ratio of magnitude of total magnetic field (B) inside a material to that of magnetic intensity (H).

$\mu = \frac{B}{H} = \frac{3H}{H} = 3$

24. (a)

Diamagnetic	Paramagnetic	Ferromagnetic
$-1 \le \chi < 0$	$0 < \chi < \varepsilon$	$\chi >> 1$
$0 \le \mu_r < 1$	$1 < \mu_r < 1 + \varepsilon$	$\mu_r >> 1$
$\mu < \mu_0$	$\mu > \mu_0$	$\mu >> \mu_0$

For vacuum $\mu_r = 1$, ε = small positive number

Hence, A-(II), B-(III), C-(I), D-(IV).

25. (c) As the source of current is switched ON, a magnetic field sets up in between the poles of the electromagnet. As we know that, a diamagnetic substance when placed in a magnetic field acquires a feeble magnetism opposite to the direction of magnetic field.

Also, in the presence of the field (non-uniform), these substances are attracted towards the weaker field, i.e. they move from stronger to weaker magnetic field.

Due to these reasons, the rod is repelled by the field produced to the current source. Hence, it is pushed up, out of horizontal field and gains gravitational potential energy. Hence, the current source is responsible for this work done.

Chapter Break Thru

1. (a) For paramagnetic material,

$$\chi \propto \frac{I}{T}$$

The graph between susceptibility and temperature will be hyperbola.

2. (d) Water is diamagnetic it's susceptibility is nearly independent of temperature.

3. (c) On increasing the temperature of a ferromagnetic material, its magnetisation decreases due to reduction of domain size of atoms having dipole moment in same direction. Above Curie temperature, a ferromagnetic substance becomes paramagnetic substance.

4. (b) According to the first condition,

$M = ml$

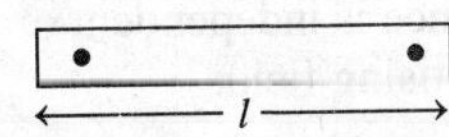

When magnet is bent into semi-circle of radius r, then $l = \pi r$

$$\Rightarrow r = \frac{l}{\pi}$$

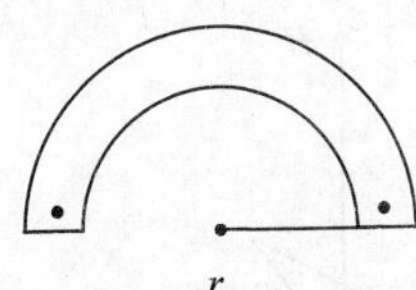

$\therefore$ Distance between the poles,

$$d = \text{diameter} = 2r = 2\frac{l}{\pi}$$

$\therefore$ Magnetic dipole moment

$$M' = m \cdot d = m\left(\frac{2l}{\pi}\right)$$

$$= \frac{2}{\pi} . ml$$

$$= \frac{2M}{\pi}$$

5. (b) Work done in rotating the magnetic dipole in uniform magnetic field B from θ_1 to θ_2 is given by

$$W = -MB(\cos\theta_2 - \cos\theta_1)$$

In case-I,

$$W_1 = -MB(\cos 90° - \cos 0°) = MB$$

$$\Rightarrow \quad W_1 = MB \quad \ldots\text{(i)}$$

In case-II,

$$W_2 = -MB(\cos 60° - \cos 0°)$$

$$= -MB\left(\frac{1}{2} - 1\right)$$

$$\Rightarrow \quad W_2 = \frac{MB}{2} \quad \ldots\text{(ii)}$$

From Eqs. (i) and (ii), we have

$$W_2 = \frac{W_1}{2}$$

$$\Rightarrow \quad W_1 = 2W_2$$

$$= nW_2 \quad \text{(given)}$$

$$\therefore \quad n = 2$$

6. (c) Area of B-H curve = Energy loss as heat per unit volume of a sample in one cycle of magnetisation and demagnetisation.

7. (d) (A)-3

The magnetic field induction (B) is directly proportional to the current flowing through the wire.

(B)-4

$$1 \text{ tesla} = 10^4 \text{ Gauss}$$

$\Rightarrow 1 \text{ Gauss} = 10^{-4} \text{ tesla} = 0.0001$ tesla

Hence, tesla is the S.I unit of magnetic field induction.

(C)-1

The S.I unit of intensity of magnetic field (H) is Am^{-1}.

(D)-2

The magnetic susceptibility $= \frac{I}{H}$ is a constant for a given substance and has no unit.

8. (b) The magnetic field lines cannot intersect each other because the lines represent the direction of magnetic field at each point. If the field lines were to intersect, it would imply that at that point, the magnetic field has two different directions, which is not physically possible. The magnetic field lines always follow a continuous path and do not cross or intersect.

9. (c) Ferromagnetic materials have large value of magnetic susceptibility, which decreases with increase in temperature.

10. (b) Magnetic permeability $(\mu) = \frac{B}{H}$

= slope of B-H curve

Slope of the graph is highest at point Q.

11. (d) Anti-ferromagnetic materials have positive value of magnetic susceptibility, which first increases with temperature and after a critical temperature starts decreasing.

12. (c) Magnetism of a magnet falls with rise of temperature and becomes practically zero above Curie temperature.

13. (a) A diamagnetic rod set itself perpendicular to the field if it is free to rotate between the poles of a magnet.

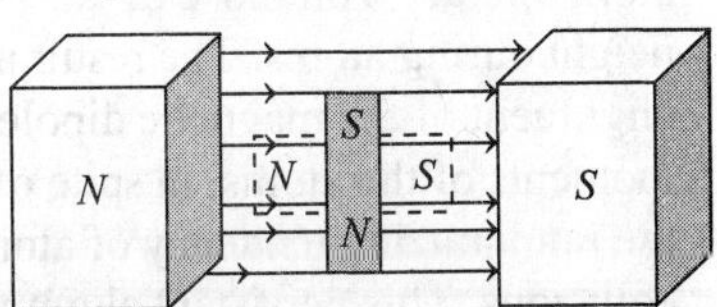

14. (b) Magnetic field at a point on axial line due to magnet (1).

$$B_1 = \frac{\mu_0}{4\pi}\frac{2M_1}{r_1^3}$$

$\therefore$ Magnetic field due to magnet (2),

$$B_2 = \frac{\mu_0}{4\pi}\frac{2M_2}{r_2^3}$$

$\therefore$ Net magnetic field at point P,

$$B = \sqrt{B_1^2 + B_2^2}$$

$$= \frac{\mu_0}{4\pi}(2)\sqrt{\frac{(3)^2}{(0.3)^6} + \frac{(4)^2}{(0.4)^6}}$$

$$= 2.54 \times 10^{-5} \text{ T}$$

15. (b) In the given figure OS refers to retentivity while OP refers to coercivity, for permanent magnets. Both retentivity and coercivity should be high.

16. (a) Diamagnetic substances are repelled by the magnetic field. The body of the lizard behaves like a diamagnetic substance, hence the smallest magnetic field placed below the body of the lizard will be strong enough to lift it.

17. (d) Torque on a bar magnet will be

$$\tau = mB\sin 60^\circ \quad \ldots\text{(i)}$$

Therefore, work done will be

$$W = mB(\cos 0^\circ - \cos 60^\circ)$$
$$= mB(1 - \cos 60^\circ) \quad \ldots\text{(ii)}$$

From Eqs. (i) and (ii),

$$\frac{\tau}{W} = \frac{\sqrt{3}/2}{1/2}$$

$$\Rightarrow \quad \tau = W\sqrt{3}$$

18. (a) Magnetic susceptibility = χ

It is negative for diamagnetic materials only.

19. (a) Cobalt exhibits ferromagnetism because of a quantum physical effect called exchange coupling in which the electron spins of one atom interact with those of neighbouring atoms. The result in alignment of the magnetic dipole moments of the atoms, in spite of the randomizing tendency of atomic collisions. This persistent alignment is what gives ferromagnetic materials their permanent magnetism. On increasing temperature, it will convert into paramagnetic material.

20. (c) The material suitable for making electromagnets should have low retentivity and low coercivity.

21. (d) In each pair of electrons, both electrons have spin in opposite direction in a diamagnetic material. Hence, the electrons of each pair completely cancel the magnetic moment of each other. Thus, the net magnetic moment of each atom of such substances is zero, i.e. $\mu_d = 0$.

The property of paramagnetism is found in those substances whose atoms or molecules have an excess of electrons spinning in the same direction.

Hence, atoms of paramagnetic substances have permanent magnetic moment, i.e. $\mu_p \neq 0$.

The property of ferromagnetism is found in substances which acquire very strong magnetism when placed in an external magnetic field. Like the paramagnetic substances, each atom of ferromagnetic substances also has a permanent magnetic moment, i.e., $\mu_f \neq 0$.

22. (c) $T = 2\pi\sqrt{\frac{I}{MB}}$

$$\therefore \frac{T_1}{T_2} = \sqrt{\frac{B_2}{B_1}}$$

$$T_2 = T_1\sqrt{\frac{B_1}{B_2}}$$

$$n_1 = 120 \text{ oscillations per minute}$$
$$= 2 \text{ oscillations per second}$$

$$\therefore T_1 = \frac{1}{2}\text{ s}$$

$$\therefore T_2 = \frac{1}{2}\sqrt{\frac{B_1}{2B_1}} = \frac{1}{2\sqrt{2}}\text{ s}$$

23. (c) $M = mL$

$$L = \frac{\pi}{6}\times r \Rightarrow r = \frac{6L}{\pi}$$

$$M' = m\times r = m\frac{6L}{\pi} = \frac{6M}{11}$$

24. (a) Repulsion is the sure test for magnetism because it occurs only when two like poles of a magnet exist while the attraction can occur between two unlike poles of magnets and also between a magnet and a magnetic material.

It means if there are two magnets they will attract each other and suppose if one material is a magnet and the other is iron then they will also attract each other. So in that case, we cannot decide which is magnet.

Therefore, both Assertion and Reason are true and Reason is correct explanation of Assertion.

25. (b) Time period for oscillation of needle in magnetic field is given as

$$T = 2\pi\sqrt{\frac{I}{MB}}$$

The magnetic moment M of each part will become one-fourth of the original moment

$$M' = \frac{M}{4}$$

Moment of inertia,

$$I' = \frac{m'(l')^2}{12}$$

$$= \frac{1}{4}, \frac{1}{16}, \frac{ml^2}{12} = \frac{I}{64}$$

For each part M becomes one-fourth while I becomes (1/64)th.

Hence, $T' = \sqrt{\frac{I/64}{(M/4)B}}$

$$= \frac{T}{4} = \frac{4}{4} = 1\text{ s}$$

26. (b) Diamagnetic substance repels external magnetic field.

27. (a) Susceptibility of a paramagnetic substance is independent of magnetising field.

28. (c) Area of hysteresis loop $\propto$ Energy lost per cycle of magnetisation and demagnetisation in form of heat.

29. (c) The given situation is shown below.

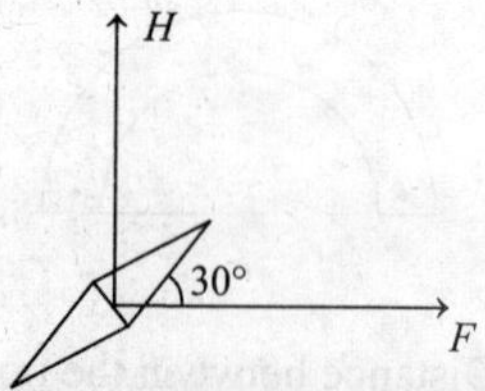

From figure at equilibrium,

$$\tan 30^\circ = \frac{H}{F} \Rightarrow \frac{1}{\sqrt{3}} = \frac{H}{F}$$

$$\Rightarrow \quad \frac{F}{H} = \frac{\sqrt{3}}{1}$$

30. (b) Work done in rotating a magnet in magnetic field is given as

$$W = MB[\cos\theta_1 - \cos\theta_2]$$
$$= MB[\cos 0^\circ - \cos 180^\circ]$$
$$\Rightarrow W = 2MB$$
$$W = 2\times 6\times 5\times 10^{-3}$$
$$= 6\times 10^{-2}\text{ J}$$

Ch-07 Electromagnetic Induction

Topical Follow Thru

Test-1

1. (c) Induced emf is given by

$$\varepsilon = \left|-\frac{d\phi}{dt}\right|_{t=2}$$

$\because \quad \phi = 30t^2 + 5$

$$\varepsilon = \left|\frac{-d\phi}{dt}\right|_{t=2} = \left|\frac{d}{dt}(30t^2+5)\right|_{t=2}$$

$$\varepsilon = |60t|_{t=2}$$

$$\varepsilon = 120 \text{ V}$$

Current in the coil,

$$i = \frac{\varepsilon}{R} = \frac{120}{100} = 1.2 \text{ A}$$

2. (b) From the diagram,

Change in flux = Area of triangle $\times R$

$$= \left(\frac{1}{2} \times 0.4 \times 14\right) \times 5$$

$$= 14 \text{ Wb}$$

3. (c) Magnetic flux is given by

$$\phi = BA\cos\theta$$

$$= \frac{5}{\pi} \times \pi(0.5)^2 \times \cos 30°$$

$$\phi = 1.08 \text{ Wb}$$

4. (c) Induced emf is given as

$$e = \frac{-(\phi_2 - \phi_1)}{t}$$

$$= \frac{-(0 - NBA)}{t} = \frac{NBA}{t}$$

Now,

$$t = \frac{NBA}{e} = \frac{100 \times 4 \times 10^{-4} \times 10}{0.5}$$

$$t = 0.8 \text{ s}$$

5. (a) When current i_2 is decreased, then flux through A decreases. According to Lenz's law, attraction occurs between A and B. Similarly, when current i_1 is increased, then loops will repel each other. As distance between the loops decreases, M decreases. Hence, loops will repel each other and current i_1 will increase, when loop 1 is moved towards loop 2. When loop 2 is moved away, loops will attract and i_2 will increase.

$\therefore \quad$ A $\rightarrow$ 2, B $\rightarrow$ 1, C $\rightarrow$ 4, D $\rightarrow$ 3.

6. (d) As magnetic field through circle is constant because current through straight wire is constant.Therefore, the magnetic flux through circle is not changing with time.

$$\therefore \quad \frac{d\phi_B}{dt} = 0$$

$$|\varepsilon| = \left|\frac{d\phi_B}{dt}\right| = 0$$

$$i = \frac{\varepsilon}{R} = \frac{0}{R} = 0$$

Hence, no current is induced and either has no direction.

7. (c) The magnitude of induced emf at any instant of time will be

$$|\varepsilon| = \frac{d\phi}{dt} = \frac{d}{dt}(3t^3 + 2t^2 + t - 4)$$

$$= 9t^2 + 4t + 1$$

At $\quad t = 2\text{s}$,

$$|\varepsilon| = 9 \times (2)^2 + 4 \times 2 + 1 = 45 \text{ V}$$

Induced current, $I = \dfrac{|\varepsilon|}{R}$

$$\Rightarrow \quad R = \frac{|\varepsilon|}{I} = \frac{45}{7.5} = 6\Omega$$

8. (a) Given, $dt = 1.5$ s

Also, $d\phi = 4 \times 10^{-4} - 0$

$$= 4 \times 10^{-4} \text{Wb}$$

The induced emf in the wire is

$$|\varepsilon| = \frac{d\phi}{dt} = \frac{4 \times 10^{-4}}{1.5}$$

$$= 2.66 \times 10^{-4} \text{ V}$$

9. (a) Given, $\dfrac{dB}{dt} = 2\text{Ts}^{-1}$

Number of turns, $N = 1500$

Side, $l = 5\text{cm} = 5 \times 10^{-2}$ m

$$\therefore Al^2 = 25 \times 10^{-4} \text{m}^2$$

Induced emf is given by

$$\frac{d\phi}{dt} = \frac{d(BA)}{dt} = \frac{dB}{dt} \cdot A$$

$$\Rightarrow \quad \frac{d\phi}{dt} = 2 \times (25 \times 10^{-4} \text{m}^2)$$

$$\Rightarrow \quad \frac{d\phi}{dt} = 50 \times 10^{-4} \text{ m}^2$$

By Faraday's law, induced emf is

$$e = -N\frac{d\phi}{dt}$$

$$e = -1500 \times 50 \times 10^{-4}$$

$$e = -75000 \times 10^{-4}$$

$$|e| = 7.5 \text{ V}$$

10. (a) The magnetic flux linked with the coil,

$$\phi = N(B \cdot A) = NBA\cos\theta \quad \text{...(i)}$$

The induced emf when the coil is rotated from $\theta_1 = 0°$ to $\theta_2 = 30°$ is

$$e = -\frac{\Delta\phi}{\Delta t} = -\frac{\Delta NBA\cos\theta}{\Delta t}$$

(from Eq. (i))

$$\Rightarrow e = -\frac{NBA}{\Delta t}(\cos\theta_2 - \cos\theta_1) \text{...(ii)}$$

Now, substitute the given value in Eq. (ii), we get

$$e = \frac{-[500 \times 1.5 \times 10^{-3} \times 0.15 \times (\cos 30° - \cos 0°)]}{0.5}$$

$$= 0.03\text{V}$$

11. (c) Given, $\phi = (6t^3 - 18t^2)$ mT, $N = 40$ and $R = 5\Omega$

Magnitude of induced emf,

$$|e| = N\left|\frac{d\phi_B}{dt}\right|$$

$$|e| = 40\frac{d}{dt}(6t^3 - 18t^2) \times 10^{-3}$$

$$= 40(18t^2 - 36t) \times 10^{-3}$$

$$= 40 \times 18(t^2 - 2t) \times 10^{-3}$$

$$= 720(t^2 - 2t) \times 10^{-3}$$

Current through coil,

$$I = \frac{|e|}{R} = \frac{720(t^2 - 2t)}{5} \times 10^{-3}$$
$$= 144\,(t^2 - 2t) \times 10^{-3}$$

For current to be maximum, $\frac{dI}{dt} = 0$

$$\frac{d}{dt} 144\,(t^2 - 2t) = 0$$
$$144\,(2t - 2) = 0$$
$$2t - 2 = 0$$
$$t = 1\,\text{s}$$

i.e. at $t = 1$ s, current is maximum. This maximum current is

$$|I_{max}| = |144\,(t^2 - 2t) \times 10^{-3}|$$
$$|I_{max}| = |144\,(1^2 - 2\times 1) \times 10^{-3}|$$
$$= 0.144\text{ A}$$

12. (a) Initial flux $= NBA \cos 0° = NBA$

Final flux $= NBA \cos 120° = -\frac{1}{2} NBA$

Change in flux $(\Delta\phi)$

$$= -\frac{1}{2} NBA - NBA$$
$$= -\frac{3}{2} NBA$$

Average induced emf

$$= \frac{|\Delta\phi|}{\Delta t}$$
$$= \frac{\frac{3}{2} NBA}{\Delta t} = \frac{3\,NBA}{2\Delta t}$$

13. (c) Emf $= -\frac{d\phi}{dt}$

So, emf is directly proportional to the rate of change of magnetic flux linked with a coil. When closed coil is used, current flows into it. Hence, option (c) is correct.

14. (c) When the switch is opened, the current in the circuit decreases. To balance it, the induction produces current in the opposite direction which produces high voltage for short term. Due to which, sound increases suddenly.

15. (d) Statement I is incorrect because flux linked with all turns is same.

Test-2

1. (d) The induced emf is given by

$$e = Bvl$$
$$e = 5 \times 10^{-4} \times 15 \times 20$$
$$e = 0.15\text{ V}$$

2. (b) $\phi = BA \cos \omega t$

Now, $e = \frac{-d\phi}{dt} = \omega BA \sin \omega t$

$$e = \omega B \pi r^2 \sin \omega t$$

Emf is zero when $\omega t = n\pi$

i.e., $\omega t = 0, \pi, 2\pi, \ldots\ldots\ldots$ etc.

So, induced emf changes direction after every half revolution.

3. (c) Eddy currents are undesirable but sometimes desirable like in inductance furnace, magnetic breaking, etc.

Statement II is correct because motion of metallic core in the magnetic field produces eddy current which opposes the motion of core and electromagnetic damping is generated.

4. (c) The direction of induced current changes periodically because the direction of induced current is based on the Lenz's law.

5. (b) Given, $B = 20$ G

$$= 20 \times 10^{-4}\text{ T}$$
$$v = 180\text{ rev/min}$$
$$\Rightarrow \omega = \frac{2\pi \times 180}{60} = 6\pi\text{ rad/s}$$

Induced emf, $\varepsilon = \frac{1}{2} B\omega r^2$

$$= \frac{1}{2}(20 \times 10^{-4})(6\pi)(1)^2$$
$$= 6\pi \times 10^{-3}\text{ V}$$

6. (b) For generating motional emf, B, l and v should be mutually perpendicular to each other. Here, the direction of velocity of cube is parallel to the direction of magnetic field, so no emf is induced.

7. (c) According to question,

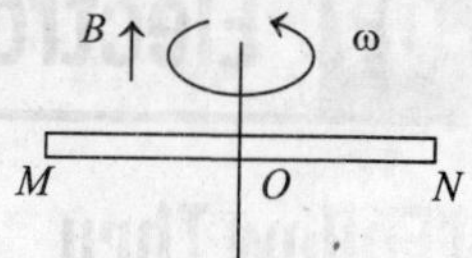

Potential difference between O and M,

$$V_O - V_M = \frac{1}{2} B\left(\frac{l}{2}\right)^2 \omega \quad \ldots\text{(i)}$$

Potential difference between O and N,

$$V_O - V_N = \frac{1}{2} B\left(\frac{l}{2}\right)^2 \omega \quad \ldots\text{(ii)}$$

From Eqs. (i) and (ii), we get

$$V_M - V_N = 0$$

8. (a) The upward force experienced by the wire is

$$F = \frac{B}{5} il = \frac{B}{5}\left(\frac{\frac{B}{5} v \frac{l}{2}}{R}\right)\frac{l}{2}$$
$$= \frac{1}{100} \frac{B^2 v l^2}{R}$$

If wire is sliding down with constant velocity, then

$$F = mg$$
$$\Rightarrow \frac{1}{100} \frac{B^2 v l^2}{R} = mg$$
$$\Rightarrow v = 100 \frac{mgR}{B^2 l^2}$$

9. (c) Vertical height, $h = L(1 - \cos\theta)$

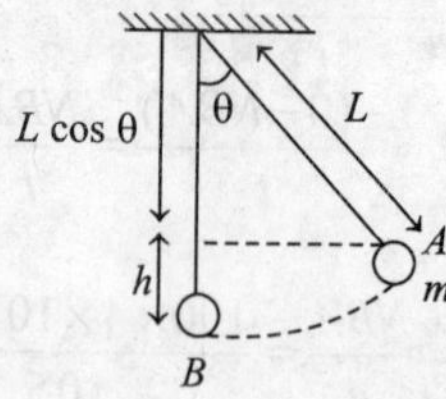

Velocity of bob at point B is v and at A is $u = 0$.

From equation, $v^2 - u^2 = 2gh$,

$$v^2 = 2gL(1 - \cos\theta) = 2gL\left(2\sin^2\frac{\theta}{2}\right)$$
$$v = 2\sqrt{gL} \sin\frac{\theta}{2}$$

Maximum induced emf,

$$\varepsilon_{max} = BvL = B \times 2\sqrt{gL}\left(\sin\frac{\theta}{2}\right)L$$

ε is maximum when $\theta = 90°$, as maximum value of θ in pendulum can never exceed 90°.

10. (b) Given, length l,

$$= 10 \text{ cm} = 10 \times 10^{-2} \text{ m}$$

Magnetic field (B) = 0.5 T

Angular velocity (ω)

$$= 200 \times 2\pi \text{ rad/s}$$

Emf induced ,

$$\varepsilon = \frac{1}{2}Bl^2\omega$$

$$= (0.5)(10\times10^{-2})^2 \pi (200)$$

$$= 3.14 \text{ V}$$

11. (b) Emf induces across the length of the wire which cuts the magnetic field. (Length of c = Length of d) > (Length of a = Length of b). So, $(e_c = e_d) > (e_a = e_b)$.

12. (c) Given, $B_V = 0.2\times 10^{-4}$ Wb/m^2

$v = 180$ km/h (given)

$$e = B_V v l$$

$$= 0.2 \times 10^{-4} \times 180 \times \frac{5}{18} \times 1$$

$$= 2 \times 10^{-5} \times 50 = 10^{-3} \text{ V}$$

13. (c) Statement I is incorrect but Statement II is correct.

Each spoke acts like an emf source

$$E = \frac{1}{2}B\omega R^2$$

So, potential difference between rim and centre is due to N such cells in parallel, i.e. $\frac{1}{2}B\omega R^2$.

14. (d) Relative velocity

$$= v - (-v) = 2v = \frac{dl}{dt}$$

Now, $e = \frac{d\phi}{dt}$

$$\Rightarrow \quad e = \frac{Bl\,dl}{dt} \quad [\because \phi = BA]$$

Induced emf, $e = 2Blv$ $\left[\because \frac{dl}{dt} = 2v\right]$

15. (c) Let at time t, the loop is placed as shown in figure.

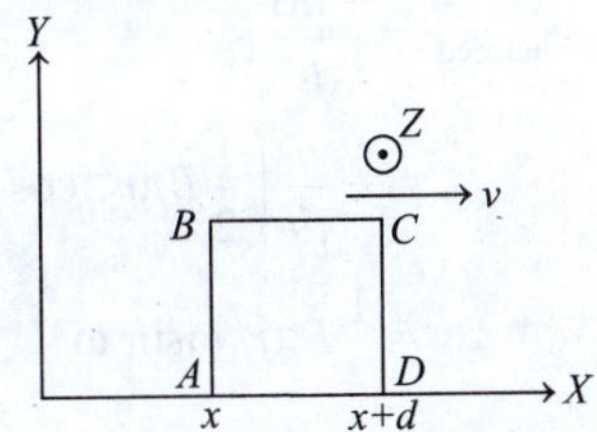

The emf induced in AB,

$$\varepsilon_{AB} = \frac{B_0(x)}{a}v_0 d$$

and the emf induced in CD,

$$\varepsilon_{CD} = \frac{B_0(x+d)}{a}v_0 d$$

So, $\varepsilon_{net} = \varepsilon_{CD} - \varepsilon_{AB} = \frac{B_0 v_0 d^2}{a}$

16. (d) Current, $I = \frac{\text{Potential difference}}{\text{Resistance}}$

$\therefore$ Potential difference

$$= 2 \times 12 = 24 \text{ V} = Bvl$$

Here, $l = AD \sin 37° = 0.3 \times \frac{3}{5}$

$$= 0.18 \text{ m}$$

$\therefore$ Velocity,

$$v = \frac{24}{Bl} = \frac{24}{4 \times 0.18} = \frac{100}{3} \text{ ms}^{-1}$$

17. (c) Circuit can be reduced as

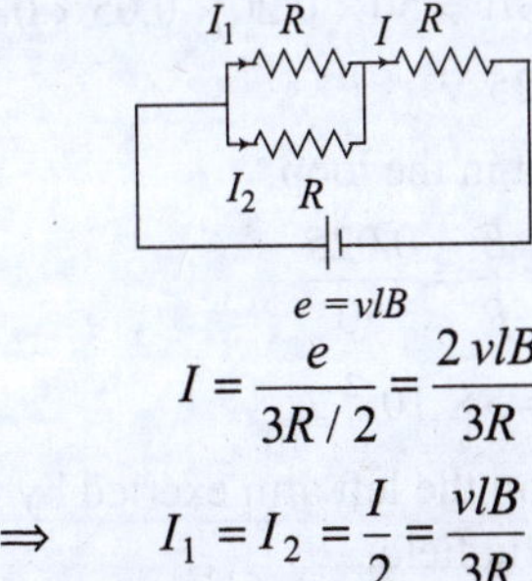

$$I = \frac{e}{3R/2} = \frac{2\,vlB}{3R}$$

$$\Rightarrow \quad I_1 = I_2 = \frac{I}{2} = \frac{vlB}{3R}$$

18. (a) Given, velocity,

$$\mathbf{v} = (2\hat{\mathbf{i}} + 3\hat{\mathbf{j}} + \hat{\mathbf{k}}) \text{ ms}^{-1},$$

and $\mathbf{B} = (\hat{\mathbf{i}} + 2\hat{\mathbf{j}})$ Wb/m^2

Length, $l = 2\hat{\mathbf{k}}$

$\therefore$ Potential difference induced between the ends of the wire,

$$e = (\mathbf{v} \times \mathbf{B})\, l$$

$$= [(2\hat{\mathbf{i}} + 3\hat{\mathbf{j}} + \hat{\mathbf{k}}) \times (\hat{\mathbf{i}} + 2\hat{\mathbf{j}})] \cdot 2\hat{\mathbf{k}}$$

$$= (4\hat{\mathbf{k}} - 3\hat{\mathbf{k}} + \hat{\mathbf{j}} - 2\hat{\mathbf{i}}) \cdot 2\hat{\mathbf{k}}$$

$$= (\hat{\mathbf{k}} + \hat{\mathbf{j}} - 2\hat{\mathbf{i}}) \cdot 2\hat{\mathbf{k}} = 2 \text{ V}$$

19. (a) Motional emf induced in the connector, $e = Blv = 2(1)(2) = 4$ V

This acts as a cell of emf 4 V and internal resistances 6 Ω and 3 Ω resistors are in parallel.

$$\therefore \quad \frac{1}{R_p} = \frac{1}{6} + \frac{1}{3} = \frac{1+2}{6} = \frac{3}{6} = \frac{1}{2}$$

$$\Rightarrow \quad R_p = 2\ \Omega$$

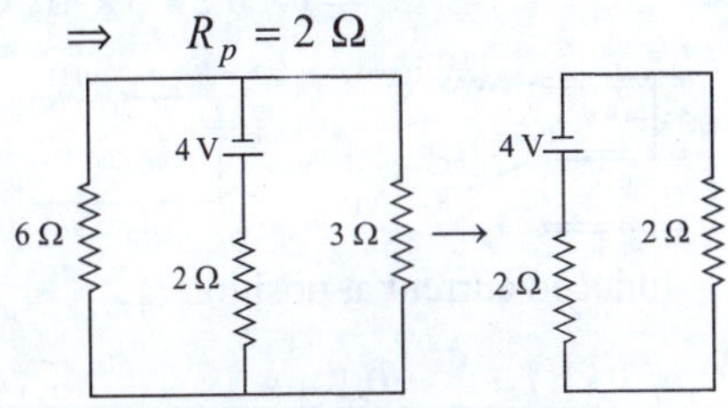

$\therefore$ Current through the connector,

$$i = \frac{E}{R_p + r} = \frac{4}{2+2} = 1 \text{ A}$$

Magnetic force on the connector

$$= Bil = 2(1)(1) = 2 \text{ N}$$

Therefore, to keep the connector moving with a constant velocity, a force of 2 N has to be applied to the right side.

20. (c) As Wheatstone bridge is balanced, then current through arm AC is zero.

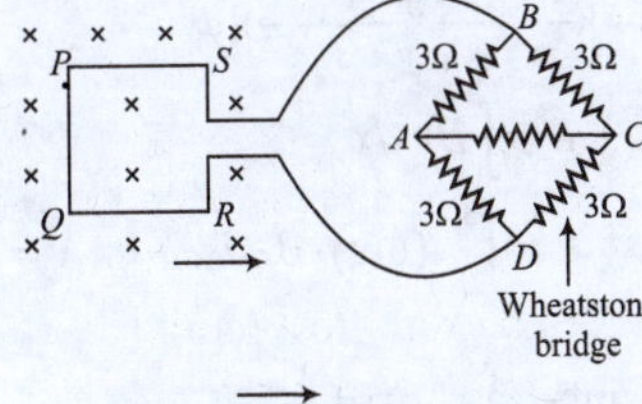

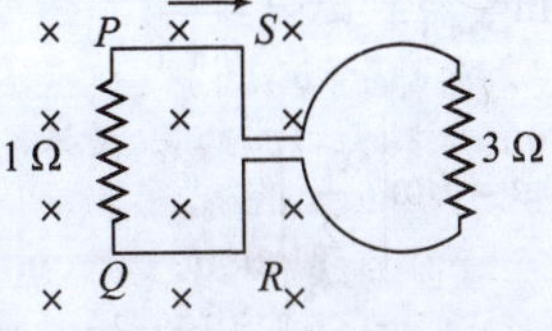

Effective resistance R of bridge,

$$\text{i.e.} \quad \frac{1}{R} = \frac{1}{6} + \frac{1}{6} = \frac{1}{3}$$

$$\Rightarrow \quad R = 3\ \Omega$$

Total resistance,

$$R_{total} = 3+1=4\,\Omega$$

So, current in the loop is

$$i = \frac{e_{induced}}{R_{total}} \Rightarrow \frac{Blv}{4}$$

$$= \frac{2\times 0.1\times v}{4} = 1\times 10^{-3}$$

$\therefore$ Speed of the loop,

$$v = 2\times 10^{-2}\ \text{ms}^{-1}$$

$$= 2\ \text{cms}^{-1}$$

21. (a) ***Case* I**

Induced emf, $e = Blv$

$$= 1\times 0.2\times 5\times 10^{-2}$$

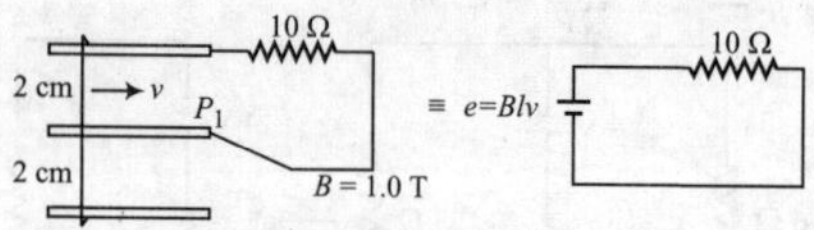

Induced current at position P_1,

$$i = \frac{e}{R} = 0.1\ \text{mA}$$

***Case* II**

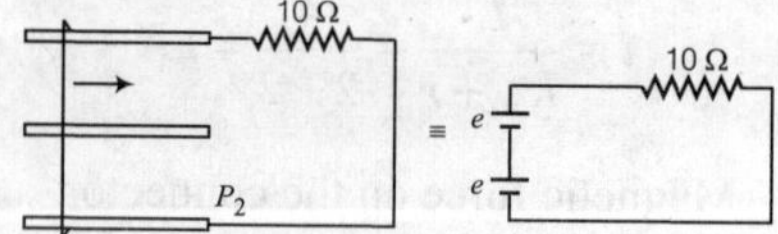

Induced current at position P_2,

$$i = \frac{2e}{R} = 0.2\ \text{mA}$$

22. (d) $\because$ Induced emf is rate of change of magnetic flux.

$\therefore \quad e = \int Bv\,dx$

$\Rightarrow \quad e = \int_{2l}^{3l} (\omega x)\cdot B\cdot dx \quad [\because v = \omega x]$

Using $\int x^n dx = \frac{x^{n+1}}{n+1}$,

$$e = B\omega\left[\frac{x^2}{2}\right]_{2l}^{3l}$$

$$\Rightarrow e = B\omega\frac{[(3l)^2-(2l)^2]}{2} = \frac{5Bl^2\omega}{2}$$

23. (b) The flux associated with coil of area A and magnetic induction B is

$$\phi = BA\cos\theta$$

$$= \frac{1}{2}B\pi r^2 \cos\omega t$$

$$\left[\because A = \frac{1}{2}\pi r^2, \text{ for semi-circle}\right]$$

$$\therefore\ e_{induced} = \frac{-d\phi}{dt}$$

$$= -\frac{d}{dt}\left(\frac{1}{2}B\pi r^2\cos\omega t\right)$$

$$= \frac{1}{2}B\pi r^2\omega\sin\omega t$$

$$\therefore \text{Power, } P = \frac{e^2_{induced}}{R}\ [\because P = V^2/R]$$

$$= \frac{B^2\pi^2 r^4\omega^2\sin^2\omega t}{4R}$$

Hence, $P_{mean} = P$

$$= \frac{B^2\pi^2 r^4\omega^2}{4R}\cdot\frac{1}{2}$$

$$\left[\because \sin^2\omega t = \frac{1}{2}\right]$$

$$= \frac{(B\pi r^2\omega)^2}{8R}$$

24. (a) Side of square,

$$l = \sqrt{2.5\times 10^{-3}} = 0.05\ \text{m}$$

As the loop of length 0.05 m is pulled out in 1.0 s, so speed of loop

$$= 0.05\ \text{m/s}$$

The emf induced in the left arm of the loop,

$$E = NBlv = 50\times 0.20\times 0.05\times 0.05$$

$$= 0.025\ \text{V}$$

Current in the loop,

$$I = \frac{E}{R} = \frac{0.025}{50}$$

$$= 5\times 10^{-3}\ \text{A}$$

Force on the left arm exerted by the magnetic field,

$$F = IlB = 5\times 10^{-3}\times 0.05\times 0.20$$

$$= 5\times 10^{-5}\ \text{N}$$

$$\therefore W = Fl = 5\times 10^{-5}\times 0.05$$

$$= 0.25\times 10^{-5}\ \text{J}$$

$$= 2.5\ \mu\text{J}$$

25. (b) As we know, conducting rod of length l is moved at constant velocity v_0, we get

Work done by external force

= Thermal energy dissipated in R

$$= \frac{B^2 l^2 v^2}{R}$$

So, we can conclude that

I. Thermal power dissipated in the resistor is equal to the rate of work done by an external person pulling the rod.

II. If applied external force is doubled, then a part of the external power increases the velocity of the rod.

IV. If resistance R is doubled, then power required to maintain the constant velocity v_0 becomes half.

So, statements I, II, IV are correct. Hence, option (b) is correct.

Test-3

1. (b) The self-inductance of solenoid is given by $L = \phi_B\cdot\frac{N}{I}$

$$= 1.2\times 10^{-2}\times\frac{1100}{2} = 6.6\,\text{H}$$

2. (d) Magnetic potential energy stored in the inductor is

$$U = \frac{1}{2}Li_0^2 = \frac{1}{2}\times 10\times(50\times 10^{-3})^2$$

$$= 12.5\times 10^{-3}\ \text{J}$$

3. (d) $L = \frac{\mu_0 N^2\pi r^2}{l}$

Length of wire $= 2\pi r$ = constant = K

$$L = \mu_0\left(\frac{K}{2\pi r}\right)^2\cdot\frac{\pi r^2}{l}$$

$$L \propto \frac{1}{l} \qquad \left(\therefore l' = \frac{l}{2}\right)$$

Self-inductance will become 2 L.

4. (d) Induced emf is given by

$$|\varepsilon|=\left|\frac{d\phi}{dt}\right|=\frac{\Delta\phi}{\Delta t}$$

$$\Rightarrow |\varepsilon|=L\frac{\Delta i}{\Delta t}=\frac{(20\,\text{mH})\times(5-1)\text{A}}{2\text{ ms}}$$
$$=40\text{ V}$$

5. (c) Self- Inductance, $L=\frac{\mu_0 N^2\pi r^2}{l}$

$\Rightarrow$ According to question,

$$\frac{L_1}{L_2}=\left(\frac{r_1}{r_2}\right)^2\left(\frac{l_2}{l_1}\right)$$
$$=\left(\frac{2}{3}\right)^2\times\left(\frac{3}{2}\right)$$
$$=\frac{2}{3}\text{ or }2:3$$

6. (d) Self-inductance is given by

$$L=\frac{\mu_0 N^2 A}{l}$$
$$\Rightarrow L=\frac{4\pi\times10^{-7}\times(10^4)^2\times10^{-6}}{20.5\times10^{-2}}$$
$$\Rightarrow L=0.61\text{ mH}$$

7. (a) Time period,

$$t=\frac{1}{\nu}=\frac{1}{50}\text{ s}$$

Emf is given as

$$|e|=\frac{Ldi}{dt}$$
$$220=\frac{L\times0.4}{1/50}$$
$$\Rightarrow \quad L=11\text{ H}$$

8. (a) Induced emf, $e=-L\frac{di}{dt}$

Putting the values of di and dt, we get

$$18=-\frac{L(-3-3)}{0.03}$$
$$\Rightarrow \quad L=\frac{18\times0.03}{6}$$
$$\Rightarrow \quad L=0.09\text{ H}$$

9. (a) We know that the magnetic flux associated with coil Y is directly proportional to current flowing in X coil,

i.e. $\phi_Y \propto I_X$

$$\phi_Y=MI_X \quad \text{...(i)}$$
$$\Rightarrow \quad 0.2=M\times14 \quad \text{[from Eq. (i)]}$$
$$\Rightarrow \quad M=\frac{0.2}{14}=0.014\text{ H}$$

10. (d)By reciprocatory theorem, $M_{12}=M_{21}$ in all practical cases.

11. (c) As, $L=\mu_0 n^2 Al$

$\therefore L\rightarrow 3\times3\times3$ times

$=27$ times

12. (d) As, $e=-M\frac{di}{dt}$

$$20\times10^3=-2\times\frac{(0-8)}{dt}$$
$$dt=\frac{16}{20\times10^3}$$
$$=0.8\times10^{-3}\text{ s}$$

13. (d) Emf induced is given as

$$\varepsilon=\frac{Mdi}{dt}=0.001(100\pi)$$
$$[-7\sin(100\pi t)]$$
$$\Rightarrow |\varepsilon_{\max}|=0.7\pi$$
$(i_{\max}$ = maximum at $\sin(100\pi t)=1)$

14. (c) At $t=1$ s,

$$i=2+3\times1=5\text{ A}$$

and $|e|=L\frac{di}{dt}$

$$\Rightarrow 9\times10^{-3}=L\times\frac{d}{dt}(2+3t)$$
$$\Rightarrow 9\times10^{-3}=L\times(3)$$
$$\Rightarrow \quad L=3\times10^{-3}\text{ H}$$
$$U=\frac{1}{2}Li^2$$
$$=\frac{1}{2}(3\times10^{-3})\times5^2$$
$$=25\times10^{-3}\times1.5$$
$$=37.5\times10^{-3}\text{ J}$$
$$U=37.5\text{ mJ}$$

15. (d) Magnetic flux due to current carrying coil is given as

$$N\phi=Li$$
$$\Rightarrow L=\frac{N\phi}{i}=\frac{500\times10^{-4}}{2}$$
$$=25\times10^{-3}\text{ H}$$
$$=25\text{ mH}$$

Chapter Break Thru

1. (a) Current I will produce ⊙ magnetic field passing through the loop. As current I increases, so ⊙ magnetic field will also increase.

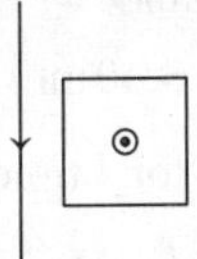

Therefore, induced current should produce cross magnetic field. For producing cross magnetic field in the loop, induced current from our side should be clockwise.

2. (a) When a conductor is moving through a uniform magnetic field with certain velocity in a perpendicular magnetic field, free electrons present in the conductor experience a magnetic force which is given as $\mathbf{F}_m=q(\mathbf{v}\times\mathbf{B})$

Due to the action of this force, the positive charge will move in the direction of $(\mathbf{v}\times\mathbf{B})$ and negative charge will move opposite to $(\mathbf{v}\times\mathbf{B})$. The direction of velocities of points P and Q is as shown in the following fig.

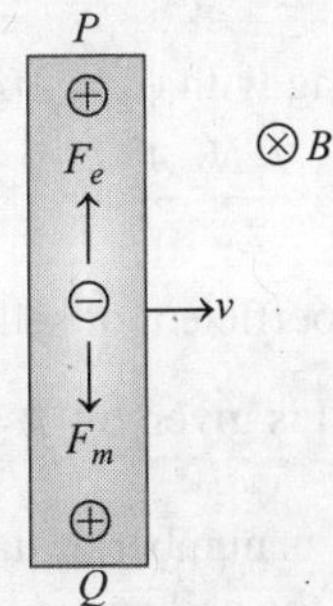

The direction of velocity of upper half part of rod is rightwards, so free electrons present in upper half part experience force according to right hand thumb rule towards point O about which rod is being rotated, leaving a net positive charge at the upper end.

Similarly, the direction of velocity of lower half part of rod is leftwards, so direction of $\mathbf{v} \times \mathbf{B}$ is downwards.

The force experienced by positive charge is towards lower end, whereas electrons experiences force towards point O.

3. (a) Given, $L = 40\,\text{mH}$

$$dt = \text{total time difference}$$
$$= t_2 - t_1 = 4\,\text{ms}$$
$$dI = I_2 - I_1 = 11 - 1 = 10\,\text{A}$$

Induced emf, $e = L\dfrac{dI}{dt}$

$$= 40 \times \left(\frac{10}{4}\right) = 100\,\text{V}$$

4. (c) When the total flux associated with one coil links with the other, i.e. a case of maximum flux linkage, then

$$M_{\max} = \sqrt{L_1 L_2}$$

Given, $L_1 = 2\,\text{mH}$, $L_2 = 8\,\text{mH}$

$$\therefore \quad M_{\max} = \sqrt{2 \times 8} = \sqrt{16} = 4\,\text{mH}$$

5. (b) Magnetic flux linked is given as

$$\phi_0 = N_2 B_1 A$$

or $\quad \phi_2 = N_2 \dfrac{\mu_0 N_1 I_2 A}{L}$

or $\quad \phi_2 = \dfrac{\mu_0 N_1 N_2 A}{L} I_2$

Comparing with $\phi_2 = MI_2$, we get

$$M = \frac{\mu_0 N_1 N_2 A}{L}$$

6. (a) The coefficient of self-inductance of the coil is given by $L = \dfrac{\mu_0 N^2 A}{l}$

where, N is number of turns, l is length of the coil and A is area of coil.

So, $\quad L \propto N^2$

Hence, both assertion and reason are true and reason is the correct explanation of assertion.

7. (b) Induced potential difference between two ends $= Blv = B_H lv$

$$= 3 \times 10^{-5} \times 2 \times 100 = 6 \times 10^{-3}\ \text{V}$$
$$= 6\,\text{mV}$$

By Fleming's right hand rule, end A becomes positively charged.

8. (b) As the magnet moves towards the coil, the magnetic flux increases (non-linearly). Also, there is a change in polarity of induced emf when the magnet passes on to the other side of the coil.

It is best represented by graph shown in option (b).

9. (c) Direction of eddy currents is given by Lenz's law.

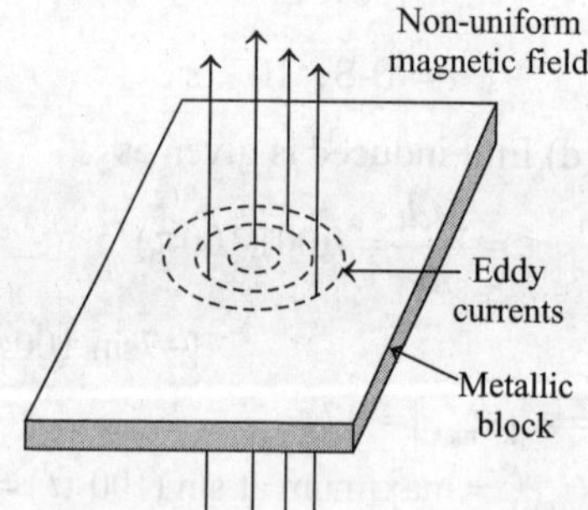

From the above figure, it is clear that the angle made by the plane of eddy currents with the plane of magnetic lines of force is 90°.

10. (d) As the magnetic field is increasing, so induced current produces a magnetic field directed out of plane of paper.

$\therefore$ Current induced is anti-clockwise.

Area of right side part is more, so emf and current induced on RHS part is more.

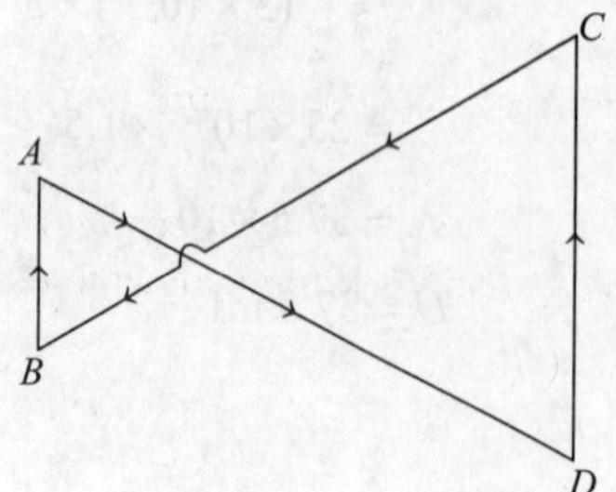

11. (a) Charge on capacitor is given by

$$q = CV = C(Bvl)$$
$$= (10 \times 10^{-6})(4)(4)(1)$$
$$= 160\,\mu\text{C} = \text{constant}$$

12. (b) Terminal velocity is attained when magnetic force is equal to $mg\sin\theta$.

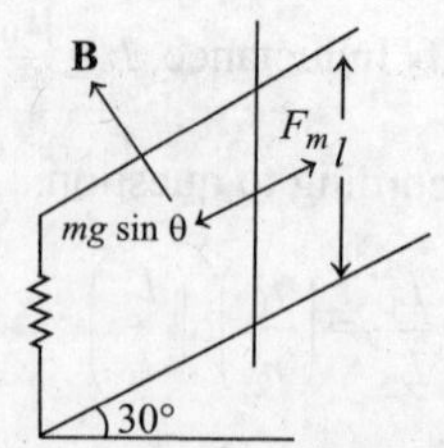

$\therefore \quad F_m = mg\sin 30°$

or $\quad ilB = mg\sin 30°$

or $\quad \left(\dfrac{e}{R}\right) lB = mg\sin 30°$

or $\quad \dfrac{(Bv_T l)}{R} \times lB = mg\sin 30°$

$$\therefore \quad v_T = \frac{mgR\sin 30°}{B^2 l^2} = \frac{mgR}{2B^2 l^2}$$

13. (b) Let $2a$ be the side of the triangle and b the length ME.

$$\frac{MH}{ME} = \frac{HG}{EO}$$

$$HG = \left(\frac{MH}{ME}\right) EO$$

or $\quad HG = \dfrac{(b - vt)}{b} \cdot a = a - \left(\dfrac{a}{b} vt\right)$

$$\therefore \quad FG = 2HG = 2\left[a - \frac{a}{b} vt\right]$$

Induced emf,

$$e = Bv(FG) = 2Bv\left(a - \frac{a}{b} vt\right)$$

$\therefore$ Induced current,

$$i = \frac{e}{R} = \frac{2Bv}{R}\left[a - \frac{a}{b} vt\right]$$

or $\quad i = k_1 - k_2 t$

Thus, i-t graph is a straight line with negative slope and positive intercept.

14. (a) Current in the inner coil,

$$i = \frac{e}{R} = \frac{A_1}{R_1}\frac{dB}{dt}$$

Length of the inner coil $= 2\pi a$

So, its resistance,

$$R_1 = 100 \times 10^{-3} \times 2\pi(a)$$

$$\therefore\ i_1 = \frac{\pi a^2}{100 \times 10^{-3} \times 2\pi(a)} \times 0.2 \times 10^{-3}$$

$$= 10^{-4}\text{ A}$$

According to Lenz's law, direction of i_1 is clockwise.

Induced current in outer coil,

$$i_2 = \frac{e_2}{R_2} = \frac{A_2}{R_2}\frac{dB}{dt}$$

$$\Rightarrow i_2 = \frac{\pi b^2}{100 \times 10^{-3} \times (2\pi b)} \times 0.2 \times 10^{-3}$$

$$= 2 \times 10^{-3} = 2 \times 10^{-4}\text{ A}$$

clockwise

15. (a) Both Statement I and Statement II are correct.

16. (d) The induced emf in side 1 of frame,

$$e_1 = B_1 vl$$

$$B_1 = \frac{\mu_0 I}{2\pi(x - a/2)}$$

The induced emf in side 2 of frame

$$e_2 = B_2 vl$$

$$B_1 = \frac{\mu_0 I}{2\pi(x + a/2)}$$

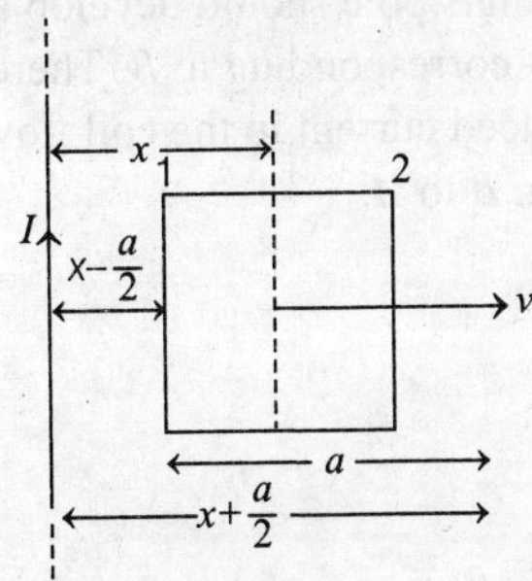

Net emf induced in square frame,

$$e = B_1 vl - B_2 vl$$

$$= \frac{\mu_0 I}{2\pi(x - a/2)} lv - \frac{\mu_0 I}{2\pi(x + a/2)} lv$$

$$\text{or } e \propto \frac{1}{(2x - a)(2x + a)}$$

Since. $I \propto$ emf, hence

$$I \propto \frac{1}{(2x - a)(2x + a)}$$

17. (a) Flux linked with each turn

$$= 4 \times 10^{-3}\text{ Wb}$$

$\therefore$ Total flux linked

$$= 500[4 \times 10^{-3}]\text{ Wb}$$

$$\phi_{\text{total}} = 2$$

$$\Rightarrow \quad Li = 2$$

$$L(2) = 2 \Rightarrow L = 1\text{ H}$$

18. (d) Fleming's left hand rule is used to find the direction of force on a current carrying conductor in a magnetic field.

$\therefore$ A $\rightarrow$ 2

Fleming's right hand rule is used to find the direction of induced current when a conductor is moved perpendicular to the magnetic field.

$\therefore$ B $\rightarrow$ 4

Magnetic field lines of a solenoid resembles like that of bar magnet and hence behaves similar to it.

$\therefore$ C $\rightarrow$ 3

Electric generator works on the principle of electromagnetic induction.

$\therefore$ D $\rightarrow$ 1

19. (b) $\dfrac{\text{Change in flux}}{\text{Area of triangle}} = R$

$$\Rightarrow \quad R = \frac{4}{0.2} = 20\,\Omega$$

20. (c) When loop is entering in the field, magnetic flux linked with the loop increases, so induced emf in it is

$$e = Bvl = 0.6 \times 10^{-2} \times 5 \times 10^{-2}$$

$$= 3 \times 10^{-4}\text{ V (negative).}$$

When loop is completely entered in the field (after 5 s), flux linked with the loop remains constant, so $e = 0$.

After 15 s, loop begins to exit out. Thus, linked magnetic flux decreases, so induced emf is $e = 3 \times 10^{-4}$ V (positive).

21. (b) Flux, $\phi = BA\cos\theta$

where, θ is the angle between area and magnetic field.

$$e = \frac{-d\phi}{dt} = BA\sin\theta\,\frac{d\theta}{dt}$$

$$= BA\left(\frac{d\theta}{dt}\right)\cos(90° + \theta)$$

Here, phase difference $= 90°$ or $(\pi/2)$.

22. (d) Given, length $(l) = 2$ m

Angular velocity $(\omega) = 10$ rad/s

Magnetic field $(B) = 0.2 \times 10^{-4}$ T

Emf developed is given by,

$$e = \frac{1}{2}B\omega l^2$$

$$= \frac{1}{2} \times 0.2 \times 10^{-4} \times 10 \times (2)^2$$

$$= 400\ \mu\text{V}$$

23. (c) Given, $\mathbf{B} = B_0(3\hat{\mathbf{i}} + 6\hat{\mathbf{j}} - 9\hat{\mathbf{k}})$T

$$B_x = (3B_0\hat{\mathbf{i}})\text{T}$$

or $B_x = (3B_0)$T = component of **B** along area **A**.

Area of the square, $A = a^2\text{ m}^2$

Magnetic flux, $\phi_B = BA\cos\theta$

$$\Rightarrow \quad \phi_B = (B\cos\theta)A$$

$$= (\text{component of } \mathbf{B} \text{ along } \mathbf{A})A$$

$\Rightarrow \phi_B$ (magnitude of magnetic flux)

$$= B_x A = 3B_0 a^2\text{ Tm}^2$$

$$= 3B_0 a^2\text{ Wb}$$

24. (d) Given, magnetic flux,

$$\phi_B = t^3 + 4t - 20$$

$$\therefore \text{Induced emf, } \varepsilon = -\frac{d\phi_B}{dt}$$

$$= -(3t^2 + 4) = -3t^2 - 4$$

At $t = 0$, $\varepsilon = 4$ V

The above equation is in the form of $y = ax^2 + b$ which represents the equation of parabola, not passing through origin.

25. (a) Given, $N = 80$, $A = 4.0\,\text{cm}^2$

$$= 4.0\times10^{-4}\ \text{m}^2$$

$$q = 2.0\times10^{-4}\ \text{C}$$

and $R = 80\Omega$

According to Faraday's law of electromagnetic induction, induced emf,

$$|\varepsilon| = \frac{d\phi_B}{dt} \quad \ldots(\text{i})$$

We know that,

$$i = \frac{dq}{dt}$$

$$\Rightarrow \quad q = \int i\,dt = \int \frac{\varepsilon}{R}\,dt$$

$$\Rightarrow \quad q = \frac{1}{R}\int \frac{d\phi_B}{dt}\cdot dt \text{ [from Eq. (i)]}$$

$$= \frac{1}{R}\int d\phi_B = \frac{\phi_B}{R}$$

For N-turns,

$$q = \frac{N\phi_B}{R} = \frac{N}{R}(BA) \quad (\because \phi_B = BA)$$

$$\Rightarrow \quad qR = NBA$$

$$\Rightarrow \quad B = \frac{qR}{NA}$$

$$= \frac{2\times10^{-4}\times80}{80\times4.0\times10^{-4}}$$

$$= 0.5\ \text{Wb m}^{-2}$$

26. (a) Given, $A = 10\times5 = 50\ \text{cm}^2$

$$= 50\times10^{-4}\text{m}^2$$

$$\frac{dB}{dt} = 0.02\ \text{Ts}^{-1},\ R = 2.0\Omega$$

$$|\varepsilon| = \frac{d\phi_B}{dt} = A\cdot\frac{dB}{dt}$$

$[\because \phi_B = BA$ and A is constant$]$

$$= 50\times10^{-4}\times0.02$$

$$= 10^{-4}\ \text{V}$$

Power dissipated in the form of heat

$$= \frac{\varepsilon^2}{R}$$

$$= \frac{10^{-4}\times10^{-4}}{2}$$

$$= 0.5\times10^{-8}\ \text{W}$$

$$= 5\times10^{-9} = 5\,\text{nW}$$

27. (a) Given, $V = 20\,\text{V}$, $R = 5\,\Omega$ and $L = 20\,\text{H}$

Current, $I = \frac{V}{R} = \frac{20}{5} = 4\ \text{A}$

Circuit switches off in 1 ms, i.e.

$$dt = 1\times10^{-3}\text{s}$$

and $dI = 4\ \text{A}$

$\therefore$ Induced emf in inductor is

$$|\varepsilon| = L\frac{dI}{dt} = 20\times\frac{4}{1\times10^{-3}}$$

$$= 8\times10^4\ \text{V}$$

28. (a) Given, length of solenoid,

$$l = 30\,\text{cm} = 30\times10^{-2}\ \text{m}$$

Area of cross-section,

$$A = 25\,\text{cm}^2 = 25\times10^{-4}\ \text{m}^2$$

Number of turns, $N = 1000$

Current, $I_1 = 2.5\text{A}, I_2 = 0$

and time, $dt = 10^{-3}\ \text{s}$

Induced emf in the solenoid,

$$\varepsilon = \frac{d\phi}{dt} = \frac{d}{dt}(BA) \quad (\because \phi = BA)$$

Magnetic field induction B at a point well inside the long solenoid carrying current I is $B = \mu_0 nI$

$\left(\text{where, n = number of turns per unit length} = \frac{N}{l}\right)$

$$\therefore \quad \varepsilon = NA\frac{dB}{dt} = NA\frac{d}{dt}\left(\mu_0\frac{N}{l}I\right)$$

$$= NA\frac{\mu_0 N}{l}\cdot\frac{dI}{dt}$$

$$\Rightarrow \quad \varepsilon = 1000\times25\times10^{-4}\times4\times3.14\times10^{-7}\times\frac{1000}{30\times10^{-2}}\times\frac{2.5}{10^{-3}}$$

$$\Rightarrow \quad \varepsilon = 26.2$$

The average back emf induced across the ends of the open switch is 26.2 V.

29. (c) Mutual inductance for a co-axial solenoid of radius r_1 and r_2 and number of turns n_1 and n_2 respectively, is given as

$$M = \mu_0 n_1 n_2 \pi r_1^2\, l \quad \ldots(\text{i})$$

(for internal coil of radius r_1)

Self-inductance for the internal coil,

$$L = \mu_0 n_1^2 \pi r_1^2 l \quad \ldots(\text{ii})$$

On dividing Eqs. (i) and (ii), we get

$$\therefore \quad \frac{M}{L} = \frac{n_1 n_2}{n_1^2} = \frac{n_2}{n_1} = 1 \quad (\because n_1 = n_2)$$

30. (b) In the rotation of magnet, N-pole moves closer to coil CD and S-pole moves closer to coil AB.

As per Lenz's law, N-pole should develop at the end corresponding to C. So, induced current flows from C to D.

Again S-pole should develop at the end corresponding to B. Therefore, induced current in the coil flows from B to A.

Ch-08 Alternating Current (AC)

Topical Follow Thru

Test-1

1. (c) For a purely inductive circuit, the current lags the voltage by $\frac{\pi}{2}$.

Hence, the correct option is (c).

2. (d) Given, $\lambda = 300\,\text{m}$

$$c = 3\times 10^8 \text{ m/s}$$

$$C = 3.6\times 10^{-6} \text{ F}$$

$$\because \quad \nu = \frac{c}{\lambda} = \frac{3\times 10^8}{300} = 10^6$$

Hz

Resonant frequency,

$$\nu = \frac{1}{2\pi\sqrt{LC}}$$

$$\sqrt{LC} = \frac{1}{2\pi\nu}$$

$$L = \frac{1}{4\pi^2 \times \nu^2 \times C}$$

$$L = \frac{1}{4\times 10\times 10^{12}\times 3.6\times 10^{-6}} \quad \{\pi^2 \approx 10\}$$

$$L = \frac{10^{-6}}{144}$$

$$L = 6.9\times 10^{-9}$$

$$L \simeq 7\,\text{nH}$$

3. (a) Capacitive reactance,

$X_C = \frac{1}{\omega C}$, when capacitance C increases, the capacitive reactance decreases. Due to decrease in value of capacitive reactance , the current in the circuit will increase $\left(I = \frac{E}{\sqrt{R^2 + X_C^2}}\right)$ and hence brightness of source (or electric lamp) will also increase.

So, both A and R are true and R is the correct explanation of A.

4. (d) Capacitive reactance is given as,

$$X_C = \frac{1}{\omega C}$$

$$= \frac{1}{2\pi f C} = \frac{1}{(2\pi)(50)\left(\frac{20}{\pi}\times 10^{-6}\right)}$$

$$= 500\,\Omega$$

$$\text{So, } i_{\text{rms}} = \frac{V_{\text{rms}}}{X_C} = \frac{110}{500} = 0.22\text{ A}$$

5. (c) Let the instantaneous current be i.

Applying KVL in circuit from P to Q,

$$V_P - iX_L - iX_C = V_Q$$

$$\Rightarrow V_P - V_Q = i(X_L + X_C)$$

$$\Rightarrow \quad i = \frac{V_P - V_Q}{X_L + X_C} \quad \ldots\text{(i)}$$

Given that, $V_P - V_Q = 30\,\text{V}$,

$$X_L = 2\Omega,\ X_C = 8\Omega$$

Putting these values in Eq. (i), we get

$$i = \frac{30}{2+8} = 3\text{ A}$$

At same instant, voltage across resistor,

$V_R = iR = 3\times 8 = 24\text{ V}$

Impedance of circuit,

$$Z = \sqrt{R^2 + (X_C - X_L)^2}$$

$$= \sqrt{8^2 + (8-2)^2} = \sqrt{64+36}$$

$= 10\,\Omega$

$\therefore$ Instantaneous source voltage,

$V = iZ = 3\times 10 = 30\text{V}$

6. (c) Given,

$$V_0 = i_0 Z \Rightarrow Z = \frac{V_0}{i_0} = \frac{300}{30} = 10\,\Omega$$

Also, $Z^2 = R^2 + X_L^2$

$$\Rightarrow \quad X_L = \sqrt{(10)^2 - (6)^2} = 8\Omega$$

$$\Rightarrow \quad X_L = \sqrt{Z^2 - R^2}$$

$$= \sqrt{(10)^2 - (8)^2} = 6\Omega$$

7. (b) Given, $R = 2 + 8 = 10\Omega$

$$X_L = \omega L = 1000\times 20\times 10^{-3} = 20\,\Omega$$

$$X_C = \frac{1}{\omega C} = \frac{1}{1000\times 100\times 10^{-6}}$$

$$= 10\Omega$$

$$Z = \sqrt{R^2 + (X_L - X_C)^2}$$

$$= \sqrt{(10)^2 + (20-10)^2}$$

$$= \sqrt{200} = 14.14\,\Omega$$

$$i_0 = \frac{V_0}{Z} = \frac{10}{14.14} = 0.707\text{ A}$$

8. (d) $A \rightarrow 2$

In purely inductive circuit, the current lags the voltage by 90°.

$B \rightarrow 1$

In purely capacitive circuit, the current leads the voltage by 90°.

$C \rightarrow 3$

In purely resistive circuit, the current and voltage are in phase.

$D \rightarrow 4$

In a series R-L circuit, the current lags behind the voltage by an angle less than 90°.

9. (a) $i_1 = 20\sin(314t + 30°)\text{A}$

$$i_2 = 40\sin(314t + 45°)\text{A}$$

$$i_0 = \sqrt{i_{02}^2 + i_{02}^2 + 2i_{01}\,i_{02}\cos(\Delta\phi)}$$

$$= \sqrt{20^2 + 40^2 + 2\times 20\times 40\times \cos 15°}$$

$$\approx 60\text{A}$$

$i_1 + i_2$ does have amplitude of 60 A.

Hence, both Statement I and Statement II are correct.

10. (b) By using, $\omega = \frac{1}{\sqrt{LC}}$

New resonant frequency,

$$\omega' = \frac{1}{\sqrt{\left(\frac{L}{2}\right) \times 8C}} = \frac{1}{2\sqrt{LC}} = \frac{\omega}{2}$$

11. (a) Resonant frequency is

$$\omega_0 = \frac{1}{\sqrt{LC}} = \frac{1}{\sqrt{64 \times 10^{-3} \times 40 \times 10^{-6}}}$$

$$= 6250 \text{ rad/s}$$

Amplitude of current

$$= \frac{V_m}{R} = \frac{V_{rms}\sqrt{2}}{R}$$

$$= \frac{220\sqrt{2}}{20} = 11\sqrt{2} \text{ A}$$

12. (c) Since, current and voltage are in phase, so

$$V_L = V_C$$

$$\Rightarrow X_L = X_C$$

$$f = \frac{1}{2\pi\sqrt{LC}}$$

$$C = \frac{1}{4\pi^2 L f^2}$$

$$= \frac{1}{4\pi^2\left(\frac{20}{\pi^2} \times 10^{-3}\right)(50)^2}$$

$$= 5 \times 10^{-3} \text{ F}$$

13. (d) As per question,

$$q(t) = q_m \cos \omega t \quad \text{...(i)}$$

Maximum charge, $q_m = CV_m$

$$= (40\,\mu\text{F})(40\,\text{V})$$

$$= 1.6 \times 10^{-3} \text{ C}$$

Resonant frequency, $\omega = \frac{1}{\sqrt{LC}}$

$$= \frac{1}{\sqrt{(4)(40) \times 10^{-6} \times 10^{-3}}}$$

$$= 2.5 \times 10^3 \text{ rad/s}$$

From Eq. (i),

$$q(t) = (1.6 \times 10^{-3}) \cos (2.5 \times 10^3 t)$$

Now, $I = \frac{-dq}{dt}$

$$I(t) = (1.6 \times 10^{-3})(2.5 \times 10^3) \sin (2.5 \times 10^3 t)$$

$$= (4) \sin (2.5 \times 10^3 t)$$

14. (a) $V = 100\sqrt{2} \sin (100t)$

$$V_0 = 100\sqrt{2}, \omega = 100 \text{ rad/s}$$

$$X_C = \frac{1}{\omega C} = \frac{1}{100 \times 10^{-6}} = 10^4\ \Omega$$

$$i_0 = \frac{V_0}{X_C} = \frac{100\sqrt{2}}{10^4}$$

$$= \sqrt{2} \times 10^{-2} \text{ A}$$

$$i_{rms} = \frac{i_0}{\sqrt{2}} = \frac{\sqrt{2} \times 10^{-2}}{\sqrt{2}} = 10 \text{ mA}$$

Reading of the ammeter is 10 mA.

15. (b) As voltage across inductor is given as

$$V_L = \frac{L dI}{dt} \text{ or } dI = \frac{1}{L} V_L\, dt$$

Integrating on both sides within limit, we get

$$\int_0^I dI = \frac{1}{L}\int_0^t V_L\, dt$$

$$[I]_0^I = \frac{1}{L}\int_0^t V_L\, dt$$

$$[I - 0] = \frac{1}{L} \times \text{Area under } V_L - t \text{ graph}$$

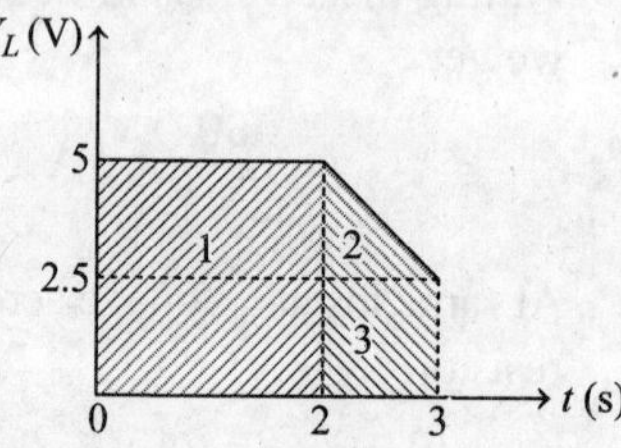

Area of V_L - t graph from $t = 0$ to $t = 3$ s,

$$A = A_1 + A_2 + A_3$$

$$= (5 \times 2) + \frac{1}{2} \times 2.5 \times 1 + 2.5 \times 1$$

$$= 13.75$$

$$\therefore I = \frac{1}{0.6} \times 13.75$$

[$\because$ Given, $L = 0.6$ H]

$$= 22.9 \text{ A}$$

16. (a) (i) As, $I = 4 \sin \omega t$

***Case* I** rms value of current from $t = 0$ to $t = \frac{\pi}{\omega}$;

$$I_{rms} = \sqrt{\frac{\int_0^{\frac{\pi}{\omega}} I_m^2 \sin^2 \omega t\, dt}{\frac{\pi}{\omega}}}$$

$$= \frac{I_m}{\sqrt{2}} \quad \text{...(i)}$$

(ii) ***Case* II** rms value of current from $t = \frac{\pi}{2\omega}$ to $\frac{3\pi}{2\omega}$;

$$I'_{rms} = \sqrt{\frac{\int_{\frac{\pi}{2\omega}}^{\frac{3\pi}{2\omega}} I_m^2 \sin^2 \omega t\, dt}{\frac{\pi}{\omega}}}$$

$$= \frac{I_m}{\sqrt{2}} \quad \text{...(ii)}$$

Dividing Eq. (i) by Eq. (ii), we get

$$\frac{I_{rms}}{I'_{rms}} = \frac{1}{1}$$

$\therefore$ Value of k is 1.

Note The rms values for one cycle and half-cycle (either positive or negative half-cycle) are same.

17. (d) Given, $I = 10$ A, $V = 80$ V

$$R = \frac{V}{I} = \frac{80}{10} = 8\ \Omega \text{ and } f = 50 \text{ Hz}$$

For AC circuit, we have

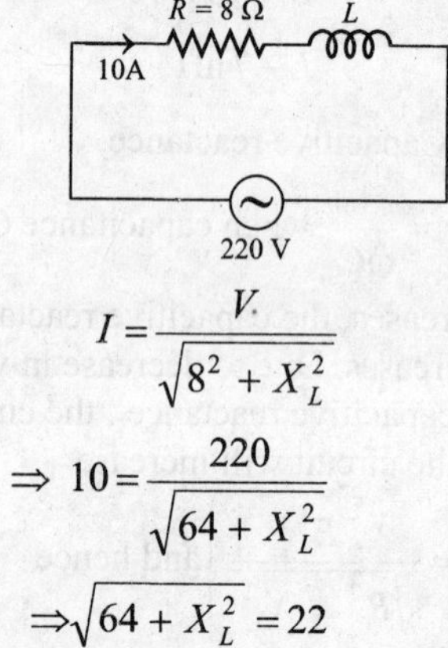

$$I = \frac{V}{\sqrt{8^2 + X_L^2}}$$

$$\Rightarrow 10 = \frac{220}{\sqrt{64 + X_L^2}}$$

$$\Rightarrow \sqrt{64 + X_L^2} = 22$$

Squaring on both sides, we get

$$64 + X_L^2 = 484$$

$\Rightarrow \quad X_L^2 = 484 - 64 = 420$

$\Rightarrow \quad X_L = \sqrt{420}$

$\Rightarrow 2\pi \times fL = \sqrt{420}$

$(\because X_L = \omega L = 2\pi fL)$

Series inductor on an arc lamp,

$$L = \frac{\sqrt{420}}{(2\pi \times 50)} = 0.065 \text{ H}$$

18. (a) $V_{\text{rms}} = 220 \text{ V}, f = 50 \text{ Hz}$

$V_{\text{peak}} = V_m = \sqrt{2}$

$V_{\text{rms}} = 220\sqrt{2} \text{ V}$

$\omega = 2\pi f = 100\pi \text{ rad s}^{-1}$

As, $V = V_m \sin \omega t$

$= 220\sqrt{2} \sin(100\pi t)$

When $V = V_{\text{rms}}$,

$220 = 220\sqrt{2} \sin(100\pi t_1)$

$\Rightarrow \sin(100\pi t_1) = \frac{1}{\sqrt{2}}$

$\Rightarrow 100\pi t_1 = \sin^{-1}\left(\frac{1}{\sqrt{2}}\right) = \frac{\pi}{4}$

$\Rightarrow \quad t_1 = \frac{\pi}{4 \times 100\pi} = \frac{1}{400}$

$= 2.5 \text{ ms}$

When $\quad I = 0$,

$0 = 220\sqrt{2} \sin(100\pi t_2)$

$\Rightarrow \sin(100\pi t_2) = 0$

$\Rightarrow \quad 100\pi t_2 = \sin^{-1}(0) = \pi$

$\Rightarrow \quad t_2 = \frac{1}{100} = 10 \times 10^{-3}$

$= 10 \text{ ms}$

$\therefore$ Time required $= 10 - 2.5 = 7.5 \text{ ms}$

$= 3 \times 2.5 \text{ ms}$

$\therefore N$ is equal to 3.

19. (c) Slope of line representing voltage line, $\quad \tan\theta = \frac{V_0}{T/2}$

Equation of line will be

$$V = \frac{V_0}{T/2} t - V_0$$

$\Rightarrow \quad V = V_0\left(\frac{2t}{T} - 1\right)$

Also, $V_{\text{av}} = \frac{\int_0^{T/2} V\, dt}{\int_0^{T/2} dt}$

$= \frac{2}{T} V_0\left(\frac{T}{4} - \frac{T}{2}\right) = \frac{-V_0}{2}$

$V_{\text{rms}} = \left(\frac{\int_0^T V^2\, dt}{\int_0^T dt}\right)^{1/2}$

$= \frac{V_0}{\sqrt{T}}\left[\int_0^T \left(\frac{4t^2}{T^2} - \frac{4t}{T} + 1\right) dt\right]^{1/2}$

$= \frac{V_0}{\sqrt{3}}$

Also, $V_0 > V_{\text{rms}} > V_{\text{av}}$

20. (a) Consider the purely capacitive circuit as shown below.

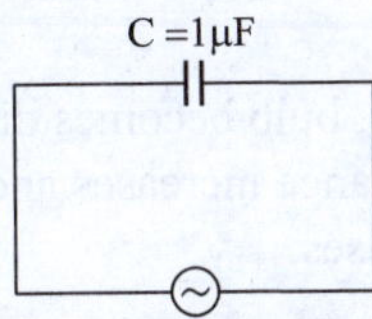

Given, $V = 200\sqrt{2} \sin(100t) \text{ V}$

Comparing it with general equation, $V = V_0 \sin(\omega t)$, we get

$V_0 = 200\sqrt{2} \text{ V}, \omega = 100 \text{ rad s}^{-1}$

$\therefore$ Reactance,

$$X_C = \frac{1}{\omega C} = \frac{1}{100 \times 10^{-6}} = 10^4 \,\Omega$$

Peak value of current,

$$I_0 = \frac{V_0}{X_C} = \frac{200\sqrt{2}}{10^4} = 2\sqrt{2} \times 10^{-2} \text{ A}$$

Rms value of current,

$$I_{\text{rms}} = \frac{I_0}{\sqrt{2}} = \frac{2\sqrt{2} \times 10^{-2}}{\sqrt{2}}$$

$= 20 \times 10^{-3} \text{ A} = 20 \text{ mA}$

Reading of the ammeter will be same as $I_{\text{rms}} = 20 \text{ mA}$.

21. (a) Mean square value of the signal, i.e.

$\frac{1}{T}\int_0^T y^2\, dt = \frac{1}{T}\int_0^T \left[10 + \frac{10}{T} t\right]^2 dt$

$= \frac{1}{T}\int_0^T \left(100 + \frac{100}{T^2} t^2 + \frac{200}{T} t\right) dt$

$= \frac{1}{T}\left[100t + \frac{100t^3}{3T^2} + \frac{100t^2}{T}\right]_0^T$

$= \frac{700}{3}$

So, rms value $= 10\sqrt{\frac{7}{3}}$

22. (a) Given, $I = I_0 + I_1 \sin \omega t$

So, root mean square value of current,

i.e. $i_{\text{rms}} = \sqrt{\langle i^2 \rangle}$

$$= \sqrt{\frac{\int_0^T (I_0^2 + I_1^2 \sin^2 \omega t + 2I_0 I_1 \sin \omega t)\, dt}{\int_0^T dt}}$$

$$= \sqrt{\frac{\int_0^T \left(I_0^2 + \frac{I_1^2}{2}(1 - \cos 2\omega t) + 2I_0 I_1 \sin \omega t\right) dt}{\int_0^T dt}}$$

$$= \sqrt{\frac{(I_0^2 + 0.5I_1^2)\,T}{T}}$$

$= \sqrt{I_0^2 + 0.5I_1^2}$

23. (c) As, $E_1 = E_0 \sin \omega t$

$E_2 = E_0 \sin[\omega t + (\pi/3)]$

According to superposition principle, we get

$E = E_1 + E_2$

$= E_0 \sin \omega t + E_0 \sin\left[\omega t + \left(\frac{\pi}{3}\right)\right]$

$\left[\text{Using, } \sin A + \sin B = 2\sin\left[\frac{A+B}{2}\right] \times \cos\left[\frac{A-B}{2}\right]\right]$

$$= E_0 \left[2 \sin \left\{ \omega t + \left(\frac{\pi}{6} \right) \right\} \cos \left(\frac{\pi}{6} \right) \right]$$

$$= \sqrt{3}\, E_0 \sin \left[\omega t + \left(\frac{\pi}{6} \right) \right]$$

24. (a) The alternating current at any instant t is given by

$$I = I_0 \sin \omega t$$

Assuming that current remains constant for a small time dt, then the amount of charge that flows through the circuit in small time dt will be $dq = Idt = I_0 \sin \omega t\, dt$

$\therefore$ The total charge that flows through the circuit in small time dt will be

$$q = \int dq = \int_0^{2\pi/\omega} I\, dt$$

$$= \int_0^{\frac{2\pi}{\omega}} I_0 \sin \omega t\, dt$$

$$= I_0 \left[\frac{-\cos \omega t}{\omega} \right]_0^{2\pi/\omega}$$

$$= \frac{-I_0}{2\pi / T} [\cos 2\pi - \cos 0°]$$

$$= \frac{-I_0 T}{2\pi} [1 - 1] = 0$$

$\therefore$ The average value of AC over one complete cycle, $I_{av} = \frac{q}{T} = 0$

25. (d) Equation of current can be written as

$$i = 2 \sin 100\pi t + 2 \sin (100\pi t + 120°)$$

$$[\because \cos \theta = \sin (90 + \theta)]$$

So, phase difference is 120°.

$$i_{peak} = \sqrt{2^2 + 2^2 + 2(2)(2) \cos 120°}$$

$$= 2 \text{ A}$$

Effective value of current,

$$i_{rms} = \frac{i_{peak}}{\sqrt{2}} = \frac{2}{\sqrt{2}} = \sqrt{2} \text{ A}$$

Test-2

1. (b) Given,

$$V = 10 \cos \omega t = 10 \sin \left(\omega t + \frac{\pi}{2} \right)$$

$$i = 5 \sin \omega t$$

$$P = V_{rms} \times i_{rms} \times \cos \phi = 0$$

$$\left[\because \phi = \frac{\pi}{2} \right]$$

2. (c) Given, $i_{WL} = i_{rms} \sin \phi$

$$\Rightarrow \sin \phi = \frac{i_{WL}}{i_{rms}} = \frac{2}{4} = \frac{1}{2}$$

$$\Rightarrow \quad \phi = \sin^{-1} \left(\frac{1}{2} \right) = 30°$$

Power factor, $\cos \phi = \cos 30° = \frac{\sqrt{3}}{2}$

3. (c) In series L-R circuit,

$$Z = \sqrt{R^2 + (\omega L)^2}$$

and $\quad I_{rms} = \frac{V_{rms}}{Z}$

Thus, $\quad P = V_{rms} \times I_{rms} \cos \phi$

$$= \frac{V_{rms}^2 \cos \phi}{Z}$$

Hence, bulb becomes dim as impedance increases and current decreases.

4. (d) Bandwidth of the system is the range of frequencies for which the total power is more than the half of maximum power. It is represented by $\Delta \omega$

$$\Delta \omega = \omega_2 - \omega_1 = \frac{R}{L}$$

or $\quad 2\pi \Delta f = \frac{R}{L}$

or $\quad \Delta f = \frac{R}{2\pi L}$

5. (c) Let the resistance of choke coil be R.

Given that, $f_1 = 180$ Hz, $\cos \phi = 0.5$ and $f_2 = 60$ Hz

Power factor, $\cos \phi = \frac{R}{Z}$

where, Z is impedance of choke coil.

or $\quad R = Z \cos \phi$

or $\quad R = Z \times 0.5 = \frac{Z}{2}$

But $\quad Z = \sqrt{R^2 + (\omega L)^2}$

or $\quad \omega L = \sqrt{Z^2 - R^2}$

or $\quad 2\pi f_1 L = \sqrt{Z^2 - \left(\frac{Z}{2} \right)^2}$

$$[\because \omega = 2\pi f]$$

or $\quad 2\pi \times 180 L = \frac{\sqrt{3}}{2} Z$

or $\quad L = \frac{\sqrt{3} Z}{720\pi}$

When frequency is changed to ω_2, then new inductive reactance,

$$X_L' = \omega_2 L = 2\pi f_2 L$$

$$= 2\pi \times 60 \times \frac{\sqrt{3} Z}{720\pi} = \frac{Z}{2\sqrt{3}}$$

New impedance,

$$Z' = \sqrt{R^2 + (X_L')^2}$$

$$= \sqrt{\left(\frac{Z}{2} \right)^2 + \left(\frac{Z}{2\sqrt{3}} \right)^2}$$

$$= \sqrt{\frac{Z^2}{4} + \frac{Z^2}{12}} = \frac{Z}{\sqrt{3}}$$

$\therefore$ New power factor, $\cos \phi_2 = \frac{R}{Z'}$

$$\cos \phi_2 = \frac{\frac{Z}{2}}{\frac{Z}{\sqrt{3}}}$$

$$\cos \phi_2 = \frac{\sqrt{3}}{2} = 0.866$$

6. (d) Given, $V = 200 \sin \left(\omega t + \frac{\pi}{3} \right)$ V

$$I = 5\sqrt{2} \cos \left(\omega t - \frac{\pi}{6} \right) \text{A}$$

or $\quad I = 5\sqrt{2} \sin \left(\frac{\pi}{2} + \omega t - \frac{\pi}{6} \right)$

$$= 5\sqrt{2} \sin \left(\omega t + \frac{\pi}{3} \right) \text{A}$$

$$\left[\because \cos \theta = \sin \left(\frac{\pi}{2} + \theta \right) \right]$$

Phase difference between voltage and current,

$$\phi = \left(\omega t + \frac{\pi}{3} \right) - \left(\omega t + \frac{\pi}{3} \right) = 0$$

Power consumption,

$$P = V_{rms} I_{rms} \cos \phi$$

$$= \left(\frac{200}{\sqrt{2}}\right)\left(\frac{5\sqrt{2}}{\sqrt{2}}\right)\cos 0^\circ$$

$$= 100\sqrt{2} \times 5 \times 1$$

$$= 500\sqrt{2}\ \text{W}$$

7. (d) Capacitive inductance,

$$X_C = \frac{1}{\omega C} = \frac{1}{340 \times 50 \times 10^{-6}}$$

$$= 58.8\,\Omega$$

$$X_L = \omega L = 340 \times 20 \times 10^{-3}$$

$$= 6.8\,\Omega$$

$$Z = \sqrt{R^2 + (X_C - X_L)^2}$$

$$= \sqrt{40^2 + (58.8 - 6.8)^2}$$

$$= \sqrt{4304}\ \Omega$$

Power loss in circuit,

$$P = i_{rms}^2 R = \left(\frac{V_{rms}}{Z}\right)^2 \times R$$

$$= \left(\frac{25/\sqrt{2}}{\sqrt{4304}}\right)^2 \times 40$$

$$= \frac{312.5 \times 40}{4304} = 2.90\ \text{W}$$

8. (a) (a) As, $X_L = \omega L = 2\pi \times 50$

$$\times \frac{100}{\pi} \times 10^{-3} = 10\,\Omega$$

and $X_C = \dfrac{1}{\omega C}$

$$= \frac{1}{2\pi \times 50 \times \dfrac{100}{\pi} \times 10^{-6}}$$

$$= 100\,\Omega$$

Impedance of the circuit, i.e.

$$Z = \sqrt{R^2 + (X_L - X_C)^2}$$

$$= \sqrt{(100)^2 + (10 - 100)^2}$$

$$= 134.5\,\Omega$$

rms value of the current through the inductor is

$$I_{rms} = \frac{220}{Z} = \frac{220}{134.5} = 1.63\ \text{A}$$

$\therefore$ C $\rightarrow$ 2

rms value of voltage drop across the capacitor is

$$V_C = I_{rms} X_C = 1.63 \times 100 = 163\ \text{V}$$

$\therefore$ D $\rightarrow$ 3

Average power dissipated across the resistor is

$$P_{av} = I_{rms}^2 \times R$$

$$= (1.63)^2 \times 100 = 265.7\ \text{W}$$

$\therefore$ A $\rightarrow$ 4

Thus, average power dissipated in inductor and capacitor would be zero.

$\therefore$ B $\rightarrow$ 1

9. (a) In an *L-C-R* circuit, in the condition of resonance, $X_L = X_C$ i.e. circuit behaves as resistive circuit. In resistive circuit, power factor is maximum.

10. (c) $\tan 60^\circ = \dfrac{\omega L}{R}$ or $\tan 60^\circ = \dfrac{\frac{1}{\omega C}}{R}$

Impedance of circuit = *R*

Current in the circuit,

$$I_0 = \frac{V_0}{Z} = \frac{V_0}{R} = 2\ \text{A}$$

Average power,

$$P = \frac{1}{2} V_0 \cdot I_0 \cdot \cos \phi$$

$$(\because \cos \phi = 1)$$

$$P = \frac{1}{2} \times 200 \times 2 \times 1$$

$$P = 200\ \text{W}$$

11. (b) Power dissipated in an *L-R* circuit is given by

$$P = Vi \cos \phi = V\left(\frac{V}{Z}\right)\left(\frac{R}{Z}\right)$$

$$= \frac{V^2 R}{Z^2} = \frac{V^2 R}{(R^2 + \omega^2 L^2)}$$

12. (a) Power consumed by lamp,

$$P = P_{peak} \cdot \cos \phi$$

$$P = 89\% \text{ of } P_{peak}$$

$$\Rightarrow 0.89 P_{peak} = P_{peak} \cos \phi$$

$$\Rightarrow \cos \phi = 0.89$$

$$\Rightarrow \phi = 27^\circ$$

13. (a) Power dissipated in the circuit is

$$P_{av} = V_{rms}\, i_{rms} \cos \phi$$

$$i_{rms} = \frac{V_{rms}}{Z} = \frac{V_{rms}}{\sqrt{R^2 + X_L^2}}$$

$$= \frac{6}{\sqrt{4^2 + 2^2}} = \frac{3}{\sqrt{5}}\ \text{A}$$

$$\cos \phi = \frac{R}{Z} = \frac{4}{\sqrt{4^2 + 2^2}} = \frac{2}{\sqrt{5}}$$

$$P_{av} = V_{rms}\, i_{rms} \cos \phi$$

$$= (6)\left(\frac{3}{\sqrt{5}}\right)\left(\frac{2}{\sqrt{5}}\right)$$

$$= \frac{36}{5} = 7.2\ \text{W}$$

14. (d) Current required for lamp

$$\frac{P}{V} = \frac{10}{50} = 0.2\ \text{A} = I_{rms}$$

The relation between I_{rms} and V_{rms} is

$$I_{rms} = \frac{V_{rms}}{X_C} = \frac{V_{rms}}{\frac{1}{2\pi f C}} = V_{rms} \times 2\pi f C$$

$$\Rightarrow \quad C = \frac{I_{rms}}{V_{rms}\, 2\pi f}$$

$$= \frac{0.2}{(240) 2\pi (50)} = 2.65\ \mu\text{F}$$

15. (c)

60 V

L

100 V, 50 Hz

For *R-L* circuit, $V = \sqrt{V_R^2 + V_L^2}$

or $V_L = \sqrt{V^2 - V_R^2}$

$$= \sqrt{(100)^2 - (60)^2}$$

$$= \sqrt{10000 - 3600}$$

$$= \sqrt{6400} = 80\text{ V}$$

Power rating of bulb, $P = VI$

or $I = \frac{P}{V} = \frac{10}{60} = \frac{1}{6}$ A

Voltage across inductor, $V_L = I X_L$

or $X_L = \frac{V_L}{I} = \frac{80}{1/6} = 480\Omega$

$2\pi f L = 480$

or $2\pi \times 50 L = 480$

$\Rightarrow L = \frac{480}{100\pi} = 1.52\text{ H}$

Test-3

1. (b) Due to change in flux, eddy current is produced in the core of the transformer. It reduces the amount of input current. Hence, to prevent this loss, the core is laminated.

Hence, option (b) is correct.

2. (d) For transformer, transformation ratio is $\frac{N_P}{N_S} = \frac{I_S}{I_P}$

$$I_P = \frac{N_S}{N_P} I_S = \frac{50}{1} \times (1) = 50\text{ A}$$

3. (d) Efficiency of transformer,

$$\eta = \frac{V_S I_S}{V_P I_P} = \frac{\text{Output power}}{V_P I_P}$$

$$= \frac{1100}{(110)(0.5)} = 20\%$$

4. (a) From transformation ratio,

$$\frac{V_S}{V_P} = \frac{N_S}{N_P}$$

$$\Rightarrow V_S = \frac{V_P \times N_S}{N_P}$$

$$= \frac{220 \times 40000}{200}$$

$$= 44000\text{ V}$$

Potential difference per turn is

$$\frac{V_S}{N_S} = \frac{44000}{40000} = 1.1\text{ V}$$

5. (b) The magnetic flux linked with the primary coil is given by

$$\phi = \phi_0 + 4t$$

So, voltage across primary coil,

$$V_P = \frac{d\phi}{dt} = \frac{d}{dt}(\phi_0 + 4t) = 4\text{ V}$$

(as ϕ_0 = constant)

Also, we have

$N_P = 50$ and $N_s = 1500$

From relation, $\frac{V_S}{V_P} = \frac{N_S}{N_P}$

$$\Rightarrow V_S = V_P \frac{N_S}{N_P}$$

$$= 4\left(\frac{1500}{50}\right) = 120\text{ V}$$

6. (a) Efficiency of a transformer is given by, $\eta = \frac{V_S I_S}{V_P I_P} \times 100$

$$I_S = \frac{\eta V_P I_P}{V_S \times 100}$$

$$= \frac{(95)(1100)(6)}{220 \times 100} = 28.5\text{ A}$$

7. (a) Given, $\frac{N_1}{N_2} = \frac{V_1}{V_2}$

$$\Rightarrow \frac{40}{1} = \frac{160}{V_2}$$

$$\Rightarrow V_2 = 40\text{ V}$$

Output power,

$$P_2 = \frac{V_2^2}{R_2} = \frac{(40)^2}{1} = 1600\text{ W}$$

8. (c) $P_{\text{in}} = 240 \times 0.7 = 168$ W,

$P_{\text{out}} = 140$ W

Efficiency of the transformer, i.e.

$$\eta = \frac{P_{\text{out}}}{P_{\text{in}}} \times 100$$

$$= \frac{140}{168} \times 100$$

$$= 83.3\%$$

9. (c) $P_o = V_S I_S$

$$6.6 \times 10^3 = 3.3 \times 10^3 I_S$$

$$I_S = 2\text{ A}$$

10. (d) Line resistance

$$= lx = 2 \times 15 \times 0.5 = 15\Omega$$

The rms value of current in line

$$= \frac{P}{V} = \frac{800 \times 1000}{4000} = 200\text{ A}$$

So, line power loss $= I_{\text{rms}}^2 R$

$$= (200)^2 \times 15 = 600\text{ kW}$$

11. (a) Here,

$N_P = 2000$, $N_S = 50$, $E_P = 120$ V, $R_S = 0.6\Omega$

By using, $\frac{E_P}{E_S} = \frac{N_P}{N_S}$

$$\Rightarrow E_S = \frac{N_S}{N_P} \times E_P$$

$$= \frac{50}{2000} \times 120 = 3\text{ V}$$

$\therefore$ Voltage across the secondary coil, i.e. $E_S = 3$ V

So, current in the bulb, i.e.

$$I_S = \frac{E_S}{R_S} = \frac{3}{0.6} = 5\text{ A}$$

As we know that, $\frac{I_P}{I_S} = \frac{N_S}{N_P}$

So, current in primary coil,

$$I_P = \frac{N_S}{N_P} \times I_S$$

$$= \frac{50}{2000} \times 5 = 0.125\text{ A}$$

As power in primary and secondary coils,

i.e. $E_P I_P = E_S I_S$

$$= 120 \times 0.125 = 15\text{ W}$$

12. (a) For a transformer, there are two circuits which have N_P and N_S (number of coil turns), I_P and I_S (currents) respectively as shown below.

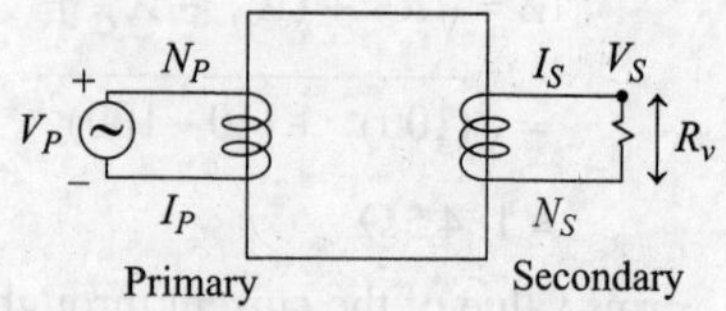

Here, input voltage, $V_P = 2300$ V

Number of turns in primary coil, $N_P = 4000$

Output voltage, $V_S = 230\,\text{V}$

Output power, $P_S = V_S \cdot I_S$

Input power, $P_P = V_P \cdot I_P$

$\therefore$ The efficiency of the transformer is

$$\eta = \frac{\text{Output (secondary) power}}{\text{Input (primary) power}}$$

$$= \frac{V_S \cdot I_S}{V_P \cdot I_P} \times 100$$

$$\Rightarrow \eta = \frac{(230)(I_S)}{(2300)(5)} \times 100$$

$$\Rightarrow 90 = \frac{230\,I_S}{(2300) \times 5} \times 100$$

$$\Rightarrow I_S = 45\,\text{A}$$

13. (a) We have, $N_S I_S = N_P I_P$

$$\Rightarrow \frac{N_S}{N_P} = \frac{I_P}{I_S}$$

$$\Rightarrow \frac{2}{3} = \frac{3}{I_S}$$

$$\Rightarrow I_S = \frac{3 \times 3}{2} = \frac{9}{2} = 4.5\,\text{A}$$

14. (a) Leclanche cell gives a DC voltage. As the input from Leclanche cell does not change with time, the magnetic flux linked with the secondary coil does not change and hence output voltage will be zero.

15. (a) Given, number of turns in primary coil, $N_1 = 300$

Number of turns in secondary coil, $N_2 = 150$

Output power,

$$P_2 = 2.2 \text{ kW} = 2.2 \times 10^3 \text{ W}$$

Current in secondary coil, $I_2 = 10\,\text{A}$

Output power,

$$P_2 = I_2 V_2$$

$$\Rightarrow V_2 = \frac{P_2}{I_2} = \frac{2.2 \times 10^3}{10} = 220\,\text{V} \quad \ldots \text{(i)}$$

We know that,

$$\frac{N_1}{N_2} = \frac{\text{Input voltage}}{\text{Output voltage}} = \frac{V_1}{V_2}$$

$$\Rightarrow V_1 = \left(\frac{N_1}{N_2}\right) V_2$$

$$\Rightarrow V_1 = \left(\frac{300}{150}\right) \times (220)$$

[using Eq. (i)]

$$\Rightarrow V_1 = 440\,\text{V} \quad \ldots \text{(ii)}$$

Again, $\frac{V_1}{V_2} = \frac{I_2}{I_1}$

$$\Rightarrow I_1 = \left(\frac{V_2}{V_1}\right) I_2 = \frac{220}{440} \times 10$$

[using Eqs. (i) and (ii)]

$$\Rightarrow I_1 = 5\,\text{A}$$

Chapter Break Thru

1. (d) In an *L-C-R* series circuit,

$$\phi = \tan^{-1} \frac{X_L - X_C}{R}$$

When $X_L = 2X_C$ and $R = X_C$, then

$$\phi = \tan^{-1} \left[\frac{2X_C - X_C}{X_C}\right]$$

$$= \tan^{-1}(1) = 45^\circ$$

2. (d) Z is minimum when $\omega = \omega_d$, at resonance.

3. (a) As we know,

$$X_L = \omega L = 3000 \times 10^{-2}\,\Omega$$

$$= 30\,\Omega$$

$$X_C = \frac{1}{\omega C} = \frac{1}{3000 \times 25 \times 10^{-6}}$$

$$= \frac{1000}{75} = \frac{40}{3}\,\Omega$$

So, $X_L - X_C = \left(30 - \frac{40}{3}\right)\Omega$

$$= \frac{50}{3}\,\Omega$$

Given, $R = 100\,\Omega$

As, $\tan\phi = \frac{|X_L - X_C|}{R}$

$$= \frac{50}{3 \times 100} = \frac{1}{6}$$

$$\phi = \tan^{-1}\left(\frac{1}{6}\right) = \tan^{-1}(0.17)$$

4. (b) Both statements are incorrect because current leads by $\frac{\pi}{2}$ in the capacitive circuit while in this Statement I ; current is lagging behind the voltage.

Statement II is incorrect because Z is the hypotenuse of the right angled triangle.

5. (d) On comparing,

$V = 100\sqrt{2}\sin(50t)$ with

$V = V_0 \sin\omega t$, we get

$V_0 = 100\sqrt{2}\,\text{V}$, $\omega = 50\,\text{rad s}^{-1}$

$$\therefore \quad V_{\text{rms}} = \frac{V_0}{\sqrt{2}} = \frac{100\sqrt{2}}{\sqrt{2}} = 100\,\text{V}$$

The capacitive reactance,

$$X_C = \frac{1}{\omega C}$$

$$X_C = \frac{1}{50 \times 2 \times 10^{-6}} = 10^4\,\Omega$$

AC ammeter reads the rms value of current. Therefore, the reading of the ammeter,

$$I_{\text{rms}} = \frac{V_{\text{rms}}}{X_C} = \frac{100}{10^4} = 10^{-2} = 10$$

mA

The average power consumed in the circuit,

$$\overline{P} = I_{\text{rms}} \cdot V_{\text{rms}} \cdot \cos\phi$$

For pure capacitive circuit,

$$\phi = 90^\circ$$

So, $\overline{P} = 0$

6. (a) At very high frequencies,

$$X_L = 2\pi f L = \infty$$

Here, inductor behaves like an open switch at very high frequency.

Capacitor behaves like pure conductor at very high frequency.

So, given circuit will be

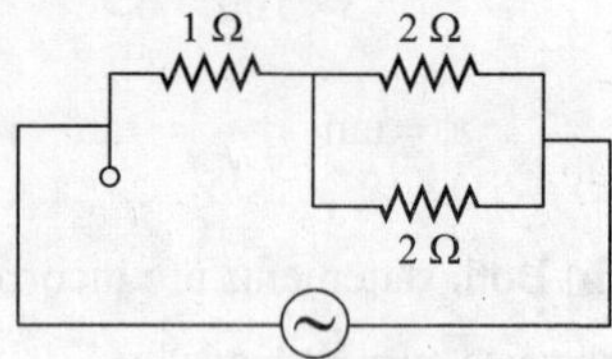

So, effective impedance

$= [1\Omega \text{ in series with } (2\Omega \,||\, 2\Omega)]$

$= 2\Omega$

7. (b) Resonance frequency is given by

$$\omega = \frac{1}{\sqrt{LC}} = \frac{1}{\sqrt{18 \times 2 \times 10^{-6}}}$$

$$= 166.7 \text{ rad/s}$$

8. (a) As average power of an AC circuit is

$$P = V_{\text{rms}} I_{\text{rms}} \cos\phi = V_{\text{rms}} I_{\text{rms}} \times \frac{R}{Z}$$

$$\left(\text{Power factor, i.e. } \cos\phi = \frac{R}{Z}\right)$$

In *R-C* series circuit with an AC source,

Net reactive impedance,

$$Z = \sqrt{R^2 + \left(\frac{1}{\omega C}\right)^2}$$

On increasing the frequency, the capacitive reactance decreases. If reactance decreases, more current will flow and the bulb will glow with more brightness.

9. (c) Root mean square value of potential difference V is given as

$$V_{\text{rms}} = \left[\frac{1}{T}\int_0^{T/4} V_0^2\, dt\right]^{1/2}$$

$$= \left[\frac{V_0^2}{T}[t]_0^{T/4}\right]^{1/2}$$

$$= \left[\frac{V_0^2}{T}\left(\frac{T}{4}\right)\right]^{1/2}$$

Thus, $V_{\text{rms}} = \dfrac{V_0}{2}$

10. (d) If $\omega = 2\pi f = 50 \times 2\pi$,

then $\omega L = 20\Omega$

$$L = \frac{20}{50 \times 2\pi} = \frac{1}{5\pi}$$

Similarly $\omega' = 100 \times 2\pi$,

then $\omega' L = \dfrac{100 \times 2\pi}{5\pi} = 40\Omega$

$$i = \frac{100}{Z} = \frac{100}{\sqrt{R^2 + (\omega' L)^2}}$$

$$= \frac{100}{\sqrt{(30)^2 + (40)^2}} = 2\text{A}$$

11. (c) Phase angle between potential and current will be given as

$$\tan\phi = \frac{X_L}{R} = \frac{2\pi f L}{R}$$

$$= \frac{2\pi \times \frac{100}{2\pi} \times 1}{100} = 1$$

$$\Rightarrow \quad \phi = \tan^{-1}(1) = 45°$$

12. (d) Given, $I_{\text{DC}} = 10\text{ A}$

$$I_{\text{AC}} = 12 \sin \omega t$$

$$I_{\text{rms}} = \frac{I_0}{\sqrt{2}} = \frac{12}{\sqrt{2}} = 6\sqrt{2}\text{A}$$

Effective value of resulting current,

$$I = \sqrt{I_{\text{DC}}^2 + I_{\text{rms}}^2}$$

$$= \sqrt{100 + 72}$$

$$\simeq 13\text{ A}$$

13. (a) [Phasor diagram: V_L upward, V_R and I_R along horizontal, V_C downward]

(a) Phase difference between current and voltage in a purely resistive AC circuit is zero.
Hence, A → 1

(b) Phase difference between current and voltage in a pure inductive AC circuit is $\frac{\pi}{2}$; current lags voltage.
Hence, B → 3

(c) Phase difference between current and voltage in a pure capacitive AC circuit is $\frac{\pi}{2}$, current leads voltage.
Hence, C → 2

(d) Phase difference between current and voltage in an *L-C-R* series circuit is

$$\tan^{-1}\left(\frac{X_C - X_L}{R}\right)$$

Hence, D → 4

14. (d) The current will lag behind the voltage when reactance of inductance is more than the reactance of condenser.

Thus, $\omega L > \dfrac{1}{\omega C}$

or $\quad \omega > \dfrac{1}{\sqrt{LC}}$

on $\quad n > \dfrac{1}{2\pi\sqrt{LC}}$ or $n > n_r$ where

n_r = resonant frequency.

15. (b) As we know that root mean square current of the sinusoidal waveform,

$$I = \frac{I_0}{\sqrt{2}}$$

So, output power of the heater, i.e.

$$P = (I_{\text{rms}})^2 R = \left(\frac{I_0}{\sqrt{2}}\right)^2 \times R = \frac{I_0^2 R}{2}$$

16. (c) $E_S = \dfrac{N_S}{N_P} E_P = \dfrac{10}{200} \times 240$

$$= 12\text{ V}$$

17. (a) Power transferred from the driving source to the driven oscillator is $P = I^2 Z \cos\phi$.
Therefore, power factor $\cos\phi \geq 0$ and $P \geq 0$. For wattless component, the driving force shall give no energy to the oscillator ($P = 0$, where $\phi = 90°$). Further, the driving force cannot syphon out energy of the oscillator, i.e. P cannot be negative.

18. (d) Wherever there's a current or moving charged particle, there is a magnetic field. So, it should not matter whether there is a direct current or an alternating current. The only difference in DC from AC is that in AC, the magnitude of the current is continuously changing and its direction changes over a period of time. So what's changing is the rate of motion of charges but anyhow charges are in motion and hence there must be any magnetic effect.

19. (c) In case of a coil, as

$$Z = \sqrt{R^2 + \omega^2 L^2}$$

i.e. $I = \frac{V}{Z} = \frac{V}{\sqrt{R^2 + \omega^2 L^2}}$

So, when DC is applied as $\omega = 0$

$I = \frac{V}{R}$, i.e. $R = \frac{12}{4} = 3\Omega$

and when AC is applied,

$I = \frac{V}{R}$,

i.e. $Z = \frac{V}{I} = \frac{12}{2.4} = 5\Omega$

Now, $Z = \sqrt{R^2 + X_L^2}$

$$Z^2 = R^2 + X_L^2$$

$$25 = (3)^2 + X_L^2$$

$$X_L^2 = 16$$

$$X_L = 4$$

We know that, $X_L = \omega L$

$$L = \frac{X_L}{\omega} = \frac{4}{50}$$

$$L = 0.08 \text{ H}$$

20. (b) Wattless component of AC

$$= I_V \sin\phi = \frac{E_V}{Z} \cdot \frac{X_L}{Z} = \frac{E_V X_L}{Z^2}$$

$$= \frac{220 \times \omega L}{(R^2 + \omega^2 L^2)}$$

As, $\omega L = 2\pi \times 50 \times 0.7 = 220\Omega$

Hence, wattless component of AC circuit

$$= \frac{220 \times 220}{(220)^2 + (220)^2}$$

$$= 0.5 \text{ A}$$

21. (a) Average power,

$$P_{av} = e_{rms} \cdot i_{rms} \cdot \cos\phi$$

$$= \frac{e_0}{\sqrt{2}} \cdot \frac{i_0}{\sqrt{2}} \cdot \cos\phi$$

Here, $e_0 = 100 \text{ V}$, $i_0 = 20 \text{ A}$, $\phi = \frac{\pi}{4}$

$$\therefore P_{av} = \frac{100}{\sqrt{2}} \cdot \frac{20}{\sqrt{2}} \cdot \cos\frac{\pi}{4}$$

$$\Rightarrow P_{av} = \frac{1000}{\sqrt{2}} \text{ unit}$$

Wattless current,

$$i_w = i_{rms} \sin\phi = \frac{i_0}{\sqrt{2}} \cdot \sin\frac{\pi}{4}$$

$$= \frac{20}{2}$$

$$\Rightarrow i_w = 10 \text{ A}$$

22. (b) For purely inductive circuit, $Z = 2\pi f L$

$$Z \propto f, \text{A} \rightarrow 4$$

For purely resistive circuit, $Z = R$ independent of frequency. B $\rightarrow$ 3

For purely capacitive circuit,

$$Z = \frac{1}{2\pi f C}$$

$$Z \propto \frac{1}{f}, \text{C} \rightarrow 2$$

The graph of Z *versus* f for an L-C-R circuit is a U-shaped curve with minimum impedance at the resonant frequency. D $\rightarrow$ 1

Hence, A-4, B-3, C-2, D-1

23. (b) Total flux in the core $= \phi_P + \phi_S = 0.2 + 0.4 = 0.6 \text{ mWb}$

Self-inductance of primary coil is

$$L_1 = \frac{N_1 \phi_1}{I_1}$$

$$\Rightarrow L_1 = \frac{500 \times 0.2 \times 10^{-3}}{5.0} = 20 \text{ mH}$$

M = coefficient of mutual induction

$$= \frac{N_2 \phi_2}{I_1} = \frac{1500 \times 0.4 \times 10^{-3}}{5}$$

$$= 120 \text{ mH}$$

and $M = \sqrt{L_1 L_2}$

$$\Rightarrow 120 \times 10^{-3} = \sqrt{20 \times L_2 \times 10^{-3}}$$

$\Rightarrow$

$$L_2 = 720 \times 10^{-3} = 720 \text{ mH}$$

$$\Rightarrow L_2 = 90 \times 8 \text{ mH}$$

$$\Rightarrow k = 8$$

24. (c) Transmission line can be made thinner. This statement is not entirely accurate. While higher voltage transmission reduces the current, which in turn reduces the power loss and potentially allows for thinner wires. Transmission lines must still be of a sufficient thickness to handle environmental factors and mechanical stresses. Hence, option (c) is the correct answer.

25. (a) In circuit (b),

Inductive reactance,

$$X_L = 2\pi f L$$

$$= 2\pi \times 50 \times 50 \times 10^{-3} \Omega$$

$$= 15.7\Omega$$

And capacitive reactance,

$$X_C = \frac{1}{2\pi f C}$$

$$= \frac{1}{2\pi \times 50 \times 0.5 \times 10^{-6}}$$

$$= 6366\Omega$$

As $X_L \neq X_C$, there is no resonance in circuit (b). So, impedance of circuit (b) is always greater than circuit (b).

$\Rightarrow I_{rms}$ is always smaller in circuit current (a).

26. (a) As, rms value of current,

$$I_{rms} = V_{rms} / Z$$

So, net impedance across L-C-R circuit,

$$Z = \sqrt{R^2 + (X_L - X_C)^2}$$

$$= \sqrt{(100)^2 + [\omega L - X_C]^2}$$

$$= \sqrt{(100)^2 + \left[\left(100 \times \pi \times \frac{1}{\pi}\right) - (X_C)\right]^2}$$

$$\left(\frac{220}{2.2}\right)^2 = (100)^2 + [(100) - (X_C)]^2 \quad \left[\because Z = \frac{V_{rms}}{I}\right]$$

$$\Rightarrow X_C = 100\,\Omega$$

As, $\tan\phi = \frac{X_C}{R} = \frac{100}{100} = 1$

$\Rightarrow \quad \phi = \tan^{-1}(1)$

$\phi = 45°$

Power factor, $\cos\phi = \frac{1}{\sqrt{2}}$

27. (b) Here, $V = 200$ V, $I = 5$ A, $\eta = ?$

$n = \frac{3000}{60} = 50$ rps, $R = 8.5\,\Omega$

If E is the back emf, then

$$I = \frac{V - E}{R}$$

or $\quad V - E = IR$

$\Rightarrow \quad E = V - IR$

$= 200 - 5 \times 8.5 = 157.5$ V

Input power,

$P_{in} = VI = 200 \times 5 = 1000$ W

Output power,

$P_{out} = VI - I^2R = I(V - IR) = IE$

$= 5 \times 157.5 = 787.5$ W

Efficiency, $\eta = \frac{\text{Output power } (P_{out})}{\text{Input power } (P_{in})}$

$= \frac{787.5}{1000} = 0.7875 = 78.75\%$

28. (d) The given circuit is under resonance as $X_L = X_C$ ($\because$ same phase change in L-R and C-R circuits)

Hence, power dissipated in the circuit is

$$P = \frac{V^2}{R} = 242 \text{ W}$$

29. (d)

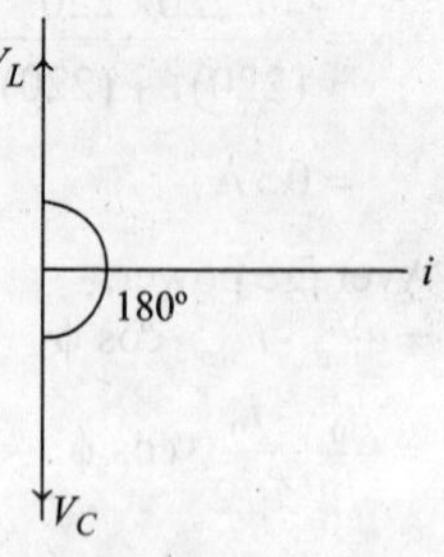

The voltage in L and in C are out of phase by 180°.

30. (d) Impedance, $(Z) = \frac{V_{AC}}{I_{AC}}$

$= \frac{100\text{ V}}{0.5\text{ A}} = 200\,\Omega$

$R = \frac{V_{DC}}{I_{DC}} = \frac{100}{1} = 100\,\Omega$

$L\omega = \sqrt{Z^2 - R^2}$

$= \sqrt{(200)^2 - (100)^2}$

$= 173.2$

$L = \frac{173.2}{\omega} = \frac{173.2}{2\pi f}$

$= \frac{173.2}{2 \times \pi \times 50} = 0.55$ H

31. (b) With DC power, $P = \frac{V^2}{R}$

$R = \frac{(10)^2}{20} = 5\,\Omega$

With AC power, $P = \frac{V_{rms}^2 R}{Z^2}$

$\Rightarrow \quad Z^2 = \frac{(10)^2 \times 5}{10} = 50\,\Omega$

The impedance,

$Z^2 = R^2 + 4\pi^2\nu^2L^2$

$\Rightarrow 50 = (5)^2 + 4(3.14)^2 \times \nu^2 \times (10 \times 10^{-3})^2$

$\Rightarrow \nu \simeq 80$ Hz

32. (b) Given: 110 V, 60 W lamp is run from a 220 V AC mains.

The lamp is close to an ideal resistance giving voltage (V_R) at phase angle $\theta = 0°$;

The capacitor is close to an ideal reactance giving voltage (V_C) at phase angle $\theta = 90°$.

The voltages across the lamp and capacitor will be in quadrature with one another, and the supply voltage (V_S) will be the phasor sum of V_r and V_C.

$\Rightarrow \quad V_S^2 = V_R^2 + V_C^2$

$\Rightarrow \quad V_C^2 = V_S^2 - V_r^2$

$\Rightarrow \quad V_C^2 = (220)^2 - (110)^2$

$\Rightarrow \quad V_C^2 = 36300$

$\Rightarrow \quad V_C = \sqrt{36300} \Rightarrow V_C \simeq 190$ V

33. (d) For instantaneous emf to be 25 V, we must have

$25 = 50\sin(314t)$

or $\quad \frac{1}{2} = \sin(314t)$ or $\frac{\pi}{6} = 314t$

or $\quad t = \frac{\pi}{6 \times 314} = \frac{1}{600}$ s

34. (a) As angular frequency,

$$\omega = \frac{1}{\sqrt{LC}} \quad \dots \text{(i)}$$

When capacitance is made one-fourth, then $\omega' = \omega$

$$\omega' = \frac{1}{\sqrt{L'\frac{C}{4}}} = \omega$$

So, $\quad L' = 4L$

35. (b) Here, $X_L = R$, $X_C = R/2$

$$\therefore \tan\phi = \frac{X_L - X_C}{R} = \frac{R - \frac{R}{2}}{R} = \frac{1}{2}$$

$\Rightarrow \quad \phi = \tan^{-1}(1/2)$

Also, $\quad Z = \sqrt{R^2 + (X_L - X_C)^2}$

$$= \sqrt{R^2 + \frac{R^2}{4}} = \frac{\sqrt{5}}{2}R$$

36. (a) In the *L-C-R* series circuit,

$R = 50\Omega, V_L = 40\text{ V}, V_C = 40\text{ V}$ and $V_{net} = 100\text{ V}$

$$V = \sqrt{V_R^2 + (V_L - V_C)^2}$$

$$100 = \sqrt{V_R^2 + (40-40)^2}$$

So, voltage across resistance,

$$V_R = 100\text{ V}$$

As we know that rms value of current,

$$I_{rms} = \frac{V_{rms}}{Z}$$

At resonating condition, $Z = R$

$$\therefore \quad I_{rms} = \frac{100}{50} = 2\text{ A}$$

37. (a) $X_L = X_C$

So, it is condition of resonance in *L-C-R* circuit.

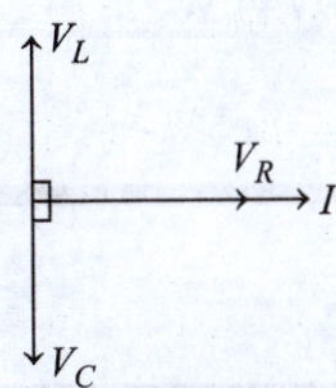

V_L leads current by 90° and V_C lags current by 90°.

Thus, current is in phase with applied voltage.

So, V_R leads V_C by 90°.

38. (d) As, voltage drop across inductance,

$$V = -\frac{LdI}{dt}$$

$V \propto$ slope in I - t graph which is constant and negative for first half (0 to $T/2$) and positive for second half ($T/2$ to T).

39. (a) Resonance frequency,

$$f_0 = \frac{1}{2\pi\sqrt{LC}}$$

In dielectric slab,

$$C = \frac{A\varepsilon_0 k}{d}$$

Capacity of capacitor increases with dielectric slab, which in turn, decreases the resonance frequency.

Hence, both Statement I and Statement II are correct.

40. (b) $P = \frac{1}{2}V_0 i_0 \cos\phi$

$$\Rightarrow 1000 = \frac{1}{2} \times 200 \times i_0 \cos 60°$$

$$\Rightarrow \quad i_0 = 20\text{ A}$$

$$\Rightarrow \quad i_{rms} = \frac{i_0}{\sqrt{2}} = \frac{20}{\sqrt{2}} = 10\sqrt{2}\text{ A}$$

41. (c) Average power dissipated in purely inductive circuit is zero.

$$P_{avg} = V_{rms}\, i_{rms} \cos\phi$$

$$\phi = 90°$$

$$\Rightarrow \quad P_{avg} = 0$$

42. (c)

i_C, i, i_R, i, $V \longrightarrow$, i_L

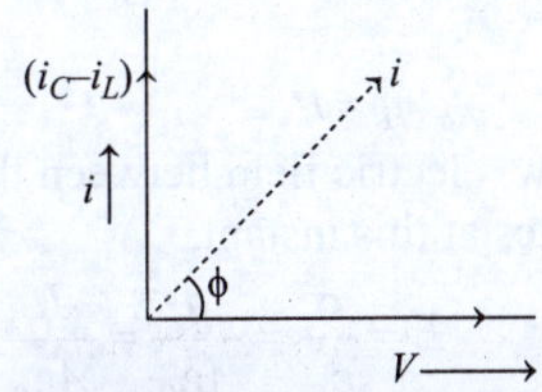

Assuming $i_C > i_L$

Resultant current,

$$i = \sqrt{i_R^2 + (i_C - i_L)^2}$$

$$\frac{V}{Z} = \sqrt{\left(\frac{V}{R}\right)^2 + \left(\frac{V}{X_C} - \frac{V}{X_L}\right)^2}$$

$$\frac{1}{Z} = \sqrt{\frac{1}{R^2} + \left(\frac{1}{X_C} - \frac{1}{X_L}\right)^2}$$

$$\frac{1}{Z} = \sqrt{\frac{1}{R^2} + \left(\omega C - \frac{1}{\omega L}\right)^2}$$

$$Z = \left[\frac{1}{R^2} + \left(\omega C - \frac{1}{\omega L}\right)^2\right]^{-\frac{1}{2}}$$

43. (b) When C is removed, circuit becomes *R-L* circuit, hence

$$\tan\frac{\pi}{3} = \frac{X_L}{R} \quad \ldots \text{(i)}$$

When L is removed, circuit becomes *R-C* circuit, hence

$$\tan\frac{\pi}{3} = \frac{X_C}{R} \quad \ldots \text{(ii)}$$

From Eqs. (i) and (ii), we obtain $X_L = X_C$.

This is condition of resonance and in resonance, $Z = R = 100\Omega$.

44. (a) $i = i_0 \cos(\omega t)$

$$i = i_0 \text{ at } t = 0 = \frac{i_0}{\sqrt{2}} \text{ at } \omega t = \frac{\pi}{4}$$

$$\Rightarrow t = \frac{\pi}{4\omega} = \frac{\pi}{4(2\pi f)} = \frac{1}{8f}$$

$$t = \frac{1}{8 \times 50} \frac{1}{400} = 2.5\text{ ms}$$

45. (c) Primary voltage,

$$V_P = 200\text{ V}$$

Secondary voltage,

$$V_S = \frac{P}{i} = \frac{50}{0.1} = 500\text{ V}$$

Hence, step-up transformer.

46. (c) $P_{out} = V_S I_S$

$$\text{Now, } V_S = \frac{N_S}{N_P} \times V_P$$

$$= \frac{1}{20} \times 2500 = 125\text{ V}$$

$$\text{Thus, } P_{out} = 125 \times 80$$

$$= 10\text{ kW}$$

(It is assumed that the load is resistive, so that the power factor is unity).

47. (c) As, $\tan\phi = \frac{V_L - V_C}{V_R}$

$$= \frac{120 - 20}{50} = 2$$

or $\quad \phi = \tan^{-1}(2) = 63.43°$

Power factor

$$= \cos\phi = \cos 63.43° = 0.4$$

48. (c) We have,

$X_L = 90\Omega, X_C = 30\Omega$

and $R = R_1 + R_2 = 44 + 36 = 80\Omega$

Impedance, $Z = \sqrt{R^2 + (X_L - X_C)^2}$

$= \sqrt{(80)^2 + (60)^2}$

$Z = \sqrt{6400 + 3600} = 100\Omega$

$I = \frac{V}{Z} = \frac{200}{100} = 2\text{ A}$

$P_{av} = I^2 R = (2)^2 \times 36 = 144\text{ W}$

49. (a) $\tan 60° = \frac{\omega L}{R}$, $\tan 60° = \frac{1/\omega C}{R}$

$\therefore \quad \omega L = \frac{1}{\omega C}$

$\therefore$ Impedance of the circuit,

$$Z = \left[R^2 + \left(\omega L - \frac{1}{\omega C}\right)^2\right]^{\frac{1}{2}} = R$$

Current in the circuit,

$i_0 = \frac{V_0}{Z} = \frac{V_0}{R} = \frac{200}{100} = 2\text{ A}$

Average power, $\overline{P} = \frac{1}{2} V_0 i_0 \cos\phi$

But, $\tan\phi = \frac{\omega L - \frac{1}{\omega C}}{R} = 0$

$\therefore \quad \cos\phi = 1$

$\therefore \quad \overline{P} = \frac{1}{2} \times 200 \times 2 \times 1 = 200\text{ W}$

50. (a) Resonant frequency,

$\omega_R = \frac{1}{\sqrt{(LC)}}$

$= \frac{1}{\sqrt{(10\times 10^{-3})\times(1\times 10^{-6})}}$

$= 10^4$ rad/s

The frequency 10% lower than this is

$\omega = 10^4 - 10^4 \times \frac{10}{100}$

$= 9\times 10^3$ rad/s

At this frequency, we have

$X_L = \omega L = 9\times 10^3 \times (10\times 10^{-3})$

$= 90\Omega$

and $X_C = \frac{1}{\omega C} = \frac{1}{9\times 10^3 \times (1\times 10^{-6})}$

$= 111.11\Omega$

$\therefore$ Impedance,

$Z = \sqrt{R^2 + (X_L - X_C)^2}$

$= \sqrt{(3)^2 + (90 - 111.11)^2}$

$= 21.32\Omega$

$\therefore$ Current amplitude is

$i_0 = \frac{E_0}{Z} = \frac{15}{21.32}$

$= 0.704$ A

Average power dissipated is

$P = \frac{1}{2} E_0 i_0 \cos\phi$

Here, $\cos\phi = \frac{R}{Z} = \frac{3}{21.32} = 0.141$

$\therefore \quad P = \frac{1}{2} \times 15 \times 0.704 \times 0.141$

$= 0.744$ W

Ch-09 Electromagnetic Waves

Topical Follow Thru

Test-1

1. (c) Only accelerating charged particle can produce electromagnetic waves. Thus, a proton moving in a non-uniform electric field is capable of producing EM waves.

2. (a) Conduction current is due to flow of charges. But inside a capacitor, charges do not flow. As a result, there is no conduction current inside a capacitor.

3. (a) An oscillating charge produces an electric field in space, which produces an oscillating magnetic field, which in turn, is a source of electric field. Thus, EM wave is a self-sustaining oscillating wave.

4. (a) The charge on capacitor plates at time t is given by

$q = It$

Now, electric field between the plates at this instant,

$E = \frac{\sigma}{\varepsilon_0} = \frac{q}{A\varepsilon_0} = \frac{It}{A\varepsilon_0}$

Flux through the area $\frac{2A}{3}$ is

$\phi_E = \left(\frac{2A}{3}\right)E = \frac{2It}{3\varepsilon_0}$

Therefore, displacement current is

$I_d = \varepsilon_0 \frac{d\phi_E}{dt}$

$= \varepsilon_0 \frac{d}{dt}\left(\frac{2It}{3\varepsilon_0}\right)$

$I_d = \varepsilon_0 \times \frac{2I}{3\varepsilon_0} = \frac{2I}{3}$

5. (a) Velocity of light in a medium is given by

$v = \frac{1}{\sqrt{\mu\varepsilon}} = \frac{c}{\sqrt{\mu_r \varepsilon_r}}$

$= \frac{3\times 10^8}{\sqrt{0.8\times 1.69}} = 2.58\times 10^8$ m/s

6. (b) Compare $\mathbf{E} = 9\sin(1.6\times 10^3 x + 48\times 10^{10} t)\hat{\mathbf{k}}$ V/m with standard equation $\mathbf{E} = E_0 \sin(kx + \omega t)\hat{\mathbf{k}}$ V/m.

From the term $(kx + \omega t)$, it is observed that the wave is propagating in negative X-axis because the argument of sine function indicates a – ve direction due to the + ve sign of kx.

Also,

$\omega = 48\times 10^{10}$ rad/s

$f = \frac{\omega}{2\pi} = \frac{48\times 10^{10}}{2\pi}$

$= 7.64\times 10^{10}$ Hz

7. (c) The standard equation is

$$B_y = B_0 \sin(kx - \omega t)$$

Comparing the given equation,

$$B_y = 4\times 10^{-6} \sin(10^3 \pi x - 2\times 10^{11} \pi t)\,\text{T}$$

with standard equation, we get

$$k = 10^3 \pi$$

$$\omega = 2\times 10^{11} \pi$$

Velocity of EM wave,

$$v = \frac{\omega}{k} = \frac{2\times 10^{11}\pi}{10^3 \pi} = 2\times 10^8 \text{ m/s}$$

8. (b) Average force,

$$F = \frac{\Delta p}{\Delta t} = \frac{2IA}{c}$$

Here, I is the intensity of light, A is the area of cross-section and c is the speed of light.

$$F = \frac{2(50\times 10^4)(30\times 10^{-4})}{3\times 10^8} = 1\times 10^{-5} \text{ N}$$

9. (a) Energy density, $v_{\text{avg}} = \dfrac{cB_0^2}{2\mu_0}$

(here, $c = 3\times 10^8$ m/s, $B_0 = 2\times 10^{-9}$T)

$$= \frac{(3\times 10^8)(2\times 10^{-9})^2}{2\times (4\pi\times 10^{-7})} = 4.77\times 10^{-4} \text{ W/m}^2$$

10. (a) Speed of EM wave,

$$v = \frac{\omega}{k} = \frac{2\times 10^{10}}{200} = 10^8 \text{ m/s}$$

Refractive index,

$$\mu = \frac{c}{v} = \frac{3\times 10^8}{10^8} = 3$$

Since, $\mu = \dfrac{c}{v} = \sqrt{\dfrac{\mu\varepsilon}{\mu_0\varepsilon_0}}$

$$\left[\because c = \frac{1}{\sqrt{\mu_0\varepsilon_0}} \text{ and } v = \frac{1}{\sqrt{\mu\varepsilon}}\right]$$

$\Rightarrow \quad \mu = \sqrt{\mu_r\,\varepsilon_r}$

$\Rightarrow \quad 3 = \sqrt{\varepsilon_r(1)} \quad (\because \mu_r = 1)$

$\Rightarrow \quad \varepsilon_r = 9$

11. (b) Displacement current,

$$i_d = \varepsilon_0 \frac{d\phi_E}{dt} = \varepsilon_0 \frac{d}{dt}(EA)$$

$$= \varepsilon_0 A\frac{dE}{dt} = \varepsilon_0 A \frac{d}{dt}\left(\frac{V}{d}\right)$$

or $\quad i_d = \dfrac{\varepsilon_0 A}{d}\times\dfrac{dV}{dt} = C\dfrac{dV}{dt}$

or $\quad \dfrac{dV}{dt} = \dfrac{i_d}{C} = \dfrac{1}{10^{-6}} = 10^6 \text{ Vs}^{-1}$

Thus, an instantaneous displacement current of 1.0 A can be set up by changing the potential difference across the parallel plates of capacitor at the rate of 10^6 Vs^{-1}.

12. (c) Capacitance,

$$C = \frac{\varepsilon_0 KA}{d} = \frac{(8.85\times 10^{-12})\times 10\times 1}{10^{-3}} = 8.85\times 10^{-8} \text{ F}$$

Now, $I_d = \dfrac{dQ}{dt} = \dfrac{d}{dt}(CV)$

$$= C\frac{dV}{dt}$$

$$= 8.85\times 10^{-8} \times 25$$

$$= 2.2\times 10^{-6}\text{ A} = 2.2\,\mu\text{A}$$

13. (c) According to the question, a parallel plate capacitor is shown in the figure below.

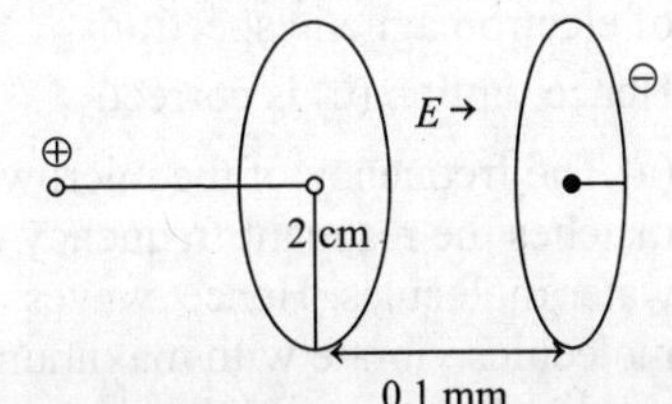

Given,

Radius = 2 cm,

Distance between plates,

$d = 0.1$ mm and $\dfrac{dV}{dt} = 5\times 10^6 \text{ Vs}^{-1}$

Displacement current in the capacitor,

$$I_d = \varepsilon_0\frac{d\phi}{dt} = \varepsilon_0\frac{d}{dt}(EA)$$

$$I_d = \varepsilon_0 A\frac{dE}{dt}$$

$\Rightarrow \quad I_d = \varepsilon_0 \dfrac{A}{d}\dfrac{dV}{dt} \quad \left(\because E = \dfrac{V}{d}\right)$

Putting the given values, we get

$$I_d = \frac{8.85\times 10^{-12}\times \pi\times (4\times 10^{-4})\times 5\times 10^6}{1\times 10^{-4}} \text{ A}$$

$\Rightarrow I_d = 555.78\times 10^{-6}$ A

or 0.556 mA

14. (d) We know that, direction of propagation of EM wave is always along the direction of vector product of electric and magnetic fields ($\mathbf{E}\times\mathbf{B}$).

Since, the direction of propagation of wave is along the Z-axis, the electric field will be perpendicular to the Z-axis and will be acting in the negative Y-axis.

Then, the associated magnetic field will be along the direction $(\hat{\mathbf{k}}\times\mathbf{E})$.

$$\mathbf{B} = B\hat{\mathbf{j}} = B(\hat{\mathbf{k}}\times\hat{\mathbf{i}})$$

$$= \frac{E}{c}(\hat{\mathbf{k}}\times\hat{\mathbf{i}})$$

$$= \frac{1}{c}(\hat{\mathbf{k}}\times \mathbf{E}\cdot\hat{\mathbf{i}})$$

$$= \frac{1}{c}(\hat{\mathbf{k}}\times\mathbf{E})$$

Now, the electric field will be along the direction $(\mathbf{B}\times\hat{\mathbf{k}})$, i.e. perpendicular to the magnetic field and direction of motion.

$\therefore \quad \mathbf{E} = E\,\hat{\mathbf{i}} = cB\,(\hat{\mathbf{j}}\times\hat{\mathbf{k}})$

$$= c\,(B\hat{\mathbf{j}}\times\hat{\mathbf{k}})$$

$$= c\,(\mathbf{B}\times\hat{\mathbf{k}})$$

The angle between the $\hat{\mathbf{k}}$ and $\mathbf{E}$ will be 90° whereas, between the $\hat{\mathbf{k}}$ and $\mathbf{B}$ will be 180°.

$$\hat{\mathbf{k}}\cdot\mathbf{E} = \hat{\mathbf{k}}\cdot(E\hat{\mathbf{i}}) = 0$$

$$\hat{\mathbf{k}}\cdot\mathbf{B} = \hat{\mathbf{k}}(B\hat{\mathbf{j}}) = 0$$

But $\hat{\mathbf{k}}\times\mathbf{E} = \hat{\mathbf{k}}\times(E\hat{\mathbf{i}}) = E\hat{\mathbf{j}}$

$$\hat{\mathbf{k}}\times\mathbf{B} = \hat{\mathbf{k}}\times(B\hat{\mathbf{j}}) = -B\hat{\mathbf{i}}$$

So, incorrect option is (d).

15. (d) Given, intensity of electromagnetic waves,

$$I = 53.1 \text{ Wm}^{-2}$$

Permittivity of free space,

$$\varepsilon_0 = 8.85\times 10^{-12} \text{ C}^2\text{N}^{-1}\text{m}^{-2}$$

Intensity of electromagnetic wave,

$$I = \frac{1}{2}\varepsilon_0 E_0^2 c$$

where, E_0 = amplitude of the electric field.

$$E_0 = \sqrt{\frac{2I}{\varepsilon_0 c}}$$

$$= \sqrt{\frac{2 \times 53.1}{8.85 \times 10^{-12} \times 3 \times 10^8}}$$

$$E_0 = 200 \text{ NC}^{-1}$$

Test-2

1. (d) Radio waves are used for TV communication system.

2. (c) Infrared rays are used to study secret writings on the ancient walls.

3. (a) Visible rays, infrared rays and ultraviolet rays can be used to study the structure of molecules and electrons in external shells.

4. (b) Ultraviolet rays are not visible, hence the correct option is from rest of the three.
From the term VIBGYOR, it is observed that green colour has the shortest wavelength.

5. (c) Frequency range for RADAR and satellite communication is 3×10^9 Hz - 3×10^{10} Hz.
Hence, correct option is (c).

6. (d) The statement given in option (d) is incorrect and it can be corrected as,
Most of ultraviolet rays are absorbed in the ozone layer in the atmosphere at an altitude of about 40-50 km.

7. (b)

A. Microwave is an electromagnetic wave used in communication satellite.

B. Ultraviolet rays are used to kill germs in water purifiers.

C. X-rays are used to detect leakage of oil in underground pipelines.

D. Infrared rays used to improve the visibility in runways during fog and mist condition.

8. (c) γ-rays are used in radio therapy for the treatment of tumor and cancer.

9. (c) Radio wave < Yellow light < Blue light < X-ray (increasing order of energy)

$\because \quad E = h\nu$

ν is frequency and is minimum for radio wave.

10. (b) Radiowaves are used in cricket to measure the speed of ball.

11. (d)

(i) Infrared waves are used to treat muscular strain.

(ii) Radio waves are used for broadcasting purposes.

(iii) X-rays are used to detect fracture of bones.

(iv) Ultraviolet rays are absorbed by the ozone layer of the atmosphere.

12. (a) The correct option is (a) because to produce heating effect, the frequency of microwave must be equal to the resonant frequency of water molecules. In this way, the maximum heat can be transferred to food items in most efficient way.

13. (c) Speed is same for all the waves of electromagnetic spectrum.
Hence, option (c) is correct.

14. (a) The frequency of the microwave matches the resonant frequency of water molecules. Hence, waves molecules vibrate with maximum amplitude, producing maximum heat energy and microwave oven heats up the food item containing water most efficiently.

15. (b) Radioactive source $\Rightarrow$ γ-rays
X-ray tube $\Rightarrow$ X-rays
Sodium vapour lamp $\Rightarrow$ Visible light
Crystal oscillator $\Rightarrow$ Microwaves
$\therefore$ The correct sequence of the increasing wavelength is
Radioactive source < X-ray tube < Sodium vapour lamp < Crystal oscillator.

Chapter Break Thru

1. (a) The displacement current arises due to time rate of change of electric flux (or electric field) between the two plates of capacitor and its magnitude is equal to
$I_d = \varepsilon_0 \frac{d\phi_E}{dt}$, where ϕ_E is electric flux.

2. (c) Given,
Area of each plate, $A = 10^{-2}$ m^2
Displacement current, $I_d = 15$ A
The displacement current across the plates,

$$I_d = \varepsilon_0 \frac{d\phi_E}{dt} = \varepsilon_0 \frac{d}{dt}(EA)$$

$$[\because \phi_E = \mathbf{E} \cdot \mathbf{A} = EA \cos\theta]$$

Here, $\theta = 0° \Rightarrow \phi_E = EA$

$$I_d = \varepsilon_0 A \frac{dE}{dt}$$

or $\frac{dE}{dt} = \frac{I_d}{\varepsilon_0 A}$

On putting the values of I_d, A and ε_0 in the above equation, we get

$$\frac{dE}{dt} = \frac{15}{8.85 \times 10^{-12} \times 10^{-2}}$$

$$= 1.69 \times 10^{14} \text{ V/m}$$

3. (b) Given that,
Radius of the plates,

$$r = 10 \text{ cm} = 0.1 \text{ m}$$

Distance between the plates,

$$d = 4 \text{ cm}$$
$$= 4 \times 10^{-2} \text{ m}$$

Charging current, $I_c = 0.2$ A
As we know that, during charging of a capacitor, the displacement current between the plates is equal to the conduction current in connecting wire, i.e.
Displacement current (I_d) = Conduction current (I_c) = 0.2 A

4. (a) Given,
Side of plates,

$$a = 8 \text{ cm} = 8 \times 10^{-2} \text{ m}$$

Distance of separation,

$$d = 2 \text{ cm} = 2 \times 10^{-2} \text{ m}$$

Charging current, $I = 0.5$ A
Area of each conducting plate,

$$A = a^2$$
$$A = (8\times 10^{-2})^2$$
$$A = 64\times 10^{-4}\,\text{m}^2$$

As, capacitance, $C = \dfrac{\varepsilon_0 A}{d}$

Substituting the given values, we get

$$C = \frac{8.85\times 10^{-12}\times 64\times 10^{-4}}{2\times 10^{-2}}$$

or $C = 2.832\times 10^{-12}$ F

Charging current, $I = \dfrac{dQ}{dt}$

$$I = \frac{d}{dt}(CV)$$
$$I = C\frac{dV}{dt}$$

or $\dfrac{dV}{dt} = \dfrac{I}{C} = \dfrac{0.5}{2.832\times 10^{-12}}$

$$\frac{dV}{dt} = 17.65\times 10^{10}\ \text{V/s}$$

5. (d) $\oint \mathbf{B}\cdot d\mathbf{l} = \mu_0 I$ is Ampere's law.

Maxwell's equation is its modified form,

$$\oint \mathbf{B}\cdot d\mathbf{l} = \mu(I_c + I_d)$$

6. (c) As we know that,

$$B_0 = \frac{E_0}{c} = \frac{E_0}{1/\sqrt{\mu_0\varepsilon_0}} = E_0\sqrt{\mu_0\varepsilon_0}$$

As the electromagnetic wave is propagating along x-direction and electric field is directed along y-direction, thus $\hat{\mathbf{E}}\times\hat{\mathbf{B}} \perp \hat{\mathbf{C}}$.
(Here, $\hat{\mathbf{C}}$ = direction of propagation of wave)
$\therefore$ $\mathbf{B}$ should be in $\hat{\mathbf{k}}$ direction.
Since,
$\mathbf{B} = E_0\sqrt{\mu_0\varepsilon_0}\cos(\omega t - kx)\,\hat{\mathbf{k}}$
At $t = 0$, $\mathbf{B} = E_0\sqrt{\mu_0\varepsilon_0}\cos(kx)\,\hat{\mathbf{k}}$

7. (d) The speed of EM wave in a medium is given by

$$v = \frac{c}{\sqrt{\mu_r\varepsilon_r}} \quad \text{... (i)}$$

where, μ_r and ε_r are relative magnetic permeability and relative electrical permittivity of the medium, respectively.
From Eq. (i), we get

$$v^2 = \frac{c^2}{\mu_r\varepsilon_r}$$

So, $\varepsilon_r = \dfrac{c^2}{v^2\mu_r} = \dfrac{(3\times 10^8)^2}{(6\times 10^7)^2\times 5}$

$\Rightarrow \varepsilon_r = 5$

8. (b) An oscillating charged particle of frequency f produces an oscillating electric field and magnetic field of same frequency f.
$\therefore$ Frequency of produced EM wave,

$$f = 2\times 10^{10}\ \text{Hz}$$

Wavelength, $\lambda = \dfrac{c}{f} = \dfrac{3\times 10^8}{2\times 10^{10}}$

$$= 1.5\times 10^{-2}\ \text{m}$$
$$\lambda = 1.5\ \text{cm}$$

This wavelength lies in microwave region.

9. (c) Given that, $E = E_0\sin(px + qt)$
and $B = B_0\sin(px + qt)$

Speed of wave, $v = \dfrac{\text{Coefficient of } t}{\text{Coefficient of } x}$

$$v = \frac{\omega}{k} = \frac{q}{p} \quad \text{... (i)}$$

Also, $v = \dfrac{E_0}{B_0}$ ... (ii)

On equating both Eqs. (i) and (ii), we get

$$\frac{q}{p} = \frac{E_0}{B_0}$$

or $pE_0 = qB_0$ ...(iii)

Also, $E_{\text{rms}} = \dfrac{E_0}{\sqrt{2}}$ ...(iv)

and $B_{\text{rms}} = \dfrac{B_0}{\sqrt{2}}$ ...(v)

From Eqs. (iii), (iv) and (v), we get

$$p\times\sqrt{2}\,E_{\text{rms}} = q\times\sqrt{2}\,B_{\text{rms}}$$

or $pE_{\text{rms}} = qB_{\text{rms}}$

10. (c) As we know, magnitude of magnetic field, $\mathbf{B} = \dfrac{|\mathbf{E}|}{c}$

Substituting the given values, we get

$$\mathbf{B} = \frac{8}{3\times 10^8}$$
$$\mathbf{B} = 2.33\times 10^{-8}\ \text{T}$$

If the direction of magnetic field is $\hat{\mathbf{n}}$, then direction of propagation of wave is along $\hat{\mathbf{E}}\times\hat{\mathbf{B}}$, i.e.

$$\hat{\mathbf{k}}\times\hat{\mathbf{n}} = \hat{\mathbf{j}}$$
$$\Rightarrow \quad \hat{\mathbf{n}} = \hat{\mathbf{i}} \qquad [\because \hat{\mathbf{k}}\times\hat{\mathbf{i}} = \hat{\mathbf{j}}]$$

$\therefore$ Magnetic field,

$$\mathbf{B} = 2.33\times 10^{-8}\,\hat{\mathbf{i}}\ \text{T}$$

11. (c) Given, equation of magnetic field,
$B_x = 6\times 10^{-8}\sin(2\times 10^3 y - 3\times 10^{10} t)$ T
The coefficient of y and t are of opposite nature and phase contains term y. Therefore, EM wave is propagating in positive y-direction.
If amplitude of electric field is E_0, then we can write

$$E_0 = B_0 c$$

where, B_0 is the amplitude of magnetic field and c is the speed of light in vacuum.

$\Rightarrow \quad E_0 = 6\times 10^{-8}\times 3\times 10^8$

or $\quad E_0 = 18$ V/m

As we know, in an EM wave, the phase of electric field and magnetic field components are the same, therefore

$$E = 18\sin(2\times 10^3 y - 3\times 10^{10} t)\ \text{V/m}$$

12. (c) Speed of EM wave is given by

$$v = \frac{\omega}{k}$$

As electric field in air is

$$E_1 = E_{01}\sin\left[\frac{\pi v x}{c} - \pi v t\right]$$

$$\therefore \text{Speed in air} = \frac{\pi v}{\left(\dfrac{\pi v}{c}\right)} = c = \frac{1}{\sqrt{\mu_0\varepsilon_0}} \quad \text{... (i)}$$

Also, speed in medium,

$$v = \frac{1}{\sqrt{\mu_0\mu_r\varepsilon_r\varepsilon_0}} \quad \text{... (ii)}$$

where, μ_r and ε_r are the relative permeability and relative permittivity of the medium, respectively.

In medium,

$$E_2 = E_{02} \sin[(2kx - kct)]$$

$\therefore$ Speed in medium $= \frac{kc}{2k} = \frac{c}{2}$

Also, $\frac{c}{2} = \frac{1}{\sqrt{\mu_0 \mu_r \varepsilon_r \varepsilon_0}}$ ... (iii)

As the medium is non-magnetic medium, so

$\mu_{\text{medium}} = \mu_{\text{air}}$

or $\mu_r = 1$

From Eq (iii),

$$\frac{c}{2} = \frac{1}{\sqrt{\mu_0 \varepsilon_r \varepsilon_0}} \quad \text{... (iv)}$$

On dividing Eqs. (i) and (iv), we get

$$2 = \sqrt{\varepsilon_r}$$

or $\varepsilon_r = 4$

13. (a) Given, equation,

$$E_y = 200 \sin \omega \left(t - \frac{x}{c}\right) \text{V/m}$$

Amplitude of electric field,

$E_0 = 200$ V/m

As amplitude of magnetic field,

$$B_0 = \frac{E_0}{c}$$

$$= \frac{200}{3 \times 10^8} \quad (\because c = 3 \times 10^8 \text{ m/s})$$

$$B_0 = 6.67 \times 10^{-7} \text{ T}$$

Maximum magnetic force,

$$F_{B\max} = B_0 qv$$

Here, $q = 2\mu\text{C} = 2 \times 10^{-6}$ C,

$v = 400$ m/s

Substituting the given values, we get

$$\Rightarrow F_{B\max} = 6.67 \times 10^{-7} \times 2 \times 10^{-6} \times 400$$

$$\Rightarrow F_{B\max} = 5.33 \times 10^{-10} \text{ N}$$

14. (c) When a wave is reflected from denser medium, only its phase changes by 180° or π radian.

Thus, for the reflected wave, $\hat{\mathbf{i}} = -\hat{\mathbf{i}}$ and $\hat{\mathbf{k}} = -\hat{\mathbf{k}}$ and additional phase of π in the incident wave.

Thus, reflected wave is given as

$$\mathbf{E}_r = (-\hat{\mathbf{k}})\, 40 \cos[k(-x) - 6 \times 10^8 t + \pi]$$

$$= -\hat{\mathbf{k}}\, 40 \cos[\pi - (kx + 6 \times 10^8 t)]$$

$$= -\hat{\mathbf{k}}\, 40[(-\cos(kx + 6 \times 10^8 t)]$$

$$[\because \cos(\pi - \theta) = -\cos\theta]$$

$$= \hat{\mathbf{k}}\, 40 \cos(kx + 6 \times 10^8 t) \text{ V/m}$$

15. (a) Since, the wavelength of microwaves is small (in the order of few millimetre), the beam signal can be transmitted in a particular direction without spread. Hence, microwaves are used in RADAR. So, both A and R are true and R is the correct explanation of A.

16. (a) The wavelength of an EM wave is given as

$$\lambda = \frac{c}{v} \quad \text{... (i)}$$

where, c is speed of wave in vacuum and v is speed of wave in medium.

As we know that speed of wave in a medium is always less than its speed in vacuum, i.e. $v < c$ or $\frac{c}{v} > 1$

From Eq. (i), $\lambda > 1$ m

17. (d) Given that,

Amplitude of electric field,

$E_0 = 80$ N/C

Frequency, $f = 30$ MHz

$= 30 \times 10^6$ Hz

As electromagnetic wave is travelling in positive x-direction, so we can write the general equation of magnetic field of wave as

$$B = B_0 \sin(\omega t - kx) \quad \text{... (i)}$$

where, B_0 is amplitude of magnetic field, k is wave constant and ω is angular frequency.

$$\because \quad B_0 = \frac{E_0}{c} = \frac{80}{3 \times 10^8}$$

$$= 2.67 \times 10^{-7} \text{ T}$$

and $\omega = 2\pi f = 2\pi \times 30 \times 10^6$

$$= 6\pi \times 10^7 \text{ rad/s}$$

and $k = \frac{\omega}{c}$

$$k = \frac{6\pi \times 10^7}{3 \times 10^8} = 0.6 \text{ m}^{-1}$$

Substituting the values of B_0, ω and k in Eq. (i), we get

$$B = 2.67 \times 10^{-7} \sin \{6\pi \times 10^7 (\text{rad/s})\, t - 0.6 (\text{m}^{-1})\, x\} \text{ T}$$

18. (b) Given electric field equation,

$$E(x,t) = 0.1 \sin \pi (3 \times 10^4 x - 7.5 \times 10^{14} t) \text{ V/m}$$

On comparing with standard equation of electric field of EM wave

$E(x,t) = E_0 \sin(kx - \omega t)$, we get

$$\omega = 7.5 \times 10^{14} \text{ rad/s}$$

$$k = 3 \times 10^4 \text{ cm}^{-1} = 3 \times 10^6 \text{ m}^{-1}$$

The speed of wave in medium,

$$v = \frac{\omega}{k} = \frac{7.5 \times 10^{14}}{3 \times 10^6}$$

$$v = 2.5 \times 10^8 \text{ m/s}$$

From the definition of refractive index, $\mu = \frac{c}{v} = \frac{3 \times 10^8}{2.5 \times 10^8}$

$$[\because c = 3 \times 10^8 \text{ m/s}]$$

$$= 1.2$$

19. (b) A point source radiates light in all directions uniformly as spheres. At a distance of 3 m, the surface area of the surrounding sphere is

$$A = 4\pi r^2$$

$$= 4\pi(3)^2$$

$$\Rightarrow \quad A = 113.04 \text{ m}^2$$

Then, intensity of the bulb/source at 3 m is

$$I = \frac{\text{Power } (P)}{\text{Area } (A)} = \frac{60 \times 0.05}{113.04}$$

[$\because$ Given, power, $P = 5\%$ of 60 W $= 0.05 \times 60$ W]

$$\Rightarrow \quad I = 0.0265 \text{ W/m}^2 \quad \text{... (i)}$$

The total intensity is the sum of individual intensity of electric field and magnetic field. Since, both the field intensities are equal in magnitude, so the electric field intensity, $I_E = \frac{\text{Total intensity}}{2}$

$$\Rightarrow \frac{1}{2} \varepsilon_0 E_{\text{rms}}^2 c = \frac{0.0265}{2}$$

[$\because$ Using Eq (i)]

or $\quad E_{\text{rms}} = \sqrt{\frac{0.0265}{\varepsilon_0 \times c}}$

$$= \sqrt{\frac{0.0265}{8.85 \times 10^{-12} \times 3 \times 10^8}}$$

$$= 3.16 \text{ V/m.}$$

Maximum value of electric field,

$E_m = \sqrt{2} \times E_{rms}$

$= \sqrt{2} \times 3.16 = 4.46\,V/m$

20. (c) Given that,

Intensity, $I = 5.9 \times 10^{-4}\ W/m^2$

Speed of light, $c = 3 \times 10^8$ m/s

The intensity of EM wave due to its electric field component is half of total intensity, i.e. $I_E = \frac{I}{2}$

$\because \quad I_E = \frac{1}{2}\varepsilon_0 E^2 c$, where E is rms value of electric field

or $\frac{I}{2} = \frac{1}{2}\varepsilon_0 E^2 c$

or $E = \sqrt{\frac{I}{\varepsilon_0 c}}$

Substituting the given values, we get

$E = \sqrt{\frac{5.9 \times 10^{-4}}{8.85 \times 10^{-12} \times 3 \times 10^8}}$

$= 0.471\,V/m$

21. (c) Electric field and magnetic field components of electromagnetic wave, both vibrate perpendicular to each other and also perpendicular to the direction of propagation of electromagnetic wave.

Since, electromagnetic wave carries both energy and radiation pressure, hence it exerts radiation pressure.

22. (c) Given expression of electromagnetic wave,

$\mathbf{E} = E_0 \hat{\mathbf{n}} \sin[\omega t + (6y - 8z)]$ ... (i)

$\Rightarrow \mathbf{E} = E_0 \hat{\mathbf{n}} \sin[\omega t - (8z - 6y)]$ ... (ii)

On comparing Eq. (ii) with Eq. (i), we get

$\mathbf{k} \cdot \hat{\mathbf{r}} = 8z - 6y$ ... (iii)

Here, $\hat{\mathbf{r}} = x\hat{\mathbf{i}} + y\hat{\mathbf{j}} + z\hat{\mathbf{k}}$

and $\mathbf{k} = k_x\hat{\mathbf{i}} + k_y\hat{\mathbf{j}} + k_z\hat{\mathbf{k}}$

$\therefore \mathbf{k} \cdot \hat{\mathbf{r}} = xk_x + yk_y + zk_z$ ... (iv)

From Eqs. (iii) and (iv), we get

$xk_x = 0 \Rightarrow k_x = 0$

$yk_y = -6y \Rightarrow k_y = -6$

$zk_z = 8z \Rightarrow k_z = 8$

Hence, $\mathbf{k} = -6\hat{\mathbf{j}} + 8\hat{\mathbf{k}}$

So, direction of propagation

$\hat{\mathbf{s}} = \hat{\mathbf{k}} = \frac{\mathbf{k}}{|\mathbf{k}|}$

$= \frac{-6\hat{\mathbf{j}} + 8\hat{\mathbf{k}}}{\sqrt{6^2 + 8^2}} = \frac{-6\hat{\mathbf{j}} + 8\hat{\mathbf{k}}}{10}$

$= \frac{-3\hat{\mathbf{j}} + 4\hat{\mathbf{k}}}{5}$

23. (a) Water molecules resonate at about 3 GHz and oscillation energy is converted into heat, which warms up food.

24. (a) $\mathbf{E} \times \mathbf{B}$ is poynting vector, $\frac{E}{B}$ is speed of electromagnetic wave, $\frac{h\nu}{c}$ is equal to momentum and $\frac{h\nu}{c^2}$ is equal to mass.

25. (a) An electron experiences both electric and magnetic forces.

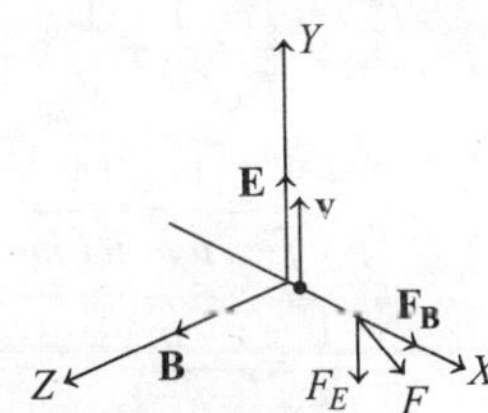

Magnetic force,

$F_B = q(\mathbf{v} \times \mathbf{B})$

$= qv\hat{\mathbf{j}} \times B\hat{\mathbf{k}} = qvB_0\hat{\mathbf{i}}$

Electric force,

$F_E = q\mathbf{E} = qE_0\hat{\mathbf{j}}$

As both electric and magnetic forces are perpendicular, so total force,

$F = \sqrt{F_B^2 + F_E^2}$

Now, $E_0 = 800$ V/m [given]

$B_0 = \frac{E_0}{c} = \frac{800}{3 \times 10^8}$ T

Magnitudes of forces are

$F_E = qE_0 = (1.6 \times 10^{-19})(800)$

$= 1.28 \times 10^{-16}$ N

and $F_B = qvB_0$

$= 1.6 \times 10^{-19} \times 3 \times 10^7 \times \frac{800}{3 \times 10^8}$

$= 1.6 \times 10^{-19} \times 80$

$= 1.8 \times 10^{-17}$ N

So, total force is

$F = \sqrt{F_E^2 + F_B^2}$

$= \sqrt{(1.28 \times 10^{-16})^2 + (1.28 \times 10^{-17})^2}$

$= 1.8 \times 10^{-17} \times \sqrt{100 + 1}$

$= \sqrt{101} \times 1.8 \times 10^{-17}$ N

$\approx 1.8 \times 10^{-16}$ N

26. (b) Faraday's law of electromagnetic induction in integral form is represented by

$\oint \mathbf{E} \cdot d\mathbf{l} = -\frac{d}{dt}\oint_s \mathbf{B} \cdot d\mathbf{S}$

27. (a) Intensity,

$I = \frac{\text{Energy}}{\text{Area} \times \text{Time}}$

$= \frac{\text{Power}}{\text{Area}}$

$= U_{av}c = \frac{1}{2}c\varepsilon_0 E_0^2$

$\Rightarrow \quad P \propto E_0^2$

$\Rightarrow \quad \frac{P_1}{P_2} = \frac{E_1^2}{E_2^2}$

$\Rightarrow \quad \frac{E_1}{E_2} = \sqrt{\frac{P_1}{P_2}}$

$\Rightarrow \quad \frac{E_1}{E_2} = \sqrt{\frac{100}{55}}$

$\Rightarrow \quad E_2 = \sqrt{\frac{11}{20}}E_1$

$= \sqrt{\frac{11}{20}}E \quad (\because E_1 = E)$

$\Rightarrow \quad E_2 = \sqrt{\frac{11}{20}} \cdot E$

28. (b) Speed of light in the medium,

$v = \frac{c}{\sqrt{\mu_r \varepsilon_r}}$

$= \frac{3 \times 10^8}{\sqrt{1.3 \times 0.9}} = 2.77 \times 10^8$ m/s

29. (a) Momentum transferred by electromagnetic wave is

$p = \frac{E}{c} = \frac{hc/\lambda}{c} = \frac{h}{\lambda}$

$= \frac{6.6 \times 10^{-34}}{5893 \times 10^{-10}}$

$= 1.1 \times 10^{-27}$ kg-m/s

30. (d) During refraction, wave speed and its wavelength $\left(\text{i.e. } k = \frac{2\pi}{\lambda}\right)$ changes. But no change in frequency and phase occurs.

Ch-10 Ray Optics and Optical Instruments

Topical Follow Thru

Test-1

1. (a) According to the question

$L =$ Light source

When the light beam is incident normally on the plane mirror, it is reflected back to the point from which it was coming. When the plane mirror is rotated by an angle θ, the reflected ray or beam of light must rotate by angle 2θ, from refraction at plane surface theory.

Angle of refraction is 2θ

$$\tan 2\theta = \frac{y}{x}$$

$$2\theta = \frac{y}{x}$$

$$\theta = \frac{y}{2x}$$

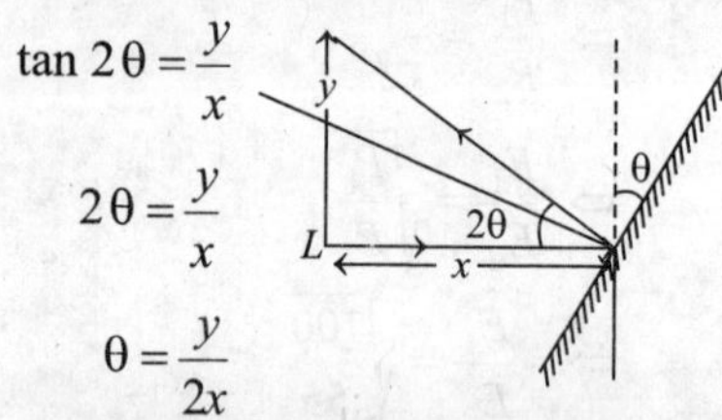

2. (d) One may think that the image will now show only half of the object, but according to the laws of reflection to be true for all points of the remaining part of the mirror, the image will be that of the whole object. However, as the area of the reflecting surface has been reduced, the intensity of the image will be low (in this case half).

3. (a) Given, $f = -20\,\text{cm}$

$\Rightarrow R = 2f = -40\,\text{cm}$

It means that end N is at the centre of curvature, hence its image will be formed at the same point.

Now, calculate the position of image of end M.

$$u = -42\,\text{cm}$$

$$\frac{1}{v} + \frac{1}{u} = \frac{1}{f} \Rightarrow v = \frac{uf}{u-f}$$

$$= \frac{(-42)(-20)}{-42-(-20)}$$

$$= -38.2\,\text{cm}$$

Length of image $= (40 - 38.2)\,\text{cm}$

$= 2.2\,\text{cm}$

4. (c) The image of object may be real in case of concave mirror.

5. (a) Number of images $= \frac{360°}{\theta} - 1$

$$= \frac{360°}{20°} - 1 = 17$$

6. (c) Magnification of the image,

$$M = -\frac{v}{u} = \frac{1}{m}$$

$$\Rightarrow \quad v = -\frac{u}{m}$$

From the mirror formula,

$$\frac{1}{f} = \frac{1}{u} + \frac{1}{v}$$

$$\frac{1}{f} = \frac{1}{u} - \frac{1}{u/m}$$

$$\frac{1}{f} = \frac{1-m}{u}$$

$$\Rightarrow \quad u = (1-m)\,f = -(m-1)f$$

7. (c) Given, $R = -10\,\text{cm}$

$\Rightarrow f = -5\,\text{cm}$

$u = -10\,\text{cm}$

Height of object, $h = 5\,\text{cm}$

From mirror formula, $\frac{1}{f} = \frac{1}{v} + \frac{1}{u}$

$$v = \frac{uf}{u-f} = \frac{-(10)(-5)}{(-10)-(-5)}$$

$$= -10\,\text{cm}$$

Also, $m = -\frac{v}{u} = \frac{-10}{10} = -1$

$$\frac{h'}{h} = -1$$

$$h' = -h = -5\,\text{cm}$$

Therefore, size of image is 5 cm.

8. (c) If the plane mirror is rotated through an angle θ, the reflected ray turns through an angle 2θ in that direction keeping the incident ray fixed.

9. (b) The first image is due to reflection from the front surface, i.e. by unpolished surface of the mirror. So, only a small fraction of the incident light energy is reflected.

The second image is due to reflection from polished surface. So, a major portion of light is reflected. Thus, the second image is the brightest.

10. (d) From $\frac{1}{v} + \frac{1}{u} = \frac{1}{f}$

$$\frac{dv}{dt} = \frac{v^2}{du^2} \cdot \frac{dv}{dt}$$

The speed of approaching car would appear to increase, since the distance between the cars decreases.

11. (a) Here, $v_{OM} = v_{IM}$

$$v_O - v_M = v_I - v_M$$

$$(+2\text{ms}^{-1}) - (-3\text{ms}^{-1}) = v_I + (-3\text{ ms}^{-1})$$

$$\Rightarrow \quad v_I = 8\,\text{ms}^{-1}$$

12. (a) Deviation at mirror M_1,

$\delta_1 = 180° - 2 \times 45° = 90° \uparrow$

Deviation at mirror M_2,

$\delta_2 = 180° - 2 \times 15° = 150° \uparrow$

Total deviation

$\delta = \delta_2 - \delta_1 = 150° - 90° = 60° \uparrow$

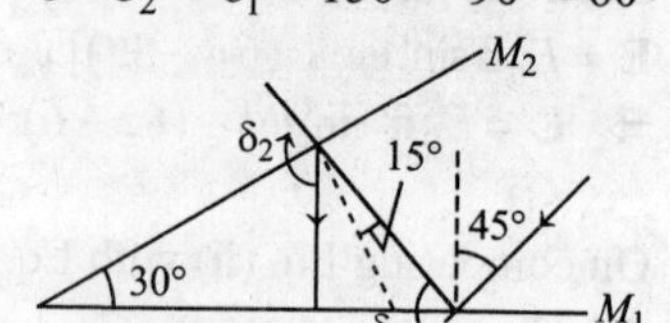

13. (a)

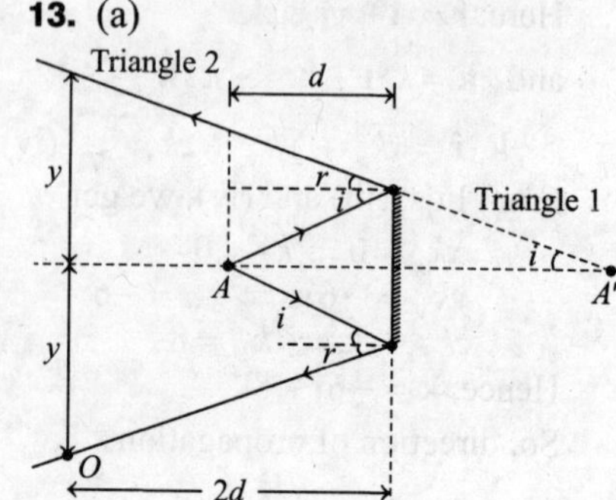

Observer can see image of A upto a distance $2y$.

Now, similarity of triangles (1) and (2) from figure; given,

$$\frac{\frac{L}{2}}{d} = \frac{y}{3d}$$

$$\Rightarrow \quad y = \frac{3L}{2}$$

$$\Rightarrow \quad 2y = 3L$$

Time for which image can be seen in mirror is

$$t = \frac{3L}{v}$$

14. (*a*) The focal length $= -f$ and $u = -1.5f$

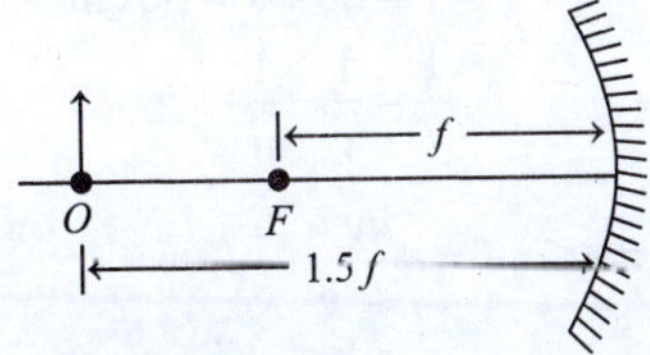

From mirror formula, we have

$$\frac{1}{u} + \frac{1}{v} = \frac{1}{f}$$

or $$\frac{1}{-1.5f} + \frac{1}{v} = -\frac{1}{f}$$

$$\frac{1}{v} = \frac{1}{1.5f} - \frac{1}{f} = -\frac{1}{3f}$$

Now, $$m = -\frac{v}{u} = -\frac{3f}{1.5f} = -2$$

or $$\frac{h_i}{h_o} = -2$$

or $$h_i = -2h_o = -5\,\text{cm}$$

The image is 5 cm long. The negative sign shows that it is inverted.

15. (a) According to given problem, for concave mirror.

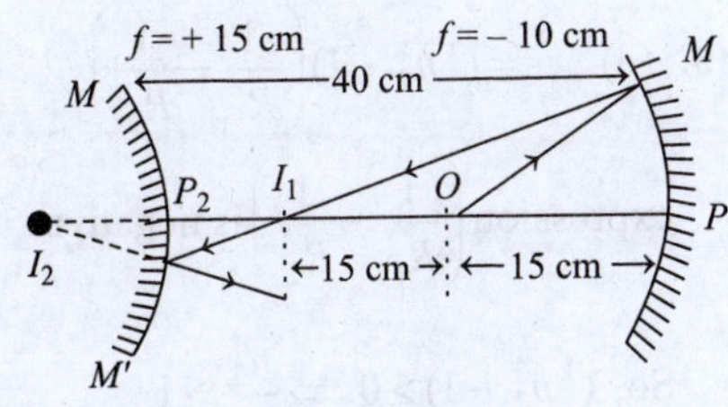

Given, $u = -15\,\text{cm}$

and $f = -10\,\text{cm}$

So, $$\frac{1}{v} + \frac{1}{-15} = \frac{1}{-10},$$

$$v = -30\,\text{cm}$$

i.e. concave mirror will form real, inverted and enlarged image I_1 of object O at a distance 30 cm from it, *i.e.* at a distance $40 - 30 = 10\,\text{cm}$ from convex mirror.

For convex mirror, the image I_1 will act as an object and so for it $u = -10\,\text{cm}$ and $f = +15\,\text{cm}$.

$$\frac{1}{v} + \frac{1}{-10} = \frac{1}{15}, \Rightarrow v = +6\,\text{cm}$$

So, final image I_2 is formed at a distance 6 cm behind the convex mirror and is virtual as shown in above figure.

Test-2

1. (a) Given, $^{w}\mu_m = \frac{7}{2} \Rightarrow {}^{w}\mu_m = \frac{v_w}{v_m}$

Here, subscript w is for water and m is for material.

$$\therefore \quad v_m = \frac{v_w}{7/2}$$

$$= \frac{21 \times 10^8}{7/2} = 6 \times 10^7 \text{ m/s}$$

2. (d) As,

$$30° + 90° + r' = 180° \quad [1° \le r \le 30°]$$

$$\Rightarrow \quad r' = 60°$$

Critical angle,

$$i_c = \sin^{-1}\left(\frac{\mu_r}{\mu_d}\right) \quad \ldots(\text{i})$$

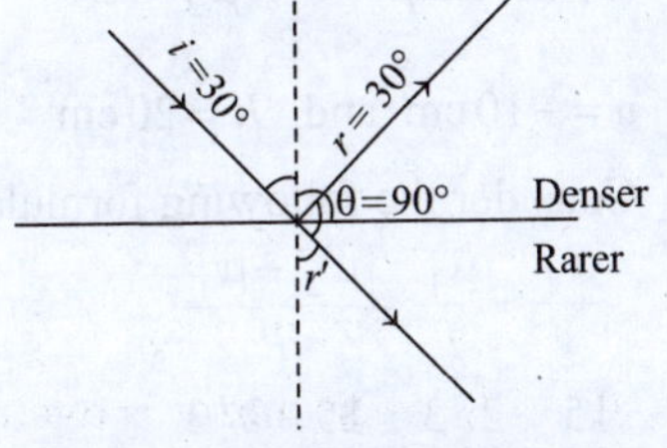

Here, μ_r is the refractive index of rarer medium and μ_d is the refractive index of denser medium.

Also, $$\frac{\mu_r}{\mu_d} = \frac{\sin i}{\sin r'}$$

Substitute this value in Eq. (i),

$$i_c = \sin^{-1}\left(\frac{\sin i}{\sin r'}\right) = \sin^{-1}\left(\frac{\sin 30°}{\sin 60°}\right)$$

$$= \sin^{-1}\left(\frac{1/2}{\sqrt{3}/2}\right)$$

$$= \sin^{-1}\left(\frac{1}{\sqrt{3}}\right)$$

3. (c) Critical angle,

$$i_c = \sin^{-1}\left(\frac{v}{c}\right) \quad \ldots(\text{i})$$

Here, v is the velocity of light in medium and c is the velocity of light in vacuum.

$$c = \frac{y}{T_1}$$

and $$v = \frac{20\,y}{T_2}$$

Substitute in Eq. (i),

$$i_c = \sin^{-1}\left[\frac{20\,y}{T_2} \times \frac{T_1}{y}\right]$$

$$= \sin^{-1}\left[\frac{20T_1}{T_2}\right]$$

4. (a) The given condition can be shown in the figure.

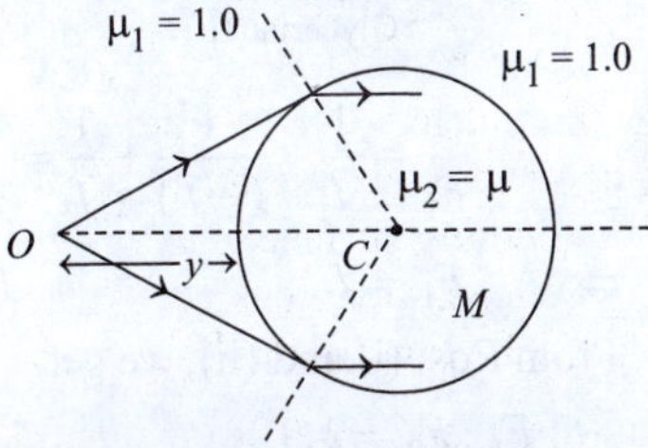

From refraction formula for curved surface, we get

$$\frac{\mu_2}{v} - \frac{\mu_1}{u} = \frac{\mu_2 - \mu_1}{M}$$

$$\frac{\mu}{\infty} - \frac{1}{(-y)} = \frac{\mu - 1}{M}$$

$$\frac{1}{y} = \frac{(\mu - 1)}{M}$$

$$y = \frac{M}{(\mu - 1)}$$

5. (d) **Case I** When two equi-convex lens are kept co-axially in contact as shown below, then the equivalent focal length of combination is

Air

$$\frac{1}{F_2}=\frac{1}{f_1}+\frac{1}{f_2}$$

$$=\frac{1}{f}+\frac{1}{f} \quad (\because f_1=f_2=f)$$

$$=\frac{2}{f}$$

$$\Rightarrow \quad F_2=\frac{f}{2} \qquad \ldots\text{(i)}$$

Case II When glycerine of same refractive index as that of the glass is filled in the space between two lenses, then the combination will now comprises of three lenses, first bi-convex, second bi-concave and third is bi-convex. So, the focal length of the combination now is given as shown below.

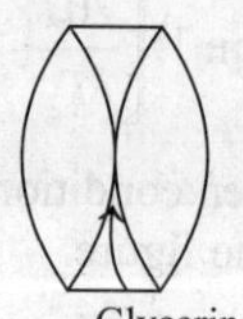

Glycerine (μ)

$$\frac{1}{F_1}=\frac{1}{f}+\frac{1}{(-f)}+\frac{1}{f}=\frac{1}{f}$$

$$\Rightarrow \quad F_1=f \qquad \ldots\text{(ii)}$$

From Eqs. (i) and (ii), we get

$$F_1:F_2=2:1$$

6. (c) As we know that,

Intensity, $I \propto A$ (Area exposed)

$$\Rightarrow \quad \frac{I_2}{I_1}=\left[\frac{A_2}{A_1}\right]$$

$$=\frac{\frac{\pi d^2}{4}-\frac{\pi d^2/4}{4}}{\frac{\pi d^2}{4}}=\frac{3}{4}$$

$$\Rightarrow \quad I_2=\frac{3}{4}I_1$$

and focal length remains unchanged.

7. (a) From lens Maker's formula, we have

$$\frac{1}{F}=\left(\frac{K-1}{1}\right)\left(\frac{1}{R_1}-\frac{1}{R_2}\right)$$

and $$\frac{1}{F'}=\left(\frac{K-K'}{K'}\right)\left(\frac{1}{R_1}-\frac{1}{R_2}\right)$$

Now, $$\frac{F'}{F}=\left(\frac{K-1}{1}\right)\left(\frac{K'}{K-K'}\right)$$

$$\Rightarrow \quad F'=\frac{FK'(K-1)}{K'-K}$$

8. (c) Consider the magnification formula,

$$m=\frac{f}{f+u}$$

$$\Rightarrow f+u=\frac{f}{m}$$

$$\Rightarrow \quad u=\frac{f}{m}-f=\left(\frac{1-m}{m}\right)f$$

Substitute $m=5,\ f=20\,\text{cm}$

we get, $u=\left(\frac{1-5}{5}\right)20=-16\,\text{cm}$

9. (a) This lens will act as a concave mirror of focal length f, which is given by

$$\frac{1}{f}=\frac{2}{f_l}+\frac{1}{f_m}$$

Here, $\frac{1}{f_l}=\frac{\mu-1}{R}=\frac{1.2-1}{6}=\frac{1}{30}$

and $\frac{1}{f_m}=\frac{1}{\infty}=0$

$$\Rightarrow \quad \frac{1}{f}=2\times\frac{1}{30}$$

$$\Rightarrow \quad f=15\,\text{cm}$$

10. (a) Given, $\mu_1=\frac{2}{3}$, $\mu_2=1.5$,

$u=-10\,\text{cm}$ and $R=20\,\text{cm}$

Consider the following formula,

$$\frac{\mu_2}{v}-\frac{\mu_1}{u}=\frac{\mu_2-\mu_1}{R}$$

$$\frac{1.5}{v}-\frac{2/3}{-10}=\frac{1.5-2/3}{20}$$

$$\frac{1.5}{v}=-\frac{1}{15}+\frac{1}{24}=\frac{-9}{15\times 24}$$

$$v=-60\,\text{cm}$$

11. (a) If $\mu_m>\mu_g$, then the medium is still rarer than the material of the lens. Hence, nature of lens will be same but focal length will increase.

12. (a)

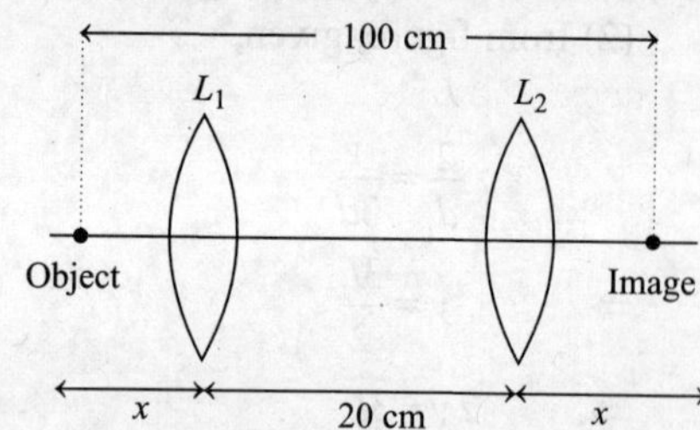

From the diagram,

$$x+20+x=100$$

$$\Rightarrow \quad x=40\,\text{cm}$$

When lens is in L_1 position,

$$u=-x=-40\,\text{cm}$$

$$v=20+x=60\,\text{cm}$$

$$\frac{1}{f}=\frac{1}{v}-\frac{1}{u}$$

$$\Rightarrow \quad f=\frac{uv}{u-v}$$

$$f=\frac{(-40)(60)}{-40-60}=24\,\text{cm}$$

13. (a) Angle of minimum deviation of a prism is

$$D_m=(\mu-1)A$$

14. (b) Given, ${}_w\mu_g=9/8$ and

$${}_a\mu_g=3/2$$

As, $${}_a\mu_g\times{}_g\mu_w\times{}_w\mu_a=1$$

and $$\frac{1}{{}_w\mu_a}={}_a\mu_w$$

$$\therefore \quad {}_a\mu_w={}_a\mu_g\times{}_g\mu_w$$

$$={}_a\mu_g\times{}_g\mu_w=\frac{{}_a\mu_g}{{}_w\mu_g}$$

∴ Refractive index of water with respect to air,

$${}_a\mu_w=\frac{3/2}{9/8}=\frac{4}{3}$$

15. (d) $\frac{1}{f}=({}^1n_2-1)\left(\frac{1}{R_1}-\frac{1}{R_2}\right)$

expression $\left(\frac{1}{R_1}-\frac{1}{R_2}\right)$ is negative.

So, $({}^1n_2-1)>0 \Rightarrow \frac{n_2}{n_1}>1$

or, $\qquad n_2 > n_1$

Thus, if the lens is filled with L_2 having refractive index n_{L_2} and placed in L_1 having refractive index n_{L_1}, the above condition will be satisfied and it will diverge a parallel beam of light.

16. (a) Here, $\sin C = \dfrac{\mu_2}{\mu_1} = \dfrac{1}{2}$

$\Rightarrow \qquad C = 30^\circ$

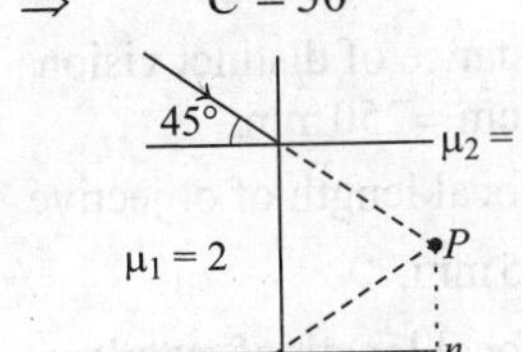

Since, angle of incident is greater than critical angle, so total internal reflection takes place. Thus, the surface behaves as plane mirror.

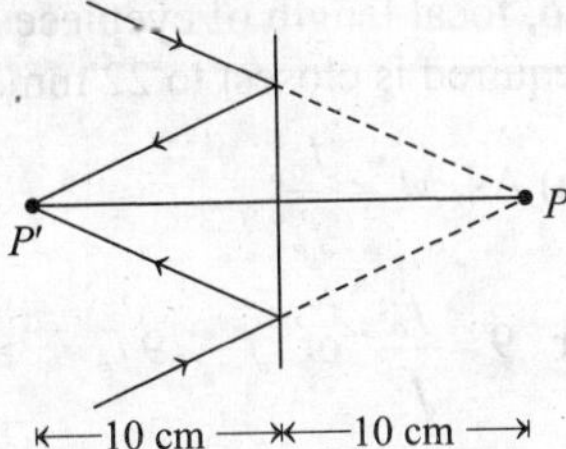

So, the new converging point is before the surface at a distance 10 cm.

17. (b) Here, $\mu_1 = 1, \mu_2 = 2, u = -\infty$, $R = +10\,\text{cm}$

$$\because \frac{\mu_2}{v} - \frac{\mu_1}{u} = \frac{\mu_2 - \mu_1}{R}$$

$$\frac{2}{v} - \frac{1}{-\infty} = \frac{2-1}{10}$$

$$\Rightarrow \qquad \frac{2}{v} = \frac{2-1}{10}$$

$$v = 20\,\text{cm}$$

$\therefore$ The beam converges at point B.

18. (a) For the fish, apparent distance of the fly from the wall of the aquarium is μx. If x is actual distance, then apparent velocity will be $= \dfrac{d(\mu x)}{dt}$.

$$(v_{\text{app}})_{\text{fly}} = \mu v_{\text{fly}}$$

Now, the fish observes the velocity of the fly to be 8 ms^{-1}. Therefore, apparent relative velocity $= 8\text{ms}^{-1}$

$$v_{\text{fish}} + (v_{\text{app}})_{\text{fly}} = 8\text{ ms}^{-1}.$$

$$3 + \mu v_{\text{fly}} = 8$$

$$v_{\text{fly}} = 5 \times \frac{3}{4} = 3.75\text{ ms}^{-1}$$

19. (c) Here, $\mu_1 = \dfrac{4}{3}, \mu_2 = 2,$

$$u = -2\,\text{m} = -200\,\text{cm}$$

and $\quad R = +40\,\text{cm}$

As, $\qquad \dfrac{\mu_2}{v} - \dfrac{\mu_1}{u} = \dfrac{\mu_2 - \mu_1}{R}$

$$\frac{2}{v} - \frac{4/3}{-200} = \frac{2 - 4/3}{40}$$

$$\frac{2}{v} + \frac{1}{150} = \frac{1}{60}$$

$$v = 200\,\text{cm}$$

20. (d) Let the focal length of one lens is x and focal length of other lens is $2x$.

Now, $P = \dfrac{1}{f_1} + \dfrac{1}{f_2}$

$$\Rightarrow \qquad 10 = \frac{1}{x} + \frac{1}{2x}$$

$$\Rightarrow \qquad \frac{3}{2x} = 10$$

$$\Rightarrow \qquad x = 0.15\text{ m or }15\text{ cm}$$

$\therefore$ Focal lengths of 1st and 2nd lenses are 15 cm and 30 cm, respectively.

21. (b) Here, $\mu_1 = \dfrac{4}{3}, \mu_2 = \dfrac{3}{2},$

$$u = -80\,\text{cm and } R = +20\,\text{cm}$$

$\mu_1 = \dfrac{4}{3}$ $\qquad \mu_2 = \dfrac{3}{2}$

80 cm

According to refractive surface formula,

$$\frac{\mu_2}{v} - \frac{\mu_1}{u} = \frac{\mu_2 - \mu_1}{R}$$

$$\frac{3}{2v} - \frac{4}{3(-80)} = \frac{\frac{3}{2} - \frac{4}{3}}{+20}$$

$$\frac{3}{2v} = \frac{1}{120} - \frac{1}{60} = -\frac{1}{120}$$

$$\frac{2v}{3} = -120$$

$$\therefore \; v = -120 \times \frac{3}{2} = -180\,\text{cm}$$

$$\text{Magnification} = \frac{\mu_1 v}{\mu_2 u}$$

$$= \frac{\left(\frac{4}{3}\right)(-180)}{\left(\frac{3}{2}\right)(-80)} = \frac{8}{9} \times \frac{180}{80} = 2$$

22. (a) Deviation is maximum at TIR ($\delta = 90^\circ - i_c$) and after that it decreases.

23. (c) Given, $f = +12\,\text{cm}$, $R_1 = +10\,\text{cm}, R_2 = -15\,\text{cm}$. Refractive index of air is taken as unity.

From the lens Maker's formula, we have

$$\frac{1}{f} = (\mu - 1)\left(\frac{1}{R_1} - \frac{1}{R_2}\right)$$

Putting the values in above expression, we get

$$\frac{1}{12} = (\mu - 1)\left(\frac{1}{10} - \frac{1}{(-15)}\right)$$

$$\frac{1}{12} = (\mu - 1)\left(\frac{1}{10} + \frac{1}{15}\right)$$

$$= (\mu - 1)\left(\frac{3+2}{30}\right) = \frac{(\mu - 1)}{6}$$

$$\Rightarrow \frac{6}{12} = \mu - 1 \Rightarrow \mu = \frac{1}{2} + 1 = \frac{3}{2} = 1.5$$

24. (a) Both Statement I and Statement II are correct.

Refractive surface formula is derived only for paraxial rays.

25. (a) A. The lens Maker's formula is given by

$$\frac{1}{f} = (\mu - 1)\left(\frac{1}{R_1} - \frac{1}{R_2}\right)$$

B. At a convex surface, light rays travelling from a rarer medium to denser medium bend towards the normal, converging to a point.

This makes convex lenses focus light to form real images.

C. At a concave surface, light rays travelling from a rarer to a denser medium bend towards the normal, diverging outward. This makes concave lenses spread out light rays, creating virtual images.

D. The critical angle is the angle of incidence in a denser medium beyond which light undergoes total internal reflection.

$$\left[\sin i_c = \frac{\mu_2}{\mu_1}\right]$$

Hence, A- (IV), B- (III), C-(II), D- (I).

Test-3

1. (a) Magnification, $m = m_0 \times m_e$

$$= m_0 \times \left(1 + \frac{D}{f_e}\right)$$

$$100 = 10\left(1 + \frac{25}{f_e}\right)$$

$$\frac{25}{f_e} = 9$$

$$f_e = \frac{25}{9}\text{ cm}$$

2. (a) For the objective,

$$\frac{1}{v_o} - \frac{1}{-1/3.8} = \frac{1}{1/4}$$

$$\frac{1}{v_o} + 3.8 = 4$$

$$\frac{1}{v_o} = 0.2 = \frac{1}{5}$$

$$v_o = 5\text{ cm}$$

Now, $M_o = \dfrac{5}{-\dfrac{1}{3.8}} = -19$

Again, $M = M_o \times M_e$

$$-95 = -19 \times M_e$$

$$M_e = \frac{95}{19} = 5$$

3. (d) For objective lens,

$$\frac{1}{f_o} = \frac{1}{v_o} - \frac{1}{u_o}$$

$$\frac{1}{2} = \frac{1}{v_o} - \frac{1}{(-3)}$$

$$\frac{1}{v_0} = \frac{1}{2} - \frac{1}{3}$$

$$v_o = 6\text{ cm}$$

Now, $m = \dfrac{v_o}{u_o}\left(1 + \dfrac{D}{f_e}\right)$

$$= \frac{6}{3}\left(1 + \frac{20}{8}\right) = 7$$

4. (b) Angle subtended by moon on objective

$$\theta_0 = \frac{3.5 \times 10^3}{3.8 \times 10^5} = 9.2 \times 10^{-3}\text{ rad}$$

$$= \left(9.2 \times 10^{-3} \times \frac{180}{\pi}\right)^\circ = 0.5^\circ$$

$$|m| = \frac{f_o}{f_e} = \frac{400}{10} = 40$$

$$m = \frac{\theta}{\theta_0} \Rightarrow 40 = \frac{\theta}{(0.5)^\circ}$$

$$\theta = 20^\circ$$

5. (a) Magnification of objective,

$$m_0 = \frac{L}{f_0} = \frac{20}{1} = 20$$

Magnification of eyepiece,

$$m_e = \frac{D}{f_e}$$

where, D is the least distance of distinct vision = 25 cm

$$m_e = \frac{25}{2} = 12.5$$

Total magnification,

$$m = m_0 \times m_e$$

$$= 20 \times 12.5 = 250$$

6. (c) Focal length of objective lens,

$$f_0 = F_1,\ f_e = F_2$$

Magnification for telescope,

$$m = \frac{f_0}{f_e} = \frac{F_1}{F_2}$$

7. (c) Separation $= f_o + \dfrac{f_e D}{f_e + D}$

$$= 80 + \frac{5 \times 25}{5 + 25} = 80 + \frac{125}{30}$$

$$= 84.16\text{ cm} = 84.2\text{ cm}$$

8. (a) In normal setting, magnification obtained by a microscope is given by

$$m = \frac{L \times D}{f_o \times f_e}$$

where, L = tube length = 150 mm,

D = distance of distinct vision = 25 cm = 250 mm,

f_o = focal length of objective = 5 mm,

f_e = focal length of eyepiece

and m = magnification = 375.

So, we have

$$375 = \frac{150 \times 250}{5 \times f_e} \text{ or } f_e = 20\text{ mm}$$

So, focal length of eyepiece required is closest to 22 mm.

9. (a) As, $M = \dfrac{f_o}{f_e}$

or $9 = \dfrac{f_o}{f_e}$ or $f_o = 9f_e$

Also, $L = f_o + f_e$

$$20 = f_o + f_e$$

$$20 = 9f_e + f_e$$

$$20 = 10f_e$$

$$f_e = 2\text{ cm}$$

$$\therefore\ f_o = 9 \times 2\text{ cm} = 18\text{ cm}$$

10. (a) For a telescope in normal setting,

$f_o + f_e = L$

(length of the tube of telescope)

and $\dfrac{f_o}{f_e} = m$ (magnification)

where, f_o and f_e are the focal lengths of the objective and eyepiece, respectively.

According to the given values in the question, we have

$$f_o + f_e = 60\text{ cm} \quad \ldots\text{(i)}$$

and $\dfrac{f_o}{f_e} = 5 \Rightarrow f_o = 5f_e$ ...(ii)

On solving Eqs. (i) and (ii), we have

$f_e = 10\,\text{cm}$

11. (a) **Case I** As,

$M = -\frac{f_o}{f_e}\left(1+\frac{f_e}{D}\right)$

$M = -\frac{200}{5}\left(1+\frac{5}{25}\right)$

$M = -40\left(1+\frac{1}{5}\right) = -40\times\frac{6}{5} = -48$

Case II

$M = \frac{f_o}{f_e} = -\frac{200}{5} = -40$

12. (a) Power of combination,

$P = P_1 + P_2 = +20 - 10 = +10\,\text{D}$

$\therefore f = \frac{1}{P} = \frac{1}{10}\,\text{m} = 10\,\text{cm}$

For image at infinity,

$M = \frac{D}{f} = \frac{25}{10} = 2.5$

13. (d) Here, $f_o = 50$ cm, $f_e = 5$ cm, $D = 25$ cm and $u_o = 200$ cm

$\therefore$ Separation between the objective and eyepiece lens is

$L = \frac{u_o f_o}{u_o - f_o} + \frac{f_e D}{(f_e + D)}$

$= \frac{200\times 50}{(200-50)} + \frac{5\times 25}{(5+25)} \simeq 71\,\text{cm}$

14. (a) When final image is formed at infinite, then

$M = \frac{v_o}{u_o}\left(\frac{d}{f_e}\right) = \frac{v_o}{f_o}\left(\frac{d}{f_e}\right)$

Now,

$v_o = 16 - f_e = 16 - 2.5 = 13.5$ cm

$\therefore\ M = \frac{13.5}{-0.4}\times\frac{25}{2.5} = -337.5$

15. (d) Distance between objective and eyepiece = Tube length

$= f_o + f_e$

$= 16 + 0.02 = 16.02$ m

Angular magnification $= \frac{f_o}{f_e}$

$= -\frac{16}{0.02} = -800$

The final image of the planet is inverted as magnification is negative.

Chapter Break Thru

1. (a) A small angled prism cannot deviate all colours brilliantly and angular dispersion is not prominent enough to form a clear spectrum.

Both Statement I and Statement II are correct.

2. (c) As we know that,

$v = \frac{c}{\mu_c} \Rightarrow v = \frac{c}{2}$

3. (c) From the relation, $m = \frac{I}{O} = \frac{v}{u}$

Here, $O = 1.39\times 10^9\,\text{m}$, $v = 0.2\,\text{m}$

$u = 1.5\times 10^{11}\,\text{m}$

$\therefore\ I = \frac{0.2}{1.5\times 10^{11}}\times 1.39\times 10^9$

$= 1.8\times 10^{-3}\,\text{m}$

4. (b) Given, $\mu_1 = 1, \mu_2 = 1.5$

$u = -30$ cm, $R_1 = 20$ cm and $R_2 = -20$ cm

Hence, using Lens maker's formula,

$\frac{1}{f} = \left(\frac{\mu_2}{\mu_1} - 1\right)\left(\frac{1}{R_1} - \frac{1}{R_2}\right)$ ... (i)

By putting all values in Eq. (i), we get

$f = 20$ cm

$\because\ \frac{1}{f} = \frac{1}{v} - \frac{1}{u}$

$\Rightarrow\ \frac{1}{20} = \frac{1}{v} + \frac{1}{30}$

$\frac{1}{v} = \frac{1}{20} - \frac{1}{30} = \frac{10}{600}$

$v = 60$ cm

$\frac{h_i}{h_o} = \frac{v}{u} = \frac{60}{-30} = -2$

$h_i = -2\times |h_o|$

$\Rightarrow\ h_i = -12$ cm

Here, image is real, inverted, magnified and the height of image is 12 cm.

5. (d) For without deviation,

$\frac{A}{A'} = \frac{\mu' - 1}{\mu - 1}$

$\frac{20°}{A'} = \frac{1.40 - 1}{1.5 - 1}$

$\frac{20°}{A'} = \frac{0.40}{0.50}$

$A' = \frac{0.50\times 20°}{0.40} = 25°$

6. (c) Focal length of the combination, $\frac{1}{f} = \frac{1}{f_1} + \frac{1}{f_2}$

Focal length in terms of radius of curvature is as follows,

$f_1 = \frac{R}{(\mu_1 - 1)}$, $f_2 = \frac{-R}{(\mu_2 - 1)}$

$\therefore\ \frac{1}{f} = \frac{(\mu_1 - 1)}{R} - \frac{(\mu_2 - 1)}{R}$

$= \frac{(\mu_1 - \mu_2)}{R}$

$f = \frac{R}{(\mu_1 - \mu_2)}$

7. (d) Apparent depth of mark as seen through a glass slab of thickness x and refractive index μ is given as,

Apparent depth $= \frac{\text{Real depth}}{\text{Refractive index}}$

$x' = \frac{x}{\mu} = \frac{6}{2} = 3$ cm

As image appears to be raised by 3 cm, therefore microscope must be moved upward by 3 cm.

8. (c)

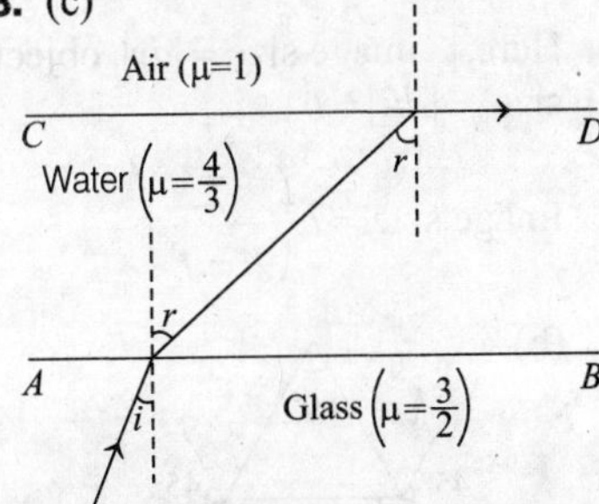

Critical angle for glass-air surface,

$\mu_g \sin C = 1\times \sin 90°$

$\sin C = \frac{1}{\mu_g} = \frac{1}{3/2} = \frac{2}{3}$.

Refraction at AB

$$\mu_g \sin C = \mu_w \sin r.$$

$$\frac{3}{2} \cdot \frac{2}{3} = \frac{4}{3} \sin r$$

$$\sin r = \frac{3}{4}$$

Refraction at water-air surface

$$\mu_w \sin r = 1 \times \sin \theta$$

$$\frac{4}{3} \cdot \frac{3}{4} = 1 \times \sin \theta$$

$$\sin \theta = 1$$

$$\sin \theta = \sin 90°$$

$$\theta = 90°$$

The ray will emerge parallel to water-air surface.

9. (a) According to question,

$u = -20\,\text{cm}$

and $v = -10\,\text{cm}$

$$\therefore \quad \frac{1}{f} = \frac{1}{v} - \frac{1}{u} = \frac{1}{-10} - \frac{1}{(-20)}$$

$$\Rightarrow \quad f = -20\,\text{cm}$$

$\therefore$ Mirror is concave.

10. (d) We know that,

$$v = \left(\frac{uf}{u-f}\right) \quad \ldots\text{(i)}$$

On differentiating Eq. (i) w.r.t. u, we get

$$\Rightarrow \quad dv = -\left(\frac{f}{u-f}\right)^2 du$$

$$\Rightarrow \quad |dv| = \left(\frac{f}{u-f}\right)^2 |du| \quad \ldots\text{(ii)}$$

Here, image size $= |dv|$, object size $= |du| = b$

$$\text{Image size} = b\left(\frac{f}{u-f}\right)^2$$

11. (b)

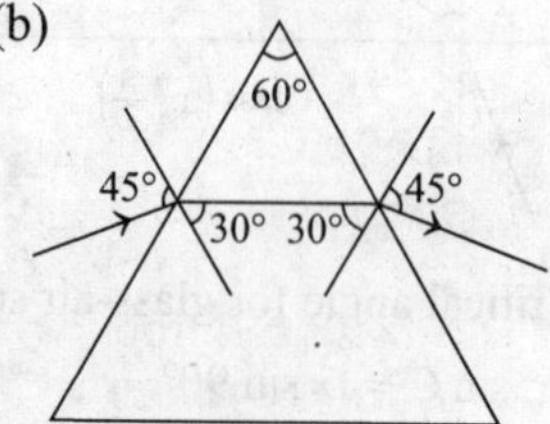

From the figure,

$i = 45°$, $A = 60°$

$$\delta_m = 2i - A = 30°$$

$$\mu = \frac{\sin\left(\frac{A+\delta_m}{2}\right)}{\sin A/2} = \frac{\sin 45°}{\sin 30°}$$

$$= \frac{1}{\sqrt{2}} \times \frac{2}{1} = \sqrt{2}$$

12. (d) As we want to correct myopia, so far point must go to infinity.

$$v = -4\text{ m}, u = -\infty, P = ?$$

$$P = \frac{1}{f} = \frac{1}{v} - \frac{1}{u} = \frac{1}{-4} - \frac{1}{\infty}$$

$$= -0.25\,\text{D}$$

negative sign implies concave lens.

13. (c)

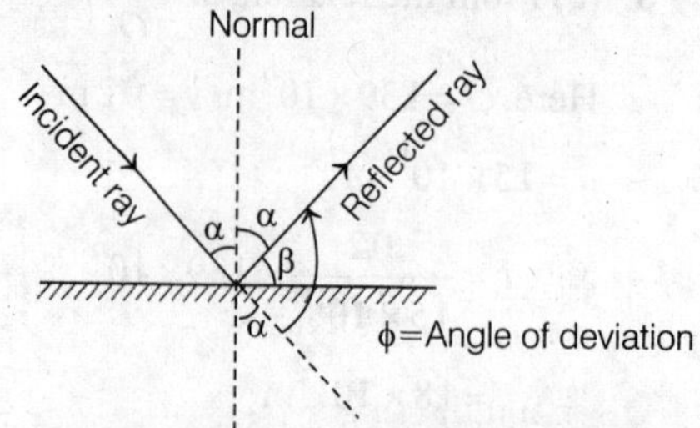

Angle of deviation, $\phi = \pi - 2\alpha$

14. (c) Suppose, water is poured up to the height, h i.e. the real depth.

Now, microscope is raised by 2 cm, hence the apparent depth should be $h-2$.

$$\text{Now, } \mu = \frac{\text{real depth}}{\text{apparent depth}} = \frac{h}{h-2}$$

$$\frac{4}{3} = \frac{h}{h-2} \Rightarrow h = 8\,\text{cm}$$

15. (d) As, $\omega = \dfrac{\delta_r - \delta_v}{\delta_w} = \dfrac{3°}{48°} = 0.0625$

16. (c) Upper part of the lens have different focal length than lower part. Hence, two images will be formed.

17. (a) Magnifying power for normal adjustment $= \dfrac{-f_o}{f_e} = -\dfrac{40}{5} = -8$

Negative sign indicates that the image is inverted.

18. (b) Angular magnification of a telescope, $m = \dfrac{\beta}{\alpha} = \dfrac{f_o}{f_e}$

Here, β is the angle subtended by the final image at the eye and α is the angle subtended by the object at the eye.

$$\frac{\beta}{0.5°} = \frac{0.3}{0.03} \Rightarrow \beta = 5°$$

19. (a) Focal length,

$$f = \frac{100}{P} = \frac{100}{25} = 4\text{ cm}$$

From lens Maker's formula,

$$\frac{1}{f} = (\mu - 1)\left(\frac{1}{R_1} - \frac{1}{R_2}\right)$$

Consider, $R_1 = +R$ and $R_2 = -R$

$$\frac{1}{f} = (\mu - 1)\left(\frac{1}{R} + \frac{1}{R}\right)$$

$$= (\mu - 1)\frac{2}{R}$$

$$\frac{1}{4} = (\mu - 1)\frac{2}{4}$$

$$\mu = \frac{1}{2} + 1 = \frac{3}{2}$$

20. (b) Apparent depth of the bottom of the beaker

$$= \frac{h_1}{n_1} + \frac{h_2}{n_2}$$

Apparent shift = Real depth − Apparent depth

$$= (h_1 + h_2) - \left(\frac{h_1}{n_1} + \frac{h_2}{n_2}\right)$$

$$= h_1\left(1 - \frac{1}{n_1}\right) + h_2\left(1 - \frac{1}{n_2}\right)$$

21. (b) From prism formula,

$$n = \frac{\sin\left(\frac{A + D_m}{2}\right)}{\sin\left(\frac{A}{2}\right)}$$

$$\Rightarrow \quad n = \frac{\sin\left(\frac{A + A}{2}\right)}{\sin\left(\frac{A}{2}\right)}$$

$$n = 2\left\{\cos\left(\frac{A}{2}\right)\right\}$$

In the given situation, value of A varies from 0 to 90°.

$$\Rightarrow \quad n_{\min} = 2\cos\left(\frac{90°}{2}\right)$$

$$= 2\cos 45° = \sqrt{2}$$

$$n_{\max} = 2\cos 0° = 2$$

22. (d) As we know that, magnification

$$m = -\frac{v}{u} \text{ or } m = \frac{-f}{u-f}$$

If the change in u and v are very small, then we can write

$$dv = -\frac{v^2}{u^2} \cdot du$$

$$dv = -\left(\frac{-f}{u-f}\right)^2 du \quad \ldots\text{(i)}$$

Given that, $f = 4$ cm, $u = 6$ cm

$du = 1$ cm

On putting these values in Eq. (i), we get

$$dv = -\left(\frac{-4}{6-4}\right)^2 \times 1$$

$$dv = -4 \text{ cm}$$

or $\quad |dv| = 4$ cm

23. (a) Given, magnification, $m = 7$

Since, we know that

$$m = 1 + \frac{D}{f_o}$$

$$7 = 1 + \frac{D}{f_o}$$

$$\Rightarrow \quad f_o = 5 \text{ cm}$$

For compound microscope, magnifying power is given by

$$m = \frac{l \cdot D}{f_o f_e} = 2m_{\text{simple microscope}}$$

$$\Rightarrow 14 = \frac{70 \times 30}{5 \cdot f_e} \Rightarrow f_e = 30 \text{ cm}$$

24. (b) When the light rays from an object have been reflected towards an observer from a standard flat mirror, then the image observed by the observer is virtual, erect, same size as the object and laterally inverted.

25. (a) In the given case, the light gets refracted twice from air to ice at A and from ice to glass at B as shown below.

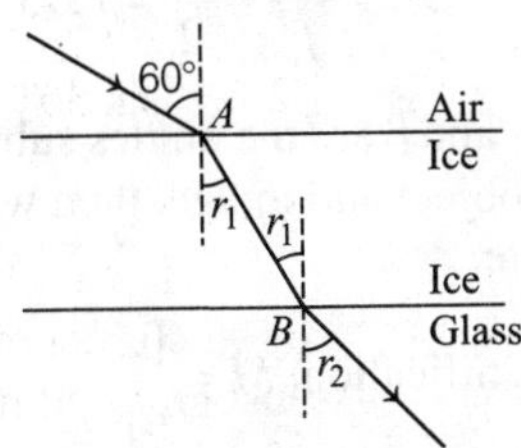

At A, air - ice interface applying Snell's law,

$$\frac{\sin i_1}{\sin r_1} = {}^{\text{air}}n_{\text{ice}} = \frac{n_{\text{ice}}}{n_{\text{air}}}$$

$$\Rightarrow \quad \frac{\sin 60°}{\sin r_1} = \frac{n_{\text{ice}}}{1} \quad \ldots\text{(i)}$$

Similarly at B, ice - glass interface applying Snell's law,

$$\frac{\sin r_1}{\sin r_2} = {}^{\text{ice}}n_{\text{glass}} = \frac{n_{\text{glass}}}{n_{\text{ice}}} \quad \ldots\text{(ii)}$$

On multiplying Eqs. (i) and (ii), we get

$$\Rightarrow \frac{\sin 60°}{\sin r_1} \times \frac{\sin r_1}{\sin r_2} = \frac{n_{\text{ice}}}{1} \times \frac{n_{\text{glass}}}{n_{\text{ice}}}$$

$$\Rightarrow \quad \frac{\sin 60°}{\sin r_2} = n_{\text{glass}}$$

$$\Rightarrow \quad \sin r_2 = \frac{\sin 60°}{n_{\text{glass}}} = \frac{\sqrt{3}/2}{3/2} = \frac{1}{\sqrt{3}}$$

26. (d) Given, focal length,

$$f = -40 \text{ cm}$$

(focal length of concave lens is negative)

Beam converges at point 20 cm. Without convex lens, it mean

$$u = +20 \text{ cm}$$

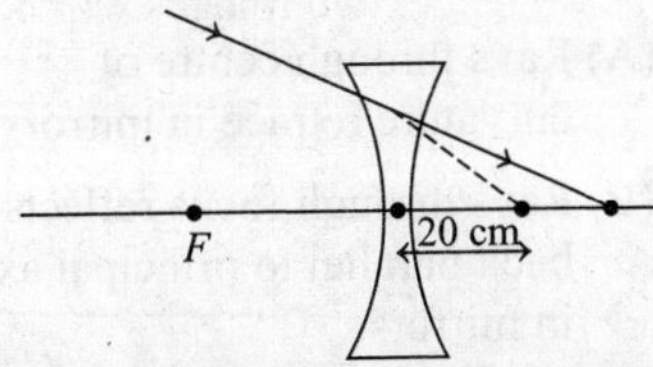

From lens formula, $\dfrac{1}{v} - \dfrac{1}{u} = \dfrac{1}{f}$

or $\dfrac{1}{v} = \dfrac{1}{u} + \dfrac{1}{f}$

$$= \frac{1}{20} + \frac{1}{(-40)}$$

$$\frac{1}{v} = +\frac{1}{40} \Rightarrow v = 40 \text{ cm}$$

27. (d) Suppose, the bubble is at a distance x from the top face of the cube. We know that,

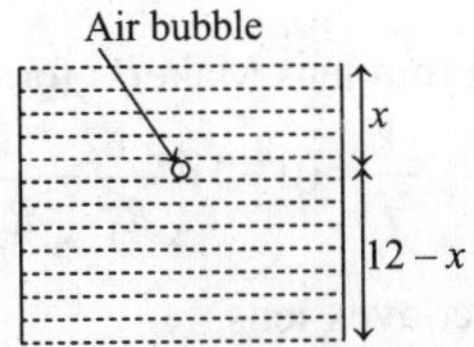

Refractive index,

$$\mu = \frac{\text{Real depth}}{\text{Apparent depth}}$$

or $\quad \mu = \dfrac{x}{3} \quad \ldots\text{(i)}$

When looking from the opposite face, then

$$\mu = \frac{12-x}{5} \quad \ldots\text{(ii)}$$

On solving Eqs. (i) and (ii), we get

$$x = \frac{9}{2} = 4.5 \text{ cm}$$

Putting the value of x in Eq. (i), we get

$$\mu = 1.5$$

28. (b) Suppose, the object is placed at O, at a height x from the surface of the liquid. For the observer at the position of the mirror inside transparent liquid, the apparent distance of the object becomes

$$= \mu x + h$$

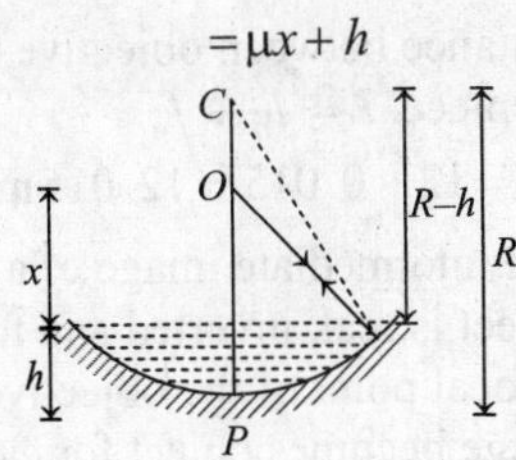

The image will form on the object itself when mirror forms virtual image at C.

i.e. at a distance R from P. Thus,

$$\mu x + h = R$$

$$\mu = \frac{R-h}{x} \quad \ldots\text{(i)}$$

Given that, $R = 15\,\text{cm}$, $h = 3\,\text{cm}$, $x = 9\,\text{cm}$.

On putting the given values in Eq. (i), we get

$$\mu = \frac{15-3}{9} = \frac{12}{9}$$

$$\mu = \frac{4}{3} = 1.33$$

29. (b) From lens Maker's formula,

$$\frac{1}{f} = (\mu - 1)\left(\frac{1}{R_1} - \frac{1}{R_2}\right)$$

For convex lens,

$$R_1 = R, R_2 = -R$$

$$\therefore \quad \frac{1}{f} = (\mu - 1)\left(\frac{1}{R} - \frac{1}{(-R)}\right)$$

$$= \frac{(\mu - 1) \times 2}{R}$$

$$\text{or} \quad f = \frac{R}{2(\mu - 1)}$$

$$= \frac{30}{2(1.5 - 1)}$$

$$\text{or} \quad f = \frac{30}{2 \times 0.5} = 30\,\text{cm}$$

30. (c) Given, focal length of objective, $f_o = 12\,\text{m}$

Focal length of eyepiece,

$$f_e = 1.5\,\text{cm}$$

Magnification of astronomical refracting telescope, $M = +\frac{f_o}{f_e}$

$$= +\frac{1200}{1.5} = +800$$

Distance between objective and eyepiece, $L = f_o + f_e$

$$= 12 + 0.015 = 12.015\,\text{m}$$

The intermediate image of a distant object is real, inverted and formed at focal point of the objective. This image becomes object for eyepiece which finally forms virtual and inverted image. Thus, statement given in option (c) is incorrect.

31. (b) Given, focal length of objective, $f_o = 50\,\text{cm}$

Focal length of eyepiece,

$$f_e = 4\,\text{cm}$$

Magnification of simple telescope,

$$M = \frac{f_o}{f_e} = \frac{50}{4} = 12.5$$

If α and β are the angles subtended by object and image, then we can write,

$$\text{magnification, } M = \frac{\beta}{\alpha}$$

Given, $\alpha = 2°$

$$\therefore \quad 12.5 = \frac{\beta}{2°}$$

$$\beta = 25°$$

32. (a) Given, focal length of objective, $f_o = 4\,\text{cm}$

Focal length of eye-piece,

$$f_e = 5\,\text{cm}$$

Length of tube, $L = 20\,\text{cm}$

When the final image is formed at infinity, then $L = v_o + f_o = 20\,\text{cm}$

$$v_o + 4 = 20\,\text{cm}$$

$$v_o = 16\,\text{cm}$$

For objective lens, using lens equation

$$\frac{1}{v_o} - \frac{1}{u_o} = \frac{1}{f_o}$$

$$\frac{1}{16} - \frac{1}{u_o} = \frac{1}{4}$$

$$\frac{1}{u_o} = \frac{1}{16} - \frac{1}{4} = \frac{1-4}{16}$$

$$\frac{1}{u_o} = \frac{-3}{16}$$

$$u_o = -\frac{16}{3} = -5.33\,\text{cm}$$

33. (a)

(A) Rays through centre of curvature retrace in mirrors.

(B) Rays through focus reflects back parallel to principal axis in mirrors.

(C) Rays from infinite distance converge at principal focus.

(D) Refracted rays to infinity emerge through principal focus.

34. (a) The magnification of astronomical telescope is given by

$$m = -\frac{f_o}{f_e}\left(1 + \frac{f_e}{D}\right)$$

where, f_o is focal length of objective, f_e is focal length of eyepiece and D is least distance of distinct vision.

From the formula, it is clear that, f_e should be least and f_o should be greatest.

Thus, the correct values for the largest magnification, f_o and f_e should be + 200 cm and +10 cm, respectively.

35. (a) Given, $R_1 = -R$ and $R_2 = +R_2$

From lens Maker's formula,

$$\frac{1}{f} = (\mu - 1)\left(\frac{1}{R_1} - \frac{1}{R_2}\right)$$

$$= (\mu - 1)\left(\frac{1}{-R} - \frac{1}{R}\right)$$

$$f = \frac{-R}{2(\mu - 1)} = \frac{-30}{2(1.5 - 1)}$$

$$= -30\,\text{cm}$$

36. (c) Refractive index for a prism is given by

$$\mu = \frac{\sin\left(\frac{A + \delta_m}{2}\right)}{\sin\frac{A}{2}} = \frac{\sin\left(\frac{A + A}{2}\right)}{\sin\frac{A}{2}}$$

$$= \frac{\sin A}{\sin\frac{A}{2}}$$

$$= \frac{2\sin\frac{A}{2}\cos\frac{A}{2}}{\sin\frac{A}{2}} = 2\cos\frac{A}{2}$$

$$\text{So, } \sqrt{3} = 2\cos\frac{A}{2}$$

$$\frac{\sqrt{3}}{2} = \cos\frac{A}{2}$$

$$\Rightarrow \quad A = 60°$$

37. (a) In total internal reflection, 100% of incident light is reflected back into the same medium and there is no loss of intensity, while in reflection from mirrors and refraction from lens, there is always some loss of intensity. Therefore, images formed by total internal reflection are much brighter than those formed by mirrors or lenses.

38. (b)

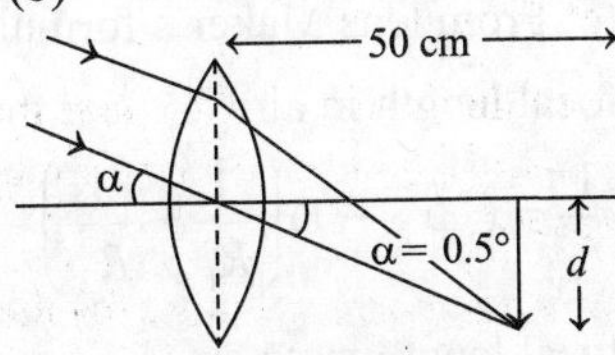

Diameter of image,

$$d = \left(0.5 \times \frac{\pi}{180}\right) \times 500 = 4.36\,\text{mm}$$

39. (c) From lens Maker's formula, we have

$$f \propto \frac{1}{\mu - 1} \text{ and } \mu \propto \frac{1}{\lambda}$$

Hence, option (c) is correct.

40. (b) Apparent depth,

$$h' = \frac{h}{_{\text{air}}\mu_{\text{liquid}}}$$

$$\Rightarrow \quad \frac{dh'}{dt} = \frac{1}{_a\mu_w}\frac{dh}{dt}$$

$$2x = \frac{1}{_a\mu_w}\frac{dh}{dt}$$

$$\frac{dh}{dt} = {_a\mu_w}\, 2x$$

Rate of drainage of water will be,

$$\frac{dV}{dt} = 4\pi R^2 \frac{dh}{dt} = 4\pi R^2 \cdot {_a\mu_w}\, 2x$$

$$= 8\,{_a\mu_w}\,\pi R^2 x = 8\frac{\mu_w}{\mu_a}\pi R^2 x$$

$$= 8\left(\frac{n_2}{n_1}\right)\pi R^2 x$$

41. (b) Here, $i > c$

$$\Rightarrow \quad \sin i > \sin c$$

$$\sin i > \frac{\mu_2}{\mu_1} \quad \text{...(i)}$$

From Snell's law,

$$\mu_1 = \frac{\sin\beta}{\sin r} \quad \text{...(ii)}$$

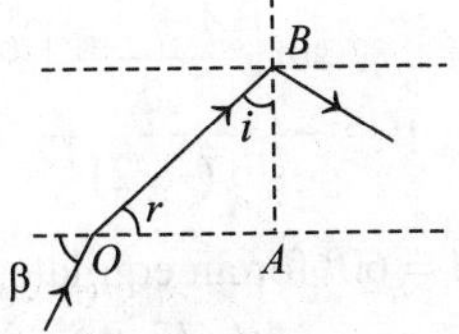

Also in ΔOBA

$$r + i = 90° \Rightarrow r = (90 - i)$$

Hence, from Eq. (ii)

$$\sin\beta = \mu_1 \sin(90 - i)$$

$$\Rightarrow \quad \cos i = \frac{\sin\beta}{\mu_1}$$

$$\sin i = \sqrt{1 - \cos^2 i}$$

$$= \sqrt{1 - \left(\frac{\sin\beta}{\mu_1}\right)^2} \quad \text{...(iii)}$$

From Eqs. (i) and (iii),

$$\sqrt{1 - \left(\frac{\sin\beta}{\mu_1}\right)^2} > \frac{\mu_2}{\mu_1}$$

$$\Rightarrow \quad \sin^2\beta < (\mu_1^2 - \mu_2^2)$$

$$\Rightarrow \quad \sin\beta < \sqrt{\mu_1^2 - \mu_2^2}$$

$$\beta_{\max} = \sin^{-1}\sqrt{\mu_1^2 - \mu_2^2}$$

42. (a) In a compound microscope, image formed by the objective is real, enlarged and inverted because objective has smaller focal length than the object distance.

The position of eyepiece is kept such that the image formed by objective lens is formed within the focal length of the eyepiece.

Hence, it forms a virtual and magnified image.

43. (c) $L_D = v_o + u_e$, and for objective lens

$$\frac{1}{f_o} = \frac{1}{v_o} - \frac{1}{u_o}$$

Putting the values with proper sign convention.

$$\frac{1}{+2.5} = \frac{1}{v_o} - \frac{1}{(-3.75)}$$

$$\Rightarrow \quad v_o = 7.5\,\text{cm}$$

For eye lens,

$$\frac{1}{f_e} = \frac{1}{v_e} - \frac{1}{u_e}$$

$$\frac{1}{+10} = \frac{1}{(-2.5)} - \frac{1}{u_e}$$

$$u_e = -7.14\,\text{cm}$$

$$|u_e| = 7.14\,\text{cm}$$

Hence, $L_D = 7.5 + 7.14 = 14.64$ cm

44. (d) For concave mirror, $m = \dfrac{f}{f - u}$

For real image,

$$m = -\frac{f}{(u - f)} = -\frac{f}{x}$$

$$\propto \frac{1}{\text{Distance of object from focus}}$$

$$\Rightarrow \quad m \propto \frac{1}{x}$$

45. (c) According to Snell's law,

$$\sin 60° = \frac{4}{3}\sin r$$

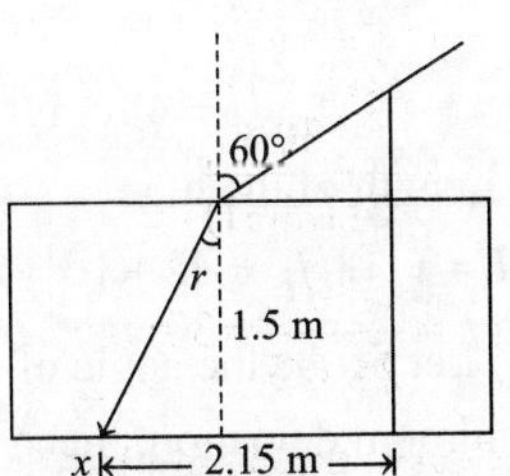

$$\sin r = \frac{3}{4} \times \frac{\sqrt{3}}{2} = \frac{3\sqrt{3}}{8} \quad \text{...(i)}$$

$$\cos r = \sqrt{1 - \frac{27}{64}} = \frac{\sqrt{37}}{8} = 0.75$$

$$\tan r = \sqrt{\frac{27}{37}} \Rightarrow \frac{x}{1.5} = 0.85$$

$$x = 0.85 \times 1.5 = 1.275\,\text{m}$$

$$\tan 30° = \frac{y}{2.15 - 1.275} = \frac{y}{0.875}$$

$$y = \frac{0.875}{1.732} = 0.50$$

So, length of pole above water surface $= 0.50\,\text{m} = 50\,\text{cm}$

46. (c) Power of system,

$$P = \frac{1}{f_1} + \frac{1}{f_2} - \frac{d}{f_1 f_2}$$

$$= \frac{1}{0.25} + \frac{1}{(-0.1)} - \frac{0.1}{(0.25)(-0.1)}$$

$$= 4 - 10 + 4 = -2$$

Since, power of the system is negative, therefore the incident parallel beam of light will diverge after emerging from the system.

47. (c) Magnifying power for relaxed eye is

$$M = \frac{v_o D}{u_o f_e}$$

Here, $M = -50$, $f_o = 2\,\text{cm}$, $f_e = 10\,\text{cm}$ and $D = 25\,\text{cm}$

$$\therefore \quad -50 = \frac{v_o}{u_o} \times \frac{25}{10} \Rightarrow \frac{v_o}{u_o} = -20$$

$$u_o = -\frac{v_0}{20} \text{ and } f_o = +2\,\text{cm}$$

$$\therefore \quad \frac{1}{v_o} - \frac{1}{u_o} = \frac{1}{f_o}$$

we get, $\frac{1}{v_o} + \frac{20}{v_o} = \frac{1}{2}$

$$v_o = 42\,\text{cm}$$

$\therefore$ Length of the tube

$$L = v_o + f_e = 42 + 10 = 52\,\text{cm}$$

48. (*a*) Let δ_m be the angle of minimum deviation, then

$$\mu = \frac{\sin\left(\frac{A+\delta_m}{2}\right)}{\sin(A/2)}$$

$\because A = 60°$ for an equilateral prism

$$\therefore \quad \sqrt{2} = \frac{\sin\left(\frac{60° + \delta_m}{2}\right)}{\sin\left(\frac{60°}{2}\right)}$$

Solving this, we get $\delta_m = 30°$

The given deviation is also 30° (i.e. δ_m).

Angle made by ray of light with the base (under minimum deviation condition) is zero, if base angles are equal.

49. (c) The formula relating *u*, *v* and *R* for concave spherical surface is

$$\frac{\mu_2}{v} - \frac{\mu_1}{u} = \frac{\mu_2 - \mu_1}{R}$$

$$\frac{2}{v} - \frac{1.2}{-20} = \frac{2-1.2}{-50}$$

$$\frac{2}{v} = -\frac{8}{500} - \frac{6}{100}$$

$$\frac{2}{v} = -\frac{38}{500}$$

$$v = -\frac{1000}{38} = -26.3\,\text{cm}$$

Therefore, the position of the image from the object is

$$v - u = -26.3 - (-20) = -6.3$$

$\therefore$ Image is 6.3 cm left to the object.

50. (c) From lens Maker's formula, focal length in air

$$\frac{1}{f_a} = ({}^a\mu_g - 1)\left(\frac{1}{R_1} - \frac{1}{R_2}\right) \quad \ldots\text{(i)}$$

focal length in water,

$$\frac{1}{f_w} = ({}^w\mu_g - 1)\left(\frac{1}{R_1} - \frac{1}{R_2}\right) \quad \ldots\text{(ii)}$$

On dividing Eq. (i) by Eq. (ii), we get

$$\frac{f_w}{f_a} = \frac{{}^a\mu_g - 1}{{}^w\mu_g - 1}$$

$$= \frac{\frac{3}{2} - 1}{\frac{3/2}{4/3} - 1} = 4$$

$$f_w = 4 \times 10 = 40\,\text{cm}$$

Ch-11 Wave Optics

Topical Follow Thru

Test-1

1. (d) $\frac{I_1}{I_2} = \beta = \frac{a^2}{b^2} \quad \left(\because \frac{a}{b} = \sqrt{\beta}\right)$

$$I_{max} = (a+b)^2$$

$$I_{min} = (a-b)^2$$

Apply componendo and dividendo rule,

$$\frac{I_{max} - I_{min}}{I_{max} + I_{min}} = \frac{(a+b)^2 - (a-b)^2}{(a+b)^2 + (a-b)^2}$$

$$= \frac{4ab}{2(a^2+b^2)} = \frac{2ab}{(a^2+b^2)}$$

$$= \frac{2 \cdot b \cdot b\sqrt{\beta}}{b^2 + \beta b^2} = \frac{2\sqrt{\beta}}{1+\beta}$$

2. (a) For phenomenon of interference, it is necessary that these light rays have constant phase difference.

3. (d) As we know,

$$n_1 = \frac{c}{v_1} = \frac{v\lambda}{v\lambda_1} = \frac{\lambda}{\lambda_1}$$

(Here, c = velocity of light, λ = wavelength in free space and v_1 = velocity of light in medium).

Similarly, $n_2 = \frac{c}{v_2} = \frac{v\lambda}{v\lambda_2} = \frac{\lambda}{\lambda_2}$

Now, $\frac{n_1}{n_2} = \frac{\lambda_2}{\lambda_1} \Rightarrow \lambda_2 = \left(\frac{n_1}{n_2}\right)\lambda_1$

4. (c) Given, $y_1 = a\sin\left(\omega t - \frac{\pi}{6}\right)$

and $\quad y_2 = b\cos\left(\omega t - \frac{\pi}{3}\right)$

$$= b\sin\left(\frac{\pi}{2} + \omega t - \frac{\pi}{3}\right)$$

Phase difference,

$$\phi = \left|\left(-\frac{\pi}{6}\right) - \left(\frac{\pi}{2} - \frac{\pi}{3}\right)\right|$$

$$\Rightarrow \quad \phi = \left|-\frac{\pi}{6} - \frac{\pi}{6}\right| = \left|-\frac{\pi}{3}\right| = \frac{\pi}{3}$$

5. (a) Here, $a_1 = 8\mu m$, $a_2 = 3\mu m$ and $a_3 = 12\mu m$.

Phase difference between a_1 and a_3 is π. Hence, their resultant amplitude is

$$A_1 = \sqrt{a_1^2 + a_3^2 + 2a_1 a_3 \cos\pi}$$
$$= \sqrt{8^2 + 12^2 + 2(8)(12)(-1)}$$
$$= 4\,\mu m$$

Now, phase difference between A_1 and a_2 is $\frac{\pi}{2}$.

Hence, their resultant amplitude is

$$A = \sqrt{A_1^2 + a_2^2 + 2A_1 a_2 \cos\frac{\pi}{2}}$$
$$= \sqrt{16 + 9 + 2\times4\times3\times0} = 5\mu m$$

6. (c) As, $\frac{I_{min}}{I_{max}} = \frac{a_2 - a_1}{a_2 + a_1}$

Ratio of slit width, $\left(\frac{a_1}{a_2}\right)^2 = \frac{49}{64}$

$$\Rightarrow \quad \frac{a_1}{a_2} = \frac{7}{8}$$

Here, a_1 and a_2 are amplitudes of wave.

$$\therefore \quad \frac{I_{min}}{I_{max}} = \frac{8-7}{8+7} = \frac{1}{15} \text{ or } 1:15$$

7. (b) Distance of nth dark fringe,

$$x_n = \frac{(2n-1)\lambda D}{2d}$$

or $x_3 = \frac{5\lambda D}{2d}$

$$\Rightarrow 0.9\times10^{-2} = \frac{5\lambda(1)}{2(0.80\times10^{-3})}$$

$$\Rightarrow \lambda = \frac{(0.9\times10^{-2})(2)(0.80\times10^{-3})}{5}$$
$$= 2.88\times10^{-6}\text{ m}$$

8. (a) By using, $d\sin\theta = n\lambda$

$$n = \frac{d\sin\theta}{\lambda}$$

For maixmum intensity, $\sin\theta = 1$

$$n = \frac{6000}{4000} = 1.5$$
$$n \le 1.5$$

Since, n must be a non-negative integer, the possible values of n are $n = 0$ and $n = 1$.

This gives as total of 2 maxima on one side of the central maximum. Including the central maximum ($n = 0$), the total number of maximum on both sides of the central fringe is 3 i.e., $n = 0, 1$ and 1.

Hence, 3 maxima will be obtained.

9. (b) Angular separation, $\theta = \frac{\lambda}{d}$

$$\theta \propto \lambda$$
$$\Rightarrow \lambda_2 = \lambda_1\frac{\theta_2}{\theta_1}$$
$$= (589)\frac{(4.2\times10^{-3} + 0.2\times4.2\times10^{-3})}{4.2\times10^{-3}}$$
$$\Rightarrow \lambda_2 = 706.8\text{ nm}$$

10. (c) Phase difference,

$$\Delta\phi = \frac{2\pi}{\lambda}\times\lambda = 2\pi$$
$$I = 4I_0\cos^2\left(\frac{2\pi}{2}\right) = 4I_0$$

When path difference $= \lambda/4$,

phase difference $= \frac{2\pi}{\lambda}\times\frac{\lambda}{4} = \frac{\pi}{2}$

$$I' = 4I_0\cos^2\left(\frac{\pi/2}{2}\right) = 2I_0$$

So, $\frac{I'}{I} = \frac{2I_0}{4I_0}$

$$I' = \frac{I}{2}$$

11. (b) Here, path difference is

$$\Delta x = \frac{Yd}{D} = \frac{d^2}{2D}$$

For first order minima,

$$\Delta x = \frac{\lambda}{2} \text{ or } \frac{d^2}{2D} = \frac{\lambda}{2}$$

$$\therefore \quad \lambda = \frac{d^2}{D}$$

12. (a) Refractive index of medium 2 with respect to medium 1 is,

$$n_{21} = \frac{v_1}{v_2} = \frac{v_1 t}{v_2 t} = \frac{BC}{AD}$$

13. (c) In a YDSE, the path difference for nth minima is given by

$$\Delta y = (2n-1)\frac{\lambda}{2}$$

For 5th minima, $n = 5$.

$$\therefore \quad \Delta y = [2(5)-1]\frac{\lambda}{2} = \frac{9\lambda}{2}$$

14. (b) Here, path difference is

$$\Delta x = d\sin\theta$$

$\therefore$ Phase difference, $\phi = \frac{2\pi}{\lambda}\Delta x$

$$= \frac{2\pi}{\lambda}(d\sin\theta) = \frac{2\pi}{\frac{c}{f}}(d\sin\theta)$$

$$\therefore \quad \phi = \frac{2\pi}{3\times10^8}\times10^6\times150\sin30^\circ$$
$$= \frac{\pi}{2}$$

$$\because \quad I = 4I_0\cos^2\frac{\phi}{2} = 4\times1\cos^2\frac{\pi}{4}$$
$$= 4\times\frac{1}{2} = 2\text{ Wm}^{-2}$$

15. (c) By Snell's law, $\frac{\sin i}{\sin r} = \frac{\mu_2}{\mu_1}$

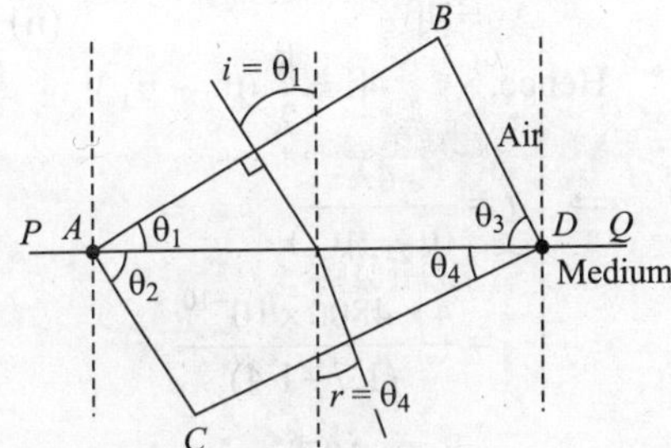

For $i = \theta_1, r = \theta_4$

and $\mu_{air} = 1$

$$\mu_{medium} = \frac{\sin\theta_1}{\sin\theta_4}$$

16. (b) For possible interference maxima on the screen, the condition is

$$d\sin\theta = n\lambda \quad \text{...(i)}$$

Given, d = slit width $= 2\lambda$

$\therefore \quad 2\lambda \sin\theta = n\lambda$

or $\quad 2\sin\theta = n$

The maximum value of $\sin\theta$ is 1, hence

$$n = 2\times 1 = 2$$

Thus, Eq. (i) must be satisfied by 5 integer values, i.e. $-2, -1, 0, 1, 2$. Hence, the maximum number of possible interference maxima is 5.

17. (c) As we know that shift due to insertion of a slab is

$$\Delta x = \frac{\beta}{\lambda}(\mu - 1)t$$

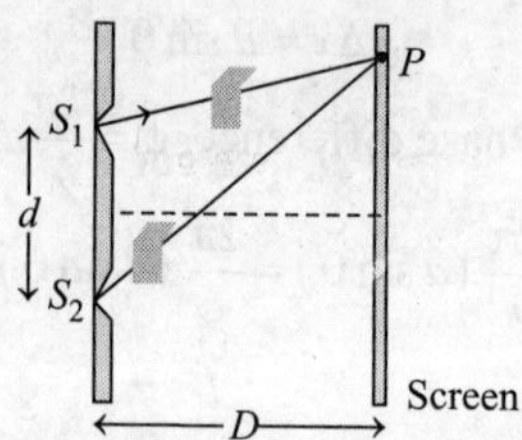

Shift due to one plate,

$$\Delta x_1 = \frac{\beta}{\lambda}(\mu_1 - 1)t$$

Shift due to another plate,

$$\Delta x_2 = \frac{\beta}{\lambda}(\mu_2 - 1)t$$

Net shift,

$$\Delta x = \Delta x_2 - \Delta x_1 = \frac{\beta}{\lambda}(\mu_2 - \mu_1)t \quad \text{...(i)}$$

Here, it is given that,

$$\Delta x = 4\beta \quad \text{...(ii)}$$

Hence, $\quad 4\beta = \frac{\beta}{\lambda}(\mu_2 - \mu_1)t$

$$\Rightarrow \quad t = \frac{4\lambda}{(\mu_2 - \mu_1)}$$

$$= \frac{4\times 4800\times 10^{-10}}{(1.7-1.4)}$$

$$= 6.4\times 10^{-6}\,\text{m} = 6.4\,\mu\text{m}$$

18. (d) Given, $a_1 = 2a_2$

$$I_2 = I_0$$

$$\Rightarrow I_1 = 4I_2 = 4I_0 \qquad [\because I \propto a^2]$$

$$\therefore I_m = (\sqrt{I_1} + \sqrt{I_2})^2 = (3\sqrt{I_2})^2$$

$$= 9I_2 = 9I_0$$

Now, $I = I_1 + I_2 + 2\sqrt{I_1 I_2}\cos\phi$

$$= 4I_0 + I_0 + 2\sqrt{4I_0 \cdot I_0}\cos\phi$$

$$= 5I_0 + 4I_0\cos\phi$$

$$= \frac{I_m}{9}(5 + 4\cos\phi) \qquad \left[\because I_0 = \frac{I_m}{9}\right]$$

$$= \frac{I_m}{9}[1 + 4(1+\cos\phi)]$$

$$= \frac{I_m}{9}\left(1 + 8\cos^2\frac{\phi}{2}\right) \qquad \left[\because 1+\cos\phi = 2\cos^2\frac{\phi}{2}\right]$$

19. (d) The frequency of light does not change due to change of media. So, colour of light does not change due to change of media. But $\lambda = \frac{\lambda_0}{\mu}$, thus wavelength of light in different media are different.

Hence, Statement II is correct but Statement I is incorrect.

20. (c) According to question,

$\mu AB = \mu' CD$

$$\Rightarrow \quad \frac{AB}{CD} = \frac{\mu'}{\mu} \quad \text{...(i)}$$

$$t_1 c_1 = AB$$

$$t_2 c_2 = CD$$

$$\therefore \quad \frac{t_1}{t_2} = \frac{AB}{CD}\times\frac{c_2}{c_1} \quad \text{...(ii)}$$

$$\mu \propto \frac{1}{c}$$

$$\frac{\mu}{\mu'} = \frac{c_2}{c_1} \quad \text{...(iii)}$$

From Eqs. (i), (ii) and (iii), we get

$$\frac{t_1}{t_2} = \frac{\mu'}{\mu}\times\frac{\mu}{\mu'}$$

$$\frac{t_1}{t_2} = 1$$

$$\Rightarrow \quad t_1 = t_2$$

Hence, Statement I is correct but Statement II is incorrect.

21. (c) The path difference at point P is

$$\Delta x = S'P + \frac{\lambda}{2} - SP$$

$$= 2l + \frac{\lambda}{2} = m\lambda$$

or $\quad 2l = m\lambda - \frac{\lambda}{2}$

$$\therefore \quad l = \frac{m\lambda}{2} - \frac{\lambda}{4} \quad \text{...(i)}$$

When the mirror is shifted downward a distance y_0

$$\Delta x' = 2(l + l_0) + \frac{\lambda}{2} = (m+1)\lambda$$

or $\quad l + l_0 = (m+1)\frac{\lambda}{2} - \frac{\lambda}{4}$

or $\quad m\frac{\lambda}{2} - \frac{\lambda}{4} + l_0 = m\frac{\lambda}{2} + \frac{\lambda}{2} - \frac{\lambda}{4}$

or $\quad l_0 = \frac{\lambda}{2} = \frac{600}{2} = 300\text{ nm}$

22. (d) Depending on the value of refractive index, the path travelled by light would be decided, which is turn, decides the shapes of wavefronts. For large refractive index, speed of light is less and hence, wavefront location would be somewhat located back side.

23. (b) The fringe width, $\beta = \frac{\lambda D}{d}$

The angular separation of the fringes is given by

$$\theta = \frac{\beta}{D} = \frac{\lambda}{d}$$

Given, $\theta = 1^\circ = \frac{\pi}{180}$ rad

$$\lambda = 589\,\text{nm}$$

$$\therefore \quad d = \frac{\lambda}{\theta} = \frac{589\times 180\times 10^{-9}}{\pi}$$

$$= 0.0337\,\text{mm}$$

24. (c) For $x = \lambda$,

phase difference $= \frac{2\pi\lambda}{\lambda} = 2\pi$

Intensity,

$$I = I_0 + I_0 + 2\sqrt{I_0 I_0}\cos 2\pi$$

$$\Rightarrow \quad I = 4I_0 = K \quad \text{...(i)}$$

For $x = \frac{\lambda}{3}$,

phase difference

$$= \frac{2\pi}{\lambda} \times \frac{\lambda}{3} = \frac{2\pi}{3}$$

Intensity,

$$I' = I_0 + I_0 + 2\sqrt{I_0 I_0} \cos \frac{2\pi}{3}$$

$$I' = I_0$$

$$\therefore \quad I' = I_0 = \frac{K}{4} \text{ [from Eq. (i)]}$$

25. (c) Given, $\lambda = 6000$ Å

$$= 6000 \times 10^{-10} \text{ m}$$

Thickness of the transparent sheet,

$$t = 3.6 \times 10^{-3} \text{ cm}$$

$$= 3.6 \times 10^{-5} \text{ m}$$

Now, $\frac{30\lambda D}{d} = \frac{D}{d}(\mu - 1)t$

$$\Rightarrow \quad (\mu - 1) = \frac{30\lambda}{t}$$

$$= \frac{30 \times 6000 \times 10^{-10}}{3.6 \times 10^{-5}} = 0.5$$

$$\Rightarrow \quad \mu = 1 + 0.5 = 1.5$$

Test-2

1. (b) Fringe width, $\beta = \frac{\lambda D}{d}$

where, D = distance of screen from the wire,

d = diameter of wire.

If diameter will increase, then fringe width will decrease.

2. (b) Angular width between first and second diffraction minima is $\theta \approx \frac{\lambda}{a}$

Angular width of fringe due to double slit is $\theta' = \frac{\lambda}{d}$

∴ Number of fringes between first and second diffraction minima,

$$n = \frac{\theta}{\theta'} = \frac{\frac{\lambda}{a}}{\frac{\lambda}{d}} = \frac{d}{a} = \frac{19.44}{4.05} = 4.8 \approx 5$$

3. (a) Distance of the central maxima from the first dark fringe is $\frac{\lambda}{a}$.

If f is the focal length of the lens, then size of the screen should be $\frac{f\lambda}{a}$.

4. (c) Intensity $\propto$ (Amplitude)^2 and when unpolarised beam passes through a polaroid, its intensity becomes half.

$\Rightarrow$ Incident intensity $= I_0 = kE_0^2$

and transmitted intensity

$$= I = \frac{I_0}{2} = k\left(\frac{E_0}{\sqrt{2}}\right)^2$$

5. (d) Most of the light will diffract at the central maxima. Hence, angular divergence = 2θ.

$$= 2\sin\theta = \frac{2\lambda}{d} \quad \left(\because \sin\theta = \frac{\lambda}{d}\right)$$

$$= \frac{2(500 \times 10^{-9})}{5 \times 10^{-4}} = 2 \times 10^{-3} \text{ rad}$$

6. (b) Position of minimum $= \frac{n\lambda D}{d}$

Position of maximum $= (2n+1)\frac{\lambda D}{2d}$

Position of first minimum = Position of fourth maximum

$$\frac{(1)\lambda_1 D}{d} = \frac{(2(4)+1)\lambda_2 D}{2d}$$

$$\Rightarrow \quad 2\lambda_1 = 9\lambda_2$$

7. (b) Distance between first dark fringe is equal to the width of the central maxima.

$$\frac{2\lambda D}{d} = \frac{2(450 \times 10^{-9})(2)}{0.5 \times 10^{-3}} = 3.6 \text{ mm}$$

8. (a) Width of central maxima in single slit diffraction pattern,

$$x = \frac{2\lambda D}{d}$$

$$\Rightarrow \frac{x'}{x} = \frac{\lambda'}{d'} \times \frac{d}{\lambda} = \frac{550}{\frac{a}{2}} \times \frac{a}{500} = 11$$

$$\Rightarrow x' = \frac{11}{5}x$$

9. (d) The phase difference (ϕ) between the wavelets from the top edge and the bottom edge of the slit is $\phi = \frac{2\pi}{\lambda}(d\sin\theta)$

where, d is the slit width.

The first minima of the diffraction pattern occurs at $\sin\theta = \frac{\lambda}{d}$.

So, phase difference,

$$\phi = \frac{2\pi}{\lambda}\left(d \times \frac{\lambda}{d}\right) = 2\pi$$

10. (c) Given, $\lambda_1 = 660$ nm

Position of minima in diffraction pattern is given by, $a\sin\theta = n\lambda$.

For first minima ($n = 1$) of wavelength λ_1, we get

$$a\sin\theta_1 = 1\lambda_1 \text{ or}$$

$$\sin\theta_1 = \frac{\lambda_1}{a}$$

For the first maxima approximately of wavelength λ_2,

$$a\sin\theta_2 = \frac{3}{2}\lambda_2 \text{ or } \sin\theta_2 = \frac{3\lambda_2}{2a}$$

The two will be coincide, if

$$\theta_1 = \theta_2 \text{ or } \sin\theta_1 = \sin\theta_2$$

$$\therefore \quad \frac{\lambda_1}{a} = \frac{3\lambda_2}{2a}$$

or $\quad \lambda_2 = \frac{2}{3}\lambda_1 = \frac{2}{3} \times 660$ nm

or $\quad \lambda_2 = 440$ nm

11. (b) Distance between first and sixth minima, $x = \frac{5\lambda D}{d}$

$$d = \frac{5 \times 5000 \times 10^{-10} \times 0.5}{0.5 \times 10^{-3}}$$

$$\Rightarrow d = 25 \times 10^{-4} \text{ m} = 2.5 \text{ mm}$$

12. (c) Let X_1 and X_2 be the distances between first minima on the right and left respectively, of central maximum.

∴ According to question,

$$X_1 + X_2 = 4 \text{ mm}$$

Also, $X_1 + X_2 = \frac{2\lambda D}{d}$

$$\therefore \quad 4 \times 10^{-3} = \frac{2 \times 6 \times 10^{-7} \times 2}{d}$$

$\Rightarrow d = 6\times10^{-4}$ m $= 0.6$ mm

$\therefore$ Width of central maximum,

$W = X_1 + X_2 = 4\times10^{-3}$ m

or $W = 4$ mm

The width of the slit and width of the central maximum are 0.6 mm and 4 mm, respectively.

13. (a) In case of a single slit diffraction pattern as shown below,

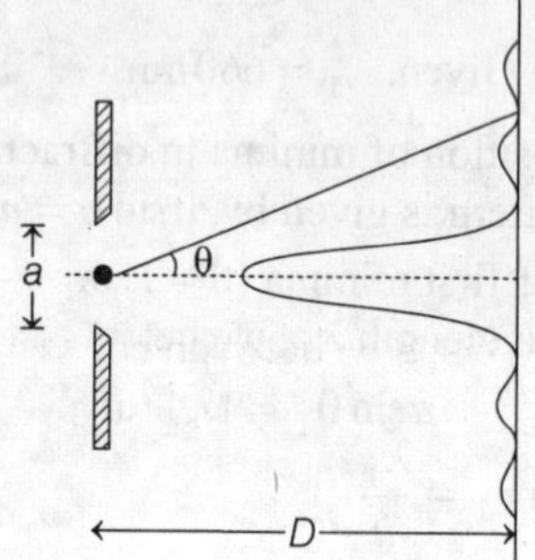

Angular position of nth minima is given by

$$\sin\theta_n = \frac{n\lambda}{D} \quad ...(i)$$

Given, $\theta_2 = 60°$ and

$\lambda = 6000\times10^{-8}$ cm

As, $\sin\theta_2 = \frac{2\lambda}{D}$

We have $\sin 60° = \frac{2\lambda}{D}$

or $\frac{\lambda}{D} = \frac{\sin 60°}{2} = 0.43 \approx \sin 25°$

[**Note** $\sin 30° = 0.5$, $\sin 25° = 0.422$ and $\sin 20° = 0.34$]

Now, if θ_1 = angular position of first minima, then

$$\sin\theta_1 = \frac{\lambda}{D}$$

[from Eq. (i), $n = 1$]

$\Rightarrow \sin\theta_1 = 0.43 \approx \sin 25°$ or $\theta_1 \approx 25°$

14. (a) Both Statement I and Statement II are correct.

15. (c) Hologram is made by using the property of diffraction of light. Hence, option (c) is correct.

16. (b) If at any instant, the axis of polariser makes angle θ with the direction of vibration of incident light.

From law of Malus,

$$I = I_0\cos^2\theta$$

As polariser is rotating, all values of θ are possible.

$$\therefore \langle I\rangle = \langle I_0\cos^2\theta\rangle = \frac{I_0}{2}$$

$$= \frac{\text{Power}}{2\times\text{Area}}$$

$$= \frac{10^{-3}}{2\times3\times10^{-4}} = \frac{5}{3}\text{ Wm}^{-2}$$

17. (b) Polarising angle = 45°

From Brewster's law,

$\mu = \tan i_p = \tan 45° = \cot 45°$

18. (b) Amplitude will be

$$A\cos 45° = \frac{A}{\sqrt2}$$

19. (a) Angle between first and second polariser = 30°

Angle between second and third polariser = 90° − 30° = 60°

Intensity of light after first polariser,

$$I_1 = \frac{I_0}{2} = \frac{30}{2} = 15\text{ Wm}^{-2}$$

Intensity of light after second polariser,

$$I_2 = I_1\cos^2 30°$$

$$= 15\left(\frac{3}{4}\right) = \frac{45}{4}\text{ Wm}^{-2}$$

Intensity of light after third polariser,

$$I_3 = I_2\cos^2 60°$$

$$= \frac{45}{4}\times\frac{1}{4} = \frac{45}{16}\text{ Wm}^{-2}$$

20. (d) A polariser-analyser set is shown below.

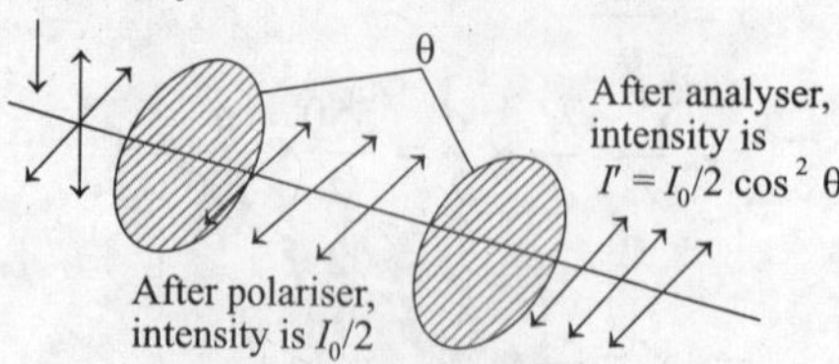

By Malus' law,

output intensity obtained from analyser, $I' = \frac{I_0}{2}\cos^2\theta \quad ...(i)$

where, θ = angle between polariser and analyser.

Now, given I' = 10% of initial intensity

$$\Rightarrow I' = \frac{1}{10}I_0 \quad ...(ii)$$

From Eqs. (i) and (ii), we get

$$\Rightarrow \cos^2\theta = \frac{1}{5} \Rightarrow \cos\theta = \frac{1}{\sqrt5}$$

$$\Rightarrow \theta = \cos^{-1}\left(\frac{1}{\sqrt5}\right) \approx 63°$$

Now, output intensity is zero, when angle between polariser and analyser is 90°.

So, analyser must be rotated by 90° − 63° = 27° to reduce output intensity to zero.

From given options, we can see that output intensity is least when analyser rotation is 18.4°.

21. (c) According to Malus' law,

$I = I_0\cos^2\theta$

Let the direction of polarisation of the light be such that it makes an angle θ′ with the X-axis.

$\therefore$ Angle between direction of polarisation and pass axis is θ′ − θ.

$$\therefore I = I_0\cos^2(\theta' - \theta) \quad ...(i)$$

Putting the values of θ one by one in Eq. (i), we get

$I_0\cos^2(\theta' - 8°) = I_0\cos^2(\theta' - 38°)$

$= I_0\cos^2(\theta' - 188°)$

$= I_0\cos^2(\theta' - 218°)$

$\therefore \cos^2(\theta' - 8°) = \cos^2(\theta' - 38°) \quad ...(ii)$

Now, putting the options one by one in Eq. (ii), we get intensities same for option (c) θ′ = 203°

$\cos^2(203° - 8°) = \cos^2(203° - 38°)$

$= \cos^2(203° - 188°)$

$= \cos^2(203° - 218°)$

$\Rightarrow \cos^2(195°) = \cos(165°)$

$= \cos^2(15°)$

$= \cos^2(-15°)$

Hence, option (c) satisfies the above equation.

22. (d) According to law of Malus,

$$I = I_0 \cos^2 \theta$$

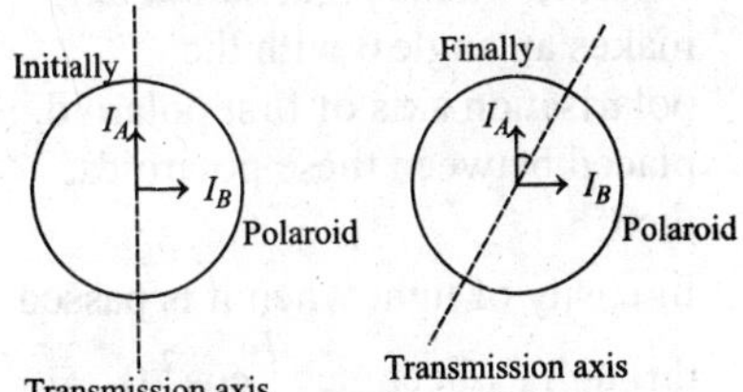

Now, $I'_A = I_A \cos^2 30°$

$I_B' = I_B \cos^2 60°$

As, $I_A' = I_B'$

$I_A \cos^2 30° = I_B \cos^2 60°$

$$\Rightarrow I_A\left(\frac{3}{4}\right) = I_B\left(\frac{1}{4}\right) \Rightarrow \frac{I_A}{I_B} = \frac{1}{3}$$

23. (a) Given, $\mu = 1.57$

According to Brewster's law,

$\mu = \tan i_p = 1.57$

$i = \tan^{-1}(1.57) = 57.5°$

As, $r = 90° - i_p$

or $r = 90° - 57.5° = 32.5°$

24. (d) Intensity observed through analyser is

$$I = \frac{I_0}{2}\cos^2 \theta$$

I_0 = Intensity of unpolarised light.

θ = angle of pass axis of polariser and analyser.

At $\theta = \frac{\pi}{2}$, intensity

$$I = \frac{I_0}{2}\cos^2 90° = 0$$

25. (c) Let I_0 be the intensity of polarised light after passing through the first polariser P_1. Then, the intensity of light after passing through second polariser P_2 will be

$$I = I_0 \cos^2 \theta$$

where, θ is the angle between pass axes of P_1 and P_2. Since, P_1 and P_3 are crossed, the angle between the pass axes of P_2 and P_3 will be $\left(\frac{\pi}{2} - \theta\right)$. Hence, the intensity of light emerging from P_2 will be

$$I = I_0 \cos^2 \theta \cos^2\left(\frac{\pi}{2} - \theta\right)$$

$$= I_0 \cos^2 \theta \sin^2 \theta$$

$$= \left(\frac{I_0}{4}\right)\sin^2 2\theta$$

Intensity of transmitted light is maximum,

when $\sin^2 2\theta = 1$

$$\Rightarrow \sin 2\theta = 1 = \sin\frac{\pi}{2}$$

$$\Rightarrow 2\theta = \frac{\pi}{2}$$

$$\Rightarrow \theta = \frac{\pi}{4}$$

Chapter Break Thru

1. (c) Angular width, $\theta = \frac{\lambda_0}{\mu d}$

If λ_0 and d are constants, then $\theta \propto \frac{1}{\mu}$.

The above dependency is similar to $y \propto \frac{1}{x}$, which have variation according to rectangular hyperbola. The variation between θ and μ can be shown as

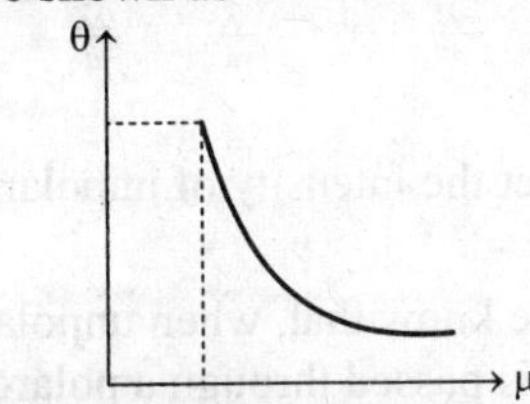

2. (c) As, $I \propto A^2$

$$\Rightarrow \frac{I_1}{I_2} = \left(\frac{A_1}{A_2}\right)^2 = \left(\frac{2}{1}\right)^2$$

or $\frac{I_1}{I_2} = \frac{4}{1} \Rightarrow \sqrt{\frac{I_1}{I_2}} = \frac{2}{1}$

Now, $I_{max} = (\sqrt{I_1} + \sqrt{I_2})^2$

$$= I_2\left(\sqrt{\frac{I_1}{I_2}} + 1\right)^2$$

and $I_{min} = (\sqrt{I_1} - \sqrt{I_2})^2$

$$= I_2\left(\sqrt{\frac{I_1}{I_2}} - 1\right)^2$$

$$\frac{I_{max}}{I_{min}} = \frac{I_2\left(\sqrt{\frac{I_1}{I_2}} + 1\right)^2}{I_2\left(\sqrt{\frac{I_1}{I_2}} - 1\right)^2} = \frac{(2+1)^2}{(2-1)^2} = \frac{9}{1}$$

$$\text{So, } \frac{I_{max} - I_{min}}{I_{max} + I_{min}} = \left(\frac{\frac{I_{max}}{I_{min}} - 1}{\frac{I_{max}}{I_{min}} + 1}\right)$$

$$= \left(\frac{9-1}{9+1}\right) = \frac{8}{10} = \frac{4}{5} \text{ or } 4:5$$

3. (a) Given, $\lambda_1 = 5800\,Å$, $\lambda_2 = \lambda$ (let)

The distance between consecutive dark fringes and bright fringes are same and is equal to

$$\beta = \frac{\lambda D}{d} \quad \text{...(i)}$$

So, $\beta_1 = 7.25$ mm and $\beta_2 = 5.075$ mm

For a particular YDSE, d and D are same.

So, we can write from Eq. (i),

$$\beta \propto \lambda \text{ or } \frac{\beta_1}{\beta_2} = \frac{\lambda_1}{\lambda_2}$$

$$\text{or } \lambda_2 = \left(\frac{\beta_2}{\beta_1}\right)\lambda_1 = \left(\frac{5.075}{7.25}\right) \times 5800$$

or $\lambda_2 = 4060\,Å$

4. (c) Given, distance between the slits, $d = 0.24$ mm or 0.24×10^{-3} m

Distance between screen and slits, $D = 0.8$ m

The position of nth dark fringe from central point is given as

$$(y_n)_{dark} = \frac{(2n-1)\lambda D}{2d}$$

and the position of mth bright fringe from central point is given as

$$(y_m)_{bright} = \frac{m\lambda D}{d}$$

For $n = 9$, $m = 6$, i.e. distance between ninth dark fringe to sixth bright fringe,

$$\Delta y = (y_9)_{dark} - (y_6)_{bright}$$

$$\Delta y = \frac{(2n-1)\lambda D}{2d} - \frac{m\lambda D}{d}$$

or $\Delta y = \left[\left(n - \frac{1}{2}\right) - m\right]\frac{\lambda D}{d}$

$$5.4 \times 10^{-3} = \frac{\left[\left(9 - \frac{1}{2}\right) - 6\right] \times \lambda \times 0.8}{0.24 \times 10^{-3}}$$

or $5.4 \times 10^{-3} = \frac{2.5 \times \lambda \times 0.8}{0.24 \times 10^{-3}}$

or $\lambda = 6480\,Å$

5. (b) The resultant intensity at a point P, where the phase difference between the light is $\Delta\phi$, can be expressed as

$$I_P = I_{max} \cos^2\left(\frac{\Delta\phi}{2}\right)$$

Here $I_P = I = I_{max} \cos^2(\pi)$

$I = I_{max}$

For $I_P = \frac{I}{4}$ or $\frac{I_{max}}{4}$

$$\frac{I_{max}}{4} = I_{max} \cos^2\left(\frac{\Delta\phi}{2}\right)$$

$\Rightarrow \cos^2\left(\frac{\Delta\phi}{2}\right) = \frac{1}{4}$

$\Rightarrow \cos\left(\frac{\Delta\phi}{2}\right) = \pm\frac{1}{2}$

$\Rightarrow \cos\frac{\Delta\phi}{2} = \cos 60° \text{ or } \cos 120°$

$\frac{\Delta\phi}{2} = 60° \text{ or } 120°$

$\Rightarrow \Delta\phi = 120° \text{ or } 240°$

$\Rightarrow \Delta\phi = \frac{2\pi}{3}, \frac{4\pi}{3}$

If $\Delta\phi = \frac{2\pi}{3}$,

$$\Delta x = \frac{\lambda}{2\pi} \times \Delta\phi = \frac{\lambda}{2\pi} \times \frac{2\pi}{3} = \frac{\lambda}{3}$$

and if $\Delta\phi = \frac{4\pi}{3}$,

$$\Delta x = \frac{\lambda}{2\pi} \times \Delta\phi = \frac{\lambda}{2\pi} \times \frac{4\pi}{3} = \frac{2\lambda}{3}$$

The correct values of path difference are $\frac{\lambda}{3}$ and $\frac{2\lambda}{3}$.

6. (b) Given, wavelength,

$\lambda = 6000\,Å = 6 \times 10^{-7}$ m

Width of slit, $a = 0.24$ mm or 2.4×10^{-4} m

Distance of slit to screen, $D = 1$ m

The width of central maxima is given as,

$$\text{width} = \frac{2D\lambda}{a} = \frac{2 \times 1 \times 6 \times 10^{-7}}{2.4 \times 10^{-4}}$$

$= 5 \times 10^{-3}$ m $= 0.5$ cm

The width of first secondary maxima is equal to half that of central maxima, i.e.

$$\Rightarrow (\text{width})_{\text{first}} = \frac{(\text{width})_{\text{central}}}{2}$$

$$= \frac{0.5}{2} = 0.25 \text{ cm}$$

7. (d) The graph between I and $\sin\theta$ due to single slit can be plotted as

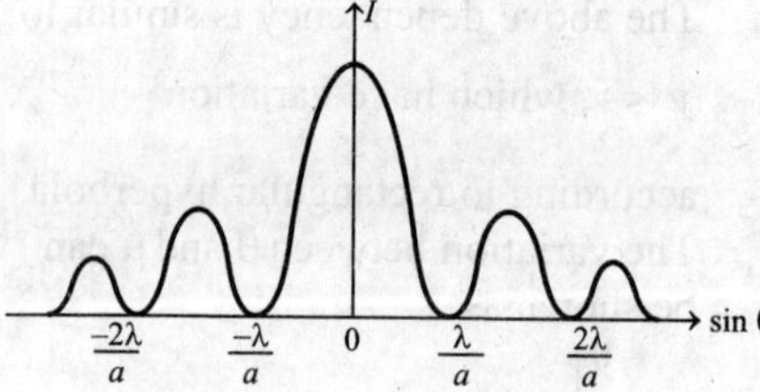

8. (a) Let the intensity of unpolarised beam $= I$

As we know that, when unpolarised light is passed through a polaroid P, the intensity of polarised light becomes $\frac{I}{2}$.

Case (i) When beam of intensity $\frac{I}{2}$ is placed through P_2, its intensity becomes

$$I' = \left(\frac{I}{2}\right)\cos^2\phi \text{ [using Malus' law]}$$

where, ϕ is angle between P_1 and P_2.

According to question, no light is emitted from the second polaroid, i.e. $I' = 0$

$\Rightarrow \left(\frac{I}{2}\right)\cos^2\phi = 0$ or $\cos\phi = 0$

or $\cos\phi = \cos 90°$

or $\phi = 90°$

Case (ii) When a third identical polaroid whose polarisation axis makes an angle θ with the polarisation axis of first polaroid, is placed between these polaroids, then

Intensity of light when it is passed through P_2 becomes $\frac{I}{2}\cos^2\theta$.

Now, angle between P_2 and $P_3 = 90° - \theta$

So, $I' = \left\{\left(\frac{I}{2}\right)\cos^2\theta\right\}\cos^2(90° - \theta)$

$= \frac{I}{2}\cos^2\theta \sin^2\theta$

$= \frac{I}{2 \times 4}(2\sin\theta\cos\theta)^2$

$= \frac{I}{8}\sin^2 2\theta$

$[\because 2\sin\theta\cos\theta = \sin 2\theta]$

9. (c) The angle of polarisation (θ_P) is given as

$$\theta_P = \tan^{-1}\left(\frac{\mu_2}{\mu_1}\right)$$

For I,

$$\theta_P = \tan^{-1}\left(\frac{\sqrt{3}}{1}\right) = 60°$$

For II,

$$\theta_P = \tan^{-1}\left(\frac{4/3}{1}\right) = 53°$$

For III, From the figure,

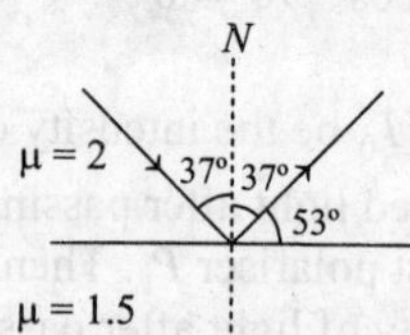

$$\theta_P = \tan^{-1}\left(\frac{1.5}{2}\right) = \tan^{-1}\left(\frac{3}{4}\right)$$

$\Rightarrow \theta_P = 37°$

For IV, Angle of polarisation,

$\theta_P = \tan^{-1}(\sqrt{2}) \Rightarrow \theta_P = 54.74°$

10. (c) For sustained interference, the positions of maxima and minima of intensity on the observation screen do not change with time and interfering waves should be in the same state of polarisation.

Hence, Assertion is true but Reason is false.

11. (c) For first minima, $\theta = \frac{\lambda}{a}$ or $a = \frac{\lambda}{\theta}$

$\therefore \quad a = \frac{6500 \times 10^{-10} \times 18}{\pi}$

(As π rad $= 180°, 10° = \frac{\pi}{18}$ rad)

$\Rightarrow a = 3.72 \times 10^{-6}$ m or $3.72\ \mu$m

12. (b) Hence, $\frac{\sin a}{\sin b} = \frac{\sin i}{\sin r} = \frac{1.6}{1} = \frac{8}{5}$

13. (d) Statement I is incorrect because the reflected light is linearly polarised perpendicular to the plane of the figure. It is represented by dots.

14. (d) Given, $\lambda = 400$ nm

$= 400 \times 10^{-9}$ m

$d = 1\text{mm} = 1 \times 10^{-3}$ m

$D = 4$ m

Width of central bright fringe ($= 2\beta$)

$$= \frac{2\lambda D}{d} = \frac{2 \times 400 \times 10^{-9} \times 4}{1 \times 10^{-3}} \text{ m}$$

$= 3.2 \times 10^{-3}$ m $= 3.2$ mm

15. (d) $\frac{I_1}{I_2} = \frac{W_1}{W_2} = \frac{1}{36}$

$$\Rightarrow \frac{I_2}{I_1} = \frac{36}{1}$$

$$\therefore \frac{I_{max}}{I_{min}} = \frac{(\sqrt{I_2} + \sqrt{I_1})^2}{(\sqrt{I_2} - \sqrt{I_1})^2}$$

$$= \left(\frac{\sqrt{\frac{I_2}{I_1}} + 1}{\sqrt{\frac{I_2}{I_1}} - 1}\right)^2$$

$$= \left(\frac{6+1}{6-1}\right)^2 = \left(\frac{7}{5}\right)^2 = \frac{49}{25}$$

16. (d) Let $\frac{I_1}{I_2} = \frac{n}{1}$

$$\frac{I_{max} - I_{min}}{I_{max} + I_{min}}$$

$$= \frac{(\sqrt{I_1} + \sqrt{I_2})^2 - (\sqrt{I_1} - \sqrt{I_2})^2}{(\sqrt{I_1} + \sqrt{I_2})^2 + (\sqrt{I_1} - \sqrt{I_2})^2}$$

$$= \frac{4\sqrt{I_1 I_2}}{2(I_1 + I_2)}$$

Dividing numerator and denominator by I_2, required ratio

$$= \frac{2\sqrt{\frac{I_1}{I_2}}}{\left(\frac{I_1}{I_2} + 1\right)} = \frac{2\sqrt{n}}{n+1}$$

17. (b) Given, f or $D = 60$ cm

For first minima,

$$y = \frac{\lambda D}{a}$$

$$= \frac{5 \times 10^{-7} \times 0.6}{2 \times 10^{-2} \times 10^{-2}}$$

$= 15 \times 10^{-4}$ m

$= 0.15$ cm

18. (c) From, $\frac{\lambda_1}{\lambda_2} = \frac{v_1}{v_2}$

$$\frac{0.6}{\lambda_2} = \frac{3 \times 10^8}{2.4 \times 10^8}$$

$$\Rightarrow \lambda_2 = \frac{(2.4 \times 10^8)(0.6)}{3 \times 10^8}$$

$= 0.48\ \mu$m

19. (d)

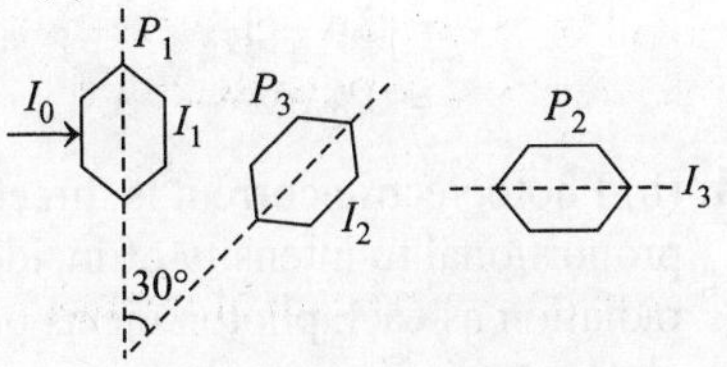

$$I_1 = \frac{I_0}{2}$$

$$I_2 = \frac{I_0}{2} \cos^2 30° = \frac{3I_0}{8}$$

$$I_3 = \frac{3I_0}{8} \cos^2 60° = \frac{3I_0}{32}$$

20. (d) For destructive interference, path difference is odd multiple of $\frac{\lambda}{2}$.

Hence, option (d) is correct.

21. (c) Since, incident wavefront makes angle 40° with horizontal. Hence, the ray makes 40° with normal.

$$\frac{\sin i}{\sin r} = \frac{4}{3}$$

$$\Rightarrow \sin r = \frac{3}{4} \sin i = \frac{3}{4} \sin 40° = 0.48$$

$\Rightarrow r = 28.8°$

22. (a) According to given condition,

$(\mu - 1)t = n\lambda$

For minimum t, $n = 1$

So, $(\mu - 1)t_{min} = \lambda$

$$\Rightarrow t_{min} = \frac{\lambda}{\mu - 1} = \frac{\lambda}{1.8 - 1} = 1.25\ \lambda$$

23. (c) Fringe width, $\beta \propto \lambda$. Therefore, λ and hence β decrease 1.5 times when immersed in liquid.

$y_n = y_0 + n\beta$

$y_6 = y_0 + 6\beta$

$9 = 6 + 6\beta \quad (y_0 = 6\text{cm})$

$\Rightarrow \quad \beta = \frac{3}{6} = \frac{1}{2}$

$\beta' = \frac{\beta}{\mu}$

$\therefore \quad \beta' = \frac{1}{3}$

$y_n' = y_0 + n\beta'$

$y_0' = y_0 = 6$ cm

$y_6' = y_0 + 6\beta'$

$= 6 + 6 \times \frac{1}{3} = 8$ cm

24. (b) Separation of nth bright fringe and central maxima is

$$x_n = \frac{n\lambda D}{d}$$

So, $x_4 = \frac{4 \times 6000 \times 10^{-10} \times 1}{0.5 \times 10^{-3}}$

$= 4.8 \times 10^{-3}$ m or 4.8 mm

25. (c) Given, $I = \frac{I_0}{2} \cos^2 (22.5°)$

$$I = \frac{I_0}{4} \cdot 2\cos^2 (22.5°)$$

$$I = \frac{I_0}{4}[1 + \cos(45°)]$$

$$I = \frac{I_0}{4} \cdot \left[1 + \frac{1}{\sqrt{2}}\right]$$

$$I = 0.42 I_0$$

which is close to option (c).

26. (d) $\beta = \frac{\lambda D}{d}$

Given, $d' = 2d$

$$D' = \frac{D}{2}$$

$$\beta' = \frac{\lambda D}{4d} = \frac{1}{4}\beta$$

$\Rightarrow$ If D becomes half and d becomes double, then β becomes one-fourth.

27. (d) New wavelength is $\frac{3}{5}$ times the old wavelength. So, the new angular separation is $\frac{3}{5} \times 0.2°$ or $0.12°$.

28. (d) Distance between the first dark fringes on either side of central maxima = width of central maxima

$$= \frac{2\lambda D}{d} = \frac{2 \times 800 \times 10^{-9} \times 4}{2 \times 10^{-3}}$$

$$= 3.2 \text{ mm}$$

29. (b) Here, $\Delta x = \frac{Yd}{D}$

$$= (2m_1 - 1)\frac{\lambda_1}{2} = n\lambda_2$$

or $(2 \times 4 - 1)\frac{400}{2} = n \times 700$

$$\Rightarrow \quad n = \frac{7}{2} \times \frac{4}{7}$$

$$\therefore \quad n = 2$$

30. (b) Width of central maximum,

$$\beta = \frac{2D\lambda}{d}$$

As, we increase d to $2d$, β becomes $\frac{\beta}{2}$.

Due to this, intensity of the central maximum increased to four times. This implies central maximum becomes much sharper. So, it becomes narrower and brighter.

Ch-12 Dual Nature of Radiation and Matter

Topical Follow Thru

Test-1

1. (b) Using the photoelectric equation,

$$hf = hf_0 + eV_0 \Rightarrow$$

$$hf = hf_0 + \frac{1}{2}mv_{max}^2$$

In case (i) $f = 2f_0$, $v_{max} = v_1$

$$h(2f_0) = hf_0 + \frac{1}{2}mv_1^2$$

$$\Rightarrow \quad \frac{1}{2}mv_1^2 = hf_0 \quad \ldots(i)$$

In case (ii) $f = 5f_0$, $v_{max} = v_2$

$$h(5f_0) = hf_0 + \frac{1}{2}mv_2^2$$

$$\Rightarrow \quad \frac{1}{2}mv_2^2 = 4hf_0 \quad \ldots(ii)$$

On dividing Eq. (i) and Eq. (ii), we get

$$\left(\frac{v_1}{v_2}\right)^2 = \frac{1}{4}$$

or $\quad \frac{v_1}{v_2} = \frac{1}{2}$

2. (a) Stopping potential (V_0) depends only upon the energy of photon and frequency of incident light but not on the intensity of the light, which only affects the number of emitted electrons.

3. (c) The maximum kinetic energy,

$$K_{max} = (E - W_0)$$

$$= (3.4 - 3)$$

$$= 0.4 \text{ eV}$$

4. (b) Photoelectric current is directly proportional to intensity of incident radiation as each photon ejects one electron constituting photocurrent.

The energy of photon E can be related to its mass *via* the mass-energy equivalence $E = mc^2$, so the mass of a photon is $\frac{E}{c^2}$.

Additionally, the momentum of a photon is given by $p = \frac{E}{c}$. So, while the reason is accurate about photon properties, it does not explain assertion.

5. (b) Given that,

Work function = 5.825 eV

Threshold wavelength,

$$\lambda_0 = \frac{12375}{5.825}$$

$$\lambda_0 = 2124.4 \text{ Å}$$

6. (d) According to Einstein's photoelectric equation,

$$h\nu = h\nu_0 + K_{max}$$

$$\Rightarrow \quad K_{max} = h\nu - h\nu_0$$

On comparing it with $y = mx + c$ (straight line equation), we find that this is the equation of straight line having positive slope h and negative intercept on KE axis.

7. (b) As we know, work function is inversely proportional to threshold wavelength, i.e. $W_0 \propto \frac{1}{\lambda}$

So, the ratio of threshold wavelength,

$$\frac{\lambda_1}{\lambda_2} = \frac{(W_0)_2}{(W_0)_1} = \frac{8.5}{4.6} = 1.847 : 1$$

8. (a) As we know, $K_{max} = h\nu - W_0$.

Hence, the maximum kinetic energy of the emitted photoelectrons depends upon frequency of incident light.

9. (d) As we know, minimum wavelength of light,

$$\lambda_{min} = \frac{1242 \text{ eV}}{6} = 207 \text{ nm}$$

Maximum wavelength,

$$\lambda_{max} = \frac{1242 \text{ eV}}{3} = 414 \text{ nm}$$

Thus, wavelength of 440 nm cannot be used for photoelectric effect.

10. (b) Work function is given by

$$\phi_0 = \frac{hc}{\lambda_0}$$

$$\phi_0 \propto \frac{1}{\lambda_0}$$

$$\frac{\phi_0}{\phi_0'} = \frac{\lambda_0'}{\lambda_0} \Rightarrow \frac{\phi_0}{\left(\frac{\phi_0}{2}\right)} = \frac{\lambda_0'}{\lambda_0}$$

$$\Rightarrow \lambda_0' = 2\lambda_0$$

11. (d) Maximum kinetic energies are given by

$$K = \frac{hc}{\lambda} - \phi_0 \quad \ldots(i)$$

$$\text{and } K' = \frac{3hc}{2\lambda} - \phi_0 \quad \ldots(ii)$$

From Eqs. (i) and (ii), we get

$$\Rightarrow \quad K' - K = \frac{3hc}{2\lambda} - \frac{hc}{\lambda}$$

$$\Rightarrow \quad K' - K = \frac{hc}{2\lambda}$$

From Eq. (i),

$$\frac{hc}{\lambda} = K + \phi_0$$

$$K' - K = \frac{K + \phi_0}{2}$$

$$\Rightarrow K' - K = \frac{K}{2} + \frac{\phi_0}{2}$$

$$\Rightarrow \quad K' > \frac{3K}{2}$$

12. (c) Higher frequency causes photoemission of electrons with largest kinetic energy, i.e.

$$f = \frac{\omega}{2\pi} = \frac{10 \times 10^{15}}{2\pi} \text{ s}^{-1}$$

Maximum kinetic energy of photoelectrons is

$$K_{max} = hf - \phi_0$$

$$= \frac{4.14 \times 10^{-15} \times 10 \times 10^{15}}{2\pi} - 4$$

$$= 6.59 - 4 = 2.59 \text{ eV}$$

13. (c) Work function, $\phi = hf_0$

$$= \frac{6.6 \times 10^{-34} \times 0.5 \times 10^{15}}{1.6 \times 10^{-19}} \text{ eV}$$

$$= 2.06 \text{ eV}$$

14. (b) Using Einstein's photoelectric equation,

$$(\text{KE})_{max} = \frac{hc}{\lambda} - \phi$$

$$\text{So,} \quad K_1 = \frac{hc}{\lambda_1} - \phi \quad \ldots(i)$$

$$K_2 = \frac{hc}{\lambda_2} - \phi \quad \ldots(ii)$$

$$\lambda_1 = 3\lambda_2 \text{ (given)}$$

Eq. (i) becomes

$$K_1 = \frac{hc}{3\lambda_2} - \phi \quad \ldots(iii)$$

From Eqs. (ii) and (iii), we have

$$K_2 - K_1 = \frac{hc}{\lambda_2} - \frac{hc}{3\lambda_2}$$

$$K_2 - K_1 = \frac{2hc}{3\lambda_2}$$

$$\Rightarrow \frac{3}{2}(K_2 - K_1) = \frac{hc}{\lambda_2}$$

On putting this in equation (ii), we get

$$K_2 = \frac{3}{2}(K_2 - K_1) - \phi$$

$$2K_2 = 3K_2 - 3K_1 - 2\phi$$

$$K_2 - 3K_1 = 2\phi$$

As, $\phi > 0 \Rightarrow K_2 - 3K_1 > 0$

Thus, $K_1 < \frac{K_2}{3}$

15. (a) Energy corresponding to 248 nm wavelength,

$$E_1 = \frac{1240}{\lambda} \text{ eV}$$

$$= \frac{1240}{248} \text{ eV} = 5 \text{ eV}$$

Energy corresponding to 310 nm wavelength,

$$E_2 = \frac{1240}{310} \text{ eV} = 4 \text{ eV}$$

$$\text{KE} = E - \text{Work function}$$

$$\therefore \quad \frac{\text{KE}_1}{\text{KE}_2} = \frac{u_1^2}{u_2^2} \Rightarrow \frac{4}{1} = \frac{5 \text{ eV} - W}{4 \text{ eV} - W}$$

Solving this equation, we get

$$W = 3.67 \text{ eV} \cong 3.7 \text{ eV}$$

Test-2

1. (a) Energy of one γ-ray

$$= \frac{10.2}{2} = 5.1 \text{ eV}$$

$$= 5.1 \times 1.6 \times 10^{-19} \text{ J}$$

$$= 8.16 \times 10^{-19} \text{ J}$$

Let λ be the wavelength.

Energy of each γ-ray,

$$E = \frac{hc}{\lambda} \text{ or } \lambda = \frac{hc}{E}$$

$$= \frac{6.63 \times 10^{-34} \times 3 \times 10^8}{8.16 \times 10^{-19}}$$

$$= 2.436 \times 10^{-7} \text{ m}$$

2. (a) As, $p = \frac{h}{\lambda} = \frac{6.6 \times 10^{-34}}{4400 \times 10^{-10}}$

$$= 1.5 \times 10^{-27} \text{ kg-m/s}$$

and mass, $m = \frac{p}{c} = \frac{1.5 \times 10^{-27}}{3 \times 10^8}$

$$= 0.50 \times 10^{-35} \text{ kg}$$

$$= 5 \times 10^{-36} \text{ kg}$$

3. (b) As we know, $E \propto \frac{1}{\lambda}$

$$\Rightarrow \frac{8.5}{E'} = \frac{1}{8000} \Rightarrow E' = 8.5 \times 8000 \text{ eV}$$

$$\Rightarrow \quad E' = 68 \text{ keV}$$

4. (c) Energy of photon,

$$E = \frac{hc}{\lambda} \text{ (Joules)}$$

$$= \frac{hc}{e\lambda} \text{ (in eV)}$$

$$\Rightarrow E(\text{eV}) = \frac{6.6 \times 10^{-34} \times 3 \times 10^8}{1.6 \times 10^{-19} \times \lambda(\text{Å})}$$

$$= \frac{12.375 \times 10^{-7}}{\lambda(\text{Å}) \times 10^{-10}}$$

$$= \frac{1.2375 \times 10^{-6}}{\lambda(\text{Å}) \times 10^{-10}}$$

$$= \frac{1.237 \times 10^{4}}{\lambda(\text{Å})}$$

$$\Rightarrow E(\text{keV}) = \frac{12.37}{\lambda(\text{Å})} \approx \frac{12.4}{\lambda}$$

5. (b) Given, $P = 10\,\text{kW}$

$\nu = 10\,\text{kHz}$

Number of photons emitted per second,

$$n = \frac{P}{h\nu} = \frac{10 \times 10^{3}}{6.6 \times 10^{-34} \times 10 \times 10^{3}}$$

$$= 0.15 \times 10^{34}$$

6. (b) The wavelength of blue light is 4800 Å, so material will emit photoelectrons when it is illuminated with light from a 40 W blue lamp.

7. (c) Energy radiated as visible light

$$= \frac{3}{100} \times 100 = 3\,\text{J/s}$$

Let n be the number of photons emitted per second, then

$$nh\frac{c}{\lambda} = E = 3$$

$$\therefore n = \frac{3\lambda}{hc} = \frac{3 \times 6.6 \times 10^{-5}}{(6.62 \times 10^{-34})(3 \times 10^{8})}$$

$$\simeq 1 \times 10^{21}$$

8. (c) Given,

$\nu = 6 \times 10^{14}$ Hz, $P = 8 \times 10^{-3}$ W

By using, $E = h\nu$

$$E = 6.63 \times 10^{-34} \times 6 \times 10^{14}\ \text{J}$$

$$= 39.8 \times 10^{-20}\ \text{J}$$

Number of photons emitted,

$$N = \frac{P}{E}$$

$$N = \frac{8 \times 10^{-3}}{39.8 \times 10^{-20}} \simeq 2 \times 10^{16}$$

9. (c) Number of photons emitted,

$$n = \frac{\text{Power}}{\text{Energy of one photon}}$$

$$n = \frac{P\lambda}{hc}$$

$$= \frac{100 \times 840 \times 10^{-9}}{(6 \times 10^{-34}) \times (3 \times 10^{8})}$$

$$= \frac{84000 \times 10^{-9}}{18 \times 10^{-26}}$$

$$\cong 4666 \times 10^{17}$$

10. (d) Power of transmitter, $P = 10\,\text{kW}$

$$P = \frac{W}{t} = \frac{nhc}{\lambda t} \Rightarrow \left(\frac{n}{t}\right) = \frac{P\lambda}{hc}$$

Putting above values,

$$\left(\frac{n}{t}\right) = \frac{10 \times 10^{3} \times 3 \times 10^{8}}{6.6 \times 10^{-34} \times 3 \times 10^{8}}$$

$$= 1.5 \times 10^{37}$$

11. (c) The energy of each photon is

$$E = \frac{hc}{\lambda} = \frac{6.6 \times 10^{-34} \times 3 \times 10^{8}}{632.8 \times 10^{-9}}$$

$$= 3.13 \times 10^{-19}\ \text{J}$$

The energy of the laser emitted per second is 10×10^{-3}.

Number of photons emitted per second

$$= \frac{10 \times 10^{-3}}{3.13 \times 10^{-19}} = 3.2 \times 10^{16}$$

12. (b) Number of photons incident on unit area in unit time

$$= \frac{I}{E_i} = \frac{2}{16.96 \times 10^{-19}} = 1.18 \times 10^{18}$$

Therefore, number of photons incident on given area

$$= (1.18 \times 10^{18})(1.0 \times 10^{-4})$$

$$= 1.18 \times 10^{14}$$

$\therefore$ Number of photoelectrons emitted per second (N),

$$N = \left(\frac{0.53}{100}\right)(1.18 \times 10^{14})$$

$$= 6.25 \times 10^{11}$$

$$K_{\max} = E_i - \text{Work function}$$

$$= (10.6 - 5.6) = 5.0\ \text{eV}$$

13. (a) As we know, intensity of the radiation is given by

$$I = \frac{E}{At} = \frac{nhc}{\lambda At} \Rightarrow \frac{n}{t} = \frac{IA\lambda}{hc}$$

$$\Rightarrow \quad \frac{n}{t} = \frac{P\lambda}{hc} \Rightarrow \frac{n}{t} \propto P\lambda$$

$$\Rightarrow \left(\frac{n}{t}\right)_2 = \left(\frac{n}{t}\right)_1 \times \frac{P_2\lambda_2}{P_1\lambda_1}$$

$$= 9 \times 10^{20} \times \frac{P}{P} \times \frac{800}{600}$$

$$= 12 \times 10^{20}$$

14. (a) Here, $I = 1.52 \times 10^{3}\ \text{Wm}^{-2}$

$\lambda = 520 \times 10^{-9}$ m

$h = 6.63 \times 10^{-34}$ J-s

Number of photons incident on the earth's surface per square metre per second is

$$n = \frac{I}{E} = \frac{I}{hc}\lambda \quad \left[\because E = \frac{hc}{\lambda}\right]$$

$$n = \frac{1.52 \times 10^{3} \times 520 \times 10^{-9}}{6.63 \times 10^{-34} \times 3 \times 10^{8}}$$

$$\simeq 4 \times 10^{21}\ \text{photons}$$

per metre^2 per second

15. (b) An electron absorbs a single photon of light and if the energy carried by photon is more than work function of the metal, then electron is emitted.

From source, total emitted power = P (total energy per second)

Energy carried by each photon = E

So, number of photons emitted by the source = P/E

Energy of a photon, $E = h\nu$.

For the cut-off or threshold frequency, the energy $h\nu_0$ of the incident radiation must be equal to work function ϕ_0, so that $h\nu_0 = \phi_0$

$$\Rightarrow \quad h = \frac{\phi_0}{\nu_0}$$

Hence, A$\rightarrow$4, B$\rightarrow$2, C$\rightarrow$3 and D$\rightarrow$1.

Test-3

1. (c) According to de-Broglie wave equation, $\lambda = \frac{h}{mv}$

As both particle and electron have same wavelength, therefore their momentum will be equal.

$$m_p v_p = m_e v_e$$

$$\Rightarrow \quad v_p = \frac{m_e v_e}{m_p}$$

$$= \frac{9.1\times10^{-31}\times5\times10^{6}}{10^{-6}}$$

$$\Rightarrow \quad v_p = 4.5\times10^{-18}\text{ m/s}$$

2. (b) According to de-Broglie wave equation,

$$\lambda = \frac{h}{\sqrt{2mE}}$$

For same energy E_1,

$$\lambda' \propto \frac{1}{\sqrt{M}}$$

So, $$\frac{\lambda'}{\lambda} = \frac{\sqrt{m}}{\sqrt{M}}$$

or $$\lambda' = \lambda\frac{\sqrt{m}}{\sqrt{M}}$$

3. (a) By using de-Broglie wave equation,

$$\lambda = \frac{h}{\sqrt{2mE}}$$

where, $E = 10^{-32}$ J

Hence, $$\lambda \propto \frac{1}{\sqrt{m}}$$

Since, $m_p > m_e$

$\therefore \quad \lambda_p < \lambda_e$

4. (a) Wavelength of neutron particle,

$$\lambda_{\text{neutron}} \propto \frac{1}{\sqrt{T}}$$

$$\Rightarrow \frac{\lambda_1}{\lambda_2} = \sqrt{\frac{T_2}{T_1}}$$

$$\frac{\lambda}{\lambda'} = \sqrt{\frac{(273+927)}{(273+27)}}$$

$$= \sqrt{\frac{1200}{300}} = 2$$

$$\therefore \quad \lambda' = \frac{\lambda}{2}$$

5. (a) According to de-Broglie wave equation,

$$\lambda = \frac{h}{p} = \frac{h}{\sqrt{2m(K)}}$$

$$\Rightarrow \quad \lambda \propto \frac{1}{\sqrt{(K)m}}$$

Now, kinetic energy (K) gained by a charge particle under potential V is $K = qV$, given V is same for the given three particles.

$\therefore \quad K_e = eV, K_p = eV$

$K_\alpha = 2eV$

$\Rightarrow \quad K_e = K_p < K_\alpha$

and $m_e < m_p < m_\alpha$

$$\Rightarrow \lambda = \frac{h}{\sqrt{2m_eK_e}} > \frac{h}{\sqrt{2m_pK_p}}$$

$$> \frac{h}{\sqrt{2m_\alpha K_\alpha}}$$

Thus, the wavelengths of all particles are given as, in which wavelength of electron is greater as compared to α-particle.

$\therefore \quad \lambda_e > \lambda_p > \lambda_\alpha$

6. (c) By using, $\lambda = \dfrac{h}{\sqrt{2mE}} = \dfrac{h}{\sqrt{2mqV}}$

$$\Rightarrow \quad \lambda \propto \frac{1}{\sqrt{mq}}$$

$$\therefore \quad \frac{\lambda_\alpha}{\lambda_p} = \sqrt{\frac{m_pq_p}{m_\alpha q_\alpha}}$$

$\because \quad q_\alpha = 2q_p$,

$m_\alpha = 4m_p$ and

$\lambda_p = \lambda$

$$\Rightarrow \quad \lambda_\alpha = \frac{\lambda}{2\sqrt{2}}$$

7. (d) As we know that wavelength of particle is inversely proportional to momentum of particles,

i.e. $$\lambda = \frac{h}{p}$$

From Statement I, momentum of broken particles will be same, hence de-Broglie wavelength will also be same.

8. (b) As we know, $\lambda = \dfrac{h}{p}$ ...(i)

Given, change in momentum,

$$\Delta p = p_0$$

Change in wavelength,

$$\frac{\Delta\lambda}{\lambda} = 0.40\%$$

$$= 0.0040$$

The change in wavelength due to the change in momentum can be expressed as

$$\frac{\Delta\lambda}{\lambda} = -\frac{\Delta p}{p}$$

$$\left|\frac{\Delta p}{p}\right| = \left|\frac{\Delta\lambda}{\lambda}\right|$$

$$\frac{p_0}{p} = 0.0040$$

$$p = \frac{1}{0.0040}\cdot p_0$$

$$p = 250p_0$$

9. (a) Wavelength of electron,

$$\lambda_e = \frac{h}{\sqrt{2mE}}$$

Wavelength of photon, $\lambda_{\text{Ph}} = \dfrac{hc}{E}$

By using $E = pc$, then ratio of both wavelengths

$$\Rightarrow \frac{\lambda_e}{\lambda_{\text{Ph}}} = \frac{h}{\sqrt{2mE}}$$

$$\times\frac{E}{hc} = \left(\frac{E}{2m}\right)^{\frac{1}{2}} \times \frac{1}{c}$$

10. (c) According to de-Broglie wavelength,

$$\lambda = \frac{h}{\sqrt{2m(\text{KE})}}$$

$$\Rightarrow \quad \lambda \propto \frac{1}{(\text{KE})}$$

The ratio of wavelengths,

$$\frac{\lambda_1}{\lambda_2} = \sqrt{\frac{(\text{KE})_2}{(\text{KE})_1}}$$

$$= \sqrt{\frac{64(x)}{(x)}} = 8$$

The percentage change in wavelength of the moving particle,

$$= \frac{\lambda_2 - \lambda_1}{\lambda_1}\times 100$$

$$= \frac{\frac{\lambda_1}{8} - \lambda_1}{\lambda_1}\times 100$$

$$= \left(\frac{1}{8} - 1\right)\times 100$$

$$= -0.875\times 100$$

$$= -87.5\%$$

i.e. de-Broglie wavelength will decrease by 87.5%.

11. (d) From momentum conservation, initial momentum = 0.

Hence, after the explosion, each

particle must have equal and opposite momentum.

So, $\lambda = \frac{h}{p}$

$\Rightarrow \frac{\lambda_1}{\lambda_2} = \frac{p_2}{p_1}$

$\because p_1 = p_2$

Hence, $\frac{\lambda_1}{\lambda_2} = 1$

12. (d) We know, $V = \frac{150}{\lambda^2}$ [λ is in Å]

$\lambda_1 = 2$ Å, $\lambda_2 = 1$ Å

$\Rightarrow V_1 = \frac{150}{4} = 37.5$ V and

$V_2 = \frac{150}{(1)^2} = 150$ V

$\therefore e(V_2 - V_1) = \Delta KE$

$\Delta KE = (150 - 37.5)$ eV

$= 112.5$ eV

13. (b) According to question,

$m_2 > m_1$ ...(i)

(m_2 is the mass of heavier particle)

As we know,

$\lambda = \frac{h}{p} = \frac{h}{mv} = \frac{h}{\sqrt{2mK}}$ ...(ii)

(i) When $p_1 = p_2$, then $\lambda_1 = \lambda_2$

(ii) $\lambda_1 = \frac{h}{\sqrt{2m_1K}}$ and

$\lambda_2 = \frac{h}{\sqrt{2m_2K}}$ [$\because K_1 = K_2 = K$]

$\because m_2 > m_1$.

So, $\lambda_1 > \lambda_2$.

(iii) When both bodies have fallen from same height h, then velocity of both bodies will be same which is

$v_1 = v_2 = v = \sqrt{2gh}$

$\because m_2 > m_1$.

So, $\lambda_1 > \lambda_2$.

(iv) When $v_1 = v_2$, then $\lambda_1 = \frac{h}{m_1 V}$

and $\lambda_2 = \frac{h}{m_2 v}$

$\because m_2 > m_1$. So, $\lambda_1 > \lambda_2$.

14. (b) Using relation, $E = \frac{p^2}{2m}$ ...(i)

(A) From Eq. (i), we get

$p = \sqrt{2mE}$

$= \sqrt{2 \times 9.1 \times 10^{-31} \times 100 \times 1.6 \times 10^{-19}}$

$= 5.4 \times 10^{-24}$ kg -ms^{-1}

(B) Speed, $v = \frac{p}{m} = \frac{5.4 \times 10^{-24}}{9.1 \times 10^{-31}}$

$= 5.9 \times 10^6$ ms^{-1}

(C) de-Broglie wavelength is given by

$\lambda = \frac{h}{p} = \frac{6.62 \times 10^{-34}}{5.4 \times 10^{-24}}$

$= 1.22 \times 10^{-10}$ m

(D) Frequency, $\nu = \frac{c}{\lambda} = \frac{3.0 \times 10^8}{1.22 \times 10^{-10}}$

$= 2.46 \times 10^{18}$ s^{-1}

Hence, A-(III), B-(II), C-(I), D-(IV).

15. (a) Maximum kinetic energy and so momentum of emitted electrons does not change by decreasing intensity.

So, their de-Broglie wavelength, $\lambda = \frac{h}{p}$ remains same.

Chapter Break Thru

1. (b) If an electron and a photon are moving in the form of wave and having same wavelength, which means that they have same momentum by de-Broglie wave equation,

$$p \propto \frac{1}{\lambda}$$

2. (d) de-Broglie wavelength,

$$\lambda \propto \frac{1}{p}$$

$$\Rightarrow \lambda \propto \frac{1}{p}$$

Wavelength of particle is inversely proportional to the momentum of particle.

3. (a) As we know,

$K = q \times V$ ...(i)

Charge on an electron is 1.6×10^{-19} C.

From Eq. (i),

$K = 1.6 \times 10^{-19} \times 200$

$= 3.2 \times 10^{-17}$ J

4. (a) Though monochromatic light is incident on a metal surface, the energies of emitted photoelectrons are different because when a monochromatic beam of light having photons of single frequency ν falls on the electron of inner layer of metal, then this electron comes out of the metal surface after multiple collisions with other atoms of its upper layer.

Hence, option (a) is correct.

5. (c) The saturation photoelectric current is directly proportional to the intensity of incident radiation but it is independent of its frequency.

6. (c) Given,

Radius of orbit, $r = 5.3 \times 10^{-11}$ m

and de-Broglie wavelength,

$\lambda = 10^{-10}$ m

From $2\pi r = n\lambda$,

$n = \frac{2\pi r}{\lambda}$

$= \frac{2 \times 3.14 \times 5.3 \times 10^{-11}}{10^{-10}}$

$\Rightarrow n = 3$

7. (b) $E_{particle} = \frac{1}{2}mv^2$, also $\lambda = \frac{h}{mv}$

$E_{particle} = \frac{1}{2}\left(\frac{h}{\lambda v}\right) \cdot v^2 = \frac{vh}{2\lambda}$ ...(i)

$E_{photon} = \frac{hc}{\lambda}$

$\therefore \frac{E_{particle}}{E_{photon}} = \frac{vh}{2\lambda} \times \frac{\lambda}{hc} = \frac{v}{2c}$

$= \frac{2.25 \times 10^8}{2 \times 3 \times 10^8} = \frac{3}{8}$

8. (a) For elastic collision, momentum is conserved, i.e.

$$p_{\text{before collision}} = p_{\text{after collision}}$$

$$mv = mv_A + \frac{m}{2} v_B$$

$$2v = 2v_A + v_B \quad \ldots \text{(i)}$$

Now, coefficient of restitution,

$$e = \frac{v_B - v_A}{u_A - u_B}$$

Here, $u_B = 0$ and for elastic collision $e = 1$

$$\therefore \quad 1 = \frac{v_B - v_A}{v}$$

$$\Rightarrow \quad v = v_B - v_A \quad \ldots \text{(ii)}$$

From Eq. (i) and Eq. (ii), we get

$$v_A = \frac{v}{3} \text{ and } v_B = \frac{4v}{3}$$

Hence, $$\frac{\lambda_A}{\lambda_B} = \frac{\left(\frac{h}{mv_A}\right)}{\frac{h}{\frac{m}{2} \cdot v_B}}$$

$$= \frac{v_B}{2v_A} = \frac{4/3}{2/3}$$

$$= 2$$

9. (c) Stopping potential is independent of intensity.

Saturation current, $i \propto I \propto \frac{1}{d^2}$

$$\frac{i_2}{i_1} = \left(\frac{d_1}{d_2}\right)^2$$

$$\frac{i_2}{i_1} = \left(\frac{0.4}{0.6}\right)^2 = \frac{4}{9}$$

$$i_2 = i_1 \times \frac{4}{9}$$

$$i_2 = 27 \times \frac{4}{9}$$

$$i_2 = 12\,\text{mA}$$

10. (a) Energy of photons is determined by using,

$$E = \frac{hc}{\lambda}$$

If there are n number of photons in a box, then energy associated with them will be

$$E = \frac{nhc}{\lambda}$$

Momentum gained by the body,

$$p = \frac{nh}{\lambda}$$

11. (d) As we know,

$$E = W_0 + K_{\max}$$

$$E = \frac{12375}{4000} = 3.093\,\text{eV}$$

$$\Rightarrow \quad K_{\max} = E - W_0$$

$$= 3.093\,\text{eV} - 2\,\text{eV}$$

$$= 1.09\,\text{eV}$$

$$\Rightarrow \frac{1}{2} mv_{\max}^2 = 1.09 \times 1.6 \times 10^{-19}\ \text{J}$$

$$\Rightarrow \quad v_{\max} = \sqrt{\frac{2 \times 1.09 \times 1.6 \times 10^{-19}}{9.1 \times 10^{-31}}}$$

$$= 0.618 \times 10^6\ \text{m/s}$$

12. (d) Net force on electron at any instant

$$F = q(\mathbf{E} + \mathbf{v} \times \mathbf{B})$$

$$= q(-E_0 \hat{\mathbf{i}} + v_0 \hat{\mathbf{i}} \times B_0 \hat{\mathbf{j}})$$

$$F = q(-E_0 \hat{\mathbf{i}} + v_0 B_0 \hat{\mathbf{k}})$$

Acceleration of electron,

$$a = \frac{F}{m} = \frac{q}{m}(-E_0 \hat{\mathbf{i}} + v_0 B_0 \hat{\mathbf{k}})$$

Velocity after t seconds $= u + at$

$$= 0 + \frac{q}{m}(-E_0 \hat{\mathbf{i}} + v_0 B_0 \hat{\mathbf{k}}) \cdot t$$

So, momentum of electron after t seconds is

$$\mathbf{p} = m\mathbf{v} = q(-E_0 \hat{\mathbf{i}} + v_0 B_0 \hat{\mathbf{k}})t$$

or $$|\mathbf{p}| = \sqrt{E_0^2 q^2 t^2 + v_0^2 B_0^2 q^2 t^2}$$

or $$\mathbf{p} = qt\sqrt{E_0^2 + (v_0 B_0)^2}$$

Thus, λ = Wavelength associated with moving electron

$$= \frac{h}{p} = \frac{h}{qt(\sqrt{E_0^2 + (v_0 B_0)^2})}$$

13. (d) As per above statements,

kinetic energy, $K = \frac{hc}{\lambda} - W$

$$K' = \frac{hc}{\left(\frac{\lambda}{2}\right)} - W = 2\left(\frac{hc}{\lambda} - W\right) + W$$

$$= 2K + W$$

i.e. $K' > 2K$

14. (c) According to question,

$$h \cdot 2\nu_0 = h \cdot \nu_0 + \frac{1}{2} m (4 \times 10^6)^2$$

$$h\nu_0 = \frac{1}{2} m (4 \times 10^6)^2 \quad \ldots \text{(i)}$$

$$h \cdot 5\nu_0 = h\nu_0 + \frac{1}{2} m v_{\max}^2$$

$$4h\nu_0 = \frac{1}{2} mv_{\max}^2 \quad \ldots \text{(ii)}$$

On dividing Eq. (i) with Eq. (ii), we get

$$\frac{1}{4} = \frac{(4 \times 10^6)^2}{(v_{\max}^2)}$$

$$v_{\max}^2 = 4 \times 16 \times 10^{12}$$

$$v_{\max}^2 = 64 \times 10^{12}$$

$$v_{\max} = \sqrt{64 \times 10^{12}}$$

$$v_{\max} = 8 \times 10^6\ \text{m/s}$$

15. (c) The de-Broglie wavelength λ associated with the electron is

$$\lambda = \frac{1.227}{\sqrt{V}}\ \text{nm}$$

$$\lambda \propto \frac{1}{\sqrt{V}}$$

$$\frac{\lambda_1}{\lambda_2} = \sqrt{\frac{V_2}{V_1}} = \sqrt{\frac{100 \times 10^3}{25 \times 10^3}} = 2$$

or $$\lambda_2 = \frac{\lambda_1}{2}$$

16. (b) Given that, charge $= 1.6 \times 10^{-19}$ C

Mass $= 1.6 \times 10^{-27}$ kg and

Potential difference $= 1\,\text{kV}$

$$\lambda = \frac{h}{p} = \frac{h}{\sqrt{2mE}} = \frac{h}{\sqrt{2mqV}}$$

$$\lambda = \frac{6.6 \times 10^{-34}}{\sqrt{2 \times (1.6 \times 10^{-27}) \times (1.6 \times 10^{-19}) \times 1000}}$$

$$\lambda = \frac{6.6 \times 10^{-34} \times 10^{22}}{1.6\sqrt{20}}$$

$$= 0.9 \times 10^{-12}\ \text{m}$$

17. (d) For photoemission

$f \geq f_{th}$ or $\lambda \leq \lambda_{th}$

18. (b) Given that,

Work function of substance,

$$\phi_0 = 19.2\,\text{eV}$$

Wavelength of light, $\lambda_0 = \dfrac{hc}{\phi_0}$

where, h is Planck's constant
c is speed of light, $c = 3 \times 10^8$ m/s

$$\lambda_0 = \frac{12400}{19.2} = 645.83\,\text{nm}$$

19. (a) de-Broglie wavelength associated with the electron,

$$\lambda = \frac{h}{\sqrt{2m(\text{KE})}}$$

$$= \frac{6.6 \times 10^{-34}}{\sqrt{2 \times 9.1 \times 10^{-31} \times 6 \times 1.6 \times 10^{-19}}}$$

$$= 4.99 \times 10^{-10}\ \text{m}$$

$$= 4.99\,\text{Å}$$

20. (b) Here, $K_{max} = h\nu - h\nu_0$

$\Rightarrow eV_0 = h\nu - h\nu_0$

$\Rightarrow V_0 = \dfrac{h}{e}\nu - \dfrac{h\nu_0}{e}$

Comparing this equation with $y = mx + c$ (straight line equation),

we get slope, $m = \dfrac{h}{e}$

$\Rightarrow \quad h = m \times e.$

21. (c) Given, slope of the graph,
$\tan\theta = 2.14 \times 10^{-14}$ V-s.

Charge on electron, $e = 1.6 \times 10^{-19}$ C

For slope of the graph, $\tan\theta = \dfrac{V}{\nu}$

We know that, $h\nu = eV$

or $\quad \dfrac{V}{\nu} = \dfrac{h}{e}$

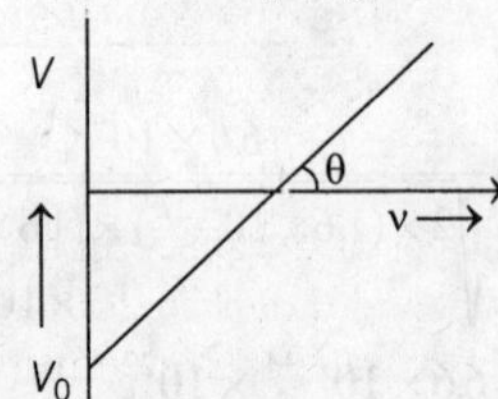

Therefore, $\dfrac{h}{e} = 2.14 \times 10^{-14}$

$$h = 1.6 \times 10^{-19} \times 2.14 \times 10^{-14}$$

$$= 3.42 \times 10^{-33}\ \text{J-s}$$

22. (a)

A. **Photocurrent *versus* Intensity** The photocurrent is directly proportional to the intensity of the incident light. As the intensity increases, more photons strike the material, releasing more electrons, hence increasing the photocurrent. It is best represented by graph 2.

B. **Photocurrent *versus* Collector potential** The photocurrent increases with the collector potential until it reaches a saturation point where all photoelectrons are collected, as shown in 4.

C. **Kinetic energy of photoelectrons *versus* Intensity** The kinetic energy of the photoelectrons does not depend on the intensity of the incident light. It depends on the frequency of the incident light. Hence, it is a straight line parallel to X-axis, as in 1.

D. **Stopping potential *versus* Frequency** The stopping potential is directly proportional to the frequency of the incident light. Higher frequency light has more energy, resulting in electrons with higher kinetic energy that requires a higher stopping potential. Graph 3 best represents it.

23. (c) Using Einstein's photoelectric equation,

$$\Rightarrow \quad \frac{hc}{\lambda} = K_{max} + \phi_0$$

we have,

$$\frac{hc}{800} = K_{max} + \phi_0 \qquad \text{...(i)}$$

and $\dfrac{hc}{500} = 2K_{max} + \phi_0 \qquad$ ...(ii)

Multiplying Eq. (i) by 2 and subtracting from Eq (ii), we get

$$\Rightarrow \quad \frac{hc}{500} - \frac{2 \times hc}{800}$$

$$= (2K_{max} + \phi_0) - 2(K_{max} + \phi_0)$$

$$\Rightarrow \quad \frac{hc}{100}\left(\frac{1}{5} - \frac{1}{4}\right) = -\phi_0$$

or $\quad -\phi_0 = \dfrac{1230\ \text{eV-nm}}{100\ \text{nm}}\left(\dfrac{4-5}{5 \times 4}\right)$

$$\Rightarrow \quad \phi_0 = 0.615\,\text{eV}$$

24. (c) According to Einstein's equation,

$$\text{KE}_{max} = h\nu - \phi$$

$$h\nu = \text{KE}_{max} + \phi$$

For Ist metal, $h\nu = 5\phi$

$\therefore \quad 5\phi = \text{KE}_1 + \phi$

$\Rightarrow \quad \text{KE}_1 = 4\phi \qquad$ ...(i)

For IInd metal, $10\phi = \text{KE}_2 + \phi$

$\Rightarrow \quad \text{KE}_2 = 9\phi \qquad$ ...(ii)

From Eqs. (i) and (ii), we get

$$\Rightarrow \quad \frac{\text{KE}_1}{\text{KE}_2} = \frac{4\phi}{9\phi}$$

$$\Rightarrow \quad \frac{\frac{1}{2}mv_1^2}{\frac{1}{2}mv_2^2} = \frac{4}{9}$$

$$\Rightarrow \quad \frac{v_1^2}{v_2^2} = \frac{4}{9} \quad \text{or} \quad v_1 : v_2 = 2:3$$

25. (a) According to photoelectric equation,

$$K_{max} = h(\nu_i - \nu_0)$$

$$= h\left(\frac{c}{\lambda_i} - \frac{c}{\lambda_0}\right) = hc\left(\frac{\lambda_0 - \lambda_i}{\lambda_0\lambda_i}\right)$$

$$= 1237\left(\frac{580 - 460}{580 \times 460}\right) = 0.5\ \text{eV}$$

26. (c) de-Broglie wavelength,

$$\lambda = \frac{h}{p} = \frac{h}{\sqrt{2mE}} = \frac{h}{\sqrt{2mqV}}$$

where, λ is wavelength of particles and p is momentum of particles.

$$\therefore \quad \lambda \propto \frac{1}{\sqrt{mq}}$$

Hence, $\dfrac{\lambda_e}{\lambda_p} = \dfrac{\sqrt{m_p q_p}}{\sqrt{m_e q_e}} = \dfrac{\sqrt{m_p}}{\sqrt{m_e}}$

$[\because q_p = q_e]$

27. (c) Given that,

$$\phi_A = 8\,\text{eV}$$
$$\phi_B = 4.5\,\text{eV}$$

Threshold wavelength of metal A,

$$\lambda_A = \frac{1242}{8}\,\text{nm}$$
$$\lambda_B = \frac{1242}{4.5}$$
$$\lambda_B - \lambda_A = \frac{1242}{4.5} - \frac{1242}{8}$$
$$= 276 - 155.25 = 120.75\,\text{nm}$$

28. (c) Lens cannot change frequency of incident light, so K_{max} remains same.

29. (c) From the relation, $eV = \frac{hc}{\lambda} - \phi$

or $$V = \left(\frac{hc}{e}\right)\left(\frac{1}{\lambda}\right) - \frac{\phi}{e}$$

This is equation of straight line.

Slope is $\tan\theta = \frac{hc}{e}$

Further $V = 0$ at $\phi = \frac{hc}{\lambda}$

$$\therefore \quad \phi_1 : \phi_2 : \phi_3 = \frac{hc}{\lambda_{01}} : \frac{hc}{\lambda_{02}} : \frac{hc}{\lambda_{03}}$$
$$= \frac{1}{\lambda_{01}} : \frac{1}{\lambda_{02}} : \frac{1}{\lambda_{03}}$$
$$= 1 : 2 : 4$$

Violet colour has wavelength 4000 Å.

So, violet colour can eject photoelectrons from metal 1 and metal 2.

30. (*a*) According to question, the wave equation of the magnetic field which produces photoelectric effect is

$$B = B_0[(\sin(3.14 \times 10^7\,ct) + \sin(6.28 \times 10^7\,ct)]$$

Here, the photoelectric effect produced by the angular frequency,

$$\omega = 6.28 \times 10^7\,c$$
$$\Rightarrow \omega = 6.28 \times 10^7 \times 3 \times 10^8$$
$$\omega = 2\pi \times 10^7 \times 3 \times 10^8\ \text{rad/s} \quad \ldots\text{(i)}$$

Using Eq. (i),

$$h\nu = \frac{h\omega}{2\pi}$$
$$= \frac{h \times 2\pi \times 10^7 \times 3 \times 10^8}{2\pi}$$
$$h\nu = 12.4\,\text{eV}$$

Therefore, according to Einstein's equation for photoelectric effect,

$$E = h\nu = \phi + \text{KE}_{max}$$
$$\Rightarrow \quad \text{KE}_{max} = E - \phi$$

(where, ϕ = work function = 4.7 eV)

$$\Rightarrow \quad \text{KE}_{max} = 12.4 - 4.7 = 7.7\,\text{eV}$$

or $$\text{KE}_{max} = 7.7\,\text{eV}$$

Ch-13 Atoms

Topical Follow Thru

Test-1

1. (c) Scattering is due to a single collision (in moderate thick sheets) and probability of a single collision increases linearly with thickness. Otherwise, if sheet is very thin, then particle go straight without any collision (zero deflection).

2. (c) Cathode rays are streams of negatively charged ions as demonstrated by J.J. Thomson's cathode ray experiment.

3. (b) The scattering of the α-particles is due to the coulombic repulsion between the positively charged α-particle and the nuclei. An α-particle like A passing through the atom at large distance from the nucleus, experiences small repulsion and passes almost undeflected. But the α-particle like B which passes closer to the nucleus, experiences large repulsive force and hence scatters through large angle.

4. (a) Since, atom is mostly empty and a very small nucleus (order of 10^{-15} m) is situated at the centre, it is more likely that α-particles go undeviated and only few α-particles trace their path backwards (almost 1%).

5. (a) The kinetic energy of the projectile is given by

$$\frac{1}{2}mv^2 = \frac{Ze(2e)}{4\pi\varepsilon_0 r_0} = \frac{Z_1 Z_2}{4\pi\varepsilon_0 r_0}$$

Thus, energy of the projectile is directly proportional to $Z_1 \times Z_2$.

6. (c) The distance of closest approach is given by

$$r_0 = \frac{2kZe^2}{E_\alpha}$$
$$= \frac{2 \times 92 \times 9 \times 10^9 \times (1.6 \times 10^{-19})^2}{5 \times 1.6 \times 10^{-13}}$$
$$r_0 = 529.92 \times 10^{-16}\ \text{m}$$
$$= 0.529 \times 10^{-13}\ \text{m} \simeq 10^{-11}\ \text{cm}$$

7. (c) Size of atom is same in both Thomson's and Rutherford's model. They differ only in arrangement of electrons.

8. (c) The distance of closest approach is $r_0 = 2 \times 10^{-14}$ m

$$Z = 79$$
$$\text{KE} = \text{PE} = \frac{(Ze)(2e)}{4\pi\varepsilon_0 . r_0}$$
$$= \frac{9 \times 10^9 \times 79 \times 2 (1.6 \times 10^{-19})^2}{2 \times 10^{-14}}$$
$$= 1.8 \times 10^{-12}\ \text{J}$$

9. (a) Most of the space in the atom is empty and only 1 in 20000 of α-particles is deflected in Rutherford's experiment, so both Statement I and Statement II are correct.

10. (c) As electron of Rutherford's atom spirals into nucleus emitting electromagnetic wave, rotational frequency of electron and so emission frequency gradually increases. So, we observe a continuous spectrum of all possible wavelengths.

11. (d) For distance of closest approach,

$$\text{KE} = \text{PE or } \frac{p^2}{2m} = \frac{1}{4\pi\varepsilon_0} \cdot \frac{q_1 q_2}{r}$$

or $r \propto \dfrac{1}{p^2}$

$\therefore \quad \dfrac{r_1}{r_2} = \dfrac{p_2^2}{p_1^2} = \dfrac{(2p)^2}{p^2}$

$$\frac{r_1}{r_2} = \frac{4}{1} \Rightarrow r_2 = \frac{r_1}{4} = \frac{r}{4}$$

i.e, when momentum p is doubled, the distance of closest approach r reduces to $r/4$.

12. (d) Impact parameter for Rutherford's scattering experiment,

$$b = \frac{Ze^2 \cot\left(\frac{\theta}{2}\right)}{4\pi\varepsilon_0 \cdot K_1} = 0$$

$$\cot\left(\frac{\theta}{2}\right) = 0 \Rightarrow \frac{\theta}{2} = 90^\circ$$

or $\theta = 180^\circ$

13. (c) Rutherford's experiment suggested the size of the nucleus to be about 10^{-15} m to 10^{-14} m. From kinetic theory, the size of an atom was known to be 10^{-10} m, about 10,000 to 1,00,000 times larger than the size of the nucleus.

Thus, the electrons would seem to be at a distance from the nucleus about 10,000 to 1,00,000 times the size of the nucleus itself. Hence, most of an atom is an empty space. Therefore, Assertion is correct but Reason is incorrect.

14. (d) At distance of closest approach,

KE = PE

$$\Rightarrow \frac{1}{2}mv^2 = \frac{k\,(Ze)\,(2e)}{v_0}$$

$$\Rightarrow v_0 \propto \frac{1}{m}$$

15. (b) In Rutherford's model,

$$\text{PE} = -\frac{ke^2}{r}$$

and centripetal force,

$$F = \frac{ke^2}{r^2} = \frac{mv^2}{r}$$

$$\Rightarrow \frac{1}{2}mv^2 = \frac{1}{2}\left(\frac{ke^2}{r}\right)$$

$$\Rightarrow \text{KE} = \frac{1}{2}\frac{ke^2}{r}$$

$\therefore$ Total energy = PE + KE

$$= -\frac{1}{2}\frac{ke^2}{r}$$

16. (a) $\frac{1}{2}mv^2 = eV$ and $v = \frac{E}{B} = \frac{V}{Bd}$

where, d = distance between capacitor plates.

$$\Rightarrow \frac{1}{2}m\left(\frac{V^2}{B^2 d^2}\right) = eV$$

$$\Rightarrow V \propto B^2$$

or $B = K\sqrt{V}$

So, magnetic field must be increased by a factor of $\sqrt{2}$.

17. (a)

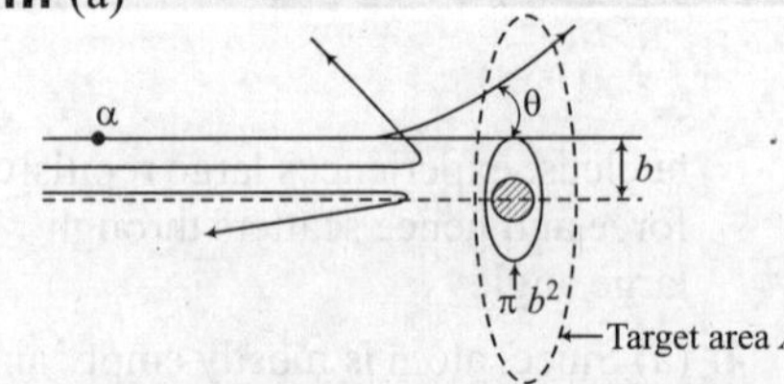

α-particle is scattered before it reaches near to nucleus and hence, it does not pass within a distance b of it.

Now, fraction of α-particles, which are scattered by angle θ or more

$$\text{is } f = \frac{\alpha\text{-particles scattered by angle } \theta \text{ or more}}{\text{Total number of incident } \alpha\text{-particles}}$$

$$= \frac{\text{Aggregate cross-section}}{\text{Target area}}$$

Now, when α-particles beam is targetted over area A, it encounters ntA nuclei. But an α-particle which is initially directed anywhere in area πb^2 is scattered through θ or more.

where, $\cot\frac{\theta}{2} = \frac{2\pi\varepsilon_0\, mv^2}{Ze^2} \cdot b$

So, $f = \dfrac{\text{Aggregate cross-section}}{\text{Area}}$

$$= \frac{ntA \times \pi b^2}{A} = nt\pi b^2$$

18. (d) Statement I is incorrect as in Rutherford's model, there is a continuous emission of energy by rotating electron and moves in orbits of gradually decreasing radii. The electron should follow a spiral path and finally it should collapse into the nucleus. Thus, the Rutherford's model cannot explain the stability of an atom. Statement II is correct, a negative total energy means a stable orbit.

19. (c) According to Rutherford's model, electrons revolve around the nucleus in circular orbit, i.e. electrons accelerate around the nucleus. The acceleration would cause the electron to radiate energy in the form of electromagnetic waves, which would imply that the electron would continuously lose energy. Thus, their velocity would decrease, causing it to spiral and eventually fall into the nucleus.

20. (a)

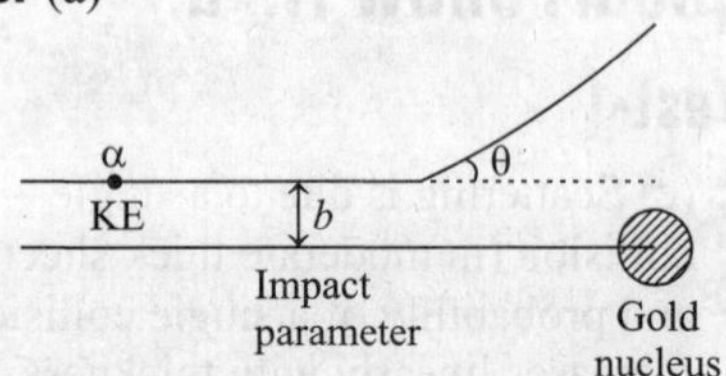

Impact parameter b is given by

$$b = \frac{Ze^2 \cdot \cot(\theta/2)}{4\pi\varepsilon_0\,(\text{KE})}$$

or $b \propto \cot\dfrac{\theta}{2}$

With given values, we get

$$\therefore \frac{\sqrt{d_1}}{\sqrt{d_2}} = \frac{\cot(60^\circ/2)}{\cot(90^\circ/2)} = \frac{\cot 30^\circ}{\cot 45^\circ}$$

or $\dfrac{\sqrt{d_1}}{\sqrt{d_2}} = \dfrac{\sqrt{3}}{1}$

On squaring both sides, we get

$$\frac{d_1}{d_2} = 3$$

21. (b) Given, $\theta = 90°$, $Z = 79$

$$E_K = 10\,\text{MeV} = 1.6\times10^{-12}\ \text{J}$$

Now, impact parameter,

$$b = \frac{Ze^2 \cot(\theta/2)}{4\pi\varepsilon_0 E_K}$$

$$= \frac{79\times9\times10^9\times(1.6\times10^{-19})^2 \times\cot 45°}{1.6\times10^{-12}}$$

$$= 79\times9\times1.6\times10^{-17}\ \text{m}$$

$$= 11\times10^{-15}\ \text{m}$$

22. (d) By law of sines,

$$\frac{\Delta p}{\sin\theta} = \frac{mv}{\sin\left(\frac{\pi-\theta}{2}\right)}$$

As, $\sin\left(\frac{\pi-\theta}{2}\right) = \cos\frac{\theta}{2}$

and $\sin\theta = 2\sin\frac{\theta}{2}\cos\frac{\theta}{2}$

We have, $\frac{\Delta p}{2\sin\frac{\theta}{2}\cos\frac{\theta}{2}} = \frac{mv}{\cos\frac{\theta}{2}}$

$$\Rightarrow \quad \Delta p = 2mv\cdot\sin\frac{\theta}{2}$$

23. (b) For no deflection,

$$\frac{e}{m} = \frac{E^2}{2VB^2}$$

When m is increased by 208 times, then keeping other things constant, B^2 must be increased 208 times, or B is increased $\sqrt{208} = 14.4$ times.

24. (d) The distance of closest approach is given by

$$r_0 = \frac{2Ze^2}{4\pi\varepsilon_0 E_K}$$

But $E_K = \frac{1}{2}mv^2 = \frac{1}{2m}(m^2v^2) = \frac{p^2}{2m}$

$$r_0 = \frac{2Ze^2 .2m}{4\pi\varepsilon_0 . p^2}$$

$$r_0 \propto \frac{1}{p^2}$$

$\therefore$ When p is increased to five times, the value of r_0 will decrease to $\frac{1}{25}$ times.

25. (d) Backward scattering is possible because nucleus is very heavy. Presence of a nucleus is not supported by Thomson's model.

Test 2

1. (a) H-atom falls from $n = 3$ to $n = 2$, energy of emitted photon,

$E = [(-1.5)-(-3.4)]\text{eV} = 1.9\ \text{eV}$

Momentum of emitted photon,

$$p = \frac{E}{c} = \frac{1.9\times1.6\times10^{-19}}{3\times10^8} = 10^{-27}\ \text{N-s}$$

To conserve momentum, H-atom must have $p = 10^{-27}$ N-s

KE of atom,

$$\text{KE} = \frac{p^2}{2m} = \frac{(10^{-27})^2}{2\times1.6\times10^{-27}} = 3.13\times10^{-28}$$

Percentage loss in energy of photon

$$= \frac{\text{Loss in energy}}{\text{Initial energy}}\times100\% = \frac{3.13\times10^{-28}}{1.9\times1.6\times10^{-19}} \approx 10^{-7}$$

2. (a) Bohr's model of Hydrogen atom is only applicable to hydrogen like atoms which means single electron atom. The study of the atoms with more than one electrons was attempted on the lines of Bohr's model for hydrogenic atom but did not meet the requirements.

3. (d) As we know that, PE = − 2KE

i.e. $E_P = -2E_K$

or $\frac{E_P}{E_K} = -2$

4. (d) For transition from

$$E_{n_1\to n_2} = -13.6\left[\frac{1}{n_2^2} - \frac{1}{n_1^2}\right];\ n_1 = 1$$

and $n_2 = 2$

$$\Rightarrow E_2 \to E_1 = 13.6\times\frac{3}{4} = 10.2\,\text{eV}$$

5. (b) As we know, the number of spectral lines observed in the spectrum is

$$n = \frac{(n_2 - n_1)(n_2 - n_1 + 1)}{2}$$

where, n = number of spectral lines

So, for $n_2 = 4$ to $n_1 = 1$,

$$n = \frac{(4-1)(4-1+1)}{2} = \frac{3\times4}{2} = 6$$

For $n_2 = 5$ to $n_1 = 3$,

$$n = \frac{(5-3)(5-3+1)}{2} = \frac{2\times3}{2} = 3$$

For $n_2 = 6$ to $n_1 = 2$,

$$n = \frac{(6-2)(6-2+1)}{2} = \frac{4\times5}{2} = 10$$

For $n_2 = 6$ to $n_1 = 1$,

$$n = \frac{(6-1)(6-1+1)}{2} = \frac{5\times6}{2} = 15$$

6. (d) Energy corresponding to a transition, between 3rd and 4th orbit given by

$$E = E_4 - E_3 = -\frac{13.6}{4^2} - \left(-\frac{13.6}{3^2}\right)$$

$$= (-0.85 + 1.51)\,\text{eV} = 0.66\ \text{eV}$$

7. (b) When electron moves from $n_2 \to n_1$ in hydrogen atom, the energy change associated with it is

$$\Delta E = \left|13.6\left(\frac{1}{n_i^2} - \frac{1}{n_f^2}\right)\right|$$

$$\left(\text{where, } E = \frac{-13.6}{n^2}Z^2\ \text{eV}\right)$$

$$\frac{13.6\left(\frac{1}{2^2} - \frac{1}{3^2}\right)}{13.6\left(\frac{1}{2^2} - 0\right)} = \frac{x}{x+4}$$

$$\Rightarrow \quad \frac{\frac{1}{4} - \frac{1}{9}}{\frac{1}{4}} = \frac{x}{x+4}$$

$$\Rightarrow \quad \frac{5}{9} = \frac{x}{x+4}$$

$$\Rightarrow \quad 5x + 20 = 9x$$

$$\Rightarrow \quad 4x = 20 \Rightarrow x = 5$$

8. (c) On the basis of Bohr's model,

$$r = \frac{n^2h^2}{4\pi^2 mKZe^2} = a_0\cdot\frac{n^2}{Z}$$

Li^{++} ion have, $Z = 3$, $n = 1$ for ground state

Now, $a_0 = 53$ pm

$$\therefore \quad r = \frac{53\times1^2}{3} \simeq 18\,\text{pm}$$

9. (c) For Balmer series, $n_1 = 2$, $n_2 = 3$ for 1st line and $n_2 = 4$ for second line

Thus, $$\frac{\lambda_1}{\lambda_2} = \frac{\left(\frac{1}{2^2} - \frac{1}{4^2}\right)}{\left(\frac{1}{2^2} - \frac{1}{3^2}\right)}$$

$$= \frac{\frac{3}{16}}{\frac{5}{36}} = \frac{3}{16} \times \frac{36}{5} = \frac{27}{20}$$

$$\lambda_2 = \frac{20}{27}\lambda_1 = \frac{20}{27} \times 6561$$

$$= 4860 \text{ Å}$$

10. (c) For hydrogen atom, when electron makes a transition from nth level to ground state, then wavelength of emitted photon is given as

$$\frac{1}{\lambda} = R\left(\frac{1}{1^2} - \frac{1}{n^2}\right)$$

For transition-1,

$$\frac{1}{\lambda_1} = R\left(\frac{1}{1^2} - \frac{1}{3^2}\right)$$

$$\Rightarrow \quad \frac{1}{\lambda_1} = R\left(1 - \frac{1}{9}\right) = \frac{8R}{9}$$

or $$\lambda_1 = \frac{9}{8R} \quad \text{...(i)}$$

For transition-2,

$$\frac{1}{\lambda_2} = R\left(\frac{1}{1^2} - \frac{1}{2^2}\right)$$

$$\Rightarrow \quad \frac{1}{\lambda_2} = R\left(1 - \frac{1}{4}\right) = \frac{3}{4}R$$

$$\Rightarrow \quad \lambda_2 = \frac{4}{3R} \quad \text{...(ii)}$$

On dividing Eq. (i) by Eq. (ii), we get

$$\frac{\lambda_1}{\lambda_2} = \frac{27}{32}$$

11. (b) From Bohr's postulate, we have

$$mv_n r_n = \frac{nh}{2\pi}$$

$\because$ $m = 10 \text{ kg}$, $r_n = 8 \times 10^6$ m (Given)

$$T = 2 \text{ h} = 2 \times 60 \times 60 = 7200 \text{ s}$$

$$v_n = \frac{2\pi r_n}{T_n}$$

Quantum number of orbit of satellite,

$$n = (2\pi r_n)^2 \times \frac{m}{T \times h}$$

$$= (2\pi \times 8 \times 10^6)^2 \times \frac{10}{7200 \times 6.64 \times 10^{-34}}$$

$$n = 5.3 \times 10^{45}$$

12. (d) Here, $h = 6.625 \times 10^{-34}$ Js,

$e = 1.6 \times 10^{-19}$ C,

$m = 9.1 \times 10^{-31}$ kg,

$c = 3 \times 10^8 \text{ ms}^{-1}$,

$\varepsilon_0 = 8.85 \times 10^{-12} \text{ C}^2 \text{ N}^{-1} \text{ m}^{-2}$, $n = 3$

Radius of the nth Bohr orbit of the hydrogen atom is given by

$$r_n = 4\pi\varepsilon_0 \cdot \frac{n^2h^2}{4\pi^2 me^2}$$

$$r_3 = 4\pi \times 8.85 \times 10^{-12} \times \frac{(3)^2 \times (6.625 \times 10^{-34})^2}{4\pi^2 \times 9.1 \times 10^{-31} \times (1.6 \times 10^{-19})^2}$$

$$= 4.777 \times 10^{-10} \text{ m}$$

$$= 4.777 \text{Å}$$

13. (c) We have, $\lambda = \dfrac{hc}{\Delta E}$

$\therefore$ So, ratio of wavelengths

$$\frac{\lambda_1}{\lambda_2} = \frac{hc/\Delta E_1}{hc/\Delta E_2} = \frac{\Delta E_2}{\Delta E_1}$$

$$= \frac{\left(\frac{4}{3}E - E\right)}{2E - E} = \frac{1}{3}$$

14. (a) According to Rydberg's formula, $\dfrac{1}{\lambda} = R\left(\dfrac{1}{n_f^2} - \dfrac{1}{n_i^2}\right)$

Here, $n_f = 1$, $n_i = n$

$$\frac{1}{\lambda} = R\left(\frac{1}{1^2} - \frac{1}{n^2}\right)$$

$$\frac{1}{\lambda} = R\left(1 - \frac{1}{n^2}\right)$$

$$\Rightarrow \quad \frac{R}{n^2} = R - \frac{1}{\lambda}$$

$$\Rightarrow \quad n = \sqrt{\frac{\lambda R}{\lambda R - 1}}$$

15. (c) As, $$\frac{\lambda_l}{\lambda_s} = \frac{R\left(\frac{1}{1^2} - \frac{1}{\infty}\right)}{R\left(\frac{1}{1^2} - \frac{1}{2^2}\right)} = \frac{4}{3}$$

$$\lambda_l = \frac{4}{3}\lambda_s = \frac{4}{3} \times 911.6$$

$$= 1215.4 \text{ Å}$$

$$\simeq 1215 \text{ Å}$$

16. (b)

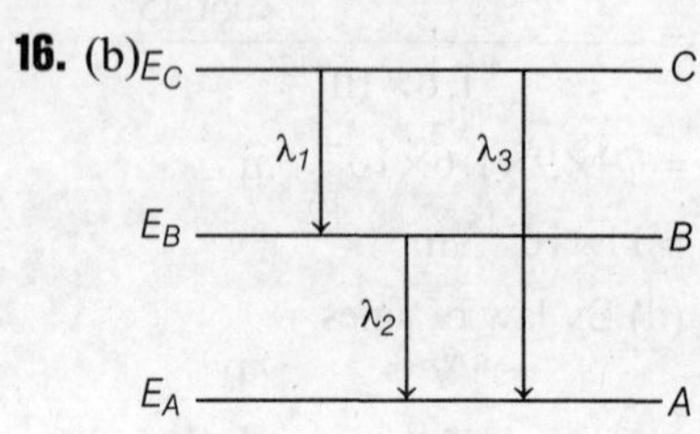

Using Bohr's postulate for radiation of spectral line, we have radiation of wavelength from C to B,

$$E_C - E_B = \frac{hc}{\lambda_1} \quad \text{...(i)}$$

Radiation of wavelength from B to A,

$$E_B - E_A = \frac{hc}{\lambda_2} \quad \text{...(ii)}$$

Radiation of wavelength from C to A,

$$E_C - E_A = \frac{hc}{\lambda_3} \quad \text{...(iii)}$$

Also, $(E_C - E_A) = (E_C - E_B) + (E_B - E_A)$

$$\therefore \quad \frac{hc}{\lambda_3} = \frac{hc}{\lambda_1} + \frac{hc}{\lambda_2}$$

or $$\frac{1}{\lambda_3} = \frac{1}{\lambda_1} + \frac{1}{\lambda_2}$$

$$\Rightarrow \quad \lambda_3 = \frac{\lambda_1\lambda_2}{\lambda_1 + \lambda_2}$$

17. (c) Given, stopping potential, $V_0 = 10$ V

Work function, $W = 2.75$ eV

According to Einstein's photoelectric equation.

$$eV_0 = h\nu - W$$

or $$h\nu = eV_0 + W$$

$$= 10 \text{ eV} + 2.75 \text{ eV}$$

$$= 12.75 \text{ eV} \quad \text{...(i)}$$

When an electron in the hydrogen atom jumps from excited state n to the ground state ($n = 1$), then the frequency ν of the emitted photon is given by

$$h\nu = E_n - E_1$$

$$\Rightarrow h\nu = -\frac{13.6}{n^2} - \left(-\frac{13.6}{1^2}\right)$$

$$\left(\because \text{For hydrogen atom, } E_n = -\frac{13.6}{n^2}\text{ eV}\right)$$

According to given problem

$$-\frac{13.6}{n^2} + 13.6 = 12.75 \text{[Using Eq. (i)]}$$

$$\frac{13.6}{n^2} = 0.85$$

$$\Rightarrow \quad n^2 = \frac{13.6}{0.85} = 16 \text{ or } n = 4$$

18. (c) From Coulomb's attraction between the positive proton and negative electron $= \frac{1}{4\pi\varepsilon_0}\frac{e^2}{r^2}$

[For neutral atom]

Centripetal force has magnitude

$$F = \frac{mv^2}{r}$$

So, the revolving electrons

$$\frac{mv^2}{r} = \frac{1}{4\pi\varepsilon_0}\frac{e^2}{r^2}$$

$$\Rightarrow \quad v^2 = \frac{1}{4\pi\varepsilon_0}\frac{e^2}{mr}$$

$$\text{or} \quad v = \frac{e}{\sqrt{4\pi\varepsilon_0 mr}}$$

For ground state of H-atom, $r = a_0$

$$\therefore \quad v = \frac{e}{\sqrt{4\pi\varepsilon_0 m a_0}}$$

19. (a) According to third postulate of Bohr's model, when an atom makes a transition from higher energy state to lower energy state, the difference of energy is carried away by a photon such that $h\nu = E_{n_i} - E_{n_f}$

$$\text{or} \quad \frac{hc}{\lambda} = Rhc\left[\frac{1}{n_f^2} - \frac{1}{n_i^2}\right]$$

[where, n_i = quantum number of higher energy state and n_f = quantum number of lower energy state.]

Energy difference between fifth and first orbit is $E_5 - E_1 = \frac{hc}{\lambda}$ and

$$Rhc - \frac{Rhc}{25} = \frac{hc}{\lambda}$$

$$\frac{24}{25}R = \frac{1}{\lambda}$$

$$\text{As,} \quad p = \frac{h}{\lambda}$$

$$\text{and} \quad v = \frac{h}{m\lambda} = \frac{24}{25}\frac{Rh}{m}$$

20. (c) We know that,

$$v \propto \frac{1}{n} \text{ and } r \propto n^2$$

$$\text{Since,} \quad \omega = \frac{v}{r}$$

$$\omega \propto \frac{1}{n.n^2}$$

$$\omega \propto \frac{1}{n^3}$$

21. (b) Electron to remain orbiting in the nth orbit of radius r_n,

$$\frac{mv^2}{r_n} = \frac{k}{r_n}$$

$$\text{or} \quad V = \sqrt{k/m} \quad \text{...(i)}$$

Using Bohr's postulate,

$$mvr_n = \frac{nh}{2\pi}$$

$$r_n = \frac{nh}{2\pi mv} = \frac{nh}{2\pi m}\sqrt{\frac{m}{k}}$$

$$\text{So,} \quad r_n \propto n$$

Further the kinetic energy of electron circulating in the nth orbit,

$$T_n = \frac{1}{2}mv^2 = \frac{1}{2}m.\frac{k}{m} = \frac{k}{2}$$

So, T_n is independent of n.

22. (a) Lyman series,

$$\frac{1}{\lambda} = R\left[1 - \frac{1}{n^2}\right]$$

where, $n = 2, 3, 4 \ldots \infty$

For series limit, $n = \infty$

$$\frac{1}{\lambda} = R \text{ or } \lambda = \frac{1}{R}$$

23. (d)

A. Ground state energy = Total energy of atom Hence, total energy of hydrogen atom is E_0. Also potential energy is 2 times of total energy i.e. PE $= 2E_0$ of hydrogen $= 2E_0$

B. Since $E \propto \frac{Z^2}{n^2}$

$\Rightarrow$ Total energy of first excited state of He^+ is $4E_0$.

C. Kinetic energy is half of negative value of total energy *i.e.* $KE_{He^+} = -2E_0$

D. Kinetic energy of hydrogen atom will be $\frac{-E_0}{2}$.

Hence, A $\rightarrow$ (III), B $\rightarrow$ (I), C $\rightarrow$ (II), D $\rightarrow$ (IV).

24. (b) Energy of electron in the 3rd orbit of He^+ is

$$E_3 = -13.6 \times \frac{Z^2}{n^2} \text{ eV}$$

$$= -13.6 \times \frac{4}{9} \times 1.6 \times 10^{-19} \text{ J}$$

From Bohr's model, $E_3 = -K$

$$E_3 = -\frac{1}{2}m_e v^2$$

$$\Rightarrow -\left(\frac{1}{2} \times 9.1 \times 10^{-31} \times v^2\right)$$

$$= -13.6 \times \frac{4}{9} \times 1.6 \times 10^{-19}$$

$$\Rightarrow \quad v^2 = \frac{136 \times 16 \times 4 \times 2 \times 10^{+11}}{9 \times 91}$$

$$\text{or,} \quad v = 1.46 \times 10^6 \text{ m/s}$$

25. (d) According to first condition,

$$\frac{hc}{\lambda_0} = \frac{-13.6}{3^2} - \left(\frac{-13.6}{2^2}\right)$$

$$\Rightarrow \quad \frac{hc}{\lambda_0} = \frac{13.6 \times 5}{36} \quad \text{...(i)}$$

According to second condition,

$$\frac{hc}{\lambda'} = \frac{-13.6}{4^2} - \left(\frac{-13.6}{3^2}\right)$$

$$\frac{hc}{\lambda'} = \frac{13.6 \times 7}{16 \times 9} \quad \text{...(ii)}$$

On dividing Eq. (i) by Eq. (ii), we get

$$\frac{hc/\lambda_0}{hc/\lambda'} = \frac{13.6 \times 5}{36} \times \frac{16 \times 9}{13.6 \times 7}$$

$$\Rightarrow \quad \frac{\lambda'}{\lambda_0} = \frac{20}{7}$$

Chapter Break Thru

1. (d) Energy required to remove electron in the $n=3$ state $= +\frac{13.6}{(3)^2}$

$$= +1.51 \text{ eV}$$

2. (a) In the revolution of electron, coulomb force provides the necessary centripetal force,

$$\frac{Ze^2}{r^2} = \frac{mv^2}{r} \Rightarrow mv^2 = \frac{Ze^2}{r}$$

Then, kinetic energy

$$\text{KE} = \frac{1}{2}mv^2 = \frac{Ze^2}{2r}$$

3. (c) The absorption lines are obtained when the electron jumps from ground state ($n=1$) to the higher energy states. Thus, only 1, 2 and 3 lines will be obtained.

4. (d) The explanation of Rutherford's α-particle experiment shows that the atom is hollow, the whole mass of atom is concentrated in small centre and nucleus is positively charged.

5. (c) For excited energy state $n=2$, By using angular momentum formula

$$L = \frac{nh}{2\pi}$$

$$L = \frac{2 \times 6.6 \times 10^{-34}}{2 \times 3.14}$$

$$L = 2.11 \times 10^{-34} \text{ J-s}$$

6. (b) Bohr's radius is given by

$$r_0 = \frac{h^2}{4\pi^2 mKe^2} = 0.53 \text{ Å}$$

or $r = \frac{n^2}{Z} \times r_0$

$$r_{(n=3)} = \frac{(3)^2}{2} \times 0.53$$

$$= 2.38 \text{ Å}$$

7. (b) Given, mass of electron,

$$m_e = 9.1 \times 10^{-31} \text{ kg}$$

Circular orbit of radius,

$$r = 0.529 \times 10^{-10} \text{ m}$$

Speed, $v = 2.2 \times 10^8$ m/s

Linear momentum of particle is given by $p = m \times v$

$$p = 9.1 \times 10^{-31} \times 2.2 \times 10^8$$

$$p = 20.02 \times 10^{-23} \text{ kg-m/s}$$

8. (d) According to classical electromagnetic theory, an accelerated charged particle continuously emits radiation. As electrons revolving in circular paths are constantly experiencing centripetal acceleration, hence they will be losing their energy continuously and the orbital radius will go on decreasing, from spiral and finally the electron will fall in the nucleus.

9. (d) If energy is radiated in transition then, $E_{R\to G} > E_{Q\to S} > E_{R\to S} > E_{Q\to R} > E_{P\to Q}$

For getting blue line, energy radiated should be maximum $\left(E \propto \frac{1}{\lambda}\right)$. Hence, (d) is the correct option.

10. (c) Potential energy $(U) = 2E$

Kinetic energy $(K) = -E$

and energy in the ground state

$$E = -\frac{13.6}{n^2}$$

So, both kinetic energy and potential energy are inversely proportional to n^2. So, for state $n=2$ to $n=1$

$K_1 = 4K_2$ and $U_1 = 4U_2$

11. (a) We know that, $N \propto \left[\frac{1}{\sin^4 \frac{\theta}{2}}\right]$

$$\Rightarrow N_1 = 7 \times \frac{1}{(\sin 30°)^4} = 112/\text{min}$$

and $N_2 = 7 \times \frac{1}{(\sin 60°)^4}$

$$= 12.5/\text{min}$$

12. (c) Given, radius of the first orbit is a_0 whereas radius of the second orbit can be determine by $r \propto n^2$ which means

$$r_n = n^2 \times a_0 \quad (\because r_1 = a_0)$$

13. (d) Given that, $n=6$

Number of spectral lines $= \frac{n(n-1)}{2}$

$$= \frac{6(6-1)}{2} = 15$$

14. (c) At closest distance of approach, Kinetic energy = Potential energy

So, PE $= 5 \times 10^6 \times 1.6 \times 10^{-19}$

$$= \frac{1}{4\pi\varepsilon_0} \times \frac{(Ze)(2e)}{r}$$

For uranium $Z = 92$,

so $r = 5.3 \times 10^{-12}$ cm

15. (c) As, for conservative fields

$$\mathbf{F} = -\left(\frac{d\,\mathbf{U}}{d\,\mathbf{r}}\right)$$

$\therefore$ Magnitude of force on particle is

$$\Rightarrow F = \frac{dU}{dr} = \frac{d}{dr}\left(\frac{1}{2}kr^2\right)$$

$$\Rightarrow F = kr$$

This force is acting like centripetal force.

$$\therefore \frac{mv^2}{r} = kr \quad \text{...(i)}$$

Multiply m on both side

So, for nth orbit,

$$\Rightarrow m^2 v_n^2 = mk\, r_n^2$$

$$\Rightarrow \frac{n^2 h^2}{4\pi^2 r^2} = mk\, r_n^2 \left[\because v_n = \frac{nh}{2\pi mr}\right]$$

Therefore, $r_n^4 \propto n^2 \Rightarrow r_n^2 \propto n$

So, $r_n \propto \sqrt{n}$

Energy of particle is

$$E_n = \text{PE} + \text{KE}$$

$$= \frac{1}{2}k\, r_n^2 + \frac{1}{2}mv_n^2$$

$$= \frac{1}{2}k\, r_n^2 + \frac{1}{2}k\, r_n^2 \text{ [using Eq. (i)]}$$

$$= k\, r_n^2$$

So, energy, $E_n \propto r_n^2$

$$\Rightarrow E_n \propto n$$

16. (a) As wave number $\bar{\nu}$ is given by

$$(\bar{\nu}) = \frac{1}{\lambda} = R\left[\frac{1}{n_1^2} - \frac{1}{n_2^2}\right]$$

$$= R\left[\frac{1}{4} - \frac{1}{16}\right] = \frac{3R}{16}$$

17. (d) $E_n = \frac{-Z^2}{n^2}(13.6 \text{ eV})$

By putting $Z=3$, we have

$$E_n = \frac{-112.4 \text{ eV}}{n^2}$$

$$E_1 = \frac{-112.4}{(1)^2} = -122.4 \text{ eV}$$

$$E_3 = \frac{-122.4}{(3)^2} = -13.6 \text{ eV}$$

$$\Delta E = E_3 - E_1 = 108 \text{ eV}$$

The corresponding wavelength is

$$\lambda = \frac{12375 \text{ Å}}{\Delta E \text{ (in eV)}} = \frac{12375}{108.8} \text{ Å}$$

$\Rightarrow \quad \lambda = 113.74$ Å

18. (b) Energy in the nth orbit is

$$E_n = \frac{13.6}{n^2}$$

$$(\text{PE})_n = 2(\text{E})_n = \frac{2 \times (13.6)}{n^2}$$

and $(\text{KE})_n = -\frac{13.6}{n^2}$

Clearly, when n increases E increases, PE increases and KE decreases.

19. (b) Transition A ($n = \infty$ to $n = 1$), series limit of Lyman series.
Transition B ($n = 5$ to $n = 2$), third spectral line of Balmer series.
Transition C($n = 5$ to $n = 3$), second spectral line of Paschen series.

20. (c) Energy of electrons

$= -13.6 + 12.1 = 1.5$ eV

Which is corresponding to third orbit, $n = 3$

Number of spectral lines

$$= \frac{n(n-1)}{2} = \frac{3(3-1)}{2} = 3$$

21. (a) Total energy of the electron in hydrogen atom is

$$E = -13.6 \text{eV}$$
$$= -13.6 \times 1.6 \times 10^{-19} \text{ J}$$

As, $E = -\frac{ke^2}{r}$

$$\therefore \quad r = \frac{-ke^2}{E}$$

$$= \frac{9 \times 10^9 \times (1.6 \times 10^{-19})^2}{13.6 \times 1.6 \times 10^{-19}}$$

$$= 5.3 \times 10^{-11} \text{ m}$$

22. (d) According to Bohr's theory,

$$mvr = n\frac{h}{2\pi}$$

Circumference, $2\pi r = n\left(\frac{h}{mv}\right) = n\lambda$

where, λ is de-Broglie wavelength for electron.

23. (d) Emission transitions take place between higher energy level to any lower energy level. While absorption transition starts from the lowest energy levels only and may end at any higher energy level.
Hence, number of absorptions transition between two given energy levels is always less than the number of emission transitions between the same two levels.

24. (d) As we know, that

$$E = \frac{hc}{\lambda} \propto \frac{Z^2}{n^2}$$

Which means that $\lambda \propto \frac{1}{Z^2}$

Thus, λ for He$^+$, $\lambda = \frac{28.397}{2}$

$$\lambda = 14.199 \text{ cm}$$

25. (d)

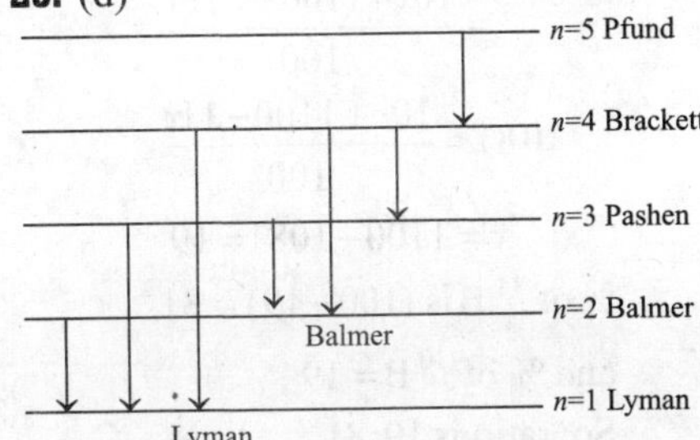

The transition $4 \to 3$ belongs to Paschen series. This is not in the ultraviolet region but this is in the infrared region.
The transition $5 \to 4$ also belongs to Brackett series and it is in the infrared region.

26. (d) For Lyman series,

$$\frac{1}{\lambda_{\text{max}}} = R\left[\frac{1}{1^2} - \frac{1}{2^2}\right] = \frac{3}{4}R$$

and $$\frac{1}{\lambda_{\text{min}}} = R\left[\frac{1}{1^2} - \frac{1}{\infty^2}\right] = \frac{R}{1}$$

$$\therefore \quad \frac{\lambda_{\text{max}}}{\lambda_{\text{min}}} = \frac{4}{3}$$

27. (c) The correct answer is (c).
The de-Broglie wavelength of an electron in nth orbit of hydrogen atom is

$$\lambda = \frac{h}{p} = \frac{h}{mv}$$

$$\Rightarrow \quad \lambda = \frac{h}{\frac{me^2}{2\varepsilon_0 hn}}$$

$$\Rightarrow \quad \lambda = \left(\frac{2h^2\varepsilon_0}{me^2}\right)n$$

$$\Rightarrow \quad \lambda \propto n$$

$$\therefore \quad \text{P} \to 2$$

Magnetic moment of electron in nth Bohr's orbit,

$$M = \frac{\text{Charge} \times \text{Area}}{\text{Time period}}$$

$$\Rightarrow M = \frac{e \times \pi r^2}{T} = \frac{e \times \pi r^2}{2\frac{\pi}{\omega}} = \frac{1}{2}e\omega r^2$$

$$M \propto r^2$$

$$\therefore \quad \text{Q} \to 4$$

Magnetic field at centre of hydrogen atom,

$$B = \frac{\mu_0 I}{2r_n}$$

$$\Rightarrow \quad B = \frac{\mu_0\left(\frac{e}{T_n}\right)}{2r_n}$$

$$\Rightarrow \quad B = \frac{\mu_0\left(\frac{e}{\frac{2\pi r_n}{v_n}}\right)}{2r_n}$$

$$\Rightarrow \quad B = \frac{\mu_0 e v_n}{2\pi r_n}$$

Using, $\quad r_n = \frac{\varepsilon_0 h^2 n^3}{\pi m e^2}$

$$v_n = \frac{e^2}{2\varepsilon_0 hn} \Rightarrow B \propto \frac{1}{n^5}$$

$$\therefore \quad \text{R} \to 1$$

Angular momentum of an electron in nth orbit of H-atom,

$$L=\frac{nh}{2\pi}$$

Also, $r=\frac{\varepsilon_0 h^2 n^2}{\pi m e^2}=\frac{4\pi\varepsilon_0}{me^2}L^2$

$$L=\left(\frac{me^2}{4\pi\varepsilon_0}\right)^{\frac{1}{2}}\times r^{\frac{1}{2}}$$

$\Rightarrow L \propto r^{1/2}$

$\therefore$ S $\rightarrow$ 3

28. (a) Wavelength number is given as

$$\frac{1}{\lambda}=R\left[\frac{1}{n_1^2}-\frac{1}{n_2^2}\right]$$

$$\Rightarrow \frac{\lambda_{min}}{\lambda_{max}}=\frac{\left[\frac{1}{2^2}-\frac{1}{3^2}\right]}{\left[\frac{1}{2^2}-\frac{1}{\infty}\right]}=\frac{5}{9}$$

29. (a) Here, $N \propto \frac{1}{\sin^4\left(\frac{\theta}{2}\right)}$

$$\Rightarrow \frac{N_2}{N_1}=\left[\frac{\sin\left(\frac{\theta_1}{2}\right)}{\sin\left(\frac{\theta_2}{2}\right)}\right]^4$$

$$\frac{N_2}{N_1}=\left[\frac{\sin\frac{90}{2}}{\sin\frac{60}{2}}\right]^4=\left[\frac{\sin 45^\circ}{\sin 30^\circ}\right]^4$$

$$N_2=(\sqrt{2})^4\times N_1=4\times 56=224$$

30. (c) Here, $E_1=-\frac{13.6(3)^2}{(1)^2}$ (for first orbit),

$E_2=\frac{13.6(3)^2}{(3)^2}$ (for third orbit)

$$\therefore \Delta E=E_2-E_1=13.6(3)^2\left[1-\frac{1}{9}\right]$$

$$=\frac{13.6\times 9\times 8}{9}=108.8\text{ eV}$$

Ch-14 Nuclei

Topical Follow Thru

Test-1

1. (c) 1 atomic mass unit

$$=1.67\times 10^{-27}\text{ kg}$$

2. (c) Ratio of masses of nuclei of hydrogen, tritium and deuterium

$$=1:3:2$$

3. (a) In free state, electrons are most stable, so they does not decay in free state.

Protons are fairly stable and neutrons are unstable at outside of nucleus. So decreasing order of stability in free state is

Electron > Proton > Neutron

4. (d) Nuclear radius is given by

$$R=R_0(A)^{\frac{1}{3}}$$

$$R_U=R_0(235)^{\frac{1}{3}}$$

$$R_{Ag}=R_0(107)^{\frac{1}{3}}$$

$$\frac{R_U}{R_{Ag}}=\frac{(235)^{\frac{1}{3}}}{(107)^{\frac{1}{3}}}\simeq 1.3$$

5. (d) Let ^{10}B be present as x%

and percentage of $^{11}\text{B}=(100-x)\%$

Average atomic mass

$$=\frac{10x+(100-x)11}{100}$$

$$10.81=\frac{10x+1100-11x}{100}$$

$$x=1100-1081=19$$

% of ^{11}B is $(100-19)=81$

and % of $^{10}\text{B}=19$

So, ratio is 19 : 81

6. (b) Radius of $^{27}_{13}\text{Al}=R_0(27)^{\frac{1}{3}}$

$$3R_0=3.6\text{ fm}$$

Radius of $^{197}_{97}\text{Au}=R_0(197)^{\frac{1}{3}}$

$$=\frac{3.6}{3}(197)^{\frac{1}{3}}\text{ fm}$$

$$=6.98\text{ fm}$$

$$\approx 7\text{ fm}$$

7. (c) Volume, $V=\frac{4}{3}\pi R^3$

$$=\frac{4}{3}\pi(R_0A^{\frac{1}{3}})^3=\frac{4}{3}\pi R_0^3\times A$$

Nuclear density, $\rho=\frac{m}{V}$

$$=\frac{3\times 107.8682\times 1.67\times 10^{-27}}{4\times\frac{22}{7}\times(1.2\times 10^{-15})^3\times 107}$$

$$=2.32\times 10^{17}\text{ kg/m}^3$$

8. (a) Each atom of $_6C^{14}$ contains 6 proton (p), 6 electron (e) and 8 neutron (n).

$\therefore$ In 14 g of $_6C^{14}$,

$$p=6\times 6\times 10^{23}=36\times 10^{23}$$

$$n=8\times 6\times 10^{23}=48\times 10^{23}$$

$$e=p=36\times 10^{23}$$

9. (c) As, $\frac{r_1}{r_2}=\left(\frac{A_1}{A_2}\right)^{1/3}=\left(\frac{64}{27}\right)^{1/3}=\frac{4}{3}$

10. (a) Mass of nucleus = Mass number × Mass of a nucleon

$$=A\times 1.67\times 10^{-27}\text{ kg}$$

Volume of nucleus $=\frac{4}{3}\pi R^3$

$$=\frac{4}{3}\pi\times(1.3\times 10^{-15}\times A^{1/3})^3$$

$= \frac{4}{3}\pi \times (1.3)^3 \times 10^{-45} \times A$

$\therefore$ Density of nucleus $= \frac{\text{Mass}}{\text{Volume}}$

$= \frac{A \times 1.67 \times 10^{-27}}{\frac{4}{3}\pi \times (1.3)^3 \times 10^{-45} \times A}$

$\approx 1.81 \times 10^{17}$ kg m^{-3}

11. (b) As, $R = R_0 A^{1/3}$

$\Rightarrow \frac{R_1}{R_2} = \left(\frac{A_1}{A_2}\right)^{1/3}$

$\Rightarrow \frac{R}{R_{He}} = \left(\frac{A}{4}\right)^{1/3}$

$\Rightarrow (14)^{1/3} = \left(\frac{A}{4}\right)^{1/3}$

$\Rightarrow \quad A = 56$ or $Z = A - N$

$\therefore \quad Z = 56 - 30 = 26$

12. (b) As radius of nucleus, $R \propto A^{\frac{1}{3}}$

$\Rightarrow \frac{R_{Ge}}{R_{Be}} = \left(\frac{X}{9}\right)^{\frac{1}{3}}$

$\Rightarrow \quad 2 = \left(\frac{X}{9}\right)^{\frac{1}{3}} \Rightarrow X = 72$

$\therefore$ Number of neutrons
$= 72 - 32 = 40$

13. (c) Most stable, $N = Z(B)$. Nucleus with more neutron number (N) is slightly more stable than nucleus which have more atomic number (Z).

So, order of stability is $B > A > C$.

14. (a) $R = R_0 (A)^{1/3}$

where, R_0 is constant and A is mass number.

For oxygen $_8O^{16}$,

$2.8 \times 10^{-15} = R_0 \times (16)^{1/3}$

$R_0 = \frac{2.8 \times 10^{-15}}{2.51} = 1.11 \times 10^{-15}$ m

For lead $_{82}Pb^{207}$;

$R = R_0 (A)^{1/3}$

$= 1.11 \times 10^{-15} \times (207)^{1/3}$

$R = 6.56 \times 10^{-15}$ m

15. (a) The density of nuclei is approximately the same for all elements becasue nuclear volume grows proportionally with the mass number, while nuclear mass also increases proportionally, resulting in a constant density.

As, $\quad R = R_0 A^{1/3}, \; R \propto A^{1/3}$

This indicates that the radius grows with the cube root of mas number.

Test-2

1. (a) The fusion reaction is

$_1H^2 + _1H^2 \rightarrow _2He^4$

In this reaction two smaller nuclei are fused together to form a single stable nuclei.

2. (c) The energy of stars is due to the fusion of light hydrogen nuclei into helium. In this process, large amount of energy is released.

3. (d) Binding energy per nucleon of nucleus A,

$E_A = 5.6$ MeV

$M_B = 105, M_C = 115$

$M_A = 220$

Binding energy per nucleon of nucleus B and C,

$E_B = E_C = E = 6.4$ MeV

$\therefore$ Released energy per fission,

$Q =$ Total binding energy of products nuclei − Total binding energy of reactants nuclei

$= (M_B + M_C)E - M_A \times E_A$

$= (105 + 115)(6.4) - 220 \times 5.6$

$= 176$ MeV

4. (b) Given, $\Delta E = 7.5 \times 234 - 6.6 \times 236$

$= 1755 - 1557.6$

$\Delta E = 197.4$ MeV

5. (a)

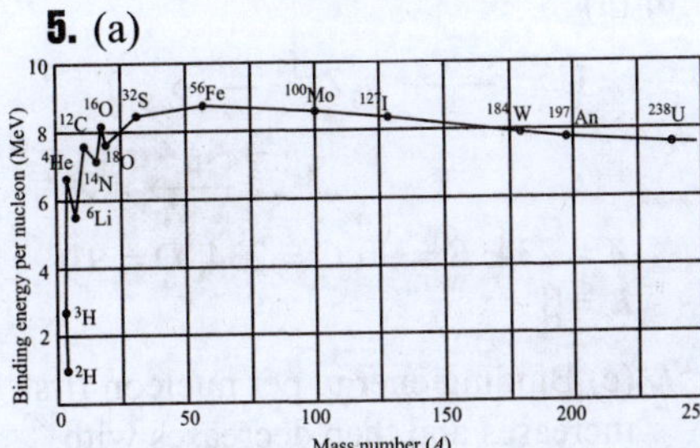

According to given figure, the binding energy per nucleon increases with atomic number and it is maximum for iron. After that, it start decreases.

6. (d) Binding energy of deuterium is 4.23 MeV, then mass defect is given by $\Delta m = \frac{4.23}{931} = 4.5 \times 10^{-3}$

7. (a) As binding energy per nucleon is about 8.5 MeV for atomic number between 50 to 80 and iron (Fe^{56}) is most stable. So, both Statement I and Statement II are correct.

8. (c) Mass of proton
$=$ mass of anti-proton
$= 1.67 \times 10^{-27}$ kg $= 1$ amu

Energy equivalent to 1 amu
$= 931$ MeV

When proton and anti-proton annihilate each other, then energy equivalent to 2 amu $= 2 \times 931$ MeV

$= 1862 \times 10^6 \times 1.6 \times 10^{-19}$

$= 2.97 \times 10^{-10}$ J

$\simeq 3 \times 10^{-10}$ J

9. (c) Mass defect,

$\Delta m = 2(m_p + m_n) - M$

$= 2(1.007277 + 1.00866) - 4.001265$

$= 0.030609$ amu

$\therefore$ Energy released,

$\Delta E = \Delta m \times 931.5$ MeV

$= 0.030609 \times 931.5$

$= 28.512$ MeV

10. (a) The arrangement of particles within U^{235} is somewhat unstable and the nucleus can disintegrate if it is excited by an outside source. When a U^{235} nucleus absorbs an extra neutron, it quickly breaks into two parts. This process is known as fission.

11. (b) Given, E_{bn} of chlorine

$= 287.67$ MeV

and E_{bn} of phosphorus

$= 262.48$ MeV

Binding energy per nucleon of $_{17}Cl^{35}$

$= \frac{\text{Binding energy}}{\text{Mass number}}$

$= \frac{287.67}{35} = 8.22\,\text{MeV}$

Similarly,
Binding energy per nucleon of ${}_{15}P^{31}$

$= \frac{262.48}{31} = 8.47\,\text{MeV}$

Since, BE per nucleon of ${}_{15}P^{31}$ is more than BE per nucleon of ${}_{17}Cl^{35}$, hence ${}_{15}P^{31}$ is more stable.

12. (c) BE of nucleus P

$= 7.6 \times 240 = 1824$ MeV

BE of nucleus Q

$= 8.5 \times 110 = 935$ MeV

BE of nucleus R

$= 8.4 \times 130 = 1092$ MeV

Energy released per fission

$= \text{BE of } R + \text{BE of } Q - \text{BE of } P$

$= 1092 + 935 - 1824 = 203$ MeV

Hence, A-(IV), B-(I), C-(II), D-(III).

13. (d) As, $3P \longrightarrow Q + E_1$

Energy relased is E_1.

Also, $2Q \longrightarrow R + E_2$.

The energy released is E_2.

To go directly from $6P \rightarrow R$ we need 2 cycles of first reaction and 1 cycle of second reaction, thus total energy relased E_2 is

$E_3 = 2E_1 + E_2$

14. (c) Binding energy per nucleon of ${}^{20}_{10}\text{Ne}$

$= \frac{M_1 - 10(m_p + m_n)}{20}$

Binding energy per nucleon of ${}^{40}_{20}\text{Ca}$

$= \frac{M_2 - 20(m_p + m_n)}{40}$

But BE per nucleon of ${}^{40}_{20}\text{Ca}$ > BE per nucleon of ${}^{20}_{10}\text{Ne}$

$\therefore \quad \frac{M_2 - 20(m_p + m_n)}{40} > \frac{M_1 - 10(m_p + m_n)}{20}$

$M_2 - 20(m_p + m_n) > 2M_1 - 20(m_p + m_n)$

$M_2 > 2M_1$

15. (c) For $m = 1$u

$E = 931\,\text{MeV}$

i.e. $1\text{u} = 931\,\text{MeV}$

Binding Energy,

$E_B = 0.42 \times 931$

$= 39.10$ MeV

Binding energy per nucleon

$= \frac{39.10}{7} = 5.58$

$\approx 5.6\,\text{MeV}$

Chapter Break Thru

1. (d) The mass number of a nucleus is more than its atomic number, but in hydrogen, atomic number and mass number are equal.

i.e. The mass number of a nucleus is sometimes more than and sometimes equal to its atomic number .

2. (b) ${}_Z X^A = {}_{88}\text{Ra}^{226} \Rightarrow Z = 88$,

So, number of protons = 88

and number of neutrons, $A - Z = 138$

3. (d) Radius of a nucleus of mass number $\propto A^{1/3}$.

4. (b) For stability in case of lighter nuclei $\frac{N}{Z} = 1$ and for heavier nuclei $\frac{N}{Z} > 1$

5. (a) Short ranged, attractive and charge independent.

6. (a)

$${}_{92}U^{238} \xrightarrow{\alpha} {}_{90}Z^{234} \xrightarrow{\beta} {}_{91}Y^{234} \xrightarrow{\beta} {}_{92}X^{234}$$

$A = 234, B = 90, C = 234, D = 91$,
$E = \beta$

7. (c) Binding energy per nucleon first increases and then decreases with increase in mass number.

8. (c) Heavy nuclei are stable only when they have more neutrons than protons because electrostatic force between protons are repulsive which may reduce stability. So, excess neutron reduce the repulsion effect of proton.

9. (a) Binding energy per nucleon for ${}^2_1X$, $BE_1 = 1.1$ MeV

For ${}^4_2Y$, $BE_2 = 7.6$ MeV

The given nuclear reaction,
${}^2_1X + {}^2_1X = {}^4_2Y$

Total no. of nucleons in the reactant, $n_1 = 2 + 2 = 4$

Total no. of nucleons in the product, $n_2 = 4$

$\therefore$ The total energy released = Change in binding energy

$= n_2 \times BE_2 - n_1 \times BE_1$

$= 4 \times 7.6 - 4 \times 1.1 = 30.4 - 4.4$

$= 26\,\text{MeV}$

10. (a) Nuclear force are short range forces because they arise from small separation of charges inside neutral atom.

11. (c) $E = \Delta mc^2$

$= 1 \times 10^{-3} \times (3 \times 10^8)^2$

$= 1 \times 10^{-3} \times 9 \times 10^{16}$

$E = 9 \times 10^{13}$ J

12. (a) The mass of nucleus formed is always less than the sum of the masses of the constituents, protons and neutrons. i.e.

$m < (A - Z)\,m_n + Zm_p$

13. (a) $P = \frac{nE}{t}$

$2 \times 10^3 = \frac{n \times 400 \times 10^6 \times 1.6 \times 10^{-19}}{t}$

$\frac{n}{t} = \frac{5}{1.6 \times 10^{-13}}$

$\frac{n}{t} = 3.1 \times 10^{13}$

14. (b) Energy released in the fission of one nucleus, $E = 200$ MeV

$= 200 \times 10^6 \times 1.6 \times 10^{-19}$ J

$E = 3.2 \times 10^{-11}$ J

As, $P = 16\text{kW}$

Now, number of nuclei required per second

$$n = \frac{P}{E} = \frac{16\times 10^3}{3.2\times 10^{-11}}$$

$$= 5\times 10^{14}$$

15. (d) Linear momentum is conserved,

$m_1 v_1 = m_2 v_2$ and $m \propto R^3$

$$\Rightarrow \frac{R_1}{R_2} = \left(\frac{m_1}{m_2}\right)^{\frac{1}{3}}$$

$$= \left(\frac{v_2}{v_1}\right)^{\frac{1}{3}} = \left(\frac{1}{2}\right)^{\frac{1}{3}}$$

16. (a) The by product is ${}^{140}_{54}\text{Xe}$ and ${}^{94}_{38}\text{Sr}$.

17. (b) During fusion, binding energy of daughter nucleus is always greater than the total energy of the parent nuclei, so energy released

$= c-(a+b) = c-a-b$

18. (d) The fusion reaction in the sun is a multi-step process in which the hydrogen is burned into helium because in fusion, lighter nuclei combine to form heavier nucleus.

19. (a) $2p + 2n \longrightarrow {}^4_2\text{He}$

$\Delta m = 2m_p + 2m_n - M\,({}^4_2\text{He})$

$= 2\times(1.0073) + 2\times(1.0087) - 4.0015$

$= 0.0305$ u

Binding Energy,

$E_b = (\Delta m \times 931.5)$ MeV

$= 0.0305\times 931.5$ MeV

$= 28.4$ MeV

20. (d) $\because$ BE $= \Delta m \times 931.5$ MeV

$\Delta m = 26\times(1.007825) + 30\times(1.008665) - 55.934939$

$= 0.528461$ u

BE $= 0.528461\times 931.5$

$= 492.26$ MeV

$$\frac{\text{BE}}{\text{nucleon}} = \frac{492.26}{56} = 8.790 \text{ MeV}$$

21. (d) Mass defect per nucleon is called the packing fraction,

i.e., $p = \dfrac{\Delta m}{A} = \dfrac{m-A}{A}$, positive value of p does not mean that Δm is large and binding energy will be calculate by $E = \Delta m\times c^2$.

Therefore, the correct option is (d), A is false but R is true.

22. (b) Total energy required to remove both electrons = BE of electron in He atom + ionisation energy of He atom

$= (24.6 + 13.6\times 2^2)$ eV

$= (24.6 + 54.4) = 79$ eV

23. (a) Number of atom in 1 g of ${}^{235}_{92}\text{U}$

$$= \frac{\text{Avogadro's number}}{\text{Mass number}}$$

$$= \frac{6.023\times 10^{23}}{235}$$

Energy released per fission = 200 MeV

Energy released by fission of 1 g of ${}^{235}_{92}\text{U}$

$$= \frac{6.023\times 10^{23}}{235}\times 200 \text{ MeV}$$

$= 5.126\times 10^{23}$ MeV

$= 5.126\times 10^{23}\times 1.6\times 10^{-13}$ J

$$= \frac{5.126\times 1.6\times 10^{10}}{3.6\times 10^6} \text{ kWh}$$

$= 2.278\times 10^4$ kWh

24. (b) Energy released = BE of products − BE of reactants

$= \text{BE}\,({}^3_2\text{He}) + \text{BE}\,(n) - 2\text{BE}({}^2_1\text{H})$

$= 7.73 + 0 - 2\times 2.23$

$= (7.73 - 4.46)$ MeV

$= 3.27$ MeV

25. (d) Let the number of fission per second be n.

Energy released per second

$= n\times 240$ MeV

$= n\times 240\times 1.6\times 10^{-13}$ J ...(i)

Energy required per second

$= P\times t = 1\text{kW}\times 1$ s

$= 1000$ J ...(ii)

Compare Eqs. (i) and (ii), we get

$n\times 240\times 1.6\times 10^{-13} = 1000$

$$\Rightarrow n = \frac{1000}{3.84\times 10^{-11}} = \frac{10}{3.8}\times 10^{13}$$

$= 2.60\times 10^{13}$

26. (c) Binding energy per nucleon of fission products is 8.5 MeV.

Binding energy per nucleon of reactants is 7.6 MeV.

Increases in binding energy per nucleon $8.5 - 7.6 = 0.9$ MeV

The energy released per nucleon in fission is 0.9 MeV.

Therefore, fractional energy released is

$$\Delta M = \frac{\Delta E}{931 \text{MeV/u}}$$

$$= \frac{0.9}{931} \simeq \frac{1}{1000}$$

Then, percentage of mass converted into energy during fission

$$= \frac{1}{1000}\times 100 = 0.1\%$$

27. (a) Kinetic energy of the molecules of a gas at a temperature T is $\frac{3}{2}kT$.

$\therefore$ To initiate the reaction,

$$\frac{3}{2}kT = 7.7\times 10^{-14} \text{ J}$$

$$\frac{3}{2}\times 1.38\times 10^{-23}\ T = 7.7\times 10^{-14}$$

$$T = 3.7\times 10^9 \text{ K}$$

Thus, the order of temperature is 10^9 K.

28. (c) Number of atoms in 3g coin

$$= \frac{N_A\times 3}{\text{Atomic mass}}$$

$$= \frac{6.023\times 10^{23}\times 3}{63}$$

$= 2.868\times 10^{22}$ atoms

Each copper atom has 29 protons and 34 neutrons.

Therefore, mass defect

$= 29\times 1.00783 + 34\times 1.00867 - 62.92960$

$= 0.59225$ u

Total mass defect of all atoms

$= 0.59225\times 2.868\times 10^{22}$

$= 1.6985 \times 10^{22}$ u

Thus, nuclear energy required

$= 1.6985 \times 10^{22} \times 931\,\text{MeV}$

$\simeq 1.6 \times 10^{25}$ MeV

29. (a) In both fission and fusion process, energy is relased. In fission, a heavy nucleus splits into lighter nuclei and releasing energy. In fusion, light nuclei, combine to form a heavier nucleus also releasing energy.

In case of fission, BE per nucleon for heavier nuclei is less than the BE per nucleon for lighter nuclei. While, in case of fusion, BE per nucleon for lighter nuclei is less than the BE per nucleon for heavier nuclei.

30. (a) Number of protons = 6

Number of neutrons = 6

Total number of nucleons

$= 6 + 6 = 12$

Mass defect $(\Delta m) = 6$(Mass of proton) + 6 (Mass of neutrons) – Mass of carbon nucleus

$\Delta m = 6[1.00783] + 6[1.00867] - 12$

$\Delta m = 0.099$ u

Binding Energy $(E_b) = \Delta M \times 931.5$ MeV

$= 0.099 \times 931.5$

$= 92.22$ MeV

Binding energy per nucleon $= \dfrac{92.22}{12}$

$= 7.68$ MeV

Ch-15 Electronic Devices

Topical Follow Thru

Test-1

1. (c) To make an n-type semiconductor like germanium doped with phosphorous, we dope neutral semiconductor unit netural atoms of impurity so an n-type crysal formed is netural. But an n-type semiconductor has more electrons in conduction band than holes in valence band.

2. (c) At room temperature, forbidden gap in the energy bands of germanium, $\Delta E_g = 0.67$ eV

3. (c) Here, $n_e n_h = n^2$

or $n_e = \dfrac{n^2}{n_h} = \dfrac{10^{16} \times 10^{16}}{4.5 \times 10^{16}}$

$= \dfrac{1}{4.5} \times 10^{16}\ \text{m}^{-3}$

$= 0.22 \times 10^{16}\ \text{m}^{-3}$

4. (a) Phosphorus is pentavalent, due to which it has excess negative charge. So, if a semiconductor is heavily doped with phosphorus, the number of electrons (n_e) is much greater than the number of holes.

5. (c) Statement I is correct and Statement II is incorrect. Electric field in junction increases with increase in doping.

6. (a) No current is obtained from a p-n junction without biasing.

7. (b) Current flow is possible and current will be

$$I = \frac{V}{R} = \frac{(6-1)\,\text{V}}{500\,\Omega} = \frac{5}{500} = 10^{-2}\ \text{A}$$

8. (d) In the formation of p-n junction diode, potential barrier offers resistance to free electrons only in n-region and holes in p-region.

9. (a) The conductivity of an intrinsic semiconductor depends on its temperature but at room temperature, its conductivity is very low. As such, no important electronic devices can be developed using these semiconductors. Hence, there is a necessity of improving their conductivity. This can be done by making use of impurities.

10. (b) In semiconductor, no covalent bond breaks at 0 K. So, no electron is free at 0 K. At room temperature, some covalent bonds break, so some electrons and holes become free. More covalent bonds break at high temperature. So, number of free electrons increases at high temperature.

11. (a) When a system of N atoms combined, we get N levels closely packed to form an energy band or a continuous distribution of energies.

12. (c) Each sodium atom has a single 3s valence electron. Each $s(l = 0)$ atomic level can have $2(2l + 1) = 2$ electrons. So, each s-band formed by n-atoms can hold $2n$ electrons. Thus 3s band in solid sodium is only half filled by electrons and hence, fermi energy level lies in middle of the band.

13. (d) In an insulator, the forbidden energy gap between the valence band and the conduction band (E_g),

$\Rightarrow \quad E_g > 3$ eV

14. (a) As we know,

$$J = \frac{i}{A} = \frac{4.8 \times 10^{-3}}{6 \times 10^{-2} \times 4 \times 10^{-3}}$$

$= 20\ \text{A/m}^2$

$$v_d = \frac{J}{ne} = \frac{20}{10^{22} \times 1.6 \times 10^{-19}}$$

$= 12.5 \times 10^{-3}$ m/s

$$\text{Time, } t = \frac{l}{v_d} = \frac{6 \times 10^{-2}}{12.5 \times 10^{-3}} = 4.8\ \text{s}$$

15. (b) When the p-n junction is forward biased, potential barrier decreases. When it is reverse biased, potential barrier increases. 3 corresponds to forward bias of junction and 1 corresponds to reverse bias of junction.

16. (a) Intrinsic semiconductors have no impurities, resulting in low conductivity n-type semiconductors are doped with donor atoms which provide extra electrons. p-type semiconductor are doped with acceptor atoms, creating more holes. Degenerate semiconductors are heavily doped leading to a very high concentration of charge carriers.

17. (d) Both the diodes are forward biased. So, they will allow current to flow from them. No current will flow through the 12 kΩ resistance and 14 kΩ resistance.

So, $I_1 = 0$

$$I_2 = \frac{10}{2000} = 5\,\text{mA}$$

18. (b) Conductivity of a semiconductor,

$$\sigma = n_e e\mu_e + n_h e\mu_h$$

Since, semiconductor is intrinsic,

$$n_e = n_h = n_i = 1.6\times 10^6\ \text{m}^{-3}$$

$$\sigma = 1.6\times 10^6 \times 1.6\times 10^{-19} \times 0.4 + 1.6\times 10^6 \times 1.6\times 10^{-19} \times 0.2$$

$$= 1.6\times 10^6 \times 1.6\times 10^{-19}(0.4+0.2)$$

$$= 1.536\times 10^{-13}\ \Omega^{-1}\ \text{m}^{-1}$$

19. (c)

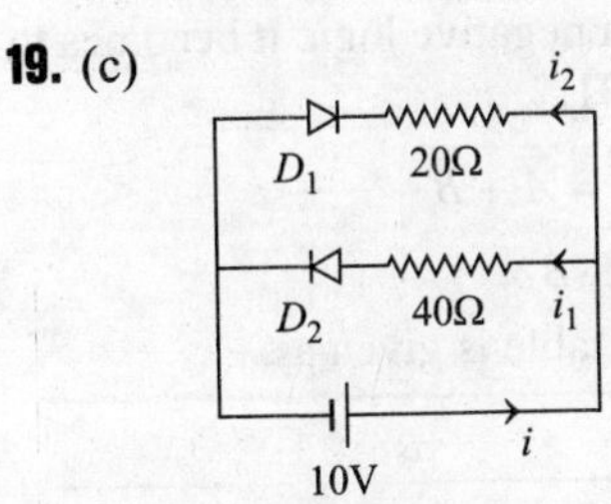

D_1 is in reverse bias, $i_2 = 0$

D_2 is in forward bias,

$$i_1 = \frac{10}{40} = 0.25\ \text{A}$$

Now, $i = i_1 + i_2$

$= 0.25 + 0 = 0.25$ A

20. (a) With increase of temperature, more electron-hole pairs are generated and so forward characteristics are more ideal. But in reverse bias region, reverse saturation current also increases with corresponding increase in reverse breakdown voltage.

So, $T_1 > T_2 > T_3$

21. (b) Option (a) is incorrect because p-n junction diode is not made by joining two different types of semiconductors, one p-type and another n-type. The p-n junction is made on a single piece of pure semiconductor by diffusing trivalent gases in one-half and pentavalent gases on another half.

Option (b) is correct, as p-n junction is formed over a single Si or Ge crystal by doping each half of crystal differently.

Option (c) is incorrect as depletion zone exists even in a p-n junction with zero bias.

Option (d) is incorrect as junction field is created by ions formed due to diffusion.

22. (b) Current density, $j = \dfrac{i}{A}$

$$= \frac{9.6\times 10^{-3}}{8\times 10^{-3} \times 12\times 10^{-2}}$$

$$= 10\ \text{A/m}^2$$

The drift speed, $v_d = \dfrac{j}{ne}$

$$= \frac{10}{10^{22} \times 1.6\times 10^{-19}}$$

$$= 6.25\times 10^{-3}\ \text{m/s}$$

23. (d) $P = Vi$

$$i = \frac{P}{V} = \frac{200\times 10^{-3}}{1} = 0.2\ \text{A}$$

Potential difference across resistor,

$V_1 = 2 - 1 = 1\text{V}$

$V_1 = iR$

$\Rightarrow 1 = 0.2R$

$\Rightarrow R = 5\Omega$

24. (a) Let V_D = potential drop across diode.

Then, V_D = 0.7 V, as diode is in forward bias.

E_1= 10 V, R_1 4.7 kΩ, V_D, R_2 2.2 kΩ, E_2= –5V

Now, current in the circuit is

$$I = \frac{E_1 - E_2 - V_D}{R_1 + R_2} = \frac{10 + 5 - 0.7}{4.7 + 2.2}$$

$$= \frac{14.3\ (\text{V})}{6.9\ (\text{k}\Omega)} \approx 2.07\ \text{mA}$$

So, potential drops across resistances are

$$V_1 = IR_1 = 2.07\times 4.7 \approx 9.74\ \text{V}$$

$$V_2 = IR_2 = 2.07\times 2.2 \approx 4.56\ \text{V}$$

Applying Kirchhoff's law in output region, we have

$$-E_2 + V_2 - V_0 = 0$$

$$\Rightarrow V_0 = 4.56 - 5$$

$$= -0.44\ \text{V}$$

25. (d) For transformer,

$$N_s \times V_p = N_p \times V_s$$

$$\Rightarrow 50\times 220 = 1000\times V_s$$

$$\Rightarrow V_s = \frac{50\times 220}{1000} = 11\,\text{V}$$

Also, $N_p \times I_p = N_s \times I_s$

$$\Rightarrow I_s = \frac{N_p \times I_p}{N_s}$$

$$= \frac{1000\times 0.25}{50}$$

$= 5\text{A} = I_{\text{rms}}$ in secondary coil.

R_L gets only half-wave supply.

$$\therefore I_{\text{av}} = \frac{I_{\max}}{\pi} = \frac{\sqrt{2}\,I_{\text{rms}}}{\pi} = \frac{\sqrt{2}}{\pi}\times 5\text{A}$$

Test-2

1. (c) If inputs are A and B, then output for NAND gate is $Y = \overline{A\cdot B}$

If $A = B = 1$

$Y = \overline{1\cdot 1} = \overline{1} = 0$

2. (a)

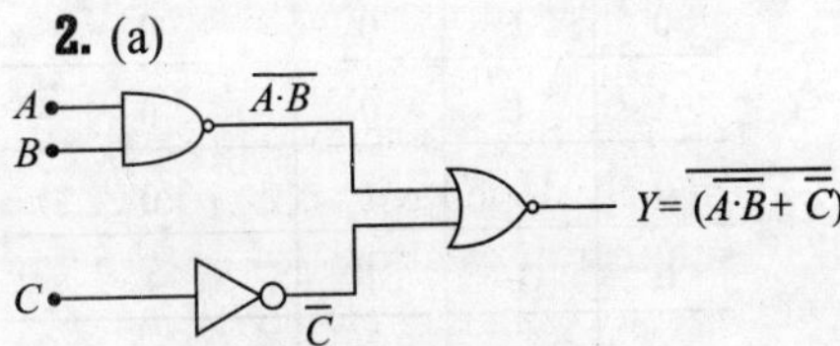

Output of the given digital circuit is

$$Y = \overline{(\overline{A\cdot B} + \overline{C})} = \overline{\overline{A\cdot B}}\cdot\overline{\overline{C}} = A\cdot B\cdot C$$

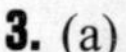

3. (a)

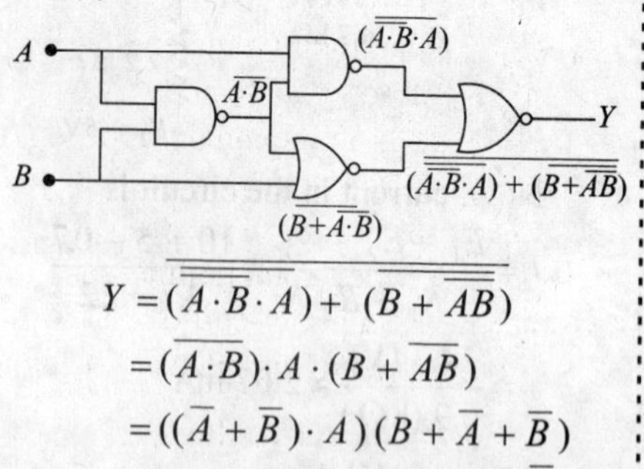

$$Y = (\overline{\overline{A \cdot B} \cdot A}) + (\overline{B + \overline{AB}})$$

$$= (\overline{A \cdot B}) \cdot A \cdot (B + \overline{AB})$$

$$= ((\overline{A} + \overline{B}) \cdot A)(B + \overline{A} + \overline{B})$$

$$[\because B + \overline{B} = 1]$$

$$= [\overline{A}A + \overline{B}A] \qquad [\therefore 1 + \overline{A} = 1]$$

$$= \overline{B}A \qquad [\therefore A\overline{A} = 0]$$

4. (a) Input (A) — Output (Y)

NOT gate is also known as inverter because it inverts the given input, also it is well establised that. If input is 1, then the output is 0 and *vice-versa*.

5. (a) It is OR gate. When input is given to either A or B (or both A and B), then an output appears across Y as the diodes are in forward bias.

6. (c) By using above circuit diagram,

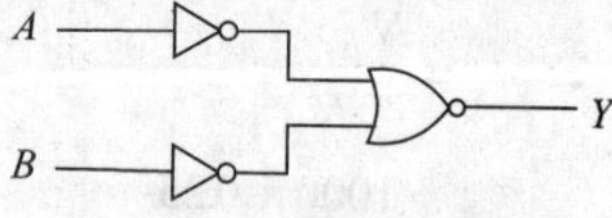

Boolean expression, $Y = \overline{\overline{A} + \overline{B}}$

According to de-Morgan's theorem,

$$Y = \overline{\overline{A} + \overline{B}} = \overline{\overline{A}} \cdot \overline{\overline{B}} = A \cdot B$$

Thus, $Y = A \cdot B$

This is the output of AND gate.

7. (b) Here, $Y = (A + B) \cdot C$

A	B	C	$Y = (A + B) \cdot C$
0	0	0	0
1	0	0	0
0	1	0	0
1	1	0	0
0	0	1	0
0	1	1	1
1	0	1	1
1	1	1	1

Therefore, $A = 1, B = 0$ and $C = 1$.

8. (a)

A. inputs 1, 1 → 0 → 0, 1 → Y

B. inputs 0, 1 → 1, 0 → 1 → Y

C. inputs 0, 1 → 1, 0 → 1 → Y

9. (a)

$C = A + B$ and $Y = \overline{A \cdot C}$

A	B	$C = A + B$	$A \cdot C$	$Y = \overline{A \cdot C}$
0	0	0	0	1
0	1	1	0	1
1	0	1	1	0
1	1	1	1	0

10. (a) A OR B is a logical function, say it is equal to X, i.e.,

$$X = A \text{ OR } B = A + B$$

Now, $D = X$ AND $B = X \cdot B$

The corresponding truth table is as under.

A	B	$X = A$ OR B	$D = (A$ OR $B)$ AND B
1	0	1	0
0	1	1	1
0	0	0	0
1	1	1	1

11. (a) According to given circuit,

$$X = \overline{\overline{A} \cdot \overline{B}}$$

$$X = \overline{\overline{A}} + \overline{\overline{B}}$$

$$X = A + B$$

which refers to OR gate.

The corresponding truth table is shown below.

A	B	$\overline{A}$	$\overline{B}$	$\overline{A} \cdot \overline{B}$	$X = (\overline{\overline{A} \cdot \overline{B}})$
0	0	1	1	1	0
0	1	1	0	0	1
1	0	0	1	0	1
1	1	0	0	0	1

12. (d) For $A = 0$ and $B = 0$ outputs given OR gates are 1.

So, outputs of 1 and 1 fed to last OR gate gives $Y = 1$.

13. (a) For upper part,

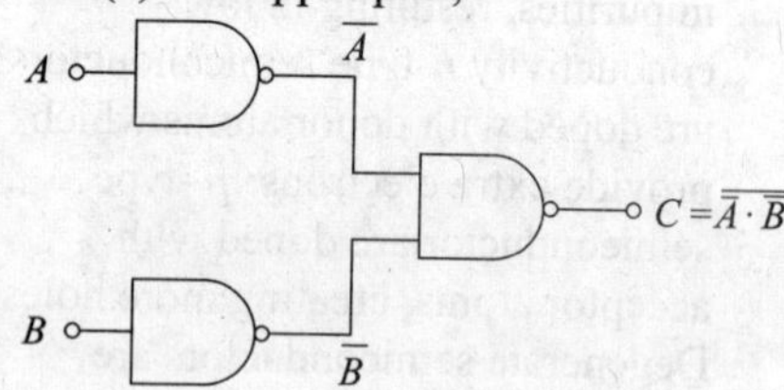

Here, $C = \overline{\overline{A} \cdot \overline{B}} = \overline{\overline{A}} + \overline{\overline{B}}$

(from de-Morgan's theorem)

$$= A + B$$

Here, output C is equivalent to OR gate.

For lower part,

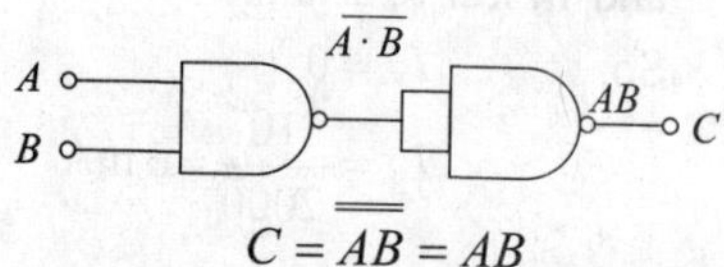

$$C = \overline{\overline{AB}} = AB$$

In this case, output C is equivalent to AND gate.

14. (c) Output of NAND gate is

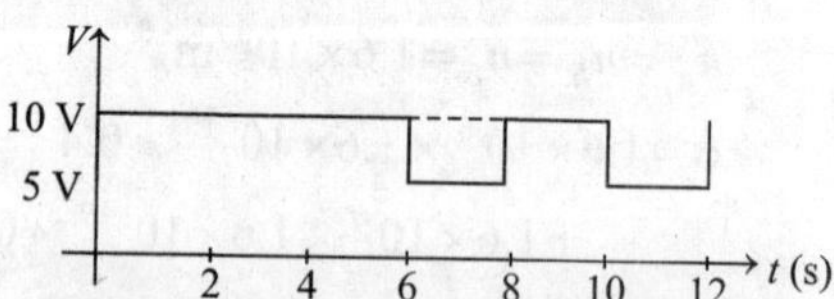

We can write this output in positive logic as 111010.

But in negative logic it becomes to 000101.

15. (d) $X = \overline{\overline{A} + \overline{B}}$

$X = A \cdot B$

Truth table is given as,

A	B	X
0	0	0
0	1	0
1	0	0
1	1	1

16. (d) An OR gate produces an output signal when any of its input signals are high (logic 1). This gate is suitable for our condition, as we want the alarm to be triggered when temperature rises above 40°C or falls below 20°C. The output of OR gate will trigger alarm.

17. (a) $Y = \overline{\overline{A} + \overline{B}} = A \cdot B$, *i.e.* it is an AND gate. For AND gate, output will be high only when both inputs are high.

Hence, option (a) is correct.

18. (d)

Truth table for above gate is

A	Y_1	Y
0	1	1
1	0	0

So, it is an inverter means NOT gate.

19. (c) When both A and B are given high potential then diodes are in reverse bias. Hence, output across Y is equals to battery voltage. It is an AND gate.

20. (b)

For OR gate, $0 + 0 \rightarrow 0$

$0 + 1 \rightarrow 1$

$1 + 0 \rightarrow 1$

$1 + 1 \rightarrow 1$

So, (ii) and (iii) are wrong.

21. (c) A digital signal has only two values of voltage variation with time. Its value is either zero or maximum (1). Hence, option (c) is correct.

22. (b) A logic gate works on a binary function. So, input must have 2 defined levels (0 and 1) which is a characteristic of a digital signal.

23. (d) From an OR gate, an output is produced, when either or both of inputs are at higher potential value. So, output waveform is

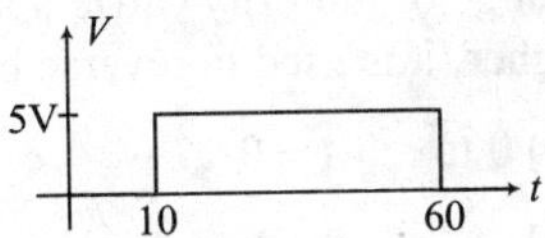

$\Rightarrow \quad V = 0$ from $t = [0, 10)$ second and $V = 5$ V from $t = [10, 60]$ second

24. (c) Waveforms of inputs are

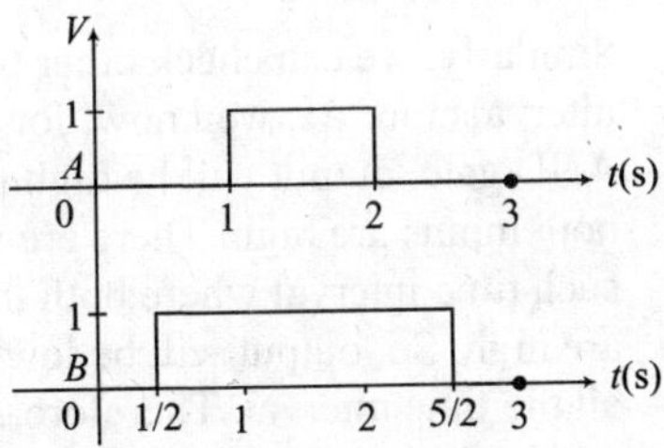

AND gate gives an output when both inputs are at higher voltage level and hence, output is

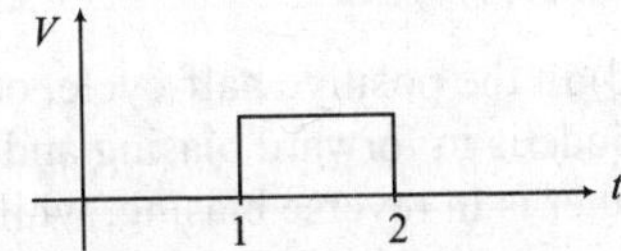

When this is fed to a NOT gate, output will be

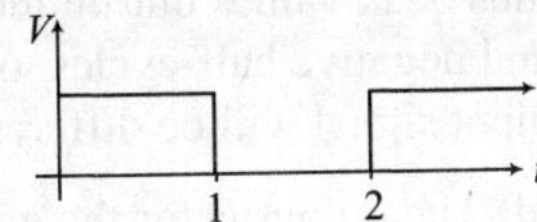

25. (a) The circuit can be redrawn as

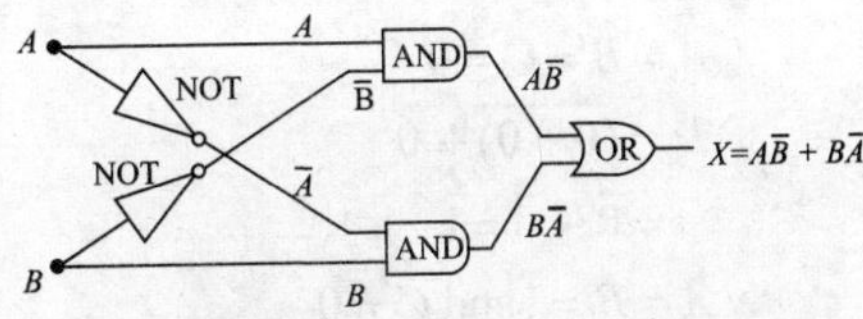

The corresponding truth table is shown below.

A	B	$\overline{A}$	$\overline{B}$	$A\overline{B}$	$B\overline{A}$	$A\overline{B} + B\overline{A} = X$
0	0	1	1	0	0	0
0	1	1	0	0	1	1
1	0	0	1	1	0	1
1	1	0	0	0	0	0

Chapter Break Thru

1. (b) When a light (wavelength sufficient to break the covalent bond) falls on the junction, new hole-electron pairs are created. Numer of produced electron hole pairs depends upon number of photons. So photo-emf or current is proportional to the intensity of light.

2. (b) A conductor facilitates the easy flow of an electron from one atom to another atom with the proper application of voltage. This is because there are no band gaps between the valence and conduction bands.

3. (b) Here, concentration of electrons,

$$n_e = 9 \times 10^{14} /\text{cm}^3$$

Concentration of holes,

$$n_h = 4 \times 10^{12} /\text{cm}^3$$

Since, concentration of electrons is greater than concentration of holes, it must be an n-type semiconductor.

4. (b) Pure germanium may be converted into an n-type semiconductor by doping with a donor impurity having 5 electrons in its outermost shell.

5. (c) Conductivity due to the breaking of covalent bond occurs in intrinsic semiconductor whereas conductivity due to breaking of covalent bond and excess of charge carriers due to impurity is occurs in extrinsic semiconductor.

6. (a) As we know, aluminium is a trivalent impurity. Trivalent impurity atoms have three valence electrons. So, to obtain p-type semiconductor, we use trivalent impurity, i.e., aluminium.

7. (a) For an electron to jump from valence band to conduction band, it needs energy equal or more than the forbidden band gap between these two bands. As the energy of band gap increases, it becomes difficult for electron to get that equivalent energy.

p-n junction dioe is a one way device. It offer a low reistance in forward bias and high reistance in reverse bias.

8. (d) Resistance in forward biasing, $R_{fr} = 10\Omega$ and resistance in reverse biasing, $R_{Rv} \cong 10^5$

Thus, $\frac{R_{fr}}{R_{Rv}} = \frac{10}{10^5} = 1:10^4$

9. (b) When a semiconductor is heated, its resistance starts to decrease with increase in temperature.

10. (d) In p - type semiconductor, holes are majority charge carriers and electrons are minority charge carriers.

11. (d) By using, $E = \frac{V}{d} = \frac{0.5}{10^{-6}}$

$= 5\times 10^5$ V/m

12. (b) By using, $E = \frac{hc}{\lambda}$

$\Rightarrow \quad \lambda = \frac{hc}{E}$

$= \frac{6.6\times 10^{-34} \times 3\times 10^8}{57\times 10^{-3} \times 1.6\times 10^{-19}}$

$= 217100$ Å

13. (b) In a p - n junction, higher potential is at n-side and lower potential is at p-side due to the concentration of doping is increased, number of charge carriers also increases.

14. (d) Photodetector is a p-n junction, it converts light intensity variation into current variation. As fractional change of minority carriers is higher, it is used in reverse bias.

15. (b) 0 to t_1, $A = 0$

and $\quad B = 1$

$\Rightarrow \quad A\cdot B = 0$

t_1 to t_2, $A = 1$

and $\quad B = 0$

$\Rightarrow \quad A\cdot B = 0$

Similarly, we can check other time intervals too. As, we know, for AND gate, output will be high if both inputs are high. There are no such time interval where both inputs are high. So, output will be low for all the time interval. Therefore, option (b) is the correct option.

16. (c) The given *p-n* junction is in reverse bias.

Hence, $i = 0$.

17. (d) In the positive half-cycle, one diode is in forward biasing and other is in reverse biasing, while in the negative half-cycle, polarity reverses. So, output is not rectified. Since, the R_1 and R_2 are different, thus peak values during the positive and negative half-cycles of the input signal will be different.

18. (d) The output D for the given combination,

$D = \overline{(A+B)\cdot C} = \overline{(A+B)} + \overline{C}$

$\because A = B = C = 0$

$\therefore D = \overline{(0+0)} + \overline{0}$

$= \overline{0} + \overline{0} = 1$

$\because A = B = 1$ and $C = 0$

$\therefore D = \overline{(1+1)} + \overline{0} = \overline{1} + \overline{0} = 1$

19. (d) This given truth table is for NAND gate. As we know, for NAND gate, output will be low only when both inputs are high.

20. (d) The truth table,

A	B	Y
1	1	0
0	0	1
0	1	1
1	0	1

It is clear from given logic circuit, that output Y is low when both the inputs are high, otherwise output is high. Thus, logic circuit is NAND gate.

21. (a) NAND gate and NOR gate are building blocks because using these gates only, we can compile all other gates also.

22. (a) An LED is a p-n junction in forward bias.

23. (c) For NAND gate, output

$= \overline{0\cdot 1} = \overline{0} = 1$

Output of NAND gate is high if either one or both inputs are low.

24. (c) A rectifier is a device which is convert AC into DC by allowing the current to flow in one direction.

A stabilizer is a device that is added to another substance to prevent retard or unwanted alternation. It is used for constant output voltage.

A transformer is a defvice that is used to transfer the electric energy from one AC circuit to another by increasing or reducing the voltage.

A filter is deive that is capable of passing a certain frequency while attenuating other frequencies in the given device.

So, A-2, B-4, C-1, d-3.

25. (a)

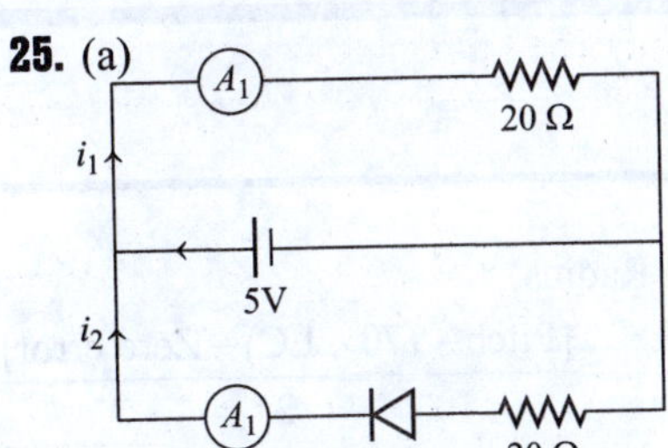

According to figure, *p-n* junction diode is in reverse bias. So, no current will flow through ammeter A_1.

$$i = 0$$

For ammeter A_2,

$$i_2 = \frac{V}{R}$$

$$i_2 = \frac{5}{20}$$

$$i_2 = 0.25\text{ A}$$

So, $i_1 = 0\text{ A},\ i_2 = 0.25\text{ A}$

26. (d) Statement I is incorrect as in a *p-n* junction or in an *n*-type semiconductor, phosphorus atoms are not isolated and there are enough free charge carriers in a semiconductor at room temperature. Last or 5th electron of pentavalent phosphorus is rotating around an ion with net +1 unit charge. Energy of this electron is nearly

$$E = -\frac{13.6}{(\varepsilon_r)^2}\text{ eV.}$$

ε_r for silicon is 12, so $E = -\ 0.1$ eV which is quite large and hence, this electron is not bounded to the core. So, ionisation is possible at room temperature.

Statement II is correct.

27. (c)

A, B, $\bar{A}$, $\bar{B}$, $\overline{\bar{A}+B}$, $\overline{A+\bar{B}}$, $X = \overline{(\bar{A}+B)} + \overline{(A+\bar{B})}$

$$X = \overline{\overline{(\bar{A}+B)} + \overline{(A+\bar{B})}}$$

$$= \overline{\overline{(\bar{A}+B)}} \cdot \overline{\overline{(A+\bar{B})}}$$

$$= (\bar{A}+B)\cdot(A+\bar{B})$$

$$= \bar{A}A + \bar{A}\bar{B} + BA + B\bar{B}$$

$$= \bar{A}\bar{B} + AB$$

Truth table for the given gate is

A	B	X
0	0	1
0	1	0
1	0	0
1	1	1

28. (c) Voltage across Zener diode remains constant.

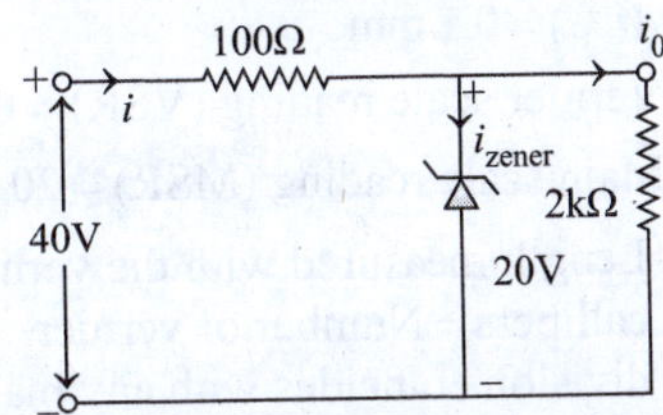

$$i_0 = \frac{20}{2\times 10^3} = 10\text{ mA}$$

$$i = \frac{40-20}{100} = \frac{1}{5}\text{ A} = 200\text{ mA}$$

$$i_{zener} = i - i_0 = 200 - 10 = 190\text{ mA}$$

29. (b) Given circuit,

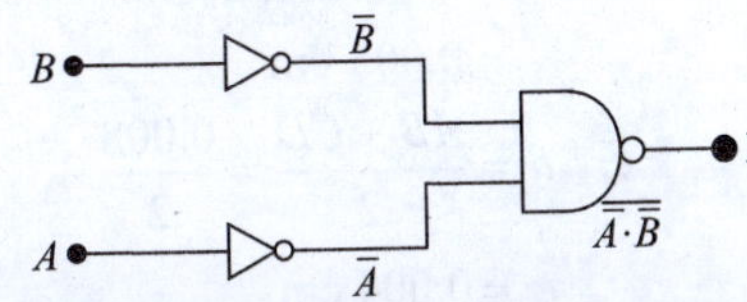

Output, $Y = \overline{\bar{A}\cdot\bar{B}} = \bar{\bar{A}} + \bar{\bar{B}} = A + B$

Corresponding truth table is shown below.

A	B	$Y = A + B$
0	0	0
0	1	1
1	0	1
1	1	1

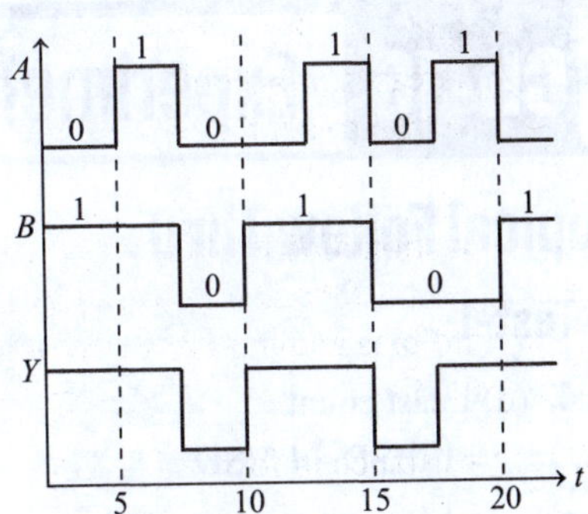

So, most appropriate option is (b).

30. (c) To calculate output, we have used truth tables of NAND and NOT gates.

NAND gate

A	B	Y
0	0	1
1	0	1
0	1	1
1	1	0

NOT gate

Y_{in}	Y_{out}
0	1
1	0

We are showing intermediate outputs on the circuit as given below.

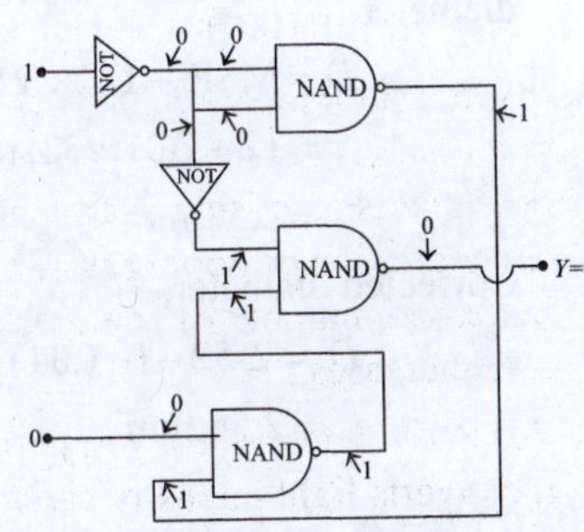

Output of above circuit at given inputs is zero.

Ch-16 Experimental Skills

Topical Follow Thru

Test-1

1. (d) Least count

$= 1\text{ MSD} - 1\text{ VSD}$

2. (a) Here, zero error is positive. So, zero correction is negative.

3. (b) Least count

$$= \frac{1\text{ MSD}}{\text{Number of divisions on vernier scale}}$$

$$= \frac{1\text{ mm}}{10} = 0.1\text{ mm}$$

4. (b) A shows positive zero error and B shows negative zero error. Zero errors are always subtracted.

$\therefore$ Correction for A is -0.4 mm and for B it is $+0.4$ mm.

5. (c) We have,

1 MSD = 1 mm

Least count = 1 MSD/Number of VSD

$= 1\text{ mm}/100 = 0.01\text{ mm}$

Zero error $= -4 \times 0.01 = -0.04$ mm

From given figure, observed diameter

$$D = \text{MSR} + \text{LC} \times \text{VSR}$$

$$= (2 + 0.01 \times 52)\text{ mm}$$

$$= 2.52\text{ mm}$$

Corrected diameter,

$$D' = 2.52 - (-0.04)$$

$$= 2.56\text{ mm}$$

6. (c) $T = 2\pi\sqrt{\dfrac{L}{g}}$

$$\Rightarrow T^2 = 4\pi^2 \frac{L}{g}$$

$$(\because \pi^2 \approx 10,\ y = mx)$$

$$\Rightarrow T^2 \approx 4\text{L}$$

$\therefore$ Slope is 4.

7. (a) We can write for balancing weight of water in a capillary tube,

$2\pi r \times T\cos\theta = \pi r^2 h\rho g$

$$\Rightarrow T = \frac{rh\rho g}{2} \quad [\because \cos\theta = 1]$$

$$= \frac{0.015 \times 10^{-2} \times 15 \times 10^{-2} \times 1000 \times 9.8}{2}$$

$$= 0.11\text{ N-m}^{-1}$$

8. (a) Given, least count (LC) = 0.1 mm

Vernier scale reading (VSR) = 0

Main scale reading (MSR) = 20 mm

Length measured with the vernier callipers = Number of vernier division coincides with any main division + Reading before the zero of vernier scale × LC

$= 20\text{ mm} + 0 \times 0.1\text{ mm} = 20\text{ mm}$

$= 2\text{ cm}$

9. (a) Here, $AB = 1.009 - 1.006$

$= 0.003$ cm

and $CD = 1.009 - 1.004$

$= 0.005$ cm

$$\therefore\ d = \frac{AB + CD}{2} = \frac{0.008}{2}$$

$$= 0.004\text{ cm}$$

$$r = \frac{d}{2} = 0.002\text{ cm}$$

10. (d) $\text{LC} = \dfrac{\text{Pitch}}{\text{Number of divisions on circular scale}}$

$$= \frac{2}{50} = 0.04\text{ mm}$$

As, zero of circular division lies 6 divisions below

Zero error $= 6 \times \text{LC} = 6 \times 0.04$

$= 0.24$ mm

Since, 1st linear scale division coincides with 70th circular scale division.

Radius,

$$r = \frac{[\text{Pitch} + (70 \times \text{LC}) - \text{Zero error}]}{2}$$

$$= \frac{2 + 70 \times 0.04 - 0.24}{2}$$

$$= 2.28\text{ mm}$$

11. (a) A concave meniscus occurs when the liquid wets the surface, resulting in a contact angle that is less than 90°.

A convex meniscus occurs when the liquid does not wet the surface, resulting in a contact angle that is greater than 90°.

If the meniscus is concave, the liquid will ascend in the capillary tube due to capillary action.

If the meniscus is convex, the liquid will descend in the capillary tube because the liquid is not strongly attracted to the tube's surface.

So, A-(iv), B-(ii), C-(i), D-(iii)

12. (d) If the length of the pendulum is large, then g is not larger and remains vertical but it will be directed towards the centre of the earth and expression of time period is given by

$$T = 2\pi\sqrt{\frac{1}{g\left(\dfrac{1}{l} + \dfrac{1}{R}\right)}}$$

where, R is the radius of the earth,

when $l \to \infty$, $\dfrac{1}{l} = 0$

$$\Rightarrow T = 2\pi\sqrt{\frac{R}{g}} = 84.6\text{ min}$$

In general, time period of a simple pendulum,

$$T = 2\pi\sqrt{\frac{l}{g}}$$

$$\Rightarrow T \propto \sqrt{l}$$

13. (c) Least count of screw gauge is much smaller than that of vernier calliper. So, screw gauge reading is more precise.

14. (a) Using, $v_T = \frac{2}{9} \cdot \frac{r^2 g}{\eta} (\rho_{ball} - \rho_{oil})$

and substituting values, we get

$$\eta = \frac{2}{9} \times \frac{(0.3)^2 \times 980}{0.5} \times 6.86$$

$$\Rightarrow \quad \eta = 268.6 \text{ g cm}^{-1} \text{ s}^{-1}$$

15. (a) Young's modulus of wire is

$$Y = \frac{\frac{W}{A}}{\frac{\Delta l}{L}}$$

From graph, $\Delta L = 2 \times 10^{-4}$ m

and $W = 40$ N

$$\text{So, } Y = \frac{\frac{40}{10^{-6}}}{\frac{2 \times 10^{-4}}{1}}$$

$$= \frac{40}{2 \times 10^{-4} \times 10^{-6}}$$

$$= 2 \times 10^{11} \text{ Nm}^{-2}$$

Test-2

1. (d) $\rho = \frac{1}{\sigma}$

$\rho \times \sigma = \text{constant}$

2. (c) A is true but R is false.

The purpose of connecting the high resistance in series with galvanometer is to protect the galvanometer from the high current i.e., high current flow through the galvanometer can damage its coil. Due to parallel resistance, total circuit resistance decreases and hence current increases.

3. (c) $\lambda = \frac{v}{f} = \frac{330}{500} = 0.66 \text{ m}$

$= 66 \text{ cm}$

Successive resonances occurs at

$\frac{\lambda}{4}, \frac{3\lambda}{4}, \frac{5\lambda}{4}, \frac{7\lambda}{4}, \ldots$

or at lengths

$\frac{66}{4}, \frac{3 \times 66}{4}, \frac{5 \times 66}{4}, \frac{7 \times 66}{4}, \ldots$

As $\frac{7 \times 66}{4}$ is more than 1.0 m, only first three resonances can occurs.

4. (c) Let,

specific heat of solid is S_s and specific heat of water is S_w

By principle of calorimetry,

$Q_{given} = Q_{used}$

$200 \times S_s \times (45° - 15°)$

$= 200 \times S_w \times (105° - 45°)$

$S_s \times 30 = S_w \times 60$

$S_s = 2 \times S_w$

$S_s =$ two times of specific heat of water

5. (c) $\frac{\theta}{i} = \frac{6}{1 \times 10^{-3}} = 6000$

$\frac{\theta}{V} = 30$

$\Rightarrow \frac{\frac{\theta}{i}}{\frac{\theta}{V}} = \frac{6000}{30}$

$\frac{V}{i} = R = 200\,\Omega$

6. (a) Both Statement I and Statement II are correct.

$v = 2f(l_2 - l_1)$

$l_2 - l_1 = \frac{v}{2f}$

It means lower frequency of tuning fork gives two resonance positions for relatively long length of air column.

So, large tube is required to obtain the two resonance positions.

7. (c) We know that, V-I curve for a linear device is a straight line passing through origin. Due to some errors/carelessness on the part of experiment all points may not come on the same line. In this situation, we draw the most appropriate curve.

From the diagram, $R = \frac{3}{3} = 1\,\Omega$.

8. (a) Heat lost by water

$= m_w s_w (T_1 - T_2)$

$= 0.30 \times 4186 \times (50 - 6.7)$

$= 54376.145$

Heat taken by ice

$= m_i L + m_i s_w (T_2 - T_0)$

$= 0.15 \times L + 0.15 \times 4186 \times (6.7 - 0)$

$= 0.15\,L + 4206.93$ J

Heat lost = Heat gain

$54376.14 = 0.15\,L + 4206.93$

$\therefore \quad L = 3.34 \times 10^5 \text{ J kg}^{-1}$

9. (a) Initially,

$\frac{R_1}{R_2} = \frac{x}{1-x}$

$\frac{12}{24} = \frac{x}{1-x}$

$\Rightarrow \quad 2x = 1 - x$

$\Rightarrow \quad x = \frac{1}{3}$

$\Rightarrow \quad x = 33.33$ cm

Finally after interchange,

$\frac{y}{1-y} = \frac{24}{12}$

$y = 2 - 2y$

$3y = 2$

$y = \frac{2}{3}$

$y = 66.66$ cm

Shifting $= y - x$

$= 66.66 - 33.33$

$= 33.33$ cm

10. (d) For full scale deflection,

$I_g = nk$

$\therefore \quad I_g = 60 \times 5 \times 10^{-4}$

$= 30 \times 10^{-3}$ A

Now, $R = \frac{V}{I_g} - G$

$= \frac{6}{30 \times 10^{-3}} - 100$

$= \frac{1000}{5} - 100$

$= 200 - 100$

$R = 100\Omega$

11. (a) Using the relation,

$R = R_0(1 + \alpha T)$

$R_1 = R_0(1 + \alpha T_1)$

$\therefore 3 = R_0(1 + 0.00145 \times 100)$ ...(i)

and $R_2 = R_0(1 + \alpha T_2)$

$\therefore 5 = R_0(1 + 0.00145 \times T_2)$ ...(ii)

On dividing Eq. (ii) by Eq. (i), we get

$$\frac{5}{3} = \frac{1 + 0.00145\,T_2}{1 + 0.00145 \times 100}$$

or $T_2 = 626.4°\text{C} \simeq 900$ K

12. (b) Initially, $I = \frac{E}{R+G} = K\theta$

$= 60 \times 10^{-6} \times 8 = 480 \times 10^{-6}$ A

$\frac{E}{R+G} = 480 \times 10^{-6}$

$\Rightarrow G = \frac{E}{480 \times 10^{-6}} - R$

$G = \frac{7.26 \times 10^6}{480} - 15 \times 10^3$

$\Rightarrow G = \frac{1}{8}$ kΩ

Finally, $\frac{I}{2} = \frac{E}{R + \frac{GS}{G+S}} \times \frac{S}{S+G}$

$\Rightarrow \frac{I}{2} = \frac{ES}{R(S+G) + GS}$

$\Rightarrow S = \frac{RG \times \frac{I}{2}}{E - \frac{(R+G)I}{2}}$

$$= \frac{15 \times 10^3 \times \frac{1}{8} \times 10^3 \times 240 \times 10^{-6}}{7.26 - \frac{7.26}{2}}$$

$\approx 124\ \Omega$

13. (b) Let S be the specific heat of aluminium.

Heat capacity of water = 1 cal/g°C

By principle of calorimetry,

$Q_{\text{given}} = Q_{\text{used}}$

$\underset{\text{(gm)}}{400} \times S \times (170° - 70°)$

$= 170 \times 1 \times (70 - 27) + \underset{\text{(gm)}}{50} \times 1 \times (70 - 27)$

$S \times 400 \times 100 = 170 \times 43 + 50 \times 43$

$S = \frac{43 \times 220}{400 \times 100}$

$S = 0.236$ cal/g°C

$S = 0.236 \times 10^3 \times 4.2$ J/kg°C

$S = 993.3$ J/kg°C

14. (d) For balanced position in a meter bridge,

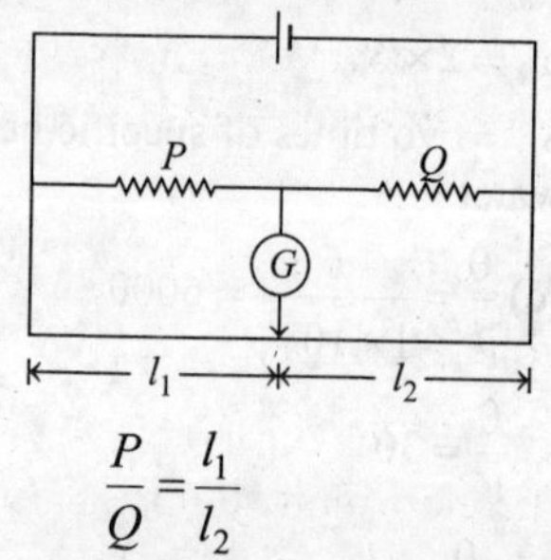

$\frac{P}{Q} = \frac{l_1}{l_2}$

Now, if position of G and cell is interchanged,

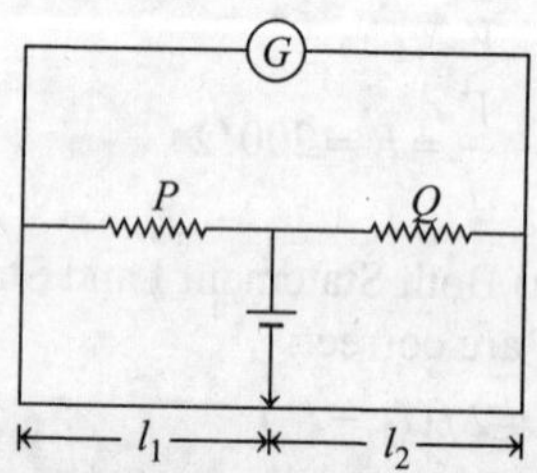

The balance condition still remains the same, if the jockey points at the same point as given in the initial condition, for which there is no deflection in the galvanometer or no current will be drawn from the cell. Thus, the bridge will work as usual and balance condition remains same, *i.e.* $\frac{P}{Q} = \frac{l_1}{l_2}$.

15. (c) Maximum percentage error in measurement of e, as given by Rayleigh's formula.

(Given, error in measurement of radius is 0.1 cm)

$e = 0.6 \times 3$

$\Delta e = 0.6 \times 0.1$

$= 0.06$ cm

Percentage error is

$\frac{\Delta e}{e} \times 100 = \frac{0.06}{0.6 \times 3} \times 100 = 3.33\%$

End correction obtained in the experiment,

$e = \frac{l_2 - 3l_1}{2}$

$= \frac{14.0 - 3 \times 4.6}{2}$

$= 0.1$ cm

So, percentage error in the calculation of e with respect to theoretical value.

Percentage error

$= \frac{0.6 \times 3 - 0.1}{0.6 \times 3} \times 100$

$= 94.44\% \simeq 94\%$

Test-3

1. (b) yellow

2. (c) Excess current is observed at 9.3 V, so breakdown must be closest to 9.3 V.

3. (a) $\mu = \frac{\sin\left(\frac{A + \delta_m}{2}\right)}{\sin\left(\frac{A}{2}\right)}$

When μ is increased, δ_m will also increase.

Hence, the deviation will also increase.

4. (a) During the experiment performed by travelling microscope of measurement of refractive index, distances are measured by vernier scale from microscope.

5. (b) Once the diode attains the breakdown voltage, then there is no change in voltage across the diode even if we change the current in circuit by changing the position of rheostat and that is why the voltage across Zener diode is constant.

6. (a) Both Statement I and Statement II are correct.

$$\because \frac{1}{f} = (\mu - 1)\left(\frac{1}{R_1} - \frac{1}{R_2}\right)$$

and $\mu \propto \frac{1}{\lambda}$

7. (a) In a prism with equal base angles, the deviation is minimum, therefore the refracted ray becomes parallel to the base of the prism. As in the case of minimum deviation, angle of incidence is equal to the angle of emergence.

8. (a) Movement of microscope = Normal shift

$$= \left(1 - \frac{1}{\mu}\right) \cdot t = \left(1 - \frac{1}{1.5}\right) \cdot 6$$

$$= \frac{6}{3} = 2 \text{ cm (upward)}$$

9. (a) The forward voltage, when current in circuit starts increasing rapidly is the knee voltage. As it is clear from the graph, current starts increasing rapidly when voltage is about 0.4 and 0.7V.

10. (c) As we observe the reverse bias data, the current remains very low ($2.0 \mu A$) for voltages upto 5.0 V, indicating the Zener diode is not in breakdown. However, when the reverse bias voltage reaches 5.5V, the current suddenly increases significantly (100.0 μA and 120.0 μA), which indicates the Zener diode has entered its breakdown region. Therefore, the reverse breakdown voltage of the Zener diode is approximately 5.3V.

11. (d) We know that, angle of prism, $A = 60°$

Angle of incidence, i = Angle of emergence e, and $e = \frac{3}{4} A$

As, $\delta = i + e - A$

$$\delta = e + e - A$$

$$\delta = 2e - A = \frac{2 \times 3}{4} A - A$$

$$\delta = \left(\frac{6-4}{4}\right) A$$

$$\delta = \frac{A}{2} = \frac{60}{2} = 30°$$

12. (b) 60 VSD = 58 MSD

$$1 \text{ VSD} = \frac{58}{60} \text{ MSD}$$

$$\text{LC} = 1 \text{ MSD} - 1 \text{ VSD}$$

$$= \left(1 - \frac{58}{60}\right) \text{MSD} = \frac{1}{30} \text{ MSD}$$

$$1 \text{ MSD} = \frac{1}{50} \text{ cm}$$

$$\text{LC} = \frac{1}{50} \times \frac{1}{30} = \frac{2}{3} \times 10^{-3} \text{ cm}$$

$$= 6.66 \times 10^{-4} \text{ cm}$$

$$\text{LC} = 6.66 \times 10^{-6} \text{ m}$$

13. (d) In convex lens, if position of object beyond $2F_1$, then size of image is diminished.

14. (c) Voltage across AB is $V_Z = 10\text{V}$

Voltage drop across R

$$= 28 - 10 = 18 \text{V}$$

Therefore, current through the resistor R_Z,

$$I = \frac{V}{R_Z} = \frac{18}{3 \times 10^3} = 6 \text{mA}$$

Voltage across load resistor,

$$= V_{AB} = 10 \text{V}$$

Current through load resistor,

$$I_L = \frac{V_{AB}}{R_L} = \frac{10}{4 \times 10^3} = 2.5 \text{ mA}$$

So, the current through the Zener diode,

$$I_Z = I - I_L = (6 - 2.5) \text{mA}$$

$$I_Z = 3.5 \text{ mA}$$

15. (b) In ideal condition, a forward biased *p-n* junction acts like a conductive path of zero resistance. So, given circuit is equivalent to circuit shown below.

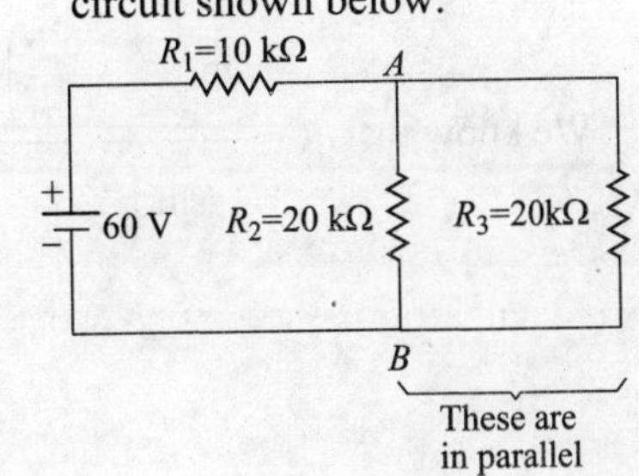

Total resistance of circuit,

$R = (R_3$ is parallel with $R_2)$ and these are in series with R_1

$$= \frac{20 \times 20}{20 + 20} + 10 = 20 \text{ k}\Omega$$

So, total current in the circuit,

$$I = \frac{V}{R} = \frac{60 \text{ V}}{20 \text{ k}\Omega}$$

$$= 3 \times 10^{-3} \text{ A}$$

So, total resistance across AB,

$$R_{AB} = 10 \text{ k}\Omega$$

$$V_{AB} = I \cdot R_{AB}$$

$$V_{AB} = 3 \times 10^{-3} \times 10 \times 10^3$$

$$V_{AB} = 30 \text{ V}$$

Chapter Break Thru

1. (a) In a meter bridge experiment when we try to obtain the null point, there are more chances of systematic or random errors due to the heating effect of electric current or fall in emf of the cell that we are using in the circuit. Hence, we always take the null point at the middle to reduce both systematic error as well as random error.

2. (a) The electrical resistance of depletion layer is large because it has no charge carriers. Depletion layer consist of mainly stationary ions.

3. (b) In an equilibrium,

$$m \times PA = M \times PB$$

$$\Rightarrow \frac{PA}{PB} = \frac{M}{m} > 1$$

Thus, $PA > PB$

4. (c) $v = 2v\,(l_2 - l_1)$

$$= 2 \times 480 \times \frac{(70 - 30)}{100}$$

(Convert cm in m)

$$= 2 \times 480 \times \frac{40}{100}$$

$$= 384 \text{ ms}^{-1}$$

5. (d) As we know,

$$v_t = \frac{2}{9} \cdot \frac{r^2 \cdot (\rho_S - \rho_F)}{\eta} \cdot g$$

$$\therefore \quad \rho = \frac{m}{v}$$

Then, $v_t = \frac{2}{9} \cdot \frac{r^2 . m}{\frac{4}{3}\pi r^3 . \eta} . g$

$$v_t \propto \frac{m}{r}$$

So, $v_t^2 \propto \frac{m^2}{r^2}$

6. (b) The least count is the smallest measurement that can be read using the Vernier calliper, which is the difference between one main scale division and one vernier scale division.

The main scale provides the primary reading in millimetres or centimetres.

Zero error is the correction needed when the zero marks of the vernier and main scales do not align when the jaws are closed.

The vernier scale provides additional decimal places to the reading from the main scale.

So, A-IV, B-I, C-III, D-II

7. (a) Cut-off voltage is the voltage applied across diode in forward bias mode to overcome the potential barrier region. Upto this, forward bias current voltage through diode is approximately zero. Thus, option (a) is correct because 0.5V is closest value.

8. (a) $\text{LC} = \frac{\text{Pitch}}{\text{Number of divisions on circular scale}}$

$$= \frac{1.0 \times 10^{-3}}{100} = 1.0 \times 10^{-5}\,\text{m} = 10\,\mu\text{m}$$

Since, circular scale is 5 units ahead of the pitch scale marking which means screw gauge has positive zero error.

9. (b) As, Young's modulus

$$Y = \frac{Fl}{A\,\Delta l}$$

Extension $\Delta l = \frac{Fl}{YA}$

$$\Delta l \propto \frac{l}{A}; \frac{\Delta l_A}{\Delta l_B} = \frac{A_B}{A_A}$$

As, $A_A > A_B$

$\therefore \quad \Delta l_B > \Delta l_A$

10. (d) Statement I is incorrect and it can be corrected as, the value of Y does not depend upon the length or the diameter of wire. It depends on nature of the material of the wire.

The Young's modulus is a measure of stiffness of the material. With rise in temperature, the length of the material increases which decreases its stiffness. Thus, we can say that with rise in the temperature the Young's modulus decreases.

11. (b) As, $T = \frac{r\left(h + \frac{r}{3}\right)\rho g}{2\cos\theta}$

$$= \frac{0.5 \times 10^{-2}\left(3 + \frac{0.5}{3}\right) \times 10^{-2} \times 10^3 \times 9.81}{2}$$

$= 0.77\ \text{Nm}^{-1}$

12. (b) We have, $\eta = \frac{2gr^2}{9v}(\rho - \sigma)$

where, η = coefficient of viscosity.

Here, $\rho = \rho_{water}$ and $\sigma = \rho_{air}$

$$= \frac{2 \times 9.81 \times (0.2 \times 10^{-2})^2 \times 999}{9 \times 8.7}$$

$= 1 \times 10^{-3}$ poise

13. (a) According to question $A = \delta_m$

We know that, $\mu = \frac{\sin\left(\frac{A + \delta_m}{2}\right)}{\sin\left(\frac{A}{2}\right)}$

We have, $\sqrt{3} = \frac{\sin\left(\frac{A + A}{2}\right)}{\sin\frac{A}{2}}$

$$\Rightarrow \sqrt{3} = \frac{\sin A}{\sin\left(\frac{A}{2}\right)} = \frac{2\sin\frac{A}{2}\cos\frac{A}{2}}{\sin\frac{A}{2}}$$

$$\therefore \cos\frac{A}{2} = \frac{\sqrt{3}}{2}$$

$$\therefore \frac{A}{2} = 30^\circ$$

or $\quad A = 60^\circ$

14. (d) Consider w is the weight of meter scale.

$$(5 \times 50) + w \times 10 = 20 \times 40$$

$$250 + 10w = 800$$

$$10w = 550$$

$$w = 55\,\text{gf}$$

15. (a) From the expression,

$$\eta = \frac{2r^2(\rho_{steel} - \rho_{glycerine})}{9 \times v} \times g$$

where, v is terminal speed.

Here, $v = \frac{0.2}{1.8}\ \text{ms}^{-1}$

$$\therefore \eta = \frac{2 \times (0.25 \times 10^{-2})^2 \times (7.8 - 1.26) \times 10^3 \times 9.81}{9 \times \frac{0.2}{1.8}}$$

$= 0.802\ \text{N-sm}^{-2}$

16. (c) Statement I is correct but Statement II is incorrect. Charging current does not damage the coil of heater.

17. (b) Volume remains same.

So, $Al = A'(2l)$

$$A' = \frac{A}{2}, R_i = \frac{\rho l}{A}$$

$$R_f = \frac{\rho \cdot 2l}{\left(\frac{A}{2}\right)}$$

$R_f = 4R_i$

Percentage change

$= \frac{4R_i - R_i}{R_i} \times 100\%$

$= 300\%$

18. (b) The intermolecular forces present in solids and liquids are stronger than that in gases. This cause the specific heat capacity of solids to be more than other forms of matter.

19. (d) $\mu = \frac{\sin \frac{(A + \delta_m)}{2}}{\sin \frac{A}{2}}$

$= \frac{\sin \frac{(60+30)}{2}}{\sin\left(\frac{60}{2}\right)}$

$= \frac{\sin 45°}{\sin 30°} = \frac{0.7070}{0.5000} = 1.414$

Now, velocity of light in glass

$= \frac{c_{air}}{\mu}$

$\Rightarrow c_g = \frac{3 \times 10^8}{1.414}$

$= 2.121 \times 10^8$ m/s

20. (d) Write KVL equation,

$-V_{BA} + IR + V_Z = 0$

[As diode is operating in breakdown region]

$\Rightarrow IR = V_{BA} - V_Z = 8 - 7$

or, $I = \frac{1\text{V}}{10\,\text{k}\Omega} = 100\,\mu\text{A}$

21. (a) Time period,

$T = 2\pi\sqrt{\frac{L}{g}}$

where, L is pendulum length and g is the acceleration due to gravity.

Also, $T^2 = 4\pi^2 \frac{L}{g}$

$g = 4\pi^2 \frac{L}{T^2}$

% error in g,

$\frac{\Delta g}{g} \times 100 = \frac{\Delta L}{L} \times 100 + \frac{2\Delta T}{T} \times 100$

$E_1 = \left(\frac{0.1}{50} + \frac{2 \times 0.1}{95}\right) \times 100$

$= 0.410\%$

$E_2 = \left(\frac{0.1}{55} + \frac{2 \times 0.1}{80}\right) \times 100$

$= 0.431\%$

$E_3 = \left(\frac{0.1}{70} + \frac{2 \times 0.1}{85}\right) \times 100$

$= 0.378\%$

So, E_3 is minimum.

So, minimum percentage error is obtained by student number 3.

22. (d) From 1,

$X = 1000 \times \frac{100 - 60}{60} = 666.67\,\Omega$

From 2,

$X = 100 \times \frac{100 - 13}{13} = 669.23\,\Omega$

From 3,

$X = 10 \times \frac{100 - 1.5}{1.5} = 656.66\,\Omega$

From 4,

$X = 1 \times \frac{100 - 1}{1} = 99\,\Omega$

4th reading is far away from other reading, so most probably it would be wrong.

23. (a) For minimum deviation

$\delta_{min} = A$,

Then, $2A = i + e$

In case of δ_{min},

$i = e$

So, $2A = 2i$,

$i = A$

$r_1 = r_2 = \frac{A}{2}$

From Snell's law

$\sin i = n \sin r_1$

$\sin A = n \sin \frac{A}{2}$

$\left(\therefore \sin\theta = 2\sin\frac{\theta}{2} \cdot \cos\frac{\theta}{2}\right)$

$2\sin\frac{A}{2} \cdot \cos\frac{A}{2} = n \sin\frac{A}{2}$

$\Rightarrow 2\cos\frac{A}{2} = n$

When, $A = 90°$

$n_{min} = \sqrt{2}$,

When $A = 0, n_{max} = 2$

24. (c) Balance is not affected by interchanging cell and galvanometer.

25. (c)

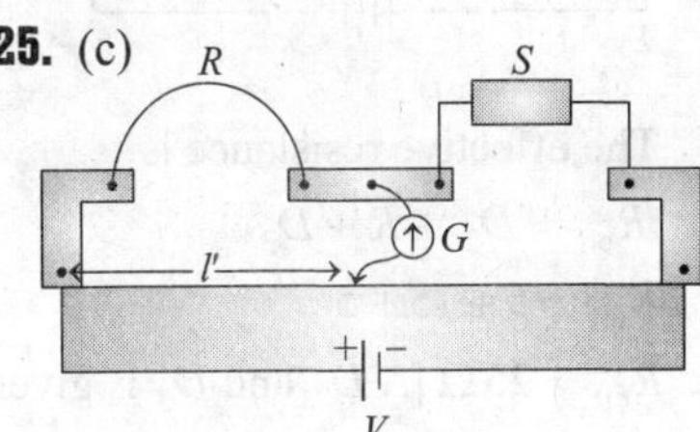

Given, balance length, $l = 40$ cm

At balance point, $\frac{R}{l} = \frac{S}{100 - l}$

$\Rightarrow \frac{R}{40} = \frac{S}{60}$

$\Rightarrow R = \frac{2S}{3}\,\Omega$ ...(i)

When R is replaced by some other resistance of half length and half diameter, then resistance in left gap,

$R' = \frac{\rho \frac{l}{2}}{\pi\left(\frac{d}{2}\right)^2}$

$= 2\left\{\frac{\rho l}{(\pi d^2)}\right\}$

$\Rightarrow R' = 2R$

Now, if balance is obtained at length l', then

$\frac{R'}{l'} = \frac{S}{(100 - l')}$

$\Rightarrow \frac{2R}{l'} = \frac{S}{100 - l'}$

Substituting the value of S from Eq. (i), we get

$\frac{2R}{l'} = \frac{3R}{(100 - l') \times 2}$

$\Rightarrow 400 - 4l' = 3l'$

or $l' = 57.14 \approx 57$ cm

26. (a) In the given circuit, D_2 and D_3 are in forward bias, so they conduct current while D_1 and D_4 are in reverse bias, so they do not conduct current. So, the equivalent circuit will be

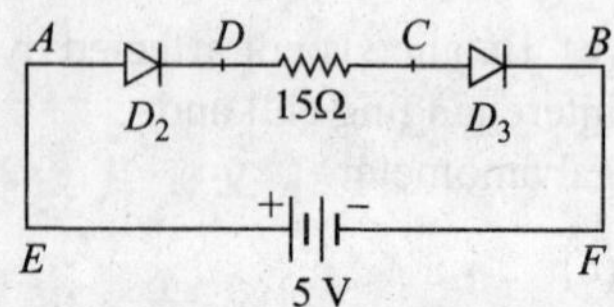

The effective resistance is

$R_{eff} = D_2 + R + D_3$

$R_{eff} = 5 + 15 + 5$

$R_{eff} = 25\Omega$ [$\because D_2$ and D_3 is given]

Here, silicon diodes are used.

$\therefore$ Barrier potential for Si is 0.7 V.

Net potential $(V_{net}) = 5 - 0.7 - 0.7$

$V_{net} = 3.6$ V

$\therefore$ Current $(I) = \dfrac{V_{net}}{R_{eff}}$

$I = \dfrac{3.6}{25}$

$\Rightarrow \quad I = 0.144$ A

27. (b) Maximum error in mass

$\left(\dfrac{\Delta m}{m}\right) = 4\% = \dfrac{4}{100}$

and maximum error in length

$\left(\dfrac{\Delta m}{m}\right) = 3\% = \dfrac{3}{100}$

Maximum error in the measurement of density.

$\dfrac{\Delta\rho}{\rho} = \dfrac{\Delta m}{m} + \left(3 \times \dfrac{\Delta l}{l}\right)$

$= \dfrac{4}{100} + 3 \times \dfrac{3}{100} = \dfrac{13}{100}$

$\dfrac{\Delta\rho}{\rho} = 13\%$

28. (a) Given,

$r = 0.4 \text{ mm} = 4 \times 10^{-4}$ m

$s = 0.55$ N/m

So, Area of 64 droplets $= 64\,(4\pi r^2)$

$= 256\pi r^2$

When drops combine, volume remains constant.

$\dfrac{4}{3}\pi R^3 = 64 \times \dfrac{4}{3}\pi r^3$

$R = 4r$

Area of big drop $= 4\pi R^2$

$= 4\pi(4r)^2$

$= 64\pi r^2$

Loss of surface area

$= 256\pi r^2 - 64\pi r^2$

$= 192\pi r^2$

$\therefore$ Loss of energy = Loss of surface area × Surface tension

$= 192 \times 3.14 \times (4 \times 10^{-4})^2 \times 0.55$

$= 5305.34 \times 10^{-8}$

$= 53.05 \times 10^{-6}$

So, loss of energy

$= 53.05\ \mu$J

29. (b) The value of Zener voltage is higher for silicon than germanium for same density of impurity atoms because reverse voltage for Si is higher than for Ge.

30. (d) Least count

$= \dfrac{\text{Value of 1 main scale division}}{\text{No. of divisions on vernier scale}}$

Here, n vernier scale divisions $= (n-1)$ main scale divisions

$1 \text{ VSD} = \dfrac{n-1}{n}$ MSD

So, LC = 1 MSD − 1 VSD

$\text{LC} = 1 \text{ MSD} - \left(\dfrac{n-1}{n}\right)\text{MSD}$

$\text{LC} = \dfrac{1 \text{ MSD}}{n}$

$\text{LC} = \dfrac{0.3°}{45}$

$\text{LC} = \dfrac{1}{150°}$

SPT1 Syllabus Part Thru 1

1. (b) If the pole strength, magnetic moment and length of each part are m', M' and L' respectively, then initially magnetic moment,

$M = m \times l$

S	N
S	N

$m' = \dfrac{m}{2}$

$L' = L$

So, $M' = m' \times L'$

$= m \times \dfrac{L}{2}$

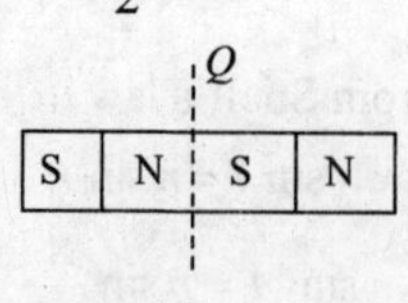

$M' = \dfrac{M}{2}$

So, all four pieces have same magnetic moment that is $\dfrac{M}{2}$.

2. (b) $V_B - V_A = \dfrac{W_{AB}}{q_0}$

$V - (-20) = \dfrac{200}{10}$

$V = 20 - 20 = 0$

3. (c) This can be achieved by connecting three in series and remaining one in parallel.

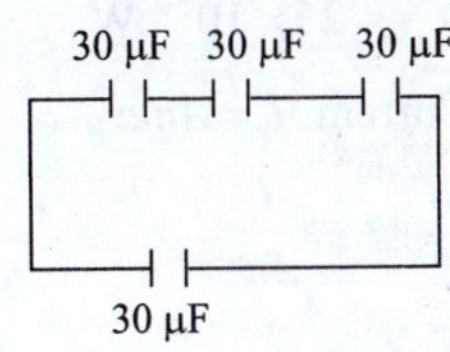

$$C_{eq} = \frac{30}{3} + 30$$
$$= 10 + 30 = 40\,\mu F$$

4. (b) Potential is constant on the surface of a sphere, so it behaves as an equipotential surface.

5. (a) Potential difference across 6Ω = Potential difference across 3Ω

$$6 \times 0.5 = 3 \times I_Z$$
$$3 = 3I_Z$$
$$I_Z = 1\,\text{A}$$

Current through $X, I_X = I_Y + I_Z$

$$I_X = 0.5 + 1$$
$$= 1.5\,\text{A}$$

6. (b) When all bulbs are working,

$$V = IR_{eq}$$
$$R_{eq} = \frac{R}{2} + R$$
$$= \frac{3R}{2}$$
$$I_{eq} = \frac{2V}{3R}$$

Current across B_2

$$I_2 = \frac{2V}{3R} \times \frac{1}{2} = \frac{V}{3R}$$

When bulb B_3 is fused,

$$R'_{eq} = 2R$$

Resistance increases.

$$I'_{eq} = \frac{V}{2R}$$

Current across $B_2, I'_2 = \dfrac{V}{2R}$

[∵ B_2 is connected in series with B_1]

∴Brightness across bulb B_1 decreases while brightness across bulb B_2 increases.

7. (d) Galvanometer resistance,

$$G = \frac{S_V}{S_i} = \frac{\frac{150}{2}\,\text{mV}}{\frac{150}{10}\,\text{mA}} = 5\,\Omega$$

Full scale deflection voltage

$$= 1 \times 150 = 150\,\text{V}$$

Now, for voltmeter,

$$V = I_g(R + G)$$
$$\Rightarrow 150 = (15 \times 10^{-3})(R + 5)$$
$$\Rightarrow \quad R = 10000 - 5$$
$$= 9995\,\Omega$$

8. (a) Induced emf, $e = \dfrac{-LdI}{dt}$

$$= -5 \times 10^{-3} \times (-10^3)$$
$$= 5\,\text{V}$$
$$V_A - 2I + 20 + 5 = V_B$$
$$V_A - 20 + 20 + 5 = V_B$$
$$V_B - V_A = 5\,\text{V}$$

9. (a) Heat produced by AC = 4 × Heat produced by DC

$$I^2_{rms}Rt = 4I^2Rt$$
$$I^2_{rms} = 4I^2 = 4 \times 4 \times 4$$
$$I_{rms} = \sqrt{64} = 8\,\text{A}$$

10. (a) Current across inductor,

$$i_L = 0.8\,\text{A}$$

Current across capacitor, $i_C = 0.4$ A

$$i_R = i_L - i_C$$
$$= 0.8 - 0.4$$
$$= 0.4\,\text{A}$$

11. (d) As we know,

$$M = K\sqrt{L_1 L_2}$$

For tight coupling, $K = 1$

$$M_{max} = \sqrt{4 \times 36} = \sqrt{144}$$
$$= 12\,\text{mH}$$

12. (b) The rotation of loop by 30° about an axis perpendicular to its plane makes no change in the angle made by magnetic moment with the direction of magnetic field. Therefore, the workdone to rotate the loop is zero.

13. (a) $V' = \dfrac{V}{3} \Rightarrow \dfrac{V}{k} = \dfrac{V}{3} \Rightarrow k = 3$

14. (c) We have,

$$\mathbf{H} = nI = \frac{N}{l} \cdot I$$
$$= \frac{100}{0.2} \times 5.2$$
$$= 2600\,\text{A/m}$$

15. (d) $T = 2\pi\sqrt{\dfrac{I}{MB}}$

and $T' = 2\pi\sqrt{\dfrac{I \times 100}{81 \times MB}} = \dfrac{10}{9}T$

$$\text{Percentage increase} = \frac{\frac{10}{9} - 1}{1} \times 100$$
$$= \frac{1}{9} \times 100 \simeq 11\%$$

16. (b) $N_S > N_P$, voltage is stepped up. This is step-up transformer.

$$\frac{V_S}{V_P} = \frac{N_S}{N_P} = \frac{I_P}{I_S}$$
$$\frac{3000}{1000} = \frac{I_P}{8}$$
$$I_P = 24\,\text{A}$$
$$\frac{V_S}{V_P} = \frac{3000}{1000}$$
$$\frac{200}{V_P} = 3$$
$$V_P = \frac{200}{3}$$

17. (b) According to Lenz's law, the direction of induced current in the loop will be clockwise because the induced current makes the ring to behave as south pole which opposes the south pole of moving magnet.

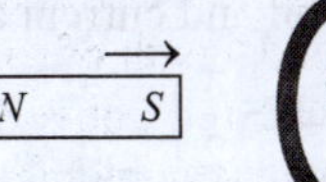

18. (d) $\mathbf{B} = B_0(2\hat{\mathbf{i}} + 3\hat{\mathbf{j}} - 8\hat{\mathbf{k}})$

$$B_y = 3B_0$$

Area of square $= a^2$

Magnetic flux, $\phi_B = B \cdot A$

$$= B_0(2\hat{\mathbf{i}} + 3\hat{\mathbf{j}} - 8\hat{\mathbf{k}}) \cdot a^2\hat{\mathbf{j}} = 3B_0a^2$$

19. (a) In configurations AB_1 and AB_2, the system is not in equilibrium because $m_B \perp B$.
In configurations AB_3 and AB_6, the system is in stable equilibrium because $m_B \| B$.
In configurations AB_4 and AB_5, the system is in unstable equilibrium because m_B is anti-parallel to B.

20. (c) Magnetic moment at point P,

$$m_{net} = \sqrt{m^2 + m^2 + m \cdot m \cos 90°}$$

$$= \sqrt{2m^2} = \sqrt{2}m$$

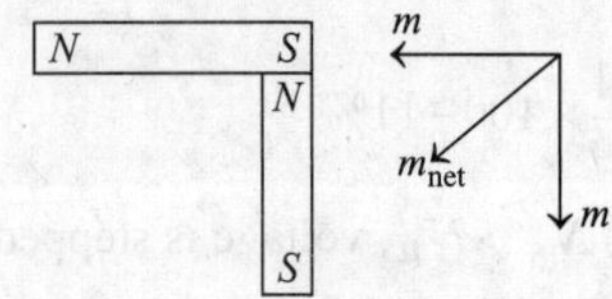

Magnetic field at P is axial, for net magnetic moment,

$$B_p = \frac{\mu_0(2m_{net})}{4\pi d^2}$$

$$= \frac{2\mu_0\sqrt{2}m}{4\pi d^2} = \frac{2\sqrt{2}\mu_0 m}{4\pi d^2}$$

21. (a) $F = q(\mathbf{v} \times \mathbf{B})$, $q = -e$

$\mathbf{B} = B\hat{\mathbf{j}}$ $\mathbf{v} = -v\hat{\mathbf{i}}$

$\mathbf{F} = -e(-v\hat{\mathbf{i}} \times B\hat{\mathbf{j}})$

$\mathbf{F} = evB\hat{\mathbf{k}}$

As force on directions is towards the face $ABCD$, the electrons will accumulate on it. Hence, it will acquire lower potential.

22. (a) When pure inductor is connected to source of an alternating emf, then instantaneous emf is given as $E = E_0 \sin \omega t$ and current as

$$I = I_0 \sin\left(\omega t - \frac{\pi}{2}\right)$$

Hence, alternating current lags behind the emf by a phase angle of $\pi/2$.

$\therefore$ Statement I is correct.

$$X_L = \omega L = 2\pi f L$$

$\therefore$Statement II is also correct.

23. (c) $R = \frac{V^2_{rated}}{P_{rated}}$

$$R_1 = \frac{(120)^2}{60} = 240\,\Omega$$

$$R_2 = \frac{(120)^2}{100} = 144\,\Omega$$

$$R_2 < R_1$$

So, Reason is incorrect.

24. (c) Distance, $d = 150$ km

Fall of potential per km,

$$V = 8\text{ V}$$

Average resistance per km,

$$R = 0.5\Omega$$

Power loss per km,

$$P_1 = \frac{V^2}{R} = \frac{8^2}{0.5} = 128\text{ W}$$

$\therefore$ Total power loss,

$$P = P_1 \times d$$
$$= 128 \times 150$$
$$= 19.2\text{ kW}$$

25. (b)

Circuit: E, i, $r = 0.2\Omega$, $V = E - ir$, $R = 4.8\Omega$

Current, $i = \frac{E}{R + r}$

$$V = E - \left(\frac{E}{R + r}\right)r$$

$$= 4 - \left(\frac{4}{0.2 + 4.8}\right) \times 0.2$$

$$= 4 - \frac{4}{5} \times 0.2$$

$$= 3.84\text{ V}$$

26. (d) Power dissipated by resistor,

$$P = I^2R$$

$$36 = (3 \times 10^{-3})^2 R$$

$$R = \frac{36}{9 \times 10^{-6}} = 4 \times 10^6\ \Omega$$

When this resistor is connected to power supply of 10 V, then power dissipated will be

$$P = \frac{V^2}{R} = \frac{10 \times 10}{4 \times 10^6}$$

$$= 25 \times 10^{-6}\text{ W}$$

27. (c) $\because$ Current, $I = Anev_d$

$$v_d = \frac{I}{Ane}$$

$$v_d \propto \frac{I}{r^2} \quad [\because A = \pi r^2]$$

Initially, $v_d \propto \frac{I}{r^2}$

$$v_d' \propto \frac{2I}{(2r)^2} \propto \frac{2I}{4r^2}$$

$$\Rightarrow v_d' \propto \frac{I}{2r^2}$$

$$v_d' = \frac{v}{2}$$

28. (c) Potential,

$$V = E_0\left(\frac{1}{3}d\right) + \frac{E_0}{K}\left(\frac{2}{3}d\right)$$

$$= E_0 d\left(\frac{1}{3} + \frac{2}{3K}\right)$$

$$V = V_0\left(\frac{K + 2}{3K}\right)$$

where, $V_0 = E_0 d$

and capacitance,

$$C = \frac{Q}{V} = \frac{Q(3K)}{(K + 2)V_0}$$

Using, $C_0 = \frac{Q}{V_0} = \frac{3KC_0}{(K + 2)}$

29. (b) Part of charge q inside the cube is $\frac{q}{4}$.

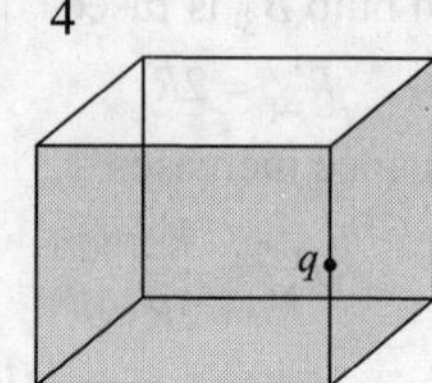

Total flux through cube is $\frac{q}{4\varepsilon_0}$.

It will be shared by only 4 faces, so flux through each of the faces is

$$= \frac{1}{4} \times \frac{q}{4\varepsilon_0} = \frac{q}{16\varepsilon_0}$$

30. (a) Electric field due to charges present at points P and R cancel each other.

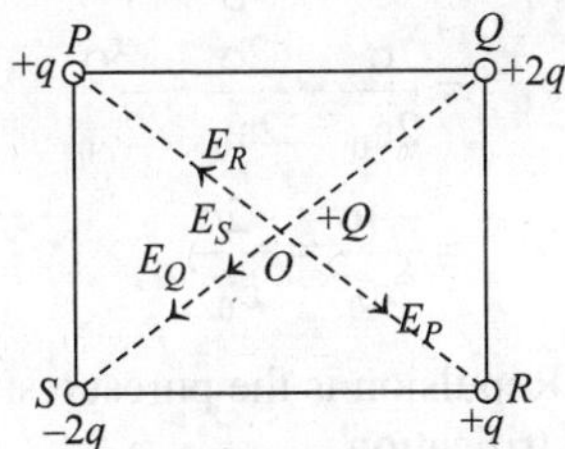

Electric field due to charges present at points Q and S are in the direction along QS.

31. (d) Changes A and B do not produce any change of magnetic flux linked with coil. So, no emf is induced in case A or B.

32. (c) To find position where E is maximum,

$$\frac{dE}{dy}=0$$

$$\Rightarrow \frac{d}{dy}\left[\frac{y}{(d^2+y^2)^{3/2}}\right]=0$$

$$\Rightarrow (d^2+y^2)^{-3/2}$$

$$-3y^2(d^2+y^2)^{-\frac{5}{2}}=0$$

On solving, we get

$$2y^2=d^2,\ y^2=\frac{d^2}{2}$$

$$y=\frac{d}{\sqrt{2}}$$

33. (c) Intensity, $I=\frac{\text{Energy}}{\text{Area}\times\text{Time}}$

$$=\frac{\text{Power}}{\text{Area}}=U_{av}=\frac{1}{2}c\varepsilon_0E_0^2$$

$$P\propto E_0^2$$

$$\frac{P_1}{P_2}=\frac{E_1^2}{E_2^2},\quad \frac{E_1}{E_2}=\sqrt{\frac{P_1}{P_2}}$$

$$\frac{E_1}{E_2}=\sqrt{\frac{200}{100}},\ E_2=\sqrt{\frac{10}{20}}E$$

$\therefore\ X=10$

34. (d) Power delivered to the capacitor per cycle is

$$P=I_mV_m\cos\theta$$

In capacitor, $\theta=90°$

$$P=I_mV_m\cos 90°=0$$

Charge on the plate is in phase with applied voltage.

$$V_{\text{rms}}=220\text{ V}$$

$$V_P=\sqrt{2}\times V_{\text{rms}}=311.13\text{ V}$$

Current and voltage have a phase difference of $\frac{\pi}{2}$. So, current is not in phase with applied voltage.

35. (b) $a=4$ cm, $b=400$ cm

$$b>>a$$

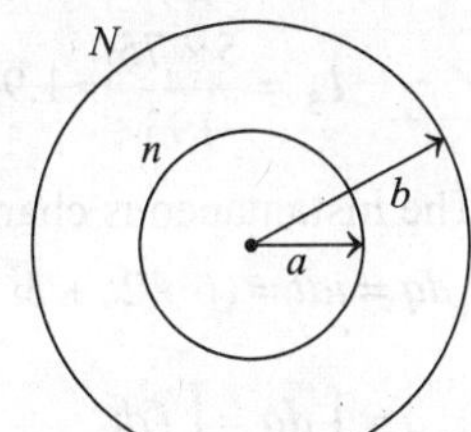

Take larger coil as primary $B=\frac{\mu_0 i_P N}{2b}$

Flux passing through secondary coil,

$$\phi_S=BA=\frac{\mu_0 i_P N}{2b}\times\pi a^2\times n$$

$$M=\frac{\phi_S}{i_P}$$

$$=\frac{\mu_0 Nn\pi a^2}{2b}$$

$$=\frac{4\pi\times10^{-7}\times100\times10\times\pi\times4^2\times10^{-4}}{2\times400\times10^{-2}}$$

$$=789\times10^{-9}\text{ H}$$

36. (a) Radius of coil,

$$r=\frac{0.04}{2}=0.02\text{ m}$$

$$B_1=4000\text{ T}$$

$$B_2=2000\text{ T},\ t=2\text{ s}$$

$$E=10\text{ V}$$

$$|E|=N\frac{(\phi_2-\phi_1)}{t}=NA\frac{(B_2-B_1)}{t}$$

$$=N\cdot\pi r^2\cdot\frac{(B_2-B_1)}{t}$$

$$10=N\times\frac{22}{7}\times(0.02)^2\frac{(2000)}{2}$$

$$N=\frac{10\times7\times2}{22\times(0.02)^2\times2000}$$

$$N\simeq8$$

37. (c) Let the magnetic moment of two magnets be M_1 and M_2.

Time period, $T=2\pi\sqrt{\frac{I}{MB}}$

$$T\propto\frac{1}{\sqrt{M}}$$

Net magnetic moment,

$$M'=M_1+M_2$$

After reversing polarity, net magnetic moment,

$$M''=M_1-M_2$$

Therefore,

$$\frac{T_1}{T_2}=\sqrt{\frac{M_1-M_2}{M_1+M_2}}$$

$$\left(\frac{8}{16}\right)^2=\frac{M_1-M_2}{M_1+M_2}$$

$$\frac{1}{4}=\frac{\frac{M_1}{M_2}-1}{\frac{M_1}{M_2}+1}$$

$$\frac{M_1}{M_2}+1=4\frac{M_1}{M_2}-4$$

$$5=\frac{3M_1}{M_2}\Rightarrow\frac{M_1}{M_2}=\frac{5}{3}$$

38. (d) Given, $B=0.168$ T

$$r=0.01\text{ m}$$

$$I=2\text{ A}$$

$$B=\mu_0 nI$$

$$B=\mu_0\frac{N}{l}\times I$$

$$N=\frac{Bl}{\mu_0 I}$$

$$L=N\times2\pi r=\frac{Bl\times2\pi r}{\mu_0 I}$$

$$=\frac{0.168\times1.4\times2\pi\times0.01}{4\pi\times10^{-7}\times2}$$

$$L=5880\text{ m}$$

39. (a) When jockey is at D, the current does not flow through galvanometer. So, potential at B and D are equal. Potentials at different points on the wire are different. The point D is unique to get null point.
$\therefore$ Statement I is correct.
When jockey is shifted to right of D, potential at D becomes smaller than at B, i.e. $V_B > V_D$. So, current flows from B to D in wire. So, Statement III is correct.
When R is increased, potential drop across R increases.
So, potential at B increases to get null point, the jockey must move to right. So, Statement IV is incorrect.

40. (b) Since, potential difference between B and D is zero, so

$$\frac{R_{AB}}{R_{BC}} = \frac{R_{AD}}{R_{CD}}$$

(using Wheatstone bridge)

$$\Rightarrow \frac{21}{\left(\frac{8x}{8+x}+3\right)} = \frac{15+3}{4+2}$$

$$\Rightarrow \frac{21}{\left[\frac{8x+24+3x}{8+x}\right]} = \frac{18}{6}$$

$$\Rightarrow 7 = \frac{8x+24+3x}{8+x}$$

$$\Rightarrow 56+7x = 11x+24$$

$$\Rightarrow 11x-7x = 56-24$$

$$\Rightarrow 4x = 32$$

$$\Rightarrow x = 8\,\Omega$$

41. (c) Let R_1, R_2 and R_3 be resistances of the wires.

$$R_1 : R_2 : R_3 = \frac{l_1}{r_1^2} : \frac{l_2}{r_2^2} : \frac{l_3}{r_3^2}$$

$$= \frac{2}{9} : \frac{3}{16} : \frac{4}{25}$$

As, $V = IR$ (Ohm's law)

$$\therefore \quad I \propto \frac{1}{R}$$

$$\Rightarrow I_1 : I_2 : I_3 = \frac{9}{2} : \frac{16}{3} : \frac{25}{4}$$

$$= 54 : 64 : 75$$

$$I_1 = \frac{5 \times 54}{193} = 1.4\text{ A}$$

$$I_2 = \frac{5 \times 64}{193} = 1.66\text{ A}$$

$$I_3 = \frac{5 \times 75}{193} = 1.94\text{ A}$$

42. (a) The instantaneous charge,

$$dq = i\,dt = (6+2t+3t^2)\,dt$$

$$q = \int dq = \int i\,dt$$

$$q = \int_2^4 (6+2t+3t^2)\,dt$$

$$q = 6t + \frac{2t^2}{2} + \frac{3t^3}{3}\Big|_2^4$$

$$= 6t + t^2 + t^3\Big|_2^4$$

$$= 6(4-2) + (4^2-2^2) + (4^3-2^3)$$

$$= 80\text{ C}$$

43. (a)

σ, −2σ, 3σ; regions I, II, III, IV

Electric field in region II,

$$= \frac{\sigma}{2\varepsilon_0} + \frac{2\sigma}{2\varepsilon_0} - \frac{3\sigma}{2\varepsilon_0} = 0$$

Electric field in region III,

$$= \frac{\sigma}{2\varepsilon_0} - \frac{2\sigma}{2\varepsilon_0} - \frac{3\sigma}{2\varepsilon_0}$$

$$= \frac{-4\sigma}{2\varepsilon_0} = \frac{-2\sigma}{\varepsilon_0}$$

44. (c) Repulsion is the purest test of electrification.
So, balls B, C, D, E are electrically charged (B and C) and (D and E) are similarly charged. A and B are oppositely charged. If ball (B, C) are positively charged, then (D, E) are negatively charged or *vice-versa*. The ball A is attracted both by B and D, i.e. by both kinds of charges. Hence, the ball A is neutral.

45. (a) As the sliding contact is being pulled, the current in the circuit changes.

Induced emf, $e = \frac{-LdI}{dt}$

Net emf, $E_{\text{net}} = 6\text{ V} - \frac{LdI}{dt}$

Current, $I = \frac{E_{\text{net}}}{R} = \frac{6 - \frac{LdI}{dt}}{12}$

As resistance increases, current will decrease.

So, $\frac{dI}{dt}$ = negative

$$I = \frac{6 + L\frac{dI}{dt}}{12} = \frac{6}{12} + \frac{L}{12}\frac{dI}{dt}$$

Thus, $I > \frac{6}{12} = 0.5\text{ A}$

$$I > 0.5\text{ A}$$

SPT2 Syllabus Part Thru 2

1. (a) $\mu = \dfrac{\sin\left(\dfrac{A+\delta_m}{2}\right)}{\sin\left(\dfrac{A}{2}\right)}$

$= \dfrac{\sin\left(\dfrac{60°+60°}{2}\right)}{\sin\left(\dfrac{60°}{2}\right)}$

$= \dfrac{\sin 60°}{\sin 30°} = \dfrac{\sqrt{3}}{2} \times \dfrac{2}{1} \Rightarrow \mu = \sqrt{3}$

Now, $v = \dfrac{c}{\mu} = \dfrac{3\times 10^8}{\sqrt{3}}$

$= \sqrt{3} \times 10^8 \text{ m/s}$

2. (b) Given, $f = 10$ cm, $d_o = 8.50$ cm.

By using the lens formula to find the image ditance,

$\dfrac{1}{f} = \dfrac{1}{d_i} + \dfrac{1}{d_o}$

$\Rightarrow \dfrac{1}{d_i} = \dfrac{1}{f} - \dfrac{1}{d_o}$

$\dfrac{1}{d_i} = \dfrac{1}{10} - \dfrac{1}{8.5}$

$\Rightarrow \dfrac{1}{d_i} = \dfrac{-1.5}{85}$

$\Rightarrow d_i = -56.67$ cm

Magnification,

$m = \dfrac{d_i}{d_o} = -\dfrac{(-56.67)}{8.50} = 6.67$

3. (b) Zener diode works as a voltage regulator in reverse bias and diode is connected in parallel with the load.

4. (c) For total internal reflection to occur, light must travel from optical denser medium to rarer medium. The angle of incidence in denser medium must be greater than the critical angle.

5. (b) When white light is passed through an unexcited gas and the transmitted light is analysed using a spectrometer, then it is found that transmitted light consists of few dark lines in bright background. These dark lines correspond precisely to those wavelengths which were found in the emission line spectrum of the gas. This is called the absorption spectrum of the material of the gas.

6. (d) Given, $\mathbf{E} = E_0 \hat{\mathbf{k}} \cos(\omega t - kx)$

The magnetic field B for an electromagnetic wave is always perpendicular to both the electric field E and the direction of propagation (which is along the x-axis in this case). The magnetic field is given by

$\mathbf{B} = \dfrac{B_0}{c} \hat{\mathbf{j}} \cos(\omega t - kx)$

For $t = 2$s,

$\mathbf{B} - \dfrac{E_0}{c} \hat{\mathbf{j}} \cos(2\omega - kx)$

As we know, $c = \dfrac{1}{\sqrt{\mu_0 \varepsilon_0}}$

So, $\mathbf{B} = E_0 \sqrt{\mu_0 \varepsilon_0} \cos(2\omega - kx)\hat{\mathbf{j}}$

7. (c) By applying calorimetry method, we get

Heat gain = Heat lost

$C_A(16-12) = C_B(19-16)$

$\Rightarrow \dfrac{C_A}{C_B} = \dfrac{3}{4}$

and $C_B(23-19) = C_C(28-23)$

$\Rightarrow \dfrac{C_B}{C_C} = \dfrac{5}{4}$

$\Rightarrow \dfrac{C_A}{C_C} = \dfrac{C_A}{C_B} \times \dfrac{C_B}{C_C}$

$= \dfrac{3}{4} \times \dfrac{5}{4} = \dfrac{15}{16}$ ...(i)

If θ is the temperature when A and C are mixed, then

$C_A(\theta - 12) = C_C(28 - \theta)$

$\Rightarrow \dfrac{C_A}{C_C} = \dfrac{28-\theta}{\theta - 12}$ ....(ii)

On solving Eqs. (i) and (ii), we have

$\dfrac{28-\theta}{\theta-12} = \dfrac{15}{16}$

$\Rightarrow 448 - 16\theta = 15\theta - 180$

$\therefore \theta = 20.2°C$

8. (b) For possible interference maxima on screen, condition is

$d \sin\theta = n\lambda$ ...(i)

Given, $d = 2\lambda$

$\Rightarrow \sin\theta = n\left(\dfrac{\lambda}{2\lambda}\right) = n\left(\dfrac{1}{2}\right)$

Now maximum value of $\sin\theta$ is 1, so $n = 2$.

Hence, Eq. (i) is satisfied with $n = -2, -1, 0, 1, 2$.

$\therefore$Maximum number of interference maximas is 5.

9. (d) $L_1L_2 = f_1 + f_2 = 10 + 15 = 25$ cm

10. (c) $\angle A = 60°$, $\mu = 1.524$, $\angle e = 90°$

$\sin\theta_C = \dfrac{1}{\mu}$

$\theta_C = \sin^{-1}\left(\dfrac{1}{1.524}\right) \approx 41.14°$

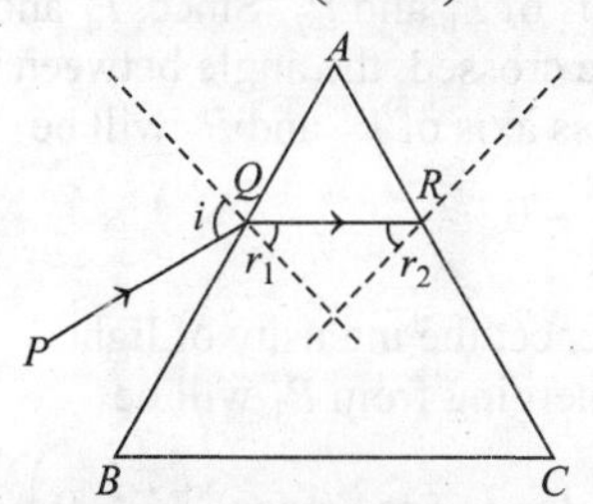

$\because r_1 + r_2 = A$ and $r_2 = \theta_C$

$\therefore r_1 = 60° - \theta_C$

$= 18.86°$

From Snell's law,

$\dfrac{\sin i}{\sin r_1} = \mu$

$\sin i \approx 1.524 \sin(18.86)$

$i = \sin^{-1}(0.493) \approx 29.54°$

11. (d) In semiconductors, the forbidden energy gap between the valence band and conduction band is very small, almost equal to KT.

Moreover valence band is completely filled, whereas conduction band is empty.

12. (a) As, $n_1 \sin\theta_1 = n_2 \sin\theta_2$

$$n_1 = 1,\ \theta_1 = 30^\circ$$
$$n_2 = \frac{3}{2},$$
$$\Rightarrow \quad 1 \sin 30^\circ = \frac{3}{2}\sin\theta_2$$
$$\Rightarrow \quad \sin\theta_2 = \frac{1}{3}$$
$$\Rightarrow \quad \theta_2 \approx 19.47^\circ$$

Lateral displacement,

$$d = t\cdot\sin(\theta_1 - \theta_2)$$
$$t = 5\,\text{cm},\ \theta_1 = 30^\circ,\ \theta_2 = 19.47^\circ$$
$$\Rightarrow \quad d = 5\times\sin(30^\circ - 19.47^\circ)$$
$$= 5\times\sin(10.53^\circ)$$
$$= 5\times 0.183$$
$$= 0.915\,\text{cm} \simeq 0.9\text{cm}$$

13. (a) Suppose I_0 be the intensity of polarised light after passing through the first polariser P_1. Then, the intensity of light after passing through second polariser will be

$$I = I_0\cos^2\theta \quad \text{[Malus's law]}$$

where, θ is the angle between pass axis of P_1 and P_2. Since, P_1 and P_3 are crossed, the angle between the pass axis of P_2 and P_3 will be $\left(\frac{\pi}{2} - \theta\right)$.

Hence, the intensity of light emerging from P_3 will be

$$I = I_0\cos^2\theta\cos^2\left(\frac{\pi}{2} - \theta\right)$$
$$= I_0\cos^2\theta\cdot\sin^2\theta$$
$$= \left(\frac{I_0}{4}\right)\sin^2 2\theta$$

Intensity is maximum, when $\sin 2\theta = 1$

$\Rightarrow 2\theta = \pi/2$

or $\theta = \pi/4$

Therefore, the transmitted intensity will be maximum when θ is $\pi/4$.

14. (d) $y = -u + v$

$$m = \frac{f}{f+u} = \frac{f-v}{f}$$

For real image, m is negative.

$$\therefore \quad -m = \frac{f}{f+u}$$

or $\quad -mf - mu = f$

$$u = \frac{-(m+1)}{m}f$$

and $\quad -m = \frac{f-v}{f}$

or $\quad -mf = f - v$

or $\quad v = (m+1)f$

$$\therefore \quad y = \left(\frac{m+1}{m}\right)f + f(m+1)$$
$$\Rightarrow \quad y = \frac{(m+1)^2}{m}f$$

or $\quad f = \dfrac{my}{(m+1)^2}$

15. (c) Energy is released in a process when total binding energy (BE) of the nucleus is increased or we can say when total BE of products is more than the reactants. By calculation, we can see that only in case of option (c), this happens.

Given, $W \to 2Y$

BE of reactants

$$= 120\times 7.5 = 900\ \text{MeV}$$

and BE of products

$$= 2\times 60\times 8.5 = 1020\,\text{MeV}$$

i.e. BE of products > BE of reactants. Hence, energy is released in the process of option (c).

In option (b), process is not possible as mass number is not conserved.

16. (a) Energy of emitted photon,

$$E = Rhc\left(\frac{1}{n_1^2} - \frac{1}{n_2^2}\right)$$
$$\Rightarrow E_{(4\to 3)} = Rhc\left(\frac{1}{3^2} - \frac{1}{4^2}\right)$$
$$= Rhc\left(\frac{7}{144}\right) = 0.05\,Rhc$$
$$E_{(4\to 2)} = Rhc\left(\frac{1}{2^2} - \frac{1}{4^2}\right)$$
$$= Rhc\left(\frac{3}{16}\right) = 0.2\,Rhc$$
$$E_{(2\to 1)} = Rhc\left[\frac{1}{(1)^2} - \frac{1}{(2)^2}\right]$$
$$= Rhc\left(\frac{3}{4}\right) = 0.75\,Rhc$$

and $E_{(1\to 4)} = Rhc\left[\frac{1}{(4)^2} - \frac{1}{(1)^2}\right]$

$$= -\frac{8}{9}Rhc = -0.9\,Rhc$$

Thus, transition III gives largest amount of energy.

17. (b)

Initial: (A) $m/3$ moving with v_0; (B) $m/4$ (rest)

Final: (A) $m/3$ moving with v_A; (B) $m/4$ moving with v_B

Applying momentum conservation,

$$\frac{m}{3}\times v_0 + \frac{m}{4}\times 0 = \frac{m}{3}\cdot v_A + \frac{m}{4}\cdot v_B$$
$$\frac{v_0}{3} = \frac{v_A}{3} + \frac{v_B}{4} \quad \text{...(i)}$$

Since, collision is elastic $(e = 1)$,

$$e = 1 = \frac{v_B - v_A}{v_0}$$
$$\Rightarrow \quad v_0 = v_B - v_A \quad \text{...(ii)}$$

On solving Eqs. (i) and (ii), we get

$$v_A = \frac{v_0}{7}$$

Now, de-Broglie wavelength of A before collision,

$$\lambda_0 = \frac{h}{m_A v_0} = \frac{h}{\left(\frac{m}{3}\right)v_0}$$
$$\lambda_0 = \frac{3h}{mv_0}$$

Final de-Broglie wavelength,

$$\lambda_F = \frac{h}{m_A v_A} = \frac{h}{\left(\frac{m}{3}\right)\frac{v_0}{7}}$$
$$\lambda_F = \frac{21h}{mv_0}$$

Now, $\Delta\lambda = \lambda_F - \lambda_0$

$$\Delta\lambda = \frac{21h}{mv_0} - \frac{3h}{mv_0}$$
$$\Delta\lambda = \frac{18h}{mv_0}$$
$$\Delta\lambda = 6\times\frac{3h}{mv_0} = 6\lambda_0$$

18. (c) When light travels from rarer medium (like air) to a denser medium (like glass or water), the speed of light decreases. Light slows down as it enters in medium with high refractive index.

$$\mu = \frac{c}{v}, \; v \propto \frac{1}{\mu}$$

$\therefore$ Assertion is correct.
Reason is incorrect because energy of photon, $E = h\nu$ remains unchanged when light enters into a different medium.

Frequency, $\nu = \frac{v}{\lambda}$

Speed v and wavelength λ changes but frequency remains same.

19. (c)

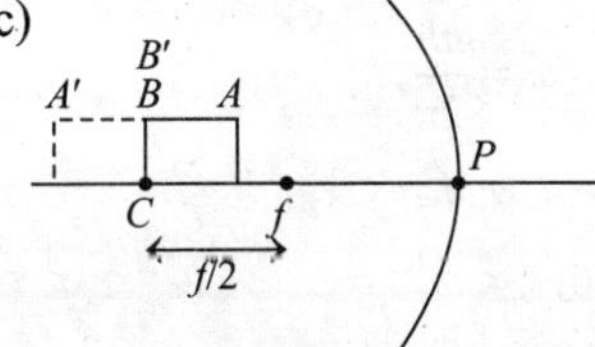

Let AB be the object and A be the near end of object and B be the far end of object.
Let $A'B'$ be the image formed.
As B' coincides with the end B at the centre of curvature, the distance of B from the mirror $= 2f$

Length $AB = \frac{f}{2}$

The end A is at a distance

$$= \left(2f - \frac{f}{2}\right) = \frac{3f}{2}$$

For concave mirror, object distance, $u = -$ ve and image is real and f is also negative.

$$\frac{1}{f} = \frac{1}{v_A} + \frac{1}{u_A}$$

$$\Rightarrow \quad -\frac{1}{f} = \frac{1}{v} - \frac{2}{3f}$$

$$\Rightarrow \quad -\frac{1}{f} + \frac{2}{3f} = \frac{1}{v} \Rightarrow v = -3f$$

Negative sign indicates the position of image at A' is at the same side of object at A.

$$B'A' = CA' = PA' - PC$$
$$= 3f - 2f = f$$

Magnification, $m = \frac{v}{u} = \frac{f}{\frac{f}{2}} = 2$

20. (a) According to graph, in forward bias voltage of p-n junction diode is 0.6 V.

In foward bias

$$V_A - 0.6 - 5I = V_B$$
$$V_A - V_B = 5I + 0.6$$
$$V_{AB} = 5I + 0.6$$

21. (b) Dynamic resistance

$$= \frac{\Delta V}{\Delta I'} = \left(\frac{2.1 - 2}{800 - 400}\right) \times 10^3$$
$$= 0.25\,\Omega$$

22. (b) Condition for maxima is

$$d \sin\theta = n\lambda$$

$$\sin\theta = \frac{n\lambda}{d}$$

$$\sin\theta = n\left(\frac{0.50}{2}\right)$$

$$\sin\theta = 0.25\,n$$

As we know, $\sin\theta$ lies between -1 and 1, so we wish to find all values of n for which

$$|0.25\,n| \le 1$$

These value are $-4, -3, -2, -1, 0, 1, 2, 3$ and 4.
For each of these, there are two different values of θ except for -4 and $+4$. A single value of θ, $-90°$ and $+90°$, is associated with $n = -4$ and $n = +4$ respectively. Thus, there are 16 different angles in all and therefore 16 maxima.

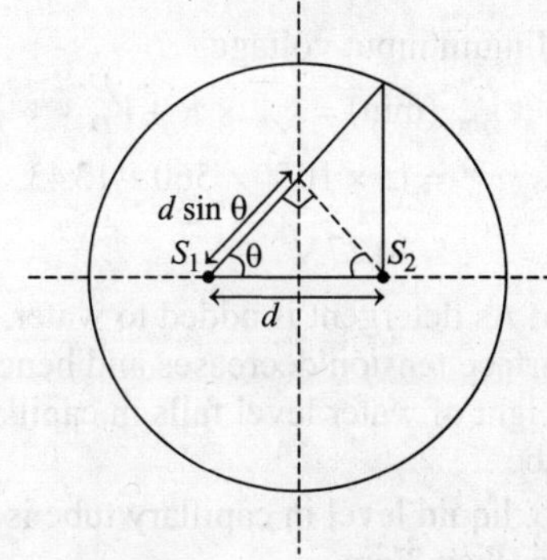

23. (c) According to question,

$$N\,\text{MSD} = (N+1)\,\text{VSD}$$

$$1\,\text{VSD} = \frac{N}{N+1}\,\text{MSD}$$

Now, LC = 1 MSD − 1 VSD

$$= \left(1 - \frac{N}{N+1}\right) \times 1\,\text{MSD}$$

$$= \left(\frac{N+1-N}{N+1}\right) \times a$$

[$\because$ 1 MSD $= a$ units]

$$= \frac{a}{N+1}\text{ units}$$

24. (d) Initially, energy corresponding to the emitted photon,

$$\Delta E = 13.6 \times 2^2\left(1 - \frac{1}{4}\right) = 40.8\text{ eV}$$

Out of 40.8 eV, 13.6 eV will be used for ionising H-atom. Hence, K_E of the photoelectron

$$= (40.8 - 13.6)\text{ eV} = 27.2\text{ eV}$$

$$\therefore \frac{1}{2}mv^2 = 27.2 \times 1.6 \times 10^{-19}$$

or $\quad v = \sqrt{\frac{2 \times 27.2 \times 1.6 \times 10^{-19}}{9.1 \times 10^{-31}}}$

or $\quad v = 3.1 \times 10^6$ m/s

25. (a) Given, for neon lamp, wavelength of monochromatic radiation,

$$\lambda = 640.2\text{ nm} = 640.2 \times 10^{-9}\text{ m}$$

Stopping voltage, $V_0 = 0.54$ V
Let ϕ_0 be the work function.

$$\therefore \quad eV_0 = \frac{hc}{\lambda} - \phi_0$$

Work function of photosensitive material,

$$\phi_0 = \frac{hc}{\lambda} - eV_0$$

$$= \frac{6.63 \times 10^{-34} \times 3 \times 10^8}{640.2 \times 10^{-9}} - 1.6 \times 10^{-19} \times 0.54$$

$$= 3.1 \times 10^{-19} - 0.864 \times 10^{-19}$$

$$= 2.236 \times 10^{-19} = \frac{2.236 \times 10^{-19}}{1.6 \times 10^{-19}}$$

$$= 1.3975 \simeq 1.4\text{ eV}$$

Now, if the material is irradiated by an iron source, then wavelength, $\lambda = 427.2$ nm

$$= 427.2 \times 10^{-9}\text{ m}$$

Let V_0' be the new stopping potential.

$$\Rightarrow eV_0' = \frac{hc}{\lambda} - \phi_0$$

$$= \frac{6.63\times 10^{-34} \times 3\times 10^8}{427.2\times 10^{-9} \times 1.6\times 10^{-19}} - 1.4$$

$$= 2.91 - 1.4$$

$$= 1.51\,\text{eV}$$

Required new stopping potential, $V_0' = 1.51\,\text{V}$

26. (a) ${}_1^2\text{H} + {}_1^2\text{H} \longrightarrow {}_2^3\text{He} + {}_0^1n$

Mass defect,

$$\Delta m = [(2.015\times 2) - (3.017 + 1.00)]$$
$$= 4\times 10^{-3}\ \text{amu}$$

Equivalent energy

$$= 4\times 10^{-3} \times 931.5\,\text{MeV}$$
$$= 3.726\,\text{MeV}$$

Number of atoms in 1 kg of ${}_1^2\text{H}$

$$= \frac{1000}{2} \times 6.023\times 10^{23}$$

In one reaction, two atoms of ${}_1^2\text{H}$ are used.

Total energy released

$$= \frac{1}{2}\left(\frac{1000}{2} \times 6.023\times 10^{23}\right) \times 3.726\times 1.6\times 10^{-13}$$

$$\simeq 9\times 10^{13}\ \text{J}$$

27. (d) Since, Q can no more be seen by adjusting ES, this means total internal reflection is occured.

$$\sin\theta_C = \frac{1}{\mu}$$

θ_C is critical angle, μ = refractive index

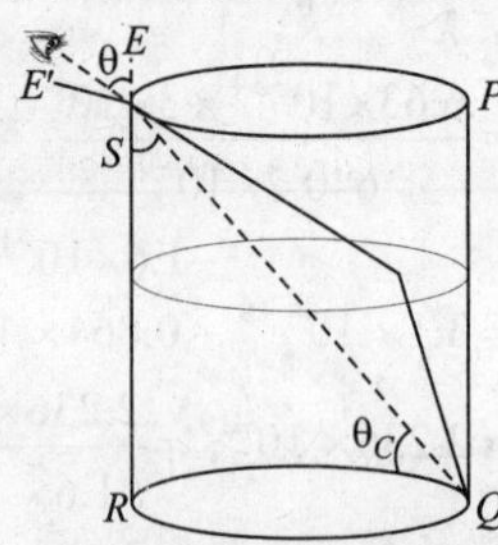

According to geometry, consider ΔSRQ

$$\sin\theta_C = \frac{SR}{QS}$$

$SR = h$, height of beaker

$RQ = d$, diameter of beaker

$h = d$ (given)

$$QS = \sqrt{h^2 + d^2} = \sqrt{2}h \quad [\because h = d]$$

$$\therefore \quad \sin\theta_c = \frac{h}{\sqrt{2}h} = \frac{1}{\sqrt{2}}$$

$$\mu = \frac{1}{\sin\theta_C} = \frac{1}{\left(\frac{1}{\sqrt{2}}\right)} = \sqrt{2}$$

So, minimum refractive index should be $\sqrt{2}$.

28. (a) $\mathbf{E} = E_0\hat{\mathbf{n}}\sin[\omega t + (8y - 4z)]$

$$\mathbf{E} = E_0\hat{\mathbf{n}}\sin[\omega t - (4z - 8y)]$$

$$\mathbf{k}\cdot\hat{\mathbf{r}} = 4z - 8y$$

$$x\cdot k_x = 0$$
$$yk_y = -8y$$
$$k_y = -8$$
$$zk_z = 4z$$
$$k_z = 4$$
$$\mathbf{k} = -8\hat{\mathbf{j}} + 4\hat{\mathbf{k}}$$

$$\text{So, } \hat{\mathbf{s}} = \hat{\mathbf{k}} = \frac{\mathbf{k}}{|\mathbf{k}|} = \frac{-8\hat{\mathbf{j}} + 4\hat{\mathbf{k}}}{\sqrt{64+16}}$$

$$= \frac{8\hat{\mathbf{j}} + 4\hat{\mathbf{k}}}{\sqrt{80}}$$

29. (a) Knee current across Zener diode

$I_{Zk} = 1.5\,\text{mA}$

Change in $I_Z = 30\,\text{mA} - 1.5\,\text{mA}$

$$= 28.5\,\text{mA}$$

voltage V across diode,

$$V_D = 14 - 20\times 28.5\times 10^{-3}$$
$$= 14 - 0.570 = 13.43\,\text{V}$$

Minium input voltage,

$$V_{\text{in}}\ (\text{min}) = I_{Zk} \times R + V_D$$
$$= 1.5\times 10^{-3} \times 560 + 13.43$$
$$= 14.27\,\text{V}$$

30. (b) As detergent is added to water, its surface tension decreases and hence height of water level falls in capillary tube.

So, liquid level in capillary tube is less than 3 cm.

31. (b) ${}_7^{14}\text{N} + {}_2^4\text{He} \longrightarrow {}_1^1\text{H} + {}_8^{17}\text{O}$

Q-value of reaction

$$= [(14.00307 + 4.00260) - (1.00783 + 16.99913)]$$
$$= -1.29\times 10^{-3}\,\text{u}$$
$$= -1.29\times 10^{-3} \times 931.5$$
$$= -1.2\,\text{MeV}$$

Q-value is negative, i.e. reaction is endothermic. Minimum kinetic energy of α-particle to initiate this reaction,

$$K\text{th} = K_{\min} = |Q|\left(\frac{M_\alpha}{M_\text{N}} + 1\right)$$

$$= 1.2\left(\frac{4.00260}{14.00307} + 1\right)$$

$$= 1.54\ \text{MeV}$$

32. (d) Angular momentum,

$$L = \frac{nh}{2\pi}$$

$$\Rightarrow \quad L \propto n \qquad \text{...(i)}$$

Also, $r \propto n^2$

$$\therefore \quad n \propto \sqrt{r} \qquad \text{...(ii)}$$

So, from Eqs. (i) and (ii)

$$L \propto \sqrt{r}$$

33. (c) As, $eV = \frac{hc}{\lambda} - W$

$$\therefore \quad V = \left(\frac{h}{e}\right)\cdot\frac{c}{\lambda} - \frac{W}{e}$$

$$\text{So,} \quad V_1 = \left(\frac{h}{e}\right)\frac{c}{\lambda_1} - \frac{W}{e} \qquad \text{...(i)}$$

$$V_2 = \left(\frac{h}{e}\right)\frac{c}{\lambda_2} - \frac{W}{e} \qquad \text{...(ii)}$$

Solving these two equations, we get

$$\frac{h}{e} = \frac{\lambda_1\lambda_2(V_1 - V_2)}{c(\lambda_2 - \lambda_1)}$$

$$= \frac{(0.6\times 0.4\times 10^{-12})\,(1.0)}{(3\times 10^8)\,(0.2\times 10^{-6})}$$

$$= 4\times 10^{-15}\ \text{Vs}$$

34. (c) $I_{\max} = (\sqrt{I_1} + \sqrt{I_2})^2$

$$I_{\min} = (\sqrt{I_1} - \sqrt{I_2})^2$$

Now, initially $I_1 = I_2 = I_0$

$$\Rightarrow \quad I_{\max} = 4I_0$$
$$I_{\min} = 0$$

After the width of one slit is made twice of the other slit,
amplitude $\propto$ slit width (s).

$$A_2 \propto s, I_2' \propto A_2^2, I_2' = I_0$$
$$A_1 \propto 2s$$
$$\Rightarrow I_1' \propto 4s^2 \propto 4A_2^2 = 4I_0$$
$$I'_{max} = (\sqrt{I_1'} + \sqrt{I_2'})^2$$
$$= (\sqrt{4I_0} + \sqrt{I_0})^2 = 9I_0$$
$$I'_{min} = (\sqrt{I_1'} - \sqrt{I_2'})^2$$
$$= (\sqrt{4I_0} - \sqrt{I_0})^2 = I_0$$

So, $I'_{max} > I_{max}$ and $I'_{min} > I_{min}$

Hence, the intensity of both maxima and the minima increases.

35. (a) ${}^a\mu_g = 1.5$ and ${}^a\mu_w = 1.3$

Deviation in air,

$$\delta_a = (\mu - 1)A$$
$$= ({}^a\mu_g - 1)A$$
$$= \left(\frac{1.5}{1} - 1\right) \times 60°$$
$$= 0.5 \times 60° = 30°$$

Deviation in water,

$$\delta_w = \left(\frac{\mu_g}{\mu_\omega}\right)$$
$$= \frac{1.5}{1.3} = 1.15$$
$$\delta = (1.15 - 1) \times 60° = 9°$$

36. (a) Truth table for 'P' is

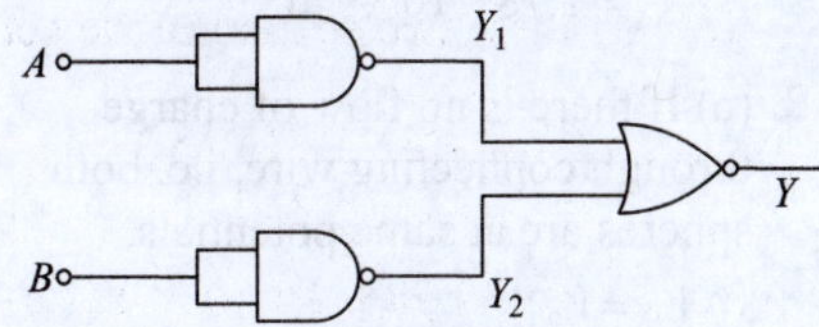

This is an OR gate

A	B	Y_1	Y_2	Y
0	0	1	1	0
1	0	0	1	1
0	1	1	0	1
1	1	0	0	1

Truth table for Q is

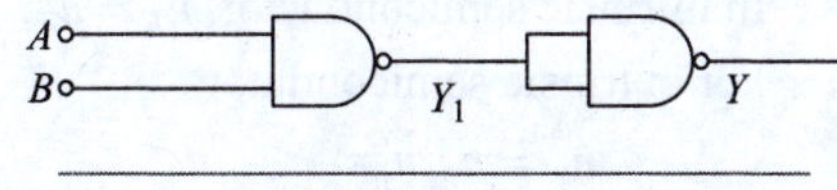

A	B	Y_1	Y
0	0	1	0
1	0	1	0
0	1	1	0
1	1	0	1

This is AND gate

37. (b) The plot corresponding to angle of deviation and angle of incidence is given as

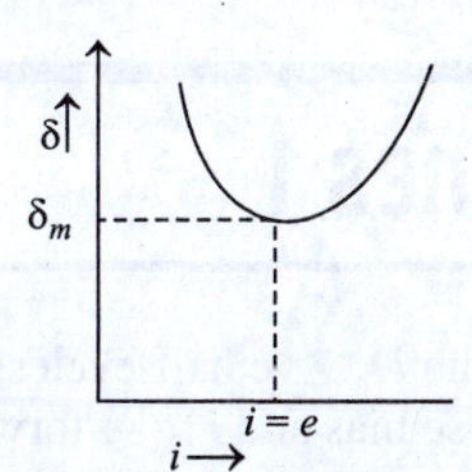

$\therefore$ δ decreases with increase in i till δ_m.

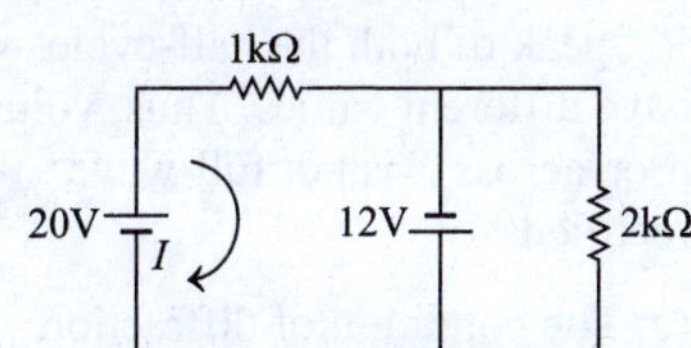

38. (c) $2I_0 = 4I_0 \cos^2 \dfrac{\phi}{2}$

$$\phi = \frac{\pi}{2} = \frac{2\pi}{\lambda} \cdot \Delta x$$
$$\frac{\pi}{2} = \frac{2\pi}{\lambda} \cdot \left(\frac{y_1 d}{D}\right)$$
$$\therefore \quad y_1 = \frac{\lambda D}{4d}$$

Further, $I_0 = 4I_0 \cos^2 \dfrac{\phi}{2}$

$$\Rightarrow \quad \phi = \frac{2\pi}{3} = \frac{2\pi}{\lambda} \Delta x$$
$$\frac{2\pi}{3} = \frac{2\pi}{\lambda}\left(\frac{y_2 d}{D}\right)$$
$$\therefore \quad y_2 = \frac{\lambda D}{3d}$$

Minimum separation,

$$\Delta y = y_2 - y_1$$
$$= \frac{1}{12}\left(\frac{\lambda D}{d}\right) = \frac{\alpha}{12}$$

39. (d) $v_1 = 2v(l_2 - l_1)$

$$v_1 = 2 \times 480 \times (70 - 20) \times 10^{-2}\ \text{ms}^{-1}$$
$$= 2 \times 48 \times 5 \times 10^2 \times 10^{-2}$$
$$= 48 \times 10\ \text{ms}^{-1}$$
$$= 480\ \text{ms}^{-1}$$

40. (b) From law of conservation of momentum,

$$m_1 v_1 = m_2 v_2$$
$$\frac{m_1}{m_2} = \frac{v_2}{v_1}$$

Also, $\quad m = \dfrac{4}{3}\pi r^3 . \rho$

$$m \propto r^3$$
$$\frac{m_1}{m_2} = \frac{r_1^3}{r_2^3} = \frac{v_2}{v_1}$$
$$\frac{r_1}{r_2} = \left(\frac{v_2}{v_1}\right)^{\frac{1}{3}}$$
$$\frac{r_1}{r_2} = \left(\frac{1}{2}\right)^{\frac{1}{3}}$$
$$r_1 : r_2 = 1 : 2^{\frac{1}{3}}$$

41. (a) The electrons might not be emitted from metal surface, rather it could be within the metal due to which it suffers collision and hence energy losses.
Also, the electrons in metals occupy different energy levels. Thus, electrons have different minimum energy required to be ejected from atom.

42. (d) $E_n = \dfrac{Z^2}{n^2} E_0$

For H atom : $Z = 1$ and $n = 2$

$$\therefore \quad E_2 = \frac{1}{2^2} E_0 = \frac{1}{4} E_0$$

For He atom : $Z = 2$ and $n = 3$

$\therefore \quad E_3 = \frac{2^2}{3^2} E_0 = \frac{4}{9} E_0$

Hence, $\frac{E_3}{E_2} = \frac{\frac{4}{9}E_0}{\frac{1}{4}E_0} = \frac{16}{9}$

$E_3 = \frac{16}{9} E_2 \quad [\because E_2 = E]$

or $\quad E_3 = \frac{16}{9} E$

43. (c) Holes are majority charge carriers in p-type semiconductor, i.e. $n_h > n_e$.

For n-type semiconductor, $n_e > n_h$.

In intrinsic semiconductor, $n_h = n_e$.

For extrinsic semicondutor,

$$n_1^2 = n_{ex} n_h$$

44. (a) During positive cycle, diode D_1 is forward biased and D_2 is reverse biased.

So, current flows through diode D_1.

So, current, $i_{max} = \frac{20}{100} = 0.2$ A

During negative cycle, diode D_1 is reverse biased and D_2 is forward biased. So, current flows through diode D_2.

Max. current, $i_{max} = -\frac{20}{200} = -0.1$ A

So, current has peak value of 0.2 A in positive half-cycle and – 0.1 A in negative half-cycle.

45. (c) $E_g = hf = \frac{hc}{\lambda}$

$= \frac{1240 \text{ eVnm}}{2480 \text{ nm}} = 0.5$ eV

NSS1 NEET Stepping Stones 1

1. (c) Given, angle between magnetic field and velocity vector, $\theta = 45°$

Pitch = P

As we know that,

$$P = \frac{2\pi}{Bq} mv \cdot \cos 45°$$

$$= \frac{2\pi}{Bq} \cdot P \cdot \frac{1}{\sqrt{2}}$$

$$\Rightarrow \quad \frac{P}{2\pi} = \frac{p}{qB} \frac{1}{\sqrt{2}} \qquad \text{...(i)}$$

where, p = momentum

Radius of helix,

$$r = \frac{mv \sin 45°}{qB} = \frac{p}{qB} \cdot \frac{1}{\sqrt{2}}$$

From Eq. (i), we get

$$r = \frac{P}{2\pi}$$

2. (b) Binding energy of ${}_1^2$H,

$$(\text{BE})_\text{H} = 2 \times 1.15 = 2.3 \text{ MeV}$$

Binding energy of ${}_2^4$He,

$$(\text{BE})_\text{He} = 4 \times 7.1 = 28.4 \text{ MeV}$$

$$Q\text{-value} = \Sigma\text{BE}_\text{product} - \Sigma\text{BE}_\text{reactant}$$

$$= 28.4 - (2.3 + 2.3) = 23.8 \text{ MeV}$$

3. (d) Given, $R_1 \neq R_2$

For the first +ve half-cycle, $D_1 \rightarrow$ forward bias and $D_2 \rightarrow$ reverse bias.

For the D_1 – ve half-cycles, $\rightarrow$ reverse bias and $D_2 \rightarrow$ forward bias. In both the half-cycles, voltage will appear across load resistance R but due to the different values of R_1 and R_2, peak of both the half-cycles will have different values. Thus, voltage drop across R is not full-wave rectified.

4. (c) The condition of diffraction minima due to single slit Fraunhofer diffraction pattern is given by

$$d \sin \theta = \pm m\lambda$$

For first diffraction minima on either side of central maxima, $m = 1$

$$\therefore \quad d \sin \theta = \pm \frac{\lambda}{d}$$

Since, θ is small,

$$\sin \theta \approx \tan \theta = \pm \frac{\lambda}{d}$$

where, $\tan \theta = \frac{5 \text{ mm}}{2 \text{ m}}$

$$= \frac{5 \times 10^{-3}}{2}$$

$$= 2.5 \times 10^{-3}$$

$$\therefore \quad \lambda = 2.5 \times 10^{-3} d$$

$$= 2.5 \times 10^{-3} \times 0.2 \text{ mm}$$

$$= 5 \times 10^{-7} \text{ m}$$

$$= 5000 \text{ Å}$$

5. (a) After annihilation, energy produced is

$$= 0.5 + 0.5 = 1 \text{ MeV}$$

The total energy of two photons

$$= (2 \times 0.2 + 1) \text{ MeV}$$

$$= 1.4 \text{ MeV}$$

Energy of each photon

$$= \frac{1.4}{2} = 0.7 \text{ MeV}$$

$$\because \quad E = h\nu = \frac{hc}{\lambda}$$

$$\lambda = \frac{hc}{E} = \frac{6.63 \times 10^{-34} \times 3 \times 10^8}{0.7 \times 10^6 \times 1.6 \times 10^{-19}}$$

$$= 1.78 \times 10^{-12} \text{ m}$$

6. (c) If there is no flow of charge through connecting wire, i.e. both spheres are at same potentials,

$$V_1 = V_2$$

$$\frac{Kq_1}{r_1} = \frac{Kq_2}{r_2}$$

$$\frac{K \times (\sigma_1 \times 4\pi r_1^2)}{r_1} = \frac{K \times (\sigma_2 \times 4\pi r_2^2)}{r_2}$$

$$\therefore \quad \sigma_1 r_1 = \sigma_2 r_2$$

7. (c) True value or average value

$$= \frac{2.63 + 2.56 + 2.42 + 2.71 + 2.80}{5}$$

$$= 2.62 \text{ s}$$

Errors, $\Delta T_1 = 2.63 - 2.62 = 0.01$

$\Delta T_2 = 0.06, \Delta T_3 = 0.20$

$\Delta T_4 = 0.09, \Delta T_5 = 0.18$

$\therefore$ Mean error $= \frac{\Sigma \Delta T}{5} = \frac{0.54}{5} = 0.11\,\text{s}$

Reported value $= (2.62 \pm 0.11)\,\text{s}$

8. (d) Refractive index of diamond w.r.t. liquid,

$$ {}^l n_d = \frac{1}{\sin i_C} = \frac{n_d}{n_l} $$

$$ \Rightarrow \quad \frac{\sqrt{6}}{\sqrt{3}} = \frac{1}{\sin i_C} $$

$$ \Rightarrow \quad \sin i_C = \frac{1}{\sqrt{2}} = \sin 45° $$

$$ \therefore \quad i_C = 45° $$

This means that when the ray of light while travelling from diamond to liquid is incident at angle of 45°, then it will show TIR.

Therefore, A is false but R is true.

9. (b) The torque acting on the dipole is given by $\tau = \mathbf{p} \times \mathbf{E}$. The potential energy of the dipole is given by $U = -\mathbf{p} \cdot \mathbf{E}$ and the resultant force on the dipole is zero.

10. (b) According to figure, it is a balanced Wheatstone bridge.

So, net resistance,

$$ R_{eq} = \frac{2R \times 2R}{2R + 2R} = \frac{4R \cdot R}{4R} = R $$

In balanced meter bridge condition, we have

$$ \frac{55}{20} = \frac{R}{(100 - 20)} $$

$$ \Rightarrow \quad R = 220\,\Omega $$

11. (c) At point of closest approach, decrease in kinetic energy of α-particle = increase in potential energy

$$ \frac{1}{2} mv^2 - 0 = \frac{K(Ze)(2e)}{r_{\min}} - 0 $$

($r_{\min}$ = minimum distance between two nuclei)

or $$ r_{\min} = \frac{4KZe^2}{mv^2} $$

From above equation, it is clear that,

$$ r_{\min} \propto Ze^2 $$

$$ r_{\min} \propto \frac{1}{v^2} $$

$$ r_{\min} \propto \frac{1}{m} $$

12. (a) Molecules of liquids and gases are always in random motion, so they cannot be ferromagnetic. Now, out of diamagnetic and paramagnetic, only paramagnetic liquids are attracted by strong magnetic fields.

13. (b) $\tau = pE \sin \theta$

Work done in rotating the dipole to an infinitesimal angle $d\theta$ in electric field is given by

$$ dW = \tau \cdot d\theta = pE \sin \theta \cdot d\theta $$

$$ W = \int_{\theta_1}^{\theta_2} pE \sin \theta \cdot d\theta $$

$$ = pE (-\cos \theta)_{\theta_1}^{\theta_2} $$

$$ = pE (\cos \theta_1 - \cos \theta_2) $$

Given, $\theta_1 = 0°$, (position of stable equilibrium) and $\theta_2 = 180°$

$$ W = pE (\cos 0° - \cos 180°) $$

$$ = pE (1 - (-1)) $$

$$ W = 2pE $$

Now, $p = q\,(2a)$

$$ = 10^{-6} \times 2 \times 10^{-2} $$

$$ = 2 \times 10^{-8}\ \text{C-m} $$

and $E = 10^5$ N/C

$$ \therefore \quad W = 2 \times 2 \times 10^{-8} \times 10^5 $$

$$ = 4 \times 10^{-3}\ \text{J} $$

14. (c) Resistance

$$ \propto \frac{1}{(\text{Cross-sectional area of wire})} $$

$$ \propto \frac{1}{(\text{Radius of wire})^2} $$

i.e., $$ R \propto \frac{1}{r^2} $$

$$ i = \frac{\Delta V}{R} $$

$$ B = \frac{\mu_0 ni}{2a} $$

$$ \therefore \quad B \propto i \propto \frac{\Delta V}{R} \propto \Delta V\,(r^2) $$

or $$ \Delta V \propto \frac{B}{r^2} $$

$$ \Delta V \propto \frac{1}{r^2} $$

$$ \therefore \quad \frac{(\Delta V)_A}{(\Delta V)_B} = \left(\frac{r_B}{r_A}\right)^2 $$

$$ = (2)^2 = 4 $$

15. (d) Radiowaves are produced by oscillating charge particles between plates of capacitor in *L-C* circuit.

16. (a) Damping in a galvanometer can be achieved by putting an aluminium plate with coil. Eddy current will be induced in plate. This will dissipate oscillation energy as heat.

17. (a) de-Broglie wavelength is given by

$$ \lambda = \frac{h}{p} $$

$$ p = \frac{h}{\lambda} $$

$$ p = \frac{6.63 \times 10^{-34}}{2 \times 10^{-6}} $$

$$ p = 3.31 \times 10^{-28}\ \text{kg-m/s} $$

18. (b) The two metallic spheres are placed far apart. Therefore, charges (if any) given to them will produce electrostatic potential on their surface and near by, but the potential on the surface of one sphere due to charge of the other sphere will be negligible, i.e. potential at the surface of each sphere is only due to its own charge.

Now, potential on the surface of first sphere (charged to $+q$) is

$$ V_1 = \frac{q}{4\pi\varepsilon_0 r_1} $$

Also, the potential on the surface of the second sphere (charged to $-q$) is

$$ V_2 = \frac{-q}{4\pi\varepsilon_0 r_2} $$

Potential difference between the spheres,

$$ V = \frac{q}{4\pi\varepsilon_0}\left[\frac{1}{r_1} - \left(-\frac{1}{r_2}\right)\right] $$

or $$V = \frac{q}{4\pi\varepsilon_0}\left(\frac{r_1 + r_2}{r_1 r_2}\right)$$

Now, $$C = \frac{q}{V} = \frac{4\pi\varepsilon_0 r_1 r_2}{r_1 + r_2}$$

19. (b) To the right of B, both fields are downwards and to the left of A, both fields are upwards. At mid-point between wires A and B, magnetic field due to current carrying wire A is equal and opposite to the magnetic field due to current carrying wire B. Hence, they cancel out each other.

20. (c) Magnetic moment $= i\,A$

Since, two charges ($+q$ each) are revolving with constant angular speed ω (say), so the orbital current produced is given as,

$$i = \frac{\text{charge}}{\text{time}} = \text{charge} \times \text{frequency}$$

$$= 2q\left(\frac{\omega}{2\pi}\right) = \frac{q\omega}{\pi}.$$

and area of the circular orbit $= \pi l^2$

Therefore, magnetic moment,

$$m = \frac{q\omega}{\pi}\cdot \pi l^2 = q\omega l^2$$

Angular momentum of the system

$$L = I\omega$$

or $L = (Ml^2 + Ml^2)\,\omega = 2Ml^2\,\omega$, where, M is the mass

Hence, $$\frac{m}{L} = \frac{q\omega l^2}{2M\,\omega l^2} = \frac{q}{2M}$$

21. (a) The total energy associated with the two H-atoms in the ground state collide inelastically,

$$E = 2 \times 13.6 \text{ eV}$$
$$= 27.2 \text{ eV}$$

The total energy associated with the two H-atoms after the collision,

$$E' = E_2 + E_1 = \left(\frac{13.6}{2^2}\right) + 13.6$$
$$= 17.0 \text{ eV}$$

Therefore, maximum loss of their combined kinetic energy,

$$\Delta E = E - E'$$
$$= 27.2 - 17.0 = 10.2 \text{ eV}$$

22. (c) If the electric field between the plates of parallel plate capacitor in air is E_0, then net electric field in dielectric medium of dielectric constant K will be $\frac{E_0}{K}$.

Or, we can say that,

$$E_{\text{medium}} \propto \frac{1}{K} \qquad \ldots\text{(i)}$$

Given, electric field is minimum for medium-3 and greatest for medium-2

$$E_3 < E_1 < E_2$$

From Eq. (i), we get

$$\frac{1}{K_3} < \frac{1}{K_1} < \frac{1}{K_2}$$

or $$K_3 > K_1 > K_2$$

23. (d) Statement I is incorrect but Statement II is correct.

As phase difference is given by

$$\tan\phi = \frac{X_L}{R}.$$

In L-R circuit, voltage leads current by an angle of $\tan^{-1}\left(\frac{X_L}{R}\right)$.

Time lag in L-R circuit,

$$t = \frac{1}{\omega}\tan^{-1}\frac{X_L}{R}$$

24. (b) Power of electric bulb,

$$P = 200 \text{ W}$$

Efficiency, $\eta = 3.5\% = 0.035$

$$r = 4 \text{ m}$$

$\therefore$ Intensity of radiation at $r = 4$ m

$$I = \frac{\text{Power}}{\text{Area}} \times \eta = \frac{200}{4\pi r^2} \times 0.035$$

$$= \frac{200}{4 \times 3.14 \times 4^2} \times 0.035$$

$$= 3.48 \times 10^{-2} \text{ W/m}^2$$

But, $$I = \frac{cB_0^2}{2\mu_0}$$

$$\Rightarrow \quad B_0^2 = \frac{2\mu_0 I}{c} \Rightarrow B = \sqrt{\frac{2\mu_0 I}{c}}$$

$$= \sqrt{\frac{2 \times 4\pi \times 10^{-7} \times 3.48 \times 10^{-2}}{3 \times 10^8}}$$

$$= 1.71 \times 10^{-8} \text{ T}$$

25. (c) Average wavelength of photons (sunlight), $\lambda = 550$ nm

So, photon flux,

$$n = \frac{P}{E} = \frac{P\lambda}{hc} \approx 4 \times 10^{21} \text{ photons per square metre per second}$$

26. (c) Resistance of 1 Ω group in parallel

$$= \frac{R}{n} = \frac{1}{3}\,\Omega$$

This is in series with $\frac{2}{3}\,\Omega$ resistor.

$$\therefore \text{Total resistance} = \frac{2}{3} + \frac{1}{3} = 1\,\Omega$$

27. (d) Given, capacitance

$$= 100 \times 10^{-6} \text{ F}$$

Resistance, $R = 40\,\Omega$

Frequency, $f = 60$ Hz

Given, the voltage lags behind the current by a phase angle of ϕ. It is given by relation, $\tan\phi = \frac{1}{\omega CR}$.

$(\because \omega = 2\pi f)$

$$\tan\phi = \frac{1}{120 \times \pi \times 10^{-4} \times 40} = 0.6635$$

$$\Rightarrow \phi = \tan^{-1}(0.6635)$$

$$\phi = 33.56° = \frac{33.56\pi}{180} \text{ rad}$$

Time lag, $$\tau = \frac{\phi}{\omega}$$

$$= \frac{33.56\,\pi}{180 \times 120\,\pi}$$

$$= 1.55 \times 10^{-3} \text{ s}$$

$$= 1.55 \text{ ms}$$

28. (c) Acceleration produced in the charged particle q of mass m in the electric field E is

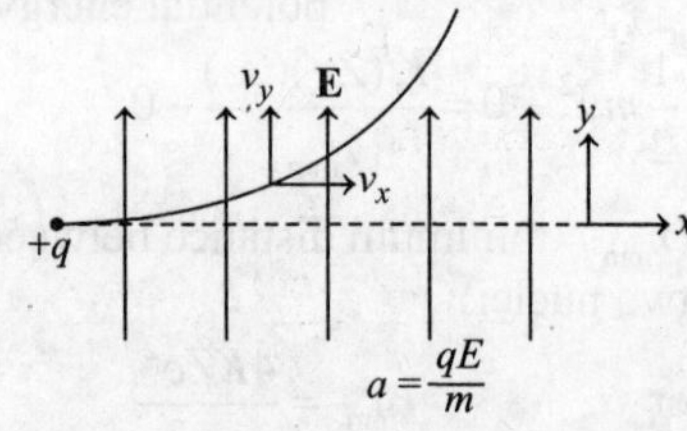

Distance travelled along X-axis in time t is

$$s_x = v_x t$$

or $t = \frac{s_x}{v_x}$ ...(i)

Distance travelled along Y-axis in time t,

$$s_y = 0 + \frac{1}{2}at^2$$

$$s_y = \frac{1}{2}\left(\frac{qE}{m}\right)\left(\frac{s_x}{v_x}\right)^2 \quad \text{[using Eq. (i)]}$$

It follows from this equation that the curvature of the trajectory is inversely proportional to m,

i.e., $s_y \propto \frac{1}{m}$

Since, q, E and v_x are the same for both the electron and proton, hence the electrons trajectory is more curved.

29. (d) $h\nu = h\nu_0 + eV_S$

$$\frac{hc}{\lambda} = \frac{hc}{\lambda_0} + eV_S$$

$$\frac{1}{\lambda_0} = \frac{1}{\lambda} - \frac{eV_S}{hc}$$

In the first case,

$$\frac{1}{\lambda_0} = \frac{1}{\lambda} - \frac{eV}{hc} \quad ...(i)$$

In the second case,

$$\frac{1}{\lambda_0} = \frac{1}{2\lambda} - \frac{eV}{3hc} \quad ...(ii)$$

On multiplying by $\frac{1}{3}$ in Eq. (i), we get

$$\frac{1}{3\lambda_0} = \frac{1}{3\lambda} - \frac{eV}{3hc} \quad ...(iii)$$

Subtracting Eq. (ii) from Eq. (iii), we get

$$\frac{2}{3}\frac{1}{\lambda_0} = \frac{1}{6\lambda}$$

$$\lambda_0 = 4\lambda$$

30. (d) Work done

$$= -q(V_f - V_i)$$

$$= -q\left[\frac{kq}{d} + \frac{kQ}{2d} - \frac{kq}{2d} - \frac{kQ}{d}\right]$$

$$= -q\left[\frac{kq}{d} + \frac{2kq}{2d} - \frac{kq}{2d} - \frac{2kq}{d}\right]$$

$$= -q\frac{kq}{d}\left(1 + 1 - \frac{1}{2} - 2\right)$$

$$= \frac{kq^2}{2d}$$

31. (a) The fringe width,

$$\beta = \frac{D\lambda}{d} \Rightarrow \beta \propto \lambda$$

As we know, $\lambda = \frac{h}{p} = \frac{h}{mv}$

$$\beta \propto \frac{1}{v}$$

$$\frac{\beta_1}{\beta_2} = \frac{v_2}{v_1} = \frac{4v_1}{v_1}$$

$$\beta_2 = \frac{1}{4}\beta_1$$

If speed of electrons is made 4 times, then central bright fringe width becomes 1/4 times

32. (c) Phase difference $= \frac{2\pi}{\lambda} \times$ Path difference

$$\phi = 2\frac{\pi}{\lambda} \cdot \Delta x$$

At, $\Delta x = \lambda$, $\phi = 2\pi$ and resultant intensity is

$$I' = I_1 + I_2 + 2\sqrt{I_1 I_2} \cdot \cos\phi$$

$$= I + I + 2I\cos 2\pi$$

[Let the two coherent sources of equal intensity I]

$$I' = 4I \quad ...(i)$$

At $\Delta x = \frac{\lambda}{3}$, $\phi = \frac{2\pi}{3}$

and $I'' = I + I + 2I\cos\frac{2\pi}{3}$

$$= 2I\left(1 + \cos\frac{2\pi}{3}\right)$$

$$= 2I(1 - \cos 60°)$$

$$= 2I\left(1 - \frac{1}{2}\right)$$

$$I'' = I = \frac{I'}{4} \Rightarrow I'' = \frac{I'}{4}$$

33. (b) For the first position of the lens, the magnification is m_1 and for the second position of the lens, which is conjugate to first position, the magnification is m_2.

So, $m_1 = \frac{v}{u}$, $m_2 = \frac{u}{v}$ and $u + v = d$ (given)

Using lens formula,

$$\frac{1}{f} = \frac{1}{v} - \frac{1}{u}$$

$$\Rightarrow \frac{v}{f} = 1 - \frac{v}{u} = 1 - m_1$$

or $v = (1 - m_1)f$ ... (i)

Also, $\frac{1}{f} = \frac{1}{v} - \frac{1}{u}$

$$\Rightarrow \frac{u}{f} = \frac{u}{v} - 1 = m_2 - 1$$

or $u = (m_2 - 1)f$ ... (ii)

On adding Eqs. (i) and (ii), we get

$$v + u = (m_2 - m_1)f$$

But, $v + u = d$

$\therefore$ $d = (m_2 - m_1)f$

or $f = \frac{d}{m_2 - m_1}$

34. (c) Energy stored in the capacitor when its plates acquire a charge q,

$$U = \frac{q^2}{2C}$$

The maximum energy stored,

$U_0 = \frac{q_0^2}{2C}$, where q_0 is the maximum charge on the capacitor plates.

Given, $\frac{q^2}{2C} = \frac{1}{2}\cdot\frac{q_0^2}{2C}$ $\left(\because U = \frac{U_0}{2}\right)$

or $q^2 = \frac{q_0^2}{2}$

$$\Rightarrow q = \frac{q_0}{\sqrt{2}} = 0.71\,q_0$$

$\because$ $q = q_0\left[1 - e^{\frac{-t}{RC}}\right]$

So, $0.71q_0 = q_0\left[1 - e^{\frac{-t}{4\times10^6\times2\times10^{-6}}}\right]$

$$= q_0\left[1 - e^{\frac{-t}{8}}\right]$$

$\therefore$ $0.71 = 1 - e^{\frac{-t}{8}}$

or $e^{\frac{-t}{8}} = 1 - 0.71 = 0.29$

$$\frac{t}{8} = \log_e\left(\frac{1}{0.29}\right) = \log_e(3.4)$$

$$t = 8 \times \log_e(3.4)$$
$$= 8 \times 1.22 = 9.76 \text{ s}$$

35. (c) Let both spheres be placed at d distance.

$$\therefore \quad F_1 = \frac{1}{4\pi\varepsilon_0} \cdot \frac{q_1 q_2}{d^2} \quad \ldots(i)$$

As we know that after touching, both spheres acquire the same charge and the acquired charge is equal to half of the total charge.

New charges on spheres,

$$q_1' = q_2' = \frac{q_1 + q_2}{2}$$

Given that, $q_1 >> q_2$

$$q_1' = q_2' = \frac{q_1}{2}$$

$$F_2 = \frac{1}{4\pi\varepsilon_0} \cdot \frac{q_1' q_2'}{d^2}$$

$$= \frac{1}{4\pi\varepsilon_0} \cdot \frac{\left(\frac{q_1}{2}\right)^2}{d^2}$$

$$F_2 = \frac{1}{4} \cdot \frac{1}{4\pi\varepsilon_0} \cdot \frac{q_1^2}{d^2} \quad \ldots(ii)$$

On dividing Eq. (i) by Eq. (ii), we get

$$\frac{F_1}{F_2} = \frac{4q_2}{q_1}$$

36. (b) Fringe width is given by

$$\beta = \frac{\lambda D}{d}$$

So that $\quad \lambda = \frac{\beta d}{D} \quad \ldots(i)$

Let u and v be the distances of the slits and the eyepiece (screen) from the lens, then

Magnification, $m = \frac{I}{O} = \frac{v}{u}$

or $\quad \frac{7 \times 10^{-3} \text{ m}}{d} = \frac{0.70 \text{ m}}{0.30 \text{ m}}$

where d is the separation between the slits (object)

or $\quad d = \frac{7 \times 0.3 \times 10^{-3}}{0.7}$

$$= 3 \times 10^{-3} \text{ m} = 3 \text{ mm}$$

Substituting in Eq. (i), we get

$$\lambda = \frac{0.194 \times 3}{100 \times 10}$$
$$= 0.582 \times 10^{-3} \text{ mm}$$
$$= 0.582 \times 10^{-3} = 5820 \text{ Å}$$

37. (d) Shift in image position due to glass plate,

$$S = \left(1 - \frac{1}{\mu}\right) t$$

$$= \left(1 - \frac{1}{1.5}\right) \times 1 \text{ cm} = \frac{1}{3} \text{ cm}$$

For focal length of the lens,

$$\frac{1}{f} = \frac{1}{v} - \frac{1}{u} = \frac{1}{12} - \frac{1}{(-240)}$$

or $\quad \frac{1}{f} = \frac{20+1}{240}$

$\Rightarrow \quad f = \frac{240}{21} \text{ cm}$

Now, to get back image on the film, lens has to form image at $\left(12 - \frac{1}{3}\right)\text{cm} = \frac{35}{3}$ cm such that the glass plate will shift the image on the film.

As $\frac{1}{f} = \frac{1}{v} - \frac{1}{u}$

$\Rightarrow \quad \frac{1}{u} = \frac{1}{v} - \frac{1}{f} = \frac{3}{35} - \frac{21}{240}$

$$= \frac{48 \times 3 - 7 \times 21}{1680} = -\frac{1}{560}$$

$\Rightarrow \quad u = -5.6 \text{ m}$

38. (b) The equivalent resistance of n resistors connected in parallel is given as

$$\frac{1}{R_{eq}} = \frac{1}{R_1} + \frac{1}{R_2} + \frac{1}{R_3} + \ldots\ldots$$

$$\frac{1}{R_{eq}} = \frac{1}{r} + \frac{1}{r} + \frac{1}{r} + \ldots$$

$$\frac{1}{R_{eq}} = \frac{n}{r}$$

$\Rightarrow \quad R_{eq} = \frac{r}{n}$

The given circuit diagram may be redrawn as

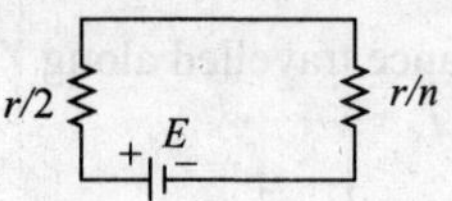

According to maximum power transfer theorem, the power consumed by all resistors of resistance r will be the largest, if the equivalent resistance of all resistors $\left(i.e. \frac{r}{n}\right)$ is equal to $\frac{r}{2}$.

$$\therefore \quad \frac{r}{2} = \frac{r}{n} \Rightarrow n = 2$$

39. (c) Induced emf e is given by

$$|e| = N\frac{d\phi}{dt}$$

Thus, $|e| \propto N \quad \ldots(i)$

Power, $\quad P = \frac{e^2}{R} \quad \ldots(ii)$

As we know,

$$R = \rho\frac{l}{A} = \frac{\rho . l}{\pi r^2}$$

$$R \propto \frac{l}{r^2}$$

Now, if the wire is stretched, its volume remains unchanged, length increases from l_1 to l_2 and radius decreases from r_1 to r_2, then

$$\pi r_1^2 l_1 = \pi r_2^2 l_2$$

or $\quad \frac{l_1}{l_2} = \left(\frac{r_2}{r_1}\right)^2$ or $l \propto \frac{1}{r^2} \quad \ldots(iii)$

$$P \propto \frac{N^2}{R}$$

or $P \propto N^2 \frac{r^2}{l} \propto N^2 r^4$

[from Eq. (iii)]

$$\therefore \frac{P_2}{P_1} = \left(\frac{N_2}{N_1}\right)^2 \left(\frac{r_2}{r_1}\right)^4$$

$$\frac{P_2}{P_1} = (4)^2 \left(\frac{1}{2}\right)^4 = 1$$

or $P_2 = P_1$

40. (d) Magnetic energy is stored in an inductor, whereas energy is dissipated through resistor.

Given, $U_m = 64$ J

$i = 8$ A

and $P = 640$ W

As, magnetic energy,

$$U_m = \frac{1}{2}Li^2$$

$$\Rightarrow \quad 64 = \frac{1}{2} \times L \times 64$$

$$\Rightarrow \quad L = 2\text{ H}$$

Energy dissipated, $P = i^2 R$

$$\Rightarrow \quad 640 = 64\,R \Rightarrow R = 10\,\Omega$$

Time constant of *R-L* circuit is given by

$$\tau = \frac{L}{R}$$

$$\Rightarrow \quad \tau = \frac{2}{10} = \frac{1}{5} = 0.2\text{ s}$$

41. (c) Given,

$$\phi = 4t^n - 3^n \quad \text{...(i)}$$

According to Faraday's law,

induced emf $= -\dfrac{d\phi}{dt}$

Magnitude of induced emf,

$$e = \left| -\frac{d\phi}{dt} \right|$$

Differentiating Eq. (i) with respect to time, we get

$$\frac{d\phi}{dt} = \frac{d}{dt}(4t^n - 3^n)$$

$$= 4nt^{n-1} - 0$$

(as 3^n is constant)

$$\frac{d\phi}{dt} = 4nt^{n-1}$$

or $\quad e = \left| -\dfrac{d\phi}{dt} \right| = 4nt^{n-1}$

If $n = 1$, then $e = 4(1)t^{1-1}$

$= 4$ (constant).

So, option (a) is correct.

If $n > 1$, $e = 4nt^{n-1}$

Let $n = 2$, $e = 8t$, i.e. $e \propto t$

With increase in time t, e also increases, so option (b) is correct and option (c) is incorrect.

If $n < 1$, $e = 4nt^{n-1}$

Let $n = 0.5$, $e = 4 \times 0.5t^{0.5-1}$

$$e = \frac{2}{\sqrt{t}}$$

or $\quad e \propto \dfrac{1}{\sqrt{t}}$

On increasing t, the value of e decreases.

$\therefore$ Option (d) is correct.

42. (b) Given, $q = \alpha t - \beta t^2$

Current, $i = \dfrac{dq}{dt} = \alpha - 2\beta t$

Let the current reduces to zero after time $t = T$ till the stored energy of the battery is consumed. Then, at $t = T$, $i = 0$

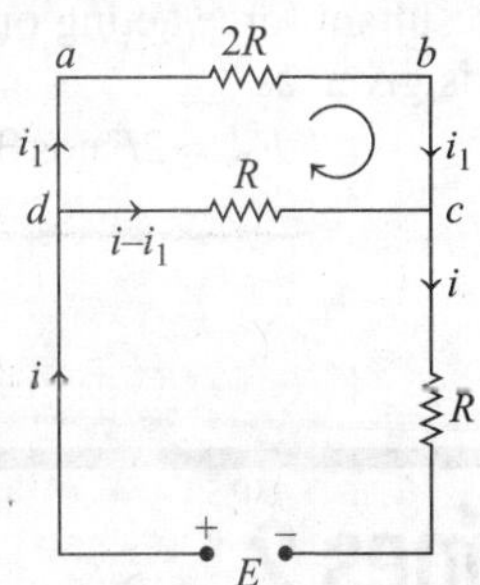

$\therefore \alpha - 2\beta T = 0$

or $\quad T = \dfrac{\alpha}{2\beta}$

Applying Kirchhoff's second law to the closed mesh *abcda*,

$$i_1(2R) - (i - i_1)R = 0$$

$$i = 3i_1$$

$$\Rightarrow \quad i_1 = \frac{i}{3}$$

or $\quad i_1 = \dfrac{1}{3}(\alpha - 2\beta t)$

Now, total heat produced in $2R$ in time T is

$$H = \int_0^T i_1^2 (2R)\,dt = \frac{2R}{9}\int_0^T (\alpha - 2\beta t)^2\,dt$$

$$= \frac{2R}{9}\int_0^T (\alpha^2 + 4\beta^2 t^2 - 4\alpha\beta t)\,dt$$

$$= \frac{2R}{9}\left[\alpha^2 t + \frac{4}{3}\beta^2 t^3 - 2\alpha\beta t^2\right]_0^T$$

$$= \frac{2R}{9}\left[\alpha^2 T + \frac{4}{3}\beta^2 T^3 - 2\alpha\beta T^2\right]$$

$$= \frac{2R}{9}\left[\alpha^2\left(\frac{\alpha}{2\beta}\right) + \frac{4}{3}\beta^2\left(\frac{\alpha^3}{8\beta^3}\right) - 2\alpha\beta\left(\frac{\alpha^2}{4\beta^2}\right)\right]$$

$$= \frac{2R}{9}\left[\frac{\alpha^3}{2\beta} + \frac{\alpha^3}{6\beta} - \frac{\alpha^3}{2\beta}\right] = \frac{\alpha^3 R}{27\beta}$$

43. (a) The current distribution has been shown in the figure *i* accordance with Kirchhoff's first law.

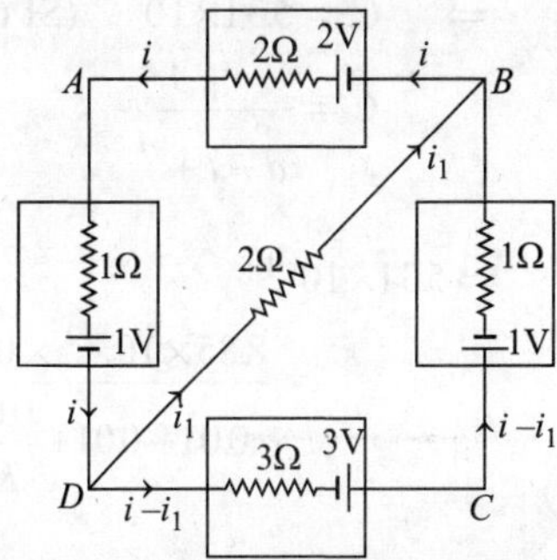

Now, applying Kirchhoff's second law to mesh *DBAD* and *DCBD*.

$$2i_1 + 2i + i = 2 - 1$$

$$2i_1 + 3i = 1 \quad \text{...(i)}$$

and $3(i - i_1) + 1(i - i_1) - 2i_1 = 3 - 1$

$$-6i_1 + 4i = 2$$

$$-3i_1 + 2i = 1 \quad \text{...(ii)}$$

Solving Eqs. (i) and (ii) for i_1 and i, we get

$$i_1 = -\frac{1}{13}\text{ A and } i = \frac{5}{13}\text{ A}$$

Now, potential difference between *B* and *D* is

$$V_D - V_B = 2i_1 = -\frac{2}{13}\text{ V}$$

or $\quad V_B - V_D = +\dfrac{2}{13}$ V

44. (c)

A. Capacitance,

$$C = \frac{\varepsilon_0 A}{d}$$

$$= \frac{8.85 \times 10^{-12} \times 0.20}{0.01}$$

$$= 1.77 \times 10^{-10}\text{ (SI unit)}$$

B. Charge on each plate, $q = CV$
$= 3000 \times 1.77 \times 10^{-10}$
$= 5.31 \times 10^{-7}$ (SI unit)

First solve for option (D) then (C).

D. Capacitance, after insertion of dielectric sheet, $C' = \dfrac{q}{V}$

$$\Rightarrow \quad C' = \frac{5.31 \times 10^{-7}}{1000}$$

$$\Rightarrow \quad C' = 5.31 \times 10^{-10} \text{ (SI unit)}$$

$$\therefore \quad C' = \frac{\varepsilon_0 A}{d - t + \dfrac{t}{K}}$$

$$\Rightarrow 5.31 \times 10^{-10} = \frac{8.85 \times 10^{-12} \times 0.20}{0.01 - 0.01 + \dfrac{0.01}{K}}$$

$$\Rightarrow K = \frac{5.31 \times 10^{-10} \times 0.01}{8.85 \times 10^{-12} \times 0.20}$$

Dielectric constant, $K = 3$

45. (b) 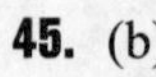

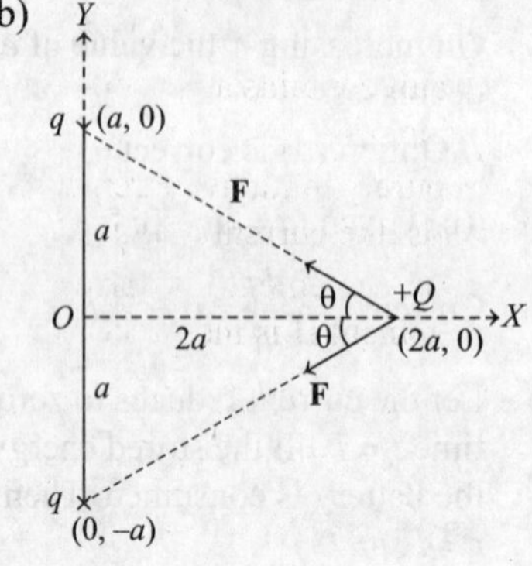

The resultant force acting on charge $(+Q)$ is given as

$$F_R = 2F\cos\theta$$

$$F_R = 2\frac{qQ}{4\pi\varepsilon_0 (a^2 + 4a^2)} \cdot \frac{2}{\sqrt{5}}$$

The charge thus moves towards X-axis. Let at instant, its position from point O is x.

Instantaneous resultant force acting over it is given as

$$F_R = 2F\cos\theta$$

$$= 2\frac{qQ}{4\pi\varepsilon_0 (a^2 + x^2)} \cdot \frac{x}{\sqrt{a^2 + x^2}}$$

$$F_R = \frac{2qQ}{4\pi\varepsilon_0} \frac{x}{(a^2 + x^2)^{\frac{3}{2}}}$$

This force is not of the form $F = kx$

Therefore, the motion of the charge Q is oscillatory but not simple harmonic.

NSS2 NEET Stepping Stones 2

1. (c) If slider moves towards A from B then, resistance decreases.

As we know, $V = IR$

$$i = \frac{V}{R} \Rightarrow I \propto \frac{1}{R}$$

So, I increases.

$$B = \frac{\mu_0}{2} \cdot \frac{I}{r}$$

$$B \propto I$$

So, B also increases.

Flux associated with small coil increases. So, induced current in coil Q is anti-clockwise.

2. (c) Induced emf $= \int_{2l}^{3l} (\omega x) B \cdot dx$

$[\because v = \omega x]$

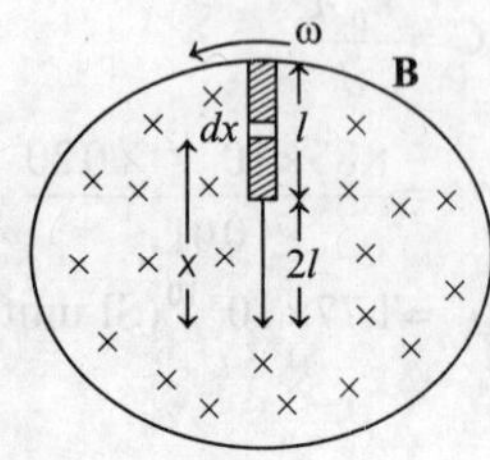

$$e = B\omega\left[\frac{x^2}{2}\right]_{2l}^{3l}$$

$$= \frac{B\omega}{2}[(3l)^2 - (2l)^2]$$

$$= \frac{5}{2} Bl^2\omega$$

3. (b) When a converging beam is incident on plane mirror, real image is formed as shown.

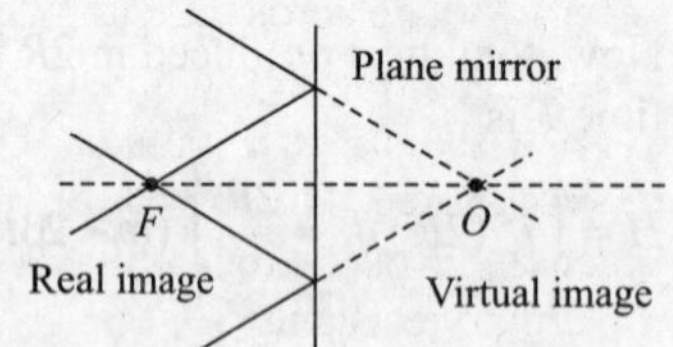

4. (d) The average power dissipated in a circuit consisting only of inductors or capacitors is zero. As we know, in pure inductive circuit, current is lagging behind the voltage by 90° i.e., phase difference (ϕ) between voltage and current is 90°.

Average power dissipated,

$$P_{avg} = \frac{V_0 i_0}{2}\cos\phi = \frac{V_0 i_0}{2}\cos 90^\circ$$

$$P_{avg} = 0$$

5. (a) Law of conservation of charge says that, charge on an isolated system remains constant. When we produce charge q_1 on a body by rubbing it against another body which gets a charge q_2, then q_1 and q_2 both are equal in magnitude but opposite in polarities. Hence, $q_1 + q_2 = 0$ because charge on an isolated system remains constant.

Therefore, A and R are correct and R is the correct explanation of A.

6. (b) Here, the resistors of $400\,\Omega$ and $10000\,\Omega$ are in parallel, so their effective resistance, R_P will be

$$R_P = \frac{400 \times 10000}{400 + 10000} = \frac{5000}{13}\,\Omega$$

Total resistance of the circuit,

$$R = \frac{5000}{13} + 800 = \frac{15400}{13}\,\Omega$$

Current in the circuit,

$$i = \frac{6}{15400/13} = \frac{39}{7700}\text{ A}$$

Potential difference across voltmeter,

$$V = iR_P$$
$$= \frac{39}{7700} \times \frac{5000}{13} = 1.95\text{ V}$$

7. (b) Initially, the time period of the magnet,

$$T = 2\pi\sqrt{\left(\frac{I}{MB}\right)}$$

For each part of magnet, its moment of inertia is $\frac{I}{27}$ and its magnetic moment $= M/3$.

When magnet is cut along its length into three equal parts and placed on each other, then new moment of inertia of system,

$$I' = \frac{I}{27} \times 3 = \frac{I}{9}$$

and magnetic moment of system,

$$M' = \frac{M}{3} \times 3 = M$$

$\therefore$ Time period of system,

$$T' = 2\pi\sqrt{\frac{I'}{M'B}} = \frac{1}{3} \times 2\pi\sqrt{\frac{I}{MB}}$$
$$= \frac{T}{3} = \frac{2}{3}\text{ s}$$

8. (b) Kinetic energy of emitted photoelectron is $\frac{1}{2}mv^2 = \frac{hc}{\lambda}$

As work function is negligible,

$$\frac{p^2}{2m} = \frac{hc}{\lambda} \text{ or } p = \sqrt{\frac{2mhc}{\lambda}}$$

$\therefore$ de-Broglie wavelength associated to photoelectrons,

$$\lambda_0 = \frac{h}{p} = \frac{h}{\sqrt{\frac{2mhc}{\lambda}}} = \sqrt{\frac{h\lambda}{2mc}}$$

or $\lambda = \lambda_0^2\left(\frac{2mc}{h}\right)$

9. (d) For a lens, $m = \frac{f-v}{f} = -\frac{1}{f}(v+1)$

Comparing it with $y = mx + c$, we have

Slope, $m = -\frac{1}{f}$

From graph, slope of the line $= \frac{b}{c}$

Hence, $-\frac{1}{f} = \frac{b}{c}$ thus, $|f| = \frac{c}{b}$

10. (c) An L-C resonance circuit have zero reactance since, $X_L = X_C$. Therefore, it is possible that the circuit contains a capacitor and an inductor.

In purely inductive circuit, voltage leads the current by 90°.

Thus, Statement I is correct but Statement II is incorrect.

11. (a) Given, energy flux,

$$\phi = 20\text{ W/cm}^2$$

Area, $A = 30\text{ cm}^2$

Time, $t = 30\text{ mins} = 30 \times 60\text{ s}$

Now, total energy falling on the surface in time t,

$U = \phi A t = 20 \times 30 \times (30 \times 60)$ J

Momentum of the incident light $= \frac{U}{c}$

$$= \frac{20 \times 30 \times (30 \times 60)}{3 \times 10^8}$$
$$= 36 \times 10^{-4}\text{ kg-m/s}$$

Momentum of the reflected light = 0

$\therefore$ Momentum delivered to the surface $= 36 \times 10^{-4} - 0$

$$= 36 \times 10^{-4}\text{ kg-m/s}$$

12. (d) Due to forward biasing during positive half-cycle of input AC voltage, the resistance of p-n junction is low. The current in the circuit is maximum. In this situation, a maximum potential difference will appear across resistance connected in series of circuit. This results in zero output voltage across p-n junction. Similarly during negative half-cycle of AC voltage, the p-n junction is reverse biased. The resistance of p-n junction becomes high which will be more than resistance in series. That's why, there will be voltage across p-n junction with negative cycles in output.

13. (c) $Q_1 = +4e$ F_2 q F_1 $Q_2 = +e$; x_1, x_2, x

For equilibrium on charge q,

$$|F_1| = |F_2|$$

which gives $x_2 = \frac{x}{\sqrt{\frac{Q_1}{Q_2}} + 1}$

$$= \frac{x}{\sqrt{\frac{4e}{e}} + 1} = \frac{x}{3}$$

14. (a) Maximum intensity is given as, $I_{max} = 4I_0$

Phase difference between two points separated by a distance equal to (1/4)th of the distance between two successive fringes is

$$\Delta\phi = \frac{1}{4} \times 2\pi = \frac{\pi}{2}$$

$$\therefore \quad I = 4I_0 \cos^2\left(\frac{\pi/2}{2}\right) = 2I_0$$

Hence, $\frac{I_{max}}{I} = \frac{4I_0}{2I_0} = 2$

15. (a) In case of hydrogen molecule, there is no unpaired electron. Thus, the net magnetic moment is zero although each atom of hydrogen has a permanent magnetic moment due to its single unpaired electron.

So, due to no unpaired electron, magnetic moment is zero and hydrogen molecules behaves as diamagnetic.

16. (b) Path difference, $\Delta x = \frac{yd}{D}$

$$= \left(\frac{1.25\lambda D}{d}\right)\left(\frac{d}{D}\right)$$
$$= 1.25\lambda = \frac{5}{4}\lambda$$

Phase difference, $\phi = \frac{2\pi}{\lambda} \cdot \Delta x$

$$= \frac{2\pi}{\lambda} \times \frac{5}{4}\lambda = \frac{5}{2}\pi$$

$$\therefore \quad \frac{\phi}{2} = \frac{5}{4}\pi = 225°$$

$\therefore$ Intensity, $I = I_{max}\cos^2\frac{\phi}{2} = \frac{1}{2}I_{max}$

17. (b) $C = \frac{\varepsilon_0 kA}{d}$

$$\Rightarrow C \propto \frac{k}{d}$$

$$\therefore \frac{C_1}{C_2} = \frac{k_1}{d_1} \times \frac{d_2}{k_2} = \frac{k}{d} \times \frac{d/2}{3k} = \frac{1}{6}$$

$$C_2 = 6C_1$$

Again for capacity of a capacitor,

$$C = \frac{k\varepsilon_0 A}{d}$$

Therefore, capacity of a capacitor depends upon the medium between the plates of capacitor.

18. (c) Let the initial full scale deflection in galvanometer be I_g and final full scale deflection be I'_g, we can write

$$I_g = 75k \text{ and } I'_g = 25k$$

where, k is the figure of merit of galvanometer.

According to the question, the circuit arrangement can be shown as

I'_g G I_g $(I_g - I_g')$ S

where, S is the resistance connected in parallel.

In parallel,

voltage across G = voltage across S

$$I'_g G = (I_g - I'_g)S$$

$$\Rightarrow \quad G = \frac{(I_g - I'_g)}{I'_g} S$$

$$= \left(\frac{75k - 25k}{25k}\right) \times 20 = 40\,\Omega$$

19. (d) According to Faraday's law, whenever the amount of magnetic flux linked with a circuit changes w.r.t. time, an emf is induced in the circuit,

The magnitude of the induced emf in a circuit is equal to the rate of change of magnetic flux w.r.t. time through the circuit,

i.e. Induced emf,

$$e = \left|\frac{d\phi_B}{dt}\right| \quad \ldots\text{(i)}$$

Given, magnetic field is varying with distance and it is not varying w.r.t. time.

Therefore, $\frac{d\phi_B}{dt} = 0$

From Eq. (i), $e = 0$

Hence, no emf is induced in triangular loop.

20. (d) The potential energy of dipole at position θ is given as

$$U = -\mathbf{M}\cdot\mathbf{B} \quad \text{or} \quad -MB\cos\theta$$

and work done in rotating dipole from position θ_1 to θ_2 is

$$W = \Delta U = U_2 - U_1$$

$$= -MB\cos\theta_2 - (-MB\cos\theta_1)$$

$$= MB\cos\theta_1 - MB\cos\theta_2$$

Given, $\theta_1 = 0°, \theta_2 = \theta$

$$W = MB[\cos 0° - \cos\theta]$$

$$= MB[1 - \cos\theta]$$

$\because \; 1 - \cos 2\theta = 2\sin^2\theta$

$$\therefore \quad W = MB[2\sin^2\theta/2]$$

$$= 2MB\sin^2(\theta/2)$$

21. (c) For rotating rod, induced emf is

$$V = \frac{1}{2}Bl^2\omega$$

× × × × × × B A O C ω

For part AO,

$$V_{OA} = V_O - V_A = \frac{1}{2}Bl^2\omega$$

For part OC,

$$V_{OC} = V_O - V_C = \frac{1}{2}B(3l)^2\omega$$

$$\therefore V_A - V_C = V_{OC} - V_{OA}$$

$$= (V_O - V_C) - (V_O - V_A) = 4Bl^2\omega$$

22. (d) Fleming's left hand rule is used to determine the direction of force. Because an electron is travelling east, the current is flowing west and the magnetic field is pointing downwards. Now, with your middle finger pointed west and your forefinger pointed downwards, your thumb will be pointing south. As a result, the direction of force on electron is along southwards.

23. (a) As we know that,

$$\lambda = \frac{hc}{eV} \Rightarrow \frac{\lambda_1}{\lambda_2} = \frac{V_2}{V_1}$$

$$\Rightarrow \quad \text{If } \lambda_2 = \frac{3}{4}\lambda_1$$

Then, $V_2 = \frac{4}{3}V_1$

As precent increase of potential difference,

$$= \frac{V_2 - V_1}{V_1} \times 100 = \frac{\frac{4}{3}V_1 - V_1}{V_1} \times 100$$

$$= \frac{100}{3} = 33.33\% \simeq 34\%$$

24. (b) Net process is,

$$3\,{}_1H^2 \longrightarrow {}_2He^4 + p + n$$

Mass defect,

$$\Delta m = (3 \times 2.014) - 4.001 - 1.007 - 1.008$$

$$= 0.026 \text{ amu}$$

Energy released by the fusion of three deuterons

$= \Delta m \times 931.48 = 0.026 \times 931.48$ MeV

$= 0.026 \times 931.48 \times 1.6 \times 10^{-13}$ J

$= 3.87 \times 10^{-12}$ J

∴ Total energy released

$$= \frac{10^{40}}{3} \times 3.87 \times 10^{-12} \text{ J}$$

$$= 1.29 \times 10^{28} \text{ J}$$

$$\text{Total time} = \frac{1.29 \times 10^{28}}{10^{16}}$$

$$= 1.29 \times 10^{12} \text{ s} \quad \left(\because \text{Power} = \frac{\text{Energy}}{\text{Time}}\right)$$

∴ The order of time is 10^{12} s.

25. (d) At the distance of closest approach r,

$$K = \frac{1}{4\pi\varepsilon_0}\frac{(2e)(Ze)}{r}$$

$$\Rightarrow \quad r = \frac{2Ze^2}{4\pi\varepsilon_0 K}$$

where, Ze = charge of the nucleus, $2e$ = charge of the α-particle and K = kinetic energy of the α-particle.

$$\because \quad K = \frac{p^2}{2m}$$

where, p is the momentum of the α-particle and m is the mass of the electron.

$$\therefore \; r = \frac{2Ze^2\,2m}{4\pi\varepsilon_0 p^2} \text{ or } r \propto \frac{1}{p^2}$$

$$\frac{r'}{r} = \left(\frac{p}{p'}\right)^2 = \left(\frac{p}{2p}\right)^2 = \frac{1}{4}$$

$$\Rightarrow \; r' = \frac{r}{4}$$

26. (a) Here, $V = (50\sin \omega t)\,\text{V}$

comparing it with general equation,

$$V = V_0 \sin \omega t$$

we get, $V_0 = 50\,\text{V}$

Given,

Load resistance,

$$R_L = 850\,\Omega$$

Internal resistance of rectifier,

$$r_d = 150\,\Omega$$

Maximum output current,

$$I_0 = \frac{V_0}{r_d + R_L} = \frac{50}{(150+850)}$$

$$= \frac{50}{1000} = 0.05\,\text{A}$$

$$= 50 \times 10^{-3}\,\text{A}$$

or $I_0 = 50\,\text{mA}$

27. (c) If a centre tap transformer is used with 2 diodes for full wave rectification, then output voltage of rectifier w.r.t. each diode is (1/2) × secondary voltage of transformer.

28. (c) Both the fields are anti-parallel to each other, so angle between them will be $\theta = 180°$.

$$\mathbf{E}_1 \times \mathbf{E}_2 = \mathbf{E}_1 \mathbf{E}_2 \sin 180°$$

$$\mathbf{E}_1 \times \mathbf{E}_2 = 0$$

and $|\mathbf{E}_1 \times \mathbf{E}_2| = 0$

29. (b) Energy,

$$U = \frac{1}{2} L i_0^2 = \frac{1}{2} L \left(\frac{V}{R}\right)^2$$

$$= \frac{1}{2} \times 50 \times 10^{-6} \left(\frac{5}{0.5}\right)^2$$

$$= 2.5\,\text{mJ}$$

Now, after switching OFF the battery, this energy is dissipated in coil (resistance = 0.5 Ω) and resistor (10 Ω) in the ratio of their resistance ($H = i^2 Rt$ or $H \propto R$). Therefore, heat generated in the coil is

$$2.5 \times \frac{0.5}{10 + 0.5} = 0.12\,\text{mJ}$$

30. (d) Given, **u** and **B** are perpendicular to each other. Force on electron due to magnetic field is

$$\mathbf{F} = -e(\mathbf{u} \times \mathbf{B})$$

Since this force acts perpendicular to **u**, therefore it does not do any work. Due to it, the magnitude of velocity of electron remains constant. It means $v = u$. Due to perpendicular magnetic field acting on the moving electron, the electron will describe a circular path in the magnetic field in clockwise direction. So, y will be less than zero and the trajectory will be as

Y X
Path of electron

Hence, option (d) $v = u$ and $y < 0$ is correct.

31. (a) Using $P = P_1 + P_2 - d \times P_1 P_2$

For equivalent power to be negative,

$$d \times P_1 P_2 > P_1 + P_2$$

$$d \times 25 > 10$$

$$d > \frac{10}{25}\,\text{m}$$

$$d > \frac{10 \times 100}{25}\,\text{cm}$$

$$\Rightarrow \quad d > 40\,\text{cm}$$

32. (c) Velocity components normal to mirror and parallel to mirror are shown in figure.

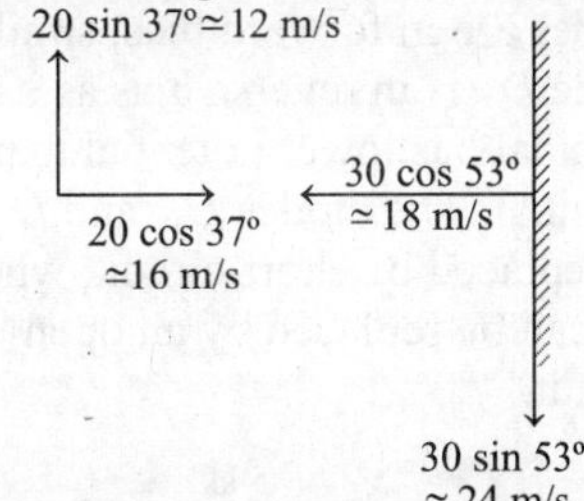

As we know,

$$\mathbf{v}_{\text{image}} = \mathbf{v}_{\text{object}} + 2\,\mathbf{v}_{\text{mirror}}$$

Now, horizontal velocity of image with respect to ground

$$= 16 + (2 \times 18) = 52\,\text{m/s}$$

Vertical velocity of image = 12 m/s

$$\mathbf{v}_{\text{image}} = (-52\hat{\mathbf{i}} + 12\hat{\mathbf{j}})\,\text{m/s}$$

33. (c) Force on wire Q due to wire R,

$$F_R = \frac{4\pi \times 10^{-7}}{4\pi} \times \frac{2 \times 20 \times 10}{0.02} \times 0.1$$

$$= 20 \times 10^{-5}\,\text{N} \quad \text{(towards right)}$$

Force on wire Q due to wire P,

$$F_P = \frac{4\pi \times 10^{-7}}{4\pi} \times \frac{2 \times 30 \times 10}{0.1} \times 0.1$$

$$= 6 \times 10^{-5}\,\text{N (towards right)}$$

Net force on Q, $F = F_R + F_P$

$$= 20 \times 10^{-5} + 6 \times 10^{-5}$$

$$= 26 \times 10^{-5}\,\text{N}$$

$$= 2.6 \times 10^{-4}\,\text{N} \quad \text{(towards right)}$$

34. (a) We know that,

$$v_d = \frac{J}{ne},\ \rho = \frac{E}{J} = \frac{E}{nev_d}$$

$$\therefore \quad v_d = \frac{E}{ne\rho} = \frac{V}{ne\rho L}$$

$$(\because E = V/L)$$

Also $\rho = \dfrac{RA}{L}$

A. If V is doubled, v_d is also doubled.

∴ A → Q

B. If L is doubled, v_d is halved, hence decreased.

∴ B → R

C. If d is doubled, drift velocity will not change.

∴ C → S

D. If temperature of wire is increased, n will increase and so v_d will decrease.

∴ D → P

35. (a) $R = \dfrac{\rho \cdot l}{A}$

$$\Rightarrow \quad \ln R = \ln \rho + \ln l - \ln A$$

$$\Rightarrow \quad \frac{dR}{R} = 0 + \frac{dl}{l} - \frac{dA}{A} \quad \text{...(i)}$$

Now, $V = l \cdot A$ and volume is constant.

$$\Rightarrow \quad \ln V = \ln l + \ln A$$

$$\Rightarrow \quad \frac{dV}{V} = \frac{dl}{l} + \frac{dA}{A}$$

$$\Rightarrow \quad 0 = \frac{dl}{l} + \frac{dA}{A} \quad \text{...(ii)}$$

Adding Eqs. (i) and (ii), we get

$$\frac{dR}{R} = 2\frac{dl}{l}$$

$$\left(\text{As, } n = 0.2\%, \frac{dl}{l} = 0.2\%\right)$$

$$\Rightarrow \quad \frac{dR}{R} = 2 \times 0.2\% \Rightarrow \frac{dR}{R} = 0.4\%$$

36. (c) Given, electric potential,

$$V = (10x^2 + 5x + 2)\,\text{V}$$

Electric potential at $x = 1\,\text{m}$,

$$V_1 = 10(1)^2 + 5(1) + 2 = 17\,\text{V}$$

Electric potential at $x = 2$ m,

$$V_2 = 10(2)^2 + 5(2) + 2 = 52\text{ V}$$

The electrostatic potential energy of a charge q in an electric field is given as $U = qV$, where V is the electric potential at that point.

Difference, $\Delta U = U_2 - U_1$

$$= qV_2 - qV_1$$
$$= q(V_2 - V_1)$$
$$= 2 \times 10^{-6} \times (52 - 17)$$
$$= 70 \times 10^{-6}\text{ J}$$

or $\Delta U = 70\mu\text{J}$

37. (b) The electric field at C due to charge $+10^{-7}$ C at A is

$$\mathbf{E}_1 = \frac{1}{4\pi\varepsilon_0}\frac{10^{-7}}{(0.2)^2} \text{ along } AC$$

The electric field at C due to charge -10^{-7} C at B is

$$\mathbf{E}_2 = -\frac{1}{4\pi\varepsilon_0}\frac{10^{-7}}{(0.2)^2} \text{ along } CB$$

As, $|\mathbf{E}_1| = |\mathbf{E}_2|$

By symmetry, the vertical components will cancel out and horizontal components will add up.

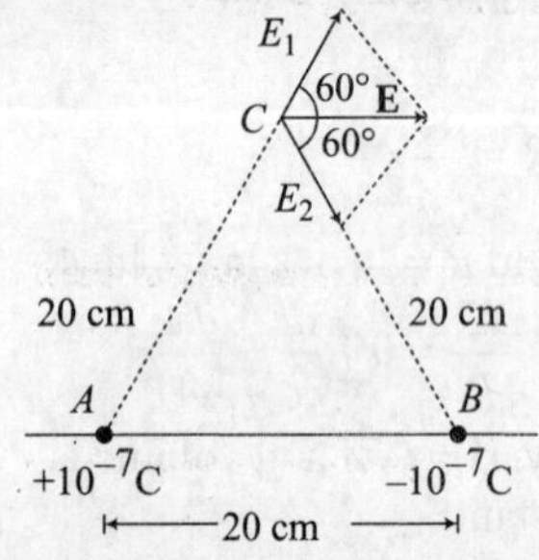

$\therefore$ The resultant electric field at C is

$$E = 2E_1 \cos 60°$$
$$= 2 \times \frac{1}{4\pi\varepsilon_0}\frac{10^{-7}}{(0.2)^2} \times \frac{1}{2}$$
$$= \frac{9 \times 10^9 \times 10^{-7}}{(0.2)^2} = 2.2 \times 10^4\text{ N/C}$$

38. (a) Let Q_1 and Q_2 be the charge on the two conducting spheres of radii $R_1 (= 3\text{ cm})$ and $R_2 (= 1\text{ cm})$, respectively.

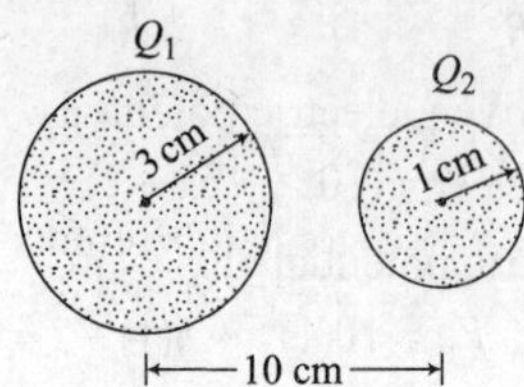

$\therefore$ Potential, $V_1 = \frac{1}{4\pi\varepsilon_0}\frac{Q_1}{R_1}$

$$\Rightarrow \quad 10 = \frac{9 \times 10^9 \times Q_1}{3 \times 10^{-2}}$$

$$\Rightarrow \quad Q_1 = \frac{10 \times 3 \times 10^{-2}}{9 \times 10^9} \quad \text{...(i)}$$

and $V_2 = \frac{1}{4\pi\varepsilon_0}\frac{Q_2}{R_2}$

$$\Rightarrow \quad 10 = \frac{9 \times 10^9 \times Q_2}{1 \times 10^{-2}}$$

$$\Rightarrow \quad Q_2 = \frac{10 \times 1 \times 10^{-2}}{9 \times 10^9} \quad \text{...(ii)}$$

According to Coulomb's law, force of repulsion between them is

$$F = \frac{1}{4\pi\varepsilon_0}\frac{Q_1 Q_2}{r^2}$$

$$= \frac{9 \times 10^9 \times 10 \times 3 \times 10^{-2} \times 10 \times 1 \times 10^{-2}}{9 \times 10^9 \times 9 \times 10^9 \times (10 \times 10^{-2})^2}$$

[using Eqs. (i) and (ii)]

$$= \left(\frac{1}{3}\right) \times 10^{-9}\text{ N}$$

39. (d) The potential at p terminal is higher than of n terminal for D_1 and D_2 diodes connected in circuit. Both diodes are in forward bias, similarly diode D_3 is in reverse bias as its p terminal has lower potential than n terminal. The diodes D_1 and D_2 can be replaced by short-circuit, where D_3 can be replaced by an open circuit.

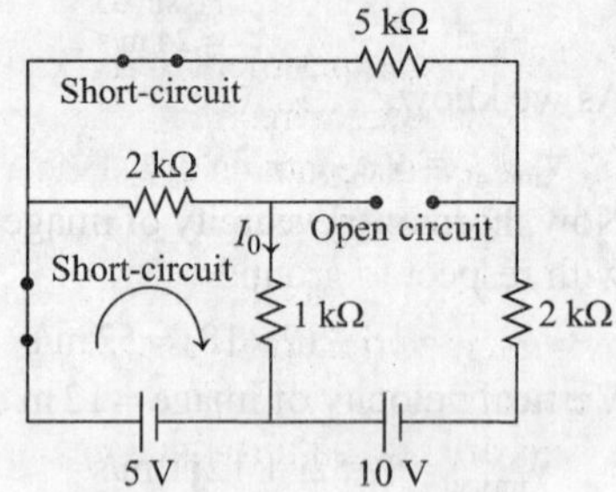

Using the KVL in loop along the direction shown,

$$5 - 2 \times 10^3 I_0 - 1 \times 10^3 I_0 = 0$$
$$\Rightarrow 3 \times 10^3 I_0 = 5$$
$$\Rightarrow \quad I_0 = 1.66 \times 10^{-3}\text{ A}$$
$$= 1.66\text{ mA}$$

40. (c) Length of tube = Separation between curves of telescope

$$= f_o + f_e \text{ (when image is at } \infty)$$
$$= 144 + 6 = 150\text{ cm}$$

41. (c) $R = \frac{80}{10} = 8\Omega$

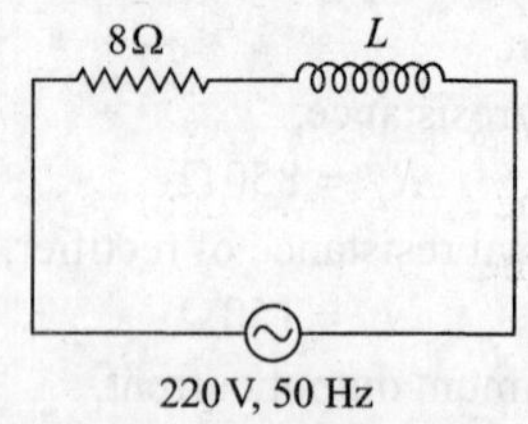

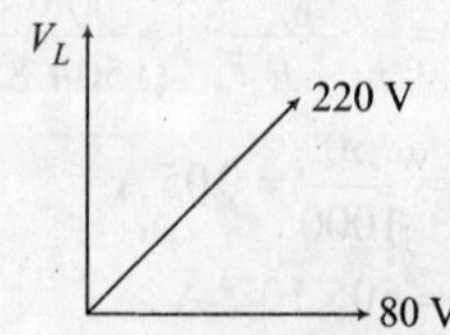

Also, $V_L^2 + 80^2 = 220^2$

$$V_L^2 = (220 + 80)(220 - 80)$$
$$= 300 \times 140$$
$$\Rightarrow \quad V_L = 204.9\text{ V}$$
$$\Rightarrow \quad I_{\text{rms}} X_L = 204.9$$
$$\Rightarrow \frac{220}{\sqrt{64 + X_L^2}} X_L = 204.9$$
$$\Rightarrow X_L = 20 \Rightarrow L = \frac{20}{2\pi f} = 0.064\text{ H}$$

42. (a) Given, $\varepsilon = 2$ V, $r = 1\ \Omega$ and $I = 1$ A

Let external resistance be R.

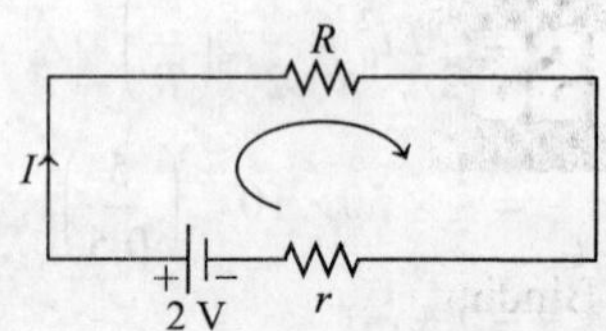

We have, $I = \frac{2}{R + r}$

or $1 = \frac{2}{R + 1}$

or $R + 1 = 2 \Rightarrow R = 1\Omega$

Now, two identical batteries are connected, then circuit

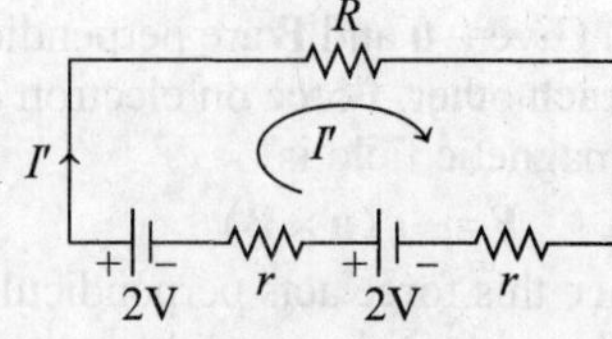

Let I' = current, then

or $I' = \dfrac{4}{(2r+R)}$

Putting the values of R and r, we get

$$I' = \frac{4}{2\times1+1} = \frac{4}{2+1} = \frac{4}{3}$$

or $I' = 1.33$ A

43. (c) The angular width of central maximum is given by

$$2\theta = \frac{2\lambda}{a} \quad \ldots(i)$$

where, λ = wavelength of light used and a = width of the slit.

Angular width, $2\theta = \theta_0$ (given)

So, $\theta_0 = \dfrac{2\lambda_1}{a}$ ...(ii) [from Eq. (i)]

For another light of wavelength λ_2 (say), the angular width decreases by 30%, so

$$2\theta = \left(\frac{100-30}{100}\right)\theta_0$$

$$2\theta = \frac{70}{100}\theta_0 = 0.7\theta_0$$

$\therefore$ Angular width, $0.7\theta_0 = \dfrac{2\lambda_2}{a}$ ...(iii)

As, slit width is constant, so on dividing Eq. (ii) by Eq. (iii), we get

$$\frac{1}{0.7} = \frac{\lambda_1}{\lambda_2}$$

$$\Rightarrow \quad \lambda_2 = \lambda_1 \times 0.7 = 6000\times 0.7 = 4200 \text{ Å}$$

44. (d) Let the separation between points P and Q is r. When the body (mass = 10^{-3} kg) is at Q, the potential at P due to charge $q = 10^{-8}$ C at Q is given as

$$V_P = \frac{q}{4\pi\varepsilon_0 r} = \frac{9\times10^9\times10^{-8}}{r} = \frac{90}{r} = 600 \text{ V (given)}$$

$$\therefore \quad r = \frac{90}{600} = \frac{3}{20} \text{ m}$$

$$F = qE = q\left(\frac{V_P - V_Q}{r}\right) = 10^{-8}\left(\frac{600-0}{\frac{3}{20}}\right)$$

$= 4\times10^{-5}$ N

Acceleration produced in the body is

$$a = \frac{F}{m} = \frac{4\times10^{-5}}{10^{-3}} = 4\times10^{-2} \text{ m/s}^2$$

Now, $v^2 = u^2 + 2ar$

$$0.04 = u^2 + 2\times4\times10^{-2}\times\frac{3}{20}$$

$(\because v = 20\times10^{-2} = 0.20$ m/s$)$

$$0.04 = u^2 + \frac{6}{5}\times10^{-2}$$

$$u^2 = 0.04 - 0.012 = 0.028$$

$$\Rightarrow \quad u = \sqrt{0.028} \text{ m/s}$$

45. (a) $Q = [m_n({}^{23}_{10}\text{Ne}) - m_n({}^{23}_{11}\text{Na}) - m_e]c^2$

$= [\{m_n({}^{23}_{10}\text{Ne}) + 10m_e\} - \{m_n({}^{23}_{11}\text{Na}) + 11m_e\}]c^2$

$= [m({}^{23}_{10}\text{Ne}) - m({}^{23}_{11}\text{Na})]c^2$

$= [22.994466 - 22.989770] \times 931.5$ MeV

$= 0.004696 \times 931.5$ MeV

$= 4.374$ MeV

Maximum kinetic energy of the electrons is 4.374 MeV.

NSS3 NEET Stepping Stones 3

1. (d) Binding energy is the amount of energy given to a nucleus, so that it can be broken into its constituent nucleons or energy released when a nucleus is formed.

Binding energy has nothing to do with the kinetic energies of the nucleons in a nucleus.

2. (d) The energy in electromagnetic waves is divided equally between the electric and magnetic fields.

The total energy per unit volume,

$$u = u_e + u_m = \frac{1}{2}\varepsilon_0 E^2 + \frac{1}{2}\frac{B^2}{\mu_0}$$

3. (d) Both Statement I and Statement II are correct.

While doing experiment, temperature of all resistance wires increases, so two consecutive values of balance lengths cannot be same.

4. (c) Cracks or faults that are present within a material are thinner than its surrounding material. Therefore, X-rays are passed through damaged area to form an image illustrating the exact location and size of the crack.

5. (b) $F = qE = ma$

$$\Rightarrow a = \frac{qE}{m} = \frac{1.6\times10^{-19}\times1\times10^3}{9\times10^{-31}} = \frac{1.6\times10^{15}}{9} \text{ ms}^{-2}$$

Given, $u = 5\times10^6$ m/s and $v = 0$

$$\therefore \quad v^2 = u^2 - 2as$$

$$\Rightarrow \quad s = \frac{u^2}{2a}$$

$$\therefore \text{ Distance, } s = \frac{(5\times10^6)^2\times9}{2\times1.6\times10^{15}} = 7\text{cm}$$

6. (d) Total current drawn from the battery, $i = \dfrac{E}{R} = \dfrac{6}{100} = 0.06$ A

Resistance of 50 cm wire,

$$R' = \frac{\rho l'}{A} = \left(\frac{\rho}{A}\right)l' = \left(\frac{R}{l}\right)l'$$

$$R' = \frac{100}{300}\times50 = \frac{50}{3}\ \Omega$$

Hence, the potential difference between two points on the wire separated by a distance 50 cm is

$$V = iR' = 0.06 \times \frac{50}{3} = 1\,\text{V}$$

7. (b) Amount of magnetic flux linked with the inductor is

$\phi = Li$

The emf induced in the inductor is

$$e = -\frac{d\phi}{dt} = -\frac{d}{dt}(Li) = -L\frac{di}{dt}$$

$$\Rightarrow |e| = L\frac{di}{dt}$$

Here, induced current $= \frac{V}{R} = \frac{10}{5} = 2\,\text{A}$

Circuit switches off in 1 ms

$\Rightarrow \; dt = 1 \times 10^{-3}$ s

$\therefore$ Induced emf in the inductor is

$$|e| = 10 \times \frac{2}{1 \times 10^{-3}} = 2 \times 10^4\ \text{V}$$

8. (b) There is always loss of energy when two capacitors share charges. This is due to loss of energy in the form of radiation due to acceleration of charges and dipoles re-alignment

9. (b) Reflecting type telescope has lenses which have chromatic aberration defect, this causes dullness of image.

10. (d) Phase difference is given by

$$\tan\phi = \frac{X_L - X_C}{R}$$

$$\Rightarrow \tan\frac{\pi}{3} = \frac{X_L - X_C}{R}$$

When L is removed,

$$\tan\frac{\pi}{3} = \frac{X_C}{R} = \sqrt{3}$$

$\therefore X_C = \sqrt{3}R$ ...... (i)

Similarly, when C is removed

$$\tan\frac{\pi}{3} = \frac{X_L}{R} = \sqrt{3}$$

$\Rightarrow \quad X_L = \sqrt{3}R$ ... (ii)

$\Rightarrow \quad X_C = X_L$ ... (iii)

Now, $\quad \phi = 0°$

$\therefore$Power factor, $\cos\phi = \cos 0° = 1$

11. (b) Here, $\mathbf{B} = 1.2 \times 10^{-8}\ \hat{\mathbf{k}}$T

The magnitude of **E**

$= Bc = (1.2 \times 10^{-8})(3 \times 10^{8})$

$= 3.6\ \text{Vm}^{-1}$

B is along z-direction and the wave propagates along x-direction.

Therefore, **E** should be in a direction perpendicular to both X and Z-axes. Using vector algebra $\mathbf{E} \times \mathbf{B}$ should be along x-direction.

Since $(+\hat{\mathbf{j}}) \times (+\hat{\mathbf{k}}) = \hat{\mathbf{i}}$

$\therefore$**E** is along the y-direction.

Thus, $\mathbf{E} = 3.6\ \hat{\mathbf{j}}\ \text{Vm}^{-1}$

12. (a) According to the Brewster,

$\mu = \tan i_p$

$\mu = \tan(53.74°)$

$\mu = \sqrt{2}$

$$\therefore \sqrt{2} = \frac{\sin i}{\sin r} \Rightarrow \sqrt{2} = \frac{\sin 45°}{\sin r}$$

$$\sin r = \frac{1}{\sqrt{2}} \times \frac{1}{\sqrt{2}} = \frac{1}{2}$$

$$r = \sin^{-1}\left(\frac{1}{2}\right)$$

$r = 30°$

13. (b)

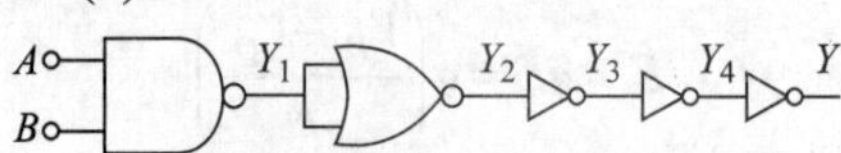

Truth table for given gate combination is

A	B	Y_1	Y_2	Y_3	Y_4	Y
0	0	1	0	1	0	1
1	0	1	0	1	0	1
0	1	1	0	1	0	1
1	1	0	1	0	1	0

So, output Y of above gate is same as that of NAND gate.

14. (d) $\because \frac{1}{f} = \frac{1}{f_1} + \frac{1}{f_2}$

$$\Rightarrow \frac{1}{80} = \frac{1}{20} + \frac{1}{f_2} \Rightarrow f_2 = -\frac{80}{3}\ \text{cm}$$

$\therefore$Power of second lens,

$$P_2 = \frac{100}{f_2} = \frac{100}{-80/3} = -3.75\,\text{D}$$

15. (b) In each case, two plano-convex lenses are placed close to each other and focal length of three lenses are

$$\frac{1}{f} = \frac{1}{f_1} + \frac{1}{f_2}$$

Hence, the plano-convex lenses have same focal length in ratio of 1:1:1.

16. (b) Number of protons = 20

Number of neutrons = 40 − 20 = 20

Total mass of 20 protons and 20 neutrons

$= 20m_p + 20m_n = 20(m_p + m_n)$

$= 20(1.007825 + 1.008665)$

$= 40.3298$ u

Mass defect,

$\Delta m = 40.3298 - 39.962589$

$= 0.367211$ u

Total BE $= 0.367211 \times 931$

$= 341.873441$ MeV

$$\text{BE/N} = \frac{341.873441}{41}$$

$= 8.34$ MeV/N

17. (d) Input, $V_{\text{rms}} = 20$ V

Peak value of input voltage,

$V_{\text{in}} = \sqrt{2}\, V_{\text{rms}}$

$= \sqrt{2} \times 20 = 28.28$ V

Since, the transformer has a transformation ratio 1 : 2. The maximum value of output voltage of the transformer applied the diode will be $V_0 = 2V_{\text{in}} = 2 \times 28.28$ V

The DC voltage in the rectified

$$\text{output} = \frac{2V_0}{\pi} = \frac{2 \times 2 \times 28.28}{\frac{22}{7}} = 36\,\text{V}$$

18. (c) Here, $L = 1$H,

$C = 20\ \mu\text{F} = 20 \times 10^{-6}$ F

$R = 300\,\Omega,\ \nu = \frac{50}{\pi}$ Hz

Inductive reactance,

$X_L = 2\pi\nu L$

$$= 2 \times \pi \times \frac{50}{\pi} \times 1 = 100\,\Omega$$

Capacitive reactance,

$$X_C = \frac{1}{2\pi\nu C}$$

$$= \frac{1}{2 \times \pi \times \frac{50}{\pi} \times 20 \times 10^{-6}} = 500\,\Omega$$

Impedance of the series L-C-R circuit,

$$Z = \sqrt{R^2 + (X_C - X_L)^2}$$

$$= \sqrt{(300)^2 + (500 - 100)^2}$$

$$= \sqrt{(300)^2 + (400)^2} = 500\,\Omega$$

19. (a) A-4, B-1, C-2, D-3.

20. (a) For step-up transformer,

$$\frac{N_P}{N_S}=\frac{V_P}{V_S}\Rightarrow\frac{1}{10}=\frac{4000}{V_S}$$

$\Rightarrow V_S = 40000\,\text{V}$

Now for step-down,

$$\frac{N_P}{N_S}=\frac{V_P}{V_S}=\frac{40000}{200}=\frac{200}{1}$$

21. (a) Magnetic field due to magnet (1),

$$B_1=\frac{\mu_0}{4\pi}\frac{2M_1}{r_1^3}=\frac{10^{-7}\times2\times2}{(0.3)^3}$$

$=1.48\times10^{-5}\,\text{T}$

Magnetic field due to magnet (2),

$$B_2=\frac{\mu_0}{4\pi}\left(\frac{2M_2}{r_2^3}\right)=\frac{10^{-7}\times2\times5}{(0.4)^3}$$

$=1.56\times10^{-5}\,\text{T}$

$\therefore$ Net magnetic field at P,

$$B=\sqrt{B_1^2+B_2^2}$$

$=2.15\times10^{-5}\,\text{T}$

22. (a) The position of 30th bright fringe,

$$y_{30}=\frac{30\lambda D}{d}$$

Now, position shift of central fringe is

$$y_0=\frac{30\lambda D}{d}$$

But we know, $y_0=\frac{D}{d}(\mu-1)t$

$$\frac{30\lambda D}{d}=\frac{D}{d}(\mu-1)t$$

$$\Rightarrow(\mu-1)=\frac{30\lambda}{t}$$

$$\text{or } \mu=\frac{30\times(6000\times10^{-10})}{(3.6\times10^{-5})}+1$$

$\therefore\ \mu=1.5$

23. (a)

Charges q, q, q, q at $x = 1, 2, 4, 8, \ldots$

$$V_0=\frac{1}{4\pi\varepsilon_0}\left[\frac{q}{1}+\frac{q}{2}+\frac{q}{4}+\ldots\infty\right]$$

$$=\frac{q}{4\pi\varepsilon_0}\left[1+\frac{1}{2}+\frac{1}{2^2}+\ldots\infty\right]$$

$$=\frac{q}{4\pi\varepsilon_0}\left[\frac{1}{1-\frac{1}{2}}\right]=\left(\frac{1}{4\pi\varepsilon_0}\right)2q$$

and

$$E_0=\frac{1}{4\pi\varepsilon_0}\left[\frac{q}{1^2}+\frac{q}{2^2}+\frac{q}{4^2}+\ldots\infty\right]$$

$$=\frac{q}{4\pi\varepsilon_0}\left[1+\frac{1}{4}+\frac{1}{16}+\ldots\infty\right]$$

$$=\frac{q}{4\pi\varepsilon_0}\left[\frac{1}{1-\frac{1}{4}}\right]=\frac{1}{4\pi\varepsilon_0}\left(\frac{4q}{3}\right)$$

24. (b) The filament of the heater reaches its steady resistance when the heater reaches the steady temperature, which is much more higher than room temperature.

The resistance at room temperature is thus much below than resistance at its steady state.

When the heater is switched ON, it draws a larger current than its steady state current. As the filament heats up, its resistance increases and current falls to its steady state value.

25. (c) In YDSE, $d\sin\theta=n\lambda$

or $\sin\theta=\frac{n\lambda}{d}$

Given that, $d=3\lambda$

$\therefore\ \sin\theta=\frac{n\lambda}{3\lambda}\Rightarrow\sin\theta=\frac{n}{3}$

For $n=0$, $\sin\theta=0\Rightarrow\theta=0^\circ$ (possible)

For $n=1$, $\sin\theta=\frac{1}{3}\Rightarrow\theta=\sin^{-1}\left(\frac{1}{3}\right)$ (possible)

For $n=2$, $\sin\theta=\frac{2}{3}\Rightarrow\theta=\sin^{-1}\left(\frac{2}{3}\right)$ (possible)

For $n=3$, $\sin\theta=1\Rightarrow\theta=90^\circ$ (possible)

Thus, there is a central maximum for $\theta=0^\circ$ and two for each $\theta=\sin^{-1}\left(\frac{1}{3}\right)$, $\theta=\sin^{-1}\left(\frac{2}{3}\right)$ and $\theta=90^\circ$

[$\because\sin\theta$ can take value between -1 to 1]

So total number of maxima are 7.

26. (b) $F_m=Bqv_0$ in upward direction.

$F_e=qE$ in downward direction.

$F_m=F_e\Rightarrow Bv_0=E$ ... (i)

$\because\ R=\frac{mv_0}{Bq}$ ... (ii)

$$4\times10^{-2}=\frac{1.6\times10^{-27}\times2\times10^5}{B\times1.6\times10^{-19}}$$

$$B=\frac{2\times10^{-3}}{4\times10^{-2}}=0.5\times10^{-1}=0.05\,\text{T}$$

From Eq. (i),

$E=0.05\times2\times10^5=10^4\,\text{N/C}$

27. (a) Given, length of solenoid

$l=30\,\text{cm}=30\times10^{-2}\,\text{m}$

Area of cross-section,

$A=25\,\text{cm}^2=25\times10^{-4}\,\text{m}^2$

Number of turns, $N=500$

Current, $I_1=2.5\,\text{A}, I_2=0$

Brief time, $dt=10^{-3}\,\text{s}$

Induced emf in the solenoid,

$$e=\frac{d\phi}{dt}=\frac{d}{dt}(BA)\qquad[\because\phi=BA]$$

Magnetic field induction B at a point inside the long solenoid carrying current I is

$B=\mu_0 nI$

(where, n = number of turns per unit length $=\frac{N}{l}$)

$$e=A\frac{dB}{dt}=A\frac{d}{dt}\left(\mu_0\frac{N}{l}I\right)$$

$$=A\frac{\mu_0 N}{l}\cdot\frac{dI}{dt}$$

$$e=500\times25\times10^{-4}\times4\times3.14\times10^{-7}\times\frac{500}{30\times10^{-2}}\times\frac{2.5}{10^{-3}}$$

$=6.5\,\text{V}$

28. (d) The magnetic moment of a current carrying loop is given as

$m=IA\,\hat{\mathbf{n}}$

where, I is current flowing through the loop, A is the area of loop and $\hat{\mathbf{n}}$ is unit vector and its direction is determined by right hand thumb rule.

For the given figure, $m=IA(-\hat{\mathbf{k}})$

[As, the current is flowing in clockwise direction]

Given, magnetic field, $\mathbf{B}=B_0(\hat{\mathbf{i}}-\hat{\mathbf{j}})$

Torque, $\tau=\mathbf{m}\times\mathbf{B}$

$=IA(-\hat{\mathbf{k}})\times B_0(\hat{\mathbf{i}}-\hat{\mathbf{j}})$

$=IAB_0[(-\hat{\mathbf{k}})\times\hat{\mathbf{i}}+\hat{\mathbf{k}}\times\hat{\mathbf{j}}]$

$$= IAB_0[-\hat{\mathbf{j}}-\hat{\mathbf{i}}]$$

Thus, the direction of torque is along $(-\hat{\mathbf{i}}-\hat{\mathbf{j}})$ and from figure, this direction is along Q to S. So, loop will rotate about an axis along QS.

29. (c) From the given figure, it is clear that, magnetic field at origin due to two parts (i.e. BC and CD) of wire will be zero, as point O is lying on the wires.

Magnetic field is only due to section parallel to Y-axis i.e. AB and is given as $\mathbf{B} = \frac{\mu_0 I}{4\pi d}\hat{\mathbf{r}}$

where, $\hat{\mathbf{r}}$ is determined by right hand rule.

$$\therefore \mathbf{B} = \frac{\mu_0 I}{4\pi(a\sqrt{2})}[\cos 45^\circ(-\hat{\mathbf{i}}) + \cos 45^\circ \hat{\mathbf{k}}]$$

$$= \frac{\mu_0 I}{4\sqrt{2}\pi a}\left(-\frac{1}{\sqrt{2}}\hat{\mathbf{i}}+\frac{1}{\sqrt{2}}\hat{\mathbf{k}}\right)$$

$$\mathbf{B} = \frac{\mu_0 I}{8\pi a}(-\hat{\mathbf{i}}+\hat{\mathbf{k}})$$

30. (c) When charge q_3 is at C, then its potential energy is

$$U_C = \frac{1}{4\pi\varepsilon_0}\left(\frac{q_1q_3}{0.4}+\frac{q_2q_3}{0.5}\right)$$

When charge q_3 is at D, then

$$U_D = \frac{1}{4\pi\varepsilon_0}\left(\frac{q_1q_3}{0.4}+\frac{q_2q_3}{0.1}\right)$$

Hence, change in potential energy.

$$\Delta U = U_D - U_C$$

$$= \frac{1}{4\pi\varepsilon_0}\left(\frac{q_2q_3}{0.1}-\frac{q_2q_3}{0.5}\right)$$

$$= \frac{q_3q_2}{4\pi\varepsilon_0}\left(\frac{1}{0.1}-\frac{1}{0.5}\right) = \frac{q_3\,q_2}{4\pi\varepsilon_0}(8)$$

as $\Delta U = \frac{q_3 K}{4\pi\varepsilon_0} \Rightarrow K = 8q_2$

31. (c) We have, $V = 10^4$ V,

$q = 2e = 2\times 1.6\times 10^{-19}$ C

$d = 0.1$ m, $B = 0.1$ T and

$m_\alpha = 6.4\times 10^{-27}$ kg

Kinetic energy,

$$K = \frac{1}{2}m_\alpha v^2 = qV = 2eV$$

$$\Rightarrow v = \sqrt{\frac{4eV}{m_\alpha}}$$

α-particle in magnetic field move in a circle of radius R which is given by

$$R = \frac{m_\alpha v}{Bq} = \frac{m_\alpha v}{2eB}$$

$$\text{Also, } \sin\theta = \frac{d}{R} = \frac{d}{\frac{m_\alpha v}{B\,2e}} = \frac{2eBd}{m_\alpha v}$$

$$= \frac{2eBd}{m_\alpha\sqrt{\frac{4eV}{m_\alpha}}} = \sqrt{\frac{e}{m_\alpha V}}\cdot Bd$$

$$= \sqrt{\frac{1.6\times 10^{-19}}{6.4\times 10^{-27}\times 10^4}}\times 0.1\times 0.1 = \frac{1}{2}$$

$$\sin\theta = \frac{1}{2}$$

$$\theta = 30^\circ$$

$\therefore$ Change in direction, $\theta = 30^\circ$

32. (c) For two successive resonance,

$$l_2 - l_1 = \frac{3\lambda}{4}-\frac{\lambda}{4} = \frac{\lambda}{2}$$

or $\lambda = 2(l_2 - l_1)$

Speed of sound,

$$v = f\cdot\lambda = f[2(l_2-l_1)]$$

$$= 480\times 2(70-30)\times 10^{-2}$$

$$= 384 \text{ m/s}$$

33. (c) According to the given question, the circuit is as shown below.

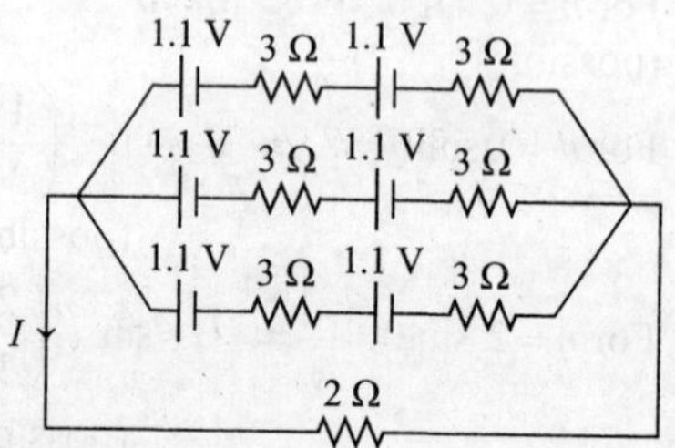

In series combination of two cells, the equivalent emf and internal resistance is given as

$$E_{eq} = E_1 + E_2$$

and $r_{eq} = r_1 + r_2$

So, the given circuit can be redrawn as

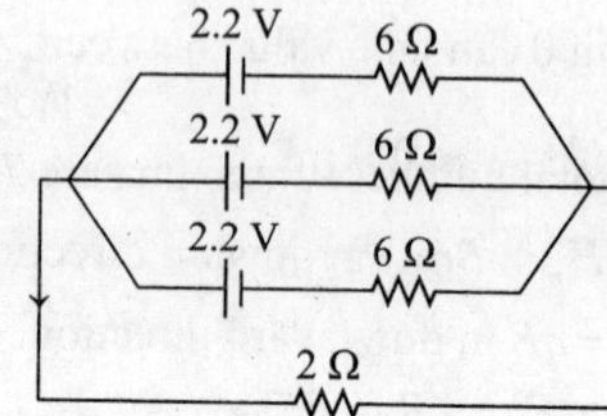

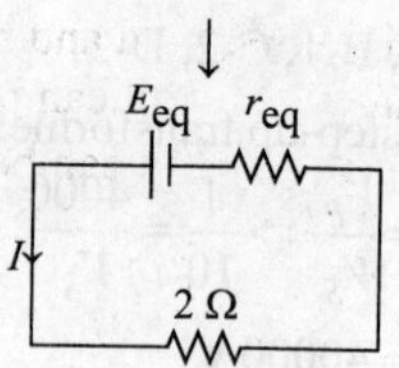

Here, equivalent emf is

$$E_{eq} = \frac{\frac{E_1}{r_1}+\frac{E_2}{r_2}+\frac{E_3}{r_3}}{\frac{1}{r_1}+\frac{1}{r_2}+\frac{1}{r_3}}$$

$$= \frac{\frac{2.2}{6}+\frac{2.2}{6}+\frac{2.2}{6}}{\frac{1}{6}+\frac{1}{6}+\frac{1}{6}} = 2.2 \text{ V}$$

$$r_{eq} = \frac{r}{3} = \frac{6}{3} = 2\Omega$$

[As, all are connected in parallel]

Current I through external resistance,

$$I = \frac{E_{eq}}{r_{eq}+R} = \frac{2.2}{2+2} = 0.55 \text{ A}$$

Power delivered to external resistance,

$$P = I^2R = (0.55)^2\times 2$$

$$= 0.605 \text{ W}$$

34. (a) $L = \frac{\mu_0 N^2\pi r^2}{l}$,

$$L' = \frac{\mu_0\left(\frac{N}{2}\right)^2\pi r^2}{\frac{l}{2}} = \frac{L}{2}$$

$$R = \frac{\rho l}{A}, R' = \frac{\rho\frac{l}{2}}{A} = \frac{R}{2}$$

$$L_{eq} = \frac{L'}{2} = \frac{L}{4}, R_{eq} = \frac{R'}{2} = \frac{R}{4}$$

$$\tau = \frac{L}{R}, \tau' = \frac{\frac{L}{4}}{\frac{R}{4}} = \frac{L}{R} = \frac{1.8\times 10^{-4}}{6}$$

$$\tau' = 0.3\times 10^{-4} = 30\,\mu\text{s}$$

$$i = \frac{E}{R_{eq}} = \frac{12}{\frac{R}{4}} = \frac{12\times 4}{6} = 8 \text{ A}$$

35. (d) The given network is symmetrical about the dotted line which is perpendicular to AB as shown in given figure below. As we know that, point lying on this line is not electrically connected and behave as a false junction and it can be lift off.

So, the given circuit can be redrawn as

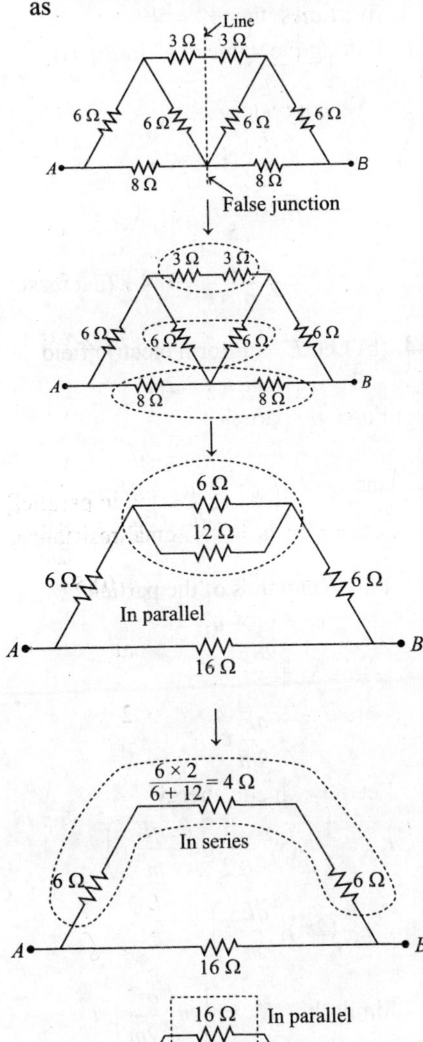

∵ In parallel combination of two resistance, $R_{AB} = \frac{R_1 R_2}{R_1 + R_2}$

$$R_{AB} = \frac{16 \times 16}{16 + 16}$$

$$R_{AB} = 8\Omega$$

36. (c) Using lens Maker's formula,

$$\frac{1}{f} = (\mu - 1)\left(\frac{1}{R_1} - \frac{1}{R_2}\right)$$

For first plano-convex lens,

$$\frac{1}{f_1} = (1.5 - 1)\left(\frac{1}{14} - \frac{1}{\infty}\right) = \frac{1}{28}$$

For second plano-convex lens,

$$\frac{1}{f_2} = (1.2 - 1)\left(\frac{1}{\infty} - \frac{1}{-14}\right) = \frac{1}{70}$$

If f is combined focal length of bi-convex lens, then

$$\frac{1}{f} = \frac{1}{f_1} + \frac{1}{f_2} = \frac{1}{28} + \frac{1}{70}$$

$$= \frac{5+2}{140} = \frac{1}{20}$$

$$f = 20\,\text{cm}$$

For this lens, $u = -40\,\text{cm}$

From, $\frac{1}{v} - \frac{1}{u} = \frac{1}{f}$

$$\frac{1}{v} = \frac{1}{f} + \frac{1}{u} = \frac{1}{20} - \frac{1}{40} = \frac{1}{40}$$

$$v = 40\,\text{cm}$$

37. (a) For electron,

$$\lambda_e = \frac{h}{m_e v_e} = \frac{h}{m_e\left(\frac{c}{100}\right)} = \frac{100h}{m_e c} \quad \dots \text{(i)}$$

According to question,

$$\lambda_p = 2\lambda_e = \frac{200h}{m_e c}$$

No, $E_p = \frac{hc}{\lambda_p} = \frac{hc}{\frac{200h}{m_e c}} = \frac{m_e c^2}{200}$

The kinetic energy of electron (E_e) is given by

$$E_e = \frac{1}{2} m_e v_e^2 = \frac{1}{2} m_e \left(\frac{c}{100}\right)^2 = \frac{m_e c^2}{20000}$$

$$\therefore \frac{E_e}{E_p} = \frac{\frac{m_e c^2}{20000}}{\frac{m_e c^2}{200}} = \frac{200}{20000} = \frac{1}{100} = 10^{-2}$$

38. (c) Given that, average power of beam, $P_{avg} = 16\text{ mW} = 16 \times 10^{-3}\text{ W}$

Diameter, $d = 4\text{ mm} = 4 \times 10^{-3}\text{ m}$

or radius, $R = 2 \times 10^{-3}\text{ m}$

Area, $A = \pi R^2 = 3.14 \times (2 \times 10^{-3})^2$

$A = 12.56 \times 10^{-6}\text{ m}^2$

As average intensity,

$$I_{avg} = \frac{P_{avg}}{A}$$

and $I_{avg} = c\varepsilon_0 E_{rms}^2$

$$\therefore \quad c\varepsilon_0 E_{rms}^2 = \frac{P_{avg}}{A}$$

and $$E_{rms} = \sqrt{\frac{P_{avg}}{Ac\varepsilon_0}}$$

Putting the given values in above expression, we get

$$E_{rms} = \sqrt{\frac{16 \times 10^{-3}}{12.56 \times 10^{-6} \times 3 \times 10^8 \times 8.85 \times 10^{-12}}}$$

$$E_{rms} = 6.92 \times 10^2\text{ V/m}$$

and rms value of magnetic field,

$$B_{rms} = \frac{E_{rms}}{c} = \frac{6.92 \times 10^2}{3 \times 10^8}$$

$$= 2.3 \times 10^{-6}\text{ T} = 2.3\,\mu\text{T}$$

39. (b) As we know that wavelength corresponding to transition, $n = n_1$ to $n = n_2$ is given by the following expression,

$$\frac{1}{\lambda} = RZ^2\left(\frac{1}{n_2^2} - \frac{1}{n_1^2}\right) \quad \dots \text{(i)}$$

For 1st line of Lyman series;

$$n_1 = 2,\ n_2 = 1$$

$$\therefore \frac{1}{\lambda_L} = RZ^2\left(\frac{1}{1^2} - \frac{1}{2^2}\right)$$

[Using Eq. (i)]

$$\frac{1}{\lambda_L} = RZ^2\left(1 - \frac{1}{4}\right)$$

$$\frac{1}{\lambda_L} = \frac{3}{4} RZ^2$$

$$\text{or } \lambda_L = \frac{4}{3RZ^2} \quad \dots \text{(ii)}$$

Similarly, for 1st line of Balmer series,

$$n_1 = 2,\ n_3 = 3$$

$$\therefore \frac{1}{\lambda_B} = RZ^2\left[\frac{1}{2^2} - \frac{1}{3^2}\right]$$

[Using Eq. (i)]

$$= RZ^2\left[\frac{1}{4} - \frac{1}{9}\right]$$

$$= RZ^2\left[\frac{9-4}{36}\right]$$

$$\frac{1}{\lambda_B} = \frac{5}{36} RZ^2$$

or $\lambda_B = \frac{36}{5RZ^2}$ ... (iii)

On dividing Eq. (ii) by Eq. (iii), we get

$$\frac{\lambda_L}{\lambda_B} = \frac{\frac{4}{3RZ^2}}{\frac{36}{5RZ^2}} = \frac{5}{27}$$

40. (b) For the capacitor shown in fig. (i).

$$= \frac{\varepsilon_0 KA}{2d} + \frac{\varepsilon_0 KA}{8d} \quad \left(\text{Given}, K_1 = K \text{ and } K_2 = \frac{K}{4}\right)$$

$$= \frac{\varepsilon_0 KA}{d}\left(\frac{1}{2} + \frac{1}{8}\right) = \frac{\varepsilon_0 KA}{d}\left(\frac{4+1}{8}\right)$$

$$\Rightarrow C_1 = \frac{5\varepsilon_0 KA}{8d} \quad ...(i)$$

and for the capacitor shown in fig. (ii),

$$C_2 = \frac{\varepsilon_0 A}{\frac{d}{2K_1} + \frac{d}{2K_2}} = \frac{\varepsilon_0 A}{\frac{d}{2K} + \frac{d}{\frac{2K}{4}}}$$

$$= \frac{(2K)\varepsilon_0 A}{5d} \quad ...(ii)$$

On dividing Eq. (i) by Eq. (ii), we get

$$\frac{C_1}{C_2} = \frac{\frac{5\varepsilon_0 KA}{8d}}{\frac{2K\varepsilon_0 A}{5d}} = \frac{5 \times 5}{2 \times 8} = \frac{25}{16}$$

41. (b) When a coil of area A having number of turns N is rotated with uniform angular speed ω in magnetic field B, then peak induced emf is given as

$$e = NAB\omega \text{ or } NAB(2\pi f)$$

Given that for coil-1, $N_1 = 100$, $f_1 = 50\,\text{Hz}$

$$\therefore \quad e_1 = 100 \times A_1 \times B \times 2\pi \times 50 \quad ... (i)$$

For coil-2, $N_2 = 50$, $f_2 = 300\,\text{Hz}$

$$e_2 = 50 \times A_2 \times B \times 2\pi \times 300 \quad ... (ii)$$

On dividing Eq. (i) by Eq. (ii), we get

$$\frac{e_1}{e_2} = \frac{100 \times A_1 \times B \times 2\pi \times 50}{50 \times A_2 \times B \times 2\pi \times 300}$$

$$\frac{e_1}{e_2} = \frac{A_1}{3A_2} \quad [\because A_1 = A_2 = A]$$

$$\therefore \quad \frac{e_1}{e_2} = \frac{1}{3}$$

42. (d) If I_g is the current for full scale deflection in voltmeter, then

$$I_g = \frac{\text{Voltage range of voltmeter}}{\text{Resistance of voltmeter}}$$

$$I_g = \frac{V}{R_V} \quad ... (i)$$

Given that $V = 5\,\text{V}$, $R_V = 300\,\Omega$

From Eq. (i),

$$I_g = \frac{5}{300} = \frac{1}{60}\,\text{A}$$

On adding a small value resistance S in parallel to voltmeter, the arrangement will be converted into an ammeter.

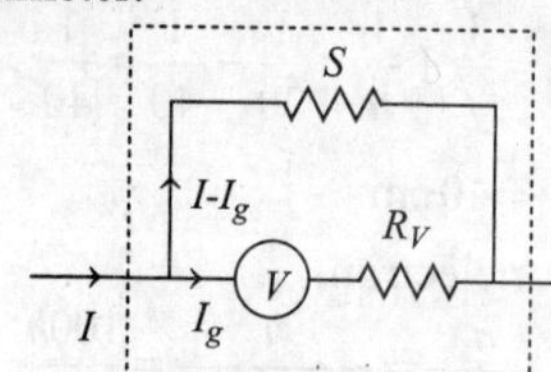

Using current division rule,

$$I_g = \frac{S}{R_V + S} \times I$$

or $$\frac{I_g}{I} = \frac{S}{R_V + S} \quad ... (ii)$$

Substituting the values in Eq. (ii), we get

$$\frac{\frac{1}{60}}{5} = \frac{S}{300 + S} \quad [\because I = 5\,\text{A}]$$

$$\frac{1}{300} = \frac{S}{300 + S}$$

$$300 + S = 300S$$

$$299S = 300$$

$$S = \frac{300}{299} = 1.003\,\Omega$$

$$S \simeq 1\,\Omega$$

43. (c) The de-Broglie wavelength of a charged particle is given as

$$\lambda = \frac{h}{\sqrt{2mqV}}$$

where, m is mass of electron, q is charge on electron and V is accelerating potential.

For electron h, m and q are constant,

$$\lambda \propto \frac{1}{\sqrt{V}}$$

At two accelerating potentials,

$$\frac{\lambda'}{\lambda} = \sqrt{\frac{V}{V'}} \quad ... (i)$$

When accelerating potential is made five times, then $V' = 5V$

Putting the value of V' in Eq. (i), we get

$$\frac{\lambda'}{\lambda} = \sqrt{\frac{V}{5V}} = \frac{1}{\sqrt{5}}$$

$$\lambda' = \frac{\lambda}{\sqrt{5}}$$

$$= \frac{\lambda}{2.23} = 0.44\,\lambda \text{ (decrease)}$$

44. (b) Let, E = uniform electric field and $m_1 = m$, $m_2 = 2m$

Force on particles,

$$F_1 = ma_1 = 2qE$$

and $$F_2 = 2ma_2 = qE$$

$$\therefore \quad a_1 = \frac{2qE}{m} \text{ and } a_2 = \frac{qE}{2m}$$

Final velocities of the particle,

$$v_1 = u_1 + a_1 t$$

$$v_1 = \frac{2qE}{m}t$$

$$v_2 = \frac{qE}{2m}t$$

Let, K = kinetic energy

$$K_1 = \frac{1}{2}m_1 v_1^2 = \frac{1}{2}m\left(\frac{2qE}{m}t\right)^2$$

$$= (2m)\left(\frac{qE}{m}t\right)^2$$

Similarly, $$K_2 = \frac{1}{2}m\left(\frac{qE}{2m}\right)^2 t^2$$

$$\frac{K_1}{K_2} = \frac{16}{1}$$

45. (c) Light ray must fall perpendicular on polished surface.

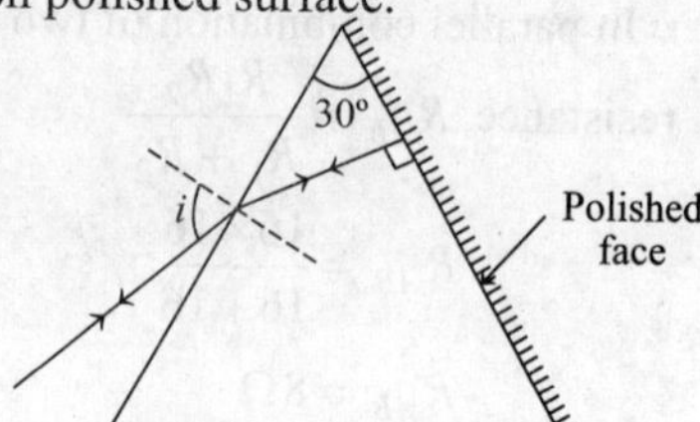

As, $A = r_1 + r_2$

$30° = r_1 + 0° \Rightarrow r_1 = 30°$

Now, $\mu = \frac{\sin i}{\sin r} \Leftrightarrow \sqrt{2} = \frac{\sin i}{\sin 30°}$

$\Rightarrow \quad i = 45°$

NK01 NEET Knock Offs 1

1. (*a*) Net force on a charged particle in electric field and magnetic field is given by

$$\mathbf{F} = q(\mathbf{v}\times\mathbf{B}) + \mathbf{E}$$

or $\mathbf{E} = \dfrac{\mathbf{F}}{q} - (\mathbf{v}\times\mathbf{B})$

$$= \frac{9.6\times10^{-19}\,(\hat{\mathbf{i}}-\hat{\mathbf{k}})}{-1.6\times10^{-19}} - (60\,\hat{\mathbf{i}})\times(0.1\,\hat{\mathbf{j}})$$

$$= -6(\hat{\mathbf{i}}-\hat{\mathbf{k}}) - 6(\hat{\mathbf{i}}\times\hat{\mathbf{j}})$$

$$= -6\,\hat{\mathbf{i}} + 6\,\hat{\mathbf{k}} - 6\,\hat{\mathbf{k}} \qquad (\because \hat{\mathbf{i}}\times\hat{\mathbf{j}} = \hat{\mathbf{k}})$$

$\Rightarrow \quad \mathbf{E} = -6\,\hat{\mathbf{i}}$ N/C

2. (*a*) A vector along angle-bisector of $\hat{\mathbf{a}}$ and $\hat{\mathbf{b}}$ is $\hat{\mathbf{a}}+\hat{\mathbf{b}}$ (using parallelogram law).

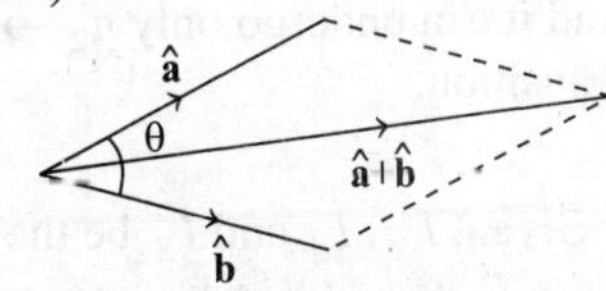

Also, magnitude of $\hat{\mathbf{a}}+\hat{\mathbf{b}}$ is

$$R = \sqrt{(\hat{\mathbf{a}})^2 + (\hat{\mathbf{b}})^2 + 2\hat{\mathbf{a}}\hat{\mathbf{b}}\cos\theta}$$

$$= \sqrt{1+1+2\cos\theta}$$

$$= \sqrt{2(1+\cos\theta)}$$

$$= \sqrt{4\cos^2\frac{\theta}{2}} = 2\cos\frac{\theta}{2}$$

So, unit vector $= \dfrac{\hat{\mathbf{a}}+\hat{\mathbf{b}}}{R} = \dfrac{\hat{\mathbf{a}}+\hat{\mathbf{b}}}{\left(2\cos\dfrac{\theta}{2}\right)}$

3. (*d*) Given, $x^2 = 4+t$ or $x = \sqrt{4+t}$

We know that,

velocity, $v = \dfrac{dx}{dt} = \dfrac{d}{dt}(\sqrt{4+t})$

$$v = \frac{1}{2\sqrt{4+t}} = \frac{1}{2x}$$

Also, acceleration, $a = v\dfrac{dv}{dx}$

$$= \frac{1}{2x}\cdot\frac{d}{dx}\left(\frac{1}{2x}\right) = \frac{1}{2x}\left(-\frac{1}{2x^2}\right)$$

$\Rightarrow \quad a = -\dfrac{1}{4x^3}$

4. (*a*) As we know,

Capacitive reactance is given by

$$X_C = \frac{1}{\omega C} \text{ or } \frac{1}{2\pi fC}$$

With decrease in frequency, X_C will increase, so current flowing through capacitor will decrease.

Also, in the case of a capacitor,

Displacement current = Conduction current

i.e. $i_d = i_c$

As i_c decreases on decreasing frequency, so i_d will also decrease

5. (*a*) From lens Maker's formula, we have

$$f = (\mu - 1)\left(\frac{1}{R_1} - \frac{1}{R_2}\right)$$

For convex lens $(R_1 = -R_2 = R)$

$$f = (\mu-1)\left(\frac{2}{R}\right)$$

Focal length of lens in air,

$$f_a = \left(\frac{\mu_{\text{glass}}}{\mu_{\text{air}}} - 1\right)\left(\frac{2}{R}\right) \quad \ldots\text{(i)}$$

Focal length of lens in liquid,

$$f_l = \left(\frac{\mu_{\text{glass}}}{\mu_{\text{liquid}}} - 1\right)\left(\frac{2}{R}\right) \quad \ldots\text{(ii)}$$

From Eqs. (i) and (ii), we get

$$\frac{f_l}{f_a} = \frac{\left(\dfrac{\mu_{\text{glass}}}{\mu_{\text{liquid}}} - 1\right)}{\left(\dfrac{\mu_{\text{glass}}}{\mu_{\text{air}}} - 1\right)}$$

or $\dfrac{f_l}{f_a} = \dfrac{\left(\dfrac{1.5}{1.25} - 1\right)}{(1.5-1)} = \dfrac{1/5}{1/2} = \dfrac{2}{5}$

$$f_l = \frac{2}{5}\times f_a$$

$$= \frac{2}{5}\times 20 \qquad [\because f_a = 20\text{ cm}]$$

$$= 8\text{ cm}$$

6. (*d*) Statement I is incorrect but Statement II is correct.

Infrared wave is not absorbed by the ozone layer of the atmosphere. It is absorbed by small dust particles and water vapours.

In EM waves, energy density for electric field is equal to that of magnetic field,

i.e. $\dfrac{1}{2}\varepsilon_0 E^2 = \dfrac{1}{2}\mu_0 B^2$

7. (*c*) Energy stored in an inductor

$$= \frac{1}{2}Li^2$$

where L is measured in henry.

Dimensions of energy = $[\text{ML}^2\text{T}^{-2}]$

Dimension of current = $[\text{QT}^{-1}]$

$$\text{Energy} = \frac{1}{2}Li^2$$

$$L = \frac{2\times\text{Energy}}{(\text{Current})^2} = \frac{[\text{ML}^2\text{T}^{-2}]}{[\text{QT}^{-1}]^2}$$

$$= [\text{ML}^2/\text{Q}^2]$$

This is the dimension of Henry unit.

8. (*b*) Since, the object is placed at focus of convex lens, so after refracting through convex lens, all rays will be parallel and these will pass through concave lens. The concave lens will diverge these rays and a virtual image will be formed at its focus which is 20 cm left from the concave lens.

So, to form final image on the object itself,

$$20 = 10 + d$$

$\Rightarrow \quad d = 10$ cm

9. (*a*) The given situation is shown below.

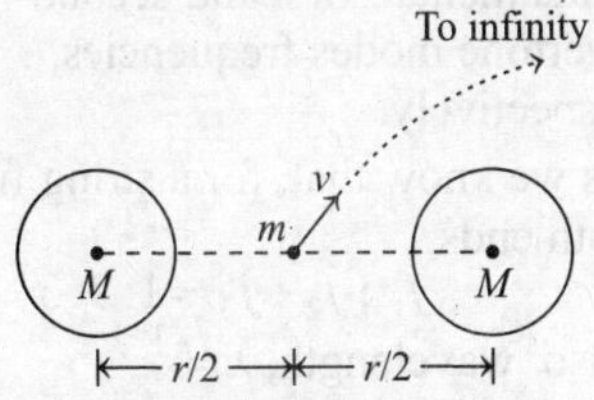

Total initial energy of rocket

$$= \frac{1}{2}mv^2 - 2\left(\frac{GMm}{r/2}\right)$$

Final energy of rocket = 0

From conservation of energy,

$$\frac{1}{2}mv^2 - \frac{4GMm}{r} = 0$$

$\Rightarrow \quad \frac{1}{2}mv^2 = \frac{4GMm}{r}$

$\Rightarrow \quad v^2 = \frac{8GM}{r} \Rightarrow v = 2\sqrt{\frac{2GM}{r}}$

10. (*b*) In the given cycle, heat is supplied in process *D* to *A* at constant volume and in process *A* to *B* at constant pressure.

∴ Heat supplied,

$Q = nC_V(\Delta T)_{DA} + nC_p(\Delta T)_{AB}$

For an ideal monoatomic gas,

$C_V = \frac{3}{2}R$ and $C_p = \frac{5}{2}R$

$\Rightarrow \quad Q = \frac{3}{2}nR\Delta T + \frac{5}{2}nR\Delta T$ $[\because nR\Delta T = p\Delta V]$

$= \frac{3}{2}(p_0V_0) + 5(p_0V_0)$

$= \frac{13}{2}p_0V_0$

11. (*a*) Diode will be in forward bias when V_i is greater than 10 V and it conducts till V_i is 12 V.

Total circuit resistance

$= 200 + 20 = 220\,\Omega$

When V_i is less than 10 V, the diode will not conduct due to its reverse biasing. Thus, initial current, $I_1 = 0$.

When $V_i = 12$ V, then diode will be in forward bias with effective voltage, $V' = 12 - 10 = 2$ V

∴ Maximum current, $I_2 = \frac{V'}{R} = \frac{2}{220}$

$= 0.009\text{A} = 9$ mA

∴ Change in current,

$\Delta I = I_2 - I_1 = 9 - 0 = 9$ mA

12. (*c*) Let f_1, f_2 and f_3 be the fundamental, first and second overtone modes frequencies, respectively.

As we know that, for a string fixed at both ends,

$f_1 : f_2 : f_3 = 1 : 2 : 3$ ...(i)

Also, wavelength, $\lambda = \frac{v}{f}$

where, *v* is the speed of wave.

$\Rightarrow \quad \lambda \propto \frac{1}{f}$

$\therefore \lambda_1 : \lambda_2 : \lambda_3 = 1 : \frac{1}{2} : \frac{1}{3}$ [from Eq. (i)]

or $\lambda_1 : \lambda_2 : \lambda_3 = 6 : 3 : 2$

13. (*c*) When electric field is applied, the random motion of all free electrons is converted into unidirectional within very short duration of time of order 10^{-9} s, which in turn sets up an electric field instantaneously.

Thus, a current through each cross-section is produced almost instantaneously.

Hence, the bulb glows very quickly.

14. (*c*) Potential energy of a bar magnet in external magnetic field is given by

$U = -MB\cos\theta$

Here, $M = 0.15$ J/T, $B = 0.4$ T, and $\theta = 180°$ as magnet is in unstable equilibrium.

$\therefore U = -0.15 \times 0.4 \times \cos 180°$

$= -0.15 \times 0.4 \times (-1)$

$= 6 \times 10^{-2}$ J

15. (*b*) Steradian is a dimensionless quantity.

A → 3

Permittivity of free space, ε_0

$= \frac{Q^2}{4\pi Fr^2}$

$= \frac{A^2T^2}{[MLT^{-2}L^2]}$

$= M^{-1}L^{-3}T^4A^2$

B → 2

Frequency $= \frac{1}{T} = [M^0L^0T^{-1}]$

C → 4

Resistivity $= \frac{R \times A}{l} = \frac{V \times A}{il} = \frac{WA}{Qil}$

$= \frac{[ML^2T^{-2}] \times [L^2]}{[ATAL]}$

$= [ML^3T^{-3}A^{-2}]$

D → 1

16. (*d*) From graph, $V = 1.5$ V at $I = 0$

∴ EMF of cell = 1.5 V

At $V = 0$, $I = 1000$ mA = 1 A

Now using, $E - V = Ir$

We have, $1.5 - 0 = 1 \times r$

$\Rightarrow \quad r = 1.5\,\Omega$

17. (*b*) Mutual inductance is given by

$M = \frac{\mu_0 N_1 \times N_2 \times A}{l}$

where, $N_1 = 500$ turns,

$N_2 = 300$ turns,

$A = 10\,\text{cm}^2 = 10 \times 10^{-4}\,\text{m}^2$

and $l = 20$ cm $= 20 \times 10^{-2}$ m

Substituting these values in the given formula, we get

$M = 3.0\pi \times 10^{-4}$ H

18. (*c*) $\phi = \frac{1}{\varepsilon_0}$ (Net enclosed charge)

$= \frac{q}{\varepsilon_0}(5 + 1 - 2) = \frac{4q}{\varepsilon_0}$

19. (*b*) $E_n = \frac{-13.6}{n^2}$ eV

⇒ Ground state energy,

$E_1 = -13.6$ eV

and first excited state energy,

$E_2 = -\frac{13.6}{4} = -3.4$ eV

As, $E_2 - E_1 = -3.4 - (-13.6)$

$= 10.2$ eV

∴ Electron is in first excited state and it can undergo only $n_2 \to n_1$ transition.

20. (*d*) Given, I_X, I_Y and I_Z be the moment of inertia of disc about *X*, *Y* and *Z*-axes. By using perpendicular axes theorem,

$I_Z = I_X + I_Y$

where, I_Z is the moment of inertia about *Z*-axis passes through its centre. $= \frac{MR^2}{2}$ and for symmetrical body, $I_X = I_Y$ (Disc in given case)

$\therefore \quad I_Z = 2I_X$

$\Rightarrow \quad I_X = I_Y = \frac{I_Z}{2} = \frac{MR^2}{4}$

Now, $\quad I_X = I_Y \neq I_Z$

As, radius of gyration, $K = \sqrt{I/M}$

$\Rightarrow \quad K \propto I$

So, radius of gyration about all axis will not be the same.

∴ Assertion is false but Reason is true because in a rigid body making rotational motion has fixed mass *M* and radius $R(I_x = I_y)$.

21. (*c*) As we know,

Slope of strain-stress curve $= \frac{1}{Y}$

where, *Y* is Young's modulus.

or $\quad \frac{(\text{Slope})_A}{(\text{Slope})_B} = \frac{Y_B}{Y_A}$

$$\Rightarrow \frac{\tan 60^\circ}{\tan 30^\circ} = \frac{Y_B}{Y_A}$$

$$\Rightarrow \frac{\sqrt{3}}{\frac{1}{\sqrt{3}}} = \frac{Y_B}{Y_A} \text{ or } Y_B = 3Y_A$$

22. (*a*) Let the final temperature of mixture be T°C.

From principle of calorimetry,

Heat given by 100 g of water = Heat taken by 100 g of ice

$$S_{\text{water}}\, m_1 (\Delta T_1) = m_2 L_f + m_2 S_{\text{water}} \Delta T_2$$

Substituting the given values, we get

$$100 \times 1 \times (80 - T) = 100 \times 80 + 100 \times 1 \times (T - 0)$$

$$\Rightarrow 80 - T = 80 + T$$

$$\Rightarrow 2T = 0 \Rightarrow T = 0^\circ\text{C}$$

23. (*d*) Escape velocity does not depend on the angle of projection, hence escape velocity will remain same.

24. (*d*) We know that,

Intensity = Energy per unit area per unit time

Energy needed for emission,

$$\phi_0 = 2\,\text{eV} = 2 \times 1.6 \times 10^{-19}\ \text{J}$$

Intensity $= 10^{-5}\ \text{Wm}^{-2}$

Effective atomic area $= 10^{-20}\ \text{m}^2$

Now, number of atoms in top 5-layers,

$$N = \frac{5 \times \text{surface area}}{\text{area of 1 atom}}$$

$$= \frac{5 \times 2 \times 10^{-4}}{10^{-20}} = 10^{17}$$

Hence, time needed for photo emission,

$$t = \frac{\phi_0}{\text{energy available for each electron}}$$

$$\Rightarrow t = \frac{\phi_0}{\left(\frac{I \times A}{N}\right)} = \frac{\phi_0 \times N}{I \times A}$$

$$= \frac{2 \times 1.6 \times 10^{-19} \times 10^{17}}{10^{-5} \times 2 \times 10^{-4}}$$

$$= 1.6 \times 10^7\ \text{s} \approx 0.5\ \text{yr}$$

25. (*a*) $E = \frac{-13.6}{n^2}$ eV

$$E_4 - E_3 = 13.6\left[\frac{1}{(3)^2} - \frac{1}{(4)^2}\right]$$

$$= 13.6\left[\frac{7}{144}\right]\text{eV}$$

$$= 0.66\ \text{eV}$$

$$\lambda = \frac{1}{R\left[\frac{1}{(3)^2} - \frac{1}{(4)^2}\right]}$$

$$= \frac{144}{1.09 \times 10^7 \times 7}\ \text{m}$$

$$= 1.88 \times 10^{-6}\ \text{m}$$

26. (*d*) Poisson's equation for an adiabatic change is given by

$$T^\gamma p^{1-\gamma} = \text{constant}$$

$$p^{1-\gamma} \propto T^{-\gamma}$$

$$p \propto T^{\frac{\gamma}{\gamma - 1}}$$

Given that $p \propto T^3$

$$\text{Hence, } \frac{\gamma}{\gamma - 1} = 3$$

$$\Rightarrow 1 - \frac{1}{\gamma} = \frac{1}{3}$$

$$\gamma = \frac{3}{2}$$

$$\therefore \frac{C_p}{C_V} = \gamma = \frac{3}{2}$$

27. (*c*) According to Einstein's photoelectric equation,

$$hf = W_0 + eV_0 \quad \ldots \text{(i)}$$

If frequency is doubled, then

$$h(2f) = W_0 + eV_0'$$

$$\text{or} \quad 2hf = W_0 + eV_0' \quad \ldots\text{(ii)}$$

Substituting hf from Eq. (i) in Eq. (ii), we have

$$V_0' = 2V_0 + \frac{W_0}{e}$$

$$\text{or} \quad V_0' > 2V_0$$

28. (*d*) Density at temperature T is given by

$$\rho = \rho_0 (1 - \gamma \Delta T)$$

$$\Rightarrow \rho = \rho_0 - \rho_0\, \gamma\, \Delta T$$

$$\Rightarrow \frac{\rho - \rho_0}{\rho_0} = -\gamma \Delta T$$

$\therefore$ Fractional change in density,

$$\frac{\Delta\rho}{\rho_0} = -\gamma \Delta T = -6 \times 10^{-5} \times 60$$

$$\Rightarrow \frac{\Delta\rho}{\rho_0} = -3.6 \times 10^{-3}$$

Note Negative sign indicates that density decreases with rise in temperature.

29. (*c*)

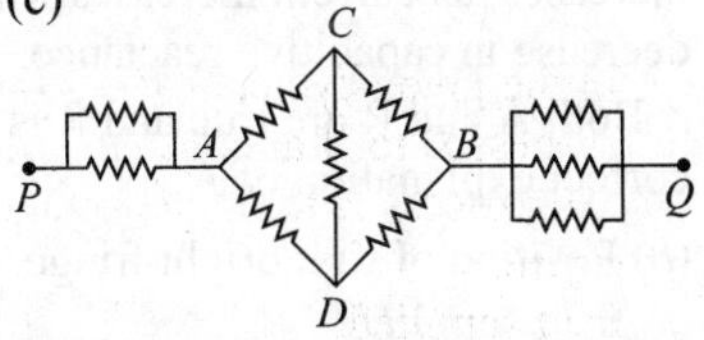

Circuit between points A and B follows Wheatstone bridge condition. So, resistor between C and D will have no current.

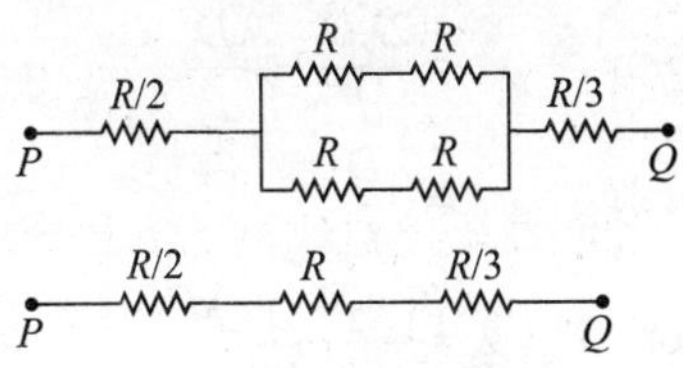

$$R_{\text{eq}} = \frac{R}{2} + R + \frac{R}{3}$$

$$= \frac{3R + 6R + 2R}{6} = \frac{11R}{6}$$

$\therefore$ Value of N is 11.

30. (*c*) Direction of current I_D is in the same direction as arrow in the diode symbol.

Si diode is in ON state while Ge diode is in OFF state.

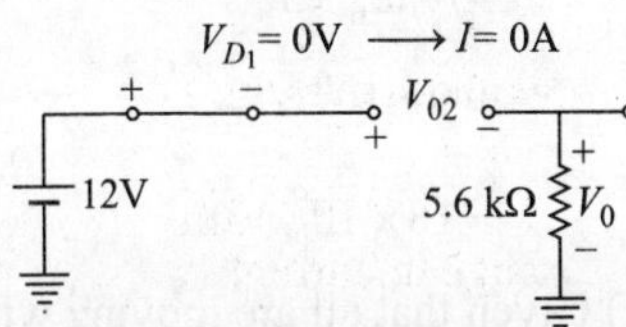

$$I_D = 0\,\text{A}, V_D = 0\,\text{V}$$

$$V_0 = I_R \times R = I_D \times R = 0\,\text{V}$$

31. (*a*) Capacitive reactance,

$$X_C = \frac{1}{\omega C}$$

As C increases, X_C decreases.

Current in the circuit is given as

$$I = \frac{E}{\sqrt{R^2 + X_C^2}}$$

As X_C increases, current decreases and *vice-versa*.

Hence, brightness of the bulb increases, as current increases with decrease in capacitive reactance.

$\therefore$ Both A and R are true and R is the correct explanation of A.

32. (*b*) Position of first bright fringe,

$$y_1 = \frac{\lambda D}{d}$$

Position of second bright fringe,

$$y_2 = \frac{2\lambda D}{d}$$

$$y_2 - y_1 = \frac{2\lambda D}{d} - \frac{\lambda D}{d}$$

$$y_2 - y_1 = \frac{\lambda D}{d}$$

or $$\lambda = \frac{(y_2 - y_1)d}{D}$$

Substituting given values, we have

$$\lambda = \frac{0.553 \times 10^{-3} \times 2.08 \times 10^{-3}}{1.8}$$

$$= 639 \times 10^{-9} \text{ m}$$

or $\lambda = 639 \text{ nm}$

33. (*a*) Given, linear charge density,

$$\lambda = 0.2 \text{ C/m}$$

Distance, $R = 2 \text{ m}$

$$\therefore \quad E = \frac{1}{4\pi\varepsilon_0} \cdot \frac{2\lambda}{R}$$

$$= 9 \times 10^9 \times \frac{2 \times 0.2}{2}$$

$$= 1.8 \times 10^9 \text{ V/m}$$

34. (*c*) Given that all are moving with same speed, let it be v.

As, $e = Blv$

Here, B and v are constants.

$\Rightarrow e \propto l$ or vertical height.

As, if the perpendicular length of a loop is more, so its induced emf will also be more.

$\therefore$ Correct order of the induced emf for the given loops is $e_3 > e_2 > e_1$.

35. (*a*) In SHM, speed of the block at equilibrium position is given by

$$v = A\omega, \text{ where } \omega = \sqrt{\frac{k}{m}} \quad \ldots \text{(i)}$$

If spring is extended to $2A$, then new amplitude, $A' = 2A$ and new velocity,

$$v' = A'\omega'$$

$$v' = (2A)\omega \quad \ldots \text{(ii)}$$

$$\left[\because \omega' = \omega = \sqrt{\frac{k}{m}}\right]$$

From Eqs. (i) and (ii), we get

$$\frac{v}{v'} = \frac{1}{2} \text{ or } v' = 2v$$

36. (*b*) When a resistor is connected to an AC source, the power drawn will be $P = V_{\text{rms}} I_{\text{rms}}$

For resistance, $I_{\text{rms}} = \frac{V_{\text{rms}}}{R}$

$$\therefore \quad P = V_{\text{rms}} \cdot \frac{V_{\text{rms}}}{R}$$

or $$V_{\text{rms}}^2 = PR \quad \ldots \text{(i)}$$

Now, an inductor is connected in series with resistor, so the power will be

$P' = V_{\text{rms}} I_{\text{rms}} \cos\phi$, where $\cos\phi$ is the power factor of circuit.

$$P' = V_{\text{rms}} \left(\frac{V_{\text{rms}}}{Z}\right)\left(\frac{R}{Z}\right)$$

Here, Z is impedance.

$$\therefore I_{\text{rms}} = \frac{V_{\text{rms}}}{Z} \Rightarrow P' = V_{\text{rms}}^2 \frac{R}{Z^2}$$

From Eq. (i), we get

$$P' = (PR)\frac{R}{Z^2} \Rightarrow P' = \frac{PR^2}{Z^2}$$

Here, $P = 150 \text{ W}$,

$R = 10\,\Omega, Z = 20\,\Omega$

$$\therefore \quad P' = 150 \times \frac{(10)^2}{(20)^2} = 37.5 \text{ W}$$

And inductive reactance,

$$X_L = \sqrt{Z^2 - R^2}$$

$$= \sqrt{(20)^2 - (10)^2} = 10\sqrt{3}\,\Omega$$

37. (*b*) We know that, power factor,

$$\cos\phi = \frac{R}{Z}$$

$$\therefore \frac{\cos\phi_1}{\cos\phi_2} = \frac{R/Z_1}{R/Z_2} = \frac{Z_2}{Z_1}$$

$$= \frac{\sqrt{X_L^2 + R^2}}{\sqrt{(X_L - X_C)^2 + R^2}}$$

$$= \frac{\sqrt{(3R)^2 + R^2}}{\sqrt{(3R - 2R)^2 + R^2}}$$

$$= \frac{\sqrt{10R^2}}{\sqrt{2R^2}} = \sqrt{5}$$

38. (*d*) Given circuit can be shown as below.

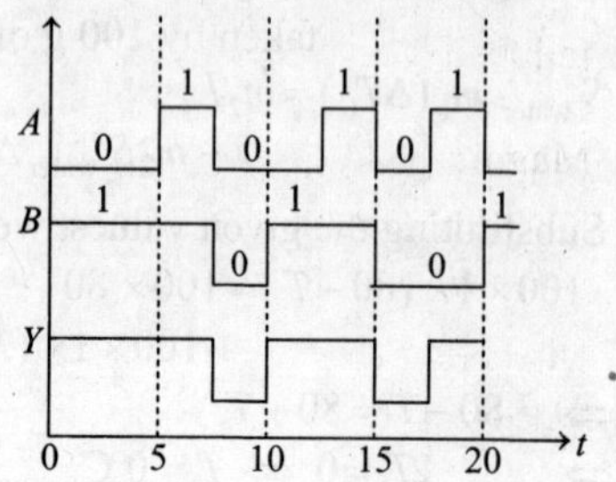

Output, $Y = \overline{\overline{A} \cdot \overline{B}} = \overline{\overline{A}} + \overline{\overline{B}} = A + B$

The corresponding input and output waveforms are shown below.

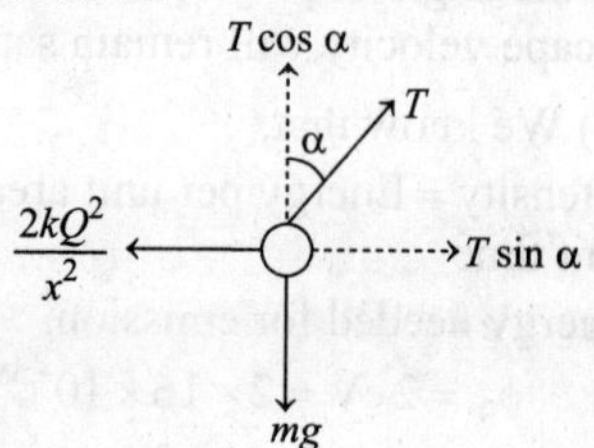

39. (*a*) FBD for pith ball with charge Q is as follows

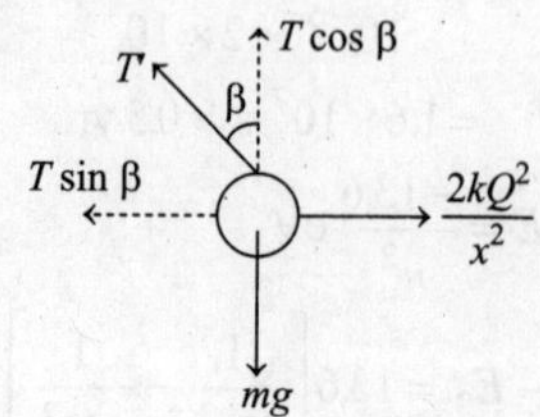

Here, x is distance between charges.

In equilibrium, $\Sigma F_x = 0$

and $\Sigma F_y = 0$

$$\Rightarrow \quad T\sin\alpha = \frac{2kQ^2}{x^2} \quad \ldots \text{(i)}$$

and $$T\cos\alpha = mg \quad \ldots \text{(ii)}$$

From Eqs. (i) and (ii), we get

$$\tan\alpha = \frac{\frac{2kQ^2}{x^2}}{mg}$$

or $$\tan\alpha = \frac{2kQ^2}{mg\,x^2} \quad \ldots \text{(iii)}$$

Similarly, FBD for pith ball with charge $2Q$ is as follows

So, $\tan\beta = \dfrac{2kQ^2}{mgx^2}$ ... (iv)

From Eqs. (iii) and (iv), we get

$$\tan\alpha = \tan\beta$$

or $\alpha = \beta$

40. (*b*) The capacitance of a parallel plate capacitor with dielectric is given as

$$C = \frac{\varepsilon_0 A}{d} K$$

The given arrangement can be treated as

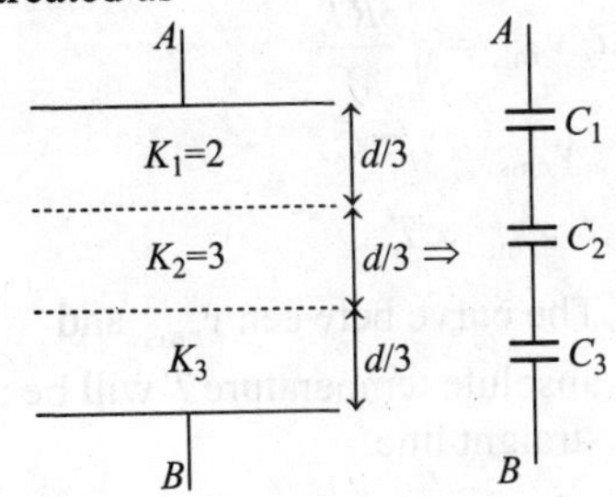

Here, $C_1 = \dfrac{2\varepsilon_0 A}{d/3} = \dfrac{6\varepsilon_0 A}{d}$

$$C_2 = \frac{3\varepsilon_0 A}{d/3} = \frac{9\varepsilon_0 A}{d}$$

$$C_3 = \frac{K_3\varepsilon_0 A}{d/3} = \frac{3K_3\varepsilon_0 A}{d}$$

Since, C_1, C_2 and C_3 are in series,

$$\frac{1}{C_{eq}} = \frac{1}{C_1} + \frac{1}{C_2} + \frac{1}{C_3}$$

$$\frac{d}{3\varepsilon_0 A} = \frac{d}{6\varepsilon_0 A} + \frac{d}{9\varepsilon_0 A} + \frac{d}{3K_3\varepsilon_0 A}$$

$$1 = \frac{1}{2} + \frac{1}{3} + \frac{1}{3K_3}$$

or $\dfrac{1}{3K_3} = \dfrac{1}{6}$ or $K_3 = 2$

41. (*b*) $I_{WL} = I_{rms}\sin\phi$

$$2 = 4\sin\phi$$

$$\sin\phi = \frac{1}{2}$$

$$\phi = 30°$$

Power factor,

$$\cos\phi = \cos 30° = \frac{\sqrt{3}}{2}$$

42. (*b*) As, acceleration is zero in downward motion.

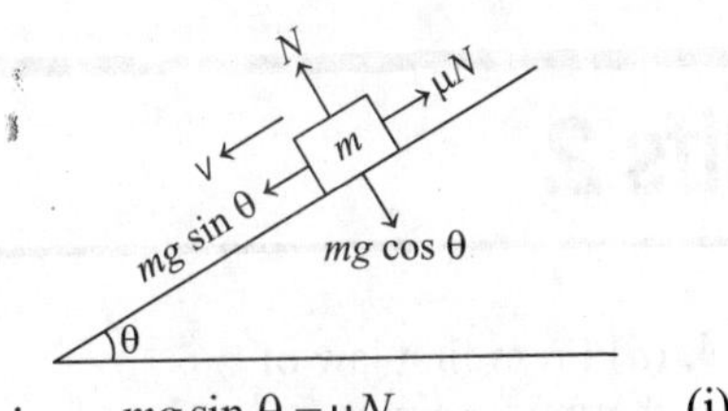

$\therefore$ $mg\sin\theta = \mu N$ ...(i)

$$mg\sin\theta = \mu mg\cos\theta$$

$(\because N = mg\cos\theta)$

or $\mu = \tan\theta$

When it is projected upward with a velocity v_0, it will be retarded by both $mg\sin\theta$ component and frictional force.

$\Rightarrow$ $ma = -(mg\sin\theta + f)$

$$ma = -(mg\sin\theta + \mu N)$$

$$ma = -(mg\sin\theta + mg\sin\theta)$$

[$\because$ using Eq. (i)]

$\Rightarrow a = -2g\sin\theta$, here negative sign implies that the block is stopped by retardation.

Now, using 3rd equation of motion along the plane,

$$v^2 = u^2 + 2as$$

$\Rightarrow$ $0^2 = v_0^2 + 2(-2g\sin\theta)s$

or $s = \dfrac{v_0^2}{4g\sin\theta}$

43. (*d*) Given, initial velocity $= u$

Acceleration due to gravity,

$$g = 9.8\text{ m/s}^2$$

Time to reach at highest point,

$t = \dfrac{u}{g}$ or $u = tg$ ...(i)

According to question,

Time taken by ball to reach ground,

$t' = 4t$ ...(ii)

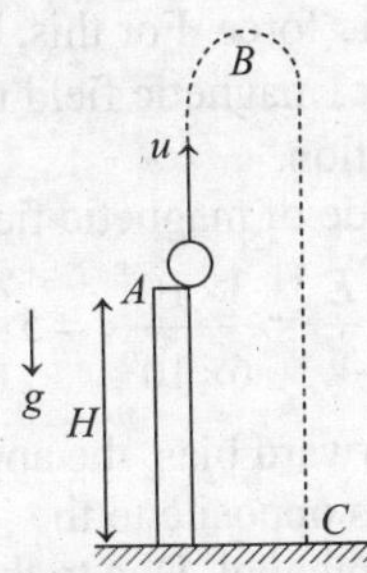

For A to C,

Using 2nd equation of motion,

$$s = ut + \frac{1}{2}gt^2$$

$\Rightarrow$ $-H = u \times t' + \dfrac{1}{2}(-g)(t'^2)$

$\Rightarrow$ $-80 = (tg) \times (4t) - \dfrac{g(4t)^2}{2}$

[using Eqs. (i) and (ii)]

$\Rightarrow$ $-80 = 4gt^2 - 8gt^2$

or $4gt^2 = 80$

or $4 \times 9.8t^2 = 80$

$$t^2 = \frac{80}{9.8 \times 4}$$

or $t = \dfrac{10}{7}$ s

and $u = tg$

$$u = \frac{10}{7} \times 9.8$$

$$= 14\text{ m/s}^2$$

Initial kinetic energy,

$$K = \frac{1}{2}mu^2$$

$$= \frac{1}{2} \times 0.5 \times (14)^2$$

$$K = 49\text{ J}$$

44. (*c*) Let u be the projection velocity of stone, where u_x and u_y be the horizontal and vertical components of u, respectively.

Horizontal distance, $x = u_x t$

or $u_x = \dfrac{x}{t} = \dfrac{30}{1} = 30$ m/s

We also know that time of flight,

$T = \dfrac{2u_y}{g}$, where u_y is the vertical component of initial velocity.

or $u_y = \dfrac{T \times g}{2} = \dfrac{8 \times 10}{2}$

or $u_y = 40$ m/s

$\therefore$ Projection velocity,

$$u = \sqrt{u_x^2 + u_y^2}$$

$$= \sqrt{(30)^2 + (40)^2}$$

$$u = 50\text{ m/s}$$

45. (*c*) As, $F_{\text{external}} = 0$

$\Rightarrow$ $a_{CM} = 0$

$\therefore$ $v_{CM} = \text{constant}$

or $v_{CM} = 20$ km/h

NK02 NEET Knock Offs 2

1. (*b*) As we know that time taken by a body to fall from a height h to reach the ground is $t=\sqrt{\dfrac{2h}{g}}$

$$\therefore \quad \frac{t_A}{t_B}=\sqrt{\frac{2h_A}{g}\times\frac{g}{2h_B}}$$

$$=\sqrt{\frac{h_A}{h_B}}$$

$$=\sqrt{9/25}$$

$$=3/5$$

2. (*b*) The first harmonic frequency is

$$f_1=\frac{v}{\lambda_i}=\frac{v}{2L} \quad \text{(open pipe)}$$

where, L is the length of the pipe.

The frequency of its nth harmonic,

$$f_n=\frac{nv}{2L} \quad \text{for } n=1,2,3.... \quad \text{(open pipe)}$$

Given, $L=20\,\text{cm}$, $v=330\,\text{ms}^{-1}$

$$f_n=\frac{n\ (330\ \text{ms}^{-1})}{0.4\ \text{m}}=825\,n\ \text{Hz}$$

The frequencies of 2nd harmonic, 3rd harmonic, 4th harmonic,... are $2\times825=1650\,\text{Hz}$, $3\times825=2475\,\text{Hz}$, $4\times825=3300\,\text{Hz}$...

Clearly, a source of frequency 1.6 kHz will resonate at f_2, i.e. the second harmonic.

3. (*c*) Let energy E in terms of momentum p, area A and time t be

$$[E]=[p^x A^y t^z]$$

$$\Rightarrow [ML^2T^{-2}]=[MLT^{-1}]^x[L^2]^y[T]^z$$

$$\Rightarrow [ML^2T^{-2}]=[M]^x[L]^{x+2y}[T]^{-x+z}$$

Equating powers of same physical quantity, we have

$$x=1,\ x+2y=2$$

and $-x+z=-2$

For these equations, we get

$$x=1,\ y=\frac{1}{2},\ z=-1$$

Hence, $[E]=[pA^{1/2}t^{-1}]$

4. (*a*) From first law of thermodynamics, $\Delta Q=\Delta U+W$

In adiabatic process, $\Delta Q=0$

$$\therefore \quad \Delta U+W=0$$

or $\quad \Delta U=-W$

In expansion, W is positive, so ΔU is negative.

So, internal energy and temperature decreases.

5. (*c*) Surface area of ${}_{13}\text{Al}^{27}=S_0$

$$S_0\propto R^2$$

$$R=R_0A^{\frac{1}{3}}$$

$$R_{\text{Al}}=R_0(27)^{\frac{1}{3}}$$

$$R_{\text{Al}}=3R_0$$

$$S_{\text{Al}}\propto(3R_0)^2$$

$$S_0\propto 9R_0^2 \quad ...(i)$$

$$R_{\text{Zn}}=R_0(64)^{\frac{1}{3}}=4R_0$$

$$S_{\text{Zn}}\propto(4R_0)^2$$

$$\propto 16R_0^2 \quad ...(ii)$$

Dividing Eq. (i) by (ii),

$$\frac{S_{\text{Zn}}}{S_0}=\frac{16R_0^2}{9R_0^2}$$

$$S_{\text{Zn}}=\frac{16}{9}S_0$$

6. (*b*) Magnetic force must be opposite to electric force. For this, by left hand rule, magnetic field must be in $+z$-direction.

Magnitude of magnetic field,

$$B=\frac{E}{v}=\frac{3\times10^4}{6\times10^6}=5\times10^{-3}\ \text{T}$$

7. (*a*) In forward bias, the applied voltage is opposite to the junction barrier potential. Due to this, effective potential barrier and depletion region decrease.

8. (*a*) We know that,

$$\text{Intensity}=\frac{\text{Power}}{\text{Area}}\Rightarrow\frac{1}{2}c\varepsilon_0E^2=\frac{P}{A}$$

$$\Rightarrow \quad E=\sqrt{\frac{2P}{Ac\varepsilon_0}}$$

$$=\sqrt{\frac{2\times27\times10^{-3}}{20\times10^{-6}\times3\times10^8\times9\times10^{-12}}}$$

$$=1\times10^3\ \text{V/m}=1\ \text{kV/m}$$

9. (*a*) $v_{\text{rms}}=\sqrt{\dfrac{3RT}{M}}$

$$v_{\text{rms}}\propto\sqrt{T}$$

$$v_{\text{rms}}^2\propto T$$

The curve between v_{rms}^2 and absolute temperature T will be a straight line.

10. (*c*) Power of source = Energy of 1 photon × Total number of photons

$$\Rightarrow \quad 6.6\times10^3=hf\times10^{20}$$

where, f = frequency of source

$$\Rightarrow \quad f=\frac{6.6\times10^3}{6.6\times10^{-34}\times10^{20}}$$

$$=10^{17}\ \text{Hz}$$

So, source is emitting X-rays and it is a coolidge tube.

11. (*a*) Wavelength of emitted photon,

$$\frac{1}{\lambda}=R\left(\frac{1}{n_f^2}-\frac{1}{n_i^2}\right) \quad ...(i)$$

and if recoil speed is v, then from

$$\lambda=\frac{h}{p}=\frac{h}{mv}$$

we have, $v=\dfrac{h}{m}\cdot\dfrac{1}{\lambda}$ ...(ii)

From Eqs. (i) and (ii), we get

$$v=\frac{h}{m}\cdot R\cdot\left(\frac{1}{n_f^2}-\frac{1}{n_i^2}\right)$$

$$=\frac{6.6\times10^{-34}}{1.67\times10^{-27}}\times1.1\times10^7\times\left(\frac{1}{1}-\frac{1}{25}\right)$$

$$=4.17\ \text{ms}^{-1}$$

12. (c) Electric field is maximum in the middle of the depletion layer of reverse biased p-n junction.

13. (*a*) Truth table by observing the waveforms is given below.

A	B	Y
0	0	1
0	1	1
1	0	0
1	1	0

It is clear that Y is complement of A.

So, $Y = \overline{A}$

14. (*a*) Let v_1 and v_2 are the speed of bodies P and Q after collision.

By using law of conservation of momentum,

$$m_1 u_1 + m_2 u_2 = m_1 v_1 + m_2 v_2$$

$$\Rightarrow \quad Mu + m \times 0 = Mv_1 + mv_2$$

$$\Rightarrow \quad \frac{M(u - v_1)}{m} = v_2 \quad \ldots \text{(i)}$$

and by using law of conservation of energy,

$$\frac{1}{2} m_1 u_1^2 + \frac{1}{2} m_2 u_2^2 = \frac{1}{2} m_1 v_1^2 + \frac{1}{2} m_2 v_2^2$$

$$\Rightarrow \quad Mu^2 + 0 = Mv_1^2 + mv_2^2$$

$$\Rightarrow \quad M(u^2 - v_1^2) = mv_2^2$$

$$\Rightarrow M(u - v_1)(u + v_1)/m = v_2^2 \quad \ldots \text{(ii)}$$

Substituting the value of $M\dfrac{(u - v_1)}{m}$ from Eq. (i) in Eq. (ii), we get

$$v_2(u + v_1) = v_2^2 \Rightarrow \quad u + v_1 = v_2$$

$\because \quad M >> m$

$\therefore \quad v_1 = u$ and $v_2 = 2u$

Hence, option (a) is correct.

15. (*b*) As we know that,

Spring constant, $k \propto \dfrac{1}{\text{Natural length}}$

As spring is cut into two parts of length $\dfrac{3l}{4}$ and $\dfrac{l}{4}$, so $k_1 = \dfrac{4k}{3}$ and $k_2 = 4k$.

The given system of spring is arranged in parallel combination,

so $\quad k_{\text{eq}} = k_1 + k_2 = \dfrac{4k}{3} + 4k = \dfrac{16k}{3}$

$\therefore$ Time period,

$$T = 2\pi\sqrt{\frac{M}{k_{\text{eq}}}} = 2\pi\sqrt{\frac{3M}{16k}}$$

16. (*a*) The given system of plates with respective charges on them can be drawn as follows.

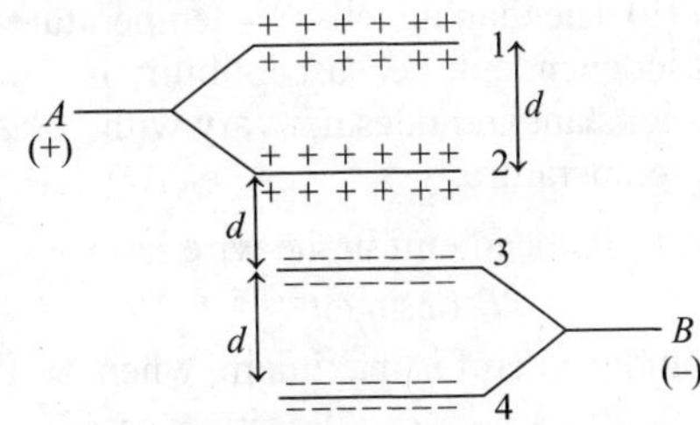

From the above figure, we can say that, there is only one capacitor between (2, 3).

So, $C_{\text{eq}} = \dfrac{\varepsilon_0 A}{d}$.

Note The answer would be the same even if polarities of A and B are reversed.

17. (*b*) From the graph, it is clear that component of initial vertical velocity,

$$v_y = 40 \text{ m/s}$$

So, maximum height,

$$H = \frac{v_y^2}{2g} = \frac{(40)^2}{2 \times 10} = 80 \text{ m}$$

18. (*b*) Given, the height of tap = 20 m

For first drop, $s = ut + \dfrac{1}{2}gt^2$

$$20 = \frac{1}{2} \times 10 \times t^2$$

$$t^2 = 4 \Rightarrow t = 2 \text{ s}$$

This means third drop leaves the tap 2 s after first drop and second drop leaves 1s after first drop.

Distance covered by second drop,

$$s = ut + \frac{1}{2}gt'^2$$

$$= \frac{1}{2} \times 10 \times 1^2 = 5 \text{ m}$$

Therefore, distance of second drop from the ground at this instant is

$$= 20 - 5 = 15 \text{ m}$$

19. (*c*) For a satellite,

$$T^2 \propto R^3 \quad \text{(Kepler's third law)}$$

or $\quad T \propto R^{3/2}$

$$T_2 / T_1 = (R_2 / R_1)^{3/2}$$

$$T_2 / T_1 = (1.02)^{3/2}$$

$$T_2 = (1.03)T_1$$

So, % change in time period

$$= \frac{T_2 - T_1}{T_1} \times 100 = 3\%$$

20. (*b*) FBD of the given rod is as shown below.

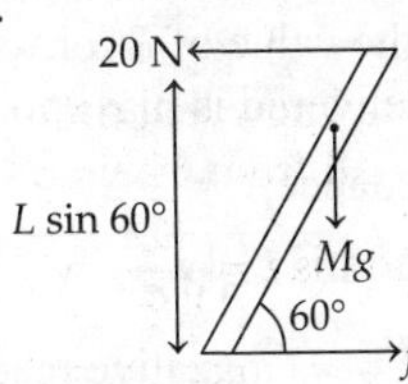

For rotational equilibrium, $\Sigma\tau = 0$.

Taking moments about bottom of rod, we have

$$20 \times L\sin 60° = Mg \times \frac{2L}{3}\cos 60°$$

$$\Rightarrow \quad 20 \times L \times \frac{\sqrt{3}}{2} = M \times 10 \times \frac{2L}{3} \times \frac{1}{2}$$

$$\Rightarrow \quad M = 3\sqrt{3} \text{ kg} = 3 \times 1.7 \approx 5 \text{ kg}$$

21. (*b*) Given, radius, $r = 3$ cm

$$= 3 \times 10^{-2} \text{ m}$$

$\because$ Maximum load = Maximum stress × Area of cross section of wire

$$= 10^{10} \times \pi r^2$$

$$= 10^{10} \times 3.14 \times (3 \times 10^{-2})^2$$

$$= 10^{10} \times 3.14 \times 9 \times 10^{-4}$$

$$= 28.2 \times 10^6$$

$$= 2.8 \times 10^7 \text{ N}$$

22. (*a*) Let angular acceleration is applied for t seconds.

Given that, $\omega_i = 0$

$$\alpha = 28 \text{ rad/s}^2$$

$$I = 10 \text{ kg-m}^2$$

Kinetic energy, KE $= \dfrac{1}{2}I\omega^2$

or $\quad \omega = \sqrt{\dfrac{2\text{KE}}{I}} = \sqrt{\dfrac{2 \times 980}{10}} = 14 \text{ rad/s}$

From first equation of rotational motion, $\omega_f = \omega_i + \alpha t$

$\Rightarrow \quad 14 = 0 + 28 \times t \qquad (\because \omega_f = \omega)$

$\Rightarrow \quad t = 0.5 \text{ s}$

23. (*d*) No field exists inside a metallic cavity.

$\therefore$ Net flux through the metal cube will be zero.

24. (*a*) The output power of cell,

$$P = I^2 R = \frac{V^2}{(r + R)^2} R$$

Maximum power is delivered to the load only when the internal resistance of the source is equal to the load resistance (R).

Hence, the value of R for which the power delivered is maximum $= 0.3\,\Omega$.

25. (*d*) Impedance,

$$Z = \sqrt{R^2 + (X_C - X_L)^2}$$

where, X_C = capacitive reactance,

X_L = inductive reactance

and $X_C = \frac{1}{\omega C}, X_L = \omega L$

$$\therefore Z = \sqrt{(60)^2 + \left(\frac{1}{314 \times 50 \times 10^{-6}} - 314 \times 30 \times 10^{-3}\right)^2}$$

$$= \sqrt{3600 + (63.69 - 9.42)^2}$$

$$= 81\,\Omega$$

$$\text{Power loss} = \left(\frac{V_{\text{rms}}}{Z}\right)^2 \cdot R$$

$$= \left(\frac{12/\sqrt{2}}{81}\right)^2 \cdot 60 = 0.66\text{ W}$$

26. (*c*) Given, current, $I = 12\text{ A}$,

radius, $R = 2\text{ cm} = 2 \times 10^{-2}\text{ m}$

Magnetic field at the centre of current carrying circular loop,

$$B_c = \frac{\mu_0 I}{2R} = \frac{\mu_0}{2\pi} \cdot \frac{\pi I}{R}$$

Magnetic field at the centre of semi-circular loop,

$$B = \frac{B_c}{2} = \frac{\mu_0}{4\pi} \frac{\pi I}{R}$$

$$= 10^{-7} \times \frac{3.14 \times 12}{2 \times 10^{-2}}$$

$$= 1.9 \times 10^{-4}\text{ T}$$

Thus, **B** is 1.9×10^{-4} T normal to the plane of the paper going inwards, i.e. ⊗ (from right hand thumb rule).

27. (*c*) Current, I = Slope of q-t graph

$$= \frac{y_2 - y_1}{x_2 - x_1} = \frac{q_0 - 0}{0 - t_0} = -\frac{q_0}{t_0}$$

Heat produced, $H = I^2 Rt$

or $$H = \frac{q_0^2 R}{t_0^2} t$$

or $$H \propto t$$

So, the graph between H and t should be straight line passing through the origin. Hence, option (c) is correct.

28. (*b*) The diamagnetism is temperature independent, i.e. susceptibility is constant and does not vary with temperature.

29. (*b*) Induced emf in the wire loop,

$$e = BA\omega \sin \omega t$$

Induced emf is maximum, when

$$\sin \omega t = \pm 1$$

$$\Rightarrow \quad \omega t = \frac{\pi}{2}$$

$$\Rightarrow \quad \frac{2\pi}{T} \cdot t = \frac{\pi}{2}$$

Here, $T = 10$ s

So, $t = \frac{10}{4} = 2.5$ s

30. (*d*) Intensity at any point is given by

$$I = I_{\max} \cos^2 \frac{\phi}{2} = 4I_0 \cos^2 \frac{\phi}{2}$$

Let the phase difference at the point where intensity is $2I_0$ be ϕ_1,

$$2I_0 = 4I_0 \cos^2 \frac{\phi_1}{2}$$

or $$\cos^2 \frac{\phi_1}{2} = \frac{1}{2} \text{ or } \cos \frac{\phi_1}{2} = \frac{1}{\sqrt{2}}$$

or $$\frac{\phi_1}{2} = \frac{\pi}{4} \text{ or } \phi_1 = \frac{\pi}{2}$$

Path difference, $\Delta x_1 = \frac{\lambda}{2\pi} \times \phi_1 = \frac{\lambda}{4}$

Let position of that point be y_1 from central maxima, then

$$\Delta x_1 = \frac{y_1 d}{D}$$

or $$y_1 = \frac{D\Delta x_1}{d} = \frac{\lambda D}{4d} \quad \text{... (i)}$$

Similarly, for a point where intensity is I_0, phase difference be ϕ_2,

$$I_0 = 4I_0 \cos^2 \frac{\phi_2}{2}$$

or $$\cos^2 \frac{\phi_2}{2} = \frac{1}{4} \text{ or } \cos \frac{\phi_2}{2} = \frac{1}{2}$$

$$\phi_2 = \frac{2\pi}{3}$$

Corresponding path difference,

$$\Delta x_2 = \frac{\lambda}{2\pi} \times \frac{2\pi}{3} = \frac{\lambda}{3}$$

$$\Delta x_2 = \frac{y_2 d}{D}$$

or $$y_2 = \frac{D\Delta x_2}{d} = \frac{\lambda D}{3d} \quad \text{... (ii)}$$

$\therefore$ Minimum separation,

$$\Delta y = y_2 - y_1 = \frac{\lambda D}{3d} - \frac{\lambda D}{4d}$$

$$= \frac{1}{12}\left(\frac{\lambda D}{d}\right) = \frac{\beta}{12} \quad \left(\because \beta = \frac{D\lambda}{d}\right)$$

31. (*d*) Coordinates of centre of mass of all four rods w.r.t. origin are as shown below.

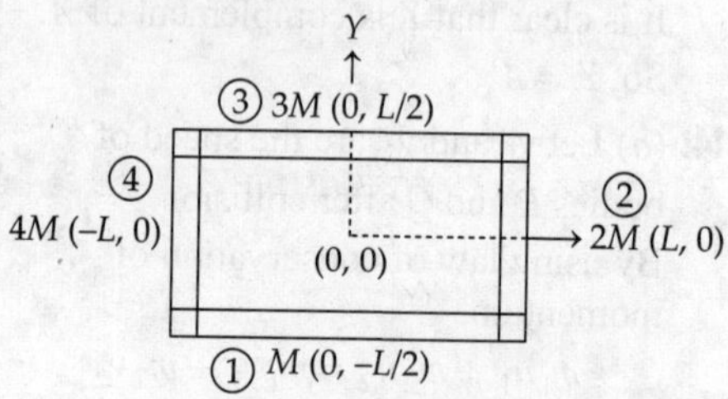

For system of rods,

$$X_{\text{CM}} = \frac{m_1 x_1 + m_2 x_2 + m_3 x_3 + m_4 x_4}{m_1 + m_2 + m_3 + m_4}$$

$$= \frac{-2}{10} L = \frac{-L}{5}$$

and similarly $Y_{\text{CM}} = \frac{L}{10}$

It is clear that X and Y-coordinates of centre of mass are negative and positive respectively, so it lies in 2nd quadrant (or IV region).

32. (*a*)

10 H 10 μF 50 Ω

200 V

Impedance, $Z = \sqrt{R^2 + (X_L - X_C)^2}$

At resonance, $X_L = X_C$

$$\Rightarrow \omega = \frac{1}{\sqrt{LC}} = \frac{1}{\sqrt{10 \times 10 \times 10^{-6}}}$$

$$= \frac{1}{\sqrt{10^{-4}}} = 100\text{ Hz}$$

$Z = R$

$Z = 50\,\Omega$

$\therefore$ A → IV

$$I_{\text{rms}} = \frac{V}{R} = \frac{200}{50} = 4\text{ A}$$

$\therefore$ B → III

$V_{R_{\text{rms}}} = 200$ V

$\therefore$ C → II

$$V_{L_{rms}} = I_{rms} \times \omega L$$
$$= 4 \times 100 \times 10$$
$$= 4 \times 10^3 = 4000 \text{ V}$$

$\therefore$ D → I

33. (*a*) As, $y_n = \dfrac{n\lambda D}{d}$

$\therefore$ $y_n \propto \lambda$ and $\lambda_{violet} < \lambda_{red}$

$\Rightarrow (y_n)_{violet} < (y_n)_{red}$

$\therefore$ Fringes come closer to centre line.

34. (*b*) The given circuit can be redrawn as

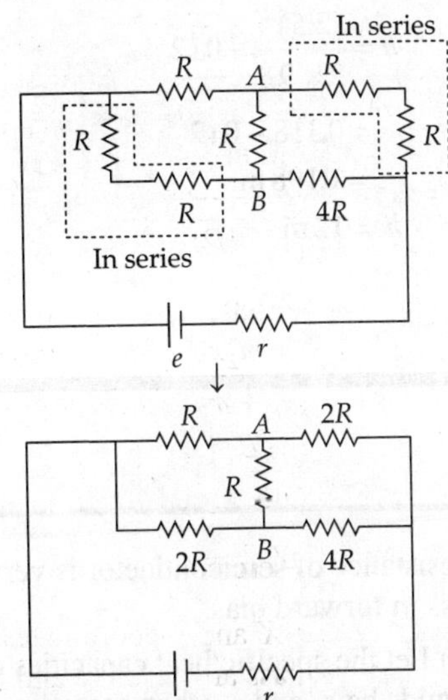

This represents a balanced Wheatstone bridge, so current will not flow through resistor R across the branch AB. It can be removed from circuit.

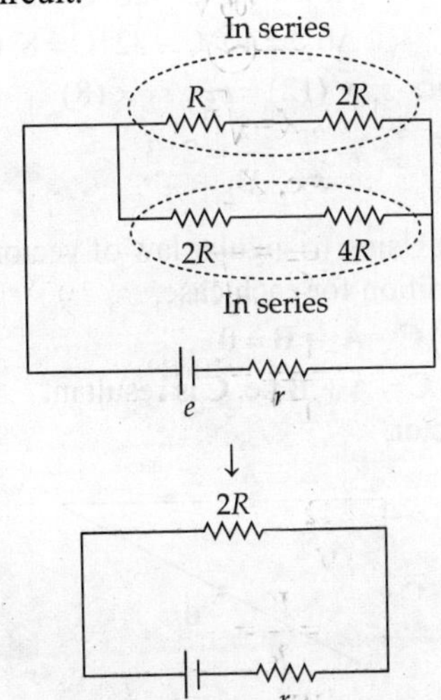

For maximum power transfer to the load, the load resistance must be equal to internal resistance of the battery.

$\therefore$ $2R = r$

or $R = \dfrac{r}{2}$

35. (*d*) Current, $I = \mathbf{J} \cdot \mathbf{A}$

$$= (2 \times 10^4 \hat{\mathbf{j}}) \cdot (2\hat{\mathbf{i}} + 3\hat{\mathbf{j}}) \times 10^{-4}$$
$$= 6 \times 10^4 \times 10^{-4} = 6 \text{ A}$$

Charge, $Q = I \times t = 6 \times 2 = 12 \text{ C}$

36. (*b*) Friction force, $F = \mu N$

and acceleration, $a = \dfrac{-F}{m} = -\dfrac{\mu mg}{m}$

$\Rightarrow$ $a = -\mu g = -10\mu$

Using third equation of motion,

$$v^2 = u^2 + 2as$$

or $0^2 = (20)^2 + 2(-10\mu)80$

or $\mu = \dfrac{(20)^2}{2 \times 10 \times 80} = \dfrac{1}{4}$

or $\mu = 0.25$

37. (*c*) Let the projection velocities of particles be u_1 and u_2.

Velocities after t seconds are

$$\mathbf{v}_1 = u_1 \hat{\mathbf{i}} - gt\,\hat{\mathbf{j}}$$

and $\mathbf{v}_2 = -u_2 \hat{\mathbf{i}} - gt\,\hat{\mathbf{j}}$

When velocities become perpendicular, i.e. $\mathbf{v}_1 \cdot \mathbf{v}_2 = 0$

$$(u_1 \hat{\mathbf{i}} - gt\,\hat{\mathbf{j}}) \cdot (-u_2 \hat{\mathbf{i}} - gt\,\hat{\mathbf{j}}) = 0$$
$$-u_1 u_2 + g^2 t^2 = 0$$

or $g^2 t^2 = u_1 u_2$

or $t = \dfrac{\sqrt{u_1 u_2}}{g}$

Here, $u_1 = 30$ m/s, $u_2 = 40$ m/s, $g = 10 \text{ m/s}^2$

$\therefore$ $t = \dfrac{\sqrt{30 \times 40}}{10}$

or $t = 2\sqrt{3}$ s

38. (*c*) Work done on dipole by external torque, $W = \Delta U = U_f - U_i$

$$= (-\mathbf{p}_f \cdot \mathbf{E}) - (-\mathbf{p}_i \cdot \mathbf{E})$$
$$= (\mathbf{p}_i - \mathbf{p}_f) \cdot \mathbf{E}$$
$$= [(3\hat{\mathbf{i}} + 4\hat{\mathbf{j}}) - (-4\hat{\mathbf{i}} + 3\hat{\mathbf{j}})] \times 10^{-30} \cdot 4000\hat{\mathbf{i}}$$
$$= (7\hat{\mathbf{i}} + \hat{\mathbf{j}}) \times 10^{-30} \cdot 4000\hat{\mathbf{i}}$$
$$= 2.8 \times 10^{-26} \text{ J}$$

39. (*a*) As we know that, the cross-sectional area of vertical pipes 1, 2 and 3 are the same.

$\therefore$ By equation of continuity,

$\Rightarrow$ $A \times v =$ constant

$\Rightarrow$ $v =$ constant

So, pressure is same at all points, i.e.

$$p_1 = p_2 = p_3$$
$$\rho g h_1 = \rho g h_2 = \rho g h_3$$
$$h_1 = h_2 = h_3$$

Hence, height of liquid will also be same.

40. (*c*)

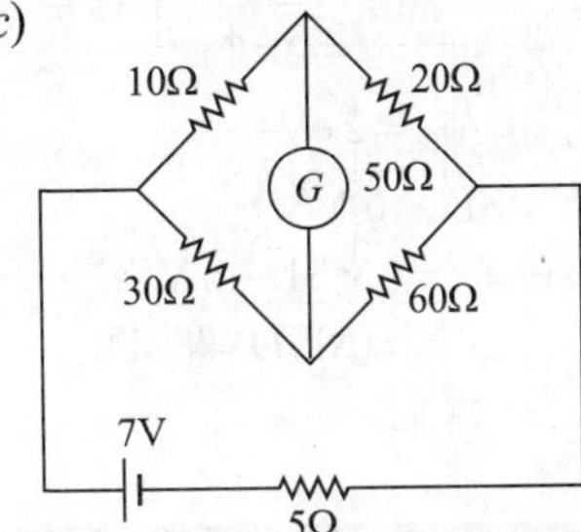

Total resistance of Wheatstone bridge

$$= \frac{30 \times 90}{30 + 90} = \frac{2700}{120} = \frac{270}{12} \Omega$$

Current through cell $= \dfrac{7}{\left(\dfrac{270}{12} + 5\right)}$

$$= 0.25 \text{ A}$$

41. (a) Magnification, $M = -\dfrac{v}{u} = -12$

Negative sign because in concave mirror, real image is always inverted.

$$v = 12u$$

Using mirror formula,

$$\frac{1}{f} = \frac{1}{v} + \frac{1}{u}$$
$$\frac{1}{f} = \frac{1}{12u} + \frac{1}{u}$$
$$\frac{1}{f} = \frac{13}{12u}$$
$$u = \frac{13f}{12}$$

Focal length, $f = +48$ cm

$$u = \frac{13 \times 48}{12} \text{ cm}$$
$$= +52 \text{ cm}$$
$$v = 12 \times 52 = 624 \text{ cm}$$
$$= 6.24 \text{ m}$$

42. (*d*) From Einstein's photoelectric equation,

$$KE = hf - \phi_0$$

$\Rightarrow \quad \frac{1}{2}mv_1^2 = 4 - \phi_0 \quad \ldots(i)$

and $\quad \frac{1}{2}mv_2^2 = 2.5 - \phi_0 \quad \ldots(ii)$

From Eqs. (i) and (ii), we get

$\therefore \quad \frac{v_1^2}{v_2^2} = \frac{4-\phi_0}{2.5-\phi_0}$

or $\quad 4 = \frac{4-\phi_0}{2.5-\phi_0} \quad \left(\text{as, } \frac{v_1}{v_2} = 2\right)$

So, $\quad \phi_0 = 2\,\text{eV}$

43. (*b*) 6 MSD = 6 VSD

Zero error = 6 MSD − 6 VSD

= 6 (MSD − VSD)

$= 6 \times 0.1 = +0.6\,\text{mm}$

44. (*a*) Both statements are correct.

As $\quad pV = nRT$

$\Rightarrow \quad p \propto T$

Hence, when temperature of a gas is increased to 3 times, then its pressure also increases 3 times.

Also, pressure of N molecules of an ideal gas contained in volume V is

$$p = \frac{2}{3}\frac{N}{V}\left(\frac{1}{2}mv^2\right)$$

45. (*b*) Using Bernoulli's equation,

$(KE)_{\text{lowered end}}$ = Pressure energy + $KE_{\text{(at the orifice)}}$

or $\quad \frac{1}{2}\rho v^2 = h_0\rho g + \frac{1}{2}\rho v_1^2 \quad \ldots(i)$

The kinetic energy at the opening is converted into the potential energy.

Thus, $\quad \frac{1}{2}\rho v_1^2 = \rho g h \quad \ldots(ii)$

From Eqs. (i) and (ii), we get

$$h = \frac{v^2}{2g} - h_0$$

Here, $v = 2.5\,\text{m/s}$

and $h_0 = 12\,\text{cm}$ or $0.12\,\text{m}$

and $g = 9.8\,\text{m/s}^2$

$\therefore \quad h = \frac{(2.5)^2}{2 \times 9.8} - 0.12$

$= 0.318 - 0.12$

$= 0.198\,\text{m}$

or $\quad h = 0.2\,\text{m}$

NK03 NEET Knock Offs 3

1. (d) Given that, $l = (16.2 \pm 0.1)\,\text{cm}$

$b = (10.1 \pm 0.1)\,\text{cm}$

Area of sheet, $A = l \times b$

$= 16.2 \times 10.1$

$= 163.62\,\text{cm}^2$

Rounding-off to three significant digits,

$$A = 164\,\text{cm}^2$$

Relative error in A,

$$\frac{\Delta A}{A} = \left(\frac{\Delta l}{l} + \frac{\Delta b}{b}\right) = \frac{0.1}{16.2} + \frac{0.1}{10.1}$$

$= 0.0061 + 0.0099 = 0.016$

So, $\Delta A = 0.016 \times A$

$= 0.016 \times 164$

$= 2.62\,\text{cm}^2$

Rounding-off to one significant figure,

$$\Delta A = 3\,\text{cm}^2$$

$\therefore \quad A = (164 \pm 3)\,\text{cm}^2$

2. (c) If a transformer is ideal, it means there is no loss of power due to flux leakage, hysteresis, eddy currents and heating of coils. So, power transferred through primary coil to secondary will be the same.

3. (a) Excess pressure in a bubble,

$$\Delta p = \frac{2T}{r} \text{ or } \Delta p \propto \frac{1}{r}$$

So, pressure in smaller bubble is greater than pressure in bigger bubble, therefore air will flow from the smaller bubble to the bigger bubble.

4. (d) As we know, ideal gas equation is given as $pV = \mu RT$

When temperature T is kept constant,

pV = constant $\quad \ldots(i)$

If volume is decreased by 5%, this means its volume becomes $\frac{95}{100}$ of the initial value, so in accordance with Eq. (i), the pressure must become $\frac{100}{95}$ of its initial value.

Thus, percentage increase in pressure

$$= \left(\frac{100-95}{95}\right) \times 100 = 5.26\%$$

5. (c) Heat is produced due to electrons transition from n to p-side or from conduction band to valence band.

Resistance of semiconductor is very less in forward bias.

6. (d) Let the specific heat capacities of liquids be s_1 and s_2, then according to the principle of calorimetry,

Heat taken (Q_1) = heat given (Q_2)

$$m_1 s_1 \Delta\theta_1 = m_2 s_2 \Delta\theta_2$$

Here, $\quad m_1 = m_2 = m \quad$ (given)

$\Delta\theta_1 = 32°\text{C} - 20°\text{C} = 12°\text{C}$

$\Delta\theta_2 = 40°\text{C} - 32°\text{C} = 8°\text{C}$

$\therefore m \times s_1 \times (12) = m \times s_2 \times (8)$

or $\quad \frac{s_1}{s_2} = \frac{2}{3} = 2:3$

7. (*b*) Using triangular law of vector addition for each case,

(A) **C** − **A** − **B** = 0

⇒ **C** = **A** + **B** i.e. **C** is resultant vector.

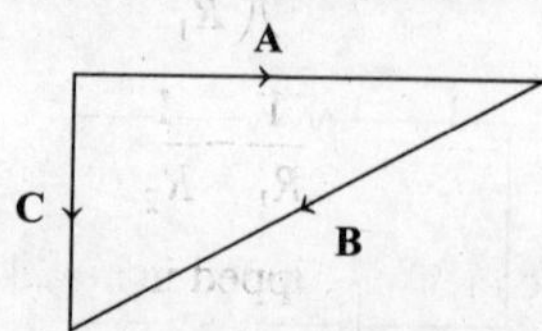

(B) **A** − **C** − **B** = 0

⇒ **A** = **C** + **B** i.e. **A** is resultant vector.

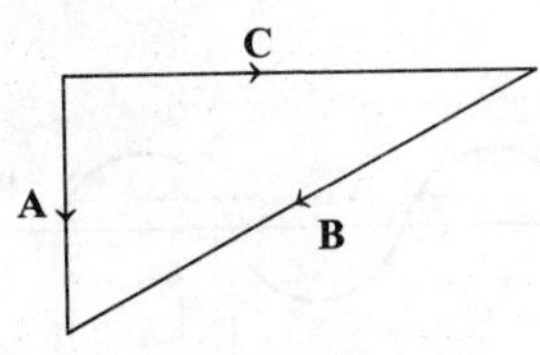

(C) $\mathbf{B}-\mathbf{A}-\mathbf{C}=0$

$\Rightarrow \mathbf{B}=\mathbf{A}+\mathbf{C}$ i.e. $\mathbf{B}$ is resultant vector.

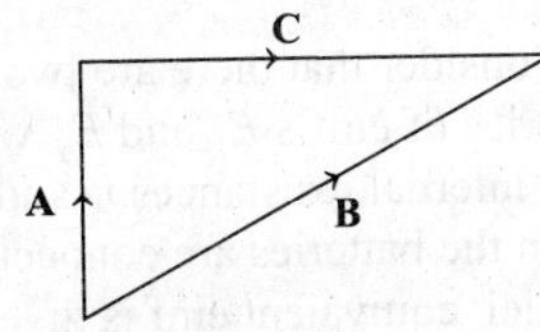

(D) $\mathbf{A}+\mathbf{B}=-\mathbf{C}$

$\mathbf{A}+\mathbf{B}+\mathbf{C}=\mathbf{0}$ i.e. these are cyclic vectors.

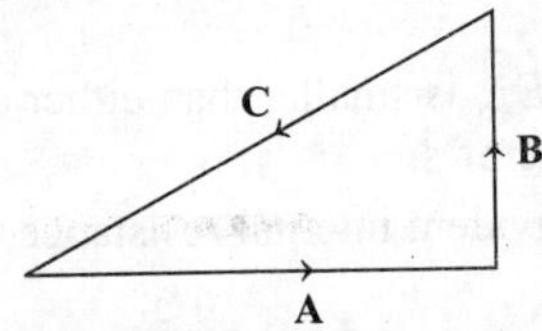

Hence, the correct match is A $\rightarrow$(4), B $\rightarrow$(3), C $\rightarrow$(1) and D $\rightarrow$(2).

8. (a) Difference in electric potential energy is given by

$$U_B - U_A = (V_B - V_A)\cdot q'$$

$$= \left(\frac{kq}{r_B} - \frac{kq}{r_A}\right)\cdot q' = a \text{ positive number}$$

Here, q' is negative, also $V_B - V_A$ is also negative. So, product is positive.

9. (b) By balanced Wheatstone bridge condition.

$$\Rightarrow \quad \frac{16}{X} = \frac{4}{0.5} \Rightarrow X = \frac{8}{4} = 2\Omega$$

10. (c) From lens Maker's formula, we have

$$\frac{1}{f_1} = \left(\frac{n_g}{n_a} - 1\right)\left(\frac{1}{R_1} - \frac{1}{R_2}\right)$$

$$\Rightarrow \quad \frac{1}{f_1} = \left(\frac{3}{2} - 1\right)\left(\frac{1}{R_1} - \frac{1}{R_2}\right)$$

or $$\frac{1}{f_1} = \frac{1}{2}\left(\frac{1}{R_1} - \frac{1}{R_2}\right) \quad \ldots(\text{i})$$

When lens is dipped in liquid of

$$n_l = \frac{7}{5}$$

then, $$\frac{1}{f_2} = \left(\frac{n_g}{n_l} - 1\right)\left(\frac{1}{R_1} - \frac{1}{R_2}\right)$$

$$\Rightarrow \quad \frac{1}{f_2} = \left(\frac{3/2}{7/5} - 1\right)\left(\frac{1}{R_1} - \frac{1}{R_2}\right)$$

$$\Rightarrow \quad \frac{1}{f_2} = \frac{1}{14}\left(\frac{1}{R_1} - \frac{1}{R_2}\right) \quad \ldots(\text{ii})$$

From Eqs. (i) and (ii), we get

$$\frac{f_2}{f_1} = 7$$

11. (b) The rate of flow of energy in an electromagnetic wave is described by poynting vector $\mathbf{s}$ which is defined by the expression, $\mathbf{s} = \frac{1}{\mu_0}(\mathbf{E}\times\mathbf{B})$

Its magnitude s is related to the rate at which energy is transported by a wave across a unit area at any instant.

Since, $\mathbf{E}$ and $\mathbf{B}$ are mutually perpendicular.

Hence, $|\mathbf{E}\times\mathbf{B}| = EB$

Thus, $s = \dfrac{EB}{\mu_0}$

12. (d) According to the question,

If $v \le v_e$, then trajectory will be parabolic.

But $v > v_e$, then it escapes the gravitational field of the earth in a hyperbolic path.

13. (c) By de-Broglie hypothesis,

$$2\pi r_n = n\lambda$$

For first orbit, $n=1, r=r_1$, then

$$2\pi r_1 = \lambda \text{ or } r_1 = \frac{\lambda}{2\pi}$$

For second orbit, $n=2, r=r_2$, then

$$2\pi r_2 = 2\lambda$$

or $$r_2 = \frac{2\lambda}{2\pi}$$

Minimum radial distance between first orbit and second orbit is

$$r_2 - r_1 = \frac{2\lambda}{2\pi} - \frac{\lambda}{2\pi}$$

$$\Rightarrow \quad r_2 - r_1 = \frac{\lambda}{2\pi}$$

14. (d) When the liquid is heated, the container will also expand along with liquid.

Thus, apparent expansion coefficient of liquid is $\gamma_a = \gamma_l - \gamma_s$

where, γ_l = coefficient of volume expansion of a liquid and

γ_s = coefficient of cubical expansion of the container.

If $\gamma_l > \gamma_s$, then $\gamma_a > 0$ and level of liquid will rise.

If $\gamma_l = \gamma_s$, then $\gamma_a = 0$ and level of liquid will not change.

If $\gamma_l < \gamma_s$ then $\gamma_a < 0$, hence level of liquid will fall.

Thus, there are three possibilities as mentioned above. All these will depend upon the coefficients of volume expansion of container and liquid.

15. (c) At $t=0$,

$$x_i = 0^3 - 6\times 0^2 + 9\times 0 = 0\,\text{m}$$

At $t = 5$s,

$$x_f = 5^3 - 6\times 5^2 + 9\times 5 = 20\,\text{m}$$

So, displacement of particle in first 5 s is

$$s = x_f - x_i = 20 - 0 = 20\,\text{m}$$

Now, velocity of particle is

$$v = \frac{dx}{dt} = 3t^2 - 12t + 9$$

$$= 3(t-1)(t-3)$$

Velocity changes its sign as shown below

Sign of v

⊕ ⊖ ⊕

$t=0$s | $t=1$s, $v=0$ | $t=3$s, $v=0$ | $t=5$s

So, particle moves in forward direction from $t=0$ to 1 s. It turns back and moves in negative direction from $t=1$s to 3s.

It again moves from $t = 3s$ to $5s$ in positive direction. Also, at $t = 3s$, position of particle is

$$x = 3^3 - 6\times 3^2 + 9\times 3 = 0 \text{ m}$$

Hence, particle moves as

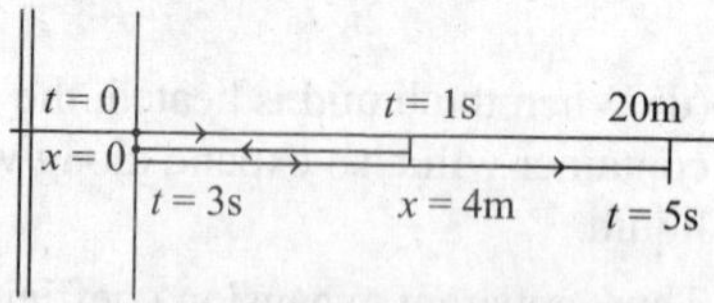

So, distance of particle in first 5 s

$$D = 4+4+20 = 28 \text{ m}$$

Hence, ratio is $\frac{28}{20} = \frac{7}{5}$

16. (d) Electric flux coming out from a surface does not depend on its surface area. It depends only on charge enclosed by surface.

As, flux, $\phi = \frac{q}{\varepsilon_0}$

17. (a) Given, time period, $t = 8$ s

amplitude, $A = 6$ cm

The time taken by a particle executing SHM from either extreme position to mean position and mean position to either extreme position is $t/4$, here $t = 2$ s.

According to the question,

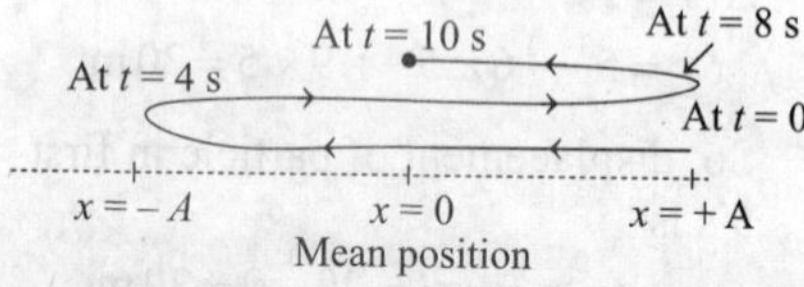

Thus, displacement of particle at $t = 10$ s is $x = 0$ cm.

18. (c) If the intensities of light coming out from slits are I_1 and I_2 respectively, then

$$I_{max} = (\sqrt{I_1} + \sqrt{I_2})^2 \quad \text{... (i)}$$

and $$I_{min} = (\sqrt{I_1} - \sqrt{I_2})^2 \quad \text{... (ii)}$$

When $I_1 = I_2 = I_0$ (Let)

then $I_{max} = (\sqrt{I_0} + \sqrt{I_0})^2 = 4I_0$

and $I_{min} = (\sqrt{I_0} - \sqrt{I_0})^2 = 0$

When width of one slit is slightly increased, then intensity due to that slit becomes greater than I_0. In that case, we can see that

$$I_{max} > 4I_0 \quad \text{[using Eq. (i)]}$$

and $$I_{min} > 0 \quad \text{[using Eq. (ii)]}$$

Thus, both maximum and minimum intensities will increase.

19. (c) As we know that, $V = V_0 \sin \omega t$

Compare with $V = 240 \sin 120t$

$$\nu = \frac{\omega}{2\pi} = \frac{120\times 7}{2\times 22} = 19 \text{ Hz}$$

$$V_{rms} = \frac{240}{\sqrt{2}} = 120\sqrt{2} = 170 \text{ V}$$

20. (b) Given,

Initial mass, $m_0 = 2000$ kg

Rate of fuel consumption,

$$\frac{dm}{dt} = 60 \text{ kg/s}$$

Relative velocity of gas,

$$v_r = 400 \text{ m/s}$$

The free body diagram of the rocket is as shown below

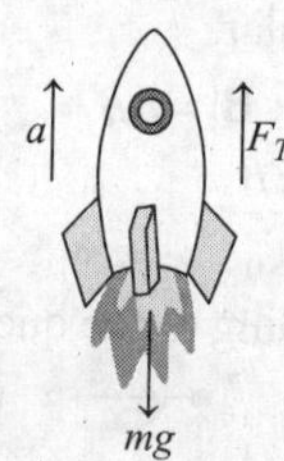

In equilibrium, $\Sigma F_y = 0$

$$\Rightarrow m_0 a = F_T - m_0 g$$

or $$a = \frac{F_T}{m_0} - g = \frac{v_r\left(\frac{dm}{dt}\right)}{m_0} - g$$

$$= \frac{400\times 60}{2000} - 10$$

$$= 12 - 10$$

$$a = 2 \text{ m/s}^2$$

21. (d) For positive half-cycle, when $V_i > 2$ V, diode is in forward bias and current will flow through the diode.

Voltage across resistance,

$$V_R = V_i - 2$$

$$V_R = 5 \sin \omega t - 2 = 3 \text{V}$$

$$[\because \sin \omega t = 1 \text{(max)}]$$

For negative half-cycle, diode is in reverse bias, so no current will flow through diode.

Voltage across resistance, $V_R = 0$ V

So, the input and output waveform for the given circuit is as shown below.

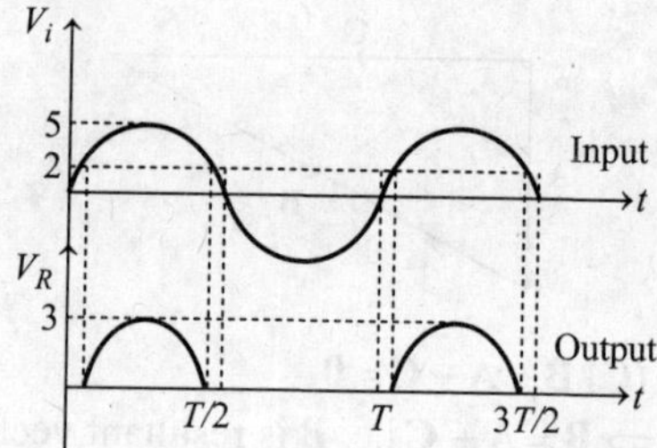

22. (a) Consider that there are two batteries of emf's E_1 and E_2 which have internal resistances r_1 and r_2. When the batteries are connected in parallel, equivalent emf is given by

$$E_{eq} = \frac{\frac{E_1}{r_1} + \frac{E_2}{r_2}}{\frac{1}{r_1} + \frac{1}{r_2}}$$

So, E_{eq} is smaller than either of the two emf's.

Equivalent internal resistance,

$$r_{eq} = \frac{r_1 r_2}{r_1 + r_2}$$

which is less than both r_1 and r_2. Hence, both Statements I and II are correct.

23. (b) Charged particles trace a circular path in a perpendicular magnetic field.

24. (c) Any two particles on different sides of a node have phase difference of 180°.

25. (b) Magnetic field due to bar magnet on its axis is given by

$$B = \frac{\mu_0}{4\pi}\cdot\frac{2m}{d^3}$$

$$\Rightarrow B = 10^{-7} \times \frac{2\times 1.2}{(0.1)^3}$$

$$(\because m = 1.2 \text{ A-m}^2)$$

$$B = 2.4\times 10^{-4} \text{ T}$$

26. (d) According to question, thickness of the slab, $t = \frac{d}{3}$

Capacitance of the capacitor before the insertion of the slab,

$$C = \frac{\varepsilon_0 A}{d} \quad \text{...(i)}$$

where, A is area of cross-section and d is the distance between the plates.

As we know, when a slab of thickness t is inserted in the capacitor, its capacitance is given as

$$C' = \frac{\varepsilon_0 A}{d - t + \frac{t}{K}}$$

$$= \frac{\varepsilon_0 A}{d - \frac{d}{3} + \frac{t}{\infty}}$$

(for conductor, $K = \infty$)

$$C' = \frac{3}{2}\frac{\varepsilon_0 A}{d} \quad \ldots \text{(ii)}$$

From Eqs. (i) and (ii), we get

$$\therefore \quad \frac{C'}{C} = \frac{3}{2}$$

27. (c) According to the question,

$$[v_c] = [\eta^\alpha \rho^\beta r^\gamma] \quad \ldots \text{(i)}$$

As we know that,

$$[v_c] = [M^0LT^{-1}]$$
$$[\eta] = [ML^{-1}T^{-1}]$$
$$[\rho] = [ML^{-3}]$$
$$[r] = [L]$$

Substituting the dimensions of above mentioned quantities in Eq. (i), we get

$$[M^0LT^{-1}] = [ML^{-1}T^{-1}]^\alpha [M^1L^{-3}]^\beta [L]^\gamma$$

$$[M^0LT^{-1}] = [M^{\alpha+\beta}L^{-\alpha-3\beta+\gamma}T^{-\alpha}]$$

On comparing the powers of M, L and T on both sides, we get

$$\alpha + \beta = 0$$
$$-\alpha - 3\beta + \gamma = 1$$
$$-\alpha = -1$$

On solving above equations, we get

$$\alpha = 1, \beta = -1, \gamma = -1$$

Thus,

$$\alpha + \beta + \gamma = 1 + (-1) + (-1) = -1$$

28. (b) For a string or wire, frequency of nth harmonic is

$$f_n = \frac{nv}{2l}$$

As per given condition,

$$450 = \frac{nv}{2l} \quad \ldots \text{(i)}$$

and $$500 = \frac{(n+1)v}{2l} \quad \ldots \text{(ii)}$$

On dividing Eq. (i) by Eq. (ii), we get

$$\frac{450}{500} = \frac{n}{n+1}$$

$$\Rightarrow \quad n = 9$$

As, $$l = \frac{nv}{2f_n}$$

$$\because \quad v = \sqrt{\frac{T}{\mu}}$$

where, T is the tension in the string and μ is the linear mass density.

$$\therefore \quad l = \frac{n}{2f_n} \times \sqrt{\frac{T}{\mu}}$$

$$= \frac{9}{2 \times 450} \times \sqrt{\frac{80}{5 \times 10^{-4}}}$$

$$l = 4 \text{ m}$$

29. (d) Binding energy,

$$\text{BE} = -\text{(Total energy)}$$

$$= \frac{13.6Z^2}{n^2} \text{ eV} \quad \ldots \text{(i)}$$

Thus, Statement I is incorrect.

Also, $$E_{\text{ionisation}} = E_\infty - E_n$$

$$= 0 - \left[-13.6\frac{Z^2}{n^2}\right]$$

$$E_{\text{ionisation}} = 13.6\frac{Z^2}{n^2} \quad \ldots \text{(ii)}$$

From Eqs. (i) and (ii), we get

$$E_{\text{ionisation}} = \text{BE}$$

Therefore, Statement I is incorrect but Statement II is correct.

30. (b) The direction of current in wire a and b is in same direction, hence they will attract each other. Let the magnitude of force of attraction between a and b be f_1.

Again, wire b and c will repel each other due to current in opposite direction. Let the magnitude of force of repulsion be f_2.

Similarly, the wire a and c repel each other with force of magnitude f_3.

$f_3 \leftarrow \odot \xrightarrow{f_1} \; \xleftarrow{f_1} \otimes \xrightarrow{f_2} \; \otimes \rightarrow f_2, f_3$

The separation between each pair of wire is

$$d_{ac} = 2d_{ab} = 2d$$

$$F = \frac{\mu_0 I_1 I_2}{2\pi d}$$

$$F_3 < F_2 \quad [\because d_{ac} > d_{ab}]$$

The magnitude of force on respective wire, $F_a = F_1 - F_3$

$$F_b = F_1 + F_2$$
$$F_c = F_2 + F_3$$

Here, the value of $(F_1 + F_2) > (F_2 + F_3)$ because $|F_2| = |F_1|$ and $|F_2| > |F_3|$

Thus order of force, $F_b > F_c > F_a$

31. (a) Given that uniform quarter disc has mass M and radius R. Let us analyse the complete disc is of same density and radius.

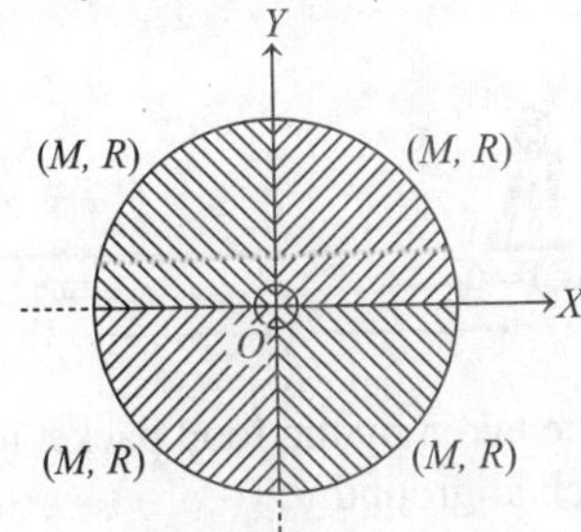

As we know that, moment of inertia of disc about axis passing through its centre and perpendicular to its plane is equal to $\frac{mR^2}{2}$.

If the moment of inertia due to quarter ring is I, then all other three parts will also be having moment of inertia I. So, we can write

$$I + I + I + I = \frac{(\text{Mass of disc})R^2}{2}$$

$$4I = \frac{(4M)R^2}{2} \text{ or } I = \frac{MR^2}{2}$$

32. (c) Output is of the logic circuit gate is given below.

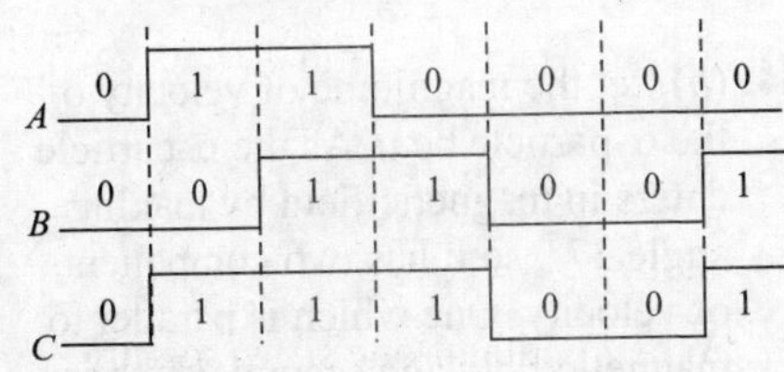

Now, the thruth table for the output is given by

A	B	C
0	0	0
1	0	1
0	1	1
1	1	1

The above table represents the OR gate.

$$Y = A + B$$

33. (c) The given situation is as shown in the figure.

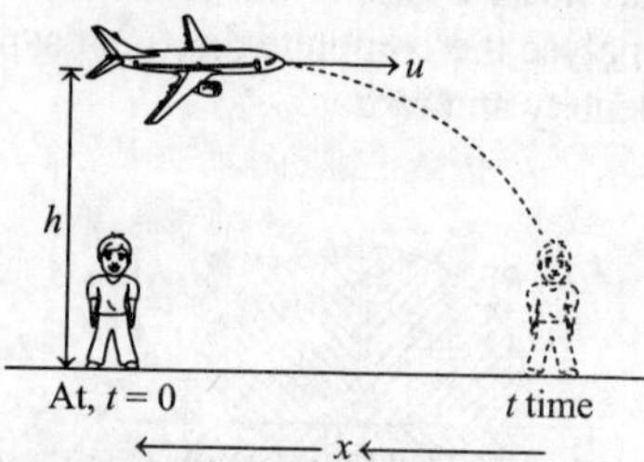

Time taken by the food packet to reach at ground,

$$t = \sqrt{\frac{2h}{g}} \quad \ldots \text{(i)}$$

and horizontal distance covered,

$$x = u \times t \quad \ldots \text{(ii)}$$

Let the man has acceleration $a_{\min}$,

then $\quad x = \frac{1}{2} a_{\min} t^2 \quad \ldots \text{(iii)}$

From Eqs. (ii) and (iii), we get

$$ut = \frac{1}{2} a_{\min} t^2$$

$$a_{\min} = \frac{2u}{t} = \frac{2u}{\sqrt{\frac{2h}{g}}} \quad \text{[using Eq. (i)]}$$

$$a_{\min} = u\sqrt{\frac{2g}{h}}$$

34. (*b*) Let the magnitude of velocity of the α-particle be u. As the α-particle enters in magnetic field by making angle 37°, so it has two components of velocity. One which is parallel to magnetic field and second which is perpendicular to it. So, we can write

$$v_\perp = u \sin 37°$$
$$v_\parallel = u \cos 37°$$

As, pitch of the helix is product of velocity component along the magnetic field and time period T.

i.e. Pitch, $P = (v_\parallel)T$

$$= (u \cos 37°)\left(\frac{2\pi m}{qB}\right) \left(\because T = \frac{2\pi m}{qB}\right)$$

$$P = \frac{2\pi mu \cos 37°}{qB} \quad \ldots \text{(i)}$$

Radius of helix, $R = \frac{mv_\perp}{qB}$

$$R = \frac{mu \sin 37°}{qB} \quad \ldots \text{(ii)}$$

On dividing Eq. (i) by Eq. (ii), we get

$$\frac{P}{R} = \frac{2\pi \cos 37°}{\sin 37°} = 2\pi \cot 37°$$

$$= 2\pi \times \frac{4}{3}$$

$$\Rightarrow \quad \frac{P}{R} = \frac{8\pi}{3}$$

or $\quad R = \frac{3P}{8\pi}$

35. (b) Given capacitor can be considered as following combination.

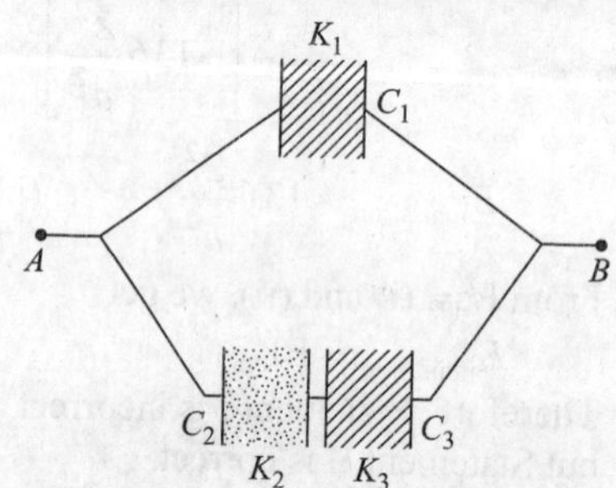

We have, $C_0 = \frac{\varepsilon_0 A}{d} = 2\,\mu\text{F} \quad \ldots \text{(i)}$

For capacitor C_1,

Distance between plates $= d$,

Area of plates $= \frac{A}{2}$

Dielectric constant, $K_1 = 2$

So, capacity $C_1 = \frac{\varepsilon_0 K_1 \left(\frac{A}{2}\right)}{d}$

$$= \frac{2}{2} \cdot \frac{\varepsilon_0 A}{d} = C_1 = 2\,\mu\text{F}$$

Similarly, $C_2 = \frac{\frac{\varepsilon_0 K_2 A}{2}}{\frac{d}{2}}$

$$= K_2 \left(\frac{\varepsilon_0 A}{d}\right) = K_2 C_1$$

$$= 3 \times 2 = 6\,\mu\text{F}$$

and $C_3 = K_3 C_1 = 5 \times 2 = 10\,\mu\text{F}$

Hence, equivalent capacity of system is,

$C_{\text{eq}} = C_1$ parallel (C_2 and C_3 series).

$$= 2 + \frac{6 \times 10}{6 + 10} = \frac{23}{4}\,\mu\text{F}$$

36. (b) The self-inductance of a long solenoid is given as

$$L = \frac{\mu_0 N^2 A}{l} \quad \ldots \text{(i)}$$

$$= \frac{\mu_0 N^2 A}{l \times A} \times A$$

$$= \frac{\mu_0 (NA)^2}{V} \quad [\because V = l \times A]$$

or $\quad L \propto \frac{1}{V} \quad [\because NA = \text{constant}]$

This means, inductance is inversely proportional to volume V.

So, the graph between L and V will be a rectangular hyperbola.

37. (c) Arsenic is pentavalent, while indium is trivalent.

Also, n (As) > n (In), so resulting crystal is n-type.

For a p-n junction, we have to dope different regions of crystal.

38. (a) Given, $V_{\text{centre}} = V_{\text{surface}} = \frac{kQ}{R} = 5$

So, $kQ = 5 \times R = 5 \times 1 = 5$

Now at a point 1 m from surface, potential will be

$$V = \frac{kQ}{r}, \text{ here } r = 2\text{ m}$$

So, $V = \frac{kQ}{2} = \frac{5}{2} = 2.5\text{ V}$

39. (c) Power available as light,

$$P = \frac{5}{100} \times 100 = 5\text{ W}$$

Intensity, $I = \frac{P}{4\pi d^2} = \frac{5}{4\pi \times 1^2}$

$= 0.398 \text{ W/m}^2$

$\approx 0.4 \text{ W / m}^2$

40. (a) From the graph,

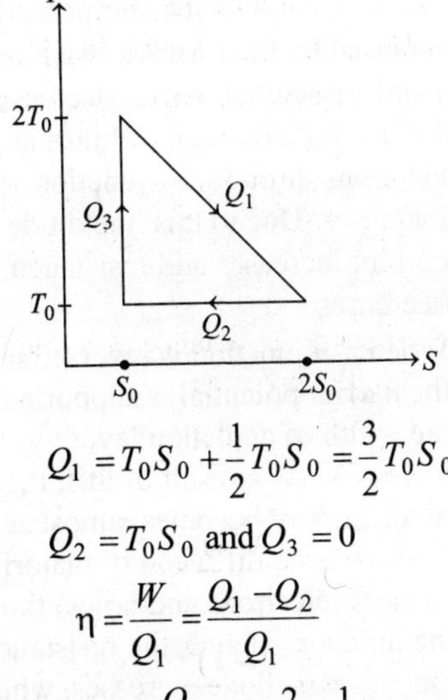

$$Q_1 = T_0 S_0 + \frac{1}{2} T_0 S_0 = \frac{3}{2} T_0 S_0$$

$$Q_2 = T_0 S_0 \text{ and } Q_3 = 0$$

$$\eta = \frac{W}{Q_1} = \frac{Q_1 - Q_2}{Q_1}$$

$$= 1 - \frac{Q_2}{Q_1} = 1 - \frac{2}{3} = \frac{1}{3}$$

41. (b) Given, displacement,

$[y] = [\text{L}]$

Velocity, $[\alpha] = [\text{LT}^{-1}]$

Acceleration, $[\beta] = [\text{LT}^{-2}]$

Amplitude, $[A] = [\text{L}]$

Now, dimensional formula is given as

$$\sqrt{\frac{y(\alpha^2 - \beta y)}{\beta}} = \frac{[y]^{\frac{1}{2}} (\alpha^2 - \beta y)^{\frac{1}{2}}}{[\beta]^{\frac{1}{2}}}$$

$$= \frac{[\text{L}]^{\frac{1}{2}} [\text{L}^2\text{T}^{-2}]^{\frac{1}{2}}}{[\text{LT}^{-2}]^{\frac{1}{2}}} = [\text{L}]$$

The physical equation is correct as dimensional formula is equal to that of amplitude.

42. (c) Let 315 Hz be the nth harmonic of the string.

Thus, $\frac{nv}{2L} = 315 \text{ Hz}$ ...(i)

and $\frac{(n+1)v}{2L} = 420 \text{ Hz}$ ...(ii)

From Eqs. (i) and (ii), we get

$$\frac{n+1}{n} = \frac{410}{315}$$

$\Rightarrow$ $n = 3$

Thus, lowest resonant frequency

$$= \frac{v}{2L} = \frac{315}{n} = 105 \text{ Hz}$$

43. (d) From the lens Maker's formula,

$$\frac{\mu_2}{v} - \frac{\mu_1}{u} = \frac{\mu_0 - \mu_1}{R_1} + \frac{\mu_2 - \mu_1}{R_2}$$

It is given that light is coming parallel to each other, then image will be formed at focus.

$\therefore$ $u = \infty, v = f$

Here, $\mu_0 = 1.5, \mu_1 = 1.2$ and $\mu_2 = 1.6$, $R_1 = +30 \text{ cm}, R_2 = -30 \text{ cm}$

Thus, $\frac{1.6}{f} = \frac{1.5 - 1.2}{30} + \frac{1.6 - 1.5}{-30}$

$$\frac{1.6}{f} = \frac{0.3}{30} - \frac{0.1}{30}$$

$$f = 240 \text{ cm}$$

44. (d) Wavelength in water and glass will be

$$\lambda_w = \frac{\lambda}{n_w} = \frac{550 \times 10^{-9}}{4/3}$$

and $\lambda_g = \frac{\lambda}{n_g} = \frac{550 \times 10^{-9}}{3/2}$

Number of waves occuring in 1 μm length of medium will be

$$N_1 \text{ (in water)} = \frac{1 \times 10^{-6}}{\lambda_w}$$

$$= \frac{10^9 \times 4 \times 10^{-6}}{550 \times 3}$$

$$= 2.4$$

and N_2 (in glass) $= \frac{10^9 \times 3 \times 10^{-6}}{550 \times 2}$

$$= 2.7$$

Difference in number of waves,

$$\Delta N = (2.7 - 2.4) = 0.3$$

So, phase difference between waves is

$$\Delta\phi = 0.3 \times 2\pi = 0.6\pi \text{ rad}$$

45. (c) The given situation is as shown in the figure below.

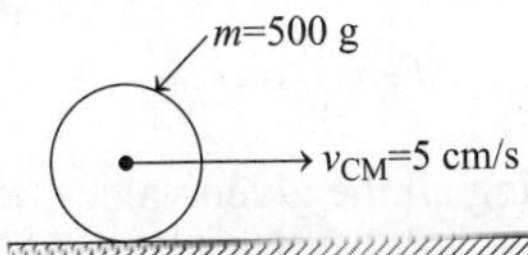

In pure rolling object possesses both translational kinetic energy and rotational kinetic energy.

So, $\text{KE}_{\text{sphere}} = \frac{1}{2} mv_{\text{CM}}^2 + \frac{1}{2} I\omega^2$

Here, $I = \frac{2}{5} mr^2$ and $\omega = \frac{v}{r}$

$[\because v_{\text{CM}} = v]$

So, $\text{KE}_{\text{sphere}}$

$$= \frac{1}{2} mv^2 + \frac{1}{2} \times \frac{2}{5} mr^2 \times \frac{v^2}{r^2}$$

$$= \left(\frac{1}{2} + \frac{1}{5}\right) mv^2$$

$$= \frac{7}{10} \times 500 \times 10^{-3} \times 25 \times 10^{-4}$$

$$= 8.75 \times 10^{-4} \text{ J}$$

NK04 NEET Knock Offs 4

1. (*a*) Given, mass of rod,

$$m = 1.5\,\text{kg}$$

Length of rod, $l = 0.6$ m

Area of cross-section,

$$A = 100\ \text{cm}^2 = 10^{-2}\ \text{m}^2$$

Young's modulus,

$$Y = 1.2 \times 10^{11}\ \text{N/m}^2$$

The effective length over which the force acts is $\frac{l}{2}$, because the average position of the weight is at the centre of mass.

Elongation produced in the rod is given as

$$\Delta l = \frac{wl}{2YA} = \frac{mgl}{2YA}$$

Putting all the given values, we get

$$\Delta l = \frac{1.5 \times 9.8 \times 0.6}{2 \times 1.2 \times 10^{11} \times 10^{-2}}$$

$$= 3.675 \times 10^{-9}\ \text{m}$$

2. (*a*) The first harmonic frequency,

$$f_1 = \frac{v}{\lambda_i} = \frac{v}{2L}$$

where, L = length of the pipe.

The frequency of nth harmonic is

$$f_n = \frac{nv}{2L}\ (\text{for } n = 1, 2, 3....)$$

Given, $L = 30\,\text{cm} = 0.3\,\text{m}$

$$f_1 = \frac{n\,(330)}{0.6} = 550\,\text{Hz}$$

$\therefore f_2, f_3$..... is 1100 Hz, 1650 Hz, etc.

Therefore, a source of frequency 1.65 kHz will resonate at f_3 i.e., the third harmonic.

3. (*b*) According to question,

$$W_A = W_B$$

$$\Rightarrow F_A d \cos\theta_A = F_B d \cos\theta_B$$

or $$\frac{F_A}{F_B} = \frac{\cos\theta_B}{\cos\theta_A} = \frac{\cos 60^\circ}{\cos 45^\circ}$$

$$= \frac{\frac{1}{2}}{\frac{1}{\sqrt{2}}} = 1 : \sqrt{2}$$

4. (*c*) Given, $F = 5\,\text{N} = \frac{5\ \text{kg} \times \text{m}}{\text{s}^2}$

Here, unit of length and time are doubled and the unit of mass is halved, then the unit of force will be

$$\frac{\frac{1}{2} \times 2}{2^2} = \frac{1}{4}\ \text{times}$$

Hence, the numerical value of the force will be 1/4 times.

5. (*d*) In case of rolling, ω = constant (without slipping)

$$v_{\text{highest}} = 2v$$

$$v_{\text{lowest}} = 0$$

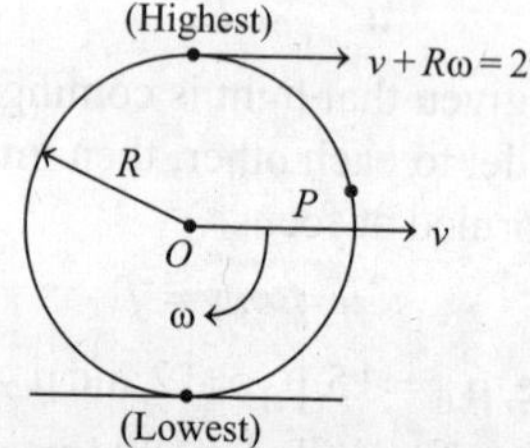

Velocity of any point, $0 \le v_p \le 2v$

Also, angular velocity is same at different points of a rigid body.

6. (*b*) The time period of a bar magnet in a magnetic field is given by

$$T = 2\pi\sqrt{\frac{I}{MB}}$$

where, I = moment of inertia,

M = moment of magnet

and B = magnetic field.

$$\therefore \quad T \propto \sqrt{I} \propto \sqrt{m}$$

Therefore, T becomes twice as mass becomes four times.

7. (*b*) Less work function means less energy is required for ejecting out the electrons. Hence, for the metal to be photosensitive, the work function should be small. Also, work function $= hf_o$, where f_o is the threshold frequency. Hence, both A and R are true but R is not the correct explanation of A.

8. (*c*) When *p-n* junction is forward biased, the width of depletion layer decreases and the barrier potential is opposed by the forward bias. In other words, potential barrier decreases. Hence, the diffusion of holes and electrons through the junction increases. Due to this, the diode current increases and resistance decreases.

When *p-n* junction is reverse biased, the barrier potential is supported and the width of depletion layer increases. As a result of this, the diode current becomes almost zero, as there is no diffusion of majority carriers (electrons and holes) through the junction. Hence, the resistance of the junction diode increases, when reverse biased.

Hence, Statement I is correct and Statement II is incorrect.

9. (*d*) As we know that,

$$Q = ms\Delta\theta$$

$$\Rightarrow \quad s = \frac{Q}{m\Delta\theta}$$

or $$[s] = \frac{[Q]}{[m][\Delta\theta]} = \frac{[\text{ML}^2\text{T}^{-2}]}{[\text{M}][\text{K}]}$$

$$[s] = [\text{M}^0\text{L}^2\text{T}^{-2}\text{K}^{-1}]$$

10. (*a*) The difference of kinetic energies will be equal to electrostatic potential energy of both the charged particles initially.

$$\therefore \quad \text{KE} = \text{PE} = \frac{1}{4\pi\varepsilon_0} \cdot \frac{q_1 q_2}{a}$$

where q_1 and q_2 are the charges of two particles and a is the distance between them.

Here, $q_1 = q_2 = q$ (let)

$$\Rightarrow \quad K = \frac{1}{4\pi\varepsilon_0} \cdot \frac{q^2}{a}$$

or $$q = \sqrt{4\pi\varepsilon_0 aK}$$

Given, $a = 0.9\,\text{m}$,

$$K = 90\,\text{mJ or } 9\times 10^{-2}\,\text{J}$$

$$q = \sqrt{\frac{1}{9\times 10^9}\times 0.9\times 9\times 10^{-2}}$$

$$= 3\times 10^{-6}\,\text{C or } 3\,\mu\text{C}$$

11. (c) Given, angle between **P** and **Q** is 60°. So, angle between **P** and 2**Q** vectors will also be 60° and angle between 3**P** and – 2**Q** vectors will be 180° – 60° = 120°.

Also, $\frac{\mathbf{P}}{4}$ is a unit vector, so $\frac{|\mathbf{P}|}{4} = 1$

or $|\mathbf{P}| = 4$

Here, $|\mathbf{P} + 2\mathbf{Q}| = |3\mathbf{P} - 2\mathbf{Q}|$

or $|\mathbf{P} + 2\mathbf{Q}| = |3\mathbf{P} + (-2\mathbf{Q})|$

Squaring on both sides, we get

$$(\mathbf{P})^2 + (2\mathbf{Q})^2 + 2\mathbf{P}\cdot 2\mathbf{Q}$$
$$= (3\mathbf{P})^2 + (-2\mathbf{Q})^2 + 2\cdot 3\mathbf{P}(-2\mathbf{Q})$$

$$P^2 + (2Q)^2 + (2P)(2Q)\cos 60^\circ$$
$$= (3P)^2 + (2Q)^2 - 2(3P)(2Q)\cos 120^\circ$$

$$\Rightarrow P^2 + 4Q^2 + 4PQ\times\frac{1}{2}$$
$$= 9P^2 + 4Q^2 - 12PQ\left(-\frac{1}{2}\right)$$

$$\Rightarrow \quad P^2 + 2PQ = 9P^2 + 6PQ$$

$$\Rightarrow \quad 8P^2 + 4PQ = 0$$

$$\Rightarrow \quad 4P(2P + Q) = 0$$

So, either $P = 0$ [Not possible, as $|\mathbf{P}| = 4$]

or $2P + Q = 0$

$$Q = -2P = -8$$

$\therefore$ $|\mathbf{Q}| = 8$

12. (d) The curve bending towards time axis represents decreasing velocity or negative velocity. So, at point III, the slope of the curve is negative. At this point, instantaneous velocity is negative.

13. (d) Buoyant force in a non-inertial frame is given by

$$B = V_l \rho_l g_{\text{eff}} \qquad \dots \text{(i)}$$

Here, V_l = volume of block immersed in liquid,

ρ_l = density of liquid and

g_{eff} = effective gravity

(Here, $g_{\text{eff}} = g + a$)

Also, $V_l = \frac{\rho_{\text{block}}}{\rho_l}\times V_{\text{block}}$

$$\Rightarrow \quad V_l = \frac{M_{\text{block}}}{\rho_l}$$

$\therefore$ Eq. (i) can be written as

$$B = \frac{M_{\text{block}}}{\rho_l}\times\rho_l\times g_{\text{eff}}$$
$$= M_{\text{block}}\times g_{\text{eff}}$$
$$= \left(\frac{w_{\text{block}}}{g}\right)\times g_{\text{eff}}$$

Substituting the given values, we get

$$B = \left(\frac{80}{10}\right)\times(10 + 2) = 96\,\text{N}$$

14. (a) Total magnetic field due to current I along A to B is

$$\mathbf{B}_{\text{net}} = \mathbf{B}_A + \mathbf{B}_B$$
$$= \frac{\mu_0 I}{4\pi a}\sin\theta_1 - \frac{\mu_0 I}{4\pi a}\sin\theta_2$$

$\because$ $\theta_1 = \theta_1$

$\theta_2 = -\theta_2$

So, $\mathbf{B}_{\text{net}} = \frac{\mu_0 I}{4\pi a}(\sin\theta_1 - \sin\theta_2)$

Therefore, the magnetic field at point P due to a current carrying straight wire, such that the ends of the wires, make angles θ_1 and θ_2 (see figure) is given by $B = \frac{\mu_0 I}{4\pi d}(\sin\theta_1 - \sin\theta_2)$

15. (a) Let the object has been given velocity u.

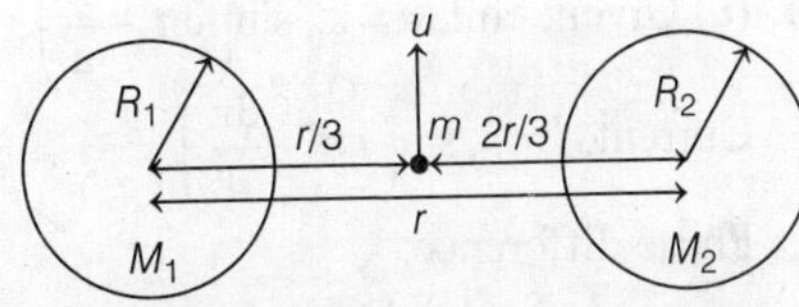

Using principle of conservation of mechanical energy,

$$\text{KE}_i + U_i = \text{KE}_f + U_f$$

$$\frac{1}{2}mu^2 + \left(-\frac{GM_1 m}{\frac{r}{3}} - \frac{GM_2 m}{\frac{2r}{3}}\right) = 0 + 0$$

$$\frac{1}{2}mu^2 - \frac{3Gm}{r}\left(M_1 + \frac{M_2}{2}\right) = 0$$

or $u^2 = \frac{3G}{r}(2M_1 + M_2)$

or $u = \sqrt{\frac{3G}{r}(2M_1 + M_2)}$

16. (c) Areal speed, $\frac{dA}{dt} = \frac{L}{2m}$

$$\Rightarrow \quad \frac{dA}{dt} = \frac{mvr}{2m} = \frac{1}{2}\omega r^2$$
$$= \frac{\pi r^2}{T} = \frac{\pi r^2}{r^{3/2}}$$
$$= \frac{\pi}{k}(r^{-\frac{1}{2}}) \propto \sqrt{r}$$

17. (a) Power consumption in series *R-L-C* circuit is maximum at resonance,

$$X_L = X_C$$
$$\frac{1}{\omega L} = \omega C$$

or $C = \frac{1}{\omega^2 L} = \frac{1}{(2\pi f)^2\times L}$

Here, $f = 50\,\text{Hz}$, $L = 2.5\,\text{H}$

$$C = \frac{1}{(2\times 3.14\times 50)^2\times 2.5}$$
$$= 4.05\times 10^{-6} \simeq 4\,\mu\text{F}$$

18. (a) The energy density in the region between the plates is given by

$$u = \frac{1}{2}\varepsilon_0 E^2$$
$$= \frac{1}{2}\varepsilon_0\left(\frac{V}{d}\right)^2 \qquad \left(\because E = \frac{V}{d}\right)$$

$$\Rightarrow \quad u = \frac{1}{2}\times 8.85\times 10^{-12}\times\left(\frac{400}{5\times 10^{-3}}\right)^2$$

$$= 283.2\times 10^{-12}\times 10^8$$
$$= 283.2\times 10^{-4}$$
$$= 2.83\times 10^{-2}\,\text{J/m}^3$$

19. (b) When intermolecular force between molecules vanishes, the water is converted into vapours. So, molecular mass of water vapours $= 18\,\text{g} = 18\times 10^{-3}\,\text{kg}$

And, volume occupied by 1 mole of vapour at STP = 22.4 litres

$\therefore$ 3.6 kg water occupies

$$= \frac{22.4\times 10^{-3}\,\text{m}^3}{18\times 10^{-3}\,\text{kg}}\times 3.6\,\text{kg}$$

$$= 4.48\,\text{m}^3$$

20. (*b*) Energy of light incident on metal surface,

$$E=\frac{12375}{\lambda}=\frac{12375}{4800}=2.57\,\text{eV}$$

Maximum kinetic energy of photon in accordance with Einstein's photoelectric equation,

$$\text{KE}_{max} = \text{Incident energy} - \text{Work function}$$

$$= E-\phi$$

where, ϕ is work function.

$$\Rightarrow \text{KE}_{max} = 2.57-1.67=0.9\,\text{eV}$$

Now, energy of electron in third excited state, i.e. $n=4$ in He^+ ion,

$$E_n=-13.6\times\frac{Z^2}{n^2}\,\text{eV}$$

For He^+, $Z=2$

$$\Rightarrow \quad E_4=-13.6\times\frac{(2)^2}{(4)^2}$$

$$E_4=-3.4\,\text{eV}$$

From conservation of energy,

Kinetic energy of photoelectron = Total energy of electron in He^+ + Energy of emitted photon

$$\text{KE}_{max}=E_4+E'$$

or $$E'=\text{KE}_{max}-E_4$$

$$=0.9-(-3.4)=4.3\,\text{eV}$$

21. (*c*) As we know that,

$$\phi_{total}=\frac{q_{enclosed}}{\varepsilon_0}$$

Here, $q_{enclosed}=0$,

$$\therefore \quad \phi_{total}=\frac{0}{\varepsilon_0}=0$$

22. (*d*) (A) Infrared rays are used to treat muscular strain.

(B) Radio waves are used for broadcasting purposes.

(C) X-rays are used to detect fracture of bones.

(D) Ultraviolet rays are absorbed by the ozone layer of the atmosphere.

23. (*d*) Given that,

$$x_A=4\sin\left(\omega t+\frac{\pi}{4}\right)+3\cos\left(\omega t-\frac{\pi}{4}\right)\text{m}$$

or $$x_A=4\sin\left(\omega t+\frac{\pi}{4}\right)+3\sin\left(\frac{\pi}{2}+\omega t-\frac{\pi}{4}\right)$$

$$\left[\because \sin\left(\frac{\pi}{2}+\theta\right)=\cos\theta\right]$$

$$=4\sin\left(\omega t+\frac{\pi}{4}\right)+3\sin\left(\omega t+\frac{\pi}{4}\right)$$

$\therefore$ Amplitude,

$$A_1=\sqrt{(4)^2+(3)^2+2(4)(3)\cos\left(\frac{\pi}{4}-\frac{\pi}{4}\right)}$$

$$=\sqrt{(4)^2+(3)^2+2(4)(3)}$$

$$=\sqrt{(4+3)^2}=7\,\text{m}$$

Similarly,

$$x_B=5\sqrt{2}(\sin 2\pi t+\cos 2\pi t)\,\text{m}$$

or $$x_B=5\sqrt{2}\sin 2\pi t+5\sqrt{2}\sin\left(\frac{\pi}{2}+2\pi t\right)$$

So, phase, $$\phi=\left(\frac{\pi}{2}+2\pi t\right)-2\pi t=\frac{\pi}{2}$$

$\therefore$ Amplitude,

$$A_2=\sqrt{(5\sqrt{2})^2+(5\sqrt{2})^2+2(5\sqrt{2})(5\sqrt{2})\cos\frac{\pi}{2}}$$

$$=10\,\text{m}$$

$$\therefore \text{Ratio}, \frac{A_1}{A_2}=\frac{7}{10}$$

24. (*c*) Given, emf, $e=e_0\sin\left(\omega t-\frac{\pi}{4}\right)$

Current, $i=i_0\sin\left(\omega t-\frac{3\pi}{4}\right)$

Phase difference,

$$\phi=\left(\omega t-\frac{\pi}{4}\right)-\left(\omega t-\frac{3\pi}{4}\right)$$

$$\phi=\frac{\pi}{2}$$

The current lags the emf by $\frac{\pi}{2}$, so the circuit should contain only inductor.

25. (*a*)

2 cm, 1, $q=9\times10^{-8}$ stat-C

4 cm, 2, $q=18\times10^{-8}$ stat-C

For charge to flow, there must be potential difference.

Potential of conducting sphere on surface, $V=\frac{kq}{r}$

Potential on sphere 1,

$$V_1=\frac{k\times9\times10^{-8}}{2}\text{ units}$$

Potential on sphere 2,

$$V_2=\frac{k\times18\times10^{-8}}{4}\text{ units}$$

$$=\frac{9k}{2}\times10^{-8}\text{ units}$$

$$V_1=V_2$$

Change in potential, $\Delta V=V_1-V_2$

So, $\Delta V=0$

$\therefore$ No charge flow will take place.

26. (*b*)

A, R, C, 3R, 3R, D, R, B

$$R_{CD}=\frac{3R}{2}$$

$$R_{AB}=R+\frac{3R}{2}+R=\frac{7R}{2}$$

$$=\frac{7\times10}{2}=35\,\Omega$$

27. (*d*) Given,

At $x=31.5$ mm, wavelengths 3600 Å and 6000 Å are absent, it means they are producing minima.

Let the slit separation be d.

As we know, path difference for minima is given by

$$\frac{xd}{D}=\left(n_1+\frac{1}{2}\right)\lambda_1$$

and $$\frac{xd}{D\lambda_1}=n_1+\frac{1}{2} \quad \ldots\text{(i)}$$

Similarly, for λ_2, path difference,

$$\frac{xd}{D\lambda_2}=n_2+\frac{1}{2} \quad \ldots\text{(ii)}$$

Subtracting Eq. (ii) from Eq. (i), we get

$$\frac{xd}{D}\left(\frac{1}{\lambda_1}-\frac{1}{\lambda_2}\right)=n_1-n_2$$

or $d = \dfrac{D(n_1 - n_2)}{x\left(\dfrac{1}{\lambda_1} - \dfrac{1}{\lambda_2}\right)}$

Given, $x = 31.5\,\text{mm or } 31.5 \times 10^{-3}\,\text{m}$

$D = 1\,\text{m}$

$\lambda_1 = 3600\,\text{Å or } 3.6 \times 10^{-7}\,\text{m}$

$\lambda_2 = 6000\,\text{Å or } 6 \times 10^{-7}\,\text{m}$

$n_1 - n_2 = 7$

Substituting these values in the above relation, we get

$$d = \frac{1 \times 7}{31.5 \times 10^{-3} \times \left(\dfrac{1}{3.6 \times 10^{-7}} - \dfrac{1}{6 \times 10^{-7}}\right)}$$

$d = 0.2\,\text{mm}$

28. (*d*) When *A* and *C* are connected, energy stored, $U_1 = \frac{1}{2}CV^2$

and charge, $q = CV$

When *B* and *C* are connected, common potential

$$V' = \frac{\text{Total charge}}{\text{Total capacity}} = \frac{CV}{4C}$$

$\Rightarrow \quad V' = \dfrac{V}{4}$

Final stored energy,

$$U_2 = \frac{1}{2}(C_{eq})V'^2$$

$$= \frac{1}{2} \times 4C \times \left(\frac{V}{4}\right)^2 = \frac{1}{8}CV^2$$

Loss of energy $= U_1 - U_2$

$$= \frac{1}{2}CV^2 - \frac{1}{8}CV^2$$

$$= \frac{3}{8}CV^2 = \frac{3}{8}\frac{q^2}{C}$$

29. (*d*) Work done by conservative force does not depend on path and for a closed loop, work done is always zero.

Hence, Statement I is incorrect and Statement II is correct.

30. (*a*) Induced electric field lines are open loops. It emerges from positive charge and goes to infinity and it enters into negative charge coming from infinity.

31. (*b*) The intensity of magnetisation varies as

$$-I \propto H$$

where, H = magnetic field strength.

So, for a diamagnetic material, the correct graph is

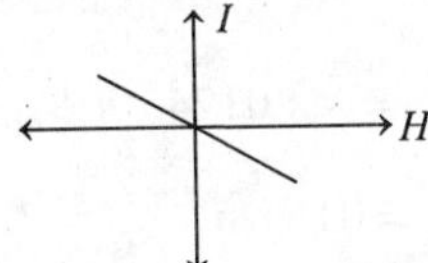

32. (*d*) Potential energy of a He^+ ion in ground state is

$$U_1 = 2E_1 = 2\left(-13.6\frac{Z^2}{n^2}\right)$$

$\because \quad n = 1 \text{ and } Z = 2$

$\Rightarrow \quad U_1 = -108.8\,\text{eV}$

But PE in ground state is given zero. So, we have to increase PE (and total energy) by 108.8 eV.

Hence, for given He^+ ion, energy of first excited state $(n = 2)$ will be

$$E(n = 2) = -13.6\frac{Z^2}{n^2} + 108.8$$

$$= -13.6 \times \frac{4}{4} + 108.8$$

$$= 95.2\,\text{eV}$$

33. (*d*) A negative temperature coefficient thermistor has a low resistance at high temperature. While a thermistor with a positive temperature coefficient has a high resistance at a high temperature. Therefore, the resistance depends on temperature coefficient.

34. (*a*) At balanced condition in a meter bridge, unknown resistance *S* is given by

$$S = \frac{100 - l}{l} \times R$$

where, R = unknown resistance,

l = balanced length from left end.

When $l = 30\,\text{cm}$,

$$S = \frac{100 - 30}{30} \times R$$

$$S = \frac{7}{3}R \quad \ldots \text{(i)}$$

Now, resistance of $2\,\Omega$ is connected in parallel with *S*, then equivalent of *S* and $2\,\Omega$ when balanced length is 40 cm, will be

$$\Rightarrow \quad \frac{2S}{2 + S} = \frac{100 - 40}{40} \times R$$

$$\frac{2S}{2 + S} = \frac{3}{2}R \quad \ldots \text{(ii)}$$

Dividing Eq. (i) by Eq. (ii), we get

$$\frac{S}{\dfrac{2S}{2 + S}} = \frac{\dfrac{7}{3}R}{\dfrac{3}{2}R}$$

$$\frac{2 + S}{2} = \frac{14}{9}$$

$$18 + 9S = 28$$

$$9S = 28 - 18 = 10$$

or $\quad S = \dfrac{10}{9} = 1.1\,\Omega$

35. (*d*) As we know that,

$$P_{\text{rated}} = \frac{V_{\text{rated}}^2}{R} \text{ or } R = \frac{(220)^2}{100}$$

Now, power consumed

$$= \frac{V^2}{R} = \frac{(110)^2 \times 100}{(220)^2} = 25\,\text{W}$$

36. (*c*) Given, initial speed, $u = 30\,\text{m/s}$

Projection angle, $\theta = 60°$

Let at an instant when velocity vector makes an angle 30° be *v*. We know that, in projectile motion, horizontal component of velocities are equal.

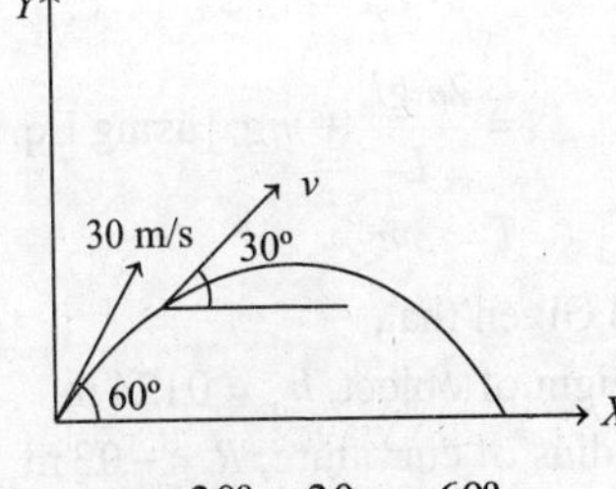

$\Rightarrow \quad v\cos 30° = 30\cos 60°$

$$v \times \frac{\sqrt{3}}{2} = 30 \times \frac{1}{2}$$

$$v = \frac{30}{\sqrt{3}}$$

or $\quad v = 10\sqrt{3}\,\text{m/s}$

37. (*a*) In circular motion, a particle have two accelerations, centripetal and tangential acceleration.

Centripetal acceleration acts towards the centre of the circular path and tangential acceleration acts either along velocity or opposite to velocity.

If the particle has acceleration along its velocity, it means its centripetal acceleration should be zero at that instant or angular velocity $\omega = 0$.

Using first equation of motion,

$$\omega_f = \omega_i + \alpha t$$

$$0 = \omega_0 + (-\alpha)t$$

or $t = \dfrac{\omega_0}{\alpha}$

38. (*d*) Let the velocity of mass at bottom of the arc be v.

Using mechanical energy conservation principle, $\Delta ME = 0$

$\Rightarrow \Delta KE + \Delta U = 0$

or $\Delta KE = -\Delta U$

$$\frac{1}{2}mv^2 - 0 = -mg\Delta h$$

$$\frac{1}{2}mv^2 = -mg(0-L)$$

or $mv^2 = 2mgL$ ...(i)

Drawing FBD of mass, when it is at bottom.

Using equation of motion,

$$\frac{mv^2}{L} = T - mg$$

or $T = \dfrac{mv^2}{L} + mg$

$= \dfrac{2mgL}{L} + mg$ [using Eq. (i)]

$T = 3mg$

39. (*b*) Given that,

Height of object, $h_o = 0.124$ m

Radius of curvature, $R = -0.3$ m

Position of object from mirror,

$u = -0.018$ m

Using mirror formula, $\dfrac{1}{v} + \dfrac{1}{u} = \dfrac{2}{R}$

or $\dfrac{1}{v} + \dfrac{1}{(-0.018)} = \dfrac{2}{(-0.3)}$

or $\dfrac{1}{v} = \dfrac{440}{9}$

or $v = +0.0204$ m

As we know that, magnification,

$$m = \frac{-v}{u} = -\frac{0.0204}{(-0.018)} = \frac{4}{3}$$

Also, $m = \dfrac{\text{Height of image}}{\text{Height of object}}$

or Height of image $= m \times$ Height of object

$$= \frac{4}{3} \times 0.124$$

$$h_i = 0.165 \text{ m}$$

or $h_i = 16.5$ cm

40. (*a*) The changing magnetic field induces an electric field which will accelerate the electron.

The acceleration of electron will be

$$a = \frac{eE}{m} \quad (\because F = qE)$$

To find electric field E, we will use Faraday's law of electromagnetic induction.

Emf, $\varepsilon = -\dfrac{d\phi}{dt} = -\dfrac{d}{dt}(B \cdot A)$

where, B is the magnetic field and A is the area of cross-section.

$\Rightarrow \varepsilon = -A \cdot \dfrac{dB}{dt} = -\pi r^2 \dfrac{dB}{dt}$

Now, electric field,

$$E = -\frac{\text{emf}}{\text{distance}} = -\frac{\varepsilon}{d} = \frac{\pi r^2}{d}\frac{dB}{dt}$$

Now, acceleration, $a = \dfrac{e}{m}\dfrac{\pi r^2}{d}\dfrac{dB}{dt}$

$$= \frac{1.6 \times 10^{-19}}{9.1 \times 10^{-31}} \times \frac{22}{7} \times \frac{(0.5)^2}{(0.3)} \times 50 \times 10^{-6}$$

$$= 23 \times 10^6 \text{ ms}^{-2}$$

41. (*b*) Given that, particle is starting from mean position, then initial phase, $\phi = 0$.

Let the particle's mean position be at origin as shown below

B (Extreme position) — O (Mean position) — A (Extreme position), OA = a

Time period for one complete oscillation,

$$T = (t_{OA} + t_{AO}) + (t_{OB} + t_{BO}) = t + t$$

$$T = 2t$$

$\because T = \dfrac{2\pi}{\omega}$

$\Rightarrow 2t = \dfrac{2\pi}{\omega}$

or $\omega = \pi / t$ ...(i)

As we know, displacement time equation for a particle executing SHM is given as

$$x = a \sin \omega t$$

Velocity, $v = \dfrac{dx}{dt} = \dfrac{d}{dt}(a \sin \omega t)$

where, a is the amplitude.

$\Rightarrow v = a\omega \cos \omega t$

$= a\omega \cos \dfrac{\pi}{t} \times t$ [using Eq. (i)]

$= a\omega \cos \pi = -a\omega$ ($\because \cos \pi = -1$)

or $v = -\dfrac{a\pi}{t}$ or $|v| = \dfrac{a\pi}{t}$

or Amplitude, $a = \dfrac{|v| \times t}{\pi} = \dfrac{1.57 \times 1.5}{3.14}$

$= 0.75$ m

42. (*a*) Using lens Maker's formula, focal length of biconvex lens is

$$\frac{1}{f_1} = (\mu - 1)\left(\frac{2}{R}\right) \quad \text{...(i)}$$

and $f_1 = 30$ cm

For plano-convex lens,

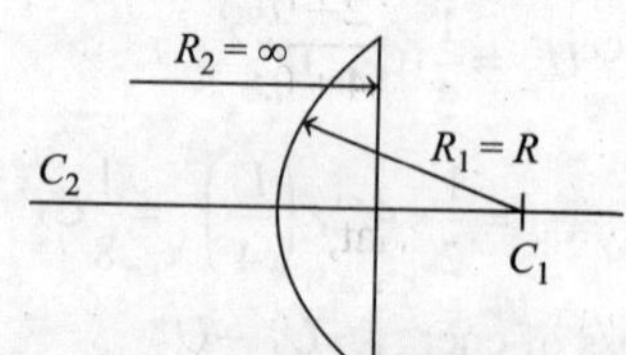

$$\frac{1}{f_2} = (\mu - 1)\left(\frac{1}{R} - \frac{1}{\infty}\right)$$

$\Rightarrow \dfrac{1}{f_2} = (\mu - 1)\left(\dfrac{1}{R}\right)$

Now, when plano-convex lenses are placed in contact, then

$$\frac{1}{f_{eq}} = \frac{1}{f_2} + \frac{1}{f_2} = \frac{2}{f_2}$$

$$= (\mu - 1)\left(\frac{2}{R}\right) \quad \text{...(ii)}$$

So, from Eqs. (i) and (ii),

$$f_{eq} = f_1 = 30 \text{ cm}$$

43. (*b*) The depletion layer consists of immobile positive and negative ions which have no free electrons and holes.

At $x=0$, number of negatively charged immobile ions increases as we move rightwards, so charge density increases but after some distance, it starts to decrease and at $x=\frac{d}{2}$, it becomes zero and the corresponding charge density becomes zero.

Now, from $x=\frac{d}{2}$, number of positively charged immobile ions starts increasing and reaches its maximum value, then at some distance, it decreases and at $x=d$, it becomes zero.

Thus, the variation of charge density and distance is best represented as in option (b).

44. (c) According to Rutherford's scattering experiment, whole of the positive charge is concentrated at the centre of atom.

45. (*a*) $R=R_0A^{\frac{1}{3}}$

$$\frac{R_1}{R_2}=\left(\frac{1}{8}\right)^{\frac{1}{3}}=\frac{1}{2}$$

Therefore, ratio of their nuclear radii is 1 : 2. Whereas, nuclear density is

$$f=\frac{\text{Mass of nucleus}}{\text{Volume of nucleus}}$$

$$\Rightarrow \quad f=\frac{m}{\frac{4}{3}\pi R_0^3}$$

or $\quad f\propto\frac{A}{R^3}$

Since, both nuclei are made of nucleons and have similar density, the density remains the same.

So, ratio of nuclear density is 1:1.

NK05 NEET Knock Offs 5

1. (*a*) The *x*-coordinate of centre of mass is given by

$$x=\frac{m_1x_1+m_2x_2}{m_1+m_2}$$

Here, $m_1=0.4$ kg, $x_1=2$ m,
$m_2=0.6$ kg, $x_2=7$ m

Hence, $x=\frac{0.4\times2+0.6\times7}{0.4+0.6}$
$=5$ m

2. (*c*) We know that,
Volume, $V=L^3$
Percentage uncertainty in volume is given by

$$\frac{\Delta V}{V}\times100=\frac{3\Delta L}{L}\times100$$
$$=\frac{3\times0.1\times100}{30}$$
$$=\frac{30}{30}=1\%$$

3. (*d*) Equivalent capacitance of the given circuit diagram,

$$C_{eq}=\frac{(2+6)\times4}{2+6+4}$$
$$=\frac{32}{12}=\frac{8}{3}\mu F$$

Charge flowing through 4 μF capacitor, $\quad q=C_{eq}\cdot V$

$$=\frac{8}{3}\times10^{-6}\times12=32\ \mu C$$

∴ Potential difference across 4 μF capacitor,

$$V=\frac{q}{C}=\frac{32}{4}=8\text{ V}$$

4. (*b*) We know that, self-inductance of a long current-carrying solenoid is given as

$$L=\frac{\mu_0N^2A}{l}\Rightarrow L\propto N^2$$

$$\Rightarrow \quad \frac{L_2}{L_1}=\left(\frac{N_2}{N_1}\right)^2$$

$$=\left(\frac{\frac{N_1}{2}}{N_1}\right)^2 \quad \left[\because N_2=\frac{N_1}{2}\right]$$

$$=\left(\frac{1}{2}\right)^2=\frac{1}{4}\Rightarrow L_2=\frac{L_1}{4}$$

Hence, its self-inductance is decreased to one-fourth.

5. (*a*) Both Statement I and Statement II are correct.

In a sum, we take least number of decimal places as that in any of term in the sum.

Hence, 123 + 5.35 = 128.35 = 128
(in three significant figures)

In a product (or ratio), the number of significant figures in final product (or ratio) are same as the number of significant figures in least accurate measurement.

So, 13.8 m → 3 significant figures
× 9.0 m → 1 significant figure
$=124.2\text{ m}^2$ ← This is actual product.
$=100\text{ m}^2$ ← Only one significant figure is reported.

6. (*b*) We know that, barrier potential of Ge, $V_{B_1}=0.3$ V

and barrier potential of Si, $V_{B_2}=0.7$ V

Redrawing the given figure as

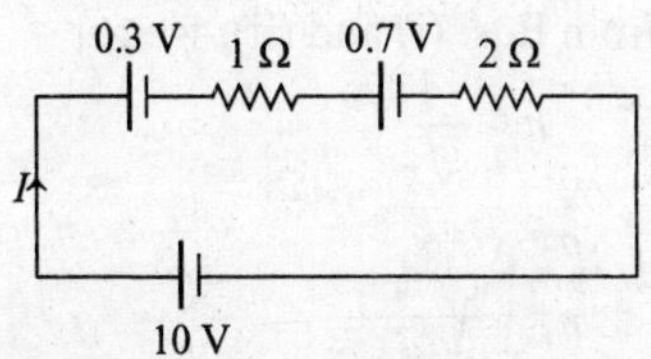

Applying KVL, we get

$$10-0.3-I\times1-0.7-2\times I=0$$
$$\Rightarrow \quad 3I=9$$
$$\Rightarrow \quad I=3\text{ A}$$

7. (*b*) Given, $r = 300\,\text{m}, \mu = 0.3,$ and $g = 10\,\text{m/s}^2$

If v is the velocity of the vehicle while turning on the road, then

$$\frac{mv^2}{r} \le \mu mg \Rightarrow v \le \sqrt{\mu rg}$$

$$\Rightarrow v_{\max} = \sqrt{\mu rg}$$

$$= \sqrt{0.3 \times 300 \times 10} = 30\,\text{m/s}$$

8. (*c*) We know that, the angle of deviation depends upon the angle of incidence. If we determine experimentally, the angle of deviation corresponding to different angles of incidence and then plot (on X-axis) and of (on Y-axis), we get a curve as shown in the figure.

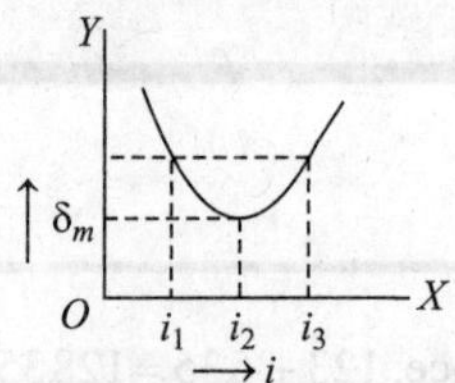

Clearly if the angle of incidence is gradually increased from a small value, the angle of deviation first decreases, becomes minimum for a particular angle of incidence and then begins to increase.

9. (*d*) We know that, time period of vibrating string,

$$T = 2\pi\sqrt{\frac{m}{k}}$$

$$\Rightarrow \frac{1}{n} = 2\pi\sqrt{\frac{m}{k}} \quad \left(\because T = \frac{1}{n}\right)$$

$$\Rightarrow n \propto \sqrt{k} \quad \text{...(i)}$$

Also for a spring,

$$k \propto \frac{1}{x} \quad \text{...(ii)}$$

From Eqs. (i) and (ii), we get

$$n \propto \frac{1}{\sqrt{x}}$$

$$\Rightarrow \frac{n_2}{n_1} = \sqrt{\frac{x_1}{x_2}}$$

$$= \sqrt{\frac{x_1}{x_1/2}} \quad \left(\because x_2 = \frac{x_1}{2}\right)$$

$$= \sqrt{2}$$

$$\Rightarrow n_2 = \sqrt{2}n_1 = \sqrt{2}\,n \quad (\because n_1 = n)$$

10. (*b*) Here, $u = 0$

Final velocity of car,

$$v = 72\,\text{km/h} = 20\,\text{m/s}$$

Time, $t = 25$ s

We know that,

$$v = u + at$$

$$\Rightarrow a = \frac{v-u}{t} = \frac{20}{25} = \frac{4}{5}\,\text{m/s}^2$$

Also, $v^2 - u^2 = 2as$

$$s = \frac{v^2 - u^2}{2a}$$

$$= \frac{(20)^2 - (0)^2}{2 \times \frac{4}{5}} = \frac{400 \times 5}{8} = 250\,\text{m}$$

11. (*b*) For the mixture of gases, specific heat at constant volume is given as

$$C_V = \frac{n_1 (C_V)_1 + n_2 (C_V)_2}{n_1 + n_2}$$

$$= \frac{2 \times \frac{5R}{2} + 8 \times \frac{3R}{2}}{2+8}$$

$$= \frac{17R}{10} = 1.7\,R$$

12. (*d*) Power output of motor = Power used by flour mill, $P = \tau\omega$

$$\Rightarrow P = 180 \times 200$$

$$= 36000$$

$$= 36\,\text{kW}$$

As motor is only 50%, efficient so, electrical power needed is

$$P' = \frac{150}{100} \times 36 = 54\,\text{kW}$$

13. (*c*) Let V be the volume of body and its density be ρ, then by law of floatation in water,

$$V\rho g = \frac{2}{3} V \times \rho_w g \quad \text{...(i)}$$

$\left[\because \frac{2}{3}V \text{ is immersed in water of density } \rho_w\right]$

Similarly, in a liquid,

$$V\rho g = \frac{1}{4} V \times \rho_l g \quad \text{...(ii)}$$

[$\because$ mass is same in both the cases]

From Eqs. (i) and (ii), we get

$$\frac{2}{3} V\rho_w g = \frac{1}{4} V\rho_l g$$

$$\Rightarrow \frac{\rho_l}{\rho_w} = \left(\frac{2}{3}\right) \times \left(\frac{4}{1}\right)$$

$$\Rightarrow \frac{\rho_l}{\rho_w} = \frac{8}{3}$$

$$\Rightarrow \rho_l = \frac{8}{3}\,\text{g/cc} \quad (\because \rho_w = 1\,\text{g/cc})$$

14. (*c*) We know that, $\frac{dV}{dx} = -\mathbf{E}$

$$\Rightarrow \int_1^{-5} dV = -\int_1^{-5} (\mathbf{E} \cdot d\mathbf{x})$$

$$\Rightarrow V_2 - V_1 = -\left[\int_1^{-5} (20x + 10)\,\hat{\mathbf{i}} \cdot dx\hat{\mathbf{i}}\right]$$

$$\Rightarrow V_1 - V_2 = \int_1^{-5} (20x + 10)\,dx$$

$$\Rightarrow V_1 - V_2 = \left[20\frac{x^2}{2} + 10x\right]_1^{-5}$$

$$= 180\,\text{V}$$

15. (*b*) When a *p-n* junction is connected in forward bias, an electric field exists which causes electrons to move from *n*-side to *p*-side (forward current).

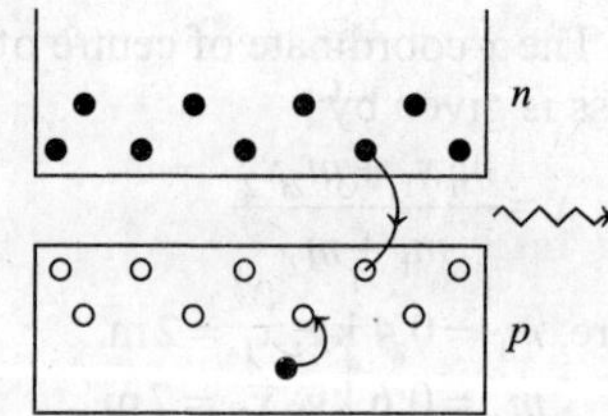

As electrons are in conduction band and holes are in valence band, thus electrons move from higher to lower energy level.

16. (*a*) Increase in surface energy = Work done

= Increase in surface area × surface tension × number of film surfaces

We know that, for liquid film, number of film surface, $n = 2$

$$\Rightarrow W = \Delta A \times T \times 2$$

$$\Rightarrow 6 \times 10^{-4} = 2(5 \times 4 - 4 \times 2) \times 10^{-4} \times T$$

$$\Rightarrow T = \frac{6 \times 10^{-4}}{24 \times 10^{-4}}$$

$$\Rightarrow T = \frac{1}{4}\,\text{N/m} = 0.25\,\text{N/m}$$

17. (*b*) As we know that,

Escape velocity,

$$v = \sqrt{\frac{2GM}{R}}$$

$$v = \sqrt{\frac{2G}{R}\left(\frac{4}{3}\pi R^3 \rho\right)}$$

$\therefore \quad v \propto R\sqrt{\rho}$

So, $\dfrac{v_e}{v_p} = \dfrac{R_e}{R_p}\sqrt{\dfrac{\rho_e}{\rho_p}}$

$\dfrac{v_e}{v_p} = 2\sqrt{2}$

$\therefore$ Ratio, $v_e : v_p = 2\sqrt{2} : 1$

18. (*b*) When a conductor moves in a magnetic field, an emf is induced in the conductor. This phenomenon is called electromagnetic induction. The Reason states that an emf can be induced by changing the magnetic field but it does not explain how this change is related to movement of the conductor.
Therefore, both Assertion and Reason are correct but Reason is not the correct explanation of Assertion.

19. (*c*) On stretching, volume of wire remains constant.

So, $\quad V = Al$ or $l = \dfrac{V}{A}$

$\therefore \quad R = \rho \cdot \dfrac{l}{A} = \dfrac{\rho V}{A^2} = \dfrac{\rho V}{\dfrac{\pi^2 D^4}{16}}$

$= \dfrac{16 \rho V}{\pi^2 D^4}$

$\therefore \quad \dfrac{\Delta R}{R} = -4\dfrac{\Delta D}{D} = -4(-0.4) = 1.6\%$

20. (*a*) As we know, $T_1 = 2\pi\sqrt{\dfrac{l}{g}}$

When $l' = 2l$, then

$T' = 2\pi\sqrt{\dfrac{2l}{g}} = 2\pi\sqrt{\dfrac{l}{g}}\sqrt{2} = \sqrt{2}T_1$

21. (*c*) **Case I** Moment of inertia of the rod (length L and mass M) about an axis perpendicular to the rod passing through the mid-point

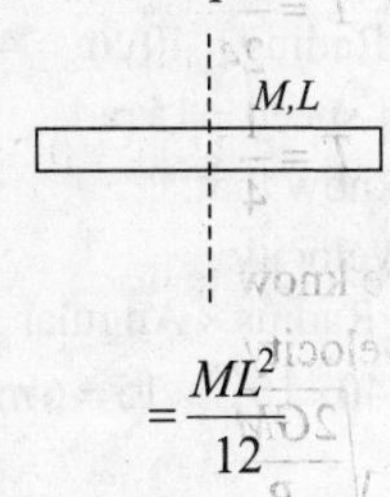

$= \dfrac{ML^2}{12}$

Case II Moment of inertia of the rod (length L and mass $2M$) about an axis perpendicular to the rod passing through one of its end

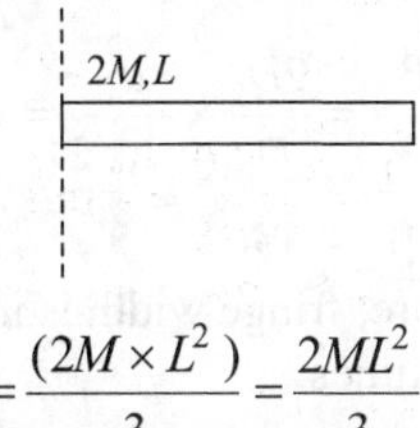

$= \dfrac{(2M \times L^2)}{3} = \dfrac{2ML^2}{3}$

Case III Moment of inertia of rod (length $2L$ and mass M) about an axis perpendicular to the rod passing through its mid-point

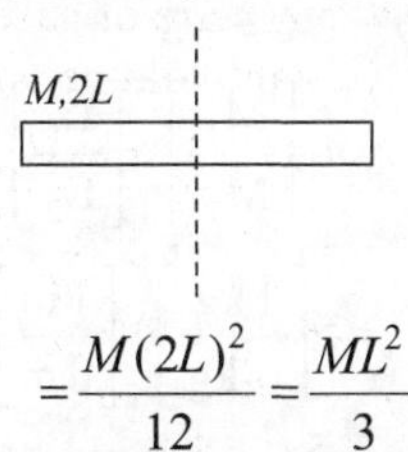

$= \dfrac{M(2L)^2}{12} = \dfrac{ML^2}{3}$

Case IV Moment of inertia of rod (length $2L$ and mass $2M$) about an axis perpendicular to the rod passing through one of its end

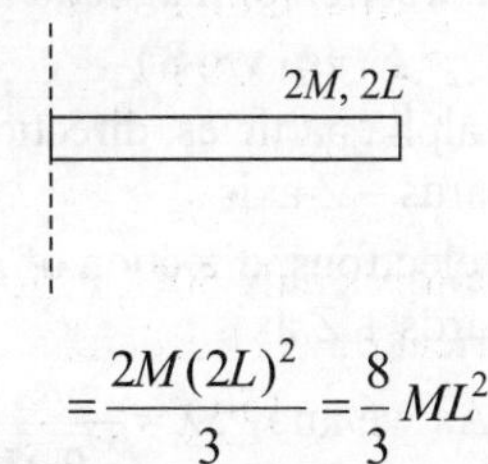

$= \dfrac{2M(2L)^2}{3} = \dfrac{8}{3}ML^2$

Hence, option (c) is correct.

22. (*c*) For slowing of a particle (in retardation), **a** and **v** must be inclined at an obtuse angle.

$\Rightarrow \quad \mathbf{a} \cdot \mathbf{v} < 0$

$\Rightarrow (a_x \hat{\mathbf{i}} + a_y \hat{\mathbf{j}}) \cdot (v_x \hat{\mathbf{i}} + v_y \hat{\mathbf{j}}) < 0$

$\Rightarrow \quad a_x v_x + a_y v_y < 0$

23. (*d*) When prism is placed in air, then deviation produced by it,

$\delta_{\text{air}} = ({}_a\mu_g - 1)\,A = (1.5 - 1)\,A = \dfrac{A}{2}$

$\Rightarrow \quad \delta_{\text{air}} = \dfrac{A}{2} = 10° \quad$ (given)

When prism is placed in water, then deviation produced by it,

$\delta_w = ({}_w\mu_g - 1)A = \left(\dfrac{{}_a\mu_g}{{}_a\mu_w} - 1\right)A$

$= \left(\dfrac{1.5}{4/3} - 1\right)A$

$= \dfrac{0.5}{4}A$

$= 0.25 \times \dfrac{A}{2}$

$= 0.25 \times \delta_{\text{air}} \quad \left[\because \delta_{\text{air}} = \dfrac{A}{2}\right]$

$= 0.25 \times 10°$

$= 2.5°$

24. (*b*) Current I_1 through path ABC

$= \dfrac{V_{AC}}{R_{AB} + R_{BC}} = \dfrac{40}{100}$

$= \dfrac{2}{5}$ A

Current, $I_2 = \dfrac{V_{AC}}{R_{AD} + R_{DC}}$

$= \dfrac{40}{200} = \dfrac{1}{5}$ A

Now, for path AB,

$V_A - V_B = I_1 \times 40$

$= \dfrac{2}{5} \times 40 = 16\text{ V}$

And for path AD,

$V_A - V_D = I_2 \times 90 = \dfrac{1}{5} \times 90$

$= 18\text{ V}$

So, $V_B - V_D = (V_A - V_D) - (V_A - V_B)$

$= 2\text{ V}$

25. (*c*) Induced emf $= Blv = B \times 2R \times v$

$= 1 \times 2 \times 1 \times 1$

$= 2\text{ V}$

26. (*c*) de-Broglie wavelength of a moving particle in terms of kinetic energy is given as

$\lambda = \dfrac{h}{\sqrt{2mK}}$

For proton,

$\lambda_p = \dfrac{h}{\sqrt{2m_p K_p}}$

For α-particle,

$\lambda_\alpha = \dfrac{h}{\sqrt{2m_\alpha K_\alpha}}$

$\therefore \quad \dfrac{\lambda_p}{\lambda_\alpha} = \sqrt{\dfrac{m_\alpha K_\alpha}{m_p K_p}}$

$$\frac{\lambda_p}{\lambda_\alpha}=\sqrt{\frac{4m_pK_p}{m_pK_p}}\quad\left(\because K_p=K_\alpha \text{ and } m_\alpha=4m_p\right)$$

$$\frac{\lambda_p}{\lambda_\alpha}=\sqrt{\frac{4}{1}}=\frac{2}{1}$$

$$\Rightarrow \frac{\lambda_\alpha}{\lambda_p}=\frac{1}{2}$$

$$\Rightarrow \lambda_\alpha:\lambda_p=1:2$$

27. (*c*) According to the given graph, Volume (V) $\propto$ Temperature (T)

or $\frac{V}{T}=$ constant

Thus, the process is isobaric.

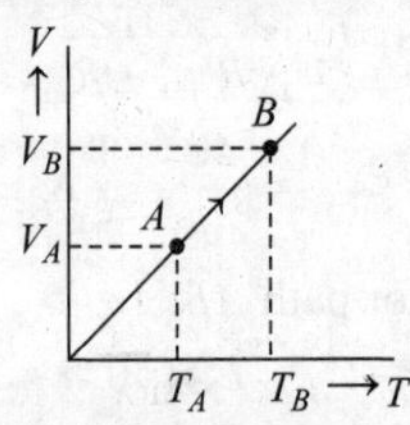

$\therefore$ Work done, $\Delta W=p\Delta V$

$$=nR\Delta T=nR(T_B-T_A)\quad \ldots\text{(i)}$$

Heat absorbed, $\Delta Q=nC_p\Delta T$

$$=nC_p(T_B-T_A)\quad \ldots\text{(ii)}$$

As, $C_p=\frac{\gamma R}{\gamma-1}\quad\left(\text{Here, } \gamma=1+\frac{2}{f}\right)$

For monoatomic gas, $f=3$

$$\Rightarrow C_p=\frac{5}{2}R$$

Substitute the value of C_p in Eq (ii), we get

$$\Delta Q=n\left(\frac{5}{2}R\right)(T_B-T_A)$$

Hence, $\frac{\Delta W}{\Delta Q}=\frac{nR\,(T_B-T_A)}{n\left(\frac{5}{2}R\right)(T_B-T_A)}=\frac{2}{5}$

28. (*a*) Conductivity of a semiconductor,

$$\sigma=e(n_e\mu_e+n_h\mu_h)$$

$$=1.6\times10^{-19}\,(5\times10^{18}\times2+5\times10^{19}\times0.01)$$

$$=1.68\ (\Omega\text{m})^{-1}$$

29. (*a*) We know that, fringe width

$$\beta=\frac{D\lambda}{d}\Rightarrow \beta\propto\frac{D}{d}$$

$$\Rightarrow \frac{\beta_2}{\beta_1}=\frac{D_2}{D_1}\times\frac{d_1}{d_2}$$

Here, $D_2=2D_1$ and $d_2=\frac{d_1}{2}$

$$\therefore \frac{\beta_2}{\beta_1}=\frac{2D_1}{D_1}\times\frac{d_1}{d_1/2}=4$$

$$\Rightarrow \beta_2=4\beta_1$$

Therefore, fringe width is increased to four times.

30. (*b*) We know that, joule is the unit of energy and the dimension formula of energy is $[\text{ML}^2\text{T}^{-2}]$.

Comparing with $[\text{M}^a\text{L}^b\text{T}^c]$, we get

$a=1, b=2, c=-2$

$$\text{As, } n_2=n_1\left[\frac{\text{M}_1}{\text{M}_2}\right]^a\left[\frac{\text{L}_1}{\text{L}_2}\right]^b\left[\frac{\text{T}_1}{\text{T}_2}\right]^c$$

$$=5\left[\frac{1\text{ kg}}{\alpha\text{ kg}}\right]^1\left[\frac{1\text{ m}}{\beta\text{ m}}\right]^2\left[\frac{1\text{s}}{\gamma\text{s}}\right]^{-2}$$

$$=\frac{5\gamma^2}{\alpha\beta^2}$$

$$n_2=5\alpha^{-1}\beta^{-2}\gamma^2$$

31. (*b*) Direction of magnetic field is

$$F=q(\mathbf{v}\times\mathbf{B})$$

For alpha particles, direction of B is towards $-Z$-axis.

For electrons, direction of B is towards $+Z$-axis.

32. (*d*) As we know, $\lambda=\frac{h}{\sqrt{2mK}}$

For same λ, $mk=$ constant

As, $m_e<m_p\simeq m_n<m_d$

$\therefore K_e>K_p\simeq K_n>K_d$

33. (*d*)

← x →	← x/4 →
T_2 k	k/2 T_1

In steady state, rate of flow of heat through two slabs will be equal.

$$H_1=H_2$$

$$\frac{kA(T_2-T)}{x}=\frac{\frac{k}{2}A(T-T_1)}{\frac{x}{4}}$$

$$(T_2-T)=2(T-T_1)$$

$$T_2-T=2T-2T_1$$

$$\frac{T_2+2T_1}{3}=T$$

$$Q=\frac{kA}{x}\left[T_2-\left(\frac{T_2+2T_1}{3}\right)\right]$$

$$=\frac{kA[2T_2-2T_1]}{3x}$$

$$=\frac{2kA}{3x}[T_2-T_1]$$

$$\therefore f=\frac{T_2-T_1}{3}$$

34. (*a*) The current in terms of drift speed is given by $I=nev_dA$

$$\Rightarrow v_d=\frac{I}{neA}\text{ or } v_d\propto\frac{1}{A}$$

So, drift velocity increases as we move from A to B.

Current remains constant, while electric potential decreases and electric field increases.

35. (*a*) We know that,

$$Y=\frac{FL}{\pi r^2 l}$$

Here, Y, F are constants

$$\therefore l\propto\frac{L}{r^2}$$

$$\Rightarrow \frac{l_1}{l_2}=\frac{r_2^2L_1}{r_1^2L_2}$$

$$=\frac{D_2^2L_1}{D_1^2L_2}=\frac{1}{4}\times\frac{2}{1}$$

$$\Rightarrow \frac{l_1}{l_2}=\frac{1}{2}\text{ or }1:2$$

36. (*a*) As we know that,

Torque, $\tau=NIAB\sin\theta$

$=800\times10\times8\times10^{-2}\times5\times\sin(90°-60°)$

$=3.2\times10^3\times\sin30°$

$=3.2\times10^3\times\frac{1}{2}=1.6\times10^3$ N-m

$=1600$ N-m

37. (*d*) Given,

Radius $=40$ cm $=40\times10^{-2}$ m

Angular speed $=15$ rad/s

As we know that,

Linear velocity

$=$ Radius $\times$ Angular speed

$=40\times10^{-2}\times15=6$ m/s

38. (*b*) Equation of motion of electron along vertical direction,

$$y=0\times t+\frac{1}{2}a_y t^2$$

$$=\frac{1}{2}\left(\frac{eE}{m}\right)\cdot t^2 \quad \left[\because a_y=a=\frac{eE}{m}\right]$$

$$=\frac{1}{2}\cdot\frac{eE}{m}\left(\frac{l}{v_0}\right)^2 \quad \left[\because t=\frac{l}{v_0}\right]$$

$$=\frac{1}{2}\frac{eE}{mv_0^2}\cdot l^2$$

$$\Rightarrow \quad y=\frac{eE}{2mv_0^2}l^2$$

This equation is in the form of $y=ax^2$, which represents the equation of parabola. Hence, path of electron in electric field is parabolic.

39. (*b*) At maximum height, $v=0$

Initial speed of stone, $u=u_0$

By the third equation of motion,

$$v^2=u^2-2gh$$

$$0=u_0^2-2gh$$

$$\Rightarrow \quad u_0=\sqrt{2gh} \quad \ldots(\text{i})$$

When $h'=3h$, then

$$0=(u_0')^2-2g(3h)$$

$$\Rightarrow \quad (u_0')^2=6gh$$

$$u_0'=\sqrt{6gh}=\sqrt{3}\sqrt{2gh}$$

$$\Rightarrow \quad =\sqrt{3}\,u_0 \quad [\text{from Eq. (i)}]$$

40. (*d*) Length of wire $=l$

Case I For square shape,

Length of side $=\frac{l}{4}$

$$\therefore \text{Area, } A_1=\left(\frac{l}{4}\right)^2=\frac{l^2}{16}$$

$\therefore$ Magnetic moment,

$$M_1=IA_1=\frac{I\cdot l^2}{16}$$

Case II For circular shape, $l=2\pi r_2$

$$\Rightarrow \quad r_2=\frac{l}{2\pi} \quad \ldots(\text{i})$$

$\therefore$ Magnetic moment,

$$M_2=IA_2=I\cdot\pi r_2^2$$

$$=I\cdot\pi\left(\frac{l}{2\pi}\right)^2 \quad [\text{using Eq. (i)}]$$

$$=I\pi\frac{l^2}{4\pi^2}$$

$$M_2=\frac{Il^2}{4\pi}$$

$$\therefore \quad \frac{M_1}{M_2}=\frac{\frac{Il^2}{16}}{\frac{Il^2}{4\pi}}=\frac{\pi}{4}$$

$$\therefore \quad M_1:M_2=\pi:4$$

41. (*d*) Volume of 8 drops = Volume of a large drop

$$\Rightarrow \quad 8\times\frac{4}{3}\pi r^3=\frac{4}{3}\pi R^3$$

$$\Rightarrow \quad 2r=R \quad \ldots(\text{i})$$

According to conservation of charge,

$$Q=8q \quad \ldots(\text{ii})$$

Potential of each small drop,

$$V=\frac{1}{4\pi\varepsilon_0}\cdot\frac{q}{r}$$

$$\Rightarrow \quad \frac{1}{4\pi\varepsilon_0}\cdot\frac{q}{r}=16 \quad \ldots(\text{iii})$$

Potential of a large drop,

$$V'=\frac{1}{4\pi\varepsilon_0}\cdot\frac{Q}{R}=\frac{1}{4\pi\varepsilon_0}\cdot\frac{8q}{2r}$$

[from Eqs. (i) and (ii)]

$$=4\times\frac{1}{4\pi\varepsilon_0}\cdot\frac{q}{r}$$

$$=4\times 16 \quad [\text{from Eq. (iii)}]$$

$$=64\text{ V}$$

42. (*a*) Given, $V=100\sin\left(100\pi t+\frac{\pi}{6}\right)$

$$\therefore \quad \phi_1=\frac{\pi}{6}$$

Since, alternating current leads by $\frac{\pi}{2}$ angle from alternating voltage in purely capacitive circuit, hence phase angle of alternating current,

$$\phi_2=\frac{\pi}{2}-\phi_1=\frac{\pi}{2}-\frac{\pi}{6}=\frac{\pi}{3}$$

$\therefore$ Instantaneous value of alternative current,

$$i=i_0\sin(100\pi t+\phi_2)$$

$$=V_0\omega C\sin\left(100\pi t+\frac{\pi}{3}\right)$$

$$=100\times 100\pi\times 1\times 10^{-6}\sin\left(100\pi t+\frac{\pi}{3}\right)$$

$$=0.01\pi\sin\left(100\pi t+\frac{\pi}{3}\right)$$

43. (*c*) In an electromagnetic wave, energy is equally shared between electric and magnetic fields.

So, $\quad u_M=u_E$

44. (*c*) Gravitational force depends on mass of two bodies and distance between their centres. It is independent of medium.

Therefore, gravitational force will remain the same.

45. (*b*) We know that, frequency,

$$\nu=Rc\left(\frac{1}{n_1^2}-\frac{1}{n_2^2}\right)$$

For series limit of Lyman series,

$$n_1=1, n_2=\infty$$

$$\nu_1=Rc\left(\frac{1}{1^2}-\frac{1}{\infty}\right)=Rc$$

For first line, $n_1=1, n_2=2$

$$\nu_2=Rc\left(\frac{1}{1^2}-\frac{1}{4}\right)=\frac{3}{4}Rc$$

For series limit of Balmer series,

$n_1=2, n_2=\infty$

$$\nu_3=Rc\left(\frac{1}{4}-\frac{1}{\infty}\right)=\frac{Rc}{4}$$

$$\Rightarrow \nu_1-\nu_2=Rc-\frac{3}{4}Rc=\frac{Rc}{4}=\nu_3$$

So, $\nu_1-\nu_2=\nu_3$

$$\nu_1=\nu_2+\nu_3$$

NC1 NEET Chronicles 1

Section-A

1. (b) The given situation is shown below.

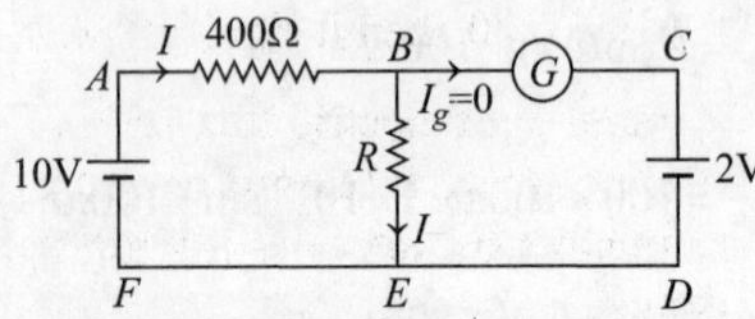

Applying Kirchhoff's voltage law in the loop *ABCDEFA*, we get

$$400I + 2 - 10 = 0$$

$$\Rightarrow \quad I = \frac{8}{400} = \frac{1}{50}\text{ A}$$

Applying Kirchhoff's voltage law in loop *ABEFA*, we get

$$400I + RI - 10 = 0$$

$$\Rightarrow \quad (400 + R)I = 10$$

$$\Rightarrow \quad (400 + R) \times \frac{1}{50} = 100$$

$$\Rightarrow \quad 400 + R = 500$$

$$\Rightarrow \quad R = 100\,\Omega$$

2. (b) When AC is converted into DC using a rectifier circuit, then converted DC is an unstable current that includes ripples. A capacitor is used to remove these ripples and maintain a constant voltage across load.

3. (d) Efficiency of Carnot engine, $\eta = 50\% = 0.5$

Temperature of source,

$$T_1 = 327°\text{C}$$

$$= (327 + 273)\text{ K} = 600\text{K}$$

Let T_2 be the temperature of sink, then $\eta = 1 - \frac{T_2}{T_1}$

$$\Rightarrow \quad 0.5 = 1 - \frac{T_2}{600}$$

$$\Rightarrow \quad \frac{T_2}{600} = 0.5$$

$$\Rightarrow \quad T_2 = 300\text{K} = (300 - 273)°\text{C} = 27°\text{C}$$

4. (c) According to given situation,

$$c = \frac{x}{t_1} \text{ and } v = \frac{10x}{t_2}$$

Since, $\sin i_c = \frac{1}{\mu} = \frac{1}{(c/v)} = \frac{v}{c}$

$$= \frac{\frac{10x}{t_2}}{\frac{x}{t_1}} = \frac{10t_1}{t_2}$$

$$\Rightarrow i_c = \sin^{-1}\left(\frac{10t_1}{t_2}\right)$$

5. (c) The direction of angular acceleration of a body moving along the circumference of the circular path is perpendicular to the plane in which rotation takes place i.e. along the axis of rotation.

6. (a) Venturimeter is a device used to measure the flow speed (flow rate) of incompressible fluid. It works on the Bernoulli's principle.

7. (c) Given, $T_{1/2} = 20$ minutes

According to given condition,

$$R = \frac{R_0}{16}$$

But, $R = R_0\left(\frac{1}{2}\right)^n$

$$\Rightarrow \quad \frac{R_0}{16} = R_0\left(\frac{1}{2}\right)^n \Rightarrow \left(\frac{1}{2}\right)^4 = \left(\frac{1}{2}\right)^n$$

$$\Rightarrow \quad n = 4 \Rightarrow \frac{t}{T/2} = 4$$

$$\Rightarrow \quad t = 4T_{1/2} = 4 \times 20 = 80\text{ minutes}$$

8. (c) Random errors can arise due to random and unpredictable fluctuations in temperature and voltage supply.

9. (c) Given, $\theta = 30°$

$$E = 2 \times 10^5\text{ NC}^{-1}$$

Dipole length, $2l = 2\text{ cm} = 2 \times 10^{-2}$ m

Torque, $\tau = 4$ N-m

We know that,

$$\Rightarrow \tau = pE\sin\theta$$

$$\Rightarrow \quad p = \frac{\tau}{E\sin\theta} = \frac{4}{2 \times 10^5 \times \sin 30°}$$

$$\Rightarrow \quad p = 4 \times 10^{-5}\text{ C-m}$$

$$\Rightarrow \quad 2l \cdot q = 4 \times 10^{-5}$$

$$\Rightarrow \quad q = \frac{4 \times 10^{-5}}{2l} = \frac{4 \times 10^{-5}}{2 \times 10^{-2}}$$

$$= 2 \times 10^{-3}\text{ C}$$

$$= 2\text{ mC}$$

10. (b) Friction force always works against the motion of the football player. Here, football player is moving in the southward direction, so friction will act in northward direction . From the Newton's law of motion, force is in the direction of change in momentum. Since, the football player is just trying to move in the east direction in which no initial momentum was present, so force will be in north-east direction.

11. (a) In hydrogen spectrum,

$$\frac{1}{\lambda} = R\left(\frac{1}{n_1^2} - \frac{1}{n_2^2}\right)$$

For shortest wavelength in the Balmer series,

$$n_1 = 2 \text{ and } n_2 = \infty$$

$$\therefore \quad \frac{1}{\lambda} = R\left(\frac{1}{2^2} - \frac{1}{\infty^2}\right)$$

$$\Rightarrow \quad \frac{1}{\lambda} = \frac{R}{4}$$

$$\Rightarrow \quad R = \frac{4}{\lambda} \quad \ldots\text{(i)}$$

For the shortest wavelength of Bracket series, $n_1 = 4$ and $n_2 = \infty$

$$\therefore \quad \frac{1}{\lambda_B} = R\left(\frac{1}{4^2} - \frac{1}{\infty^2}\right)$$

$$= \frac{R}{16} = \frac{4/\lambda}{16}$$

$$\Rightarrow \quad \frac{1}{\lambda_B} = \frac{1}{4\lambda} \Rightarrow \lambda_B = 4\lambda$$

12. (a) The circuit diagram is shown as

Applying KVL in the closed loop *AEBCDA*,

$$2I - 10 + 5 + I \cdot 1 + 7I = 0$$

$$\Rightarrow \quad 10I = 5$$

$$\Rightarrow \quad I = 0.5\,\text{A}$$

Since, current is positive, hence direction of current is from *A* to *B* through *E*.

13. (d) According to given situation,

$$V_S = 12\,\text{V},$$

$$\therefore \quad I_S = \frac{P}{V_S} = \frac{60}{12} = 5\,\text{A}$$

$\therefore$ Given, $V_P = 220$ V

For ideal transformer.

$$I_P V_P = I_S V_S$$

$$\Rightarrow \quad I_P = \frac{I_S V_S}{V_P} = \frac{5 \times 12}{220} = 0.27\,\text{A}$$

14. (d) For photoelectric emission, energy of incident electromagnetic radiation must be greater than or equal to work function of photosensitive surface. Thus, only Cs can emit photoelectrons.

15. (c) Given, when $x_1 = 2\,\text{cm}$

Then, $U_1 = U \Rightarrow \frac{1}{2} k x_1^2 = U$

$$\Rightarrow \quad K = \frac{2U}{x_1^2} \qquad \ldots\text{(i)}$$

When $x_2 = 8\,\text{cm}$, then $U = \frac{1}{2} k x_2^2$

$$= \frac{1}{2} \times \frac{2U}{x_1^2} \times x_2^2 \qquad \text{[From Eq. (i)]}$$

$$= U \cdot \left(\frac{x_2}{x_1}\right)^2 = U\left(\frac{8}{2}\right)^2 = 16U$$

16. (d) Net magnetic flux through a closed surface is zero because the number of field lines leaving the surface are equal to the number of field lines entering the surface.

17. (b) Given, surface tension,

$T = 0.03\,\text{Nm}^{-1}$

Radius of soop bubble, $r = 2\,\text{cm}$
$= 2 \times 10^{-2}\,\text{m}$

$\therefore$ Amount of energy required,

$$E = 2TA = 2 \times 0.03 \times 4\pi\,(2 \times 10^{-2})^2$$

$$= 3.01 \times 10^{-4}\,\text{J}$$

18. (a) Longitudinal stress $= \frac{\text{Weight}}{\text{Area}} = \frac{w}{A}$

19. (b) The given situation is shown below.

$$(m) \xleftarrow{\;x\;} O \xrightarrow{\;R-x\;} (9m)$$

Since, gravitational field at point *O* is zero, hence

$$\frac{Gm}{x^2} = \frac{G(9m)}{(R-x)^2}$$

$$\Rightarrow \quad \left(\frac{1}{x}\right)^2 = \left(\frac{3}{R-x}\right)^2$$

$$\Rightarrow \quad \frac{1}{x} = \frac{3}{R-x} \Rightarrow 3x = R - x$$

$$\Rightarrow \quad x = \frac{R}{4}$$

$\therefore$ Gravitational potential at point *O*,

$$V = \frac{-Gm}{x} + \left[\frac{-G(9m)}{R-x}\right]$$

$$= \frac{-Gm}{\frac{R}{4}} - \frac{9Gm}{R - \frac{R}{4}}$$

$$= -\frac{4Gm}{R} - \frac{12Gm}{R} = -\frac{16Gm}{R}$$

20. (a) Initial temperature of the gas,
$= (-50 + 273)\,\text{K} = 223\,\text{K}$

Final temperature of the gas,

$T_2 = ?$

$(v_{\text{rms}})_1 = v$

At the speed is increased by 3 times, so the final speed beocmes

$(v_{\text{rms}})_2 = 4v$

We know that,

$$v_{\text{rms}} = \sqrt{\frac{3RT}{m}} \Rightarrow v_{\text{rms}} \propto \sqrt{T}$$

$$\Rightarrow \quad \frac{(v_{\text{rms}})_2}{(v_{\text{rms}})_1} = \sqrt{\frac{T_2}{T_1}} \Rightarrow \frac{4v}{v} = \sqrt{\frac{T_2}{223}}$$

$$\Rightarrow 16 = \frac{T_2}{223} \Rightarrow T_2 = 3568\,\text{K}$$

In °C,

$$T_2 = (3568 - 273)\,°\text{C} = 3295\,°\text{C}$$

21. (d) Photovoltaic devices can convert optical radiation into electricity. The basic example of such device is solar photovoltaic system which converts solar energy directly into electrical energy.

Zener diode is heavily doped *p-n* junction diode operating in reverse biased condition in breakdown region.

22. (d) According to Gauss's law, $\oint \mathbf{E} \cdot d\mathbf{S}$ represents total electric flux passing through a closed surface.

If $\oint \mathbf{E} \cdot d\mathbf{S} = 0$, then it signifies that the number of electric flux lines entering the surface must be equal to the number of flux lines leaving the surface.

23. (c) In series *L-C-R* circuit,

$$L = 10\,\text{mH} = 10^{-2}\,\text{H}$$

$$C = 1\,\text{F} = 10^{-6}\,\text{F}$$

$$R = 100\,\Omega$$

$\therefore$ Resonance frequency, $f = \frac{1}{2\pi\sqrt{LC}}$

$$= \frac{1}{2\pi\sqrt{10^{-2} \times 10^{-6}}}$$

$$= \frac{1}{2\pi \times 10^{-4}} = \frac{10^4}{2\pi}$$

$$= 1.59 \times 10^3\,\text{Hz} = 1.59\,\text{kHz}$$

24. (b) We know that, capacitive reactance,

$$X_C = \frac{1}{\omega C} = \frac{1}{2\pi f C}$$

i.e., due to decrease in operating frequency (f), X_C increases. As X_C increases, the conduction current decreases.

Since, in case of capacitor, conduction current is equal to displacement current.

Thus, with the decrease of operating frequency, displacement current decreases.

25. (b) Given, $u = 280\,\text{ms}^{-1}, \theta = 30°$

$\therefore$ Maximum height attaiend by the bullet.

$$H_{\text{max}} = \frac{u^2 \sin^2\theta}{2g}$$

$$= \frac{(280)^2 \sin^2 30°}{2 \times 9.8}$$

$$= \frac{(280)^2 \times (0.5)^2}{2 \times 9.8} = 1000\,\text{m}$$

26. (b) $\overset{A}{\longleftarrow}\frac{s}{2}\overset{v\;\;C\;\;2v}{\longleftrightarrow}\frac{s}{2}\longrightarrow B$

Time taken by vehicle to cover first half,

$$t_1 = \frac{s/2}{v} = \frac{s}{2v}$$

Time taken by vehicle to cover second half,

$$t_2 = \frac{s/2}{2v} = \frac{s}{4v}$$

$\therefore$ Average speed,

$$v_{avg} = \frac{\text{Total distance covered}}{\text{Total time taken}}$$

$$= \frac{\frac{s}{2}+\frac{s}{2}}{t_1 + t_2} = \frac{s}{\frac{s}{2v}+\frac{s}{4v}} = \frac{4v}{3}$$

27. (b) Given, $R = (22000 \pm 5\%)\Omega$

$$= (22 \times 10^3 \pm 5\%)\Omega$$

Here, colours of four bands are

Red	Red	Orange	Gold
↓	↓	↓	↓
2	2	3	± 5%

Thus, colour of third band is orange.

28. (d) Equivalent capacitance of the system,

$$C_{AB} = \frac{3 \times (3+3)}{3 + (3+3)} = \frac{18}{9} = 2\,\mu\text{F}$$

29. (a) The minimum wavelength of X-rays produced by an electron accelerated through a potential difference V is given as

$$\lambda_{min} = \frac{hc}{eV}$$

$$\Rightarrow \lambda_{min} \propto \frac{1}{V}$$

30. (c) Stored magnetic energy,

$$U = \frac{1}{2} LI^2$$

Here, $L = 4\,\mu\text{H} = 4 \times 10^{-6}$ H

$$I = 2\text{ A}$$

$$\therefore \quad U = \frac{1}{2} \times 4 \times 10^{-6} \times 2^2$$

$$= 8 \times 10^{-6}\text{ J}$$

$$= 8\,\mu\text{J}$$

31. (b) Angular separation of fringes,

$$\theta = \frac{\lambda}{d}$$

i.e., Angular separation does not depend on the distance between screen and plane of slits. Thus, statement I is correct.

Since, $\theta \propto \lambda$

Thus, if the monochromatic source is replaced by another monochromatic source of larger wavelength, then angular seperation of fringes increases. Hence, statement II is incorrect.

32. (d) Radius of gyration of solid sphere and hollow sphere are K_1 and K_2 respectively, then

$$MK_1^2 = \frac{2}{5} MR^2$$

$$\Rightarrow \quad K_1 = \sqrt{\frac{2}{5}} R$$

and $MK_2^2 = \frac{2}{3} MR^2$

$$\Rightarrow \quad K_2 = \sqrt{\frac{2}{3}} R$$

$$\therefore \quad \frac{K_1}{K_2} = \frac{\sqrt{2/5}R}{\sqrt{2/3}R} = \sqrt{\frac{3}{5}}$$

$$K_1^2 : K_3^2 = 3:5$$

33. (b) Given, $E_0 = 48\text{ Vm}^{-1}$

$$c = 3 \times 10^8 \text{ m/s}$$

$\therefore$ Amplitude of oscillating magnetic field,

$$B_0 = \frac{E_0}{c}$$

$$= \frac{48}{3 \times 10^8} = 1.6 \times 10^{-7}\text{ T}$$

34. (b) Given, $M = (0.4 \pm 0.002)$ g

$$R = (0.3 \pm 0.001)\text{ mm}$$

$$L = (5 \pm 0.02)\text{ cm}$$

$\therefore$ Density of wire, $\rho = \frac{M}{\pi r^2 L}$

$\therefore$ Maximum percentage error in the measurement of density of wire

$$\frac{\Delta\rho}{\rho} \times 100 = \frac{\Delta M}{M} \times 100 + 2 \times \frac{\Delta r}{r} \times 100 + \frac{\Delta L}{L} \times 100$$

$$= \frac{0.002}{0.4} \times 100 + 2 \times \frac{0.001}{0.3} \times 100 + \frac{0.02}{5} \times 100$$

$$= 0.5 + 0.67 + 0.4$$

$$= 1.57\% \approx 1.6\%$$

35. (a) Fundamental frequency of an open pipe, $f_0 = \frac{v}{2l}$

and fundamental frequency of an closed pipe,

$$f_c = \frac{v}{4l}$$

$$\therefore \quad \frac{f_0}{f_c} = \frac{v/2l}{v/4l} = \frac{2}{1}$$

$$\therefore \quad f_0 : f_c = 2:1$$

Section-B

36. (c) Focal length of convex lens,

$$f_1 = +f$$

Focal length of concave lens,

$$f_2 = -f$$

When both lenses are kept in contact, then equivalent focal length (F) is given by

$$\frac{1}{F} = \frac{1}{f_1} + \frac{1}{f_2} = \frac{1}{f} + \frac{1}{-f}$$

$$= 0 \Rightarrow F = \infty$$

37. (a) Time period of satellite,

$$T = \frac{2\pi r}{v_0}$$

$$\Rightarrow \quad T = \frac{2\pi(R_e + h)}{v_0} \quad \text{...(i)}$$

Orbital velocity, $v_0 = \sqrt{\frac{GM_e}{r}}$

$$\Rightarrow \quad v_0 = \sqrt{\frac{GM_e}{(R_e + h)}} \quad \text{...(ii)}$$

From Eqs. (i) and (ii), we get

$$T = \frac{2\pi(R_e + h)}{\sqrt{\frac{GM_e}{R_e + h}}}$$

$$T = 2\pi\sqrt{\frac{(R_e + h)^3}{GM_e}} \quad \text{...(iii)}$$

Since, $M_e = \frac{4}{3}\pi R_e^3 d$

$\therefore$ Putting the value of M_e in Eq. (iii), we get

$$T = 2\pi\sqrt{\frac{(R_e + h)^3}{G \cdot \frac{4}{3}\pi R_e^3 d}} = \sqrt{\frac{3\pi(R_e + h)^3}{GdR_e^3}}$$

Since, satellite is orbiting just above the surface of the earth, hence $h = 0$

$$\therefore \quad T = \sqrt{\frac{3\pi R_e^3}{GdR_e^3}} = \sqrt{\frac{3\pi}{Gd}}$$

38. (b) The given situation is shown below.

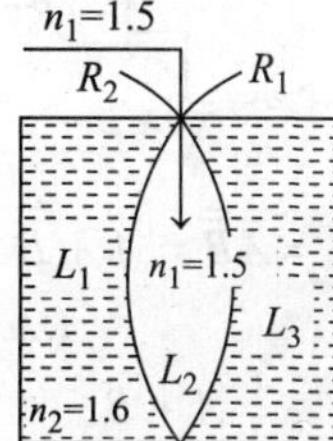

$$\therefore \quad R_1 = 20\,\text{cm}$$

$$R_2 = -20\,\text{cm}$$

Lens L_1 and L_3 are plano concave lens.

Focal length of lens L_1 is given as

$$\frac{1}{f_1} = (n_2 - 1)\left(\frac{1}{\infty} - \frac{1}{R_1}\right)$$

$$= (1.6 - 1)\left(-\frac{1}{20}\right) = \frac{-6}{200}$$

$$\Rightarrow \quad f_1 = \frac{-3}{100}\,\text{cm}$$

Similarly, focal length of lens L_3,

$$f_3 = \frac{-3}{100}\,\text{cm}$$

Now, focal length of convex lens L_2 is given as

$$\frac{1}{f_2} = (n_1 - 1)\left(\frac{1}{R_1} - \frac{1}{R_2}\right)$$

$$= (1.5 - 1)\left(\frac{1}{20} - \frac{1}{-20}\right) = \frac{1}{20}$$

$$\Rightarrow \quad f_2 = 20\,\text{cm}$$

If F be the focal length of combination, then

$$\frac{1}{F} = \frac{1}{f_1} + \frac{1}{f_2} + \frac{1}{f_3}$$

$$= \frac{-3}{100} + \frac{1}{20} + \frac{-3}{100}$$

$$= -\frac{1}{100}$$

$$\Rightarrow \quad F = -100\,\text{cm}$$

39. (d) The given situation is shown below.

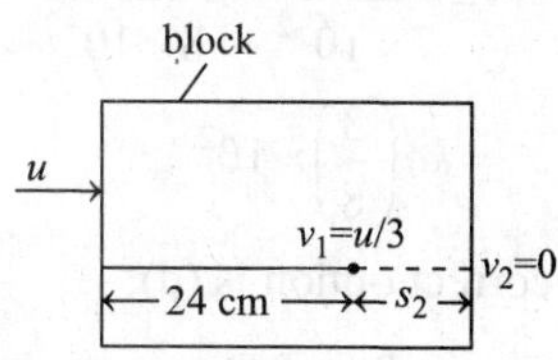

$$s_1 = 24\,\text{cm}$$

Using, $v^2 = u^2 - 2as$

$$\Rightarrow \quad v_1^2 = u^2 - 2as$$

$$\Rightarrow \left(\frac{u}{3}\right)^2 = u^2 - 2a \times 0.24$$

$$\Rightarrow 0.48a = \frac{8}{9}u^2$$

$$\Rightarrow \quad a = \frac{8u^2}{9 \times 0.48} = \frac{u^2}{0.54}$$

According to second condition,

$$0 = v_1^2 - 2as_2$$

$$\Rightarrow \quad 0 = \left(\frac{u}{3}\right)^2 - 2 \times \frac{u^2}{0.54} \times s_2$$

$$\Rightarrow \quad \frac{u^2}{9} = \frac{2u^2}{0.54} s_2$$

$$\Rightarrow \quad s_2 = \frac{0.54}{9 \times 2} = 0.03\,\text{m} = 3\,\text{cm}$$

$\therefore$ Total length of the block $= s_1 + s_2$

$$= 24 + 3 = 27\,\text{cm}$$

40. (a) When 10 resistors, each of resistance R is connected in series, then equivalent resistance.

$$R_s = R + R + R + \ldots \text{10 times}$$

$$\Rightarrow \quad R_s = 10R$$

$\therefore$ Current drawn from the battery,

$$I_s = \frac{E}{R_S} = \frac{E}{10R}$$

$$\Rightarrow \quad I_s = \frac{E}{10R} \quad \text{...(i)}$$

In second case, when resistors are connected in parallel, then equivalent resistance,

$$\frac{1}{R_p} = \frac{1}{R} + \frac{1}{R} + \frac{1}{R} + \ldots \text{10 times}$$

$$= \frac{10}{R} \Rightarrow \quad R_p = \frac{R}{10}$$

$\therefore$ Current drawn from the battery,

$$I_p = \frac{E}{R_p} = \frac{E}{R/10} = 10 \times \frac{E}{R}$$

$$= 100 \times \frac{E}{10R} \Rightarrow I_p = 100I$$

$$\therefore \quad n = 100$$

41. (b) Given, $L = \frac{50}{\pi}\,\text{mH} = \frac{5}{\pi} \times 10^{-2}\,\text{H}$

$$C = \frac{10^3}{\pi}\,\mu\text{F} = \frac{1}{\pi} \times 10^{-3}\,\text{F}$$

$$R = 10\,\Omega, f = 50\,\text{Hz}, V = 220$$

V

$$\therefore \quad X_L = 2\pi fL$$

$$= 2\pi \times 50 \times \frac{5}{\pi} \times 10^{-2} = 5\,\Omega$$

$$X_C = \frac{1}{\omega C} = \frac{1}{2\pi fC}$$

$$= \frac{1}{2\pi \times 50 \times \frac{1}{\pi} \times 10^{-3}}$$

$$= \frac{1}{10^{-1}} = 10\,\Omega$$

$\therefore$ Net impedance the circuit,

$$Z = \sqrt{R^2 + (X_C - X_L)^2}$$

$$= \sqrt{10^2 + (10 - 5)^2}$$

$$= \sqrt{125} = 5\sqrt{5}\,\Omega$$

42. (c) The motion of the particle performing S.H.M. is represented by

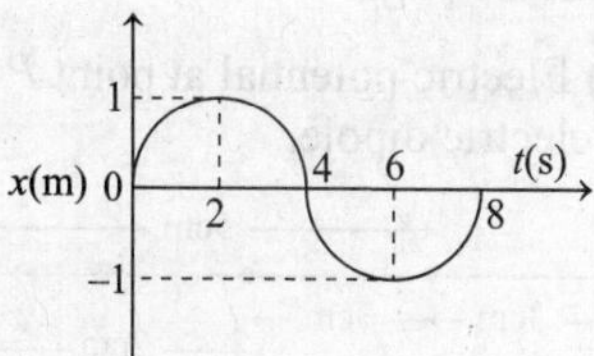

$$x = A \sin \omega t = 1 \sin \frac{2\pi}{T} t$$

$$= 1 \sin \frac{2\pi}{8} t$$

$$\Rightarrow \quad x = \sin\left(\frac{\pi}{4} t\right)$$

$\therefore$ velocity, $v = \frac{dx}{dt}$

$$= \frac{d}{dt}\sin\left(\frac{\pi}{4}\right)t$$

$$= \frac{\pi}{4}\cos\left(\frac{\pi}{4}\right)t$$

$\therefore$ Acceleration of the particle,

$$a = \frac{dv}{dt} = \frac{d}{dt}\left[\frac{\pi}{4}\cos\left(\frac{\pi}{4}\right)t\right]$$

$$= -\frac{\pi}{4}\cdot\frac{\pi}{4}\cdot\sin\left(\frac{\pi}{4}t\right)$$

$$\Rightarrow \quad a = -\frac{\pi^2}{16}\sin\left(\frac{\pi}{4}\cdot t\right)$$

At $\quad t = 2s$

$$a = -\frac{\pi^2}{16}\cdot\sin\left(\frac{\pi}{4}\cdot 2\right)$$

$$= -\frac{\pi^2}{16}\ \text{ms}^{-2}$$

43. (b)

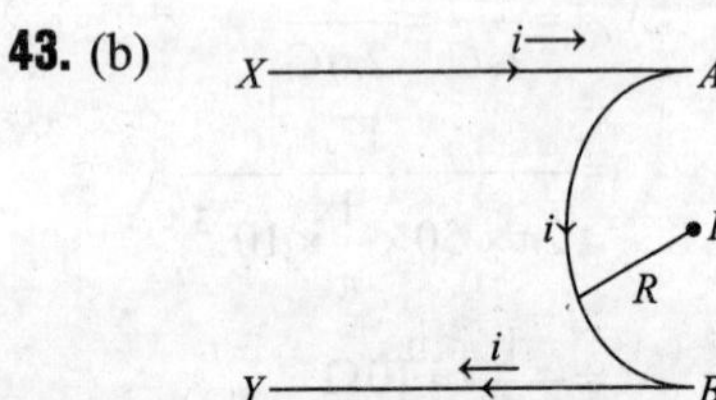

Net magnetic field at point P,

$$B = B_{\text{semicircle}} - B_{XA} - B_{YB}$$

$$= \frac{\mu_0 i}{4R} - \frac{\mu_0 i}{4\pi R} - \frac{\mu_0 i}{4\pi R}$$

$$= \frac{\mu_0 i}{4R}\left[1 - \frac{2}{\pi}\right] \text{ pointed away}$$

from the page.

44. (d) Electric potential at point P due to electric dipole.

5cm

$-q$ ← 3cm →← 3cm → q ← 2cm →

← 8cm →

$$V = \frac{1}{4\pi\varepsilon_0}\cdot\frac{q}{r^2}$$

$$= K\cdot\frac{p}{r^2}$$

From the figure,

$$V = \frac{kq}{2\times 10^{-2}} - \frac{kq}{8\times 10^{-2}}$$

$$= kq\left(\frac{3}{8}\right)\times 10^2$$

So, correct option is (d).

45. (b) Given, $R_0 = 2\Omega$

At $t = 80°\text{C}, R_t = 6.8\ \Omega$

We know that,

$$R_f = R_0(1 + \alpha t)$$

$$\Rightarrow \quad R_t = R_0 + R_0\alpha t$$

$$\therefore \quad \alpha = \frac{R_t - R_0}{R_0 t}$$

$$= \frac{6.8 - 2}{2\times 80} = \frac{4.8}{2\times 80} = 0.03$$

$$= 3\times 10^{-2}\ °\text{C}^{-1}$$

46. (b) Given, $\mathbf{L} = L\hat{\mathbf{i}}$

$$\mathbf{B} = 2\hat{\mathbf{i}} + 3\hat{\mathbf{j}} - 4\hat{\mathbf{k}}$$

$$\therefore \quad \mathbf{F} = \mathbf{I}(\mathbf{L}\times\mathbf{B})$$

$$= I[L\hat{\mathbf{i}}\times(2\hat{\mathbf{i}} + 3\hat{\mathbf{j}} - 4\hat{\mathbf{k}})]$$

$$= I[L(\hat{\mathbf{i}}\times\hat{\mathbf{i}}) + 3L(\hat{\mathbf{i}}\times\hat{\mathbf{j}}) - 4L(\hat{\mathbf{i}}\times\hat{\mathbf{k}})]$$

$$= I[0 + 3L\hat{\mathbf{k}} + 4L\hat{\mathbf{j}}]$$

$$= I[4L\hat{\mathbf{i}} + 3L\hat{\mathbf{k}}]$$

$$\therefore \quad F = |\mathbf{F}| = \sqrt{(4LI)^2 + (3LI)^2} = 5LI$$

47. (b) Given, $\mu = 0.15$

For the given situation,

$$F = ma = \mu mg$$

$$\Rightarrow \quad a = \mu g$$

$$= 0.15\times 10$$

$$= 1.5\ \text{ms}^{-2}$$

48. (c) Radius of innermost orbit of H-atom $\quad r_0 = 5.3\times 10^{-11}$ m

$\therefore$ Radius of third allowed orbit of H-atom,

$$r_3 = r_0 n^2 = r_0(3)^2 = 9r_0$$

$$= 9\times 5.3\times 10^{-11}$$

$$= 47.7\times 10^{-11}$$

$$= 4.77\times 10^{-10}\ \text{m}$$

$$= 4.77\ \text{Å}$$

49. (a) Output of the logic circuit is

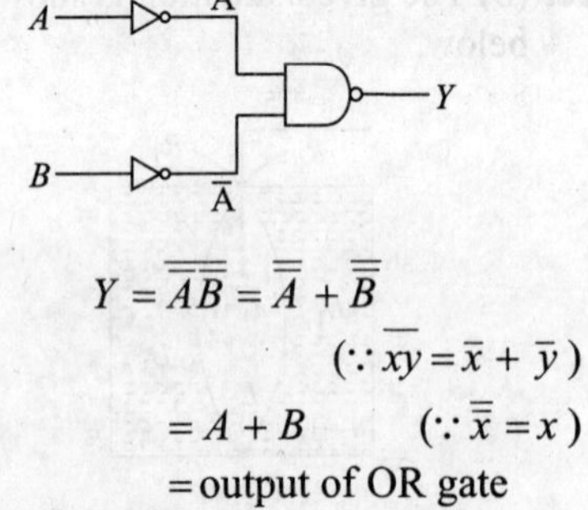

$$Y = \overline{\overline{A}\,\overline{B}} = \overline{\overline{A}} + \overline{\overline{B}}$$

$$(\because \overline{xy} = \overline{x} + \overline{y})$$

$$= A + B \qquad (\because \overline{\overline{x}} = x)$$

= output of OR gate

Truth table is

A	B	$Y = A + B$
0	0	0
0	1	1
1	0	1
1	1	1

50. (b) Maximum height attained by the ball, $h' = \frac{v^2}{2g} = \frac{4^2}{2\times 10} = 0.8$ m

Time of flight from bridge to bridge

$$t_1 = \frac{2v}{g} = \frac{2\times 4}{10} = 0.8\ \text{s}$$

Total time of flight is given as 4 s. Time taken by the ball to reach at the surface of water from highest point,

$$t_2 = 4 - \frac{t_1}{2} = 4 - \frac{0.8}{2} = 3.6\ \text{s}$$

$$\therefore \quad h = 0\times t_2 + \frac{1}{2}gt_2^2$$

$$= 0 + \frac{1}{2}\times 10\times(3.6)^2 = 64.8\ \text{m}$$

$\therefore$ The height of bridge above surface of water

$$= h - h'$$

$$= 64.8 - 0.8 = 64\ \text{m}$$

NC2 NEET Chronicles 2

Section-A

1. (b) The tension in the string will be equal to centripetal force is,

$$F_c = \frac{mv^2}{r} = m\omega^2 r$$

According to question, $T = m\omega^2 r$

and $T' = m(2\omega)^2 r$

$$\frac{T'}{T} = \frac{m(4\omega^2)r}{m\omega^2 r}$$

$\Rightarrow \quad T' = 4T$

2. (d) The direction of motion changes continuously in a circular motion, therefore circular motion is an accelerated motion.

So, uniform circular motion have varying velocity as well as varying acceleration.

3. (c) Output from the truth table

$$Y = \overline{A}\overline{B} + A\overline{B}$$
$$= \overline{B}(A + \overline{A})$$
$$Y = \overline{B}$$

So, correct option is (c).

4. (a) The direction of induced current is always such that it opposes the cause which created it. For solenoid-1, the magnet is moving away. Thus, near the B-point, S-pole will be generated.

Thus, the current in solenoid-1 will be from A to B.

Similarly, the current in the solenoid-2 will be from D to C.

5. (c) We know that, potential at point due to an ideal point at any point on axial line is given

$$V = \pm \frac{1}{4\pi\varepsilon_0} \frac{p}{r^2}$$

Putting the values of p and r, we get

$$V = \pm 9 \times 10^9 \times \frac{4 \times 10^{-6}}{(2)^2}$$

$$= \pm 9 \times 10^3 \text{ V}$$

Hence, A is true but R is false.

6. (a) For a diamagnetic material magnetic susceptibility χ is small and negative, is, $0 > \chi \geq -1$.

For a ferromagnetic material, $\chi >> 1$.

For a paramagnetic material, $0 < \chi < \varepsilon$ (ε is a small positive number) and for non-magnetic material, $\chi = 0$.

Hence, correct option is (a).

7. (d) Given, magnetic field

$B = 0.049$ T

Time period, $T = \frac{5}{20} = \frac{1}{4}$ s

Moment of inertia,

$I = 9.8 \times 10^{-6}$ kg m^2

The time period of oscillation of a magnetic needle in a magnetic field is given by $T = 2\pi\sqrt{\frac{I}{MB}}$

where, M is the magnetic moment of the needle.

Thus, $T = 2\pi\sqrt{\frac{9.8 \times 10^{-6}}{M \times 0.049}}$

$$\Rightarrow \left(\frac{1}{4}\right)^2 = (2\pi)^2\left(\frac{9.8 \times 10^{-6}}{M \times 4.9 \times 10^{-2}}\right)$$

$$\Rightarrow \frac{1}{16} = \frac{4\pi^2 \times 2 \times 10^{-4}}{M}$$

$$\Rightarrow M = 16 \times 8 \times \pi^2 \times 10^{-4}$$

$$= 128\pi^2 \times 10^{-4} \text{ Am}^2$$

$$= 1280\pi^2 \times 10^{-5} \text{ Am}^2$$

8. (b) We know that, transformation ratio, $r = \frac{N_s}{N_p} = \frac{V_s}{V_p}$

$$\because \frac{N_p}{N_s} = \frac{1}{2} = \frac{V_p}{V_s}$$

$$\Rightarrow V_s : V_p = 2:1$$

9. (b) Given, 1 MSD = 0.1 mm

$(N+1)$ VSD $= N$ MSD

$$\therefore \text{ 1 VSD} = \left(\frac{N}{N+1}\right)\text{MSD}$$

Least count or vernier constant,

$$\text{1MSD} - \text{1VSD} = \left[1 - \frac{N}{N+1}\right]\text{MSD}$$

$$= \left(\frac{1}{N+1}\right)\text{MSD} = \left(\frac{0.1}{N+1}\right)\text{mm}$$

$$= \frac{1}{100(N+1)} \text{ cm}$$

10. (c) Net force on A and $B = 10$ N

Acceleration of both A and $B = \frac{F}{m}$

F=10 N → A | B

$$a = \frac{10}{5} = 2 \text{ ms}^{-2}$$

For block A,

F = 10 N → [2 kg] ← F_B ($\vec{a}$)

F_B = force exerted by block B on block A.

$$F - F_B = 2 \times a$$

$$\Rightarrow 10 - F_B = 2 \times 2 \Rightarrow F_B = 6 \text{ N}$$

For block B,

F_A → [3 kg] ($\vec{a}$)

Force exerted by A on B,

$$F_A = 3a = 6 \text{ N}$$

11. (b) Given, $x = 5\sin\left(\pi t + \frac{\pi}{3}\right)$ m ...(i)

The standard Eq. for SHM is

$$x = A\sin(\omega t + \phi) \quad \text{...(ii)}$$

Thus, comparing Eqs. (i) and (ii), we get

$$A = 5 \text{ m and } \omega = \pi$$

$$\Rightarrow \frac{2\pi}{T} = \pi$$

$$\Rightarrow T = 2 \text{ s}$$

Hence, option (b) is correct.

12. c) Given, EMF, $\varepsilon = 10\,V$

Internal resistance, $r = 1\Omega$

Externl resistance, $R = 4\,\Omega$

Terminal voltage, $V = \varepsilon - Ir$

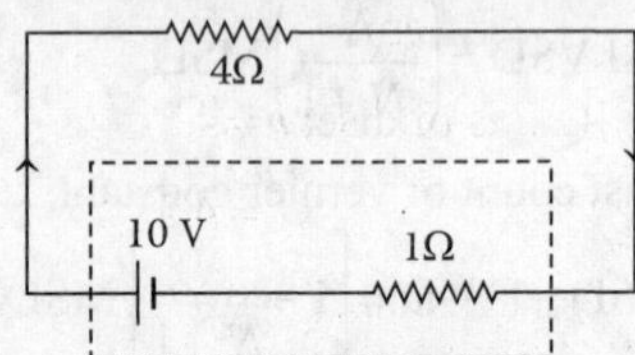

and $I = \dfrac{\varepsilon}{R+r} = \dfrac{10}{4+1} = 2\,A$

Thus, $V = 10 - 2\times 1 = 8\,V$

13. (c) Atoms are electrically neutral as they contain equal number of protons and electrons. Statement II is incorrect because atom of radioactive elements are not stable.

So, option (c) is correct.

14. (b) Photon is quanta of energy. It is a massless and chargeless particle. The rest mass of photon is zero. In free space, it moves with velocity c and energy of photon is equal to hv. The momentum of the photon is given as $p = \dfrac{E}{c} = \dfrac{hv}{c}$.

15. (b) The wavelength of spectral line is given by

$$\frac{1}{\lambda} = R\left[\frac{1}{n_1^2} - \frac{1}{n_2^2}\right]$$

A. $\dfrac{1}{\lambda} = 1.09737\times 10^7\left[\dfrac{1}{2^2} - \dfrac{1}{3^2}\right]$

$= 1.09737\times 10^7\left[\dfrac{1}{4} - \dfrac{1}{9}\right]$

$= 1.09737\times 10^7\left[\dfrac{5}{36}\right]$

$\Rightarrow \lambda = \dfrac{36\times 10^{-7}}{5\times 1.09737}$

$= 6.56114\times 10^{-7}$

$\simeq 656.3\,nm$

B. $\lambda = \dfrac{10^{-7}}{1.09737\left[\dfrac{1}{2^2} - \dfrac{1}{4^2}\right]}$

$= \dfrac{10^{-7}\times 16}{1.09737\times 3}$

$= 4.8601\times 10^{-7}\,m$

$\simeq 486.1\,nm$

C. $\lambda = \dfrac{10^{-7}}{1.09737\times\left[\dfrac{1}{2^2} - \dfrac{1}{5^2}\right]}$

$= \dfrac{10^{-7}\times 100}{1.09737\times 21}$

$= 4.3393\times 10^{-7}\,m$

$\simeq 434.1\,nm$

D. $\lambda = \dfrac{10^{-7}}{1.09737\times\left[\dfrac{1}{2^2} - \dfrac{1}{6^2}\right]}$

$= \dfrac{10^{-7}\times 144}{1.09737\times 32} \simeq 410.2\,nm$

Hence, A - III, B - IV, C - II, D - I

16. (c) Given, number of turns $N = 100$

radius, $r = 10\,cm = 10\times 10^{-2}\,m$

current, $I = 7A$

Magnetic field at the centre of a solenoid,

$B = \dfrac{\mu_0 NI}{2r}$

$= \dfrac{4\pi\times 10^{-7}\times 100\times 7}{2\times 10\times 10^{-2}}$

$= 44\times 10^{-4}$

$= 4.4\times 10^{-3}\,T$

$= 4.4\,mT$

17. (d) The given combination of gates can be taken as

$\overline{A.A} = \overline{A}$

A, B, $Y = \overline{\overline{A}+\overline{B}}$

$\overline{B+B} = \overline{B}$

$Y = \overline{\overline{A}+\overline{B}} = \overline{\overline{A}}\cdot\overline{\overline{B}} = A\cdot B$

Hence, the output Y of the given logic gate is similar to AND gate.

18. (b) Given,

wire of length l is divided into 10 parts

each having $\dfrac{100}{10}\Omega = 10\,\Omega$

resistance.

According to question, 5 parts are connected in series

i.e., $R_1 = 5\times 10 = 50\Omega$

5 parts are connected in parallel

i.e., $R_2 = \dfrac{R}{5} = \dfrac{10}{5} = 2\Omega$

Then, both R_1 and R_2 are connected in series

Thus, $R_{net} = R_1 + R_2$

$= 50 + 2 = 52\Omega$

19. (d) Given,

$${}^{290}_{82}X \xrightarrow{\alpha} Y \xrightarrow{e^+} Z \xrightarrow{\beta^-} P \xrightarrow{e^-} Q$$

From $X \to Y$, α-particle is emitted thus ${}^{286}_{80}Y$.

Now, $Y \to Z$, e^+ is emitted, thus ${}^{286}_{79}Z$.

Again $Z \to P$, β^- is emitted thus ${}^{286}_{80}P$.

Again $P \to Q$, e^- is emitted thus ${}^{286}_{81}Q$.

20. (a) Length of wire $= 1\,m$

Elastic limit, $E = 8\times 10^8\ Nm^{-2}$

Young's modulus $Y = 2\times 10^{11}\ Nm^{-2}$

We know that, $Y = \dfrac{F}{A}\dfrac{l}{\Delta l}$

Here, $\dfrac{F}{A} =$ Elastic limit E

$\Rightarrow \quad Y = E\dfrac{l}{\Delta l}$

$\Rightarrow \quad \Delta l = \dfrac{E}{Y}l$

$\Rightarrow \quad \Delta l = \dfrac{8\times 10^8}{2\times 10^{11}}\times 1 = 4\times 10^{-3}\,m$

$= 4\,mm$

21. (c) When YDSE is performed in white light instead of monochromatic light, all wavelengths shows their maxima and minima in order of their wavelength. Thus, a central bright is observed along with few fringes that will be different colours.

22. (a) Given,

$$x = 2t - 1\,\text{unit}$$

Force, $F = 5\,\text{N}$

Instantaneous power, $P = F.v$

Thus, $P = F\dfrac{dx}{dt}$

$$= 5 \times \frac{d(2t-1)}{dt}$$

$$= 5 \times 2 = 10\,\text{unit}$$

23. (a) A is correct but B is incorrect.

In reverse biased *p-n* junction, the current is due to minority charge carriers, which is very small and hence measured in terms of μA.

24. (b) Let both masses be m

A →v_1 B (Before) AB →v_2 (After)

Thus, applying conservation of momentum, we get

$$m_1u_1 + m_2u_2 = m_1v_1 + m_2v_2$$

Both masses A and B stick together as a system.

So, $mv_1 = 2mv_2$ $\quad [\because u_2 = 0]$

$$v_1 = 2v_2$$

$$\Rightarrow \frac{v_1}{v_2} = \frac{2}{1}$$

Hence, option (b) is correct.

25. (b) Given, the rays in the prism is parallel to base.

$$A = r_1 + r_2$$

i.e., $r_2 = 90 - r_1$ $\quad$ ...(i)

For AB interface, $\sin 30° = \mu \sin r_1$

$$\Rightarrow \sin r_1 = \frac{1}{2\mu} \quad \text{...(ii)}$$

For AC interface,

$$\mu \sin r_2 = 1 \sin 90°$$

$$\Rightarrow \sin r_2 = \frac{1}{\mu}$$

$$\Rightarrow \sin(90 - r_1) = \frac{1}{\mu}$$

$$\cos r_1 = \frac{1}{\mu} \quad \text{...(iii)}$$

We know that, $\sin^2\theta + \cos^2\theta = 1$

From Eqs. (ii) and (iii), we get

$$\sin^2 r_1 + \cos^2 r_1 = 1$$

$$\Rightarrow \left(\frac{1}{2\mu}\right)^2 + \left(\frac{1}{\mu}\right)^2 = 1$$

$$\Rightarrow \frac{1}{4\mu^2} + \frac{1}{\mu^2} = 1$$

$$\Rightarrow \frac{1}{\mu^2}\left(\frac{1}{4} + \frac{1}{1}\right) = 1$$

$$\Rightarrow \mu^2 = \frac{5}{4} \Rightarrow \mu = \frac{\sqrt{5}}{2}$$

26. (d) We know that $\lambda = \dfrac{h}{p} = \dfrac{h}{\sqrt{2mE}}$

Here, E = kinetic energy

Thus, $\lambda^2 = \dfrac{h^2}{2mE} \Rightarrow \dfrac{1}{\lambda^2} = \dfrac{2mE}{h^2}$

$$\propto E$$

Hence, option (d) is correct.

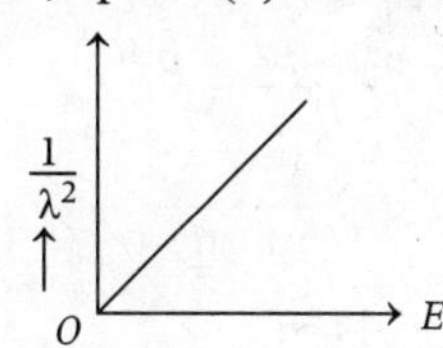

27. (a) Strain and angle are dimensionless quantities as solid angle.

Arc has dimension of length.

Stress has dimension of pressure.

28. (d) At Brewster's angle, the angle between refracted and reflected rays is 90°. The reflected ray is completely linearly polarised and the refracted rays is partially polarised.

29. (a) Given, moment of inertia

$I = 2400\,\text{g cm}^2$

mass of rod, $m = 400\,\text{g}$

We know that moment of inertia of a thin rod,

$$I = \frac{ml^2}{12}$$

$$\Rightarrow \frac{12 \times I}{m} = l^2$$

$$\Rightarrow l^2 = \frac{12 \times 2400}{400}$$

$$\Rightarrow l^2 = 12 \times 6$$

$$\Rightarrow l = \sqrt{72} = 8.48$$

$$\simeq 8.5\,\text{cm}$$

30. (a) Radius of disc, $r = 4.5\,\text{cm}$

$$= 4.5 \times 10^{-2}\,\text{m}$$

Surface tension, $S = 0.07\,\text{Nm}^{-1}$

The force required to take away circular disc from the surface of water,

$$F = S \times 2\pi r$$

$$= 0.07 \times 2 \times 3.14 \times 4.5 \times 10^{-2}$$

$$= 1.9782 \times 10^{-2}\,\text{N} = 19.8\,\text{mN}$$

31. (a) Work done in an isochoric process is always zero.

32. (b) In rolling motion, wheel is rolling with velocity v. All the points move with different velocity as shown

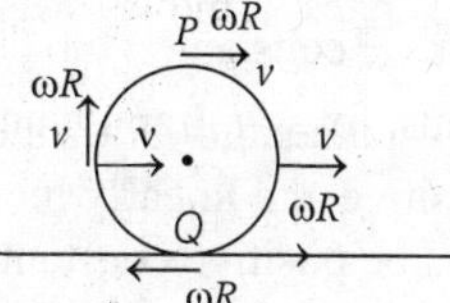

Thus, the velocity of P is greater than velocity at Q.

33. (d) We know that,

$$g = \frac{GM}{R^2}$$

According to question,

$$g = \frac{G\left(\frac{M}{10}\right)}{\left(\frac{R}{2}\right)^2} = \frac{GM \times 4}{R^2 \times 10} = \frac{GM}{R^2} \times \frac{2}{5}$$

Hence, $\dfrac{g'}{g} = \dfrac{\dfrac{GM}{R^2} \times \dfrac{2}{5}}{\dfrac{GM}{R^2}}$

$$\Rightarrow g' = \frac{2}{5} \times g = \frac{2}{5} \times 9.8$$

34. (a) Given combination of capacitors represent Wheatstone bridge, thus central capacitor can be removed.

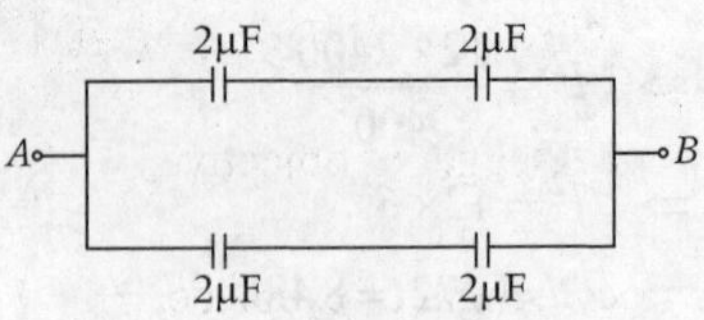

Capacitance of each branch,

$$C = \frac{2}{2} = 1\mu\text{ F}$$

Capacitance between A and B,

$$C_{\text{net}} = 1 + 1 = 2\mu\text{F}$$

35. (d) Since, there is no electric field inside the shell the potential at any point inside the shell is equal to the potential on the surface of the shell is

$$V = \frac{1}{4\pi\varepsilon_0}\frac{q}{r}$$

$$V_C - V_P = 0$$

Section-B

36. (c) We know that

$$a = \frac{dv}{dt}$$

For $v =$ constant, $a = 0$

Thus, for v- t graph when v is positive and linearly increasing a will be positive constant and if v is decreasing linearly a will be negative constant.

Hence, option (c) is correct.

37. (b) Time period of a bob is given by,

$$T = 2\pi\sqrt{\frac{l}{g}}$$

According to question,

$$T' = 2\pi\sqrt{\frac{l}{2g}} = \frac{2\pi\sqrt{l}}{\sqrt{2g}}$$

Thus, $\dfrac{T'}{T} = \dfrac{T}{\sqrt{2}} = \dfrac{x}{2}T$

Hence, $x = \sqrt{2}$

38. (b) Given, $C = 10\mu\text{F} = 10\times 10^{-6}$ F

Potential, $V = 210$ V

Frequency, $f = 50$ Hz

Reactance of circuit,

$$X_C = \frac{1}{\omega C} = \frac{1}{2\pi f C}$$

$$= \frac{1}{2\times 3.14\times 50\times 10\times 10^{-6}}$$

$$= \frac{10^3}{3.14}$$

Peak current, $I_m = \dfrac{V\sqrt{2}}{X_C} = \dfrac{210\times\sqrt{2}}{\frac{10^3}{3.14}}$

$$= \frac{3.14\times 210\times\sqrt{2}}{1000} \simeq 0.93\text{ A}$$

39. (d) Charle's law states that volume of a gas is proportional to its temperature on Kelvin scale at constant pressure.

It is clear for p_1, T is higher.

Thus, $p_1 > p_2 > p_3$.

Alternate Solution

We know that $pV = nRT$

$$\frac{T}{V} = \frac{p}{nR}$$

$$\text{Slope} = \frac{p}{nR}$$

i.e., slope $\propto p$

Hence, $p_1 > p_2 > p_3$

40. (b)

$-m$ [L, M] $+m$ $\frac{l}{2}$ 60° $\frac{l}{2}$ $-m$ $+m$ $\frac{l}{2}$

The magnetic moment is given by

$M = m\cdot L$

New magnetic moment,

$$M' = m\cdot L' = m\cdot\frac{l}{2} = \frac{ml}{2}$$

Thus, $M' = \dfrac{M}{2}$

41. (a) Given altitude, $h = 2R$

From surface, $r_1 = R$

and $r_2 = 2R + R = 3R$

Then, energy required to launch a satellite from orbit r_1 to r_2 is sum of difference in energies in the orbit (ΔE) and energy on the surface of the earth.

$$\Delta E = GMm\left(\frac{1}{r_1} - \frac{1}{r_2}\right)$$

$$= GMm\left(\frac{1}{R} - \frac{1}{3R}\right)$$

$$= \frac{2}{3}\left(\frac{GMm}{R}\right)$$

Energy on surface $= \dfrac{1}{2}mv^2$

$$v^2 = \frac{GM}{r_{\text{orbit}}} = \frac{GM}{3R}$$

$\therefore$ Minimum energy

$$= \Delta E + \frac{GMm}{6R}$$

$$= \frac{2}{3}\left(\frac{GMm}{R}\right) + \left(\frac{GMm}{6R}\right) = \frac{5}{6}\frac{GMm}{R}$$

42. (b) When a capacitor is charged through a battery, its opposite plates are charged to a maximum value. There is displacement current as the capacitor is being charged,

$$I_d = \varepsilon\cdot\frac{d\phi_E}{dt}$$

Due to charging, ϕ_E changes and hence displacement current equal to conduction current arises while charging. When capacitor gets fully charged, the displacement current became zero.

43. (d) Electromagnetic waves are generated by accelerated charged particles.

Hence, option (d) is incorrect.

44. (b) Given,

Young's modulus,

$Y = 0.5\times 10^{11}\text{ Nm}^{-2}$

Coefficient of liner thermal expansion, $\alpha = 10^{-5}\ ^\circ\text{C}^{-1}$

Length, $l = 1$ m

Area of cross-section,

$$A = 10^{-3}\text{ m}^2$$

$$\Delta T = 100^\circ\text{C}$$

We know that, stress $= Y\cdot\dfrac{\Delta l}{l}$

Here, $\Delta l = l\alpha\Delta T$

$$= 1\times 10^{-5}\times 100 = 10^{-3}$$

$$\Rightarrow \quad \frac{F}{A} = Y\cdot\frac{10^{-3}}{1}$$

Compressive force,

$$F = 0.5\times 10^{11}\times 10^{-3}\times 10^{-3}$$

$$= 0.5\times 10^5 = 50\times 10^3\text{ N}$$

45. (a) For a diode to be active it must be forward biased. In option (b) and (d), diode is reverse biased.

Hence, option (b) and (d) cannot achieve bridge balance.

For option (a) :

Balance bridge condition is

$$\frac{10}{15}=\frac{10}{5+r}$$

If $r = 10\Omega$, bridge can be balanced.

For option (c) : $\frac{10}{15}=\frac{10}{5\,||\,r}$

In this case, the resistance of 5Ω branch can only decrease.

∴This circuit can not achieve balance condition.

46. (b) If the sheet is magnetic in nature, then the flux will be linked through the sheet and a small amount of force will be needed to held the sheet. The pole will apply a force on the sheet.

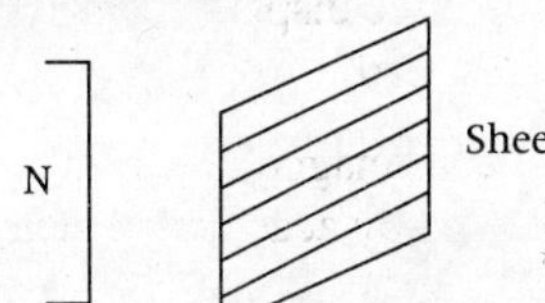

Also, to move the sheet towards or away from the magnetic pole, a force will be required.

If sheet is non-magnetic then no force will be required either to hold it or move it when the sheet is non-conducting.

47. (b) We know that, $C=\frac{\varepsilon_0 A}{d}$

$$E=\frac{1}{2}CV^2$$

and $\quad Q = C.V$

As the distance between the plates decreases capacitance increases, therefore energy increases and also charge stored is increased.

Hence, A, C, and E are correct.

48. (b) Given, $P_1 = 1\text{kW}$

$P_2 = 2\text{kW}$

$P_{\text{Series}}=\frac{P_1P_2}{P_1+P_2}$ and

$P_{\text{Parallel}} = P_1 + P_2$

According to question,

$$\frac{P_{\text{Series}}}{P_{\text{Parallel}}}=\frac{\frac{1\times 2}{1+2}}{1+2}=\frac{2}{3\times 3}=\frac{2}{9}$$

49. (b) Given,

Focal length of objective,

$f_0 = 140\,\text{cm}$

Focal length of eyepiece, $f_e = 5\,\text{cm}$

Magnifying power,

$$M=\left[\frac{f_0}{f_e}\right]=\left[\frac{140}{5}\right]=28$$

50. (b) Given, $F=\alpha t^2+\beta t$

We know that dimensions on the both sides will be the same, i.e.,

$$[\text{F}]=[\alpha t^2]=[\beta t]$$

$\Rightarrow [\alpha][\text{T}^2]=[\text{ML}^1\text{T}^{-2}]$

$\Rightarrow \quad \alpha=[\text{M}^1\text{L}^1\text{T}^{-4}]$

and $[\beta][\text{T}]=[\text{M}^1\text{LT}^{-2}]$

$\Rightarrow \quad \beta=[\text{M}^1\text{L}^1\text{T}^{-3}]$

(a) $\frac{[\beta t]}{[\alpha]}=\frac{[\text{M}^1\text{L}^1\text{T}^{-2}]}{[\text{M}^1\text{L}^1\text{T}^{-4}]}=[\text{T}^{+2}]$

(b) $\frac{[\alpha t]}{[\beta]}=\frac{[\text{M}^1\text{L}^1\text{T}^{-4}][\text{T}]}{[\text{M}^1\text{L}^1\text{T}^{-3}]}$

$$=[\text{M}^0\text{L}^0\text{T}^0]$$

Hence, option (b) is correct.

PHYSICS VOLUME II

MIND MAP

MED+ACE

Test 1

Syllabus

- Conservation of Charge
- Coulomb's Law, Forces between Two Point Charges
- Forces between Multiple Charges
- Superposition Principle

NCERT Page 1 to 9, Page 11 to 12

For deeper insight **Scan the QR Code**

Chapter 01

Electric Charge

Electric charge is an intrinsic property of elementary particles of matter which gives rise to electric force between various objects. It is a scalar quantity. Its SI unit is coulomb (C).

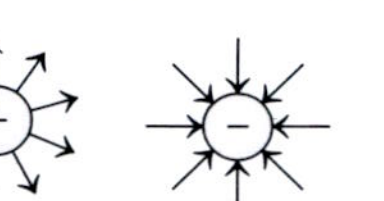

Important Points Regarding Electric Charge

(i) Like charges repel each other and unlike charges attract each other.

(ii) The property which differentiates two kinds of charge is called the **polarity of charge**. If an object possesses an electric charge, then it is said to be **electrified** or **charged**. When its net charge is zero, then it is said to be **neutral (just like neutron).**

(iii) Charge is a scalar quantity as it has magnitude but no direction. It can be of two types as positive and negative. When some electrons are removed from the atom, it acquires a positive charge and when some electrons are added to the atom, it acquires a negative charge.

(iv) Charge can be transferred from one body to another.

(v) Charge is invariant, *i.e.*, it does not depend on the velocity of charged particle.

(vi) A charged particle at rest produces electric field. A charged particle with unaccelerated motion produces both electric and magnetic fields but does not radiate energy. But an accelerated charged particle not only produces an electric and magnetic fields but also radiates energy in the form of electromagnetic waves.

(vii) 1 coulomb $= 3 \times 10^9$ esu $= 1/10$ emu of charge, where esu is electrostatic unit of charge. Its CGS unit is stat coulomb.

(viii) The dimensional formula of charge is $[q] = [AT]$.

(ix) Frankline is the smallest unit of charge. It is also known as esu.
1 Frankline = 1esu = 1/10 emu

(x) Charge is always associated with mass.

Basic Properties of Charge

- **Additivity**
  The total charge of a system is the algebraic sum of all the individual charges located at different points inside the system. If a system contain charges $q_1, q_2, \ldots q_n$, then its total charge is $q = q_1 + q_2 + \ldots + q_n$
- **Quantisation of electric charge**
  The total charge (q) of a body is always an integral multiple of a basic quantum of charge (e), i.e., $\pm q = ne$
  where, $n = 0, \pm 1, \pm 2, \pm 3 \ldots$
- **Conservation of Charge**
  The law of conservation of charge states that
  (i) The total charge of an isolated system remains constant.
  (ii) The electric charge can neither be created nor destroyed, they can only be transferred from one body to another.

Conductors and Insulators

- **Conductors** The substances through which electric charges can flow easily are called conductors.
  Metals, human body and animal bodies, graphite, acids, etc. are examples of conductors.
- **Insulators** The substances through which electric charges cannot flow easily are called insulators. Most of the non-metals like glass, diamond, porcelain, plastic, nylon, wood, mica, etc. are examples of insulators

Relative Permittivity

- **Permittivity** Permittivity is a property of the medium which determines the electric force between two charges situated in that medium.
- **Dielectric constant or relative permittivity**
  It is a measure of how much a material can resist the electric field within it compared to vacuum. It is the ratio of the permittivity of a material ε to the permittivity of free space(vacuum) ε_0.

$$\varepsilon_r = k = \varepsilon/\varepsilon_0$$
$$k_{(air)} = 1.00054$$
$$k_{(vacuum)} = 1$$
$$k_{(water)} = 80$$

Coulomb's Law

If two stationary point charges q_1 and q_2 are kept at a distance r, then force of attraction or repulsion between them is

$$F \propto \frac{q_1 q_2}{r^2} \Rightarrow F = \frac{1}{4\pi\varepsilon_0} \cdot \frac{q_1 q_2}{r^2} \text{ newton}$$

$\mathbf{F}_{12} \leftarrow$ (q_1) - - $q_1q_2>0$, r_{21} - - (q_2) $\rightarrow \mathbf{F}_{21}$

Coulomb's Law in vector Form

Consider two point charges q_1 and q_2 placed in vacuum at a distance r from each other, repel each other.

$\mathbf{F}_{12} \leftarrow +q_1$ - - - r - - - $+q_2 \rightarrow \mathbf{F}_{21}$; $\hat{\mathbf{r}}_{12} \leftarrow$, $\rightarrow \hat{\mathbf{r}}_{21}$

Repulsive Coulombian force for $q_1, q_2 > 0$

In vector form, Coulomb's law may be expressed as

$\mathbf{F}_{12}$ = Force on charge q_1 due to q_2

$$= \frac{1}{4\pi\varepsilon_0} \frac{q_1 q_2}{r^2} \hat{\mathbf{r}}_{12}$$

where, $\hat{\mathbf{r}}_{12} = \frac{\mathbf{r}_{12}}{r}$ is a unit vector in the direction from q_2 to q_1.

Similarly, $\mathbf{F}_{21}$ = Force on charge q_2 due to q_1

$$= \frac{1}{4\pi\varepsilon_0} \frac{q_1 q_2}{r^2} \hat{\mathbf{r}}_{21}$$

where, $\hat{\mathbf{r}}_{21} = \frac{\mathbf{r}_{21}}{r}$ is a unit vector in the direction from q_1 to q_2.

Similar case arises for attraction between two charges.

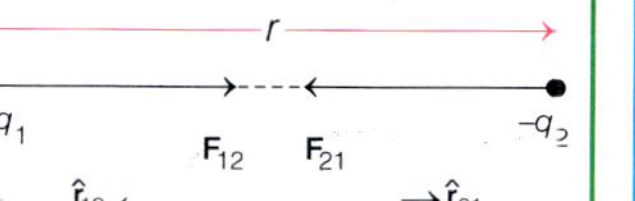

Attractive Coulombian forces for q_1, $q_1 < 0$

The Superposition Principle

When a number of charges are interacting, the total force on a given charge is the vector sum of the force exerted on it due to all other charges. The force between two charges is not affected by the presence of other charge. The total force on charge q_1 is given by

$$\mathbf{F}_1 = \mathbf{F}_{12} + \mathbf{F}_{13} + \ldots + \mathbf{F}_N$$

$$F_1 = \frac{q_1}{4\pi\varepsilon_0}\left[\frac{q_2\hat{\mathbf{r}}_{12}}{r_{12}^2} + \frac{q_3\hat{\mathbf{r}}_{13}}{r_{13}^2} + \ldots\ldots + \frac{q_n\hat{\mathbf{r}}_{1n}}{r_{1n}^2}\right]$$

$$= \frac{q_1}{4\pi\varepsilon_0} \sum_{i=2}^{n} \frac{q_i \hat{\mathbf{r}}_{1i}}{r_{1i}^2}$$

Force between the charge $q_1, q_2, q_3, \ldots\ldots q_n$

Important Points Related to Coulomb's Law

Important points related to Coulomb's law are given below

(i) The electric force is an action reaction pair, i.e the two charges exert equal and opposite forces on each other. Thus, Coulomb's law obeys Newton's third law.

$$\mathbf{F}_{12} = -\mathbf{F}_{21}$$

(ii) The electric force is conservative in nature.

(iii) Coulomb's law as we have stated above can be used for point charges in vacuum. When a dielectric medium is completely filled in between charges, rearrangement of the charges inside the dielectric medium takes place and the force between the same two charges decreases by a factor of k(dielectric constant).

$$F'_e = \frac{F_e}{K} = \frac{1}{4\pi\varepsilon_0 K} \cdot \frac{q_1 q_2}{r^2}$$
$$= \frac{1}{4\pi\varepsilon} \cdot \frac{q_1 q_2}{r^2} \text{ (in medium)}$$

Here, $\varepsilon = \varepsilon_0 K$ is called **permittivity of the medium.** For vacuum $K = 1$, for metal $K = \infty$.

(iv) The electric force is much stronger than gravitational force, $F_e >> F_g$.
As value of $1/4\pi\varepsilon_0 = 9 \times 10^9$ N-m²/C², which is much more than the value of gravitational constant,
$G = 6.67 \times 10^{-11}$ N-m²kg⁻²

Applications of Electric Force (Coulomb's Law)

Two identical charged balls are suspended from same point

The balls repel and come into equilibrium at separation r. The ball is in equilibrium under the following forces :

(i) Weight of the ball,

$$w = mg$$

(ii) Electric force,

$$F_e = \frac{1}{4\pi\varepsilon_0} \frac{q \cdot q}{r^2} = \frac{q^2}{4\pi\varepsilon_0 r^2}$$

(iii) Tension in the string

FBD of right ball

$$T = \sqrt{(T\sin\theta)^2 + (T\cos\theta)^2}$$
$$= \sqrt{F_e^2 + (mg)^2}$$

From geometry of the figure,

$$\tan\theta = \frac{r/2}{\sqrt{L^2 - \frac{r^2}{4}}}$$

Formation of a triangle through $r/2$ and L

If θ is small,

$$\tan\theta \cong \sin\theta = \frac{r/2}{L}$$

Test 2

Syllabus

- Electric Field due to a Point Charge, Electric Field Lines
- Continuous Charges Distribution
- Electric Dipoles and Electric Field due to a Dipole
- Torque on a Dipole in a Uniform Electric Field

NCERT
Page 14,15
Page 19 to 21
Page 23 to 29

For deeper insight **Scan the QR Code**

Chapter 01

Electric Field

The electric field intensity at any point is defined as the force experienced by a unit positive charge placed at that point.

$$E = \frac{F}{q_o} = \frac{kq}{r^2}$$

SI unit $= \frac{\text{newton}}{\text{coulomb}} = \frac{\text{volt}}{\text{metre}}$

Dimension : $[E] = [MLT^{-3} A^{-1}]$

Basic Characteristics

- Fields lines start from positive charge and end at negative charges.
- Electrostatic fields lines do not form any closed loops.
- Two fields lines can never cross each other.

Electric Field Lines

An electric field line is an imaginary line or curve drawn through a region of space, so that its tangent at any point is in the direction of the electric field vector at that point.

- **Properties of electric field lines**

(i) The tangent to a field line at any point gives the direction of **E** at that point.

Electric field points P and Q

(ii) Electric field lines always begin from a positive charge and end on a negative charge and do not start or stop in mid-space.

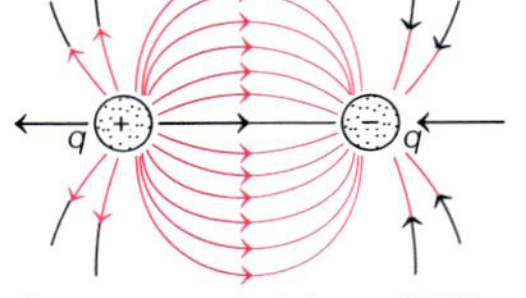

(iv) Two lines can never intersect. If it happens, then two tangents can be drawn at their point of intersection, i.e. intensity at that point will have two directions which is not possible.

(v) In a uniform field, the field lines are straight, parallel and uniformly spaced.

(vi) The electric field lines can never form closed loops as a field line can never start and end on the same charge.

Line Charge Distribution

The line charge density at any point on this line as the charge per unit length of the line at that point,

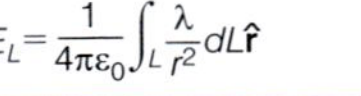

i.e., $\lambda = \frac{dq}{dL}$

The SI unit for λ is Cm^{-1}.

Electric field due to the line charge distribution at the location of charge q_0 is

$$E_L = \frac{1}{4\pi\varepsilon_0}\int_L \frac{\lambda}{r^2} dL\hat{r}$$

Surface Charge Density

It is a charge distribution spread over a two-dimensional surface S in space, as shown in figure. We define the surface charge density at any point on this surface as the charge per unit area at that point, i.e.

$dq = \sigma dS$

$$\sigma = \frac{dq}{dS}$$

The SI unit for σ is Cm^{-2}.

Electric field due to the surface charge distribution at the location of charge q_0 is

$$E_S = \frac{1}{4\pi\varepsilon_0}\int_S \frac{\sigma}{r^2} dS\hat{r}$$

Volume Charge Distribution

It is a charge distribution spread over a three dimensional volume or region V of space as shown in figure. We define the volume charge density at any point in this volume as the charge contained per unit volume at that point, i.e. $\rho = \frac{dq}{dV}$

$dq = \rho dV$

The SI unit for ρ is coulomb per cubic metre (Cm^{-3}).

Electric field due to the volume charge distribution at the location of charge q_0 is

$$E_V = \frac{1}{4\pi\varepsilon_0}\int_V \frac{\rho}{r^2} dV\hat{r}$$

Electric Field of a Charged Ring

Electric field at a distance x from the centre of uniformly charged ring of total charge q on its axis is given by $E_x = \left(\frac{1}{4\pi\varepsilon_0}\right)\frac{qx}{(x^2+R^2)^{3/2}}$

Direction of this electric field is along the axis and away from the ring in case of positively charged ring and towards the ring in case of negatively charged ring.

Electric field of positively and negatively charged rings

Special Cases

From the above expression, we can see that

(i) $E_x = 0$ at $x = 0$, i.e. field is zero at the centre of the ring.

(ii) $E_x = \frac{1}{4\pi\varepsilon_0}\cdot\frac{q}{x^2}$ for $x >> R$ i.e. when the point P is much farther from the ring, its field is the same as that of a point charge.

(iii) E_x will be maximum, where $dE_x/dx = 0$. Differentiating E_x with respect to x and putting it equal to zero, we get $x = \pm\frac{R}{\sqrt{2}}$ and E_{max} comes out to be, $\frac{2}{3\sqrt{3}}\left(\frac{1}{4\pi\varepsilon_0}\frac{q}{R^2}\right)$

Graph between Electric Field and Distance from Centre (x) for Uniformly Charged Ring

$E_{max} = \frac{2}{3\sqrt{3}}\left(\frac{1}{4\pi\varepsilon_0}\cdot\frac{Q}{R^2}\right)$, $x_m = \frac{R}{\sqrt{2}}$

Electric field at the centre of uniformly charged arc An arc of radius R is charged uniformly with linear charge density of λ and angle subtended at centre is α Electric field at centre of this arc is as

$$E = \frac{2k\lambda}{R}\left(\sin\frac{\alpha}{2}\right)$$

If charge on arc is Q, then $Q = \lambda R\alpha$, $\lambda = Q/R\alpha$

$\lambda = \frac{Q}{R\alpha}$ (α in radian) and $E = \frac{2kQ}{R^2\alpha}\left(\sin\frac{\alpha}{2}\right)$

Electric Dipole

Every dipole is associate with a dipole moment **p** whose magnitude is equal to the product of the magnitude of either charge (q) and the distance $2a$ between the charges, i.e., $\mathbf{p} = q \times (2a)$

Axial Point

Electric field at any axial point of the dipole acts along the dipole axis from negative to positive charge i.e., in the direction of dipole moment **p**.

$$\mathbf{E}_{axial} = \frac{1}{4\pi\varepsilon_0}\cdot\frac{2p}{r^3}\cdot\mathbf{p}$$

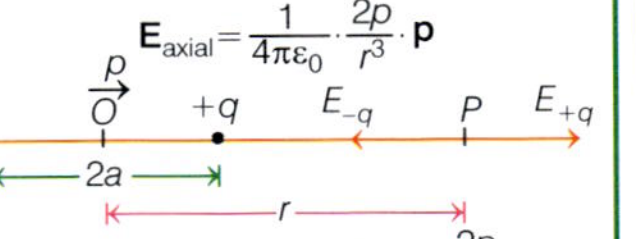

For short dipole, $r >> a$, $\mathbf{E} = -\frac{2p}{4\pi\varepsilon_0 r^3}$

Direction **E** is same as **p**

Equatorial Point

The direction of electric field at any point on the equatorial line will be anti-parallel to the dipole moment **p.**

$$\mathbf{E}_{eq} = -\frac{1}{4\pi\varepsilon_0}\cdot\frac{p}{r^3}\hat{\mathbf{p}}$$

Electric Field at the Position (r,θ)

Due to the positive charge of the dipole, electric field at point P will be in radially outward direction and due to the negative charge it will be radially inward.

Now, we have considered the radial component E_r and transverse component of the net electric field E as shown in figure.

$$E_r = \frac{1}{4\pi\varepsilon_0}\cdot\frac{2p\cos\theta}{r^3}\quad E_\theta = \frac{1}{4\pi\varepsilon_0}\cdot\frac{p\sin\theta}{r^3}$$

$\therefore$ Net electric field at P is $E = \sqrt{E_r^2 + E_\theta^2}$

$$\Rightarrow \mathbf{E} = \frac{1}{4\pi\varepsilon_0}\frac{p}{r^3}\sqrt{1+3\cos^2\theta}$$

Direction of the electric field,

$$\tan\alpha = \frac{E_\theta}{E_r} = \frac{1}{2}\tan\theta$$

Force on Dipole

For an electric dipole of dipole moment $\mathbf{p} = 2aq$ is placed in an uniform electric field **E** at an angle θ, where θ is the angle between **p** and **E.** A force $\mathbf{F}_1 = q\mathbf{E}$ will act on positive charge and $\mathbf{F}_2 = -q\mathbf{E}$ on negative charge. Since, $\mathbf{F}_1$ and $\mathbf{F}_2$ are equal in magnitude but opposite in direction.

Electric dipole in a uniform electric field

Hence, $\mathbf{F}_1 + \mathbf{F}_2 = 0$ or $\mathbf{F}_{net} = 0$

Thus, net force on a dipole in uniform electric field is zero. While in a non-uniform electric field, it may or may not be zero.

Torque

- **Uniform Electric Field**

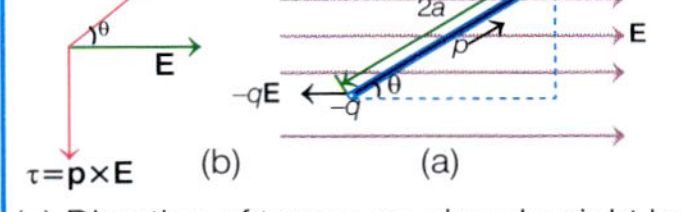

$\tau = \mathbf{p}\times\mathbf{E}$ (b)

(a) Direction of torque as given by right hand screw rule. The torque on the dipole will be maximum when the dipole is held perpendicular to **E**.

Thus, $\tau_{max} = pE \sin 90° = pE$

The direction of torque is perpendicular to the plane of paper inwards. Further this torque is zero at $\theta = 0°$ or, $\theta = 180°$ i.e. when the dipole is parallel or anti-parallel to **E** and maximum at $\theta = 90°$. Thus, variation of τ with θ is as shown in graph below.

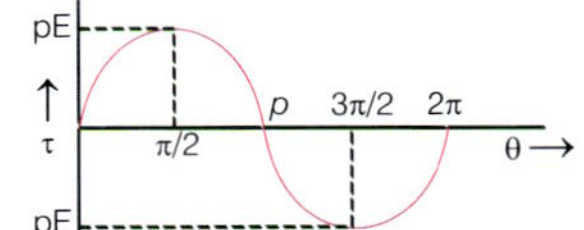

variation of τ with θ

- **Non-Uniform Electric Field**

In a non-uniform electric field, the $+q$ and $-q$ charges of a dipole experience different forces (not equal and opposite) at slightly different positions in the field and hence, a net force acts on the dipole in a non-uniform field. Also, a net torque acts on the dipole which depends on the location of the dipole in the non-uniform field. $\tau = \mathbf{p}\times\mathbf{E}(\mathbf{r})$

Test 3

Syllabus

- Electric Flux
- Gauss's Law and Its Application to Find Electric Field due to Infinitely Long Uniformly Charged Straight Wire
- Uniformly Charged Infinite Plane Sheet and Thin Spherical Shell

NCERT Page 21 to 23, Page 29 to 36

For deeper insight **Scan the QR Code**

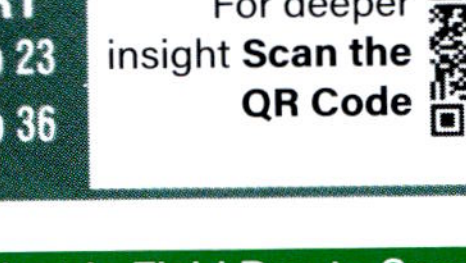

Chapter 01

Electric Flux

The total number of electric lines of force passing normally through that area.

If an electric field **E** passes normally through an area element ΔS, then the electric flux through this area is $\Delta\phi_E = E\Delta S$. The flux is a scalar quantity having SI unit V-m or Nm^2C^{-1}.

Area Vector

Area vector is a vector quantity. The direction of a planar area vector is specified by normal to the plane, e.g. in case of closed surface like cube, sphere, etc., direction of area vector in outward direction is considered to be positive. In case of open surface, any normal direction can be considered positive

(a) Closed surface (b) Open surface

Direction of area vector.

The flux of electric field passing through an area is the dot product of electric field vector and area vector.

i.e. $\phi = \mathbf{E}\cdot\mathbf{S} = ES\cos\theta$

It is scalar physical quantity with units (volt × m) and dimensions

$$[\phi_E] = [\mathbf{E}d\mathbf{A}] = \left[\frac{\mathbf{F}}{q}d\mathbf{A}\right] = \left[\frac{MLT^{-2}}{AT}L^2\right] = [ML^3T^{-3}A^{-1}]$$

Gauss's Law

According to this law, the total flux linked with a closed surface is $\frac{1}{\varepsilon_0}$ times the charge enclosed by the surface (gaussian surface).

Mathematically

$$[\phi_E] = \oint[\mathbf{E}\cdot d\mathbf{S}] = \frac{q_{enclosed}}{\varepsilon_0}$$

Important Points Regarding Gauss' Law

(i) Flux through a closed surface is independent of its shape, size and position of charge inside it.

(ii) Electric field intensity at any gaussian surface depends on all charges in and around it.

(iii) If $E = 0$, then $\phi_E = 0$ but if $\phi = 0$, then E may or may not be zero.

Electric flux Calculation of Some Specific Structure

Using, $\phi_E = \int E\cdot ds$ and $\phi_E = \frac{q_{enclosed}}{\varepsilon_o}$

- **Cylinder in uniform E**

$\phi_{in} = \pi R^2E$ and $\phi_{Out} = -\pi R^2E$ $\Rightarrow \phi_{total} = 0$

- **Hemisphere in uniform E**

$\phi_{in} = \phi_{circular} = -\pi R^2E$, $\phi_{Out} = \phi_{curved} = \pi R^2E$ $\Rightarrow \phi_{total} = 0$

- **Cube in uniform E**

$\phi_{in} = -a^2E$ and $\phi_{out} = a^2E$ $\Rightarrow \phi_{total} = 0$

- **Charge q in a hemisphere**

Electrical field is radial

$\phi_{total} = \frac{q}{2\varepsilon_0}$

- **Charge placed at the centre of the cube**

$\phi_{total} = \frac{q}{\varepsilon_0}$

- **Charge placed at the face centre of cube**

$\phi_{one\ side} = \frac{q}{6\varepsilon_0}$

- **Charge placed at the centre of face of the cube**

$\phi_{cube} = \frac{q}{2\varepsilon_0}$

Electric Field Due to Special Charge Distribution

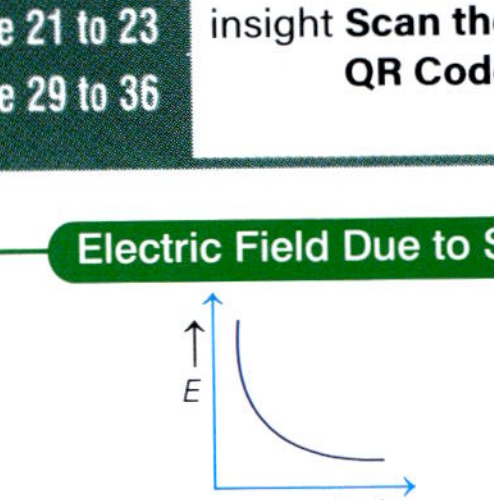

- **Point charge**

$E = \frac{kq}{r^2}$

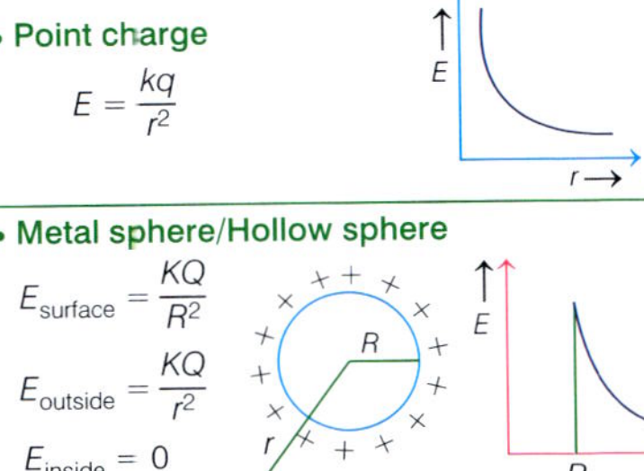

- **Metal sphere/Hollow sphere**

$E_{surface} = \frac{KQ}{R^2}$

$E_{outside} = \frac{KQ}{r^2}$

$E_{inside} = 0$

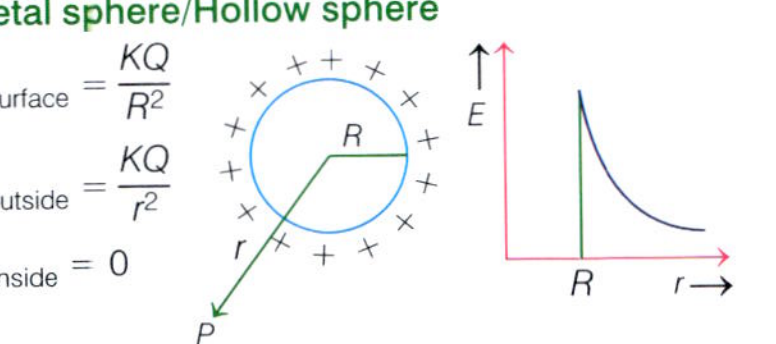
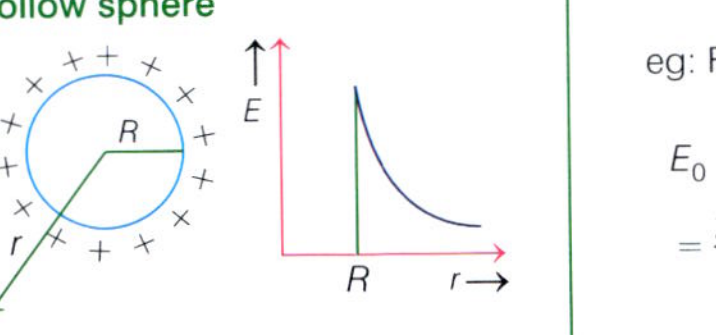
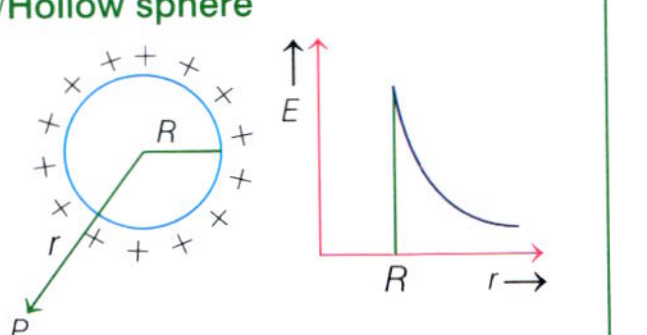
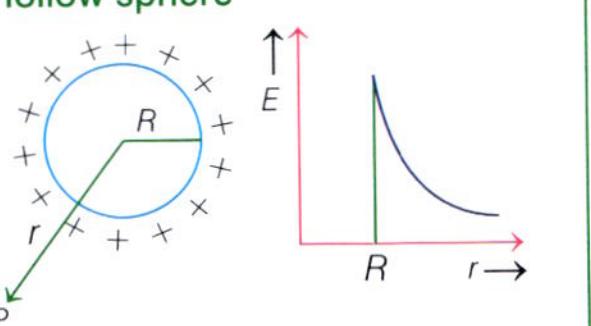
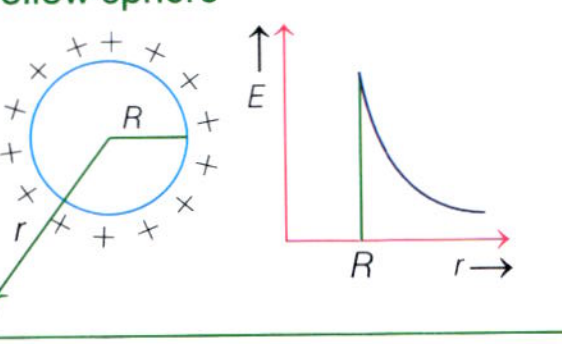
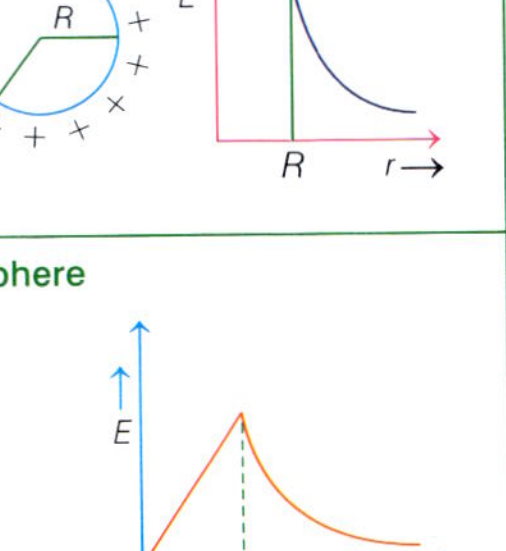

- **Non-Conducting sphere**

$E_{inside} = \frac{KQr}{R^3}$

$E_{surface} = \frac{KQ}{R^2}$

$E_{outside} = \frac{KQ}{r^2}$

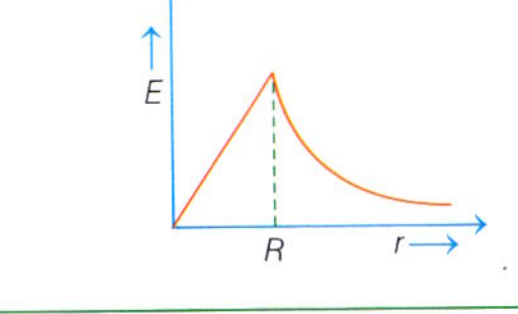

- **Conducting sheet**

$E = \frac{\sigma}{\varepsilon_0}$

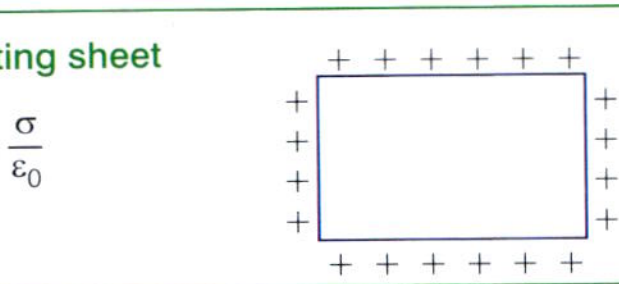

- **Non-conducting sheet**

$E = \frac{\sigma}{2\varepsilon_0}$

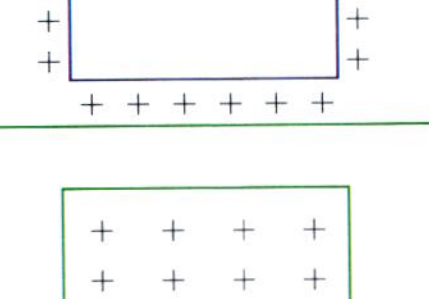
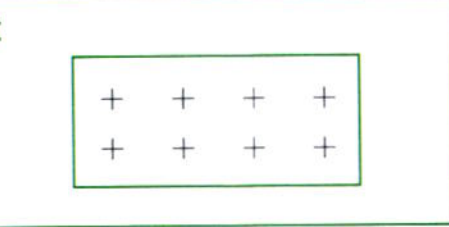

- **Electric field due to a finite linear charge distribution**

$E = \frac{2k\lambda}{r}\sin(\theta/2)$

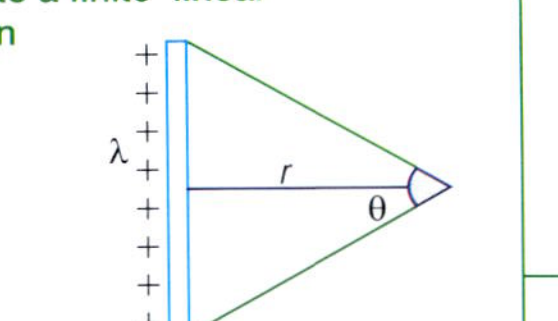
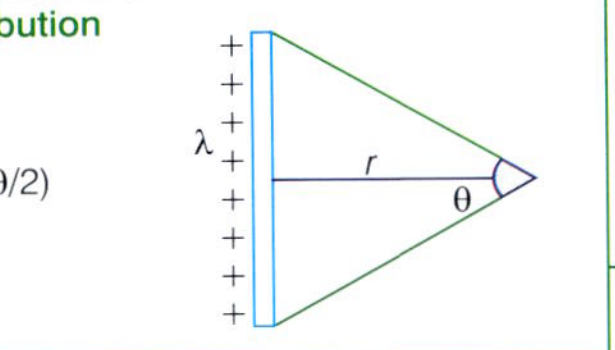
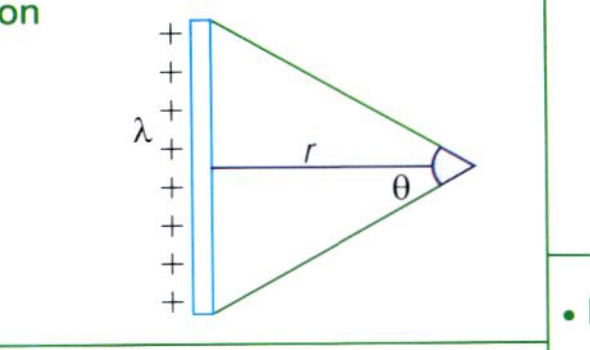

- **Electric field due to a charge disc**

$E_p = \frac{\sigma}{2\varepsilon_0}\left(1 - \frac{r}{\sqrt{R^2+r^2}}\right)$

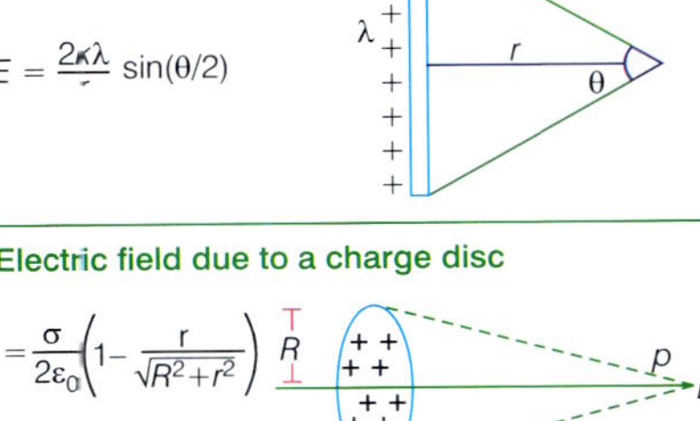
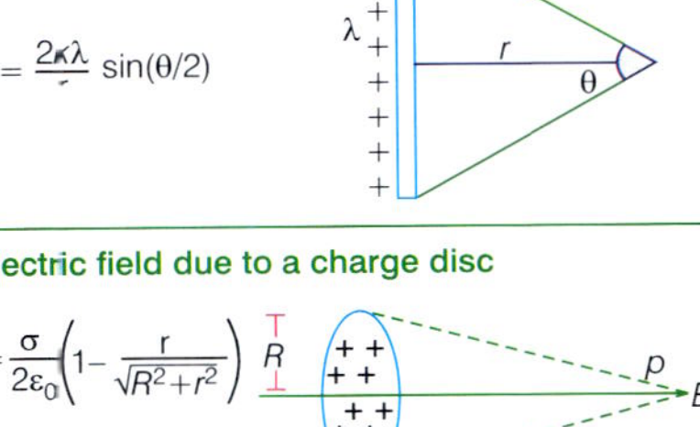
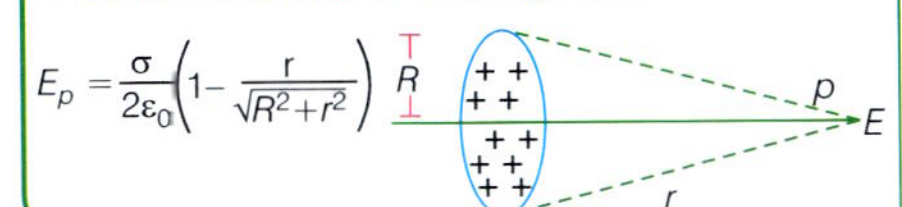
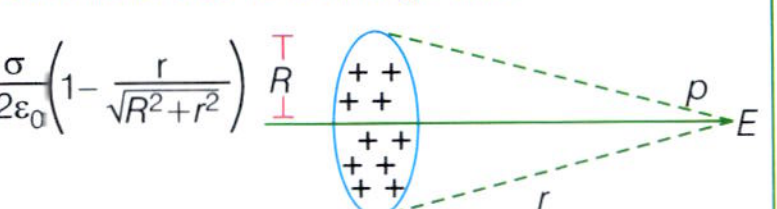

- **Electric field due to circular arc at its enter**

$E = \frac{2k\lambda}{r}\sin(\theta/2)$

eg: For a semicircle $\theta = 180°$

$E_0 = \frac{2k\lambda}{r}\sin(180/2) = \frac{2k\lambda}{r}$

- **Electric field due to a infinite linear charge distribution**

$E = \frac{2k\lambda}{r}$

- **Electric field due to a circular ring of charge**

$E = \frac{1}{4\pi\varepsilon_0}\frac{qx}{(x^2+r)^{3/2}}$

$E = \frac{1}{4\pi\varepsilon_0}\frac{q}{x^2}$ (if x>>r)

- **If a charge q is placed at a corner of cube**

$\phi_{cube} = \frac{q}{8\varepsilon_0}$

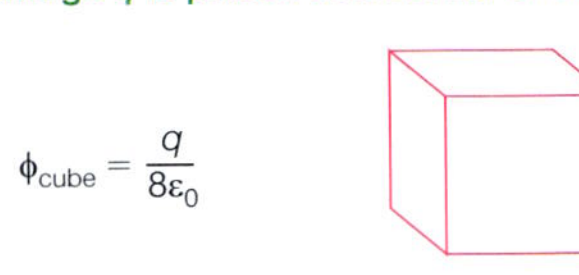
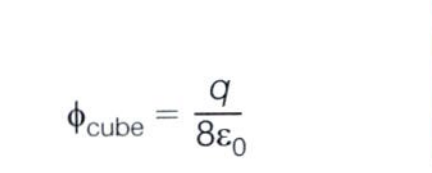

Test 1

Syllabus

- Electric Potential and its Calculation for a Point Charge
- Electric Dipole and System of Charge
- Potential Difference, Equipotential Surface

NCERT Page 45 to 55

For deeper insight **Scan the QR Code**

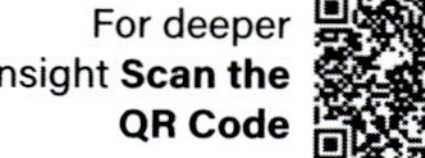

Chapter 02

Electric Potential

The electric potential at any point in the region of electric field is defined as the amount of work done in bringing a unit positive test charge from infinity to that point along any arbitrary path. It is a scalar quantity and is denoted by V.

Electric potential $(V) = \frac{\text{Work done}(W)}{\text{Charge}(q)}$

Its SI unit is volt (V).

$$1 \text{ volt} = \frac{1 \text{ joule}}{1 \text{ coulomb}}$$

Its dimensional formula is $[ML^2T^{-3}A^{-1}]$.

Potential Difference

Source charge $+q$ O — B — A Test charge $+q_0$

Potential difference between points A and B, $V = V_B - V_A = \frac{W_{AB}}{q_0}$

The SI unit of potential difference is volt (V).

Potential Due to a Point Charge

Electric potential due to a point charge at point P.

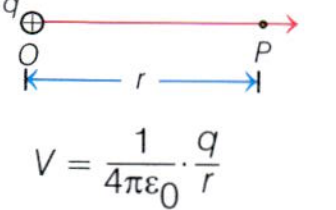

$$V = \frac{1}{4\pi\varepsilon_0} \cdot \frac{q}{r}$$

- Variation of potential with distance is shown in graph

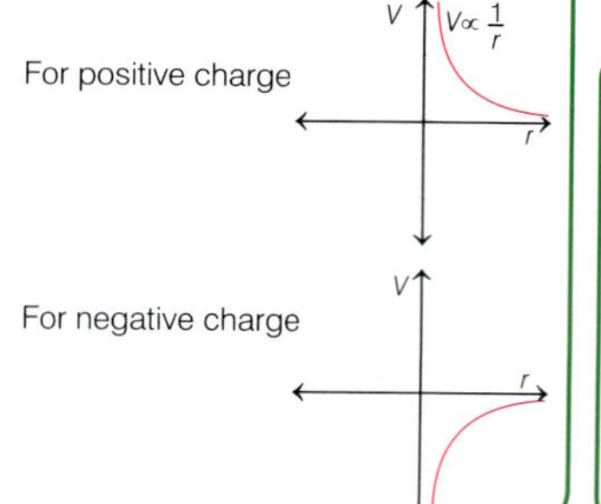

Potential Due to a System of Charges

Potential at a point due to a system of N point charges.

$$V = \frac{1}{4\pi\varepsilon_0} \sum_{i=1}^{N} \frac{q_i}{r_i}$$

The electric potential at a point whose position vector is **r**, would be

$$V = \frac{1}{4\pi\varepsilon_0} \sum_{i=1}^{N} \frac{q_i}{|\mathbf{r} - \mathbf{r}_i|}$$

Potential Due to an Axial Point

Potential at an axial point of a dipole.

$$V = \frac{1}{4\pi\varepsilon_0} \cdot \frac{p}{r^2} \quad (\text{for } a^2 << r^2)$$

Potential Due to an Equatorial Point

Electric potential at equatorial point P due to the dipole,

$$V = V_1 + V_2 = \frac{1}{4\pi\varepsilon_0} \cdot \frac{-q}{AP} + \frac{1}{4\pi\varepsilon_0} \cdot \frac{q}{BP}$$

$$= -\frac{1}{4\pi\varepsilon_0} \cdot \frac{q}{\sqrt{r^2 + a^2}} + \frac{1}{4\pi\varepsilon_0} \cdot \frac{q}{\sqrt{r^2 + a^2}} = 0$$

Potential Due to an any General Point

$$V = \frac{1}{4\pi\varepsilon_0} \cdot \frac{p\cos\theta}{r^2}$$

$$V = \frac{1}{4\pi\varepsilon_0} \frac{\mathbf{p} \cdot \mathbf{r}}{r^3} = \frac{1}{4\pi\varepsilon_0} \frac{\mathbf{p} \cdot \hat{\mathbf{r}}}{r^2}$$

Here, $p = q \times 2a$, is the dipole moment and $\hat{\mathbf{r}} = \mathbf{r}/r$, is a unit vector along the positive vector $\mathbf{OP} = \mathbf{r}$

Uniformly Charged Thin Spherical Shell

Consider a uniformly charged spherical shell of radius R and carrying charge q.

(i) When the point P lies outside the shell,

$$V = \frac{1}{4\pi\varepsilon_0} \frac{q}{r} \quad [r > R]$$

(ii) When point P lies on the surface of the shell,

$$V = \frac{1}{4\pi\varepsilon_0} \frac{q}{R} \quad [r = R]$$

(iii) When point P lies inside the shell,

$$V = \frac{1}{4\pi\varepsilon_0} \frac{q}{R} \quad [r < R]$$

Electric Potential Due to Uniformly Charged Disc

$$V = \frac{1}{4\pi\varepsilon_0} \left[\sqrt{R^2 + x^2} - x\right]$$

Potential at the centre, $x = 0$

$\Rightarrow V = 2\pi K\sigma R$

$= \frac{\sigma R}{2\varepsilon_0}$

Electric Potential Due to Uniformly Charged Ring

Potential at point P, $V = \frac{1}{4\pi\varepsilon_0} \frac{q}{\sqrt{R^2 + x^2}}$

Potential at the centre, $x = 0$

$\Rightarrow V = \frac{1}{4\pi\varepsilon_0} \frac{q}{R}$

Potential Due to Uniformly Charged Long Wire

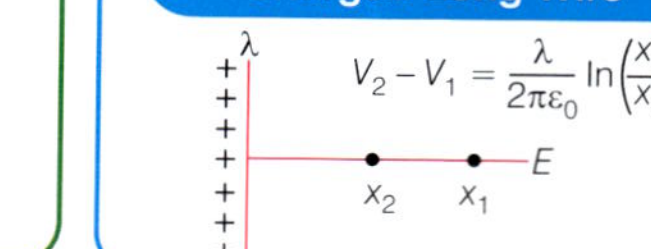

$$V_2 - V_1 = \frac{\lambda}{2\pi\varepsilon_0} \ln\left(\frac{x_1}{x_2}\right)$$

Electric Potential due to Concentric Shells

For two concentric conducting shells of radii r_1 and r_2 ($r_2 > r_1$) carrying uniformly distributed charges Q_1 and Q_2 respectively. Potential at the surface of each shell is

Potential on inner shell, $V_1 = \frac{Q_1}{4\pi\varepsilon_0 r_1} + \frac{Q_2}{4\pi\varepsilon_0 r_2}$

Potential on outer shell, $V_2 = \frac{Q_1}{4\pi\varepsilon_0 r_2} + \frac{Q_2}{4\pi\varepsilon_0 r_2}$

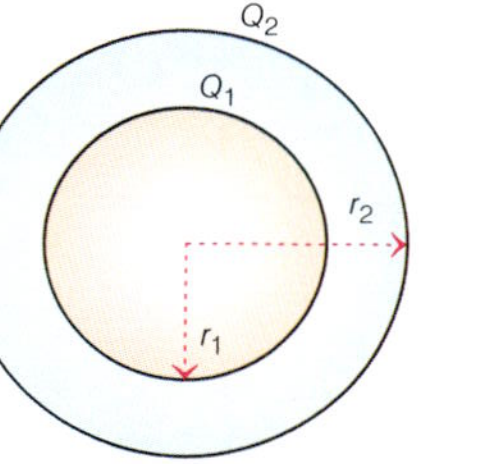

Electric Field and Potential

$$E = \frac{-dV}{dr} \quad E_x = \frac{-\partial V}{\partial x}$$

$$E_y = \frac{-\partial V}{\partial y} \quad E_z = \frac{-\partial V}{\partial z}, \quad \Delta V = -\int \mathbf{E} \cdot d\mathbf{r}$$

The variation of electric potential (V) and electric field (E) with distance (r) for a point charge is given below.

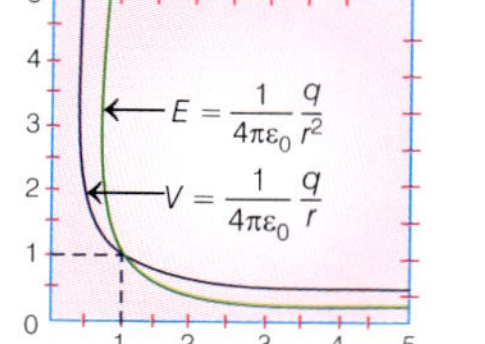

Charge Under Electric Field

If a charge moves under only the effect of electric field, then ΔKE = Work done by electric force. If a charged particle accelerates by a potential difference ΔV, then

$$q\Delta V = \frac{1}{2} mv^2$$

Equipotential Surface and their Properties

Any surface that has same electric potential at every point on it, is called an equipotential surface.

Properties

(i) No work is done in moving a test charge on an equipotential surface.

(ii) Electric field is always normal to the equipotential surface at every point.

(iii) Equipotential surfaces are closer together in the regions of strong field and farther apart in the regions of weak field.

(iv) No two equipotential surfaces can intersect each other.

Equipotential Surface of Various Charge Systems

(i) Equipotential surfaces of a positive point charge.

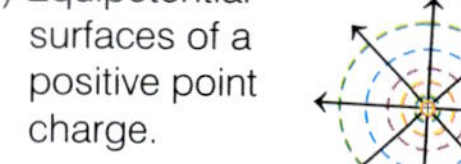

(ii) Equipotential surfaces of two equal and opposite point charges.

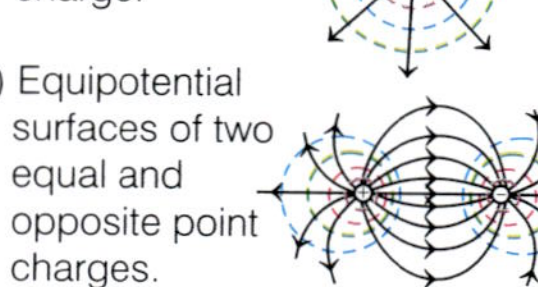

(iii) Equipotential surfaces of two equal positive charges.

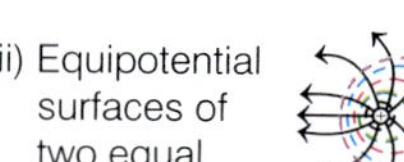

(iv) The electric lines of force are parallel straight lines and equipotential surfaces are equidistant parallel planes perpendicular to the electric field lines.

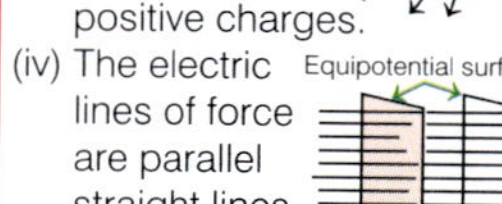

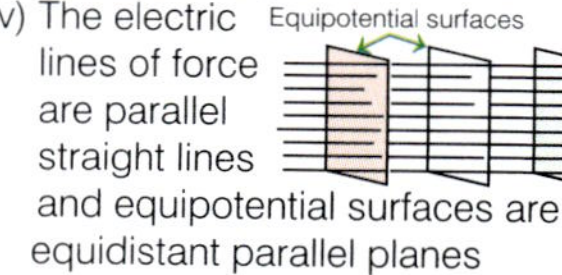

Test 2

Syllabus

- Electrical Potential Energy of a System of two Point Charges
- Electric Dipole in an Electrostatic Fields

NCERT Page 55 to 61

For deeper insight **Scan the QR Code**

Chapter 02

Electric Potential Energy

The electrostatic potential energy of a system of point charges is the work needed to bring the charges from an infinite separation to their final positions.

It represented by U.

It is defined only in a conservative field.

Potential Energy of Two Point Charges in an External Field

$$U = q_1V_A + q_2V_B + \frac{1}{4\pi\varepsilon_0}\frac{q_1q_2}{r}$$

where, V_A and V_B are electric potentials at point A and B respectively.

Potential Energy of a System of Charges

Electrostatic potential energy of a system of two point charges is given by

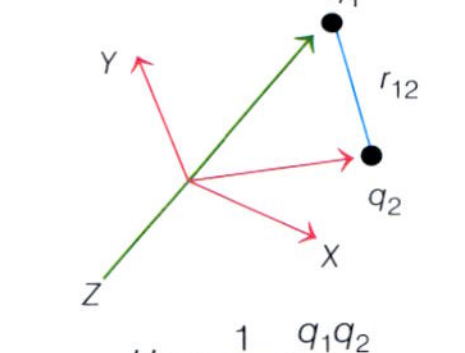

$$U = \frac{1}{4\pi\varepsilon_0}\cdot\frac{q_1q_2}{r_{12}}$$

The potential energy of the system of three charges is given by

$$U = \frac{1}{4\pi\varepsilon_0}\left(\frac{q_1q_2}{r_{12}} + \frac{q_1q_3}{r_{13}} + \frac{q_2q_3}{r_{23}}\right)$$

Potential energy for a system of n point charges is given by

$$U = \frac{1}{2}\frac{1}{4\pi\varepsilon_0}\sum_{i=1}^{n}\left[\sum_{j=1}^{n}\frac{q_iq_j}{r_{ij}}\right]$$

Relation between Work and Energy

If a force **F** is conservative, the work done by **F** can always be expressed in terms of a potential energy U.

When a charge particle moves from a point, where the potential energy is U_a to a point where it is U_b, the change in potential energy is $\Delta U = U_b - U_a$.

This is related by the work $W_{a\to b}$ as

$$W_{a\to b} = U_a - U_b = -(U_b - U_a) = -\Delta U$$

Here, $W_{a\to b}$ is the work done in displacing the charge particle from a to b by the conservative force.

Electron Volt

One electron volt (1 eV) is the energy equal to the work done in moving a single elementary charge particle, such as the electron or the proton through a potential difference of exactly one volt (1 V).

$1\text{ eV} = e\,(1\text{V}) = (1.6\times10^{-19}\text{ C})\,(1\text{V})$
$= (1.6\times10^{-19}\text{ C})\,(\text{J})$

Work done in Uniform Electric Field

Let's look at the electric potential energy when we move a charge q by a distance d in a constant electric field.

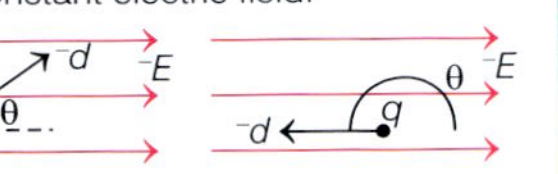

The definition of work is $W = F\times d$

For a constant electric field the force is $F = q\mathbf{E}$

So, the work done by the electric field on the charge is $W = q\mathbf{E}\times d = qEd\cos\theta$

Note, θ = angle between **E** and **d**

Work Done in Rearrangement of the System

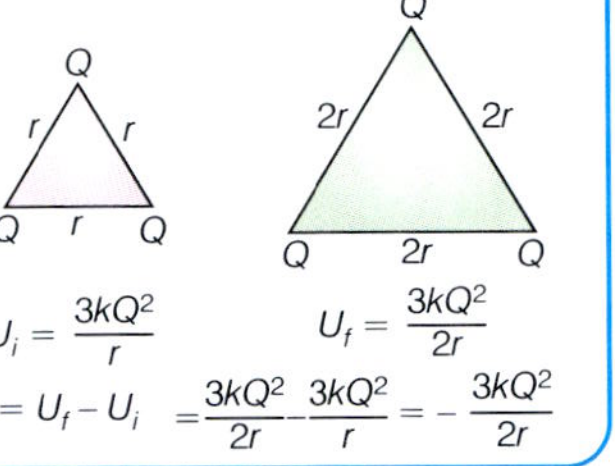

$U_i = \frac{3kQ^2}{r}$ $\quad U_f = \frac{3kQ^2}{2r}$

$$W = U_f - U_i = \frac{3kQ^2}{2r} - \frac{3kQ^2}{r} = -\frac{3kQ^2}{2r}$$

Potential Energy of a Dipole in a Uniform Electric Field

Electrostatic potential energy of a dipole placed in a uniform electric field is defined as the work done in rotating a dipole from a direction perpendicular to the field to the given direction, i.e.

$$U = -pE\cos\theta = \mathbf{p}\cdot\mathbf{E}$$

When an electric dipole is placed in uniform electric field, then

(i) **If $\theta = 0°$** $\cos\theta = 1$

$F = 0$, $\tau = 0$, $U = -pE$ (minimum)

$\Rightarrow$ So, dipole is in stable equilibrium.

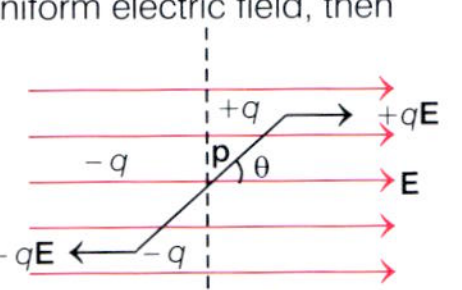

Potential energy of a dipole in a electric field

(ii) **If $\theta = 90°$**

$\cos\theta = 0$

$F = 0$, $\tau = pE$, $U = 0$

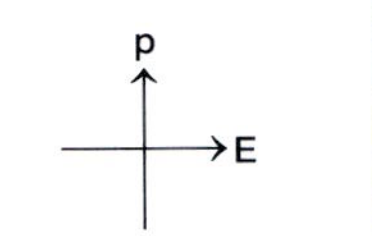

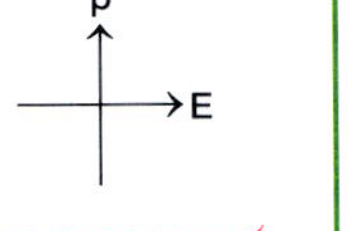

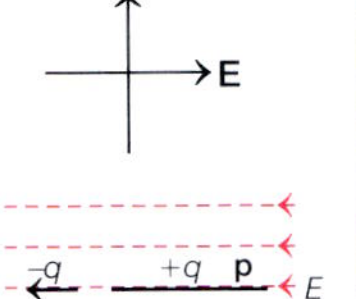

(iii) **If $\theta = 180°$**

$\cos\theta = -1$

$F = 0$, $\tau = 0$, $U = pE$ (maximum)

$\Rightarrow$ So, dipole is in unstable equilibrium.

- **Graph between potential energy and angle θ is shown below**

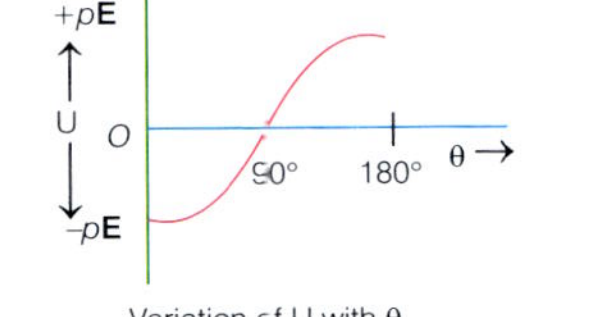

Variation of U with θ

Force on an Electric Dipole in Non-uniform Electric Field

- When a short dipole is placed in a non-uniform electric field it will experience a force.
- The interaction energy of the dipole in electric field E is $U = -\mathbf{p}\cdot\mathbf{E}$.
- If $E = f(r) \Rightarrow U = f(r)$, so the force on dipole due to electric field is $F = -\frac{\Delta U}{\Delta r}$
- If the dipole is placed in the direction of electric field, then

$$\mathbf{F} = -\mathbf{p}\cdot\frac{d\mathbf{E}}{dr}$$

Equilibrium of Dipole

Work done, when $\theta = 0°$

$$U = -pE\cos0° = -pE$$

Thus, the potential energy of a dipole is minimum when its dipole moment is parallel to the external field. This is the position of stable equilibrium.

(ii) When $\theta = 180°$

$$U = -pE\cos180° = +pE$$

Thus, the potential energy of a dipole is maximum when its dipole moment is antiparallel to the external field. This is the position of unstable equilibrium.

$\theta = 0°$
U = minimum $= -pE$
$\mathbf{F}_{net} = 0$, $t = 0$

When displaced from mean position, a restoring torque acts on the dipole

$\theta = 180°$
U = minimum $= +pE$
$\mathbf{F}_{net} = 0$, $t = 0$

When displaced from mean position, the torque acts in opposite direction

Potential Energy in Constant Electric Field

If the displacement is in the same direction as the electric field.

$$W = qEd$$

So, $\quad \Delta U = -qEd$

A positive charge loses potential energy when it moves in the direction of the electric field.

If the displacement is in the direction opposite to the electric field, then

$$W = -qEd \text{ so } \Delta U = qEd$$

A positive charge gains potential energy when it moves in the direction opposite to the electric field.

Test 1

Syllabus • Dielectric, Capacitance and their Types

NCERT Page 61 to 71

For deeper insight **Scan the QR Code**

Chapter 03

Conductor

The substances such as metals in which the charge can flow through them are called conductors. Conductors contain large number of free electrons which can move inside it.

Conductor Placed in Electric Field

Whenever a conductor is placed in an external electric field, the free electrons in it experience a force due to it and start moving opposite to the field. This movement makes one side of conductor positively charged and the other as negatively charged. This creates an electric field in the conductor in a opposite direction to external electric field (called induced field). The movement of electrons continues till the net electric field (resultant of external electric field and induced field) becomes zero. This is a state of electrostatic equilibrium.

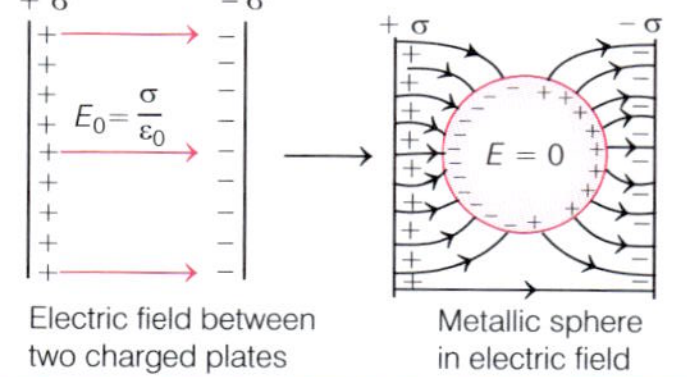

Electric field between two charged plates

Metallic sphere in electric field

Properties of Charged Conductor

(i) When a conductor is charged by induction, induced charge (which is free to move) is equal and opposite to the inducing charge, i.e. $q' = -q$.

(ii) In electrostatic, conductors are equipotential surfaces, i.e. potential on the surface or inside the conductor is same.

(iii) Charge given to conductor resides on its outer surface. However, distribution of charge on the surface is such that surface density of charge varies inversely as the radius of curvature of that part of the conductor, i.e., $\sigma \propto 1/R$.

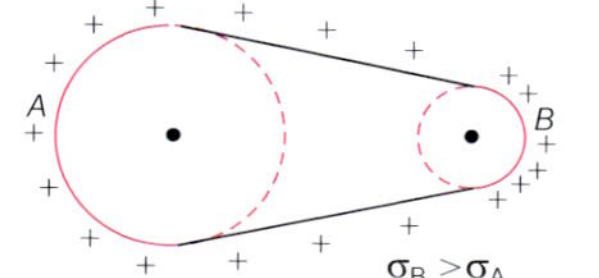

(iv) The dielectric constant of conductors in electrostatics is infinite, i.e., $\varepsilon_r = \infty$.

(v) Electric field intensity inside a conductor is zero, so electrostatic field lines never exist within the conducting object.

(vi) Electric field lines of force are normal to the surface of a conductor.

(vii) Electric field intensity near a conducting surface is given as $\mathbf{E} = \frac{\sigma}{\varepsilon_0}\hat{\mathbf{n}}$

Dielectrics

Dielectrics are insulating (non-conducting) materials that can produce electric effect without conduction. Movement of free charges is not possible in a dielectric. So, they behave differently. When a dielectric material is kept in an external electric field, then the field induces dipole moment. Due to which, net charge on the surface of the dielectric appears and as a result electric field is produced that opposes the external field. Induced field is less in magnitude than the external field, so field inside the dielectric gets reduced.

Polarised dielectric Slab

$$\mathbf{E} = |\mathbf{E}_0| - |\mathbf{E}_{ind}|$$

where, **E** = resultant electric field in the dielectric, $\mathbf{E}_0$ = external electric field between two plates and $\mathbf{E}_{ind}$ = induced electric field inside the dielectric.

Polar Dielectrics

A polar molecule is one in which the centres of positive and negative charges are separated (even when there is no external field). Such molecules have permanent dipole moment, e.g. HCl, H_2O. So, a polar dielectric is one which is having a net dipole moment zero in the absence of electric field due to the random orientation of polar molecules as shown in figure.

Non-polar Dielectrics

In a non-polar molecule, the centres of positive and negative charges coincide. The molecule thus has no permanent (or intrinsic) dipole moment, e.g., oxygen (O_2) and hydrogen (H_2) molecules. In an external electric field, the positive and negative charges of a non-polar molecules are displaced in opposite direction. This occurs till the point where external force is balanced by the restoring force (due to internal field in the molecule). Thus, dipole moment is induced in non-polar molecules and dielectric is said to be polarised. The induced dipole moments of different molecules add up giving a net dipole moment of the dielectric in the presence of the external field.

Polarisation (P)

It is a process of inducing equal and opposite charges on the two surfaces of the dielectrics on the application of electric field. In other words, the induced dipole moment developed per unit volume in a dielectric slab on placing it, in an electric field is called **polarisation**. It is denoted by *P*.

- Electric Susceptibility (χ)

The **polarisation** density of dielectric slab is directly proportional to the reduced value of the electric field and may be expressed as

$$P = \chi\varepsilon_0 E_0$$

Capacitor

A capacitor is a device which is used to store electric charge or potential energy. It is made up of two isolated conductors carrying equal and opposite charges placed at small separation.

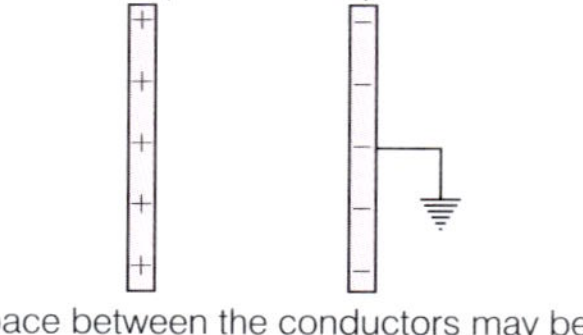

The space between the conductors may be vacuum or an insulating material. Capacitor is represented as

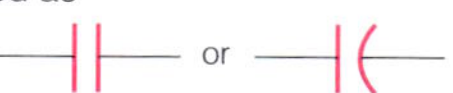

Capacitance

Capacitance is the capacity of the material object to hold electric charge.

$$Q = CV \Rightarrow C = \frac{Q}{V}$$

This *C* is constant of proportionality and is called the capacitance of the conductor. The SI unit of capacitance is farad (F).

1 Farad = 1 coulomb/volt (1 C/V)

Its dimensional formula is $[M^{-1}L^{-2}T^4A^2]$.

It depends upon the following factors:

(i) Size and shape of the conductor.

(ii) Nature (permittivity) of the surrounding medium.

(iii) Presence of the other conductors in its neighbourhood.

Parallel Plate Capacitor

The simplest and the most widely used capacitor is the parallel plate capacitor. It consists of two large plane parallel conducting plates separated by a small distance.

The capacitance of parallel plate capacitors is given by $C = \frac{\varepsilon_0 A}{d}$

Area = A   E = 0

$E = \frac{\sigma}{\varepsilon_0}$ d

Charge density +σ

Charge density −σ

E = 0

Capacitance of a Capacitor Partially Filled with Dielectric

When the space between parallel plates of capacitor is partially filled with a dielectric (dielectric constant = *K*) of thickness $t < d$, then the filling thickness between the plates is *t* in the dielectric and $(d-t)$ in vacuum (or air).

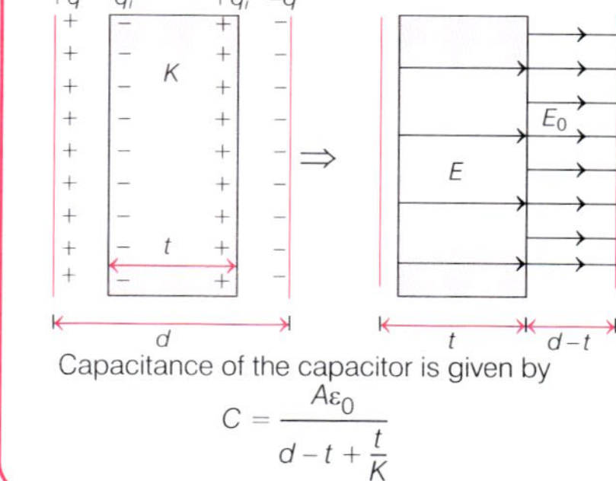

Capacitance of the capacitor is given by

$$C = \frac{A\varepsilon_0}{d - t + \frac{t}{K}}$$

Capacitance of an Isolated Spherical Capacitor

The potential at any point on the surface of the spherical conductor will be capacitance of the spherical conductor situated in vacuum is

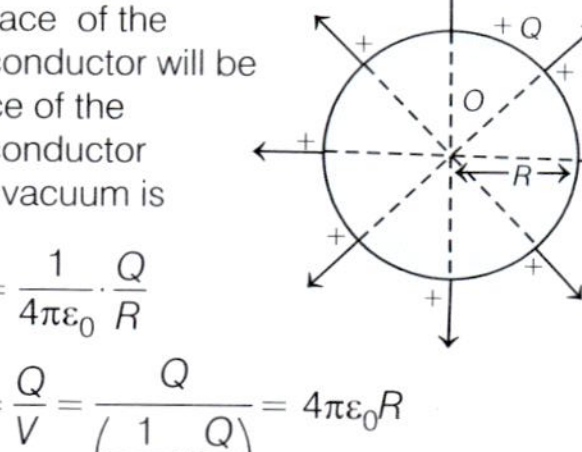

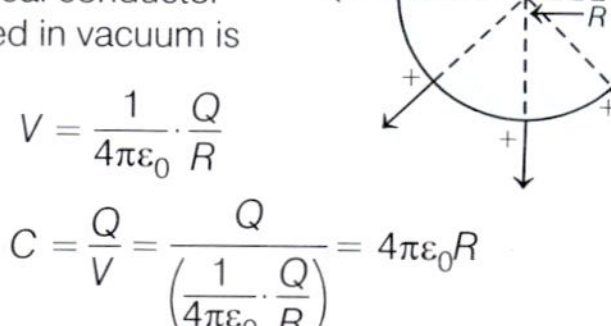

$$V = \frac{1}{4\pi\varepsilon_0}\cdot\frac{Q}{R}$$

or $$C = \frac{Q}{V} = \frac{Q}{\left(\frac{1}{4\pi\varepsilon_0}\cdot\frac{Q}{R}\right)} = 4\pi\varepsilon_0 R$$

Test 2

Syllabus • Combination of Capacitors

NCERT Page 71 to 72

For deeper insight **Scan the QR Code**

Chapter 03

Capacitors in Series

In a series connection, charge on each capacitor remains same and equals to the charge supplied by the battery but potential difference across each capacitor is different, such that $V = V_1 + V_2 + V_3$.
where, V_1, V_2, V_3, are the potential difference across capacitor C_1, C_2 and C_3, respectively.

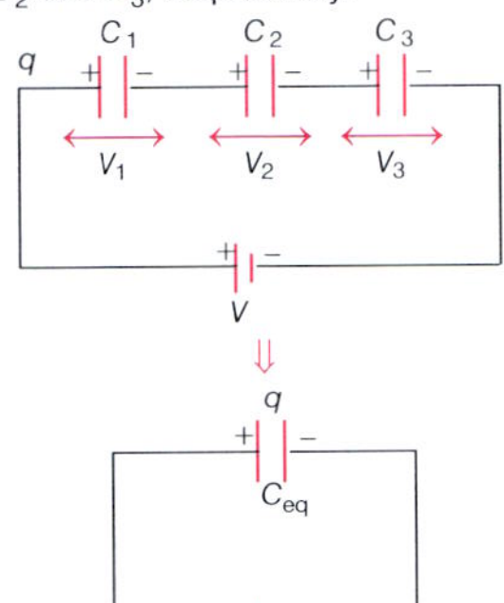

The arrangement shown above in series connection. Here, the equivalent capacitance is

$$\frac{1}{C_{eq}} = \frac{1}{C_1} + \frac{1}{C_2} + \frac{1}{C_3}$$

Following points are important in case of series combination of capacitors

(i) In series combination, potential difference distributes in the inverse ratio of capacitance, i.e., $V \propto \frac{1}{C}$

(ii) If two capacitors having capacitances C_1 and C_2 are connected in series, then

$$C = \frac{C_1 C_2}{C_1 + C_2}$$

$$V_1 = \left[\frac{C_2}{C_1 + C_2}\right] V$$

$$V_2 = \left[\frac{C_1}{C_1 + C_2}\right] V$$

(iii) If n capacitors of equal capacity C are connected in series, with supply voltage V, then their equivalent capacitance is $\frac{C}{n}$ and potential difference across each capacitor is $V' = \frac{V}{n}$.

Capacitors in Parallel

In a parallel connection, potential difference across each capacitor remains same and equal to be applied potential difference but charge gets distributed,

i.e., $q = q_1 + q_2 + q_3$

where, q_1, q_2 and q_3, are the charges across capacitor C_1, C_2 and C_3, respectively and q is the net charge flowing across the circuit.

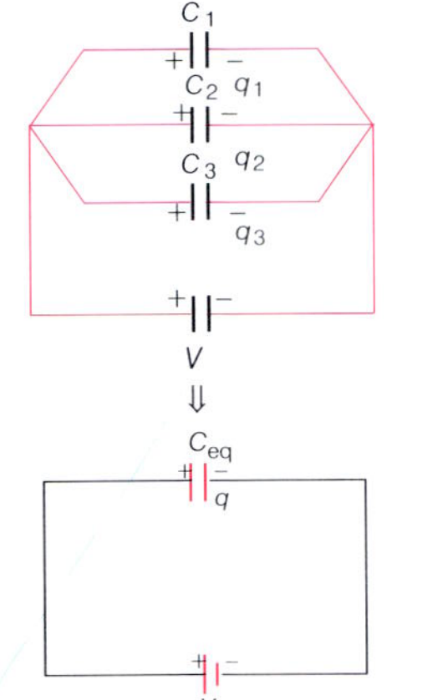

The arrangement shown in figure is called a parallel connection. Here, the equivalent capacitance is equal to $C_{eq} = C_1 + C_2 + C_3$

Following points are important in case of parallel combination of capacitors

(i) In parallel combination, charge and energy distributes in the ratio of their capacitance, *i.e.*, $q \propto C$.

If two capacitors having capacitance C_1 and C_2, respectively are connected in parallel, then $C_{eq} = C_1 + C_2$

$$q_1 = \left(\frac{C_1}{C_1 + C_2}\right) q$$

and $$q_2 = \left(\frac{C_1}{C_1 + C_2}\right) q$$

(ii) If n identical capacitors are connected in parallel, then equivalent capacitance is $C_{eq} = nC$ and charge on each capacitor is $q' = \frac{q}{n}$

Combination of n Capacitors

If n identical plates are arranged such that even numbered of plates are connected together and odd number of plates are connected together as shown in figure, then $(n - 1)$ capacitors are formed and will be in parallel.

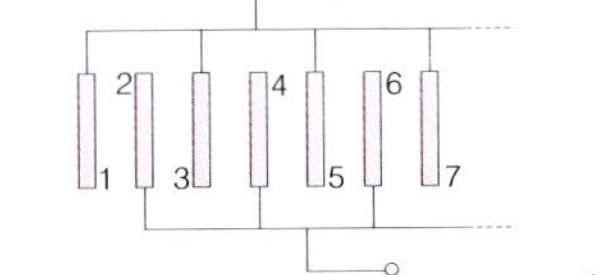

The capacitance of each capacitor is $\frac{\varepsilon_0 A}{d}$

Equivalent capacitance $C_{eq} = \frac{(n-1)\varepsilon_0 A}{d}$

If there are n identical capacitors, then $\frac{C_p}{C_s} = n^2$

where, C_p and C_s are the equivalent capacitances when capacitors are connected in parallel and series, respectively. Below are some of the examples of combination of capacitors arranged in parallel.

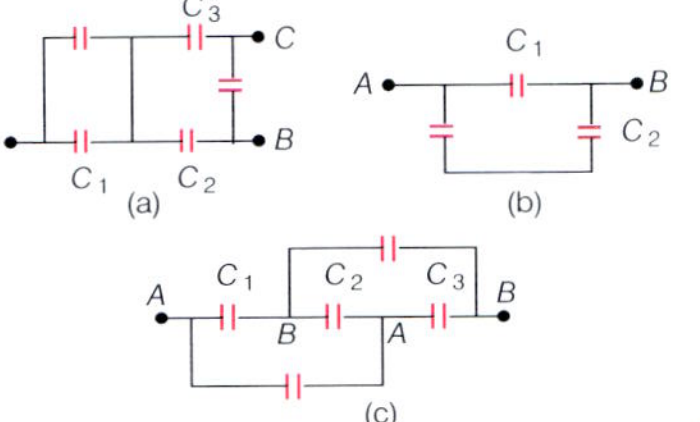

Combinations of Dielectric Filled Capacitors

Dielectrics filled inside the capacitor can be assumed as series/parallel combinations as follows

- K_1, K_2 and K_3 are in series
- K_1, K_2 and K_3 are in parallel
- K_1 and K_2 are in series and K_3 is parallel to K_1 and K_2

Wheatstone's Bridge Circuits

Wheatstone bridge consists of five capacitors, or a number of capacitors which can be reduced to five as shown in the following arrangement

- **For balanced condition**

$$\frac{C_1}{C_2} = \frac{C_3}{C_4}$$

$$V_C = V_D \text{ or } V_C - V_D = 0 \text{ or } V_{CD} = 0$$

i.e. no charge is stored in C_5. Hence, it can be removed from the circuit.

Some of the different forms of the Wheatstone bridge are given below.

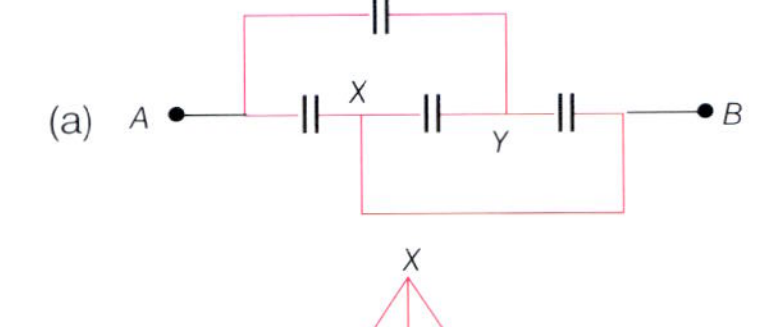

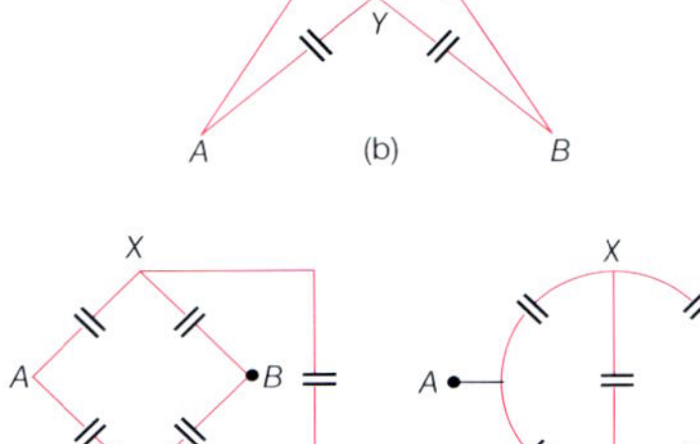

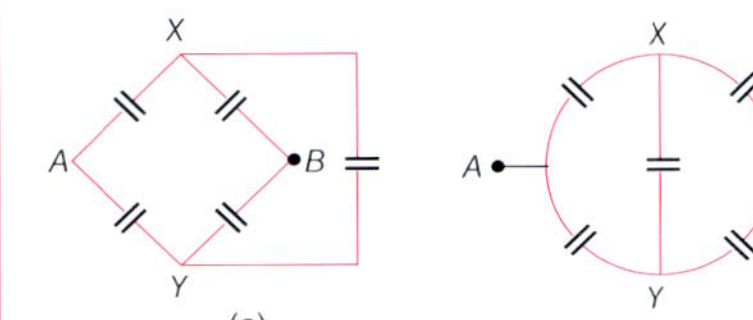

Test 3

Syllabus • Energy of Capacitors

NCERT Page 73 to 75

For deeper insight **Scan the QR Code** 

Chapter 03

Energy stored in a Capacitors

The total work done to charge a capacitor is stored as electric potential energy in the capacitor. At a given time t, if the charge on the capacitor is q and the potential across the capacitor is V, then bringing an additional small charge dq onto the capacitor requires work against the electric field created by the existing charge. The work needed to add this small charge dq is given by the product of the potential V and the charge dq.

$$dW = (dq)\,V = \frac{q}{C} \qquad (\text{as } V = q/C)$$

Total work done to charge a capacitor to a value q_0, can be obtained by integrating additional work from limits 0 to q_0, we get

$$W = \frac{q_0^2}{2C}$$

∴ Energy stored by a charged capacitor,

$$U = W = \frac{q_0^2}{2C}$$

$$= \frac{1}{2}CV_0^2$$

$$= \frac{1}{2}q_0V_0$$

Thus, if a capacitor is given a charge q, then the potential energy stored in it is,

$$U = \frac{1}{2}CV^2$$

$$= \frac{1}{2}\cdot\frac{q^2}{C}$$

$$= \frac{1}{2}\cdot qV$$

The above relation shows that the charged capacitor is the electrical analog of a stretched spring whose elastic potential energy is $\frac{1}{2}kx^2$.

The charge q is analogous to the elongation x and the reciprocal of capacitance, *i.e.* $\frac{1}{C}$ to the force constant k.

Total energy stored in series combination or parallel combination of capacitors is equal to the sum of the energies stored in individual capacitors, *i.e.*,

$$U = U_1+U_2+U_3$$

Energy Density Between the Plates

The energy density u of the electric field between the plates of a capacitor is the amount of energy stored per unit volume in the electric field. It can be derived from the formula for the total energy stored in the capacitor and the relationship between the electric field and the geometry of the capacitor.

Energy density,

$$u = \frac{\text{Energy stored}}{\text{Volume of capacitor}} = \frac{U}{Ad} \qquad \text{......(i)}$$

Energy on either plate of capacitors is

$$Q = \sigma A = \varepsilon_0 EA \qquad \text{......(ii)}$$

Energy stored in the capacitor is

$$U = \frac{Q^2}{2C} = \frac{(\varepsilon_0 EA)^2}{2\varepsilon_0 A/d} = \frac{1}{2}\varepsilon_0 E^2 . Ad \qquad \text{......(iii)}$$

Put the value of U in Eq (i), we get

$$u = \frac{1}{2}\varepsilon_0 E^2$$

Dielectric Slab When Battery is Connected

Change in energy on introducing a dielectric slab.

- When a dielectric slab is inserted between the plates of a charged capacitor, with battery connected to its plates. Then, the capacitance and energy stored in the capacitor becomes K (dielectric constant) times.
- Capacitance increase by a factor of K *i.e.*, $C = KC_o$
- Voltage remains same *i.e.*, $V = V_o$
- Energy stored increase by a factor of K *i.e.*, $U = U_oK$

Dielectric When battery is Disconnected

When a dielectric slab is inserted between the plates of a charged capacitor and battery is disconnected. Then, the charge on this plates remains unchanged and energy stored in the capacitor becomes U_o/K. *i.e.* energy decreases.

- Capacitance increase by a factor of C *i.e.*, $C = KC_o$
- Charge remains constant *i.e.*, $Q = Q_o$
- Energy stored decrease by a factor of K *i.e.*, $U = U_o/K$

Common Potential

When two charged conductors or capacitors are joined together by a conducting wire and having different potentials, then charge flows from capacitor at higher potential to the capacitor at lower potential. This flow of charge continues till their potential becomes equal, this equal potential is called common potential.

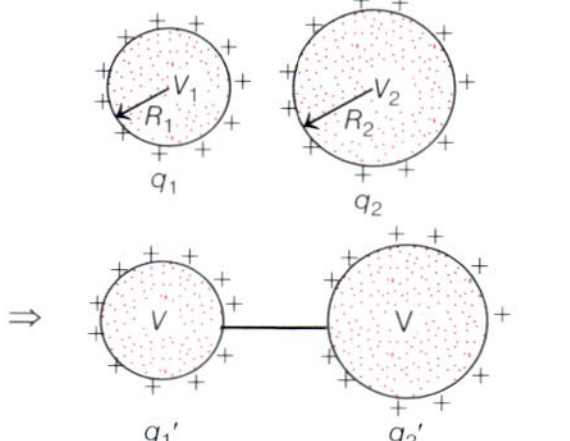

Suppose two conductors of capacities C_1 and C_2 have charges q_1 and q_2 respectively and raised to potential V_1 and V_2 respectively are joined together by a conducting wire, then charge redistributes in these conductors in the ratio of their capacities. Charge redistributes till potential of both the conductors becomes equal. Thus, let q'_1 and q'_2 be the final charges on them, then

$$q'_1 = C_1V \text{ and } q'_2 = C_2V$$

$$\text{or} \quad \frac{q'_1}{q'_2} = \frac{C_1}{C_2}$$

and if they are spherical conductors, then

$$\frac{C_1}{C_2} = \frac{R_1}{R_2}$$

$$\therefore \quad \frac{q'_1}{q'_2} = \frac{C_1}{C_2} = \frac{R_1}{R_2}$$

Here R_1 and R_1 are radius of capacitors

Since, the total charge is (q_1+q_2). therefore,

$$q'_1 = \left(\frac{C_1}{C_1+C_2}\right)(q_1+q_2)$$

$$q'_2 = \left(\frac{C_2}{C_1+C_2}\right)(q_1+q_2)$$

$$\text{Common potential, } V = \frac{\text{Total charge}}{\text{Total capacity}}$$

$$V = \frac{q_1+q_2}{C_1+C_2} = \frac{C_1V_1+C_2V_2}{C_1+C_2}$$

Loss of energy Redistribution of charge

The initial charge on the capacitor C_1 is q and after joining it becomes q'. The transferred charge from the capacitor C_1 to the capacitor C_2 is $q - q'$.

$$q - q' = C_1V_1 - C_1V$$

$$= C_1\left(V_1 - \frac{C_1V_1+C_2V_2}{C_1+C_2}\right) \Rightarrow q - q' = \frac{C_1C_2(V_1-V_2)}{C_1+C_2}$$

This is the quantity of the transferred charge.

The loss of energy due to redistribution of charge is given by

$$\Delta U = \frac{C_1C_2}{2(C_1+C_2)}(V_1-V_2)^2$$

Now, as C_1, C_2 and $(V_1-V_2)^2$ are always positive.

$U_i > U_f$,

i.e., there is a decrease in energy. Hence, energy is always lost in redistribution of charge. Further,

$$\Delta U = 0, \text{ if } V_1 = V_2$$

This is because no flow of charge takes place when both the conductors are at same potential.

If capacitors are connected with plates of opposite polarities together *i.e.*, positive plate of A is connected to negative plate of B, then

$$\text{Common potential, } V = \frac{|Q_1 - Q_2|}{C_1+C_2} = \frac{|C_1V_1 - C_2V_2|}{C_1+C_2}$$

$$\text{Loss of energy, } \Delta U = \frac{1}{2}\frac{C_1C_2}{C_1+C_2}(V_1+V_2)^2$$

The phenomenon of redistribution of charge is similar to completely inelastic collision

$\longrightarrow u_1$ (m_1) $\quad u_2 \longrightarrow$ (m_2) $\quad \longrightarrow \quad \longrightarrow V$ (m_1+m_2)

$$\text{Common velocity, } V = \frac{m_1u_1 + m_2u_2}{m1 + m2}$$

$$\text{Loss of K.E. } \Delta K = \frac{1}{2}\frac{m_1m_2}{m_1+m_2}(u_1-u_2)^2$$

$\longrightarrow u_1$ (m_1) $\quad u_2 \longleftarrow$ (m_2) $\quad \longrightarrow \quad \longrightarrow v$ (m_1+m_2)

$$\text{Common velocity, } V = \frac{|m_1u_1 - m_2u_2|}{m_1+m_2}$$

$$\text{Loss KE, } \Delta K = \frac{1}{2}\frac{m_1m_2}{m_1+m_2}(u_1+u_2)^2$$

Test 1

Syllabus

- Electric Current
- Drift Velocity, Mobility and their Relation with Electric Current
- Ohm's Law and Electrical Resistance
- *V-I* Characteristics of Ohmic and Non-Ohmic Conductors
- Electrical Resistivity, Conductivity and Temperature Dependence of Resistance

NCERT Page 81 to 91

For deeper insight **Scan the QR Code**

Electric Current

- The rate of flow of electric charge through any cross-sectional area of a conductor is known as electric current.
- If electric current through a conductor is steady, then current,

$$I = \frac{q}{t} = \frac{ne}{t}$$

- Currents are not always steady and hence more generally, we define the current as $I(t) = \lim_{\Delta t \to 0} \left(\frac{\Delta Q}{\Delta t}\right)$

Ampere

One ampere is the current through a wire, if a charge of one coulomb flows through any cross-section of the wire in one second, i.e.

$$1\text{ampere(A)} = \frac{1\text{ coulomb (C)}}{1\text{ second (s)}}$$

Direction of Current

As a matter of convention, the direction of flow of positive charge gives the direction of current. This is called **conventional current**. The direction of flow of electrons gives the direction of **electronic current**. Therefore, the direction of electronic current is opposite to that of conventional current.

Current Density

The amount of charge flowing per second through a unit area held normal to the direction of the flow of charge at that point is called current density. Current density is a vector quantity and its direction is along the motion of the positive charge as shown in Fig. (a).

Current density, $\mathbf{J} = \frac{q/t}{\mathbf{A}} = \frac{I}{\mathbf{A}}$

If the cross -sectional area A is not perpendicular to the current and normal to the area makes an angle θ with the direction of the current as shown in fig.(b), then $A_n = A\cos\theta$

$\therefore$ Current density, $J = \frac{I}{A_n} = \frac{I}{A\cos\theta}$

Drift Velocity

It is defined as "the average velocity with which the free electrons in a conductor get drifted towards the positive end of the conductor under the influence of an electric field applied across the conductor".

$$v_d = \frac{eE}{m}\tau$$

The electric current relates with drift velocity as

$$I = neAv_d$$

$$\Rightarrow v_d = \frac{I}{neA} = \frac{J}{ne}$$

Current density is also given by

$$J = \frac{I}{A} = nev_d$$

The direction of drift velocity for electrons in a metal is opposite to that of applied electric field. The drift velocity of electrons is very small of the order of 10^{-4} ms^{-1} as compared to thermal speed ($\approx 10^5$m/s) of electron at room temperature.

Mobility

Drift velocity of free electron per unit electric field represensts mobility.

$$\mu = \frac{v_d}{E}$$

$$\Rightarrow \mathbf{v}_d = \mu\mathbf{E} = \frac{eE\tau}{m} \Rightarrow \mu = \frac{e\tau}{m}$$

Its unit is m^2/V-s.

Relaxation Time

Average time taken by free electron between two successive collisions is called time of relaxation. ($\tau \approx 10^{-14}$ s in metals) With increase in temperature, relaxation time decreases.

Ohmic Conductors

The conductors which obey Ohm's law are called ohmic conductors.

Thus the *V-I* graph for Ohmic conductor is a straight line passing through the origin.

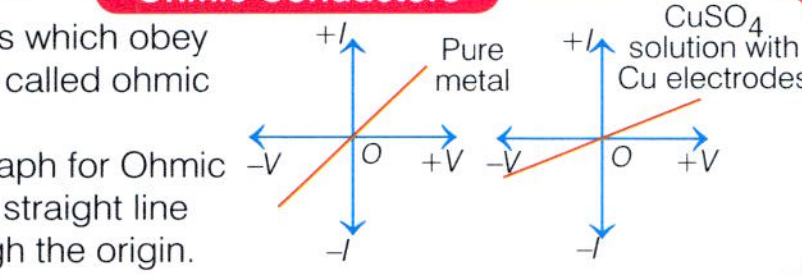

Non-ohmic Conductors

The conductors which do not obey Ohm's law are called non-ohmic conductors.

The *V-I* graph for non-ohmic conductors does not pass through the origin.

V-I relationship is non-linear.

V-I relationship is non-unique.

V-I relationship depends on the sign of V for the same absolute value of *V*.

Ohm's Law

The current *I* flowing through a conductor is always directly proportional to the potential difference *V* across the ends of the conductor", provided that the physical conditions (temperature, mechanical strain, etc)are kept constant. $V = IR$

where, *R* is resistance of the conductor. Graph between *V* and *I* for a metallic conductor is a straight line as shown. At different temperature, *V-I* curves are different.

(a) Slope of the line $= \tan\theta = \frac{V}{I} = R$

(b) Here, $\tan\theta_1 > \tan\theta_2$

So, $R_1 > R_2$ i.e. $T_1 > T_2$

Resistance

The resistance of a conductor is the property by virtue of which it opposes the flow of charges through it. SI unit of resistance is ohm. $R = \frac{V}{I}$

The resistance of the conductor depends upon the following factors

(i) It is directly proportional to the length of the conductor,

i.e. $R \propto l$ ...(i)

(ii) It is inversely proportional to the area of the cross-section of the conductor,

i.e. $R \propto \frac{1}{A}$ ...(ii)

From Eqs. (i) and (ii), we get

$$R \propto \frac{l}{A} \Rightarrow R = \rho\frac{l}{A}$$

where, ρ s resistivity of material

Conductance

The conductance of a conductor is the ease with which electric charges flow through it. It is equal to the reciprocal of its resistance and is denoted by *G*.

$$\text{Conductance} = \frac{1}{\text{Resistance}}$$

$$G = \frac{1}{R}$$

Conductivity

The reciprocal of the resistivity of a material is called its conductivity and is denoted by σ.

$$\text{Conductivity} = \frac{1}{\text{Resistivity}} \quad \sigma = \frac{1}{\rho}$$

Chapter 04

Temperature Dependence of Resistivity

Resistivity of a material depends on relaxation time as follows. $\rho \propto \frac{1}{\tau}$

When temperature increases in a conductor, average speed of free electrons increases, hence relaxation time decreases. Thus, resistivity increases. Resistivity of a metal conductor is given by

$$\rho = \rho_0 [1 + \alpha (T - T_0)]$$

where, ρ = resistivity at temperature T,

ρ_0 = resistivity at temperature T_0 and

α = temperature coefficient of resistance.

i.e. $\alpha = \frac{\rho - \rho_0}{\rho_0 (T - T_0)}$

In terms of resistance, $R \propto \rho$

$\therefore R_t = R_0 [1 + \alpha (T - T_0)]$

$$\Rightarrow \alpha = \frac{R_t - R_0}{R_0(T - T_0)}$$

where, R_0 = resistance of conductor at 0°C and R_t = resistance of conductor at t°C.

Temperature *versus* Resistivity Curve

- **For metals**, α is positive as their resistivity increases with rise in temperature. The graph of ρ plotted against *T* would be a straight line as shown in figure.

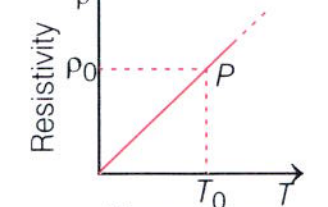

- **For semiconductors**, α is negative as their resistivity decreases with rise in temperature. Variation in resistivity with the temperature for semiconductor is shown in figure.

- The resistivity of **alloys** also increases with rise in temperature. The graph between resistivity and temperature is shown in figure.

Test 2

Syllabus
- Series and Parallel Combination of Resistors
- Internal Resistors
- Potential Difference and Emf of a Cell
- A Combination of Cells in Series and Parallel

NCERT Page 92 to 97

For deeper insight **Scan the QR Code**

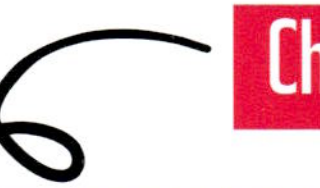

Series Combination

In this combination, resistors are connected end-to-end, *i.e.* second end of first resistor is connected to first end of the second resistor and so on. In series combination, same current flows through each resistor but potential difference distributes in the ratio of their resistances, *i.e.* $V \propto R$. So, the total potential difference is equal to the sum of potential difference applied across the combination of resistors. Equivalent resistances in series combination is given by $R_{eq} = R_1 + R_2 + R_3$

i.e. equivalent resistance is greater than the maximum value of resistance in the combination.

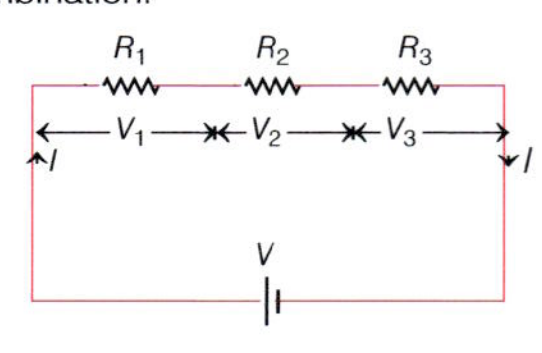

Parallel Combination

In this combination, first end of all resistors are connected to one point and second end of all resistors are connected to other point. Same potential difference appears across each resistor but current distributes in the reverse ratio of their resistances, *i.e.* $I \propto \frac{V}{R}$

So, the total current is equal to the sum of currents through each resistance.

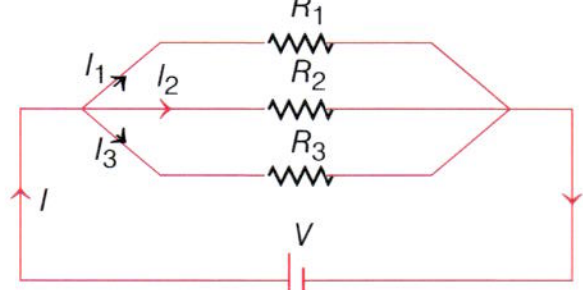

Equivalent resistance in parallel combination is given by

$$\frac{1}{R_{eq}} = \frac{1}{R_1} + \frac{1}{R_2} + \frac{1}{R_3}$$

i.e. equivalent resistance is less than the minimum value of resistance in the combination.

Combination of Series and Parallel Resistors

The combination of four resistors has both series and parallel parts. Each is identified and reduced to an equivalent resistance, and these are further reduced until a single equivalent resistance is reached.

Cell

An electric cell is a source of energy that maintains a continuous flow of charge in a circuit. Electric cell changes chemical energy into electrical energy. It is a device which provides constant potential difference.

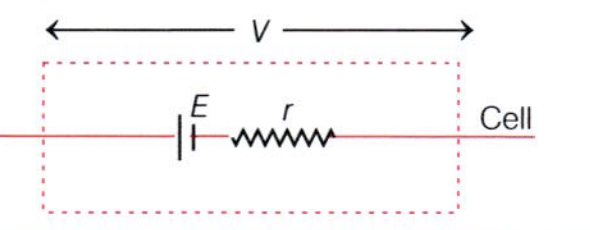

Electromotive Force [EMF]

When a cell is in open circuit or no current associates with it, then potential difference across the terminals of cell represent emf of the cell.

$$V_A - E + 0 = V_B$$

$$\Rightarrow \quad V_A - V_B = E$$

It depends upon nature of electrode and concentration of electrolyte.

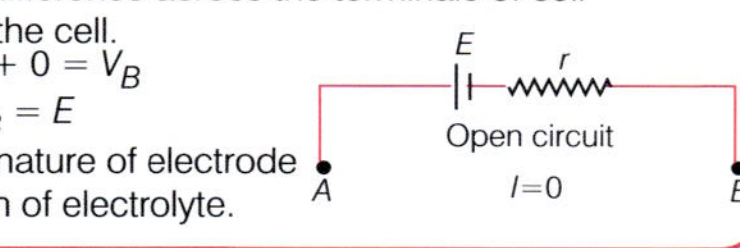

Internal Resistance (r)

It is opposition provided by electrolytes of a cell to the flow of ions through it. Dependence of internal resistance (r) with various factors of a battery is given below.

(i) $r \propto$ distance between electrodes and concentration of electrolyte.

(ii) $r \propto \frac{1}{\text{temperature and area of electrode}}$

(iii) r depends on the nature, concentration and temperature of the electrolyte. It increases with increment in concentration of electrolyte.

Cells in Series

In series grouping of cells, anode of one cell is connected to cathode of other cell and so on as shown below.

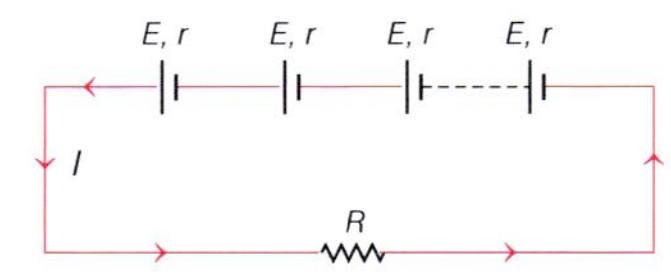

If n identical cells of emf E and internal resistance r each, are connected in series, then

(i) equivalent emf of the combination, $E_{eq} = nE$.

(ii) equivalent internal resistance of the combination, $r_{eq} = nr$.

(iii) main current = current from each cell $= I = \frac{nE}{R + nr}$

(iv) potential difference across external resistance, $V = IR$.

(v) potential difference across each cell, $V' = \frac{V}{n}$.

Cells in Parallel

In parallel grouping of cells, all anodes of cells are connected at one point and all cathodes of cells are connected together at other point as shown below.

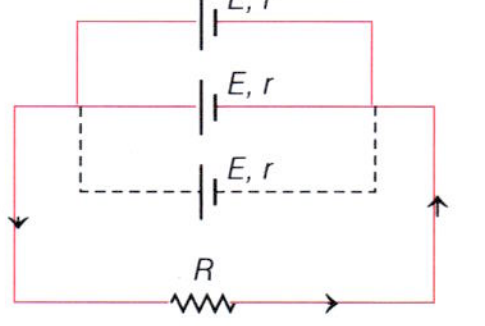

If n identical cells of emf E and internal resistance r each, are connected in parallel, then

(i) equivalent emf of the combination, $E_{eq} = E$.

(ii) equivalent internal resistance, $r_{eq} = r/n$.

(iii) main current, $I = \frac{E}{R + r/n}$

(iv) current from each cell, $I' = \frac{I}{n}$

(v) potential difference across external resistance = potential difference across each cell i.e, $V = IR$.

If external resistance is much smaller than the total internal resistance, then cells should be connected in parallel to get the maximum current.

Mixed Grouping

If n identical cells of emf E and internal resistance r each, are connected in a row and such m rows are connected in parallel as shown in figure, then

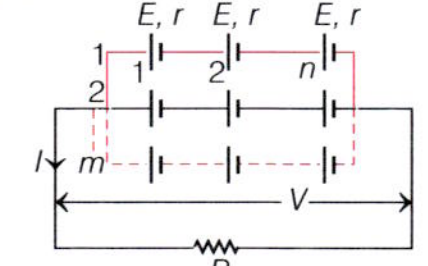

(i) equivalent emf of the combination, $E_{eq} = nE$

(ii) equivalent internal resistance, $r_{eq} = \frac{nr}{m}$

(iii) main current flowing through the load,

$$I = \frac{nE}{R + \frac{nr}{m}} = \frac{mnE}{mR + nr}$$

(iv) potential difference across load,

$$V = IR$$

(v) current from each cell,

$$I' = \frac{I}{n}$$

(vi) potential difference across each cell, $V' = \frac{V}{n}$

(vii) total number of cells = mn

In mixed grouping of cells, the current through the external resistance would be maximum, if the external resistance is equal to the total internal resistance of the cells, *i.e*

$$R = \frac{nr}{m}$$

Electrical Energy

It is defined as the total work done W by the source of emf V in maintaining the electric current I in the circuit for a specified time t.

$$E = \left(\frac{V}{R}\right)^2 Rt = \frac{V^2 t}{R} \qquad \left[\because I = \frac{V}{R}\right]$$

The SI unit of electrical energy is joule (J), where

1 joule = 1volt × 1ampere × 1second

= 1watt × 1second

1 kilowatt hour (kWh) = 3.6×10^6 joule

Electrical Power

It is defined as the rate of electrical energy supplied per unit time to maintain the flow of electric current through a conductor.

Mathematically, $P = \frac{W}{t} = VI = I^2R = \frac{V^2}{R}$

The SI unit of power is watt (W),

where 1 watt = 1volt × 1ampere = 1ampere-volt.

Test 3

Syllabus

- Kirchhoff's Rule and their Applications
- Wheatstone Bridge
- Meter Bridge

NCERT Page 97 to 101

For deeper insight **Scan the QR Code**

Kirchhoff's Laws

Many complex electric circuits cannot be reduced to simple series-parallel combinations. Kirchhoff's laws are used to solve these complicated electric circuits. These rules are basically the expressions of conservation of electric charge and of energy. e.g. two circuits that cannot be broken down are shown in figure.

(a) (b)

However, it is always possible to analyse such circuits by applying two rules.

- **Junction** A junction in a circuit is a point, where three or more conductors meet. Junctions are also called **nodes** or **branch points.** In figure (*a*), point *D* and *C* are junctions
- **Loop** A loop is any closed conducting path. In figure (*a*), *DCEFD, ABEFA* are loops.

Junction Rule

At any junction, the sum of the currents entering the junction is equal to the sum of currents leaving the junction, i.e. $\Sigma I = 0$. This rule is based on the law of **conservation of charges**.

From the given figure, $I_1 - I_2 - I_3 + I_4 + I_5 = 0$

Loop Rule

The algebraic sum of change in potential around any closed loop involving resistors and cells in the loop is zero, i.e. $\Sigma IR + \Sigma \varepsilon = 0$.

From the figure, $\varepsilon - IR_1 - IR_2 = 0$

This rule is based on the law of **conservation of energy.**

Sign Conventions

For the application of Kirchhoff's laws, the following sign conventions are used

(i) The change in potential in traversing a resistance in the direction of current is $-IR$, while in the opposite direction is $+IR$.

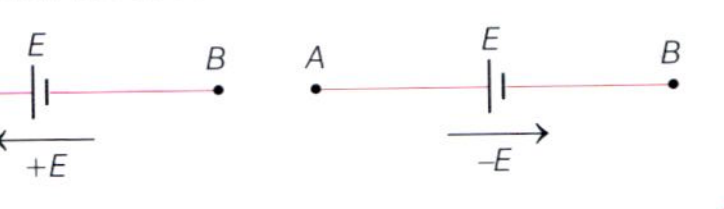

(ii) The change in potential in traversing an emf source from negative to positive terminal is $+E$, while in the opposite direction is $-E$, irrespective of the direction of current in the circuit.

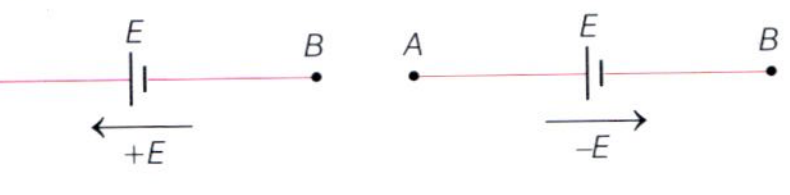

Potential Difference

While using Kirchhoff's laws to calculate the potential difference, the following points should be considered

(i) Start from a point on the loop and go along the loop, either anti-clockwise or clockwise, to reach the same point again, but balance currents at junction as per KCL.

(ii) If moving along the direction of the current, there will be potential drop across a resistance and if moving in the opposite direction, there will be potential gain.

(iii) The net sum of all these potential differences should be zero, using the KVL rule.

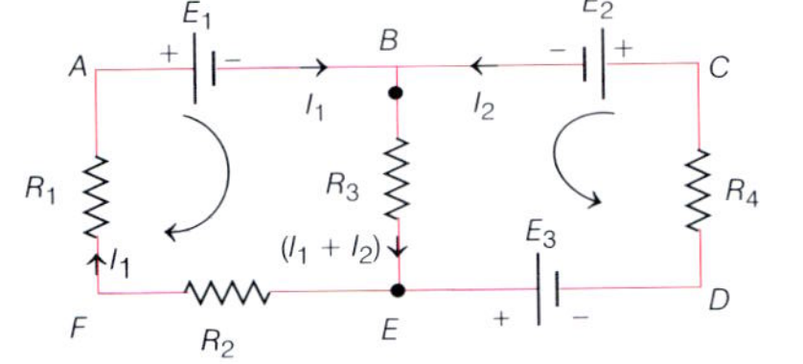
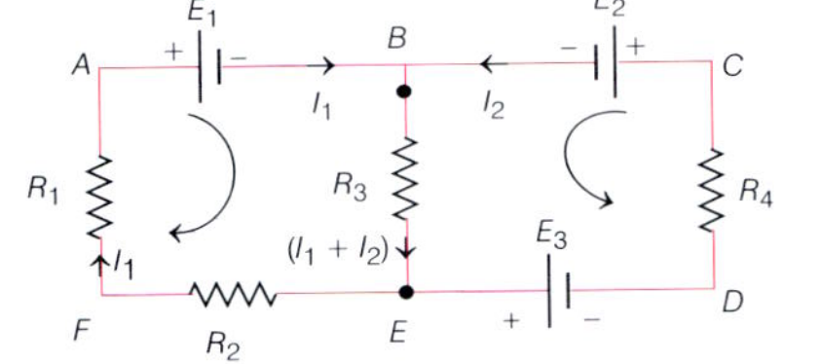

In closed loop, *ABEFA*,

$$-E_1 - (I_1 + I_2) R_3 - I_1 R_2 - I_1 R_1 = 0$$

In closed loop, *BCDEB*,

$$E_2 + I_2 R_4 + E_3 + (I_1 + I_2) R_3 = 0$$

Wheatstone Bridge

It is an application of Kirchhoff's rules. The bridge has four resistors R_1, R_2, R_3 and R_4. Across one pair of diagonally opposite points (*A* and *C* in the figure) a source is connected. This (i.e., *AC*) is called the battery arm. Between the other two vertices. *B* and *D*, a galvanometer *G* (which is a device to detect currents) is connected. This line, shown as *BD* in the figure is called the galvanometer arm.

In general, there will be currents flowing across all the resistors as well as a current I_g through *G*. Of special interest, is the case of a balanced bridge where the resistors are such that $I_g = 0$. We can easily get the balance condition, such that there is no current through *G*. In this case, the Kirchhoff's junction rule applied to junctions *D* and *B* (see the figure) immediately gives us the relations $I_1 = I_3$ and $I_2 = I_4$. Next, we apply Kirchhoff's loop rule to closed loops ADBA and CBDC. The first loop gives

$$-I_1 R_1 + 0 + I_2 R_2 = 0 \qquad (I_g = 0)$$

$$\frac{I_1}{I_2} = \frac{R_2}{R_1}$$

and the second loop gives, upon using $I_3 = I_1, I_4 = I_2$

$$I_2 R_4 + 0 - I_1 R_3 = 0$$

$$\frac{I_1}{I_2} = \frac{R_4}{R_3}$$

Hence, we obtain the condition

$$\frac{R_2}{R_1} = \frac{R_4}{R_3}$$

This last equation relating the four resistors is called the **balance condition** for the galvanometer to give zero or null deflection.

Meter Bridge

The meter bridge is a practical application of Wheatstone bridge. It consists of a wire of length 1 m and of uniform cross-sectional area stretched taut and clamped between two thick metallic strips bent at right angles, as shown. The metallic strip has two gaps across which resistors can be connected. The end points where the wire is clamped are connected to a cell through a key. One end of a galvanometer is connected to the metallic strip midway between the two gaps. The other end of the galvanometer is connected to a jockey. The jockey is essentially a metallic rod whose one end has a knife-edge which can slide over the wire to make electrical connection.

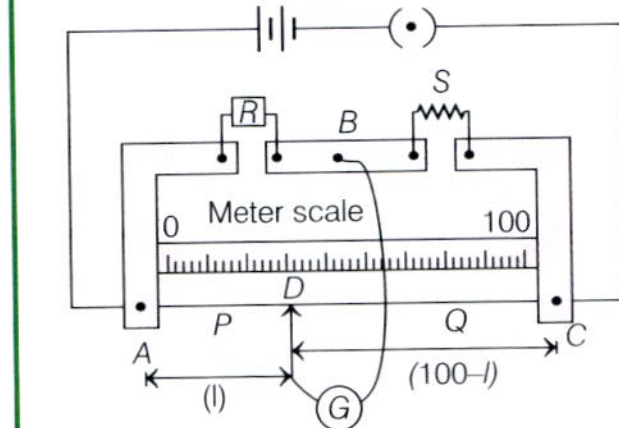

At balance point be $l = l_1$. The four resistances of the bridge at the balance point are *R*, *S*, $R_{cm} l_1$ and $R_{cm}(100 - l_1)$. The balance condition gives

$$\frac{R}{S} = \frac{R_{cm} l_1}{R_{cm}(100 - l_1)} = \frac{l_1}{100 - l_1}$$

Thus, once we have found out l_1, the unknown resistance *R* is known in terms of the standard known resistance *S* by

$$R = S \frac{l_1}{100 - l_1}$$

By choosing various values of *S*, we would get various values of l_1 and calculate *R* each time. An error in measurement of l_1 would naturally result in an error in *R*. It can be shown that the percentage error in *R* can be minimised by adjusting the balance point near the middle of the bridge, i.e. when l_1 is close to 50 cm. (This requires a suitable choice of *S*).

Test 1

Syllabus

- Biot-Savart's Law and Its Applications to Current - Carrying Loop
- Ampere's Law and Its Applications to Long Current - Carrying Loop Straight Wire
- Solenoid

NCERT Page 113 to 116

For deeper insight **Scan the QR Code**

Chapter 05

Biot-Savart law

The magnetic field dB at a point P due to current elements of length is

$$dB \propto \frac{Idl\sin\theta}{r^2}$$

$$dB = \frac{\mu_0}{4\pi}\frac{Idl\sin\theta}{r^2}$$

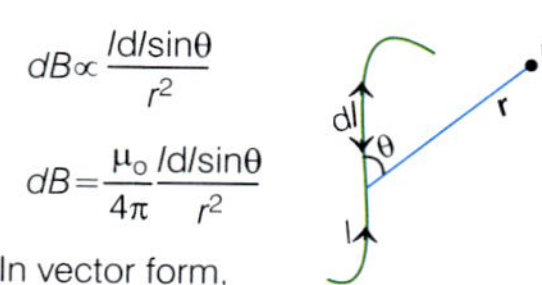

In vector form,

$$d\mathbf{B} = \frac{\mu_0}{4\pi} I \frac{d\mathbf{l}\times\mathbf{r}}{r^3}$$

$d\mathbf{B}$ is perpendicular to both side $d\mathbf{l}$ and $\mathbf{r}$. By using right hand screw rule we can find direction of magnetic field. Here, $\mathbf{B}$ is into the plane

Magnetic Field for Different Configurations of the Circular Coil

Magnitude and direction of magnetic fields associated with different configurations of the circular coil are given below.

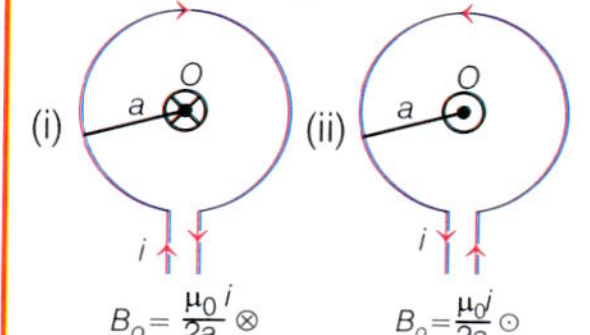

(i) $B_o = \frac{\mu_0 i}{2a} \otimes$ (ii) $B_o = \frac{\mu_0 i}{2a} \odot$

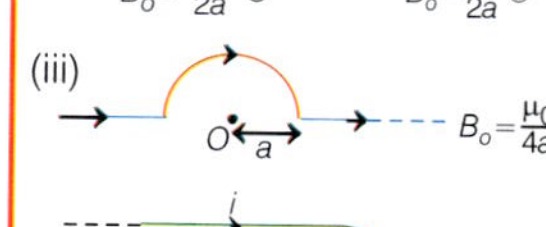

(iii) $B_o = \frac{\mu_0 i}{4a} \otimes$

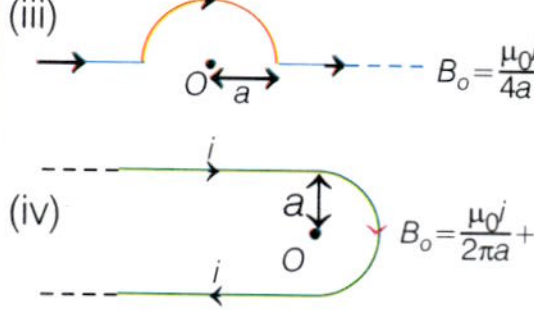

(iv) $B_o = \frac{\mu_0 i}{2\pi a} + \frac{\mu_0 i}{4a} \otimes$

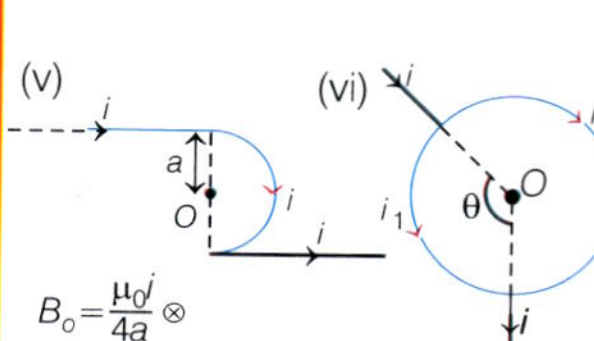

(v) $B_o = \frac{\mu_0 i}{4a} \otimes$

(vi) $B_o = 0$ (for any value of θ)

Magnetic Field Due to Long Straight Conducting Wire

At point P, B is into the plane.

$$B = \frac{\mu_0 I}{4\pi r}(\sin\alpha + \sin\beta)$$

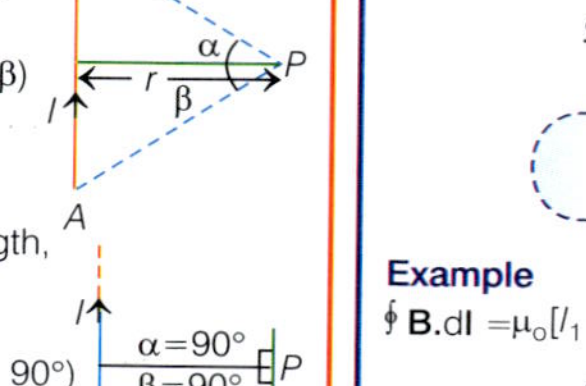

Cases:

a) Wire of infinite length, $\alpha = 90°$ and $\beta = 90°$.

$$B = \frac{\mu_0 I}{4\pi r}(\sin 90° + \sin 90°) = \frac{\mu_0 I}{2\pi r}, \otimes$$

b) Wire of semi-infinite length,

$$B = \frac{\mu_0 I}{4\pi r}(\sin 90° + \sin 0°) = \frac{\mu_0 I}{4\pi r}$$

Magnetic Field Due to Circular Coils

- **Field at the axis of the ring**

$$B_p = \frac{\mu_0 I R^2}{2(x^2 + R^2)^{3/2}}$$

- **Field at the centre of the ring,**

$$B_C = \frac{\mu_0 I}{2R}$$

Magnetic field lines

- **Relation between field at axis and field at centre**

$$B_{axis} = \frac{B_C}{\left(1 + \frac{x^2}{R^2}\right)^{3/2}}$$

Ampere Circuital Law

The line integral of magnetic field over a closed loop is equal to μ_0 times the total current enclosed by the loop

$$\oint \mathbf{B}.d\mathbf{l} = \mu_0 I_{enclosed}$$

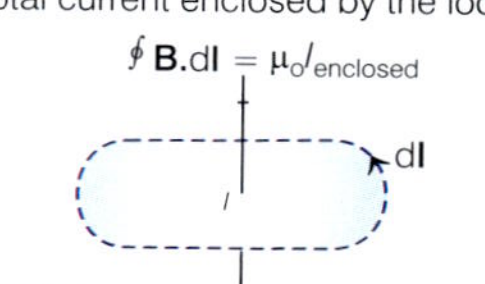

Example

$$\oint \mathbf{B}.d\mathbf{l} = \mu_0[I_1 - I_2 + I_3]$$

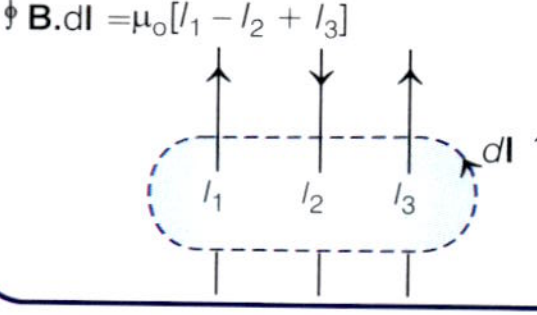
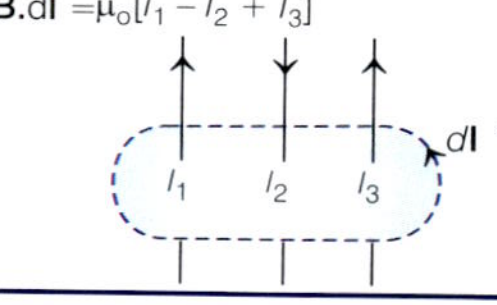

Magnetic Field due to an Arc

Magnetic field due to an arc of a circular current-carrying coil at the centre is given by

$$B = \left(\frac{\theta}{2\pi}\right)\frac{\mu_0 i}{2a} = \frac{\mu_0}{4\pi}\left(\frac{i}{a}\right)\theta$$

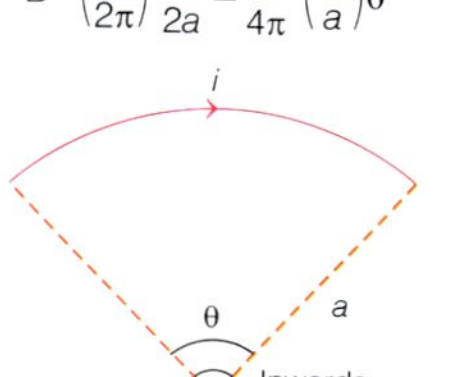
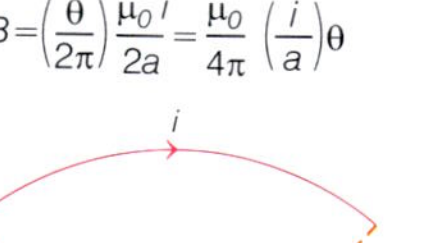

Here, θ is to be substituted in radians.

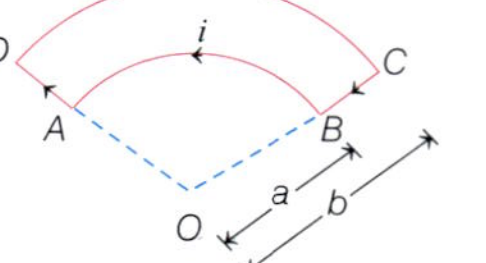
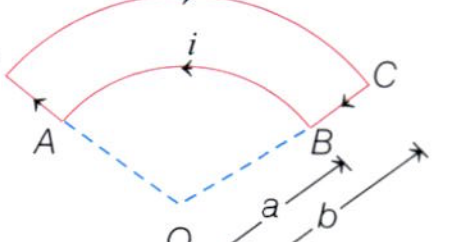

The resultant field at O,

$$B = B_1 - B_2 = \frac{\mu_0 i\theta(b-a)}{4\pi ab}$$

out of the plane

Magnetic Field of Solenoid

- Magnetic field produced around and within the solenoid in shown below

Solenoid

- Magnetic field outside the ideal solenoid is zero

$B = 0$

Magnetic field outside due to ideal solenoid

(i) Finite length solenoid If N = total number of turns, l = length of the solenoid and n = number of turns per unit length = N/l.

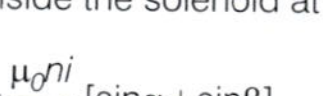

Magnetic field due to finite length solenoid

Magnetic field inside the solenoid at point P is given by

$$B = \frac{\mu_0 ni}{2}[\sin\alpha + \sin\beta]$$

(ii) Infinite length solenoid If the solenoid is of infinite length and the point is well inside it,

i.e. $\alpha = \beta = (\pi/2)$,

Then $B_{in} = \mu_0 ni$

If the solenoid is of infinite length and the point is near one end, i.e. $\alpha = 0$ and $\beta = (\pi/2)$, then

$$B_{end} = \frac{\mu_0 ni}{2}$$

Magnetic Field of a Cylindrical Wire

(I) Outside the cylinder ($r > R$)

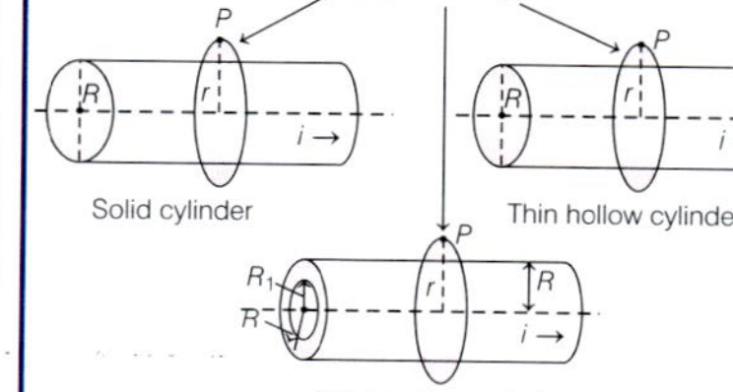

In all the above cases, magnetic field outside the wire at P,

$$\oint \mathbf{B}.d\mathbf{l} = B(2\pi r)$$

$$\Rightarrow B_{surface} = \frac{\mu_0 i}{2\pi r}$$

In all above cases, $B_{out} = \frac{\mu_0 i}{2\pi R}$

(ii) Inside the hollow cylinder ($r < R$) Magnetic field inside the hollow cylinder is zero because no current is enclosed by Amperian loops as shown below.

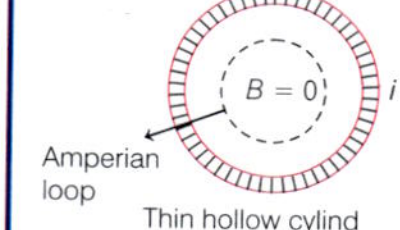

(iii) Inside the solid cylinder ($r < R$) Current i' enclosed by Amperian loop is less than the total current i. Current density is uniform, i.e. $J = J'$

$$\Rightarrow i' = i \times \frac{A'}{A} = i\left(\frac{r^2}{R^2}\right)$$

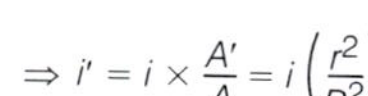
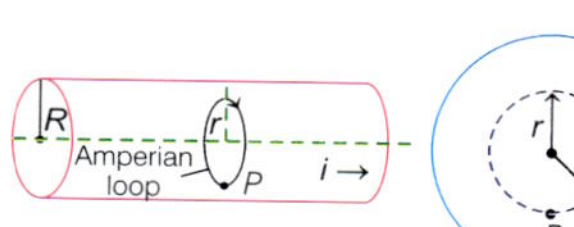

$$\oint \mathbf{B}_{in}.d\mathbf{l} = \mu_0 i' \Rightarrow B_{in} = \frac{\mu_0}{2\pi}\frac{ir}{R^2}$$

Test 2

Syllabus

- Force on a Moving Charge in Uniform Magnetic and Electric Fields
- Lorentz, Force
- Force on a Current-Carrying Conductor in a Uniform Magnetic Field
- The Force between Two Parallel Current-Carrying Conductor

NCERT Page 117 to 121

For deeper insight **Scan the QR Code**

Chapter 05

Force on a Moving Charge in a Magnetic Field

The electric charges moving in a magnetic field experience a force, while there is no such force on static charges. The charge q moving in the magnetic field B experiences a force F such that, $F \propto v \sin\theta$, $\mathbf{F} = q(\mathbf{v} \times \mathbf{B})$

$\therefore F = qvB \sin\theta$

Fleming's Left Hand Rule

Stretch the thumb and the first two fingers of the left hand mutually perpendicular to each other. If the forefinger points in the direction of the magnetic field, central finger in the direction of current, then the thumb gives the direction of the force on the charged particle.

Forces Between Two Parallel Current-Carrying Conductors

Consider two long parallel wires carrying currents I_1 and I_2. Let r be the separation between them.

The magnetic field produced by current I_1 at any point on wire is force per unit length,

$$B_1 = \frac{\mu_0 I_1}{2\pi r}\ f = \frac{F_2}{L} = \frac{\mu_0 I_1 I_2}{2\pi r}$$

Motion in Magnetic Field

Case I When the initial velocity is parallel to the magnetic field.

Here, $\theta = 0°$, so

$F = qvB \sin 0° = 0$.

Case II When the initial velocity is perpendicular to the magnetic field.

Here, $\theta = 90°$, so $F = qvB \sin 90°$

$= qvB =$ maximum force.

The radius of circular path $r = \frac{mv}{qB}$

Period of revolution $= \frac{\text{Circumference}}{\text{Speed}}$

or $T = \frac{2\pi r}{v} = \frac{2\pi}{v} \cdot \frac{mv}{qB} = \frac{2\pi m}{qB}$

The frequency of revolution is $f_c = \frac{1}{T} = \frac{qB}{2\pi m}$

Case III When the initial velocity makes an arbitrary angle with the field direction. The radius of the circular path is

$$r = \frac{mv_\perp}{qB} = \frac{mv \sin\theta}{qB}$$

The period of revolution, $T = \frac{2\pi m}{qB}$

- Angular speed of the particle, $\omega = \frac{2\pi}{T} = \frac{Bq}{m}$

$$\omega = \frac{Bq}{m}$$

- Frequency of rotation, $f = \frac{1}{T}$, $f = \frac{Bq}{2\pi m}$

- When a charged particle is projected perpendicular to a magnetic field, then
  (i) its path is circular in a plane perpendicular to the plane of magnetic field.
  (ii) the speed and kinetic energy of the particle remain constant.
  (iii) the velocity and momentum of the particle change only in direction.
  (iv) the time period of revolution, angular velocity and frequency of revolution are independent of velocity of the particle and radius of circular path.

Motion of a Charge in Perpendicular Magnetic and Electric Fields

A beam of charged particles, say electrons, possessing a range of speeds passes through a slit S_1 and then enters a region in which crossed electric and magnetic field exist. The electric field **E** acts in the downward direction and deflects the electrons in the upward direction. The magnetic field **B** acts normally into the plane of paper and deflects the electrons in the downward direction.

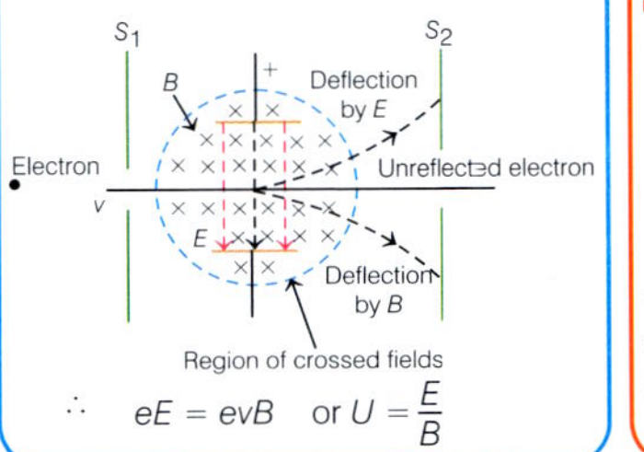

$\therefore\ eE = evB$ or $U = \frac{E}{B}$

Lorentz Force

The total force experienced by a charged particle moving in a region where both electric and magnetic fields are present is called Lorentz force. $\therefore \mathbf{F} = q(\mathbf{E} + \mathbf{v} \times \mathbf{B})$

Case I When v, E and B are all Collinear The magnetic force on it will be zero and only electric force will act.

So, acceleration,

$$a = \frac{F_e}{m} = \frac{qE}{m}$$

The particle will pass through the field following a straight line path (parallel field) with change in its speed.

Case II When v, E and B are Mutually Perpendicular If E and B are such that, $F = F_e + F_m = 0$, i.e, $a = (F/m) = 0$

Motion of a charged particle with $\mathbf{v} \perp \mathbf{E} \perp \mathbf{B}$

The particles will passes through the field with same velocity without any deviation in its path $F_e = F_m$, i.e, $qE = qvB$

$$v = E/B$$

Magnetic Force on different Configurations of the Curve

Magnetic force on a straight wire placed in magnetic field.

$F = BiL$

(a) Straight wire

Magnetic force on a semiconductor wire placed in magnetic field.

$F = i(2a)B$

(b) Semicircular wire

Magnetic force on a sinusoidal wire placed in magnetic field.

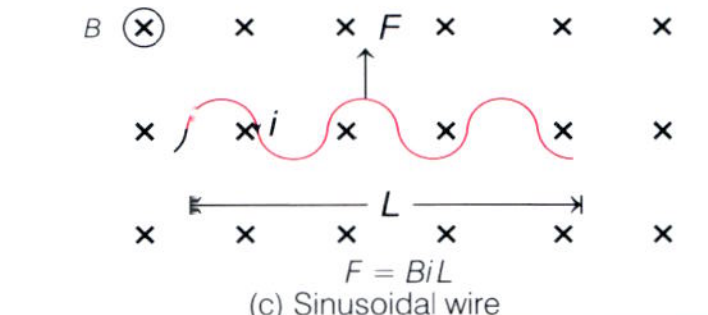

$F = BiL$

(c) Sinusoidal wire

Definition of Ampere

One ampere is the current which flows through each of the two parallel uniform long linear conductors, which are placed in free space at a distance of 1 m from each other and attract or repel each other with a force of 2×10^{-7} N/m.

Right Hand Palm Rule

If we spread our right hand in such a way that thumb is towards the direction of current and fingers are towards that point where we have to find the direction of magnetic field, then direction of magnetic field will be perpendicular to the palm.

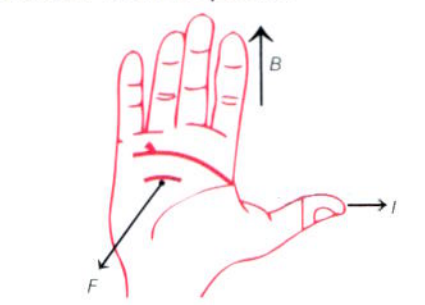

Neutral point

Point at which magnetic field becomes zero are called neutral point

Case 1: Parallel wires carrying current in same direction ($I_1 > I_2$),

$\therefore x = \frac{I_1 r}{I_1 - I_2}$

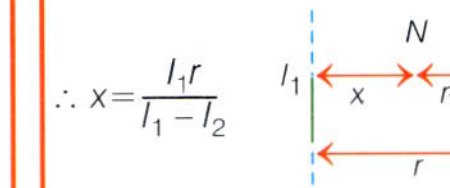

If y is the distance from 2nd conductor, then $y = \frac{I_1 r}{I_1 - I_2}$

Case 2 : Parallel wires carrying current in opposite direction ($I_1 > I_2$)

$x = \frac{I_1 r}{I_1 - I_2}$

Case 3 : Wires perpendicular to each other, field will be zero on all points of the line OP.

Slope, $m = \frac{I_y}{I_x}$

Test 3

Syllabus
- Torque Experienced by a Current Loop in a Uniform Magnetic Field
- Moving Coil Galvanometer, its Sensitivity and Conversion to Ammeter and Voltmeter

NCERT Page 108 to 112, Page 122 to 131

For deeper insight **Scan the QR Code**

Chapter 05

Magnetic Dipole Moment

- Magnetic dipole moment associated with a current-carrying loop is given as
  $M = NiA \Rightarrow |M| = NiA$
  where, N = number of turns in the loop
  i = current in the loop
  and A = area of cross-section of the loop
- It is a vector quantity directed along area vector **A** of the loop with anti-clockwise sense as positive.
- Its SI unit is A-m^3.

Torque Experienced by a Current Loop

When a current carrying coil is placed in a magnetic field, the coil experiences a torque.

For a rectangular current carrying coil $PQRS$ having turns and area A. When this coil is placed in a uniform field **B** in such a way that the normal $\hat{\mathbf{n}}$ to the coil makes an angle θ with the direction of **B**. The coil experiences a torque which is given by

$$\tau = NBiA \sin\theta$$

In vector form, τ = **M.B**

Special cases

(i) τ is zero when $\theta = 0$, i.e. the plane of the coil is perpendicular to the field.

(ii) τ is maximum when $\theta = 90$, i.e. the plane of the coil is parallel to the field,

$$\tau_{max} = NBiA$$

The direction of the torque τ is such that it rotates the loop anti-clockwise about the axis of suspension.

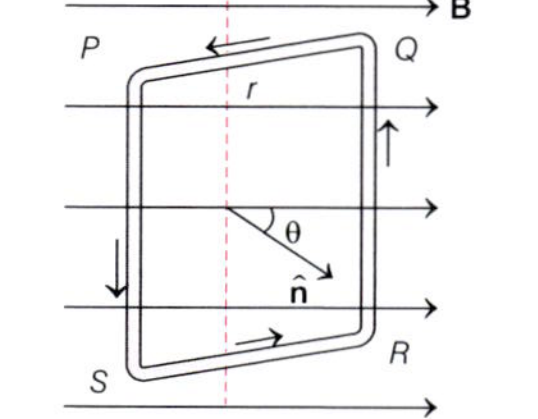

Torque on a Current Carrying Loop

Moving Coil Galvanometer

A device which is based on the principle that when a current carrying coil is placed in a uniform magnetic field, then it experiences a torque. Consists of a multi-turn coil free to rotate about a vertical axis, in a uniform radial magnetic field. There is a cylindrical soft iron core to increase the sensitivity of the MCG.

The plane of the coil always remains parallel to the direction of magnetic field, therefore $\theta = 90$. The deflecting torque has maximum value,

$$\tau = NIAB \quad \ldots(i)$$

where, the symbols have their usual meaning. Since, the magnetic field is radial by design, we have taken $\sin\theta = 1$ in the above expression for the torque.

As the coil deflects, a restoring torque is set-up in the suspension fibre. If α is the angle of twist, the restoring torque,

$$\tau_{rest} = k\alpha \quad \ldots(ii)$$

where, k is the torsional constant of the fibre.

When the coil is in equilibrium,

$$NIAB = k\alpha$$
$$I = G\alpha \quad \alpha \propto I$$

where, $G = \dfrac{k}{NBA}$ is the galvanometer constant.

This linear relationship between I and α makes the moving coil galvanometer useful for current measurement and detection.

Sensitivity of Moving Coil Galvanometer

- **Current Sensitivity**

The current sensitivity of a meter is the deflection of the meter per unit i.e, α/I, it is given by

$$I_s = \frac{\alpha}{I} = \frac{NBA}{K}$$

The sensitiveness can be increased by increasing N, A and B and decreasing the value of k. But N and A cannot be increased much because this will increase the length and consequently the resistance of the coil. In that case, the galvanometer will not respond to weak electric currents.

B can be increased by using a strong magnet. k can be decreased by using phosphor-bronze for suspension. k can be further reduced by using quartz suspension fibre.

- **Voltage Sensitivity**

It is defined as the deflection of the meter per unit voltage

$$V_s = \frac{\alpha}{V} = \frac{\alpha}{IR} = \frac{NBA}{kR}$$

Conversion of Galvanometer to Ammeter

A current measuring instrument is called an **ammeter**. A galvanometer can be converted into an ammeter by connecting a small resistance S (called shunt) in parallel with it. If G is the resistance of a galvanometer and it give full scale deflection for current i_g, then required low resistances, connected in its parallel for converting it into an ammeter of range i is given by

$$i_g \times G = (i - i_g) \times S$$

$$S = \left(\frac{i_g}{i - i_g}\right) G$$

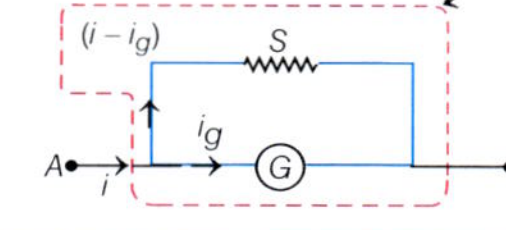

Conversion of Galvanometer to Voltmeter

A voltage measuring device is called a **voltmeter**. It measures the potential difference between two points. A galvanometer can be converted into voltmeter by connecting a high resistance R in series with it.

If a galvanometer of resistance G shows full scale deflection for current I_g, then required high resistance, connected in series for converting it into a voltmeter of range V is given by

$$V = i_g(G + R)$$

$$R = \frac{V}{i_g} - G$$

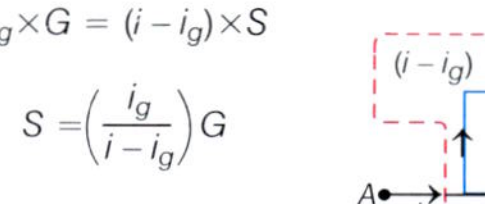

Summarising

S. No	Ammeter	Voltmeter
1.	It is a low resistance instrument	It is a high resistance instrument.
2.	Resistance $= GS/G + S$	Resistance $= G + R$
3.	Shunt resistance $= \dfrac{G\, I_g}{I - I_g}$	Series resistance $= \dfrac{V}{I_g} - G$
4.	It is always connected in series.	It is always connected in parallel.
5.	The resistance of an ideal ammeter is zero.	The resistance of an ideal voltmeter is infinity.
6.	Since, ammeter is a parallel combination of galvanometer and shunt resistance, therefore, the resistance of the ammeter is less than that of the galvanometer.	Since, voltmeter is a series combination of galvanometer and resistance, therefore, the resistance of the voltmeter is greater than that of the galvanometer.
7.	It is not possible to decrease the range of given ammeter.	It is not possible to decrease the range of given voltmeter.

Shunt Resistance

A low resistance which is connected in parallel with a galvanometer (or ammeter) to protect, it from strong currents.

Uses of Shunt Resistance

(i) To prevent a galvanometer from being damaged due to large current.

(ii) To convert a galvanometer into ammeter.

(iii) To increase the range of an ammeter.

Advantages Of Moving Coil Galvanometer

(I) The galvanometer can be made extremely sensitive.

(ii) Since the magnetic field B is very high, therefore, the external magnetic fields cannot appreciably alter the deflection of the coil. So, the galvanometer can be used in any position.

(iii) Since the deflection of the coil is proportional to current, therefore, linear scale can be used.

(iv) Since the coil is wound over metallic frame, therefore, damping is produced by eddy currents. So, the galvanometer coil comes to rest quickly. This type of galvanometer is called aperiodic or dead beat galvanometer. The galvanometer can be made ballistic by winding the coil on a non-conducting frame of ivory or ebonite.

(v) The lamp and scale arrangement used to measure the deflection of the coil makes the galvanometer very sensitive.

Test 1

Syllabus

- Bar Magnet as an Equivalent Solenoid and Magnetic Field Lines
- Magnetic Field Due to a Magnetic Dipole (Bar Magnet) Along its axis and Perpendicular to Its Axis.
- Torque on a Magnetic Dipole in a Uniform Magnetic Field

NCERT Page 137 to 146

For deeper insight **Scan the QR Code**

Chapter 06

Bar Magnet

A bar magnet is a circular or rectangular cross-section. It is made up of iron, steel or any other ferromagnetic substance or ferromagnetic composite, having permanent magnetic properties.

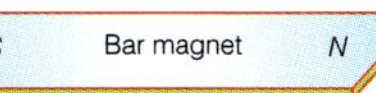

Properties of Magnet

- **Directive Property**
  When a magnet is suspended freely, it aligns itself in the geographical north-south direction.

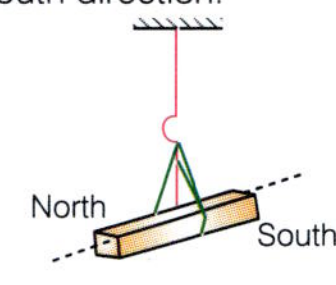

- **Monopole Non-existence Property**
If a magnet is broken into number of pieces, then each piece behaves as an individual magnet rather than isolated poles. This means that monopoles do not exist.

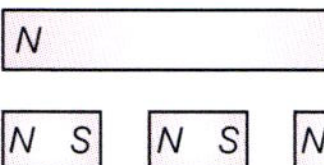

- **Attractive/Repulsive Property**
  Like magnetic poles repel each other and unlike magnetic poles attract each other.

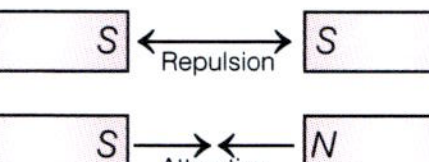

- Earth behaves like a magnet with magnetic field from south to north (approx.)
- Magnets can be made using iron and its alloys.

Magnetism

A magnet is a material that has both attractive and directive properties. It attracts small pieces of iron, nickel, cobalt, etc. This property of attraction is called magnetism.

Magnetic Field Lines

The curve whose tangent at any point gives the direction of the magnetic field or the path along which a unit north pole would tend to move, if free to do so.

Properties of Magnetic Field Lines

(i) The magnetic field lines of a magnet form closed continuous loops. This property is unlike electric field lines, which begin from a positive charge and terminate at the negative charge or escape to infinity.

(ii) At any point, tangent to the magnetic field line represents the direction of net magnetic field (**B**) at that point.

(iii) Larger the number of field lines crossing per unit area, stronger is the magnitude of the magnetic field B.

(iv) Magnetic field lines do not intersect each other, if they did, the direction of the magnetic field would not be unique at the point of intersection.

(a) Magnetic field lines due to a bar magnet (form closed loops)

(b) Magnetic field lines due to a horse shoe magnet (form closed loops)

(c) Magnetic field lines between two unlike poles (contract longitudinally)

(d) Magnetic field lines between two like poles (repel each other laterally)

Coulomb's Law of Magnetic Force

This law states that the force of attraction or repulsion between two magnetic poles is directly proportional to the product of their pole strengths and inversely proportional to the square of the distance between them.

$$F = \frac{\mu_0}{4\pi} \cdot \frac{q_{m_1} q_{m_2}}{r^2}$$

Magnetic Dipole Moment

It is the product of the strength of either of the pole strength and the magnetic length of the magnet. It is a vector quantity and it is represented by **M**.

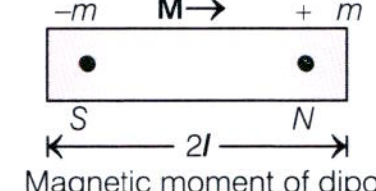

Magnetic moment of dipole

The direction of magnetic dipole moment is same as that of $2l$.

Therefore, $M = m(2l)$

Its SI unit is ampere-(metre)^2(A-m)^2.

Magnetic field of a bar magnetic on axial point, $\mathbf{B}_{\text{axial}} = \frac{\mu_0}{4\pi} \cdot \frac{2\mathbf{M}}{r^3}$

At an equatorial point, $\mathbf{B}_{\text{equa}} = \frac{-\mu_0}{4\pi} \frac{\mathbf{M}}{r^3}$

Solenoid as Equivalent Bar Magnet

- Each turns of the solenoid can be regarded as a small magnetic dipole, then the solenoid becomes a small magnetic dipole.
- The number of magnetic dipole is equal to the number of turns in the solenoid.
- For a solenoid of length $2l$ and radius a consisting n per unit length, the magnetic field is given by $B = \frac{\mu_0 2M}{4\pi r^3}$

Bar Magnet in Magnetic Field

Torque on a magnetic dipole (bar magnet),

τ = force x perpendicular distance between coupled forces

$$\tau = MB \sin\theta$$

$\theta = 90° \Rightarrow \tau = MB$ (Max)

$\theta = 0° \Rightarrow \tau = 0$ (Min)

Potential energy of magnetic moment dipole,

$$U = -MB\cos\theta$$

Clockwise, $F_m = mB$, $\vec{B}$ (uniform), Clockwise, $F_m = mB$

Special Shapes of Bar Magnet

- When two identical bar magnets are joined perpendicular to each other

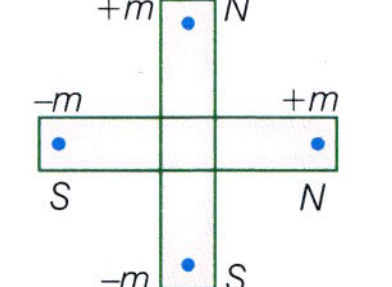

$$M = \sqrt{M_1^2 + M_2^2} = \sqrt{2}M$$

- If a bar magnet is bent in the form of semi-circle

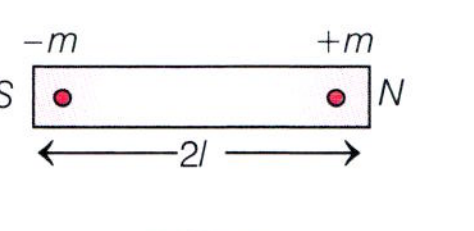

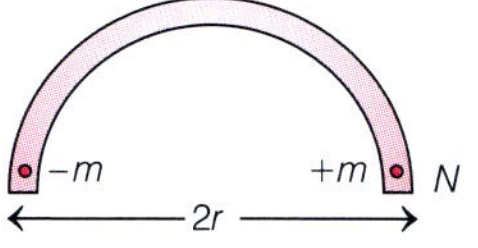

$M' = m(2r)$ $\quad [\because 2l = \pi r]$

$$M' = m \times 2\left(\frac{2l}{\pi}\right) = \frac{2M}{\pi}$$

$\left(\text{Become } \frac{2}{\pi} \text{ times}\right)$

Gauss's Law in Magnetism

The surface integral of a magnetic field over a closed surface is always zero. i.e. the net magnetic flux through any closed surface is always zero $\oint \mathbf{B}.d\mathbf{s} = 0$

Consequences of Gauss Law

(i) Consider a Gaussian surface (any closed surface) enclosing one of the poles (say south) of the magnet as shown in figure. Here, the number of field lines entering the Gaussian surface is same as the number of lines leaving it. *i.e.* Net magnetic flux for the whole Gaussian surface is zero.

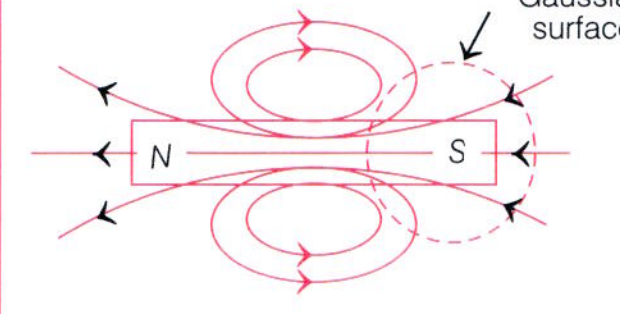

(ii) The Gauss's theorem in magnetism implies that isolated magnetic poles do not exist.

(iii) In case of open surface,
$\int \mathbf{B} \cdot d\mathbf{S} = \phi_B$
(magnetic flux associated with the surface)

(iv) The magnetic poles always exist as unlike pairs of equal strengths.

Bar magnet Inclined at an Angle

When two bar magnetic are inclined at an angle θ, then the resultant magnetic moment of the system is given by

Resultant magnetic moment,

$$M = \sqrt{M_1^2 + M_2^2 + 2M_1M_2\cos\theta}$$

Angle made by resultant magnetic moment (M') with M_1 is given by

$$\tan\phi = \frac{M_2\sin\theta}{M_1 + M_2\cos\theta}$$

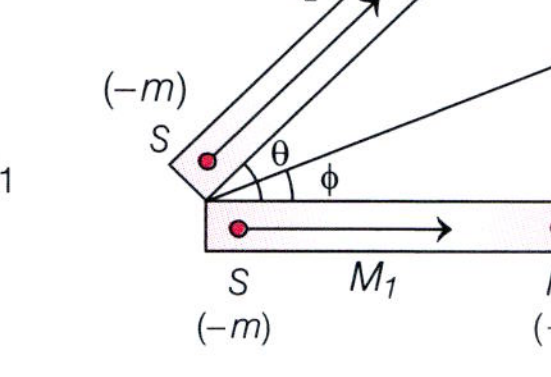
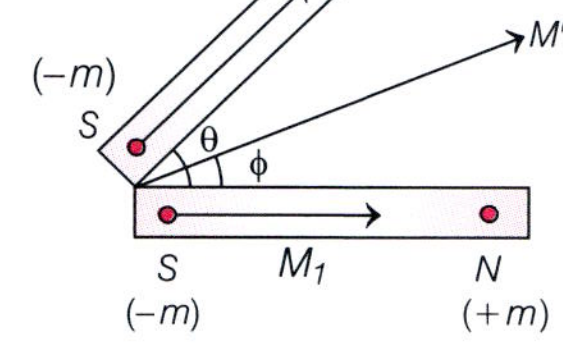
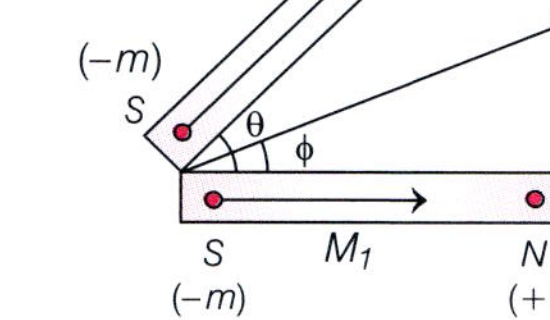

Test 2

Syllabus

- Para, Dia and Ferromagnetic Substances with Examples
- Effect of Temperature or Magnetic Properties

NCERT Page 147 to 149

For deeper insight **Scan the QR Code**

Chapter 06

Magnetising Field

The magnetic field that exists in vacuum and induces magnetism is called magnetising field. $B_0 = \mu_0 nI$

Magnetic Induction

The total number of magnetic lines of force crossing per unit area normally through a material. The SI unit of magnetic induction is tesla (T).

Magnetising Field Intensity

The ability of a magnetising field to magnetise a material medium is expressed by a vector **H**, called magnetising field intensity or magnetic intensity. $H = nI$

$\therefore \quad B_0 = \mu_0 nI = \mu_0 H$ or $H = \dfrac{B_0}{\mu_0}$

Intensity of Magnetisation

The magnetic moment developed per unit volume of a material when placed in a magnetising field is called intensity of magnetisation.

$$\mathbf{I} = \frac{\mathbf{M}}{V}$$

Its SI units is ampere/meter (A/m).

For bar magnet, $I = m/A$

Magnetic Permeability

The magnetic permeability of a material defined as the ratio of its magnetic induction B to the magnetic intensity H.

$$\mu = \frac{B}{H}$$

Relative Magnetic Permeability

The ratio of the magnetic permeability of the medium to the magnetic permeability of free space. $\therefore \mu_r = \dfrac{\mu}{\mu_0}$

In vacuum, its value is 1

Magnetic Susceptibility

It is the property of the substance which shows how easily a substance can be magnetised when kept in a magnetising field. It can also be defined as the ratio of intensity of magnetisation (I) in a substance to the magnetic intensity (H) applied to the substance,

i.e. $\quad \chi_m = \dfrac{\mathbf{I}}{\mathbf{H}}$

It is a scalar quantity with no units and dimensions.

Relation between μ_r and χ_m

We have, $\mathbf{B} = \mu_0(\mathbf{I}+\mathbf{H})$

or $\quad B = \mu_0 H\left[\left(\dfrac{\mathbf{I}}{\mathbf{H}}\right)+1\right]$ or $B = B_o(\chi_m + 1)$

$\Rightarrow \quad \dfrac{B}{B_o} = \chi_m + 1$

But $\quad \dfrac{B}{B_o} = \dfrac{\mu}{\mu_o} = \mu_r =$ relative permeability

$\therefore \quad \mu_r = \chi_m + 1$

Paramagenetic Substances

Paramagnetic substances are those which are attracted by a magnetic field.

- When a rod of paramagnetic material is suspended freely between two magnetic poles, then its axis becomes parallel to the magnetic field. The poles produced at the ends of the rod are opposite to the nearer magnetic poles.
- These substances are attracted towards regions of stronger magnetic field when placed in a non-uniform magnetic field.

Thus, they move from weaker to stronger parts of the field.

- A paramagnetic liquid is filled in a narrow U-tube and one limb is placed in between the pole pieces of an electromagnet, the liquid is feebly attracted by the magnet. Therefore, the level of the solution in the arm rises
- For paramagnetic substances, the relative permeability μ_r is slightly greater than one.
- Magnetic susceptibility is positive.
- The magnetic susceptibility of a paramagnetic material varies inversely as the absolute temperature.

i.e., $\chi_m = \dfrac{C}{T}$

- As soon as the magnetising field is removed, a paramagnetic substance looses its magnetism.

Diamagnetic Substances

- When a rod of diamagnetic material is suspended freely between two magnetic poles, then its axis becomes perpendicular to the magnetic field.

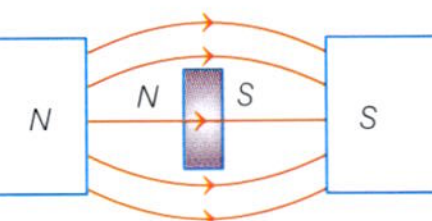

(ii) In a non-uniform magnetic field, these substances move from stronger to weaker parts of the external magnetic field. As, they acquire magnetisation in opposite direction, hence these are weakly repelled by the magnetic field.

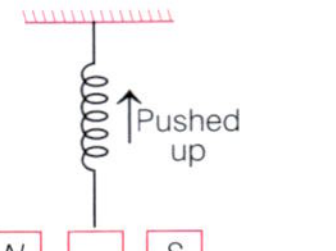

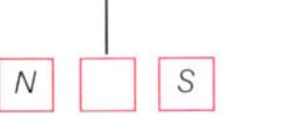

- Diamagnetic is present in all the substances. However, the effect is so weak that it gets shifted by other effects like paramagnetism, ferromagnetism etc.
- The relative permeability μ_r is slightly less than 1, i.e. $\mu_r < 1$.
- If a diamagnetic solution is poured into a U-tube and one arm of this U-tube is placed between the poles of a strong magnet, the level of the solution in that arm is depressed.

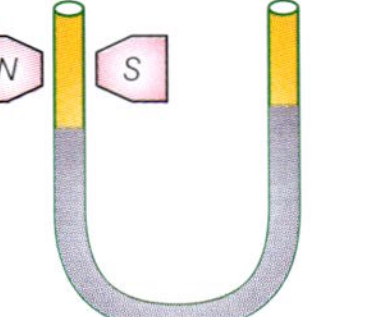
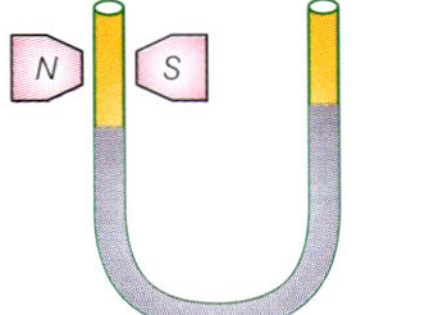

- The susceptibility of a diamagnetic substance is independent of the magnetising field and the temperature.

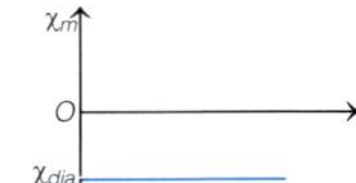

- The magnetisation of a diamagnetic substance lasts so long as the magnetising field is applied.

Ferromagnetic Substances

- They are strongly attracted towards the magnetic field.
- These are strongly magnetised in the direction of applied magnetic field.
- Liquid level in that limb rises up very much.
- A ferromagnetic substance retains magnetism even after the magnetising field is removed.

Curie's Law

According to this law, the magnetic susceptibility of paramagnetic substances is inversely proportional to its absolute temperature, i.e.

$$\chi_m \propto \frac{1}{T} \Rightarrow \chi_m = \frac{C}{T}$$

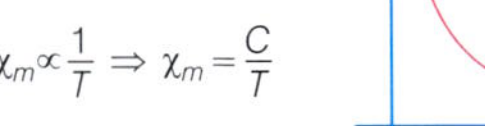
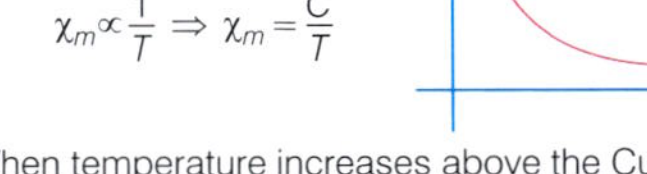

When temperature increases above the Curie temperature, a ferromagnetic substance becomes an ordinary paramagnetic substance whose magnetic susceptibility obeys the Curie-Weiss law as given below.

$$\chi_m = \frac{C'}{T - T_C}$$

Variation of χ_m *versus* T is shown below.

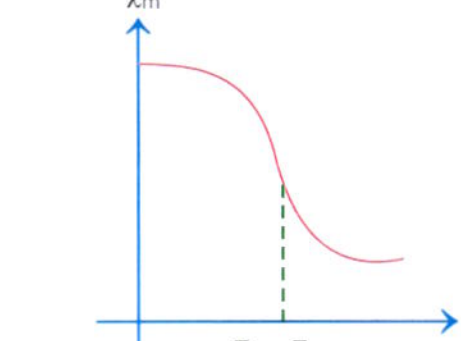
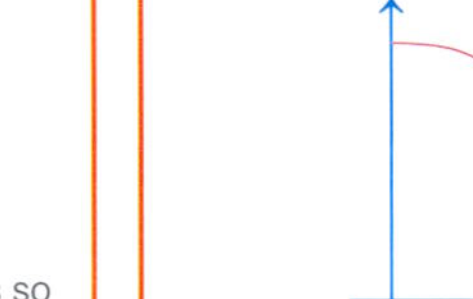

Test 1

Syllabus
- Magnetic Flux and Laws of EMI

NCERT Page 154 to 161

For deeper insight **Scan the QR Code**

Magnetic Flux

The magnetic flux through any surface placed in a magnetic field is the total number of magnetic lines of force crossing this surface normally. SI unit of magnetic flux is weber (Wb).

$\phi = \mathbf{B} \cdot \mathbf{A}$ or $\phi = BA \cos\theta$

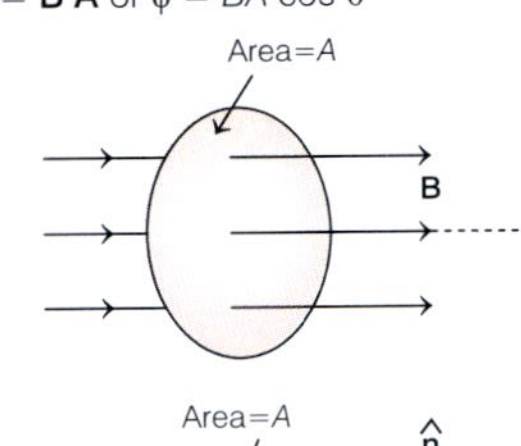

In uniform magnetic field B

(i). If $\theta = 0°$, maximum flux, $\phi = BA$

(ii). If $\theta = 90°$, minimum flux, $\phi = 0$

(iii). If $\theta = 180°$, minimum flux, $\phi = BA$

Unit and Dimensions of Magnetic Flux

(i) Magnetic flux is a scalar quantity.

(ii) The SI unit of magnetic flux is tesla-meter square (T-m^2). This unit is also called weber (Wb). 1 Wb = 1 T-m^2 = 1 N-m/A. The CGS unit of magnetic flux is Maxwell.

(iii) Dimensions of magnetic flux = $ML^2T^{-2}A^{-1}$

Methods of Generating Induced EMF

An induced emf can be produced by changing the magnetic flux linked with a circuit. The magnetic flux,

$\phi = BA \cos\theta$

Induced EMF by Changing the Magnetic Field B

(i) Moving a magnet towards a stationary coil.

(ii) Moving a coil towards a stationary magnet.

(iii) Varying current in the neighbouring coil.

Methods for Changing Magnetic Flux

The magnetic flux can be changed in the following ways

(i) The magnitude of **B** can be changed with time, i.e. time-varying magnetic field, $\mathbf{B} = B(t)$

(ii) The current producing the magnetic field can be changed with time, i.e. time varying current, $i = i(t)$.

(iii) The area enclosed by the loop can be change with time. This can be done by pulling a loop inside or outside a magnetic field. By doing, so the area enclosed by loop (hatched area) can be changed.

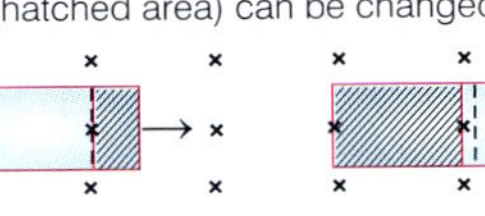

(iv) The angle θ between **B** and the normal to the loop can be changed with time. This can be done by rotating a loop in a magnetic field.

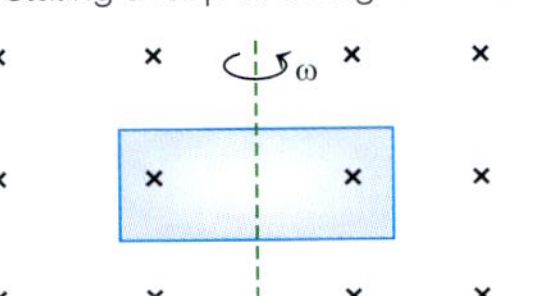

(v) Any combination of the above can be taken to change magnetic flux

Faraday's Law

(i) Whenever the magnetic flux linked with a conducting loop or coil changes, an emf is induced in it.

(ii) The induced emf is directly proportional to the rate of change of magnetic flux through the coil.

$$\varepsilon = -N \times \frac{d\phi}{dt}$$

The negative sign indicates that the induced emf opposes the cause that produces it.

The induced emf can be increased by increasing the number of turns N of a closed coil.

Lenz's Law

The direction of the induced emf is always such as to oppose the cause that produces it.

From Faraday's law,

$$\varepsilon = -N\frac{d\phi}{dt}$$

$$I = \frac{\text{Induced emf}}{\text{Resistance}} = -\frac{1}{R}\frac{d\phi}{dt}$$

Expression for induced charge,

$$dq = i_{in}\,dt = -\frac{1}{R}\left(\frac{d\phi}{dt}\right)dt = -\frac{d\phi}{R}$$

$$\Delta q = -\frac{\Delta\phi}{R}$$

It is a consequence of the law of conservation of energy.

- To apply Lenz's law, you can remember **RIN** or ⊗ **IN** (when the loop lies on the plane of paper).

(Increasing) i — Induced current

(i) In **RIN**, **R** stands for Right, **I** stands for Increasing and **N** for North pole (anti-clockwise). It means, if a loop is placed on the right side of a straight current-carrying conductor and the current i in the conductor is increasing, then induced current in the loop is anti-clockwise(↺).

(ii) In ⊗ **IN**, suppose the magnetic field in the loop is perpendicular to paper inwards (⊗) and this field is increasing, then induced current in the loop is anti-clockwise(↺).

⊗ Increasing

Induced Current

When the magnetic flux passing through a loop is changed, an induced emf and hence an induced current is produced in the circuit.

If R is the resistance of the circuit, then induced current is given by

$$i = \frac{V}{R} = \frac{1}{R}\left(\frac{-d\phi}{dt}\right)$$

Induced charge When the current starts flowing in the circuit, flow of charges also takes place. Charge flown in a circuit in time dt will be given by

$$dq = i\,dt = \frac{1}{R}(-d\phi)$$

Direction of Induced emf

(i) Conducting loop is being pulled inside and outside of magnetic field

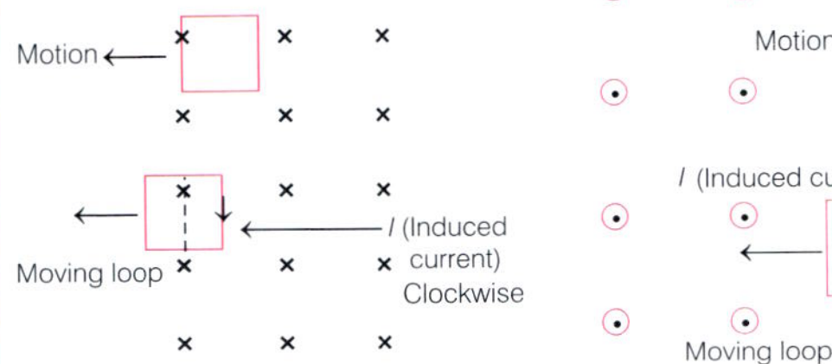

(ii) Loop bought near and move away from current - carrying wire

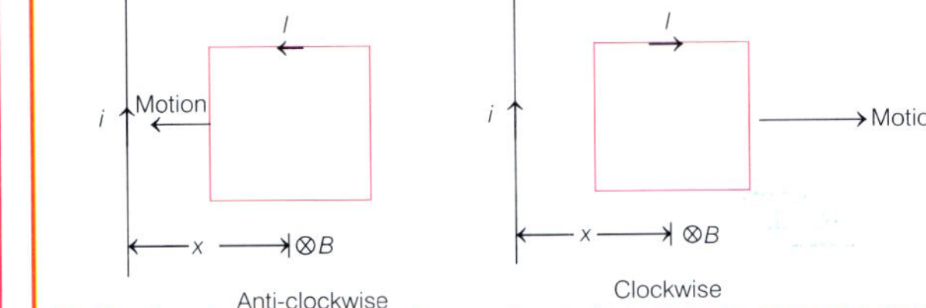

(iii) North pole of the magnet move towards and away from the ring

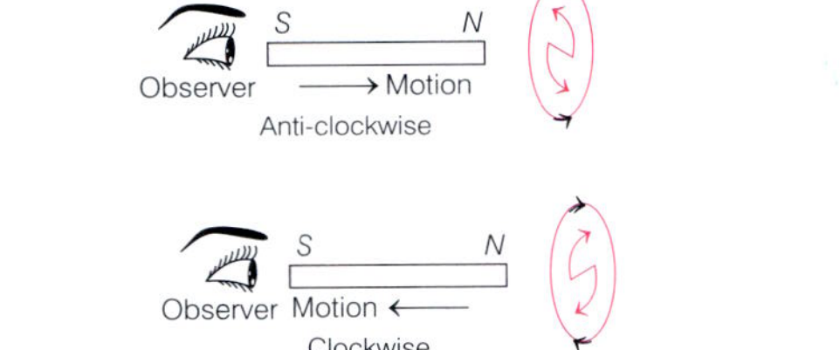

Test 2

Syllabus
- Motional EMF and Eddy Current

NCERT Page 162 to 164

For deeper insight **Scan the QR Code**

Chapter 07

Motional EMF

The emf induced across the ends of a conductor due to its motion in a magnetic field is called motional emf.

$$\varepsilon = Blv$$

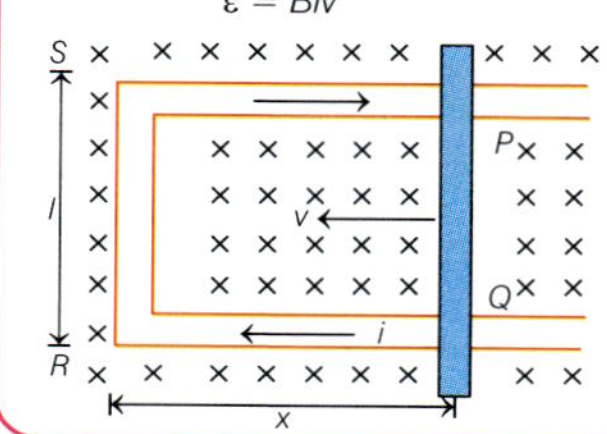

Fleming's Right Hand Rule

If we stretch the thumb and the first two fingers of our right hand in mutually perpendicular directions and if the forefinger points in the direction of the magnetic field, thumb in the direction of motion of the conductor, then the central finger points in the direction of current induced in the conductor.

This rule is also called the dynamo or generator rule and has wide practical applications.

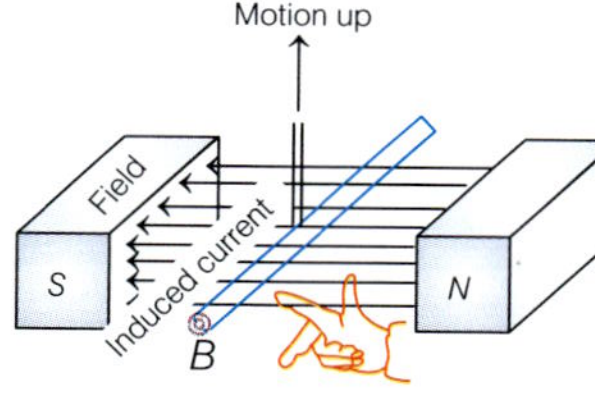

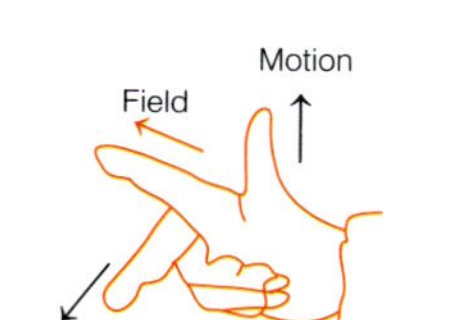

Important Points Related to Motional EMF

- For a semi-circular conducting loop (PQ) of radius R with the centre at O and moving with velocity v, then the emf is given by

$$e = Bv\,(2R)$$
$$V_P - V_Q = 2BvR$$

P (+), O, R, Q (–), v

$\Rightarrow$ P —|— Q, e

If a conducting rod PQ moves with a velocity v in XY-plane,

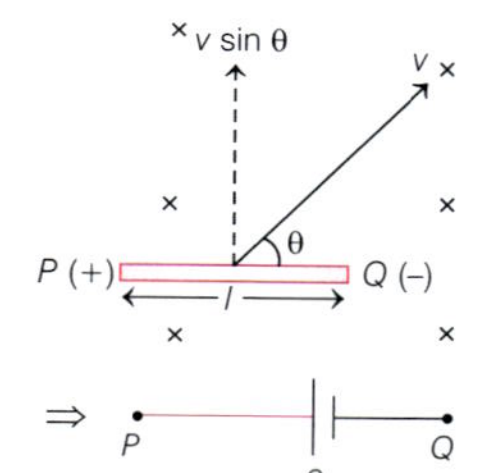

$\Rightarrow$ P —|— Q, e

No emf will be induced, due to $v\cos\theta$. So, the net effect of emf will be due to $v\sin\theta$, which is given by $e = B\,(v\sin\theta)\,l$.

Motional EMF for Circular Loop

For a circular loop of radius R moving with velocity v, we can replace its two ends lying on opposite sides of diameter with a battery of emf e. The emf is given by $e = Bv(2R) = 2BvR$

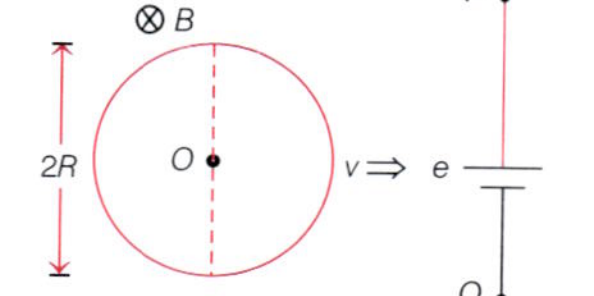

Motional EMF from Lorentz Force and Energy Consideration

A conductor has a large number of free electrons. When it moves through a magnetic field, a Lorentz force acting on the free electrons can set up a current.

$F_m = F_e$ or $qvB = qE$ or $vB = E$

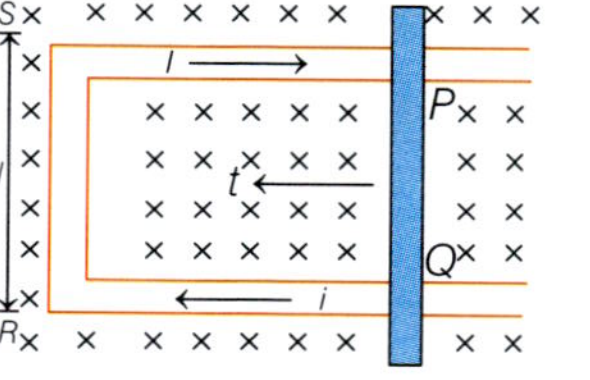

Current induced in the loop

$$I = \frac{\varepsilon}{R} = \frac{Blv}{R}$$

Force on the movable arm

$$F = \frac{B^2l^2v}{R}$$

Power delivered by the external force

$$P = Fv = \frac{B^2l^2v^2}{R}$$

Power dissipated as joule loss,

$$P_J = I^2R = \left(\frac{Blv}{R}\right)^2 R = \frac{B^2l^2v^2}{R}$$

Instantaneous value of Induced EMF

When the normal to the coil is at an angle θ with the field, the flux through the coil is given by

$$\phi = NBA\cos\theta$$
$$= NBA\cos\omega t$$
$$\varepsilon_{ind} = \frac{d\phi}{dt}$$
$$\varepsilon_{ind} = NBA\omega\sin\omega t$$
$$\varepsilon_0 = NBA\omega$$
when $t = 0$
$$\varepsilon_{ind} = \varepsilon_0\sin\omega t$$

The instantaneous value of induced EMF is directly linked to how rapidly the magnetic flux changes with time.

Motional EMF Induced in a Rotating Bar

(i) A conducting rod of length l rotates with a constant angular speed ω about a pivot at one end. A uniform magnetic field B is directed perpendicular to the plane of rotation as shown in figure.

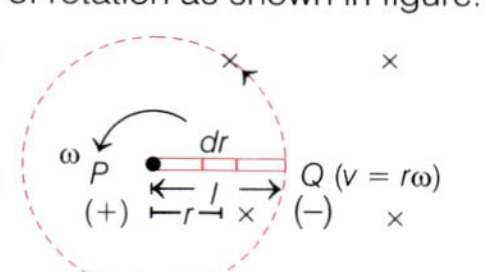

Let us suppose an element of length dr at a distance r from P. The induced emf in this segment is

$$de = Bvdr = B(r\omega)dr$$
$$e = \int de = \int_0^l B r\omega\, dr$$
$$e = \frac{B\omega l^2}{2}$$

(ii) A conducting disc of radius r rotates with constant angular velocity ω about its axis in a uniform magnetic field parallel to its axis of rotation as shown in figure.

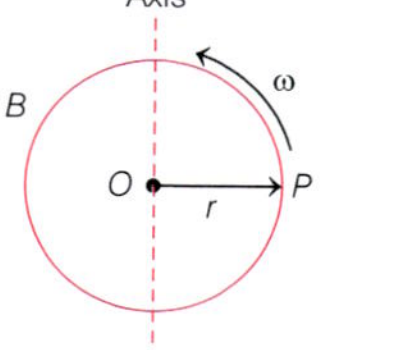

Take a rod between centre and point P.

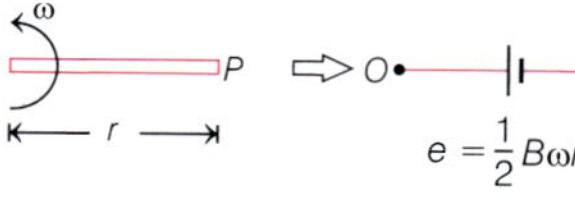

$\Rightarrow$ O —|— P

$$e = \frac{1}{2}B\omega r^2$$

So, the induced emf is given by $e = \frac{1}{2}B\omega r^2$

Methods to Reduce Eddy Current

Eddy currents are minimised by using laminations of metal to make a metal core. The laminations are separated by an insulating material. The plane of the laminations must be arranged parallel to the magnetic field, so that they cut across the eddy current paths. This arrrangement reduces the strength of eddy currents.

Eddy Current

Whenever the magnetic flux linked with a metal sheet changes, induced currents are produced in it. The flow of these current look like swirling eddies. This is known as eddy current.

Applications of Eddy Current

- **Induction furnace** If a metal specimen is placed in a changing magnetic field, very large eddy currents are set up. The heat produced is sufficient to even melt the metal.
- **Electric brakes** A strong magnetic field is applied to the rotating drum attached to the wheel. Eddy currents set up in the drum exert a torque on the drum, so as to stop the train.
- **Inductothermy** Eddy currents can be used to heat localised tissues of the human body. This branch is called inductothermy.
- **Energy meters** the energy meters used for measuring electric energy, the eddy currents induced in an aluminium disc are used for converting electrical power into mechanical power

General form of Motional EMF

To find motional emf for a conductor of any shape, moving in a uniform or non-uniform magnetic field, we will consider any small element dl of a conductor, then the magnitude of induced emf ($d\varepsilon$) is the magnitude of $d\,\mathbf{l}$ multiplied by the component of $(\mathbf{v} \times \mathbf{B})$ which is parallel to $d\,\mathbf{l}$.

i.e. $d\varepsilon = (\mathbf{v} \times \mathbf{B}).\,d\mathbf{l}$

$\Rightarrow \varepsilon = \int (\mathbf{v} \times \mathbf{B}).d\mathbf{l}$ [motional emf, closed conducting loop]

Relation Between Induced Charge and Magnetic Flux

According to Faraday's law, the magnitude of induced emf is given by

$$\varepsilon = \Delta\phi/\Delta t$$

if R is the total resistance of the closed loop then, $I = \varepsilon/R$ or $\Delta q/\Delta t = \Delta\phi/\Delta t \cdot 1/R$

Hence, the charge induced in the circuit in time Δt

$$\Delta q = \Delta\phi/R$$

The induced charge depends on the net change in the magnetic flux.

Test 3

Syllabus
- Inductance - Self and Mutual Inductance

NCERT Page 165 to 172

For deeper insight **Scan the QR Code**

Chapter 07

Inductance

Flow of charge (in form of induced current) in a coil due to change in flux through the coil is known as inductance. The flux associated to a coil is proportional to the current flowing in same coil or another coil.

$$\phi_B \propto I$$

Also, $\frac{d\phi_B}{dt} \propto \frac{dI}{dt}$

The constant of proportionality in the above equation is known as inductance. It is a scalar quantity and its unit is henry.
Its dimensions are $[M^1L^2T^{-2}A^{-2}]$.
Inductance is of two types : Self-inductance and mutual inductance.

Self - Inductance

The phenomenon of electromagnetic induction in which on changing the current in a coil, an opposing induced emf is set up in that every coil is called self inductance.

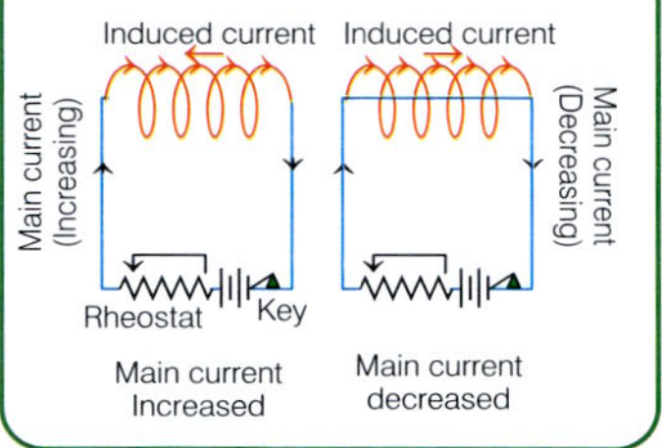

Coefficient of Self-Inductance

The magnetic flux ϕ linked with a coil is proportional to the current i through it,
i.e. $\phi \propto i$, $\phi = Li \therefore \varepsilon = \frac{d\phi}{dt} = -L\frac{di}{dt}$

Combination of self-inductances

In series Equivalent inductance,

$$L = L_1 + L_2 + L_3$$

In parallel Equivalent inductance,

$$\frac{1}{L} = \frac{1}{L_1} + \frac{1}{L_2} + \frac{1}{L_3}$$

Self-Inductance of a Coil

For a coil of radius r and current i is flowing through the coil. If number of turns in the coil is N, then magnetic field at the centre is given as

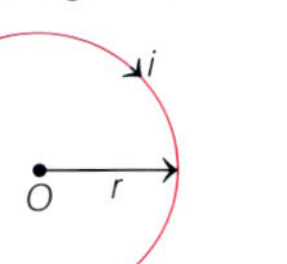

$\Rightarrow B_{centre} = \frac{\mu_0 Ni}{2r}$ and $\phi_B = BS$

where S = area of cross-sectional of the coil $= \pi r^2$

So, $\phi_B = \frac{\mu_0 Ni}{2r} \times \pi r^2 \Rightarrow \phi_B = \frac{\mu_0 \pi Nir}{2}$

Now, net flux for the coil of N number of turns

$$\Rightarrow \phi = N\phi_B = \frac{N \times \mu_0 \pi Nir}{2} = \frac{\mu_0 \pi N^2 ir}{2}$$

We know that,

$$L = \frac{\phi}{i}$$

$$L = \frac{\mu_0 N^2 \pi r}{2} \text{ henry}$$

Self inductance of a Long Solenoid

Consider a long solenoid of length l and radius r with $r << l$ and having n turns per unit length.
$B = \mu_0 nI$
$\therefore$ Self inductance of the long solenoid is

$$L = \mu_0 n^2 lA$$

$$\therefore \quad L = \frac{\mu_0 N^2 A}{l}$$

Factors Affecting Self-Inductance

- **Number of turns**
  Larger the number of turns in the solenoid, larger is its self-inductance.
- **Area of cross-section**
  Larger the area of the cross-section of the solenoid, larger is its self-inductance.
- **Permeability of the core material**
  The self-inductance of a solenoid increases μ_r times, if it is wound over an iron core of relative permeability μ_r.

Mutual Induction

The phenomenon of production of induced emf in one coil due to a change of current in the neighbouring coil.

B K P S G Rh

Coefficient of mutual induction
Here, $\varepsilon = -d\phi/dt = -M dI/dt$

Mutual Inductance of Two Long Solenoids

Mutual inductance will be
$M = \mu_0 N_1 N_2 A_1 / l = \mu_0 n_1 n_2 A_1 l = \mu_0 n_1 n_2 \pi r_1^2 \, l$

I_2 S_2 I_2 r_1 r_2 I_1 S_1 l I_1

Factors Affecting Mutual Inductance

- **Number of turns** Larger the number of turns in the two solenoids, larger will be their mutual inductance.

$$M \propto N_1 N_2$$

S S P P

- **Relative separation** Larger the distance between two solenoids, smaller will be the magnetic flux linked with secondary coil due to current in the primary coil.
- **Common cross-sectional area**
  Larger the common cross-sectional area of two solenoids, larger will be their mutual inductance.
- **Relative orientation of the two coils**
  Mutual inductance will be maximum, when they are parallel to each other whereas minimum, when they are perpendicular to each other.

P S

Mutual Inductance of Two Long Co-axial Solenoids

Figure shows two long co-axial solenoids, each of length l. Let n_1 be the number of turns per unit length of inner solenoid S_1 of radius r_1 and n_2 is number of turns per unit length of outer solenoid S_2 of radius r_2.

i S_2 S_1 l

Magnetic field due to S_1, $B_1 = \mu_0 n_1 i$
Flux through S_2, $\phi_B = (n_2 l) B_1 \pi r_1^2$
$= (n_2 l)\mu_0 n_1 i \pi r_1^2 = Mi \Rightarrow M = \mu_0 n_1 n_2 \pi r_1^2 l$

$$M = \frac{\mu_0 n_1 n_2 \times S}{l}$$

where, S is the area of cross-section of inner solenoid.

Mutual Inductance for Two Concentric Coils

A coil having N_1 turns and of radius r surrounded by another coil having N_2 turns and of radius R as shown in the figure ($R >> r$).

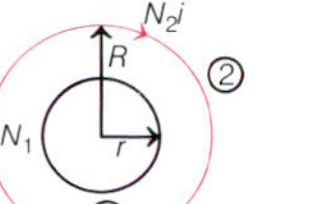

Magnetic field due to coil 2 at centre, $B_2 = \frac{\mu_0 N_2 i}{2R}$

Flux through coil 1,

$$\phi_{B_1} = N_1 B_2 S = \frac{N_1 \mu_0 N_2 i}{2R} \pi r^2 = Mi$$

$$\Rightarrow M = \frac{\mu_0 N_1 N_2 \pi r^2}{2R}$$

Combination of Inductors

- If two coils of self-inductances L_1 and L_2 having mutual inductance M are **in series** and placed close to each other, then net inductance will be
  $$L_S = L_1 + L_2 \pm 2M$$
- If two coils of self-inductances L_1 and L_2 having mutual inductance M, are connected **in parallel**, pl aced close to each other, then
  $$L_P = \frac{L_1 L_2 - M^2}{L_1 + L_2 \pm 2M}$$

Method of Generating induced EMF

Induced emf by changing relative orientation of the coil and magnetic field

A coil $PQRS$ free to rotate in a uniform magnetic field **B**. The axis of rotation of the coil is perpendicular to the field **B**.
$\phi = BA \cos\theta$

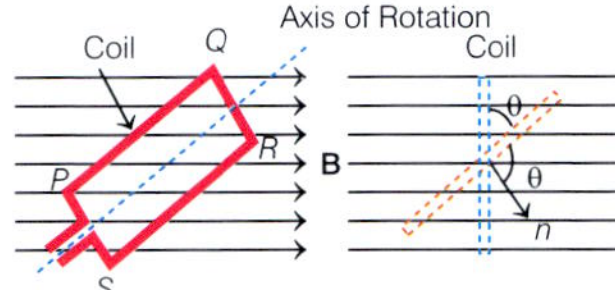

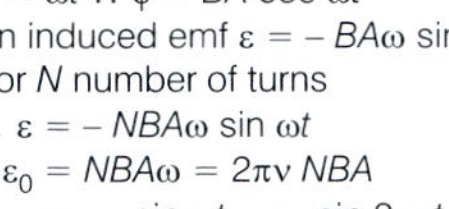

$\theta = \omega t \therefore \phi = BA \cos \omega t$
An induced emf $\varepsilon = -BA\omega \sin \omega t$
For N number of turns
$\therefore \varepsilon = -NBA\omega \sin \omega t$
$\varepsilon_0 = NBA\omega = 2\pi\nu NBA$
$\varepsilon = \varepsilon_0 \sin \omega t = \varepsilon_0 \sin 2\pi\nu t$

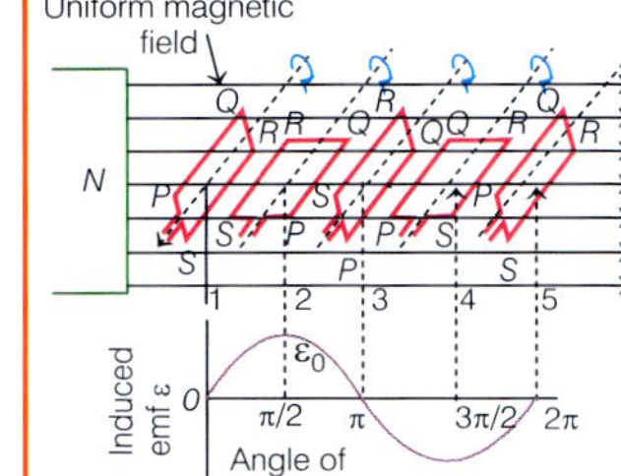

Reciprocity Theorem

This theorem states that mutual inductance due to secondary coil on primary coil is equal to the mutual induction due to primary coil on secondary coil. *i.e.* $M_{21} = M_{12} = M$.

Energy Stored in an Inductor

The energy of a capacitor is stored in the electric field between its plates. Similarly, an inductor has the capability of storing energy in its magnetic field.

$$W = U = \frac{1}{2}Li^2$$

Test 1

Syllabus
- Alternating Current
- Peak and RMS values of Alternating Current / Voltage
- Reactance and Impedance
- *L-C-R* Circuit, Resonance

NCERT Page 178 to 189

For deeper insight **Scan the QR Code**

Chapter 08

Alternating Current and Direct Current

An alternating current is that current whose magnitude changes continuously with time and direction reverses periodically.
A direct current is that current which flows with a constant magnitude in the same direction,

$$\varepsilon = \varepsilon_0 \sin \omega t, I = \frac{\varepsilon}{R} = \frac{\varepsilon_0}{R} \sin \omega t \quad (\varepsilon = \text{emf of alternating current})$$

- **Amplitude** The maximum value attained by an alternating current in either direction is called its amplitude. It is denoted by I_0.
- **Time period** $\quad \text{Time Period} = \dfrac{2\pi}{\text{Angular velocity}}$

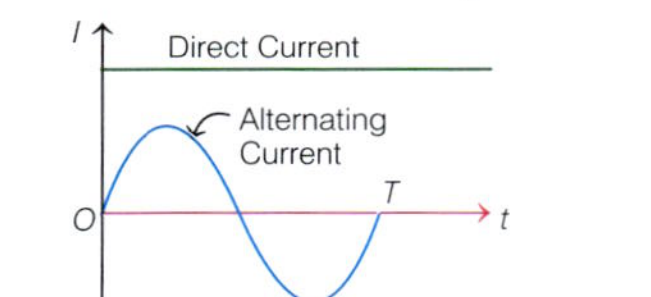

Average Value of an AC

Average value of AC is defined as the value of direct current which sends the same amount of charge in a circuit in the same time as is sent by the given alternating current in its half-cycle (*i.e.* $T/2$). It is denoted by I_{av} or I_m.

Thus, $\quad I_{av} = \dfrac{2}{\pi} I_0 = 0.637 I_0 = 63.7\%$ of I_0

$$E_{av} = \frac{2E_0}{\pi} = 0.637 E_0 = 63.7\% \text{ of } E_0$$

Similarly, for negative half-cycle, the mean value of alternating current is $-2I_0/\pi$ and the average value of emf for negative half-cycle is $-2E_0/\pi$.

RMS Value of AC

It is defined as that value of a direct current which produces the same amount of heating effect in a given resistor as is produced by the given alternating current when passed for the same time during a complete cycle. It is denoted by I_{rms}, I_v or I_{eff}.

$$I_{rms} = \frac{I_0}{\sqrt{2}}$$
$$I_{rms} = 0.707 I_0$$
$$I_{rms} = 70.7\% \text{ of } I_0$$

Average value of alternating emf,

$$E_{rms} = \frac{E_0}{\sqrt{2}} = 0.707\, E_0 = 70.7\% \text{ of } E_0$$

AC Circuit Containing Only a Capacitor

- A pure capacitor C connected across a source of alternating emf ε is given by $\varepsilon = \varepsilon_0 \sin \omega t$
- Potential Difference across the capacitor plates applied emf
  $V = \varepsilon = \varepsilon_0 \sin \omega t$
  $Q = CV = C\varepsilon_0 \sin \omega t$
  $\therefore$ Current at any instant is
  $I = I_0 \cos \omega t = I_0 \sin(\omega t + \pi/2)$
  where, $I_0 = \omega C \varepsilon_0 = \dfrac{\varepsilon_0}{1/\omega C}$
- **Phase relationship between ε and *I***
  The current leads the emf in phase by $\pi/2$ rad, so the current phasor I makes an angle $\pi/2$ rad, with phasor ε in anti-clockwise direction.

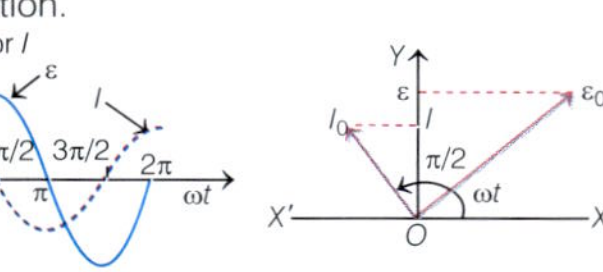

Capacitive Reactance (X_C)

- The capacitive reactance is the effective opposition offered by a capacitor to the flow of current in the circuit.
- $X_C = \dfrac{1}{\omega C} = \dfrac{1}{2\pi f C}$

AC Circuit Containing Only an Inductor

- Suppose an inductor of inductance L is connected to a source of alternating emf given by $\varepsilon = \varepsilon_0 \sin \omega t$.
- Net instantaneous emf, $\varepsilon = -L\dfrac{dI}{dt}$
- **Phase relationship between ε and *I*.**
  The voltage is ahead of the current in phase by 90°.

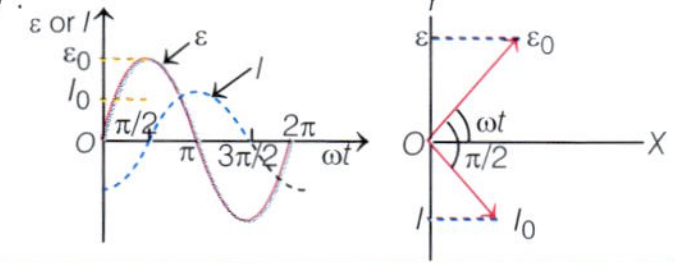

Inductive Reactance (X_L)

- The inductive reactance is the effective opposition offered by the inductor to the flow of current in the circuit.
- $X_L = \omega L = 2\pi f L$

AC Circuit Containing Only a Resistor

- A resistor of resistance R is connected to a source of alternating current ε given by $\varepsilon = \varepsilon_0 \sin \omega t$
- Instantaneous current of the source, $I = I_0 \sin \omega t$
- **Phase relationship between ε and *I*.**

R
$\varepsilon_0 \sin \omega t$

The emf ε and current I are in same phase in a purely resistive circuit. This means that both attain their zero, minimum and maximum values at the same respective times.

Resistor and Capacitor in Series

A resistor and capacitor connected in series to a source of alternating emf given by $\varepsilon = \varepsilon_0 \sin \omega t$.
- Voltage ($V_R = RI$) across the resistance R will be in phase with the current I. Thus, $V_{0R} = I_{0R}$
- Voltage ($V_C = X_C I$) across the capacitance C lags behind the current I by $\pi/2$ rad.
  Thus, $V_{0C} = I_0 X_C$

Resistor and Inductor in Series

A resistor and inductor connected in series to a source of alternating emf given by $\varepsilon = \varepsilon_0 \sin \omega t$
- Voltage $V_R = RI$ across the resistance R will be phase with the current I. $V_{0R} = I_0 R$
- Voltage $V_L = X_L$ across the inductance L leads the current I by $\pi/2$ rad.
  Thus, $V_{0L} = I_0 X_L$

Series *L-C-R* Circuit

A resistance R, an inductance L and capacitance C are connected in series to a source of alternating emf given by $\varepsilon = \varepsilon_0 \sin \omega t$
- Voltage $V_R = RI$ across the resistance R will be phase with the current I. $V_0 = I_0 R$
- Voltage $V_C = X_C I$ across the capacitance C lags behind the current I in phase by $\pi/2$ rad. $V_{OC} = I_0 X_C$
- Voltage $V_L = X_L I$ across the inductance L is ahead of current I in phase by $\pi/2$ rad. So, phasor V_L lies $\pi/2$ rad anti-clockwise w.r.t the phasor I. Its amplitude is $V_{OL} = I_0 X_L$

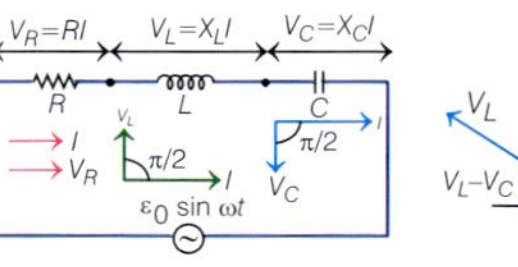

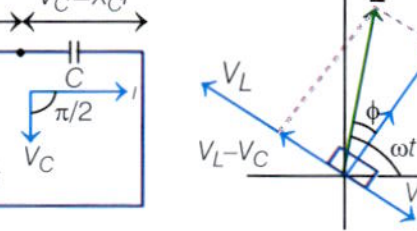

Resonance in *L-C-R* Series Circuit

– In series RLC circuit impedance of circuit is minimum & equal to resistance $\Rightarrow Z = R$ and current is maximum
- **Condition for resonance**

$X_L = X_C \Rightarrow L\omega = \dfrac{1}{C\omega}$

$\omega = \omega_r = \dfrac{1}{\sqrt{LC}}$ rad/s

$\omega_r \rightarrow$ resonant frequency (angular)

$f = f_r = \dfrac{1}{2\pi\sqrt{LC}}$ Hz

f_r = resonant frequency

Graph

$\omega < \omega_r$, $X_C > X_L$ current leads

$\omega > \omega_r$, $X_L > X_C$ current lags

In resonance, $V = V_R$ (applied voltage = voltage across resistance) $Z = R$ (impedance is minimum and equal to resistance) voltmeter connected across V_L & V_C will show the same reading, voltmeter connected commonly across inductor and capacitor show no reading.

Here, $V = 0$

$V_L = V_C$

$V_{net} = V_R$

$i_{max} = \dfrac{V_{net}}{Z} = \dfrac{V_R}{R}$

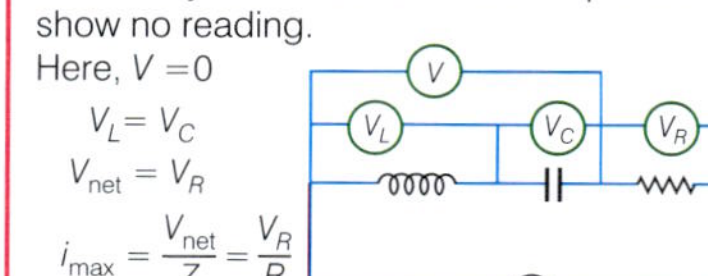

Test 2

Syllabus
- Power in AC Circuits
- Wattless Current

NCERT Page 190 to 191

For deeper insight **Scan the QR Code**

Chapter 08

Power in AC Circuits

For electric circuits power is defined as the product of voltage and current.

$$P = VI$$

Its SI unit is watt.

– The **instantaneous power** dissipated in a component is a product of the instantaneous voltage and the instantaneous current.

– **Average power** is the average of the instantaneous power over one period.

$$P_{av} = V_{rms} I_{rms} \cos\phi$$
$$= (V_0 I_0 /2) \cos\phi$$

Power factor

– It may be defined as cosine of the angle of lag or lead (i.e. cos ϕ)

- **In Series *RC* circuit**
  Power factor,
  $$\cos\phi = \frac{R}{\sqrt{R^2 + X_C^2}}$$
- **In Series *RL* circuit**
  Power factor,
  $$\cos\phi = \frac{R}{\sqrt{R^2 + X_L^2}}$$
- **In Series *LCR* circuit**
  Power factor,
  $$\cos\phi = \frac{R}{\sqrt{R^2 + (X_L - X_C)^2}}$$

Energy in Inductor and Capacitor

Energy stored in inductor

When an inductor is connected to a source of emf, the current starts growing through it. An induced emf is set up in the inductor which opposes the growth of current through it. The external source has to expand energy in building up the current through the inductor against the induced emf. This energy is stored in the inductor as magnetic field energy is given by

$$U = 1/2\, L I_0^2$$

Energy stored in capacitor

It is due to the work done to separate charges and create an electric field between plates of the capacitor. This stored energy can be released when the capacitor discharges. The work done is stored as the electrostatic energy given by

$$U = 1/2\, CV^2$$

Power in Resistive Components

The phase difference between instantaneous current and instantaneous emf is zero, therefore,

$$\text{Average Power, } P = \frac{1}{2} V_P I_P = \frac{V_P}{\sqrt{2}} \times \frac{I_P}{\sqrt{2}} = VI$$

$$P_{av} = I_{rms} V_{rms} \text{ (Maximum)}$$

– where *V* and *I* are the rms voltage and current

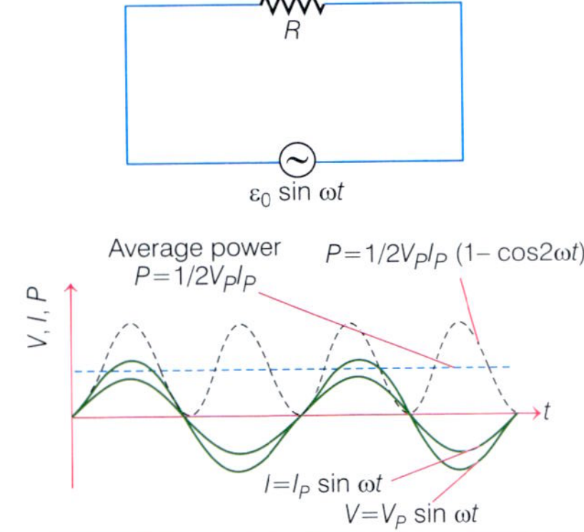

Power in Capacitor

The capacitive current leads the voltage by 90° voltage $V = V_p \sin\omega t$ is applied across a capacitance *C*, the current will be given by $I = I_p \cos\omega t$.

- Then, $P = VI$
  $= V_P \sin\omega t \times I_P \cos\omega t$
  $= V_P I_P (\sin\omega t \times \cos\omega t) = V_P I_P \left(\frac{\sin^2 \omega t}{2}\right)$

Again the average power is zero

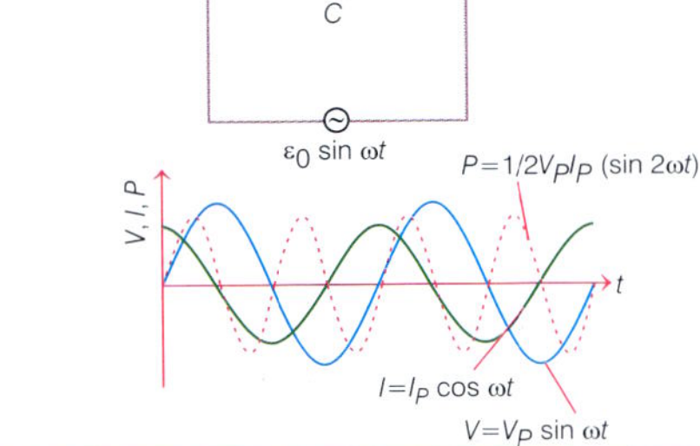

Power in Inductors

In pure inductor circuit current lags the voltage by 90° voltage $V = V_p \sin\omega t$ is applied across an inductance *L*, the current will be given by $I = -I_p \cos\omega t$.

- Therefore
  $P = Vi$
  $= V_p \sin\omega t \times I_p \cos\omega t$
  $= -V_p I_p (\sin\omega t \times \cos\omega t)$
  $= -V_p I_p \left(\frac{\sin^2 \omega t}{2}\right)$

Again the average power is zero

$P = -1/2 V_P I_P$ (sin 2ωt)

$I = I_P \cos\omega t$

$V = V_P \sin\omega t$

Power in AC Circuit Containing *L* and *R*

In a series circuit consisting of inductance and resistance, the current lags the voltage by an angle (ϕ) that is less than 90°.

$$\tan\phi = \frac{\omega L}{R}$$

$$\Rightarrow \cos\phi = \frac{R}{\sqrt{R^2 + \omega^2 L^2}}$$

$$\Rightarrow P_{av} = V_{rms} I_{rms} \cdot \frac{R}{\sqrt{R^2 + \omega^2 L^2}}$$

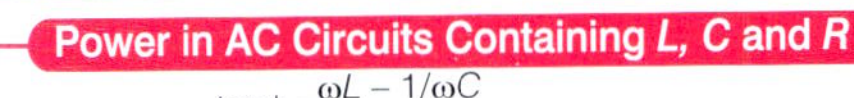

Power in AC Circuits Containing *C* and *R*

The average power supplied to the circuit is a positive quantity and this represents the power dissipated in the resistance.

$$\tan\phi = \frac{1/\omega C}{R}$$

$$\Rightarrow \cos\phi = \frac{R}{\sqrt{R^2 + 1/\omega^2 C^2}}$$

$$\Rightarrow P_{av} = V_{rms} I_{rms} \cdot \frac{R}{\sqrt{R^2 + \omega^2 C^2}}$$

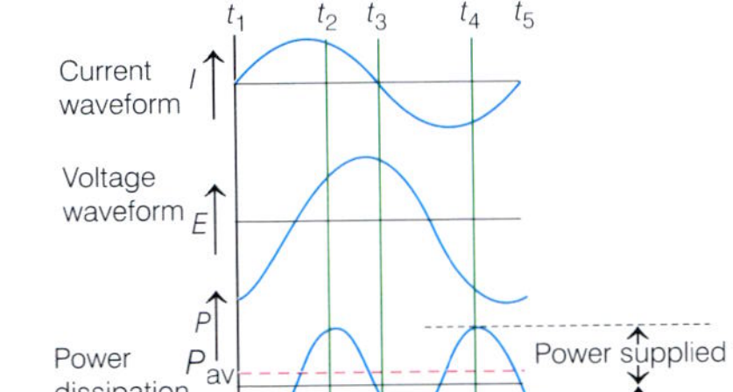
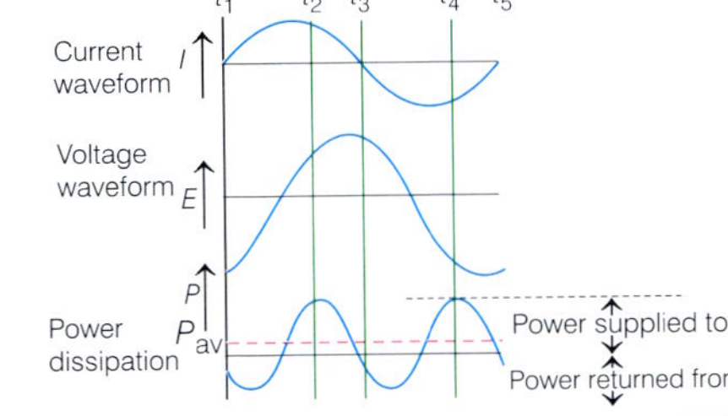

Power in AC Circuits Containing *L*, *C* and *R*

$$\tan\phi = \frac{\omega L - 1/\omega C}{R}$$

$$\Rightarrow \cos\phi = \frac{R}{\sqrt{R^2 + (\omega L - 1/\omega C)^2}}$$

$$\Rightarrow P_{av} = V_{rms} I_{rms} \frac{R}{\sqrt{R^2 + \left(\omega L - \frac{1}{\omega C}\right)^2}}$$

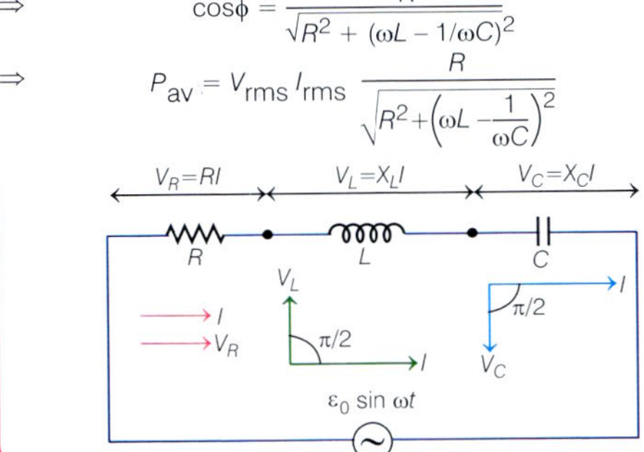

Wattless Current

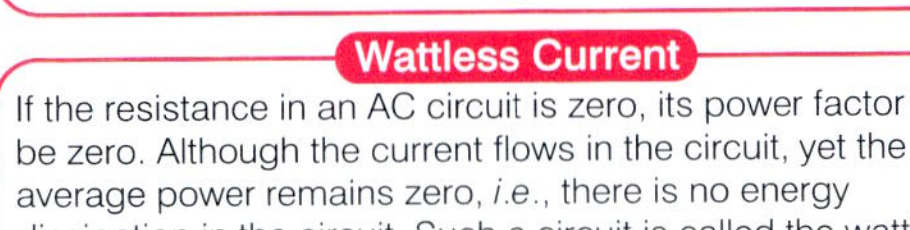

If the resistance in an AC circuit is zero, its power factor will be zero. Although the current flows in the circuit, yet the average power remains zero, *i.e.*, there is no energy dissipation in the circuit. Such a circuit is called the wattless circuit and the current flowing is called the wattless current.

Test 3

Syllabus
- AC Generators
- Transformers

NCERT Page 170 to 172, Page 194 to 196

For deeper insight **Scan the QR Code**

Chapter 08

Transformer

- It is a device which converts low voltage (high current) into high voltage (low current) and *vice versa*. It is based on the principle of electromagnetic induction. It consists of two sets of coil, insulated from each other. They are wound on a soft-iron core as given in the figure.

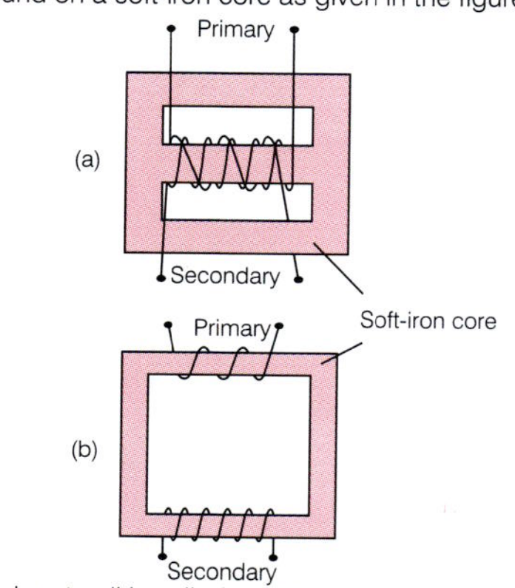

The input coil is called **primary coil** with number of turns N_p and the output coil is called **secondary coil** with number of turns N_s.

- When an alternating voltage is applied to the primary, the resulting current produces an alternating magnetic flux which links with secondary and induces an emf in it. The value of this emf depends on the number of turns in the secondary. For an ideal transformer,

$$\frac{\varepsilon_s}{\varepsilon_p}=\frac{V_s}{V_p}=\frac{N_s}{N_p}=\frac{I_p}{I_s}$$

Efficiency:- It is defined as the ratio of output power to the input power

$$\eta=\frac{\text{Output power}}{\text{Input power}}=\frac{V_s I_s}{V_p I_p}$$

Uses of Transformers

Transformers are used in almost all AC operations. Some of them are given below

- In the induction furnace.
- In voltage regulators for TV, computers, refrigerators etc.
- A stepdown transformer is used for the purpose of weldings.

Types of Transformer

- **Step up transformer** If it increases the input voltage it is called step up transformer.

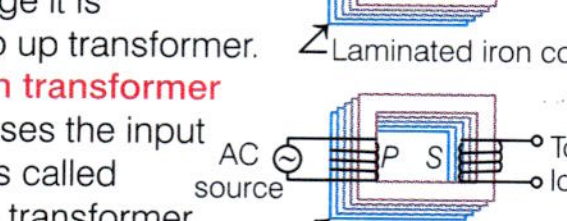

- **Step down transformer** If it decreases the input voltage it is called step down transformer.

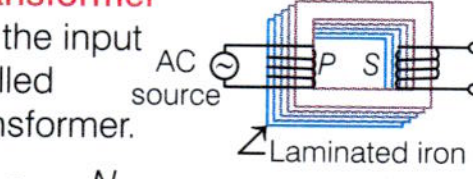

- **Induced emf,** $\frac{\varepsilon_2}{\varepsilon_1}=\frac{N_2}{N_1}$
- **Current,** $\frac{I_1}{I_2}=\frac{\varepsilon_2}{\varepsilon_1}=\frac{N_2}{N_1}$
- **Efficiency** Efficiency of transformer is defined as the ratio of output power to the input power

$$=\frac{\text{Output power}}{\text{Input power}}\times 100\%$$

The efficiency of real transformers is fairly high (80 to 95%) though not 100%

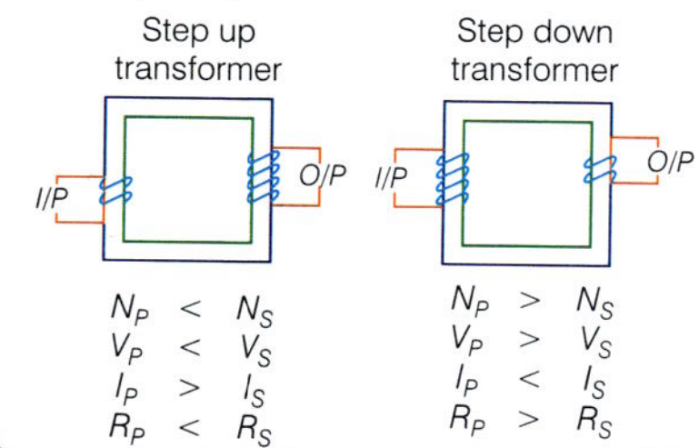

Step up transformer	Step down transformer
$N_P < N_S$	$N_P > N_S$
$V_P < V_S$	$V_P > V_S$
$I_P > I_S$	$I_P < I_S$
$R_P < R_S$	$R_P > R_S$

Types of Electric Generator

There are **various types of generator** depending on the source of mechanical energy

(i) **Hydroelectric generators** The mechanical energy required for rotation of the armature is provided by water falling from a height, e.g. dams.

(ii) **Thermal generators,** Water is heated to produce steam using coal or other sources. The steam at high pressure produces the rotation of the armature.

(iii) **Nuclear power generators,** Instead of coal, nuclear fuel is used as a source.

If instantaneous induced emf produced in a coil is $e = e_0 \sin\omega t = nBA\omega\sin\omega t$, then

(a) when $\omega t = 0, \pi$, i.e. coil is vertical, emf, $e = 0$

(b) when $\omega t = \frac{\pi}{2}$, i.e. coil is horizontal, emf, $e > 0$ (+ve) (maximum)

Energy Losses in Transformers

In actual transformers, small energy losses occurs due to following reasons,

- **Flux leakage** There is always some leakage i.e., not all of the flux that the primary passes through the secondary, due to poor design of core, or the air gap in the core. It can be reduced by winding the primary and secondary coils one over another.
- **Resistance of the winding** The wire used for the winding has some resistance and so, energy lost due to heat produced in the wire. In high current low voltage winding, this is minimized by using thick wire.
- **Eddy current** The alternating magnetic flux induces eddy currents in the iron core and causes heating. The effect is reduced by having a laminated core.
- **Hysteresis** The magnetisation of the core is reapeatedly reversed by an alternating magnetic field. The resulting ecpediture of energy in the core appears as heat and is kept to a minimum by using a magnetic material which has low hysteresis loss.
- **Magnetostriction** It is a humming noise of a transformer.

Electric Generator or Dynamo

Electric generator is a device which is used to convert mechanical energy to electrical energy. Generator provide nearly all of the power for electric power grids.
The reverse conversion of electrical energy to mechanical energy is done by electric motor.

AC Generator

- It is an electrical machine which produces a current that alternates or changes its direction regularly after a fixed interval of time and is used to convert mechanical energy into electrical energy.
- The essential parts of the AC generator are coil or armature, field magnets (N and S), slip ring and brushes as shown in figure below.
- **Principle** It is based on the principle of electromagnetic induction and the magnitude of induced emf is given by

$$\varepsilon = N\frac{d\phi}{dt}=NBA\omega\sin t = \varepsilon_0 \sin\omega t$$

where, $\varepsilon_0 = NBA\omega$

- The **current induced in the circuit** is given by

$$i=\frac{\varepsilon}{R}=\frac{\varepsilon_0}{R}\sin\omega t = i_0 \sin\omega t$$

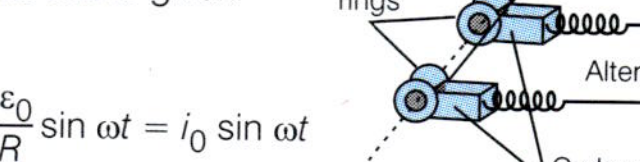

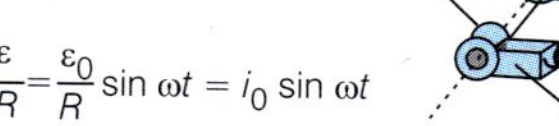

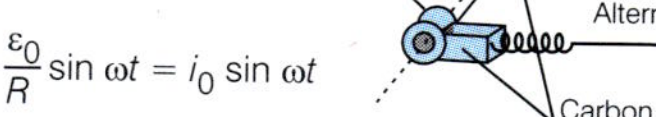

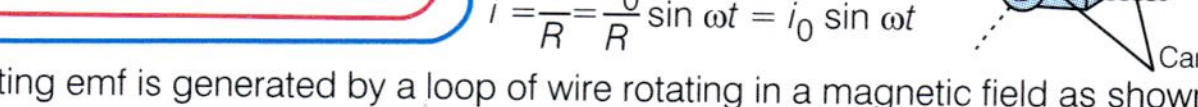

Working An alternating emf is generated by a loop of wire rotating in a magnetic field as shown in figure below.

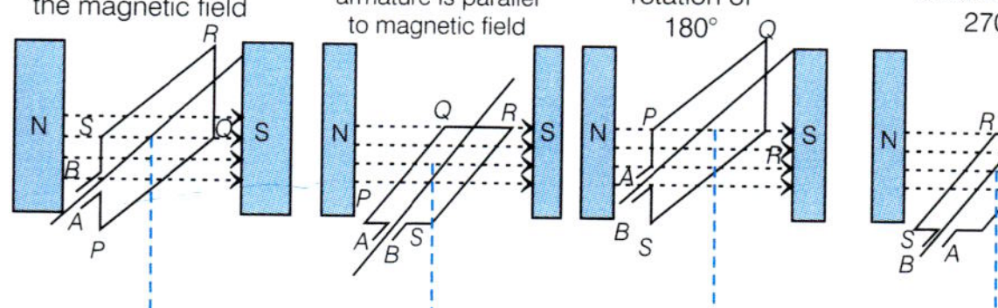

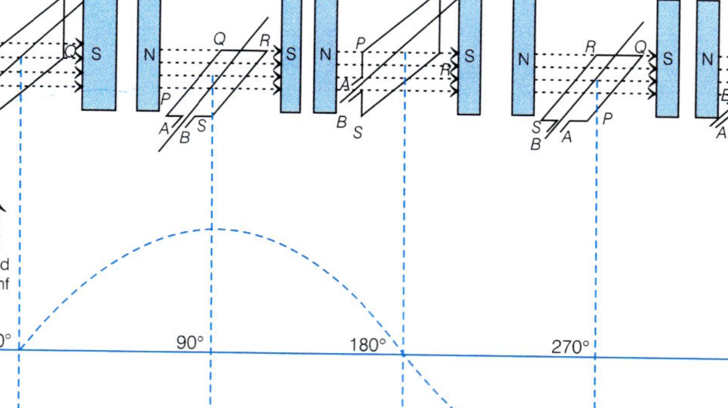

Test 1

Syllabus

- Displacement Current, Electromagnetic Wave and its Characteristics.
- Transverse Nature of Electromagnetic Wave

NCERT Page 202 to 207

For deeper insight **Scan the QR Code**

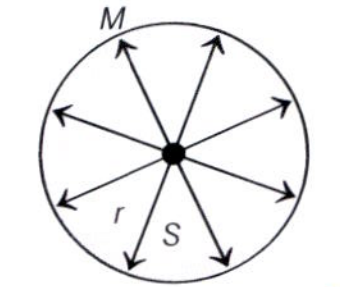
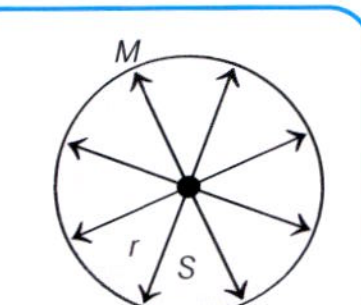

Chapter 09

Displacement Current

It is a current which is produced due to the rate of change of electric flux w.r.t. time.

$$I_D = \varepsilon_0 \frac{d\phi_E}{dt}$$

- The conduction and displacement currents are individually discontinuous but these together possess the property of continuity through any closed electric circuit.
- The displacement current is precisely equal to the conduction current when both are present in different parts of the circuit.
- The displacement current arises due to rate of change of electric flux (or electric field) between the two plates of the capacitor.
- Just as the conduction current, the displacement current is also the source of varying magnetic field.

Ampere's Circuital Law

The line integral of magnetic field around any closed path in vacuum is equal to the μ_0 times the total current passing through that closed path.

$$\oint \mathbf{B}\cdot d\mathbf{l} = \mu_0 \mathbf{I}$$

Maxwell's Equations in Vacuum

Maxwell's equations gives the description about all the electromagnetic interaction. These equations are fundamental to electromagnetic phenomenon.
Maxwell's four equations in vacuum can be written in differential form as follows

(i) $\nabla \cdot \mathbf{E} = \frac{\rho}{\varepsilon_0}$

(ii) $\nabla \cdot \mathbf{B} = 0$

(iii) $\nabla \times \mathbf{E} = -\frac{\partial \mathbf{B}}{\partial t}$

(iv) $\nabla \times \mathbf{B} = \mu_0 \left(\mathbf{J} + \varepsilon_0 \frac{\partial \mathbf{E}}{\partial t}\right)$

where, ρ is charge density and J is current density).

Gauss's Law in Electrostatics

This law states that "the total electric flux through any closed surface is always equal to $\frac{1}{\varepsilon_0}$ times the net charge enclosed by that surface". This law relates electric field with a charge distribution.
It is given by $\oint \mathbf{E}\cdot d\mathbf{S} = q/\varepsilon_0$
This equation is called Maxwell's first equation.

Gauss's Law in Magnetism

This law states that "the net magnetic flux through any closed surface is always zero". It is given by $\oint \mathbf{B} \times d\mathbf{S} = 0$
This equation is called Maxwell's second equation.
This law implies that isolated magnetic poles does not exist i.e, it explain the absence of magnetic monopole.

Faraday's Law of Electromagnetic Induction

This law states that "the line integral of electric field along a closed path is equal to the rate of change of magnetic flux through the surface bounded by that closed path". It is given by

$$\oint \mathbf{E}\cdot d\mathbf{l} = \frac{d\phi_E}{dt}$$

This equation is called Maxwell's third equation.

Ampere-Maxwell's Circuital Law

This law states that "the line integral of the magnetic field along a closed path is equal to μ_0 times the total current (i.e. sum of conduction current and displacement current) threading the surface bounded by that closed path." It is given by

$$\oint \mathbf{B}.d\mathbf{l} = \mu_0 \left(\varepsilon_0 + I_c \frac{d\phi_E}{dt}\right)$$

This equation is called Maxwell's fourth equation.
This law implies that not only a conduction current but a displacement current, associated with a changing electric field, also produced a magnetic field.

Production of Electromagnetic Waves

An electromagnetic wave consists of oscillating electric and magnetic fields
The various possible frequencies of electromagnetic waves form a spectrum, and a small part of which is visible light.
Electromagnetic waves along
X-axis : $E_x = E_o \sin(kx - \omega t)$
Y-axis : $B_y = B_o \sin(kx - \omega t)$

Transverse Nature of Electromagnetic Waves

A changing electric field produces a changing magnetic field and *vice-versa* which give rise to a transverse wave known as electromagnetic wave.
The variation of electric field (E) and magnetic field (B) are mutually perpendicular to each other as well as the direction of the propagation of the wave i.e., the electromagnetic waves are transverse in nature.

X E Direction of propagation → Z B Y

A plane EM wave travelling along Z-axis

Intensity of Electromagnetic Waves

Intensity of electromagnetic wave is defined as the energy crossing per unit area per unit time perpendicular to the direction of propagation of the wave

$$\text{Intensity} = \frac{\text{Energy}}{\text{Area x Time}}$$

$c\Delta t$ Area $= A$ c

Physical Quantities Associated with EM waves

(i) Speed of electromagnetic waves in a medium is given by

$$v = \frac{1}{\sqrt{\mu\varepsilon}}$$

where, μ and ε are the permeability and permittivity of any medium.

(ii) Speed of electromagnetic wave in a free space or vacuum is given by

$$c = \frac{1}{\sqrt{\mu_0\varepsilon_0}} = 3 \times 10^8 \text{ ms}^{-1}$$

(iii) The amplitudes of electric field (E_0) and amplitude of magnetic field (B_0) are related to each other by relation.

$$c = \frac{E_0}{B_0}$$

(iv) Electromagnetic waves carry energy as they travel from one point to another point in the space without any material medium or actual transfer of material medium. The average energy densities of an electromagnetic wave is given by.

$$U_{av} = U_E + U_B = \frac{1}{2}\varepsilon_0 E_0^2 + \frac{B_0}{2\mu_0^2}$$

(v) Intensity of an EM wave depends upon the amplitude of electric field $I = \frac{1}{\mu_0} B_{rms}^2 c$

magnetic field $I = \frac{1}{2} c\varepsilon_0 E_0^2$

Momentum

EM waves carry momentum. If a portion of EM wave of energy U propagating with speed c, then

$$\text{linear momentum} = \frac{\text{energy}(U)}{\text{speed}(c)}$$

If wave is incident on a completely absorbing surface, then momentum delivered, $p = U/c$.
If wave is incident on a totally reflecting surface, then momentum delivered, $p = \frac{2U}{c}$

Characteristics of Electromagnetic Waves

(i) These waves do not require any material medium for propagation.
(ii) These waves travel in free space with the speed of light ($\cong 3.0 \times 10^8$ m/s).
(iii) Electromagnetic waves are transverse in nature.
(iv) The oscillating electric and magnetic field vectors of an EM wave are oriented along mutually perpendicular directions and are in phase.
(v) These waves are not deflected by electric field or magnetic field.
(vi) EM waves are polarised.

Energy Density of Electromagnetic Waves

Energy density of electromagnetic wave is defined as the energy per unit volume of the space in which it travels.

$$U_E = \frac{1}{2}\varepsilon_0 E^2, \quad U_B = \frac{B^2}{2\mu_0}$$

$$U_{av} = \frac{1}{2}\varepsilon_0 E^2 \text{rms} + \frac{B^2 \text{rms}}{2\mu_0}$$

$$U_{av} = \frac{\varepsilon_0 E_0^2}{4} + \frac{\varepsilon_0 E_0^2}{4} = \frac{1}{2}\varepsilon_0 E_0^2 = \varepsilon_0 E^2 \text{rms}$$

$$U_E = U_B$$

Radiation Pressure

It is the mechanical pressure exerted upon any surface due to the exchange of momentum between the surface and the EM wave.
For a perfectly reflecting surface, $p_r = \frac{2\mathbf{S}}{c}$
where, $\mathbf{S}$ = Poynting vector and c = speed of light.
For a perfectly absorbing surface, $p_a = \frac{\mathbf{S}}{c}$

Polynting Vector

The rate of flow of energy in EM waves is described by $\mathbf{S}$.$\mathbf{S} = \frac{1}{\mu_0}(\mathbf{E} \times \mathbf{B})$

Intensity Due to a Point Source

Consider a point source S, emanating electromagnetic waves (light) in all directions. If power of the source is P, then intensity of light at any point M is $I = \frac{4}{A \times t} = \left(\frac{P}{A}\right)$W/m^2
Intensity of a line source, $I \propto 1/r$ and for a plane source, intensity is independent of r.

M r S

Test 2

Syllabus

- Electromagnetic Spectrum, Radiowave, Microwave, Infrared, Visible, Ultraviolet, X-rays, Gamma ray,
- Applications of Electromagnetic Waves

NCERT Page 208 to 211

For deeper insight **Scan the QR Code**

Chapter 09

Electromagnetic Spectrum

Frequency (Hz): 10^{23}, 10^{22}, 10^{21}, 10^{20}, 10^{19}, 10^{18}, 10^{17}, 10^{16}, 10^{15}, 10^{14}, 10^{13}, 10^{12}, 10^{11}, 10^{10}, 10^{9}, 10^{8}, 10^{7}, 10^{6}, 10^{5}, 10^{4}, 10^{3}, 10^{2}, 10

Gamma-rays, X-ray, Ultraviolet, Visible, Infrared, Microwaves, Short-radio-waves, Television-and FM radio, AM-radio, Long-radio-waves

Wavelength,(m): 10^{-14}, 10^{-13}, 10^{-12}, 10^{-11}, 10^{-10}, 10^{-9}, 10^{-8}, 10^{-7}, 10^{-6}, 10^{-5}, 10^{-4}, 10^{-3}, 10^{-2}, 10^{-1}, 1, 10^{1}, 10^{2}, 10^{3}, 10^{4}, 10^{5}, 10^{6}, 10^{7}

400 nm, 450 nm, 500 nm, 550 nm, 600 nm, 650 nm, 700 nm

Violet, Blue, Green, Yellow, Orange, Red

Gamma (γ)-Rays

These rays were discovered by **Rutherford**. They have high penetration power.

It is radiated from radioactive nuclei and nuclear reactions, Co-60 is a pure γ-rays source.

Uses of gamma (γ)-rays are given below

(i) These are used to produce nuclear reaction.
(ii) These are used in radiotherapy for the treatment of tumour and cancer.
(iii) These are used in food industry to kill pathogenic microorganism.
(iv) These are used to provide valuable information about the structure of atomic nucleus.

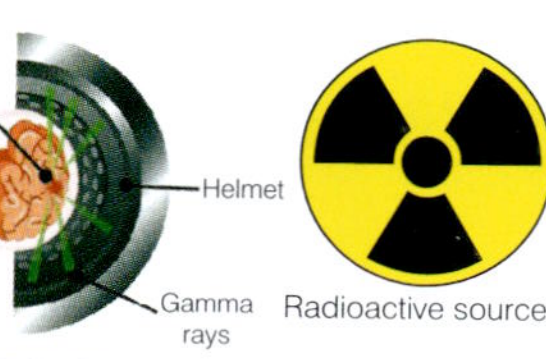

X-Rays

These rays were discovered by German professor **Roentgen**.

It is radiated from sudden deceleration of fast moving electron by a metal target.

Uses of X-rays are given below

(i) These are used in surgery to detect the fracture, diseased organs, stones in the body.
(ii) These are used in engineering to detect fault, crack on bridges, testing of welds.
(iii) These are used at metro station to detect metal or explosive material.
(iv) These are used in scientific research.

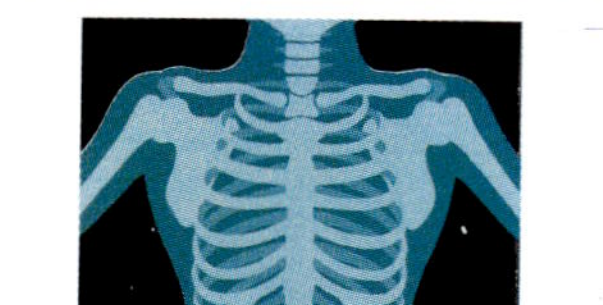

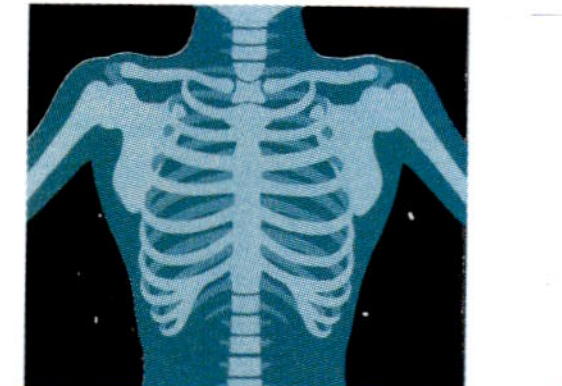

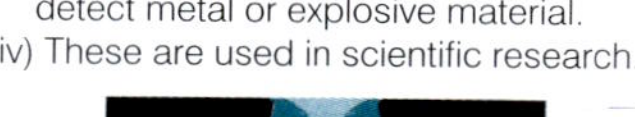

Ultraviolet Rays

These rays were discovered by **Johann Ritter** in 1801. UV-rays are produced by special lamps and very hot bodies. The sun is an important source of UV-rays but fortunately these rays are absorbed by ozone layer. This region of EM waves spectrum has wavelength just shorter than visible light.

Uses of ultraviolet rays are given below

(i) These are used in burglar alarm.
(ii) These are used to study molecular structure and in detection of invisible writing.
(iii) These are used to kill germs in minerals.
(iv) These are used to sterilise surgical instruments. Can cause many chemical reactions, e.g., the tanning of the human skin. Ionise atoms in atmosphere, resulting in the ionosphere.

Infrared Waves

These waves were discovered by **Herschel**. These radiation lie close to low frequency of visible spectrum. Infrared waves are also called heat waves. These waves are produced by heat radiating bodies and molecules. They have high penetration power.

Uses of infrared waves are given below

(I) These are used in heat therapy to heat muscular pain or sprain.
(ii) These are used in satellite for army purpose.
(iii) These are used in weather forecasting.
(iv) These are used for producing dehydrated fruits.
(v) These are used in solar water heater, solar cells and cooker.
(vi) These are used in TV remote as signal carrier.
(vii) These are used in night vision or infrared photography.

Visible Rays

These rays were discovered by **Sir Isaac Newton**. It is that part of spectrum which is visible by human eye.

Visible rays are related by excited atoms in ionised gas and incandescent bodies.

Visible rays are used by the optical organs of humans and animals for three primary purposes given below

(i) To see things, avoid bumping from them and escape danger.
(ii) To find stuff to eat.
(iii) To find other living things with which to consort, so as to prolong the species.

Radio Waves

These waves were first predicted by **James Clerk Maxwell.**

Radio waves are produced due to oscillating charge particles between plates of capacitor in *L-C* circuit.

These waves have longest wavelength and minimum frequency.

Uses of radio waves are given below

(i) These are used in AM (Amplitude Modulation) from 530 kHz to 1710 kHz. These are also used in ground wave propagation.
(ii) These are used in TV waves ranging from 54 MHz to 890 MHz.
(iii) These are used in FM (Frequency Modulation) ranging from 88 MHz to 108 MHz.
(iv) UHF (Ultra High Frequency) waves are used in cellular phones.

Microwaves

These waves were also predicted by **James Clerk Maxwell.** Microwaves are called short wavelength radio waves which are produced by vacuum tubes.

Uses of microwaves are given below

(i) These are used in RADAR systems for aircraft navigation.
(ii) These are used in microwave oven for cooking purpose.
(iii) These are used in the study of atomic and molecular structures.
(iv) These are used to measure the speed of vehicle, speed of cricket ball, etc.

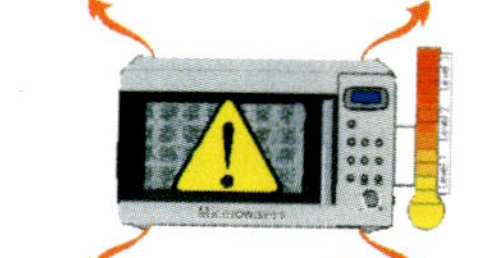

Test 1

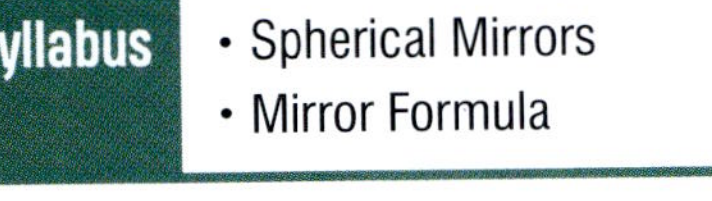

Syllabus
- Reflection of Light
- Spherical Mirrors
- Mirror Formula

NCERT Page 221 to 227

For deeper insight **Scan the QR Code**

Chapter 10

Reflection of Light

When light is incident on a polished smooth surface, then most of the incident light returns to the same medium.

This phenomenon of returning of light after striking a smooth polished surface is called reflection of light.

(i) **Reflecting surface** The surface, after striking which, light reflects is called reflecting surface (MM').

(ii) **Incident ray** The striking ray (AO) on the reflecting surface is called incident ray.

(iii) **Reflected ray** The reflected ray (OB) after striking the reflecting surface is called reflected ray.

(iv) **Point of incidence** It is the point (O) on the reflecting surface at which incident light strikes.

(v) **Normal** It is the normal (ON) to the surface drawn from point of incidence (O) on the reflecting surface.

(vi) **Angle of incidence** It is the angle (i) between incident ray (AO) and the normal (ON). In the given figure, $\angle AON = i$.

(vii) **Angle of reflection** It is the angle (r) between reflected ray (OB) and the normal (ON). In the given figure, $\angle NOB = r$.

Laws of Reflection

There are two laws for reflection of light from a smooth reflecting surface.

(i) **First law** The angle of incidence is equal to the angle of reflection, i.e. $\angle i = \angle r$.

(ii) **Second law** The incident ray, the reflected ray and the normal at the point of incidence all lie in the same plane.

These laws are valid for plane as well as curved surfaces as shown in the figure given below.

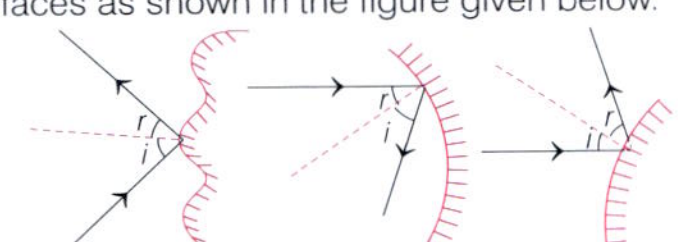

- In geometrical optics, angles are measured with normal.
- Also in geometrical optics, we deal with plane and spherical surfaces. In case of spherical surface, normal to surface will pass through centre of sphere.

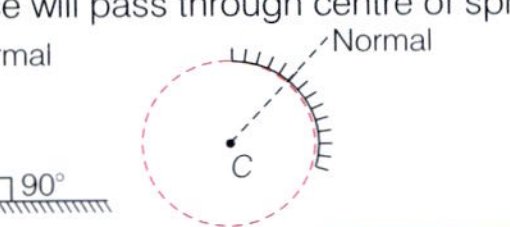

Plane Mirror

The mirror whose reflecting surface is plane is called plane mirror. It's one side is silvered and reflection takes place from other side as shown in the figure.

Reflecting surface
Polished surface
Plane mirror

Spherical Mirror

It is the part of a spherical transparent medium. One of the curved surfaces is polished and reflection takes place from other side.

Spherical mirrors are of two types

(i) **Concave mirror** A spherical mirror whose reflecting surface is towards the centre of the sphere is called concave mirror. In this mirror, outer curved surface is polished and reflection takes place from inner curved surface as shown in figure.

Reflecting surface, A, R, C, P (Pole), B, Polished surface

(ii) **Convex mirror** A spherical mirror whose reflecting surface is away from the centre of the sphere is called convex mirror. In this mirror, inner curved surface is polished and reflection takes place from outer curved surface as shown in figure.

Reflecting surface, A, R, C, P (Pole), B, Polished surface

Sign Convention

- All the distances are measured from pole (P) of mirror
- The distances measured in the direction of incident ray are taken positive, otherwise negative.
- Heights measured upward and perpendicular to the principal axis are +ve and otherwise –ve.

Height upwards positive; Direction of incident light; Mirror; C (–ve), F (–ve); P (Pole); X-axis; Height downwards negative; Distances against incident light negative; Distances along incident light positive; +ve; –ve; F (+ve) C (+ve); Concave mirror; Convex mirror

Image Formation by Concave Mirrors

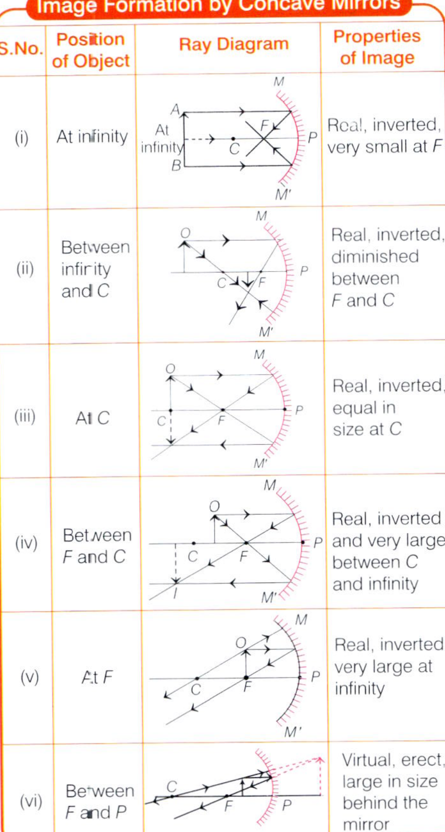

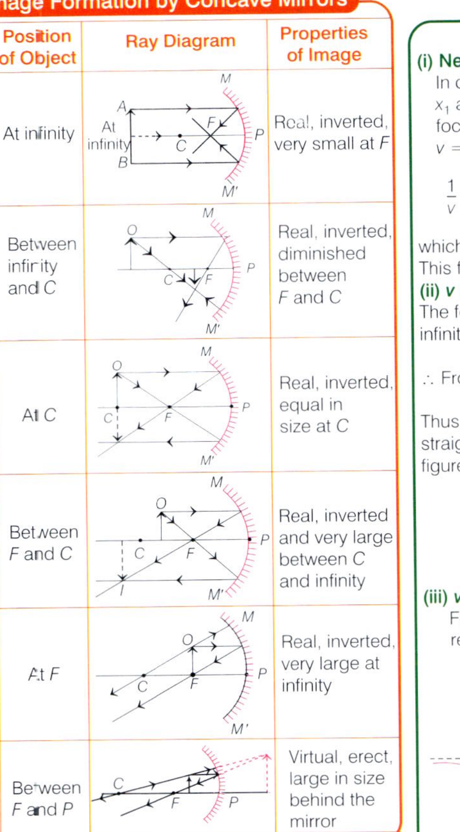

S.No.	Position of Object	Ray Diagram	Properties of Image
(i)	At infinity		Real, inverted, very small at F
(ii)	Between infinity and C		Real, inverted, diminished between F and C
(iii)	At C		Real, inverted, equal in size at C
(iv)	Between F and C		Real, inverted and very large between C and infinity
(v)	At F		Real, inverted, very large at infinity
(vi)	Between F and P		Virtual, erect, large in size behind the mirror

Image Formation by Convex Mirrors

S.No.	Position of Object	Ray Diagram	Properties of Image
(i)	At infinity		Virtual, erect, very small in size at F
(ii)	In front of mirror (at finite distance)		Virtual, erect, diminished between P and F

Important Informations Related to Mirror Formula

(i) Newton's Formula

In case of spherical mirrors, if object distance x_1 and image distance x_2 are measured from focus instead of pole, then $u = (f + x_1)$ and $v = (f + x_2)$. The mirror formula,

$$\frac{1}{v} + \frac{1}{u} = \frac{1}{f} \text{ reduces to, } \frac{1}{f + x_2} + \frac{1}{f + x_1} = \frac{1}{f}$$

which on simplification gives $x_1 x_2 = f^2$

This formula is called **Newton's formula**.

(ii) v versus u Graph for a Plane Mirror

The focal length and the radius of curvature are infinite for a plane mirror.

$\therefore$ From mirror formula, $\frac{1}{v} + \frac{1}{u} = 0 \Rightarrow v = -u$

Thus, v versus u graph for a plane mirror is a straight line with slope equal to -1 as shown in figure.

v, 135°, O, u

(iii) v versus u Graph for a Spherical Mirror

For a spherical mirror v versus u graph is a rectangular hyperbola as shown in figure.

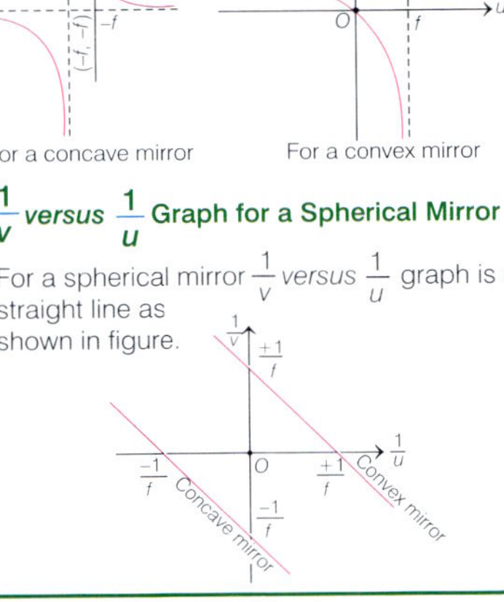

For a concave mirror For a convex mirror

(iv) $\frac{1}{v}$ versus $\frac{1}{u}$ Graph for a Spherical Mirror

For a spherical mirror $\frac{1}{v}$ versus $\frac{1}{u}$ graph is a straight line as shown in figure.

$\frac{1}{v}$, $\frac{+1}{f}$, $\frac{1}{u}$, $\frac{-1}{f}$, O, $\frac{+1}{f}$, $\frac{-1}{f}$, Concave mirror, Convex mirror

Test 2

Syllabus

- Reflection of Light at Plane and Spherical Surfaces
- Thin Lens Formula and Lens Maker's Formula
- Total Internal Reflection and Its Applications
- Magnification and Power of a Lenses in Contact
- Refraction of Light Through a Prism

NCERT Page 228 to 240

For deeper insight **Scan the QR Code**

Chapter 10

Refraction of Light

The phenomenon of the change in the path of light as it passes obliquely from one transparent medium to another is called refraction of light.

Laws of Refraction of Light

- **First Law** The incident ray, the refracted ray and the normal to the interface at the point of incidence all lie in the same plane.
- **Second Law** The ratio of the sine of the angle of incidence and the sine of the angle of refraction is constant for a given pair of media.

$$\frac{\sin i}{\sin r} = {}_1\mu_2$$

Refractive Index

The refractive index of a medium for a light of given wavelength may be defined as the ratio of the speed of light in vacuum to its speed in that medium.

$$\mu = \frac{c}{v}$$

Real and Apparent Depths

It is on account of refraction of light that the apparent depth of an object placed in denser medium is less than the real depth.

$$\text{Apparent depth} = \frac{\text{Real depth}}{\text{Refractive Index}}$$

Refraction Through Lateral Shift

Lateral shift is the perpendicular distance between the incident and emergent rays, when light is incident obliquely on a refracting slab with parallel faces.

Critical Angle

Whenever a ray of light goes from a denser medium to a rarer medium, it bends away from the normal. As angle of incidence in denser medium increases, angle of refraction also increases in rarer medium.

The angle of incidence ($\angle i$) in denser medium for which the angle of refraction ($\angle r$) in rarer medium is 90° is called the critical angle ($\angle C$ or $\angle\theta_C$). $\mu_d > \mu_r$

$$\Rightarrow \frac{\sin C}{\sin 90^\circ} = \frac{\mu_{rarer}}{\mu_{denser}} = \frac{\mu_r}{\mu_d} = \sin C$$

Total Internal Reflection

The phenomenon in which a ray of light travelling from denser to a rarer medium at an angle of incidence greater than the critical angle is totally reflected back into denser medium is called total internal reflection.

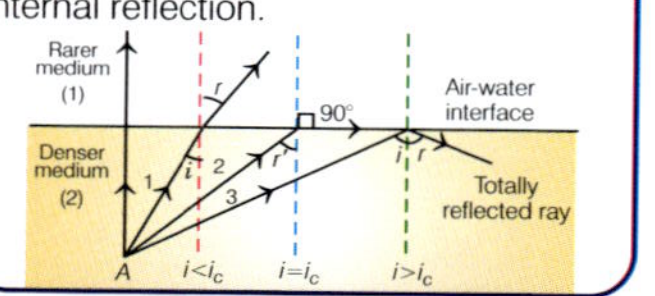

Totally Refracting Prisms

These prisms are right-angled isosceles triangle which turn light ray by 90° or 180°. They are based on the phenomenon of total internal reflection. Refractive index of crown glass is 3/2.

$$\text{Hence, } C = \sin^{-1}\left(\frac{1}{\mu}\right) = \sin^{-1}\left(\frac{2}{3}\right) \approx 42^\circ$$

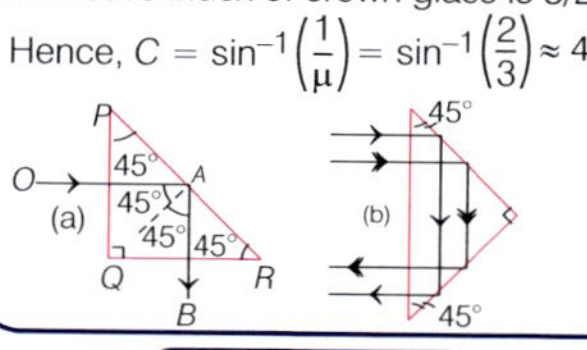
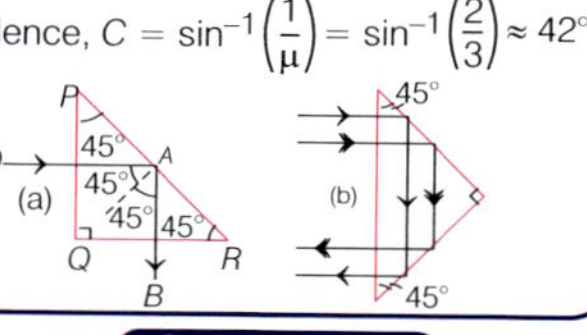

Optical Fiber

An optical fiber is a flexible glass or plastic fiber that can transmit light from one end to the other.

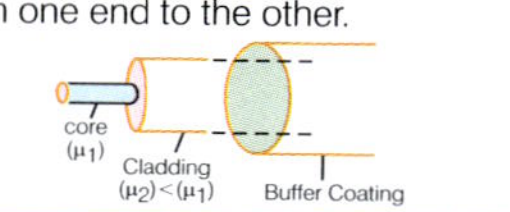

Lenses

Lens is a transparent medium (material) bounded by two surfaces atleast one of which should be spherical. Refractive index of the medium (material) should also be different from the surroundings.

Lenses are of two types.

(i) **Convex or converging lens** In this lens, a transparent medium is bounded by two surfaces such that it is thicker in the middle.

(ii) **Concave or diverging lens** In this lens, a transparent medium is bounded by two surfaces such that it is thinner in the middle.

Lens Maker's Formula

This formula relates the focal length of a lens to the refractive index of the lens material and the radii of curvature of its two surfaces.

$$\frac{1}{f} = (\mu - 1)\left[\frac{1}{R_1} - \frac{1}{R_2}\right]$$

Power of Lens

The tangent of the angle by which it converges or diverges a beam of light falling at unit distance from the optical centre

$$P = \frac{1}{f}$$

Refraction Through a Prism

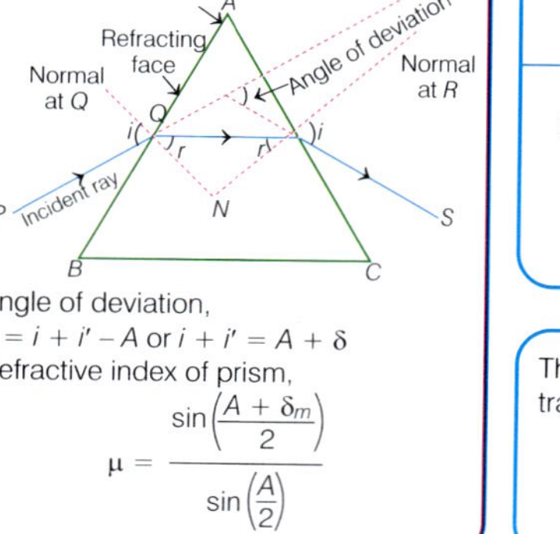

Angle of deviation,

$\delta = i + i' - A$ or $i + i' = A + \delta$

Refractive index of prism,

$$\mu = \frac{\sin\left(\frac{A + \delta_m}{2}\right)}{\sin\left(\frac{A}{2}\right)}$$

Formation of Image by Convex Lens

S.No.	Position of object	Ray diagram	Position of image	Nature and size of image
(i)	At infinity		At the principal focus (F_2) or in the focal plane	Real, inverted and extremely diminished
(ii)	Beyond $2F_1$		Between F_2 and $2F_2$	Real, inverted and diminished
(iii)	At $2F_1$		At $2F_2$	Real, inverted and of same size as the object
(iv)	Between F_1 and $2F_1$		Beyond $2F_2$	Real, inverted and highly magnified

Formation of Image by Concave Lens

S.No.	Position of object	Ray diagram	Position of image	Nature and size of image
(i)	At infinity		At F_2	Virtual, erect and point sized
(ii)	Anywhere on the principle axis		Between optical centre and F_2	Virtual, erect and diminished

Magnification Produced by a Lens

The ratio of the size of the image to the size of object is called magnification. The lateral, transverse or linear magnification (m) produced by a lens is defined by

$$\text{Magnification } (m) = \frac{\text{Height of Image}}{\text{Height of Object}}$$

Test 3

Syllabus
- Microscope and Astronomical Telescope (Reflecting and Refracting) and their Magnifying Power

NCERT Page 240 to 246

For deeper insight **Scan the QR Code**

Chapter 10

Simple Microscope

A microscope is a converging lens of small focal length. It consists of a convex lens with object placed between its focus and optical centre and eye close to it. The image formed by simple microscope will be erect, virtual, enlarged and on the same side of the lens between object and infinity as shown in figure below.

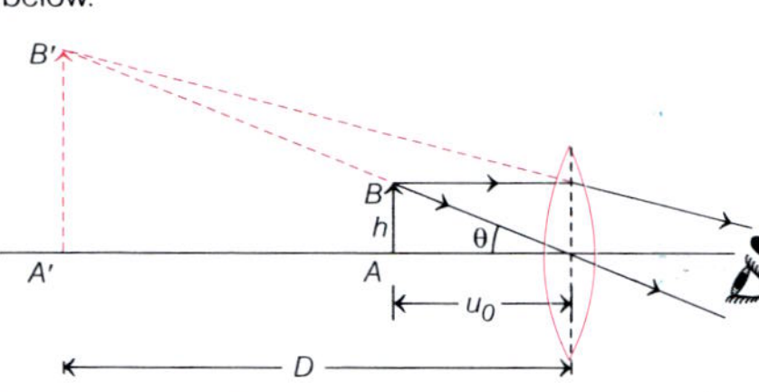

The linear magnification m for the image formed at near point D by a simple microscope can be obtained by using the relation

$$m = \left(1 - \frac{v}{f}\right)$$

or

$$m = \left(1 + \frac{D}{f}\right)$$

When the image is at infinity, the angular magnification is

$$m = \frac{D}{f}$$

A simple microscope has a limited maximum magnification (≤ 9) for realistic focal lengths.

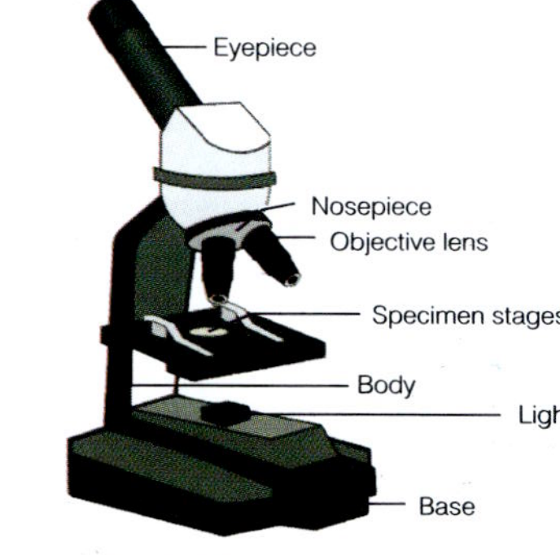

Simple Microscope

Compound Microscope

- Compound microscope is used for much larger magnifications, one uses two lenses, one compounding the effect of the other.

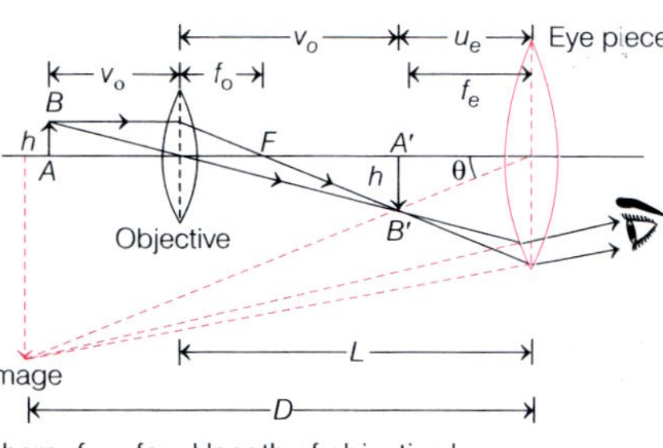

where, f_o = focal length of objective lens and f_e = focal length of eyepiece lens.

- The lens nearest to the object, called the **objective**, forms a real, inverted, magnified image of the object. This serves as the object for the second lens, the **eyepiece**, which functions essentially like a simple microscope or magnifier, produces the final image, which is enlarged and virtual.
- The magnification due to a compound microscope is $m = m_0 m_e$
- The magnification m and the length of tube L of a compound microscope, when the final image is formed at least distance of distinct vision D are given by

$$m = m_0 m_e = \left(\frac{v_o}{u_o}\right)\left(1 + \frac{D}{f_e}\right) = \left(\frac{L}{f_o}\right)\left(1 + \frac{D}{f_e}\right) \quad L = v_o + \left(\frac{f_e D}{f_e + D}\right)$$

The magnification m and the length of the tube L of a compound microscope, when the final image is formed at infinity (normal adjustment) are given by

$$m = m_0 m_e = \left(\frac{v_o}{u_o}\right)\left(\frac{D}{f_e}\right) = \left(\frac{L}{f_o}\right)\left(\frac{D}{f_e}\right) \text{ and } \quad L = f_o + f_e$$

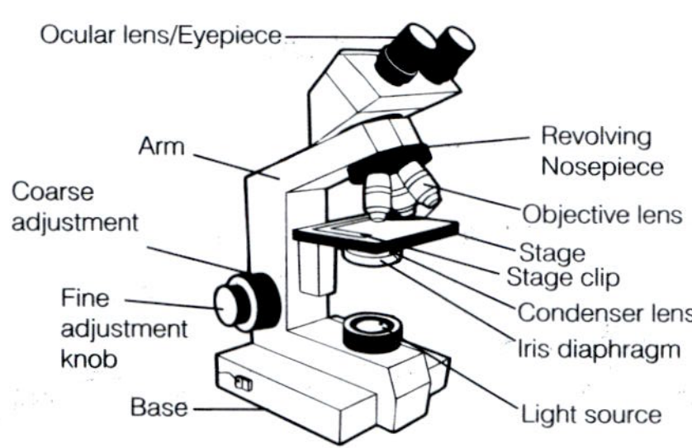

Compound Microscope

Telescope

A telescope is an instrument used to look at the distant objects such as stars, planets or space activities.

There are three types of refracting telescopes in use

(i) Astronomical telescope

(ii) Terrestrial telescope and

(iii) Galilean telescope

Reflecting Telescope

This type of telescope is based upon the same principle at which the astronomical telescope works except that the formation of images takes place by reflection instead of by refraction. It consists of concave mirror of large aperture and large focal length (objective). A plane mirror is placed between the concave mirror and its focus. A small convex lens works as eye-piece.

Eye-piece

M_1 = Parabolic mirror

Rays parallel from a very distant object

M_2 = Plane mirror

If f_o is focal length of the concave spherical mirror and f_e the focal length of the eye-piece, then magnifying power of the reflecting telescope is given by

$$m = \frac{f_o}{f_e}$$

Astronomical Telescope

It is used to see the heavenly bodies. It consists of two converging lenses placed coaxially. The one facing the distant object is called the objective and has a large aperture and large focal length. The other is called the eye piece, as the eye is placed closed to it.

Objective lens, Parallel rays from object at infinity, f_o, f_e, Eyepiece, Eye, Final image at infinity

The intermediate image formed by objective is real, inverted and small and final image formed by eye piece is real, inverted and highly magnified.

Magnifying Power

(i) When object is at infinity

Magnifying power, $M = \frac{\beta}{\alpha} = \frac{f_o}{u_e}$

where, α = angle subtended by object on objective and β = angle subtended by final image at eye-piece.

$$\therefore M_\infty = \frac{f_o}{f_e} \text{ and } L_\infty = f_o + f_e \qquad (\because u_e = f_e)$$

(ii) When the final image is at D

Magnifying Power, $M_D = \frac{f_0}{f_e}\left(1 + \frac{f_e}{D}\right)$

and $L_D = f_0 + \frac{Df_e}{D + f_e}$

Formulae For Simple Microscope Compound Microscope and Astronomical/Telescope

Name of optical instrument	M	L	M_∞	M_D	L_∞	L_D
Simple microscope	$\frac{D}{u_o}$	–	$\frac{D}{f}$	$1 + \frac{D}{f}$	–	–
Compound microscope	$\frac{v_o}{u_o}\frac{D}{u_e}$	$v_o + u_e$	$\frac{v_o}{u_o}\frac{D}{f_e}$	$\frac{v_o}{u_o}\left(1 + \frac{D}{f_e}\right)$	$v_o + f_e$	$v_o + \frac{Df_e}{D + f_e}$
Astronomical telescope	$\frac{f_o}{u_e}$	$f_o + u_e$	$\frac{f_o}{f_e}$	$\frac{f_o}{f_e}\left(1 + \frac{f_e}{D}\right)$	$f_o + f_e$	$f_o + \frac{Df_e}{D + f_e}$

Syllabus
- Wavefront and Huygens' Principle
- Laws of Reflection and Refraction using Huygens' Principle
- Young's Double Slit Experiment and Expension for Fringe Width, Coherent Source and Sustained Interference of Light

NCERT Page 255 to 266

For deeper insight **Scan the QR Code**

Chapter 11

Huygens' Wave Theory of Light

Wave theory of light was propounded by Christian Huygens'.
(i) Light travels in the form of waves.
(ii) These waves travel in all the directions with the velocity of light.
(iii) The waves of light of different colours have different wavelengths.
(iv) Initially, the light waves were assumed to be longitudinal. But later on while explaining the phenomenon of polarisation, the light waves were considered to be transverse.
(v) The whole universe with all matter and space is filled with a luminiferous medium called **ether**, of very low density and very high elasticity.
(vi) Huygens' theory could explain reflection, refraction, interference, diffraction, polarisation but could not explain photoelectric effect and compton's effect.
(vii) Wave theory introduced the concept of wavefront.

Wavefronts

The continuous locus of all such particles of the medium which are vibrating in the same phase at any instant.

- **Spherical Wavefront** In case of waves travelling in all directions from a point source, the wavefronts are spherical in shape.
- **Cylindrical Wavefront** When the source of light is linear in shape, the wavefronts are cylindrical.
- **Plane Wavefront** At very large distances from the source, a portion of spherical or cylindrical wavefront is plane wavefront.

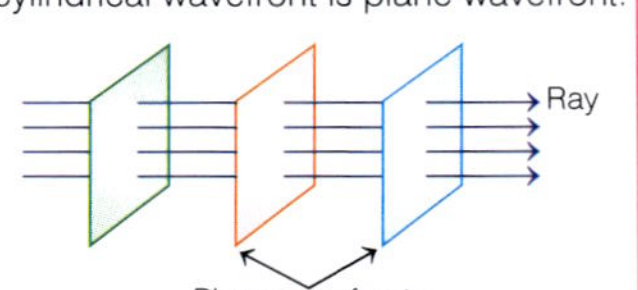

Huygens' Principle of Secondary Wavelets

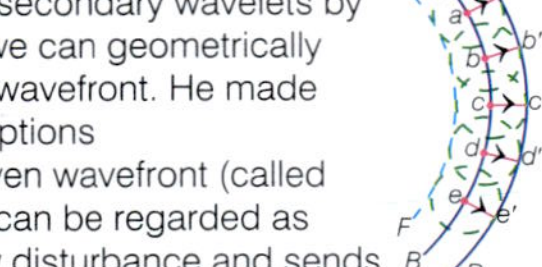

Huygens' propounded a principle known as Huygens' principle of secondary wavelets by which at any instant, we can geometrically obtain the position of wavefront. He made following three assumptions
(i) Every point on a given wavefront (called primary wavefront) can be regarded as fresh source of new disturbance and sends out its own spherical wavelets called secondary wavelets.
(ii) The secondary wavelets spread in all directions with the velocity of wave (i.e. velocity of light).
(iii) A surface touching these secondary wavelets, tangentially in the forward direction at any instant (Δt) gives the position and shape of the new wavefront at the instant. This is called secondary wavefront.

Interference of Light Waves

When two light waves of exactly equal frequency having constant phase difference with respect to time travelled in same direction and superimpose (overlap) with each other, then intensity of resultant wave does not remain uniform in space. This phenomenon of formation of maximum intensity at some points and minimum intensity at some other points by the two identical light waves travelling in same direction is called the interference of light.

Types of Interference

(i) Constructive Interference
When the two waves meet in same phase, i.e. the intensity of light is maximum, is called the constructive interference.

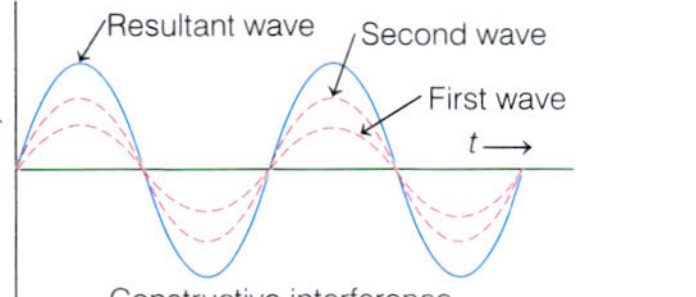

Constructive interference

Maximum intensity, $I_{max} = (\sqrt{I_1} + \sqrt{I_2})^2 = k(a_1 + a_2)^2$

(ii) Destructive Interference When the two waves meet in opposite phase, i.e. the intensity of light is minimum, is called the destructive interference.

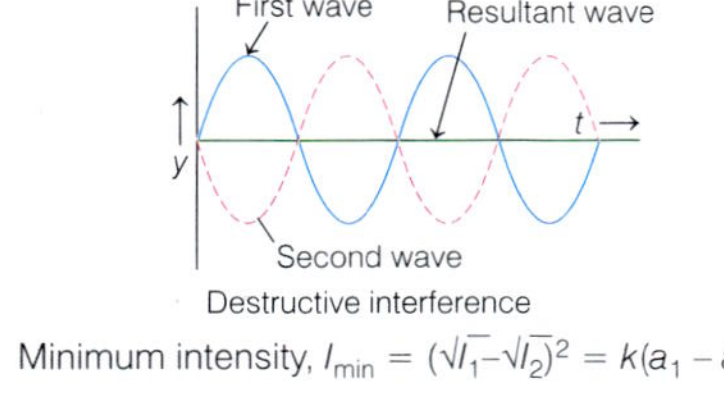

Destructive interference

Minimum intensity, $I_{min} = (\sqrt{I_1} - \sqrt{I_2})^2 = k(a_1 - a_2)^2$

Coherent and Incoherent Sources

- **Coherent sources** Two sources of light which continuously emit light waves of same frequency (or wavelength) with a zero or constant phase difference between them.
- **Incoherent sources** Two sources of light which do not emit light waves with a constant phase difference.

Coherent and Incoherent Addition of Waves

Resultant intensity, $I_R = I_1 + I_2 + 2\sqrt{I_1 I_2}\cos\phi$

For bright fringes,
$I_{max} = (\sqrt{I_1} + \sqrt{I_2})^2$ at $\phi = 0°, 2\pi, 4\pi, \ldots$

For dark fringes,
$I_{min} = (\sqrt{I_1} - \sqrt{I_2})^2$ at $\phi = \pi, 3\pi, 5\pi, \ldots$

For $I_1 = I_2 = I_0$; $I_R = 4I_0\cos^2\frac{\phi}{2}$

If the sources are incoherent $I_R = 2I_0$

Condition for Sustained Interference

The interference pattern in which the positions of maxima and minima of intensity on the observation screen do not change with time is called a sustained or permanent interference pattern.

- Intensity ratio of maxima and minima,

$$\frac{I_{max}}{I_{min}} = \frac{(a_1 + a_2)^2}{(a_1 - a_2)^2} = \frac{(r+1)^2}{(r-1)^2}$$

where, $r = \frac{a_1}{a_2}$

Necessary Conditions for Interference of Light

(i) Sources must be coherent For a stable interference pattern, the individual waves must maintain a constant phase relationship with one another.

(ii) Same frequency or wavelength Phase relationship between two waves can be kept constant only when their frequencies are same. Thus we can say that, two coherent sources must have the same frequency.

(iii) Equality of amplitudes The amplitudes of two interfering waves should be equal or approximately equal. Otherwise the difference between the intensities of maxima and minima will be too small and the contrast will be poor. Maximum contrast is, however obtained when $A_1 = A_2$, because, then minimum intensity will be zero.

Young's Double Slit Experiment

Two identical narrow slits S_1 and S_2 are placed symmetrically with respect to narrow slit S illuminated with monochromatic light. The interference pattern is obtained on an observation screen placed at large distance D from S_1 and S_2.

The position of nth bright fringe from the centre of screen is

$$x_n = n\frac{D\lambda}{d}$$

The position of nth dark fringe from the centre of the screen is

$$x'_n = (2n-1)\frac{D\lambda}{2d}$$

Expression for Fringe Width

Fringe width is the separation between two successive bright or dark fringes and is given by

$$\beta = \frac{D\lambda}{d}$$

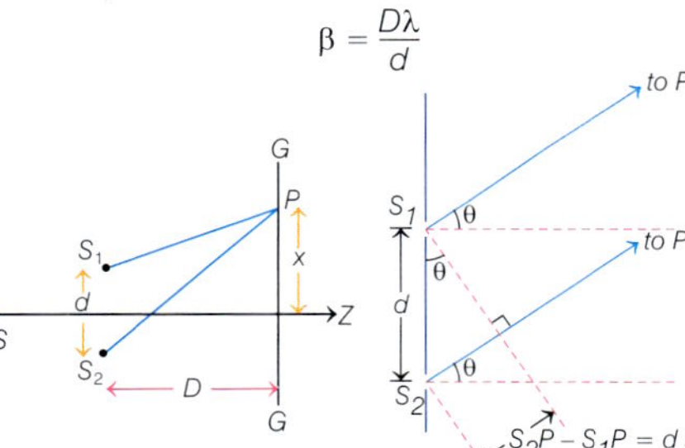

- **Angular fringe width**

The angular fringe width is given by

$$\theta = \frac{\lambda}{d} = \frac{\beta}{D}$$

- **Distribution of Intensity**

The distribution of intensity in Young's double slit experiment is shown below

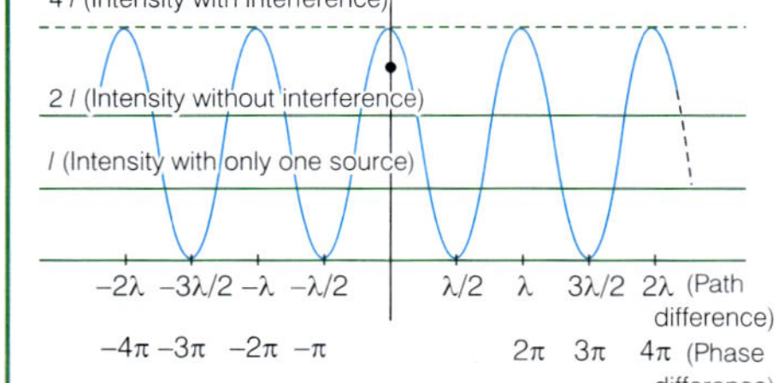

Test 2

Syllabus

- Diffraction due to Single Slit, Width of Central Maximum.
- Polarisation, Plane – Polarised Light:
- Brewster's Law, Uses of Plane – Polarised Light and Polaroids

NCERT Page 266 to 271

For deeper insight **Scan the QR Code**

Diffraction of Light

The phenomenon of bending of light around the corners of small obstacles or apertures and their consequent spreading into the regions of geometrical shadow is called diffraction of light.

Diffraction of light around corner of (a) a small aperture (b) a small object

Fresnel Diffraction

If source and screen are at finite distance from the obstacle or aperture, then diffraction observed is known as Fresnel diffraction

Fresnel diffraction through a slit

Fraunhofer Diffraction

When all the rays passing through a narrow slit are approximately parallel to one another, this can be achieved experimentally either by placing the screen far from the opening used to create the diffraction or by using a converging lens to focus the rays once they pass through the opening. The diffraction produced in such an arrangement is called Fraunhofer diffraction.

Fraunhofer diffraction pattern of a single slit. The pattern consists of a central bright fringe flanked by much weaker maxima alternating with dark fringes.

Diffraction due to a Single Slit

When a plane wave passes through a narrow slit, it suffers diffraction producing a central bright fringe and obtained flanked of maxima and minima.

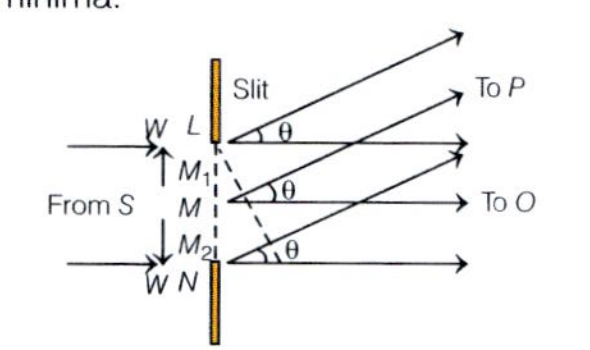

- For nth minimum

$a \sin\theta_n = n\lambda$, where $n = 1, 2, 3, \ldots$

- For nth secondary maximum

$a \sin\theta_n = (2n+1)\lambda/2, n = 1, 2, 3 \ldots$

- Width of a secondary maximum

$$\beta = \frac{D\lambda}{a}$$

- Width of central maximum

$$\beta_0 = 2\beta = \frac{2D\lambda}{a}$$

Intensity of Single Slit Diffraction Pattern

$$I = I_0\left[\frac{\sin(\pi a \sin\theta)/\lambda}{(\pi a \sin\theta)/\lambda}\right]^2 \text{ (at angle } \theta)$$

Here, I_0 is the intensity at $\theta = 0°$ (the central maximum). From this result, we see that minima occurs, when

$\frac{\pi a \sin\theta}{\lambda} = m\pi$ or $\sin\theta = m\frac{\lambda}{a}$

where, $m = \pm 1, \pm 2, \ldots$ (not zero)

Intensity Distribution Curve

Intensity distribution curve on the screen in diffraction pattern with sinθ is given below

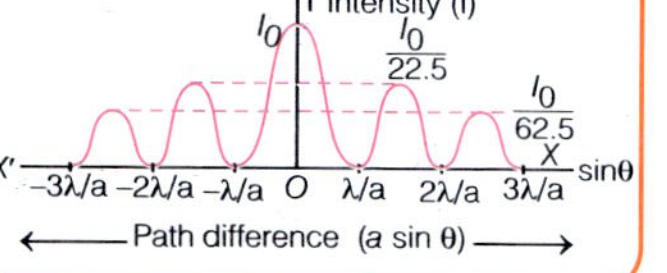

Polarisation of Waves

The phenomenon of restricting the oscillations of a wave to just one direction in the transverse plane is called polarisation of waves.

Polarised Light

If the vibrations of a wave are present in one direction, perpendicular to the direction of propagation.
In a linearly polarised wave, the vibrations at all points, at all times, lie in the same plane, so it is also called a plane polarised wave.

Pictorial representation of polarised light

Brewster's Law

This law states that the tangent of the polarising angle of incidence of a transparent medium is equal to its refractive index.

$\mu = \tan i_p$

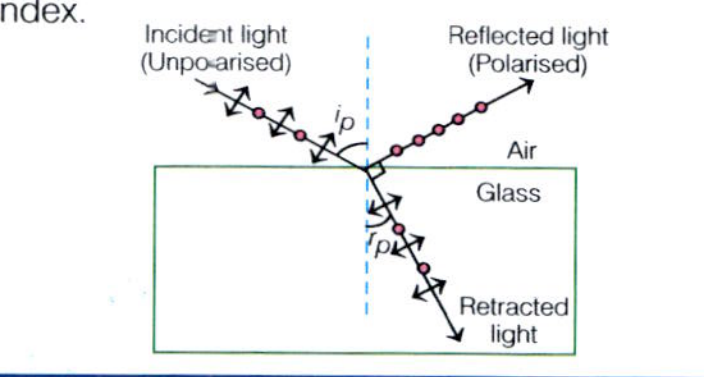
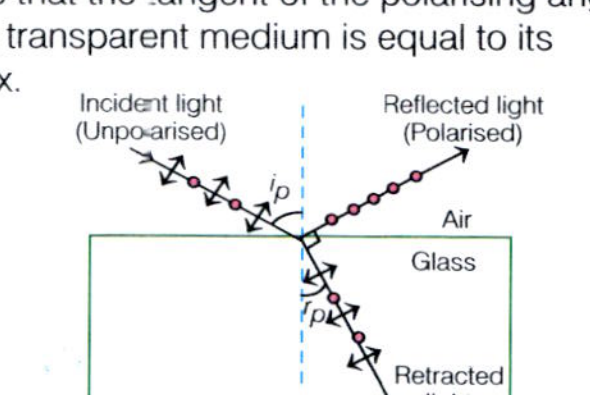

Malus' Law

The intensity of transmitted light passed through an analyser is

$$I = I_0 \cos^2\theta$$

(θ = angle between transmission directions of polariser and analyser).

Polaroids

Polaroids are thin commercial sheets which make use of the property of selective absorption to produce an intense beam of plane polarised light.

Uses of Polaroids

(i) Polaroids are used in goggles and cameras to avoid glare of light.
(ii) Polaroids are useful in three dimensional motion pictures, i.e. in holography.
(iii) They are used to eliminate the head light, glare in motor cars.
(iv) They are used to improve contrast in old oil paintings.
(v) They are used as window glasses to control the intensity of incoming light.

Polarisation of Light by Scattering

When a beam of white light passes through a medium consisting of small particles of size of the order of the wavelength of light (dust, smoke, air molecules), then the light seen in a direction perpendicular to the incident beam appears bluish. This phenomenon is known as **scattering of light** and the particles causing scattering are called **scatterers.** The scattering of light is, infact, absorption and re-radiation of light by the scatterers.

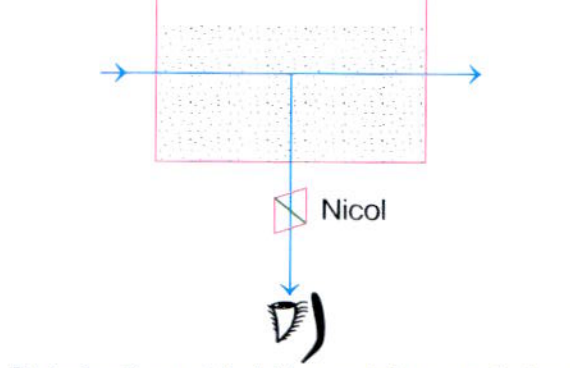

Polarisation of light by sulphur particles

Test 1

Syllabus
- Photoelectric Effect
- Einstein's Photoelectric Equation
- Hertz and Lenard's Observations

NCERT Page 274 to 283

For deeper insight **Scan the QR Code**

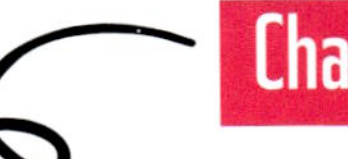

Chapter 12

Electron Volt (eV)

- It is the kinetic energy gained by an electron when it is accelerated through a potential difference of 1 volt. $1 eV = 1.6 \times 10^{-19} J$
- The work function of a metal is generally measured in electron volt (eV).

Electron Emission

The phenomenon of emission of electrons from a metal surface is called electron emission.

- **Thermionic emission**
  The electrons are emitted from the metal surface with the help of thermal energy.
- **Field or cathode emission**
  Electrons are emitted from a metal surface by subjecting it to a very high electric field.
- **Photoelectric emission**
  Electrons are emitted from a metal surface with the help of suitable electromagnetic radiations.
- **Secondary emission**
  Electrons are ejected from a metal surface by striking fast moving electrons over it.

Work Function

The minimum amount of energy required by an electron to just escape from the metal surface is called work function of the metal. The work function depends on
(i) the nature of the metal
(ii) the conditions of its surface.

Free Electrons in Metals

In metals, the electrons in the outer shells of the atoms are loosely bound. They move about freely throughout the lattice of positive ions. Such loosely bound electrons are called free electrons.

Photoelectric Effect

The phenomenon of emission of electrons from the surface of metal, when radiations of suitable frequency fall on it, is known as photoelectric effect.
The emitted electrons (as shown in figure) are called photoelectrons and the current, so produced is called photoelectric current.

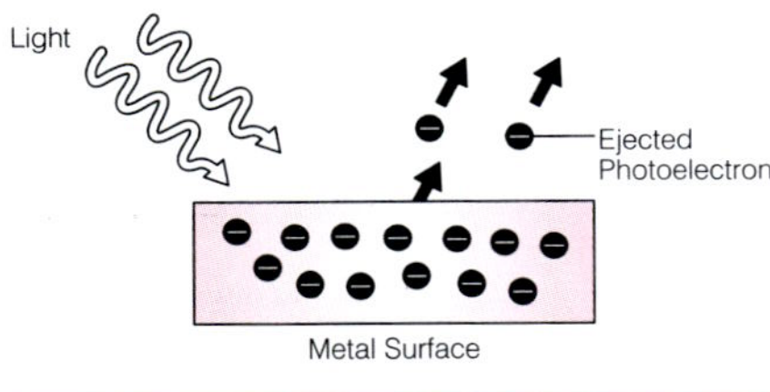

Hertz's Observation

- Hertz experimentally investigated on production of electromagnetic waves using spark discharge method.
- He found high voltage sparks (electrons) across metal when illuminated by UV light.
- Electrons escape from the surface into the surrounding environment are findings of Hertz's observations.

Lenard's Observation

- UV radiations incidented on metal plate (emitter) placed inside an evacuated glass tube which had two electrodes.
- It is found that current flows through the electrodes in the closed circuit (see experimental study of photoelectric effect).
- Lenard established that current flows confirmly due to incident light.
- Lenard studied how this current varies with collector plates, potential difference with frequency and with intensity of incident light.

Laws of Photoelectric Emission

(i) For a given metal and a radiation of fixed frequency, the rate of emission of photoelectrons is proportional to the intensity of incident radiation.
(ii) For every metal, there is a certain minimum frequency below which no photoelectrons are emitted.
(iii) The photoelectric emission is an instantaneous process.
(iv) For the radiation of frequency higher than the threshold frequency, the maximum kinetic energy of the photoelectrons is directly proportional to the frequency of incident radiation and is independent of the intensity of incident radiation.

Experimental Setup of Photoelectric Effect

Quartz window, S, Evacuated glass tube, W, Photosensitive plate, Collector, Electrons, C, A, μA, V, Potential divider, H.T.B, Key

Photoelectric Current

The current constituted by photoelectrons is called photoelectric current. Its value depends on
(i) the intensity of light
(ii) the potential difference applied between the two electrodes,
(iii) the nature of the cathode material

Threshold Frequency

The minimum value of the frequency of incident radiation below which the photoelectric emission stops altogether is called threshold frequency. It is denoted by ν_0 and is a characteristic of the metal.

Effect of Intensity of Light on Photocurrent

As the photoelectric current is directly proportional to the number of photoelectrons emitted per second.

Photoelectric current → ; O ; Intensity →

So, for constant frequency of incident radiation, the number of photoelectrons emitted per second is directly proportional to the intensity of the incident radiations, *i.e.* intensity $\propto$ photoelectric current $\propto$ number of photo electrons emitted/second $\propto \frac{1}{(\text{Distance})^2}$

Effect of Potential

The photoelectric current increases with the increase in accelerating potential till a stage is reached when the photoelectric current becomes maximum and does not increase further with the increase in the accelerating potential.

$K_{max} = 1/2\, mv_{max}^2 = eV_0$

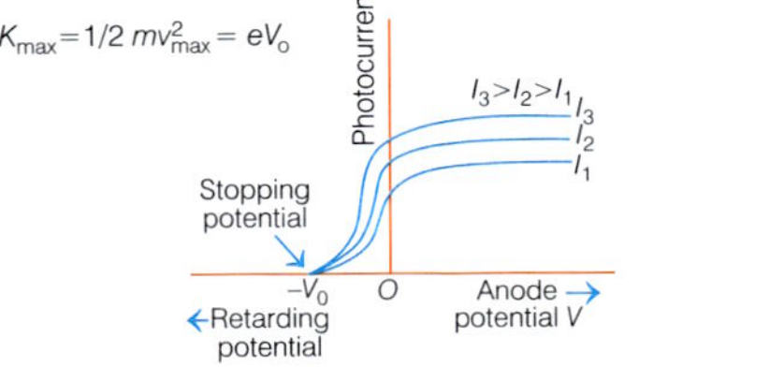

Effect of Frequency of Incident Radiation on Stopping Potential

The greater frequency of the incident radiation, greater is the maximum kinetic energy of the photoelectrons and hence, greater is the retarding potential required to stop such electrons completely.

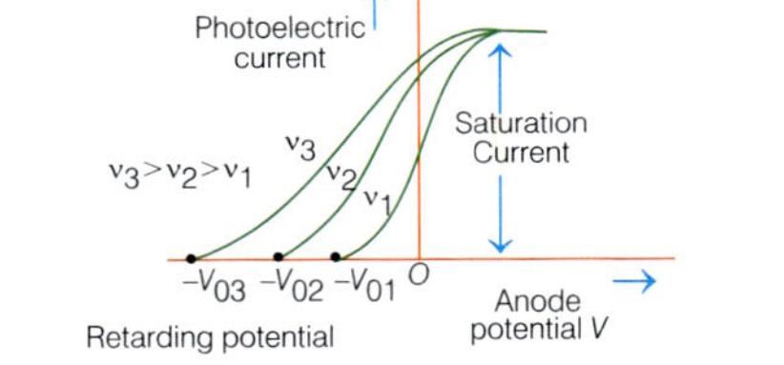

Stopping Potential *versus* frequency graph

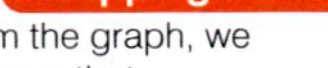
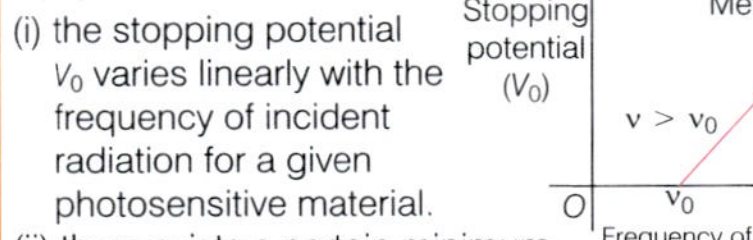

From the graph, we observe that
(i) the stopping potential V_0 varies linearly with the frequency of incident radiation for a given photosensitive material.
(ii) there exists a certain minimum cut-off frequency ν_0 for which the stopping potential is zero. This minimum frequency is called **threshold frequency**.

It can be defined as the minimum frequency of light which can emit photoelectrons from a material is called **threshold frequency** or **cut-off frequency** of that material. It is a characteristic property of material. If frequency of incident radiation is more than the threshold frequency, then the photoelectric emission starts instantaneously without any apparent time lag ($\sim 10^{-9}$ s or less), even when the incident radiation has low intensity.

Test 2

Syllabus • Particle Nature of Light : The Photon

NCERT Page 283 to 284

For deeper insight **Scan the QR Code**

Chapter 12

Particle Nature of light: The Photon

According to this theory, the energy of an electromagnetic wave is not continuously distributed over the wave front, instead it travels in the form of discrete packets or bundles of energy called **quanta.** One quantum of light radiation is called a **photon,** which travels with the speed of light. Photoelectric effect, thus gave evidence that light consists of packets of energy. Energy of a photon is given by

$$E = h\nu = \frac{hc}{\lambda}$$

The momentum of photon is given by

$$p = \frac{E}{c} = \frac{h\nu}{c} = \frac{h}{\lambda}$$

Properties of Photons

Different characteristic properties of photons are given below.

(i) In interaction of radiation with matter, radiation behaves as it is made up of particles called **photons**.

(ii) A photon in vacuum travels with a speed of light c (i.e. $3 \times 10^8 \text{ms}^{-1}$) in straight line.

(iii) According to the theory of relativity, the mass m of a particle moving with velocity v, comparable with the velocity of light c is given by

$$m = \frac{m_0}{\sqrt{1 - \frac{v^2}{c^2}}} \Rightarrow m_0 = m\sqrt{1 - \frac{v^2}{c^2}}$$

(iv) The inertial mass of a photon is given by $m = \frac{E}{c^2} = \frac{h}{c\lambda} = \frac{h\nu}{c^2}$

(v) Irrespective of the intensity of radiation, all the photons of a particular frequency ν or wavelength λ have the same energy

$$E = h\nu = \frac{hc}{\lambda}$$

and momentum, $p = \frac{h\nu}{c} = \frac{h}{\lambda}$

(vi) Energy of a photon depends upon frequency of the photon, so the energy of the photon does not change when photon travels from one medium to another.

(vii) As, velocity of a photon is different in different media, so wavelength of the photon also changes in different media.

Intensity of Photons

A moving photon carries momentum with it. Therefore, pressure and intensity are also associated with photons.

Total Energy of photons, $E = Nh\nu = N\left(\frac{hc}{\lambda}\right)$

Power of source, $P = \frac{E}{t} = \frac{Nh\nu}{t} = nh\nu = \frac{nhc}{\lambda} \left(\because n = \frac{N}{t}\right)$

Also, we can write $n = P/E = \frac{P}{h\nu} = \frac{P\lambda}{hc}$

As, intensity or energy flux is defined as the energy crossing per unit area normally per second.

$\Rightarrow$ Intensity, $I = \frac{P}{A} = \frac{E}{tA} = \frac{nh\nu}{A} = n\frac{hc}{A\lambda}$

where, A = area normal to incidental light,

N = number of photons

and n = number of photons/second.

- At a distance r from a point source of power P, intensity of photons is given by $I = \frac{P}{4\pi r^2} \Rightarrow I \propto \frac{1}{r^2}$
- For a line source of power P, intensity of photons is given by

$$I = \frac{P}{2\pi r l} \Rightarrow I \propto \frac{1}{r}$$

Relation between Stopping Potential (V_0), Frequency (ν) and Wavelength (λ) of Incident Light

Maximum kinetic energy is given by

$$K_{max} = h(\nu - \nu_0)$$

If stopping potential is V_0, then

$$K_{max} = eV_0$$

$\therefore$ $$eV_0 = h(\nu - \nu_0) \quad \text{.......(i)}$$

If λ = wavelength of the incident radiation,

λ_0 = threshold wavelength for the metal surface

and c = velocity of light.

Then, $\nu = \frac{c}{\lambda}$ and $\nu_0 = \frac{c}{\lambda_0}$

Putting these values in Eq. (i), we get ....(i)

$$eV_0 = h\left(\frac{c}{\lambda} - \frac{c}{\lambda_0}\right) \Rightarrow eV_0 = hc\left(\frac{1}{\lambda} - \frac{1}{\lambda_0}\right)$$

Einstein's Photoelectric Equation

Albert Einstein explained the various laws of photoelectric emission on the basis of Planck's quantum theory. According to Planck's quantum theory, light radiations consist of tiny packets of energy called **quanta.** One quantum of light radiation is called a **photon** which travels with the speed of light. The energy of a photon is given by

$$E = h\nu$$

When a photon of energy $h\nu$ falls on a metal surface, the energy of the photon is absorbed by the electron and is used in following two ways.

(i) A part of energy is utilised to overcome the surface barrier and come out of the metal surface. This part of energy is called **work function**. It is expressed as

$$\phi_0 = h\nu_0$$

(ii) The remaining part of the energy is used in giving a velocity v to the emitted photoelectron. This is equal to the maximum kinetic energy of the photoelectron $= \frac{1}{2}mv^2_{max}$, where m is the mass of the photoelectron. This can be seen in the figure given below.

hν (Photon) — (1/2) mv^2_{max} (Photoelectron) — $\phi_0 = h\nu_0$ — Metal

According to the law of conservation of energy,

$$K_{max} = h\nu - \phi_0$$

This equation is called **Einstein's photoelectric equation**. From Einstein's equation, it is clear that K_{max} does not depend on intensity of incident light.

Graph of stopping potential and frequency

Consider the equation,

$$eV_0 = hc\left(\frac{1}{\lambda} - \frac{1}{\lambda_0}\right) \Rightarrow V_0 = \frac{h}{e}\left(\frac{c}{\lambda} - \frac{c}{\lambda_0}\right)$$

or $$V_0 = \frac{h}{e}\nu - \frac{h\nu_0}{e}$$

The slope of this line is given by $\tan\theta = h/e$ and intercept on V_0 axis is given by $\frac{h\nu_0}{e}$ as shown in the graph.

V_0; Slope = $\tan\theta = \frac{h}{e}$; θ; $\nu = \nu_0$; ν; O; $\frac{h\nu_0}{e}$

Graph of V_0 versus ν

In terms of wavelength, we can write

$$V_0 = \frac{hc}{\lambda_e} - \frac{hc}{\lambda_0 e}$$

The slope of this line is given by $\tan\theta = hc/e$ and intercept on V_0 axis is given by $\frac{hc}{\lambda_0 e}$ as shown in the graph.

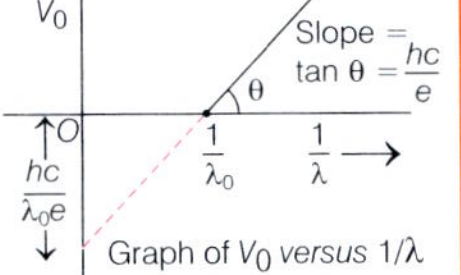

Graph of V_0 versus $1/\lambda$

Explanation of Photoelectric Effect from Einstein's Equation

Einstein explained all the observations of photoelectric effect using Einstein's photoelectric equation. These are as follow

(i) From photoelectric equation, it is clear that K_{max} is independent of intensity of radiation but depends linearly on ν.

(ii) Photoelectric emission is possible only, if $h\nu > \phi_0$.

or $h\nu > h\nu_0$ $(\because \phi_0 = h\nu_0)$

$\Rightarrow$ $\nu > \nu_0$

where, ν_0 is threshold frequency. If $\nu < \nu_0$, then kinetic energy of electron comes out to be negative, which is not possible, so no photoelectric emission is possible below ν_0, even if the incident radiation is of high intensity falls on the surface for long duration.

(iii) Intensity of radiation (I) is proportional to the number of energy quanta per unit area per unit time (n). Higher the value of n, higher the number of electrons emitted (for $\nu > \nu_0$). That is the reason (for $\nu > \nu_0$),

photocurrent $\propto$ intensity

(iv) The absorption of photon by electron is instantaneous process, hence emission of electrons is instantaneous. **Note** Practically only one electron is ejected by 1 million photons.

$$\text{Quantum effciency} = \frac{\text{Number of electrons ejected per sec}}{\text{Number of photons incident per sec}}$$

$$\Rightarrow \eta = \frac{n'}{n} \times 100\%$$

Syllabus
- Matter Waves
- Wave Nature of Particle
- de-Broglie Relation

NCERT Page 284 to 286

For deeper insight Scan the QR Code

Matter Waves : de-Broglie Waves

According to de-Broglie, a wave is associated with moving material particle which controls the particle in every respect. The wave associated with moving particle is called matter waves or de-Broglie wave and it propagates in the form of wave packets with group velocity. Wavelength associated with de-Broglie wave is called **de-Broglie wavelength** and is given by

$$\lambda = \frac{h}{mv} = \frac{h}{p}$$

According to Planck's quantum theory, the energy of the photon is given by

$$E = h\nu = \frac{hc}{\lambda}$$

According to Einstein's theory, the energy of the photon is given by $E = mc^2$

$$\lambda = \frac{h}{mc} = \frac{h}{p}$$

where, $p = mc$ is momentum of a photon.

Importance of de-Broglie wave

(i) de-Broglie wavelength of the electron is large enough to be observed. Because of their small mass, electrons can have a small momentum and in turn a large wavelength $\left(\lambda = \frac{h}{p}\right)$ Diffraction effects have been obtained with streams of protons, neutrons and alpha particles. It is evident from de-Broglie's equation that greater the mass of the moving particle, the smaller is the wavelength associated with the particle. Hence, detection is difficult. Ordinary objects have extremely small wavelengths.

(ii) If m is the mass and v is the velocity of the material particle, then $p = mv$ or $\lambda = h/mv$

(iii) If E is the kinetic energy of the material particle, then

$$E = \frac{1}{2}mv^2 = \frac{p^2}{2m} \text{ or } p = \sqrt{2mE}$$

Therefore, the de-Broglie wavelength is given by $\lambda = \frac{h}{\sqrt{2mE}}$

(iv) If a charged particle carrying charge q is accelerated through a potential difference of V volt, then Kinetic energy K.E$=qV$

In that case, $\lambda = \frac{h}{\sqrt{2mqV}}$

(v) When the material particles like neutrons are in thermal equilibrium at absolute temperature T, then they possess Maxwellian distribution of velocities and so their average kinetic energy is given by $E = \frac{1}{2}mv_{rms}^2 = \frac{3}{2}kT$

where k is Boltzmann's constant whose value is 1.38×10^{-23} m^{2}kg s^{-2}K^{-1}, so that

$$\lambda = \frac{h}{\sqrt{3mkT}}$$

de-Broglie Wavelength Associated with Uncharged Particles

For neutron, de-Broglie wavelength is given as

$$\lambda_{neutron} = \frac{0.286 \times 10^{-10}}{\sqrt{E \text{ (in eV)}}} \text{ m} = \frac{0.286}{\sqrt{E \text{ (in eV)}}} \text{Å}$$

Energy of thermal neutrons or gas molecules at ordinary temperature is given by

$$E = \frac{3}{2}kT \Rightarrow \lambda = \frac{h}{\sqrt{3mkT}}$$

where, T = absolute temperature

k = Boltzmann's constant $= 1.38 \times 10^{-23}$ J/K

Also, $\lambda_{\text{thermal neutrons}} = \frac{25.17}{\sqrt{T}}$ Å

de-Broglie Wavelength of an Accelerating Electron

Let an electron of charge e having mass m be accelerated from rest through a potential difference V, then gain in kinetic energy of electron is given by $K = \frac{1}{2}m_e v^2$

Work done on electron $= eV$

$$\therefore \quad \frac{1}{2}m_e v^2 = eV \Rightarrow v = \sqrt{\frac{2eV}{m_e}}$$

Momentum is given by $p = m_e v = \sqrt{2eVm_e}$

The wavelength associated with moving electrons is given by $\lambda = \frac{h}{\sqrt{2eVm_e}}$

$$\lambda = \frac{6.63 \times 10^{-34}}{\sqrt{2 \times 9.1 \times 10^{-31} \times 1.6 \times 10^{-19} V}} = \frac{12.27}{\sqrt{V}} \text{Å}$$

Similarly, de-Broglie wavelength for the charged particles can be given by $\lambda = h/p$

where, $p = \sqrt{2m(\text{KE})} = \sqrt{2mqV}$

- **For proton,** $\lambda = \frac{h}{\sqrt{2m_p q}}$

On putting the values of h, m_p and q, we get

$$\lambda = \frac{0.286}{\sqrt{V}} \text{Å}$$

- **For deuteron,** $\lambda = \frac{0.202}{\sqrt{V}}$ Å
- **For α-particle,** $\lambda = \frac{0.101}{\sqrt{V}}$ Å
- **For gas,** $\lambda = \frac{h}{mv_{rms}}$

Characteristics of Matter Waves

(i) Matter waves are not electromagnetic waves in nature.

(ii) These waves are non-mechanical waves, i.e. they can travel in vacuum.

(iii) Matter waves are independent of charge, i.e. they are associated with every moving particle (whether charged or uncharged).

(iv) Observation of matter waves is possible only when the de-Broglie wavelength is of the order of size of the particle (i.e. the waves are diffracted).

(v) The phase velocity of the matter waves can be greater than the speed of the light.

(vi) The number of de-Broglie waves associated with nth orbital electron is n.

Relationship between wavelength of photon and that of electron

- Ratio of wavelength of photon to that of electron with same energy E

$$\frac{\lambda_{photon}}{\lambda_e} = c\sqrt{\frac{2m}{E}} \quad \lambda_{photon} \propto \lambda_e^2$$

- Ratio of KE of electron to that of photon with same wavelength

For Same $\frac{\text{KE}_{electron}}{\text{KE}_{photon}} = \frac{V}{2c}$

- A particle formed due inelastic collision of particles 'x' and 'y' having de-broglie wavelength λ_x and λ_y respectively.

If they are moving in opposite directions, then

$$\Delta p = p_x - p_y \qquad \overrightarrow{P_x} \quad \overleftarrow{P_y}$$

$$\frac{h}{\lambda} = \frac{h}{\lambda_x} - \frac{h}{\lambda_y} \qquad \lambda = \frac{\lambda_x \lambda_y}{\lambda_x - \lambda_y}$$

If they are moving at right angle to each other

$$\Rightarrow p = \sqrt{p_x^2 + p_y^2} \Rightarrow \frac{h}{\lambda} = \sqrt{\frac{h^2}{\lambda_x^2} + \frac{h^2}{\lambda_y^2}}$$

$$\frac{1}{\lambda} = \sqrt{\frac{1}{\lambda_x^2} + \frac{1}{\lambda_y^2}}$$

λ_x, p_x; p_y, λ_y

Summarized Properties of de-Broglie Wavelength of particles

- **de-Broglie wavelength associated with charged particles**

(i) For electrons ($m_e = 9.1 \times 10^{-31}$kg)

$$\lambda = \frac{h}{\sqrt{2mqV}} = \frac{6.62 \times 10^{-34}}{\sqrt{2 \times 9.1 \times 10^{-31} \times 1.6 \times 10^{-19} V}} \text{m} = \frac{12.27}{\sqrt{V}} \text{Å}$$

Note: The potential difference required to have an election of wavelength λ Å is

$$V = \frac{150.6}{\lambda^2} \quad \text{(from above equation)}$$

(ii) For protons ($m_p = 1.67 \times 10^{-27}$kg)

$$\lambda = \frac{0.286}{\sqrt{V}} \text{Å}$$

(iii) For deuterons ($m_d = 2 \times 1.67 \times 10^{-27}$kg)

$$\lambda = \frac{0.202}{\sqrt{V}} \text{Å}$$

(iv) For α-particles ($m_\alpha = 4 \times 1.67 \times 10^{-27}$kg)

$$\lambda = \frac{0.101}{\sqrt{V}} \text{Å}$$

- **de Broglie wavelength associated with uncharged particles**

(i) For neutrons ($m_n = 1.67 \times 10^{-27}$kg)

$$\lambda = \frac{h}{\sqrt{2mE}} = \frac{6.62 \times 10^{-34}}{\sqrt{2 \times 1.67 \times 10^{-27} E}}$$

$$\lambda = \frac{0.286}{\sqrt{E(eV)}} \text{Å}$$

(ii) For thermal neutrons at ordinary temperatures,

$$E = \frac{3}{2}kT$$

$$\lambda = \frac{h}{\sqrt{3mkT}} = \frac{25.17}{\sqrt{T}} \text{Å}$$

(iii) For gas molecules

$$\lambda = \frac{h}{m \times C_{rms}}$$

$\Rightarrow$ For gas molecules at T K

$$E = \frac{3}{2}kT \quad \therefore \lambda = \frac{h}{\sqrt{3mkT}}$$

Test 1

Syllabus
- α-particle Scattering Experiment
- Rutherford's Model of Atom

NCERT Page 291 to 296

For deeper insight **Scan the QR Code**

Chapter 13

Rutherford's α-Particle Scattering Experiment

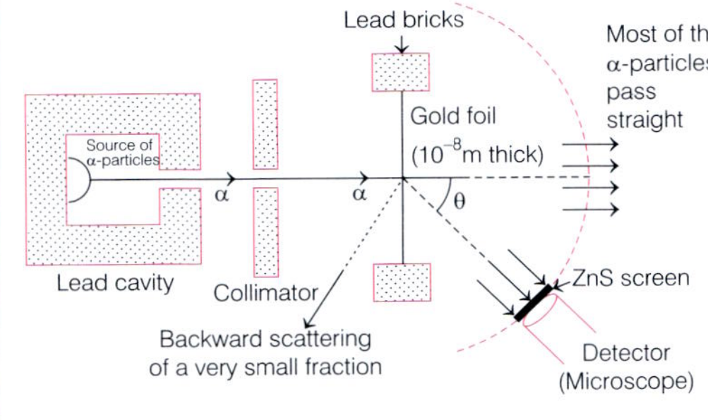

When an α-particle strikes the screen, it produces a flash of light which were observed by the microscope.

Observations of Rutherford Experiment

Rutherford made following observations from the experiment

(i) Most of the α-particles pass through the foil remains undeflected.

(ii) Some of them are deflected through small angles.

(iii) Few α-particles (about 1 in 8000) are deflected through an angle more than 90°.

(iv) A very few α-particles return back, *i.e.* deflected by 180°. Thus, few α-particles reverse their motion without actually touching the gold foil.

(v) The scattering of α-particles is proportional to the thickness of target for thin targets.

(vi) The number of α-particles scattered per unit area $N(\theta)$ at scattering angle θ varies inversely as $\sin^4(\theta/2)$,

i.e., $$N(\theta) \propto \frac{1}{\sin^4(\theta/2)}$$

This number $[N(\theta)]$ as a function of θ can be represented by following graph.

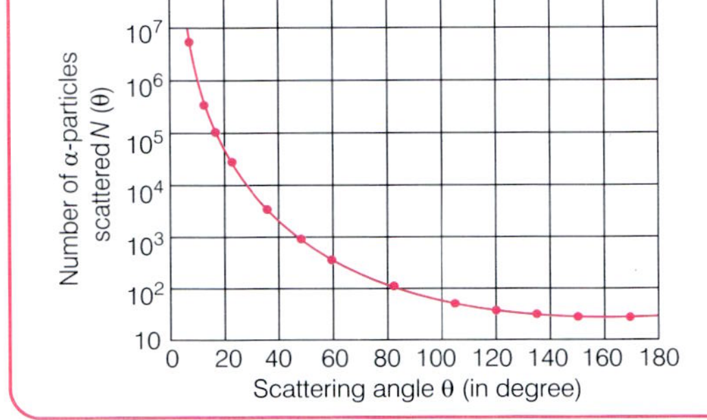

Rutherford's Atomic Model

The essential features of Rutherford's model of the atom or planetary model of the atom are as follows

(i) Most of the mass (at least 99.95%) and all of the charge of an atom is concentrated in a very small region of atom called atomic nucleus.

(ii) Nucleus is positively charged and its size is of the order of 10^{-15}m ≈ 1 fermi. The nucleus occupies only about 10^{-12} of the total volume of the atom or less.

(iii) In an atom, maximum space is empty and the electrons revolve around the nucleus in the same way as the planets revolve around the sun (i.e. in elliptical orbits).

Distance of Closest Approach

The minimum distance from the nucleus upto which the α-particle approaches is called the distance of closest approach (r_0). At this distance (when particle deflect by 180°), whole of the KE of α-particle converts into electrostatic potential energy,

$$\frac{1}{2}mv^2 = \frac{1}{4\pi\varepsilon_0}\frac{(Ze)2e}{r_0}$$

[∵ charge on α-particle is $+2e$ and charge on target nucleus is Ze, where Z is atomic number]

$$\Rightarrow r_0 = \frac{1}{4\pi\varepsilon_0}\frac{2Ze^2}{\left[\frac{1}{2}mv^2\right]} = \frac{4kZe^2}{mv^2}$$

This distance of closest approach (r_0) can be seen in the figure below.

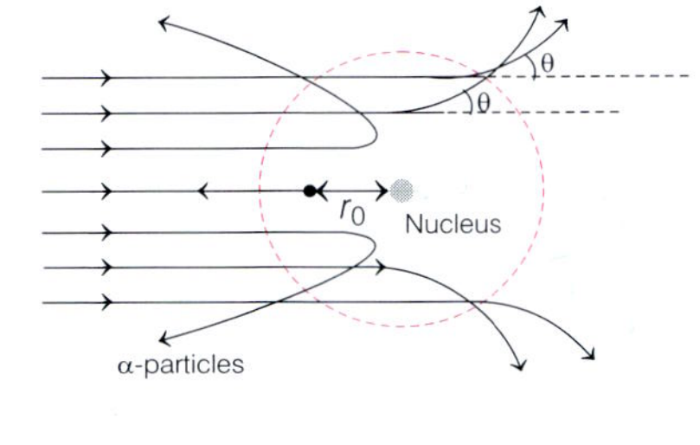

Impact Parameter

The perpendicular distance of the velocity vector of the α-particle from the centre of the nucleus, when it is far away from the atom.

$$b = \frac{1}{4\pi\varepsilon_0}\cdot\frac{Ze^2\cot\frac{\theta}{2}}{E}$$

$$= \frac{1}{4\pi\varepsilon_0}\cdot\frac{Ze^2\cot\frac{\theta}{2}}{\frac{1}{2}mv^2}$$

b
θ
Nucleus

α-Particle Trajectory

The α-particle which passes through the atom at a large distance from the nucleus experience a small electrostatic force of repulsion due to the nucleus and hence, undergoes a very small deflection. However, the α-particle which passes through the atom at a smaller distance from the nucleus suffer a large deflection. On the other hand, α-particle which travel towards the nucleus directly, slow down and ultimately comes to rest and then after being deflected through 180° retrace their path.

The trajectory of the α-particle at various scattering angles, is shown in the figure below.

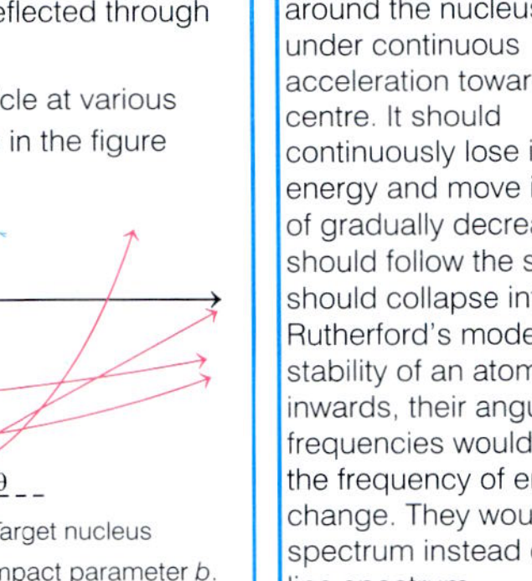

Trajectory of α-particles and impact parameter *b*.

Electron Orbits

In the Rutherford's nuclear model of the atom, the atom as an electrically neutral sphere consisting of a very small, massive and positively charged nucleus at the centre surrounded by the revolving electrons in their respective dynamically stable orbits. The electrostatic force of attraction F_e between the revolving electrons and the nucleus provides the requisite centripetal force F_c to keep them in their orbits. Thus, for a dynamically stable orbit in a H-atom,

$$F_c = F_e \Rightarrow \frac{mv^2}{r} = \frac{1}{4\pi\varepsilon_0}\cdot\frac{e^2}{r^2} \quad (\because Z = 1)$$

Thus, the relation between the orbit radius and the electron velocity,

$$r = \frac{e^2}{4\pi\varepsilon_0 mv^2}$$

The kinetic energy K and electrostatic potential energy U of the electron in H-atom are

$$K = \frac{1}{2}mv^2 = \frac{e^2}{8\pi\varepsilon_0 r} \quad \left(\because mv^2 = \frac{e^2}{4\pi\varepsilon_0 r}\right)$$

$$\text{and } U = -2K = -\frac{e^2}{4\pi\varepsilon_0 r}$$

(the negative sign in U signifies that the electrostatic force is in the $-r$ direction or attractive in nature.) Thus, the total mechanical energy E of the electron in a H-atom is

$$E = K + U = \frac{e^2}{8\pi\varepsilon_0 r} - \frac{e^2}{4\pi\varepsilon_0 r} = -\frac{e^2}{8\pi\varepsilon_0 r}$$

Limitations of Rutherford's Atomic Model

An electron revolving around the nucleus is under continuous acceleration towards the centre. It should continuously lose its energy and move in orbits of gradually decreasing radii. The electron should follow the spiral path and finally, it should collapse into the nucleus. Thus, the Rutherford's model cannot explain the stability of an atom. As the electrons spiral inwards, their angular velocities and frequencies would change continuously and the frequency of emitted light will also change. They would emit a continuous spectrum instead of the actually observed line spectrum.

Test 2

Syllabus
- Bohr Model, Energy Levels
- Hydrogen Spectrum

NCERT Page 297 to 302

For deeper insight **Scan the QR Code**

Chapter 13

Bohr's Atomic Model

Bohr proposed a model for hydrogen atom which is applicable for some lighter atoms in which a single electron revolves around a stationary nucleus of positive charge which are usually known as hydrogen like atom, *e.g.* $_1H^1$, $_1H^2$, He^+, Li^{++}, etc.

Bohr's model is based on the following three postulates

(i) Bohr postulated that an electron in an atom can move around nucleus in certain circular stable orbits without emitting radiations.

(ii) Electrons can revolve only in those orbits in which their angular momentum is an integral multiple of $h/2\pi$, where h is Planck's constant. If the mass of the electron be m and it is revolving with velocity v in an orbit of radius r, then its angular momentum will be mvr. According to Bohr's postulate, we have angular momentum, $mvr = nh/2\pi$ where, n is an integer ($n = 1, 2, 3, \ldots$) and is called the principal quantum number of the orbit. This equation is called Bohr's quantisation condition.

(iii) When the atom receives energy from outside, then one (or more) of its outer electrons leaves its orbit and goes to some higher orbit. This state of the atom is called excited state.

The electron in the higher orbit stays only for 10^{-8} s and returns back to lower orbit. While returning back, the electron radiates energy in the form of electromagnetic waves.

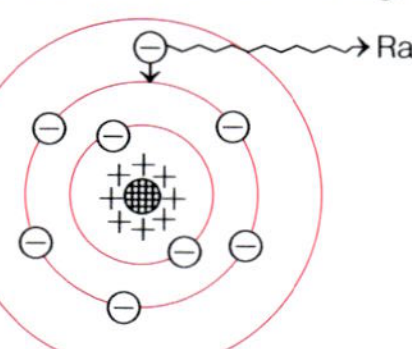

Electron falls down to lower orbit and emits energy

If the energy of electron in the higher orbit be E_2 and that in the lower orbit be E_1, then the frequency ν of the radiated waves is given by

$$h\nu = E_2 - E_1$$

or

$$\nu = \frac{E_2 - E_1}{h}$$

This equation is called Bohr's frequency condition.

Unit Time Period

Speed of electron and time period of electron in nth orbit,

$$\text{Speed, } v_n = \frac{Ze^2}{2h\varepsilon_0}\frac{1}{n}$$

$$\text{Time period, } T_n = \frac{1}{v_n} = \frac{nhr_n}{kZe^2}$$

Analysis of Bohr's Atomic Model

A hydrogen like atom consists of a tiny positively charged nucleus and an electron revolving in a stable circular orbit around it as shown in the figure below.

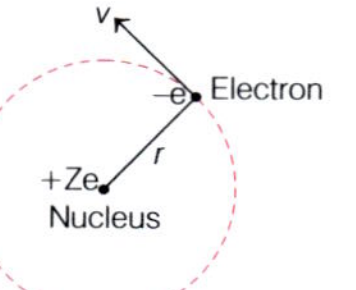

An electron is revolving around a nucleus of hydrogen like atoms

From the first postulate, the angular momentum of the electron,

$$mvr = n\frac{h}{2\pi}$$

Radius of Electron in nth Orbit

$$r_n = n^2\frac{h^2\varepsilon_0}{\pi mZe^2} \quad (\because r = r_n)$$

This is the equation for the radii of the permitted orbits. According to this equation, $r_n \propto n^2$.

Bohr's Radius

The radius of the first orbit ($n = 1$) of H-atom ($Z = 1$) will be

$$r_1 = \frac{h^2\varepsilon_0}{\pi me^2}$$

Radius of nth orbit is,

$$r_n = 0.53\frac{n^2}{Z}\text{ Å} = \frac{n^2}{Z}r_1$$

- **Variations of r_n**

(i) Using the relation, $r_n = \frac{n^2}{Z}r_1$ we can plot the following graphs

Here, $r_n \propto 1/Z$

Nature of graph will be rectangular hyperbola.

r_n - Z graph

(ii) Here, $\sqrt{r_n} \propto n$

Nature of graph will be parabola.

r_n - n graph

(iii) Here, $r_n \propto n^2$

Nature of graph will be straight line.

r_n versus n^2 graph

Energy of Electron in nth Orbit

The energy E of an electron in an orbit is the sum of kinetic and potential energies.

Kinetic Energy Electron possess kinetic energy because of its motion. Inner orbits have greater kinetic energy than outer ones.

$$KE_n = \frac{RhcZ^2}{n^2}$$

$$R = \frac{me^4}{8\varepsilon_0^2ch^3} = \text{Rydberg's contant}$$

Potential Energy The potential energy of the electron in an orbit is due to the electrostatic attraction by nucleus.

$$U_n = -\frac{2RhcZ^2}{n^2}$$

Total Energy This is the expression for the total energy of the electron in the nth orbit

$$E_n = \frac{-RhcZ^2}{n^2}$$

$$U_n = -2KE_n \Rightarrow |U_n| = 2|KE_n|$$

$$\therefore En = KE_n - 2KE_n = -KE_n$$

Limitations of Bohr's Model

The limitation of Bohr's model are as follows

(i) Bohr's model is applicable only to a single electron atoms/ions.

(ii) It does not explain the fine structure of spectral lines. Application of external magnetic field (Zeeman effect) and external electric field (Stark effect) to radiating atoms could not be explained.

(iii) Bohr's assumption regarding stationary orbits is against Heisenberg uncertainty principle.

(iv) No explanation is given regarding principle of quantisation of angular momentum.

(v) This model does not explain why orbits of electrons are taken as circular whereas elliptical orbits are also possible.

Quantisation Condition

(i) **Quantum Condition** All the possible circular orbits allowed by the classical theory, the electrons are permitted to circulate only in such orbits in which the angular momentum of an electron is an integral multiple of $\frac{h}{2\pi}$, h being Planck's constant.

$$L = mvr = \frac{nh}{2\pi}, n = 1, 2, 3 \ldots$$

(ii) **Stationary Orbit** While revolving in the permissible orbits, an electron does not radiate energy. These non-radiating orbits are called stationary orbits.

(iii) **Frequency Condition** An atom can emit or absorb radiation in the form of discrete energy photons only when an electron jumps from a higher to a lower orbit or from a lower to a higher orbit. $h\nu = E_2 - E_1$

Excitation and Ionisation Potential

- **Excitation Potential**

It is that accelerating potential which gives to a bombarding electron sufficient energy to excite the target atom by raising one of its electrons from an inner to an outer orbit. First excitation potential of hydrogen = – 3.4 – (– 13.6) = 10.2 V Second excitation potential of hydrogen = – 1.51 – (– 13.6) = 12.09 V.

- **Ionisation Potential**

It is that accelerating potential which gives to a bombarding electron sufficient energy to ionise the target atom by knocking one of its electrons completely out of the atom.

Ionisation potential of hydrogen = 0 – (– 13.6) = 13.6 V.

Hydrogen Line Spectrum

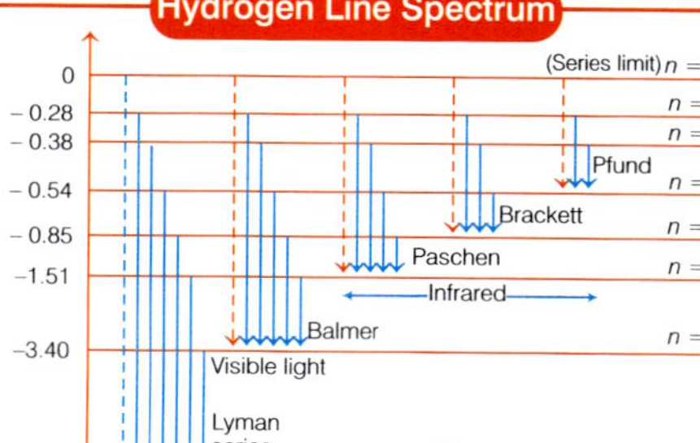

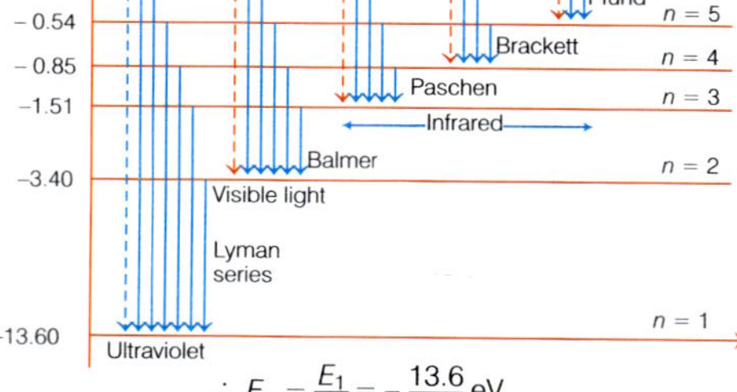

$$\therefore E_n = \frac{E_1}{n^2} = -\frac{13.6}{n^2}\text{ eV}$$

Syllabus
- Composition and Size of Nucleus, Atomic Masses.
- Mass Energy Relation, Mass Defect, Binding Energy Per Nucleon and its Variation with Mass Number

NCERT Page 306 to 313

For deeper insight **Scan the QR Code**

Nucleus

As per the Rutherford's experiment, it was concluded that the entire positive charge and mass of an atom was present at its very tiny centre known as nucleus.

Composition of Nucleus

Nucleus is composed of two types of particles
(i) Protons Positively charged particles
(ii) Neutrons Neutral particles
Mass of neutron is slightly greater than the mass of the proton.
Mass of proton, m_p
$= 1.6726231 \times 10^{-27}$kg
Mass of neutron, m_n
$= 1.6749286 \times 10^{-27}$kg
$m_p \sim 1840 m_e$
where, m_e = mass of electron

Atomic Number

Atomic number of an element is the number of proton present inside the nucleus of a neutral atom. It is also equal to the number of electrons revolving in various orbits around the nucleus of an uncharged atom.
It is represented by Z.
Atomic number, Z = Number of proton
= Number of electron

Mass Number

The total number of neutrons and protons, *i.e.* number of nucleons present inside the nucleus of an element is called its mass number A.
Number of neutrons is represented by N.
So, mass number $(A) = Z + N$
It is symbolically represented as (chemical symbol)^A or $_Z X^A$.
Total charge of the nucleus is equal to the total charge on all protons Z in it
i.e. Ze, where $e = 1.6 \times 10^{-19}$ C.

Nuclear Size and Density

- **Nuclear Size**
  The volume of a nucleus is directly proportional to the number of nucleons in it.
  $R = R_0 A^{1/3}$
- **Nuclear density**
  The density of a nucleus is independent of the size of the nucleus and is given by

$$\rho_{nu} = \frac{\text{Nuclear mass}}{\text{Nuclear volume}} = \frac{m_{nu}}{\frac{4\pi R^3}{3}}$$

The nuclear density is of the order of 10^{17}kg m^{-3}.

Mass Defect

The difference between the rest mass of a nucleus and the sum of the rest masses of its constituent nucleons.

$$\Delta m = Zm_p + (A - Z)m_n - m$$

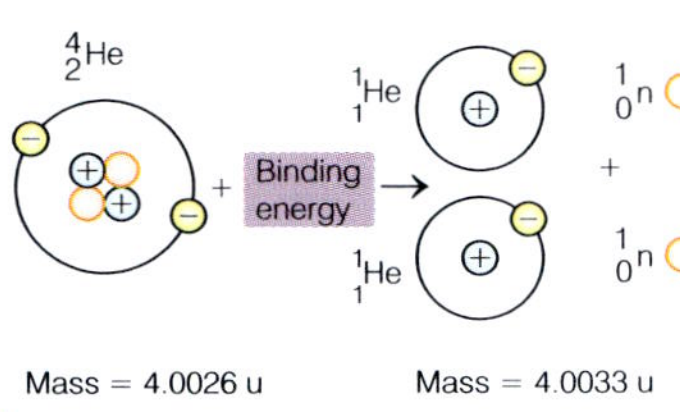

Packing Fraction

The packing fraction of a nucleus is its mass defect per nucleon.

$$\text{P.F. of a nucleus} = \frac{\text{Mass defect}}{\text{Mass number}} = \frac{\Delta m}{A}$$

It is directly related to the availability of nuclear energy and the stability of the nucleus.

Binding Energy

The energy required to break up a nucleus into its constituent protons and neutrons and to separate them to such a large distance that they may not interact with each other.
The binding energy of a nucleus $^A_Z X$ is given by

$$\Delta E_b = [Zm_p + (A - Z)m_n - m]c^2$$

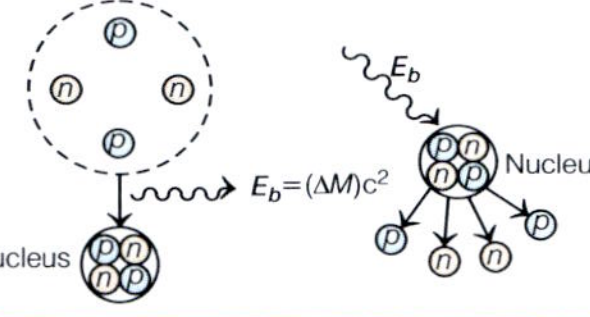

Binding Energy Per Nucleon

Average energy required to extract one nucleon from the nucleus. It is obtained by dividing the binding energy of a nucleus by its mass number.

$$\Delta E_{bn} \text{ or } \bar{B} = \frac{\text{BE}}{A}$$

$$= \frac{[Zm_H + (A - Z)m_n - m]\, c^2}{A}$$

Binding Energy Curve

The value of binding energy per nucleon of a nucleus gives a measure of the stability of that nucleus. Greater is the binding energy per nucleon of a nucleus, more stable is the nucleus.

Nuclear Force

It is one of the strongest force in nature.
It acts only in the range of the order of few fermi metres ($\approx 4.2 \times 10^{-15}$m).
It balances the electrostatic force between protons in the nucleus.

Properties of nuclear forces are given below.

(i) Nuclear forces are charge independent.
(ii) Nuclear forces are short range forces. These do not exist at large distances greater than 10^{-15} m.
(iii) These are attractive force and cause stability of the nucleus.
(iv) Nuclear forces are non-central forces.
(v) Nuclear forces are the strongest force in nature.
(vi) Nuclear forces depends on the direction of the spins of the nucleons. The force is stronger, if the spin of nucleons is parallel and is weak, if it is anti-parallel.
(vii) Electrical and gravitational forces follow inverse square law (i.e. $F \propto 1/r^2$) but nuclear forces are complicated in nature and does not follow it.

Nuclear Stability

The stability of a nucleus is determined by the value of its binding energy per nucleon. Higher the binding energy of nucleon, more stable is the nucleus. The stability of nucleus is also determined by its neutron to proton ratio.
A plot of number of neutrons and number of protons is shown in the figure below.

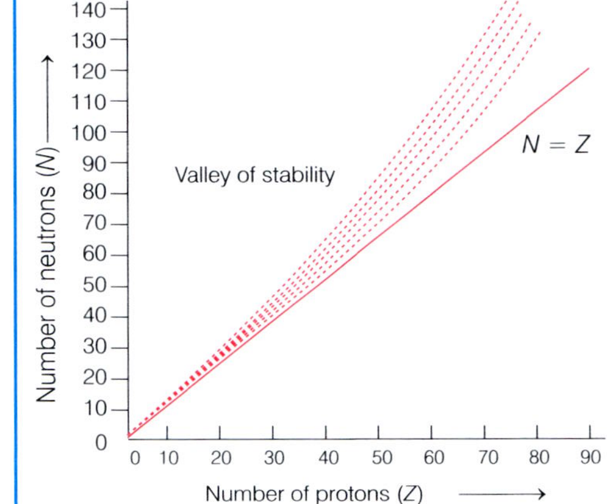

In the figure, the solid line shows the nuclei with equal number of protons and neutrons ($N = Z$). Only light nuclei are on this line, *i.e.* they are stable if they contain approximately same number of protons and neutrons.
Heavy nuclei are stable, only when they have more neutrons than protons.
The long narrow region shown in the figure, which contains the cluster of short lines representing stable nuclei is referred to as the valley of stability.
The nuclide $^{209}_{83}$Bi is the heaviest stable nucleus.
Experimental study shows that the stable nuclei contain even number of protons or neutrons or both.

Nuclear Unstability

When the atom of an element have extra neutrons or protons, it create extra energy in the nucleus and causes the atom to become unbalanced or unstable.

Test 2

Syllabus • Nuclear Reaction and Energy

NCERT Page 314 to 317

For deeper insight **Scan the QR Code**

Chapter 14

Nuclear Reaction

The process by which involves the change of stable nucleus of one element into the nucleus of another element is called nuclear reaction. The general expression for the nuclear reaction is a follows.

$$\underset{\text{(Parent nucleus)}}{X} + \underset{\text{(Incident particle)}}{a} \longrightarrow \underset{\text{(Compound nucleus)}}{C} \longrightarrow \underset{\text{(Product nucleus)}}{Y} + \underset{\text{(Daughter nucleus)}}{b} + \underset{\text{(Energy)}}{Q}$$

Here, X and a are the reactants, Y and b are the products and Q is the kinetic energy released in the nuclear reaction.

Conservation Laws

(i) Mass number and electric charge is conserved.
i.e. $\Sigma Z_{\text{initial}} = \Sigma Z_{\text{final}}$, $\Sigma A_{\text{initial}} = \Sigma A_{\text{final}}$

(ii) Linear momentum and angular momentum are conserved.

(iii) Total energy of the reaction remains conserved, here the term Q helps to balance the total energy of reaction.

Q-value

Q-value is the difference between the sum of the rest mass energy of initial constituents and the sum of the rest mass energy of final constituents of a nuclear reaction.

Q-value of nuclear reaction

As considered, $X + a \longrightarrow Y + b + Q$

where, $Q = U_i - U_f$

Here, U_i = rest mass energy of initial constituents

and U_f = rest mass energy of final constituents

$$= (M_X + M_a - M_Y - M_b)c^2$$

If $Q = +$ ve, reaction is exothermic

and $Q = -$ ve, reaction is endothermic.

e.g. For α-decay, ${}_ZX^A \rightarrow {}_{Z-2}Y^{A-4} + {}_2He^4$ (alpha particle)$+Q$

So, Q -value will be

$$Q = [m({}_ZX^A) - m({}_{Z-2}Y^{A-4}) - m({}_2He^4)] \cdot c^2$$

which represents the kinetic energy available to the products.

For β^- decay, ${}_ZX^A \rightarrow {}_{Z+1}Y^A + e^- + \bar{\nu}$

$$U_i = [m({}_ZX^A) - Zm_e] . c^2$$

$$U_f = [m({}_{Z+1}Y^A) - (Z+1)m_e + m_e] \cdot c^2$$

Kinetic energy available to the products,

$$Q = U_i - U_f = [m({}_ZX^A) - m({}_{Z+1}Y^A)] \cdot c^2$$

For β^+ decay, ${}_ZX^A \rightarrow {}_{Z-1}Y^A + e^+ + \nu$

$$U_i = [m({}_ZX^A) - Zm_e] . c^2$$

$$U_f = [m({}_{Z-1}Y^A) - (Z-1)\, m_e + m_e]\, c^2$$

Kinetic energy available to the products,

$$Q = [m({}_ZX^A) - m({}_{Z-1}Y^A) - 2m_e] . c^2$$

For electron capture, ${}_ZX^A + e^- \rightarrow {}_{Z-1}Y^A + \nu$

$$Q = [m({}_ZX^A) - m({}_{Z-1}Y^A)] . c^2$$

Nuclear Energy

The energy released during nuclear reaction is called nuclear energy.

Generally, there is loss of mass in nuclear reaction, which results (according to Einstein's equation) into release of energy.

In a nuclear reaction, the energy released is of the order of MeV. For same quantity of matter, nuclear sources produces a million times more energy than a chemical source.

Two distinct ways of obtaining energy from nucleus are as

(i) Nuclear fission (ii) Nuclear fusion

Nuclear Fission

It is the process in which a heavy nucleus ($A > 230$), when excited gets split up into two smaller nuclei of nearly comparable masses.

Example

$${}^{235}_{92}U + {}^1_0n \longrightarrow {}^{141}_{56}Ba + {}^{92}_{36}Kr + 3\,{}^1_0n + Q.$$

Neutron
Target nucleus
Neutron
Fission product
Neutron
Fission product
Neutron

Nuclear Fission as a Source of Energy

The sum of the masses of the final products is less than the sum of the masses of the reactant components. The difference in masses is called mass defect, is converted into energy according to Einstein's mass-energy relationship ($E = mc^2$).

$${}^{235}_{92}U + {}^1_0n \longrightarrow {}^{140}_{54}Xe + {}^{94}_{38}Sr + 2\,{}^1_0n$$

• **Necessary Conditions for Nuclear Fission**

The mass of the compound nucleus must be greater than the sum of masses of fission products.

The $\dfrac{\text{binding energy}}{A}$ of compound nucleus must be less than that of the fission products. Hence, mass difference, *i.e.* mass defect, is converted into energy ($E = mc^2$). Thus, tremendous amount of energy is released, first appears as kinetic energy of the fragments and neutrons, then it is transferred to the surrounding appearing as heat.

Nuclear Fusion

It is the process of fusion of two light nuclei into a heavier nucleus with the liberation of large amount of energy.

Example

$${}^2_1H + {}^2_1H \longrightarrow {}^3_2He + {}^1_0n + 3.27\,\text{MeV}$$

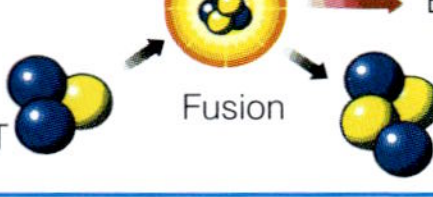

Necessary Conditions for Nuclear Fusion

The high temperature is necessary for the light nuclei to have sufficient kinetic energy, so that they can overcome their mutual coulombic repulsions and come closer than the range of nuclear force. That is why, the fusion reaction is also called thermonuclear reaction.

Chain Reaction

In nuclear fission, many neutrons are produced along with the release of large energy. Under favourable conditions, these neutrons can cause further fission of other nuclei, producing large number of neutrons.

Thus, a chain of nuclear fissions is established which continues until the whole of the uranium is consumed. In the chain reaction, the number of nuclei undergoing fission increases very fast, so the energy produced takes a tremendous magnitude very soon.

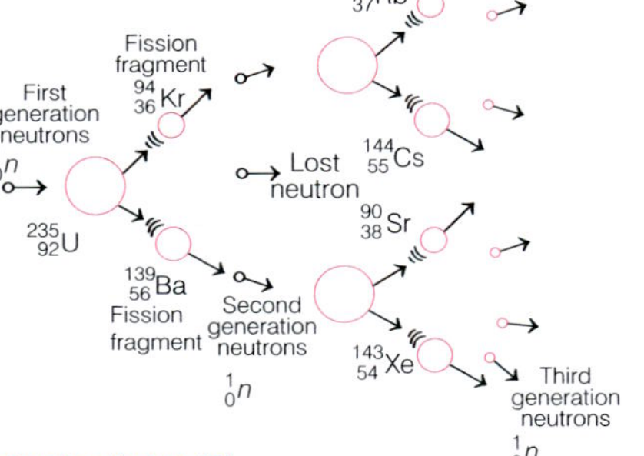

• **Multiplication factor (R)**

A chain reaction once started will remain steady, accelerate or retard depends upon neutron reproduction factor or multiplication factor (R) which is defined as

$$R = \frac{\text{Rate of production of neutrons}}{\text{Rate of loss of neutrons}}$$

If $R = 1$, then chain reaction will be steady. The size of the fissionable sample used is said to be the **critical size** and its mass, the **critical mass.**

• If $R > 1$, then chain reaction grows faster. Size of the material is said to be **supercritical.**

• If $R < 1$, then chain reaction comes to hault. Size of the material is said as **sub-critical.**

Type of Chain Reaction

(i) **Controlled chain reaction** The reaction which can be controlled by absorbing suitable number of neutrons at each stage of the reaction, so that all neutrons are absorbed except one, which is available for further fission. This type of reaction is called controlled chain reaction. The rate of this reaction is slow and the energy liberated is always less than the explosive energy. The reproduction factor is $R = 1$. Nuclear reactor works on this principle.

(ii) **Uncontrolled chain reaction** The reaction which cannot be controlled externally because there are more than one neutron taking part in reaction. So, the reaction will accelerate at such a rapid rate that the whole material will explode within few micro-seconds, liberating tremendous amount of energy. The reproduction factor is $R > 1$. Atom bomb works on this principle.

Test 1

Syllabus
- Semiconductor; Semiconductor Diode: *I-V* Characteristics in Forward and Reverse Bias; Diode as a Rectifier,
- *I-V* Characteristics of LED the Photodiode, Solar cell, Zener Diode; Zenor Diode as a Voltage Regulator

NCERT Page 324 to 340

For deeper insight **Scan the QR Code**

Chapter 15

Semiconductor

A solid substance that allows heat or electricity to pass through it. They have much higher resistivity than metals. They have considerably lower number density of charge carriers than metals. Semiconductors may be elemental (Si, Ge) and compound (GaAs, CdS, etc.)

Classification of Semiconductors

- **Intrinsic Semiconductor** The pure semiconductors are called intrinsic semiconductors. The numbers of excited electrons is equal to number of holes.
- **Extrinsic Semiconductor** When a small amount few parts per million (ppm) impurity is added to the pure semiconductor, the conductivity of semiconductor is increased.
- **Doping** When some suitable impurity is added to intrinsic semiconductors, then this process is called doping.
  (i) Pentavalent dopants such as Sb and P, these are also called donors.
  (ii) Trivalent dopants such as In (indium), B (boron) and Al (aluminium).

Types of Extrinsic Semiconductor

- ***n*-type semiconductors**

The pentavalent impurity is used in this type of semiconductor. In *n*-type semiconductor, electrons are the majority charge carriers and holes are the minority charge carriers.

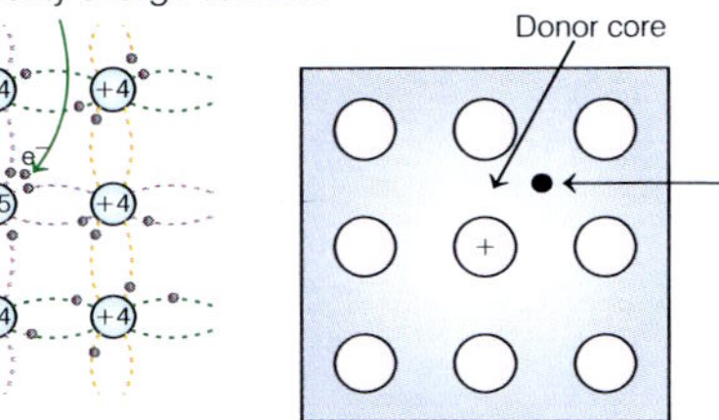

- ***p*-type semiconductors**

The trivalent impurity atoms are called acceptors because they create holes which can accept electrons from the nearby bonds. In *p*-type semiconductor, holes are the majority charge carriers and electrons are the minority charge carriers.

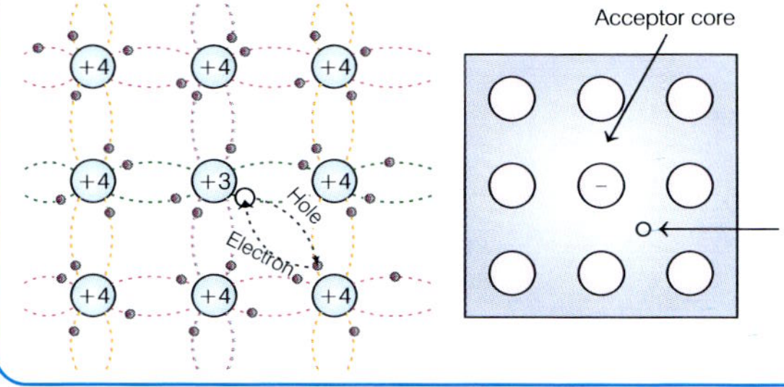

Energy Bands in Solids

- **Valence band (VB)**
  – It is the range of energies of valence electron.
- **Conduction band (CB)**
  – It is the range of energies of conduction electron.

(i) For insulators $E_g \approx 15\text{eV}$
(ii) For conductors $E_g \approx 0$
(iii) For semiconductor $E_g \approx 1\text{eV}$

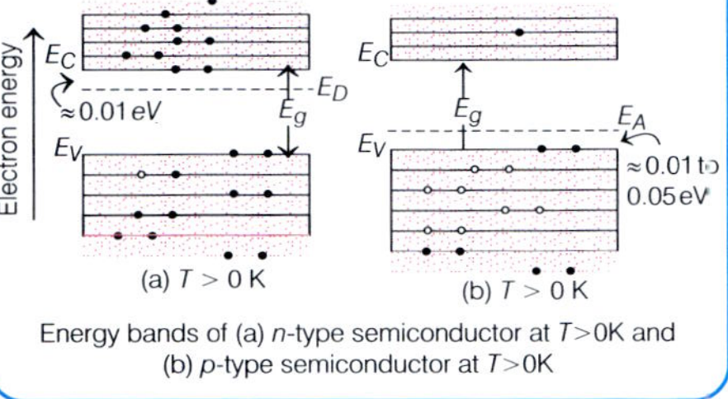

Energy bands of (a) *n*-type semiconductor at $T>0$K and (b) *p*-type semiconductor at $T>0$K

Classification of Solids on the Basis of Their Electrical Properties

(i) Metals have very low resistivity or high conductivity.

$$\rho \approx 10^{-2} - 10^{-8}\ \Omega\text{-m}$$
$$\sigma \approx 10^{2} - 10^{8}\ \text{Sm}^{-1}$$

(ii) Insulators have high resistivity or low conductivity.

$$\rho \approx 10^{11} - 10^{19}\ \Omega\text{-m}$$
$$\sigma \approx 10^{-11} - 10^{-19}\ \text{Sm}^{-1}$$

(iii) Semiconductor possess resistivity or conductivity intermediate to metals and insulators.

$$\rho \approx 10^{-5} - 10^{+6}\ \Omega\text{-m}$$
$$\sigma \approx 10^{5} - 10^{-6}\ \text{Sm}^{-1}$$

p-n Junction

it is formed at boundary between *p*-type and *n*-type semiconductor, where the *p*-type contains excess of holes and *n*-type contains an excess of electrons. This junction results in the creating of depletion region with an internal electric field.

Electron diffusion
Electron drift
p
n
Hole diffusion
Hole drift
Depletion region

Semiconductor Diode

A semiconductor diode is basically a *p-n* junction with metallic contacts provided at the ends for the application of an external voltage. It is a two terminal device.

Depletion region
p *n*
Metallic contact
(a)
Anode *p* *n* Cathode
(b)

Forward Biasing

p connected to (+) terminal of battery.
n connected to (–) terminal of battery.
Till the applied voltage exceeds the potential barrier, the current increases very slowly with increase in applied voltage (*OA* portion of the graph).

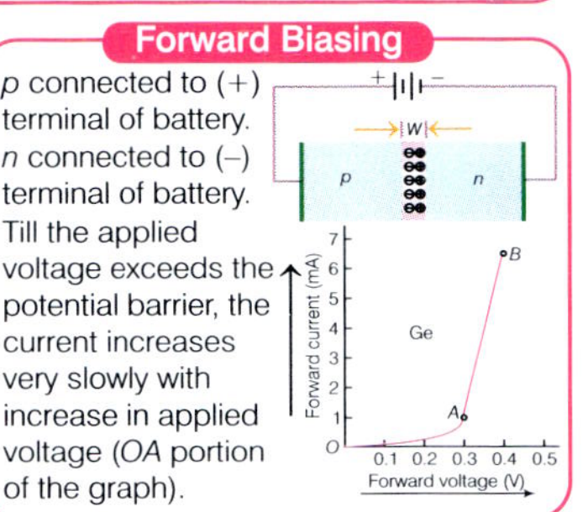

Reverse Biasing

p connected to (–) terminal of battery.
n connected to (+) terminal of battery.
Therefore, the small reverse current almost remains constant over a sufficiently long range of reverse bias voltage, increasing very little with increasing voltage (*OC* portion of the graph).

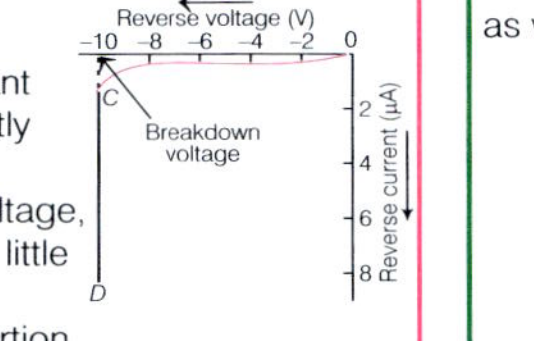

Solar Cell

It is a junction diode which converts solar energy into electricity and is based on photovoltaic effect.

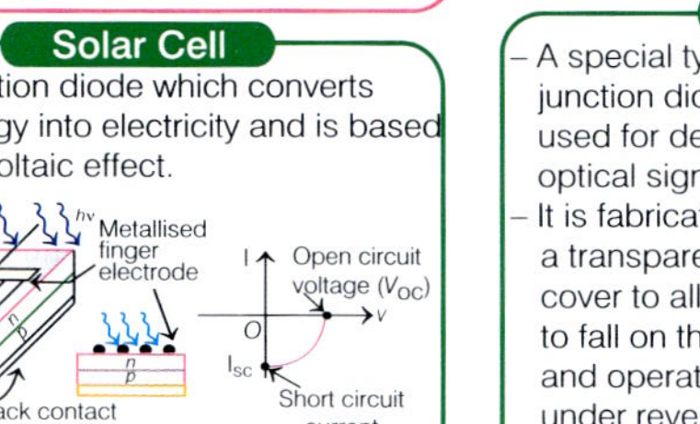

Diode as a Rectifier

A device which rectifies AC to DC.

- **Half wave rectifier**
  – Average output per cycle
  $I_{DC} = \frac{I_o}{\pi}; V_{DC} = \frac{V_o}{\pi}$
  – Ripple frequency = Frequency of AC input

Input Voltage at A
Input AC
Output Voltage across R_L
Output voltage

- **Full wave rectifier**
  – Average output per cycle
  $I_{DC} = \frac{2I_o}{\pi}; V_{DC} = \frac{2V_o}{\pi}$
  – Ripple frequency = 2 x frequency of AC input

Input at A
Input at B
Output voltage (across R_L)
Due to D_1 | Due to D_2 | Due to D_1 | Due to D_2

Zener Diode

A junction diode specially designed to operate only in the reverse breakdown region continuously (without getting damaged).

Anode *p* *n* Cathode

Zener Diode as a Voltage Regulator

When a zener diode is operated in the reverse breakdown region, the voltage across it remains constant for a large change in the reverse current. This will used as voltage regulator.

Unregulated voltage (V_{in})
R_S
I_L
I_Z
R_L
Regulated voltage (V_Z)

Photodiode

– A special type of junction diode used for detecting optical signal.
– It is fabricated with a transparent cover to allow light to fall on the diode and operated under reverse bias.

hν
Anode *p* *n* Cathode
(mA)
Reverse bias
(volt)
I_1 I_2 I_3 I_4
Reverse current
(μA)
$I_4 > I_3 > I_2 > I_1$

Test 2

Syllabus • Logic Gates

NCERT Page 501 to 505

For deeper insight **Scan the QR Code**

Chapter 15

Logic Gate

Logic gates are the building blocks of digital circuit that makes use of diodes and transistors to perform switching function. It is used for performing a particular logical operation. In other words, a gate is a digital circuit that follows certain logical relationship between the input and output voltages.

A logic gate has one output but one or more inputs. There are three basic gates named as OR gate, AND gate and NOT gate. Each basic logic gate is indicated by a logic symbol and its function is defined and described either by a truth table or by a Boolean expression.

Boolean Expression

Boolean algebra is a different kind of algebra in which only two states of variables (0 and 1) called boolean variables are allowed. Hence, to describe the functioning of a logic gate in terms of an equation, we use boolean expression. It is defined as the expression showing the combination of two boolean variables resulting into a new boolean variable.

Some Useful Postulates and Laws of Boolean Algebra

(i) Boolean postulates

(a) $0 + A = A$ (b) $1 + A = 1$

(c) $0 \cdot A = 0$ (d) $1 \cdot A = A$

(e) $A + \overline{A} = 1$

(ii) Identity law

(a) $A + A = A$

(b) $A \cdot A = A$

(iii) Negation law $\overline{\overline{A}} = A$

(iv) De-Morgan's theorem It states that, the complement of the whole sum is equal to the product of individual complements and *vice-versa*. i.e.

(a) $\overline{A + B} = \overline{A} \cdot \overline{B}$

(b) $\overline{A \cdot B} = \overline{A} + \overline{B}$

De-Morgan's theorem also states that

(a) $\overline{\overline{A} + \overline{B}} = \overline{\overline{A}} \cdot \overline{\overline{B}} = A \cdot B$

(b) $\overline{\overline{A} \cdot \overline{B}} = \overline{\overline{A}} + \overline{\overline{B}} = A + B$

(v) Commutative law

(a) $A + B = B + A$ (b) $A \cdot B = B \cdot A$

(vi) Associative law

(a) $A + (B + C) = (A + B) + C$

(b) $A \cdot (B \cdot C) = (A \cdot B) \cdot C$

(vii) Distributive law

(a) $A \cdot (B + C) = A \cdot B + A \cdot C$

(b) $(A + B) \cdot (A + C) = A + BC$

(viii) Absorption law

(a) $A + A \cdot B = A$ (b) $A \cdot (A + B) = A$

(c) $A \cdot (A + \overline{A}) = A$ (d) $\overline{A} \cdot (A + B) = \overline{A} \cdot B$

(ix) Boolean identities

(a) $A + \overline{A}B = A + B$ (b) $A(\overline{A} + B) = AB$

(c) $A + BC = (A + B)(A + C)$

NOT Gate

It inverts the input signal. It is described by the Boolean expression,

$\overline{A} = Y$

Logic symbol of NOT Gate

Truth Table

A	Y
0	1
1	0

Input and output wave form

OR Gate

It gives a high output, if either input A or B or both are high (1)

$A + B = Y$

Logic symbol of OR Gate

Truth Table

A	B	Y=A+B
0	0	0
0	1	1
1	0	1
1	1	1

Input and output wave form

AND Gate

It gives a high output (1), if inputs A and B are both high (1). It is described by the Boolean expression,

$A.B = Y$

Logic symbol of AND Gate

Truth Table

A	B	Y=A·B
0	0	0
0	1	0
1	0	0
1	1	1

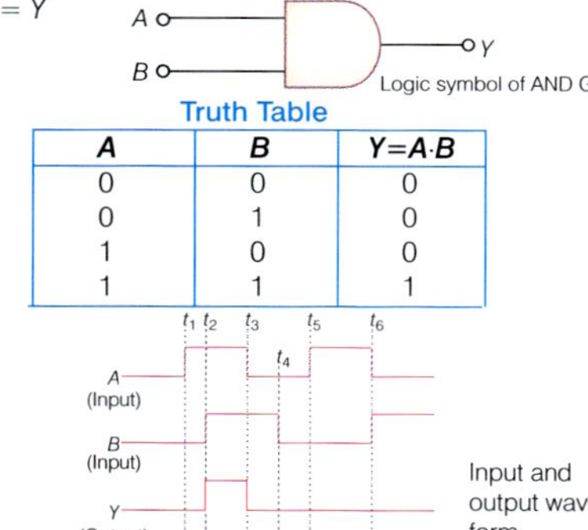

Input and output wave form

NAND and NOR Gates as Digital Building Blocks

The repeated use of the OR, AND or the NOT gates alone cannot give a different gate. But the repeated use of the NAND or the NOR gates alone can give all basic gates like OR, AND and NOT gates. Hence, the NAND and the NOR gates are also called **universal gates**. In digital circuits, these gates serve as digital building blocks.

NAND Gate

Its input is high, if both inputs A and B are not high. It is described by the Boolean expression,

$\overline{A \cdot B} = Y$

Logic symbol of NAND gate

Truth table

A	B	Y
0	0	1
0	1	1
1	0	1
1	1	0

Input and output wave form

NOR Gate

In this gate, if all the inputs are 0, then only output will be 1, otherwise it is 0. Let the two inputs be A and B respectively and its output be Y.

Boolean Expression

$Y = \overline{A + B}$

Logic Symbol

$Y' = A + B$ NOT $Y = \overline{A+B}$

Truth Table

Input		Output	
A	B	Y′ = A + B	Y = $\overline{A+B}$
0	0	0	1
0	1	1	0
1	0	1	0
1	1	1	0

Input and Output Waveforms of NOR Gate

The output waveform for NOR gate will be as shown in figure.

Input and output wave form

XOR Gate

It is also called the exclusive OR function. It is a function of two logical variables A and B which evaluates to 1, if one of two variables is 0 and the other is 1. The output is zero, if both the variables are 0 or 1.

Boolean Expression

$Y = \overline{A \oplus B} = A$ XOR B or $Y = A \oplus B$ or $Y = \overline{A}B + A\overline{B}$

Logic Symbol

$Y = \overline{A} \cdot B + A \cdot \overline{B}$

Truth Table

Input						Output
A	B	$\overline{A}$	$\overline{B}$	$A \cdot \overline{B}$	$\overline{A} \cdot B$	$Y = A \cdot \overline{B} + \overline{A} \cdot B$
0	0	1	1	0	0	0
0	1	1	0	0	1	1
1	0	0	1	1	0	1
1	1	0	0	0	0	0

XNOR Gate

It is also called exclusive NOR function. It is a function of two logical variables A and B which evaluates to 0, if one of two variable is 0 and the other is 1. The output is one, if both the variables are 0 or 1.

Boolean Expression

$Y = A \oplus B =$ or $Y = \overline{A}\overline{B} + AB$

Logic Symbol

$Y = \overline{A}\overline{B} + AB$

Truth Table

Input		Output
A	B	$Y = \overline{A}\overline{B} + AB$
0	0	1
0	1	0
1	0	0
1	1	1

Input and output waveforms of XNOR gate

The output waveform Y for XNOR gate is as shown in figure.

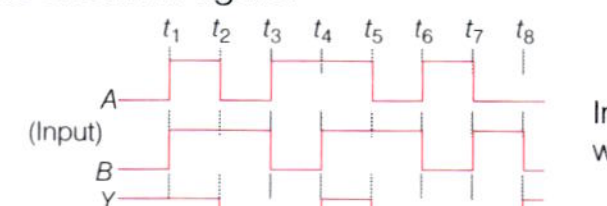

Input and output wave form

Test 1

Syllabus

- Vernier Calipers, Screw Gauge, Simple Pendulum
- Meter Scale, Young's Modulus, Surface Tension
- Coefficient of Viscosity

For deeper insight **Scan the QR Code**

Chapter 16

Experiment 1

Vernier Caliper It is used to measure internal and external diameter and depth of vessel.

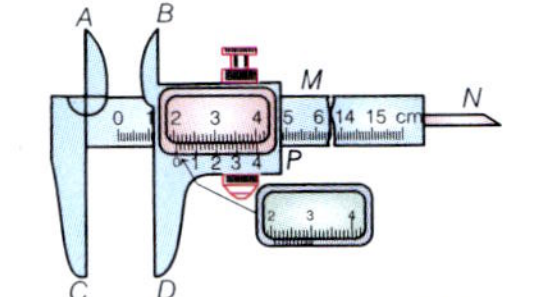

Least count of vernier calliper (LC)

$$= \frac{M}{x} = \frac{\text{1Main scale division}}{\text{Number of division in vernier scale}}$$

Zero Error When the jaws are made to touch each other, the zero mark of the main scale and vernier does not coincide. Reading in this case is known as zero error.

- Positive zero error = (Number of the vernier division coinciding with the main scale) × (LC)
- Corrected reading = Observed reading + Positive zero error.
- Negative zero error = (Number of vernier division coinciding with the main scale) × (LC) - (Smallest main scale units)
- Corrected reading = Observed reading + Negative zero error
- Negative of zero error is also known as zero correction. Zero correction = – (Zero error)

Experiment 2

Micrometer Screw Gauge It is used to measure thickness/diameter of thin sheet/wire. Least count of screw gauge

$$= \frac{\text{Pitch}}{\text{Total Number of division on circular scale}}$$

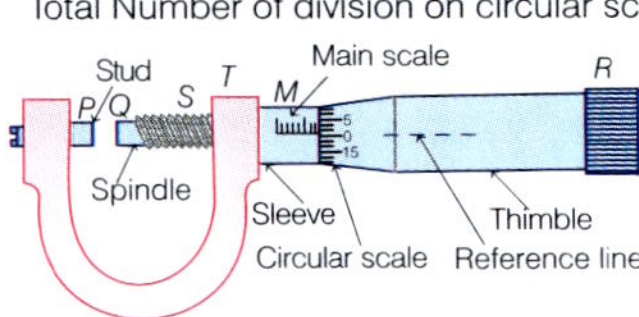

Zero Error In case of positive zero error, zero of (Circular scale) is below the reference line.

ZE = n × LC (n = circular deflection)

Corrected reading = Observed reading – Zero error. In case of negative zero error, zero of CS (circular scale) is above the reference line.

ZE = (n –100) × LC

Experiment 3

Dissipation of energy by plotting graph between the square of amplitude and time

- Restoring force (SHM), F = – kx
- Damping force (drag force), F = – bv

  Equation of damped motion,

$$\frac{md^2x}{dt^2} + b\frac{dx}{dt} + kx = 0$$

Solution of above equation,

$$x = A_0 e^{-bt/2m}\cos(\omega' t + \phi)$$

$$\text{Where, } \omega' = \sqrt{\frac{k}{m} - \frac{b^2}{4m^2}}$$

- *x versus t graph*

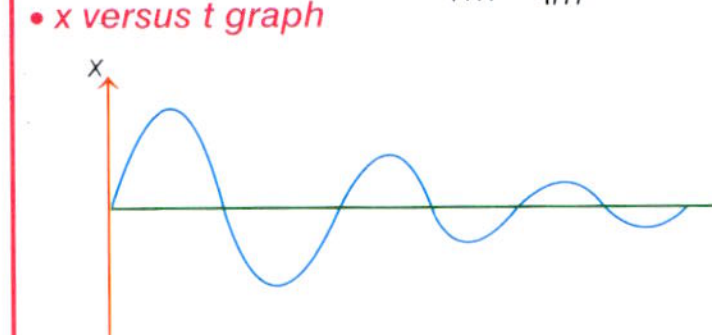

- **Damped Oscillation**

(i). (Amplitude)^2 , $A^2 = A_0^2\, e^{-bt/m}$

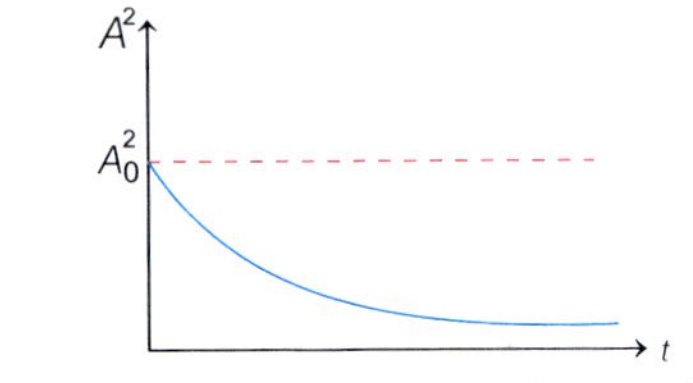

(ii). Total energy, $E = \frac{1}{2}kA^2 = \frac{1}{2}k\left[A_0 e^{\frac{-bt}{m}}\right]^2$

$$E = \left(\frac{1}{2}kA_0^2\right)e^{-bt/m} = E_0 e^{-bt/m} = E_0 e^{(-2\lambda)t}$$

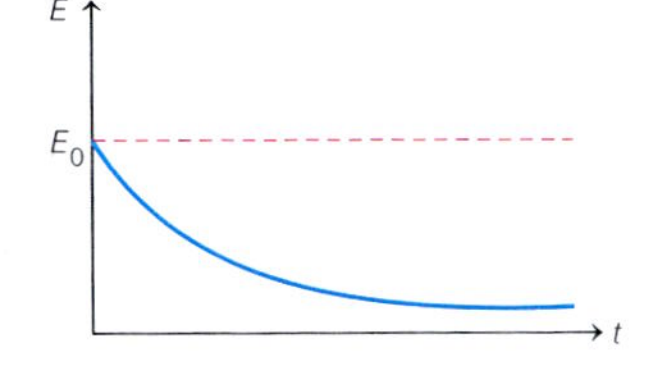

- Graph of (amplitude)^2 *versus* time is same as energy-time graph.
- All three graphs (amplitude) *versus* time, energy *versus* time and (amplitude)^2 *versus* time decay exponentially with time.

Experiment 4

Meter Scale

Mass of given object by the principle of moments. A meter rod is supported at its centre of gravity on a wedge as shown.

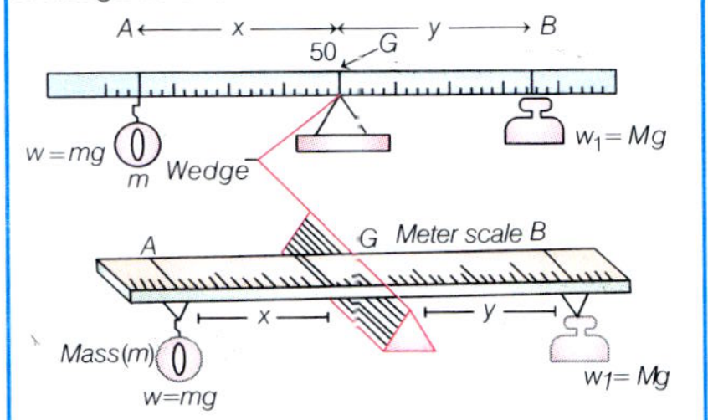

As unknown mass m is suspended from the left arm at a distance x and known as standard mass M is suspended from the right arm at a distance y. The distances are measured from the knife edge. For equilibrium, the moments of forces about the fulcrum of knife edge is equal, so we have

$$mg \times x = Mg \times y$$

$$m = M\left(\frac{y}{x}\right)$$

Experiment 5

Young's modulus of elasticity of the material of a metallic wire when a wire of length L is stretched by a force F. Its cross-section is A and it extends by l.

$$\text{Young's modulus, } Y = \frac{FL}{Al} = \frac{mgL}{\pi r^2 l}$$

where, r is radius of wire.

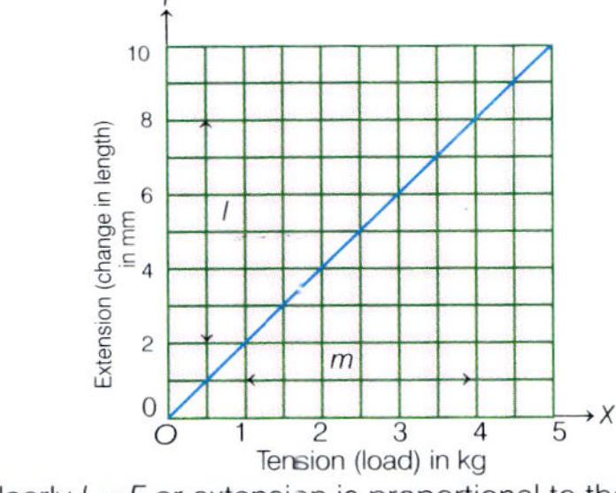

Clearly $l \propto F$ or extension is proportional to the tension

Experiment 6

Surface tension of liquid by capillary rise method and effect of detergents.

$$\text{Weight of meniscus} = \left(\frac{\pi r^3}{3}\right)\rho g, \text{if } r \text{ is small}$$

where, ρ is the density of liquid and r is the radius of capillary.

$$\text{Surface tension, } T = \frac{rh\rho g}{2\cos\theta}$$

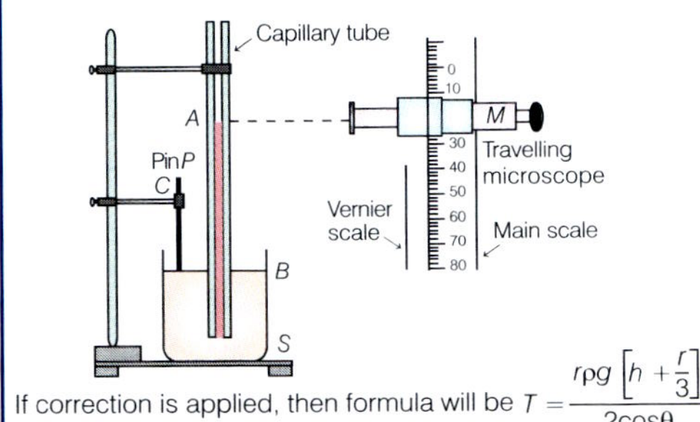

If correction is applied, then formula will be $T = \frac{r\rho g\left[h + \frac{r}{3}\right]}{2\cos\theta}$

$$\text{For water, } T = \frac{h\rho g r}{2}$$

Experiment 7

Coefficient of viscosity of a given viscous liquid by measuring terminal velocity of a given spherical body.

Stoke's force, $F = 6\pi\eta r v$

where,

η = coefficient of viscosity,

r = radius of sphere

v = velocity of sphere

$$\eta = \frac{2}{9}g\left(\frac{\rho - \sigma}{v_T}\right)$$

$$\Rightarrow v_T = \frac{2}{9}\frac{r^2 g(\rho - \sigma)}{\eta}$$

where,

η = viscosity of liquid

r = radius of sphere

ρ = density of sphere

σ = density of liquid

v_T = terminal velocity

velocity $v_T = v_0\left[1 + \frac{2.4r}{R}\right]$

R = radius of vessel

v_0 = Velocity of sphere in viscous fluid in vessels.

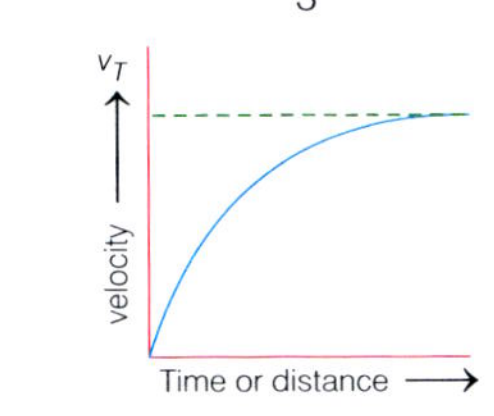

Test 2

Syllabus
- Resonance Tube, Specific Heat Capacity
- Meter Bridge, Resistance using Ohm's Law
- Galvanometer

For deeper insight **Scan the QR Code**

Experiment 8

Speed of sound in air at room temperature using a resonance tube.

The resonance tube apparatus is an instrument used to measure the speed of sound in air.

It consists of a glass tube with one end closed and the other end open, a water reservoir and a tuning fork.

The closed end submerged in the water and the tuning fork is struck and held over the open end of the tube.

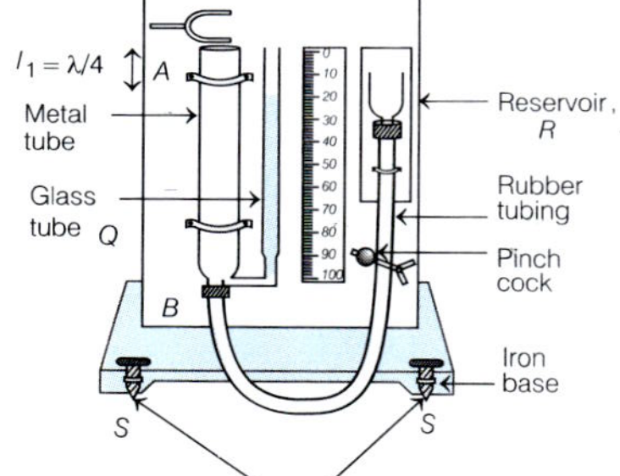

If l_1 and l_2 are the lengths of the air columns for the first and the second positions of resonance, respectively.

$$l_1 + x = \frac{\lambda}{4} \quad \text{...(i)}$$

$$\text{and } l_2 + x = \frac{3\lambda}{4} \quad \text{...(ii)}$$

x = end correction, l = wavelength of the sound wave.

So, $l_2 - l_1 = \frac{\lambda}{2}$

or $\lambda = 2(l_2 - l_2)$

$\because$ $v = n\lambda$

where, v and n are the velocity and frequency of the sound wave, respectively.

So, $v = 2n\,(l_2 - l_1)$

The velocity at 0°C is given by

$v_0 = (v_t - 0.61 \times t)$ in ms^{-1} where, v_t is velocity at room temperature t°C.

Also by eliminating λ from Eqs. (i) and (ii), the end correction.

$$x = \frac{l_2 - 3l_1}{2}$$

Experiment 9

Specific heat capacity of a given (i) solid and (ii) liquid by method of mixture.

Law of mixtures i.e.,

Heat gained by cold substance = Heat loss by hot substance

(Assuming no heat loss to the atmosphere)

- **For solids**

Mass of calorimeter + Stirrer + Lid = m_1g.

Mass of calorimeter + Lid + Cold water = m_2g.

Temperature of cold water in calorimeter = θ_1°C.

Steady temperature of solid in hypsometer by thermometer = θ_2°C.

Final, i.e. equilibrium temperature of the mixture = θ_e°C.

Mass of calorimeter + Stirrer + Liq. + water + Solid = m_3g.

Water equivalent of calorimeter+stirrer, $W=m$ (mass of calorimeter) $\times S_c/S_w$

Applying law of mixtures, keeping in view the conditions, heat lost = heat gained

$$(m_3 - m_2) \times S_c(\theta_2 - \theta_e) = (m_w + W) \times S_w\,(\theta_e - \theta_1)$$

$$\therefore S_c = \frac{(m_w + W)}{(m_3 - m_2)} \frac{(\theta_e - \theta_1).S_w}{(\theta_2 - \theta_e)} \text{ J/g}^{-1}\text{°C}^{-1}$$

- **For Liquids**

Mass of calorimeter + Stirrer = m_1g.

Mass of calorimeter + Stirrer + Oil = m_2g.

Temperature of oil in the calorimeter = θ_1°C.

Mass of the cylindrical piece tied to thread = m_3g

Temperature of boiling water in the beaker, i.e., temperature of metal piece θ_2=100°C.

Steady equilibrium temperature of mixture = θ_e°C.

Water equivalent of calorimeter,

$$W = \text{Mass} \times \frac{\text{Specific heat of material of calorimeter}}{\text{Specific heat of water}}$$

Mass of oil, $m = m_2 \times 0.095$ (for copper calorimeter)

Applying law of mixtures,

$$(\theta_e - \theta_1)\,(W + mS_l) = m_3 \times S \times (100 - \theta_e)$$

Specific heat of liquid,

$$S_l = \frac{m_3.S(100 - \theta_e)}{m(\theta_e - \theta_1)} - \frac{W}{m}\ (\text{Jg}^{-1}\,\text{°C}^{-1})$$

Experiment 10

Resistivity of the material of a given wire using meter bridge.

Meter bridge is based on Wheatstone bridge. Diagram of meter-bridge and its comparison with Wheatstone bridge are shown below.

The resistance R, the unknown resistance X, the wire length l and the wire of length $100 - l$ acts as four arms of the Wheatstone bridge.

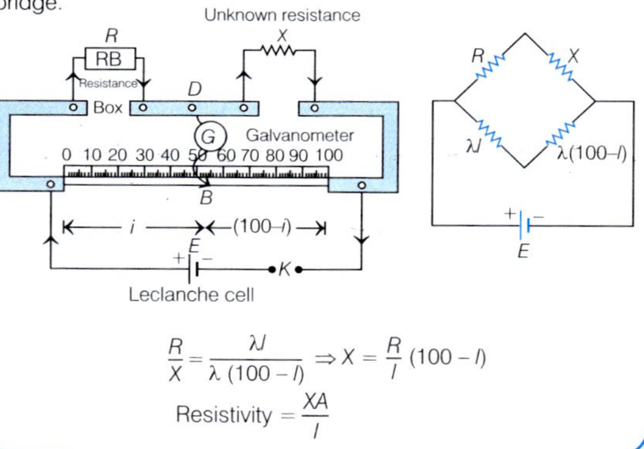

$$\frac{R}{X} = \frac{\lambda l}{\lambda\,(100 - l)} \Rightarrow X = \frac{R}{l}\,(100 - l)$$

$$\text{Resistivity} = \frac{XA}{l}$$

Experiment 11

The resistance of a given wire using Ohm's law.

The following arrangement is used in this method.

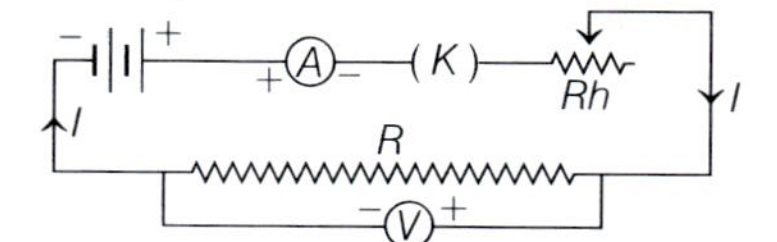

If I be the current flowing through a conductor and V be the potential difference across its ends, then according to Ohm's law,

$$V \propto I \Rightarrow V = RI$$

where, R is the constant of proportionality. It is known as resistance of the conductor.

or $\frac{V}{I} = R$

The graph of V versus I is shown below.

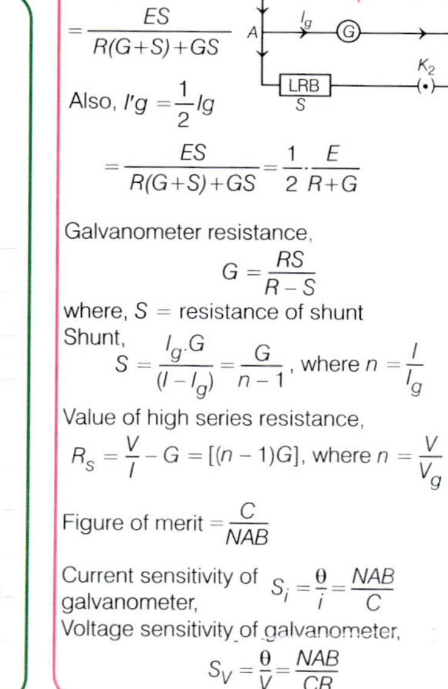

Experiment 12

Resistance and figure of merit of a galvanometer by half-deflection method

Galvanometer constant, is given by

$$K = \left(\frac{c}{NAB}\right)$$

Resistance of galvanometer by half deflection method.

When a high resistance R is applied in the circuit with K_1 closed and K_2 open, the galvanometer draws a current I_g and shows a deflection θ such that $I_g = \frac{E}{R + G}$

Now, K_2 is closed. Adjust the resistance, in LRB such that galvanometer deflection becomes equal to $\theta/2$.

Now, the galvanometer draw the current.

$$I'g = \frac{IS}{G+S} = \frac{ES}{R(G+S)+GS}$$

Also, $I'g = \frac{1}{2}Ig$

$$= \frac{ES}{R(G+S)+GS} = \frac{1}{2}\cdot\frac{E}{R+G}$$

Galvanometer resistance,

$$G = \frac{RS}{R - S}$$

where, S = resistance of shunt

Shunt, $S = \frac{I_g.G}{(I - I_g)} = \frac{G}{n - 1}$, where $n = \frac{I}{I_g}$

Value of high series resistance,

$R_s = \frac{V}{I} - G = [(n-1)G]$, where $n = \frac{V}{V_g}$

Figure of merit $= \frac{C}{NAB}$

Current sensitivity of galvanometer, $S_i = \frac{\theta}{i} = \frac{NAB}{C}$

Voltage sensitivity of galvanometer,

$$S_V = \frac{\theta}{V} = \frac{NAB}{CR}$$

Test 3

Syllabus

- Focal length of Mirrors and Lenses,
- Triangular Prism, Travelling Microscope, Semi-conductor and Electronic Devices

For deeper insight **Scan the QR Code**

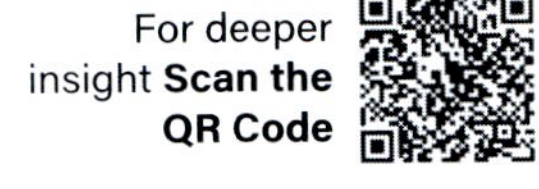

Experiment 13

Focal length of Concave mirror, Convex mirror and Convex lens

Concave Mirror

Formula for focal length, $f = \frac{uv}{u+v}$

(a) Graph between u and v

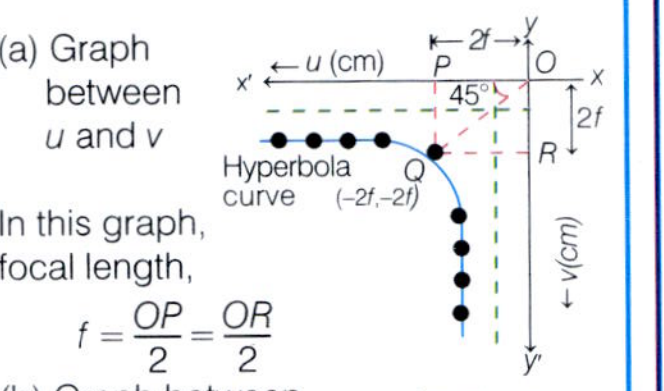

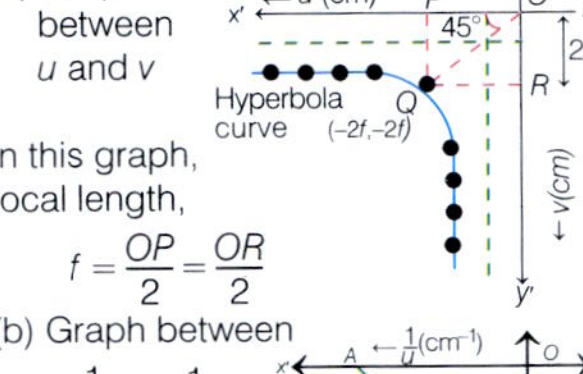

In this graph, focal length,

$f = \frac{OP}{2} = \frac{OR}{2}$

(b) Graph between $\frac{1}{u}$ and $\frac{1}{v}$

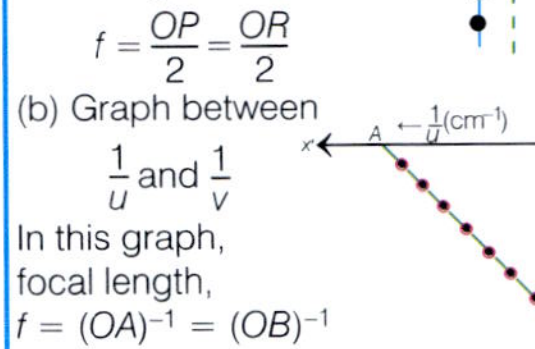

In this graph, focal length,

$f = (OA)^{-1} = (OB)^{-1}$

Convex Mirror

Formula for focal length, $f = \frac{uv}{u+v}$

Here, u is negative and v is positive.

(a) Graph between u and v

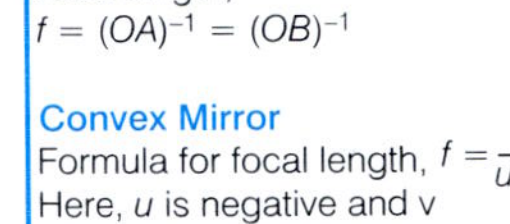
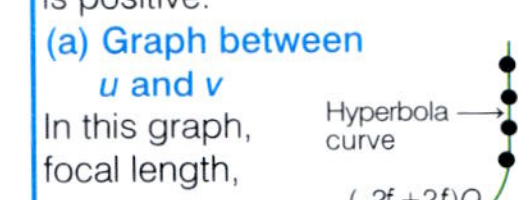
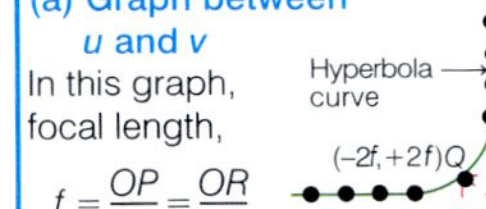
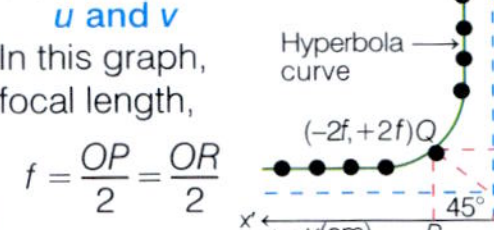
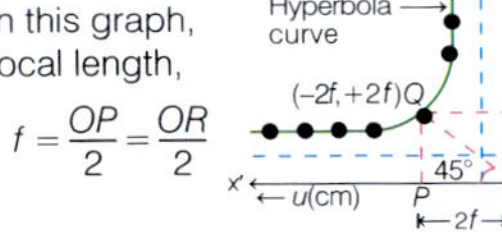

In this graph, focal length,

$f = \frac{OP}{2} = \frac{OR}{2}$

(b) Graph between $\frac{1}{u}$ and $\frac{1}{v}$

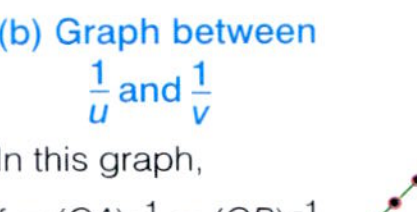

In this graph,

$f = (OA)^{-1} = (OB)^{-1}$

Convex Lens

Focal length, $f = \frac{uv}{u-v}$

Here, u is negative and v is positive.

Graphs between u and v, $\frac{1}{u}$ and $\frac{1}{v}$ are similar to that of convex mirror.

Note:- Bench error (of optical bench) is given by

Bench error = Actual distance − Observed distance

Experiment 14

Plot of angle of the deviation *versus* angle of incidence for a triangular prism. Deviation of ray through prism is shown below

Incident ray — Incident angle — 90° — Deviation angle — Emerging ray — Emerging angle

This experiment is performed for different incident angles (30° to 60°, in increments of 5°)

Graph between i and δ

Angle of deviation (δ) — 30, 35, δ_m, 40, 45, 50 — Angle of incidence (i) 35° 40° 45° 50° 55° 60°

Here, δ_m is known as angle of minimum deviation.

Experiment 15

Refractive index of a glass slab using a travelling microscope.

r_3, r_2, r_1, A, B, C, D, N, R, S, P_1, P, t, r, i

Formula $\mu = \frac{\text{Real depth (thickness)}}{\text{Apparent depth (thickness)}}$

Refractive index (in this case)

$\mu = \frac{r_3 - r_1}{r_2 - r_1}$

Experiment 16

Characteristic curves of a p-n junction diode in forward and reverse bias.

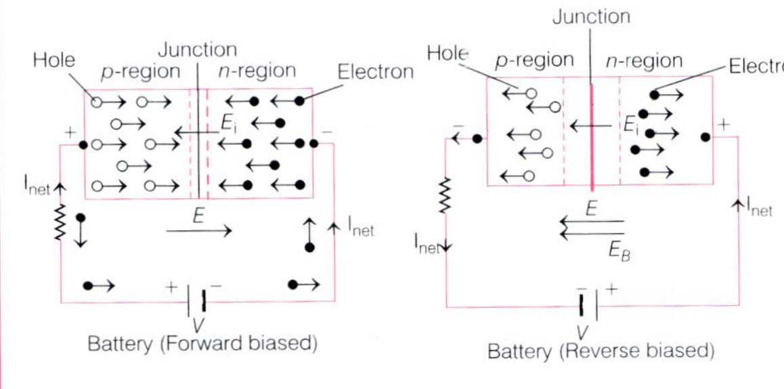

Forward biased	Reverse biased
$p \rightarrow$ positive, $n \rightarrow$ negative	$p \rightarrow$ negative, $n \rightarrow$ positive
Potential barrier reduces.	Potential barrier increases.
Width of depletion layer decreases.	Width of depletion layer increases.
p-n junction provides very small resistance.	p-n junction provides high resistance.
Order of forward current is milliampere.	Order of current is micro-ampere (Ge) or nanoampere (Si).
Current flows mainly due to majority charge carrier.	Current flows mainly due to minority charge carrier.

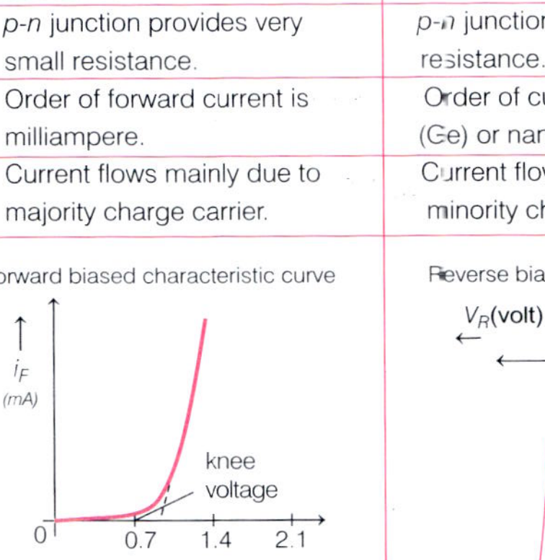

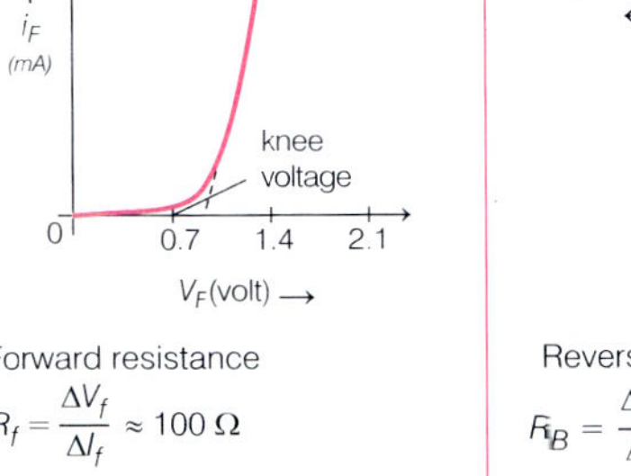

Forward resistance

$R_f = \frac{\Delta V_f}{\Delta I_f} \approx 100\,\Omega$

Reverse resistance

$R_B = \frac{\Delta V_B}{\Delta I_B} \approx 10^6\,\Omega$

Experiment 14

Characteristics curve of a zener diode and finding reverse breakdown voltage.

Circuit diagram and Characteristic curve.

(V) — Zener diode — p n — (μA) — (K)

Circuit parametres in the circuit as shown in the figure above.

V(volt) −12 −10 −8 −6 −4 −2 0 — V_z — −20 −40 −60 −80 −100 — I(μA)

Potential divider — 10V — K — R_I — mA — I_I — I_L — I_Z — R_L — V_I — V_2 V_O

Relations

$I_L = I_I - I_Z$ ...(i)

$V_O = V_I - R_I I_I$ ...(ii)

$V_O = I_L R_L$

Initially as V_I is increased, I_I increases a little, then V_0 increases. At breakdown, increase of V_I, increases I_I by large amount, so that $V_0 = V_L = R_L I_L$ becomes constant. This constant value of V_0 which is the reverse breakdown voltage is called zener voltage.

Experiment 18

Identification of Diode, LED, Resistor, Capacitor from a mixed collection of such items.

For the identification, appearance and working of each item will is considered.

(i) **Diode** is a two terminal device. It conducts in forward bias and does not conduct when connected in reverse biased.

(ii) **LED** stands for light emitting diode. It consists of two terminals and conducts when connected in forward bias and does not conduct in reverse biased. While conducting, LED emits light.

(iii) **Resistor** is also a two terminal device. It conducts equally in both directions. It conducts in AC and DC voltage.

(iv) **Capacitor** It is a device that store electric charge. A capacitor blocks the passage of DC while it allows AC to pass through it.

MEDACE

OMR SHEET

ROLL No.

1	1	1	1	1	1	1	1	1	1
2	2	2	2	2	2	2	2	2	2
3	3	3	3	3	3	3	3	3	3
4	4	4	4	4	4	4	4	4	4
5	5	5	5	5	5	5	5	5	5
6	6	6	6	6	6	6	6	6	6
7	7	7	7	7	7	7	7	7	7
8	8	8	8	8	8	8	8	8	8
9	9	9	9	9	9	9	9	9	9
0	0	0	0	0	0	0	0	0	0

TEST BOOKLET No.

1	1	1	1	1	1	1
2	2	2	2	2	2	2
3	3	3	3	3	3	3
4	4	4	4	4	4	4
5	5	5	5	5	5	5
6	6	6	6	6	6	6
7	7	7	7	7	7	7
8	8	8	8	8	8	8
9	9	9	9	9	9	9
0	0	0	0	0	0	0

TEST BOOKLET Code

DECLARATION BY THE CANDIDATE

I declare that particulars and signature on this OMR Answer sheet are mine and are Name as in Attendance Sheet. I fruther declare that particulars filled in and Signature as well as the circles darkened on this ORIGINALCOPY is same as in OFFICE COPY.

Signature with time (in running handwriting)

CANDIDATE's NAME (in running handwriting)

Q No.	Response				Q No.	Response			
001	a	b	c	d	051	a	b	c	d
002	a	b	c	d	052	a	b	c	d
003	a	b	c	d	053	a	b	c	d
004	a	b	c	d	054	a	b	c	d
005	a	b	c	d	055	a	b	c	d
006	a	b	c	d	056	a	b	c	d
007	a	b	c	d	057	a	b	c	d
008	a	b	c	d	058	a	b	c	d
009	a	b	c	d	059	a	b	c	d
010	a	b	c	d	060	a	b	c	d
011	a	b	c	d	061	a	b	c	d
012	a	b	c	d	062	a	b	c	d
013	a	b	c	d	063	a	b	c	d
014	a	b	c	d	064	a	b	c	d
015	a	b	c	d	065	a	b	c	d
016	a	b	c	d	066	a	b	c	d
017	a	b	c	d	067	a	b	c	d
018	a	b	c	d	068	a	b	c	d
019	a	b	c	d	069	a	b	c	d
020	a	b	c	d	070	a	b	c	d
021	a	b	c	d	071	a	b	c	d
022	a	b	c	d	072	a	b	c	d
023	a	b	c	d	073	a	b	c	d
024	a	b	c	d	074	a	b	c	d
025	a	b	c	d	075	a	b	c	d
026	a	b	c	d	076	a	b	c	d
027	a	b	c	d	077	a	b	c	d
028	a	b	c	d	078	a	b	c	d
029	a	b	c	d	079	a	b	c	d
030	a	b	c	d	080	a	b	c	d
031	a	b	c	d	081	a	b	c	d
032	a	b	c	d	082	a	b	c	d
033	a	b	c	d	083	a	b	c	d
034	a	b	c	d	084	a	b	c	d
035	a	b	c	d	085	a	b	c	d
036	a	b	c	d	086	a	b	c	d
037	a	b	c	d	087	a	b	c	d
038	a	b	c	d	088	a	b	c	d
039	a	b	c	d	089	a	b	c	d
040	a	b	c	d	090	a	b	c	d
041	a	b	c	d	091	a	b	c	d
042	a	b	c	d	092	a	b	c	d
043	a	b	c	d	093	a	b	c	d
044	a	b	c	d	094	a	b	c	d
045	a	b	c	d	095	a	b	c	d
046	a	b	c	d	096	a	b	c	d
047	a	b	c	d	097	a	b	c	d
048	a	b	c	d	098	a	b	c	d
049	a	b	c	d	099	a	b	c	d
050	a	b	c	d	100	a	b	c	d

MOTHER's NAME (in running handwriting)	FATHER's NAME (in running handwriting)

CANDIDATE LEFT HAND IMPRESSION	SIGNATURE OF INVIGILATOR'S WITH TIME
	1
	2

MEDACE

OMR SHEET

ROLL No.

1	1	1	1	1	1	1	1	1	1
2	2	2	2	2	2	2	2	2	2
3	3	3	3	3	3	3	3	3	3
4	4	4	4	4	4	4	4	4	4
5	5	5	5	5	5	5	5	5	5
6	6	6	6	6	6	6	6	6	6
7	7	7	7	7	7	7	7	7	7
8	8	8	8	8	8	8	8	8	8
9	9	9	9	9	9	9	9	9	9
0	0	0	0	0	0	0	0	0	0

TEST BOOKLET No.

1	1	1	1	1	1	1
2	2	2	2	2	2	2
3	3	3	3	3	3	3
4	4	4	4	4	4	4
5	5	5	5	5	5	5
6	6	6	6	6	6	6
7	7	7	7	7	7	7
8	8	8	8	8	8	8
9	9	9	9	9	9	9
0	0	0	0	0	0	0

TEST BOOKLET Code

Q No.	Response				Q No.	Response			
001	a	b	c	d	051	a	b	c	d
002	a	b	c	d	052	a	b	c	d
003	a	b	c	d	053	a	b	c	d
004	a	b	c	d	054	a	b	c	d
005	a	b	c	d	055	a	b	c	d
006	a	b	c	d	056	a	b	c	d
007	a	b	c	d	057	a	b	c	d
008	a	b	c	d	058	a	b	c	d
009	a	b	c	d	059	a	b	c	d
010	a	b	c	d	060	a	b	c	d
011	a	b	c	d	061	a	b	c	d
012	a	b	c	d	062	a	b	c	d
013	a	b	c	d	063	a	b	c	d
014	a	b	c	d	064	a	b	c	d
015	a	b	c	d	065	a	b	c	d
016	a	b	c	d	066	a	b	c	d
017	a	b	c	d	067	a	b	c	d
018	a	b	c	d	068	a	b	c	d
019	a	b	c	d	069	a	b	c	d
020	a	b	c	d	070	a	b	c	d
021	a	b	c	d	071	a	b	c	d
022	a	b	c	d	072	a	b	c	d
023	a	b	c	d	073	a	b	c	d
024	a	b	c	d	074	a	b	c	d
025	a	b	c	d	075	a	b	c	d
026	a	b	c	d	076	a	b	c	d
027	a	b	c	d	077	a	b	c	d
028	a	b	c	d	078	a	b	c	d
029	a	b	c	d	079	a	b	c	d
030	a	b	c	d	080	a	b	c	d
031	a	b	c	d	081	a	b	c	d
032	a	b	c	d	082	a	b	c	d
033	a	b	c	d	083	a	b	c	d
034	a	b	c	d	084	a	b	c	d
035	a	b	c	d	085	a	b	c	d
036	a	b	c	d	086	a	b	c	d
037	a	b	c	d	087	a	b	c	d
038	a	b	c	d	088	a	b	c	d
039	a	b	c	d	089	a	b	c	d
040	a	b	c	d	090	a	b	c	d
041	a	b	c	d	091	a	b	c	d
042	a	b	c	d	092	a	b	c	d
043	a	b	c	d	093	a	b	c	d
044	a	b	c	d	094	a	b	c	d
045	a	b	c	d	095	a	b	c	d
046	a	b	c	d	096	a	b	c	d
047	a	b	c	d	097	a	b	c	d
048	a	b	c	d	098	a	b	c	d
049	a	b	c	d	099	a	b	c	d
050	a	b	c	d	100	a	b	c	d

DECLARATION BY THE CANDIDATE

I declare that particulars and signature on this OMR Answer sheet are mine and are Name as in Attendance Sheet. I fruther declare that particulars filled in and Signature as well as the circles darkened on this ORIGINALCOPY is same as in OFFICE COPY.

Signature with time (in running handwriting)

CANDIDATE's NAME (in running handwriting)

MOTHER's NAME (in running handwriting)

FATHER's NAME (in running handwriting)

CANDIDATE LEFT HAND IMPRESSION

SIGNATURE OF INVIGILATOR'S WITH TIME

1

2

MEDACE

OMR SHEET

ROLL No.

1	1	1	1	1	1	1	1	1	1
2	2	2	2	2	2	2	2	2	2
3	3	3	3	3	3	3	3	3	3
4	4	4	4	4	4	4	4	4	4
5	5	5	5	5	5	5	5	5	5
6	6	6	6	6	6	6	6	6	6
7	7	7	7	7	7	7	7	7	7
8	8	8	8	8	8	8	8	8	8
9	9	9	9	9	9	9	9	9	9
0	0	0	0	0	0	0	0	0	0

TEST BOOKLET No.

1	1	1	1	1	1	1
2	2	2	2	2	2	2
3	3	3	3	3	3	3
4	4	4	4	4	4	4
5	5	5	5	5	5	5
6	6	6	6	6	6	6
7	7	7	7	7	7	7
8	8	8	8	8	8	8
9	9	9	9	9	9	9
0	0	0	0	0	0	0

TEST BOOKLET Code

Q No.	Response				Q No.	Response			
001	a	b	c	d	051	a	b	c	d
002	a	b	c	d	052	a	b	c	d
003	a	b	c	d	053	a	b	c	d
004	a	b	c	d	054	a	b	c	d
005	a	b	c	d	055	a	b	c	d
006	a	b	c	d	056	a	b	c	d
007	a	b	c	d	057	a	b	c	d
008	a	b	c	d	058	a	b	c	d
009	a	b	c	d	059	a	b	c	d
010	a	b	c	d	060	a	b	c	d
011	a	b	c	d	061	a	b	c	d
012	a	b	c	d	062	a	b	c	d
013	a	b	c	d	063	a	b	c	d
014	a	b	c	d	064	a	b	c	d
015	a	b	c	d	065	a	b	c	d
016	a	b	c	d	066	a	b	c	d
017	a	b	c	d	067	a	b	c	d
018	a	b	c	d	068	a	b	c	d
019	a	b	c	d	069	a	b	c	d
020	a	b	c	d	070	a	b	c	d
021	a	b	c	d	071	a	b	c	d
022	a	b	c	d	072	a	b	c	d
023	a	b	c	d	073	a	b	c	d
024	a	b	c	d	074	a	b	c	d
025	a	b	c	d	075	a	b	c	d
026	a	b	c	d	076	a	b	c	d
027	a	b	c	d	077	a	b	c	d
028	a	b	c	d	078	a	b	c	d
029	a	b	c	d	079	a	b	c	d
030	a	b	c	d	080	a	b	c	d
031	a	b	c	d	081	a	b	c	d
032	a	b	c	d	082	a	b	c	d
033	a	b	c	d	083	a	b	c	d
034	a	b	c	d	084	a	b	c	d
035	a	b	c	d	085	a	b	c	d
036	a	b	c	d	086	a	b	c	d
037	a	b	c	d	087	a	b	c	d
038	a	b	c	d	088	a	b	c	d
039	a	b	c	d	089	a	b	c	d
040	a	b	c	d	090	a	b	c	d
041	a	b	c	d	091	a	b	c	d
042	a	b	c	d	092	a	b	c	d
043	a	b	c	d	093	a	b	c	d
044	a	b	c	d	094	a	b	c	d
045	a	b	c	d	095	a	b	c	d
046	a	b	c	d	096	a	b	c	d
047	a	b	c	d	097	a	b	c	d
048	a	b	c	d	098	a	b	c	d
049	a	b	c	d	099	a	b	c	d
050	a	b	c	d	100	a	b	c	d

DECLARATION BY THE CANDIDATE

I declare that particulars and signature on this OMR Answer sheet are mine and are Name as in Attendance Sheet. I fruther declare that particulars filled in and Signature as well as the circles darkened on this ORIGINALCOPY is same as in OFFICE COPY.

Signature with time (in running handwriting)

CANDIDATE's NAME (in running handwriting)

MOTHER's NAME (in running handwriting)

FATHER's NAME (in running handwriting)

CANDIDATE LEFT HAND IMPRESSION

SIGNATURE OF INVIGILATOR'S WITH TIME

1

2

MEDACE

OMR SHEET

ROLL No.

1	1	1	1	1	1	1	1	1	1
2	2	2	2	2	2	2	2	2	2
3	3	3	3	3	3	3	3	3	3
4	4	4	4	4	4	4	4	4	4
5	5	5	5	5	5	5	5	5	5
6	6	6	6	6	6	6	6	6	6
7	7	7	7	7	7	7	7	7	7
8	8	8	8	8	8	8	8	8	8
9	9	9	9	9	9	9	9	9	9
0	0	0	0	0	0	0	0	0	0

TEST BOOKLET No.

1	1	1	1	1	1	1
2	2	2	2	2	2	2
3	3	3	3	3	3	3
4	4	4	4	4	4	4
5	5	5	5	5	5	5
6	6	6	6	6	6	6
7	7	7	7	7	7	7
8	8	8	8	8	8	8
9	9	9	9	9	9	9
0	0	0	0	0	0	0

TEST BOOKLET Code

Q No.	Response			
001	a	b	c	d
002	a	b	c	d
003	a	b	c	d
004	a	b	c	d
005	a	b	c	d
006	a	b	c	d
007	a	b	c	d
008	a	b	c	d
009	a	b	c	d
010	a	b	c	d
011	a	b	c	d
012	a	b	c	d
013	a	b	c	d
014	a	b	c	d
015	a	b	c	d
016	a	b	c	d
017	a	b	c	d
018	a	b	c	d
019	a	b	c	d
020	a	b	c	d
021	a	b	c	d
022	a	b	c	d
023	a	b	c	d
024	a	b	c	d
025	a	b	c	d
026	a	b	c	d
027	a	b	c	d
028	a	b	c	d
029	a	b	c	d
030	a	b	c	d
031	a	b	c	d
032	a	b	c	d
033	a	b	c	d
034	a	b	c	d
035	a	b	c	d
036	a	b	c	d
037	a	b	c	d
038	a	b	c	d
039	a	b	c	d
040	a	b	c	d
041	a	b	c	d
042	a	b	c	d
043	a	b	c	d
044	a	b	c	d
045	a	b	c	d
046	a	b	c	d
047	a	b	c	d
048	a	b	c	d
049	a	b	c	d
050	a	b	c	d

Q No.	Response			
051	a	b	c	d
052	a	b	c	d
053	a	b	c	d
054	a	b	c	d
055	a	b	c	d
056	a	b	c	d
057	a	b	c	d
058	a	b	c	d
059	a	b	c	d
060	a	b	c	d
061	a	b	c	d
062	a	b	c	d
063	a	b	c	d
064	a	b	c	d
065	a	b	c	d
066	a	b	c	d
067	a	b	c	d
068	a	b	c	d
069	a	b	c	d
070	a	b	c	d
071	a	b	c	d
072	a	b	c	d
073	a	b	c	d
074	a	b	c	d
075	a	b	c	d
076	a	b	c	d
077	a	b	c	d
078	a	b	c	d
079	a	b	c	d
080	a	b	c	d
081	a	b	c	d
082	a	b	c	d
083	a	b	c	d
084	a	b	c	d
085	a	b	c	d
086	a	b	c	d
087	a	b	c	d
088	a	b	c	d
089	a	b	c	d
090	a	b	c	d
091	a	b	c	d
092	a	b	c	d
093	a	b	c	d
094	a	b	c	d
095	a	b	c	d
096	a	b	c	d
097	a	b	c	d
098	a	b	c	d
099	a	b	c	d
100	a	b	c	d

DECLARATION BY THE CANDIDATE

I declare that particulars and signature on this OMR Answer sheet are mine and are Name as in Attendance Sheet. I fruther declare that particulars filled in and Signature as well as the circles darkened on this ORIGINALCOPY is same as in OFFICE COPY.

Signature with time (in running handwriting)

CANDIDATE's NAME (in running handwriting)

MOTHER's NAME (in running handwriting)

FATHER's NAME (in running handwriting)

CANDIDATE LEFT HAND IMPRESSION

SIGNATURE OF INVIGILATOR'S WITH TIME

1

2

MEDACE

OMR SHEET

ROLL No.

1	1	1	1	1	1	1	1	1	1
2	2	2	2	2	2	2	2	2	2
3	3	3	3	3	3	3	3	3	3
4	4	4	4	4	4	4	4	4	4
5	5	5	5	5	5	5	5	5	5
6	6	6	6	6	6	6	6	6	6
7	7	7	7	7	7	7	7	7	7
8	8	8	8	8	8	8	8	8	8
9	9	9	9	9	9	9	9	9	9
0	0	0	0	0	0	0	0	0	0

TEST BOOKLET No.

1	1	1	1	1	1	1
2	2	2	2	2	2	2
3	3	3	3	3	3	3
4	4	4	4	4	4	4
5	5	5	5	5	5	5
6	6	6	6	6	6	6
7	7	7	7	7	7	7
8	8	8	8	8	8	8
9	9	9	9	9	9	9
0	0	0	0	0	0	0

TEST BOOKLET Code

Q No.	Response			
001	a	b	c	d
002	a	b	c	d
003	a	b	c	d
004	a	b	c	d
005	a	b	c	d
006	a	b	c	d
007	a	b	c	d
008	a	b	c	d
009	a	b	c	d
010	a	b	c	d
011	a	b	c	d
012	a	b	c	d
013	a	b	c	d
014	a	b	c	d
015	a	b	c	d
016	a	b	c	d
017	a	b	c	d
018	a	b	c	d
019	a	b	c	d
020	a	b	c	d
021	a	b	c	d
022	a	b	c	d
023	a	b	c	d
024	a	b	c	d
025	a	b	c	d
026	a	b	c	d
027	a	b	c	d
028	a	b	c	d
029	a	b	c	d
030	a	b	c	d
031	a	b	c	d
032	a	b	c	d
033	a	b	c	d
034	a	b	c	d
035	a	b	c	d
036	a	b	c	d
037	a	b	c	d
038	a	b	c	d
039	a	b	c	d
040	a	b	c	d
041	a	b	c	d
042	a	b	c	d
043	a	b	c	d
044	a	b	c	d
045	a	b	c	d
046	a	b	c	d
047	a	b	c	d
048	a	b	c	d
049	a	b	c	d
050	a	b	c	d

Q No.	Response			
051	a	b	c	d
052	a	b	c	d
053	a	b	c	d
054	a	b	c	d
055	a	b	c	d
056	a	b	c	d
057	a	b	c	d
058	a	b	c	d
059	a	b	c	d
060	a	b	c	d
061	a	b	c	d
062	a	b	c	d
063	a	b	c	d
064	a	b	c	d
065	a	b	c	d
066	a	b	c	d
067	a	b	c	d
068	a	b	c	d
069	a	b	c	d
070	a	b	c	d
071	a	b	c	d
072	a	b	c	d
073	a	b	c	d
074	a	b	c	d
075	a	b	c	d
076	a	b	c	d
077	a	b	c	d
078	a	b	c	d
079	a	b	c	d
080	a	b	c	d
081	a	b	c	d
082	a	b	c	d
083	a	b	c	d
084	a	b	c	d
085	a	b	c	d
086	a	b	c	d
087	a	b	c	d
088	a	b	c	d
089	a	b	c	d
090	a	b	c	d
091	a	b	c	d
092	a	b	c	d
093	a	b	c	d
094	a	b	c	d
095	a	b	c	d
096	a	b	c	d
097	a	b	c	d
098	a	b	c	d
099	a	b	c	d
100	a	b	c	d

DECLARATION BY THE CANDIDATE

I declare that particulars and signature on this OMR Answer sheet are mine and are Name as in Attendance Sheet. I fruther declare that particulars filled in and Signature as well as the circles darkened on this ORIGINALCOPY is same as in OFFICE COPY.

Signature with time (in running handwriting)

CANDIDATE's NAME (in running handwriting)

MOTHER's NAME (in running handwriting)

FATHER's NAME (in running handwriting)

CANDIDATE LEFT HAND IMPRESSION

SIGNATURE OF INVIGILATOR'S WITH TIME

1

2

MEDACE

OMR SHEET

ROLL No.

1	1	1	1	1	1	1	1	1	1
2	2	2	2	2	2	2	2	2	2
3	3	3	3	3	3	3	3	3	3
4	4	4	4	4	4	4	4	4	4
5	5	5	5	5	5	5	5	5	5
6	6	6	6	6	6	6	6	6	6
7	7	7	7	7	7	7	7	7	7
8	8	8	8	8	8	8	8	8	8
9	9	9	9	9	9	9	9	9	9
0	0	0	0	0	0	0	0	0	0

TEST BOOKLET No.

1	1	1	1	1	1	1
2	2	2	2	2	2	2
3	3	3	3	3	3	3
4	4	4	4	4	4	4
5	5	5	5	5	5	5
6	6	6	6	6	6	6
7	7	7	7	7	7	7
8	8	8	8	8	8	8
9	9	9	9	9	9	9
0	0	0	0	0	0	0

TEST BOOKLET Code

Q No.	Response				Q No.	Response			
001	a	b	c	d	051	a	b	c	d
002	a	b	c	d	052	a	b	c	d
003	a	b	c	d	053	a	b	c	d
004	a	b	c	d	054	a	b	c	d
005	a	b	c	d	055	a	b	c	d
006	a	b	c	d	056	a	b	c	d
007	a	b	c	d	057	a	b	c	d
008	a	b	c	d	058	a	b	c	d
009	a	b	c	d	059	a	b	c	d
010	a	b	c	d	060	a	b	c	d
011	a	b	c	d	061	a	b	c	d
012	a	b	c	d	062	a	b	c	d
013	a	b	c	d	063	a	b	c	d
014	a	b	c	d	064	a	b	c	d
015	a	b	c	d	065	a	b	c	d
016	a	b	c	d	066	a	b	c	d
017	a	b	c	d	067	a	b	c	d
018	a	b	c	d	068	a	b	c	d
019	a	b	c	d	069	a	b	c	d
020	a	b	c	d	070	a	b	c	d
021	a	b	c	d	071	a	b	c	d
022	a	b	c	d	072	a	b	c	d
023	a	b	c	d	073	a	b	c	d
024	a	b	c	d	074	a	b	c	d
025	a	b	c	d	075	a	b	c	d
026	a	b	c	d	076	a	b	c	d
027	a	b	c	d	077	a	b	c	d
028	a	b	c	d	078	a	b	c	d
029	a	b	c	d	079	a	b	c	d
030	a	b	c	d	080	a	b	c	d
031	a	b	c	d	081	a	b	c	d
032	a	b	c	d	082	a	b	c	d
033	a	b	c	d	083	a	b	c	d
034	a	b	c	d	084	a	b	c	d
035	a	b	c	d	085	a	b	c	d
036	a	b	c	d	086	a	b	c	d
037	a	b	c	d	087	a	b	c	d
038	a	b	c	d	088	a	b	c	d
039	a	b	c	d	089	a	b	c	d
040	a	b	c	d	090	a	b	c	d
041	a	b	c	d	091	a	b	c	d
042	a	b	c	d	092	a	b	c	d
043	a	b	c	d	093	a	b	c	d
044	a	b	c	d	094	a	b	c	d
045	a	b	c	d	095	a	b	c	d
046	a	b	c	d	096	a	b	c	d
047	a	b	c	d	097	a	b	c	d
048	a	b	c	d	098	a	b	c	d
049	a	b	c	d	099	a	b	c	d
050	a	b	c	d	100	a	b	c	d

DECLARATION BY THE CANDIDATE

I declare that particulars and signature on this OMR Answer sheet are mine and are Name as in Attendance Sheet. I fruther declare that particulars filled in and Signature as well as the circles darkened on this ORIGINALCOPY is same as in OFFICE COPY.

Signature with time (in running handwriting)

CANDIDATE's NAME (in running handwriting)

MOTHER's NAME (in running handwriting)

FATHER's NAME (in running handwriting)

CANDIDATE LEFT HAND IMPRESSION

SIGNATURE OF INVIGILATOR'S WITH TIME

1

2

MEDACE

OMR SHEET

ROLL No.

1	1	1	1	1	1	1	1	1	1
2	2	2	2	2	2	2	2	2	2
3	3	3	3	3	3	3	3	3	3
4	4	4	4	4	4	4	4	4	4
5	5	5	5	5	5	5	5	5	5
6	6	6	6	6	6	6	6	6	6
7	7	7	7	7	7	7	7	7	7
8	8	8	8	8	8	8	8	8	8
9	9	9	9	9	9	9	9	9	9
0	0	0	0	0	0	0	0	0	0

TEST BOOKLET No.

1	1	1	1	1	1	1
2	2	2	2	2	2	2
3	3	3	3	3	3	3
4	4	4	4	4	4	4
5	5	5	5	5	5	5
6	6	6	6	6	6	6
7	7	7	7	7	7	7
8	8	8	8	8	8	8
9	9	9	9	9	9	9
0	0	0	0	0	0	0

TEST BOOKLET Code

Q No.	Response				Q No.	Response			
001	a	b	c	d	051	a	b	c	d
002	a	b	c	d	052	a	b	c	d
003	a	b	c	d	053	a	b	c	d
004	a	b	c	d	054	a	b	c	d
005	a	b	c	d	055	a	b	c	d
006	a	b	c	d	056	a	b	c	d
007	a	b	c	d	057	a	b	c	d
008	a	b	c	d	058	a	b	c	d
009	a	b	c	d	059	a	b	c	d
010	a	b	c	d	060	a	b	c	d
011	a	b	c	d	061	a	b	c	d
012	a	b	c	d	062	a	b	c	d
013	a	b	c	d	063	a	b	c	d
014	a	b	c	d	064	a	b	c	d
015	a	b	c	d	065	a	b	c	d
016	a	b	c	d	066	a	b	c	d
017	a	b	c	d	067	a	b	c	d
018	a	b	c	d	068	a	b	c	d
019	a	b	c	d	069	a	b	c	d
020	a	b	c	d	070	a	b	c	d
021	a	b	c	d	071	a	b	c	d
022	a	b	c	d	072	a	b	c	d
023	a	b	c	d	073	a	b	c	d
024	a	b	c	d	074	a	b	c	d
025	a	b	c	d	075	a	b	c	d
026	a	b	c	d	076	a	b	c	d
027	a	b	c	d	077	a	b	c	d
028	a	b	c	d	078	a	b	c	d
029	a	b	c	d	079	a	b	c	d
030	a	b	c	d	080	a	b	c	d
031	a	b	c	d	081	a	b	c	d
032	a	b	c	d	082	a	b	c	d
033	a	b	c	d	083	a	b	c	d
034	a	b	c	d	084	a	b	c	d
035	a	b	c	d	085	a	b	c	d
036	a	b	c	d	086	a	b	c	d
037	a	b	c	d	087	a	b	c	d
038	a	b	c	d	088	a	b	c	d
039	a	b	c	d	089	a	b	c	d
040	a	b	c	d	090	a	b	c	d
041	a	b	c	d	091	a	b	c	d
042	a	b	c	d	092	a	b	c	d
043	a	b	c	d	093	a	b	c	d
044	a	b	c	d	094	a	b	c	d
045	a	b	c	d	095	a	b	c	d
046	a	b	c	d	096	a	b	c	d
047	a	b	c	d	097	a	b	c	d
048	a	b	c	d	098	a	b	c	d
049	a	b	c	d	099	a	b	c	d
050	a	b	c	d	100	a	b	c	d

DECLARATION BY THE CANDIDATE

I declare that particulars and signature on this OMR Answer sheet are mine and are Name as in Attendance Sheet. I fruther declare that particulars filled in and Signature as well as the circles darkened on this ORIGINALCOPY is same as in OFFICE COPY.

Signature with time (in running handwriting)

CANDIDATE's NAME (in running handwriting)

MOTHER's NAME (in running handwriting)

FATHER's NAME (in running handwriting)

CANDIDATE LEFT HAND IMPRESSION

SIGNATURE OF INVIGILATOR'S WITH TIME

1

2

OMR SHEET

ROLL No.

1	1	1	1	1	1	1	1	1	1
2	2	2	2	2	2	2	2	2	2
3	3	3	3	3	3	3	3	3	3
4	4	4	4	4	4	4	4	4	4
5	5	5	5	5	5	5	5	5	5
6	6	6	6	6	6	6	6	6	6
7	7	7	7	7	7	7	7	7	7
8	8	8	8	8	8	8	8	8	8
9	9	9	9	9	9	9	9	9	9
0	0	0	0	0	0	0	0	0	0

TEST BOOKLET No.

1	1	1	1	1	1	1
2	2	2	2	2	2	2
3	3	3	3	3	3	3
4	4	4	4	4	4	4
5	5	5	5	5	5	5
6	6	6	6	6	6	6
7	7	7	7	7	7	7
8	8	8	8	8	8	8
9	9	9	9	9	9	9
0	0	0	0	0	0	0

TEST BOOKLET Code

Q No.	Response				Q No.	Response			
001	a	b	c	d	051	a	b	c	d
002	a	b	c	d	052	a	b	c	d
003	a	b	c	d	053	a	b	c	d
004	a	b	c	d	054	a	b	c	d
005	a	b	c	d	055	a	b	c	d
006	a	b	c	d	056	a	b	c	d
007	a	b	c	d	057	a	b	c	d
008	a	b	c	d	058	a	b	c	d
009	a	b	c	d	059	a	b	c	d
010	a	b	c	d	060	a	b	c	d
011	a	b	c	d	061	a	b	c	d
012	a	b	c	d	062	a	b	c	d
013	a	b	c	d	063	a	b	c	d
014	a	b	c	d	064	a	b	c	d
015	a	b	c	d	065	a	b	c	d
016	a	b	c	d	066	a	b	c	d
017	a	b	c	d	067	a	b	c	d
018	a	b	c	d	068	a	b	c	d
019	a	b	c	d	069	a	b	c	d
020	a	b	c	d	070	a	b	c	d
021	a	b	c	d	071	a	b	c	d
022	a	b	c	d	072	a	b	c	d
023	a	b	c	d	073	a	b	c	d
024	a	b	c	d	074	a	b	c	d
025	a	b	c	d	075	a	b	c	d
026	a	b	c	d	076	a	b	c	d
027	a	b	c	d	077	a	b	c	d
028	a	b	c	d	078	a	b	c	d
029	a	b	c	d	079	a	b	c	d
030	a	b	c	d	080	a	b	c	d
031	a	b	c	d	081	a	b	c	d
032	a	b	c	d	082	a	b	c	d
033	a	b	c	d	083	a	b	c	d
034	a	b	c	d	084	a	b	c	d
035	a	b	c	d	085	a	b	c	d
036	a	b	c	d	086	a	b	c	d
037	a	b	c	d	087	a	b	c	d
038	a	b	c	d	088	a	b	c	d
039	a	b	c	d	089	a	b	c	d
040	a	b	c	d	090	a	b	c	d
041	a	b	c	d	091	a	b	c	d
042	a	b	c	d	092	a	b	c	d
043	a	b	c	d	093	a	b	c	d
044	a	b	c	d	094	a	b	c	d
045	a	b	c	d	095	a	b	c	d
046	a	b	c	d	096	a	b	c	d
047	a	b	c	d	097	a	b	c	d
048	a	b	c	d	098	a	b	c	d
049	a	b	c	d	099	a	b	c	d
050	a	b	c	d	100	a	b	c	d

DECLARATION BY THE CANDIDATE

I declare that particulars and signature on this OMR Answer sheet are mine and are Name as in Attendance Sheet. I fruther declare that particulars filled in and Signature as well as the circles darkened on this ORIGINALCOPY is same as in OFFICE COPY.

Signature with time (in running handwriting)

CANDIDATE's NAME (in running handwriting)

MOTHER's NAME (in running handwriting)

FATHER's NAME (in running handwriting)

CANDIDATE LEFT HAND IMPRESSION

SIGNATURE OF INVIGILATOR'S WITH TIME

1

2

MEDACE

OMR SHEET

ROLL No.

1	1	1	1	1	1	1	1	1	1
2	2	2	2	2	2	2	2	2	2
3	3	3	3	3	3	3	3	3	3
4	4	4	4	4	4	4	4	4	4
5	5	5	5	5	5	5	5	5	5
6	6	6	6	6	6	6	6	6	6
7	7	7	7	7	7	7	7	7	7
8	8	8	8	8	8	8	8	8	8
9	9	9	9	9	9	9	9	9	9
0	0	0	0	0	0	0	0	0	0

TEST BOOKLET No.

1	1	1	1	1	1	1
2	2	2	2	2	2	2
3	3	3	3	3	3	3
4	4	4	4	4	4	4
5	5	5	5	5	5	5
6	6	6	6	6	6	6
7	7	7	7	7	7	7
8	8	8	8	8	8	8
9	9	9	9	9	9	9
0	0	0	0	0	0	0

TEST BOOKLET Code

Q No.	Response				Q No.	Response			
001	a	b	c	d	051	a	b	c	d
002	a	b	c	d	052	a	b	c	d
003	a	b	c	d	053	a	b	c	d
004	a	b	c	d	054	a	b	c	d
005	a	b	c	d	055	a	b	c	d
006	a	b	c	d	056	a	b	c	d
007	a	b	c	d	057	a	b	c	d
008	a	b	c	d	058	a	b	c	d
009	a	b	c	d	059	a	b	c	d
010	a	b	c	d	060	a	b	c	d
011	a	b	c	d	061	a	b	c	d
012	a	b	c	d	062	a	b	c	d
013	a	b	c	d	063	a	b	c	d
014	a	b	c	d	064	a	b	c	d
015	a	b	c	d	065	a	b	c	d
016	a	b	c	d	066	a	b	c	d
017	a	b	c	d	067	a	b	c	d
018	a	b	c	d	068	a	b	c	d
019	a	b	c	d	069	a	b	c	d
020	a	b	c	d	070	a	b	c	d
021	a	b	c	d	071	a	b	c	d
022	a	b	c	d	072	a	b	c	d
023	a	b	c	d	073	a	b	c	d
024	a	b	c	d	074	a	b	c	d
025	a	b	c	d	075	a	b	c	d
026	a	b	c	d	076	a	b	c	d
027	a	b	c	d	077	a	b	c	d
028	a	b	c	d	078	a	b	c	d
029	a	b	c	d	079	a	b	c	d
030	a	b	c	d	080	a	b	c	d
031	a	b	c	d	081	a	b	c	d
032	a	b	c	d	082	a	b	c	d
033	a	b	c	d	083	a	b	c	d
034	a	b	c	d	084	a	b	c	d
035	a	b	c	d	085	a	b	c	d
036	a	b	c	d	086	a	b	c	d
037	a	b	c	d	087	a	b	c	d
038	a	b	c	d	088	a	b	c	d
039	a	b	c	d	089	a	b	c	d
040	a	b	c	d	090	a	b	c	d
041	a	b	c	d	091	a	b	c	d
042	a	b	c	d	092	a	b	c	d
043	a	b	c	d	093	a	b	c	d
044	a	b	c	d	094	a	b	c	d
045	a	b	c	d	095	a	b	c	d
046	a	b	c	d	096	a	b	c	d
047	a	b	c	d	097	a	b	c	d
048	a	b	c	d	098	a	b	c	d
049	a	b	c	d	099	a	b	c	d
050	a	b	c	d	100	a	b	c	d

DECLARATION BY THE CANDIDATE

I declare that particulars and signature on this OMR Answer sheet are mine and are Name as in Attendance Sheet. I fruther declare that particulars filled in and Signature as well as the circles darkened on this ORIGINALCOPY is same as in OFFICE COPY.

Signature with time (in running handwriting)

CANDIDATE's NAME (in running handwriting)

MOTHER's NAME (in running handwriting)

FATHER's NAME (in running handwriting)

CANDIDATE LEFT HAND IMPRESSION

SIGNATURE OF INVIGILATOR'S WITH TIME

1

2

MEDACE

OMR SHEET

ROLL No.

1	1	1	1	1	1	1	1	1	1
2	2	2	2	2	2	2	2	2	2
3	3	3	3	3	3	3	3	3	3
4	4	4	4	4	4	4	4	4	4
5	5	5	5	5	5	5	5	5	5
6	6	6	6	6	6	6	6	6	6
7	7	7	7	7	7	7	7	7	7
8	8	8	8	8	8	8	8	8	8
9	9	9	9	9	9	9	9	9	9
0	0	0	0	0	0	0	0	0	0

TEST BOOKLET No.

1	1	1	1	1	1	1
2	2	2	2	2	2	2
3	3	3	3	3	3	3
4	4	4	4	4	4	4
5	5	5	5	5	5	5
6	6	6	6	6	6	6
7	7	7	7	7	7	7
8	8	8	8	8	8	8
9	9	9	9	9	9	9
0	0	0	0	0	0	0

TEST BOOKLET Code

Q No.	Response	Q No.	Response
001	a b c d	051	a b c d
002	a b c d	052	a b c d
003	a b c d	053	a b c d
004	a b c d	054	a b c d
005	a b c d	055	a b c d
006	a b c d	056	a b c d
007	a b c d	057	a b c d
008	a b c d	058	a b c d
009	a b c d	059	a b c d
010	a b c d	060	a b c d
011	a b c d	061	a b c d
012	a b c d	062	a b c d
013	a b c d	063	a b c d
014	a b c d	064	a b c d
015	a b c d	065	a b c d
016	a b c d	066	a b c d
017	a b c d	067	a b c d
018	a b c d	068	a b c d
019	a b c d	069	a b c d
020	a b c d	070	a b c d
021	a b c d	071	a b c d
022	a b c d	072	a b c d
023	a b c d	073	a b c d
024	a b c d	074	a b c d
025	a b c d	075	a b c d
026	a b c d	076	a b c d
027	a b c d	077	a b c d
028	a b c d	078	a b c d
029	a b c d	079	a b c d
030	a b c d	080	a b c d
031	a b c d	081	a b c d
032	a b c d	082	a b c d
033	a b c d	083	a b c d
034	a b c d	084	a b c d
035	a b c d	085	a b c d
036	a b c d	086	a b c d
037	a b c d	087	a b c d
038	a b c d	088	a b c d
039	a b c d	089	a b c d
040	a b c d	090	a b c d
041	a b c d	091	a b c d
042	a b c d	092	a b c d
043	a b c d	093	a b c d
044	a b c d	094	a b c d
045	a b c d	095	a b c d
046	a b c d	096	a b c d
047	a b c d	097	a b c d
048	a b c d	098	a b c d
049	a b c d	099	a b c d
050	a b c d	100	a b c d

DECLARATION BY THE CANDIDATE

I declare that particulars and signature on this OMR Answer sheet are mine and are Name as in Attendance Sheet. I fruther declare that particulars filled in and Signature as well as the circles darkened on this ORIGINALCOPY is same as in OFFICE COPY.

Signature with time (in running handwriting)

CANDIDATE's NAME (in running handwriting)

MOTHER's NAME (in running handwriting)

FATHER's NAME (in running handwriting)

CANDIDATE LEFT HAND IMPRESSION

SIGNATURE OF INVIGILATOR'S WITH TIME

1

2

OMR SHEET

ROLL No.

1	1	1	1	1	1	1	1	1	1
2	2	2	2	2	2	2	2	2	2
3	3	3	3	3	3	3	3	3	3
4	4	4	4	4	4	4	4	4	4
5	5	5	5	5	5	5	5	5	5
6	6	6	6	6	6	6	6	6	6
7	7	7	7	7	7	7	7	7	7
8	8	8	8	8	8	8	8	8	8
9	9	9	9	9	9	9	9	9	9
0	0	0	0	0	0	0	0	0	0

TEST BOOKLET No.

1	1	1	1	1	1	1
2	2	2	2	2	2	2
3	3	3	3	3	3	3
4	4	4	4	4	4	4
5	5	5	5	5	5	5
6	6	6	6	6	6	6
7	7	7	7	7	7	7
8	8	8	8	8	8	8
9	9	9	9	9	9	9
0	0	0	0	0	0	0

TEST BOOKLET Code

Q No.	Response				Q No.	Response			
001	a	b	c	d	051	a	b	c	d
002	a	b	c	d	052	a	b	c	d
003	a	b	c	d	053	a	b	c	d
004	a	b	c	d	054	a	b	c	d
005	a	b	c	d	055	a	b	c	d
006	a	b	c	d	056	a	b	c	d
007	a	b	c	d	057	a	b	c	d
008	a	b	c	d	058	a	b	c	d
009	a	b	c	d	059	a	b	c	d
010	a	b	c	d	060	a	b	c	d
011	a	b	c	d	061	a	b	c	d
012	a	b	c	d	062	a	b	c	d
013	a	b	c	d	063	a	b	c	d
014	a	b	c	d	064	a	b	c	d
015	a	b	c	d	065	a	b	c	d
016	a	b	c	d	066	a	b	c	d
017	a	b	c	d	067	a	b	c	d
018	a	b	c	d	068	a	b	c	d
019	a	b	c	d	069	a	b	c	d
020	a	b	c	d	070	a	b	c	d
021	a	b	c	d	071	a	b	c	d
022	a	b	c	d	072	a	b	c	d
023	a	b	c	d	073	a	b	c	d
024	a	b	c	d	074	a	b	c	d
025	a	b	c	d	075	a	b	c	d
026	a	b	c	d	076	a	b	c	d
027	a	b	c	d	077	a	b	c	d
028	a	b	c	d	078	a	b	c	d
029	a	b	c	d	079	a	b	c	d
030	a	b	c	d	080	a	b	c	d
031	a	b	c	d	081	a	b	c	d
032	a	b	c	d	082	a	b	c	d
033	a	b	c	d	083	a	b	c	d
034	a	b	c	d	084	a	b	c	d
035	a	b	c	d	085	a	b	c	d
036	a	b	c	d	086	a	b	c	d
037	a	b	c	d	087	a	b	c	d
038	a	b	c	d	088	a	b	c	d
039	a	b	c	d	089	a	b	c	d
040	a	b	c	d	090	a	b	c	d
041	a	b	c	d	091	a	b	c	d
042	a	b	c	d	092	a	b	c	d
043	a	b	c	d	093	a	b	c	d
044	a	b	c	d	094	a	b	c	d
045	a	b	c	d	095	a	b	c	d
046	a	b	c	d	096	a	b	c	d
047	a	b	c	d	097	a	b	c	d
048	a	b	c	d	098	a	b	c	d
049	a	b	c	d	099	a	b	c	d
050	a	b	c	d	100	a	b	c	d

DECLARATION BY THE CANDIDATE

I declare that particulars and signature on this OMR Answer sheet are mine and are Name as in Attendance Sheet. I fruther declare that particulars filled in and Signature as well as the circles darkened on this ORIGINALCOPY is same as in OFFICE COPY.

Signature with time (in running handwriting)

CANDIDATE's NAME (in running handwriting)

MOTHER's NAME (in running handwriting)

FATHER's NAME (in running handwriting)

CANDIDATE LEFT HAND IMPRESSION

SIGNATURE OF INVIGILATOR'S WITH TIME

1

2

OMR SHEET

ROLL No.

1	1	1	1	1	1	1	1	1	1
2	2	2	2	2	2	2	2	2	2
3	3	3	3	3	3	3	3	3	3
4	4	4	4	4	4	4	4	4	4
5	5	5	5	5	5	5	5	5	5
6	6	6	6	6	6	6	6	6	6
7	7	7	7	7	7	7	7	7	7
8	8	8	8	8	8	8	8	8	8
9	9	9	9	9	9	9	9	9	9
0	0	0	0	0	0	0	0	0	0

TEST BOOKLET No.

1	1	1	1	1	1	1
2	2	2	2	2	2	2
3	3	3	3	3	3	3
4	4	4	4	4	4	4
5	5	5	5	5	5	5
6	6	6	6	6	6	6
7	7	7	7	7	7	7
8	8	8	8	8	8	8
9	9	9	9	9	9	9
0	0	0	0	0	0	0

TEST BOOKLET Code

Q No.	Response				Q No.	Response			
001	a	b	c	d	051	a	b	c	d
002	a	b	c	d	052	a	b	c	d
003	a	b	c	d	053	a	b	c	d
004	a	b	c	d	054	a	b	c	d
005	a	b	c	d	055	a	b	c	d
006	a	b	c	d	056	a	b	c	d
007	a	b	c	d	057	a	b	c	d
008	a	b	c	d	058	a	b	c	d
009	a	b	c	d	059	a	b	c	d
010	a	b	c	d	060	a	b	c	d
011	a	b	c	d	061	a	b	c	d
012	a	b	c	d	062	a	b	c	d
013	a	b	c	d	063	a	b	c	d
014	a	b	c	d	064	a	b	c	d
015	a	b	c	d	065	a	b	c	d
016	a	b	c	d	066	a	b	c	d
017	a	b	c	d	067	a	b	c	d
018	a	b	c	d	068	a	b	c	d
019	a	b	c	d	069	a	b	c	d
020	a	b	c	d	070	a	b	c	d
021	a	b	c	d	071	a	b	c	d
022	a	b	c	d	072	a	b	c	d
023	a	b	c	d	073	a	b	c	d
024	a	b	c	d	074	a	b	c	d
025	a	b	c	d	075	a	b	c	d
026	a	b	c	d	076	a	b	c	d
027	a	b	c	d	077	a	b	c	d
028	a	b	c	d	078	a	b	c	d
029	a	b	c	d	079	a	b	c	d
030	a	b	c	d	080	a	b	c	d
031	a	b	c	d	081	a	b	c	d
032	a	b	c	d	082	a	b	c	d
033	a	b	c	d	083	a	b	c	d
034	a	b	c	d	084	a	b	c	d
035	a	b	c	d	085	a	b	c	d
036	a	b	c	d	086	a	b	c	d
037	a	b	c	d	087	a	b	c	d
038	a	b	c	d	088	a	b	c	d
039	a	b	c	d	089	a	b	c	d
040	a	b	c	d	090	a	b	c	d
041	a	b	c	d	091	a	b	c	d
042	a	b	c	d	092	a	b	c	d
043	a	b	c	d	093	a	b	c	d
044	a	b	c	d	094	a	b	c	d
045	a	b	c	d	095	a	b	c	d
046	a	b	c	d	096	a	b	c	d
047	a	b	c	d	097	a	b	c	d
048	a	b	c	d	098	a	b	c	d
049	a	b	c	d	099	a	b	c	d
050	a	b	c	d	100	a	b	c	d

DECLARATION BY THE CANDIDATE

I declare that particulars and signature on this OMR Answer sheet are mine and are Name as in Attendance Sheet. I fruther declare that particulars filled in and Signature as well as the circles darkened on this ORIGINALCOPY is same as in OFFICE COPY.

Signature with time (in running handwriting)

CANDIDATE's NAME (in running handwriting)

MOTHER's NAME (in running handwriting)

FATHER's NAME (in running handwriting)

CANDIDATE LEFT HAND IMPRESSION

SIGNATURE OF INVIGILATOR'S WITH TIME

1

2

OMR SHEET

ROLL No.

1	1	1	1	1	1	1	1	1	1
2	2	2	2	2	2	2	2	2	2
3	3	3	3	3	3	3	3	3	3
4	4	4	4	4	4	4	4	4	4
5	5	5	5	5	5	5	5	5	5
6	6	6	6	6	6	6	6	6	6
7	7	7	7	7	7	7	7	7	7
8	8	8	8	8	8	8	8	8	8
9	9	9	9	9	9	9	9	9	9
0	0	0	0	0	0	0	0	0	0

TEST BOOKLET No.

1	1	1	1	1	1	1
2	2	2	2	2	2	2
3	3	3	3	3	3	3
4	4	4	4	4	4	4
5	5	5	5	5	5	5
6	6	6	6	6	6	6
7	7	7	7	7	7	7
8	8	8	8	8	8	8
9	9	9	9	9	9	9
0	0	0	0	0	0	0

TEST BOOKLET Code

Q No.	Response	Q No.	Response
001	a b c d	051	a b c d
002	a b c d	052	a b c d
003	a b c d	053	a b c d
004	a b c d	054	a b c d
005	a b c d	055	a b c d
006	a b c d	056	a b c d
007	a b c d	057	a b c d
008	a b c d	058	a b c d
009	a b c d	059	a b c d
010	a b c d	060	a b c d
011	a b c d	061	a b c d
012	a b c d	062	a b c d
013	a b c d	063	a b c d
014	a b c d	064	a b c d
015	a b c d	065	a b c d
016	a b c d	066	a b c d
017	a b c d	067	a b c d
018	a b c d	068	a b c d
019	a b c d	069	a b c d
020	a b c d	070	a b c d
021	a b c d	071	a b c d
022	a b c d	072	a b c d
023	a b c d	073	a b c d
024	a b c d	074	a b c d
025	a b c d	075	a b c d
026	a b c d	076	a b c d
027	a b c d	077	a b c d
028	a b c d	078	a b c d
029	a b c d	079	a b c d
030	a b c d	080	a b c d
031	a b c d	081	a b c d
032	a b c d	082	a b c d
033	a b c d	083	a b c d
034	a b c d	084	a b c d
035	a b c d	085	a b c d
036	a b c d	086	a b c d
037	a b c d	087	a b c d
038	a b c d	088	a b c d
039	a b c d	089	a b c d
040	a b c d	090	a b c d
041	a b c d	091	a b c d
042	a b c d	092	a b c d
043	a b c d	093	a b c d
044	a b c d	094	a b c d
045	a b c d	095	a b c d
046	a b c d	096	a b c d
047	a b c d	097	a b c d
048	a b c d	098	a b c d
049	a b c d	099	a b c d
050	a b c d	100	a b c d

DECLARATION BY THE CANDIDATE

I declare that particulars and signature on this OMR Answer sheet are mine and are Name as in Attendance Sheet. I fruther declare that particulars filled in and Signature as well as the circles darkened on this ORIGINALCOPY is same as in OFFICE COPY.

Signature with time (in running handwriting)

CANDIDATE's NAME (in running handwriting)

MOTHER's NAME (in running handwriting)

FATHER's NAME (in running handwriting)

CANDIDATE LEFT HAND IMPRESSION

SIGNATURE OF INVIGILATOR'S WITH TIME

1

2

MEDACE

OMR SHEET

ROLL No.

1	1	1	1	1	1	1	1	1	1
2	2	2	2	2	2	2	2	2	2
3	3	3	3	3	3	3	3	3	3
4	4	4	4	4	4	4	4	4	4
5	5	5	5	5	5	5	5	5	5
6	6	6	6	6	6	6	6	6	6
7	7	7	7	7	7	7	7	7	7
8	8	8	8	8	8	8	8	8	8
9	9	9	9	9	9	9	9	9	9
0	0	0	0	0	0	0	0	0	0

TEST BOOKLET No.

1	1	1	1	1	1	1
2	2	2	2	2	2	2
3	3	3	3	3	3	3
4	4	4	4	4	4	4
5	5	5	5	5	5	5
6	6	6	6	6	6	6
7	7	7	7	7	7	7
8	8	8	8	8	8	8
9	9	9	9	9	9	9
0	0	0	0	0	0	0

TEST BOOKLET Code

Q No.	Response				Q No.	Response			
001	a	b	c	d	051	a	b	c	d
002	a	b	c	d	052	a	b	c	d
003	a	b	c	d	053	a	b	c	d
004	a	b	c	d	054	a	b	c	d
005	a	b	c	d	055	a	b	c	d
006	a	b	c	d	056	a	b	c	d
007	a	b	c	d	057	a	b	c	d
008	a	b	c	d	058	a	b	c	d
009	a	b	c	d	059	a	b	c	d
010	a	b	c	d	060	a	b	c	d
011	a	b	c	d	061	a	b	c	d
012	a	b	c	d	062	a	b	c	d
013	a	b	c	d	063	a	b	c	d
014	a	b	c	d	064	a	b	c	d
015	a	b	c	d	065	a	b	c	d
016	a	b	c	d	066	a	b	c	d
017	a	b	c	d	067	a	b	c	d
018	a	b	c	d	068	a	b	c	d
019	a	b	c	d	069	a	b	c	d
020	a	b	c	d	070	a	b	c	d
021	a	b	c	d	071	a	b	c	d
022	a	b	c	d	072	a	b	c	d
023	a	b	c	d	073	a	b	c	d
024	a	b	c	d	074	a	b	c	d
025	a	b	c	d	075	a	b	c	d
026	a	b	c	d	076	a	b	c	d
027	a	b	c	d	077	a	b	c	d
028	a	b	c	d	078	a	b	c	d
029	a	b	c	d	079	a	b	c	d
030	a	b	c	d	080	a	b	c	d
031	a	b	c	d	081	a	b	c	d
032	a	b	c	d	082	a	b	c	d
033	a	b	c	d	083	a	b	c	d
034	a	b	c	d	084	a	b	c	d
035	a	b	c	d	085	a	b	c	d
036	a	b	c	d	086	a	b	c	d
037	a	b	c	d	087	a	b	c	d
038	a	b	c	d	088	a	b	c	d
039	a	b	c	d	089	a	b	c	d
040	a	b	c	d	090	a	b	c	d
041	a	b	c	d	091	a	b	c	d
042	a	b	c	d	092	a	b	c	d
043	a	b	c	d	093	a	b	c	d
044	a	b	c	d	094	a	b	c	d
045	a	b	c	d	095	a	b	c	d
046	a	b	c	d	096	a	b	c	d
047	a	b	c	d	097	a	b	c	d
048	a	b	c	d	098	a	b	c	d
049	a	b	c	d	099	a	b	c	d
050	a	b	c	d	100	a	b	c	d

DECLARATION BY THE CANDIDATE

I declare that particulars and signature on this OMR Answer sheet are mine and are Name as in Attendance Sheet. I fruther declare that particulars filled in and Signature as well as the circles darkened on this ORIGINALCOPY is same as in OFFICE COPY.

Signature with time (in running handwriting)

CANDIDATE's NAME (in running handwriting)

MOTHER's NAME (in running handwriting)

FATHER's NAME (in running handwriting)

CANDIDATE LEFT HAND IMPRESSION

SIGNATURE OF INVIGILATOR'S WITH TIME

1

2

MEDACE

OMR SHEET

ROLL No.

1	1	1	1	1	1	1	1	1	1
2	2	2	2	2	2	2	2	2	2
3	3	3	3	3	3	3	3	3	3
4	4	4	4	4	4	4	4	4	4
5	5	5	5	5	5	5	5	5	5
6	6	6	6	6	6	6	6	6	6
7	7	7	7	7	7	7	7	7	7
8	8	8	8	8	8	8	8	8	8
9	9	9	9	9	9	9	9	9	9
0	0	0	0	0	0	0	0	0	0

TEST BOOKLET No.

1	1	1	1	1	1	1
2	2	2	2	2	2	2
3	3	3	3	3	3	3
4	4	4	4	4	4	4
5	5	5	5	5	5	5
6	6	6	6	6	6	6
7	7	7	7	7	7	7
8	8	8	8	8	8	8
9	9	9	9	9	9	9
0	0	0	0	0	0	0

TEST BOOKLET Code

Q No.	Response				Q No.	Response			
001	a	b	c	d	051	a	b	c	d
002	a	b	c	d	052	a	b	c	d
003	a	b	c	d	053	a	b	c	d
004	a	b	c	d	054	a	b	c	d
005	a	b	c	d	055	a	b	c	d
006	a	b	c	d	056	a	b	c	d
007	a	b	c	d	057	a	b	c	d
008	a	b	c	d	058	a	b	c	d
009	a	b	c	d	059	a	b	c	d
010	a	b	c	d	060	a	b	c	d
011	a	b	c	d	061	a	b	c	d
012	a	b	c	d	062	a	b	c	d
013	a	b	c	d	063	a	b	c	d
014	a	b	c	d	064	a	b	c	d
015	a	b	c	d	065	a	b	c	d
016	a	b	c	d	066	a	b	c	d
017	a	b	c	d	067	a	b	c	d
018	a	b	c	d	068	a	b	c	d
019	a	b	c	d	069	a	b	c	d
020	a	b	c	d	070	a	b	c	d
021	a	b	c	d	071	a	b	c	d
022	a	b	c	d	072	a	b	c	d
023	a	b	c	d	073	a	b	c	d
024	a	b	c	d	074	a	b	c	d
025	a	b	c	d	075	a	b	c	d
026	a	b	c	d	076	a	b	c	d
027	a	b	c	d	077	a	b	c	d
028	a	b	c	d	078	a	b	c	d
029	a	b	c	d	079	a	b	c	d
030	a	b	c	d	080	a	b	c	d
031	a	b	c	d	081	a	b	c	d
032	a	b	c	d	082	a	b	c	d
033	a	b	c	d	083	a	b	c	d
034	a	b	c	d	084	a	b	c	d
035	a	b	c	d	085	a	b	c	d
036	a	b	c	d	086	a	b	c	d
037	a	b	c	d	087	a	b	c	d
038	a	b	c	d	088	a	b	c	d
039	a	b	c	d	089	a	b	c	d
040	a	b	c	d	090	a	b	c	d
041	a	b	c	d	091	a	b	c	d
042	a	b	c	d	092	a	b	c	d
043	a	b	c	d	093	a	b	c	d
044	a	b	c	d	094	a	b	c	d
045	a	b	c	d	095	a	b	c	d
046	a	b	c	d	096	a	b	c	d
047	a	b	c	d	097	a	b	c	d
048	a	b	c	d	098	a	b	c	d
049	a	b	c	d	099	a	b	c	d
050	a	b	c	d	100	a	b	c	d

DECLARATION BY THE CANDIDATE

I declare that particulars and signature on this OMR Answer sheet are mine and are Name as in Attendance Sheet. I fruther declare that particulars filled in and Signature as well as the circles darkened on this ORIGINALCOPY is same as in OFFICE COPY.

Signature with time (in running handwriting)

CANDIDATE's NAME (in running handwriting)

MOTHER's NAME (in running handwriting)

FATHER's NAME (in running handwriting)

CANDIDATE LEFT HAND IMPRESSION

SIGNATURE OF INVIGILATOR'S WITH TIME

1

2

MEDACE

OMR SHEET

ROLL No.

1	1	1	1	1	1	1	1	1	1
2	2	2	2	2	2	2	2	2	2
3	3	3	3	3	3	3	3	3	3
4	4	4	4	4	4	4	4	4	4
5	5	5	5	5	5	5	5	5	5
6	6	6	6	6	6	6	6	6	6
7	7	7	7	7	7	7	7	7	7
8	8	8	8	8	8	8	8	8	8
9	9	9	9	9	9	9	9	9	9
0	0	0	0	0	0	0	0	0	0

TEST BOOKLET No.

1	1	1	1	1	1	1
2	2	2	2	2	2	2
3	3	3	3	3	3	3
4	4	4	4	4	4	4
5	5	5	5	5	5	5
6	6	6	6	6	6	6
7	7	7	7	7	7	7
8	8	8	8	8	8	8
9	9	9	9	9	9	9
0	0	0	0	0	0	0

TEST BOOKLET Code

Q No.	Response	Q No.	Response
001	(a) (b) (c) (d)	051	(a) (b) (c) (d)
002	(a) (b) (c) (d)	052	(a) (b) (c) (d)
003	(a) (b) (c) (d)	053	(a) (b) (c) (d)
004	(a) (b) (c) (d)	054	(a) (b) (c) (d)
005	(a) (b) (c) (d)	055	(a) (b) (c) (d)
006	(a) (b) (c) (d)	056	(a) (b) (c) (d)
007	(a) (b) (c) (d)	057	(a) (b) (c) (d)
008	(a) (b) (c) (d)	058	(a) (b) (c) (d)
009	(a) (b) (c) (d)	059	(a) (b) (c) (d)
010	(a) (b) (c) (d)	060	(a) (b) (c) (d)
011	(a) (b) (c) (d)	061	(a) (b) (c) (d)
012	(a) (b) (c) (d)	062	(a) (b) (c) (d)
013	(a) (b) (c) (d)	063	(a) (b) (c) (d)
014	(a) (b) (c) (d)	064	(a) (b) (c) (d)
015	(a) (b) (c) (d)	065	(a) (b) (c) (d)
016	(a) (b) (c) (d)	066	(a) (b) (c) (d)
017	(a) (b) (c) (d)	067	(a) (b) (c) (d)
018	(a) (b) (c) (d)	068	(a) (b) (c) (d)
019	(a) (b) (c) (d)	069	(a) (b) (c) (d)
020	(a) (b) (c) (d)	070	(a) (b) (c) (d)
021	(a) (b) (c) (d)	071	(a) (b) (c) (d)
022	(a) (b) (c) (d)	072	(a) (b) (c) (d)
023	(a) (b) (c) (d)	073	(a) (b) (c) (d)
024	(a) (b) (c) (d)	074	(a) (b) (c) (d)
025	(a) (b) (c) (d)	075	(a) (b) (c) (d)
026	(a) (b) (c) (d)	076	(a) (b) (c) (d)
027	(a) (b) (c) (d)	077	(a) (b) (c) (d)
028	(a) (b) (c) (d)	078	(a) (b) (c) (d)
029	(a) (b) (c) (d)	079	(a) (b) (c) (d)
030	(a) (b) (c) (d)	080	(a) (b) (c) (d)
031	(a) (b) (c) (d)	081	(a) (b) (c) (d)
032	(a) (b) (c) (d)	082	(a) (b) (c) (d)
033	(a) (b) (c) (d)	083	(a) (b) (c) (d)
034	(a) (b) (c) (d)	084	(a) (b) (c) (d)
035	(a) (b) (c) (d)	085	(a) (b) (c) (d)
036	(a) (b) (c) (d)	086	(a) (b) (c) (d)
037	(a) (b) (c) (d)	087	(a) (b) (c) (d)
038	(a) (b) (c) (d)	088	(a) (b) (c) (d)
039	(a) (b) (c) (d)	089	(a) (b) (c) (d)
040	(a) (b) (c) (d)	090	(a) (b) (c) (d)
041	(a) (b) (c) (d)	091	(a) (b) (c) (d)
042	(a) (b) (c) (d)	092	(a) (b) (c) (d)
043	(a) (b) (c) (d)	093	(a) (b) (c) (d)
044	(a) (b) (c) (d)	094	(a) (b) (c) (d)
045	(a) (b) (c) (d)	095	(a) (b) (c) (d)
046	(a) (b) (c) (d)	096	(a) (b) (c) (d)
047	(a) (b) (c) (d)	097	(a) (b) (c) (d)
048	(a) (b) (c) (d)	098	(a) (b) (c) (d)
049	(a) (b) (c) (d)	099	(a) (b) (c) (d)
050	(a) (b) (c) (d)	100	(a) (b) (c) (d)

DECLARATION BY THE CANDIDATE

I declare that particulars and signature on this OMR Answer sheet are mine and are Name as in Attendance Sheet. I fruther declare that particulars filled in and Signature as well as the circles darkened on this ORIGINALCOPY is same as in OFFICE COPY.

Signature with time (in running handwriting)

CANDIDATE's NAME (in running handwriting)

MOTHER's NAME (in running handwriting)

FATHER's NAME (in running handwriting)

CANDIDATE LEFT HAND IMPRESSION

SIGNATURE OF INVIGILATOR'S WITH TIME

1

2

OMR SHEET

ROLL No.

1	1	1	1	1	1	1	1	1	1
2	2	2	2	2	2	2	2	2	2
3	3	3	3	3	3	3	3	3	3
4	4	4	4	4	4	4	4	4	4
5	5	5	5	5	5	5	5	5	5
6	6	6	6	6	6	6	6	6	6
7	7	7	7	7	7	7	7	7	7
8	8	8	8	8	8	8	8	8	8
9	9	9	9	9	9	9	9	9	9
0	0	0	0	0	0	0	0	0	0

TEST BOOKLET No.

1	1	1	1	1	1	1
2	2	2	2	2	2	2
3	3	3	3	3	3	3
4	4	4	4	4	4	4
5	5	5	5	5	5	5
6	6	6	6	6	6	6
7	7	7	7	7	7	7
8	8	8	8	8	8	8
9	9	9	9	9	9	9
0	0	0	0	0	0	0

TEST BOOKLET Code

DECLARATION BY THE CANDIDATE

I declare that particulars and signature on this OMR Answer sheet are mine and are Name as in Attendance Sheet. I fruther declare that particulars filled in and Signature as well as the circles darkened on this ORIGINALCOPY is same as in OFFICE COPY.

Signature with time (in running handwriting)

CANDIDATE's NAME (in running handwriting)

Q No.	Response				Q No.	Response			
001	a	b	c	d	051	a	b	c	d
002	a	b	c	d	052	a	b	c	d
003	a	b	c	d	053	a	b	c	d
004	a	b	c	d	054	a	b	c	d
005	a	b	c	d	055	a	b	c	d
006	a	b	c	d	056	a	b	c	d
007	a	b	c	d	057	a	b	c	d
008	a	b	c	d	058	a	b	c	d
009	a	b	c	d	059	a	b	c	d
010	a	b	c	d	060	a	b	c	d
011	a	b	c	d	061	a	b	c	d
012	a	b	c	d	062	a	b	c	d
013	a	b	c	d	063	a	b	c	d
014	a	b	c	d	064	a	b	c	d
015	a	b	c	d	065	a	b	c	d
016	a	b	c	d	066	a	b	c	d
017	a	b	c	d	067	a	b	c	d
018	a	b	c	d	068	a	b	c	d
019	a	b	c	d	069	a	b	c	d
020	a	b	c	d	070	a	b	c	d
021	a	b	c	d	071	a	b	c	d
022	a	b	c	d	072	a	b	c	d
023	a	b	c	d	073	a	b	c	d
024	a	b	c	d	074	a	b	c	d
025	a	b	c	d	075	a	b	c	d
026	a	b	c	d	076	a	b	c	d
027	a	b	c	d	077	a	b	c	d
028	a	b	c	d	078	a	b	c	d
029	a	b	c	d	079	a	b	c	d
030	a	b	c	d	080	a	b	c	d
031	a	b	c	d	081	a	b	c	d
032	a	b	c	d	082	a	b	c	d
033	a	b	c	d	083	a	b	c	d
034	a	b	c	d	084	a	b	c	d
035	a	b	c	d	085	a	b	c	d
036	a	b	c	d	086	a	b	c	d
037	a	b	c	d	087	a	b	c	d
038	a	b	c	d	088	a	b	c	d
039	a	b	c	d	089	a	b	c	d
040	a	b	c	d	090	a	b	c	d
041	a	b	c	d	091	a	b	c	d
042	a	b	c	d	092	a	b	c	d
043	a	b	c	d	093	a	b	c	d
044	a	b	c	d	094	a	b	c	d
045	a	b	c	d	095	a	b	c	d
046	a	b	c	d	096	a	b	c	d
047	a	b	c	d	097	a	b	c	d
048	a	b	c	d	098	a	b	c	d
049	a	b	c	d	099	a	b	c	d
050	a	b	c	d	100	a	b	c	d

MOTHER's NAME (in running handwriting)

FATHER's NAME (in running handwriting)

CANDIDATE LEFT HAND IMPRESSION

SIGNATURE OF INVIGILATOR'S WITH TIME

1

2

MEDACE

OMR SHEET

ROLL No.

1	1	1	1	1	1	1	1	1	1
2	2	2	2	2	2	2	2	2	2
3	3	3	3	3	3	3	3	3	3
4	4	4	4	4	4	4	4	4	4
5	5	5	5	5	5	5	5	5	5
6	6	6	6	6	6	6	6	6	6
7	7	7	7	7	7	7	7	7	7
8	8	8	8	8	8	8	8	8	8
9	9	9	9	9	9	9	9	9	9
0	0	0	0	0	0	0	0	0	0

TEST BOOKLET No.

1	1	1	1	1	1	1
2	2	2	2	2	2	2
3	3	3	3	3	3	3
4	4	4	4	4	4	4
5	5	5	5	5	5	5
6	6	6	6	6	6	6
7	7	7	7	7	7	7
8	8	8	8	8	8	8
9	9	9	9	9	9	9
0	0	0	0	0	0	0

TEST BOOKLET Code

Q No.	Response				Q No.	Response			
001	a	b	c	d	051	a	b	c	d
002	a	b	c	d	052	a	b	c	d
003	a	b	c	d	053	a	b	c	d
004	a	b	c	d	054	a	b	c	d
005	a	b	c	d	055	a	b	c	d
006	a	b	c	d	056	a	b	c	d
007	a	b	c	d	057	a	b	c	d
008	a	b	c	d	058	a	b	c	d
009	a	b	c	d	059	a	b	c	d
010	a	b	c	d	060	a	b	c	d
011	a	b	c	d	061	a	b	c	d
012	a	b	c	d	062	a	b	c	d
013	a	b	c	d	063	a	b	c	d
014	a	b	c	d	064	a	b	c	d
015	a	b	c	d	065	a	b	c	d
016	a	b	c	d	066	a	b	c	d
017	a	b	c	d	067	a	b	c	d
018	a	b	c	d	068	a	b	c	d
019	a	b	c	d	069	a	b	c	d
020	a	b	c	d	070	a	b	c	d
021	a	b	c	d	071	a	b	c	d
022	a	b	c	d	072	a	b	c	d
023	a	b	c	d	073	a	b	c	d
024	a	b	c	d	074	a	b	c	d
025	a	b	c	d	075	a	b	c	d
026	a	b	c	d	076	a	b	c	d
027	a	b	c	d	077	a	b	c	d
028	a	b	c	d	078	a	b	c	d
029	a	b	c	d	079	a	b	c	d
030	a	b	c	d	080	a	b	c	d
031	a	b	c	d	081	a	b	c	d
032	a	b	c	d	082	a	b	c	d
033	a	b	c	d	083	a	b	c	d
034	a	b	c	d	084	a	b	c	d
035	a	b	c	d	085	a	b	c	d
036	a	b	c	d	086	a	b	c	d
037	a	b	c	d	087	a	b	c	d
038	a	b	c	d	088	a	b	c	d
039	a	b	c	d	089	a	b	c	d
040	a	b	c	d	090	a	b	c	d
041	a	b	c	d	091	a	b	c	d
042	a	b	c	d	092	a	b	c	d
043	a	b	c	d	093	a	b	c	d
044	a	b	c	d	094	a	b	c	d
045	a	b	c	d	095	a	b	c	d
046	a	b	c	d	096	a	b	c	d
047	a	b	c	d	097	a	b	c	d
048	a	b	c	d	098	a	b	c	d
049	a	b	c	d	099	a	b	c	d
050	a	b	c	d	100	a	b	c	d

DECLARATION BY THE CANDIDATE

I declare that particulars and signature on this OMR Answer sheet are mine and are Name as in Attendance Sheet. I fruther declare that particulars filled in and Signature as well as the circles darkened on this ORIGINALCOPY is same as in OFFICE COPY.

Signature with time (in running handwriting)

CANDIDATE's NAME (in running handwriting)

MOTHER's NAME (in running handwriting)

FATHER's NAME (in running handwriting)

CANDIDATE LEFT HAND IMPRESSION

SIGNATURE OF INVIGILATOR'S WITH TIME

1

2

MEDACE

OMR SHEET

ROLL No.

1	1	1	1	1	1	1	1	1	1
2	2	2	2	2	2	2	2	2	2
3	3	3	3	3	3	3	3	3	3
4	4	4	4	4	4	4	4	4	4
5	5	5	5	5	5	5	5	5	5
6	6	6	6	6	6	6	6	6	6
7	7	7	7	7	7	7	7	7	7
8	8	8	8	8	8	8	8	8	8
9	9	9	9	9	9	9	9	9	9
0	0	0	0	0	0	0	0	0	0

TEST BOOKLET No.

1	1	1	1	1	1	1
2	2	2	2	2	2	2
3	3	3	3	3	3	3
4	4	4	4	4	4	4
5	5	5	5	5	5	5
6	6	6	6	6	6	6
7	7	7	7	7	7	7
8	8	8	8	8	8	8
9	9	9	9	9	9	9
0	0	0	0	0	0	0

TEST BOOKLET Code

Q No.	Response	Q No.	Response
001	a b c d	051	a b c d
002	a b c d	052	a b c d
003	a b c d	053	a b c d
004	a b c d	054	a b c d
005	a b c d	055	a b c d
006	a b c d	056	a b c d
007	a b c d	057	a b c d
008	a b c d	058	a b c d
009	a b c d	059	a b c d
010	a b c d	060	a b c d
011	a b c d	061	a b c d
012	a b c d	062	a b c d
013	a b c d	063	a b c d
014	a b c d	064	a b c d
015	a b c d	065	a b c d
016	a b c d	066	a b c d
017	a b c d	067	a b c d
018	a b c d	068	a b c d
019	a b c d	069	a b c d
020	a b c d	070	a b c d
021	a b c d	071	a b c d
022	a b c d	072	a b c d
023	a b c d	073	a b c d
024	a b c d	074	a b c d
025	a b c d	075	a b c d
026	a b c d	076	a b c d
027	a b c d	077	a b c d
028	a b c d	078	a b c d
029	a b c d	079	a b c d
030	a b c d	080	a b c d
031	a b c d	081	a b c d
032	a b c d	082	a b c d
033	a b c d	083	a b c d
034	a b c d	084	a b c d
035	a b c d	085	a b c d
036	a b c d	086	a b c d
037	a b c d	087	a b c d
038	a b c d	088	a b c d
039	a b c d	089	a b c d
040	a b c d	090	a b c d
041	a b c d	091	a b c d
042	a b c d	092	a b c d
043	a b c d	093	a b c d
044	a b c d	094	a b c d
045	a b c d	095	a b c d
046	a b c d	096	a b c d
047	a b c d	097	a b c d
048	a b c d	098	a b c d
049	a b c d	099	a b c d
050	a b c d	100	a b c d

DECLARATION BY THE CANDIDATE

I declare that particulars and signature on this OMR Answer sheet are mine and are Name as in Attendance Sheet. I fruther declare that particulars filled in and Signature as well as the circles darkened on this ORIGINALCOPY is same as in OFFICE COPY.

Signature with time (in running handwriting)

CANDIDATE's NAME (in running handwriting)

MOTHER's NAME (in running handwriting)

FATHER's NAME (in running handwriting)

CANDIDATE LEFT HAND IMPRESSION

SIGNATURE OF INVIGILATOR'S WITH TIME

1

2

MEDACE

OMR SHEET

ROLL No.

1	1	1	1	1	1	1	1	1	1
2	2	2	2	2	2	2	2	2	2
3	3	3	3	3	3	3	3	3	3
4	4	4	4	4	4	4	4	4	4
5	5	5	5	5	5	5	5	5	5
6	6	6	6	6	6	6	6	6	6
7	7	7	7	7	7	7	7	7	7
8	8	8	8	8	8	8	8	8	8
9	9	9	9	9	9	9	9	9	9
0	0	0	0	0	0	0	0	0	0

TEST BOOKLET No.

1	1	1	1	1	1	1
2	2	2	2	2	2	2
3	3	3	3	3	3	3
4	4	4	4	4	4	4
5	5	5	5	5	5	5
6	6	6	6	6	6	6
7	7	7	7	7	7	7
8	8	8	8	8	8	8
9	9	9	9	9	9	9
0	0	0	0	0	0	0

TEST BOOKLET Code

DECLARATION BY THE CANDIDATE

I declare that particulars and signature on this OMR Answer sheet are mine and are Name as in Attendance Sheet. I fruther declare that particulars filled in and Signature as well as the circles darkened on this ORIGINALCOPY is same as in OFFICE COPY.

Signature with time (in running handwriting)

CANDIDATE's NAME (in running handwriting)

Q No.	Response				Q No.	Response			
001	a	b	c	d	051	a	b	c	d
002	a	b	c	d	052	a	b	c	d
003	a	b	c	d	053	a	b	c	d
004	a	b	c	d	054	a	b	c	d
005	a	b	c	d	055	a	b	c	d
006	a	b	c	d	056	a	b	c	d
007	a	b	c	d	057	a	b	c	d
008	a	b	c	d	058	a	b	c	d
009	a	b	c	d	059	a	b	c	d
010	a	b	c	d	060	a	b	c	d
011	a	b	c	d	061	a	b	c	d
012	a	b	c	d	062	a	b	c	d
013	a	b	c	d	063	a	b	c	d
014	a	b	c	d	064	a	b	c	d
015	a	b	c	d	065	a	b	c	d
016	a	b	c	d	066	a	b	c	d
017	a	b	c	d	067	a	b	c	d
018	a	b	c	d	068	a	b	c	d
019	a	b	c	d	069	a	b	c	d
020	a	b	c	d	070	a	b	c	d
021	a	b	c	d	071	a	b	c	d
022	a	b	c	d	072	a	b	c	d
023	a	b	c	d	073	a	b	c	d
024	a	b	c	d	074	a	b	c	d
025	a	b	c	d	075	a	b	c	d
026	a	b	c	d	076	a	b	c	d
027	a	b	c	d	077	a	b	c	d
028	a	b	c	d	078	a	b	c	d
029	a	b	c	d	079	a	b	c	d
030	a	b	c	d	080	a	b	c	d
031	a	b	c	d	081	a	b	c	d
032	a	b	c	d	082	a	b	c	d
033	a	b	c	d	083	a	b	c	d
034	a	b	c	d	084	a	b	c	d
035	a	b	c	d	085	a	b	c	d
036	a	b	c	d	086	a	b	c	d
037	a	b	c	d	087	a	b	c	d
038	a	b	c	d	088	a	b	c	d
039	a	b	c	d	089	a	b	c	d
040	a	b	c	d	090	a	b	c	d
041	a	b	c	d	091	a	b	c	d
042	a	b	c	d	092	a	b	c	d
043	a	b	c	d	093	a	b	c	d
044	a	b	c	d	094	a	b	c	d
045	a	b	c	d	095	a	b	c	d
046	a	b	c	d	096	a	b	c	d
047	a	b	c	d	097	a	b	c	d
048	a	b	c	d	098	a	b	c	d
049	a	b	c	d	099	a	b	c	d
050	a	b	c	d	100	a	b	c	d

MOTHER's NAME (in running handwriting)	FATHER's NAME (in running handwriting)

CANDIDATE LEFT HAND IMPRESSION	SIGNATURE OF INVIGILATOR'S WITH TIME
	1
	2